A COMPLETE HISTORY OF
WORLD CUP
CRICKET

A COMPLETE HISTORY OF
WORLD CUP
CRICKET

Mark Browning and James Grapsas

NEW
HOLLAND

This edition published in 2014 by New Holland Publishers Pty Ltd
London • Sydney • Cape Town • Auckland

The Chandlery Unit 114 50 Westminster Bridge Road London SE1 7QY United Kingdom
1/66 Gibbes Street Chatswood NSW 2067 Australia
Estuaries No. 4 Oxbow Crescent Century Avenue Century City 7441 South Africa
218 Lake Road Northcote Auckland New Zealand

www.newhollandpublishers.com

A record of this book is held at the British Library and the National Library of Australia.

ISBN 9781742575070

Managing Director: Fiona Schultz
Publisher: Alan Whiticker
Project Editor: Jason Mountney
Designer: Peter Guo
Production Director: Olga Dementiev
Printer: Toppan Leefung Printing Limited

10 9 8 7 6 5 4 3 2 1

Keep up with New Holland Publishers on Facebook
www.facebook.com/NewHollandPublishers

I dedicate my work on this book to my wife Vicky. Her continual support and encouragement made this project a reality. This work is also a tribute to my children Olive and Joseph, who continue to inspire by word and deed.

— James Grapsas

This book was written in memory of my father, Douglas James Browning. I also dedicate this book to my wonderful wife and best friend for over 40 years, Chris.

— Mark Browning

Acknowledgments

We would like to acknowledge the assistance of the following people in the compilation of this book. We are grateful to Rodney Hogg for preparing a lively and insightful foreword. We appreciate the help of Bob Simpson, who contributed the foreword for the first edition of the book in 1999 and who assisted Mark with queries about the 1987, 1992 and 1996 World Cup campaigns. Our thanks to Rick McCosker, Doug Walters, Bob Taylor, Mike Veletta, Asanka Gurusinha, Brad Hogg, Nathan Bracken and Tilan Samaraweera for their recollections of World Cup Finals. Ken Piesse, Kersi Meher-Homji, Rick Smith and Roger Page also provided some vital assistance.

We would like to reiterate our appreciation for two people who provided crucial help with the first edition. Ben Browning for compiling the statistical section up to 1999 and Carl Harrison-Ford for his encouragement and vigilance in examining and correcting the manuscript.

Finally, we would like to thank Alan, Jason and the team at New Holland for supporting this project and for their on-going assistance.

— James Grapsas and Mark Browning

Contents

Foreword

The World Cup is cricket's premier tournament; the one true stage for the limited-overs game. Many 50-over competitions are held around the world, seemingly year round. For many cricket followers, these contests fade from the memory quickly as one limited-overs competition appears to blend into the next one.

Rising above the treadmill of limited-overs contests around the globe is the World Cup. Held every four years, it is cricket's closest equivalent to the Olympic Games. It is the cricket tournament that the general public remembers most and that resonates deepest with cricket enthusiasts. A high-quality performance at the World Cup will often linger in the memory bank and will usually earn a player much more credit than a similar feat in another one-day competition.

The World Cup will celebrate its 40th birthday when the tournament returns Down Under in 2015. Despite the interest in the Twenty20 format in recent years and many controversies in international cricket since the 1970s, the World Cup has endured and retained its status as the pinnacle of limited-overs cricket. The World Cup has seen a cricket evolution. In 1975, a team's best Test players generally were picked for the one-day side and most captains had yet to develop tactics tailored to the demands of the shorter format. World Cup matches were played in white clothing, with a red ball, during daylight hours, and without field restrictions. This seems light years from the colour and pizzazz of recent tournaments, where sides have picked 50-over specialists, sophisticated tactics have been developed, captains have had to negotiate fielding restrictions, powerplays and Duckworth-Lewis calculations, and the matches have been played with a white ball, often under lights well into the evening.

In an ever-changing cricket landscape, it is pleasing to see that the cream of world cricket has risen to the top on many World Cup stages, providing lasting memories. Who could forget Viv Richards' superb hundred in the 1979 final? Wasim Akram's sensational bowling to secure victory for Pakistan in 1992? The nerve-jangling Australia-South Africa semi-final from 1999? Or Adam Gilchrist's masterclass in the rain-shortened final in Barbados in 2007?

My first World Cup experience was in England in June 1979, a short time after the post-World Series Cricket reconciliation. We had a tough challenge ahead of us, as none of the World Series Cricket representatives were in the squad. On the 1979 tour, my appreciation of the World Cup was dampened by a cold, wet English summer, which played real havoc with my asthma. I made it to one more World Cup, back in England in 1983, where we fancied our chances of making the semi-finals with India, Zimbabwe and the West Indies in our group. We were unable to do ourselves justice and our campaign was over at the pool stage. A loss to Zimbabwe in our opening match proved very costly in the end.

Despite these challenges, the World Cup offered me a vital opportunity to pit my skills against the world's best, including Richards, Greenidge, Haynes, Marshall, Garner, Holding, Botham, Gower, Gavaskar and Kapil Dev. The World Cup also gave me a taste of the emerging cricket nations, such as Canada in 1979 and Zimbabwe in 1983. The expansion of cricket beyond the traditional Test teams is an important, although gradual, process that has been adopted by the World Cup.

An understanding of the events at the World Cup over the years is a key factor in appreciating the tournament and the history of international cricket. With this in mind, the cricket community across the world is fortunate that James and Mark have written an authoritative history of this great tournament. They have done a sterling job in recapturing the mood of, and the main performances in, each game played in an interesting and insightful way.

This book will be an invaluable resource in following the World Cup in Australia-New Zealand in 2015, and beyond.

Rodney Hogg

CHAPTER 1:

Something Had To Be Done

When Frank Woolley dismissed the last Australian batsman at The Oval on 22 August 1912, everyone breathed a collective sigh of relief. Even Woolley, who had a brilliant match, taking 10-49 with his left-arm spinners, would have been grateful that the sodden, ill-fated Triangular Tournament had finally been laid to rest. The sinking of the *Titanic* was the greatest disaster of 1912, but this bad-tempered, poorly attended first attempt at a cricket world cup came a close second.

Even today, the suggestion by the Imperial Cricket Conference of 1909 that Test matches should be regulated by a regular program of tours, including a four-yearly triangular tournament between Australia, England and South Africa, seems meritorious. The prospect of a World Test Championship is growing by the day and, although it is still at the embryonic stage, it is generating plenty of passionate discussion at official and unofficial levels. However, everything conspired against that first brave attempt and instead of an epoch-making occasion it is remembered as one of cricket's greatest failures.

When the idea was conceived Australia and South Africa were both worthy adversaries of the English team. The idea of three Test teams doing battle in one English summer had first been mooted by Sir Abe Bailey, who by his encouragement and money, had already done a great deal to get South Africa up and running as a competitive Test nation. By 1912, though, their playing strength had, temporarily at least, waned badly.

The Australians were more doubtful of the worth of the enterprise. They knocked back the original proposal for the tournament to be held in 1909 on the grounds that a traditional Ashes tour of England would be more profitable to all concerned, particularly the Australians. This upset the English counties, who favoured the concept, and put the tour by Monty Noble's Australians at risk. It took a letter to *The Times* by F.S. (later Sir Stanley) Jackson to placate everybody.

Eventually the Australians had a successful tour in 1909, but three years later Australian cricket was plagued by internal strife. The players demanded that they be allowed to choose their manager for the trip as they had in the past. The board, unhappy with the players' man, Frank Laver, wanted to make their own choice. Their appointment of G.S. Crouch meant that six of Australia's best players—Clem Hill, Warwick Armstrong, Hanson Carter, Vernon Ransford, Albert Cotter and, saddest of all, Victor Trumper—did not make the trip to England. A number of their replacements were hardly great ambassadors. There were reports of "unpleasantness" and the tourists behaved so badly that they were "socially ostracised". Despite the latter-day efforts of the likes of Rod Marsh, Doug Walters and David Boon, Syd Gregory's side still probably holds the record for alcoholic consumption on an Australian tour of England. Perhaps they were overwhelmed by the English team that confronted them. It contained the bulk of the side that had just returned from a triumphant tour of Australia. In addition to the all-round skills of Woolley, the hosts boasted names such as Jack Hobbs, Wilfred Rhodes, Charles Fry, Frank Foster and Syd Barnes.

It rained and rained in 1912. Australia vs South Africa without a lot of stars was already a doubtful attraction. Most Mancunians found it an even more unappetising prospect when Old Trafford remained cold, grey and damp throughout late May. Forty-four thousand attended the four days of the Oval Test, the third of the series between England and Australia and, being the decider, the first to be scheduled to be played to a finish, but overall lots of money was lost that terrible summer. *Wisden* said, "Such a combination of adverse conditions could not be imagined."

A second triangular tournament was originally scheduled for 1916. However, the failure of the first one and an intrusive event called the Great War ensured that it did not occur. There was no thought of another cricket world cup for 60 years.

Former English captain Ted Dexter has always been considered something of a semi-eccentric character. He is full of ideas. Some have had merit; others could often be dismissed as fanciful. His early 1969 prediction that "one-day Test matches" were "just around the corner" seemed to fit into the latter category, but within two years his crystal-ball gazing proved to be accurate. At the MCG on 5 January 1971, as a substitute for the abandoned Third Test between Australia and England, 46,000 spectators watched an international match restricted to 40 eight-ball overs per side.

In an instant, Test cricket, the pride of the Commonwealth's summer game, had a fresh-faced, exciting and very marketable competitor. The sun shone warmly that day and the crowd loved the energetic approach of the players. They in turn relished the opportunity for some exercise after they had been cooped up inside a damp dressing-room watching the rain fall for several days. In addition, the happy patrons saw a result, and it was the one most of them wanted; a win to Australia.

Although Dexter's one-day Test call had been dismissed by traditionalists as extremist rubbish, it had as its basis the fact that at that time first-class and Test cricket was at a low ebb as a sporting attraction. Following the postwar boom period of the late 1940s and early 1950s, crowds at first-class and Test matches in both England and Australia had begun to decrease alarmingly. Many economic and social factors contributed to this, but the game did not help itself in either country when the

Ashes contests, for so long the showpiece of world cricket, turned into series after series of grinding attritional matches relished by the devotee, but hardly anyone else.

As the money coming in each season dwindled, the game's authorities started to look for ways to regain the lost ground. From committees were formed subcommittees, which discussed and researched this and that and forwarded proposals. These proposals were further debated back at full committee level and usually, whatever their merits, thrown out at some stage or so watered down as to be rendered useless by the notoriously conservative cricket establishment in both Australia and England. So the problem of falling attendances continued.

As early as 1944 there had been a recommendation by an MCC Committee headed by famous Yorkshireman and former England captain, Sir Stanley Jackson, that upon the resumption of postwar cricket, a county knockout competition be established along the lines of the fabulously successful Football Association (FA) Cup. Much of the cricket played during the Second World War was by necessity of the one-day variety, although the proposal put forward by Jackson's committee was for a tournament of three-day matches. Their suggestion was temporarily shelved because of the talk of a possible government ban on mid-week sport to help lift the country's industrial productivity.

By 1956, attendances at English county matches were half those of 1947. They continued to decline. Another committee, led by the respected Harry Altham, again recommended a county knockout cup. This time it was suggested the games be in one-day format. In 1961, when hardly anybody was watching county championship cricket, the concept was finally accepted.

A sponsored cup competition was to be fitted into a reduced first-class program. The number of overs per side was to be restricted to 65 per innings.

So in 1963 the Gillette Cup began. It was an immediate success. Sussex, who had never won the County Championship, took the first title. Their captain was Ted Dexter. Lord's filled for the final and has done so on each succeeding year. The matches also created a lot of interest through the various knockout rounds.

Once the Gillette Cup was established as a moneymaker the amount of one-day county cricket was quickly expanded. The John Player Sunday League started in 1969 and another tournament, the zonal-based Benson and Hedges Cup, increased the chances of sides winning some sort of silverware even further in 1972.

In Australia by the end of the 1960s there had been limited-overs matches at club level. The prospects for a financially productive summer in 1969-70 were not good. The Test team was away on what proved to be a near impossible twin tour assignment in India and South Africa. Attendances during the visits by India in 1967-68 and in 1968-69 by the West Indies had been modest. A knockout cup, to include all the Sheffield Shield-playing states plus Tasmania and New Zealand, was inaugurated. Vehicle and General were the sponsors and each innings was to be restricted to 40 eight-ball overs per innings. Richie Benaud was the public relations director.

New Zealand, to the relief of a nation with Test match status, won a lacklustre first final. The competition, without New Zealand and under the latest of several different sponsors, continues to this day.

South Africa, soon to be totally ostracised from official international cricket, also began their domestic limited-overs competition in 1969-70. It was another Gillette Cup and was restricted to 60 six-ball overs per innings. Gillette in England eventually dropped their sponsorship in 1980 because their name was becoming publicly associated more with a limited-over cricket final than with shaving. The razor company handed out sponsorship cash again when the West Indies started their inter-island limited-over competition in 1976. This immediately went to a 50-over-per-side format. Indian spectators got their first taste of limited-overs cricket in 1973. The Deodhar Trophy was a 60-over-per-side zonal competition. The Wills Trophy got under way in Pakistan in 1980-81, nine years later than New Zealand, who even before they had pulled out of the Australian competition, had started their own interprovincial tournament in 1971-72.

Limited-over internationals were well established before one-day cricket was embraced domestically in Pakistan and the West Indies. However, cricket administrators around the world were still reluctant to undermine the "authority of first-class cricket" with the shortened game. They have long been criticised for this and in some ways, mostly for economic reasons and player treatment, this is justified. By the same token, Test and first-class cricket is still seen by the cricket purist and the majority of the players both at club and first-class level as the superior form of the game. In most respects they are right. It will never be abandoned casually.

Despite the apparent success of the fill-in match now recognised as the first limited-overs international in Melbourne in January 1971; the next recognised limited-overs international was not played until August 1972. That match, again at the MCG, was not a totally isolated event, though.

When England were making short work of India and South Africa in 1959 and 1960, players were made to fill in the rest of the day after an early finish with a limited-overs exhibition match. No-one enjoyed these empty contests and it was during one such exhibition game that Sid Buller no balled South African Geoff Griffin out of cricket for throwing.

The Australian authorities were not totally blind to the success of the one-off game against England. When the South African tour of 1971-72 was replaced by a Rest of the World side, they sprinkled the program with one-day games. A few were originally scheduled, others were fitted in to fill days in the same way they had been in England a decade before. One limited-overs match in Melbourne was finished so quickly, a second 15-overs-per-side slog was scheduled on the same afternoon!

The Prudential Assurance Company sponsored the little festival of games at the conclusion of the Test series in England in 1972, 1973 and 1974.

It was the women cricketers who first revived the idea of a world cup, however. The most significant female innovation to the game since the introduction of round-arm bowling was largely funded by the players themselves. Teams from Trinidad and Tobago and Jamaica received government assistance and a benefactor named Jack Hayward put in some money, but then as now, the women proved to be wonderfully resourceful.

The tournament was played all over England in June and July 1973. Australia and England dominated and then contested the final at Edgbaston on 28 July. A fine century by Enid Bakewell led the home side to a comfortable 92-run victory. To date the England's male palyers have never been able to emulate the success of their female counterparts.

Two days before the women's final, the International Cricket Conference at their annual meeting at Lord's approved a plan put forward by the Test and County Cricket Board that a 60-overs-a-side tournament involving all current Test playing sides be played in England in 1975. The competition was to be organised around a round robin between two sets of four sides, followed by two semi-finals and a final at Lord's. Unlike the women, there was never any doubt the men would be able to play their first World Cup final at the home of cricket.

The tournament would cost £100,000 to run over a two-week period. A sponsor was sought to cover the expenses. Prudential again came forward. The ICC and certain renowned scribes like E.W. Swanton did not want the tournament to be called the World Cup. This was a fall back to the status of the one-day game against Test matches. In the 1976 Wisden it was called the Prudential Cup. But everywhere else it was accepted in common parlance as, indeed, the World Cup.

South Africa were scheduled to tour England that year, but in 1975 the government of that country remained intransigent in its apartheid policy and there was never a chance they would be allowed to visit. With no South African tour, English cricket officials were unsure of the likely public support of their program. So as an added insurance Australia were invited to stay on after the World Cup to play a four-Test Ashes series.

South Africa's exclusion meant two extra teams had to be found to raise the number of competitors to eight. Sri Lanka, soon to be the eighth Test-playing nation, were an obvious choice, while East Africa literally and figuratively made up the numbers. England and Australia were placed in separate groups. This was another indication of the uncertainty surrounding the venture. A semi-final or even final clash between the traditional rivals would be likely from such a draw. That might be needed to compensate for the lack of interest in games like East Africa vs India and Pakistan vs Sri Lanka. Three days were to be set aside for each game. That was wise. They would be played in England in June and nobody wanted a repeat of the fiasco of 1912. Another failed World Cup might have seen the concept disappear forever.

CHAPTER 2:

The First Prudential World Cup: The Glory of 1975

If the 1912 Triangular Tournament was doomed from the outset, the 1975 Prudential Cup was equally blessed. When the authorities set aside three days for each of the 60-overs-per-side matches they were not being overly pessimistic.

May and June of 1972 had been diabolically wet; 1973 cold, grey and damp; and in 1974, everyone got soaked. Days before the tournament got under way there were frost, snow and washouts. Yet every one of the games in the 1975 World Cup was completed in a day and they were all, for the most part, played in the most glorious sunshine imaginable.

The winners of the Prudential Cup would split £9000 between them. The runners-up £2000 and the semi-finalists would pocket £1000 each. In addition, each game would have a Man of the Match award, the winner to receive £50 in the first-round games, £100 in the semi-finals and £200 for the Man of the Match in the final. Radio and newspaper commentator Henry Blofeld, having witnessed the recent Ashes Test series, imagined the pace bowling of Lillee and Thomson would be irresistible and made Australia outright favourites.

Former England spinner and esteemed television commentator Jim Laker believed England would win every one of their matches, including the final. John Arlott was far less confident. Betting agency Ladbrokes had the West Indies at 9-4 official favourites, with England second at 11-4. Pakistan were third and Australia fourth. A punter could get 1500-1 on East Africa winning the tournament. There is no evidence that Rod Marsh or Dennis Lillee wagered any money on the team whose manager is alleged to have said that his side were in England "to enjoy our cricket and drink plenty of booze".

Although there was fear of the unknown, the cricketing prospects were really quite tantalising. England had not long returned from Australia where they received a hiding from Ian Chappell's aggressive, slightly rough-edged, but immensely talented side. The cornerstone of their success was the fast-bowling duo of Dennis Lillee and Jeff Thomson. Bristling with intimidating intent, they had cut a bruising swathe through the touring Englishmen. They were trumped up as long-haired anti-heroes. Cricketers for the new era, they arrived in England to a media response befitting pop stars. Their experience of local conditions, the draw, and all the limited-overs cricket played in the three county competitions seemed likely to be, to the advantage of the English side. Most of the West Indians also played county cricket so they were similarly advantaged. Indeed their captain Clive Lloyd had already made one-day Lord's finals something of his speciality, his 126 for Lancashire against Warwickshire in the 1972 Gillette Cup final being a typically thrilling knock.

Lloyd brought a West Indian side to the World Cup that was just coming out of a period of transition. The majority of the old guard from the successful teams of the 1960s were gone. Garry Sobers had originally been selected in the squad of 14. Sadly, the 38-year-old champion all-rounder had to withdraw with a groin injury. The first World Cup might have been a fitting swansong to a fantastic career. But Sobers had played his last international match. Lloyd had taken over the captaincy from Rohan Kanhai for the tour of India, Sri Lanka and Pakistan from November 1974 to March 1975. Included in that party were several newcomers, such as Gordon Greenidge, Viv Richards and Andy Roberts.

In Roberts, Lloyd had a fast bowler fit to challenge Lillee and Thomson for speed and aggression. Another West Indian figure familiar to English cricket followers, he had taken 111 wickets for Hampshire at an outstanding average of 13.45 during the 1974 County Championship. Roberts gained a reputation as a cold, unsmiling assassin. At Basingstoke he had felled 41-year-old Colin Cowdrey with a vicious bouncer. Soon after, despite the fact that his arm was always ramrod straight, accusations were made in the English tabloid press that Roberts threw. These theories soon died a natural death.

Equally exciting was the West Indian batting line-up. Their array of strokeplayers, three of them left-handers, as much as anything made them favourites with the punters. Roy Fredericks and Gordon Greenidge formed a powerful opening partnership. Alvin Kallicharran at the time was rated not far short of being the best batsman in the world, with a Test average of 57. Sobers' replacement, another veteran from the previous era, Kanhai, had lost none of his steely wristed timing and Lloyd himself had a fantastic tour of the subcontinent, gorging himself on the local spinners with his long reach and awesomely heavy bat. At number six in the order came the young Viv Richards, oozing still largely untapped potential.

With a large expatriate West Indian contingent in the country, they would prove to be almost as big a drawcard as England. Indeed the match between the West Indies and Australia, scheduled for The Oval on Saturday 14 June was sold out before the tournament commenced.

England's greatest advantage, after their one-day county experiences, was seen to be the support of the crowds. The pressure on the captaincy of Mike Denness had been intense since his appointment at the end of 1973. He was not blamed for the hammering England had received in Australia, where he had scored 188, 181 and 59 not out in his last three Test innings. These knocks allowed him to cling onto the job. Early in the season, classy Yorkshire opening batsman Geoff Boycott announced he would continue his controversial self-imposed exile from the England team. He preferred to score his runs for 'his' Yorkshire and Barnsley.

At the time it was suggested Boycott might be trying to avoid having to face the extreme pace of the likes of Lillee, Thomson and Roberts. That was not the case. Rather, he was dissatisfied with playing under a captain he did not consider worthy of a Test place. However, the other English problem child, veteran fast bowler John Snow, was set to return. Denness had wanted him in his side all along, but had not been able to sway the selectors. Despite being 34, Snow was still considered the best fast bowler in the country.

England's squad had a solid look, and it was expected that the likes of Keith Fletcher and Dennis Amiss would find runs easier to come by in the one-day environment than they had in the boiling cauldrons of the Australian Test match grounds. In a tall South African, Tony Greig, the home side had an all-rounder the equal of any in the world, while seamers such as Geoff Arnold and Chris Old could be a handful in cloudy conditions on green wickets.

Bushy haired, moustachioed and brash, the Australians almost had a pre-punk image in their disdain of certain conventions. They arrived having re-established their position at the top of the Test match tree. Ian Chappell led a side that had restored the popularity of cricket in Australia. In addition to Lillee and Thomson, they had a fine batting side led by the fighting capabilities of the captain, the stylish authority of his brother Greg and the enigmatic brilliance of Doug Walters.

It was believed big strong inswing bowler Max Walker would relish the wickets in England, while the belligerent left-handed batting of wicketkeeper Rod Marsh in the middle order could be a key to the chances of Australian success. However, Australia missed the stability of Ian Redpath's solid technique at the top of the order. Like Boycott, he had withdrawn his services. One of the least outspoken players in the game's history, no-one questioned his right to stay at home in Geelong to ensure the success of his antique shop.

Ian Chappell said that the main objective of his side was to retain the recently hard won Ashes later in the summer, but that they would fight all the way to win the Cup.

Pakistan, as ever, were the wild card of the tournament. They had been unbeaten on their 1974 tour of England and had made short work of the home side in two limited-over internationals. But they were in the hard side of the draw and had to overcome Australia and the West Indies to reach the semi-finals. Laden with quality batting and valuable all-rounders, their temperament at crucial times might be called into question if things got tight.

Nevertheless, their team boasted a fine array of talent. The strokeplay of Asif Iqbal, Zaheer Abbas, Majid Khan and the Mohammad brothers, Sadiq and Mushtaq, was the equal of any. Their bowling attack was less impressive, but in Imran Khan and Javed Miandad, Pakistan could point to some unparalleled junior talent. Asif Iqbal had just replaced Intikhab Alam as captain, but his fitness did not see him through the tournament. Majid took over the reins. Both those players were stood aside and Mushtaq was the new man in charge by the time New Zealand arrived in Pakistan in October the following year. Some things in cricket never change.

Despite their Test match status, neither India nor New Zealand was thought to have the depth of ability to go all the way and win the Prudential Cup. India had bowed to the philosophy that spinners made little impact in the shortened game and filled their team with medium pacers who could bat a bit. Eknath Solkar, Abid Ali, Mohinder Amarnath, Madan Lal and Karsan Ghavri were thought unlikely to keep the best sides to a losing score. Gundappa Viswanath, Farokh Engineer and Sunil Gavaskar led the batting capably, but India's batting was notably unreliable and in contrast to Pakistan they had been annihilated in England the previous year.

New Zealand's batting was built around their prolific opener and captain Glenn Turner. Another player with extensive experience in English county cricket, Turner had been turned from a strokeless wonder into a stylish shot maker by the need to adapt his game to the more urgent demands of limited-overs cricket. He had reliable run-making support in Brian Hastings, John Morrison and Worcestershire team-mate, John Parker. Dayle Hadlee, Richard Collinge and Hedley Howarth were all to be respected rather than feared. Dayle's younger brother, Richard, was raw, but it was thought he might make a reasonable bowler of international standard at some stage, too. The unavailability of the likes of Mark Burgess, Vic Pollard, Bevan Congdon and Bruce Taylor told against a team already struggling to find enough quality players from their small population base.

Outside the Indian subcontinent, little was known about the Sri Lankan side. The country had only had its new name for three years. The majority of the names of the players had a fairly new ring to them, too. But some like Sunil Wettimuny, young Duleep Mendis and leg-spinner Somachandra de Silva would eventually be able to look back at the 1975 World Cup as the moment when their country launched them onto the road of full international recognition. That recognition reached fruition when they and their nation made their Test debut in February 1982.

If little was known of the Sri Lankans, virtually none of the players from Kenya, Zambia, Tanzania and Uganda had been heard of in the wider cricketing community. The only players from the region with first-class experience—Basharat Hassan of Nottinghamshire and John Solanky of Glamorgan—were left out in favour of locally based players. Don Pringle, a landscape consultant from Kenya and already 42 years old, was father of future England Test cricketer, Derek, but that was hardly a cause for renown in 1975. Like Hassan and Solanky, he had at one point been offered the chance to play county cricket. Wicketkeeper Hamish McLeod, a Slazenger representative from Zambia, stood out on the team sheet because he did not have a very East African name. That was almost the extent of it. They played mostly one-day cricket but were still lambs to the slaughter.

One thing that would help them was an ICC ruling that any bouncer that passed over the head of the batsman would be called a wide and that non-recognised batsmen were not to be submitted to facing such deliveries. Lillee and Thomson were not impressed, while Andy Roberts called the ruling "ridiculous".

The sides did not arrive en masse at Heathrow. A number of New Zealanders, Pakistanis and West Indians were already involved with county cricket. The 10 remaining Kiwis touched down on 27 May, the Australians two days later following a short stopover in Canada where they suffered a surprising defeat. The following day, the three West Indians not on county contracts landed.

All teams tried to acclimatise with practice matches against various county sides and among themselves. Such was the interest in the Australians that 15,000 attended one such game against Middlesex at Lord's, much to the delight of the club's beneficiary, stalwart wicketkeeper John Murray.

On Friday 6 June all eight sides met the Queen at Buckingham Palace. Then it was down Park Lane and Baker Street, past Hyde Park and Sherlock Holmes and Madame Tussaud's territory, along Park Road, left into St John's Wood Road to the Grace Gates of Lord's cricket ground. There, the players mingled with each other, numerous cricket officials and Prince Philip, who had followed them. A sense of excitement, nervousness and anticipation prevailed during the luncheon. Ties were loosened, the sun was out and the weather was warm. Lord's under blue skies is at its grandest and Saturday 7 June was D-Day for the 112 cricketers playing in the first World Cup.

SATURDAY 7 JUNE 1975
THE PRUDENTIAL CUP: ROUND ONE
GROUP A: ENGLAND VS INDIA
LORD'S: ENGLAND WON BY 202 RUNS

The best and worst features of limited-overs cricket were evident in this showcase game on the first day of the Prudential Cup. After England, led by Dennis Amiss, had pulverised India's array of tame medium pacers to the tune of 4-334 in their 60 overs India admitted immediate defeat and crawled their way to 3-132 in reply, also off 60 overs. A cursory glance at the scoreboard would suggest interference from rain. Instead, as Tony Lewis called it, India's batting was a display of "senseless perversity". Richie Benaud's critique amounted to "one of the most astonishing games of limited-overs cricket I've ever seen".

The 16,274 spectators who paid £19,000, basked in the early-afternoon warmth of English batsmen scoring at will against inadequate bowling. It was far closer to their cricketing ideal than watching them dodging the firepower of Lillee and Thomson. Amiss relished the downgrading of the physical threat more than anyone as he unleashed his fluent array of off-side strokes. He raced to his 50 in 66 balls, promptly hit Mohinder Amarnath for three fours in three balls between third man and cover point, then went on to his century in 112 deliveries.

He lost his opening partner, the recalled John Jameson, when the score was 54 but then added 176 for the second wicket with Keith Fletcher. At the time such things meant nothing, but 24 years later this stand remains the best for the second wicket in the World Cup. Amiss was 98 out of 1-150 at lunch and by the time he was bowled for 137, slogging at Madan Lal in the 51st over with the total on 245, he had hit 18 sumptuous boundaries.

Fletcher had already been dismissed for 68 in the same way and Tony Greig went cheaply, giving Abid Ali's figures a modicum of respectability. But that only unleashed the batting mayhem of a Chris Old-Mike Denness partnership which yielded 89 runs in 10 overs, including 63 in the last five. Old, picked for his bowling, belted 51 in 28 balls. A couple of his best smites went for six, one over the short Mound Stand boundary, the other straight to the Nursery End sightscreen. Fletcher, accelerating as his innings progressed, and Denness had also made good use of that inviting short boundary, depositing the ball once each among the spectators.

Feast was followed by famine and the chief culprit was Sunil Gavaskar, who carried his bat throughout the innings for 36. He faced 174 balls and kept everyone out on the ground until 7.30 pm. No-one was really sure why. Tony Lewis suggested it might have been a protest at the omission of Bishen Bedi from the team. The actions, or in this case inactions, of Gavaskar himself invited plenty of protests. Demonstrators continually ran on to the ground imploring their countrymen to play some shots. One Indian supporter became so irate he punched two policemen and was sentenced to six months' jail.

Those who weren't protesting were either drinking themselves into a stupor or quietly dozing off in the afternoon sunshine.

Neither the Indian manager, Gulabrai Ramchand, nor his captain, Srinivas Venkataraghavan could offer a reason for Gavaskar's approach. It probably did not make any difference to the result of this match, but it massacred India's run rate, which meant that on the first day of competition they had severely reduced their chances of reaching the semi-finals.

The man who went on to become the game's greatest century maker in Test cricket later said he was just completely and utterly out of form. He couldn't even get out when he tried and considered standing aside and letting a straight ball bowl him. In his defence, he was dropped a couple of times. Also, Gavaskar in 1975 was not yet the confident and complete player he would later become. Since his astonishing debut series in the Caribbean in 1971 the 26-year-old opener had made just one more Test hundred in 13 Tests. Nevertheless, this was a bizarre performance. Ramchand admitted to being disappointed but he said it would not lead to disciplinary action against Gavaskar.

ENGLAND		INDIA	
J. A. Jameson c Venkat b Amarnath	21	S. M. Gavaskar not out	36
D. L. Amiss b Madan Lal	137	E. D. Solkar c Lever b Arnold	8
K. W. R. Fletcher b Abid Ali	68	A. D. Gaekwad c Knott b Lever	22
A. W. Greig lbw b Abid Ali	4	G. Viswanath c Fletcher b Old	37
M. H. Denness (capt) not out	37	B. P. Patel not out	16
C. M. Old not out	51	Extras (lb 3, w 1, nb 9)	13
Extras (lb 12, w 2, nb 2).	16	(60 overs)	3-132
(60 overs)	4-334	Did not bat: M. Amarnath, F. M. Engineer (wk), S. Abid Ali,	
Did not bat: B. Wood, A. P. E. Knott (wk), J. A. Snow,		Madan Lal, S. Venkataraghavan (capt), K. Ghavri	
P. Lever, G. G. Arnold		1/21 2/50 3/108	
1/54 2/230 3/237 4/245		Bowling: Snow 12-2-24-0; Old 12-4-26-1; Greig 9-1-26-0;	
Bowling: Madan Lal 12-1-64-1; Amarnath 12-2-60-1;		Lever 10-0-16-1; Jameson 2-1-3-0; Arnold 10-2-20-1;	
Abid Ali 12-0-58-2; Ghavri 11-1-83-0; Venkataraghavan		Wood 5-2-4-0	
12-0-41-0; Solkar 1-0-12-0			

Umpires: D.J. Constant, J.G. Langridge.

Toss: England.   Points: England 4, India 0

GROUP A: NEW ZEALAND vs EAST AFRICA
EDGBASTON: NEW ZEALAND WON BY 181 RUNS

The scoreboards of the first two Group A matches look remarkably similar. There was little surprise, however, at the turn of events at Edgbaston. As most people had suspected, East Africa were totally out of their depth against New Zealand. If the century from Amiss showed up the inadequacy of the Indian bowling, Glenn Turner was clinical in his destruction of the hopes of the East African combine. He won the toss, batted then occupied the crease for the duration of the 60 overs, scoring 171 runs in the meantime.

The Edgbaston wicket was on the slow side and it required a period of adjustment from the Kiwi batsman. Turner offered sharp chances at 16 and 27, one to left-arm spinner P.G. Nana who impressed with his control, and another to a slow-moving mid off fieldsman. New Zealand was 2-145 from 40 overs at lunch and the match remained competitive until John Parker joined his captain and Worcestershire team-mate in a 149-run partnership for the third wicket in 23 overs. They continually pierced the field with strong drives, lifting the run rate almost at will.

Parker was dismissed at 252 but Turner by this time had reached his hundred and was starting to belt the forlorn bowlers to all parts. Two sixes sailed over the mid wicket boundary in one over. Normally very correct, the New Zealand opener had struck 16 fours including a series of hoicks and swipes, by the time the innings closed on 5-309. The final 20 overs had seen the addition of 164 runs.

For the 4000 faithful patrons in the ground, the fun was now over. East Africa never challenged the New Zealand total. Their openers looked solid enough and Frasat Ali lasted 39 overs for his 45. He even managed a big straight six off left-arm spinner Hedley Howarth. But Howarth soon had his revenge, young Brian McKechnie, later to face the infamous grubber on the MCG in 1981, scored a direct-hit run out; and Dayle Hadlee picked up three cheap victims. Mehmood Quraishy and Zulfiqar Ali ensured the total reached three figures and that the humiliation of not batting out the overs was avoided. Zulfiqar hit a rare boundary and two young boys ran out on to the ground to congratulate him. Unfortunately they went up to Quraishy instead and were then escorted away by the police. In the end East Africa was 21 runs closer to victory than India had been. I don't know if that was any consolation to them.

NEW ZEALAND		EAST AFRICA	
G. M. Turner (capt) not out	171	Frasat Ali st Wadsworth b H. J. Howarth	45
J. F. M. Morrison c & b Nana	14	Sam Walusimba b D. R. Hadlee	15
G. P. Howarth b Quraishy	20	Ramesh Sethi run out	1
J. M. Parker c Zulfiqar b Sethi	66	Shiraz Sumar b D. R. Hadlee	4
B. F. Hastings c Sethi b Zulfiqar	8	Jawahir Shah c & b H. J. Howarth	5
K. J. Wadsworth (wk) b Nagenda	10	Harilal R. Shah (capt) lbw, H. J. Howarth	0
R. J. Hadlee not out	6	Mehmood Quraishy not out	16
Extras(b 1, lb 8, w 5)	14	Zulfiqar Ali b D. R Hadlee	16
(60 overs)	5-309	H. M. Leod (wk) b Collinge	5
Did not bat: B. J. McKechnie, D. R. Hadlee, H. J. Howarth,		P. G. Nana not out	1
R. O. Collinge		Extras (lb 5, nb 1)	6
1/51 2/103 3/252 4/278 5/292		(60 overs)	8-128
Bowling: Nagenda 9-1-50-1; Nana 12-2-34-1;		Did not bat: J. Nagenda	
Zulfiqar 12-0-71-1; Frasat 9-0-50-0; Sethi 10-1-51-1;		1/30 2/32 3/36 4/59 5/59 6/84 7/121 8/126	
Quraishy 8-0-39-1		Bowling: Collinge 12-5-23-1; McKechnie 12-2-39-0;	
		H. J. Howarth 12-3-29-3; R. J. Hadlee 12-6-10-0;	
		D. R. Hadlee 12-1-21-3	

Umpires: H.D. Bird, A.E. Fagg.

Toss: New Zealand.   Points: New Zealand 4, East Africa 0

GROUP B: WEST INDIES vs SRI LANKA
OLD TRAFFORD: WEST INDIES WON BY 9 WICKETS

When the West Indies toured the Indian subcontinent early in 1975, they had played a few games in Sri Lanka between their Test commitments in India and Pakistan. Then, the locals had given a fairly decent account of themselves. They held Clive Lloyd's side to draws in two three-day representative games, taking a big first innings lead in the second match. On the neutral territory of Old Trafford in Manchester, though, their resistance against the tournament favourites lasted until just 3.30 in the afternoon.

Sent in to bat by Clive Lloyd on a sunny morning in front of 5000 fans, the Sri Lankan batsmen were badly found out by the West Indian pace attack, even though the pitch offered no real assistance. Left-arm swing bowler Bernard Julien began the demolition in the fourth over. Opener/wicketkeeper Edwards Fernando was caught behind and then in the biggest blow of all, captain Anura Tennekoon, who had scored a century against this attack in Colombo, was also dismissed by the Murray/Julien combination with the score still on five. After fewer than 40 overs, it was the West Indies' turn to bat. Even the final Sri Lankan total of 86 was only boosted by a last-wicket partnership of 28 between Somachandra de Silva and Lalith Kaluperuma. It was fortunate that the last three wickets had doubled the score or the match might have been embarrassingly completed before lunch. Sri Lanka had lost three wickets moving from 41 to 42 and had been 9-58 at the break. Sri Lanka's total was the first under 100 in limited-over internationals.

As in the England-India game, the pitch was occasionally disrupted by demonstrators during the Sri Lankan innings. This time the protests were politically motivated. The pitch invaders might have added to their 'racist' placards something about the fact that the Sri Lankan batting performance was a setback to their country's plan to receive full recognition by the ICC. Julien and Keith Boyce did the bulk of the damage, but the Sri Lankans showed a lack of technique against all four West Indian fast bowlers. Only from ageing off spinner Lance Gibbs were they able to score a few worthwhile runs.

Leg spinner de Silva opened the bowling and claimed the only wicket to fall in the 21 overs the West Indies needed to score the 87 runs they required for victory. He had Roy Fredericks caught at point before Alvin Kallicharran and wicketkeeper Deryck Murray, promoted to opener, completed the formalities. For anyone who wanted to stay, an exhibition match filled in an extra couple of hours following the abbreviated main event.

SRI LANKA		WEST INDIES	
E. R. Fernando (wk) c Murray b Julien	4	R. C. Fredericks c Warnapura b de Silva	33
B. Warnapura c Murray b Boyce	8	D. L. Murray (wk) not out	30
A. Tennekoon (capt) c Murray b Julien	0	A. I. Kallicharran not out	19
P. O. Heyn c Lloyd b Roberts	2	Extras (b 2, lb 1, w 1, nb 1)	5
M. Tissera c Kallicharran b Julien	14	(20.4 overs)	1-87
L. R. D. Mendis c Murray b Boyce	8	Did not bat: R. B. Kanhai, C. H. Lloyd (capt),	
A. Ranasinghe b Boyce	0	I. V. A. Richards, B. D. Julien, K. D. Boyce, V. A. Holder,	
H. S. M. Peris c Lloyd b Julien	3	A. M. E. Roberts, L. R. Gibbs	
A. R. M. Opatha b Roberts	11	1/52	
D. S. de Silva c Lloyd b Holder	21	Bowling: Opatha 4-0-19-0; de Silva 8-0-33-1;	
L. W. S. Kaluperuma not out	6	Peris 2-0-13-0; Kaluperuma 6.4-1-17-0	
Extras (b 3, lb 3, nb 3)	9		
(37.2 overs)	86		

1/5 2/5 3/16 4/21 5/41 6/41 7/42 8/48 9/58
Bowling: Roberts 12-5-16-2; Boyce 8-1-22-3; Holder
1.2-0-2-1; Julien 12-3-20-4; Gibbs 4-0-17-0

Umpires: W.L. Budd, A Jepson;

Toss: West Indies.   Points: West Indies 4, Sri Lanka 0

GROUP B: AUSTRALIA vs PAKISTAN
HEADINGLEY: AUSTRALIA WON BY 73 RUNS

This game justified its Match of the Day status by the fact that it was a contest between two evenly matched teams. And like a quality Aussie rules match, it was tight all day until the last quarter, when a champion took the game by the scruff of the neck and carried his side to what, on paper, looked like a comfortable victory.

Headingley was full to capacity when Ian Chappell won the toss and elected to bat. There was some early new-ball movement for Sarfraz Nawaz, Naseer Malik and Asif Masood, but Alan Turner and Rick McCosker, both from New South Wales and both new to English conditions, rode their luck well. Turner, who was surprised at his inclusion ahead of Bruce Laird, in particular hit aggressively to the on side and the pair had put on 63 by the 15th over. The large crowd, mainly made up of local Pakistani immigrants and Yorkshiremen and probably keen to see Australia get beaten, had been relatively restrained until then.

Asif Iqbal, once his country's leading paceman, now just a change bowler, then had Turner caught at square leg. This led to a period of dominance by the Pakistanis and Australia slipped to 4-124. McCosker was becalmed until being caught behind from the last ball before lunch, Ian Chappell was caught deep on the leg side after a couple of fine shots, and Doug Walters' appalling record in England was continued when he was caught at slip for two.

Greg Chappell was also struggling for timing and it took some fine positive batting by Ross Edwards to restore Australia's momentum. The West Australian added 60 with Greg Chappell until the younger Chappell brother was caught trying to hit the ball over cover from the 22-year old all-rounder Imran Khan. Edwards put on 48 with Max Walker, then 35 with Jeff Thomson. Walker had batted brilliantly in the recent Ashes series in Australia and he used his long reach to good effect again in this innings. Thomson's style was one more normally associated with tail enders. He trusted his eye and hit the ball powerfully to unguarded areas of the outfield.

Edwards, having survived an early lbw scare against Asif Masood, ran brilliantly between wickets and remained unbeaten on 80. Seventy-nine runs were added in the final 10 overs. Seven for 278 was a lot more than had seemed likely at 6-195.

Scoring 20 not out was just about the highlight of Jeff Thomson's day. In his first over in international cricket in England the new terror of the cricketing world sprayed the ball, his limbs and his invective all over the place. As Umpire Torn Spencer continued to call no-ball after no-ball and once also, wide, the crowd roared as loudly as they had done all day. Thomson rewarded their 'encouragement' with a two-fingered salute at the end of his 11-ball over. He eventually overstepped 12 times during his eight-over spell, giving the local scribes plenty to write about.

The whole crowd appreciated the batting of Majid Khan, who carried on against the world's fastest bowlers in his usual unhurried fashion as if they were mere trundlers. He lost Sadiq and Zaheer early, the latter to a mishook off Thomson. Majid reached 65 out of 104 before being fourth out to a faint leg-side tickle from the bowling of off spinner Ashley Mallett. Ian Chappell had introduced Mallett and the medium pace of Doug Walters as first and second change, holding the extra paceman, Max Walker, in reserve.

The captain, Asif Iqbal, and Wasim Raja rallied the Pakistanis to 4-181. Asif, hands apart on the bat handle, nudging and improvising while Wasim, left-handed and flamboyant, took risks and got away with them. At the 40-over mark they were actually 24 runs ahead of what Australia's total had been. The enthusiastic waving of flags and banners by their supporters added to the atmosphere as the game seemed to be building towards a thrilling climax. Just under 100 runs in more than 15 overs with six wickets in hand looked achievable, but the return of Lillee in the 43rd over changed the course of the match again, this time irrevocably. He removed Asif's off-stump as clean as a whistle and, well supported by Walker, promptly cleaned up the tail. The Australians, still slightly suspicious of limited-overs cricket, had maintained their recent dominance over Pakistani teams. For Asif Iqbal's team the loss meant they were already unlikely to reach the semi-finals.

PAKISTAN		AUSTRALIA	
Sadiq Mohammad b Lillee	4	A. Turner c Mushtaq b Asif Iqbal	46
Majid Khan c Marsh b Mallett	65	R. B. McCosker c Wasim Bari b Malik	25
Zaheer Abbas c Turner b Thomson	8	I. M. Chappell (capt) c Wasim Raja b Sarfraz Nawaz	28
Mushtaq Mohammad c G. Chappell b Walters	8	G. S. Chappell c Asif Iqbal b Imran Khan	45
Asif Iqbal (capt) b Lillee	53	K. D. Walters c Sarfraz Nawaz p Malik	2
Wasim Raja c Thomson b Walker	31	R. Edwards not out	80
Imran Khan c Turner b Walker	9	R. W. Marsh (wk) c Wasim Bari b Imran Khan	1
Sarfraz Nawaz c Marsh b Lillee	0	M. H. N. Walker b Asif Masood	18
Wasim Bari (wk) c Marsh b Lillee	2	J. R. Thomson not out	20
Asif Masood c Walker b Lillee	6	Extras (lb 7, nb 6)	13
Naseer Malik not out	0	(60 overs)	7-278
Extras (lb 4, w 3, nb 12)	19		
(53 overs)	205		

Did not bat: A. A. Mallett, D. K. Lillee

1/15 2/27 3/68 4/104 5/181 6/189 7/189 8/195 9/203

1/63 2/99 3/110 4/124 5/184 6/195 7/243

Bowling: Lillee 12-2-34-5; Thomson 8-2-25-1; Mallett 12-1-49-1; Walters 6-0-29-1; Walker 12-3-32-2; G. S. Chappell 3-0-17-0

Bowling: Malik 12-2-37-2; Sarfraz 12-0-63-1; Imran Khan 10-0-44-2; Asif Masood 12-0-50-1; Asif Iqbal 12-0-58-1; Wasim Raja 2-0-13-0

Umpires: T.W. Spencer, W.E. Alley.

Toss: Australia.   Points: Australia 4, Pakistan 0

WEDNESDAY 11 JUNE 1975
THE PRUDENTIAL CUP: ROUND TWO
GROUP A: ENGLAND vs NEW ZEALAND
TRENT BRIDGE: ENGLAND WON BY 80 RUNS

Sunny Saturday turned into blazing Wednesday as the Prudential Cup began to take real shape under perfect, clear blue skies. It was a cutthroat day during which most of the semi-final positions in both groups would be determined.

Lancastrian fast bowler Peter Lever took just one wicket in the game in Nottingham, yet in most people's minds it won the match for England. New Zealand's main hope of scoring the 267 runs they needed to defeat Mike Denness' side was for Glenn Turner to build another major innings like the one he had on the Saturday. When Lever bowled him for 12 in the 10th over with the score on 30 the Kiwis were in very big trouble.

England still had to work a bit harder for their points than they had against India. They left out John Snow and Barry Wood for the spin of Derek Underwood and for another batsman, Frank Hayes. Turner won the toss and sent England in, hoping to take advantage of the heavy, misty atmosphere. His big left-arm seamer Richard Collinge responded well, bowling Dennis Amiss with an in-swinger, then having John Jameson caught behind in his next over to leave England 2-28. However the sun beat down, the shirts came off in the crowd and the conditions soon settled. So did Frank Hayes and Keith Fletcher, who added 83 for the third wicket before Hayes badly misjudged a pull shot in the 32nd over.

The loss of a third wicket on 111 may have been a bad omen for England, but Fletcher was now well entrenched and Denness, at his stylish and aggressive best, put on another 66 in 16 overs with him. The run rate was steady rather than spectacular until Denness on-drove Hedley Howarth for six, then swept him for four next ball. The English captain soon perished, caught in the deep at mid wicket, and Tony Greig, wearing silly batting gloves, was bowled swinging across the line.

England still had wickets and Fletcher in hand. The Essex 'gnome' stepped away and clipped Collinge through point for three to bring up his century in the 55th over. Chris Old again chimed in with a very handy 20, once smacking young Richard Hadlee out of the ground over mid wicket. Fifty-three runs had been scored in the final five overs.

When Fletcher was run out going for a second suicidal run off the last ball of the innings, New Zealand knew they had their work cut out for them. Despite the loss of Turner they got to 1-83, but the run rate became an increasing problem as the innings progressed. Barry Hadlee, the third Hadlee brother in the New Zealand side playing the second of his two limited-over internationals, supported John Morrison who went on to complete a solid half century before being caught at square leg off Underwood.

Tony Greig, bowling his mixture of off-cutters and seamers, did most damage as the Kiwi challenge subsided. Chris Old came as close as is humanly possible to claiming a hat rick without actually getting one. He had Brian Hastings caught by Derek Underwood, bowled Richard Hadlee next ball, then brushed Dayle Hadlee's stumps without removing a bail on the third ball. Dayle Hadlee and Brian McKechnie then added 48, but the match was over as a contest. In such situations the interest of all concerned quickly subsides. The last wicket did not fall until the final ball of the innings, Underwood bowling Richard Collinge perhaps looking for a way to score the 81 runs required for victory.

ENGLAND		NEW ZEALAND	
D. L. Amiss b Collinge	16	J. F. M. Morrison c Old b Underwood	55
J. A. Jameson c Wadsworth b Collinge	11	G. M. Turner (capt) b Lever	12
K. W. R. Fletcher run out	131	B. G. Hadlee c Old b Greig	19
F. E. Hayes lbw b R. J. Hadlee	34	J. M. Parker b Greig	1
M. H. Denness (capt) c Morrison b D. R. Hadlee	37	B. F. Hastings c Underwood b Old	10
A. W. Greig b D. R. Hadlee	9	K. J. Wadsworth (wk) b Arnold	25
C. M. Old not out	20	R. J. Hadlee b Old	0
Extras (lb 6, w 1, nb 1)	8	B. J. McKechnie c Underwood b Greig	27
(60 overs)	6-266	D. R. Hadlee c Arnold b Greig	20
Did not bat: A. P.E. Knott (wk), D. L. Underwood,		H. J. Howarth not out	1
G. G. Arnold, P. Lever		R. O. Collinge b Underwood	6
1/27 2/28 3/111 4/177 5/200 6/266		Extras (b 1, lb 4, w 1, nb 4)	10
Bowling: Collinge 12-2-43-2; R. J Hadlee 12-2-66-1;		(60 overs)	186
D. R. Hadlee 12-1-55-2; McKechnie 12-2-38-0;		1/30 2/83 3/91 4/95 5/129 6/129 7/129 8/177 9/180	
Howarth 12-2-56-0		Bowling: Arnold 12-3-35-1; Lever 12-0-37-1; Old 12-2-29-2;	
		Underwood 12-2-30-2; Greig 12-0-45-4	

Umpires: W.E. Alley, T.W. Spencer.

Toss: New Zealand.　　Points: England 4, New Zealand 0

GROUP A: INDIA vs EAST AFRICA
HEADINGLEY: INDIA WON BY 10 WICKETS

The official attendance figure said 6000, but only 720 people actually paid to see this second East African mismatch at Leeds. Harilal Shah won the toss and his side batted and lasted 55.3 overs, but even so they could only muster 120 runs against a similar attack to the one that had conceded 334 to England on the Saturday.

There was one change to the Indian bowling line-up. Sikh left-arm spinner Bishen Bedi returned for young Karsan Ghavri. He claimed only one wicket, but otherwise mesmerised the hapless East Africans with his beautifully concealed variations, conceding just six runs in his 12-over spell. The score stumbled along to 5-56 in the 39th over. The captain was caught behind for his second first-ball duck and his side were looking at an embarrassingly low total. Jawahir Shah and Ramesh Sethi then added 42 to, temporarily at least, slow the Indians' progress. Shah put a few nice shots through the covers and Sethi completed a couple of effective leg-side hits.

It kept the 720 paying Headingley customers a bit longer in their warm sunny seats and allowed Sunil Gavaskar and Farokh Engineer enough scope to each pass the half-century mark in the 179 balls it took them to pass their target of 120. Madan Lal had polished off the East African tail to finish with the best bowling figures, but it was Engineer who received the Man of the Match award from former Yorkshire and England wicketkeeper, Jimmy Binks. Gavaskar had actually outscored Engineer at the batting crease, but Binks may have wanted to reward a fellow member of the wicketkeepers' union. Or perhaps he felt it inappropriate for Gavaskar to be recognised in such a way just a couple of days after his debacle against England at Lord's. Engineer's was quite a brave effort—the veteran was playing with a torn hamstring and he had to walk most of his runs. He was, however, rarely stretched by the East African bowlers or their fieldsmen.

EAST AFRICA		INDIA	
Frasat Ali b Abid Ali	12	S. M. Gavaskar not out	65
Sam Walusimba lbw b Abid Ali	16	F. M. Engineer (wk) not out	54
Praful Mehta (wk) run out	12	Extras (b 4)	4
Yunus Badat b Bedi	1	(29.5 overs)	0-123
Jawahir Shah b Amarnath	37	Did not bat: A. D. Gaekwad, G. R. Viswanath, B. P. Patel,	
Harilal R. Shah (capt) c Engineer b Amarnath	0	E. D. Solkar, S. Abid Ali, Madan Lal, M. Amarnath,	
Ramesh Sethi c Gaekwad b Madan Lal	23	S. Venkataraghavan (capt), B. Bedi	
Mehmood Quraishy run out	6	Bowling: Frasat Ali 6-1-17-0; Pringle 3-1-14-0;	
Zulfiqar Ali not out	2	Zulfiqar 11-3-32-0; Nana 4.5-0-36-0; Sethi 5-0-20-0	
P. G. Nana lbw Madan Lal	0		
D. Pringle b Madan Lal	2		
Extras (lb 8, nb 1)	9		
(55.3 overs)	120		
1/27 2/36 3/37 4/56 5/56 6/98 7/116 8/116 9/116			
Bowling: Abid Ali 12-5-22-2; Madan Lal 9.3-2-15-3;			
Bedi 12-8-6-1; Venkataraghavan 12-4-29-0; Amarnath 10-0-39-2			

Umpires: H.D. Bird, A. Jepson.

Toss: East Africa.   Points: India 4, East Africa 0

GROUP B: AUSTRALIA vs SRI LANKA
THE OVAL: AUSTRALIA WON BY 52 RUNS

His friends and colleagues are quick to point out that Jeff Thomson was and is basically a fairly placid fellow with no cross to bear and a love of the outdoor life. This is despite the infamous article that bore his name in 1974 claiming that he enjoyed seeing batsmen screaming in pain on the pitch after being struck by him. He was probably pining very much for some quiet outdoor Australian activity after just a couple of weeks and two games of cricket in England.

After his no-ball problems at Leeds and the negative press reactions, Thomson had to bear close scrutiny at the nets at Lord's in preparation for the match against Sri Lanka. When the cameras were lined up with the bowling crease his team-mates encouraged Thomson to deliberately overstep. His captain, Ian Chappell said, "He's had a gutful of this business."

History has shown that an angry fast bowler can be a dangerous fast bowler and there is no doubt the Sri Lankan batsmen who faced the wrath of Jeff Thomson at The Oval on 12 June 1975 wish that he had been left alone. Thomson's figures from the match seem modestly respectable. He claimed 1-22 from 12 overs. Sri Lanka's 4-276 looks a case of bat dominating ball. Bat did dominate ball, too, except when it was in Thomson's hands. Then it was a case of ball dominating body.

In addition to taking one wicket, Thomson put two Sri Lankan batsmen into St Thomas's Hospital, Lambeth. He bowled a wide at the start of his second spell, which raised his ire. Duleep Mendis was concussed after being hit on the side of the head by a bouncer. He stayed for a little longer, but a second deflected blow to his forehead finished him.

"I'm going boss, I'm going," he replied to his captain's inquiry as to his intentions.

Sunil Wettimuny compiled a brave half century. However, he was beaten about the body by Thomson's phenomenally quick bowling, and retired after chopping the ball into the same battered foot for the second time.

Many in the 6000-strong crowd at The Oval started jeering, especially when Thomson threw down the stumps and appealed for a run out with Wettimuny still hopping around. If the Queenslander was hoping to avoid attention he was going the wrong way about it. The initial reaction of the Sri Lankan manager, K.M.T. Pereira, was that bouncers were not allowed at unrecognised batsmen and that all Sri Lankans fell into that category. The next day, having had time to reflect, he revised that opinion. As Fred Bennett the Australian manager pointed out; "What do you expect Thomson to do ... bowl underarm?"

All of which detracted from a game that featured a feast of runs. Over the day 604 runs were scored for the loss of nine wickets. Alan Turner and Rick McCosker got Australia away to a flyer after Tennekoon won the toss and invited Ian Chappell's side to bat. The decision seemed to be based as much on wanting to give the spectators close to a full day's cricket as on gaining any special tactical advantage. The pair of New South Welshmen had put on 178 in 34 overs by lunch. Turner had already completed his century, the first by an Australian in any limited-over internationals. "I don't think I've hit the ball better, and you certainly didn't have to worry about life and limb with those guys," he said.

He hit one big six over long on, a mighty stroke on the large playing field. But immediately after the interval leg spinner, Somachandra de Silva struck twice and three wickets fell for nine runs in 11 balls. Greg Chappell and Doug Walters responded to the collapse by adding 117 runs in 19 overs, leaving the Sri Lankans an awesome chase.

They didn't get there and there was no feature innings, but their consistency and determination frustrated the Australians and gained Sri Lanka great admiration and plenty of sympathy from neutrals. They really got stuck into Ashley Mallett's off-spin and Greg Chappell's and Doug Walters' medium pace. Wettimuny passed 50, so did Michael Tissera. The bruises became badges of courage. *Wisden* said Australia did not gain many admirers. Even the Australian players believed they had been a bit lucky.

AUSTRALIA		SRI LANKA	
R. B. McCosker b de Silva	73	S. R. de S. Wettimuny retired hurt	53
A. Turner c Mendis b de Silva	101	R. Fernando (wk) b Thomson	22
I. M. Chappell (capt) b Kaluperuma	4	B. Warnapura st Marsh b Mallett	31
G. S. Chappell c Opatha b Pieris	50	L. R. D. Mendis retired hurt	32
K. D. Walters c Tennekoon b Pieris	59	A. Tennekoon (capt) b I. M. Chappell	48
J. R. Thomson not out	9	M. Tissera c Turner b I. M. Chappell	52
R. W. Marsh (wk) not out	9	A. Ranasinghe not out	14
Extras (lb 20, b 1, w 1, nb 1)	23	H. S. M. Pieris not out	0
(60 overs)	5-328	Extras (b 6, lb 8, w 8, nb 2)	24
Did not bat: R. Edwards, M. H. N. Walker, D. K. Lillee,		(60 overs)	4-276
A. A. Mallett		Did not bat A. R. M. Opatha, D. S. de Silva, L. W. S. Kaluperuma	
1/182 2/187 3/191 4/308 5/308		1/30 2/84 3/246 4/268	
Bowling: Opatha 9-0-32-0; Pieris 11-0-68-2;		Bowling: Lillee 10-0-42-0; Thomson 12-2-22-1;	
Warnapura 9-0-40-0; Ranasinghe 7-0-55-0; de		Mallett 12-0-72-1; Walters 6-0-33-0; Walker 12-1-44-0;	
Silva 12-3-60-2; Kaluperuma 12-0-50-1		G. S. Chappell 4-0-25-0; I. M. Chappell 4-0-14-2	

Umpires: W.L. Budd, A.E. Fagg.

Toss: Sri Lanka.　　Points: Australia 4, Sri Lanka 0

GROUP B: PAKISTAN vs WEST INDIES
EDGBASTON: WEST INDIES WON BY 1 WICKET

The superiority of the World Cup and the significance of the games ahead of all other limited-over internationals could not be better emphasised than by this encounter at Edgbaston which remains an all-time classic.

Clive Lloyd has gone so far as to suggest the match signalled the start of the West Indies' self-belief that they had the talent to win the tournament and to then emerge as the best team in the world. Whether that was the case, this was a great game of cricket. The result seemed for most of the day to be going one way only for the plot to have a late and unpredictable twist, like the very best drama. If there was a down side it was that the result condemned the talented Pakistanis to an early finish in the tournament. They made all the running, but lacked enough killer instinct to finish off the Caribbean players.

In one way the quality and closeness of the game should not have been a total surprise. Over the years the West Indies and Pakistan have been remarkably evenly matched, even through the West Indies halcyon years in the 1980s.

Not that the Pakistanis were at full strength. Their captain, Asif Iqbal, was in a hospital in Birmingham having a haemorrhoid operation and Imran Khan was also unavailable, as he was taking exams at Oxford University. Despite missing both players and the early loss of Sadiq to Bernard Julien, they got away to an excellent start after acting captain Majid Khan won the toss and elected to bat in front of a healthy mix of Pakistani and West Indian expatriates and a few English locals.

The crowd of 16,000 saw a typically graceful half century from Majid. Under a sunhat that was darker than the colour of his bat he hit the ball with exquisite timing before being caught behind off his opposite number. Zaheer chipped in with a solid 31 before future captain, Mushtaq Mohammad, and Wasim Raja added an important 62 runs for the fourth wicket. Mushtaq barely scored in front of square, twirling his bat and flicking the ball on both sides of the wicket with incredible effectiveness. Wasim, who seemed to relish West Indian bowling, benefited from some sloppy fielding, after earlier brilliance from the likes of Keith Boyce. Boyce also revealed the West Indians' sense of growing frustration when he bowled a 'beamer' at Mushtaq for daring to charge and slice him for four over covers.

Pakistan's 7-266 was healthy rather than insurmountable on a flat track in beautiful weather. Clive Lloyd said his side were confident of reaching their target. Sarfraz Nawaz had other ideas. Perhaps he was annoyed by the strange, coloured towelling hats worn by the West Indian top order. Whatever the motivation the big, lumbering medium pacer made short work of Greenidge, Fredericks and Kallicharran. Each was beaten on merit as the West Indies tumbled to 3-36. Sarfraz by then had 3-10 in 3.4 overs. Lloyd made a half century, being upset when given out caught behind off 17-year-old Javed Miandad. The West Indies kept up with the required run rate, but regularly lost wickets. On 8-166 they seemed destined to lose. BBC Television commentator Richie Benaud confirmed the feeling when, after Boyce played on, he said, "The West Indies surely cannot win."

However the Pakistan bowling ranks were thinning and the West Indies batted right down to number 11. Wicketkeeper Deryck Murray, an experienced and fighting campaigner, gave his team a glimmer of hope. Vanburn Holder, choking down low on the bat handle stayed just long enough for the 200 to be passed. When last man Andy Roberts walked to the crease 64 runs were required for the last wicket in 14 overs.

Clive Lloyd's accountant put £150 on the West Indies to win at 66-1. Lloyd himself started drinking a crate of pale ale and told Gordon Andrews he was very unwise with his money. He was still stewing over the decision that had gone against him.

As the overs passed the stack of pale ale empties grew, as did the tension inside the West Indies dressing-room. Murray hit sweet boundaries through mid wicket and the covers. Roberts clubbed the full-pitched deliveries off the back foot straight and to the cover boundary. Sarfraz finished his overs. A win was possible. The target was reduced to 29 runs off six overs, then 16 off four. Parvez Mir bowled a critical maiden. But someone had miscalculated and Wasim Raja, normally a fastish leg-spinner, was called on to bowl medium pace for the 60th over. He had five runs to play with. Roberts and Murray scrambled a tight leg bye, but Pakistan saw their great victory chance slipping away and instead of a run out, there was an overthrow. The Hollies Stand vibrated with the excitement of the West Indian supporters. A quiet little push to mid wicket off the fourth ball and it was all over. The ground was invaded, Murray was swamped. Clive Lloyd, drunk, ecstatic but still smarting charged out of the dressing-room and yelled into the members' enclosure, "That will teach you ... you cheats!" It had been a wonderful, pressure-packed occasion.

PAKISTAN		WEST INDIES	
Majid Khan (capt) c Murray b Lloyd	60	R. C. Fredericks lbw b Sarfraz Nawaz	12
Sadiq Mohammad c Kanhai b Julien	7	C. G. Greenidge c Wasim Bari b Sarfraz Nawaz	4
Zaheer Abbas lbw b Richards	31	A. I. Kallicharran c Wasim Bari b Sarfraz Nawaz	16
Mushtaq Mohammad b Boyce	55	R. B. Kanhai b Naseer	24
Wasim Raja b Roberts	58	C. H. Lloyd (capt) c Wasim Bari b Javed Miandad	53
Javed Miandad run out	24	I. V. A. Richards c Zaheer b Parvez	13
Parvez Mir run out	4	B. D. Julien c Javed Miandad b Asif Masood	18
Wasim Bari (wk) not out	1	D. L. Murray (wk) not out	61
Sarfraz Nawaz not out	0	K. D. Boyce b Naseer	7
Extras (b 1, lb 15, w 4, nb 6)	26	V. A. Holder c Parvez b Sarfraz Nawaz	16
(60 overs)	7-266	A. M. E. Roberts not out	24
Did not bat: Asif Masood, Naseer Malik		Extras (lb 10, w 1, nb 8)	19
1/21 2/83 3/1404/202 5/249 6/263 7/265		(59.4 overs)	9-267
Bowling: Roberts 12-1-47-1; Boyce 12-2-44-1;		1/6 2/31 3/36 4/84 5/99 6/145 7/151 8/166 9/203	
Richards 4-0-21-1; Julien 12-1-41-1; Holder 12-3-56-0;		Bowling: Asif Masood 12-1-64-1; Sarfraz Nawaz 12-1-44-4;	
Lloyd 8-1-31-1		Naseer Malik 12-2-42-2; Parvez Mir 9-1-42-1; Javed	
		Miandad 12-0-46-1; Mushtaq Mohammad 2-0-7-0; W,asim	
		Raja 0.4-0-3-0	

Umpires: DJ. Constant, J.G. Langridge.

Toss: Pakistan.   Points: West Indies 4, Pakistan 0

SATURDAY 14 JUNE 1975
THE PRUDENTIAL CUP: ROUND THREE
GROUP A: ENGLAND vs EAST AFRICA
EDGBASTON: ENGLAND WON BY 196 RUNS

Edgbaston went from the sublime to the ridiculous in a matter of three days. East Africa's total inadequacy at this level was again cruelly exposed. It was time for them to go home and lick their wounds. There were many who questioned the wisdom of including a side so far below the strength of all others. Uganda, Tanzania and Zambia have not been back, but Kenya returned 20 years later and made a far greater impact than this combine ever did.

Harilal Shah won the toss and sent England in. Dennis Amiss and Barry Wood, in for John Jameson, responded with an opening stand of 158. Amiss gave a couple of chances and concentration may have been a bit difficult, especially as England were assured of their semi-final place. He got to 88 before someone actually held a chance.

Wood also missed his hundred, hitting across one from Quraishy. It was Wood's Lancashire team-mate, Frank Hayes, who provided the day's highlight. In 14 overs, Hayes belted his way to hit two sixes, straight towards the pavilion, and six fours. Tony Greig missed out for the third time and 290 was a smaller total than it might have been. But it was always going to be far too many for the East Africans.

John Snow showed no mercy. Back in place of Geoff Arnold, Snow took 4-5 in his first six overs. Straight and fast was enough, two victims were bowled, two were lbw. Before long, East Africa was 4-21. A quick finish would have been merciful, but it took 52.3 overs for England to finish the contest. The captain, Harilal Shah, scored his first runs for the tournament and Ramesh Sethi, showing admirable application, lasted for 32 overs. Peter Lever finally bowled him, Zulfiqar and Harnish McLeod. Not all of the crowd of 5000 saw that.

England had had a nice workout in the sunshine as a lead-up to their semi-final. The question remained whether this match, or even the previous two encounters, had been tough enough work-outs to prepare them to take on the West Indies or Australia.

ENGLAND		EAST AFRICA	
B. Wood b Quraishy	77	Frasat Ali b Snow	0
D. L. Amiss c Nana b Zulfiqar	88	S. Walusimba lbw b Snow	7
F. E. Hayes b Zulfiqar	52	Yunus Badat b Snow	0
A. W. Greig lbw b Zulfiqar	9	Jawahir Shah lbw b Snow	4
A. P. E. Knott (wk) not out	18	Ramesh Sethi b Lever	30
C. M. Old b Quraishy	18	Harilal R. Shah (capt) b Greig	6
M. H. Denness (capt) not out	12	Mehmood Quraishy c Amiss b Greig	19
Extras [b 7, lb 7, w 1, nb 1]	16	Zulfiqar Ali b Lever	7
(60 overs)	5-290	H. M. Leod (wk) b Lever	0
Did not bat: K. W.R. Fletcher, J. A. Snow, P. Lever,		P. G. Nana not out	8
D. L. Underwood		D. Pringle b Old	3
1/158 2/192 3/234 4/244 5/277		Extras (lb 6, w 1, nb 3)	10
Bowling: Frasat 9-0-40-0; Pringle 12-0-41-0; Nana 12-2-46-0;		(52.3 overs)	94
Sethi 5-0-29-0; Zulfiqar 12-0-63-3; Quraishy 10-0-55-2		1/7 2/7 3/15 4/21 5/42 6/72 7/76 8/79 9/88 10/94	
		Bowling: Snow 12-6-11-4; Lever 12-3-32-3;	
		Underwood 10-5-11-0; Wood 7-3-10-0; Greig 10-1-18-2;	
		Old 1.3-0-2-1	

Umpires: W.E. Alley, J.G. Langridge.

Toss: East Africa.   Points: England 4, East Africa 0

GROUP A: NEW ZEALAND vs INDIA
OLD TRAFFORD: NEW ZEALAND WON BY 4 WICKETS

If there was any injustice about the structure and results of the Prudential World Cup, it was that in Round Three India and New Zealand were playing for a spot in the semi-finals while the Pakistani side would just be going through the motions against Sri Lanka, then heading home. Neither team at Old Trafford had done anything except defeat East Africa, but the groupings designed to ensure England's progress also favoured one of these two teams.

The contest attracted only 4000 patrons to Old Trafford. For a time it seemed they might see a fairly one-sided contest. Through a slightly superior showing against England, New Zealand started the match as favourites and with the Hadlee brothers, Dayle and Richard, and Hedley Howarth putting in good spells they reduced India to a very uncomfortable 6-101 just before lunch. The Hadlee brothers had combined early on to remove the prize victim of Sunil Gavaskar.

Finally India's policy of selecting a heap of all-rounders paid some dividends. Madan Lal and the more experienced Abid Ali turned the tide with a stand of 55. Madan Lal became McKechnie's second victim, but Abid Ali stayed on, turning a good start into a major limited overs innings in his final international. He hit some nice shots through the covers and a couple of effective slogs, one over mid wicket from the left-armer Collinge going all the way for six. Venkataraghavan also made an important contribution with the bat, adding 60 with Abid Ali. Their stand ensured India ended with a competitive total.

As had been the case for New Zealand in the previous two games, the innings of Glenn Turner was crucial. Probably in his hands rested the fate of who would reach the semi-finals. He and John Morrison made a positive start. In 10 overs they rattled up 45 runs, then Bishen Bedi was introduced into the attack. The folly of not selecting him against England was again soon obvious. He choked off the scoring, dismissing Morrison with his second ball and conceded only 11 runs in eight overs before tea. Geoff Howarth was unluckily run out when a Turner straight drive was deflected from the bowler's hand onto the stumps at the non-striker's end. When Abid Ali trapped John Parker lbw, New Zealand were 3-70 and anything but certainties.

That was as close as India got, though. Turner could not be shifted. Bedi was seen off and Brian Hastings joined his captain in a 65-run partnership for the fourth wicket. Wicketkeeper, the ill-fated Ken Wadsworth, and Richard Hadlee also contributed. At no stage did New Zealand break free, but Turner completed his hundred in 163 minutes and following two boundaries from Dayle Hadlee the Kiwis reached their target with seven balls and four wickets to spare. Turner had struck 13 boundaries in his 114 not out.

INDIA		NEW ZEALAND	
S. M. Gavaskar c R. J. Hadlee b D. R. Hadlee	12	G. M. Turner (capt) not out	114
F. M. Engineer (wk) lbw b R.J. Hadlee	24	H. M. Morrison c Engineer b Bedi	17
A. D. Gaekwad c Hastings b R. J. Hadlee	37	G. P. Howarth run out	9
G. R. Viswanath lbw b McKechnie	2	J. M. Parker lbw b Abid Ali	1
B. P. Patel c Wadsworth b H. J. Howarth	9	B. F. Hastings c Solkar b Amarnath	34
L. D. Solkar c Wadsworth b H. J. Howarth	13	K. J. Wadsworth (wk) lbw Madan Lal	22
S. Abid Ali c H. J. Howarth b McKechnie	70	R. J. Hadlee b Abid Ali	15
Madan Lal c & b McKechnie	20	D. R. Hadlee not out	8
M. Amarnath c Morrison b D. R. Hadlee	1	Extras (b 8, lb 5)	13
S. Venkataraghavan (capt) not out	26	(58.5 overs)	6-233
B. Bedi run out	6	Did not bat: B. J. McKechnie, H. J. Howarth, R. O. Collinge	
Extras (b 5, w 1, nb 4)	10	1/45 2/62 3/70 4/135 5/185 6/224	
(60 overs)	230	Bowling: Madan Lal 11.5-1-62-1; Amarnath 8-1-40-1;	
1/17 2/48 3/59 4/81 5/94 6/101 7/156 8/157 9/217 10/230		Bedi 12-6-28-1; Abid Ali 12-2-35-2;	
Bowling: Collinge 12-2-43-0; R.J. Hadlee 12-2-48-2;		Venkataraghavan 12-0-39-0; Solkar 3-0-16-0	
D. R. Hadlee 12-3-32-3; McKechnie 12-1-49-3; H. J.			
Howarth 12-0-48-2			

Umpires: W.L. Budd, A.E. Fagg.

Toss: India.   Points: New Zealand 4, India 0

GROUP B: AUSTRALIA vs WEST INDIES
THE OVAL: WEST INDIES WON BY 7 WICKETS

The sell-out crowd that packed into the old south London ground witnessed a feast of exciting cricket, albeit virtually all of it was from one side. The West Indies, in what was for them almost a home game, demolished the Australians with a brilliant display of calypso cricket in its purest form; incisive fast bowling followed by spectacular strokeplay. Neither side could forfeit its semi-final berth by losing this match, but the Australians must have been worried by their second-rate showing.

Riding high on the excitement of their wonderful win against Pakistan, Clive Lloyd's side played with exhilaration and supreme confidence right from the moment the West Indian captain won the toss and sent Australia in to bat. The third day of World Cup cricket, although starting cloudy and a bit cooler, again encouraged shirtsleeves and later bare torsos. The crowd was in a very buoyant mood well before the start of play. Some paid scalpers 10 times the face value for a ticket while others had found their entrance by less-accepted means, such as hiding in the back of beer trucks. They absolutely exploded into life in the first over when Rick McCosker failed to keep down a lifting Julien delivery on the leg side and Roy Fredericks dived forward at leg slip to scoop up the low catch. Alan Turner found Andy Roberts an altogether more difficult proposition from the Sri Lankan trundlers and probably imagined his pads were made of paper when he got his knee in front of a very fast, straight delivery.

On what was really a fairly slow wicket Ian and Greg Chappell responded in their best fighting-family traditions. Both fell within seven runs and six balls of each other to Keith Boyce, who sent down a fine spell of quick outswing. At 4-56 the West Indies were riding high and better still when a left-hand pick and lightning right-hand throw by Gordon Greenidge found Doug Walters short of his ground. Run out for seven was hardly a score to crown the day you had been awarded an MBE.

This was cricket at breakneck speed and it could not last. West Australian pair Rod Marsh and Ross Edwards restored a sense of sanity to proceedings without quite putting the game back on an even keel, adding 99 for the sixth wicket. Strangely, considering their reputations, it was Edwards who dominated the scoring, a, leg-side pick-up shot off Lloyd registering the first Australian boundary just prior to lunch. Salad was taken at 5-76, after which the West Australian rebuilding exercise continued. It lasted until the introduction of young Viv Richards. Edwards twice lofted him for four, deep towards the boundary at wide mid-on. He gave himself room for a third such blow, only to miss a faster straight ball. Roberts was recalled. He struck Thomson on the forearm and smashed out Lillee's leg-stump stump. Again the crowd exploded, Englishmen just as jubilant as the West Indians this time at seeing the Aussie pacemen receive some of their own medicine. Roberts had Ashley Mallett caught behind the next ball, leaving Rod Marsh stranded on 52 with no partners left to help him push the total beyond 192. His side had wasted 6.2 overs.

A target of 193 at just over three runs per over might have produced a sedate response from many sides. Not from the West Indians on this day, however. Once Lillee and Thomson fired in a few bouncers the challenge was always going to be met. Greenidge was trapped by a big inswinger from Max Walker with the total on 29. The left-handed Guyanese pair of Alvin Kallicharran and Roy Fredericks then took the game by the scruff of the neck with a series of flashing shots; cuts, hooks and back-foot drives sending the ball in all directions.

It was all great entertainment and it built to a tremendous climax. In an astonishing display, little 160cm tall 'Kalli' belted Dennis Lillee for 35 runs from 10 balls. He got himself moving with a cracking drive through the covers and reached his 50 with a slash that sent the ball high, wide and handsome to the third-man boundary. Lillee continued to bowl short. Kallicharran kept hooking. One he picked up and hit finer, ever so sweetly over the boundary at the Pavilion End. When at last he finally mistimed a hook he had somewhat dented the Australian fast bowler's reputation. Kallicharran's 78 included a six and 13 fours. He had added 124 for the second wicket with his fellow Guyanese left-hander.

Forty runs and a few overs later Viv Richards pulled Ian Chappell away to Compton's corner for four, heralding another joyous black invasion of an English cricket ground. The West Indies had romped home by seven wickets, leaving them to return to The Oval in four days time to play New Zealand in the supposedly easier semi-final. As they filed out of the ground the West Indian supporters sang, "We killed a kangaroo . . . we killed a kangaroo; eeeiii-adio, we killed a kangaroo." The Australians were criticised for having a naïve approach to limited-overs cricket. They had to travel to Leeds to tackle a confident, strongly supported England team.

AUSTRALIA		WEST INDIES	
R. B. McCosker c Fredericks b Julien	0	R. C. Fredericks c Marsh b Mallett	58
A. Turner lbw b Roberts	7	C. G. Greenidge lbw b Walker	16
I. M. Chappell (capt) c Murray b Boyce	25	A. I. Kallicharran c Mallett b Lillee	78
G. S. Chappell c Murray b Boyce	15	I. V. A. Richards not out	15
K. D. Walters run out	7	R. B. Kanhai not out	18
R. Edwards b Richards	58	Extras [b 4, lb 2, w 3, nb 1]	10
R. W. Marsh (wk) not out	52	(46 overs)	3-195
M. H. N. Walker lbw b Holder	8	Did not bat: C. H. Lloyd (capt), B. D. Julien, D. L. Murray (wk),	
J. R. Thomson c Holder b Richards	1	K. D. Boyce, V. A. Holder, A. M. E. Roberts	
D. K. Lillee b Roberts	3	1/29 2/153 3/159	
A. A. Mallett c Murray b Roberts	0	Bowling: Lillee 10-0-66-1; Thomson 6-1-21-0; Walker	
Extras [lb 9, w 1, nb 6]	16	12-2-41-1; G. S. Chappell 4-0-13-0; Mallett 11-2-35-1;	
(53.4 overs)	192	I. M. Chappell 3-1-9-0	

1/0 2/21 3/49 4/56 5/61 6/160 7/173 8/1749/192 10/192
Bowling: Julien 12-2-31-1; Roberts 10.4-1-39-3;
Boyce 11-0-38-2; Holder 10-1-31-1; Lloyd 4-1-19-0;
Richards 6-0-18-2

Umpires: H.D. Bird, D.J. Constant.
Toss: West Indies.   Points: West Indies 4, Australia 0

GROUP B: PAKISTAN vs SRI LANKA
TRENT BRIDGE: PAKISTAN WON BY 192 RUNS

The Sri Lankans came back to earth with a thud in Nottingham after their fine showing against Australia. They were unable to contain the talented Pakistani stroke-players and when they batted could make little of the array of wrist spinners confronting them. In front of the smallest crowd of the tournament there was only token satisfaction for Majid Khan's side, as well. When Imran Khan returned to the team dressing room following his exams at Oxford, he found there was still an atmosphere of stunned disbelief at the loss against the West Indies. The pros and cons were being debated endlessly. They had a place in the semi-finals at their beck and call but had failed to grasp it.

When Sadiq Mohammad and Majid went out to open the batting at the invitation of Tennekoon it was quickly evident the pressure was off. Sadiq was dropped on one run, but it was the Sri Lankans' only look-in. Against friendly bowling the pair traded shot for shot, adding 159 in 32 overs. Once the openers were separated Zaheer took centre stage, caressing the ball square on both sides as he raced towards his century in 27 overs. He dominated a stand of 88 with Mushtaq. Eventually Zaheer fell just three runs short, playing on from Opatha late in the innings. Imran missed out on the run feast altogether. Perhaps his focus was still on his university papers.

Faced with a daunting target of 331, Sri Lanka went bravely for their shots as they had against Australia. However, this time it didn't work. They missed the injured Duleep Mendis and Sunil Wettimuny, not yet recovered from their pounding from Thomson, and slipped quickly from 1-44 to 6-79. Somachandra de Silva, who had a solid tournament, offered a little late resistance before Imran cleaned up what Javed Miandad and the other spinners had left behind. The Sri Lankan innings closed when Imran had last man, Ginigalgodagede Silva caught by Wasim Raja from the first ball of his eighth over, finishing the Prudential Cup for themselves and their unfortunate opponents.

PAKISTAN		SRI LANKA	
Sadiq Mohammad c Opatha b Warnapura	74	E. R. Fernando (wk) c & b Javed Miandad	21
Majid Khan (capt) c Tennekoon b D. S. de Silva	84	B. Warnapura b Imran Khan	2
Zaheer Abbas b Opatha	97	A. P. B. Tennekoon (capt) lbw Naseer	30
Mushtaq Mohammad c Heyn b Warnapura	26	M. H. Tissera c Wasim Bari b Sadiq	12
Wasim Raja c Opatha b Warnapura	2	P. O. Heyn c Zaheer b Javed Miandad	1
Javed Miandad not out	28	A. N. Ranasinghe b Wasim Raja	9
Imran Khan b Opatha	0	H. S. M. Pieris lbw b Parvez	16
Parvez Mir not out	4	A. R. M. Opatha c Zaheer b Sadiq	0
Extras (b 4, lb 4, w 2, nbS)	15	D. S. de Silva b Imran Khan	26
(60 overs)	6-330	L. W. S. Kaluperuma not out	13
Did not bat: Wasim Bari (wk), Asif Masood, Naseer Malik		G. R. A. de Silva c Wasim Raja b Imran Khan	0
1/159 2/168 3/256 4/268 5/318 6/318		Extras (lb 1. w 3. nb 4)	8
Bowling: Opatha 12-0-67-2; Pieris 9-0-54-0;		(50.1 overs)	138
G. R.A. de Silva 7-1-46-0; D. S. de Silva 12-1-61-1;		1/5 2/44 3/60 4/61 5/75 6/79 7/90 8/113 9/135 10/138	
Kaluperuma 9-1-35-0; Warnapura 8-0-42-3;		Bowling: Asif Masood 6-2-14-0; Imran Khan 7.1-3-15-3;	
Ranasinghe 3-0-10-0		Javed Miandad 7-2-22-2; Naseer Malik 6-1-19-1;	
		Sadiq Mohammad 6-1-20-2; Wasim Raja 7-4-7-1;	
		Mushtaq Mohammad 5-0-16-0; Parvez Mir 6-1-17-1	

Umpires: A. Jepson. T.W. Spencer.

Toss: Sri Lanka.   Points: Pakistan 4. Sri Lanka 0

WEDNESDAY 18 JUNE 1975
THE PRUDENTIAL CUP SEMI FINALS

The tables at the end of the preliminary rounds of the Prudential Cup were as follows:

GROUP A					GROUP B			
	P	W	L	Pts		P	W	L	Pts
England	3	3	0	12	West Indies	3	3	0	12
New Zealand	3	2	1	8	Australia	3	2	1	8
India	3	1	2	4	Pakistan	3	1	2	4
East Africa	3	0	3	0	Sri Lanka	3	0	3	0

FIRST SEMI-FINAL: AUSTRALIA vs ENGLAND
HEADINGLEY: AUSTRALIA WON BY 4 WICKETS

This abrupt 65-over game of cricket will forever be known as 'Gilmour's Match'. The young Newcastle all-rounder, coming into the Australian side for the first time in the tournament, fully exploited conditions which were favourable to his bowling style. Almost single-handedly Gilmour dashed the hope of the home supporters that England would win the Prudential Cup. It was a sad day for Yorkshire and England, especially as their exit came courtesy of the dreaded warriors in baggy green caps.

Headingley, or more particularly their ground staff, had a habit of turning out some rather strange wickets for major matches in the 1970s and this one was up there with the weirdest of them. In 1972, the previously little known disease fuserium became an identity overnight when it shaved … I mean, destroyed … all the grass on the pitch for the deciding Test against Australia. In a happy coincidence, at the same time England recalled Derek Underwood, a bowler perfectly suited to the grassless and bounceless, turning pitch.

There was no sign of fuserium or Underwood this day. The wicket, the same one used for the Australia vs Pakistan match 10 days earlier, was emerald green. It looked badly underprepared, as if the ground staff had only found out the day before that they had to make a pitch at all and had to quickly water, roll and cut an old one. Underwood was left out and England's attack included John Snow, Geoff Arnold, Peter Lever and Chris Old—the types of bowlers who relish such conditions. As if to order, the early-morning sunshine disappeared and a cool wind sprung up, sending low grey scudding clouds over Headingley. The ground filled to capacity—this time there were few Pakistanis or West Indians—and the home side could be assured of crowd support. A couple of things then put a glitch in the plans of the locals. Australia recognised a green top wicket as a green top, too, and omitted spinner Ashley Mallett for left-arm swing bowler Gary Gilmour. In addition Ian Chappell won the toss and asked England to bat in those typically northern English conditions.

Gilmour shared the new ball with Dennis Lillee ahead of Jeff Thomson and Max Walker. The 23-year-old had never expected such a quick promotion, but Chappell's reading of the situation was perfect. Gilmour immediately began darting the ball very late in to the right-handers. Lillee got bounce and cut, repeatedly passing the edge. Gilmour kept a fuller length and with the first ball of his second over he pinned the hapless Dennis Amiss to his stumps. The crack of a cover drive to the boundary by Barry Wood gave the crowd their first chance for a big cheer, only for them to be quietened again when another full-length Gilmour delivery cannoned off the opener's pads onto his stumps to make the score 2-11.

Tony Greig, who had a miserable tournament with the bat, tried to counterattack. Gilmour responded with one that went the other way. Greig drove, edged and Marsh, diving horizontally at full length past Ian Chappell, provided photographer Patrick Eagar with one of the game's best-known action shots.

Frank Hayes, hitting one sweet on drive, and Keith Fletcher, hanging on for grim death, took the total to 33 before Gilmour, obviously bowling his 12-over spell in one hit, utterly broke the back of the England innings. Hayes, Fletcher and Alan Knott were all trapped lbw by balls straightening down the line. The crowd groaned, but each batsman gave umpire David Constant an easy decision by falling across the crease. Knott said the static sightscreen at the grandstand end gave the batsman a poor view of a left-arm, over-the-wicket bowler. Gilmour just gave a contented smile. The bank clerk had 6-14.

Chris Old edged Max Walker to Greg Chappell to make it 7-37. A sub-50 total looked a possibility, but Gilmour's spell was soon finished and the maligned English captain, Mike Denness, was trying to make a fight of it. He lost John Snow caught behind down the leg-side on the stroke of lunch, but managed to take the total to 73 before an exaggerated Walker inswinger bowled him. Each run was precious and Geoff Arnold's method of hanging out a vertical bat proved as effective as any of the more accepted techniques. A couple of edged fours frustrated the Australians until Walker found favour from Bill Alley against Peter Lever. England all out 93. England stunned.

But just as Gilmour, Walker and Lillee revelled in the strange Headingley surface, so, too, would Snow, Old and Arnold. Alley and Constant were soon called on to adjudicate again on balls seaming late and thumping into pads. In the eighth over, with Australia's score on 17, Geoff Arnold received an affirmative answer against Turner. On 24, Snow, after no-balling and running on the pitch problems, got it right against Ian Chappell. Eight runs later he repeated the dose to Greg.

If 3-32 gave the Yorkshire faithful some cheer, the start of local boy Chris Old's spell then sent them into ecstasy. Old required no umpire's assistance as he smashed the stumps of Rick McCosker, Ross Edwards and Rod Marsh in eight balls. The three dismissals, particularly the sight of Edward's middle stump flying, induced a sort of stolid Yorkshire-style hysteria. Despite the odds, England now looked likely winners.

Doug Walters remained, phlegmatic, gum chewing, joking. Out to join him came the Newcastle bank clerk. Like Walters, Gilmour wore a long-sleeved jumper to keep out the chilly wind, yet he immediately warmed to his task. He felt he had nothing to lose. His day had already been quite a good one.

"I always assumed if I went out and hit the ball, nothing could go wrong," he later commented. So when the ball was overpitched or off line he swung hard. England had taken their six wickets without the involvement of a fieldsman. When the ball started flying, their slips could not catch it. Gilmour struck five boundaries. Walters hit a terrific straight drive to the Kirkstall Lane end and struck a perfect square cut off Arnold. The pressure eased. A scampered leg bye from the fourth ball of the 29th over took the seventh wicket stand to 55, and this exciting sudden-death semi-final was over. Australia, criticised from pillar to post throughout the tournament, were relieved to be through. They may not have shown too much knowledge about one-day cricket, except for one fairly important thing: under Ian Chappell they knew how to win.

England was devastated by its inability to again make runs against Australian pacemen. Their selectors were within a couple of weeks of making wholesale changes to the make-up of the national team. The post-mortems included plenty of criticism of the pitch. Denness did not like the uneven bounce. Jim Laker wrote, "I don't like condemning wickets … but …" George Cawthray, the head groundsman, defended his creation suggesting the atmosphere was responsible for the way the seam and swing bowlers dominated. Other Englishmen bemoaned their bad luck with the toss.

ENGLAND		AUSTRALIA	
D. L. Amiss lbw b Gilmour	2	A. Turner lbw Arnold	7
B. Wood b Gilmour	6	R. B. McCosker b Old	15
K. W. R. Fletcher lbw b Gilmour	8	I. M. Chappell (capt) lbw Snow	2
A. W. Greig c Marsh b Gilmour	7	G. S. Chappell lbw b Snow	4
F. E. Hayes lbw Gilmour	4	K. D. Walters not out	20
M. H. Denness (capt) b Walker	27	R. Edwards b Old	0
A. P. E. Knott (wk) lbw b Gilmour	0	R. W. Marsh (wk) b Old	5
C. M. Old c G. S. Chappell b Walker	0	G. J. Gilmour not out	28
J. A. Snow c Marsh b Lillee	2	Extras (b 1, lb 6, nb 6)	13
G. G. Arnold not out	18	(28.4 overs)	6-94
P. Lever lbw Walker	5	Did not bat: M. H. N. Walker, D. K. Lillee, J. R. Thomson	
Extras (lb 5, w 7, nb 2)	14	1/17 2/24 3/32 4/32 5/32 6/39	
(36.2 overs)	93	Bowling: Arnold 7.4-2-15-1; Snow 12-0-30-2; Old 7-2-29-3;	
1/2 2/11 3/26 4/33 5/35 6/36 7/37 8/52 9/73 10/93		Lever 2-0-7-0	
Bowling: Lillee 9-3-26-1; Gilmour 12-6-14-6; Walker 9.2-3-22-3; Thomson 6-0-17-0			

Umpires: W.E. Alley, D.J. Constant.
Toss: Australia

SECOND SEMI-FINAL: NEW ZEALAND vs WEST INDIES
THE OVAL: WEST INDIES WON BY 5 WICKETS

Not unnaturally, there was less attention paid to the semi-final in the south of the country than the one holding the nation riveted at Leeds. Yet a goodly 12,000 turned up at The Oval to witness the West Indies continue their inexorable progress into the final at Lord's. This game failed to go the full distance either, but it lasted more than 90 overs and had a pace to it more akin to what is usual at a cricket match. New Zealand just about did the sum of their talents justice against Clive Lloyd's powerful unit without totally convincing anyone that they deserved to be there ahead of Pakistan.

Lloyd won the toss and asked the Kiwis, who were without Richard Hadlee, to bat. This was a decision of habit rather than one based on the conditions. The south of England was bathed in sunshine and the pitch at The Oval was flat and hard. Bernard Julien struck quickly, trapping John Morrison lbw with an inswinger that straightened down the line. At the same time further up the M1 Gary Gilmour was making that type of dismissal a habit and the day his own. Julien, too, would end with excellent figures, but nothing as spectacular as the Australian's.

Certainly there was no sign of a collapse at this stage. Andy Roberts started with a fiery spell, but Glenn Turner and Geoff Howarth, who was enjoying the familiar surroundings of his county home, consolidated. They took the total to 1-92 at the lunch break off 29 overs, an excellent platform from which to build a total to really challenge the West Indies. But while they had withstood the Roberts barrage once, they failed to do so a second time. A brilliant diving slips catch by Rohan Kanhai removed Turner and the dismissal of the New Zealand captain once more precipitated disaster. Howarth just made it to his half century before becoming Roberts' second victim. Then Julien ripped through the middle order. With the exception of Brian Hastings, the Kiwi resistance crumbled. Only 66 runs were added after lunch in 23 overs while nine wickets fell to a succession of fairly soft strokes. Julien and Vanburn Holder had the figures, but Roberts had done the psychological damage.

The West Indies was 159 runs away from a place in the final. They, too, lost their first wicket with eight runs on the board, Roy Fredericks holing out at square leg off Dayle Hadlee. Gordon Greenidge was in his best form of the tournament, however, and Alvin Kallicharran was again irrepressible. The pair had to overcome an accurate spell by Richard Collinge. Once he was seen off the shots started flowing.

Greenidge was relieved to be back to something approaching his best form, while Kallicharran batted as beautifully as he had against Australia without resorting to quite the same artistic savagery even when Dayle Hadlee, against all logic, tried him out with a few short deliveries. They were promptly dealt with. Greenidge and Kallicharran added 125 for the second wicket, taking their side to within 26 runs of victory. The never-say-die spirit of New Zealand had kept them in the tournament and even though their fate was now sealed they were not quite finished. Big Collinge came back, banging the ball hard into and, more than once, through the top of the wicket.

He got his large frame down low to hold a checked drive from Kallicharran, forced Greenidge into a hook from a ball too far up to him, and got the last lbw of the tournament when Viv Richards, like so many others that day, misjudged an inswinger from a left-arm paceman. When young Brian McKechnie had Clive Lloyd caught at square leg they had lost four wickets while advancing just 18 runs. Given another 40 to chase there might have been some drama, but Rohan Kanhai and Julien only needed to put together a stand of eight runs, which they duly did with 20 overs still to spare. The New Zealanders, with a couple of exceptions, packed their bags and headed for home with their heads held high. The West Indies prepared for a Lord's final they believed had been their destiny since the day the sun shone on the welcoming Duke of Edinburgh's shining silver pate.

NEW ZEALAND		WEST INDIES	
G. M. Turner (capt) c Kanhai b Roberts	36	R. C. Fredericks c Hastings b Hadlee	6
J. F. M. Morrison lbw b Julien	5	C.G. Greenidge lbw b Collinge	55
G. P. Howarth c Murray b Roberts	51	A. I. Kallicharran c & b Collinge	72
J. M. Parker b Lloyd	3	I. V. A. Richards lbw b Collinge	5
B. F. Hastings not out	24	R. B. Kanhai not out	12
K. J. Wadsworth (wk) c Lloyd b Julien	11	C. H. Lloyd (capt) c Hastings b McKechnie	3
B. J. McKechnie lbw b Julien	1	B. D. Julien not out	4
D. R. Hadlee c Holder b Julien	0	Extras (lb 1, nb 1)	2
B. L. Cairns b Holder	10	(40.1 overs)	5-159
H. J. Howarth b Holder	0	Did not bat D. L. Murray (wk), K. D. Boyce, V. A. Holder,	
R. O. Collinge b Holder	2	A. M. E. Roberts	
Extras (b 1, lb 5, w 2, nb 7)	15	1/82/133 3/139 4/142 5/151	
(52.2 overs)	158	Bowling; Collinge 12-4-28-3; D. R. Hadlee 10-0-54-1;	
1/8 2/98 3/105 4/106 5/125 6/133 7/139 8/155 9/155		Cairns 6.1-2-23-0; McKechnie 8-0-37-1; H. J.	
10/158		Howarth 4-0-15-0	
Bowling; Julien 12-5-21-4; Roberts 11-3-18-2; Holder			
8.2-0-30-3; Boyce 9-0-31-0; Lloyd 12-1-37-1			

Umpires: W.L. Budd, A.E. Fagg.

Toss: West Indies

SATURDAY 21 JUNE 1975
THE PRUDENTIAL CUP FINAL
AUSTRALIA vs WEST INDIES
LORD'S: WEST INDIES WON BY 17 RUNS

The lead up to the greatest cricketing show on earth was everything the promoters would have wished. NW8 buzzed with excitement as ticket touts, newsmen, photographers, officials and, somewhere in there, players practising, were caught up in the thrills and tension of a true cup final. There was even a little bit of controversy to add some extra spice. Derrick Robbins, a wealthy promoter of private tours to South Africa, called the Prudential Cup "rubbish" and a "travesty". He claimed to have first proposed a world cup of first-class matches more along the lines of the 1912 fiasco. He was especially upset at what happened in the game at Headingley: "If that match had gone over two innings, we would have had a true result." Robbins was speaking from Cape Town, but he was an Englishman.

All that was quickly forgotten when Saturday 21 June dawned with the bluest skies and an unending sun that demanded cricket. Satellites were not numerous or sophisticated enough to make the World Cup final the significant global television event it later became. Fans in the Caribbean had to be content with radio coverage. In Australia the Australian Broadcasting Commission made a special satellite booking allowing them to televise the majority of the match live and in colour into every household. In 1975, that was an occasion as historic as the game itself. Those who settled for the evening in front of their television or radio knew they would be in for a long night. One hundred and twenty overs of cricket looked likely to extend well into the early morning in Australia, especially when the team selections revealed both sides were packed with pacemen. There was not a short run-up, nor a spinner, in sight.

Lord's was filled to its 27,000 capacity as Gordon Greenidge and Roy Fredericks made their way out behind Ian Chappell's Australians as the clock approached 11am. Chappell had won the toss and asked the West Indies to bat. Chasing a target seemed to be becoming the favoured option of the toss-winning captain. Clive Lloyd also tended to follow that practice, although he stated he was a little surprised by his counterpart's decision because the conditions seemed so favourable to batsmen.

The West Indies, as crowd and bookmakers' favourites, were perhaps under a little more pressure than the Australians.

Even by this stage of the tournament Doug Walters felt the Aussies had a fairly relaxed attitude, admitting "we did not have any team meetings or make any special plans for the final".

"Ian Chappell won the toss, sent the West Indies in and hoped Lillee, Thomson, Gilmour and Walker would blast them out for 120," he says. "Failing that, I suppose he wanted to know the target we would have to chase."

Walters was on his third tour of England. For Rick McCosker on his first trip, everything was new and exciting. "It was all a fairy story to me," McCosker says. "I was just chuffed to be there. There was a special atmosphere brought about by this huge din that lasted all day. It was like a carnival."

In contrast to the Australians, Clive Lloyd said everyone in his side was quite tense. Greenidge admits to being so nervous and excited, his entry onto the ground is now a bit of a blur, but he and Fredericks didn't have much trouble getting the score to 12. The wicket was true and there was no perceptible movement off the seam or in the air.

Then Lillee, bowling from the Nursery End, sent down a bouncer to the left-handed Fredericks. An instinctive hooker, he struck it sweetly and fine, rocketing the ball over the fine-leg boundary. The West Indian supporters broke into a spontaneous roar. Fredericks, though, started to walk towards the pavilion. Lillee's bouncer had just angled back into him, causing Fredericks to have to lean back further and then overbalance slightly on the pivot with the shot. That, his decision to wear rubber-soled shoes, and the English habit of leaving the grass uncut and unrolled within the batting creases threw his feet' from under him and onto the.stumps. It was an astonishing, genuine and classic case of six and out and it occurred on the game's greatest and newest stage.

Kallicharran announced his arrival by starting off where he finished at The Oval. A glorious cover drive off Gilmour was followed by a pull to the grandstand. But Greenidge, perhaps becoming even more overcome by the occasion, had stalled. The team's momentum went with him and Kallicharran, perhaps for just a moment, was distracted. He tried an off-balance cut against Gilmour and only succeeded in edging the ball to Rod Marsh. In the 10th over the West Indies were 2–27.

Rohan Kanhai, having seen it all, looked in command of his emotions. Lloyd has stated how important his experience was in controlling the situation within the team. He got off the mark with a boundary, too; a classic cover drive on the up off Thomson, who had relieved Lillee. He also hit another fine cover shot off Walker before the big medium pacer quietened him with balls that jumped and struck the splice of his bat. The total was taken to 50 in the 18th over, but it had progressed no further when Greenidge edged a low catch behind off Thomson. The opener, still in his funny blue towelling hat, was disappointed, but he consoled himself with the fact that the sting had been taken out of the new ball for the strokeplayers to follow.

Whatever Greenidge's thoughts, the West Indian innings at 3-50 was in the balance. Ian Chappell recognised this and immediately brought back Lillee into the attack. Lloyd responded with a clip off his toes to the square-leg boundary in front of the Tavern Stand. Lillee challenged with a bouncer and Lloyd hooked him for a perfect six in the same direction. Another pull/hook was mistimed, but Ross Edwards failed to hold the low chance at mid wicket; a crucial miss. The West Indies went to lunch at 3-91 off 28 overs.

Kanhai remained scoreless for 11 overs either side of the interval. Lloyd, however, kept the runs coming single-handedly. A fine leg glance to the pavilion off Thomson brought up the 100 and the 50-run partnership in 49 minutes, Kanhai having contributed just six of those. Ten minutes later the West Indian captain lofted Walker down the ground to record his own half century in under an hour with seven fours and that one six.

Big 'Tangles' Walker's tidy first seven-over spell became a distant memory as Lloyd took it upon himself to lift the run rate. There were more dropped catches, another to Edwards at deep point off Greg Chappell and one to Lillee at fine leg off the now despairing Walker. Both times Kanhai was the beneficiary. Lloyd needed no further assistance. He smacked Walker, now bowling around the wicket, off the front foot over square leg into the waving, cheering throng in the grandstand for his second six. That brought up the 100 partnership in 85 minutes and was followed by two slashing square cuts and a lofted cover drive all to the boundary off the same bowler. Walker, thought of as someone suited to English conditions, conceded 71 runs from his allotted 12 overs, including 49 from his last five.

No bowler was immune. Gilmour was lifted to mid wicket for another four to take Lloyd to 99. A stunning square drive, just for a single to the now protected point boundary, raised the most amazing century in 100 fantastically entertaining minutes off just 82 balls with two sixes and 12 fours.

"I guess you would call my fielding position off side sweeper now," Rick McCosker says. "I remember Lloyd hitting that ball straight to me. I was right on the boundary and it was struck with such power I am certain that a yard either side of me I wouldn't have been able to cut it off. I thought, 'How hard did he hit that?' He had so much power."

Television commentator, Jim Laker, normally very restrained, was in uncontained rapture at Lloyd's superb exhibition. Of course, he was still slightly more subdued than the spontaneous Caribbean festival that was erupting among the West Indian fans. Even the Australian team acknowledged Lloyd's mastery. "At the time Ross Edwards missed that catch, we weren't too pleased," Doug Walters says. "At this distance I don't mind so much, though. Lloyd's innings still holds up as one of the best ever seen in one-day cricket. He certainly played magnificently."

English batting legend Denis Compton compared Lloyd's innings to Australian Stan McCabe's startling 232 in the Trent Bridge Test of 1938. Tony Lewis wrote of an innings of "surpassing talent and power". John Arlott's tribute spoke of "relaxed majesty" and Lloyd's ability to strike the ball "mightily and as he willed". Soon after the cacophony of cans and bugles died down Kanhai got them going again when he drove Walters wristily to the point boundary to complete his own invaluable fifty. Then, after 36 overs and a 149-run stand with Kanhai, Lloyd's magnum opus was over. Unfortunately its ending was a bit anti-climactic. A leg-side flick off Gilmour, a low take by Marsh, an appeal, the umpires consulted and 'Dickie' Bird raised his finger. Lloyd was unsure, but he proudly ambled away to a thunderous standing ovation befitting the performance.

Suddenly, Gilmour was on song from the Nursery End. He bowled Kanhai through the gate and repeated the dose to young Viv Richards. At 6-209 in the 46th over the West Indies were in danger of not seeing out their overs. It was Keith Boyce who regained the initiative. He took a liking to Thomson's bowling and hit up a quickfire 34 before mistiming a full toss off the same bowler. With Bernard Julien holding firm, Boyce and then Deryck Murray struck out with freedom. The wicketkeeper pulled Lillee over square leg for another six before a leading edge made him Gilmour's fifth victim.

Vanburn Holder's cue-end swipe and an overthrow from the final ball of the innings left the Australians a massive 8-291 to chase. At 4pm, Gilmour, rightly content again with his efforts, led the side from the field. He was followed by 10 furrowed brows all of which registered the enormity of the task in front of them.

The Australians required 4.86 runs per over for the duration of their innings if they were to reach their target. Rick McCosker and Alan Turner opened with a stand of 25 before Boyce ran a leg-cutter up the slope to have McCosker caught at second slip for seven.

Ian Chappell immediately settled in with typical fidgety determination and found that Turner had warmed to his task. The Australian captain could hardly hope to emulate his West Indian counterpart, but still unleashed some fine shots. A pull off Julien was followed by a cracking cover drive. Chappell lofted Boyce over mid-on for another four and Turner hooked Holder down to the Tavern boundary.

At 1-81 from 20 overs Australia had built the foundation they needed. Seeing his fast medium bowlers punished, Lloyd brought himself into the attack. Chappell played his first ball quietly to the on side and called Turner for a single. The left-hander hesitated a moment, then took off. Viv Richards raced in and in one movement picked up the ball and with an underarm flick scored a direct hit on the stumps. It was close, but 'Dickie' Bird gave Turner out.

That signalled the start of the most bizarre period of the match. Clive Lloyd said his side noticed quite early that the Australians had some suicidal running tendencies. After Turner's demise the Chappell brothers added 26 runs in four overs up to tea, Greg Chappell hitting a terrific on drive and a pull for four. The break was taken at 2-107 from 25 overs. It was already 6 pm in St John's Wood and 3am in the eastern states for the bleary-eyed still watching on television in Australia.

Soon after the interval Ian Chappell glanced Andy Roberts to the pavilion rails. A couple of stolen singles took the partnership to 34. When Ian Chappell pushed a Roberts delivery to point there was a momentary misfield, a change in the call, then a brilliant recovery by Richards who this time picked up, swivelled and threw down the stumps from side on. Greg Chappell just kept running towards the pavilion.

An Ian Chappell straight drive for three off Roberts brought up the Australian captain's 50 in 100 minutes with four fours. Now, though, he was playing second fiddle to Walters who was in prime form. Pulls and cuts brought boundaries off Holder. One deflected off umpire Tom Spencer's leg. Such was its force it left him with a bleeding cut for the rest of the game.

Again Australia fought back to level terms, only to muck up between wickets. After 38 overs it was 3-162 when Lloyd began his 10th over. Ian Chappell pushed to mid wicket. There was hesitation. The fieldsman, inevitably, was Richards. Chappell went through but the throw to Lloyd found him a metre short. The cans and bugles rang out.

"A lot has been made of our running between wickets," Doug Walters says. "But the need to chase such a big total meant we had to chance short singles. Then run outs are always on. Especially when someone like Viv Richards is in such good form with their throwing arm."

"It wasn't just the number of run outs," Rick McCosker says. "It was who they were and when they occurred. Richards ran out three key players. I believe it made the difference in the end. It's funny, probably the two best outfieldsmen on the ground were Richards and Ross Edwards. Roscoe had a bad day, Richards was brilliant. If the game had been played again the situation could just as easily have been reversed."

From that point the Australian innings started to subside. After another beautiful cover drive Walters took one chance too many off Lloyd: "I was happy with the way I batted. All the time, though, the match seemed to be slipping away. I tried to hit a straight one to the on side and missed."

Ross Edwards, Rod Marsh, Gary Gilmour and Max Walker hit out as effectively as they could, but succumbed to Keith Boyce and the pressure of the required run rate.

When Walker became the fourth batsman to be run out in the innings, another direct-hit victim looking for a run to square leg that wasn't there, Australia were 9-233. The crowd was already charging onto the ground at every opportunity. They had danced all over the place when Marsh was clean bowled, and Rohan Kanhai was swamped when he caught Gary Gilmour at deep square leg just in front of the grandstand. Now it seemed half the 27,000 were lined up at the boundary rope anticipating the end.

The last wicket pair of Dennis Lillee and Jeff Thomson required 59 runs from just 43 balls, supposedly an impossible task. Just as impossible as the one Murray and Roberts tackled at Edgbaston. Thomson straight drove the first ball of Roberts' ninth over for four, then clipped him off his toes to square leg for another. Lillee lofted Holder over mid-on for still another boundary and the field spread to all corners. A sharp single to square leg gave Richards the opportunity for another direct-hit run out, but he missed and the resultant overthrow brought up the Australian 250.

Every appeal by the fieldsmen led to another pitch invasion. When Thomson was caught at cover by Fredericks off a no ball there was absolute mayhem. Fredericks threw at the stumps for a run out, missed and there was no sign of anyone backing up. Nobody could find the ball. Jim Laker suggested the Australians could have run 10! When the crowd was finally persuaded to leave the arena and the ball was returned, Thomson was given three runs. Lloyd, who had not heard Tom Spencer's no ball call, had to ask what was going on.

Even the neutral English spectators found it hard to bear the tension. With the field spread and the ground now mostly in evening shadow, the requirement was getting steeper. Eighteen were needed off nine balls when Thomson swung and missed at Holder. He just sort of wandered out of his crease looking for the ball and the chance of a run at the same time. When he saw that Murray had it in his gloves he dived back for his crease. Too late. Murray scored yet another direct hit. Thomson was the fifth run out victim and the Prudential Cup had a winner at 8.43pm on the longest day of the year.

No-one dwelt on that thought. Despite their obvious exhaustion, players and umpires sprinted for safety, Murray risking self-impalement with a clutch of stumps as he ran. An area in front of the pavilion was secured by rope and police enforcement. The Duke of Edinburgh stepped forward. Clive Lloyd was called up to the podium. He received both the Man of the Match award and the World Cup. The latter trophy was held aloft. The West Indian captain admits to this being his greatest moment in cricket.

"We were disappointed at having got so close and not quite making it," McCosker says. "But there was also the feeling that we had competed well and we were proud to be there on such a fantastic day in front of such a fantastic crowd. We were also absolutely exhausted. We had got there early in the morning and by the time we left the ground after having showers and a few drinks it was midnight. 'The two teams stayed together and had a few beers. It was a nice moment, with both sides feeling they had been part of a special event."

WEST INDIES		AUSTRALIA	
R. C. Fredericks hit wicket b Lillee	7	R. B. McCosker c Kallicharran b Boyce	7
C. G. Greenidge c Marsh b Thomson	13	A. Turner run out	40
A. I. Kallicharran c Marsh b Gilmour	12	I. M. Chappell (capt) run out	62
R. B. Kanhai b Gilmour	55	G. S. Chappell run out	15
C. H. Lloyd (capt) c Marsh b Gilmour	102	K. D. Walters b Lloyd	35
I. V. A. Richards b Gilmour	5	R. W. Marsh (wk) b Boyce	11
K. D. Boyce c G. S. Chappell b Thomson	34	R. Edwards c Fredericks b Boyce	28
B. D. Julien not out	26	G. J. Gilmour c Kanhai b Boyce	14
D. L. Murray (wk) c & b Gilmour	14	M. H. N. Walker run out	7
V. A. Holder not out	6	J. R. Thomson run out	21
Extras (lb 6, nb 11)	17	D. K. Lillee not out	16
(60 overs)	8-291	Extras (b 2, lb 9, nb 7)	18
Did not bat: A. M. E. Roberts		(58.4 overs)	274

1/12 2/27 3/50 4/199 5/206 6/209 7/261 8/285

Bowling: Lillee 12-1-55-1; Gilmour 12-2-48-5; Thomson 12-1-44-2; Walker 12-1-71-0; G. S. Chappell 7-0-33-0; Walters 5-0-23-0;

1/25 2/81 3/115 4/162 5/170 6/195 7/221 8/231 9/233 10/274

Bowling: Julien 12-0-58-0; Roberts 11-1-45-0; Boyce 12-0-50-4; Holder 11.4-1-65-0; Lloyd 12-1-38-1

Umpires: H.D. Bird, T.W. Spencer.

Toss: Australia

POST-MORTEM

The cricketing world was unanimous in its approval of the 1975 World Cup final. Jack Fingleton, a hard-bitten Australian cricketer journalist who had played in the Bodyline series, called it "a game never to be forgotten, in line with the Brisbane tied Test against the West Indies".

"The entertainment was prodigious," said John Arlott. Nobody could disagree.

Australia had less time to wait than even Clive Lloyd to forget the World Cup. The next Wednesday they began preparation for the main objective of their tour, with a match against Kent at Canterbury. They went on to win the four-Test series against England 1-0, thus retaining the Ashes. That was also a well-attended series, further boosting the coffers of the TCCB during an almost ideal summer. Once all the sums had been done the Prudential World Cup registered a surplus of £244,784. Takings from the Lord's final itself were £117,000. A tidy profit for what was considered a risky venture. A subcommittee set up by the International Cricket Conference decided the future of the World Cup. That was easy, too. Everyone would be back in four years, although there was consideration given to lifting the number of contestants to 10.

CHAPTER 3:

The Second Prudential World Cup, 1979: Richards Lightens The Gloom

The cricket world of the Prudential World Cup in 1979 was a very different place to the one it had been in 1975. Some would say the sport had finally started to grow up. Others might suggest it had lost some of its essential charm and aspects that were unique and valuable. Both arguments are correct in their own right. Certainly after the events of 1977 cricket would never be the same again.

I refer, of course, to the setting up of World Series Cricket by Australian media magnate Kerry Packer. In a bid to take control of televised cricket in Australia, Packer signed the best players in the world for sums of money far in excess of anything the game's established authorities believed they could afford to give them.

The problems associated with the meagre financial rewards of the leading cricketers in the world could be no better exemplified than by the events that immediately followed the 1975 World Cup. The whole tournament was an unqualified success with 160,000 spectators filing through the turnstiles to witness the 15 cricket matches. This included the full house at the Lord's Final, all 27,000 of whom were right royally entertained by the 22 protagonists on the day.

Yet the fantastic efforts of the winning side over the concentrated and enervating two weeks were rewarded with a mere £350 pounds per man, plus the splitting of the £4000 prize money and the honour and glory. The captain for one was not impressed at the non-recognition from the admittedly always cash-strapped West Indian Board. Lloyd was then at least partly satisfied when the Guyanese Government organised a motorcade through Georgetown and presented each team member with a commemorative gold chain.

When Packer came along with his chequebook, the West Indians signed almost en masse. So, too, did most of the Australians who had also started to wonder at their recompensation in relation to the massive crowds they attracted to cricket grounds and the enormous television audiences that followed them. Packer was not buying into a game that was in its death throes, even though his media empire has perpetuated that myth over the years. He was mainly concerned with the lucrative television rights. When he secured those, he was prepared to hand back the control of international cricket and cricketers to the original authorities. So poorly paid were the players, though, that it is now obvious that if Packer had not stepped another entrepreneur soon would have. They were ripe for the picking.

The 'Cricket War' as it has been called split the game's fraternity, ruptured many friendships and created a lot of ill will. In the cut throat competitive business world of 1999 it all seems small potatoes in comparison to the wheeling and dealing that goes on now. A modern cut throat economic rationalist would wonder how the game ever ran as it did before 1977.

The truce was called in May 1979, only a couple of weeks before the second Prudential World Cup. It came as no surprise. ICC officials had spoken with Packer early in 1979 and the big man had gone to "have lunch" with the Australian authorities during the poorly attended Australia vs Pakistan Test at the MCG in March.

The second World Cup, like the first one, was to be fought out in England over the period of a fortnight in early to mid June. Some suggested the West Indies, as the holders of the trophy should have been the hosts the second time around. But even Clive Lloyd felt that the geography and climate of the Caribbean might make the effective running of the tournament difficult. The Indian authorities quickly revealed their interest in taking a turn at being hosts, but had to wait a little longer.

A similar format and time frame to that used in 1975 was agreed upon. The tournament would again constitute a schedule of 15 matches, contested between eight teams over two weeks in June. In the first round, matches each side in two groups of four would play against each other. The top two teams in each group would then contest the semi-finals followed by a final at Lord's three days later between the semi-final winners. Prudential Assurance as major sponsor again, kicked in £250,000. Six of the eight teams were the current Test playing nations. South Africa, even more isolated than in 1975, were not considered.

Sri Lanka, as they did in 1975, and Canada, made up the numbers. They earned their spot by being finalists in the International Cricket Conference Trophy. That tournament, played on grounds in the English Midlands, preceded the World Cup by only a couple of weeks. It was purpose initiated by the ICC to fill those World Cup places and to encourage associate member countries to strive for recognition against the major cricketing nations. Despite their loss to Israel in a walkover, Sri Lanka's victory in the ICC final surprised no-one. They were getting very close to full Test status and followed their 1979 World Cup campaign with a nine-match, first-class tour of England. The promotion of Canada, on the other hand, was quite a shock.

Innings would be 60 overs. Bowlers were permitted a maximum of 12 overs. Any bouncer that flew above the batsman's head was to be called a no ball. The weather, so kind four years previous was still not to be trusted. Each game had two reserve days attached to it. In 1975, not one reserve day was used. This time it was to be quite a different story.

The ICC at their 1978 meeting, offered no guidance to individual countries as to what their selection policy should be regarding players contracted to World Series Cricket. The game's authorities had lost out badly when taken to court by some Packer players in 1977 for restraint of trade. They had no desire to return there again. Any real chance of embarrassment in the matter receded further when Packer and the Australian authorities signed their truce. It meant that every side, with the exception of the Australians, would virtually be at full strength for the tournament.

The West Indies were red-hot favourites to retain the title. Since their great victory in 1975, they had built a side with awesome fast bowling firepower. In support of the still very formidable Andy Roberts were Michael Holding, Joel Garner and Colin Croft. All four were fast bowlers of the most intimidating type, capable of devastating pace. Batsmen had their composure challenged on a number of levels, not least being that each paceman had such a long run-up matches might not be finished until the dulled light of late evening. To compensate with this new found threat of four express fast bowlers in the one side, batsman had just recently started to wear helmets regularly.

The West Indian batting, too, had matured into something to be envied. Left-handed opener Roy Fredericks had retired, but into his place had stepped the aggressive young Barbadian, Desmond Haynes. Clive Lloyd had lost none of his powers either as batsman or astute captain and motivator. Most imposing of all when assessing the West Indies' prospects was that their line-up now contained clearly the best batsman in the world. Four years on, Viv Richards had emerged as the most entertaining, powerful and aggressive strokeplayer imaginable. He had stamped his presence on the previous tournament with his fielding in the Final. This time he would be able to let his bat do the talking.

The West Indies of 1979 were arguably as good as any side that has ever played the game. In 1984, with the addition of the superb Malcolm Marshall to the starting 11, they were pretty special, too, but hardly more so than this squad for the second World Cup. The young Marshall was in the party, but could not break into the final line-up. The likes of Wayne Daniel and Sylvester Clarke did not even get that far. The captain initially was concerned as to how his three non-WSC members would blend in with the bulk of the side. He need not have worried.

The West Indies' worthy opponents in the 1975 final could boast no such equal development. Despite the settlement with Packer, the Australian authorities were obliged to stay with the players who had remained faithful to their cause between 1977 and 1979. That meant they were captained by the inexperienced 25-year-old Western Australian, Kim Hughes. Hughes had only recently secured the job when he replaced the injured Graham Yallop for the second Test of the brief series against Pakistan. He led what amounted to a 'B' side, considered 20-1 outsiders to win the tournament. It was a team that was supposed to have loads of potential. Most of that was never realised and many had only a couple of weeks left as Australian players. Some of the names from that World Cup squad and the follow up tour of India do make for excellent quiz questions for cricket trivia buffs. Is all-rounder Graeme Porter the most obscure cricketer to wear a baggy green cap this side of the Second World War? Maybe so, but he did top the bowling averages for the whole tournament.

Not all of the side were without a future. Fast bowler Rodney Hogg, who had taken a record-breaking 41 wickets in the recent Ashes series did have his moments of success in the early 1980s. He arrived in England with an anti-hero fanfare to rival Jeff Thomson from the previous World Cup. Hogg bowled very fast and very straight and had fair hair like Thomson. But it was curly and he also had a great tendancy to fall over in his follow through which never was a concern for 'Thommo'.

Kim Hughes batted brilliantly at times and captained Australia off and on between 1979 and 1984, without ever totally convincing everyone of his suitability for the role. Eventually he resigned in tears in Brisbane after a bitter defeat by the West Indies. And a lower-profiled left-handed batsman named Allan Border was emerging from the second-string pack on way to a reasonably respectable career of 156 Tests and 11,000 runs. This was the first of seven eventual trips to England for Border wearing Australian colours.

The names left out of the Australian line-up were far more impressive than those in it. Greg and Ian Chappell, Dennis Lillee and Jeff Thomson, and Rod Marsh would have to wait until the next southern summer to reclaim their rightful places at the forefront of Australian cricket.

England under Mike Brearley looked a much stronger contender this time around. They had demolished Australia 5-1 in the Test series in Australia, having lost just a handful of players to World Series Cricket. They had been defeated 2-1 in a three-match one-day series 'down under', though. This time they were drawn in the same group as their traditional rivals and were scheduled to meet them on the opening day of the tournament at Lord's in a sell-out match. But in all reality it was Pakistan, not Australia who posed the greatest threat to English progress in Group B.

England have probably never had a better side since than the one which represented them between 9 June and 23 June, 1979. Geoff Boycott was properly rehabilitated and well man-managed by Brearley. Ian Botham had emerged as a match-winning all-rounder. He and Bob Willis gave the English pace attack a bite it has often lacked in the two decades since. David Gower and Graham Gooch added class to the middle order batting and some youthful zest. Members of the support cast such as Derek Randall, Mike Hendrick and Chris Old were also quite worthy.

Much attention surrounded the young Ian Botham. The powerful Somerset all-rounder had completed an almost unbroken sequence of fantastic feats since his debut on the international stage against Australia at Trent Bridge in 1977. He had belted centuries, smashed stumps and taken blinding catches seemingly at will over a two-year period. Some English supporters almost believed he would win them the World Cup by himself. Such was Botham's confidence he might just about have imagined it, too.

New Zealand's semi-final berth in 1975 had accelerated their growing stature as a force to be reckoned with in international cricket. In 1979 Glenn Turner had just returned to the side after a self-imposed break, but he was no longer captain. The veteran batsman, Mark Burgess assumed that role. Nor could Turner take his position as number one in the batting order for granted. The left-handed opening combination of John Wright and Bruce Edgar had recently done sterling service and they offered a far better long term bet than the older and sometimes reluctant Turner.

The most obvious sign of progress in New Zealand cricket, however, had been the growth in status and expertise of the fast bowler, Richard Hadlee. Hadlee was now a fast bowler and hard-hitting lower-order batsman of the highest calibre. It was a stunning spell by Hadlee at Wellington in February 1978 that had led to England being skittled for 64. That effort had given New Zealand cricket the filip of an historic and long-awaited first Test win against the mother country. It was a superb effort by Hadlee and there would be many more to follow.

Pakistan did a full circle by reinstating Asif Iqbal as captain just prior to the tournament. In 1975 he took over the role from Intikhab Alam. This time he replaced Mushtaq Mohammad. Pakistan, like the West Indies picked virtually all their World Series Cricket players. As such, they would again be a formidable contender.

They also had a brilliant fast bowling all-rounder as their spearhead and inspiration. Imran Khan had elevated his rating almost in unison with Hadlee and Botham. The turning point in Imran's career had been a mighty 12-wicket bowling return in a Test in Sydney early in 1977 which, like Hadlee's spell in Wellington a year later, led his side to a first even win over a previously revered opponent.

Pakistan still boasted their collection of fine batsmen like Majid Khan, Zaheer Abbas and Sadiq Mohammad. Added to that was the precocious talent of Javed Miandad, already at 22 a veteran of his second World Cup. This aggressive, cheeky, irritating fellow sought to rival Viv Richards as the best batsman in the world.

India, too, had reinstated their captain from the previous tournament. Srinivas Venkataraghavan assumed the leadership role from Sunil Gavaskar. Gavaskar by now was his side's number one batsman and most obvious choice as captain. He was in the midst of a prolific couple of years of Test century making, but there had been rumours of him flirting with the professional troupe of Kerry Packer. He had the captaincy taken away, but kept his place in the side. Wicketkeeper Syed Kirmani, who Packer had also attempted to woo, was dropped from the side altogether. He responded to the news by jumping in a taxi and asking the driver to take him anywhere at all. Wherever they drove, Kirmani did eventually come back.

Poor old Venkat had hardly inspired his team to any great degree four years before. Now his role was further compromised because his selection was based more on a political decision rather than cricketing merit. He knew that and so did his team.

Gavaskar would be the batting key to any prospective Indian success. Gundappa Vishwanath was still a fine player and Dilip Vensarkar had established his place in the middle order. But the Indian bowling resources looked thin, despite the emergence of a young all-rounder whose talent matched that of Botham, Hadlee and Imran. Unlike the other three emerging champions, the Kapil Dev of 1979 was new to English wickets and weather conditions and he would only have a few days to acclimatise for the concentrated program of limited-over Iinternationals in a side which was unlikely to be full of help and harmony.

After the World Cup, though, he would immediately have the opportunity to further that experience in a meaningful way. With the English authorities now confident of the success of the World Cup, India, rather than Australia, would compete in the follow-up four-match Test series. Australia were not needed as back-up guarantee. Nor, with their current emaciated line-up, were they an assured attraction anyway.

Sri Lanka completed their four-year cycle from one World Cup preparation to the next with another unofficial mini-Test series against the West Indies. Anura Tennekoon retained the nucleus of the talent he had four years earlier. This time they were more worldly wise in the cricketing sense. They had established themselves as the dominant team amongst the Associate countries and felt ready to compete with the best the rest of the world could offer. Besides which, Jeff Thomson would not be bowling to them.

Canada's line-up boasted names with a cricketing ring to them, such as Chappell, Marshall, Patel and Walters. But this team, largely made up of expatriate West Indians, were expected to make about the same impact as the East Africans had in 1975. That is, none. A school-teaching left-arm medium pacer, John Valentine, had bowled impressively throughout the ICC Trophy matches and the team had fought hard by scoring a losing 264 in the final against Sri Lanka. Despite the nature of the tournament, the trip was costing the Canadian players money. Kerry Packer hadn't come near them.

The weather throughout the ICC Trophy matches had been miserable, but so it had been in the lead up four years before. That was not necessarily a bad omen. Talk of worldwide petrol shortages might have been less encouraging and the split caused by World Series Cricket had hardly had time to heal. The feelings between the teams and players variously affected and variously cashed up was an unknown, potentially volatile quantity. Dennis Lillee, working as a journalist, had all sorts of trouble getting into Lord's when he tried to wish the Australians good luck before their opening day clash with England. He was three times denied entry by various officials and when he was finally received into the Australian dressing room the response of several players was distinctly chilly.

When non-WSC Australia played the WSC-enriched Pakistan side in March there was a lot of ill-temper between the teams. At least everyone was on their best behaviour at Buckingham Palace and in the Long Room at Lord's where the players enjoyed their wine, roast beef and Prince Phillip in fine form. All the teams lined up together for a massed photograph the type of which has now become almost as big a tradition as the tournament itself, but unlike 1975 there was no loosened ties. That had nothing to do with a greater acceptance of formality. It was just too overcast and chilly. But once Australia and England lined up against each other at Lord's in their traditional garb in front of a full house only one thing really mattered.

SATURDAY 9 JUNE 1979
THE PRUDENTIAL CUP: ROUND ONE
GROUP B: ENGLAND vs AUSTRALIA
LORD'S: ENGLAND WON BY 6 WICKETS

When England meet Australia at Lord's, the ground will fill to capacity. It will fill for a limited-over international or a Test match. It will fill if the weather is hot or cold. I have seen it full when soaked in glorious sunshine and I have seen it filled when most people in the crowd were just getting a thorough soaking.

This capacity gathering had to endure a continuance of the cold, drizzly and cloudy weather that seemed in a permanent holding pattern over the whole country. But despite the unbroken steel grey canopy they still created a special buzz of anticipation. It wasn't just brought about by the cheery confrontational T-shirts on the chests of the opposing supporters. England were going in to the match as red-hot favourites and that at the game's headquarters is a very rare occurrence. Whatever the strength of Kim Hughes' side they most likely would have won if this had been a Test. Australia have lost only one such an encounter there in the entire century.

With 12 of the 14 players in the English squad recent Australian tourists, some in the dressing room commented that it was like the start of the Ashes tour again. Mike Brearley won the toss and sent the Australians in to bat. He said he thought the wicket contained some moisture. The decision may also have been influenced after his county side Middlesex had been demolished for 107 by Yorkshire just three days before when they batted first in a Benson and Hedges quarter-final match.

The inexperienced Australians had their pre-tournament preparations badly interrupted by the weather. In their warm-up games they thrashed New Zealand, lost to strong County side, Kent, and had matches against Hampshire and Middlesex ruined by rain. Not surprisingly Andrew Hilditch and Rick Darling were tentative against Mike Hendrick and Bob Willis armed with the new ball. In the still gloomy conditions they scratched around for just 14 runs in the first 10 overs before settling properly to their task and lifting the total to 56 from 21 overs.

Willis then returned to trap the increasingly aggressive Darling for 25. Border, who would end up with a Test average of just on 100 at Lord's, fought tenaciously to keep his wicket intact and stayed with the more comfortable Hilditch until lunch was reached at 1-97 after 36 overs. Brearley's decision had seemingly backfired and many thought the English captain was becoming desperate when he resorted to bringing Geoff Boycott and his gentle seamers into the attack.

The controversial opening batsman from Yorkshire had had a miserable Test tour of Australia and at age 38, his selection in the World Cup squad had been no certainty. Now he looked almost ridiculous charging in still wearing his England cap at a silly angle. But lo and behold, in the first over after the interval Hilditch, still three runs short of a deserved half century, dragged a delivery into his stumps. The crowd erupted for the first time. Boycott stood mid-pitch his arms aloft. Border and Kim Hughes took the total to 111. Hughes saw an opportunity to lift the scoring. He belted Boycott towards the mid wicket boundary where Mike Hendrick ran in dived forward and held an excellent low outfield catch. After a spell of six overs, Brearley was finished with him but Boycott had served a very useful purpose.

Border and Graham Yallop lifted the score to 131, however it was still a hard graft and now the dwindling overs became something of an issue. Run outs had bedevilled the young Australians during the recent Ashes series. They had escaped unscathed until lunch even though 'Kamikaze Kid' Darling had riskily taken on David Gower's arm a couple of times. Now Yallop challenged Derek Randall at cover and lost. The Australian innings continued its downward spiral when Bob Taylor, who had a bad day and earlier missed two stumpings, finally held an edge off the left-arm spin of Phil Edmonds. Edmonds bowled a very tidy spell, but he hurt his back so badly he was assisted from the field at the end of the Australian innings.

A mix up left Gary Cosier stranded in the middle of the pitch when Taylor removed the bails. All-rounder Trevor Laughlin and Rodney Hogg were also run out victims, leaving many to wonder what it was about Australians, Prudential World Cup matches, Lord's and run outs. Hogg's dismissal made it nine such dismissals in two starts at this venue. Since lunch eight wickets had fallen for 56 and it was left to tailenders Alan Hurst and Geoff Dymock to hold on and bat out the overs. When the 60th had been completed they had only pushed the total up to a fairly inadequate 9-159. The English bowling had been tight and done its job, but the fielding and outcricket had been brilliant, which is not something English teams have often had as an advantage over Australia.

Australia looked to have blown their chances by setting a target of just 160 in 60 overs. But Rodney Hogg and Alan Hurst had other ideas. Boycott was trapped in front by Hogg whose first burst of four overs was very fast. David Frith noted the irony of a cricket match where Boycott took more wickets than he scored runs. The English glitch became a tremour when Hurst, an underrated back up to Hogg, but such an appalling batsman he would fit beautifully into the current England lower order, had Derek Randall caught behind wafting outside the off-stump.

England at 2-5 suggested a fight to the finish. Hogg, though, was prone to fizzle out as quickly as he fired up. Graham Gooch joined Mike Brearley and their stand of 108 virtually settled the issue. Gooch had already scored 1000 runs for his County in all competitions throughout April and May and was soon into his stride. He struck the ball powerfully to the boundary six times on way to a half century in two and three quarter hours. Gooch's strike rate was excellent, but the tempo of the game was slowed by Kim Hughes' meticulous and persistent field adjustments. Australia had gone in without a spinner and Hogg in particular was slow to complete an over.

Perhaps Hughes was praying for the rain that always threatened, but never came. Australian hope only flickered again when bustling all-rounder Trevor Laughlin had Brearley caught behind by Kevin Wright and won an lbw decision in his next over against Gooch. Four for 124 was a worse position than Australia had been in. However, David Gower and Ian Botham had no intention of running out themselves or anyone else. They added the 36 runs required for victory in brisk time, Gower scoring elegantly, Botham in muscular fashion. The target was reached with nearly 13 overs to spare.

Wisden, giving the English point of view, suggested the day was an absorbing one. For the Australian supporters there, or at home, watching television this time on the Ten Network because Kerry Packer said the BBC coverage was not up to the required standard, it was cold grey and depressing and made them pine once more for the return of their WSC stars. They had witnessed this second-string team choke too often like this to hold any more faith in their ability.

Gooch was named Man of the match by Fred Titmus.

AUSTRALIA		ENGLAND	
A. M. J. Hilditch b Boycott	47	J. M. Brearley (capt) c Wright b Laughlin	44
W. M. Darling lbw b Willis	25	G. Boycott lbw b Hogg	1
A. R. Border c Taylor b Edmonds	34	D. W. Randall c Wright b Hurst	1
K. J. Hughes (capt) c Hendrick b Boycott	6	G. A. Gooch lbw b Laughlin	53
G. N. Yallop run out	10	D. I. Gower not out	22
G. J. Cosier run out	6	I. T. Botham not out	18
T. J. Laughlin run out	8	Extras lb10 nb11	21
K. J. Wright (wk) lbw b Old	6	(47.1 overs)	4-160
R. M. Hogg run out	0	Did not bat: P. H. Edmonds, R. W. Taylor (wk), C. M. Old,	
A. G. Hurst not out	3	M. Hendrick, R. G. D. Willis	
G. Dymock not out	4	1/4 2/5 3/113 4/124	
Extras b4 lb5 w1	10	Bowling: Hogg 9-1-25-1; Hurst 10-3-33-1;	
(60 overs)	9-159	Dymock 11-2-19-0; Cosier 8-1-24-0; Laughlin 9.1-0-38-2	
1/56 2/97 3/111 4/131 5/132 6/137 7/150 8/153 9/153			
Bowling: Willis 11-2-20-1; Hendrick 12-2-24-0;			
Old 12-2-33-1; Botham 8-0-32-0; Edmonds 11-1-25-1;			
Boycott 6-0-15-2			

Umpires: D.J. Constant B.J. Meyer

Toss: England   Points: England 4 Australia 0

GROUP B: PAKISTAN vs CANADA
HEADINGLEY: PAKISTAN WON BY 8 WICKETS

The Canadian team that confronted Pakistan at Headingley contained such a strong West Indian contingent it should have been no surprise that they relished fast bowling. Barbados-born, 39-year-old Glenroy Sealy exhibited typical Caribbean enthusiasm when he put away the first ball of the match from Imran Khan for a leg-side four. After their captain and wicketkeeper Bryan Mauricette had won the toss and elected to bat, Sealy and Chris Chappell went on to add an impressive 54 runs for the first wicket. Chappell later stated that making runs against the likes of Imran and fellow paceman Sarfraz Nawaz made all the personal expense of travelling to England worthwhile.

Like Australia in the other Group B match, Canada built a really useful platform, reaching 2-103 at one point. But progress was eventually slowed, especially by Majid Khan's slow-medium off-spin. Majid conceded just one run per over, while Asif Iqbal's little in-swingers made quite a mess of Canada's middle order. Opener Sealy went on to make 45, but again like Australia, the Canadian innings really went nowhere in its later stages. They were pleased to last their allotted 60 overs, however their last seven wickets added a meagre 36 runs and 139 was never likely to challenge a Pakistani team desperate to make up for the shocking disappointments of 1975.

Left-armer John Valentine, who had done so well in the ICC Trophy matches and ended this game with very respectable figures, soon yorked Majid. Then Sadiq Mohammad and Zaheer Abbas added 57 before Chappell ran out Zaheer with a direct hit throw to the bowler's end. That was the Canadians' last success. Sadiq remained firm, Haroon Rashid dominated the scoring and the 140 runs required for victory were achieved with eight wickets and 20 overs to spare when a single was taken from the first ball of Patel's final over.

Sadiq's sound effort puncutated with his trademark shots square of the wicket, earned him the Man of the Match Award. Always an entertainer, the youngest Mohammad brother could give the bat handle a vigorous twirl between deliveries. On the 1978 tour of England he became one of the first players to bat in a helmet in a Test match. Whether it would have afforded him much protection if struck is debateable, though. He batted with the motorbike style headgear on back to front for quite some time.

CANADA		PAKISTAN	
C. J. D. Chappell c & b Sikander Bakht	14	Majid Khan b Valentine	1
G. R. Sealy c & b Asif Iqbal	45	Sadiq Mohammad not out	57
F. A. Dennis c Wasim Bari b Sarfraz Nawaz	25	Zaheer Abbas run out	36
M. P. Stead c Zaheer Abbas b Asif Iqbal	10	Haroon Rashid not out	37
C. A. Marshall b Imran	8	Extras b1 lb3 w1 nb4	9
J. C. B. Vaughan c & b Asif Iqbal	0	(40.1 overs)	2-140
B. M. Mauricette (capt/wk) c Zaheer Abbas b Sarfraz Nawaz	15	Did not bat: Javed Miandad, Asif Iqbal (capt),	
Tariq Javed st Wasim Bari b Majid Khan	3	Mudassar Nazar, Imran Khan, Sarfraz Nawaz,	
J. M. Patel b Sarfraz Nawaz	0	Wasim Bari (wk), Sikander Bakht	
C. C. Henry not out	1	1/4 2/61	
Extras lb10 w5 nb3	18	Bowling: Valentine 9-3-18-1; Vaughan 5-1-21-0;	
(60 overs)	9-139	Henry 5-0-26-0; Patel 11.1-0-27-0; Sealy 6-0-21-0;	
Did not bat: J. N. Valentine		Stead 4-0-18-0	

1/54 2/85 3/103 4/110 5/110 6/129 7/134 8/138 9/139
Bowling: Imran Khan 11-1-27-1; Sarfraz Nawaz 10-1-26-3;
Mudassar Nazar 4-1-11-0; Sikander Bakht 12-5-18-1; Majid
Khan 11-4-11-1; Asif Iqbal 12-2-28-3;

Umpires: H.D. Bird   A.G.T. Whitehead
Toss: Canada   Points: Pakistan 4 Canada 0

GROUP A: INDIA vs WEST INDIES
EDGBASTON: WEST INDIES WON BY 9 WICKETS

The first century of the 1979 Prudential World Cup by Gordon Greenidge swept the West Indies to an easy nine-wicket victory over India in their opening encounter at Edgbaston. The pattern of the whole match was fairly predictable from the moment Clive Lloyd won the toss and sent the Indian batsmen in to cope with his awesome battery of fast bowlers.

Gavaskar had come a long way since his bizarre batting display on the corresponding day four years before. He had emerged as a superb opening batsman and was now a wonderful technician with the ability to counter any form of bowling, including West Indian speed. In the Caribbean early in 1976, he had scored centuries in two of the four Tests. Then in six Tests back in India between December and February, Gavaskar had amassed an astonishing 732 runs from the West Indians, who were admittedly without their WSC players.

The little opener started confidently putting away Andy Roberts' first delivery for four. He rated the Antiguan the best bowler he ever faced. Soon a mistimed hook off the same bowler steepled the ball and Michael Holding safely judged the catch. The multitude of flags which were waved vigorously by the thousands of Indian supporters after that first ball now went sadly limp. And they were just about at half mast soon after when Holding removed Anshuman Gaekwad and Dilip Vengsarkar caught low at third slip with the total still only 29. It was the turn of the equally enthusiastic West Indians to lift the roof of the Hollies Stand.

Gundappa Vishwanath handled the situation and the frequent short of a length deliveries well, defending competently and scoring freely with flicks, cuts and glides. But he lost Brijesh Patel to a foolish run out and when Mohinder Amarnath was brilliantly caught behind by Deryck Murray off Colin Croft, half the Indian side was gone for 77 and a total rout seemed on the cards.

Some previous Indian sides might have folded completely to the onslaught of such pace. There was never any prospect of a full recovery, however, Vishwanath eventually found a couple of worthy partners in the all-rounders, young Kapil Dev and Kharsan Ghavri. They pushed the total beyond 150, then a clinking delivery from Holding breached Vishwanath's defence and all resistance seemed over. It wasn't quite because skipper Venkataraghaven and the unlikely figure of Bishen Bedi added a joyous 27 runs for the last wicket. Bedi who liked to give himself quite a bit of room when facing fast bowling hit Holding for a boundary which got the flags going again. There were still seven overs of the Indian innings remaining when Roberts spoiled the fun by having Bedi caught at slip, leaving the West Indies a straightforward target of 191 to win.

The simplicity of the task was exemplified by the ease with which Gordon Greenidge and Desmond Haynes added 138 for the first wicket. The Indian attack, so lacking in firepower, still sent down more no balls than their West Indian counterparts. Greenidge, often a solemn character, was determined to make up for a modest first World Cup and this was his best opportunity. After settling himself for a few overs, he hit the ball with fearsome strength off the back foot through the off-side and dominated the scoring during his stand with Haynes.

Kapil Dev, in front of the wider cricketing audience for the first time, impressed as a bowler with a lot more spunk than is normally associated with Indian pacemen. He trapped Haynes lbw three short of a half century. That, of course, only brought in Richards who cruised along to ensure Greenidge reached his deserved century. He really enjoyed the hundred, but perhaps not the buffeting he received from the dozens of well wishers who invaded the ground supposedly to congratulate him. Greenidge would be named Man of the Match. Everyone thought the choice obvious despite Holding's devastating exploits with the ball.

Bedi had lost his mesmeric powers. Ghavri, Amarnath and Venkataraghaven lacked penetration. The West Indies reached their objective with eight and a half overs to spare. India, humiliated in 1975 looked to be in deep trouble again. The flags were down. It was the sound of Caribbean bugles, drums, whistles and hand held bells that filled the Birmingham evening air. Twenty-one-year-old Malcolm Marshall sitting in the pavilion, who had suffered recent bowling humiliations in India wrote that he found the ease of his team's win particularly satisfying.

INDIA		WEST INDIES	
S. M. Gavaskar c Holding b Roberts	8	C. G. Greenidge not out	106
A. D. Gaekwad c King b Holding	11	D. L. Haynes lbw b Kapil Dev	47
D. B. Vengsarkar c Kallicharran b Holding	7	I. V. A. Richards not out	28
G. R. Vishwanath b Holding	75	Extras lb6 nb7	13
B. P. Patel run out	15	(51.3 overs)	1-194
M. Amarnath c Murray b Croft	8	Did not bat: A. I. Kallicharran, C. H. Lloyd (capt),	
Kapil Dev b King	12	C. L. King, D. L. Murray (wk), A. M. E. Roberts, J. Garner,	
S. C. Khanna (wk) c Haynes b Holding	0	M. A. Holding, C. E. H. Croft	
K. D. Ghavri c Murray b Garner	12	1/138	
S. Venkataraghaven (capt) not out	13	Bowling: Kapil Dev 10-1-46-1; Ghavri 10-2-25-0;	
B. S. Bedi c Lloyd b Roberts	13	Venkataraghaven 12-3-30-0; Bedi 12-0-45-0; Amarnath	
Extras b6 lb3 w3 nb4	16	7.3-0-35-0	
(53.1 overs)	190		

1/10 2/24 3/29 4/56 5/77 6/112 7/119 8/155 9/163
10/190

Bowling: Roberts 9.1-0-32-2; Holding 12-2-33-4;
Garner 12-1-42-1; Croft 10-1-31-1; King 10-1-36-1

Umpires: D.G.L. Evans   J.G. Langridge

Toss: West Indies   Points: West Indies 4 India 0

GROUP A: NEW ZEALAND vs SRI LANKA
TRENT BRIDGE: NEW ZEALAND WON BY 9 WICKETS

The remarkable similarity in the scores in the two Group A matches meant that a close result was nowhere to be found on the opening day of the 1979 Prudential World Cup.

At Trent Bridge everyone nodded approvingly and noted the improved Sri Lankan batting. But the subcontinental side did not last their 60 overs and the total of 189 proved as inadequate as that of the other three countries who had gone in first on this typically overcast and chilly early English summer's day. Wisely, in view of their battering at the hands of Jeff Thomson in 1975, the Sri Lankans wore batting helmets after Mark Burgess had won the toss and invited Anura Tennekoon's side to bat.

That did cause a problem or two for the scorers who had all sorts of difficulty identifying one busy Sri Lankan from another. It is still fairly safe to assume that Tennekoon did complete a competent half century which seemed to set his side up for a competitive total. He and Roy Dias added 50 runs for the third wicket, taking the score to a very promising 2-107. But like Australia at Lord's and Canada at Headingley, the underdogs flattered to deceive. Both Tennekoon and Dias fell to Warren Stott, bowling in his sole international appearance. The rest of the batsmen had no real idea how to boost the run rate later in the innings and stumbled and fell from 4-149 to 8-154. Tony Opatha and D.L.S. de Silva gave the total a bit of a boost, although it hardly seemed enough.

The Sri Lankan medium pacers made little impression on Glenn Turner and John Wright, as the Kiwis began their reply. The total had already reached 64 before Wright mistimed a catch to the Sri Lankan captain at mid-on off left-arm spinner Ginigalgodage de Silva. A further 126 runs were required when Geoff Howarth joined Turner and this pair were able to achieve their objective with more than 12 overs to spare. Turner never missed an opportunity to spend time at the crease when there were easy runs to be made. He was always likely to be not out at the end of this innings. Howarth's main difficulty arose from a strained hamstring that required a runner. He scored as freely as Turner and even belted Somachandra de Silva for a clean six on way to an unbeaten 63. His stylish pulling and driving in the face of some physical adversity earned Howarth the Man of the Match Award just ahead of his more experienced batting partner.

SRI LANKA		NEW ZEALAND	
B. Warnapura c & b McKechnie	20	G. M. Turner not out	83
S. R. de S. Wettimuny b Cairns	16	J. G. Wright c Tennekoon b G. R.A. de Silva	34
A. P.B. Tennekoon (capt) b Stott	59	G. P. Howarth not out	63
R. L. Dias c & b Stott	25	Extras lb7 w2 nb1	10
L. R. D. Mendis c Turner b Troup	14	(47.4 overs)	1-190
D. S. de Silva c Burgess b Stott	6	Did not bat: J. V. Coney, M. G. Burgess (capt), W. K. Lees (wk),	
S. A. Jayasinghe (wk) run out	1	B. J. McKechnie, B. L. Cairns, R. J. Hadlee, L. W. Stott,	
S. P. Pasqual b Hadlee	1	G. B. Troup	
A. R. M. Opatha b McKechnie	18	1/64	
D. L. S. de Silva c Wright b McKechnie	10	Bowling: Opatha 7-1-31-0; D. L.S. de Silva 8-2-18-0;	
G. R. A. de Silva not out	2	Warnapura 7-0-30-0; D. S.de Silva 9-0-42-0; G. R. A.	
Extras lb13 w2 nb2	17	De Silva 12-1-39-1; Pasqual 4.4-0-20-0	
(56.5 overs)	189		

1/26 2/57 3/107 4/137 5/149 6/150 7/150 8/154 9/178
10/189

Bowling: Hadlee 12-3-24-1; Troup 10-0-30-1;
Cairns 12-1-45-1; McKechnie 10.5-2-25-3; Stott 12-0-48-3

Umpires: W.L. Budd   K.E. Palmer

Toss: New Zealand   Points: New Zealand 4 Sri Lanka 0

WEDNESDAY
13 JUNE, THURSDAY 14 JUNE 1979
THE PRUDENTIAL CUP: ROUND TWO
GROUP B: ENGLAND vs CANADA
OLD TRAFFORD: ENGLAND WON BY 8 WICKETS

The ghost of Abe Bailey, still smarting from the disasters of 1912, finally took out his wrath on Round Two of the 1979 tournament. What had threatened in Round One became an unpleasant reality four days later in Round Two. Rain covered the country, worse in the west and south than the north. Only the game at Headingley could be completed in a day.

Across the Penines, though, at Old Trafford, no play was possible on the Wednesday. Heavy rain soon caused Barry Meyer and John Langridge to abandon proceedings and when everyone, including a mere sprinkling of spectators turned up on the Thursday, there was a further delay of an hour.

For some unexplained reason Canadian captain, Mauricette elected to bat first in what *Wisden* called "farcical conditions". Bob Willis said none of the England team could believe Bryan Mauricette's decision and that they felt sorry for their opponents. That pity did not extend to the generosity of the bowling, however. In an astonishing display of miserly economy the English seamers dismissed Canada for 45. Perhaps coming from the 1975 Sunil Gavaskar school for batting in limited-over internationals, survival was the Canadians' only objective and they at least managed to do this for 40 overs. Number three batsman Franklin Dennis lasted for 31 of those overs before misjudging the bounce of a short ball from Bob Willis. That caused him to overbalance and fall on his wicket.

Willis had superb figures, but Chris Old's were even better. His 4-8 from 10 overs remains one of the best analyses from any World Cup tournament. The Canadian innings lasted just 157 minutes and they became the first and still the only World Cup side to be dismissed for less than 60. On another miserable Manchester day only Ian Botham held a catch. It did not matter much because six of the last seven batsmen were bowled, the stumps flying spectacularly in all directions from the rain softened turf. The last six wickets fell for eight runs. Extras were equal second-top score.

More heavy rain delayed the start of the England innings for another three-and-a-half hours. It was 7.00pm before Geoff Boycott and Mike Brearley made their way out to the wicket in brief but welcome sunshine and not long after the hour when

Brearley was on his way back. The Canadians had no hope of protecting their total, but they retained their unadulterated enthusiasm. That was quickly rewarded when John Valentine straightened one on the English captain. Callender then bowled the out-of-form Derek Randall. England were 2-11 and potential embarrassment loomed.

Again it was Graham Gooch who ended the fuss, hitting out effectively in the gathering gloom. The match aggregate of 91 runs is a World Cup all time low, as is the playing time of just three hours and thirty-five minutes. Old was named Man of the Match.

CANADA		ENGLAND	
G. R. Sealey c Botham b Hendrick	3	J. M. Brearley (capt) lbw b Valentine	0
C. J. D. Chappell lbw b Botham	5	G. Boycott not out	14
F. A. Dennis hit wicket b Willis	21	D. W. Randall b Callender	5
Tariq Javed lbw b Old	4	G. A. Gooch not out	21
J. C.B. Vaughan b Old	1	Extras w3 nb3	6
C. A. Marshall b Old	2	(13.5 overs)	2-46
B. M. Mauricette (capt/wk) b Willis	0	Did not bat: D. I. Gower, I. T. Botham, G. Miller,	
M. P. Stead b Old	0	R. W. Taylor (wk), C. M. Old, R. G. D. Willis, M. Hendrick	
J. M. Patel b Willis	1	1/3 2/11	
R. G. Callender b Willis	0	Bowling: Valentine 7-2-20-1; Callender 6-1-14-1;	
J. N. Valentine not out	3	Stead 0.5-0-6-0	
Extras lb4 nb1	5		
(40.3 overs)	45		

1/5 2/13 3/25 4/29 5/37 6/38 7/41 8/41 9/42 10/45
Bowling: Willis 10.3-3-11-4; Hendrick 8-4-5-1;
Botham 9-5-12-1; Miller 2-1-1-0; Boycott 1-0-3-0;
Old 10-5-8-4

Umpires: J.G. Langridge B.J. Meyer
Toss: Canada   Points: England 4 Canada 0

GROUP B: AUSTRALIA vs PAKISTAN
TRENT BRIDGE: PAKISTAN WON BY 89 RUNS

As it did four years ago, the clash between these two countries loomed as a crucial contest to see who would progress through to the semi-finals. Unlike 1975, this time nearly all the best cricket came from Pakistan and on the second day they emerged comfortable and relieved winners by 89 runs.

Rain delayed the start for an hour. Then Kim Hughes won the toss and invited Asif Iqbal and his side to bat. Hughes' major spearhead, Rodney Hogg was out of the starting 11. The continuing cold and damp was causing all sorts of bronchial problems for the asthmatic fast bowler, although some reports suggested a muscle strain stopped him from playing. His partner in crime, Alan Hurst, now led the way. Hurst had bowled brilliantly in the ill-tempered two-match Test series against Pakistan in Australia in March, but here, just a couple of months later, the responsibility of being the number one fast bowler seemed to distract him.

"I'd got it into my head that I could get a few of these guys out by bowling short," Hurst later said to Gideon Haigh in *The Cricket War*. "I kept at them and they kept hammering me. I was stupid and I don't use it as an excuse, but it was really made worse by the inexperience of the side. I had the adrenalin flowing and I got no guidance at all."

Trent Bridge was certainly not the WACA. Majid Khan could not believe his luck and took a heavy toll on the wayward Hurst who sent down a quota of five wides and four no balls as well as the misplaced short stuff. Hughes might have despaired, but fortunately Hogg's replacement, that obscure West Australian, Graeme Porter, and left-armer Geoff Dymock stemmed the run flow with some sensible line and length bowling. Both Majid and his opening partner Sadiq were dismissed when the total was on 99. Then Gary Cosier, bowling medium-paced swing, removed Zaheer Abbas and Haroon Rashid cheaply.

When Pakistan were 4-152 Australia thought they were back in the contest. At selection Australia had brought in left-handed batsman Jeff Moss for all-rounder Trevor Laughlin. That meant Graham Yallop and Allan Border had to make up a 12-over stint between them. The idea was a poor one. Both left-armers were caned. Yallop conceded 56 runs from eight overs, Border 38 runs from just four.

Javed Miandad and Asif Iqbal made the most of these innocuous offerings. They lifted the score to 239 with some fine strokes and sharp running in 14 overs before being parted. The Australians were tested by Javed and Asif's energetic batting and found wanting. Ginger-haired wicketkeeper, Kevin Wright, another with injury problems, had a bad day behind the stumps.

Another 47 runs from the last five overs left the Australians needing 287 to have any hope of progressing to the semi-finals. Andrew Hilditch and Rick Darling scored 17 runs while they negotiated five overs of a Pakistan attack without the injured Sarfraz Nawaz, before play was halted for the day.

Kim Hughes' team had everything to play for on a cold grey Thursday at Trent Bridge but they were never really in the hunt. Imran Khan soon had Darling caught behind and when Sikander Bakht bowled Allan Border for a duck Australia were 2-24 and right behind the eight-ball. Hilditch had batted well at Lord's and it was Hughes' vice-captain who again held the innings together as best he could. He added 71 with Graham Yallop in 21 overs, giving the scoreboard respectability without causing the Pakistanis any real angst. Eventually Hilditch fell to Mudassar's persistence and Yallop missed a straight one from Majid.

The Australian innings limped along from there until Kevin Wright trying to score the 90 runs still required from three overs, edged Imran to Wasim Bari from the first ball of the 58th over. The result had long been a formality. At least there had only been one run out.

Asif Iqbal's sprightly innings, his tidy bowling and astute captaincy earned him the Man of the Match Award.

PAKISTAN		AUSTRALIA	
Sadiq Mohammad c Moss b Porter	27	W. M. Darling c Wasim Bari b Imran Khan	13
Majid Khan b Dymock	61	A. M. J. Hilditch c Sadiq Mohammad b Mudassar Nazar	72
Zaheer Abbas c & b Cosier	16	A. R. Border b Sikander Bakht	0
Haroon Rashid c Wright b Cosier	16	K. J. Hughes (capt) lbw b Sikander Bakht	16
Javed Miandad c Border b Cosier	46	G. N. Yallop b Majid Khan	37
Asif Iqbal (capt) c sub (D. F. Whatmore) b Hurst	61	J. K. Moss run out	7
Wasim Raja c Moss b Border	18	G. J. Cosier c & b Majid Khan	0
Imran Khan not out	15	K. J. Wright (wk) c Wasim Bari b Imran Khan	23
Mudassar Nazar not out	1	G. D. Porter c Sadiq Mohammad b Majid Khan	3
Extras b6 lb4 w5 nb10	25	G. Dymock lbw b Sikander Bakht	10
(60 overs)	7-286	A. G. Hurst not out	3
Did not bat: Wasim Bari (wk), Sikander Bakht		Extras b1 lb5 w8	14
1/99 2/99 3/133 4/152/5/239 6/268 7/274		(57.1 overs)	197

Bowling: Porter 12-3-20-1; Dymock 12-3-28-1; Cosier 12-1-54-3; Hurst 12-0-65-1; Yallop 8-0-56-0; Border 4-0-38-1

1/22 2/24 3/46 4/117 5/136 6/137 7/172 8/175 9/193 10/197

Bowling: Asif Iqbal 12-0-36-0; Majid Khan 12-0-53-3; Mudassar Nazar12-0-31-1; Imran Khan10.1-2-29-2; Sikander Bakht 11-1-34-3

Umpires: H.D. Bird   K.E. Palmer

Toss: Australia   Points: Pakistan 4 Australia 0

GROUP A: INDIA vs NEW ZEALAND
HEADINGLEY: NEW ZEALAND WON BY EIGHT WICKETS

In the only second-round match to be completed on the scheduled playing day, India's complete inadequacy at 60-overs-per-side cricket was again cruelly exposed, this time by New Zealand at Headingley.

Venkataraghaven lost the toss once more and his team were required to bat when the wicket gave the greatest assistance to New Zealand's competent pace attack. The Indians had to graft nearly all the way. Richard Hadlee made the first breakthrough, but Brian McKechnie, only available because he had no rugby commitments with the All Blacks, and burly in-swinger Lance Cairns did the most damage.

Gavaskar batted for 44 overs at a pace not much above his crawl at Lord's in 1975. He had greater cause to be circumspect than during that debacle, though. There was a damp and heavy atmosphere over Leeds and Gavaskar's wicket was obviously a key to the result. He had an early let off; Hadlee missing a sharp caught and bowled, then settled down to play an anchor role. Gundappa Vishwanath's early dismissal was a blow. After 20 overs, India were 2-50. Soon they were 3-53.

It took an enterprising knock by Brijesh Patel to give the innings a bit of momentum. At 3-104, India had almost fought back on level terms only for big left-arm paceman, Gary Troup, a direct replacement for Richard Collinge, to bowl both Patel and Mohinder Amarnath in quick succession.

Kapil Dev and Kharsan Ghavri chipped in with runs of value, lifting the total from the pathetic to the vaguely competitive. Hadlee finally got Gavaskar caught behind and this time there was no last wicket bonus from Bedi. The omission of accomplished wicketkeeper batsman, Syed Kirmani, again looked a costly move by the Indian selectors. India were again unable to bat out their 60 over allocation and could only set New Zealand 183 for victory.

The heavy cloud cover had lifted and batting conditions had eased by the time left-handed pair Bruce Edgar and John Wright established themselves at the crease in pursuit of the runs that would assure New Zealand of a semi-final berth. None of the Indian bowlers could make any impact as Wright and Edgar gradually built a solid platform for victory. It was sensible rather than exciting stuff from the young pair. They put on exactly 100 before Wright hit a return catch to Mohinder Amarnath. Burgess must have been a little concerned about the run rate because he sent in Lance Cairns to smack the ball around a bit. That came unstuck when Cairns was quickly run out, but Glenn Turner had enough experience of limited-overs cricket to know what was required.

He moved positively into his work and with Edgar becoming more fluent, saw New Zealand to victory with no further alarms and three overs to spare. The opener's unbeaten 84 was considered the feature of a fairly plain day and thus earned him the Man of the Match Award.

INDIA			NEW ZEALAND	
S. M. Gavaskar c Lees b Hadlee	55		J. G. Wright c & b Amarnath	48
A. D. Gaekwad b Hadlee	10		B. A. Edgar not out	84
D. B. Vengsarkar c Lees b McKechnie	1		B. L. Cairns run out	2
G. R. Vishwanath c Turner b Cairns	9		G. M. Turner not out	43
B. P. Patel b Troup	38		Extras lb3 nb3	6
M. Amarnath b Troup	1		(57 overs)	2-183
Kapil Dev c & b Cairns	25		Did not bat: J. V. Coney, M. G. Burgess (capt),	
K. D. Ghavri c Coney b McKechnie	20		J. F. M. Morrison, B. J. McKechnie W. K. Lees (wk) R. J.	
S. C. Khanna (wk) c Morrison b McKechnie	7		Hadlee G. B. Troup	
S. Venkataraghaven (capt) c Lees b Cairns	1		1/100 2/103	
B. S. Bedi not out	1		Bowling: Amarnath 12-1-39-1; Bedi 12-1-32-0;	
Extras lb8 w5 nb1	14		Venkataraghaven 12-0-34-0; Ghavri 10-1-34-0; Kapil	
(55.5overs)	182		Dev 11-3-38-0	

1/27 2/38 3/53 4/104 5/107 6/147 7/153 8/180 9/181 10/182

Bowling: Hadlee 10-2-20-2; Troup 10-2-36-2; Cairns 11.5-0-36-3; McKechnie 12-1-24-3; Coney 7-0-33-0; Morrison 5-0-19-0

Umpires: W.L. Budd A.G.T. Whitehead

Toss: New Zealand   Points: New Zealand 4 India 0

GROUP A:WEST INDIES vs SRI LANKA THE OVAL:MATCH ABANDONED

On a clear day at The Oval you can see three planes in the sky following the Thames as their flight path. One is about to touch down at Heathrow, the other is straight over head and the third is beginning its landing approach. On a bad day you cannot see any planes in the sky. Rather you look up at three big black clouds. One has just rained on you and drifted away, one is currently dousing you and the cricket ground and one is getting ready to pour some more on you.

On 13, 14 and 15 June 1979 when the cricketers of West Indies and Sri Lanka gazed up into the sky they saw black clouds not planes. There were, in fact, a couple of breaks in the weather, but each successive downpour soon dampened the thought of any prospect of play.

Each side was given two points for turning up. In their own way these were historic. Sri Lanka received their first ever points in the World Cup and also became the first team to take any off the West Indies. There were a few smiles amongst the Sri Lankan players at that. Although unlikely, mathematically it was now possible for Clive Lloyd's side to miss a place in the semi-finals. This was the only no result match in the World Cup until rain arrived at an opportune time for Pakistan when they were playing England in Adelaide on 1 March 1992.

SATURDAY 16 JUNE 1979
THE PRUDENTIAL CUP: ROUND THREE
GROUP B: ENGLAND vs PAKISTAN
HEADINGLEY: ENGLAND WON BY 14 RUNS

This tight fluctuating encounter played before a full house, proved to be the best round robin match of the tournament. Both England and Pakistan were assured of a semi-final berth, but a win would to either side would probably see them avoid the West Indies in the semi-finals and therefore improve their chances of reaching the final itself.

Like many games between England and Pakistan, this one had a special edge to it. The supporters of both sides on the terraces added plenty of enthusiasm and noise and increased the tension for the players. There were so many Pakistani fans,

Bob Willis suggested the entire city of Bradford must be closed. Later in the day, unfortunately, police dogs would be needed to separate the worst elements of both sides when fighting broke out. While the weather had improved from mid-week, the conditions still favoured the bowlers. Asif Iqbal sent England in to bat when he won the toss.

Irregular bounce and movement off the seam proved his reading of the wicket correct. Even without the services of the still injured Sarfraz Nawaz, Pakistan quickly broke through. In a trice the home side were 2-4, Mike Brearley and Derek Randall both edging seaming deliveries to Wasim Bari.

Geoff Boycott was fairly familiar with such conditions. He held firm for an hour-and-a-half and put on 47 valuable runs with the more enterprising Graham Gooch. They appeared to have weathered the worst of the storm when Boycott was trapped in front by Majid Khan. That was rarely a popular decision in Yorkshire. Sadiq Mohammad then held an excellent catch at deep gully from a Gooch slash off Sikander Bakht. Ian Botham and David Gower got going, but each in turn became the second and third victims of Majid's seemingly innocuous flat off-spin. Asif Iqbal had England in further trouble when he removed Phil Edmonds and held a return catch off Chris Old.

Bob Willis came to the wicket to the noise and chanting of Pakistani supporters delirious at an England scoreline of 8-118. With the ball still moving around, Willis plonked his long left leg down the wicket so far across his off-stump that he often played the ball inside out. As many deliveries were missed and edged as were struck, but with Bob Taylor holding fast at the other end a few overs were consumed and the total began to rise a little.

Imran was champing at the bit trying to convince Asif to put him on and finish the innings. Willis was dropped by Sikander Bakht, skewed a few more runs in unlikely directions between extra cover and third man and then was bowled by Sikander for an invaluable 24. He had added 43 with Taylor, who with Mike Hendrick batted out the innings.

England had set Pakistan a target of 166 from their allotted 60 overs. Despite the on-going assistance for seam bowlers from the wicket Sadiq and Majid promptly took the score to 27. Derbyshire seamer, Hendrick, who had beaten the bat more than once, suddenly began putting the ball in exactly the right spot. In five phenomenal overs six wickets fell for seven runs. There was panic in the Pakistani dressing room with players running in all directions and equipment flying through the air. Hendrick, well supported by Botham, took four wickets in eight balls, each one a batsman of real quality. This time the English sections of the crowd were ecstatic as Pakistan at 6-34 seemed beyond recall.

But there was great batting depth in their line-up and Hendrick was finally seen off by Asif, playing with a stick of rhubarb, according to Bob Willis, and Wasim Raja. They re-established a semblance of sanity to the Pakistani innings adding 52 runs in the process. Raja went lbw to Old, but Imran, suffering badly from nerves, then stayed with his captain leaving Asif to play the shots while he held firm. The Pakistani captain reached his invaluable half century, the only one of the match, in an hour and three quarters. Each run was now greeted with wild cheering, but Bob Willis' next delivery to Asif after he completed his 50 was a brutish lifter, which was edged to Mike Brearley at slip.

Pakistan, now at 8-115, looked to Imran as their main hope. He and Wasim Bari had plenty of overs in hand. Brearley reverted to his part-time seamers rather than entrust the ball to his spinner Phil Edmonds. The tension became almost unbearable as Imran and Wasim added 30, closing the target to within 20 runs. Brearley's use of Geoff Boycott as a bowler would have been seen as a sign of desperation if Pakistan had got home. As it turned out the England captain was hailed as a genius. On 145, still bowling in his cap around the wicket, Boycott induced an ill-advised cut shot to an in-swinger from Wasim Bari. Bob Taylor had had another poor day behind the stumps but this time he held the inside edge superbly.

Brearley set the field back on the boundary for Imran and brought it in for last man Sikander Bakht. Imran took the singles on offer. The Pakistanis crept to within 14 runs. Imran said the tension was so great and the crowd so silent at times you could hear a pin drop. The last ball of Boycott's fifth over was a widish half volley. Sikander launched himself at it. He hit it well, but in the air towards deep mid off. There stood Hendrick. He leapt in the air and clutched at the ball with his right hand. It stuck, giving England their precious and thrilling victory. Imran unbeaten on 21 was distraught, as was Sikander. The Pakistanis had been unable to secure victory in another close World Cup match. Imran believed he batted with great determination, others thought he looked out of form. After the game many inconsolable Pakistani supporters questioned the approach of the great all-rounder. Whatever the rights and wrongs at least Pakistan knew they had not forfeited a semi-final place this time.

Mike Hendrick for his sensational spell of bowling and grand finale catch was named Man of the Match by Brian Close.

ENGLAND		PAKISTAN	
J. M. Brearley (capt) c Wasim Bari b Imran Khan	0	Majid Khan c Botham b Hendrick	7
G. Boycott lbw b Majid Khan	18	Sadiq Mohammad b Hendrick	18
D. W. Randall c Wasim Bari b Sikander Bakht	1	Mudassar Nazar lbw b Hendrick	0
G. A. Gooch c Sadiq Mohammad b Sikander Bakht	33	Zaheer Abbas c Taylor b Botham	3
D. I. Gower b Majid Khan	27	Haroon Rashid c Brearley b Hendrick	1
I. T. Botham b Majid Khan	22	Javed Miandad lbw b Botham	0
P. H. Edmonds c Wasim Raja b Asif Iqbal	2	Asif Iqbal (capt) c Brearley b Willis	51
R. W. Taylor (wk) not out	20	Wasim Raja lbw b Old	21
C. M. Old c & b Asif Iqbal	2	Imran Khan not out	21
R. G. D. Willis b Sikander Bakht	24	Wasim Bari (wk) c Taylor b Boycott	17
M. Hendrick not out	1	Sikander Bakht c Hendrick b Boycott	2
Extras lb3 w7 nb5	15	Extras lb8 w1 nb1	10
(60 overs)	9-165	(56 overs)	151
1/0 2/4 3/51 4/70 5/99 6/115 7/115 8/118 9/161		1/27 2/27 3/28 4/30 5/31 6/34 7/86 8/115 9/145 10/151	
Bowling: Imran Khan 12-3-34-1; Sikander Bakht 12-3-32-3; Mudassar Nazar 12-4-30-0; Asif Iqbal 12-3-37-2; Majid Khan 12-2-27-3		Bowling: Willis 11-2-37-1; Hendrick 12-6-15-4; Botham 12-3-38-2; Old 12-2-28-1; Edmonds 3-0-8-0; Boycott 5-0-14-2; Gooch 1-0-1-0	

Umpires: W.L. Budd D.G.L. Evans

Toss: Pakistan   Points: England 4 Pakistan 0

GROUP B: AUSTRALIA vs CANADA
EDGBASTON: AUSTRALIA WON BY 7 WICKETS

The Australians and Canadians filled in the Saturday before their flights back home with a cricket match. Even though the weather was half decent, only about 1200 people filed into Edgbaston and a number of those might have turned up to see if even Canada would be too good for Kim Hughes' forlorn team.

Hughes won the toss and sent in the Canadians. Opener Glenroy Sealy reacted by smashing four boundaries off the first over of the match from Rodney Hogg. He defended the opening two deliveries before unleashing three powerful pull shots in a row and an exquisite leg glance from the sixth ball. Hogg conceded another 10 runs from his second over before he took his long-sleeved sweater and retired to the outfield, his reputation somewhat damaged by a 39-year-old.

Sealy and Chris Chappell extended their opening stand to 44, but again what followed them was inadequate. Geoff Dymock and Graeme Porter showed far greater control than Hogg and Alan Hurst, a schoolteacher by profession, showed he had learnt quickly from his excesses against Pakistan. He reaped the reward of bowling a much fuller length, his pace eventually proving too much for five of the Canadians. Hurst was eventually named Man of the Match. After the breakneck start only Vaughan provided any real resistance and the Canadians having lost their last five wickets for eight runs were all out by lunch.

Australia's reply started with a flurry as well, 12 came from the first over before John Valentine removed Rick Darling with a shooter. He also took an excellent catch at square leg to dismiss Andrew Hilditch, but by then the Australians were halfway towards their target of 106. That was achieved in just 26 overs for the further loss of Allan Border, allowing both teams to pay their respects to each other and organise their departures nice and early. The Australians were leaving with their tail between their legs.

CANADA		AUSTRALIA	
G. R. Sealy c Porter b Dymock	25	A. M. J. Hilditch c Valentine b Henry	24
C. J. D. Chappell lbw b Hurst	19	W. M. Darling lbw b Valentine	13
F. A. Dennis lbw b Hurst	1	A. R. Border b Henry	25
Tariq Javed c Wright b Porter	8	K. J. Hughes (capt) not out	27
S. Baksh b Hurst	0	G. N. Yallop not out	13
J. C. B. Vaughan b Porter	29	Extras lb1 nb3	4
B. M. Mauricette (capt/wk) c Hilditch b Cosier	5	(26 overs)	3-106
J. M. Patel b Cosier	2	Did not bat: G. J. Cosier, K. J. Wright (wk), G. D. Porter,	
R. G. Callender c Wright b Hurst	0	R. M. Hogg, G. Dymock, A. G. Hurst	
C. C. Henry c Hughes b Hurst	5	1/23 2/53 3/72	
J. N. Valentine not out	0	Bowling: Valentine 3-0-28-1; Callender 3-0-12-0;	
Extras b4 lb5 w1 nb1	11	Henry 10-0-27-2; Vaughan 6-0-15-0; Patel 4-0-20-0	
(33.2 overs)	105		
1/44 2/50 3/51 4/51 5/78 6/97 7/97 8/98 9/104 10/105			
Bowling: Hogg 2-0-26-0; Hurst 10-3-21-5; Dymock 8-2-17-1;			
Porter 6-2-13-2; Cosier 7.2-2-17-2			

Umpires: D.J. Constant   J.G. Langridge

Toss: Australia   Points: Australia 4 Canada 0

GROUP A: INDIA vs SRI LANKA
OLD TRAFFORD: SRI LANKA WON BY 47 RUNS

In some ways this match provided the most significant result of the tournament. Although the game had no bearing on the World Cup itself, Sri Lanka's win, the first by an associate ICC member over a full ICC member, gave a lot of weight to that country's push for full Test status, something they achieved within a couple of years. It also condemned India to a pointless tournament, leaving them on a level pegging with lowly Canada. At that moment it was probably a fair assessment of India's achievements in limited-over internationals.

Further rain delayed the start of the match, and when proceedings got underway, Venkataraghaven won the toss and sent the Sri Lankans in. They were without their respected captain, Anura Tennekoon, who had strained a hamstring at practice the day before the match, but still had no trouble coping with the unimpressive Indian bowling.

Sidath Wettimuny and Roy Dias added an enterprising 96 runs in 25 overs, charming a small crowd with their wristy strokeplay. Duleep Mendis, another like Wettimuny, who had suffered at the hands of Jeff Thomson four years before, made sure their efforts were not wasted. He belted the Indian medium pacers for three big sixes on way to the third half century of the innings. Mohinder Amarnath picked up three wickets, but that hardly stemmed the run flow as 52 were added in seven overs by Mendis and the young left hander, Pasqual.

At the end of their 60 overs, Sri Lanka had made 5-238, a worthy total. However, it was not necessarily one to daunt the Indians. Sri Lanka's bowling also had few credentials and was considered far inferior to their batting.

The Indians had all of Sunday to stew over their run chase. It did not appear to concern them unduly early on, though, when Sunil Gavaskar and Anshuman Gaekwad had an opening partnership of 60. India went to lunch on 2-117 requiring a further 122 runs from the remaining 25 overs.

It was soon after the interval that things started to go amiss. Gundappa Viswanath's wicket was pivotal to the Indian effort. He foolishly ran himself out and Sri Lanka saw an opening. Somachandra de Silva, a fast leg-spinner of a style not dissimilar to India's own recent champion, Bhagwat Chandrasaker, took advantage. He dismissed Dilip Vengsarkar and then bowled Brijesh Patel and Mohinder Amarnath. The Indian middle order started to crumble under the pressure. They were unable to establish any sort of a partnership and the innings began to subside, much as it had in every World Cup match so far.

Tony Opatha had made no impact with the new-ball, but now, stand in captain Bandula Warnapura brought him back into the attack at just the right time. Opatha bowled with increased pace and picked up the wickets of Kharsan Ghavri and wicketkeeper Surinder Khanna. Then, from the first ball of his eleventh over, the opening bowler had last man Bishen Bedi caught behind. India were all out with nearly six overs still to go. Sri Lanka had claimed a merited and historic 47-run victory. The small cluster of Sri Lankan enthusiasts who came to Old Trafford this special Monday celebrated with their proud team. Duleep Mendis was named Man of the Match.

India quietly eased themselves off the arena. Behind the closed doors of their dressing room there was a lengthy and fairly sombre post mortem. They had lots to talk about. India's sole success in six World Cup starts in 1975 and 1979 had been their win over East Africa. Their innings totals this time had all been similar and inadequate: 190, 182 and 191 in 53.1, 55.5 and 54.1 overs respectively.

SRI LANKA		INDIA	
B. Warnapura (capt) c Gaekwad b Amarnath	18	S. M. Gavaskar c Dias b Warnapura	26
S. R. de Wettimuny c Vengsarkar b Kapil Dev	67	A. D. Gaekwad c sub (G. R.A. de Silva) b D. L.S. de Silva	33
R. L. Dias c & b Amarnath	50	D. B. Vengsarkar c D. L.S. de Silva b D. S. de Silva	36
L. R. D. Mendis run out	64	G. R. Vishwanath run out	22
R. S. Madugalle c Khanna b Amarnath	4	B. P. Patel b D. S. de Silva	10
S. P. Pasqual not out	23	Kapil Dev c Warnapura b D. L.S. de Silva	16
D. S. de Silva not out	1	M. Amarnath b D. S. de Silva	7
Extras lb8 w2 nb1	11	K. D. Ghavri c Warnapura b Opatha	3
(60 overs)	5-238	S. C. Khanna (wk) c Dias b Opatha	10
Did not bat: S. A. Jayasinghe (wk), A. R.M. Opatha,		S. Venkataraghaven (capt) not out	9
D. L.S. de Silva, F. R.M. Goonatillake		B. S. Bedi c Jayasinghe b Opatha	5
1/31 2/127 3/147 4/175 5/227		Extras lb10 w3 nb1	14
Bowling: Kapil Dev 12-2-53-1; Ghavri 12-0-53-0;		(54.1 overs)	191
Amarnath 12-3-40-3; Bedi 12-2-37-0;		1/60 2/76 3/119 4/132 5/147 6/160 7/162 8/170 9/185	
Venkataraghaven 12-0-44-0		10/191	
		Bowling: Opatha 10.1-0-31-3; Goonatillake 9-1-34-0;	
		Warnapura 12-0-47-1; D. L.S. de Silva 12-0-36-2; D. S. de Silva 11-1-29-3	

Umpires: K.E. Palmer A.G.T. Whitehead

Toss: India   Points: Sri Lanka 4 India 0

GROUP A: NEW ZEALAND vs WEST INDIES
TRENT BRIDGE: WEST INDIES WON BY 32 RUNS

It is a measure of the general estimation of the qualities of these two sides that New Zealand were considered to have done quite well to get within 32 runs of the mighty West Indians. The Kiwis were described as "plucky", "efficient", "competent", "underrated" and "good fighters". The trouble was Clive Lloyd's side was all that and a whole lot more and only early on and very briefly did this game for top spot in Group A look like being close.

New Zealand were still without Geoff Howarth, whose hamstring had not healed. Mark Burgess won the toss and sent the West Indies in to bat. The belief was that the Caribbean team preferred to chase runs than bat first. That and the prospect of Richard Hadlee taking advantage of any favourable bowling conditions on the ground where he played County Cricket would have been the determining factors in Burgess' decision.

Hadlee was a little erratic early, but he won an lbw decision against Desmond Haynes. Jeremy Coney's gentle little swing deliveries always looked easy pickings for quality batsmen. When he came on, second change Viv Richards' eyes probably lit up. But the great man underestimated Coney's worth and with the total on 61 he holed out to the New Zealand captain.

Burgess kept deep set, defensive fields and tried to unsettle the West Indies with constant bowling changes. Gordon Greenidge and Alvin Kallicharran built a worthwhile stand of 58 ,which took the West Indies to 2-117. The opener felt in good fettle, got to 65 in 33 overs and saw no reason why he should not complete his second century in as many innings. But Greendige, too, paid insufficient heed to Coney's wiles and edged to Bruce Edgar.

Hadlee returned and bowled a fiery spell which thrilled the crowd. The West Indian total built steadily without their strokemakers ever really breaking loose. At the 55-over mark, Clive Lloyd was still at the crease with his side on 7-204. An easily forgotten aspect of the great West Indian sides of this era is the fact that most of their fast bowlers were quite competent batsmen. The West Indian captain, who was later named Man of the Match, finally found a worthy partner in big Joel Garner. Lloyd took control, Garner held firm and 40 runs were added in the final five overs.

Without Howarth's attractive strokeplay 245 was always going to be too many for New Zealand against the West Indies' prize attack. They kept Lloyd's side out in the field for the full 60 overs, but battled to maintain a run rate above three per over rather than the required four. Michael Holding proved particularly difficult to get away.

Coney and Glenn Turner had a promising stand, Burgess played some nice shots and Hadlee clubbed the ball around for a while to take the score above the 200 run respectability mark. When the innings concluded Brian McKechnie and Ewen Chatfield were at the crease. They were unable to make any real attempt to score the runs necessary, but were probably not overly concerned. New Zealand conceded top place in their group to their opponents, however their place in the semi-finals had already been assured and they knew they would not be facing the West Indies again at least until the final.

WEST INDIES		NEW ZEALAND	
C. G. Greenidge c Edgar b Coney	65	B. A. Edgar run out	12
D. L. Haynes lbw b Hadlee	12	J. G. Wright c Lloyd b Garner	15
I. V. A. Richards c Burgess b Coney	9	J. V. Coney c Garner b King	36
A. I. Kallicharran b McKechnie	39	G. M. Turner c Lloyd b Roberts	20
C. H. Lloyd (capt) not out	73	J. F. M. Morrison c Murray b Garner	11
C. L. King lbw b Cairns	12	M. G. Burgess (capt) c Richards b Roberts	35
D. L. Murray (wk) c Coney b Chatfield	12	W. K. Lees (wk) b Croft	5
A. M. E. Roberts c Lees b Cairns	1	R. J. Hadlee b Roberts	42
J. Garner not out	9	B. J. McKechnie not out	13
Extras b5 lb7	12	B. L. Cairns b Holding	1
(60 overs)	7-244	E. J. Chatfield not out	3
Did not bat: M. A. Holding, C. E.H. Croft		Extras lb14 w4 nb1	19
1/23 2/61 3/117 4/152 5/175 6/202 7/204		(60 overs)	9-212
Bowling: Hadlee 11-2-41-1; Chatfield 11-0-45-1;		1/27 2/38 3/90 4/91 5/138 6/143 7/160 8/199 9/202	
Cairns 12-1-48-2; Coney 12-0-40-2; McKechnie 11-0-46-1;		Bowling: Roberts 12-2-43-3; Holding 12-1-29-1;	
Morrison 3-0-12-0		Croft 12-1-38-1; Garner 12-0-45-2; King 12-1-38-1	

Umpires: H.D. Bird B.J. Meyer

Toss: New Zealand   Points: West Indies 4 New Zealand 0

WEDNESDAY 20 JUNE 1979
THE PRUDENTIAL CUP SEMI-FINALS.

At the end of the preliminary rounds of the 1979 World Cup the Group tables finished as follows:

GROUP B	P	W	L	Pts	GROUP A	P	W	L	NR	Pts
England	3	3	0	12	West Indies	3	2	0	1	10
Pakistan	3	2	1	8	New Zealand	3	2	1	0	8
Australia	3	1	2	4	Sri Lanka	3	1	1	1	6
Canada	3	0	3	0	India	3	0	3	0	0

IST SEMI FINAL: ENGLAND vs NEW ZEALAND
OLD TRAFFORD: ENGLAND WON BY 9 RUNS

The weather finally turned on its 1975 best for the two mid-week semi-finals and the cricketers of the four teams involved responded accordingly with a fine display of all the best aspects of the limited-overs game.

Old Trafford was filled to its 22,000 capacity for the clash between England and New Zealand. The English supporters crammed into the saucer shaped arena were hoping to cheer their side one step further than they had gone four years before. They eventually got what they wanted. The Kiwis made them apprehensive on more than one occasion, though, before the favourites sneaked home by a mere nine runs.

Unlike Headingley 1975, there was no *Pitchus horribilis* for this encounter. Sunshine and a dry flat wicket ensured most if not all the days allocation of 120 overs would be needed. Mark Burgess won the toss and, as was his and every other captain's habit, inserted the opposition. His spearhead, Richard Hadlee responded with a superb opening spell. Geoff Boycott survived a sharp chance to wicketkeeper, Warren Lees from the second ball he faced off Gary Troup before Hadlee had the opener well caught at third slip by the fit again Geoff Howarth in the fifth over of the day.

It was the start New Zealand wanted. England had included debutant batsman Wayne Larkins at the expense of their spinner, Phil Edmonds, and it was the newcomer who joined Mike Brearley with the score on 13. Larkins middled the ball well from the moment he arrived at the crease. His placement, though, was lacking. His captain, too, was fairly circumspect and the pair occupied 16 overs while adding 21 before Larkins tough initiation ended when he holed out at cover off Brian McKechnie.

Burgess had put in place his deep field setting by now, ensuring few if any boundaries were conceded. Brearley, who would take Burgess' deep set field theory to excess in Australia the following winter, continued to accumulate in singles. Gooch arrived and played shots. Often he had to be content with singles, as well. One straight six off McKechnie altered the pattern. Gooch danced down the wicket and thumped the ball straight. It soared towards and then through the sightscreen at Stretford End leaving a neat hole that Gooch says he checked every time he played on the ground and was not mended for 10 years.

Brearley now helmetless and hatless went to his solid half century, but he could barely extend it and in the 34th over was caught behind cutting at Jeremy Coney. 3-96 suggested a game in the balance. That balance swung the way of the Kiwis almost immediately when David Gower took on Lance Cairns arm going for a sharp second run and lost. Gooch and Ian Botham lifted the tempo of the England innings and levelled the game's pendulum by adding 47 runs in just 10 overs. Cairns then struck again, this time as a bowler. A loud appeal for lbw against Botham when he essayed a massive hook at a ball that kept low was answered in the affirmative as he and Gooch set off for a leg bye.

Derek Randall had probably held his place in the side through his brilliant fielding. His tournament scores in the preliminary rounds batting at number three had been 1, 5 and 1. 'Arkle' came in now at 5-145 and played his chip and run role to perfection. Gooch finally chopped a wide one from McKechnie onto his stumps and Troup had Chris Old caught behind for a duck. England were now 7-178 and a sub-standard total loomed as a possibility.

As he did against Pakistan, Bob Taylor came in at a crucial time to play an important small innings. The 38-year-old greying, immaculate little keeper ran well with the busy Randall and once lifted Cairns over long on for six to the delight of the big Mancunian crowd. Randall also put one into the crowd off Cairns. The suffering bowler would eventually run out Taylor in the last over with a direct under arm hit, but New Zealand had conceded 25 runs in their final three overs. England finished on 8-221 and knew now they were well in the contest.

Some English scribes were not confident that the required run rate of 3.7 per over was quite enough of an ask and the ease with which John Wright and Bruce Edgar got the Kiwi reply underway suggested their pessimism could be well founded. They put on 47 in 16 overs and then Edgar became the first of four batsmen in the New Zealand innings to be given out lbw. Chris Old won that decision. Geoff Howarth was the next eleven runs later, his dismissal being a real blow to the Kiwis' chances. Geoff Boycott came on as second change. He went around the wicket. Howarth received a full toss. He went to sweep the ball to square leg, missed and was given out. Even the Lancastrians were pleased with yet another bonus Boycott wicket.

Coney and Wright lifted the score into three figures. But Coney became the third lbw victim and Wright after a fine display was sent back on a second run by Glenn Turner and fell foul of a superb throw from the revitalised Randall. He rocketed the ball in 60 yards from deep square leg. Bob Willis related how relieved he was to catch it and successfully remove the bails.

New Zealand were now struggling a little at 4-112. Another Randall inspired run out, this time Mark Burgess making the misjudgement, left them an even worse 5-132. Bob Willis wrenched his knee in a bowling foothold so badly it would eventually keep him out of the final, but he had time to complete his twelve over spell and win a critical lbw decision against the experienced Glenn Turner.

The game was slipping away, but Hadlee, Lees, and Cairns would not give in. Forty-three runs were required from the last five overs. Lees hit Hendrick long, hard and high to mid-on. Boycott manoeuvred under the ball then held the catch. However with his feet over the boundary rope the shot counted for six. Botham bowled Hadlee, another crucial dismissal. Cairns, an immensely powerful man, retaliated by hoisting the English all-rounder into the crowd at mid wicket. Twenty-five runs were still needed from the final 18 deliveries.

Botham and Hendrick were both limping, yet they managed to keep the ball right up on a yorker length at the business end of the innings. Cairns smacked a catch hard and low to mid wicket off Hendrick. Brearley held on without fuss. McKechnie and Lees pushed on, scraping together another 13 precious runs until the second last over of the match, when Hendrick sent down the perfect yorker to the New Zealand wicketkeeper. McKechnie and Troup needed 14 runs off the final over from Botham. If Greg Chappell had witnessed McKechnie's failure to get more than four runs with his partner from this over he may later have refrained from his regrettable underarm instruction to his younger brother in a later limited overs tournament. Six more well-directed deliveries and England could celebrate their advance into the final.

For the second consecutive World Cup New Zealand bowed out at the semi-final stage. This time they had got to within an agonising nine runs of their objective. There was plenty of "hard luck old boy" attitude amongst the press to their efforts, but the Kiwis' final total of 9-212 was identical to the one they scored off the West Indies at Trent Bridge four days before. As it did in that game, the score indicated a batting line-up that was not quite good enough.

Graham Gooch's important innings earned him his second Man of the Match Award in 11 days.

ENGLAND		NEW ZEALAND	
J. M. Brearley (capt) c Lees b Coney	53	J. G. Wright run out	69
G. Boycott c Howarth b Hadlee	2	B. A. Edgar lbw b Old	17
W. Larkins c Coney b McKechnie	7	G. P. Howarth lbw b Boycott	7
G. A. Gooch b McKechnie	71	J. V. Coney lbw b Hendrick	11
D. I. Gower run out	1	G. M. Turner lbw b Willis	30
I. T. Botham lbw b Cairns	21	M. G. Burgess (capt) run out	10
D. W. Randall not out	42	R. J. Hadlee b Botham	15
C. M. Old c Lees b Troup	0	W. K. Lees (wk) b Hendrick	23
R. W. Taylor (wk) run out	12	B. L. Cairns c Brearley b Hendrick	14
R. G. D. Willis not out	1	B. J. McKechnie not out	4
Extras lb 8 w3	11	G. B. Troup not out	3
(60 overs)	8-221	Extras b5 w4	9
Did not bat: M. Hendrick		(60 overs)	9-212

England: 1/13 2/38 3/96 4/98 5/145 6/177 7/178 8/219

New Zealand: 1/47 2/58 3/104 4/112 5/132 6/162 7/180 8/195 9/208

Bowling: Hadlee 12-4-32-1; Troup 12-1-38-1; Cairns 12-2-47-1; Coney 12-0-47-1; McKechnie 12-1-46-2

Bowling: Botham 12-3-42-1; Hendrick 12-0-55-3; Old 12-1-33-1; Boycott 9-1-24-1; Gooch 3-1-8-0; Willis 12-1-41-1

Umpires: J.G. Langridge and K.E. Palmer

Toss: New Zealand

2ND SEMI-FINAL: PAKISTAN vs WEST INDIES
THE OVAL: WEST INDIES WON BY 43 RUNS

If the semi-final at Old Trafford provided a classic limited-overs, nip-and-tuck contest, then the match at The Oval was the sumptuous batting feast. The West Indian side must have marvelled at the transformation of the south London ground from the wet, gloomy hole of 10 days earlier to the sun-drenched buzzing venue that greeted them this time.

An almost equal mix of West Indians, Pakistanis and neutrals created a fantastic, noisy cosmopolitan atmosphere which demanded great cricket. The 20,000 fans saw Asif Iqbal win the toss and predictably send the West Indies in. The Pakistani captain had Sarfraz Nawaz back at the helm with Imran Khan and he must have been hopeful his new ball pair could provide an early breakthrough. Sarfraz had been brilliant against the West Indies in 1975. On this day, though, he was obviously underdone and could find neither line nor length. David Lemmon compared his profligacy with that of Alan Hurst against Pakistan at Trent Bridge. Imran bowled with genuine pace, but in Gordon Greenidge's estimation, was too short.

Greenidge and Desmond Haynes took full advantage, punishing anything loose with the utmost vigour. Greenidge continued his especially fine form. Mudassar Nazar was introduced into the attack and Haynes on 32 top-edged him towards Imran at fine leg. The all-rounder momentarily could not sight the ball against the crowd background and moving late he missed the important catch. It was Pakistan's only real opportunity for 30 overs as Greenidge and Haynes put on 132 for the first wicket. Finally Asif brought himself on and got Greenidge to edge the ball to Wasim Bari standing up.

Viv Richards and Clive Lloyd played some blazing strokes as the bowlers conceded on average five or six runs an over. Asif caught Haynes off his own bowling and later bowled Richards. However, it was Majid Khan who did most to stem the torrent of runs. In the midst of the batting carnage going on all around him Majid sent down his quiet little off-spinners at no more than two an over.

Collis King dominated a stand of 49 with Alvin Kallicharran. King's aggressive cameo would prove the perfect warm up for Saturday's festivities, but in this case it was a material help towards the West Indies 60 over total of 6-293, which was easily the best of the tournament so far.

The West Indies had started this match as clear favourites with the bookmakers and, after setting Pakistan 294 to win, were virtually unbookable. Michael Holding started with a very fast spell, including a few bouncers to soften the batsmen's resolve. The tactic worked when Sadiq Mohammad was caught behind with the score on just 10. But Greenidge at second slip dropped Majid and soon the West Indian pacemen were finding the wicket as slow and unresponsive as had Sarfraz and Imran.

Majid and Zaheer Abbas took full advantage. In a dazzling display the pair added 166 runs in 36 overs. On their day either could be the most enchanting strokeplayer in the world. At The Oval their sublime batting thrilled all except the West Indians. For the first time in any World Cup contest, Clive Lloyd was worried. Pakistan got themselves into a position where they required five runs an over with nine wickets in hand. On such a day this was a very gettable target. Lloyd admitted that the tea break arrived at just the right time. It allowed his side to regroup and re-assess their tactics.

They agreed to concentrate on a restrictive leg-stump line of attack. Colin Croft the meanest and, regards action, ugliest member of the Caribbean pace quartet and Viv Richards were entrusted with the job. Both responded magnificently. Richards' first over cost 12 runs, but next over Zaheer's superb 93 was ended by a brilliant diving leg-side catch by wicketkeeper Deryck Murray. Imran believes Asif then made a grave tactical error at this point by sending in the inexperienced Haroon Rashid. He could not give Majid enough of the strike and eventually it was the established batsman who mistimed a ball to Kallicharran in the covers.

Croft then picked up his third wicket from 12 balls in his spell from the Vauxhall End when he trapped Javed Miandad lbw first ball. From 1-176 Pakistan had promptly slipped to 4-187. Asif came in and tried to resurrect the run rate. He attempted to blast Richards for six and was dropped on the boundary. He tried again and was caught by Holding. Finally with the total on 6-220 Imran walked to the wicket. At Headingley everything had depended on him. Now it did again. Already, though, he felt defeated and soon became Richards third victim when the off-spinner held a spectacular caught and bowled chance.

Andy Roberts made the denouement a brief one and at 8.10pm, Pakistan were all out 43 runs short of the West Indies total in the 57th over of their innings. Imran and perhaps most of his teammates felt sickened by the result. Their compatriots filed out of the ground on a beautiful evening wondering what had gone wrong. With a sensational win within their grasp, they had lost 9-74. Like the corresponding fixture in1975, Pakistan's temperament had failed them at exactly the wrong moment.

The West Indies were relieved, but believed, as did most cricket followers, that justice was being done by them progressing to the Final. Whether justice was done by John Edrich's choice of the Man of the Match is another matter. Greenidge, who admittedly played a fine innings, got the nod ahead of Majid, who also bowled well, and Zaheer who made 20 extra runs. It is rare that the Man of the Match comes from the losing side and frequent that the adjudicator picks someone who fulfils the same team role that he used to.

WEST INDIES		PAKISTAN	
C. G. Greenidge c Wasim Bari b Asif Iqbal	73	Majid Khan c Kallicharran b Croft	81
D. L. Haynes c & b Asif Iqbal	65	Sadiq Mohammad c Murray b Holding	2
I. V. A. Richards b Asif Iqbal	42	Zaheer Abbas c Murray b Croft	93
C. H. Lloyd (capt) c Mudassar Nazar b Asif Iqbal	37	Haroon Rashid run out	15
C. L. King c sub (Wasim Raja) b Sarfraz Nawaz	34	Javed Miandad lbw b Croft	0
A. I. Kallicharran b Imran Khan	11	Asif Iqbal (capt) c Holding b Richards	17
A. M. E. Roberts not out	7	Mudassar Nazar c Kallicharran b Richards	2
J. Garner not out	1	Imran Khan c & b Richards	6
Extras b1 lb17 w1 nb4	23	Sarfraz Nawaz c Haynes b Roberts	12
(60 overs)	6-293	Wasim Bari (wk) c Murray b Roberts	9
Did not bat: D. L. Murray (wk), M. A. Holding, C. E.H. Croft		Sikander Bakht not out	1
1/132 2/165 3/233 4/236 5/285 6/285		Extras lb9 w2 nb1	12
Bowling: Imran Khan 9-1-43-1; Sarfraz Nawaz 12-1-71-1;		(56.2 overs)	250
Sikander Bakht 6-1-24-0; Mudassar Nazar 10-0-50-0; Majid		1/10 2/176 3/187 4/187 5/208 6/220 7/221 8/228 9/246	
Khan 12-2-26-0; Asif Iqbal 11-0-56-4		10/250	
		Bowling: Roberts 9.2-2-41-2; Holding 9-1-28-1;	
		Croft 11-0-29-3; Garner 12-1-47-0;	
		King 7-0-41-0; Richards 8-0-52-3	

Umpires: W.L.Budd D.J.Constant
Toss: Pakistan

SATURDAY 23 JUNE 1979
THE PRUDENTIAL WORLD CUP FINAL
ENGLAND VS WEST INDIES
LORDS: WEST INDIES WON BY 92 RUNS

Phil Edmonds returned to London from Old Trafford in the same car as his captain. The two did not always see eye to eye. Edmonds was not selected in the semi-final so it was not surprising that the atmosphere in the vehicle was tense.

Edmonds has indicated that his captain was clearly intimidated by the pressure of leading his country against the might of the West Indies. It was something he never had to do in a Test match. The left-arm spinner reveals that Brearley kept repeating, "How can we possibly beat the West Indies?"

Edmonds does not go any further than this or indicate what suggestions he might have offered except to say that he thought Brearley had a poor match tactically. From the word go he was up against it, though. In addition to the quality of the opposition Brearley had to try and cover shortcomings in his own side. Bob Willis, try as he might, had insufficient time to recuperate from his knee injury. He agonised over the decision right up to the morning of the big match and even tried his knee out in the nets before he succumbed to the discomfort and had to inform Chairman of Selectors, Alec Bedser of his withdrawl.

That left the English selectors in something of a quandary. At the time of the nomination of their 14-man squad, there were many who chastised them for including an extra batsman at the expense of another pace bowler such as in-form Essex left-armer, John Lever. The folly of their policy was quickly apparent because Mike Gatting was not selected in any games. Nor was there any confidence in the second spinner, Geoff Miller. England, with the extra batsman in the final would have to make do with overs from the likes of Geoff Boycott and Graham Gooch again. Boycott had done a sterling job during the tournament, taking five important and inexpensive wickets. But he had not had to bowl against the West Indies and was also now troubled by a sore back.

He had tried wearing a helmet for the first time in the nets prior to the big match. His decision whether to use it had to wait, however, as Mike Brearley won the toss. He had asked a few of his closest lieutenants what he should do and then, like everyone else in the tournament except the Canadian captain Mauricette, he asked the opposition to bat.

An air of expectancy filled the ground. The weather, although not as good as 1975, promised to be fine throughout. There would be high cloud with some sunny breaks. It would be a day very comfortable for players and spectators alike. The West Indian players who were lucky enough to be involved for the second time were just as exhilarated and nervous as they had been four years before. They had no real selection or injury problems and maintained the same 11 for the entire tournament. The West Indies went into the game as clear cut favourites. A punter could get 9-4 on England taking out the final. Once they were at the ground the Englishteam really believed they could win. "We knew the West Indies had a great side," England wicketkeeper Bob Taylor recalls. "But because it was a one-day game we thought we had a very good chance."

The match had long been a sell-out, with 25,000 crammed into Lord's. The bells and rhythms of the West Indian fans rang through the ground early and then continued non-stop. People milled outside Lord's in St Johns Wood Road, hoping to buy a stray ticket from a tout, to just catch a glimpse of the players or action, or even to absorb some of the atmosphere of the great event.

"It was a fantastic atmosphere," says Bob Taylor. "There were plenty of West Indians in the crowd, a lot more than seem to go to matches in England today. But the majority were still right behind us and that helped. It was a big day, a cricketer's equivalent of the football World Cup. There were a few nerves before the game in the dressing room, however, once you are on the ground and into the game you just get on with it."

Brearley's decision to bowl had met with a mixed reaction, but there was plenty of movement off the seam early on and the ball regularly beat the edge of the bats of Gordon Greenidge and Desmond Haynes. Mike Hendrick was moving his leg-cutter up the slope. Maiden overs were enthusiatically applauded by hopeful English supporters. Greenidge had batted beautifully throughout the tournament. Today, though, he seemed slightly overawed by the occasion as he had in 1975. A call for a short single to mid wicket was misjudged. Randall swooped and scored a direct hit with his underarm throw. Greenidge did not even have to look at the umpire to know his fate.

Viv Richards was another who failed with the bat at the previous World Cup final. His form in this tournament had been patchy and off his second ball he had to withstand a confident lbw shout. A clip off his pads to the Grandstand boundary off Chris Old was an isolated stroke of quality as the champion batsman struggled to find his touch.

Richards was able to hang on, but Haynes after working his way to 20, edged Old to Hendrick at second slip. The West Indies were an uneasy 2-36. Brearley thought it a good opportunity to use up some overs from Boycott. When he conceded just one run in his first over, it seemed the veteran, bad back and all, could once more do the job required. The pattern of limited-over internationals today is that batting becomes more restrained in the 15th over as it signals the end of fielding restrictions outside the circle. Richards saw the 15th over of this match as the time to open up. He smashed Old to mid-on with a stand up pull and next ball played a perfect cover drive to the Mound Stand boundary.

Spinner Phil Edmonds was introduced. He concentrated on a leg-side attack and once more Richards was obliged to go on the defensive. The 50 was passed, but Alvin Kallicharran, almost a shadow of the batsman who dominated in 1975, soon misjudged the line of a ball from Hendrick and was bowled behind his legs.

The comparisons to 1975 continued. Then Lloyd had come in at 3-50. Today the total was 3-55 and another rescue job was required. He grabbed a single first ball, but at no time looked to take control as he had against the Australians. Instead he let Richards, who had been on 22 when Lloyd came in, continue to dominate. Boycott came back on from the pavilion end. This time Richards relished his around the wicket in-swing. A short ball was crashed into the Tavern concourse for six. The next was a full toss struck sweetly through square leg for four more.

The fourth wicket stand carried the total to 99 when Old lifted English spirits once more. Lloyd finally unleashed a powerful straight drive. The Yorkshireman stooped, put down his left hand and came up with an astonishing caught and bowled. It was no more than his side deserved. They had fielded in exemplary fashion all morning. The home crowd sensed an upset and the possibility of a complete West Indian collapse. Collis King was coming in at number six and his record was hardly imposing.

"We thought we had one end open," Bob Taylor says. "But how wrong we were. Collis got going straight away." Richards passed his 50 with an edge off Ian Botham, wide of second slip to the pavilion rail. It had been scored out of 109 from 71 balls in 89 minutes. King started fluently enough with 19 runs off five overs including one cracking back foot drive through the covers and the West Indies were 4-125 at lunch off 34 overs leaving the game nicely poised.

Brearley still had get through more overs with his 'fill in' bowlers. He brought them on straight after lunch. It would prove the crucial phase of the match. Richards and King turned their attention first to Gooch. King swept him for four and Richards, also playing a sweep, hit him for his second six, this time into the Mound Stand. Next Richards stepped right away from his leg stump and cracked Edmonds through the covers for four more.

The stand was growing quickly and alarmingly for the English team and its supporters. And things would get a whole lot worse for them before they got better. King, who had struggled in a short stint as a County player with Glamorgan, had been impressive in his matching Richards stroke for stroke. Now, though, with Richards just six short of his century, the Barbadian all-rounder took total control.

As expensive as Gooch and Boycott had been, Brearley was expecting too much by asking Wayne Larkins to bowl. The English captain could not have done worse if he had used himself. Larkins came on and in the 47th over of the innings conceded 16 runs. King twice deposited juicy long hops into the Grandstand for six, the first one bringing King to his wonderful half century and raising the 200. From the second Randall was lucky to get the ball back from the excited dancing crowd. On television Jim Laker spoke of the futility of England not picking a recognised fifth bowler. Boycott returned and received similar treatment. King crashed him off the back foot through the covers, clipped him off his toes over square leg for six and "using every shot in the book", belted a front foot cover drive for four more towards the Mound Stand. Fifteen runs came from that over.

Edmonds was recalled and soon put an end to the mayhem, King holing out to Randall on the deep square leg boundary. The fieldsman joined the applause for King as soon as the catch was held. Randall knew his unbelievable innings of 86 off 67 balls in 77 minutes including three sixes and 10 fours, had ruined England's chances. King had added 139 with Richards in just 21 overs, leaving the score on 5-238. He left the arena to a great ovation. This was the greatest moment of King's career.

"It's easy after the event, I know," says Bob Taylor. "However it really was asking too much of second string bowlers to keep a tight rein on Viv Richards and Co. in a World Cup Final. Goochie maybe, but never Geoff Boycott and Wayne Larkins. It turned the game. You sensed even as they came on to bowl that Richards and King were going to get into them. They played shots all around the wicket, every shot in the book."

King was dismissed in the 51st over of the innings. In the 52nd Richards went to the hundred that had temporaily been put on hold. An on-drive from an Old full toss raised the three figures in 129 balls. Richards raised his bat and cap as the sun shone. An Antiguan flag fluttered at the front of the Tavern in proud response.

It was a magic moment. Richards knew, though, that his job was not done. For the rest of the innings only five more runs were scored by batsmen other than the Antiguan champion. Andy Roberts, Joel Garner and Michael Holding were all dismissed for ducks. Roberts was brilliantly caught by Brearley on the mid-boundary. Richards took his turn to blaze. Hendricks conceded 14 runs in the 60th over. A flat-bat straight drive had nearly decapitated the umpire, Barry Meyer, as well as the bowler. Then from the final ball of the innings came his *piece de resistance*. Hendricks fired in the ball full and straight. Richards was already moving straight across his stumps. He picked the ball up and swatted it straight over square leg for a most ridiculous six. "A front foot straight drive executed at right angles," was how *World of Cricket 1980* described it.

The West Indies had finished on 9-286, just five runs short of their wonderful effort in 1975. Eighty-six of those runs had been conceded by Boycott, Gooch and Larkins, although Clive Lloyd believed nobody would have been able to contain King on that day. Richards batted three-and-a-half hours for his unbeaten 138 and hit three sixes and 11 fours.

England began their reply at 3.35pm. The pairing of Boycott and Brearley had been a dismal failure in this World Cup, but the wicket was now dry and sound and the obdurate pair got themselves entrenched. Boycott looked in trouble against Holding who was again fearsome with the new ball. In the seventh over, the England captain struck Roberts to the point boundary. Then a pull shot went square through Garner's fingers for four more, lifting the pressure for the moment.

Brearley was let off again in the 15th over when Lloyd dropped him at second slip. Boycott, who had taken 17 overs to reach double figures, hooked Croft and after 19 overs England were 0-55. Richards was becoming agitated at the missed opportunities and lack of a breakthrough. He was brought on to bowl and snatched his cap off umpire 'Dickie' Bird. Next over he threw the ball back like a bullet at Deryck Murray behind the stumps.

Both batsmen were reduced to scoring mostly in singles so that England went to tea at 0-79 from 25 overs. At that point, 208 runs were needed from 35 overs. The West Indian fans had gone quiet, but Lloyd was not concerned. "I thought they would have opened with Gooch," he told 'Dickie' Bird at tea. "They are scoring only at three an over and that's not bad for us."

A foundation had been established, but the need to accelerate straight after the interval was obvious. Yet inside the England dressing room the sentiment acccording to Brearley was "keep it going like it is". He says that Botham told him not to take too many chances and that Randall assured him with, "It's magic." Edmonds, as was often the case, was a dissenter and voiced his disapproval of the scoring rate.

After the break, with the light gradually starting to deteriorate, the runs continued to come in singles. The hundred partnership was raised in the 32nd over. Boycott advanced on Richards and hit him to Lloyd at mid-on. He leapt and dropped his second catch. The cynical suggested he had done so on purpose. In 13 overs after tea, Boycott and Brearley added a further 50 runs. It was good solid stuff, but it made the task of the following batsmen impossible. Brearley knew Richards should have been attacked, however he conceded only 35 runs from his 10 overs. Gooch wrote in his autobiography, "In hindsight they should never have opened together."

Bob Taylor agrees: "Boycott and Mike Brearley were too much the same in their batting styles. We should have opened with at least one strokeplayer, like Gooch, himself."

Boycott hit Roberts through the covers on the up and guided him to third man for boundaries. Both men reached their half century. But the run rate was creeping up all the time. Every single increased it further. Lloyd said he knew that each over the pair stayed together it was "another nail in the English coffin".

Brearley finally hooked Holding straight high to King at square leg and Boycott, too, could not control a cross-batted shot off the same bowler. Gooch, England's best batsman in the competition came in to join Randall facing the awesome task of scoring 151 runs in 20 overs.

He gave it his best shot. Garner was struck hard and high to the mid-on boundary. Gooch unleashed pulls and further drives. In 43 balls he and Randall put on 48 runs in energetic fashion lifting the score to 2-183 and the faint prospect of an English miracle. Then Joel Garner snuffed it out in an instant. Gooch had hit a couple of fine drives while scoring 32 in 28 balls. Then Randall swiped once too often at Colin Croft and was bowled. From the first ball of the next over Gooch played all over a Garner yorker and England were 4-183. Four balls and three runs later David Gower backed away, making room for a cut, and saw his off stump knocked back. Then from the final ball of this sensational over Garner completed Larkins' misery for the day by delivering yet another spot on yorker.

Botham intended to go down fighting and he hooked hard and high to fine leg. There was his Somerset colleague and friend Viv Richards running hard and taking a brilliant catch. Botham's miserable four were the only runs scored by a fast bowler in the entire match. England 7-188. Now Garner went to work again. From the fourth ball of his next over he flattened Old's off stump. Like Gower he had totally misjudged the line and length of the ball. Did he see it? Perhaps not. It was now quite late in the evening and the hand of the giant Barbadian was coming down from above the sightscreen at the Nursery End. Gooch said the ball was coming out of the darkening trees. When Bob Taylor was caught behind first ball, Garner with that heavy footed run and galumphing action had taken 5-4 in 11 balls. "By the time I got in, we were already dead and buried," says Bob Taylor. England were 9-192 and the World Cup was in effect over.

Croft completed the last rites a few moments later when he bowled Hendrick. The Derbyshire seamer became the fifth English batsman out for no score. The last eight wickets had fallen for 11 runs. The West Indies had won the Prudential Cup for the second time, on this occasion defeating England by 92 runs. West Indian supporters who had overflowed onto the ground with some regularity during the afternoon now charged from every direction in joyous celebration.

"We participated in the celebrations," says Bob Taylor. "I don't know about now, but then all the teams fraternised. The one gap in my career was that I never got to play a Test against the West Indies even though I was picked 57 times for England. This was the only big match I got to compete against that great side, so that made it special for me, too."

Young Malcolm Marshall, watching in the dressing room had been tense and nervous all day, more so, he admitted, than the actual players in the game. He was exultant when he received his winners' medal with the rest of the team. Gordon Greenidge reveals the celebrations were as hectic and joyous as they had been four years before. He felt prouder this time because his own contribution throughout the four matches played had been far more significant.

Clive Lloyd believed the win totally unified West Indian cricket again in the post-Packer era. He wondered, though, how much the game's authorities had learned when he was originally offered a captain's winning bonus of just £50 by the Board's representative, Clyde Walcott.

England, the majority of the 25,000 crowd and everyone else watching on the BBC, felt disappointed but proud. Brearley later wrote of his opponents, "I cannot believe that in the history of the game, there had been a side better equipped for one-day cricket." The English have always revered the gallant defeat. By 1992, when they had lost two more finals, pride at just participating in the event was starting to wear thin. By then only the result mattered.

Viv Richards was named Man of the Match. Dennis Compton called it a 'joyous exhibition' and also wrote, "The Don at his best could not have been more impudently superior."

WEST INDIES		ENGLAND	
C. G. Greenidge run out	9	J. M. Brearley (capt) c King b Holding	64
D. L. Haynes c Hendrick b Old	20	G. Boycott c Kallicharran b Holding	57
I. V. A. Richards not out	138	D. W. Randall b Croft	15
A. I. Kallicharran b Hendrick	4	G. A. Gooch b Garner	32
C. H. Lloyd (capt) c & b Old	13	D. I. Gower b Garner	0
C. L. King c Randall b Edmonds	86	I. T. Botham c Richards b Croft	4
D. L. Murray (wk) c Gower b Edmonds	5	W. Larkins b Garner	0
A. M. E. Roberts c Brearley b Hendrick	0	P. H. Edmonds not out	5
J. Garner c Taylor b Botham	0	C. M. Old b Garner	0
M. A. Holding b Botham	0	R. W. Taylor (wk) c Murray b Garner	0
C. E. H. Croft not out	0	M. Hendrick b Croft	0
Extras b1 lb10	11	Extras lb12 w2 nb3	17
(60 overs)	9-286	(51 overs)	194

1/22 2/36 3/55 4/99 5/238 6/252 7/258 8/260 9/272

Bowling: Botham 12-2-44-2; Hendrick 12-2-50-2; Old 12-0-55-2; Boycott 6-0-38-0; Edmonds 12-2-40-2; Gooch 4-0-27-0; Larkins 2-0-21-0

1/129 2/135 3/183 4/183 5/186 6/186 7/192 8/192 9/194 10/194

Bowling: Roberts 9-2-33-0; Holding 8-1-16-2; Croft 10-1-42-3; Garner 11-0-38-5; Richards 10-0-35-0; King 3-0-13-0

Umpires: H.D. Bird   B.J. Meyer

Toss: England

POST-MORTEM

Whatever the weather miseries of the second round of the 1979 Prudential World Cup, the tournament was once more considered a fantastic success overall. The ICC certainly liked it enough to announce a limited-overs world cup would now be a regular tournament, played every four years.

The financial returns were attractive to the officials from every country. Prudential had put in their £250,000, while gate receipts were up from £188,000 to £359,000. Attendance was down from 160,000 to 132,000, a factor blamed entirely on the inferior weather. The West Indies took away £10,000 pounds in prizemoney, plus the £100 pound bonus for Clive Lloyd being winning captain—Walcott had come back later and doubled his original offer.

Although celebrations had been wholehearted, within a few days everyone was back to the treadmill. The next Thursday, 27 June, Ian Botham, Viv Richards and Joel Garner were teammates again as Somerset tackled Worcestershire.

CHAPTER 4:

Prudential World Cup 1983: Tournament of the Boilovers

Just as the 1979 World Cup followed in the immediate wake of the controversial World Series Cricket 'Cricket War', the 1983 tournament also took place in the shadow of a greater issue.

South African authorities, frustrated by their ongoing cricketing isolation, had been flying incognito to various countries, bringing out their chequebooks and signing players to tour their country. They secured the services of 'rebel' teams from England early in 1982 and side from Sri Lanka and the West Indies 12 months later. The players involved were banned by their home boards for varying amounts of time. The English players, including Graham Gooch and John Emburey, would miss three years of Test and limited-overs cricket for a fistful of rand. The West Indian and Sri Lankan players originally received 25-year and lifetime bans, so seriously did their countries view players venturing into the then forbidden territory.

This was a completely different matter to the World Series Cricket ruckus over television and cricket. The cricket world risked being split between black and white nations. Further complications arose from the fact that Zimbabwe, formerly Rhodesia, now had a democratically elected majority government and their representative teams were welcome all over the cricketing world. On At the same time, conservative elements within the Marylebone Cricket Club were calling for a side representing them to be sent to South Africa. In a final twist, South African-born players such as Allan Lamb had qualified for England and were establishing themselves in the Test side in the absence of the banned rebels.

The problem of these clandestine signings remained until the end of the decade. England, the West Indies and Sri Lanka had reduced resources to draw upon for the 1983 Prudential Cup, although none would be as decimated as the Australians of 1979.

The scheduling of limited-over internationals had grown dramatically since the previous World Cup. Between the first two tournaments there had been 28 recognised matches. In the four years since England had met the West Indies at Lord's, until the first match of the 1983 Prudential World Cup, 122 encounters had taken place. Many of those were among the plethora of matches played in Australia each year under the title of the World Series Cup. Now the other Test nations had embraced the concept, as well. They relished the instant popularity of the one-day games and the money they brought in. In Australia, one-day cricket reached the peak of its appeal in the early 1980s and doubts about the future of Test cricket were at their most serious.

The time was right to increase the number of World Cup matches. At their 1982 meeting, the ICC agreed in each group every side should play each other twice. This was to reduce the chances of a "freak result caused by the weather". No mention of money there. A couple of extra days were added to the fixture list and the number of days available for each match was reduced from three as it had been in 1979 to just two. The semi-finals and final were an exception to this with three days still available. It was felt the 1979 finalists should be seeded into two separate groups. This meant that England, for the third time, did not have to meet the West Indies in the preliminary rounds. The groups would be made up of the seven current Test playing nations, Sri Lanka being added to that company, and Zimbabwe, who had defeated Bermuda in the 1982 ICC Trophy Final.

Games were unchanged at 60 overs per innings with bowlers limited to 12 overs. They were due to start at 10.45 a.m. each day. For the first time in the World Cup, fielding restrictions were enforced. In this tournament they took the form of two 30-yard semi-circles with the fieldsmen inside and outside set at specific numbers at various times during an innings. Umpires were told to be strict in their interpretation of wides and bouncers to prevent negative bowling tactics.

The extra matches meant that venues away from the major Test grounds would have to be used this time. The best of the county grounds, such as Swansea, Taunton, Leicester, Bristol, Worcester, Southampton, Tunbridge Wells and Chelmsford were to be used to spread the World Cup gospel further around the country.

Prudential Assurance lifted their sponsorship to £500,000, double that of 1979. But at the same time, the company announced that three times was enough and they would have no involvement in 1987. This left the door open to other countries that were keen to stage the tournament.

The members of the winning team would go home £20,000 richer. Most people believed, with justification, that the West Indies would collect that cash, continue their dominance of the competition and secure the World Cup for the third time. The Caribbean juggernaut had sustained its run of success in an almost unbroken fashion since their 1979 win. They clearly stood head and shoulders above every other side in the world, despite the fact their squad did not include a specialist spinner.

Clive Lloyd returned as leader for the last time, seeking to complete a hat trick of trophies, a precedent unlikely ever to be matched. While the batting remained a real attraction, it was the quartet of pacemen that seemed likely to dominate all comers. A couple of the faces had changed, but the formula was the same; sustained blistering speed that eventually wore down a batsman's resolve. Colin Croft had gone the way of the South African rebels, but into his place stepped Malcolm Marshall, if anything faster than Croft, and probably more skilful.

Andy Roberts, Michael Holding and Joel Garner remained. Graham Gooch thought too much county cricket had blunted Roberts' edge in 1979 and soon he would be replaced. But he was now a canny bowler who had adapted beautifully to the demands of the limited-overs game. Holding, despite a knee operation, and Garner had several years of batting demolition ahead of them yet. Wayne Daniel and Winston Davis squeezed into the squad as heirs apparent to the next two spots in the fast-bowling production line. The West Indies completed their bowling quota now with the tight straight breaks of Viv Richards and Larry Gomes rather than the medium pace of Collis King. King, like Croft, was prepared to take the consequences of accepting South African rand.

One thing that had unchanged since 1979 was that Viv Richards stood at the top of the tree as the batsman with the world's highest rating. Now carrying the title the 'Master Blaster', the tremendous range and power of Richards' strokes were undiminished from four years before. Lloyd was now pushing 40, but his form was better in 1983 than it had been four years before. Gordon Greenidge and Desmond Haynes remained firmly entrenched as the world's premier pair of opening batsman, while left-hander Larry Gomes had come into the line-up to provide middle order stability.

Lloyd's right-hand man, Deryck Murray had been replaced in 1980, much to the disgust of his fans in Trinidad. But the man who now stood in his stead, Jeffrey Dujon was a more than worthy replacement. The Jamaican bore comparison with Murray as a wicketkeeper, but was in a higher class as a stylish middle-order batsman. He injected further quality into a side which had more right to start the World Cup as favourites that even their worthy predecessors. Most thought that way. Bookmakers had them 11-8 on. The West Indies arrived in England having just completed fairly comprehensive Test and limited-over series victories in the Caribbean over India.

England had overcome the loss of the loss of their South African rebels with moderate success. Fast-bowling veteran Bob Willis was at the helm of a team that had to plug several holes over the previous 18 months. Willis himself was in form as consistent as any from his long and distinguished career and he was closing in fast on the 300-Test-wicket mark. He had led an unsuccessful campaign in Australia, although he was not likely to have his position as captain questioned in the immediate future.

Test series against Australia were not yet the demoralising contests for England they became in the 1990s and Willis' side returned home with some definite positives. David Gower had responded to his appointment as deputy skipper with a brilliant Ashes tour, scoring prolifically in Tests and limited-overs internationals alike. Gower's premier batting won him the honour of the International Cricketer of the Year in Australia for 1982-83.

South African Allan Lamb had also proven himself a genuine run-making acquisition while Ian Botham's powers, in England at least, were as threatening as ever. The limited-over game almost seemed custom-made for a man of Botham's belligerent talents, yet his record in the shorter game remained far inferior to that in Tests. The 1983 World Cup would be another opportunity for him to redress that balance. His team, despite the loss of their defectors, attracted a lot of local money which made them 7-2 second favourites to go one step further than 1979 and claim the trophy at Lord's on 25 June.

The top-order English batting was less settled despite the obduracy of Chris Tavare, but quality pace bowling support for the ageing Willis seemed to be flowering. Graham Dilley's progress would be watched with interest, while young Norman Cowans had created a big impression in Australia.

Pakistan's two previous World Cup campaigns had been marred by the frustration of missed opportunities. This one was in trouble before the team even assembled in England. Imran Khan remained Pakistan's main strike bowler and his batting had developed to the point where he was now a major contributor in the middle order. Since his appointment as captain, he had unified his team into a force in world cricket. Such a mighty effort was starting to take a toll by 1983, though. Imran had been diagnosed as having stress fractures of the shin and despite a two-month rest in the lead up to the World Cup, he would not be able to bowl in the tournament. Imran had all sorts of advice about whether to go or not until he finally decided to make himself available just as a batsman.

His fast in-swing bowling would be missed as the pace back up of Tahir Naqqash and Rashid Khan was modest. Not that the Pakistani attack would be totally without merit. The last word used to describe Sarfraz Nawaz as a cricketer would be modest, and there was much interest around Abdul Qadir. His wheeling, fizzing legbreaks had revitalised the belief that wrist-spin could be a viable commodity at the top level of the game. Qadir had attracted rave reviews during the tight series between England and Pakistan in 1982.

Also emerging as a star during that three match contest was opening batsman, Mohsin Khan, who made an attractive, match-winning 200 in the Lord's Test. Mohsin assumed the mantle of number one opener following the departure of

Majid Khan. Majid's partner, Sadiq, the last of the Mohammad clan, was also gone, but Zaheer Abbas, Wasim Raja and the ever present nuisance, Javed Miandad remained.

Another fixture to return was New Zealand opener, Glenn Turner. There was not much international cricket left in him and he had made himself unavailable for the follow up Test series against England, but there is no doubting in 1975 and 1979 he had made a significant contribution to New Zealand's admirable progress. Geoff Howarth led the Kiwis this time and they looked as competent as their predecessors, if not more so.

Richard Hadlee's powers had not waned in any way and his seam support in Ewen Chatfield, Lance Cairns and Martin Snedden was more than respectable. Howarth himself was an accomplished middle-order batsman with a fine blend of experience and achievement in English conditions. The Crowe brothers, Jeff and Martin, were establishing their reputations on the world stage and John Wright and Bruce Edgar had become a solid fixture as an opening combination.

The cricketing world of Kim Hughes had fluctuated quite vigorously since 1979, both as captain and batsman, with worse to come. But in 1983 he was back in England as leader of Australia again with a second, far more realistic chance at glory. This time Dennis Lillee would not have to request entry into any dressing room. He would be trying to make his mark on the tournament on the playing field. It would be his last tour of England and his first lengthy outing since knee surgery the previous November.

His mates from the 1970s, wicketkeeper Rod Marsh and Sri Lankan scourge Jeff Thomson were also in the Australian squad this time. Lillee, Thomson, Rod Hogg and newcomer Geoff Lawson formed a pace quartet which was supposed to challenge the West Indian fast-bowling supremacy. Lawson, tall with a long toe drag and plenty of speed, was the bowler who now arrived with the big reputation. He had just secured 34 wickets for himself in the recently completed Ashes series. The clearest assessment of Australia's improved chances was shown by their rating as 6-1 equal third favourites with Pakistan. The one doubt was the threat to team harmony. The cloud of World Series Cricket had not yet properly dissipated from over the Australian dressing. In addition South African authorities were looking for new recruits. A number of Australian players were targets and the South Africans were offering them substantial amounts of money which would have been something of a distraction. Meantime the Australian Cricket Board was trying to protect its men from such temptations.

Greg Chappell had a neck injury and decided to stay with his family in Queensland, but if Hughes maintained his recent form, Chappell would hardly be missed. Hughes had topped the averages and aggregates against England and had as his vice-captain David Hookes, also successful against England, and Allan Border, quietly emerging as the grittiest batsman in world cricket. Graham Yallop, Graham Wood and South African Kepler Wessels, along with Border, Hookes and Marsh, completed the largest set of left-handed batsmen ever to wear the baggy green cap in one team. Trevor Chappell ensured his famous Australian cricket family did not completely miss out on all the fun of the World Cup. He had an important spare parts role within Hughes' side. Tom Hogan beat Bruce Yardley for the sole spinner's place. Yardley promptly retired when his fellow West Australian took the spot.

Little wonder India would begin the 1983 Prudential Cup as 66-1 outsiders. Their limited-overs form guide made depressing reading. There had been a sprinkling of victories since Kapil Dev had taken over the leadership reigns from Sunil Gavaskar, but nothing to suggest that the embarrassments of 1975 and 1979 could be turned into victory in the whole competition. The very idea seemed ludicrous. David Frith's preview in *Wisden Cricket Monthly* suggested: "If their pride is not important enough to spur them to wholehearted effort this time, they might as well give way to other would-be participants in 1987."

Their new captain, Kapil Dev, had, like Botham, Hadlee and Imran before him, developed into a fantastic all-rounder full of charisma and wonderful attacking cricket. By himself he should have ensured at least an improved performance from India. Sunil Gavaskar, with the departure of Geoff Boycott, now stood alone as the world's greatest batting technician. He was not pleased to lose the captaincy again, but did not let that stand in the way of his thirst for big scores.

His brother-in-law Gundappa Vishwanth was no longer in the team and would be missed. However, there were consolations. Mohinder Amarnath's batting recently in the West Indies had been a revelation, Sandeep Patil's strokeplay was exciting and handsome enough to attract movie producers and Kris Srikkanth had an approach to opening the batting that was 13 years ahead of its time. His attitude was that the harder and shinier the ball, the further it was meant to be hit.

Spin and guile were out, medium-pace and swing were in. Kapil Dev and a variety of support staff such as Amarnath, Roger Binny, Madan Lal and Balwindersingh Sandhu would do the bulk of the Indian bowling this time.

Of the three countries so far affected, Sri Lanka could least afford to lose their South African 'rebels'. Despite their country's elevation to full Test match status, a lack of depth remained an issue and the loss of talents such as Tony Opatha and Bandula Warnapura would be felt. They had, however, under the guidance of former Australian spinner and coach, Peter Philpott and West Indian legend Sir Garfield Sobers, already made some impact on the limited-over international stage with wins over Australia, India, Pakistan and England.

Their bowling lacked any real speed and would rely more on accuracy, Somachandra de Silva's wrist spin offering the most serious test of anyone's batting technique. Duleep Mendis, now captain, and Roy Dias had dabbled with the South African prospectus. This pair of short, stocky strokeplayers, were clearly Sri Lanka's best batsmen and their eventual availability was crucial to their team being able to make any impact on the competition at all.

In previous World Cups the eighth team, East Africa in 1975 and Canada in 1979, did little more than make up the numbers. Indications were that, although Zimbabwe might struggle to win the tournament, and they were rated at 1000-1 outsiders, they would be competitive and might, like Sri Lanka before them, give a few frights to any of the big boys who were off their guard.

Their captain, Duncan Fletcher was a very capable all-rounder, batting left-handed and bowling tight medium pace. He led a side several of whose members had first-class experience with Rhodesia in the South African Currie Cup. Wicketkeeper-batsman Dave Houghton would go onto become a stalwart of Zimabawe's earliest forays into the international cricketing brotherhood, while John Traicos, an Egyptian-born off-spinner with Greek parents, had played in South Africa's last few Tests before isolation in 1970. Kevin Curran was an all-rounder who went onto a long and successful career with English County sides Gloucestershire and Northhamptonshire. And on the trip for experience was a very talented 17-year-old schoolboy batsman named Graeme Hick.

The now traditional Buckingham Palace reception made a big impression on the teenage Zimbabwean. He nervously forgot his protocol and said, "Hi" when introduced to the queen and spent the afternoon drinking champagne and scoffing his beloved cashew nuts.

When the Australians practised against New Zealand at Arundel prior to the tournament, they had to call off the game because of a hailstorm that covered the ground in ice in 15 minutes. Bats were put away for cameras. English batsman David Gower in *Wisden Cricket Monthly* described his occupation as a cricketer as a 'joke' so little play was there in the month of May. Once again there was the fear the World Cup might be drenched out of existence if 9 June did not bring about a change. Some were not even optimistic that there would be enough time for grounds to dry before the start of the tournament, even if the rain did stop in time.

But when the four sides involved on the first day at The Oval and Swansea turned up at the grounds they must have wondered what all the fuss was about. The weather was perfect for cricket.

England opened their campaign at The Oval on a Thursday rather than Lord's on a Saturday. It made no real difference to Bob Willis' side, who ran out convincing winners. Unlike 1975 and 1979 the ground was nowhere near full for the host country's opening match, with only 9,500 people turning up.

Fielding restrictions undermined New Zealand's restrictive tactics of the previous tournament, and when the Kiwis had to bowl first, they conceded runs freely. One in particular, was thoroughly hammered. Those restrictions had been an innovation first tried in the Australian World Series Cup. Another gimmick imported from Australia was the setting up of a replay screen at The Oval for this match, but it caused some problems, only received mixed acceptance and by the end of the day was being switched off when left-handers were facing the Vauxhall End.

New Zealand had defeated England five times in limited-overs matches during the southern summer and must have approached this contest with some confidence. Bob Willis won the toss and batted, but Lance Cairns soon broke through for the Kiwis, sending Graeme Fowler back to the pavilion caught at slip from a late-moving delivery when there were just 13 runs on the board.

Richard Hadlee, less of a tear-away paceman now, was as testing and accurate as ever, but David Gower and Chris Tavare added 66 for the second wicket. Gower was caught on the mid wicket boundary. Then the generally stolid Kent opener stayed with Allan Lamb until Ewen Chatfield dismissed him with the total on 117. That set loose Mike Gatting and Lamb, who demolished the New Zealand attack in a fourth-wicket partnership of 115 in just 16 overs. Martin Snedden came in for some severe punishment. Once Lamb pulled him high into the crowd. Young Martin Crowe was also very expensive, conceding 23 runs in one wayward over.

A brief interruption for rain failed to stem the batting momentum. On resumption, Gatting hit the next two balls for four. He had been in and out of the England side for the past five years, only scraping into this squad ahead of Derek Randall because of his part-time bowling. Gatting was exhilarated by the energy of the partnership. He and Lamb were taking twos from hits straight to fieldsman on the boundary in a fashion Dean Jones would later become famous for.

Finally Snedden, the first bowler ever to concede a hundred runs in a World Cup match, gained a modicum of revenge by bowling both Gatting and Lamb, but that was not before the South African had completed his powerful century in 103 balls. It was Lamb's third in limited-over internationals, and, like the other two, it won him the Man of the Match Award.

Hadlee won the points in his personal duel with Ian Botham, but Graham Dilley's late flurry of hitting meant England added a phenomenal 203 from their last 25 overs. Ninety runs came from the last 10 overs while Gatting and Dilley had added 44 in 23 balls.

Any hope New Zealand had of scoring the 323 runs they needed for victory soon evaporated. Willis and Dilley sent down very fast opening spells which were too much for Glenn Turner, Bruce Edgar and John Wright. Edgar was the first to go, caught behind by Ian Gould diving in front of first slip, and when Turner was trapped in front and Wright, mistiming a pull, fell within three runs of each other New Zealand were 3-31. From that point there was really nowhere to go. Geoff Howarth succumbed to Vic Marks before tea. At the break New Zealand were 4-71 from 25 overs.

The wickets continued to fall at regular intervals in the last session and when New Zealand were 8-138 an early finish seemed likely. But Martin Crowe, assisted by Martin Snedden, kept the match going, without ever looking likely to alter the result. They had conceded an astonishing 156 runs in 18 overs between them. Now they added 52 runs for the ninth wicket, giving the 20-year-old Crowe an outside chance to make his first international hundred. When Gatting snaffled Snedden, last man Ewen Chatfield held firm too, and the landmark got closer. Finally, however, just three runs short of his personal target, Crowe was run out backing up too far.

ENGLAND		NEW ZEALAND	
G. Fowler c Coney b Cairns	8	G. M. Turner lbw b Willis	14
C. J. Tavare c Edgar b Chatfield	45	B. A. Edgar c Gould b Willis	3
D. I. Gower c Edgar b Coney	39	J. G. Wright c Botham b Dilley	10
A. J. Lamb b Snedden	102	G. P. Howarth (capt) c Lamb b Marks	18
M. W. Gatting b Snedden	43	J. V. Coney run out	23
I. T. Botham c Lees b Hadlee	22	M. D. Crowe run out	97
I. J. Gould (wk) not out	14	W. K. Lees (wk) b Botham	8
G. R. Dilley not out	31	R. J. Hadlee c Lamb b Marks	1
Extras lb12 w1 nb5	18	B. L. Cairns lbw b Botham	1
(60 overs)	6-322	M. C. Snedden c Gould b Gatting	21
Did not bat: V. J. Marks, P. J.W. Allott, R. G.D. Willis (capt)		E. J. Chatfield not out	9
1/13 2/79 3/117 4/232 5/271 6/278		Extras b2 lb4 w4 nb1	11
Bowling: Hadlee 12-4-26-1; Cairns 12-4-57-1;		(59 overs)	216
Snedden 12-1-105-2; Chatfield 12-1-45-1; Coney 6-1-20-1;		1/3 2/28 3/31 4/62 5/85 6/123 7/136 8/138 9/190	
Crowe 6-0-51-0		10/216	
		Bowling: Willis 7-2-9-2; Dilley 8-0-33-1; Botham 12-0-42-2;	
		Allott 12-1-47-0; Marks 12-1-39-2; Gatting 8-1-35-1;	

Umpires: B.J. Meyer D.O. Oslear

Toss: England   Points: England 4 New Zealand 0

GROUP A: PAKISTAN vs SRI LANKA
St.HELENS, SWANSEA: PAKISTAN WON BY 50 RUNS

The people of Wales were provided with an absolute run feast when World Cup cricket came to Swansea. Pakistan and Sri Lanka hit 626 runs in the 120 overs of cricket during the day, batsman after batsman enjoying the favourable conditions and the less than imposing bowling on offer.

The match aggregate of 14 wickets for 626 runs is still the second-highest ever in the World Cup, while Pakistan's 5-338 was at the time the highest innings total ever recorded in that competition.

What made it seem especially meritorious at the time was that Duleep Mendis won the toss and sent Pakistan in on a wicket that contained a lot of early moisture. But neither the wicket nor the bowling of Ashantha de Mel and big Vinothen John gave the opening batsmen Mudassar Nazar and Mohsin Khan any significant trouble.

They put on 88 in 26 overs before Mohsin and Zaheer Abbas added a further 68 in 14 overs. The stylish opener was finally removed just after lunch for 82, but Javed Miandad and Zaheer comfortably lifted the total to 229. Zaheer was also dismissed for 82. It was then that the fun began. Imran joined Javed and for nine overs there was batting mayhem.

John had come back for his second spell and bowled Mohsin. As if to punish him for that impudence, Javed and his captain smashed John for 42 runs from his last three overs. One of those went for 23, Imran, obviously trying to limit the amount of running on his sore shin, belted 22 of those including four fours and one six. Some of the shots were out of the textbook, others were the invention of the batsmen. Ninety-six runs were put on for the fourth wicket in what seemed like an instant. De Mel finally won an lbw shout against Javed, but he too had been punished severely, his last two overs costing 30. Javed's 72 lasted 54 balls and contained three sixes.

It was great entertainment and few expected Sri Lanka to seriously challenge a target of 339. However, they showed, as they had bravely against Australia eight years before, that chasing large totals did not overwhelm them. The wicket was now in excellent condition and most of the bowling was unthreatening. Even Zaheer Abbas was called on to send down a few deliveries, which he and probably the batsmen all would have enjoyed.

The Sri Lankans were never up with the required run rate, nor were there any big partnerships. Twenty-one-year-old opener Brendon Kuruppu did best with a fighting innings that lasted 33 overs and included two more sixes. His stand with Arjuna

Ranatunga took the score to a promising 3-142 before Zaheer ran out the youngster with a direct hit from mid wicket. Roy Dias and Duleep Mendis had both missed out so that once Ranatunga and Kuruppu were dismissed the challenge slipped badly. At 7-180 the margin of defeat seemed likely to be a large one. But wicketkeeper Guy de Alwis batted through the remainder of the innings. He and John were still unbeaten when the 60 overs were up. It was 8.15pm and Sri Lanka were still 50 runs short of their requirement. Their 9-288 was the highest losing World Cup score at the time.

Six batsmen completed half centuries in this match. Mohsin Khan's name was the one eventually picked from the hat to receive the Man of the Match Award. Yet on a day and in a form of the game custom made for batsmen, who could deny that Sarfraz Nawaz's figures of 3-40 from his 12 overs was not the most impressive performance?

PAKISTAN		SRI LANKA	
Mudassar Nazar c de Silva b Ratnayake	36	S. Wettimuny c Rashid Khan b Sarfraz Nawaz	12
Mohsin Khan b John	82	D. S. B. P. Kuruppu run out	72
Zaheer Abbas c Kuruppu b de Mel	82	R. L. Dias b Rashid Khan	5
Javed Miandad lbw b de Mel	72	L. R. D. Mendis (capt) b Tahir Naqqash	16
Imran Khan (capt) not out	56	A. Ranatunga c & b Mudassar Nazar	31
Ijaz Faqih run out	2	M. A. R. Samarasekera run out	0
Tahir Naqqash not out	0	D. S. de Silva c Wasim Bari b Sarfraz Nawaz	35
Extras b4 lb4	8	A. L.F. de Mel c Tahir Naqqash b Shahid Mahboob	11
(60 overs)	5-338	R. G. de Alwis (wk) not out	59
Did not bat: Wasim Bari (wk), Rashid Khan,		R. J. Ratnayake c Mudassar Nazar b Sarfraz Nawaz	13
Shahid Mahboob, Sarfraz Nawaz		V. B. John not out	12
1/88 2/156 3/229 4/325 5/332		Extras lb8 w10 nb4	22
Bowling: de Mel 12-2-69-2; John 12-2-58-1;		(60 overs)	9-288
Ratnayake 12-0-65-1; Ranatunga 9-0-53-0;		1/34 2/58 3/85 4/142 5/143 6/157 7/180 8/234 9/262	
de Silva 10-0-52-0; Samarasekera 5-0-33-0		Bowling: Sarfraz Nawaz 12-1-40-3; Shahid Mahboob 11-0-48-1;	
		Tahir Naqqash 8-0-49-1; Rashid Khan 12-1-55-1;	
		Ijaz Faqih 12-1-52-0; Mudassar Nazar 4-0-18-1;	
		Zaheer Abbas 1-0-4-0	

Umpires: K.E. Palmer   D.R. Shepherd

Toss: Sri Lanka   Points: Pakistan 4 Sri Lanka 0

GROUP B: AUSTRALIA vs ZIMBABWE
TRENT BRIDGE: ZIMBABWE WON BY 13 RUNS

According to Australian wicketkeeper, Rod Marsh, Australia just about got what they deserved in this historic World Cup upset. Kim Hughes' side apparently had been lackadaisical in their preparation and they felt turning up at Trent Bridge would be enough for them to win. It wasn't.

They fell foul of a more determined Zimbabwe side who looked as though they had more to play for. After the match Kim Hughes admitted Australia had been "outplayed". Certain members of the Australian side were very embarrassed that they had been caught so badly unawares. The Zimbabwean amateurs had defeated the best that Australia could put in the field against them. Most scribes had to go back to the loss against Holland in 1964 for a result of equal humiliation.

Nothing extraordinary looked likely at lunch after Hughes had won the toss and sent Zimbabwe in to bat at Trent Bridge. Hughes started confidently with three slips to Lawson, but it was Dennis Lillee, coming on first change, who got the breakthrough. He claimed his 100th wicket in limited-over internationals when in the 18th over he severed the solid opening partnership between Ali Shah, who knicked an outswinger and Grant Paterson who top edged a hook. The clouds rolled in after a sunny start and even Graham Yallop and Allan Border, those bowling bunnies of 1979, took three wickets between them. Yallop had the dangerous Dave Houghton caught behind for a duck. Marsh juggled the catch and it took a conference between

Hughes, Marsh and umpire David Constant before Houghton was sent on his way. He had also removed Jack Heron in the same fashion the previous ball to give Rod Marsh his 100th catch in limited-over internationals. The fifth wicket fell right on the interval. Zimbabwe were 5-94 and the small crowd, remembering the authentic minnow efforts of East Africa and Canada, must have imagined a straightforward result for Australia. Ladbrokes by now had Australia at unbackable odds.

In the session after lunch, though, the mood of the game began to change. The Australians had not been fielding at their best and, as the innings progressed, it got worse. Much to the frustration of all the fieldsmen and bowlers concerned, five chances were missed during the 60 overs. The Zimbabwean captain, Duncan Fletcher, benefitted twice and he eventually was able to take advantage of the let offs.

He put on 70 runs with young Kevin Curran in 15 overs and an unbroken 75, then a World Cup record, with Iain Butchart in 12 overs. Fletcher took the attack up to the bowlers. The left-hander hit hard and effectively. The reputations of the four Australian fast bowlers counted for little as the Zimbabwean batted through to the end of the innings at 6-239.

Australia's fielding and bowling efforts had got them into some strife, conceding 31 extras during the Zimbabwean innings. They must have still imagined they had the resources to score at four runs per over for 60 overs against a lowly rated attack. Graham Wood and Kepler Wessels started comfortably enough. Their opening stand realised 61 until Fletcher had Wood caught behind, umpire Merv Kitchen, in his first international, sending the West Australian on his way. Two runs later and captain removed captain. Hughes, brilliantly caught by a diving Shah on the leg-side, found his day had gone from bad to worse. It was 2-77 at tea from 25 overs and after the interval Wessels and David Hookes lifted the score to 2-114. Once more Australia seemed well on course.

But Zimbabwe were much sharper in the field than Australia had been. They maintained the pressure on the batsmen, ensuring the run rate was always a factor in the progress of the Australians, and made the most of their chances. Wessels, who had got bogged down by a leg-stump attack after a solid innings was run out by a marvellous throw from Heron. Fletcher picked up two more victims in Hookes, well caught at cover, and Graham Yallop. When Yallop went to an amazing catch on the boundary by Pycroft, who juggled the ball while looking into the sun, the score was 5-138 and Australia required nearly eight an over to win. Curran and Butchart got rid of Border and Geoff Lawson cheaply. In the cool late afternoon Nottingham sunlight the underdogs gathered in groups were all smiles, while one after another the Australians bowed their heads and trudged away.

Marsh, standing at the non-striker's end, was disgusted by what he saw. Australia were 7-176 and staring absolute humiliation in the face. Rodney Hogg, who despite the doubts about his resilience was now on his third visit to England in Australian colours, found the necessary competitive edge to hang in with Marsh. They had to fight for every run they could muster as the Zimbabweans threw themselves around in the field. The score mounted beyond 200, but the overs dwindled away. The run requirement got harder and harder. Fifty-three runs were needed from five overs. Then 23 had to be hit from the last one. Marsh reached his 50 with a six, however, when the 360th ball had been delivered Australia were still 13 runs short of the Zimbabwean total.

Fletcher's team had reaped the benefit of all the determined preparation they had put in. The captain, himself, was rewarded for his efforts with the Man of the Match Award. In the Australian dressing room the cloud still hanging overhead from the World Series Cricket split grew darker and larger.

ZIMBABWE		AUSTRALIA	
A. H. Shah c Marsh b Lillee	16	G. M. Wood c Houghton b Fletcher	31
G. A. Paterson c Hookes b Lillee	27	K. C. Wessels run out	76
J. G. Heron cMarsh b Yallop	14	K. J. Hughes (capt) c Shah b Fletcher	0
A. J. Pycroft b Border	21	D. W. Hookes c Traicos b Fletcher	20
D. L. Houghton (wk) c Marsh b Yallop	0	G. N. Yallop c Pycroft b Fletcher	2
D. A. G. Fletcher (capt) not out	69	A. R. Border c Pycroft b Curran	17
K. M. Curran c Hookes b Hogg	27	R. W. Marsh (wk) not out	50
I. P. Butchart not out	34	G. F. Lawson not out	0
Extras lb18 w7 nb6	31	R. M. Hogg not out	19
(60 overs)	6-239	Extras b2 lb7 w2	11
Did not bat: P. W. E. Rawson, A. J. Traicos, V. R. Hogg		(60 overs)	7-226
1/55 2/55 3/86 4/86 5/94 6/164		Did not bat: D. K. Lillee, J. R. Thomson	
Bowling: Lawson 11-2-33-0; Hogg 12-3-43-1;		1/61 2/63 3/114 4/133 5/138 6/168 7/176	
Lillee 12-1-47-2; Thomson 11-1-46-0; Yallop 9-0-28-2;		Bowling: Hogg 6-2-15-0; Rawson 12-1-54-0;	
Border 5-0-11-1		Butchart 10-0-39-1; Fletcher 11-1-42-4; Traicos 12-2-27-0;	
		Curran 9-0-38-1;	

Umpires: D.J. Constant   M.J. Kitchen

Toss: Australia   Points: Zimbabwe 4 Australia 0

GROUP B: INDIA vs WEST INDIES
OLD TRAFFORD: INDIA WON BY 34 RUNS

In its own way this result was as just as big a surprise as the match at Trent Bridge. It took a little longer as a delayed start meant the game lasted into the second day, but it was no less warmly received for that.

India, the great World Cup underachievers, were thought no match for the West Indies. Even they probably approached this game in Manchester with apprehension. Their only glimmer of optimism came from an isolated victory in a limited-over international in Guyana just a couple of months prior to this encounter.

The conditions encountered that day could not have been more different than what greeted both sides at Old Trafford. The Guyanese heat and humidity had been replaced by Mancunian grey. This was not a venue nor a colour normally associated with Indian batting heroics.

There was nothing in the early stages to suggest that the status quo of 1975 and 1979 would be altered, either. Damp weather and conditions held up play until shortly after the scheduled lunch interval. Then Clive Lloyd won the toss and, with a smile, told Kapil Dev his side could bat. Kapil demanded his top order blunt the firepower of the West Indian pacemen, but it would be no easy task as light was poor and the wicket remained moist and conducive to sideways movement.

Sunil Gavaskar, Kris Srikkanth and Mohinder Amarnath, who had batted brilliantly against this attack in the Caribbean, all fought hard before falling to catches by the athletic wicketkeeper Jeffrey Dujon. After 22 overs India were 3-76 and a total of around 180-190, India's par in a World Cup match, seemed likely. The next 10 overs saw Sandeep Patil and Yashpal Sharma take the attack up to the West Indians, paying particular attention to Viv Richards and Larry Gomes. The runs came freely before Gomes struck twice, bowling Patil and having the Indian captain caught by Richards.

There was to be no turning back this time, though. Sharma was playing the innings of his life and he found a worthy partner in Roger Binny. Pulling fiercely and driving whenever the ball was up Sharma raced past his 50 and added an invaluable 73 runs in 15 overs for the sixth wicket with Binny. After Binny shuffled in front of his stumps, the recovery continued when Madan Lal joined Sharma. By the time Michael Holding ended the number five's superb 120-ball effort, India were well on the way to 262, their highest score in this competition.

"It gave us something to defend. Defend it we were going to—with body and soul," said Kapil Dev in his autobiography *By God's Decree*. As the day drew to a close, rain clouds built up again on the horizon. However, West Indian openers Gordon

Greenidge and Desmond Haynes were making more than satisfactory progress. They put on 49 runs in even time. Then Haynes was run out going for a sharp single in the 14th over and seven runs and four overs later, Greenidge was bowled by one from Balwindersingh Sandhu that cut back.

The West Indies ended the day on 2-67 from 22 overs, pretty much equal with India at the same point of their innings. However, the press the next morning looked at the West Indian batting line-up and still reckoned Lloyd's team would win.

Conditions on the Friday were improved, but there was no drying from a weak sun and the West Indian batsmen found it hard to time the succession of medium pacers on a wicket that was not conducive to flamboyant strokeplay. Roger Binny put in a superb spell, lifting his team's spirits immeasurably when he had Richards caught behind early on. It was a key wicket which set the pattern for most of the rest of the innings. Richards' dismissal left the West Indies at 3-76. Soon they were 8-130 and the game appeared over. Binny had removed Lloyd, then Dujon, caught at mid off, cheaply. Gomes was run out going for a third run and Marshall was stumped off a ball from the left-arm spin of Ravi Shastri that turned a long way.

Michael Holding survived a chance on the boundary and held on with Andy Roberts for a while until Shastri struck again. Roberts and Garner needed to add 106 for the 10th wicket if the West Indies were to steal the match. There were still lots of overs left and Roberts was already settled at the crease. Garner, too, established himself and soon the runs began to flow. Both batsmen used their height to get well forward and their strength to give the ball an occasional hefty thump. Garner hit Shastri for a four then a six next ball and Kapil removed him from the attack.

Against the odds they took the total to 200, completing their 50-run stand soon after. Garner hit Sandeep Patil for another six. Eventually thoughts turned to the West Indies' magnificent win over Pakistan in 1975 when Roberts and Deryck Murray guided their side home. Murray and Roberts had put on 64. Garner and Roberts added 71, still a World Cup record for the last wicket, and were within 35 runs of a miracle. Indian brows were furrowed. Gavaskar suggested Kapil bring back his young spinner Shastri, into the attack forcing the two tailenders to hit against the spin.

It was a risk, there were 36 balls remaining, but from the first delivery of Shastri's sixth over Garner swung hard. Syed Kirmani had the bails off in a flash. The wicketkeeper jumped in instantaneous glee. Big Joel just lowered his head and walked away. He had only been out of his ground for an instant. India had completed their best win in limited-over internationals. It was only their second ever victory in this competition. The West Indies had suffered their first ever defeat. Yashpal Sharma was named Man of the Match.

INDIA		WEST INDIES	
S. M. Gavaskar c Dujon b Marshall	19	C. G. Greenidge b Sandhu	24
K. Srikkanth c Dujon b Holding	14	D. L. Haynes run out	24
M. Amarnath c Dujon b Garner	21	I. V. A. Richards c Kirmani b Binny	17
S. M. Patil b Gomes	36	S. F. A. F. Bacchus b Madan Lal	14
Yashpal Sharma b Holding	89	C. H. Lloyd (capt) b Binny	25
Kapil Dev (capt) c Richards b Gomes	6	P. J. L. Dujon (wk) c Sandhu b Binny	7
R. M. H. Binny lbw b Marshall	27	H. A. Gomes run out	8
Madan Lal not out	21	M. D. Marshall st Kirmani b Shastri	2
S. M.H. Kirmani (wk) run out	1	A. M. E. Roberts not out	37
R. J. Shastri not out	5	M. A. Holding b Shastri	8
Extras b4 lb10 w1 nb8	23	J. Garner st Kirmani b Shastri	37
(60 overs)	8-262	Extras b4 lb17 w4	25
Did not bat: B. S. Sandhu		(54.1 overs)	228

1/21 2/46 3/76 4/125 5/141 6/214 7/243 8/246

Bowling: Holding 12-3-32-2; Roberts 12-1-51-0; Marshall 12-1-48-2; Garner 12-1-49-1; Richards 2-0-13-0; Gomes 10-0-46-2

1/49 2/56 3/76 4/96 5/107 6/124 7/126 8/130 9/157 10/228

Bowling: Kapil Dev 10-0-34-0; Sandhu 12-1-36-1; Madan Lal 12-1-34-1; Binny 12-1-48-3; Shastri 5.1-0-26-3; Patil 3-0-25-0

Umpires: B. Leadbeater A.G.T. Whitehead

Toss: West Indies   Points: India 4 West Indies 0

SATURDAY 11 JUNE
THE PRUDENTIAL CUP: ROUND TWO
GROUP A: ENGLAND vs SRI LANKA
TAUNTON: ENGLAND WON BY 47 RUNS

Sri Lanka stayed out west, this time in the cider country of Somerset. And, as they did at Swansea, the Sri Lankans turned on a great spectacle against England, this time for a sell-out crowd. The formula was the same. Weak bowling that was belted in all directions and a spirited batting reply that entertained, but inevitably fell significantly short of the required target.

The ground was packed. People had been queuing since the early hours of the morning. Bob Willis won the toss and, bucking what had been the limited-overs norm, elected to bat as he did at The Oval. His openers, Graeme Fowler and Chris Tavare gave England another positive start on a very friendly batting surface. Neither player was able to turn that start into anything substantial and it was only when the in form Allan Lamb joined David Gower that the fireworks really began.

The pair traded stroke for stroke while adding 96 runs. Lamb was first to his 50 but went no further as he became over ambitious against Rumesh Ratnayake. Mike Gatting did not last long, finding himself in the middle of the pitch looking for a second run to square leg which Gower had no interest in. That brought Ian Botham to the wicket on his home county ground. The capacity crowd responded enthusiastically to his entrance, expecting something special from their favourite all-rounder.

In a way they got it, but not as they would have wished. Botham had been in only a couple of balls and had still not scored when there was confusion between himself and Gower. A mad scramble for the stumps and a charge for the crease found the local hero short of his ground. England, 2-174 prior to Lamb's dismissal, were now 5-194.

Ian Gould had won a place in the side ahead of specialist wicketkeeprs such as Bob Taylor for his bubbly enthusiasm and busy batting. This day, the favourite of his brief England career, he fulfilled his obligations to perfection, supporting Gower and giving him the strike as often as possible while the left-hander continued to flay the bowling. The left-handed combination worked perfectly and added 98 runs for the sixth wicket. Gower completed his thrilling century and went on to 130. He hit 12 fours and five glorious sixes, three of which sailed over long on into the new grandstand at Taunton. Two were from successive deliveries from Rumesh Ratnayake.

Gower and Gould fell within a few runs of each other, but again Graham Dilley, as he did at The Oval, was able to flog a tiring attack to good effect. His 17-ball innings included five fours. England scored 105 runs from their final 10 overs and finished on 9-333, another massive score for Sri Lanka to chase. No bowler came in for special treatment, they were all unable to stem the run flow and conceded on average between five and six runs per over. The whole innings contained just three maidens, all sent down by Asantha de Mel.

The Sri Lankans began their reply against a fired-up Willis and Dilley. Soon the latter was making in roads. Brendon Kuruppu, who had batted so well against Pakistan, was caught at first slip by Gatting. Roy Dias, aiming a furious flat-footed drive, was brilliantly held two-handed at second slip by a high-leaping Botham. At 2-17, all hope for Sri Lanka was really lost, but they pressed on regardless. Duleep Mendis and Sidath Wettimuny were able to fashion a recovery and keep up with the required run rate. Mendis hooked Willis for six, giving the members in the new pavilion another close look at the ball. Paul Allott found out how difficult it was for a medium pacer to bowl on the flat Taunton wicket. Nor could Botham make any impression.

But it was another hometown boy, off-spinner Vic Marks, who settled the issue once and for all. He broke the 75-run Wettimuny and Mendis stand and when he removed Ranjan Madugalle, Sri Lanka were 5-117 in the 32nd over. From that point the batsmen were generally in control. Arjuna Ranatunga, Somachandra de Silva, de Mel and the consistent Guy de Alwis all made good runs, the bulk of which still came from the bowling of Allott and Botham. Marks on the other hand continued to pick up wickets. By the conclusion of his 12-over spell he had sent five upper- and middle-order batsmen to the dressing rooms. de Silva was stumped by the beaming Gould. A rare treat, Gould's success was only the sixth stumping in World Cup matches to that date.

Dilley finally ended the game from the final ball of his 11th over when he bowled Vinothen John. Sri Lanka, who finished 47 runs short of their target, had played in two matches within three days where 1245 runs had been scored. It was a run orgy enough to make bowlers wonder at the reason for their existence.

ENGLAND		SRI LANKA	
G. Fowler b John	22	S. Wettimuny lbw b Marks	33
C. J. Tavare c de Alwis b Ranatunga	32	D. S. B. P. Kuruppu c Gatting b Dilley	4
D. I. Gower b de Mel	130	R. L. Dias c Botham b Dilley	2
A. J. Lamb b Ratnayake	53	L. R. D. Mendis (capt) c Willis b Marks	56
M. W. Gatting run out	7	R. S. Madugalle c Tavare b Marks	12
I. T. Botham run out	0	A. Ranatunga c Lamb b Marks	34
I. J. Gould (wk) c Ranatunga b Ratnayake	35	D. S. de Silva st Gould b Marks	28
G. R. Dilley b de Mel	29	R. G. de Alwis(wk) not out	58
V. J. Marks run out	5	A. L.F. de Mel c Dilley b Allott	27
P. J. W. Allott not out	0	R. J. Ratnayake c Lamb b Dilley	15
Extras lb11 w9	20	V. B. John b Dilley	0
(60 overs)	9-333	Extras lb12 w2 nb3	17
Did not bat: R. G. D. Willis (capt)		(58 overs)	286

England: 1/49 2/78 3/174 4/193 5/194 6/292 7/298 8/333 9/333

Bowling: de Mel 12-3-62-2; John 12-0-55-1; Ratnayake 12-0-66-2; Ranatunga 12-0-65-1; de Silva 12-0-65-0

Sri Lanka: 1/11 2/17 3/92 4/108 5/117 6/168 7/192 8/246 9/281 10/286

Bowling: Willis 11-3-43-0; Dilley 11-0-45-4; Allott 12-1-82-1; Botham 12-0-60-0; Marks 12-3-39-5

Umpires: M.J. Kitchen K.E. Palmer

Toss: England   Points: England 4 Sri Lanka 0

GROUP A: NEW ZEALAND vs PAKISTAN
EDGBASTON: NEW ZEALAND WON BY 52 RUNS

This was another two-day 'one-day' match. Persistent Birmingham drizzle delayed the start of play until 1.45pm, while another 90-minute delay meant only 56 overs could be completed on the Saturday. So on Sunday the 12th, New Zealand asserted their dominance over Pakistan with a win that threw Group A wide open.

Every Round One match had been won by the side batting first. However, Imran sent New Zealand in to bat when he won the toss, even though he was unavailable to bowl at them.

His opening attack could not make the early breakthrough, although they would have if Wasim Bari uncharacteristically had not put down two catches off Bruce Edgar. The left-hander and Glenn Turner provided the Kiwi innings with an excellent platform during their opening stand of 57. It was the introduction of Abdul Qadir, brought into the side at the expense of Tahir Naqqash, that created some anxiety amongst the New Zealanders for the first time.

In a superb spell the leg-spinner not only stemmed the run flow, but he snapped up four prize wickets. The Kiwis were not used to this form of bowling, and had no idea which way the ball would turn. John Wright was caught behind, while Lance Cairns, promoted to belt the spinner out of the attack, was bowled having a slog. Geoff Howarth became the seventh batsman to be stumped in a World Cup game.

New Zealand slipped to 5-120, but the rain returned for another 90 minutes. Qadir was restricted by the wet ball; besides which he could not bowl forever. On the resumption, Jeremy Coney and Martin Crowe were able to fashion a reasonable recovery. By the close, New Zealand had fought their way to 8-211 from 56 overs.

They were able to make the most of their remaining four overs on the Sunday, adding a further vital 27 runs. Wicketkeeper, Warren Lees, scored the bulk of those running and hitting furiously and New Zealand had a competitive 238 on the board.

There were plenty of Pakistani supporters at Edgbaston and they cheered the arrival Mohsin Khan and Mudassar Nazar to the crease. The noise quickly subsided, though, in Richard Hadlee's first over. By its completion Pakistan was 2-0, Mohsin and Zaheer Abbas both falling to the champion fast bowler. Mohsin was given out lbw to the third ball, Zaheer lost his off stump on the sixth. Two hundred and thirty-eight had quickly moved from competitive to mountainous. In the next over the peak got even higher when Lees pulled off a fantastic catch to send Mudassar on his way, still without a run on the board.

Imran, who was completely frustrated by his being unable to match himself properly against another champion all-rounder, could do little to improve his side's fortunes before hooking loosely and becoming Hadlee's third victim. At 6-60, Pakistan looked like they were due for an early and embarrassing finish. Their aggrieved fans vented their anger inappropriately by throwing the occasional missile at New Zealand fieldsmen.

Once more Qadir saved face, this time with the bat. Wasim Bari and Shahid Mahboob had pushed the total to more than three figures, but it was Qadir who ensured the teams' overall runs per over coefficient was not damaged beyond repair. He was never going to win the game and ran out of partners in the 56th over, however, Qadir topscored for Pakistan, was only three runs short of the highest score in the match and batted well enough after his great bowling spell to lift his standing above all the other Man of the Match contenders.

After the game Imran was critical of just about everyone, including his batsmen and the umpire, Barrie Leadbeater. He had a bad day.

NEW ZEALAND		PAKISTAN	
G. M. Turner c Wasim Bari b Rashid	27	Mohsin Khan lbw b Hadlee	0
B. A. Edgar c Imran b Qadir	44	Mudassar Nazar c Lee b Cairns	0
J. G. Wright c Wasim Bari b Qadir	9	Zaheer Abbas b Hadlee	0
B. L. Cairns b Qadir	4	Javed Miandad lbw b Chatfield	35
G. P. Howarth (capt) st Wasim Bari b Qadir	16	Imran Khan (capt) c Chatfield b Hadlee	9
J. V. Coney c Ijaz b Shahid	33	Ijaz Faqih cEdgar b Coney	12
M. D. Crowe c Mohsin b Rashid	34	Shahid Mahboob c Wright b Coney	17
R. J. Hadlee c Wasim b Sarfraz	13	Wasim Bari (wk) c Edgar b Coney	34
J. G. Bracewell lbw b Rashid	3	Abdul Qadir not out	41
W. K. Lees (wk) not out	24	Sarfraz Nawaz c Crowe b Chatfield	13
E. J.Chatfield not out	6	Rashid Khan c & b Cairns	9
Extras lb20 w4 nb1	25	Extras b5 lb6 w3 nb2	16
(60 overs)	9-238	(55.2 overs)	186

1/57 2/68 3/80 4/109 5/120 6/166 7/197 8/202 9/223

1/0 2/0 3/0 4/22 5/54 6/60 7/102 8/131 9/158 10/186

Bowling: Sarfraz Nawaz 11-1-49-1; Shahid Mahboob 10-2-38-1; Rashid Khan 11-0-47-3; Mudassar Nazar 12-1-40-0; Abdul Qadir 12-4-21-4; Ijaz Faqih 1-0-6-0; Zaheer Abbas 3-0-12-0

Bowling: Hadlee 9-2-20-3; Cairns 9.2-3-21-2; Chatfield 12-0-50-2; Crowe 2-0-12-0; Coney 12-3-28-3; Bracewell 11-2-39-0

Umpires: H.D. Bird B. Leadbeater

Toss: Pakistan   Points: New Zealand 4 Pakistan 0

GROUP B: AUSTRALIA vs THE WEST INDIES
HEADINGLEY: WEST INDIES WON BY 101 RUNS

The last thing the disgruntled Australians needed was to meet the West Indies on the rebound on a wicket that was an uneven greentop. Kim Hughes might suggest such luck was the story of his life as Australian captain, because that is exactly what happened to them.

This was another match affected by bad weather on the Saturday. In complete contrast to the rain and general misery that delayed the start until 3.30pm the first day, Australia's batting capitulation occurred during a spell of brilliant sunshine on Sunday.

What quickly became obvious was that the improvement in the weather had not changed the character of the wicket. It remained firmly entrenched in the 'brute' class. The modern era has shown such tracks are almost custom made for tall aggressive West Indian fast bowlers.

Not that they got first use of it. In fact Malcolm Marshall and Joel Garner did not get any use of it at all, missing out on the match with injuries. They were replaced by Wayne Daniel and debutant, the ultimately ill-fated, Winston Davis. By the end of the game the Australians might have preferred it if Garner and Marshall had been fit.

Australian players who had inspected the pitch before the match were reminded of the surface provided for the astonishing Test at Headingley in 1981. Then their bogeys were Ian Botham and Bob Willis. When the match got underway after Kim Hughes had won the toss, it seemed the main problem was getting the ball and the bowler's feet within the legal parameters of a cricket pitch. Wide followed no ball, followed wide as the new ball was sprayed about. Jeff Thomson often guilty of such sins could not be held responsible. He sat watching from the pavilion, replaced in the Australian eleven by Ken MacLeay.

There would be more interruptions for bad light and drizzle and so difficult were the conditions that even the occasional delivery in the right place brought a result. Rodney Hogg broke through first, having Gordon Greenidge caught at square leg and when Geoff Lawson had Desmond Haynes caught behind and removed Viv Richards' off stump the West Indies were 3-32 and in real trouble. Clive Lloyd and Larry Gomes began the recovery, but the total was still only 78 when the West Indian captain was trapped lbw by Ken MacLeay.

Faoud Bacchus had limited success as a West Indian player, but at Headingley this day he put together a precious innings of 47 which turned the match in the favour of his team. He and the imperturbable if lucky Gomes added 76 as the day drew to a close. Bacchus didn't quite make it to stumps, becoming another victim of part-timer Graham Yallop, but by then the West Indies on 5-160 from 42 overs were well back in the contest.

On the Sunday, Gomes pushed and deflected his way to 78 as the West Indies increased their score by 92 runs in the 18 overs available. Michael Holding and Daniel hit out in muscular fashion and added 41 runs in four belligerent overs before Holding was run out from the final ball of the innings.

Australia needed 253 to win and they were none too confident. In that famous Test match two years before, they had failed to chase 130 against an attack less lethal than the one they were about to face. The intention was to come out with all guns blazing, but all that Graeme Wood did was go down in a screaming heap. With the score on 18 a Holding delivery leapt off a length and hit Wood flush on the cheekbone. Hughes recalls that although Wood was wearing a helmet he had no visor. The opener was knocked unconscious and had to be carried from the field on a stretcher. The Australians were critical of the time it had taken for on-field assistance to arrive for Wood.

He was taken straight to Leeds Infirmary where he was diagnosed with concussion and kept in overnight for observation. Fortunately there was no bone damage. Back at Headingley, Hughes counter-attacked with two sensational hooked sixes off Wayne Daniel's first two balls. Winston Davis came on and quickly had Hughes edging to Clive Lloyd at first slip. Kepler Wessels was out of sorts and soon left. However, David Hookes and Graham Yallop took up where Hughes left off. The two strokeplayers traded blow for blow for eight exhilarating overs which realised 59 runs and seemed to place Australia in a position where they might reach 253.

Alas their batting was an act of desperation rather than one of calculated aggression. Both were dismissed within two runs of each other, Yallop to a desperate hook, and the remaining executions were swift. Davis was nigh on unplayable as the ball flew at all angles. The Australian tail had no stomach for such an unequal contest and halfway through their 31st over the match had ended. Eight wickets fell for 37 runs. Davis had 1-37 at one stage from five overs. He finished with 7-51, and became the first bowler to take seven wickets in a limited-over international. He was named Man of the Match by Brian Close. The next day the headlines read, 'The Davis Cup'.

Both captains complained that the wicket was totally unsuitable for the game. "What are they trying to do to sides containing genuine fast bowlers by playing the match up here?" Lloyd said. "Getting us to knock each other out?"

After the game it was decided that the pitch used should be dug up, relaid and not used again until the following season. Graeme Wood thought the idea a sensible one.

WEST INDIES		AUSTRALIA	
C. G. Greenidge c Wood b Hogg	4	G. M. Wood retired hurt	2
D. L. Haynes c Marsh b Lawson	13	K. C. Wessels b Roberts	11
I. V. A. Richards b Lawson	7	K. J. Hughes (capt) c Lloyd b Davis	18
H. A. Gomes c Marsh b Lillee	78	D. W. Hookes c Dujon b Davis	45
C. H. Lloyd (capt) lbw b MacLeay	19	G. N. Yallop c Holding b Davis	29
S. F. A. F. Bacchus c Wessels b Yallop	47	A. R. Border c Lloyd b Davis	17
P. J. L. Dujon (wk) lbw b Lawson	12	K. H. MacLeay c Haynes b Davis	1
A. M. E. Roberts c Marsh b Lillee	5	R. W. Marsh (wk) c Haynes b Holding	8
M. A. Holding run out	20	G. F. Lawson c Dujon b Davis	2
W. W. Daniel not out	16	R. M. Hogg not out	0
Extras b1 lb9 w10 nb11	31	D. K. Lillee b Davis	0
(60 overs)	9-252	Extras b1 lb4 w5 nb8	18
Did not bat: W. W. Davis		(30.3 overs)	151
1/7 2/25 3/32 4/78 5/154 6/192 7/208 8/211 9/252		1/18 2/55 3/114 4/116 5/126 6/137 7/141 8/150 9/151	
Bowling: Lawson 12-3-29-3; Hogg 12-1-49-1;		Bowling: Roberts 7-0-14-1; Holding 8-2-23-1; Davis	
MacLeay 12-1-31-1; Lillee 12-0-55-2; Yallop 5-0-26-1;		10.3-0-51-7; Daniel 3-0-35-0; Gomes 2-0-10-0	
Border 7-0-31-0			

Umpires: D.J. Constant   D.G.L. Evans

Toss: Australia   Points: West Indies 4 Australia 0

GROUP B: INDIA vs ZIMBABWE
GRACE ROAD: INDIA WON BY 5 WICKETS

After yet another delayed start, Zimbabwe were totally unable to reproduce the batting and bowling form that took them to their sensational victory in the first round. In the 'battle of the giant killers' India came out on top very comfortably.

Again there was drizzle and again the spectators, including the large Indian contingent inside the ground had to wait until after lunch for some action. They made up such a large percentage of the crowd that some PA announcements were in Hindi. What cricket they did eventually see only provided mediocre entertainment.

Kapil Dev sent Zimbabwe in on a very green wicket after winning the toss and their batsmen really struggled against the seaming and swinging ball. Madan Lal in particular achieved plenty of late movement. Zimbabwe received the benefit of a few chances as they did against Australia, but could not capitalise on them or lift the run rate significantly. After Ali Shah became the first of a record-equalling five vicitms behind the wicket for Syed Kirmani, Grant Paterson and Jack Heron lifted the score to 1-55. Neither batsman looked in total control, so it was no surprise when wickets began to fall with some regularity.

Dave Houghton and Iain Butchart did best down the order without ever increasing the run rate to a point that seemed likely to worry India. It took 34 overs to reach 100. Houghton was caught behind trying to accelerate. Curran was run out while still in the middle of the pitch. When John Traicos was run out from the fourth ball of the 52nd over, Zimbabwe were all out for 155. India required just over 2.5 runs per over from their 360-ball allocation to go to the top of Group B.

Zimbabwe had to take early wickets if they were to make a game of it. They were without one fast bowler, Vince Hogg, who was suffering a back strain. Peter Rawson, who as ordered quickly got rid of Sunil Gavaskar and Kris Srikkanth, went down with a similar complaint at the start of his sixth over. Zimbabwe continued to impress with their fielding, but once Mohinder Amarnath and Sandeep Patil began to build their 69-run partnership it was never enough.

Patil scored his 50 at a run a ball. Curran conceded 15 runs in one over. The Indians began to race to their target. A couple more wickets fell, but halfway through the 38th over, Yashpal Sharma hit Ali Shah to the boundary and Kapil Dev's side had completed a comfortable win. The Indian captain, leading a team that had previously been World Cup easybeats, noted that the Indian fielding had been poor and that his players were starting to get a little complacent. Madan Lal beat Patil for the Man of the Match Award.

ZIMBABWE		INDIA	
A. H. Shah c Kirmani b Sandhu	8	K. Srikkanth c Butchart b Rawson	20
G. A. Paterson lbw b Madan Lal	22	S. M. Gavaskar c Heron b Rawson	4
J. G. Heron c Kirmani b Madan Lal	18	M. Amarnath c sub (G. E.Peckover) b Traicos	44
A. J. Pycroft c Shastri b Binny	14	S. M. Patil b Fletcher	50
D. L. Houghton (wk) c Kirmani b Madan Lal	21	R. J. Shastri c Brown b Shah	17
D. A. G. Fletcher (capt) b Kapil Dev	13	Yashpal Sharma not out	18
K. M. Curran run out	8	Kapil Dev (capt) not out	2
I. P. Butchart not out	22	Extras w2	2
R. D. Brown c Kirmani b Shastri	6	(37.3 overs)	5-157
P. W. E. Rawson c Kirmani b Binny	3	Did not bat: R. M. H. Binny, Madan Lal, S. M. H. Kirmani,	
A. J. Traicos run out	2	B. S. Sandhu	
Extras lb9 w9	18	1/13 2/32 3/101 4/128 5/148	
(51.4 overs)	155	Bowling: Rawson 5.1-1-11-2; Curran 6.5-1-33-0;	
1/13 2/55 3/56 4/71 5/106 6/114 7/115 8/139		Butchart 5-1-21-0; Traicos 11-1-41-1; Fletcher 6-1-32-1;	
9/148 10/155		Shah 3.3-0-17-1	
Bowling: Kapil Dev 9-3-18-1; Sandhu 9-1-29-1; Madan Lal			
10.4-0-27-3; Binny 11-2-25-2; Shastri 12-1-38-1			

Umpires: J. Birkenshaw   R. Palmer

Toss: India   Points: India 4 Zimbabwe 0

MONDAY 13 JUNE 1983
THE PRUDENTIAL CUP: ROUND THREE
GROUP A: ENGLAND vs PAKISTAN
LORD'S: ENGLAND WON BY 8 WICKETS

Unusually for a Monday, Lord's was filled to capacity for this clash of World Cup arch rivals, England and Pakistan. The crowd, who at least got plenty of sunshine for their troubles, expected another tooth-and-nail struggle, but a goodly number of them, particularly the Pakistani supporters, were to be sadly disappointed. England were at their best and steamrollered Imran's side by eight wickets with plenty of overs to spare.

The players were constantly on the go. The number of preliminary matches may have been doubled, but the time frame had not. One match quickly followed another so that there was little time to savour or enjoy an achievement. No wonder some cricketers find it hard to recollect what happened in games during their limited-overs career.

Imran elected to bat this day, but his side hit trouble almost immediately as Bob Willis and Graham Dilley took advantage of a fast wicket. It was the English captain who twice struck early; Mohsin Khan mishooked to a diving Tavare at mid-on after struggling for 45 minutes and Mansoor Akhtar edged behind. He had been brought in to allow Zaheer Abbas to slip down the order. Both Mohson and Mansoor were back in the grand old pavilion by the time the score reached 33. Willis' first spell realised 2-12 from 9 overs.

It could have been worse. The camera showed Mudassar had been short of his ground following a run out attempt by Ian Botham at the bowler's end. The umpire, though, gave the batsman the benefit of the doubt. Javed Miandad struck Paul Allott for two consecutive fours. Then wicketkeeper Ian Gould, who had caught Mansoor, snapped up Javed, beaten by Botham, and Mudassar, swinging too hard at Allott as his second and third victims. That left Pakistan a precarious 4-67. They were 4-72 at lunch off 33 overs.

Javed was back on the ground soon after his dismissal. As if a stress fractured shin was not enough, Imran was hit on the toe, had to call for a runner and later was unable to field. Dilley exerted enormous pressure in his four-over spell from the pavilion end after lunch. He failed to take a wicket, however, his pace was extreme and his accuracy exemplary. After one express delivery Imran was so surprised he turned to Allan Lamb and said in amazement, "What's going on, then?"

Although Imran survived the Dilley onslaught and a chance to Gould, he could not get going and then suffered the indignity of being a passive witness to his own run out. His runner, Javed, on way for a second run was sent back too late by Zaheer. England were once more jubilant to have Pakistan 5-96 with fewer than 20 overs remaining.

Zaheer was now in good touch, but still Pakistan struggled. Off-spinner, Vic Marks, who had again been tidy, picked up Wasim Raja and when Abdul Qadir became the second run out victim of the day Pakistan were 7-118. Finally Sarfraz Nawaz and Wasim Bari held on with Zaheer. The bespectacled champion attacked to good affect so that the run rate for the first time was lifted above three per over. At the 40-over mark the score had been 4-87, 20 overs later the total had been increased by 106.

Graeme Fowler and David Gower soon had England progressing comfortably towards their target of 194. Fowler had lost his opening partner, Chris Tavare, at 15, but he could sit back and watch his new partner again unveil his wide array of exquisite strokes. Gower scored 48 of the 78-run partnership he had with his fellow left-hander in 22 overs. The lack of bowling depth was a problem for Pakistan. The rarely used Mansoor had to send down a full quota of 12 overs, although He, in fact took the second wicket of the English innings, the last captured by Pakistan, when David Gower, his concentration finally deserting him, holed out to Sarfraz at mid wicket.

Fowler found difficulty in timing his strokes and was missed three times, but it hardly mattered. He just kept giving the in form batsmen the strike as much as possible. Allan Lamb, after a close call for lbw against a Qadir wrong 'un, took up where Gower left off. Abdul Qadir often troubled Lamb. On this day, though, the South African scored freely off him.

The game was finished when Lamb put the leg-spinner over long off for six, lifting his tournament average above the 100 mark in the process. On the day England had asserted a clear dominance over their opponents, although one, Zaheer Abbas was recognised by adjudicator John Murray as Man of the Match.

PAKISTAN		ENGLAND	
Mohsin Khan c Tavare b Willis	3	G. Fowler not out	78
Mudassar Nazar c Gould b Allott	26	C. J. Tavare lbw b Rashid Khan	8
Mansoor Akhtar c Gould b Willis	3	D. I. Gower c Sarfraz Nawaz b Mansoor Akhtar	48
Javed Miandad c Gould b Botham	14	A. J. Lamb not out	48
Zaheer Abbas not out	83	Extras b1 lb12 w2 nb2	17
Imran Khan (capt) run out	7	(50.4 overs)	2-199
Wasim Raja c Botham b Marks	9	Did not bat: M. W. Gatting, I. T. Botham, I. J. Gould (wk),	
Abdul Qadir run out	0	V. J. Marks, G. R. Dilley ,P. J. W. Allott, R. G. D. Willis (capt)	
Sarfraz Nawaz c & b Botham	11	1/15 2/93	
Wasim Bari (wk) not out	18	Bowling: Rashid Khan 7-2-19-1; Sarfraz Nawaz 11-5-22-0;	
Extras b5 lb8 w3 nb3	19	Wasim Raja 3-0-14-0; Mudassar Nazar 8-0-30-0; Abdul	
(60 overs)	8-193	Qadir 9.4-0-53-0; Mansoor Akhtar 12-2-44-1	
Did not bat: Rashid Khan			

1/29 2/33 3/49 4/67 5/96 6/112 7/118 8/154
Bowling: Willis 12-4-24-2; Dilley 12-1-33-0; Allott 12-2-48-1; Botham 12-3-36-2; Marks 12-1-33-1

Umpires: B.J. Meyer A.G.T. Whitehead
Toss: Pakistan   Points: England 4 Pakistan 0

GROUP A: NEW ZEALAND vs SRI LANKA
PHOENIX COUNTY GROUND, BRISTOL: NEW ZEALAND WON BY 5 WICKETS

New Zealand made three changes to the side which defeated Pakistan on the Saturday and Sunday. It did not undermine their strength. On the back of a sensational bowling spell by Richard Hadlee, New Zealand cruised home by five wickets with more than 20 overs to spare.

The Sri Lankans, still hanging about in the west country, were sent in and might have hoped, after their batting efforts against Pakistan and England, that they could set the Kiwis a big total to chase. But hey had lost Sidath Wettimuny by the time the score reached 16, thanks to Hadlee striking in his first spell. Brendon Kuruppu and Roy Dias set about establishing the innings base, but it was not until Duleep Mendis and Ranjan Madugalle got together that Sri Lanka really looked like getting anything close to the 280's they had hit at Swansea and Taunton.

Madugalle completed a pleasing half century. He and Mendis had seen their side through to 3-144 when Hadlee struck again soon after lunch, ending a productive 71-run partnership in 20 overs. Sri Lanka's tail had boosted their previous efforts.

However, this time they were not able to quell the threat of New Zealand's champion. Hadlee dismissed the young left-hander Ranatunga before he had scored and stage-managed a late collapse which saw four wickets fall for 10 runs. In addition to Hadlee's outstanding spell, Ewen Chatfield's economy played an important part in Sri Lanka being restricted to 206.

New Zealand were concerned by the threat of rain, so Glenn Turner and John Wright cracked 89 runs in 17 overs off an inadequate Sri Lankan pace attack. The Kiwis had a hiccup, slipping to 3-110, when Asantha de Mel and Somachandra de Silva combined for a triple breakthrough.

But neither really looked like getting rid of Geoff Howarth. The New Zealand captain was at his stylish, stroke filled best, scoring very freely. His side were 3-120 from 25 overs at tea and his 66-run partnership with Jeff Crowe sealed the result, although neither was at the wicket when the win was achieved. It was left to Ian Smith, brought in as wicketkeeper for Warren Lees, to hit the winning boundary off Vinothen John.

Five weeks after the match the Sri Lankan manager wrote to the English Test and County Cricket Board announcing that Ashantha de Mel and not Rumesh Ratnayake had dismissed Howarth. But both scorers were convinced that they had observed Ratnayake perform the deed. Perhaps the Sri Lankans were unsure of the identity of some New Zealand batsmen.

No one had any real trouble identifying Hadlee as Man of the Match.

SRI LANKA		NEW ZEALAND	
S. Wettimuny lbw b Hadlee	7	G. M. Turner c Mendis b de Silva	50
D. S. B. P. Kuruppu c Hadlee b Chatfield	26	J. G. Wright lbw b de Mel	45
R. L. Dias b Chatfield	25	G. P. Howarth (capt) c Madugalle b Ratnayake	76
L. R. D. Mendis (capt) b Hadlee	43	M. D. Crowe c de Alwis b de Mel	0
R. S. Madugalle c Snedden b Coney	60	J. J. Crowe lbw b John	23
A. Ranatunga lbw b Hadlee	0	J. V. Coney not out	2
D. S. de Silva b Coney	13	I. D. S. Smith (wk) not out	4
R. G. de Alwis(wk) c Howarth bSnedden	16	Extras lb6 w3	9
A. L.F. de Mel c & b Hadlee	1	(39.2 overs)	5-209
R. J. Ratnayake b Hadlee	5	Did not bat: R. J. Hadlee, B. L. Cairns, M. C. Snedden,	
V. B. John not out	2	E. J. Chatfield	
Extras lb6 w1 nb1	8	1/89 2/99 3/110 4/176 5/205	
(56.1 overs)	206	Bowling: de Mel 8-2-30-2; John 8.2-0-49-1;	

1/16 2/56 3/73 4/144 5/144 6/171 7/196 8/199 9/199 10/206

Ratnayake 12-0-60-1; de Silva 9-0-39-1; Ranatunga 2-0-22-0

Bowling: Hadlee 10.1-4-25-5; Snedden 10-1-38-1; Chatfield 12-4-24-2; Cairns 7-0-35-0; Coney 12-0-44-2; M. D.Crowe 5-0-32-0

Umpires: H.D. Bird   D.R. Shepherd

Toss: New Zealand   Points: New Zealand 4 Sri Lanka 0

GROUP B: AUSTRALIA vs INDIA
TRENT BRIDGE: AUSTRALIA WON BY 162 RUNS

The cricketing world seemed to be returning to a state of equilibrium after Australia thrashed India in Nottingham. Despite the upheavals of the first day of the tournament, there was only ever one side in this contest, as India were totally outclassed. The only real surprise came from the fact that the Australian heroes were the largely previously unsung third Chappell brother, Trevor, and West Australian swing bowler Ken MacLeay.

Kim Hughes won the toss and elected to bat. He left out Jeff Thomson again and also, this time, the great Dennis Lillee, who was still underdone after his injury-affected southern summer. At 34, there were those who considered this a sign the great man's career was almost at an end. Lillee and Hughes were not on the best of terms. At one net session, the legendary fast bowler sent down nothing but bouncers at his captain.

India had their worries, too. Sunil Gavaskar reported unfit and was left out of the side. He and Kapil Dev were not seeing eye to eye.

Of more immediate concern to the Indian captain, though, was that Chappell, in the side as a replacement opener for the concussed Graeme Wood, got Australia away to a flyer. He lost his out-of-form opening partner Kepler Wessels to a poor stroke in the third over with the score on just 11. But when Hughes joined him, Chappell went on a spree that rattled the Indians.

The sun shone, the wicket was good and Chappell and Hughes ran for everything. There was an element of risk involved, but the Indians were way off the mark in the field. Roger Binny put down a caught and bowled chance when Chappell was on 27. None of the throws could hit the stumps.

The partnership prospered and 144 runs were added in 29 overs. Hughes had been badly out of form in the lead-up matches and had failed against Zimbabwe and the West Indies. He was under pressure from team manager, Phil Ridings, to elevate Graham Yallop in the order and demote himself to number five. To his great relief at Trent Bridge he went to his 50 in 80 balls, with three fours.

The relief might just have broken his concentration, because he was out soon after. Four runs later, David Hookes was caught at cover misjudgung a Madan Lal slower ball and Australia looked at risk of another collapse.

Chappell, though, was set upon a bigger milestone. He raced on to his century, his first in international cricket and the second by an Australian in World Cup matches. By the time he holed out at point off Mohinder Amarnath, he had seen the 200 raised in 40 overs and hit 13 fours in 131 balls.

Kapil Dev was not suffering from complacency. He kept the pressure on for the remainder of the innings and finished with five wickets, but his teammates were below par. Allan Border, who gave two chances, stayed until the score was 254 and Yallop batted through, ensuring a 300-plus total from the previously beleaguered Australians.

Without Gavaskar, India's task of chasing 321 was always going to be tough. Kris Srikkanth hit about with his usual dash, scoring five boundaries in the first six overs of the innings.

But while Geoff Lawson and Rodney Hogg were quite expensive, the Indians were always in trouble. Lillee's replacement, West Australian leg-spinner Tom Hogan, fired in darts at leg stump from around the wicket that restricted the freedom of India's strokeplayers.

Rain and bad light interruptions interfered with any momentum that the Indians tried to build, and MacLeay took great advantage. He kept the ball on a full length, moved it a little and waited for the batsmen to overreach. Sandeep Patil was bowled between bat and pad and Yashpal Sharma found out how high the tall MacLeay could reach to take a caught and bowled.

The Indians were 6-66 after 22 overs, having lost 4-9 at the start of MacLeay's spell. They were all out after 37.5 overs for 158. Kapil Dev had hit out and top scored. Generally, though, it was a reminder of the bad old days. At least the complacency was gone. Trevor Chappell received the Man of the Match Award.

AUSTRALIA		INDIA	
K. C. Wessels b Kapil Dev	5	R. J. Shastri lbw b Lawson	11
T. M. Chappell c Srikkanth b Amarnath	110	K. Srikkanth c Border b Hogan	39
K. J. Hughes (capt) b Madan Lal	52	M. Amarnath run out	2
D. W. Hookes c Kapil Dev b Madan Lal	1	D. B. Vengsarkar lbw b MacLeay	5
G. N. Yallop not out	66	S. M. Patil b MacLeay	0
A. R. Border c Yashpal b Binny	26	Yashpal Sharma c & b MacLeay	3
R. W. Marsh (wk) c Sandhu b Kapil Dev	12	Kapil Dev (capt) b Hogan	40
K. H. MacLeay c & b Kapil Dev	4	Madan Lal c Hogan b MacLeay	27
T. G. Hogan b Kapil Dev	11	R. M.H. Binny lbw b MacLeay	0
G. F. Lawson c Srikkanth b Kapil Dev	6	S. M.H. Kirmani (wk) b MacLeay	12
R. M. Hogg not out	2	B. S. Sandhu not out	9
Extras b1 lb14 w8 nb2	25	Extras b1 lb4 w3 nb2	10
(60 overs)	9-320	(37.5 overs)	158

1/11 2/155 3/159 4/206 5/254 6/277 7/289 8/301 9/307

Bowling: Kapil Dev 12-2-43-5; Sandhu 12-1-52-0; Binny 12-1-52-1; Shastri 2-0-16-0; Madan Lal 12-0-69-2; Patil 6-0-36-0; Amarnath 4-0-27-1

1/38 2/43 3/57 4/57 5/64 6/66 7/124 8/126 9/136 10/158

Bowling: Lawson 5-1-25-1; Hogg 7-2-23-0; Hogan 12-1-48-2; MacLeay 11.5-3-39-6; Border 2-0-13-0

Umpires: D.O. Oslear R. Palmer

Toss: Australia   Points: Australia 4 India 0

GROUP B: WEST INDIES vs ZIMBABWE
NEW ROAD, WORCESTER: WEST INDIES WON BY 8 WICKETS

Zimbabwe came out of this game with nearly as much credit as the winners. For much of the day at the one of the world's most beautiful cricket grounds, the Africans challenged the world champions before the West Indies' depth in quality saw them through. In the end the margin was substantial, yet when Clive Lloyd's side were 2-23 chasing 218, another massive upset was being contemplated. Again Zimbabwe proved their worth as competitors in the World Cup.

Lloyd won the toss and would not even have had to tell his opposite number, Duncan Fletcher, that his side would be sent in to bat. The move paid immediate dividends. Ali Shah chopped a ball from Andy Roberts onto his stumps and when Grant Paterson edged a Michael Holding screamer to Jeff Dujon Zimbabwe were 2-7 and a complete rout was on the cards.

That possibility had been quelled by lunch, but the Zimbabweans were still struggling at 4-70 from 33 overs. Andy Pycroft had hit the first boundary of the day, a nice drive through the covers off Winston Davis. Davis and Wayne Daniel held their places with Joel Garner's side strain and Malcolm Marshall's injury still a worry. With the score on 35 Pycroft tried to take a sharp single to Viv Richards. Not wise. Jack Heron hung on for 41 minutes before scoring, and batted 108 minutes for 12 before being stumped off Larry Gomes third ball.

Against Australia, Zimbabwe had gone to lunch in trouble and recovered. Now, as then, it was captain Fletcher who led the way. He and Dave Houghton added 92 runs for the fifth wicket, 55 of their runs coming from the slows of Gomes and Richards. Fletcher was dropped twice, by Davis on 25 then Dujon on 44, but he went to a fine 50 in 48 balls. Houghton finally edged a Roberts outswinger in the 50th over. The Zimbabwean captain once more batted until the end of the innings. Zimbabwe added 34 runs from the last four overs to ensure they were in with a chance.

Vince Hogg was still suffering from his back complaint, but Peter Rawson had recovered. He quickly had Desmond Haynes caught behind and after a brief flurry of strokes trapped Viv Richards in front.

By now poor light interrupted play a couple of times. Gordon Greenidge and Larry Gomes needed to be at their best. Gomes was regularly beaten outside the off-stump and Greenidge was subdued. Like the Australia's Chappell and Hughes at Trent Bridge, they initially built the scoreboard with a series of sharply taken singles. They had no other choice as the pressure was maintained.

After the 50 was passed in 19 overs strokes began to replace pushes and the Zimbabwean bowlers lost a little of their edge. Greendige powered ahead of his partner. Partnership landmarks were passed, 50, 100, and 150. Greenidge completed his second World Cup century. He had hit one six and just five fours. He and Gomes completed an unbroken 195 run partnership which was then an all wicket record for the World Cup, beating Rick McCosker and Alan Turner's 182 run effort against Sri Lanka at The Oval in 1975.

The West Indies finally romped home with more than 11 overs to spare. Greenidge, perhaps starting a medal collection, was the nominated Man of the Match.

ZIMBABWE		WEST INDIES	
A. H. Shah b Roberts	2	C. G. Greenidge not out	105
G. A. Paterson c Dujon b Holding	4	D. L. Haynes c Houghton b Rawson	2
J. G. Heron st Dujon b Gomes	12	I. V. A. Richards lbw b Rawson	16
A. J. Pycroft run out	13	H. A. Gomes not out	75
D. L. Houghton (wk) c Dujon b Roberts	54	Extras b1 lb8 w9 nb2	20
D. A. G. Fletcher (capt) not out	71	(48.3 overs)	2-218
K. M. Curran b Roberts	7	Did not bat: S. F. A. F. Bacchus, C. H. Lloyd (capt),	
I. P. Butchart lbw b Holding	0	P. J.L. Dujon (wk), W. W. Daniel, A. M. E. Roberts,	
G. E. Peckover not out	16	M. A. Holding, W. W. Davis	
Extras b1 lb23 w7 nb 7	38	1/3 2/23	
(60 overs)	7-217	Bowling: Rawson 12-1-39-2; Curran 10.3-1-37-0;	
Did not bat: P. W. E. Rawson, A. J. Traicos		Butchart 9-1-40-0; Fletcher 4-0-22-0; Traicos 9-0-37-0;	
1/7 2/7 3/35 4/65 5/157 6/181 7/183		Shah 4-0-23-0	
Bowling: Roberts 12-4-36-3; Holding 12-2-33-2;			
Daniel 12-4-21-0; Davis 12-2-34-0; Gomes 8-0-42-1;			
Richards 4-1-13-0			

Umpires: J. Birkenshaw D.G.L. Evans

Toss: West Indies   Points: West Indies 4 Zimbabwe 0

WEDNESDAY 15 JUNE 1983
THE PRUDENTIAL CUP: ROUND FOUR
GROUP A: ENGLAND vs NEW ZEALAND
EDGBASTON: NEW ZEALAND WON BY 2 WICKETS

Following six days on the merry go round the eight sides were back to the starting point again. There had been a lot of cricket and there was a lot more to come. Realistically seven sides remained in the hunt for a semi-final berth. Only Sri Lanka were without a win and mathematically, if they won all their last three games, they could make it, too.

As the teams entered the mid-week round four, the only unbeaten side was England. By the end of the day, though, they also had tasted defeat. At Edgbaston, New Zealand turned the tables, converting a 106-run defeat on the opening day of he tournament into an exciting two-wicket victory. It was their first ever win over England in any international in an English venue.

Graeme Fowler, more confident after his innings against Pakistan, and Chris Tavare gave England a positive start of 63 from 19 overs. Bob Willis, after winning the toss, saw an opportunity for Ian Botham to regain a bit of batting confidence and score some quick runs against the slower bowling of Jeremy Coney and John Bracewell. The all-rounder made every attempt to bludgeon the ball, but after making 12, which included one chance as well as one four and one six, he hit a low scorcher straight back at Bracewell, which the off-spinner held.

The change in the order made no difference to David Gower who continued on his merry way. He and Fowler put England in a position where another 250 plus total seemed likely. From 2-117, though, the innings sort of lost its way.

The England captain blamed over confidence, Gower suggested the innings was poorly paced. He was in the best position to judge as he saw eight partners come and go, their failures almost certainly denying him yet another century.

Lance Cairns, bowling wrong-footed in swing, put the Kiwis on top, disposing of Allan Lamb, Mike Gatting and Ian Gould in quick succession and leaving England on 6-162.

Gower finally found support from Vic Marks and Graham Dilley. He cruised into the 90s in 96 balls hitting four sixes and six fours on the way. Gower dominated the scoring in the latter part of the innings, compiling 52 runs out of the 72 scored.

At 7-233 with a few overs left, England still had the chance of a very decent total. But that was as far as it got. Richard Hadlee and Ewen Chatfield quickly polished off the last three wickets for one run to leave Gower high and dry. England were all out and had wasted 28 deliveries.

New Zealand had plenty of work to reach 235, especially as no Kiwi side had ever won an international in England. Bob Willis, perhaps annoyed at making a duck, gave the Kiwis a double set back by getting rid of Glenn Turner in his first over and Bruce Edgar in his second with only three runs on the board. Both decisions prompted some debate, especially the second where there was doubt whether the ball carried.

The wicket was not entirely to be trusted, so it was hard work to bring about a recovery. Willis finished his spell, but Paul Allott bowled Jeff Crowe to make it 3-47. The younger Crowe, Martin, made 20 out of a stand of 28 with his resilient captain before he was bowled by Vic Marks. It was 4-75 and at that point England were in control.

It was Jeremy Coney who finally became the kind of partner Geoff Howarth had been looking for. The New Zealand captain, who was recovering from a bout of dysentry, and the future Kiwi skipper, added a very important 71 runs in 15 overs before Howarth's fine innings of 60 came to an unfortunate end, run out when trying to take a second run to Dilley's strong throw from fine leg.

Ian Smith soon went, but Coney was still there as a potential matchwinner. He and Hadlee changed the direction of the game. They put on 70 at five runs per over to take New Zealand to the brink of victory. Willis wasn't finished, though. He came back to bowl Hadlee and won an lbw decision against Cairns with four runs still needed. Allott bowled the last over of the match. Bracewell and Coney contrived three runs from four balls including two byes from the second delivery, to level the scores. Then Bracewell cracked the Lancastrian seamer to the mid-on boundary to give Geoff Howarth's side victory in the closest match of the tournament so far. For his guiding light innings, Jeremy Coney won the Man of the Match award.

England's award was a post match chastisement from their Chairman of Selectors, Peter May. He called them "arrogant" and "undisciplined".

ENGLAND		NEW ZEALAND	
G. Fowler c J. J.Crowe b Chatfield	69	G. M.Turner lbw b Willis	2
C. J. Tavare c Cairns b Coney	18	B. A. Edgar c Gould b Willis	1
I. T. Botham c & b Bracewell	12	G. P. Howarth (capt) run out	60
D. I. Gower not out	92	J. J. Crowe b Allott	17
A. J. Lamb c J. J.Crowe b Cairns	8	M. D. Crowe b Marks	20
M. W. Gatting b Cairns	1	J. V. Coney not out	66
I. J. Gould (wk) lbw b Cairns	4	I. D. S. Smith (wk) b Botham	4
V. J. Marks b Hadlee	5	R. J. Hadlee b Willis	31
G. R. Dilley b Hadlee	10	B. L. Cairns lbw b Willis	5
P. J.W. Allott c Smith b Hadlee	0	J. G. Bracewell not out	4
R. G.D. Willis (capt) not out	0	Extras b2 lb22 w1 nb3	28
Extras b4 lb10 w1	15	(59.5 overs)	8-238
(55.2 overs)	234	Did not bat: E. J. Chatfield	

England: 1/63 2/77 3/117 4/143 5/154 6/162 7/203 8/233 9/233 10/234

New Zealand: 1/2 2/3 3/47 4/75 5/146 6/151 7/221 8/231

Bowling (England): Hadlee 10-3-32-3; Cairns 11-0-44-3; Coney 12-2-27-1; Bracewell 12-0-66-1; Chatfield 10.2-0-50-2

Bowling (New Zealand): Willis 12-1-42-4; Dilley 12-1-43-0; Botham 12-1-47-1; Allott 11.5-2-44-1; Marks 12-1-34-1

Umpires: J. Birkenshaw K.E. Palmer

Toss: England   Points: New Zealand 4 England 0

GROUP A: PAKISTAN vs SRI LANKA
HEADINGLEY: PAKISTAN WON BY 11 RUNS

Although Round Four did not quite provide the upsets of Round One, there was plenty of excitement in Group A. The day after England and New Zealand fought out their thriller in Birmingham further up the M1 in Leeds Sri Lanka made life very uncomfortable for Imran Khan and his Pakistani team.

Twice during the match the Sri Lankans appeared to be well on the road to a great victory. They were unable to sustain the pressure, however, and much to the relief of the stressed captain of Pakistan, his side hung on by 11 runs.

It was a grey morning at Headingley when Duleep Mendis won the toss and elected to bowl. While not the dangerous minefield that the Australians and West Indians had played on, there was still plenty of assistance for the bowlers and Ashantha de Mel took full advantage. He moved the ball around and got rid of both openers. When Rumesh Ratnayake replaced de Mel he got Javed Miandad lbw and then won another decision against Ijaz Faqih. Pakistan were 5-43 and in big trouble.

Shahid Mahboob only ever played one Test, so he is not well remembered. He was selected for a number of limited-over internationals in this period, though, and put in some useful performances. None were more valuable than this one. He and Imran lifted Pakistan out of their precarious position by adding 144 runs in 36 overs.

At the end of the 1996 tournament this was still a World Cup record for the sixth wicket and it could not have come at a more opportune time. They both offered sharp chances, but the Sri Lankan fieldsmen could not take advantage. By the time de Mel came back to claim his fourth wicket by dismissing Shahid, Pakistan were back in the contest.

As the 60-over mark closed in, Imran dominated the scoring and completed a vital century. It was the first by a Pakistani in the World Cup and contained 11 fours. de Mel's five-wicket haul was the first by a Sri Lankan in the World Cup—a far cry from the days when the entire team battled to get five wickets in the whole 60 overs.

Despite the early loss of Brendon Kuruppu, Sri Lanka batted confidently in their pursuit of 236.

Lacking Imran, the Pakistani attack still lacked punch and by now had completely lost its radar. Mansoor, proving what a part-timer he really was, sent down five wides in one over. The batting conditions had settled down and Sidath Wettimuny, Roy Dias and Duleep Mendis showed composure in taking their side to 1-86 at tea off 25 overs and later 2-162. They were just 74 runs away from a win with 13 overs to play.

But if the Pakistani pace attack lacked bite, there could be no such criticism of its spinner. Imran had to fight to get the unfashionable leggie, Abdul Qadir, into his side for a limited-overs tournament. Qadir repaid his captain's faith by bowling Pakistan to victory over New Zealand at Edgbaston and he now turned this match around decisively.

With Wasim Bari an ever-present threat and accomplice behind the stumps, Qadir grabbed five cheap wickets, including 4-16 in his last four overs. Sri Lanka lost 7-37 in a terrible hurry. de Silva was run out from mid wicket and de Alwis edged Qadir to slip. Sri Lanka slumped to 9-199. They now seemed certain to lose, but de Mel was not going to waste his five-wicket haul without a fight. He and Vinothen John got stuck in and put on 25 runs for the last wicket. Twelve more were needed with nine balls remaining and de Mel drove hard at Sarfraz. Imran was at long off and he held the catch. There was a collective sigh in Urdu.

Qadir's match-winning spell got him the nod for the Man of the Match award ahead of other candidates such as Imran, Shahid and the brave de Mel.

PAKISTAN			SRI LANKA	
Mohsin Khan c Ranatunga b de Mel	3		S. Wettimuny c Shahid Mahboob b Rashid Khan	50
Mansoor Akhtar c de Alwis b de Mel	6		D. S. B. P. Kuruppu b Rashid Khan	12
Zaheer Abbas c Dias b de Mel	15		R. L. Dias st Wasim Bari b Abdul Qadir	47
Javed Miandad lbw b Ratnayake	7		L. R. D. Mendis (capt) c Wasim Bari b Abdul Qadir	33
Imran Khan (capt) not out	102		R. J. Ratnayake st Wasim Bari b Abdul Qadir	1
Ijaz Faqih lbw b Ratnayake	0		R. S. Madugalle c Abdul Qadir b Shahid Mahboob	26
Shahid Mahboob c de Silva b de Mel	77		A. Ranatunga c Zaheer Abbas b Abdul Qadir	0
Sarfraz Nawaz c Madugalle b de Mel	9		D. S. de Silva run out	1
Abdul Qadir not out	5		R. G. de Alwis(wk) c Javed Miandad b Abdul Qadir	4
Extras b1 lb4 w4 nb2	11		A. L. F. de Mel c Imran Khan b Sarfraz Nawaz	17
(60 overs)	7-235		V. B. John not out	6
Did not bat: Wasim Bari (wk), Rashid Khan			Extras lb8 w17 nb2	27
1/6 2/25 3/30 4/43 5/43 6/187 7/204			(58.3 overs)	224
Bowling: de Mel 12-1-39-5; John 12-1-48-0;			1/22 2/101 3/162 4/162 5/166 6/166 7/171 8/193 9/199	
Ratnayake 12-2-42-2; Ranatunga 11-0-49-0;			10/224	
de Silva 12-1-42-0; Wettimuny 1-0-4-0			Bowling: Rashid Khan 12-4-31-2; Sarfraz Nawaz 11.3-2-25-1;	
			Shahid Mahboob 10-1-62-1; Mansoor Akhtar 1-0-8-0;	
			Ijaz Faqih 12-0-27-0; Abdul Qadir 12-1-44-5	

Umpires: D. Oslear A.G.T. Whitehead

Toss: Sri Lanka Points: Pakistan 4 Sri Lanka 0

GROUP B:
AUSTRALIA vs ZIMBABWE
COUNTY GROUND, SOUTHAMPTON: AUSTRALIA WON BY 32 RUNS

On the south coast, the Australians recovered a little of the pride they'd lost a week earlier at the hands of Zimbabwe. They won comfortably enough by 32 runs, without convincing anyone they were likely to make much impression against better sides.

Like Pakistan and Sri Lanka, Australia and Zimbabwe played on the Thursday instead of Wednesday. There was no sign of interruption after Kim Hughes won the toss and batted. He had originally said that Graeme Wood might be unfit to play, but it was the West Australian who walked to the centre at the start of play with Trevor Chappell. Kepler Wessels was dropped.

Wood showed no ill-effects as he and Chappell started brightly with 46 runs in 10 overs. Wood could have been run out on 16, but it was Monday's centurion who went first. Wood continued on with his captain in a productive second wicket partnership of 78. Hughes fell to the accurate off-spin of John Traicos and Australia went to lunch on 2-145 from 37 overs. They briefly forfeited their sound position straight after the interval when Traicos ended Wood's worthy effort and David Hookes was caught on the same total at mid off from a wild uncultured swing at Duncan Fletcher.

Sensible batting and running by Allan Border and the consistent Graham Yallop was the feature of their 69-run stand that took the score from 4-150 to 5-219. Then Rod Marsh was able to swing his arms with some freedom and hit two sixes on way to an invaluable 35 not out, guiding Australia to a score of 7-272 and a position of some strength.

That was always going to be enough, even though Grant Paterson and Robin Brown put on 48 in 13 overs for the first wicket. Andy Pycroft and Jack Heron were both victims of poor running between the wickets. Pycroft was run out going for a quick single by a throw from Rod Marsh to the bowler's end.

When Tom Hogan bowled the bogeyman from the first match, Duncan Fletcher, Zimbabwe were 5-109. They would never get 273 from there. But Dave Houghton and Kevin Curran were not going let the Australians have an early finish to the afternoon, putting on 103 in 17 overs. Houghton showed just what a good player he was; in 110 minutes he hit nine fours and one six off Chappell.

There were a few furrowed brows amongst the Australians and the 4,000-strong crowd was brought to life until three lbw shouts were upheld within seven balls, ruining any lingering Zimbabwean hopes in the gathering gloom. From the last ball of an over Chappell finally got rid of the determined Kevin Curran. One run later in the next over, Rodney Hogg got the umpire's nod against Ian Butchart and Peter Rawson off successive deliveries. With Houghton, caught at short mid off, also gone Zimbabwe slipped to 9-213. Vince Hogg and John Traicos held on until the second-last ball of the 60 overs, but they were a source of frustration, not a threat to victory.

Houghton's 84 was considered the highlight of the day. Roy Marshall gave him the Man of the Match award.

AUSTRALIA		ZIMBABWE	
G. M. Wood c Rawson b Traicos	73	R. D. Brown c Marsh b Hogan	38
T. M. Chappell c Traicos b Rawson	22	G. A. Paterson lbw b Hogg	17
K. J. Hughes (capt) b Traicos	31	J. G. Heron run out	3
D. W. Hookes c Brown b Fletcher	10	A. J. Pycroft run out	13
G. N. Yallop c Houghton b Curran	20	D. L. Houghton (wk) c Hughes b Chappell	84
A. R. Border b Butchart	43	D. A. G. Fletcher (capt) b Hogan	2
R. W. Marsh (wk) not out	35	K. M. Curran lbw b Chappell	35
K. H. MacLeay c Rawson b Butchart	9	I. P. Butchart lbw b Hogg	0
T. G. Hogan not out	5	P. W. E. Rawson lbw b Hogg	0
Extras lb16 w2 nb6	24	A. J. Traicos b Chappell	19
(60 overs)	7-272	V. R. Hogg not out	7
Did not bat: D. K. Lillee, R. M. Hogg		Extras b1 lb10 w1 nb10	22
1/46 2/124 3/150 4/150 5/219 6/231 7/249		(59.5 overs)	240
Bowling: Hogg 9-2-34-0; Rawson 9-0-50-1;		1/48 2/53 3/79 4/97 5/109 6/212 7/213 8/213 9/213	
Fletcher 9-1-27-1; Butchart 10-0-52-2; Traicos 12-1-28-2;		10/240	
Curran 11-0-57-1		Bowling: Hogg 12-0-40-3; Lillee 9-1-23-0; Hogan 12-0-33-2;	
		MacLeay 9-0-45-0; Border 9-1-30-0; Chappell 8.5-0-47-3	

Umpires: D.G.L. Evans   R. Palmer

Toss: Australia   Points: Australia 4 Zimbabwe 0

GROUP B: INDIA vs WEST INDIES
THE OVAL: WEST INDIES WON BY 66 RUNS

A sunny Kennington Oval and a fast wicket were seemingly tailor made for a West Indian side continuing to build their momentum as the Prudential Cup moved into its business phase. They comfortably accounted for India in this, the Wednesday Group B fixture. The key Caribbean batsmen hit form and their pace attack was too much for the Indians.

India were without Sunil Gavaskar again. This time he was just left out of the side, a decision as controversial inside and outside the team as had been Australia's omission of Lillee. In Joel Garner's case injury was still the problem.

Clive Lloyd won the toss and for the first time in the World Cup, elected to bat. This decision was greeted with immense pleasure by the large West Indian contingent out of the 12,000 who were attracted to The Oval by the prospect of revenge against India and a warming, almost Caribbean sun.

Those West Indian fans did not enjoy the prompt dismissal of Gordon Greenidge, caught at first slip off Kapil Dev. They were far better entertained by a century partnership between Desmond Haynes and the previously out-of-form Viv Richards. The wicket had pace, but the bounce was unreliable the mighty Antiguan was circumspect. It took quite a while for him to play with any freedom and even as he asserted himself, his strokes were more restrained than normal.

Haynes eventually got a ball from the innocuous looking Amarnath which lifted alarmingly and Richards was joined by Clive Lloyd, another batsman yet to make in an impression in this World Cup. The powerful left-hander once lifted Roger Binny over mid wicket for six and in 14 overs added 80 runs with Richards.

Their stand took the West Indies to a very healthy 2-198 in the 45th over. Then Lloyd was left stranded in mid pitch after a misunderstanding with his partner as Kirmani threw down the stumps. The West Indies now struggled to accelerate. Richards went to his deserved century and also deposited one delivery onto the roof of the Surrey Members pavilion. Eventually he was caught behind in the 52nd over, his 119 containing just six fours and the one six, a low rate of boundaries for the 'Master Blaster'.

The four West Indian fast bowlers found it just as hard to play big shots and only 59 runs came from the final 10 overs. Larry Gomes again held things together as the innings concluded on 9-282 from 60 overs.

It was a worthy total and India had a very difficult chase. The wicket was rock hard and the ball flew when Andy Roberts, Malcolm Marshall, Michael Holding and Winston Davis bent their backs. The West Indian supporters loved that. Roberts had openers Kris Srikkanth and Ravi Shastri caught behind by the time the scoreboard reached 21.

Amarnath, displaying the fortitude he had shown in the Caribbean a few months earlier, was joined by Dilip Vengsarkar in a brave 68-run stand in 21 overs.

Then the spite in the pitch finally took its toll. Marshall unleashed a ball to Vengsarkar which reared and struck him in the chin. Marshall has indicated Vengsarkar was never a favourite opponent, although there was no suggestion he gained any pleasure from decking him.

Vengsarkar took no further part in the match; or the rest of the tournament. But Amarnath went on. Battered from pillar to post, struck about the elbow, knuckles and even the face, he resisted and hooked bravely at every opportunity for three hours. His captain rated him the best player of express fast bowling in the world. It was an opinion he would not change even after Amarnath scored one run from six innings in the Test series in India against the West Indies four months later.

Sandeep Patil also fought hard and Kapil Dev continued to strive for victory. India got to 5-193, however the overs were starting to run out. Michael Holding returned and picked up a couple of quick wickets. When Kapil Dev was dismissed India needed 71 runs from just eight overs. Haynes, Dev's catcher, showed the delight of a man who believed a match was won.

He was right. India scored only four of the 71 runs they needed. Sandhu was run out from the first ball, of the 54th over, leaving the West Indies winners by 66 runs. Only those at the ground were witnesses to this West Indian revenge. The television coverage was blacked out by a strike by the Association of Broadcasting Staffs.

Everyone outside The Oval had to be told that Viv Richards was Man of the Match.

WEST INDIES		INDIA	
C. G. Greenidge c Vengsarkar b Kapil Dev	9	K. Srikkanth c Dujon b Roberts	2
D. L. Haynes c Kapil Dev b Amarnath	38	R. J. Shastri c Dujon b Roberts	6
I. V. A. Richards c Kirmani b Sandhu	119	M. Amarnath c Lloyd b Holding	80
C. H. Lloyd (capt) run out	41	D. B. Vengsarkar retired hurt	32
S. F. A. F. Bacchus b Binny	8	S. M. Patil c & b Gomes	21
P. J. L. Dujon (wk) c Shastri b Binny	9	Yashpal Sharma run out	9
H. A. Gomes not out	27	Kapil Dev (capt) c Haynes b Holding	36
A. M. E. Roberts c Patil b Binny	7	R. M.H. Binny lbw b Holding	1
M. D. Marshall run out	4	Madan Lal not out	8
M. A. Holding c sub (K. Azad) b Madan Lal	2	S. M. H. Kirmani (wk) b Marshall	0
W. W. Davis not out	0	B. S. Sandhu run out	0
Extras lb13 w5	18	Extras b3 lb13 nb5	21
(60 overs)	9-282	(53.1 overs)	216

1/17 2/118 3/198 4/213 5/239 6/240 7/257 8/270 9/280

1/2 2/21 3/130 4/143 5/193 6/195 7/212 8/214 9/216

Bowling: Kapil Dev 12-0-46-1; Sandhu 12-2-42-1;
Binny 12-0-71-3; Amarnath 12-0-58-1; Madan Lal 12-0-47-1

Bowling: Roberts 9-1-29-2; Holding 9.1-0-40-3;
Marshall 11-3-20-1; Davis 12-2-51-0; Gomes 12-1-55-1

Umpires: B.J. Meyer   D.R. Shepherd

Toss: West Indies   Points: West Indies 4 India 0

SATURDAY 18 JUNE 1983
THE PRUDENTIAL CUP: ROUND FIVE
GROUP A: ENGLAND vs PAKISTAN
OLD TRAFFORD: ENGLAND WON BY 7 WICKETS

Saturday provided beautiful weather and reassurement for English fans that everything really was on course in their World Cup campaign. Most of England's cricket was disciplined and displayed only the positive aspects of arrogance. Pakistan, in contrast, looked lacklustre and rarely seemed to have the upper hand.

If it is sunny in Manchester, then the whole of England is usually basking and that brings out the fans. The gates were closed soon after the start of play and 20,000, many of them baring their chests—a couple of streakers showing a little more—saw Pakistan struggle to build a competitive score only for their bowlers to fail to make any impression on the in-form English batsmen.

The wicket was a little low and slow, but the outfield was fast and Imran Khan decided to bat after he won the toss. As at Lord's, Mudassar Nazar and Mohsin Khan were merely intent on survival as they withstood an early barrage from Bob Willis and Graham Dilley. The English captain, in prime bowling form, conceded just seven runs in his first six overs, while Dilley picked up the first two wickets, despite straining a muscle at the top of his right thigh in his third over. He had Mudassar caught behind down the leg-side and then removed Zaheer Abbas, the Man of the Match at Lord's, with a beauty that lifted and separated, one run later.

At 2-34, Pakistan had more securing work to do. Mohsin wanted to be the backbone and scored at barely a run an over. Javed Miandad, however, was in good touch. He alone kept the score rate reasonable. After 30 overs he finally lost Mohsin, well caught by Vic Marks. Three overs later it was lunch and Pakistan were 3-101. Imran was not on song this day at all, nor was Wasim Raja. Both were caught at long off, choosing the wrong ball from off-spinner Marks to try and boost the scoring.

Javed finally found a partner of equal intent in Ijaz Faqih, only ever called Ijaz on western television and radio.

Ian Botham's bowling had looked very ordinary again. His fielding, as it had been at Taunton, would be his day's saviour. Javed and Ijaz were looking in control when in the 51st over Ijaz guided Willis behind point. Javed called for a single. Botham moved to his left, picked the ball up in his right hand and in one motion threw down the stumps with a mighty 20-metre pelt that caught Javed short of his ground.

It was an inspirational piece of work that thrilled the crowd, the England players and Botham himself, in equal measure. Botham's joy was evidenced by the fact that he thought the effort worth a punch of the air and a spit on the ground. Pakistan were 6-169 and again battling to set a worthy target.

Ijaz kept going until the end of the innings playing some energetic cover drives with his left foot pointing at mid-on. He added valuable runs with Sarfraz Nawaz and Abdul Qadir. Pakistan put on 43 from their last six overs, enabling them to reach 8-232.

Imran's side needed early wickets, but without their captain's pace and skill they never looked like getting any. Graeme Fowler and Chris Tavare had an opening partnership of 115 in 30 overs. Their work was effective rather than exciting. The tackling of a streaker by umpire Don Oslear provided as much entertainment as any of the strokeplay by the Lancastrian and his partner from Kent. Fowler completed his third half century of the tournament. Tavare got his first before falling to the wiles of Zaheer. Qadir's leg-spin had been Pakistan's main hope and he was introduced as soon as it was obvious the pacemen would have little impact. However, there was precious little in the wicket for him, either.

A 52-run partnership between Allan Lamb and Mike Gatting saw England home in the 58th over. Lancastrian Roy Tattersall made home town hero, Graeme Fowler, Man of the Match.

PAKISTAN		ENGLAND	
Mohsin Khan c Marks b Allott	32	G. Fowler c Javed Miandad b Mudassar Nazar	69
Mudassar Nazar c Gould b Dilley	18	C. J. Tavare c Wasim Raja b Zaheer Abbas	58
Zaheer Abbas c Gould b Dilley	0	D. I. Gower c Zaheer Abbas b Mudassar Nazar	31
Javed Miandad run out	67	A. J. Lamb not out	38
Imran Khan (capt) c Willis b Marks	13	M. W. Gatting not out	14
Wasim Raja c Willis b Marks	15	Extras b1 lb15 w7	23
Ijaz Faqih not out	42	(57.2 overs)	3-233
Sarfraz Nawaz b Willis	17	Did not bat: I. T. Botham, I. J. Gould (wk), V. J. Marks,	
Abdul Qadir run out	6	G. R. Dilley, P. J.W. Allott, R. G.D. Willis(capt)	
Wasim Bari (wk) not out	2	1/115 2/165 3/181	
Extras b3 lb14 w2 nb1	20	Bowling: Rashid Khan 11-1-58-0; Sarfraz Nawaz 10.2-2-22-0;	
(60 overs)	8-232	Abdul Qadir 11-0-51-0; Ijaz Faqih 6-0-19-0; Mudassar	
Did not bat: Rashid Khan		Nazar 12-2-34-2; Zaheer Abbas 7-0-26-1	

1/33 2/34 3/87 4/116 5/144 6/169 7/204 8/221

Bowling: Willis 12-2-37-1; Dilley 12-2-46-2; Allott 12-1-33-1;
Botham 12-1-51-0; Marks 12-0-45-2

Umpires: H.D. Bird   D.O. Oslear

Toss: Pakistan   Points: England 4 Pakistan 0

GROUP A: NEW ZEALAND vs SRI LANKA
COUNTY GROUND, DERBY: SRI LANKA WON BY 3 WICKETS.

At Derby, on arguably the ugliest cricket ground in the world, New Zealand blew what looked an obvious chance to secure a semi-final berth when they lost to Sri Lanka. The Sri Lankans, who had been thrashed in New Zealand in both Test and limited-over internationals in March, were overjoyed to notch up their second World Cup win.

Derbyshire is the spiritual home of the English medium-pace seamer and this Saturday produced the sort of steamy, sunny weather and green wicket that used to delight the Les Jacksons and Cliff Gladwins of this world. So Duleep Mendis won the toss and send New Zealand in to bat. Sure enough Ashantha de Mel got the ball to start hooping and darting around. John Wright, a Derbyshire player, should have been familiar with the conditions. A loose shot and a diving Guy de Alwis removed him for a duck.

With Glenn Turner caught off an out-swinger in the same over, New Zealand had made a horrendous start at 2-8. Rumesh Ratnayake also got into the act providing a double breakthrough, getting rid of Geoff Howarth and Martin Crowe after they had briefly hinted at a recovery.

That left New Zealand 4-47 and Bruce Edgar and Jeremy Coney had to rebuild the innings. They were never able to bat with any real confidence against the unerring accuracy of wrist-spinner Somachandra de Silva, whose economy rate of less than one run per over was remarkable. They still put together 41 runs' worth of recovery when de Silva gained another double breakthrough. Both Edgar and Coney were caught in his leg trap, the latter being wonderfully held by a diving substitute, Susil Fernando.

At 6-91, hopes of that recovery were disappearing fast, especially when de Mel came back on after lunch and in quick succession got rid of the dangerous hitters, Richard Hadlee and Lance Cairns, in addition to wicketkeeper Warren Lees, who had reclaimed his spot from Ian Smith. That made it 10-71 in the last two games for the Sri Lankan paceman, a sensational couple of days work.

New Zealand were 9-116 and almost out of the contest. However, de Mel's spell was finished so Sri Lanka's second-string bowlers were charged with the responsibility of getting out either Martin Snedden or Ewen Chatfield. Snedden would later open the batting in the 1987 World Cup. This time he and his poorly credentialled partner approached their task with real aggression to put on 65 precious runs for the last wicket. The left-handed Snedden dominated the scoring until charging for a second run he failed to beat a spot on throw from mid-on. The fielder, de Mel, could almost claim it as his 11th wicket since Thursday.

The hundreds of Sri Lankan supporters in the healthy crowd watched nervously as their team began the pursuit of the 182 runs they needed. Sidath Wettimuny was an early casualty to a swinging Cairns yorker and on 49 Crowe got through the defence of Arjuna Rantunga. The New Zealand bowlers did not seem to be getting the same assistance as their Sri Lankan counterparts, though. Hadlee had been seen off without taking a wicket.

Brendon Kuruppu and Duleep Mendis added a crucial 80 runs for the third wicket. Kuruppu reached his 50 in 32 hard fought overs. He hit ten fours and with Dias had taken Sri Lanka to a position where victory seemed inevitable when Snedden held a hard hit caught and bowled. Chatfield trapped Mendis one run later suggesting the Sri Lankan middle order choke had started again. The colliwobbles lasted until they were 7-161 and defeat loomed as a real possiblity.

Fortunately Dias had held on throughout the 5-32 collapse. He continued to bat sensibly and with de Alwis made sure the win was not thrown away this time. From the second-last ball of the 53rd over Sri Lanka completed their win. De Alwis had made unbeaten 50s in the first two World Cup matches, but his 11 runs at Derby were far more valuable. Certainly those happy flag-waving Sri Lankan supporters appreciated them.

De Mel was David Allen's choice for the Man of the match Award.

NEW ZEALAND		SRI LANKA	
G. M. Turner c Dias b de Mel	6	S. Wettimuny b Cairns	4
J. G. Wright c de Alwis b de Mel	0	D. S. B. P. Kuruppu c & b Snedden	62
G. P. Howarth (capt) b Ratnayake	15	A. Ranatunga b Crowe	15
M. D. Crowe lbw b Ratnayake	8	R. L. Dias not out	64
B. A. Edgar c Samarasekera b de Silva	27	L. R. D. Mendis (capt) lbw b Chatfield	0
J. V. Coney c sub (E. R. N. S. Fernando) b de Silva	22	R. S. Madugalle c Lees b Snedden	6
R. J. Hadlee c Madugalle b de Mel	15	M. A. R. Samarasekera c Lees b Hadlee	5
W. K. Lees (wk) c Ranatunga b de Mel	2	D. S. de Silva run out	2
B. L. Cairns c Dias b de Mel	6	R. G. de Alwis (wk) not out	11
M. C. Snedden run out	40	Extras b1 lb4 w10	15
E. J. Chatfield not out	19	(52.5 overs)	7-184
Extras b4 lb5 w11 nb1	21	Did not bat: A. L. F. de Mel, R. J. Ratnayake	
(58.2 overs)	181	1/15 2/49 3/129 4/130 5/139 6/151 7/161	

1/8 2/8 3/32 4/47 5/88 6/91 7/105 8/115 9/116 10/181

Bowling: de Mel 12-4-32-5; Ratnayake 11-4-18-2; Ranatunga 10-2-50-0; de Silva 12-5-11-2; Samarasekera 11.2-2-38-0; Wettimuny 2-0-11-0

Bowling: Hadlee 12-3-16-1; Cairns 10-2-35-1; Snedden 10.5-1-58-2; Chatfield 12-3-23-1; Crowe 4-2-15-1; Coney 4-1-22-0

Umpires: D.J. Constant   B Leadbeater

Toss: Sri Lanka   Points: Sri Lanka 4 New Zealand 0

GROUP B: AUSTRALIA vs WEST INDIES
LORD'S: WEST INDIES WON BY 7 WICKETS

Lord's was packed to the rafters on a sunny Saturday for a big clash between Australia and the West Indies. It could have been the 1975 final all over again. Only seven players—three Australians and four West Indians—remained in the two teams from that magical day eight years before.

This day they would participate in another run-filled and entertaining game of cricket, if not one that was anywhere near as close at the finish. Much to the Australians' relief, they found the wicket at Lord's flat, encouraging players to play strokes. Kim Hughes won the toss and, unlike in Headingley, had no problem with batting first.

Docile pitch or not, Malcolm Marshall, the world's fastest bowler, conjured up something to test the opening batsmen. By the 10th over he had Trevor Chappell caught behind with the total on 10 and, when Australia was 37, Graeme Wood was bowled.

David Hookes and Kim Hughes responded as they did at Headingley with a counterattack full of aggressive, daring shots. Hughes, still batting at number three, had strained a hamstring muscle stretching for overthrows in the ninth over so badly that he required a runner for the remainder of his innings. Hookes struck out at anything loose, dominating the scoring for 26 overs. Captain and vice-captain, their differences temporarily put aside, added 101 runs in that time, both completing half centuries.

Jeff Dujon had just failed to grasp a difficult chance off Hookes when the South Australian was on 10. It was costly. The score was 138 before he took one risk too many and skied a ball from Winston Davis.

The innings lost some impetus following Hookes' dismissal. Hughes lasted while 38 more runs were scored, but was bowled as he tried to take advantage of flat off-spin from Larry Gomes. Allan Border made little progress and Graham Yallop was circumspect after two lucky let offs. Desmond Haynes and Marshall failed to grasp lofted opportunities.

When only 40 runs were put on between the 40th and 50th overs, Australia seemed headed for a sub-par total in batsman-friendly conditions. It was left to the veteran wicketkeeper, Rod Marsh, to strike the telling blows the Australians required from the final overs. Out of a 64-run stand with Yallop, he belted 37 runs from 26 balls, picking of all people, Michael Holding as his unlikely target. He pulled Holding into the Mound Stand for six, hooked the next easily anticipated shorter faster ball into the Tavern for another six, then straight drove the following ball to the Nursery End boundary to make it 16 runs from three balls. A "perfect postscript" said *Wisden Cricket Monthly*. Australia had added 77 in the last 10 overs.

That Marsh's hitting and Yallop's unbeaten 52 were very much required quickly became evident as the West Indies began their reply. Geoff Lawson was out of the Australian side with a groin strain and Ken MacLeay, the hero at Trent Bridge, had been dropped. Dennis Lillee and Jeff Thomson would share an international stage together for the last time.

Sadly, it was no triumph. Thomson shared the new ball with Rod Hogg. Hogg earned respect, while Thomson conceded runs freely to Haynes and Gordon Greenidge. If the West Indian speed quartet could get little help from the wicket then there was not much hope for the ageing Lillee and Thomson. It was Tom Hogan who finally broke the opening stand. After 18 overs, with the score on 79 the left-arm spinner caused Haynes to drag a ball onto his stumps.

Haynes may have been disappointed, but few in the crowd were. The Barbadian's dismissal allowed them to be treated to 27 overs of sublime batsmanship from two of the best players in the world. Viv Richards announced his arrival with a straight hit that sailed over the boundary at long on. He would later deposit another Hogan delivery to the same spot and heaped the ignominy onto Thomson by stepping away and clouting a leg-side delivery for another six over extra cover. Greenidge, whose this time was sporting an unlabelled baggy maroon hat, was just as impressive hitting eight fours during his three-hour stay at the wicket.

After the 200 was raised and 124 runs had been added, Greenidge finally rewarded Hogg for his perseverance. "We didn't bowl all that badly," said Rod Marsh. "It was simply that they batted so beautifully."

There was no follow-up collapse to revive Australian hopes. Larry Gomes played second fiddle to Richards while another 38 runs were added, then Lloyd, knowing there were overs to spare, tried to give the Antiguan enough strike to reach his 100. When that was no longer possible the West Indian captain promptly finished the match with a trademark big lofted drive off Chappell's medium pace. Richards had to be satisfied with an unbeaten 95 from 117 balls striking nine fours along with those three sixes. It was enough to win him the Man of the Match Award.

The spectators, many of them neutral, walked away content. During the day of unbroken sunshine, they had seen nine wickets for 549 runs off 120 overs, less 13 balls. It was the type of cricket that once made Hogg suggest that to save a lot of sweat and pain, bowlers should be replaced in one-day games with bowling machines.

AUSTRALIA		WEST INDIES	
G. M. Wood b Marshall	17	C. G. Greenidge c Hughes b Hogg	90
T. M. Chappell c Dujon b Marshall	5	D. L. Haynes b Hogan	33
K. J. Hughes (capt) b Gomes	69	I. V. A. Richards not out	95
D. W. Hookes c Greenidge b Davis	56	H. A. Gomes b Chappell	15
G. N. Yallop not out	52	C. H. Lloyd (capt) not out	19
A. R. Border c & b Gomes	11	Extras b3 lb18 w1 nb2	24
R. W. Marsh (wk) c Haynes b Holding	37	(57.5 overs)	3-276
T. G. Hogan not out	0	Did not bat: S. F. A. F. Bacchus, P. J. L. Dujon (wk),	
Extras b1 lb18 w6 nb1	26	M. D. Marshall, A. M. E. Roberts, M. A. Holding, W. W. Davis	
(60 overs)	6-273	1/79 2/203 3/228	
Did not bat: J. R. Thomson, D. K. Lillee, R. M. Hogg		Bowling: Hogg 12-0-25-2; Thomson 11-0-64-0;	
1/10 2/37 3/138 4/176 5/202 6/266		Hogan 12-0-60-1; Lillee 12-0-52-0; Chappell10.5-0-51-1	
Bowling: Roberts 12-0-51-0; Marshall 12-0-36-2;			
Davis 12-0-57-1; Holding 12-1-56-1; Gomes 12-0-47-2			

Umpires: K.E. Palmer A.G.T. Whitehead

Toss: Australia   Points: West Indies 4 Australia 0

GROUP B: INDIA vs ZIMBABWE
NEVILL GROUND, TUNBRIDGE WELLS: INDIA WON BY 31 RUNS

Tucked away in a lovely setting in the provincial town of Tunbridge Wells in Kent, India and Zimbabwe played out one of the more remarkable games of cricket of any World Cup. The transformation of the Indian innings from ruination to success and the legendary innings by Kapil Dev that got them there are part of the folklore of this premier limited-overs cricket competition.

It is still hard to imagine how a side that was 5-17 after 13 overs could recover to make 8-266 and then go on to win the match and stay in the competition.

Kapil Dev indicated from the start of the tournament that he was a man on a mission and on this day his resolve was put to its most severe test. To his and his countrymen's great delight, he came through with flying colours. The Zimbabweans had to suffer a disappointment of equal magnitude.

On the colourful, rhododendron-encircled ground, Kapil Dev won the toss and chose to bat. Even the moisture in the wicket could not distract him from his objective to bat first and build a total that would bring India's run rate up to India's main challenger for a semi-final berth, Australia.

Kapil admitted to a slight nagging doubt about his side's chances of getting 300 on that wicket. At the start of play, it looked like such ambitions were mere fantasy. Peter Rawson's first ball of the day lifted and ripped past the outside edge of Sunil Gavaskar's bat. From the last delivery in that first over, the recalled Gavaskar played across the line and the Zimbabwean shout for lbw was answered in the affirmative.

It was the beginning of a procession. Mohinder Amarnath and Kris Srikkanth could not score a run until the third over, then in Rawson's third over Amarnath was given out caught behind. On the same score Srikkanth, still not off the mark, tried to hit Kevin Curran straight down the ground. The shot was badly mistimed and skied over mid off. Iain Butchart ran around and held a nicely judged catch. India were 3-6. Three runs later Sandeep Patil touched a ball from Curran down the leg-side.

Kapil said he came in at this stage in a trance-like state. More likely he was stunned to have his World Cup dreams almost in tatters. Soon he lost Yashpal Sharma, the hero of the first-round win against the West Indies, as well. Rawson had found another outside edge in his seventh over. India had reached their nadir of 5-17.

It was Roger Binny who joined his captain in stopping the rot, bringing the contest back to being a fair one between bat and ball. They put on 60 in 14 overs, the wicket slowly drying and easing all the time. There were no fireworks at this stage. Both batsmen were content to build their partnership with pushes and deflections.

Then Binny went lbw to the off-spinner, John Traicos and with Ravi Shastri caught behind playing a reckless stroke one run later India were 7-78 and again heading for ignominious defeat. The spectre of the inglorious campaigns of 1975 and 1979 must have haunted the veteran, Madan Lal as he approached his skipper. He promised to stay put while Kapil scored the runs and up to lunch was as good as his word.

India's 100 and Kapil's 50 were reached from the same shot in the 36th over and India lunched on 7-106. Kapil entered the dressing room, intent on blasting his top order batsmen, only to find they had anticipated his wrath and disappeared into the dining room leaving him with a glass of water to cool down.

The lunch break had further eased the wicket and upon the resumption Kapil changed his original plans which had been to just try and last out the 60 overs. The small ground and the better batting conditions encouraged him to counterattack. Almost immediately the runs began to flow. Another 34 were added in brisk time until Curran struck again, having Madan Lal caught behind. Syed Kirmani, the hairless wicketkeeper, entered with the score still precarious on 8-140.

Kapil said by now he had progressed from a trance to a daze. So he unleashed a furious assault on all the bowlers. From the next 18 deliveries he faced, the Indian captain struck three fours and three sixes. Kapil admitted one pull for six off Curran into the hospitality tents was mistimed. The Zimbabwean gave him a verbal serve. Kapil replied with the suggestion Curran should try another short ball. He did. It sailed right out of the ground and Kapil showed Curran his bat.

The onslaught continued. So brutal was Kapil's strokeplay it became too much for his first bat. The ninth-wicket pair added an unbroken 126 runs in 16 overs. Kirmani's share was 24.

There was no real sign of a mistimed hit until Kapil had reached 140, and soon after the crowd were applauding. Kapil asked the umpire, Barry Meyer, why peopel were clapping. Meyer explained that Kapil had hit the highest score ever in the World Cup. His 175 not out was India's first ever World Cup century and beat Glenn Turner's 171 against East Africa in 1975. His innings, containing six sixes and 16 fours, was spread over three hours. The highest individual score has since been passed, however the ninth-wicket partnership record remains unbeaten.

Zimbabwe, full of hope when India were 5-17, now needed 267 to keep their semi-final aspirations alive. There was no reason to think they could not achieve that target except that the Indians had gained a big psychological boost from their captain's performance.

Pressure and run outs haunted the Zimbabweans throughout their brave pursuit. Robin Brown and Grant Paterson put on 44 for the first wicket then two wickets fell in three overs. The second was after a scramble that found Jack Heron short of his ground for the second game in a row. Brown, too, was badly run out and Duncan Fletcher was beautifully caught on the boundary by Kapil Dev.

At 6-113 Zimbabwe should have accepted defeat. But Curran could not. As if trying to match Kapil's display he struck the ball with increasing vigour. He and Iain Butchart put on 55 for the seventh wicket. Briefly the game flickered as Zimbabwe made it to 8-230. Finally Curran had to take one risk too many and when Kapil held Traicos off his own bowling, a remarkable day was over with India 31 runs in front.

Wrapped up in two sweaters against the cool of the evening Kapil accepted his Man of the Match Award from Mike Denness without a word. Perhaps he was still in a trance.

INDIA		ZIMBABWE	
S. M. Gavaskar lbw b Rawson	0	R. D. Brown run out	35
K. Srikkanth c Butchart b Curran	0	G. A. Paterson lbw b Binny	23
M. Amarnath c Houghton b Rawson	5	J. G. Heron run out	3
S. M. Patil c Houghton b Curran	1	A. J. Pycroft c Kirmani b Sandhu	6
Yashpal Sharma c Houghton b Rawson	9	D. L. Houghton (wk) lbw b Madan Lal	17
Kapil Dev (capt) not out	175	D. A. G. Fletcher (capt) c Kapil Dev b Amarnath	13
R. M. H. Binny lbw b Traicos	22	K. M. Curran c Shastri b Madan Lal	73
R. J. Shastri c Pycroft b Fletcher	1	I. P. Butchart b Binny	18
Madan Lal c Houghton b Curran	17	G. E. Peckover c Yashpal b Madan Lal	14
S. M.H. Kirmani (wk) not out	24	P. W. E. Rawson not out	2
Extras lb9 w3	12	A. J. Traicos c & b Kapil Dev	3
(60 overs)	8-266	Extras lb17 w7 nb4	28
Did not bat: B. S. Sandhu		(57 overs)	235

1/0 2/6 3/6 4/9 5/17 6/77 7/78 8/140

Bowling: Rawson 12-4-47-3; Curran 12-1-65-3; Butchart 12-2-38-0; Fletcher 12-2-59-1; Traicos 12-0-45-1

1/44 2/48 3/61 4/86 5/103 6/113 7/168 8/189 9/230 10/235

Bowling: Kapil Dev 11-1-32-1; Sandhu 11-2-44-1; Binny 11-2-45-2; Madan Lal 11-2-42-3; Amarnath 12-1-37-1; Shastri 1-0-7-0

Umpires: M.J. Kitchen B.J. Meyer

Toss: India   Points: India 4 Zimbabwe 0

MONDAY 20 JUNE 1983
THE PRUDENTIAL CUP: ROUND SIX
GROUP A: ENGLAND vs SRI LANKA
HEADINGLEY: ENGLAND WON BY 9 WICKETS

Interest in the final preliminary round of the 1983 World Cup was centred elsewhere than Leeds. Sri Lanka could not make semi-finals and England could not miss out.

In this match Sri Lanka batted and bowled as if their thoughts had already turned to home. Bob Willis won the toss and sent the side led by Duleep Mendis into bat. Sidath Wettimuny made the bulk of the early runs with the first wicket falling at 25.

Willis, and Norman Cowans, brought in for the injured Graham Dilley and given the downhill run, had offered the batsmen little freedom. When the wickets started to fall they did so with a clatter. Ian Botham, too, was fired up. He had been irked by criticism of his World Cup performances in the press, while Kapil Dev's innings might have been a bit of a spur, as well.

When a confident caught behind appeal against Wettimuny was turned down, Botham indicated some disappointment. But ultimately he would not be denied and Ranatunga, whose World Cup day would eventually come, was dismissed for his third duck of the tournament. Botham also snared Wettimuny lbw.

Paul Allott took a couple of quick wickets, so Sri Lanka lost 6-29 as they slipped to 6-54. The lower half of the order showed some fight. Mike Gatting had a bit of a bowl. Vic Marks got two wickets before anything got serious. Rumesh Ratnayake and Vinothen John added 33 for the last wicket which allowed the innings to last beyond the 50-over mark.

England needed 137 to win. Ashantha de Mel again got some movement, but this time the edges were missed. Chris Tavare and Graeme Fowler were soon moving towards the target. Fowler looked in good touch. He swung one ball from Ratnayake over square leg for six and hit a number of other fine shots. David Gower also played a nice little cameo when he came to the wicket in the 16th over following the demise of Tavare to the worthy de Mel. From that point the end came quickly. Somachandra de Silva, who had conceded less than one run per over from a full spell against New Zealand, was now clouted for 29 runs from three overs. A single off Ranatunga's first ball and the game had finished prior to the tea break. England had won with 215 balls to spare.

Richard Hutton, who is prone to occasional eccentricities, gave the Man of the Match Award to Willis for his "leadership".

SRI LANKA		ENGLAND	
S. Wettimuny lbw b Botham	22	G. Fowler not out	81
D. S. B. P. Kuruppu c Gatting b Willis	6	C. J. Tavare c de Alwis b de Mel	19
A. Ranatunga c Lamb b Botham	0	D. I. Gower not out	27
R. L. Dias c Gould b Cowans	7	Extras b1 lb3 w3 nb3	10
L. R. D. Mendis (capt) b Allott	10	(24.1 overs)	1-137
R. S. Madugalle c Gould b Allott	0	Did not bat: A. J. Lamb, M. W. Gatting, I. T. Botham,	
D. S. de Silva c Gower b Marks	15	I. J. Gould (wk), V. J. Marks, P. J.W. Allott,	
R. G. de Alwis (wk) c Marks b Cowans	19	R. G. D. Willis (capt), N. G. Cowans	
A. L. F. de Mel c Lamb b Marks	10	1/68	
R. J. Ratnayake not out	20	Bowling: de Mel 10-1-33-1; Ratnayake 5-0-23-0;	
V. B. John c Cowans b Allott	15	John 6-0-41-0; de Silva 3-0-29-0; Ranatunga 0.1-0-1-0	
Extras b5 lb2 w3 nb2	12		
(50.4 overs)	136		
1/25 2/30 3/32 4/40 5/43 6/54 7/81 8/97 9/103 10/136			
Bowling: Willis 9-4-9-1; Cowans 12-3-31-2; Botham 9-4-12-2;			
Allott 10.4-0-41-3; Gatting 4-2-13-0; Marks 6-2-18-2			

Umpires: B. Leadbeater   R. Palmer

Toss: England   Points: England 4 Sri Lanka 0

GROUP A: NEW ZEALAND vs PAKISTAN
TRENT BRIDGE: PAKISTAN WON BY 11 RUNS

This was a winner-take-all contest. For both sides victory, plus in Pakistan's case a slight improvement in their run rate, would ensure second place in Group A behind England. New Zealand would have been kicking themselves for losing to Sri Lanka and not securing their spot prior to this match. Pakistan, although weakened, still had plenty of mercurial talent capable of dominating any side. By the end of the day New Zealand would have some more self-kicking to do.

Imran Khan, hardly able to believe his side were still viable finalists after their up-and-down form, won the toss and elected to bat in front of a 5,000-strong crowd full of Pakistani supporters.

The top order struggled to get the run rate up against accurate bowling from Richard Hadlee and Lance Cairns, so openers Mudassar Nazar and Mohsin Khan took 20 overs to reach 48. Mohsin then tried to smash Jeremy Coney out of the ground, only to get as far as Lance Cairns at deep mid-on.

Javed Miandad also struggled for timing. Mudassar left six runs after Mohsin, deflecting another Coney delivery into his stumps and Javed spoilt his lunch playing Hadlee on after surviving for 19 overs. At the break Pakistan were 3-126 from 42 overs, well below their run requirement.

Whatever Imran and Zaheer consumed during the interval certainly fortified them. Upon the resumption they suddenly and very effectively went on the attack. Imran hit out, Zaheer played his graceful shots. It was brilliant batting that thrilled the crowd and came at a perfect time for Pakistan.

Zaheer completed a century in exactly two hours. Imran scored at faster than a run per minute. They took an astonishing 47 runs from Hadlee's last five overs. One hundred and forty-seven runs were scored in 75 minutes. In 60 overs, Pakistan reached 3-261. Their run rate was 4.01 for the tournament, higher than New Zealand's. The Kiwis had to win.

The New Zealanders did not get the start they wanted. Glenn Turner, in his final appearance for his country, was caught behind off Sarfraz Nawaz with the score on just 13. Thirty-one runs later, John Wright hit out at Abdul Qadir and was held by Imran. At tea New Zealand were 2-76 from 25 overs. Geoff Howarth looked in good form and perhaps he held the destiny of his side in his own hands.

He added a further nine runs with Martin Crowe at the start of the last session, then Imran brought on Zaheer. 'Zed' loosened up with an authentic first-ball loosener, a chest high full toss. Howarth swiped it away straight to Javed at square leg.

Commentator Jack Bannister called it "the 'sucker dismissal' of the competition". It was a big set back for the Kiwis, who really struggled after that.

Crowe got to 43 before hitting across the line against Mudassar's medium pace. Bruce Edgar missed out and Richard Hadlee completed what by his standards was an ordinary day when he, too, fell to the underrated Mudassar. From 7-152 Coney and Warren Lees had to stop the procession. They did by adding 35. However, progress slowed and 75 runs were needed from just eight overs when John Bracewell joined Coney.

Pakistan were almost planning their semi-final strategies when Bracewell started to strike out at the medium pace of Sarfraz and Rashid Khan. Fifty-three runs were added in five overs. Bracewell and Coney had reduced the target to a gettable 22 from three overs when the off-spinner hooked hard and high at Sarfraz. The last ball of the 58th over sailed into the deep at square leg. Bracewell's timing was better than his placement. He picked out Mohsin right on the boundary.

Now only one wicket remained. Coney needed to farm the strike. He completed his 50. It was a meaningless milestone. At the start of the last over, 13 runs were required for victory. Coney and Chatfield took a single from the Sarfraz's first ball. Javed's throw missed the stumps. The 10th-wicket pair looked for another run, but hesitated. Imran quickly retrieved the ball and threw it to Wasim Bari who gleefully removed the bails. Coney was stranded.

The Pakistani supporters did not have to be told of the significance of the result. They ran, joyously laughing and bouncing from all directions straight at the players and umpires. David Evans was knocked flying. Merv Kitchen found a brandished stump was a useful deterrent to the invaders.

Imran Khan, thrilled with the turn of events, gratefully received the Man of the Match Award. New Zealand had missed a semi-final berth in World Cup for the first time.

PAKISTAN		NEW ZEALAND	
Mohsin Khan c Cairns b Coney	33	G. M. Turner c Wasim Bari b Sarfraz Nawaz	4
Mudassar Nazar b Coney	15	J. G. Wright c Imran Khan b Abdul Qadir	19
Javed Miandad b Hadlee	25	G. P. Howarth (capt) c Javed Miandad b Zaheer Abbas	39
Zaheer Abbas not out	103	M. D. Crowe b Mudassar Nazar	43
Imran Khan (capt) not out	79	B. A. Edgar lbw b Shahid Mahboob	6
Extras b1 lb2 w2 nb1	6	J. V. Coney run out	51
(60 overs)	3-261	R. J. Hadlee c Mohsin Khan b Mudassar Nazar	11
Did not bat: Ijaz Faqih, Shahid Mahboob, Sarfraz Nawaz,		B. L. Cairns c Imran Khan b Qadir	0
Abdul Qadir, Wasim Bari (wk), Rashid Khan		W. K. Lees (wk) c sub (Mansoor Akhtar) b Mudassar Nazar	26
1/48 2/54 3/114		J. G. Bracewell c Mohsin Khan b Sarfraz Nawaz	34
Bowling: Hadlee 12-1-61-1; Cairns 12-1-45-0;		E. J. Chatfield not out	3
Chatfield 12-0-57-0; Coney 12-0-42-2; Bracewell 12-0-50-0;		Extras lb8 w5 nb1	14
		(59.1 overs)	250
		1/13 2/44 3/85 4/102 5/130 6/150 7/152 8/187 9/246 10/250	
		Bowling: Rashid Khan 6-1-24-0; Sarfraz Nawaz 9.1-1-50-2; Abdul Qadir 12-0-53-2; Ijaz Faqih 6-1-21-0; Shahid Mahboob 10-0-37-1; Mudassar Nazar 12-0-43-3; Zaheer Abbas 4-1-8-1	

Umpires: D.G.L. Evans   M.J. Kitchen
Toss: Pakistan   Points: Pakistan 4 New Zealand 0

GROUP B: AUSTRALIA vs INDIA
COUNTY GROUND: CHELMSFORD INDIA WON BY 118 RUNS

To the Australians it was unthinkable, to the Indians a cricketing delight, literally against the odds. A full house at the well-appointed Essex County Ground in Chelmsford witnessed an inglorious batting display by Kim Hughes' side which condemned them to an unexpected early departure from the 1983 Prudential Cup.

Despite their obvious improvement from 1975 and 1979, India were not expected to win this match. Certainly the Australians were confident. They had thrashed India seven days earlier and several of their players felt they would remain a very manageable combination. Kim Hughes must have been one. He withdrew from the match to rest his injured thigh, so that it would be ready for the semi-final clash, handing the captaincy to David Hookes.

Kapil Dev won the toss and he elected to bat on what seemed an excellent wicket. Geoff Lawson, back in the side at the expense of Dennis Lillee, began proceedings with a wide; the first of 24 illegal deliveries. Kris Srikkanth was quickly into his stride and 27 runs were briskly accumulated. His partner was still out of sorts, though, and Gavaskar soon mistimed a ball to Trevor Chappell in the covers. The 50 was up in the 11th over when Srikkanth drove Thomson for four through the off-side. Then the aggressive opener from Tamil Nadu pulled the same bowler hard to midwicket where Allan Border held the catch at the second attempt.

Thomson struck again to have Mohinder Amarnath caught behind, leaving India at 3-65. It was a good comeback by the blond-haired slinger as, like Lawson, he had also started with a wide. However the worst culprit in that regard was Rodney Hogg whose indiscretions during the Indian innings included 15 no balls and three wides.

Right on the lunch break, Sandeep Patil was removed. India went into the pavilion on 4-119 from 30 legitimate overs. Kapil Dev used the approach that worked at Tunbridge Wells after lunch, but it only worked until the total was 157. He then mishooked a fast lifter from the inaccurate Hogg and was easily caught at mid off.

Seventeen runs later, anchorman and top scorer Yashpal Sharma was gone, also caught at mid off. India were 6-174 and the innings threatened to fade away. It didn't fade and didn't rally, either. Everyone got a few runs. No-one got a lot. There was a run out, there was an lbw. One partnership was worth 33, another 17. Kim Hughes tried to control field placings from the pavilion. Rod Marsh told him where he could go. The upshot was that after 56 overs, less one ball, India were all out for 247.

Australia felt up to the task ahead of them. They had smashed India for 320 at Trent Bridge. Then Chappell had made a fine century. This time Balwindersingh Sandhu had the same batsman caught in the gully from a ball that lifted off a length in his first over. That displeased the youngest Chappell brother, who was another on his final international outing. He was so enraged he demolished an entre set of cups and saucers on the dressing room table with his bat and ruptured a water cooler with another piece of crockery. He was fined and later apologised.

Graeme Wood and Graham Yallop seemed to consolidate Australia's push for the necessary 248 runs. They added 43 to take the total to 1-46 by the start of the 16th over when Roger Binny was introduced.

Kapil Dev knew the medium pacer could trouble left-handers; dismissing three of them within three overs. Wood was caught behind in the first, Hookes bowled by pearler in the second and Yallop caught and bowled off a skied shot in the third. When Madan Lal had Rod Marsh lbw from the first ball of the next over, Australia had collapsed to 5-52. Madan Lal struck once more when Macleay hit out and Gavaskar held a sharp slips catch. The afternoon tea must have tasted bitter to the Australians and got worse when Tom Hogan hit a catch straight to cover straight after the break.

India had recovered from 7-78 to 8-266 at Tunbridge Wells. Australia were now 7-78, as well, and Allan Border would need to play an innings as great as Kapil's if Australia were to survive. Great player as Border was, it was never on. Border never gave up, but the wicket was keeping low now and he could not do the impossible. Australia's last hope vanished when the future captain was bowled from the first ball of Madan Lal's ninth over. Thomson was also bowled from the next delivery leaving India victorious by 118 runs. The whole fiasco had taken less than 40 overs.

There was no joy in the Australian camp. David Hookes' only day ever as captain of his country had not gone very well. To make matters worse, the next day Hughes disappeared back to Australia without saying goodbye to most of his team. He blamed his team for the mess that their World Cup campaign had become. Many of his team blamed him for poor and uncommunicative captaincy. It was hardly a climate for success.

Roger Binny was probably not even aware of his opponents' problems. He just cherished his Man of the Match Award and the opportunity he would have to play England in the semi-finals.

INDIA		AUSTRALIA	
S. M. Gavaskar c Chappell b Hogg	9	T. M. Chappell c Madan Lal b Sandhu	2
K. Srikkanth c Border b Thomson	24	G. M. Wood c Kirmani b Binny	21
M. Amarnath c Marsh b Thomson	13	G. N. Yallop c & b Binny	18
Yashpal Sharma c Hogg b Hogan	40	D. W. Hookes (capt) b Binny	1
S. M. Patil c Hogan b MacLeay	30	A. R. Border b Madan Lal	36
Kapil Dev (capt) c Hookes b Hogg	28	R. W. Marsh lbw b Madan Lal	0
K. Azad c Border b Lawson	15	K. H. MacLeay c Gavaskar b Madan Lal	5
R. M.H. Binny run out	21	T. G. Hogan c Srikkanth b Binny	8
Madan Lal not out	12	G. F. Lawson b Sandhu	16
S. M.H. Kirmani (wk) lbw b Hogg	10	R. M. Hogg not out	8
B. S. Sandhu b Thomson	8	J. R. Thomson b Madan Lal	0
Extras lb13 w9 nb15	37	Extras lb5 w5 nb4	14
(55.5 overs)	247	(38.2 overs)	129

1/27 2/54 3/65 4/118 5/157 6/174 7/207 8/215 9/2332
10/247

1/3 2/46 3/48 4/52 5/52 6/69 7/78 8/115 9/129 10/129

Bowling: Lawson 10-1-40-1; Hogg 12-2-40-3; Hogan 11-1-31-1; Thomson 10.5-0-51-3; MacLeay 12-2-48-1

Bowling: Kapil Dev 8-2-16-0; Sandhu 10-1-26-2; Madan Lal 8.2-3-20-4; Binny 8-2-29-4; Amarnath 2-0-17-0; Azad 2-0-7-0

Umpires: J. Birkenshaw   D.R. Shepherd

Toss: India   Points: India 4 Australia 0

GROUP B: WEST INDIES vs ZIMBABWE
EDGBASTON: WEST INDIES WON BY 10 WICKETS

Little hinged on this game except that the West Indies needed a decent work out in the lead up to the semi-finals. They had to send down their full compliment of overs so the six bowlers worked up a decent sweat. The batting was a different story. No-one below number four even got their pads on.

There were three changes to the most recent West Indies line-up. Gordon Greenidge, Andy Roberts and Michael Holding were all rested for Gus Logie, Wayne Daniel and the recovered Joel Garner. It was Garner who did the early damage after Duncan Fletcher had won the toss and elected to bat on what looked a fine wicket. The total had reached 17 when, in the fourth over, 'Big Bird' had Grant Paterson caught by Viv Richards and next ball Jack Heron found one of the worst ways possible to avoid being run out.

There were a few wides and no balls floating around which helped Robin Brown and Andy Pycroft lift the total from 2-17 to 2-41. Then Malcolm Marshall and Daniel ripped out three more batsmen while one run was being added. In the 23rd over, Zimbabwe were 5-42 and their final innings in the tournament looked in ruins.

Fletcher and Kevin Curran developed a hard-fought stand that temporarily halted the slide. They had put on 37 for the sixth wicket when Richards claimed the Zimbabwean captain as the first of his three victims. Curran was not one of them. The all-rounder again impressed with his determination and ability to score runs against quality bowling. He smacked Garner for six over long off, a rare feat, put on 55 for the ninth wicket with Peter Rawson and reached a fine 62 before being bowled in the final over of the innings. Rawson's ineffective last-ball slog against Daniel neatly terminated the Zimbabwean effort right at the end of the 60th over for 171.

Haynes and Bacchus put the Zimbabwean batting into perspective. They were rarely troubled on a sound batting surface. Runs were taken freely off the pace bowlers, Haynes scoring the bulk of his off the front foot, Bacchus concentrating on back foot strokes. Only John Traicos' off-spin really stemmed the flow, his full quota of 12 overs costing just 24 runs.

Either batsman could have made a century, neither quite did. It was Barbadian who had his nose in front when the winning run was scored from the first ball of the 46th over of the innings, but the Guyanan beat him for the Man of the Match Award.

The West Indies won with nearly 15 overs to spare. Next up with a semi-final with Pakistan at The Oval.

ZIMBABWE		WEST INDIES	
R. D. Brown c Lloyd b Marshall	14	D. L. Haynes not out	88
G. A. Paterson c Richards b Garner	6	S. F. A. F. Bacchus not out	80
J. G. Heron c Dujon b Garner	0	Extras lb1 w3	4
A. J. Pycroft c Dujon b Marshall	4	(45.1 overs)	0-172
D. L. Houghton (wk) c Lloyd b Daniel	0	Did not bat: A. L. Logie, I. V. A. Richards, H. A. Gomes,	
D. A. G. Fletcher (capt) b Richards	23	C. H. Lloyd (capt), P. J. L. Dujon (wk), J. Garner,	
K. M. Curran b Daniel	62	M. D. Marshall, W. W. Daniel, W. W. Davis	
I. P. Butchart c Haynes b Richards	8	Bowling: Rawson 12-3-38-0; Butchart 4-0-23-0;	
G. E. Peckover c & b Richards	3	Traicos 12-2-24-0; Curran 9-0-44-0; Fletcher 8.1-0-39-0	
P. W. E. Rawson b Daniel	19		
A. J. Traicos not out	1		
Extras b4 lb13 w7 nb7	31		
(60 overs)	171		

1/17 2/17 3/41 4/42 5/42 6/79 7/104 8/115 9/170
10/171

Bowling: Marshall 12-3-19-2; Garner 7-4-13-2;

Davis 8-2-13-0; Daniel 9-2-28-3; Gomes 12-2-26-0;

Richards 12-1-41-3

Umpires: H.D. Bird   D.J. Constant

Toss: Zimbabwe   Points: West Indies 4 Zimbabwe 0

WEDNESDAY 22 JUNE 1983
THE PRUDENTIAL CUP SEMI-FINALS

At the end of the preliminary rounds of the 1983 World Cup the group tables finished as follows:

GROUP A						GROUP B			
	P	W	L	Pts	Run Rate		P	W	L	Pts
England	6	5	1	20	4.6706	West Indies	6	5	1	20
Pakistan	6	3	3	12	4.0139	India	6	4	2	16
New Zealand	6	3	3	12	3.9273	Australia	6	2	4	8
Sri Lanka	6	1	5	4	3.7525	Zimbabwe	6	1	5	4

Both tables had a nice symmetrical look to them, but New Zealanders must cry every time they study the Group A table; missing the semi-finals by a run rate of 0.08 has got to hurt. With the preliminary rounds as a form guide, England and the West Indies would start the semi-finals as big favourites.

FIRST SEMI FINAL: ENGLAND vs INDIA
OLD TRAFFORD: INDIA WON BY 6 WICKETS

Of all the let downs that English cricket teams and supporters have suffered during the various World Cups, and there have been plenty, none could have more demoralising than this six-wicket defeat at Old Trafford. The Bob Willis-led side had been utterly convincing in the preliminary rounds, yet were so comfortably beaten by the underdogs.

The result provided the opportunity for a bit of a whinge. The wicket provided for the occasion was bare of grass, low and slow. Some English players felt the ground staff had unintentionally played into India's hands with conditions similar to those when Kapil Dev's side defeated the West Indies in the first round. Not that there was a soul in the packed ground that considered it would have a significant influence on the result when Graeme Fowler and Chris Tavare smoothly took England to 0-69 after 17 overs.

Bob Willis had won the toss and all was set fair on a sunny day. Fowler had been in great form throughout the tournament, with Tavare playing a sound, if unspectacular, back-up role to the Lancastrian. On semi-final day both were at their best, striking seven boundaries between them and running smartly for ones and twos. Balwindersingh Sandhu conceded runs freely.

As at Chelmsford, Binny's introduction altered the match's direction. He immediately had Tavare caught behind from a defensive push and 15 runs later, Fowler was bowled middle stump by one that kept low. England's batting became more hesitant. Kapil Dev introduced Mohinder Amarnath and Kirti Azad. Their captain had originally meant for them to share a spell of 12 overs, but they so completely choked off England's supply of runs either side of lunch and picked a few wickets that Kapil was thrilled to be able to keep them going. All through he kept them going over by over and just waited until they were hit around. That moment never came.

David Gower, so productive in the preliminary games, flashed outside the off-stump at Amarnath, edged and was well taken by wicketkeeper Syed Kirmani. It was 3-107 and the home team's position was just starting to deterioate. Allan Lamb in 1982 had feasted on the tame offerings of the Indian bowlers. He and Mike Gatting added 34 and promised more to put England back in a position where again they could push towards a formidable score. Then Lamb swept at a ball which rolled away off his pad. Gatting called his South African-born partner through for single. There was a slight hesitation and Yashpal Sharma at short fine leg swooped and threw down the wicket with Lamb short of his ground at the bowler's end.

It was an unnecessary dismissal that provided India with a real opening. Ian Botham stepped away to thump the ball through point only to miss a delivery that nearly bounced twice before it hit his leg-stump. Gatting left a gap between bat and pad and an Amarnath off-cutter cartwheeled his off-stump. The situation for England was now becoming critical. Slow, low wicket or not, they were making a hash of their later overs. At the 50-over mark they were 6-169, that added up to a sorry tale of 6-100 from their last 33 overs. Only 55 runs were scored from the 24 overs sent down by Azad and Amarnath. At one stage there was an hour's cricket without one shot piercing the five men stationed on the boundary. Ian Gould's run out and Vic Mark's inablity to keep out Kapil Dev saw a further slump to 8-177.

Only the fast bowlers were left. Fortunately one of those was Graham Dilley, whose broad-shouldered, left-handed batting had already been a contributing factor to England's success in the previous couple of weeks.

With Paul Allott and Bob Willis in tow, Dilley gave the England innings a boost when it appeared they may fall short of the 200 mark. No English supporters minded that the bulk of these were runs were scored off the edge. For the first time, the Indian fielding lagged with a few errors and overthrows. Kapil Dev's final over contained four wides and, when Willis had his off stump neatly removed by his opposite number from the last ball of the 60th over, England had 213 runs to protect.

Like England, India had a good start, then stumbled. Sunil Gavaskar showed his best form of competition, even outpacing the normally frenetic Kris Srikkanth. The slow wicket dulled the new-ball threat of Willis and Dilley and they moved easily to 46 in the 14th over. As if in sympathy with each other both were gone in consecutive overs, Paul Allott and Ian Botham doing the important damage. India were 2-50 and the game lay in the balance.

Mohinder Amarnath and Yashpal Sharma had to resurrect the chase. It was no easy task while Botham, Allott and Marks kept it tight and either side of tea the runs dried up. The tension was perceptible as both teams strove to achieve the advantage over their opponents that would carry them through to the World Cup Final. There were big shouts against Sharma for a run out and then a caught behind. India fought to 2-107 from 38 overs, but despite the half century stand neither batsman was comfortable. Amarnath survived two close shaves in the next over when he mishit off-spinner Marks into space and then substitute fieldsman, Derek Randall dived at square leg only to disclaim what at first looked a catch.

It was as if England had missed their chances. Amarnath and Sharma now began the necessary acceleration. Amarnath hit Allott straight for six and Sharma bravely swiped the first ball of a new spell from Willis over mid wicket for another six. They had built their stand to 92 in 29 overs when Amarnath became the third run out victim of the day, trying for a second run that was not there.

India still required 72 for victory. It could have been difficult, however Sandeep Patil's entrance changed the game's complexion one last time. On the same ground where he had caned Willis for 24 runs off one over a year before, the Indian movie star made people wonder why so many other batsmen had struggled. He drove with impressive freedom, rapidly closing in on the target and bringing dejection into the English ranks. Patil and Sharma had lifted the total by 63 runs in nine overs when the latter slashed a short ball from Willis towards third man. Allott, in front of his home crowd, took a fantastic catch, but it was too little too late. Sharma had had a great day and victory was nine runs away.

Lots of Indian fans miscounted, because when eight of those runs had been scored they charged onto the field in premature celebration. Don Oslear, remembering what happened to Merv Kitchen and his fellow semi-final umpire, David Evans two days before at Trent Bridge, grabbed a stump to protect himself. Neither he nor the spectators came to any real harm and after a few minutes clearing time, the game was able to restart.

India had six wickets and more than five overs to spare when Willis put all his fieldsmen on the boundary on the pavilion side of the ground and let Patil hit the ball to the rope towards the outer so that everyone could get off in safety.

A small contingent of English hooligans tried to disrupt the Indian celebrations, but luckily any nastiness was avoided and the players could shower their delirious fans with champagne. Those few thousand were able to share the moment with their heroes, while in India millions more were thrilled at the prospect of their team playing in a final they'd never come close to reaching in the past.

To top off the Indian joy Mohinder 'Jimmy' Amarnath was named Man of the Match.

ENGLAND		INDIA	
G. Fowler b Binny	33	S. M. Gavaskar c Gould b Allott	25
C. J. Tavare c Kirmani b Binny	32	K. Srikkanth c Willis b Botham	19
D. I. Gower c Kirmani b Amarnath	17	M. Amarnath run out	46
A. J. Lamb run out	29	Yashpal Sharma c Allott b Willis	61
M. W. Gatting b Amarnath	18	S. M. Patil not out	51
I. T. Botham b Azad	6	Kapil Dev (capt) not out	1
I. J. Gould (wk) run out	13	Extras b5 lb6 w1 nb2	14
V. J. Marks b Kapil Dev	8	(54.4 overs)	4-217
G. R. Dilley not out	20	Did not bat: K. Azad, R. M. H. Binny, Madan Lal,	
P. J. W. Allott c Patil b Kapil Dev	8	S. M.H. Kirmani (wk), B. S. Sandhu	
R. G. D. Willis (capt) b Kapil Dev	0	1/46 2/50 3/142 4/205	
Extras b1 lb17 w7 nb4	29	Bowling: Willis 10.4-2-42-1; Dilley 11-0-43-0;	
(60 overs)	213	Allott 10-3-40-1; Botham 11-4-40-1; Marks 12-1-38-0	
1/69 2/84 3/107 4/141 5/150 6/160 7/175 8/177 9/202			
10/213			
Bowling: Kapil Dev 11-1-35-3; Sandhu 8-1-36-0;			
Binny 12-1-43-2; Madan Lal 5-0-15-0; Azad 12-1-28-1;			
Amarnath 12-1-27-2;			

Umpires: D.G.L. Evans D.O. Oslear

Toss: England

SECOND SEMI-FINAL: PAKISTAN vs WEST INDIES
WEST INDIES WON BY 8 WICKETS

Pakistan were not only without their captain's bowling; their fighting batting hero, Javed Miandad, was stricken down by influenza. So the Asian team played their semi-final against the West Indies as if they had already run their race in this tournament. The great win against New Zealand really turned out to be their final because the West Indies, seemingly en route to their third world crown, were rarely troubled to win by eight wickets.

Few teams would select The Oval as a venue to face the West Indies. It has the fastest and bounciest wicket in England and in 1983, with the West Indies having the fastest and bounciest bowlers in the world, making runs was going to be a difficult assignment. Many of the capacity crowd who filled the historic old ground would have hoped for a repeat of the classic run feast of 1979. It soon became obvious that was not going to be the case.

Unlike four years before, winning the toss in 1983 did not mean an automatic insertion of the opposition. When Clive Lloyd made the correct call on a fine, but humid, south London morning the prospect of early moisture, pace bounce and lateral movement proved too great a temptation and he reverted to his old habit. Almost immediately it was evident he'd made the right choice. Joel Garner, back in the side and wanting to keep the likes of Winston Davis and Wayne Daniel at arm's length, was a very difficult proposition for Mudassar Nazar and Mohsin Khan. He repeatedly beat the outside edge and both batsmen looked at nothing more than survival against the new ball. Mohsin took a single from a leg-glance in the sixth over. It was his first run.

After another six overs, the total had limped to 23 when Mudassar offered a tame caught-and-bowled chance to Garner, who gratefully accepted. Pakistan's problems were magnified when Ijaz Faqih came in at number three. He was never going to be an adequate replacement for Javed and despite a couple of brave hook shots, was soon edging Michael Holding behind to leave Pakistan struggling at 2-34.

Zaheer Abbas's best innings in an illustrious career were against flat bowlers on flat wickets, when he could compile the most attractive centuries and double centuries imaginable. Dodging and weaving bullets fired by express West Indians on fiery surfaces was never his strong point. With Mohsin playing a purely passive role he came in to withstand the awesome firepower of Holding and Malcolm Marshall. Often his head was not behind the line of the ball, but he survived and in the 25th over, along with all the Pakistani supporters, relaxed a little for the first time when Larry Gomes' off-spin was introduced into the attack.

The runs began to tick over at last and, on the verge of the lunch break, Mohsin and Zaheer had taken their stand to 54 in 12 overs and the total to 2-88. Then, in the 31st over, the last prior to the break all the Pakistanis were put off their food when Zaheer moved down the wicket tried to drive Gomes to mid wicket, missed and was bowled off his pads.

After the interval, Mohsin and Imran continued to make use of the pace respite. They put on 51 in 16 overs and Pakistan reached 3-139 which gave the illusion of mild strength.

However, they were merely in the eye of the storm. Marshall returned and in his second over set Pakistan right back on their heels. From the second ball, the Pakistani captain nicked an outswinger and from the fifth left-hander Wasim Raja was caught in front of his stumps.

Five overs and 20 runs later, Marshall ended Shahid Mahboob's World Cup when the all-rounder hit softly to mid wicket. Shahid had already been pinged on the helmet by the same bowler and seemed relieved to get off the ground. Marshall had taken three for three in 14 balls to really break the back of the Pakistani effort. It was fast bowling of the highest quality. Sarfraz was caught off a skier. Mohsin hung on until there were just three overs remaining. Finally, after four hours' vigilance, 70 runs, one four, which resulted from a misfield, 43 singles and plenty of barracking, he swung across the line at Andy Roberts and was bowled.

Pakistan's tailenders also managed to hold out against the fearsome late innings pace onslaught. However, after 60 overs, despite being only eight wickets down, they finished with their lowest total in the competition.

The whole innings contained just two boundaries.

The West Indies only needed 185 to reach their third final in three attempts. Pakistan required a miracle. Unfortunately, there was no-one qualified to provide it. Rashid Khan put in a fine effort with the new ball and in the 11th over, trapped Gordon Greenidge lbw with a delivery that kept low. By then the total had reached 34. It had been 29 when Abdul Qadir was introduced to a loud fanfare in the 10th over.

The leg-spinner's early overs were impressive. He troubled both Desmond Haynes and Viv Richards. They failed to spot his wrong 'un and Richards was nearly caught at short leg. Haynes hit two fours to mid wicket before misreading another wrong 'un, driving over the top of the ball and being bowled.

That was 2-56 in 20 overs. At tea it was 2-72. In the last session, the Qadir threat seemed to have evaporated. His percentage of loose deliveries increased, or at least Richards made it appear they had. In front of a big noisy crowd on a warm day at one of his most productive venues Richards turned up the batting heat in the final session. He blasted the bowling in his most masterly fashion. Imran set two mid wickets and two mid-ons to curb his strength and stop the run flow. Richards still cracked the ball through and over the fieldsmen with immense power.

He reached his 50 in 30 overs and went on to an unbeaten 80, which contained 11 fours and one six. Richards eased back to allow Larry Gomes to reach his 50, a noble gesture which made his Man of the Match Award all the more deserved. When the ball was engulfed by the charging West Indian fans following the winning boundary hit off Zaheer, Richards and Gomes had put on 132 and carried their side to an emphatic victory with 12 overs to spare.

As well as complaining about The Oval crowd's joyous reaction to news of England's demise at Old Trafford, editor of *The Cricketer*, Christopher Martin-Jenkins wrote the was result a dress rehearsal for what would happen at Lord's the next Saturday. He said the West Indies had looked a half a class above their opposition. The one glitch on the horizon was the groin injury sustained by Lloyd when in the field.

Once again, the witnesses to this game were restricted to those who actually attended. The people at home were frustrated by another strike which caused a television blackout.

PAKISTAN		WEST INDIES	
Mohsin Khan b Roberts	70	C. G. Greenidge lbw b Rashid Khan	17
Mudassar Nazar c & b Garner	11	D. L. Haynes b Abdul Qadir	29
Ijaz Faqih c Dujon b Holding	5	I. V. A. Richards not out	80
Zaheer Abbas b Gomes	30	H. A. Gomes not out	50
Imran Khan (capt) c Dujon b Marshall	17	Extras b2 lb6 w4	12
Wasim Raja lbw b Marshall	0	(48.4 overs)	2-188
Shahid Mahboob c Richards b Marshall	6	Did not bat: C. H. Lloyd (capt), S. F. A. F. Bacchus,	
Sarfraz Nawaz c Holding b Roberts	3	P. J. L. Dujon (wk), A. M. E. Roberts, M. D.Marshall,	
Abdul Qadir not out	10	J. Garner, M. A. Holding	
Wasim Bari (wk) not out	4	1/34 2/56	
Extras b6 lb13 w4 nb5	28	Bowling: Rashid Khan 12-2-32-1; Sarfraz 8-0-23-0;	
(60 overs)	8-184	Abdul Qadir 11-1-42-1; Shahid Mahboob 11-1-43-0;	
Did not bat: Rashid Khan		Wasim Raja 1-0-9-0; Zaheer Abbas 4.4-1-24-0; Mohsin	
1/23 2/34 3/88 4/139 5/139 6/159 7/164 8/171		Khan 1-0-3-0	
Bowling: Roberts 12-3-25-2; Garner 12-1-31-1;			
Marshall12-2-28-3; Holding 12-1-25-1; Gomes 7-0-29-1;			
Richards 5-0-18-0			

Umpires: D.J. Constant   A.G.T. Whitehead

Toss: West Indies

SATURDAY 25 JUNE 1983
THE PRUDENTIAL CUP FINAL: INDIA vs WEST INDIES
LORD'S: INDIA WON BY 43 RUNS.

There could hardly have been a cricket fan in the world who was not pleased for the previously maligned Indians for making it to a World Cup final. Against all predictions, they had defeated Australia, Zimbabwe and the West Indies in the preliminary rounds, then upset scribes and pundits by knocking out England in the Old Trafford semi-final.

It was good for them and good for cricket, because they were a lovely bunch of fellows who had done jolly well for themselves and their country. But now it would be all over. This was the final and underdogs do not win finals against juggernauts. It was a miracle that Kapil Dev's side had made it to Lord's on Saturday 25 June, 1983. Lightning would not strike twice and by the early evening or even the middle of the afternoon the West Indies would have another Prudential World Cup.

So confident was West Indian fast bowler Malcolm Marshall of the outcome that he put on order a BMW sports car that he intended to pay for with his World Cup winnings. No-one told him not to. He was only echoing the sentiments of the rest of the cricket community. Marshall's actions hinted at arrogance. Did they also suggest a modicum of complacency? If they had Kapil Dev, would have identified them.

Many Indians were satisfied just to have made it to Lord's. Fans flew in from all corners of the globe so they could say they saw their team play in a World Cup final. Four came from Belgium and paid 70 pounds each for their precious tickets. Three more had hidden all night in the Lord's toilets only to be found by police tracking dogs and ejected. Others risked life and limb on the ground's outer wall, perhaps briefly fooling police who are more used to people trying to get out of a walled establishment rather than into it.

Not everyone made it or found a ticket tout; Lord's still only held 25,000. Those who were successful were overjoyed. The original odds on India even reaching Lord's had been very long. The Indian team hastily arranged a cocktail party to which friends and ex-players were invited. They didn't have much notice. Early in the tournament the Indian players and management couldn't assume they would still be in London at that time.

There had been early morning rain in St Johns Wood and the streets were still wet when those fans who were too excited to sleep arrived at the ground bright and early. The gates were opened at 9.15 and everyone started to file in. Well before 11am, the ground was completely full and by then the sun was shining in all its glory.

Neither side changed their semi-final line-ups. A question mark hung over Clive Lloyd's groin, but he strode confidently to the wicket at the appointed time with Kapil Dev, called correctly at the toss and sent India into bat. Sunil Gavaskar and Kris Srikkanth followed out the West Indians to a rousing reception, a great, if nerve-wracking, moment for both of them.

Gavaskar took strike. Andy Roberts, the most experienced of the Caribbean pace quartet, was entrusted with the new ball. He opened from the Nursery End. Gavaskar, a tiny figure, looked incongruous facing big powerful fast bowlers. They seemed sure to break him in half.

Often the little Indian champion relished the split second contest against the best and fastest in the world. He had taken double centuries off them and would do so again, but this was not his day. Nor his tournament. Both batsmen strove to do nothing more than survive the opening salvos from Roberts and Joel Garner. The score was only two in the fifth over when the bravely helmetless and hatless, Gavaskar checked an off-drive and was caught behind. It was Roberts' first wicket in three finals.

Gavaskar's dismissal was a blow both for the confidence of the Indian team and its fans. Mohinder Amarnath, such an accomplished batsman against fast bowling, was greeted with a Garner bouncer. Srikkanth took that as a cue to begin to return fire. Soon he cut Garner over the slips for the first four of the match. Then he turned his attention to Roberts. An on drive raced into the milling spectators in the Grandstand. A few balls later and the Antiguan was hooked for six into the Warner Stand, bringing a vigorous flagwaving response from several quarters. He climaxed his trio of brilliant shots in Roberts' next over when he crouched on one knee and drove the ball forward of point to the boundary at the speed of light.

With Amarnath settling in to his task, momentarily at least, India suggested a competitive total could be within their capabilities. The match at Lord's the week before between the West Indies and Australia had produced 549 runs and there was no reason to think this might not also be a high-scoring affair. India reached 1-59 in 19 overs and Srikkanth, who ran a second run backwards all the way, had scored 38 in 57 balls.

Then Malcolm Marshall started to cause trouble as soon as he replaced Roberts, sending Srikkanth walking in front of a very fast and straight delivery.

Scoring runs was harder work; at least until Larry Gomes' off-spin brought its usual relief. His first over was a maiden, but soon Amarnath hit him through the covers for four and moving down the wicket drove him for another. Michael Holding bowled a wild one that eluded Jeffrey Dujon and went unhindered for four wides to the Nursery End. Faoud Bacchus might have run out Yashpal Sharma with a direct hit. A vibrant crowd danced, sang and whistled. The atmosphere inside the ground was fantastic.

Amarnath and Sharma lasted until the 30th over, their 31-run stand lifting the total to a neat 90. Lunchtime loomed and India could brag they had done a fair morning's work. However, quality fast bowlers are always capable of producing an unplayable delivery out of nowhere and Michael Holding did just that. Bowling from his short run, the Jamaican sent down a ripsnorter that cut back and succinctly removed Amarnath's off stump. As if that was not enough to ruin the Indians' midday meal, two runs later Sharma tried to belt Gomes through the off-side, only to hit a catch straight at Gus Logie who was substituting for Desmond Haynes. Two for 90 had slipped to 4-92.

At lunch it was 4-100 from 32 overs and consensus suggested India were doing no more than they could against superior opposition. The growing dominance of the West Indies continued after the interval. Gomes was still on and Kapil Dev eased him twice to the on-side boundary, then unwisely tried to belt him for six, reaching only as far as the safe hands of Holding in the deep. One run and one over later, Kirti Azad hit a simple catch to square leg off Roberts. India was 6-111 in the 36th over, having lost 4-21. Their innings was sagging badly.

Sandeep Patil, late hero of the semi-final and always aggressive in intent, tried to regain some Indian initiative and showed his captain how to put Gomes into the crowd for six. There was no significant partnership, however. Roger Binny soon went the same way as Azad and after Madan Lal hit Gomes for another six, Patil thoroughly mistimed a pull shot off Garner to leave India 8-153. Eight runs later Marshall broke through Madan Lal's defence and India had lost 7-71 in 15 inglorious overs.

Syed Kirmani and Balwindersingh Sandhu had 15 overs available for their last-wicket partnership. To the surprise of many, they used 10 of them. The stand featured 22 runs and a thump on the helmet for Sandhu courtesy of another Marshall fireball. Sandhu survived and 'Dickie' Bird told Marshall what he thought of bouncers to a number-11 batsmen. In fact the Sikh finally outlasted Kirmani, when, like Amarnath, he received a delivery from Holding, bowling from the Nursery End, that would have challenged any batsman on earth. India was all out for 183 in the 55th over.

It was 3.15pm. The West Indies were sure to win, but at least the paying customers could feel satisfied that close to six hours of cricket would be provided. A slight haze covered the afternoon sun as Haynes and Gordon Greenidge began the pursuit of 184. It cooled proceedings slightly and quelled the atmosphere a little. Kapil Dev kept his dressing-room speech short, admitting to limited confidence for the task ahead. In the other dressing room Marshall was relaxing and taking it easy. He did not expect to have to bat and settled back to dream about his new BMW. India were now at odds of 100-1 to win.

Greenidge had missed out in the 1975 and 1979 finals. Another chance now presented itself and Sandhu appeared to offer the chance of a few early comfortable runs. Haynes thought so and drove him to the extra cover boundary. Then the man in the maroon patka sent down his second over to the man in the baggy maroon cap. Greenidge lifted his bat out of the way of a ball outside the off-stump. Suddenly it jagged back and hit his off stump. The opener could not believe his own error of judgement. The West Indies were 1-5 and Greenidge's three finals had realised 13, 9 and 1; a poor return for such a great batsman.

A champion took the place of the great batsman at the wicket and almost from the moment he arrived assumed his trademark role of dominance. Sandhu dropped short. Richards silently and sweetly pulled the ball to mid wicket for four. He had been made Man of the Match in 1979 for his supreme 138 not out and this time was coming out of the blocks as if he wanted to top that performance. Two drives, one to the off and one to the on reduced the margin by eight more runs and showed the Indian captain who was in charge.

Madan Lal was introduced. Richards welcomed him by sending the ball to all points for three more fours in four balls. The 50 was raised in no time, then out of the blue Haynes, wanting a piece of the boundary action, drove loosely at Madan Lal and was caught by Binny in the covers. It was thought that might stem the run flow for a while, especially when Lloyd pulled up lame going for his first single, a simple trot to a shot to third man. Haynes came back straight away as his captain's runner. It was easy to believe the Barbadian knew straight away he would be needed and that Lloyd had carried the injury into the match. Even if that were so, Kapil made no fuss and allowed the runner.

Besides which he soon had other things to occupy him. 'Dickie' Bird says that when Haynes was caught, Kapil came up to him and said, "Do you know, we will win after all. They think it is too easy." Most would have thought he was still being a bit optimistic, but they may have had their first doubts a few moments later.

Madan Lal bowled the 14th over of the innings. Richards pulled at a short ball and sent it sailing over mid wicket towards the noisy throng in the Grandstand. They roared their approval just as Kapil turned, eyes skyward following its trajectory. Quickly the inadequacy of Richards' timing was evident. Kapil ran hard for 25 metres and judged the ball's descent perfectly. His eyes never left their objective and he held a very important catch. Richard's innings of 33 had contained seven stunning boundaries. Each shot to the rope seemed to indicate his side's superiority, his dismissal gave the first glimpse of their fragility. The West Indies were 3-57 and for the first time since Srikkanth's early assault Indian noise drowned out West Indian noise.

It was a pivotal moment. Lloyd was really struggling. 'Dickie' Bird thought he should have retired hurt. Lloyd was intent on helping his side win a match that now, unbelieveably was no longer there for the taking. He and Larry Gomes took their time for a few overs and added nine runs, just trying to consolidate things. Gomes had been shackled by Binny. Now he took a liberty outside the off-stump at Madan Lal, edged the ball and Gavaskar held the slips catch into his stomach.

The twist was quickly gaining momentum. Gomes had gone in the18th over. From the first ball of the 19th Lloyd lunged painfully at Binny. The attempted drive was ill conceived and lobbed straight to mid off. The West Indies were 5-66 and a cricket a match had been turned on its head. The medium pacers were swinging the ball and Lloyd's batsmen were not handling them well. Bacchus and Dujon batted in rearguard mode, surviving six overs until the tea break where the West Indies could regroup and re-focus. Marshall was no longer dreaming of BMWs, he had the pads on and had to think about batting.

Three balls into the final session of the 1983 Prudential Cup Final, Marshall was thinking very hard about his batting. He was the incoming batsman crossing over with the outgoing Bacchus, who without addition had slashed at a wide ball from Sandhu, only to edge a catch to the diving Kirmani. The West Indies had lost 5-16 to plummet to 6-76.

Dujon hit Sandhu over square leg for the fourth and last six of this low-scoring match. It was the sole boundary in a 43-run partnership with Marshall that revived West Indian hopes.

"This is going to be tough," Dujon had told the fast bowler when he arrived at the wicket. They took no more risks than their three runs per over requirement necessitated.

Playing straight and running hard they seemed to have everything under control when Kapil re-introduced Amarnath for the 42nd over at the Nursery End. Dujon went to play his first delivery, then pulled his bat away, only for the ball to follow him a little. It glided off the edge of the bat and down into his stumps. Dujon was devastated, not being able to believe his misfortune. He bent over and thumped his open palm on the ground.

It was 7-119 and all the recognised batsmen were gone. Soon Marshall joined them. His 73-minute vigil ended when he moved down the wicket to Amarnath, followed the ball as it moved away down the slope and guided it to Gavaskar at slip. The bowler whom Lloyd had hoped would provide the easiest runs for his side was winning the game for India. The West Indies were 60 runs short of their objective when Garner joined Roberts. These two had put on 71 in the opening match of the tournament against India with some uninhibited free hitting.

This time there was a lot more at stake and two runs after Marshall was out Roberts, the cool calm Antiguan, so often the lower-order batting hero in a tight situation, shuffled in front to Kapil and was adjudged lbw. Now it was 9-126 and India were on the verge of the greatest boilover in what had been a competition full of upset results.

It did not come straight away. Garner and Holding clung on to the hope of another Caribbean miracle for seven overs and 28 minutes. They pushed a few runs here and there edging 14 closer to the target. The requirement was 44 runs from 49 balls as Amarnath ran in to deliver the final ball of his seventh over. It was short of a length. Holding swung hard across it and was struck on the pads. Amarnath, Kirmani and 750 million watching the special telecast live in India let out an almighty appeal. 'Dickie' Bird acknowledged the irresistible plea. Up came a crooked right finger. India were the winners of the 1983 Prudential Cup.

Everyone ran in every direction except poor Holding who stood rooted at the crease, not stunned at the decision, but at his fate. It was a mistake because the invading hordes knocked him flying, resulting in a twisted ankle which kept the fast bowler out of county cricket for several days.

The contrast between Indian joy and West Indian despair could not have been more marked. Some West Indian players broke down and cried.

"We were dreadful," Lloyd lamented. He retired on the spot and had to be talked into continuing by his teammates and the West Indian Board of Control. Gradually the pain dulled amongst the vanquished, but it would not be forgotten. They gathered their composure and went to acknowledge and share a drink with the team that had defeated them on the day on their merits.

Kapil announced the moment of victory as the most joyous in his life. The celebrations started instantly and were to last for quite some time. There was more joy yet. Amarnath, who had charged straight down the wicket and grabbed a stump once 'Dickie' Bird had given Holding out was presented with an even more valuable souvenir; the Man of the Match Award from Mike Brearley for his important innings and carpet-sweeping, seven-over spell of 3-12. Not all the rewards were silverware, either. As a bonus the Indian Board gave each player £1150. In India it was 1am on the Sunday morning when the match finished. Instantly June 26th became a public holiday.

The Indian team danced and sang all night at the Westmoreland Hotel. In the streets of London there was much the same tune as thousands of Indian expatriates revelled in the proud moment. And the mood was the same all over India, with sitars, drums, whistles, rhythmic handclapping all beating out the same happy tune. Mihir Bose in *A History of Indian Cricket* wrote of the cohesion within the team, resulting, partially at least, from the success of players from the northern part of the India and their support for a captain from the same region. That may be so, but to an outsider the 1983 final will always be a game where a 66-1 underdog turned the tables on the acknowledged best team in the world in another wonderful game of limited-overs cricket.

INDIA		WEST INDIES	
S. M. Gavaskar c Dujon b Roberts	2	C. G. Greenidge b Sandhu	1
K. Srikkanth lbw b Marshall	38	D. L. Haynes c Binny b Madan Lal	13
M. Amarnath b Holding	26	I. V. A. Richards c Kapil Dev b Madan Lal	33
Yashpal Sharma c sub (A. L. Logie) b Gomes	11	C. H. Lloyd (capt) c Kapil Dev b Binny	8
S. M. Patil c Gomes b Garner	27	H. A. Gomes c Gavaskar b Madan Lal	5
Kapil Dev (capt) c Holding b Gomes	15	S. F. A. F. Bacchus c Kirmani b Sandhu	8
K. Azad c Garner b Roberts	0	P. J. L. Dujon (wk) b Amarnath	25
R. M. H. Binny c Garner b Roberts	2	M. D. Marshall c Gavaskar b Amarnath	18
Madan Lal b Marshall	17	A. M. E. Roberts lbw b Kapil Dev	4
S. M.H. Kirmani (wk) b Holding	14	J. Garner not out	5
B. S. Sandhu not out	11	M. A. Holding lbw b Amarnath	6
Extras b5 lb5 w9 nb1	20	Extras lb4 w10	14
(54.4 overs)	183	(52 overs)	140
1/2 2/59 3/90 4/92 5/110 6/111 7/130 8/153 9/161 10/183		1/5 2/50 3/57 4/66 5/66 6/76 7/119 8/124 9/126 10/140	
Bowling: Roberts 10-3-32-3; Garner 12-4-24-1; Marshall 11-1-24-2; Holding 9.4-2-26-2; Gomes 11-1-49-2; Richards 1-0-8-0		Bowling: Kapil Dev 11-4-21-1; Sandhu 9-1-32-2; Madan Lal 12-2-31-3; Binny 10-1-23-1; Amarnath 7-0-12-3; Azad 3-0-7-0	

Umpires: H.D. Bird   B.J. Meyer
Toss: West Indies

POST-MORTEM

After the 1983 World Cup, the editor of *Wisden Cricket Monthly*, David Frith, literally ate his own words. He said he was doing so on behalf of everyone who maligned the Indians prior to the tournament. After a reader of his magazine challenged him to do so, Frith consumed the offending piece with good grace.

The 'boilover' World Cup, the last to be held in England for 16 years, had been an outstanding success. The increase in the number of games had been a worthwhile innovation as the figures revealed. 232,000 people attended the matches, up from 132,000 and gate takings amounted to over one million pounds.

The growing prestige of the World Cup meant there was close scrutiny of teams and players who underperformed. Kim Hughes' Australians were perhaps the most disappointing combination over the two weeks and the flak flew when they returned home. David Hookes copped a hefty fine for airing his thoughts publicly on whom he thought should be in charge of the side. Worse than that, he was left out of the Test team for the next two summers. Australian cricket had still not bottomed out. Despite the efforts of Phil Ridings in England, several of their stars had already been secured for the next controversial 'Rebel' tour of South Africa.

That the West Indies were hurting there was no doubt. They soon rallied, however, and under Clive Lloyd the following October they thrashed India 3-0 in a six-match Test series and hammered them 5-0 in the limited-over internationals. It may have given the Caribbean champions some satisfaction to exact such a revenge. I am not sure, though, that they would not have willingly swapped any of those victories for a winner's medal at Lord's on Saturday June 25th.

The ICC had a meeting following the tournament where they called for tenders to be submitted by the end of the year to host the 1987 competition.

CHAPTER 5

The Reliance World Cup, 1987: The Australian Revival

peak to any Australian, New Zealand or English player about their tours of the sub-continent in the 1950s and 1960s and they will regale you with horror stories of illness and poor hygiene. Former Australian Test batsman and current Test match referee, Peter Burge said his greatest achievement on three tours of India and Pakistan was to arrive home each time with his health intact. Others revelled in the cultural exotica of the two countries and all had enough bizarre experiences to provide plenty of material for their various biographies.

By the 1980s, the situation had improved, but there were still problems with transport, climate and accommodation, especially outside the major cities. In addition a siege mentality lingered amongst many western players as to the treatment they had received at the hand of the umpires from that part of the world.

So when the July 1984 ICC meeting voted 16-12 in favour of the fourth World Cup being staged in India and Pakistan, there were doubters who feared the whole thing could be an organisational fiasco. An example of the type of difficulties that might arise occurred when Australia met India at Jamshedpur in October 1984. The match started three hours late because the baggage of both sides was still in transit on the road from Trivandrum.

The behaviour of volatile crowds were also a concern and both India and Pakistan had a history, some of it quite recent, of games being disrupted and even ruined by poorly behaved elements in big crowds.

The authorities from India and Pakistan worked hard to win the votes they needed at the ICC meeting. What clinched the deal ahead of England's bid to again stage the tournament was the guarantee that all full ICC member countries involved would receive £75,000 plus expenses from participating in the tournament. The English Test and County Cricket Board could not match that.

That was the easy part settled. The greatest issue to be resolved was whether English players who had toured, played or coached in South Africa would be allowed into India or Pakistan by the governments of the day. There was lots of to-ing and fro-ing and political grandstanding over this.

Graham Gooch was a particular target. He had a rotten tour of the West Indies in 1986, being subjected to much local criticism for his visits to the forbidden land. There was no guarantee he or John Emburey would be granted visas to enter India. If they had been refused, England would not have participated in the 1987 World Cup and Australia and New Zealand might have also withdrawn in support. Then the cricket world would have been split into two along lines of race and colour, something still too awful to contemplate.

Eventually sanity sort of prevailed. The Indian government said they would accept players with South African connections if they publicly denounced Apartheid. This allowed the tournament to go ahead with all teams participating. The problem did not go away, though. When Graham Gooch was made captain of England for the 1988-89 tour of India, local politicians considered him unacceptable and the tour was called off.

The ICC had to address the issue of the shorter daylight hours in that part of the world. The first idea was that each innings would be limited to 60 overs, as previously, and that every game would go into a second day. The folly of this was obvious and two years later was corrected. Each innings was reduced from 60 to 50 overs in the hope each game would be completed in a day, so establishing in the premier competition the now standard length of an innings in all limited-over internationals. Two days were still available for each game.

Play was scheduled to start at 9am to help finish the matches before dark. Each side was required to complete their 50 overs within an allotted three-and-a-half hours or face financial penalties. The West Indies had to pay close attention to that if they were not to return home out of pocket.

Neutral umpires were selected to officiate for the first time, also. Each preliminary round match would be controlled by one specially appointed official from an overseas panel and a leading Indian umpire for matches in Pakistan and a leading Pakistani umpire for the games in India.

What all this did was stimulate extra interest and perhaps a greater sense of anticipation than if the tournament had been held once more in England. In August 1986 the Indian and Pakistan authorities had secured the big sponsor they needed in the Indian company Reliance, which provided sponsorship the winner's trophy. This was a lavish product of gold, silver and diamonds and would be the featured prize of the Reliance Cup World Cup Final.

Further world wide interest arose from the fact that there were no clear cut favourites to win the trophy and that India in 1983 had set a precedent for outsiders to come from nowhere, hit their straps over the concentrated two-week period, and snatch victory against the odds.

India had not emerged as a powerhouse since their triumph under Kapil Dev. There had been moments of triumph, but equally plenty of defeats and frustrations. A win in the World Championship of Cricket limited overs tournament in Australia early in 1985 echoed the Prudential Cup success. At other times, particularly at home against England in 1984-85, their performances were poor. One noticeable and seemingly permanent change following the 1983 win was that Indian crowds had ditched the slower, more sophisticated spectacle of Test cricket for the thrills and spills of the limited overs game.

Their challenge would be led by their charismatic captain and leading all-rounder, Kapil Dev. He had lost the captaincy and even his place in the side against England, only to regain it and then the leadership soon after. He carried a lot on his shoulders as his team's leader, most penetrative bowler, and fastest scoring batsman. He would finish the tournament as hero or villain. The passionate Indian fans would allow nothing in between.

The great Sunil Gavaskar used the Reliance Cup as his swansong. This little champion had pushed himself to the top of the Test tree in terms of run aggregate and centuries. Gavaskar passed Sir Donald Bradman's 29 Test century record in 1984 and by the time of the World Cup had lifted his quota to 34 tons, beaten only in 2005 by Sachin Tendulkar. He had become the first batsman to clock more than 10,000 Test runs and finished with an average of over 50, a true measure of a batsman's quality. There had been plenty of limited-over achievements, too, but his World Cup record was modest in comparison to everything else. The greying 38-year-old opener had one last chance to correct that situation.

India's attack in 1983 was successfully based on medium-paced bowlers who could move the ball around in English conditions. On their home turf they would return to their traditional dependence on spinners. Left-arm Sikh, Maninder Singh and blossoming all-rounder Ravi Shastri, also left-arm orthodox, were key players in the side. Dilip Vengsarkar and Mohammad Azharuddin were attractive and successful middle-order batsmen who ensured India's rating with the bookmakers was much higher than the 66-1 it had been prior to the 1983 tournament.

What threw open the competition more than anything else was the diminishing power of the West Indies as a force in limited-overs internationals. Now led by Viv Richards, the Caribbean side remained the best around in the longer-form of the game. But the gap between the two forms of cricket was widening. Bouncers were now outlawed by the ruling that deemed any ball above the batsman's shoulder be called a no ball, nullifying some of the threat of the West Indian pacemen. In addition, almost a completely new set of speedsters had to be found. Michael Holding was recently retired and Joel Garner and Malcolm Marshall were unavailable due to injury. The second line of pacemen such as Tony Gray, Winston Benjamin and Patrick Patterson would have to make plenty of adjustments to foreign wickets and conditions very quickly.

Clive Lloyd had been two-and-a-half years out of the game. He would be missed and so would Gordon Greenidge, not retired, but nursing a gammy knee. Since the heady days of the early 1980s Richie Richardson had developed into a fine back foot slayer of wayward bowlers and the little Trinidadian, 'Gus' Logie thrilled crowds, but as much with his athletic catching as his stylish run making.

Much would depend on Greenidge's reliable opening partner, Desmond Haynes and the captain, Richards, who was still considered the world's premier batsman.

His side had missed out in the two limited-over tournaments held in Australia in the first months of 1987. Those losses indicated a reduction of West Indian dominance and the seeming emergence of a quality England side. They had a fine time of it 'down under' led by Mike Gatting, winning everything on offer against an admittedly demoralised Australian team.

Like the West Indies they would have to do without a couple of important players. David Gower and Ian Botham decided a winter at home was more desirable than this four-week sojourn, although the follow-up Test tour of Pakistan was possibly more of a discouraging factor. Gower had not taken a break from the game since the start of the 1978 English season. so he was entitled to a bit of long service leave.

Botham had let slip a quip about not wanting to send his mother-in-law to Pakistan after he returned from the country in 1984. His decision not to make the trip may have been mutually appreciated. The English tabloid journalists did not really want to go and made their feelings plain and the BBC, wrongly thinking the facilities would be inadequate, at first refused to televise the matches until the final.

One player who did agree to attend was sometimes reluctant tourist, Graham Gooch. A match winning opener, especially in limited-over internationals, Gooch had his ups and downs as an international batsman. When on song, though, he could win a match off his own very ample bat. Gatting's hold on the captaincy in the lead up to the World Cup looked much more secure than it actually was. He was at his peak as a thumping middle-order batsman and had been a big success in India three years previous.

English supporters might have been more apprehensive about their bowling attack. The pace of Phil DeFreitas, Gladstone Small and Neil Foster suggested honest competence, not blistering firepower. John Emburey could be relied upon for accuracy in the spin department. His ability to claim wickets was more open to question. As England's chief spinner he had taken a total of none in five Tests against Pakistan.

England were in Group B. This time they would have to face the West Indies in the preliminary rounds, as well as Pakistan and Sri Lanka.

Pakistan, like India, had the burden of extra pressure matched by homeground advantage as Imran led them into another campaign where their likely level of success was very hard to assess. The 35-year-old Pakistani captain also suggested the month long concentration of limited-over internationals would see him out of international cricket. This added to the romance of the occasion.

Imran had taken some time to recuperate from his 1983 injuries. He was bowling effectively again, if at a slightly reduced pace than in his prime. Imran's ability to send down lethal, prodigious in-swingers was unaffected, however.

Imran now had at his side an heir apparent in Wasim Akram, a left-handed all rounder of immense potential as a pace bowler and lower-order hitter. With Abdul Qadir's leg-spin expected to be a handful on Pakistan's own pitches, it was thought Imran's attack was the best equipped in the competition.

Zaheer Abbas and Mohsin Khan were finished, which put pressure on Javed Miandad. There was no suggestion he did not relish that opportunity. Javed was in a rich vein of form and prior to the tournament had threatened to pull out if he did not receive a pay rise. His most recent Test innings prior to the World Cup was 260 against England at The Oval. Salim Malik had emerged as a typically precocious Pakistani middle-order talent and since his return from injury, Imran was a far more reliable run maker. Jack Bannister, an English cricket commentator and bookmaker thought Pakistan were 2-1 favourites to win the final.

Allan Border brought an Australian side whose recent cricket had been as low as at any time in its history. They had not won a Test series since January 1984. In the years since there had been mass retirements, tearful captaincy resignations and South African defections which decimated the quality of the side. The West Indies, England and even New Zealand had all triumphed over this once proud cricketing nation. At times it seemed only their tough little captain was holding the team together and he had threatened to quit a couple of times, too.

Border's batting during this period was often astonishing in its resilience against overwhelming odds. Fast bowling or slow, he sold his wicket dearly and on several occasions rescued losing causes almost single-handedly.

Border now had Bob Simpson as team coach to try and give the side direction and to develop a strong cooperative work ethic. It remained to be seen if Simpson's tactics and approach would have any impact.

Border seemed to have the nucleus of a team blossoming with talent. Dean Jones had already made his mark, Geoff Marsh was noted for his dedication and had been an instant success at international level in both forms of the game. Steve Waugh carried a reputation as an excellent limited-overs all-rounder and David Boon, despite a poor 1986-87 Ashes series, remained the batting pride of Tasmania.

Less certain were the bowling resources at Border's disposal. Beanpole, left-arm paceman, Bruce Reid had quickly established his rating as the team's main strike bowler. Craig McDermott was the fastest bowler in the party and still young enough to be a developing talent. That also meant much of his potential was as yet unfulfilled. Beyond that pair the bowling responsiblities would be shared between all-rounders Waugh and Simon O'Donnell; Border himself; and his off-spinners Peter Taylor and Tim May.

On paper the Australians looked to have the easier run in Group A, having to overcome two of India, New Zealand and their 1983 nemisis, Zimbabwe to reach the semi-finals. Of course, everyone thought they had a fairly easy draw in 1983 and that did not do them any good. Such was the pessimissm pervading throughout the Australian cricket community that Channel Nine, despite having the Australian television rights to the 1987 World Cup showed no inclination to provide any direct telecasts of the tournament. They touted the feeble excuse that the expected picture quality was too low.

Of all the teams missing players from the Reliance Cup, none were harder hit than New Zealand who had to strive for victory without the services of their premier bowler, Richard Hadlee. As well as Hadlee, whose decision was controversial because he told the press before informing New Zealand's cricket authorities of his unavailability, Bruce Edgar and Jeremy Coney had retired. Jeff Crowe was the captain of a team still expected to give a good account of themselves.

Crowe's younger brother Martin, about to embark upon his second World Cup tournament, was rated in the top-five batsmen in the game at the time. A real stylist, Crowe had shown an ability to compile centuries against top quality opposition of varying types. His would be the wicket most wanted by opposing attacks. John Wright's stability at the top of the batting order could have an influence and Ken Rutherford, in limited-overs internationals at least, was revealing his talent for positive batting.

Without Hadlee, medium-pacers Ewen Chatfield, Martin Snedden and Willie Watson would share a greater burden. Chatfield, the cricketer who literally came back from the dead after a bouncer to the head, had uncanny accuracy and was rarely collared. He was the most experienced of the trio. Danny Morrison was sharp, but untried, raw in the ways of containment and unlikely to be used often in this form of cricket just yet.

Since the 1983 World Cup, Sri Lanka had secured their first couple of Test victories, one each over India and Pakistan. Duleep Mendis retained the captaincy, becoming a more rounded figure as the seasons progressed. He, fellow batting aggressor, Roy Dias, and rotund young left-hander, Arjuna Ranatunga, would be expected to score the bulk of the quick runs needed by Sri Lanka to make up for lack of penetration in their bowling.

They would still be calling the likes of Rumesh Ratnayake, Vinothen John and Ashantha de Mel to threaten their opposition. It was an unlikely prospect on England's fairly sympathetic wickets and was even less so on the hard-baked surfaces of India and Pakistan.

Holland had given Zimbabwe a decent run for their money in the ICC Trophy Final in July 1986, but there was never any real doubt that the African nation would make their deserved return to their second World Cup. Their prodigy from 1983, Graeme Hick, had decided to follow his cricketing destiny in England, first with Worcestershire and later with England. His talent would be missed as would that of retired captain and important all-rounder, Duncan Fletcher.

Thirty-nine-year-old off-spinner, John Traicos had assumed the leadership mantle. His experience was an asset to the Zimbabweans and he could expect to trouble batsmen with his accuracy on the finger spinner-friendly wickets of the subcontinent.

Dave Houghton was Traicos' vice-captain. Equally he had a key role to play as wicketkeeper batsman. Others back four years on for more run making fun were openers Grant Paterson, Robin Brown and Ali Shah, Andy Pycroft, all-rounder Iain Butchart and the fiercely competitive Kevin Curran. Curran and Butchart would be required to do plenty of bowling. Peter Rawson was remembered as Zimbabwe's best new-ball exponent in 1983. He retained his place in the line-up, but had a new off-sider to nurture in the developing Eddo Brandes.

The venues for each of the World Cup games had been carefully selected to assuage fears about hygiene and organisation. The Indians and Pakistanis were determined that their showpiece tournament would be a success. They were leaving nothing to chance. Each venue had to receive a stamp of approval from a TCCB or an ACB representative if it was to be added to the venue list. Once these locations had been accepted the policy was to take the matches all over the subcontinent. That would involve the players travelling far greater distances than they had in the tournaments in England. To compensate for this and the need to recover from long, perhaps arduous journeys, the 27 Reliance Cup matches were extended over four weeks rather than crammed into two as they had been in 1983. Again, everyone would play each other twice as they had four years before.

The extent of the travel was yet another worry and there were still plenty of frowns as the sides began to file into India and Pakistan at the end of September. Sri Lanka, who hardly had to move from match to match in 1983, had a very strenuous World Cup itinerary this time as they had to flit from one corner of Pakistan to the next. The Australians impressed all observers with their willingness to get out and practise in the heat, acclimatising themselves with prevailing conditions. It immediately contrasted with the attitude that had gone before them.

Another more obvious contrast was the match selected to open the Reliance Cup. Instead of England leading the way at beautiful Lord's or the austerely traditional Oval it would be Pakistan doing battle with Sri Lanka at the Niaz Stadium in Hyderabad. This ground was put on the world cricketing map when Mudassar Nazar and Javed Miandad put on 451 against India in 1982-83. The greatest threat to an interruption of play was not chilly May rain in this notably hot location, but maybe a dust storm from the Thar Desert.

THURSDAY 8 OCTOBER, FRIDAY 9 OCTOBER and SATURDAY 10 OCTOBER 1987
THE RELIANCE CUP: ROUND ONE
GROUP B: PAKISTAN vs SRI LANKA
NIAZ STADIUM, HYDERABAD: PAKISTAN WON BY 15 RUNS

Although an unlikely venue for the opening of the world's major cricket tournament, Hyderabad turned on an excellent cricket match for the start of the Reliance Cup.

Pakistan was in the grip of World Cup fever. The whole country seemed to stop to watch Imran's side fight it out with their Group B opponents. There was a passionate belief that this side would have the honour of bringing that gold and silver trophy to Pakistan after the Final in Calcutta on 8 November, with Sri Lanka just the first stepping stone to that national triumph. So it eventually proved, but the Sri Lankans put up a great fight and their trio of up-and-coming batsmen nearly ruined the Pakistani plan at the first time of asking.

A 9am start did not deter Imran and he had no hesitation in electing to bat after he won the toss. It proved the correct decision. The Sri Lankan opening bowlers betrayed some nervousness, conceding 18 extras in the first nine overs. Ijaz Ahmed and Ramiz Raja opened capably enough with a stand of 48 before Ijaz was caught behind off Rumesh Ratnayake. Nineteen runs later Rumesh caught Mansoor Akhtar off his namesake, Ravi Ratnayake, to leave Pakistan 2-67. Rameez and Javed Miandad then took control of the innings with a stand of 113. Ramiz provided the solidity, taking 30 overs to reach his 50, while Javed attacked and improvised his way to an excellent century in 96 balls.

Javed's 103 was his fifth 100 in limited-over internationals, but his first in the World Cup. He hit six fours and won the Man of the Match Award. After the departure of this pair, the run-making momentum was maintained to the completion of the 50 overs. The two Ratnayakes had each picked up a couple of wickets. Neither they nor the other Sri Lankans were able to halt the steady run flow.

Pakistan had finished with 6-267, the equivalent of which off 60 overs would have been 320. It was an imposing chase for the Sri Lankans, many of whom were inexperienced. And it did not start off well. Roshan Mahanama, quickly into his stride, lost partners, Brendon Kuruppu caught behind at 29, Roy Dias bowled by the mesmerising Abdul Qadir at 57, Arjuna Ranatunga, also bowled, this time by off-spinner Tauseef Ahmed on 100, and his captain, Duleep Mendis, disastrously run out just three runs later. Sri Lanka, at 4-103, were quickly slipping to defeat.

Twenty-one-year-old Mohanama was joined by the equally youthful left-hander Asanka Gurusinha. They added 79 runs for the fifth wicket in impressive fashion. Mudassar Nazar was made to suffer, conceding seven runs per over throughout his spell. Imran became annoyed as the standard of fielding slipped. Mohanama had guided his side to within 86 runs of their target and hit seven fours and the first six of the tournament when he was caught from a long hop off Mansoor Akhtar's only over.

Gurusingha was bowled by the deserving Abdul Qadir which meant that only Aravinda de Silva, another 21 year old, stood between Pakistan and victory. He pressed on adding valuable runs with the two Ratnayakes. The Sri Lankans closed in, but the overs available were running dangerously low. Imran returned and settled the issue when he bowled de Silva with a full toss, his 100th wicket in limited-over internationals. The challenge had gone and Don Anurasiri's run out from the second ball of the final over was merely academic. Pakistan had the start they needed.

PAKISTAN		SRI LANKA	
Ramiz Raja c R. J. Ratnayake b Anurasiri	76	D. S. B. P. Kuruppu (wk) c Salim Yousuf b Imran Khan	9
Ijaz Ahmed c Kuruppu b R. J. Ratnayake	16	R. S. Mahanama c Javed Miandad b Mansoor Akhtar	89
Mansoor Akhtar c R. J. Ratnayake b J. R. Ratnayake	12	R. L. Dias b Abdul Qadir	5
Javed Miandad b J. R.Ratnayake	103	A. Ranatunga b Tauseef Ahmed	24
Wasim Akram run out	14	L. R. D. Mendis (capt) run out	1
Salim Malik not out	18	A. P. Gurusinha b Abdul Qadir	37
Imran Khan (capt) b R. J.Ratnayake	2	P. A. de Silva b Imran Khan	42
Salim Yousuf (wk) not out	1	J. R. Ratnayake c Salim Yousuf b Wasim Akram	7
Extras lb15 w1 nb9	25	R. J. Ratnayake c Mudassar Nazar b Wasim Akram	8
(50 overs)	6-267	V. B. John not out	1
Did not bat: Mudassar Nazar, Abdul Qadir, Tauseef Ahmed		S. D. Anurasiri run out	0
1/48 2/67 3/180 4/226 5/259 6/266		Extras b7 lb14 w7 nb1	29
Bowling: John 10-2-37-0; R. J.Ratnayake 10-0-64-2;		(49.2 overs)	252
J. R.Ratnayake 9-0-47-2; de Silva 10-0-44-0;		1/29 2/57 3/100 4/103 5/182 6/190 7/209 8/223 9/251	
Anurasiri 10-0-52-1; Gurusingha 1-0-8-0		10/252	
		Bowling: Imran Khan 10-2-42-2; Wasim Akram 9.2-1-41-2;	
		Mudassar Nazar 9-0-63-0; Abdul Qadir 10-1-30-2;	
		Tauseef Ahmed 10-0-48-1; Mansoor Akhtar 1-0-7-1	

Umpires: V.K. Ramaswamy S.J. Woodward

Toss: Pakistan   Points: Pakistan 4 Sri Lanka 0

GROUP B: ENGLAND vs WEST INDIES
MUNICIPAL STADIUM: GUJRANWALA, ENGLAND WON BY 2 WICKETS

Limited-overs cricket is almost designed to provide exciting finishes. This fluctuating encounter in a small ground rarely used in international cricket was one of two thrillers played on the first Friday of the tournament. England won in unlikely fashion from the third ball of the last over of the match, giving the West Indies their second consecutive World Cup defeat. Following the poor performances in Australia, there was no doubt that for the first time in years the West Indies were not insurmountable.

Not that they really should have lost this match. An English middle-order collapse left them needing 34 runs with two wickets left from the last three overs. Unbelievably, Courtney Walsh cracked and Allan Lamb hit England home.

For those making the 200km journey from Lahore it was an early start on the road to Gujranwala, 5am for some to make the impressive Municipal Stadium on time. By the start of play a healthy neutral crowd was in. Soon the heat, pollution and humidity of the holiday Friday would affect the players of the two sides as they strove to gain the ascendancy over each other. The wicket, bare apart from an occasional tuft of grass, was so hard the umpires had trouble getting the stumps into it. There was no chance it would deteriorate, so Mike Gatting had no problem with sending the opposition in to bat after he won the toss.

His bowlers were the ones with problems. They were sweating so profusely they struggled to find a dry spot on their whites to shine the ball. Nevertheless Phil DeFreitas soon got through Carlisle Best with the new ball. His partner and fellow Barbadian, Desmond Haynes was also subdued taking 18 overs to make 19 before being run out by a diving John Emburey who made good a wayward throw from Chris Broad.

The West Indian total was 2-53 by then, Richie Richardson being quickly into his stride. He was joined by his captain Viv Richards, who began the acceleration when he hit Derek Pringle's second and third deliveries to the boundary, both trademark on drives. Pringle undid all the good work of DeFreitas, who was so affected by the heat he vomited in the middle of one spell, and Emburey who bowled with impeccable control, if still not taking a wicket.

The Antiguans have played some awesome partnerships. This, though, would not be one of them. Neil Foster had bowled them both by the time the score was 122, Richards' dismissal, playing on a back foot off-side drive, was almost as trademark as his boundary shots.

The loss of wickets slowed the run rate. It was 4-151 after 40 overs, Jeff Dujon and Gus Logie were concentrating on consolidation. Dujon had one lucky escape when a sweep off the back of his bat was caught by Downton only for the token appeal to be rejected. Then, as if a bell had gone for a final lap, the strokes were unleashed again. The bowlers and fielders began to wilt in the Gujranwala heat. Foster, despite bowling Logie, lost control for an over and Pringle was treated like a novice.

He bowled the 49th over of the innings to Roger Harper. Chris Broad at mid off failed to stop the first ball going through his legs for four. Two balls later Harper smacked him for six over the leg-side and hit two more boundaries—one off a no ball to third man and the other straight past the bowler. The over cost 22. Nine more runs for the wicket of Harper were contrived from Gladstone Small in the 50th over to leave England a target of 244 for victory. Ninety-two had come from the final 10 overs.

The heat of the day was at its fiercest as England began their chase. Broad did not have to suffer it for long. Courtney Walsh quickly had him caught behind. Tim Robinson was also making little headway when Harper ran him out in the 17th over. It was another astonishing display of the Guyanan's fielding talents. Immediately upon his arrival, Gatting added some urgency to the batting. His aggression infected Gooch and the runs began to flow freely from the pacemen who were as badly affected by the heat as their English counterparts.

They added 58 in nine overs to put their team in a strong position. Then, within four balls, they undid all their good work. Not for the first time Carl Hooper benefitted from the batsmen relaxing mentally after having seen off the fast bowling threat. Now, sending down medium pacers he had developed while playing club cricket in Melbourne, Hooper had Gatting dancing over and around a straight ball and Gooch chasing a wide delivery. Allan Lamb looked out of sorts and Pringle hit the ball with about 10 per cent of the power that had been dealt out to him. Paul Downton was run out after Lamb turned down a call for a leg-bye. The wicketkeeper gave up the cause when he might have made his ground. That mix-up left England 6-131 from 37 overs, a long way from their objective.

Emburey is credited with kick starting the innings again. His ungainly whacking brought him 22 runs in 13 balls, including a flat pull for a straight six off Patrick Patterson. Ninety-one runs were still needed from 10 overs and an attempt at another six saw Patterson knock back Emburey's leg stump. With Lamb pushing singles DeFreitas took over Emburey's role and he hit 23 from five overs. From the last ball of the 47th over he also emulated the off-spinner's dismissal so when Foster joined Lamb the equation was 34 from three overs.

It looked an unlikely propostion, but Walsh was really suffering now and Lamb had set a personal precedent some months before in Australia when he took 18 runs from the final Bruce Reid over to win a World Series Cup match. He took 15 from the tiring Jamaican's six deliveries. Patterson conceded just six from the 49th over, allowing Walsh 13 runs to play with in the last.

Lamb scored two from the first ball, then slip drove the second, a full toss, for four to third man. The third delivery was meant to follow Lamb as he stepped away to hit the ball through the gaps in the off-side. Walsh over compensated and the ball shot past Dujon down the leg-side to the boundary for four wides. Walsh's next ball was a no ball and Lamb took the single on offer. It was down to two runs from four balls. Only one was needed. Foster moved down the wicket, played another cultured slip drive and the ball went away to third man for the four that won the match for England.

Walsh bent over distraught and tearful, his hands on his knees. The future captain, taker of more than 400 Test wickets and possibly most level headed member of the side, had conceded 29 runs from his last nine balls. Derek Pringle would have been sympathetic. Lamb finished on 67 from 68 balls. He, too was exhausted, had to be helped from the ground and later said he would not have lasted another over. He won the Man of the Match Award.

WEST INDIES		ENGLAND	
D. L. Haynes run out	19	G. A. Gooch c Dujon b Hooper	47
C. A. Best b DeFreitas	5	B. C. Broad c Dujon b Walsh	3
R. B. Richardson b Foster	53	R. T. Robinson run out	12
I. V. A. Richards (capt) b Foster	27	M. W. Gatting (capt) b Hooper	25
P. J. L. Dujon (wk) run out	47	A. J. Lamb not out	67
A. L. Logie b Foster	49	D. R. Pringle c Best b Pringle	12
R. A. Harper b Small	24	P. R. Downton (wk) run out	3
C. L. Hooper not out	1	J. E. Emburey b Patterson	22
W. K.M. Benjamin not out	7	P. A. J. DeFreitas b Patterson	23
Extras lb9 nb3	12	N. A. Foster not out	9
(50 overs)	7-243	Extras lb14 w6 nb3	23
Did not bat: C. A. Walsh, B. P. Patterson		(49.3 overs)	8-246
1/8 2/53 3/105 4/122 5/205 6/235 7/235		Did not bat: G. C. Small	
Bowling: DeFreitas 10-2-31-1; Foster 10-0-53-3;		1/14 2/40 3/98 4/99 5/123 6/131 7/162 8/209	
Emburey 10-2-22-0; Small 10-0-45-1; Pringle 10-0-83-0		Bowling: Patterson 10-0-49-2; Walsh 9.3-0-65-1;	
		Harper 10-0-44-0; Benjamin 10-1-32-0; Hooper 10-0-42-3	

Umpires: A.R. Crafter   R.B. Gupta

Toss: England   Points: England 4 West Indies 0

GROUP A: INDIA vs AUSTRALIA
CHEPAUK GROUND: MADRAS (CHENNAI), AUSTRALIA WON BY ONE RUN

In contrast to their celebrating rivals across the western frontier, India had to suffer an agonising single-run defeat as their World Cup defence got underway. The sight of Maninder Singh's off stump cartwheeling out of the ground with two runs needed for victory stunned into silence the capacity crowd, but sent the Australian party into raptures.

Almost exactly a year before a game on the same ground between the same two countries had ended in Test cricket's second only ever tie. The last batsman dismissed in that emotional cauldron was also Maninder Singh.

The heat in Madras was no less forgiving than that in Gujranwala when Kapil Dev won the toss and told Allan Border his side could take the 9am batting start. The early morning dew which prompted the decision of the Indian captain had no apparent slowing effect on the batting of the Australian openers Geoff Marsh and David Boon. They launched the Australian innings in very impressive fashion, raising 110 runs in 25 overs, until Ravi Shastri had Boon lbw with the Tasmanian one short of his 50. Boon didn't agree with umpire Dave Archer's decision and discussed it heatedly with a few Indian players on his way out.

Dean Jones lifted the run tempo even further. He attacked the bowling from the moment of his arrival and dominated the 64-run partnership with the reliable Marsh. His 35-ball innings included several big hits, one of which was changed from a four to a six by Hanif Mohammad, the match adjudicator, during the lunch break. That became a far more significant event in retrospect than it seemed at the time. After Jones had fallen to the spin of Maninder Singh, Marsh and Allan Border lifted the total beyond the 200 mark by the 40th over. A really massive score loomed, but the Australian middle order stumbled as they tried to accelerate.

Marsh fell to Manoj Prabhakar after completing his third century in limited-over internationals. All three had been against India. This one, worth a Man of the Match Award, had taken three-and-a-half hours and included one six and seven fours. His stamina in the hot airless stadium while facing 141 deliveries was phenomenal. When Simon O'Donnell was run out from the last ball of the innings Australia had set India 271 to win.

Sunil Gavaskar began as if reaching that requirement was the simplest thing in the world. His strokeplay delighted Henry Blofeld, who called the Mumbaiker's back foot drive off McDermott's first over "the stroke of the year". McDermott's third over contained three more boundaries, a drive through mid wicket, a square cut and a square drive. Off-spinner Peter Taylor came on for the 10th over of the innings. Gavaskar sweetly drove his first ball over mid off for four and in his second over the little Indian champion swatted Taylor back over his head for a big six. Fifty thousand supporters roared as one. In the same over Taylor had a modicum of revenge when Gavaskar holed out to Bruce Reid. India, through the efforts of the same man who once batted through 60 overs for 36 runs, had got away to a flying 69 in 12 overs.

Kris Srikkanth and limited-over international debutant, Navjot Singh Sidhu, took up where Gavaskar left off, continuing to trade in fours and sixes. Sidhu, in sensational form, hit five balls over the boundary, including three big drives off the suffering Taylor. He and Srikkanth added a further 52 then Dilip Vengsarkar stayed with the debutant until the score reached 207. They added 76 in just 11 overs and India were cruising, needing just 64 more runs in 13 overs with eight wickets standing.

McDermott had conceded 31 in his first four overs. Now he yorked Sidhu and bowled Mohammad Azharuddin slogging across the line. Vengsarkar was caught at mid-on and Shastri offered a simple caught and bowled to the Queenslander.

Despite the Australian comeback, the equation still got down to 15 runs from four overs with four wickets standing. In 1983 the outcome would have been obvious. This Australian side, though, had maintained its standards in the field throughout and they would not relent.

Jones and Border ran out Roger Binny and Prabhakar respectively with direct hits. When the last over started, Maninder and Kiran More needed to score six more runs for the final wicket. Twenty-two-year-old Steve Waugh, building his reputation as the 'iceman' in tight finishes, was given the responsibility of bowling the 50th over of the innings. Maninder got two to fine leg from the first ball and two more to third man from the third ball. He tried to win it from the fifth with a big drive. The clatter of timber was followed by the silence of 50,000.

Australia celebrated after the match at the Taj Coromandel Hotel in a fashion so enthusiastic they might have won the whole tournament in one game. Expatriate Australians turned up from everywhere in the hotel lobby after the match to share in the success. Border's team had been strongly motivated by Zaheer Abbas' newspaper call that the Australians were no better than "a schoolboy side". They had also developed a bit of niggling rivalry with India in recent times and were well prepared by their coach Bobby Simpson. This was not a reverse of the upset that befell Australia in 1983, but it did give them some real momentum, not unlike India's win over the West Indies in Round One of the last Prudential Cup.

AUSTRALIA		INDIA	
D. C. Boon lbw b Shastri	49	S. M. Gavaskar c Reid b Taylor	37
G. R. Marsh c Azahruddin b Prabhakar	110	K. Srikkanth lbw b Waugh	70
D. M. Jones c Sidhu b Maninder	39	N. S. Sidhu b McDermott	73
A. R. Border (capt) b Binny	16	D. B. Vengsarkar c Jones b McDermott	29
T. M. Moody c Kapil Dev b Prabhakar	8	M. Azharuddin b McDermott	10
S. R. Waugh not out	19	Kapil Dev (capt) c Boon b O'Donnell	6
S. P. O'Donnell run out	7	R. J. Shastri c & b McDermott	12
Extras lb18 w2 nb2	22	K. S. More (wk) not out	12
(50 overs)	6-270	R. M.H. Binny run out	0
Did not bat: G. C. Dyer (wk), P. L. Taylor, C. J. McDermott,		M. Prabhakar run out	5
B. A.Reid		Maninder Singh b Waugh	4
1/110 2/174 3/228 4/237 5/251 6/270		Extras lb7 b2 w2	11
Bowling: Kapil Dev 10-0-41-0; Prabhakar 10-0-47-2;		(49.5 overs)	269
Binny 7-0-46-1; Maninder Singh 10-0-48-1;		1/69 2/131 3/207 4/229 5/232 6/246 7/256 8/256 9/265	
Shastri 10-0-50-1; Azharuddin 3-0-20-0		10/269	
		Bowling: McDermott 10-0-56-4; Reid 10-0-35-0;	
		O'Donnell 9-1-32-1; Taylor 5-0-46-1; Waugh 9.5-0-52-2;	
		Border 6-0-39-0	

Umpires: D.M. Archer   H.D. Bird
Toss: India   Points: Australia 4 India 0

GROUP A: NEW ZEALAND vs ZIMBABWE
FATEH MAIDAN: HYDERABAD, NEW ZEALAND WON BY 3 RUNS

The Saturday fixture of the first round provided a match the equal of the two last over thrillers played on the Friday. The Indian Hyderabad could hardly boast they had the feature event of the tournament. However, there would be no complaints at the Saturday afternoon entertainment put on by the New Zealanders and Zimbabweans.

New Zealand tried to shore up their limited resources by opening with Martin Snedden after John Traicos had won the toss and sent them in to bat. At the first time of asking it proved a real success. Taking the opportunity to exploit the open spaces while the fieldsmen were kept up close by the restrictive circle, Snedden used his ungainly left-handed technique to pinch hit some early runs. He scored the majority of a 59 opening stand with John Wright and then helped his side to an impressive 1-143 in partnership with the stylish Martin Crowe.

Peter Rawson finally ended Snedden's 95-ball escapade and his 84-run stand with Crowe. John Traicos then applied the brakes to the New Zealand scoring. He choked off Crowe's run flow and wickets began to fall. Once Snedden had gone the Kiwis only added a further 99 for the rest of the innings. Their final total of 7-242 looked no better than par for the course.

It seemed much better than that once Snedden and Ewen Chatfield began to knock over the Zimbabwean top order. The openers Robin Brown and Ali Shah were removed with only 10 on the board. Andy Pycroft stayed with Dave Houghton for a 51 run stand until suffering a recurrence of the 1983 run out disease and six runs later Willie Watson dismissed the dangerous Kevin Curran.

The wickets continued to tumble to Watson and left-arm spinner Stephen Boock, so that in the 23rd over Zimbabwe were an inglorious 7-104. Curly-haired wicketkeeper/batsman Houghton was unbeaten and had reached an accomplished 50 in 62 balls with his second driven six off John Bracewell. He was joined by Iain Butchart, who was capable, but not more so than those who had come before him. In the next 20 overs Butchart showed his teammates how to support a batsman in prime form.

Houghton was racing towards his 100, taking runs at will from an attack that had lost its earlier edge. Another six, this time a pull from off-spinner Dipak Patel, took him to 80. Soon after he swept Boock for four to bring him his worthy 100 in 107 balls out of 156. By the 40th over the target was a far more accessible 69 runs.

A chance to long off allowed Houghton to continue his heroic assault. He faced Snedden at the start of the 47th over with 36 runs still required. Four balls later and the target was 22. Houghton hit three leg-side boundaries and a straight drive for two then lofted the fifth ball over mid-on. Martin Crowe turned, ran and at full stretch held what was acknowledged as the catch of the tournament.

Eddo Brandes was immediately run out. Butchart passed his 50 and he and Traicos took the game into the final over when, like India's last wicket pair, six runs had to be squeezed out. They had only made two of those by the fourth ball. A big swing by Butchart missed, the ball hit his pad, there was confusion and the all-rounder was run out.

His side's brave revival failed by just three runs.

Dave Houghton's 141 runs, and one stone loss of weight in the heat, had been in vain. The Man of the Match Award was his sole consolation.

NEW ZEALAND		ZIMBABWE	
M. C. Snedden c Waller b Rawson	64	R. D. Brown c J. J.Crowe b Chatfield	1
J. G. Wright c Houghton b Traicos	17	A. H. Shah lbw b Snedden	5
M. D. Crowe c & b Rawson	72	D. L. Houghton (wk)c M. D.Crowe b Snedden	141
A. H. Jones c Brandes b Shah	0	A. J. Pycroft run out	12
J. J. Crowe (capt) c Brown b Curran	31	K. M. Curran c Boock b Watson	4
D. N. Patel b Shah	0	A. C. Waller c Smith b Watson	5
J. G. Bracewell not out	13	G. A. Paterson c Smith b Boock	2
I. D. S. Smith (wk) c Brown bCurran	29	P. W. E. Rawson lbw b Boock	1
S. L. Boock not out	0	I. P. Butchart run out	54
Extras b4 lb5 w4 nb3	16	E. A. Brandes run out	0
(50 overs)	7-242	A. J. Traicos (capt) not out	4
Did not bat: W. Watson, E. J. Chatfield		Extras lb8 w1 nb1	10
1/59 2/143 3/145 4/166 5/169 6/205 7/240		(49.4 overs)	239
Bowling: Curran 10-0-51-2; Rawson 10-0-62-2;		1/8 2/10 3/61 4/67 5/86 6/94 7/104 8/221 9/221 10/239	
Brandes 7-2-23-0; Traicos10-2-28-1; Butchart 4-0-27-0;		Bowling: Chatfield 10-2-26-1; Snedden 9-0-53-2;	
Shah 9-0-42-2		Watson 10-2-36-2; Bracewell 7-0-47-0; Patel 5-0-27-0;	
		Boock 8.4-0-42-2	

Umpires: Mahboob Shah   P.W.Vidanagamage

Toss: Zimbabwe   Points: New Zealand 4 Zimbabwe 0

TUESDAY 13 OCTOBER and WEDNESDAY 14 OCTOBER
THE RELIANCE CUP: ROUND TWO
GROUP B: ENGLAND vs PAKISTAN
CLUB GROUND, RAWALPINDI: PAKISTAN WON BY 18 RUNS

Originally scheduled for the Monday this match was postponed until Tuesday the 13th after a downpour left the outfield totally saturated. The England management complained at the early abandonment, but should have been more unhappy with the late batting panic that cost them the match the next day when it appeared they would win.

They had no excuses. Mike Gatting won the toss and asked Pakistan to bat when the outfield was still damp and slow. He had beaten Javed Miandad rather than Imran Khan at the call of the coin. The Pakistani captain was suffering from food poisoning and although he batted, he was not fit to bowl.

At the home of the Pakistani President, General Zia, half an hour away from the Presidential Palace in Islamabad, England put on an early fielding display unfit to show any spectator let alone a powerful military leader. While their bowlers tried to take advantage of helpful conditions two straightforward catches were missed.

Gladstone Small and Derek Pringle moved the new ball around and Neil Foster quickly had Mansoor Akhtar edging to the keeper. Rameez Raja and Salim Malik took some advantage of the fielding lapses before Chris Broad drilled a direct hit throw from mid off to run out Rameez at the bowler's end.

Salim, playing to win, and Javed had to work hard to add a further 61 runs. They lasted until the 31st over when Australian umpire, Tony Crafter, gave Javed out lbw to Phil DeFreitas. This was a rare form of dismissal for Javed in Pakistan and he quickly showed his dislike for it, indicating that he had been struck above the pad. He dwelt at the crease for some time and found that the gathered English players were advising him where he could find the pavilion. Javed raised his bat at Gatting in a repeat of the pose he adopted in 1981 against Dennis Lillee pose. Bill Athey finally ushered him gently away in the direction Crafter had originally intended.

Pakistan were still struggling when the ailing Imran came in at 4-123 two overs after Javed's incident. He held firm, in more ways than one, while Ijaz Ahmed attacked. The youngster scored his 59 at a run a ball and hit a six and six fours. He nearly cleaned up Gatting with the bat when it slipped from his hands playing a sweep and flew out to square leg. The fifth wicket pair added 79, lifting the total beyond 200. Both were dismissed by Gladstone Small, Imran leaving the ground and going straight back to bed.

John Emburey began the final over of the innings with figures of 0-36 from nine overs. The total was 9-224. Six balls later, Pakistan were 15 runs better off. Abdul Qadir hit a four and a straight six and Pakistan, so long struggling with their run rate, had somehow finished with a competitive 239.

Graham Gooch and Broad launched the reply with a solid opening of 52 in 14 overs. Neither of the two left-arm pacemen, Wasim Akram nor Salim Jaffer could break through. But Qadir, his confidence already high, bowled Gooch. Broad struggled once Qadir and off-spinner Tauseef were working in tandem. He and Robinson added a further 40 runs, but when the left-hander was bowled by Tauseef, half England's quota of overs had been consumed and they were still 148 runs from their target.

Even though Gatting injected the batting with some greater urgency, Robinson was still sluggish so that the runs per over requirement was kept constantly around seven. Finally the Nottinghamshire opener's 21-over vigil ended when he was bowled by Qadir. Lamb's entrance boosted the game's tempo. He and his captain silenced the large crowd with some vigorous strokeplay and daring running between wickets. Gatting was stranded mid pitch in the 42nd over, only for Mansoor Akhtar's throw to miss the stumps at the bowler's end. Next ball Lamb had to dive back to regain his ground to avoid being run out.

Fifty-four runs were needed from eight overs when Gatting stepped right away from his stumps to hit Salim Jaffer through the off side and was bowled. The English press groaned at his misjudgement. Martin Johnson blamed Gatting's stroke for setting England on the road to defeat. However, there was no immediate sign that it would prove to be so costly. Lamb and Pringle reduced the equation to 34 runs from four overs with six wickets standing. A tight finish seemed in prospect. Sixteen balls later the match was over.

Lamb fell lbw trying to sweep Qadir. Emburey was run out going for a second run. Paul Downton swept also, only to top edge a catch to the keeper Salim Yousuf. Three wickets fell in four balls and England had slipped from 4-206 to 7-207. The three England fast bowlers, caught up in the frenzy hit and dived around the place which resulted in two more run outs and an lbw.

Pakistan, who had suffered all those disappointments against England in the Prudential World Cups were thrilled their opponents could also panic when under the pressure of closing overs. Abdul Qadir added to the local joy by being named Man of the Match.

General Zia enjoyed the result. He gave the Pakistani players a cheque for 100,000 rupees as a sign of gratitude for the win.

PAKISTAN		ENGLAND	
Mansoor Akhtar c Downton b Foster	6	G. A. Gooch b Abdul Qadir	21
Rameez Raja run out	15	B. C. Broad b Tauseef Ahmed	36
Salim Malik c Downton b DeFreitas	65	R. T. Robinson b Abdul Qadir	33
Javed Miandad lbw b DeFreitas	23	M. W. Gatting (capt) b Salim Jaffer	43
Ijaz Ahmed c Robinson b Small	59	A. J. Lamb lbw b Abdul Qadir	30
Imran Khan (capt) b Small	22	D. R. Pringle run out	8
Wasim Akram b DeFreitas	5	J. E. Emburey run out	1
Salim Yousuf (wk) not out	16	P. R. Downton (wk) c Salim Yousuf b Abdul Qadir	0
Abdul Qadir not out	12	P. A. J. DeFreitas not out	3
Extras lb10 w3 nb3	16	N. A. Foster run out	6
(50 overs)	7-239	G. C. Small lbw b Salim Jaffer	0
Did not bat: Tauseef Ahmed, Salim Jaffer		Extras b6 lb26 w8	40
1/13 2/51 3/112 4/123 5/202 6/210 7/210		(48.4 overs)	221
Bowling: DeFreitas 10-1-42-3; Foster 10-1-35-1;		1/52 2/92 3/141 4/186 5/206 6/207 7/207 8/213 9/221	
Small 10-1-47-2; Pringle 10-0-54-0; Emburey 10-0-51-0		10/221	
		Bowling: Wasim Akram 9-0-32-0; Salim Jaffer 9.4-0-42-2;	
		Tauseef Ahmed 10-0-39-1; Abdul Qadir 10-0-31-4;	
		Salim Malik 7-0-29-0; Mansoor Akhtar 3-0-16-0	

Umpires: A.R. Crafter R.B. Gupta

Toss: England   Points: Pakistan 4 England 0

GROUP B: SRI LANKA vs WEST INDIES
NATIONAL STADIUM, KARACHI: WEST INDIES WON BY 191 RUNS

West Indian captain, Viv Richards, was probably very annoyed by his side's narrow loss against England. Four days later he found the perfect way to exorcise his frustration; beat an innocuous Sri Lankan attack into utter submission. In 125 scintillating balls he put Kapil Dev's remarkable 175 at Tunbridge Wells in the previous Prudential Cup into second place on the list of highest ever World Cup scores. He added 182 with Desmond Haynes for the third wicket and 116 with Gus Logie for the fourth. Despite the reduction in this tournament of each innings to 50 overs, the West Indies made 4-360, at the time the highest ever World Cup total.

Duleep Mendis gave his opposite number first use of the wicket in the National Stadium in front of the smallest crowd of the tournament. When Ravi Ratnayake bowled Carlisle Best and then had Richie Richardson caught behind first ball Mendis must have nodded his head in self approval. Later there might have been greater regret.

Richards joined Haynes at 2-45. The West Indian captain avoided the hat trick then took control. He and Haynes used common sense at first to ensure the Sri Lankans were kept at bay. Once their position was established they let loose and the Sri Lankans lost all semblance of control. Richards reached his first 50 in 62 balls, 35 balls later he was celebrating his century. Still the mayhem continued, along the ground or in the air, Richards was unerring in his ability to strike the ball with immense power right off the middle, although he ensured the majority of his strokes were played with a straight bat. Ratnayake conceded 44 runs in two overs. Ashantha de Mel, so effective in England, was treated with contempt. Ninety-seven runs flowed during his 10-over stint.

Overshadowed by his captain's innings Haynes reached his own 100 at almost a run per ball. When Asanka Gurusinha finally bowled him, the Barbadian had hit one six and nine fours. His partnership with Richards had taken 177 balls. The stand between Richards and Logie lasted less than an hour. Logie gave his captain the strike and Richards raced from 100 to 150 in just 15 balls. Finally, going for his seventh six, the Antiguan holed out to Roshan Mohanama. His final 81 runs had come from just 33 deliveries. In addition to his six sixes Richards had struck 16 wonderful fours.

Sri Lanka needed 7.2 runs per over to win. As if to continue the day's theme, Mohanama and Brendon Kuruppu hit 24 runs from the first eight balls of the innings. When Mohanama was caught behind from Courtney Walsh's third ball Sri Lanka's charge ceased. They slipped to 3-57 and then opted for batting practice. Richards thought to save his main bowlers for more important contests so that even Richardson bowled some overs. Off spinner Roger Harper conceded 1.5 runs per over during his stint.

The futility of limited-overs matches when one side gives up was again in evidence during much of the Sri Lankan innings.

Richards' display was something special, but it ruined the second half of the game. The West Indian captain was made Man of the Match.

WEST INDIES		SRI LANKA	
D. L. Haynes b Gurusinha	109	R. S. Mahanama c Dujon b Walsh	12
C. A. Best b Ratnayake	18	D. S. B. P. Kuruppu (wk) lbw b Patterson	14
R. B. Richardson c Kuruppu b Ratnayake	0	A. P. Gurusinha b Hooper	36
I. V. A. Richards (capt) c Mahanama b de Mel	181	P. A. de Silva c Dujon b Hooper	9
A. L. Logie not out	31	A. Ranatunga not out	52
R. A. Harper not out	5	L. R. D. Mendis (capt) not out	37
Extras b4 lb8 w4 nb4	20	Extras b1 lb2 w6	9
(50 overs)	4-360	(50 overs)	4-169

Did not bat: P. J. L. Dujon (wk), C. L. Hooper, W. K. M. Benjamin, C. A. Walsh, B. P. Patterson

1/45 2/45 3/227 4/343

Bowling: John 10-1-48-0; Ratnayake 8-0-68-2; Anurasiri 10-0-39-0; de Mel 10-0-97-1; de Silva 6-0-35-0; Ranatunga 2-0-18-0; Gurusinha 4-0-43-1

Did not bat: R. S. Madugalle, J. R. Ratnayake, A. L. F. de Mel, V. B. John, S. D. Anurasiri

1/24 2/31 3/57 4/112

Bowling: Patterson 7-0-32-1; Walsh 7-0-23-1; Harper 10-2-15-0; Benjamin 4-0-11-0; Hooper 10-0-39-2; Richards 8-0-22-0; Richardson 4-0-22-0

Umpires: V.K. Ramaswamy S.J. Woodward

Toss: Sri Lanka   Points: West Indies 4 Sri Lanka 0

GROUP A: AUSTRALIA vs ZIMBABWE
CHEPAUK GROUND, MADRAS (CHENNAI): AUSTRALIA WON BY 96 RUNS

Talk prior to this match centred on the possibility of Zimbabwe repeating their shock victory from the opening round in 1983. It was not to be. Australia were a totally different outfit to the rabble from four years before and had no trouble in comfortably accounting for the Africans.

Not only did Australia play on the same arena where they had beaten India on the previous Friday, they were sent in to bat by John Traicos on exactly the same wicket. Again the early start offered the bowlers morning moisture and Kevin Curran quickly had David Boon caught behind. Ten runs later it was 2-20 when Dean Jones, for once, overestimated his running ability. Then, left-arm debutant, Malcolm Jarvis, dropped a dollied caught and bowled chance from Allan Border who was on one.

Border was too fine a player to not take advantage of such a let off. With the reliable and in-form Geoff Marsh he put on 113 in 20 overs. The left-handed Australian captain repeatedly punched the ball through the on side as the Zimbabwean bowling drifted on to his pads. He faced 88 balls and passed 4000 runs in limited-over internationals before being caught in the deep off Iain Butchart. Marsh and Simon O'Donnell fell soon after, then wicketkeeper Greg Dyer and Steve Waugh rallied the cause with a well-timed 47-run stand. Waugh finished with 45 in 40 balls before becoming the third of four run out victims. A few runs from Peter Taylor at the end of the innings lifted Australia to 9-235 from their 50 overs.

That was almost the total Zimbabwe had set Australia at Trent Bridge in 1983. Then it proved just enough. This, time on a wicket of variable bounce, it was enough with plenty to spare. The opening partnership between Grant Paterson and Robin Brown realised 13 runs in nine overs. O'Donnell bowled Brown as soon as he came on, Paterson was run out and so, almost inevitably, was Andy Pycroft.

Kevin Curran, fighting all the way, top scored, but he became the second of O'Donnell's four victims. Debutant Tim May's off-spin was more rewarding than Peter Taylors'. When the South Australian picked up a couple of wickets, including Hyderabad hero Dave Houghton, Zimbabwe were quickly sliding to defeat. They were able to hang on until the 43rd over, however their run rate was barely above three an over when it needed to be at least four and a half.

Captain Traicos promoted himself from 11 to 10 in the batting order. It made no difference. Craig McDermott and Steve Waugh shared 13 overs and conceded just 20 runs between them. Waugh's all-round effort won him the Man of the Match Award.

AUSTRALIA		ZIMBABWE	
G. R. Marsh c Curran b Shah	62	R. D. Brown b O'Donnell	3
D. C. Boon c Houghton b Curran	2	G. A. Paterson run out	16
D. M. Jones run out	2	D. L. Houghton (wk) c O'Donnell b May	11
A. R. Border (capt) c Shah b Butchart	67	A. J. Pycroft run out	9
S. R. Waugh run out	45	K. M. Curran b O'Donnell	30
S. P. O'Donnell run out	3	A. C. Waller c & b May	19
G. C. Dyer (wk) c Paterson b Butchart	27	A. H. Shah b McDermott	2
P. L. Taylor not out	17	P. W. E. Rawson b Reid	15
C. J. McDermott c Brown b Curran	1	I. P. Butchart c Jones b O'Donnell	18
T. B. A. May run out	1	A. J. Traicos (capt) c & b O'Donnell	6
Extras w8	8	M. P. Jarvis not out	1
(50 overs)	9-235	Extras b2 lb3 w3 nb1	9
Did not bat: B. A. Reid		(42.4 overs)	139

1/10 2/20 3/133 4/143 5/155 6/202 7/228 8/230 9/235

1/13 2/27 3/41 4/44 5/79 6/97 7/97 8/124 9/137 10/139

Bowling

Curran 8-0-29-2; Jarvis 10-0-40-0; Rawson 6-0-39-0; Butchart 10-1-59-2; Traicos 10-0-36-0; Shah 6-0-32-1

Bowling: McDermott 7-1-13-1; Reid 7-1-21-1; O'Donnell 9.4-1-39-4; Waugh 6-3-7-0; May 8-0-29-2; Taylor 5-0-25-0

Umpires: Khizar Hayat   D.R. Shepherd

Toss: Zimbabwe   Points: Australia 4 Zimbabwe 0

GROUP A: INDIA vs NEW ZEALAND
KARNATAKA STATE CA GROUND, BANGALORE: INDIA WON BY 16 RUNS

India left their disappointing defeat at Madras behind and travelled west into the hills to meet New Zealand at Bangalore. They had another 50,000 supporters in the ground to noisily urge them on and this time the fans did not go home disappointed.

The result of this match was seen as crucial to the fate of both sides. India could hardly afford to go down a second time, while New Zealand were lucky to get away with a win over Zimbabwe and had to prove they were a finals prospect.

After Jeff Crowe had won the toss and sent India in to bat, Kris Srikkanth ran out Sunil Gavaskar then himself in the opening overs of the match. Again the early start meant the outfield was slow when India began their innings. With the bounce in the wicket inconsistent the top order stressed itself. Srikkanth, who was coasting up the pitch when Ken Rutherford threw down the stumps, had committed his double kamikaze by the eighth over. Two overs and five runs later Dilip Vengsarkar checked a drive and hit the ball straight back to Willie Watson. India were teetering at 3-21.

Navjot Sidhu led the recovery. Uninhibited in his strokeplay as he had been at Madras, he dominated a 65 run stand with Mohammad Azharuddin, no mean feat in itself. A sweet straight drive off left-arm spinner Stephen Boock was one of four sixes struck by Sidhu in 71 balls. Each one brought a big roar from the crowd, but they went as quiet as they had been during the early collapse, when Dipak Patel started to eat his way through the Indian middle order. The off-spinning Kenyan, recruited by New Zealand from Worcestershire, dismissed Azharuddin, Sidhu and Ravi Shastri to leave India a still precarious 7-170 from 42 overs.

Kapil Dev, in his best Tunbridge Wells trancelike state, and Kiran More had eight overs to try and raise a worthy target. They got 82 in 51 balls. Kapil went to 72 in 58 balls with one six and four fours.

Kiwi opener Rutherford had replaced John Wright, suffering from influenza. He batted well and Martin Snedden proved to be of value as a restrained pinch hitter. Even when Martin Crowe was drawn out of his crease by Maninder Singh and controversially given out stumped by West Indian umpire, Dave Archer, the Kiwis kept in touch. Rutherford and Andrew Jones took them to 2-146. However, the spin trio of Maninder, Laxman Shivaramakrishnan and Ravi Shastri kept the runs in check.

Batting had to become more reckless, which led to rash shots and run outs. Of the last six batsmen who made it to the crease only wicketkeeper, Ian Smith got into double figures. The charismatic Kapil Dev won the Man of the Match Award for his important captain's innings.

INDIA		NEW ZEALAND	
K. Srikkanth run out	9	M. C. Snedden c Shastri b Azharuddin	33
S. M. Gavaskar run out	2	K. R. Rutherford c Srikkanth b Shastri	75
N. S. Sidhu c Jones b Patel	75	M. D. Crowe st More b Maninder	9
D. B. Vengsarkar c & b Watson	0	A. H. Jones run out	64
M. Azharuddin c Boock b Patel	21	J. J. Crowe (capt) c Vengsarkar b Maninder	7
R. J. Shastri c & b Patel	22	D. N. Patel run out	1
Kapil Dev (capt) not out	72	J. G. Bracewell c Maninder b Shastri	8
M. Prabhakar c & b Chatfield	3	I. D. S. Smith (wk) b Prabhakar	10
K. S.More (wk) not out	42	S. L. Boock not out	7
Extras lb4 w2	6	W. Watson not out	2
(50 overs)	7-252	Extras b5 lb9 w5 nb1	20
Did not bat: L. Shivaramakrishnan, Maninder Singh		(50 overs)	8-236
1/11 2/16 3/21 4/86 5/114 6/165 7/170		Did not bat: E. J. Chatfield	
Bowling: Chatfield 10-1-39-1; Snedden 10-1-56-0;		1/67 2/86 3/146 4/168 5/170 6/189 7/206 8/225	
Watson 9-0-59-1; Boock 4-0-26-0; Bracewell 7-0-32-0;		Bowling: Kapil Dev 10-1-54-0; Prabhakar 8-0-38-1;	
Patel 10-0-36-3		Azharuddin 4-0-11-1; Shivaramakrishnan 8-0-34-0;	
		Maninder 10-0-40-2; Shastri 10-0-45-2	

Umpires: D.M.Archer H.D.Bird

Toss: New Zealand   Points: India 4 New Zealand 0

FRIDAY 16 OCTOBER, SATURDAY 17 OCTOBER, SUNDAY 18 OCTOBER and MONDAY 19 OCTOBER
THE RELIANCE CUP: ROUND THREE
GROUP B: PAKISTAN vs THE WEST INDIES
GADDAFI STADIUM, LAHORE: PAKISTAN WON BY ONE WICKET

On the previous Tuesday Pakistan had enjoyed laying to rest the disappointments they had suffered at the hands of England in the previous World Cups. Now, three days later, they stole the show against the West Indies, whom they also could not beat in 1975, 1979 or 1983. What is more this was another thriller and it was the West Indies who succumbed to the pressure of a tense finish.

Abdul Qadir emerged as a late hero by hitting a six in the final over and scoring the winning two runs from the last ball of the match. Courtney Walsh, who was again the suffering bowler, was developing into some kind of unfortunate tragic figure.

The queues had formed tightly and early. Soon Gaddafi Stadium was filled for this clash between two of the most talented and exciting cricket teams in the world. Desmond Haynes and debutant, Phil Simmons kept the crowd pretty quiet during the first part of the day with an impressive opening partnership. Neither the rehabilitated Imran Khan nor Wasim Akram could shift the in form Barbadian or the newcomer, selected to replace Carlisle Best. Simmons hit eight fours during his run per ball 50 and he shared in a partnership of 91 with Haynes.

Both openers fell within six runs of each other and the rest of the West Indians struggled to build on the excellent base provided for them. Richards was an exception. He never threatened a repeat of his Karachi massacre, but batted fluently to reach another half century. When the West Indies reached 4-169 a testing total looked likely. Imran, though, showed the food poisoning had not affected his fitness and he returned to have his opposite number caught and then bowled Roger Harper next ball. Akram also had a better second spell, securing the important wickets of Carl Hooper and Jeff Dujon. Eventually the West Indies fell three balls short of batting out their overs.

Pakistan needing 217 to win, lost Mansoor Akhtar and Salim Malik cheaply before Rameez Raja and Javed Miandad added 64 runs for the third wicket in a struggling partnership. Harper dismissed Rameez to claim his 50th wicket in limited over internationals, Walsh bowled Ijaz Ahmed and when Carl Hooper held a catch off his own bowling six runs later to get rid of Miandad Pakistan were 5-110 from 35 overs and in deep trouble.

Imran, as he had at Rawalpindi, then played a steadying role while wicketkeeper Salim Yousuf went for his shots. He amazingly survived three chances in three balls from the luckless Eldine Baptiste before reviving his side's fortunes, dominating a 73-run stand with Imran in 11 overs. Yousuf went on to 56, the highest score in the match, in 49 balls with seven telling fours. He got his side within 21 runs of victory with four wickets in hand when Hooper finally held a chance off Walsh in the 48th over. Patrick Patterson then sent down a classic 49th over which saw Akram caught and Tauseef Ahmed run out while only two runs were conceded.

That left Qadir and Salim Jaffer with the unlikely task of hitting 14 runs from the final over for the last wicket. Walsh would have thought he had little to worry about when only two singles were scored from his first two balls. The equation was reduced to 10 runs required from three balls when Qadir launched into Walsh and hit him back down the ground and over the boundary for six. The crowd were ecstatic.

Walsh and Richards now feared the worst. Qadir squeezed two more runs from the fifth ball. Two more were needed from the last ball to win the match, although one would have tied the scores and given Pakistan victory on the fewer wickets lost rule.

Walsh ran in to Qadir who had scored all but one run from the final over so far. He arrived at the bowling crease and stopped. Jaffer was already half way up the wicket. Walsh could have ended the match there and then with a simple flick of the wrist. Instead he warned the number 11 for his transgression and went back to bowl again. This time it was delivered and Qadir sliced the ball behind point for the two runs that gave Pakistan a wonderful victory.

Walsh's hands were on his knees again. Richards lay flat on the ground. Soon they both had to charge towards the sanctuary of the dressing room as the invading hordes took over the arena. Qadir was their objective and without some aid he could have been trampled by the army of well-wishers. Despite the leg-spinner's heroics, Salim Yousuf received the Man of the Match Award.

Qadir had to be satisfied with a gift worth £20,000 from a very happy and wealthy businessman.

WEST INDIES		PAKISTAN	
D. L. Haynes b Salim Jaffer	37	Rameez Raja c Richards b Harper	42
P. V. Simmons c & b Tauseef Ahmed	50	Mansoor Akhtar b Patterson	10
R. B. Richardson c Ijaz Ahmed b Salim Jaffer	11	Salim Malik c Baptiste b Walsh	4
I. V. A. Richards (capt) c Salim Malik b Imran Khan	51	Javed Miandad c & b Hooper	33
A. L. Logie c Akhtar b Salim Jaffer	2	Ijaz Ahmed b Walsh	6
C. L. Hooper lbw b Wasim Akram	22	Imran Khan (capt) c Logie b Walsh	18
P. J. L. Dujon (wk) lbw b Wasim Akram	5	Salim Yousuf (wk) c Hooper b Walsh	56
R. A. Harper c Akhtar b Imran Khan	0	Wasim Akram c Richardson b Patterson	7
E. A.E. Baptiste b Imran Khan	14	Abdul Qadir not out	16
C. A. Walsh lbw b Imran Khan	7	Tauseef Ahmed run out	0
B. P. Patterson not out	0	Salim Jaffer not out	1
Extras b1 lb14 w2	17	Extras b5 lb12 w7	24
(49.3 overs)	216	(50 overs)	9-217

1/91 2/97 3/118 4/121 5/169 6/184 7/184 8/196 9/207
10/216

Bowling: Imran Khan 8.3-2-37-4; Wasim Akram 10-0-45-2;
Abdul Qadir 8-0-42-0; Tauseef Ahmed 10-2-35-1;
Salim Jaffer 10-0-30-3; Malik 3-0-12-0

1/23 2/28 3/92 4/104 5/110 6/183 7/200 8/202 9/203

Bowling: Patterson 10-1-51-2; Walsh 10-1-40-4;
Baptiste 8-1-33-0; Harper 10-0-28-1; Hooper 10-0-38-1;
Richards 2-0-10-0;

Umpires: A.R. Crafter S.J. Woodward

Toss: West Indies   Points: Pakistan 4 West Indies 0

GROUP B: ENGLAND vs SRI LANKA
SHAHI BAGH STADIUM, PESHAWAR: ENGLAND WON ON FASTER SCORING RATE

Playing in 21 different venues around India and Pakistan meant there was plenty of travelling to do for those involved in the 1987 Reliance Cup. Sri Lanka had to cope with more packing and travelling than anyone else, this time scooting from the southern coast of Pakistan in Karachi to Peshawar in the northwest corner of the country, near the Khyber Pass. The fatigue brought on by the constant disruption and annoyance of uncomfortable travelling may have partially accounted for Duleep Mendis' side performing so poorly in the tournament.

Certainly, on the Saturday of Round Three, England had as much trouble with the weather as they did with the friendly bowling and tame batting of their opponents. Even as Gatting won the toss and elected to bat, thunder clouds were building up to the west of the city. Three quarters of an hour into the contest a few big spots of rain landed on Gupta and Ramaswamy. It looked like Graham Gooch had to convince the two umpires that it was worth staying out on the ground.

Meantime he and Chris Broad were setting England up for a big score with strong opening partnership. Gooch was at his fluent and powerful best on a flat wicket. Broad again struggled for timing and eventually after taking 60 balls to make 28 misjudged a slog at Ravi Ratnayake. Gatting not only changed his habit of bowling first and his line-up, he also promoted himself in the batting order to good effect. While Gooch went on to 84 in 100 balls with eight fours, Gatting clubbed and clipped his way to 58 in 63 balls.

The England captain added 76 in 12 overs with Allan Lamb to take the England innings well beyond 200 with plenty of overs to come. The ground was bathed in sunshine, but the clouds swelled and closed in. In this volatile part of the world a big clap of thunder during the lunch break had nervous patrons worrying about terrorist attacks. Outside the ground there was a political demonstration.

Indeed, the crowd in the ground was a small one, leaving plenty of room on the bare concrete terraces. They might have been entertained by the ongoing slaughter of the bowlers. Gatting was bowled by Rumesh Ratnayake to make it 3-218. Emburey came in ahead of Bill Athey and with Lamb stepped up the tempo even further. In five overs the South African and the South African Rebel added 66. Lamb was at his punishing best, hitting two sixes and three fours in just 58 balls. Emburey faced just 19 balls and hit a six and three fours. One hundred and one runs came from the final 10 overs.

The Sri Lankans looked out of their depth. They were never likely to get the 297 runs needed to win. The only real chance they had was for the match to get washed out and that remained a possibility. Another part of Peshawar was awash. If the Sri Lankan innings did not contain 25 overs the game would be declared to have 'no result' and would be started again the following day. England moved at great speed, running between overs and refusing to take drinks breaks. Sri Lanka still lost three early wickets. Then when Gooch completed the 25th over of the innings, everything could go back to a regular 1987 on-field pace.

Then the rains arrived and everyone beat a hasty retreat. However, there was no washout and after having their innings reduced by five overs and their target to 267 Sri Lanka resumed batting. Arjuna Ranatunga and Ranjan Madugalle put on 62 for the fourth wicket either side of the interruption. On a wicket that stayed lower as the day wore on neither they nor the batsmen that followed could score with the necessary energy, though. Emburey and fellow off-spinner, Eddie Hemmings conceded just 57 runs between them from 20 overs.

Gatting even gave Bill Athey, Chris Broad and eventual Man of the Match, Allan Lamb a bowl. That might have entertained the English team. Otherwise the cricket was pointless and it might have been better if the rain had returned.

ENGLAND		SRI LANKA	
G. A. Gooch c & b Anurasiri	84	R. S. Mohanama c Gooch b Pringle	11
B. C. Broad c de Silva b J. R.Ratnayake	28	D. S. B. P. Kuruppu (wk) c Hemmings b Emburey	13
M. W. Gatting (capt) b R. J.Ratnayake	58	A. P. Gurusinha run out	1
A. J. Lamb c de Silva b J. R.Ratnayake	76	R. S. Madugalle b Hemmings	30
J. E. Emburey not out	30	A. Ranatunga lbw b DeFreitas	40
C. W. J. Athey not out	2	L. R. D. Mendis (capt) run out	14
Extras lb13 w5	18	P. A. de Silva c Emburey b Hemmings	6
(50 overs)	4-296	J. R. Ratnayake c Broad b Emburey	1
Did not bat: D. R. Pringle, P. R. Downton (wk),		R. J. Ratnayake not out	14
P. A. J. DeFreitas, E. E. Hemmings, G. C. Small		V. B.J ohn not out	8
1/89 2/142 3/218 4/289		Extras b2 lb9 w6 nb3	20
Bowling: J. R.Ratnayake 9-0-62-2; John 10-0-44-0;		(45 overs)	8-158
de Silva 7-0-33-0; R. J.Ratnayake 10-0-60-1;		Did not bat: S. D. Anurasiri	
Anurasiri 8-0-44-1; Ranatunga 6-0-40-0		1/31 2/32 3/37 4/99 5/105 6/113 7/119 8/137	
		Bowling: DeFreitas 9-2-24-1; Small 7-0-27-0;	
		Pringle 4-0-11-1; Emburey 10-1-26-1; Hemmings 10-1-31-2;	
		Gooch 2-0-9-0; Athey 1-0-10-0; Broad 1-0-6-0;	
		Lamb 1-0-3-0	

Umpires: R.B. Gupta   V.K. Ramaswamy
Toss: England   Points: England 4 Sri Lanka 0

GROUP A: INDIA vs ZIMBABWE
WANKHEDE STADIUM, BOMBAY(MUMBAI): INDIA WON BY 8 WICKETS.

A clatter of wickets, a burst of runs and by 2pm everyone could pack up and go home as India made short work of Zimbabwe in perhaps the most featureless contest of the 1987 Reliance Cup. The 22,000 who turned up at Wankhede stadium made no complaints at being short changed. They were gratified enough by their heroes' dominance of the Africans.

John Traicos thought batting first would give his side their best chance of victory. The other four Group A matches in India had all been won so far by the team who had set a target. What was essential to success was that top order wickets were not lost while there was early humidity, moisture and movement. Zimbabwe failed to achieve that prerequisite. All-rounder, Manoj Prahakar, took the new-ball, swung it appreciably and in a devastating spell claimed four wickets in 17 balls to leave Zimbabwe in tatters. Dave Houghton had quickly come down to earth being bowled for a duck. Kevin Curran was caught behind and also failed to score.

Only Andy Pycroft stood firm. So often a disappointment, he was the only Zimbabwean batsman to do himself justice this day. Pycroft came in at 2-12 and was last out in the 45th over after making a gallant 61 in 102 balls. He and second-game left-arm seamer, Malcolm Jarvis, took the score from 9-99 to 135, before Ravi Shastri finally had Pycroft stumped. The wicket had flattened out and after Prabhakar's burst every other wicket in the match was taken by a spinner. The 10th-wicket stand of 36 was the highest of the innings. Nevertheless Zimbabwe had made their lowest total in World Cup competition.

It made little impression on India. They wanted to lift their run rate, conscious of the fact that if things got tight on their group table a strong rate might be valuable. Sunil Gavaskar began the assignment by dealing solely in boundaries for his first 36 runs. He lasted 51 balls and put on 76 for the first wicket with Kris Srikkanth before becoming the day's third stumping victim.

Traicos also removed Srikkanth and withstood the Indian onslaught well. The other bowlers were flayed and after an hour and 40 minutes in the 28th over India had completed their second Reliance Cup victory. Prabhakar, at the crease with a rampant Dilip Vengsarkar when the winning runs were scored, was named Man of the Match.

ZIMBABWE		INDIA	
G. A. Paterson b Prabhakar	6	K. Srikkanth c Paterson b Traicos	31
K. J. Arnott lbw b Prabhakar	1	S. M. Gavaskar st Houghton b Traicos	43
D. L. Houghton (wk) b Prabhakar	0	M. Prabhakar not out	11
A. J. Pycroft st More b Shastri	61	D. B. Vengsarkar not out	46
K. M. Curran c More b Prabhakar	0	Extras lb1 w4	5
A. C. Waller st More b Maninder	16	(27.5 overs)	2-136
I. P. Butchart c Shivaramakrishnan b Maninder	10	Did not bat: N. S. Sidhu, M. Azharuddin, Kapil Dev (capt),
A. H. Shah c More b Maninder	0	R. J. Shastri ,K. S. More ,L. Shivaramakrishnan,
M. A. Meman run out	19	Maninder Singh
A. J. Traicos c Gavaskar b Shivaramakrishnan	0	1/76 2/80
M. P. Jarvis not out	8	Bowling: Curran 6-0-32-0; Jarvis 4-0-22-0;
Extras b2 lb6 w6	14	Butchart 3-0-22-0; Traicos 8-0-27-2; Meman 6.5-0-34-0
(44.2 overs)	135		

1/3 2/12 3/13 4/13 5/47 6/67 7/67 8/98 9/99 10/135
Bowling: Kapil Dev 8-1-17-0; Prabhakar 8-1-19-4;
Maninder 10-0-21-3; Azharuddin 1-0-6-0;
Shivaramakrishnan 9-0-36-1; Shastri 8.2-0-28-1

Umpires: Mahboob Shah   D.R. Shepherd
Toss: Zimbabwe   Points: India 4 Zimbabwe 0

GROUP A: AUSTRALIA vs NEW ZEALAND
NEHRU STADIUM, INDORE: AUSTRALIA WON BY 3 RUNS

A 30-overs-per-side slather-and-whack contest reached a thrilling climax from which Australia once more emerged victorious. The breakneck cricket was brought about by heavy rain, the first at Indore in October for 35 years, which flooded the ground on the Sunday and made it still unfit at the start of the Monday. Even when play began over three hours late the run-ups and outfield were very wet.

New Zealand's assistant manager Glenn Turner argued that the match should be abandoned. The day before groundsmen had been knee-deep in water as they used picks and an assortment of other implements to clear blocked drains.

Jeff Crowe sent the Australians in to bat. Soon the in-form Geoff Marsh drove at Snedden and was caught by the sole slip, John Wright. That brought together Dean Jones and David Boon who batted with uninhibited freedom to add 117 runs in 98 balls. They reached their century stand in 11 overs and were very severe on off-spinners John Bracewell and Dipak Patel.

Boon clubbed Patel down ground, while a pull sweep by Jones off Bracewell sent the ball sailing over the admittedly short mid wicket boundary and out of the stadium. He had got off the mark by playing a reverse sweep from the same bowler.

Fieldsman lost their footing on a few occasions, but there was never any risk of serious injury. Patel exacted a modicum of revenge when Jones, after making 52 in 49 balls, lofted a full toss to a juggling Ken Rutherford deep on the on side. Boon continued on at a run a ball to 87 until he lofted Martin Snedden straight, only for Wright to take a fine diving catch to the left of the sightscreen. The Tasmanian had added 37 with Allan Border. The captain played all sorts of strokes for 26 balls to take his side to the verge of 200 when the overs ran out. Steve Waugh, just 22 years old and already a limited-overs-international veteran passed the 1000 run landmark less than two years after his debut.

Two hundred was New Zealand's target. It would require 6.66 runs per over. They were given a perfect start, too, by Rutherford and Wright, who put on 83 in just 12 overs. Rutherford danced at Craig McDemott and cracked him over mid-on for six. He danced again at Simon O'Donnell, but failed to pick his slower ball and was bowled. O'Donnell had Wright caught behind eleven runs later which left much of the responsibility for scoring with Martin Crowe. He responded magnificently racing to 58 in 46 balls and shared short productive partnerships with Andrew Jones and Patel.

When the final over began, Crowe was on strike and seven runs were needed with four wickets in hand. If the bowler had been the 1987 version of Courtney Walsh the Kiwi win would have been a formality. Waugh was a different proposition. He had already bowled his magical final 'iceman' over against India. He said he had watched Kapil Dev bowling at the end of an innings for India and had learned from that champion all-rounder how to approach the pressure task.

Crowe admits he 'choked' on the first ball failing to decide whether to hit the ball straight or over the off-side. The compromise was a lofted drive which swirled over cover. Geoff Marsh ran around from his off-side sweeping position and held a running catch.

"What had I done?" Crowe lamented in his autobiography *Out on a Limb*. He confessed that on his return to the dressing room he put his head in his hands and sulked and that he was so distressed he did not bat well for the rest of the tournament.

Despite Crowe's departure the game was still there to be won. But Waugh fired in a quicker yorker. Ian Smith played over and around the ball; it cannoned off his pads and onto his stumps. Seven runs were still needed with only four balls and two wickets left. Singles were scored from the third and fourth balls. From the fifth, Willie Watson backed away and slapped the ball hard. He made contact but hit the ball straight back up the pitch to Waugh. Snedden, backing up, as he had to, had no chance of getting back. Watson needed to hit a six to win the match from the final ball. An underarm would have ensured against that.

Instead Waugh bowled straight and full and restricted Watson to a single. The Australian hero was surrounded by his teammates. Border admitted Waugh was the only one in the side who did not seem to have legs of jelly at the climax.

David Boon received the Man of the Match Award.

AUSTRALIA		NEW ZEALAND	
D. C. Boon c Wright b Snedden	87	K. R. Rutherford b O'Donnell	37
G. R. Marsh c J. Crowe b Snedden	5	J. G. Wright c Dyer b O'Donnell	47
D. M. Jones c Rutherford b Patel	52	M. D. Crowe c Marsh b Waugh	58
A. R. Border (capt) c M. Crowe b Chatfield	34	A. H. Jones c Marsh b McDermott	15
S. R. Waugh not out	13	J. J. Crowe (capt) c & b Reid	3
T. M. Moody not out	0	D. N. Patel run out	13
Extras b1 lb5 w2	8	J. G. Bracewell c & b Reid	6
(30 overs)	4-199	I. D. S. Smith (wk) b Waugh	1
Did not bat: S. P. O'Donnell, G. C. Dyer (wk),		M. C. Snedden run out	1
C. J. McDermott, T. B. A. May, B. A. Reid		E. J. Chatfield not out	0
1/17 2/134 3/171 4/196		W. Watson not out	2
Bowling: Snedden 6-0-35-2; Chatfield 6-0-28-1;		Extras b4 lb5 w4	13
Watson 6-0-34-0; Patel 6-0-45-1; Bracewell 6-0-51-0		(30 overs)	9-196
		1/83 2/94 3/133 4/140 5/165 6/183 7/193 8/193 9/195	
		Bowling: McDermott 6-0-30-1; Reid 6-0-38-2; May 6-0-39-0;	
		O'Donnell 6-0-44-2; Waugh 6-0-36-2	

Umpires: D.M. Archer   Khizar Hayat

Toss: New Zealand   Points: Australia 4 New Zealand 0

TUESDAY 20 OCTOBER, WEDNESDAY 21 OCTOBER, THURSDAY 22 OCTOBER and FRIDAY 23 OCTOBER
RELIANCE CUP: ROUND FOUR
GROUP B: PAKISTAN vs ENGLAND
NATIONAL STADIUM, KARACHI: PAKISTAN WON BY 7 WICKETS

Pakistan ensured their place in the semi-finals in front of an enthusiastic, if at times badly behaved, gathering in Karachi.

It was a victory based around the performances of two quality bowlers, a partnership between two quality batsmen and two ill-advised sweep shots by Englishmen. The day before the game the sweeping was being done by soldiers with metal detectors which reminded everyone that the security and efficiency of the tournament could not be taken for granted. The conscientiousness of the local organisers was commendable and may have spilled over to Imran Khan who generously offered England the chance to bat first on a flat wicket on a very warm morning.

If Salim Yousuf had held an edge from Tim Robinson, Imran would have made the breakthrough he sought in the first over. Instead he had to wait until Graham Gooch, after a couple of powerful strokes, top edged a shovel hook to Wasim Akram, one of two fieldsmen out for the shot, at 26. Robinson struggled on without ever looking in form until in Abdul Qadir's second over his cut missed a straight top-spinner. So England were an unimpressive 2-52 when Mike Gatting joined Bill Athey. In the next 24 overs it seemed as if the third wicket pair had put their side into a match-winning position. After Yousuf had missed a stumping and Javed Miandad dropped him in slips, the English captain put on 135 with his stylish Yorkshire partner.

Athey was in particularly fine form. Noted journalist Scyld Berry rated his 86 the equal of any English innings in the tournament. He got off the mark first ball with a boundary glided through slips off Wasim Akram. Later he drove Tauseef Ahmed for six over long on and pulled Salim Malik for another six.

Gatting, who had further unpleasant words with Javed during his 65 ball innings, hit Qadir for six over long on and England reached 2-187 with 13 overs to go. Finally Athey incurred the wrath of the entire English press contingent when he hit two boundaries and then played a reverse sweep at Tauseef and was bowled. That one rash moment spoiled 102 balls of exquisite batting that included four fours as well as the two sixes. In the next over Gatting swept in orthodox fashion at Qadir and top edged a simple catch to Yousuf. Now Imran and Qadir really went to work.

John Emburey was bemused by the spinner and hit on the full in front of his stumps, Paul Downton nicked a well pitched outswinger from the Pakistani captain and Allan Lamb had his leg stump removed by one that swung in late as he attempted a cut. 2-187 had become 7-206. The capacity crowd were very pleased. Imran stood tall and wiped his brow. Neil Foster and Phil DeFreitas halted a complete collapse, but England could hardly have been satisfied with a return of 7-57 from those final 13 overs. The wicket showed no sign of dying as had occurred in other games and the weather remained good for batsmen.

England had to get an early breakthrough if they were to protect 244. Foster had Rameez Raja lofting a shot to square leg when he was six, only for Gatting to drop the straightforward chance. This allowed Rameez and Mansoor Akhtar to put on 61 for the first wicket which gave Pakistan exactly the start they wanted. Salim Malik and Rameez were then able to take full control against an out-of-sorts English attack. Rameez had two more let-offs, a close stumping call off Emburey and another dropped chance on 62 to Athey at mid-on off Eddie Hemmings. He took full advantage of the opportunities he had been given by going on to complete his first limited-overs-international 100 and added 167 in 29 overs with the polished Malik.

The Pakistani pair ran England ragged. Rameez's innings of 113 included 62 singles as well as five fours. Malik hit 43 singles and seven stylish boundaries in an innings which lasted 92 balls. The greatest threat to Pakistan's progress towards victory came from some of their own irresponsible spectators who, perhaps tiring of seeing one single after another, started throwing substantial missiles on to the playing field. Play was held up for 10 minutes while the boundary edge was cleared. Gatting handed one rock to umpire Ramaswamy who held it up as if it were a second new ball. The English bowlers might have shown more penetration if such a change had been made. DeFreitas had been ill after his first spell, although it was Gladstone Small whose accuracy had been most off-colour.

Rameez and Malik clinically reduced the target. With twenty overs to go Pakistan required 128. Ten overs later 65 were required and the rate was almost identical. Neither batsman made it right through to the end. It did not matter. Ijaz Ahmed hit the winning run from the last ball of the 49th over to give Pakistan their fourth victory in four starts. For once a bowler was recognised ahead of batsmen, Imran receiving the Man of the Match Award. More cash flowed the way of the Pakistanis.

ENGLAND		PAKISTAN	
G. A. Gooch c Wasim Akram b Imran Khan	16	Rameez Raja c Gooch b DeFreitas	113
R. T. Robinson b Abdul Qadir	16	Mansoor Akhtar run out	29
C. W. J. Athey b Tauseef Ahmed	86	Salim Malik c Athey b Emburey	88
M. W. Gatting (capt) c Salim Yousuf b Abdul Qadir	60	Javed Miandad not out	6
A. J. Lamb b Imran Khan	9	Ijaz Ahmed not out	4
J. E. Emburey lbw b Abdul Qadir	3	Extras lb6 w1	7
P. R. Downton (wk) c Salim Yousuf b Imran Khan	6	(49 overs)	3-247
P. A. J. DeFreitas c Salim Yousuf b Imran Khan	13	Did not bat: Imran Khan (capt), Salim Yousuf (wk),	
N. A. Foster not out	20	Wasim Akram, Abdul Qadir, Tauseef Ahmed, Salim Jaffer	
G. C. Small run out	0	1/61 2/228 3/243	
E. E. Hemmings not out	4	Bowling: DeFreitas 8-2-41-1; Foster 10-0-51-0;	
Extras lb7 w4	11	Hemmings 10-1-40-0; Emburey 10-0-34-1; Small 9-0-63-0;	
(50 overs)	9-244	Gooch 2-0-10-0	

1/26 2/52 3/187 4/187 5/192 6/203 7/206 8/230 9/230

Bowling: Imran Khan 9-0-37-4; Wasim Akram 8-0-44-0;
Tauseef Ahmed 10-0-46-1; Abdul Qadir 10-0-31-3;
Salim Jaffer 8-0-44-0; Salim Malik 5-0-35-0

Umpires: A.R. Crafter   V.K. Ramaswamy

Toss: Pakistan   Points: Pakistan 4 England 0

GROUP B: SRI LANKA vs WEST INDIES
GREEN PARK, KANPUR: WEST INDIES WON BY 25 RUNS

Unlike the earlier Viv Richards exhibition match in Karachi this clash was reasonably close at certain stages. Eventually the West Indies won which meant their clash with England at Jaipur would in effect be a knockout quarter final. Sri Lanka's long south eastern journey seemed to agree with a few of their players who put up their best performance since Round One. Possibly it was because they were a little bit closer to home than they had been.

Richards won the toss and batted. His side found that the wicket was very slow and that the Sri Lankan finger spinners Don Anurasiri, Aravinda de Silva and Sridharan Jeganathan were difficult to score from. Between them they picked up four good wickets and conceded just 122 runs from their combined 30 overs. It was de Silva, later to emerge as one of the best batsmen in the world, who claimed the prize scalp of Richards.

Desmond Haynes and Phil Simmons got the West Indies away to steady start of 62. Haynes became the first victim of the spin trio and Richie Richardson could make little progress against the slow low turn. However, Simmons without ever breaking loose, hit strongly when the opportunity presented itself. He batted 37 overs, faced 122 balls and hit 11 fours before being fourth out at 155. Into Simmons' shoes stepped Gus Logie. He batted throughout the remainder of the innings using a wide range of shots, some with names, others without. The 22 put on in the final overs by Logie and Courtney Walsh were invaluable.

Sri Lanka's reply took a long time to get going. Almost immediately Patrick Patterson bowled Roshan Mahanama for a duck. There were no further shocks and Brendon Kuruppu batted steadily if a little slowly. It was not until the short robust left-hander, Arjuna Ranatunga, asserted himself that Sri Lanka looked at all likely to get anywhere near 237. He hit Courtney Walsh for two consecutive sixes. Ranatunga's assault was almost single handed. Apart form Simmons and Logie, no West Indians passed 24 and Ranatunga's brave fight was the only Sri Lankan innings over 33. The man who would later captain his country to their greatest triumph in international cricket reduced the target to 72 runs in eight overs then 37 from 24 deliveries.

Then at such a crucial time, he was deprived of the strike and the run flow was stemmed. From the next 18 balls only nine runs were scored. Sri Lanka required 28 from the 50th and last over of the innings. Ranatunga was still in and Walsh had an over left to bowl. Sparing himself and Walsh, Richards called on Winston Benjamin. The over cost two.

Ranatunga's 92-ball innings had been a mighty effort, but Simmons was named Man of the Match.

WEST INDIES		SRI LANKA	
D. L. Haynes b Anurasiri	24	R. S. Mahanama b Patterson	0
P. V. Simmons c Madugalle b J. R.Ratnayake	89	D. S. B. P. Kuruppu (wk) c & b Hooper	33
R. B. Richardson c Mahanama b Jeganathan	4	J. R. Ratnayake lbw b Benjamin	15
I. V. A. Richards (capt) c R. J.Ratnayake b de Silva	14	R. S. Madugalle c Haynes b Harper	18
A. L. Logie not out	65	A. Ranatunga not out	86
C. L. Hooper st Kuruppu b de Silva	6	L. R. D. Mendis (capt) b Walsh	19
P. J. L. Dujon (wk) c Kuruppu b J. R.Ratnayake	6	P. A. de Silva b Patterson	8
R. A. Harper b J. R.Ratnayake	3	R. J. Ratnayake c Walsh b Patterson	5
W. K.M. Benjamin b R. J.Ratnayake	0	S. Jeganathan run out	3
C. A. Walsh not out	9	V. B. John not out	1
Extras b2 lb7 w7	16	Extras b2 lb11 nb10	23
(50overs)	8-236	(50 overs)	8-211
Did not bat: B. P. Patterson		Did not bat: S. D. Anurasiri	
1/62 2/80 3/115 4/155 5/168 6/199 7/213 8/214		1/2 2/28 3/66 4/86 5/156 6/184 7/200 8/209	
Bowling: J. R.Ratnayake 10-1-41-3; John 5-0-25-0;		Bowling: Patterson 10-0-31-3; Walsh 9-2-43-1;	
R. J.Ratnayake 5-0-39-1; Jeganathan 10-1-33-1;		Benjamin 10-0-43-1; Harper 10-1-29-1; Hooper 8-0-35-1;	
Anurasiri 10-1-46-1; de Silva 10-0-43-2		Richards 3-0-17-0	

Umpires: Amanullah Khan   Mahboob Shah

Toss: Sri Lanka   Points: West Indies 4 Sri Lanka 0

GROUP A: INDIA vs AUSTRALIA FEROZ SHAH KOTLA, NEW DELHI: INDIA WON BY 56 RUNS

Australia came back to earth with a thud as they were totally outbatted by the Indians in front of an excited packed house at the Feroz Shah Kotla ground on the Thursday match of Round Four.

The Australians got a few things wrong for this particular match. Allan Border won the toss and, even though his side had been successful in each of their three matches batting first, elected to bowl. Then, in the belief that Indian batsmen play spin better then pace and because the boundaries were short, Tim May was omitted for the 20-year-old seamer, Andrew Zesers.

Neither tactic worked and later Border admitted that perhaps he and his fellow selectors were wrong. Right from ball one the Indians went for their shots and showed themselves to be in prime form. When Kris Srikkanth was caught behind off Craig McDermott's second ball in the 10th over the total was already 50. He had played the shot of the morning. A square drive off Bruce Reid, reminiscent of the one that he crashed to the point boundary in the 1983 final off Andy Roberts. Sunil Gavaskar continued to sign off from international cricket with a series of beautiful shots. This innings amounted to 61 before he chopped a Simon O'Donnell delivery onto his stumps, bent down, handed over a bail and left contentedly to tumultuous applause from an appreciative throng of more than 40,000.

Navjot Sidhu also took advantage of the fast outfield and short boundaries. His third consecutive half century included a trademark straight six off young Zesers, who despite the onslaught, was as economical as any of the Australian bowlers. Sidhu was third out at 167, and Kapil Dev did not last long before becoming McDermott's third victim. The third and fourth half centuries of the innings were scored by Dilip Vengsarkar and Mohammad Azharuddin. Their 65 run stand for the fourth wicket in 10 overs was a treat. Vengsarkar's 63 lasted 59 balls. Azharuddin's 54 not out, which included a memorable on-drive off Reid in the final over and one six, another straight drive, this time off Steve Waugh, took just 47 balls.

He was still going strong when the 50 overs was up and it was to be wondered what sort of a total India would have finished with if the matches were still 60 overs. Australia had an awesome task in front of them if they were to score the 290 required to keep their unbeaten record intact. For a time Geoff Marsh and David Boon gave the impression that such an assignment was quite reasonable. They had no more trouble with medium pace than had the Indians and added 88 in 18 overs. Boon was his usual pugnacious self, using hooks, pulls and cuts to good effect.

The spinners were much harder to handle. Maninder Singh was introduced by Kapil Dev in the 16th over, Ravi Shastri in the

17th. Maninder immediately looked threatening. In his second over the Sikh lured Marsh out to drive with a beautifully flighted delivery that spun a long way past the outisde edge of his bat and presented Kiran More with a straightforward stumping. Sixteen runs later Boon, who had hit seven fours in 55 balls, backed away to cut Shastri. The ball went through to More and there was a confident appeal for a catch. Umpire Khalid Aziz gave Boon out.

The Tasmanian showed his astonishment at the decision and when he slowly walked away he was booed by sections of the crowd and had something to say back to a few spectators. Australia never really made a serious challenge to India's total from that point. The two spinners slowed the run rate, conceding just 69 from their combined allocation of 20 overs. Maninder had Border caught at long on and Australia in the 32nd over were slipping at 3-135. Kapil rested his main spinner for a couple of overs, brought him back on and Maninder instantly had Dean Jones caught at cover. Once more he had beaten a quality batsman with flight. Australia were 4-164 in the 36th over.

Steve Waugh after a worthwhile 53-ball innings became Kapil's first victim of the tournament. He had watched Azharuddin, brought into the attack after paceman Chetan Sharma broke down, remove O'Donnell's leg stump with a yorker. The future Indian captain went on to claim the Man of the March Award and the best bowling figures with 3-19. His catch off his own bowling had stopped a very hot straight drive from McDermott from drilling him between the eyes. When Azharuddin removed Reid, Australia were all out with an over to go for 233, the game long since out of their reach.

The Feroz Shah Kotla ground can be a featureless stadium of high wire fences and bland concrete terraces. On this day, with 40,000 celebrating an important win, it was a sea of noise, colour and happiness. India, like their western neighbours, now seemed certain of their semi-final place.

INDIA		AUSTRALIA	
K. Srikkanth c Dyer b McDermott	26	G. R. Marsh st More b Maninder	33
S. M. Gavaskar b O'Donnell	61	D. C. Boon c More b Shastri	62
N. S. Sidhu c Moody b McDermott	51	D. M. Jones c Kapil Dev b Maninder	36
D. B. Vengsarkar c O'Donnell b Reid	63	A. R. Border (capt) c Prabhakar b Maninder	12
Kapil Dev (capt) c Dyer b McDermott	3	S. R. Waugh c Sidhu b Kapil Dev	42
M. Azharuddin not out	54	T. M. Moody run out	2
R. J. Shastri c & b Waugh	8	S. P. O'Donnell b Azharuddin	5
K. S. More not out	5	G. C. Dyer (wk) c Kapil Dev b Prabhakar	15
Extras b1 lb6 w11	18	C. J. McDermott c & b Azharuddin	4
(50 overs)	6-289	A. K. Zesers not out	2
Did not bat: M. Prabhakar, Chetan Sharma, Maninder Singh		B. A. Reid c Sidhu b Azharuddin	1
1/50 2/125 3/167 4/178 5/243 6/274		Extras lb11 w8	19
Bowling: O'Donnell 9-0-45-1; Reid 10-0-65-1;		(49 overs)	233
Waugh 10-0-59-1; McDermott 10-0-61-3; Moody 2-0-15-0;		1/88 2/104 3/135 4/164 5/167 6/182 7/214 8/227 9/231	
Zesers 9-1-37-0		10/233	
		Bowling: Kapil Dev 8-1-41-1; Prabhakar 10-0-56-1;	
		Maninder 10-0-34-3; Shastri 10-0-35-1; Sharma 7.1-0-37-0;	
		Azharuddin 3.5-0-19-3	

Umpires: Khalid Aziz   D.R. Shepherd
Toss: Australia   Points: India 4 Australia 0

GROUP A: NEW ZEALAND vs ZIMBABWE
EDEN GARDENS, CALCUTTA: NEW ZEALAND WON BY 4 WICKETS

Zimbabwe once more challenged New Zealand without being able to clinch their first victory of the Reliance Cup. A contest in many parts of the world between these two sides would be hard to sell. Not in Calcutta. Fifty thousand cricket-mad inhabitants of the massive crowded city would front up to Eden Gardens to watch a match between Greenland and Liechtenstein.

Jeff Crowe sent Zimbabwe into bat and his side had an immediate breakthrough, Grant Paterson being run out for a duck. There were no further early dramas as the other opener, Ali Shah, settled in to play a solid innings. He let his partner, Kevin Arnott, do the bulk of the scoring. The pair had added 81 and Arnott had completed his half century when Shah changed his call mid-run and left his partner stranded. Still Shah soldiered on, lasting until the 35th over, by which time the score was only 121. The New Zealanders may have been disappointed by his dismissal because it opened the way for Dave Houghton and Andy Pycroft to up the tempo of the innings. Houghton once more demonstrated his relish for Kiwi bowling by racing to 50 in 58 balls. This time he went no further, but his confidence rubbed off on Pycroft who took over the major role towards the closure of the innings.

Zimbabwe's 227 was hardly an imposing total to pursue, especially when Kevin Curran and Malcolm Jarvis failed to make an early breakthrough. Then Eddo Brandes and Ali Shah gave the match a shake as New Zealand slipped from 0-37 to 3-56. The Crowe brothers, Martin and captain, Jeff, responded with a partnership of 69. Martin was seen as the key and he cruised to 58 off as many deliveries. His dismissal, caught in the deep by Iain Butchart when sweeping Ali Shah, the best of the Zimbabwean bowlers, left New Zealand 4-125. The game looked wide open again and it might have been if Jeff Crowe had not played his best innings of the competition.

Crowe was able to let his side cling to a faint hope of making the semi-finals. He batted two hours for his 88, hit eight fours in 105 balls and was still at the crease with Ian Smith when the winning runs were scored off Jarvis in the 48th over. The New Zealand captain was an obvious choice for the Man of the Match Award.

ZIMBABWE		NEW ZEALAND	
G. A. Paterson run out	0	K. R. Rutherford b Brandes	22
A. H. Shah c M. Crowe b Watson	41	J. G. Wright b Shah	12
K. J. Arnott run out	51	M. D. Crowe c Butchart b Shah	58
D. L. Houghton (wk) c M. Crowe b Boock	50	D. N. Patel c Arnott b Brandes	1
A. J. Pycroft not out	52	J. J. Crowe (capt) not out	88
K. M. Curran b Boock	12	A. H. Jones c Jarvis b Traicos	15
A. C. Waller not out	8	M. C. Snedden b Jarvis	4
Extras lb7 w6	13	I. D. S. Smith (capt) not out	17
(50 overs)	5-227	Extras b1 lb5 w4 nb1	11
Did not bat: I. P. Butchart, E. A. Brandes, A. J. Traicos (capt),		(47.4 overs)	6-228
M. P. Jarvis		Did not bat: S. L. Boock, W. Watson, E. J. Chatfield	
1/1 2/82 3/121 4/180 5/216		1/37 2/53 3/56 4/125 5/158 6/182	
Bowling: Snedden 10-2-32-0; Chatfield 10-2-47-0;		Bowling: Curran2-0-12-0; Jarvis 7.4-0-39-1;	
Patel 10-0-52-0; Watson 10-1-45-1; Boock 10-1-44-2		Brandes 10-1-44-2; Shah 10-0-34-2; Butchart 8-0-50-0;	
		Traicos 10-0-43-1	

Umpires: Khizar Hayat P.W. Vidanagamage

Toss: New Zealand   Points: New Zealand 4 Zimbabwe 0

SUNDAY OCTOBER 25th, MONDAY 26 OCTOBER and TUESDAY 27 OCTOBER
RELIANCE2 CUP: ROUND FIVE
GROUP B: PAKISTAN vs SRI LANKA
THE IQBAL STADIUM, FAISALABAD: PAKISTAN WON BY 113 RUNS

Sri Lanka went back over the western border to Pakistan just so their bowlers could suffer another merciless caning. Only briefly were they in the hunt at the Iqbal Stadium as the superior depth in talent of the Pakistanis became more and more obvious as the day wore on. This win by the home side ensured they would top Group B and could play their semi-final at Lahore.

Salim Malik followed up his fine innings against England with an even 100 at Faisalabad. He saw his team through a mini collapse when they lost three wickets between 64 and 77 and went on to complete his century in 85 balls with 10 fours.

Imran Khan elected to bat in the hope that his strokeplayers would score quickly enough to put Sri Lanka out of the contest. Once more Duleep Mendis got very little bite out of his new-ball bowlers as Mansoor Akhtar and Rameez Raja moved through the opening overs in relative comfort. It was the spinners, Don Anurasiri and Sridharan Jeganathan, who caused the brief flutter by removing an opener each. Javed Miandad's run out then lifted Sri Lankan hopes further.

Almost as quickly Malik and Wasim Akram dampened them down again. Promoted up the order, Akram boosted the run rate and twice hit the ball for six with mighty left-handed swipes. Malik added 60 with Akram, a further 60 with Ijaz Ahmed, whose 30 runs took just 18 balls, and 67 with Imran. Pakistan put on 154 in their final 15 overs and their total of 297 was their highest in the tournament to date.

Imran was unable to complete his fourth over because of an injured ankle, but he had already put Sri Lanka on the back foot by having Brendon Kuruppu caught behind. Nor did his absence from the bowling crease inspire the Sri Lankan batsmen to deeds of great daring. The innings just stuttered along. No-one was able to score with enough freedom to get anywhere near Pakistan's total. Tauseef Ahmed bowled with great economy, Arjuna Rantunga completed his second consecutive half century and added 80 runs with his captain for the fifth wicket. Both fell to Abdul Qadir's wrist spin, whose fascinating bowling was the just about the best feature of some tame afternoon cricket. Salim Malik received the Man of the Match Award.

PAKISTAN		SRI LANKA	
Rameez Raja c & b Anurasiri	32	R. S. Mahanama run out	8
Mansoor Akhtar b Jeganathan	33	D. S. B. P. Kuruppu c Salim Yousuf b Imran Khan	0
Salim Malik b Ratnayake	100	J. R. Ratnayake run out	22
Javed Miandad run out	1	R. S. Madugalle c Salim Yousuf b Manzoor Elahi	15
Wasim Akram c Ranatunga b de Silva	39	A. Ranatunga c & b Abdul Qadir	50
Ijaz Ahmed c & b John	30	L. R. D. Mendis (capt) b Abdul Qadir	58
Imran Khan (capt) run out	39	P. A. de Silva not out	13
Manzoor Elahi not out	4	A. L. F. de Mel b Abdul Qadir	0
Salim Yousuf (wk) not out	11	S. Jeganathan c Salim Yousuf b Javed Miandad	1
Extras lb6 w2	8	V. B. John not out	1
(50 overs)	7-297	Extras b4 lb4 w6 nb2	16
		(50 overs)	8-184

Did not bat: Abdul Qadir, Tauseef Ahmed
1/64 2/72 3/77 4/137 5/197 6/264 7/285
Bowling: Ratnayake 10-0-58-1; John 8-0-53-1; de Mel 10-0-53-0; Jeganthan 9-1-45-1; Anurasiri 7-0-45-1; de Silva 6-0-37-1

Did not bat: S. D. Anurasiri
1/4 2/11 3/41 4/70 5/150 6/173 7/173 8/179
Bowling: Imran Khan 3.2-1-13-1; Wasim Akram 7-0-34-0; Manzoor Elahi 9.4-0-32-1; Tauseef Ahmed 10-0-23-0; Abdul Qadir 10-0-40-3; Salim Malik 7-1-29-0; Javed Miandad 3-0-5-1

Umpires: R.B. Gupta S.J. Woodward
Toss: Pakistan   Points: Pakistan 4 Sri Lanka 0

GROUP B: ENGLAND vs WEST INDIES
SAWAI MAN SINGH STADIUM, JAIPUR: ENGLAND WON BY 34 RUNS

The was great English joy in Jaipur as a second win over the West Indies virtually ensured Mike Gatting's team a place in the semi-finals. Even though both sides had one more match, this game amounted to what was virtually a quarter final and England's pleasure was matched by West Indian disappointment, especially as a large proportion of the margin of defeat could be attributed to a surfeit of wides.

Some of those were illegal bouncers from fast bowlers, while Carl Hooper totally lost control of his slow medium swingers during his short and unsuccessful spell. Viv Richards had sent England in to bat on a wicket that was greener than most and contained a lot of early morning moisture. Gatting would also have bowled if he had won.

Rather than take advantage of the wicket, Patrick Patterson and Winston Benjamin sprayed the ball around. Courtney Walsh, on the other hand, conceded fewer runs in his 10-over spell than he had off those horrendous 10 deliveries at Gujranwala and Lahore. He cut the ball off the wicket prodigiously without having any luck.

Patterson achieved the first breakthrough when he got through Robinson's defence after half an hour and snapped his off stump in half. Robinson had been missed by Jeff Dujon when he was six and the West Indian wicketkeeper also dropped a catch off Bill Athey.

In the stifling heat of Rajastan, Gooch settled to build an important innings. He dominated an opening stand of 35 with Robinson, one of 55 with Athey for the second wicket and another of 64 runs with Mike Gatting for the third. England were 2-151 at the start of the 31st over, having scored 71 runs from their previous 10 overs, and potentially on target for a score of around 300. Richards having lost some faith in his bowlers, used the captain's perogative and claimed the ball, himself.

It paid immediate dividends. The sweep shot again proved a dangerous choice for the English captain, Gatting missing a straight ball. Gooch and Allan Lamb were then becalmed so that by the 40th over only another 35 runs had been added. At least another collapse had been avoided.

Patterson came back to dismiss Gooch eight short of his century after seven fours in 137 balls and Lamb. By now, though, the runs were flowing again. John Emburey and Phil DeFreitas unleashed an assault on some more loose deliveries. The big off-spinner hit four fours in sixteen balls. 83 runs were made in the final 10 overs, including 51 in the last five.

Only DeFreitas kept the pressure on the West Indian top order as they began their pursuit of the 270 runs they required for victory. Neil Foster and Gladstone Small were expensive early and the runs were being conceded at five per over. DeFreitas removed Desmond Haynes and Emburey bowled Phil Simmons with an arm ball in the 13th over with the total already on 65.

In partnership with his fellow Antiguan, Richie Richardson, the West Indian captain Richards thrilled the crowd for the next 17 overs while 82 runs were added. They brought up the 100 in the 21st over which was quicker than England had. The wicket had dried into a batsman's paradise. Off-spinner, Eddie Hemmings, and a more controlled Foster suddenly found their line and length to dry up all but nine runs for five overs. Then Richards and Richardson broke loose again. Richards had already hit Emburey for one six when he swept Hemmings hard and high for six more. Off the next ball he repeated the dose, this time a top edge just clearing the fieldsman on the boundary.

The captain had just reached his 50 and the West Indies were 2-147, needing 123 to win off 20 overs. The heat remained intense, several bowlers were unwell and there were thoughts that England might start to wilt. Instead Richards stepped back to cut Hemmings, missed a ball that was tossed up slower and higher and was bowled.

Gus Logie joined Richardson in the middle and there were no immediate signs of tremors in the West Indian camp. They reduced the target to 88, when Logie played the tournament's favourite shot off Emburey only to top edge the ball to Hemmings.

At the start of the 41st over the West Indies still appeared to be in control. Another 65 runs and they would condemn England to an early exit from the competition. Six wickets were still in hand, one of them being Richardson. Six runs later and both Carl Hooper and Jeff Dujon had been caught behind by Paul Downton, the one to dismiss Hooper off DeFreitas being a fine diving effort.

The pressure was now starting to build. Roger Harper guided the ball to backward point. Richardson called him for a sharp run to Hemmings, the oldest and chubbiest player on the field. In the middle of a sweltering afternoon with everything to play for Hemmings moved quickly, picked up the ball one handed and threw down the stumps at the bowler's end with the agile Harper still stretching for the crease. The West Indian challenge was fading.

Richardson went on to top score in the match, beating Gooch's total by one run in 130 balls with one six and eight fours. The he fell to another fine catch behind by Downton.

From the first ball of the 49th over, with his side still needing another 35 runs Winston Benjamin was caught by Foster off DeFreitas. The West Indies had lost 6-30 in eight overs to hand over the match.

Beneath one of the 'Pink' City's ancient castles, which overlooks the ground, Graham Gooch received his Man of the Match Award. It was a worthy reward for a fine innings. The English supporters also celebrated the contribution of the unfashionable Eddie Hemmings with enthusiasm.

ENGLAND		WEST INDIES	
G. A. Gooch c Harper b Patterson	92	D. L. Haynes c Athey b DeFreitas	9
R. T. Robinson b Patterson	13	P. V. Simmons b Emburey	25
C. W. J. Athey c Patterson b Harper	21	R. B. Richardson c Downton b Small	93
M. W. Gatting (capt) lbw b Richards	25	I. V. A. Richards (capt) b Hemmings	51
A. J. Lamb c Richardson b Patterson	40	A. L. Logie c Hemmings b Emburey	22
J. E. Emburey not out	24	C. L. Hooper c Downton b DeFreitas	8
P. A. J. DeFreitas not out	16	P. J. L. Dujon (wk) c Downton b Foster	1
Extras b5 lb10 w22 nb1	38	R. A. Harper run out	3
(50 overs)	5-269	W. K. M. Benjamin c Foster b DeFreitas	8
Did not bat: P. R. Downton (wk), N. A. Foster,		C. A. Walsh b Hemmings	2
E. E. Hemmings, G. C. Small		B. P. Patterson not out	4
1/35 2/90 3/154 4/209 5/250		Extras lb7 w1 nb1	9
Bowling: Patterson 9-0-56-3; Walsh 10-0-24-0;		(48.1 overs)	235

England bowling figures / West Indies fall of wickets:

Bowling: Patterson 9-0-56-3; Walsh 10-0-24-0;
Benjamin 10-0-63-0; Harper 10-1-52-1; Hooper 3-0-27-0;
Richards 8-0-32-1

1/18 2/65 3/147 4/182 5/208 6/211 7/219 8/221 9/224
10/235
Bowling: DeFreitas 9.1-2-28-3; Foster 10-0-52-1;
Emburey 9-0-41-2; Small 10-0-61-1; Hemmings 10-0-46-2

Umpires: Mahboob Shah   P.W. Vidanagamage

Toss: West Indies   Points: England 4 West Indies 0

GROUP A: INDIA vs ZIMBABWE
GUJARAT STADIUM, AHMEDABAD: INDIA WON BY 7 WICKETS

While England and the West Indies fought out their fluctuating 'quarter final' at Jaipur, India and Zimbabwe were engaged in a lacklustre affair to the south. There was little attractive batting from either side even though India were supposed to be striving to lift their run rate above Australia's.

The wicket that Kapil Dev asked John Traicos' side to bat on was slow and low. It made stroke making difficult, especially against the intelligent left-arm spin of Ravi Shastri and Maninder Singh. Not that they were required to break the opening partnership, Ali Shah took his turn to be the victim of a Zimbabwean top order run out in the second over of the match. Kevin Arnott joined the recalled Robin Brown and he stuck around for 43 overs while compiling a sound if unadventurous 60.

There were no prospects of a major collapse, however, there was no major acceleration, either. Dave Houghton, capable of the aggression required, got out just at the wrong time and Kevin Curran, also potentially a fast scorer, was out of form and out of the side. Chris Waller helped Arnott add 67 for the fourth wicket which ensured the spectators would have their fill of cricket for the day.

Chasing 192, the only 50 over sub 200 first innings total of the Reliance Cup, Kapil Dev ordered his team try and win in 38 overs so as to lift their run rate above Australia. Strangely Sunil Gavaskar, who had been batting in such positive fashion, reverted to Lord's 1975 type and occupied the crease for 114 balls for his 50. Kapil twice sent out messages to the veteran opener to increase his scoring, but to no avail. The old feud between India's two greatest players briefly simmered again. The crowd were also a bit annoyed and behaved in such an unruly fashion that play had to be held up. '

Gavaskar had lost his opening partner, Kris Srikkanth early. He might have felt encumbered by the turgid pitch and the need to establish a platform for victory. In such circumstances John Traicos was almost inevitably miserly in his run concessions. Navjot Sidhu completed his fourth consecutive half century, batting altogether more fluently than his partner. Peter Rawson, another recalled to the Zimbabwean side, dismissed Sidhu and, in the 35th over, Gavaskar. By then India were 3-132 and well on the way to victory. Kapil still had a point to prove. Coming in at number five he put his bat where his mouth was and in 25 balls smashed the game towards its obvious destiny. Three sixes helped dissipate the anger of the Indian captain, even if they were not quite enough to lift his team's run rate above that of the Australians. With eight overs still to be bowled Kapil could claim his Man of the Match Award and announce to the press his disappointment with Gavaskar's tardiness.

ZIMBABWE		INDIA	
R. D. Brown c More b Sharma	13	K. Srikkanth lbw b Jarvis	6
A. H. Shah run out	0	S. M. Gavaskar c Butchart b Rawson	50
K. J. Arnott b Kapil Dev	60	N. S. Sidhu c Brandes b Rawson	55
A. J. Pycroft c More b Sharma	2	D. B. Vengsarkar not out	33
D. L. Houghton (wk) c Kapil Dev b Shastri	22	Kapil Dev (capt) not out	41
A. C .Waller c Shastri b Maninder	39	Extras lb6 w3	9
I. P. Butchart b Kapil Dev	13	(42 overs)	3-194
P. W. E. Rawson not out	16	Did not bat: M. Azharuddin, R. J. Shastri, K. S. More,	
E. A. Brandes not out	3	M. Prabhakar, Chetan Sharma, Maninder Singh	
Extras b1 lb12 w9 nb1	23	1/11 2/105 3/132	
(50 overs)	7-191	Bowling: Brandes 6-0-28-0; Jarvis 8-1-21-1; Shah 8-0-40-0;	
Did not bat: A. J. Traicos (capt), M. P. Jarvis		Traicos 10-0-39-0; Rawson 8-0-46-2; Butchart 2-0-14-0	

Did not bat: A. J. Traicos (capt), M. P. Jarvis
1/4 2/36 3/40 4/83 5/150 6/155 7/184
Bowling: Kapil Dev 10-2-44-2; Prabhakar 7-2-12-0;
Sharma 10-0-41-2; Maninder 10-1-32-1; Shastri 10-0-35-1;
Azharuddin 3-0-14-0

Umpires: D.M. Archer H.D. Bird
Toss: India   Points: India 4 Zimbabwe 0

GROUP A: AUSTRALIA vs NEW ZEALAND
CHANDIGARH: AUSTRALIA WON BY 17 RUNS

Allan Border's 'bunch of club cricketers' secured their place in the Reliance Cup semi-finals with this 17-run win over the disappointing New Zealanders at Chandigarh. Through their hard work and determination they had gone further than the better credentialled 1983 team which was all credit to their captain and to their coach, Bobby Simpson.

There was also great Aussie satisfaction in the humidity of the northern Indian city with the success of Geoff Marsh. His work ethic and support of Border in his new role as vice-captain, was beyond reproach. Without Marsh's individual contribution of 126 not out it is quite possible that Australia would have been defeated and their finals spot placed in jeopardy.

There was not much thought of that while Dean Jones and Marsh were building a powerful second wicket partnership of 126 in 26 overs. Allan Border had restored the batting first option after winning the toss and would have been gratified at the response of his vice-captain and the brash Victorian. Marsh and David Boon had opened against Martin Snedden and Ewen Chatfield in their usual competent fashion until the 10th over when the West Australian hit the ball to point, Boon went looking for a run, was sent back and found well short when Jeff Crowe threw to the bowler, Chatfield.

Jones soon made light of the Australian disappointment with his usual busy aggression. The run rate remained an issue and despite the form of Marsh and Jones, Australia struggled to keep ahead of India. Jones reached his 50, then in the 36th over struck Willie Watson for a huge six over mid wicket. That might have been the signal for him to cut loose, but from the next ball, his 80th of the innings, Jones essayed a drive and was caught behind. Border too, wanted to boost that run rate and seven runs later he unleashed a big drive at Snedden that only deflected the ball onto his off stump. Mike Veletta on his international debut dropped his first ball beside the pitch, got into a terrible muddle with his partner and was run out as Martin Crowe ran in and broke the bowler's stumps.

The Australian middle order had flopped. Six wickets went down for 50 as the total reached an unimposing 7-201after 45 overs. Tim May added a few useful runs lifting his side to 8-232 at the start of the final over of the innings. It was to be bowled by Chatfield, considered to be among the most frugal bowlers in the world. That opinion was confirmed by his figures at that stage of 9-2-33-2.

On his second century of the tournament, Marsh was looking to attack. And Chatfield offered him every chance. A delivery drifted onto Marsh's pads. The batsman lifted it high over the leg-side boundary for six. The next ball was in the same place and achieved the same result. Chatfield conceded 19 runs in his desperate final over. Marsh finished 126 not out and became the third player after Glenn Turner and Sunil Gavaskar to carry his bat through a World Cup innings. He hit three sixes and 12 fours.

New Zealand had a chase that was their last chance to resurrect their campaign. They needed to get 252 and started well. Martin Snedden opened again instead of Rutherford. The left-handed coupling—one an orthodox batsman and the other a promoted tailender—realised 72 runs in 17 overs. Snedden was not afraid to use the old-fashioned slog. He belted Craig McDermott for four through mid-on, using a horizontal bat to a ball pitched short of a length outside the off-stump. Snedden finally deflected Steve Waugh onto his stumps, which was a setback, although not as big as the one that occurred 10 runs later. Martin Crowe was still regarded as the Kiwis' leading batsman and most obvious match-winner. At Indore he had failed his team at a crucial moment with an error of judgement. In front of 25,000 at Chandigarh he was again dismissed at a critical moment, this time, however, without any blame to himself.

John Wright hit a straight drive off Waugh as sweet as a nut. The all-rounder put down his hand. The ball flicked through his fingers and cannoned into the stumps at the bowler's end. Crowe saw the danger an instant too late and, backing up, was about five centimeteres out of his ground when the bails came off. Wright and Ken Rutherford maintained the healthy challenge. They added a further 45 runs and Wright completed his 50.

Shot making and risk taking had to be maintained if the target was to be reached in time. Eventually that took its toll on the batsmen. On 127 Wright hit a full toss straight back at Andrew Zesers off a leading edge. Even while Rutherford and Jeff Crowe put on 46 the pressure was still evident. Rutherford hooked McDermott, only to pick out Jones running in at fine leg. Border brought himself on to bowl left-arm spin. In seven tidy overs he caught and bowled his opposite number, Crowe, and had Dipak Patel stumped. Now the Kiwis were 6-186 and their challenge was starting to falter.

From the last 10 overs 72 runs had been required. John Bracewell, Ian Smith and Stephen Boock would not give up and took the total within 30 of their target. Now risks had to be taken with running, as well. Bracewell and Boock were run out. Last-wicket pair Willie Watson and Ewen Chatfield put on another precious 13. They were within 18 of victory but only nine balls remained when Waugh sent down the fourth delivery of the 49th over. It was full. Watson dug it out and the ball rolled towards mid-on. The last-wicket pair had to run on everything. Both batsmen took off, Border swooped and, with one stump to aim at, threw down the wicket underarm from close range. New Zealand's last seven wickets had gone down for 61 in 11 overs.

Australia's middle-order collapse had forfeited their top position in Group A, but they felt little disappointment. An assured semi-final berth was achievement enough.

AUSTRALIA		NEW ZEALAND	
G. R. Marsh not out	126	M. C. Snedden b Waugh	32
D. C. Boon run out	14	J. G. Wright c & b Zesers	61
D. M. Jones c Smith b Watson	56	M. D. Crowe run out	4
A. R. Border (capt) b Snedden	1	K. R. Rutherford c Jones b McDermott	44
M. R. J. Veletta run out	0	J. J. Crowe (capt) c & b Border	27
S. R. Waugh b Watson	1	D. N. Patel st Dyer b Border	3
G. C. Dyer (wk) b Chatfield	8	J. G. Bracewell run out	12
C. J. McDermott lbw b Chatfield	5	I. D. S. Smith (wk) cBoon b Waugh	12
T. B. A. May run out	15	S. L. Boock run out	12
A. K. Zesers not out	8	W. Watson run out	8
Extras lb10 w7	17	E. J. Chatfield not out 5	
(50 overs)	8-251	Extras b1 lb7 w4 nb2	14
Did not bat: B. A. Reid		(48.4 overs)	234
1/25 2/151 3/158 4/158 5/175 6/193 7/201 8/228		1/72 2/82 3/127 4/173 5/179 6/186 7/206 8/208 9/221 10/234	
Bowling: Snedden 10-0-48-1; Chatfield 10-2-52-2; Boock 10-1-45-0; Bracewell 4-0-24-0; Patel 8-0-26-0; Watson 8-0-46-2		Bowling: McDermott 10-1-43-1; Reid 6-0-30-0; Waugh 9.4-0-37-2; Zesers 6-0-37-1; May 10-0-52-0; Border 7-0-27-2	

Umpires: Khizar Hayat D.R. Shepherd

Toss: Australia   Points: Australia 4 New Zealand 0

FRIDAY OCTOBER 30th and SATURDAY OCTOBER 31st
RELIANCE CUP: ROUND SIX
GROUP B: ENGLAND vs SRI LANKA
NEHRU STADIUM, PUNE: ENGLAND WON BY 8 WICKETS

England suffered few moments of uncertainty as they marched through to their rightful place in the semi-finals. They comfortably accounted for Sri Lanka who packed their bags for home without a point for all their travelling and efforts. At Pune they mostly looked a tired and uninspired team, something for which England were extremely grateful.

They were less grateful at having to field first after having lost the toss on a rough outfield in front of a restless crowd that half filled the Nehru Stadium.

Duleep Mendis' correct call was virtually his last success as his country's captain. The Sri Lankan openers, batting first for the only time in the tournament, were restrained early by the accuracy of Phil DeFreitas and Gladstone Small. They might have been in a parlous position if the England fieldsmen had been in any sort of catching form. After Roshan Mahanama hit DeFreitas' first ball of the day through the leg-side for four, Graham Gooch dislocated a finger while dropping a slips catch from the fifth ball of the opening over.

In the 14th over, with the crowd booing and the total on a subdued 2-31 wicketkeeper, Paul Downton dropped the struggling Roy Dias. Dias had just been recalled to the side and offered Downton the most straightforward of chances. The afternoon's entertainment may have been sadly curtailed if the catch had been held for Dias went on to provide the Sri Lankan innings with its only real degree of substance. Just when everyone was starting to lose interest he swept Jaipur hero, Eddie Hemmings, for six. Later, a drive off John Emburey cleared the boundary at long off and then Dias picked up a ball from Small so perfectly that it sailed over mid wicket for his third six. Some critics rated that shot the best of the competition.

Dias added 88 in 22 overs with the tall, accomplished Asanka Gurusinha. When Sri Lanka reached 2-113 there was a possibility of them setting England a testing target. The partnership was broken when the 'Guru' hit the ball to mid-on and ran a single. Unfortunately Dias did not move and when Gatting's throw to Downton left Gurusinha run out by the length of the pitch the Sri Lankans went into their shell again.

They were 4-144 at the start of the 40th over, struggling to get their run rate up to four per over. The Sri Lankans managed to achieve that at least by adding 74 from the final 60 deliveries. Dias completed his 105 ball innings, containing six fours as well as the three sixes, and Ranjan Madugalle, Aravinda de Silva and Sridharan Jeganathan chipped in. England's contribution amounted to four dropped catches.

The wicket had provided some turn, but there was nothing to suggest England would not make the 219 they required to win.

Gooch's early-morning finger injury had been repaired well enough by the team physiotherapist, Laurie Brown, for him to open with Tim Robinson. He immediately hit Ravi Ratnayake's first ball through mid off for four and then settled in to play a typically powerful innings. Robinson, too, was in prime form and the pair rattled up a partnership of 123 in 23 overs. They struck 14 boundaries between them. Gooch's sharp chance to mid wicket was the only blemish before he hit a return catch off the leading edge to the accurate Jeganathan from his 79th ball. Jeganathan also bowled Robinson on the sweep for his equally impressive 55. That double breakthrough was the end of Sri Lankan success for the Reliance Cup.

Bill Athey and Gatting quickly took up where the opening pair had left off. They attacked with confidence and raced towards their objective. Aravinda de Silva was crunched, Ashantha de Mel was pulverised and when the partnership had put on 87 by the second ball of the 42nd over England had completed their victory. Graham Gooch, with a knack for being recognised, beat all other contenders for the Man of the Match Award.

SRI LANKA		ENGLAND	
R. S. Mahanama c Emburey b DeFreitas	14	G. A. Gooch c & b Jeganthan	61
J. R. Ratnayake lbw b Small	7	R. T. Robinson b Jeganathan	55
A. P. Gurusinha (wk) run out	34	C. W. J. Athey not out	40
R. L. Dias st Downton b Hemmings	80	M. W. Gatting (capt) not out	46
L. R. D. Mendis b DeFreitas	7	Extras b1 lb13 w3	17
R. S. Madugalle c sub (P. W. Jarvis) b Hemmings	22	(41.2 overs)	2-219
P. A. de Silva not out	23	Did not bat: A. J. Lamb, J. E. Emburey, P. R. Downton (wk),
A. L.F. de Mel c Lamb b Hemmings	0	P. A. J. DeFreitas, N. A. Foster, E. E. Hemmings, G. C. Small
S. Jeganathan not out	20	1/123 2/132
Extras lb3 w3 nb5	11	Bowling
(50 overs)	7-218	Ratnayake 8-1-37-0; John 6-2-19-0; de Mel 4.2-0-34-0;
Did not bat: V. B. John, S. D. Anurasiri		Jeganathan 10-0-45-2; Anurasiri 10-0-45-0; de Silva 3-0-25-0

1/23 2/25 3/113 4/125 5/170 6/177 8/180
Bowling: DeFreitas 10-2-46-2; Small 10-1-33-1;
Foster 10-0-37-0; Emburey 10-1-42-0; Hemmings 10-0-57-3

Umpires: D.M. Archer Khizar Hayat

Toss: Sri Lanka   Points: England 4 Sri Lanka 0

GROUP B: PAKISTAN vs WEST INDIES
NATIONAL STADIUM, KARACHI: WEST INDIES WON BY 28 RUNS

The West Indies did everything they could to reassert pressure on England in their best performance of the Reliance Cup. Their 28-run win however was too little too late and this excellent victory would finish as merely a consolation for a team that let their destiny fall into the hands of others.

The West Indian loss in the 1983 final had been seen as a temporary aberration. The form of the side under Viv Richards in the 1987 Reliance Cup revealed that in the shorter form of the game the Caribbean decline was real enough. This was the first time they had failed to reach the final, let alone the semi-finals.

Richards won the toss and elected to bat. Phil Simmons was dismissed early, but Richie Richardson was soon demonstrating he had retained his form from Jaipur. His stand of 65 with Desmond Haynes provided the innings with the type of base which Viv Richards is able to brutally exploit. He and his fellow Antiguan tore into the Pakistani attack to the tune of 137 runs in 23 overs. They were assisted by some lackadaisical fielding which resulted in dropped catches and bonus runs for the West Indies. Perhaps the Pakistani fieldsmen were distracted by the clashes between police and students in the crowd and the teargas that drifted over the ground.

Richardson struck Imran down the ground for a rare six off the Pakistani captain. He hit one other ball into the crowd and eight fours as he stroked his way to 110 in 136 balls. Richards brought up his 1000th World Cup run during his 74-ball innings. Finally he was bowled by left-arm paceman, Wasim Akram. He and Abdul Qadir would prove the best of the Pakistani bowlers.

Imran also came back strongly to pick up three wickets, while also concerning himself with his team's slow over rate. Heavy fines loomed at one stage, a problem exacerbated by wayward bowling and plenty of wides. The West Indies could only add a further 37 runs after Richards and Richardson were separated, although this was enough to temporarily lift their run rate above England who were listening hard to the goings on at the National Stadium during their own match in Pune.

Pakistan's tardiness with their over rate carried over into the early batting of their openers. Mudassar Nazar and Rameez Raja had put on just 26 after 10 overs. From there they were able to accelerate and they had got their rate up to four per over by the time Mudassar was bowled by off-spinner Roger Harper with the total on 78. Rameez and Salim Malik put on another 50 and Pakistan reached 1-128. It was an excellent platform, but this was the sort of day Imran had come to dread. His later batsmen were not on task and could not maintain the challenge. A few sharp shocks by Patrick Patterson and Winston Benjamin saw Pakistan decline from 5-202 to 9-208.

Both camps would have been dissatisfied with the eventual result. Pakistan could not have been happy with such a performance as a lead up to a semi-final clash and the West Indies must have wondered what could have been if they had consistently played as well as they did this day. Still, it was an impressive way to finish. Especially as this was Viv Richards' farewell World Cup match.

Richie Richardson was a clear-cut choice for the Man of the Match Award.

WEST INDIES		PAKISTAN	
D. L. Haynes c Imran Khan b Mudassar Nazar	25	Mudassar Nazar b Harper	40
P. V. Simmons b Wasim Akram	6	Rameez Raja c Hooper b Patterson	70
R. B. Richardson c Abdul Qadir b Imran Khan	110	Salim Malik c Richards b Walsh	23
I. V. A. Richards (capt) b Wasim Akram	67	Javed Miandad b Benjamin	38
A. L. Logie c Mudassar Nazar b Imran Khan	12	Ijaz Ahmed b Benjamin	6
R. A. Harper b Wasim Akram	2	Imran Khan (capt) c Harper b Walsh	8
C. L. Hooper not out	5	Salim Yousuf (wk) b Patterson	7
W. K.M. Benjamin c Mudassar Nazar b Imran Khan	0	Wasim Akram lbw b Patterson	0
P. J. L. Dujon (wk) not out	1	Abdul Qadir not out	8
Extras b3 lb10 w16 nb1	30	Shoaib Mohammad b Benjamin	0
(50 overs)	7-258	Salim Jaffer not out	8
Did not bat: C. A. Walsh, B. P. Patterson		Extras b4 lb6 w10 nb2	22
1/19 2/84 3/221 4/242 5/248 6/255 7/255		(50 overs)	9-230
Bowling: Imran Khan 9-0-57-3; Wasim Akram 10-0-45-3;		1/78 2/128 3/147 4/167 5/186 6/202 7/202 8/208 9/208	
Abdul Qadir 10-1-29-0; Mudassar Nazar 10-0-47-1;		Bowling: Patterson 10-1-34-3; Walsh 10-1-34-2;	
Salim Jaffer 6-0-37-0; Salim Malik 5-0-30-0;		Harper 10-0-38-1; Benjamin 10-0-69-3; Richards 10-0-45-0	

Umpires: R.B. Gupta V.K. Ramaswamy

Toss: West Indies   Points: West Indies 4 Pakistan 0

GROUP A: AUSTRALIA vs ZIMBABWE
BARABATI STADIUM, CUTTACK: AUSTRALIA WON BY 70 RUNS

The third Friday match in Round Six of the Reliance Cup saw Australia comfortably account for Zimbabwe. It was a solid pre semi-final workout, however the Australians still had to wait for the result of the India-New Zealand game on the Saturday to find out whether they would finish in top or second place in Group A.

Allan Border called incorrectly, but found that his side were still going to bat first. John Traicos wanted them to take first use of the green and lively track prepared at the Barabati Stadium. Geoff Marsh and David Boon were unfazed by the juice in the wicket, nor did Peter Rawson or Malcolm Jarvis cause them much concern with the new ball. Maintaining their excellent tournament record they added 90 in 23 overs before Marsh was run out.

With such a good start Dean Jones was an ideal man to come in at number three. He and Boon had to work for their runs as Traicos extracted some turn from the moist surface. They still added 58 in 10 overs until Iain Butchart and wicketkeeper Dave Houghton ended Boon's resistance which had included a six and nine fours.

Craig McDermott's pinch hitting promotion failed and Border soon rewarded Traicos' persistance so that Australia had slid from 1-148 to 4-170. Jones was still in, ticking the score over rather than taking control. Mike Veletta was to the forefront with a busy innings during which he put on 78 with Jones. His 43 was of real benefit to his side and his own cause.

They batted just quickly enough to lift Australia's rate one hundredth of a run per over ahead of India's. Jones completed his 50, his third of the competition, hitting just one six and one four, on the way. Australia put 266 on the board, which considering the conditions was no mean feat.

Zimbabwe were quickly in trouble. Chris Waller was cracked on the bridge of the nose by a ball from Bruce Reid that lifted from a length and forced him to temporarily retire hurt. Ali Shah and Kevin Curran, back in the side again, were then put on the defensive by the Australian pacemen who were threatening on the grassy wicket. The Africans took nearly 30 overs to reach a reasonable platform of 1-89. Then they threw the position away.

Off-spinner Tim May had Curran caught in the 27th over and then trapped Dave Houghton lbw in the 29th. Zimbabwe were 4-97, chasing runs at nine per over against the fastest improving team in the competition. Soon it was obvious this was another example of a limited-overs match that would benefit from some sort of forfeiture rule being available to bail everyone out from having to play over after over of pointless cricket.

Boon was given a bowl. It was for entertainment rather than tactical reasons and cost 17 runs. Waller did return to the batting crease showing no serious ill effects from the blow to his nose and he finished equal top score for his side.

After Australia had won by 70 runs David Boon was announced as Man of the Match.

Back in Australia there was another announcement. Cricket fans up to this final match had had to be satisfied with nothing more than a 60-second report on the sports section of the news. At last Channel Nine agreed to show an hour of delayed highlights of both semi-finals.

AUSTRALIA		ZIMBABWE	
D. C. Boon c Houghton b Butchart	93	A. H. Shah b Waugh	32
G. R. Marsh run out	37	A. C. Waller c Waugh b McDermott	38
D. M. Jones not out	58	K. M. Curran c Waugh b May	29
C. J. McDermott c Rawson b Traicos	9	A. J. Pycroft c Dyer bMcDermott	38
A. R. Border (capt) st Houghton b Traicos	4	D. L. Houghton (wk) lbw b May	1
M. R. J. Veletta run out	43	I. P. Butchart st Dyer b Border	3
S. R. Waugh not out	10	P. W. E. Rawson not out	24
Extras b3 lb3 w6	12	E. A. Brandes not out	18
(50 overs)	5-266	Extras lb5 w6 nb2	13
Did not bat: S. P. O'Donnell, G. C. Dyer (wk), T. B. A. May		(50 overs)	6-196
B. A. Reid		Did not bat: K. J. Arnot, A. J. Traicos (capt), M. P. Jarvis	
1/90 2/148 3/159 4/170 5/248		1/55 2/89 3/92 4/97 5/139 6/156	
Bowling: Rawson 9-0-41-0; Jarvis 6-0-33-0; Shah 7-0-31-0;		Bowling: McDermott 10-0-43-2; Reid 9-2-30-0;	
Brandes 10-1-58-0; Traicos 10-0-45-2; Butchart 8-0-52-1		Waugh 4-0-9-1; O'Donnell 7-1-21-0; May 10-1-30-2;	
		Border 8-0-36-1; Jones 1-0-5-0	

Umpires: Mahboob Shah P.W. Vidanagamage

Toss: Zimbabwe   Points: Australia 4 Zimbabwe 0

GROUP A: INDIA vs NEW ZEALAND
VIDARBHA C.A.GROUND, NAGPUR: INDIAWON BY 9 WICKETS

In front of a big crowd, three Indian batsmen turned on fireworks for 32.1 overs so that their side charged to the top position of their group and could look forward to a home semi-final in the Wankhede Stadium in Bombay, now Mumbai. Chasing a respectable, if modest, 221, Kris Srikkanth, Mohammad Azharuddin and a supposedly ailing Sunil Gavaskar struck boundary after boundary to completely demoralise the Kiwi attack. India had needed to reach their target in 42.2 overs. That was more than enough time.

There was little prospect of anything remarkable while New Zealand steadily built their total after Jeff Crowe won the toss and chose to bat first. John Wright, again a consistent performer, and another left-hander in for his first game in the tournament, Phil Horne, gave New Zealand a steady opening. That stayed the nature of the innings up until the 42nd over. The Kiwis reached 4-181. Each batsman had got a start without properly capitalising. Ravi Shastri had just dismissed top scorer, the stylish Dipak Patel, when paceman Chetan Sharma began his sixth over. The first three balls contained little of real note, from the fourth, though, Ken Rutherford was bowled. 6-182 suggested a few problems arising and they worsened when Sharma bowled wicketkeeper Ian Smith first ball.

Ewen Chatfield joined Martin Snedden. The innings was quickly disintegrating and Chatfield faced a hat trick ball from a rampant Sharma with the frenzied crowd behind him. A charging run, a whipping action and a set of shattered stumps followed immediately by an explosion of special Indian joy meant that Sharma had completed the first hat trick in six world cups.

That ended the 42nd over. After the euphoria had subsided Snedden and Willie Watson rallied and added 39 from the last eight overs to give their side's total a modicum of substance.

Once India got underway it was shown up to really only be a modicum, too. Eighteen runs came off the first two overs. Then from Chatfield's third over Gavaskar, supposedly ill with a temperature, lifted the innings into warp speed. The same man that five days earlier had earned his captain's wrath by batting too slowly, put his foot down the wicket and with a scything sweep of the bat clouted the ball over the mid wicket boundary for six. Next ball an effortless straight drive registered another six that scattered a few patrons in a VIP box. Gavaskar followed that with another drive, this time the result was a one bounce four over mid off. Finally, he clipped a full toss to the square leg boundary to make it 20 runs from four balls.

From that point the tempo rarely eased. The 50 was raised after eight overs. While Gavaskar continued to charm as he raced towards his first ever century in 106 one-dayers, Srikkanth became even more dominant. The arms of umpires Bird and Shepherd must have tired such was the regularity that they had to signal fours and sixes.

Willie Watson, who came out of the massacre best, claimed, "It was just like bowling in the TV highlights."

Six overs after the 50 mark had been reached the crowd was cheering the Indian 100. Finally Srikkanth's 58-ball extravaganza ended when Watson had him caught by Rutherford in the 17th over. He had hit three sixes and nine fours and the total was 136.

Azharuddin maintained the tempo, as he had to. Gavsakar, by now feeling the effects of his illness, slowed a little in the 90s. Then from his 85th ball the most prolific century maker in Test cricket pushed the New Zealand debutant, young paceman Danny Morrison, through mid wicket for two to complete his 100. It was the second-fastest century ever scored in the World Cup. Azharuddin hit the first ball of Chatfield's fifth over, the 33rd of the innings, over mid wicket for four to terminate India's astonishing batting heroics. They had comfortably achieved both their objectives.

Gavskar had hit three sixes and 10 fours in his 103 not out. He still had to share the Man of the Match Award with the hat trick man, Sharma.

NEW ZEALAND		INDIA	
J. G. Wright run out	35	K. Srikkanth c Rutherford b Watson	75
P. A. Horne b Prabhakar	18	S. M. Gavaskar not out	103
M. D. Crowe c Pandit b Azharuddin	21	M. Azharuddin not out	41
K. R. Rutherford b Sharma	26	Extras lb1 w2 nb2	5
J. J. Crowe (capt) b Maninder	24	(32.1 overs)	1-224
D. N. Patel c Kapil Dev b Shastri	40	Did not bat: N. S. Sidhu, D. B. Vengsarkar, Kapil Dev,	
M. C. Snedden run out	23	R. J. Shastri, C. S. Pandit, M. Prabhakar, C. Sharma,	
I. D. S. Smith (wk) b Sharma	0	Maninder Singh	
E. J. Chatfield b Sharma	0	1/136	
W. Watson not out	12	Bowling: Morrison 10-0-69-0; Chatfield 4.1-1-39-0;	
Extras lb14 w7 nb1	22	Snedden 4-0-29-0; Watson 10-0-50-0; Patel 4-0-29-0	
(50 overs)	9-221		

Did not bat: D. K. Morrison

1/46 2/84 3/90 4/122 5/181 6/182 7/182 8/182 9/221

Bowling: Kapil Dev 6-0-24-0; Prabhakar 7-0-23-1;
Sharma 10-2-51-3; Azharuddin 7-0-26-1; Maninder
Singh 10-0-51-1; Shastri 10-1-32-1

Umpires: H.D. Bird D.R. Shepherd

Toss: New Zealand   Points: India 4 New Zealand 0

WESDNESDAY 4 NOVEMBER AND THURSDAY 5 NOVEMBER 1987
THE RELIANCE CUP SEMI-FINALS

At the conclusionof the preliminary rounds of the 1987 World Cup the Group tables finished as follows:

GROUP A					GROUP B				
	P	W	L	Pts	R/R	P	W	L	Pts	R/R
INDIA	6	5	1	20	5.39	PAKISTAN	6	5	1	20	5.01
AUSTRALIA	6	5	1	20	5.19	ENGLAND	6	4	2	16	5.12
NEW ZEALAND	6	2	4	8	4.88	WEST INDIES	6	3	3	12	5.16
ZIMBABAWE	6	0	6	0	3.76	SRI LANKA	6	0	6	0	4.04

1st SEMI-FINAL
AUSTRALIA vs PAKISTAN
GADDAFI STADIUM, LAHORE: AUSTRALIA WON BY 18 RUNS

The case for Pakistan winning this semi-final seemed irresistable. Excellent lead-up form, a side laden with talent, home ground and home crowd advantage and an opponent with little success behind them prior to this competition. Many felt Australia had done well to reach the semi-finals and that sub-consciously they would be satisfied with that.

This semi-final was a very special event for the Pakistani team and the people of their country. The intensity and the passion was tangible. Nothing mattered in the streets of the cities and the villages other than the Reliance Cup would be theirs after the final at Eden Gardens. The cricket fans of Pakistan, and that was virtually the entire population, saw the win as the destiny of their side. Imran reiterated his belief, that his main ambitions centred around Test cricket. He knew how much this tournament meant to the people of his country, though, and he wanted to go out of the game with this one final honour. The only doubts arose from the thought that previous Pakistani teams had fallen at the semi-final hurdle and that the enormous local enthusiasm may have added extra pressure to a team with an occasionally questionable collective temperament.

The concrete terraces were covered early by 40,000 plus fans when Allan Border won the toss and elected to bat. Australia made no change to the team that won at Cuttack while Pakistan brought in Mansoor Akhtar for Mudassar Nazar who had a neck injury, and off-spinner Tauseef Ahmed for Shoaib Mohammad. Imran believed the need to change the side and the loss of the toss were bad omens.

Geoff Marsh and David Boon gave Imran even further worries by getting Australia away to yet another excellent start. Salim Jaffer was very expensive and fellow left-armer, Wasim Akram, who had been in doubt because of a foot injury, also struggled. Marsh showed the occasion effected him when he was nearly out to the second ball of the day. He edged Imran to second slip only for Mansoor to take the ball on the half volley. A flowing cover drive by the same batsman for four off a wide Akram half volley indicated the malady was temporary.

The Australian openers had put together a partnership of 73 in 18 overs when Marsh pushed Tauseef to square leg. He took off for a single, but Boon sent him back. Salim Malik threw down the stumps with Marsh still well short. That brought the day's first big cheer and made Malik a very popular fellow.

Dean Jones had to survive a close lbw shout when Abdul Qadir's leg-spin was introduced. Boon then put the Pakistani in his place by crashing him through the covers for four with a perfect front foot drive. The run out had not improved the fortunes of Imran's team. A top-spinning Qadir wrong 'un flipped up off Jones' pad and whacked wicketkeeper Salim Yousuf in the mouth. He had to leave the ground for treatment. Javed Miandad took over his role with a smile and a bit to say. When there was a close call for a run out he smashed all three stumps out of the ground, sending them flying metres. It was spectacular, but Jones had made his ground.

Pakistan had even more troubles. Boon danced down the wicket and drove the ball straight back at Tauseef. The caught and bowled chance burst through the off-spinner's fingers, cracking his left thumb on the way. More time was consumed while Tauseef was repaired. There was still plenty of noise coming from the stands. The ladies cheered and squealed at Imran even when he was not directly involved with the play. "Imran we'll miss you" and "King Khan" they waved on homemade signs, but the 'Tiger' of Pakistan was only interested in the cricket.

Jones and Boon brought up the Australian 100 from 135 balls. Jones twice square cut the wayward Jaffer for four and Boon raised his 50 with a two to fine leg off, Malik. Malik's unlikely little cutters provided the breakthrough in the 31st over to end the second-wicket partnership of 82 between the stocky Tasmanian and his Victorian partner. Boon went walking to a ball that drifted down leg side. Javed was just quick enough to punch out the middle stump ending Boon's 91-ball resistance.

Next over Jones stepped away to cut Tauseef, missed and was bowled. 3-155 looked a bit better than 1-155 for the locals. Border and Mike Veletta repaired the damage with a fourth wicket stand 60, allbeit at a slower run rate, only 56 runs came between the 30th and 40th overs. Veletta was the busier of the two, although Border's square cut off Imran for four was a feature shot. In the 42nd over the Australian captain drove Akram into the covers. He took off for a single, but had hit the ball too well and straight at Mansoor. When the stumps were thrown down Border kept on running towards the pavilion.

Steve Waugh and Veletta added another 21, until in the 47th over the West Australian gave himself room to drive Imran and lost his leg stump. He could have been proud of his 50-ball knock. Instead Veletta walked away holding his head and grimacing. He might have known what was to follow. In the same over Simon O'Donnell was struck on the pad and the ball fell at his feet. Waugh ran for a single, O'Donnell did not move. Imran rolled the ball back to Malik who removed a bail, then put it back on the stumps. Waugh kept walking, however the umpires ruled that the batsmen had crossed and that O'Donnell was out.

Waugh neatly edged a four past the outstretched glove of Miandad, then in the same over Dyer was bowled off stump by a full length delivery. In the 49th over Imran completed the set by taking out Craig McDermott's middle stump to leave Australia 8-249. It was a mighty fightback by the Pakistani captain.

He still had to find a bowler to finish the innings and had miscalculated so that the expensive nervous Jaffer would be required to finish the job. Final over 'Master', Waugh, awaited the left armer with relish. His first delivery landed on off stump on a length. Waugh made a mighty swing and lofted the ball over long on for six. Jaffer's next ball was wide of off stump. Waugh dragged it through mid-on with a cross bat thump that gave the boundary fielders no chance. Two full tosses brought two more twos, then from the final delivery Waugh clipped a leg-stump half volley square. The fieldsman ran around, lost his white hat and let the ball through his hands for four. Eighteen runs had come from the 50th over and Imran's disgust as he led his team off the field was obvious to all.

Pakistan's passage to the Reliance Cup Final was no longer a certainty. They required 268 to win at 5.36 per over. Their strong batting line-up was capable enough, although the Australians now scented a chance at a boilover akin to the 1983 Lord's final. The bubbling soon intensified, too, when disaster struck from the third ball of the innings. Mansoor clipped McDermott off the back foot to cover. Rameez took off. Mansoor who had gone a few steps sent him back. Border returned the ball to the bowler, who turned around and broke the stumps with Rameez struggling to get back. It was a costly mistake as Rameez's recent scores had been 42, 113, 32 and 70.

Malik had also been in form and in Reid's first over he followed an edged four with an authentic cover drive. He did the bulk of the scoring while the total reached 37 in the ninth over. Mansoor totally out of sorts, then tried to hit to square leg a full pitched McDermott delivery which struck his off-stump. The silence that dismissal caused was, if anything, greater when Malik chipped Waugh's first ball straight to mid off off the bat's leading edge. Pakistan after 10.1 overs were 3-38. Imran was coming in to a crisis.

It was not the farewell he was hoping for and it could have got much worse the very next ball. An lbw shout was turned down. Replays showed the decision could easily have gone the way of the bowler. Miandad was also lucky when a catch off Reid flew between the keeper and Boon standing at about third slip. Pakistan's requirement had increased to 6.5 runs per over.

The captain knew the time was nigh. He glanced Waugh for four and lofted him with just enough force to clear mid wicket for another boundary. An on-driven four by Imran off O'Donnell brought up the 100 in the 27th over. Imran completed his 50 in 73 balls with four fours. He reached 58 and had put on 112 with Miandad when Border came on to bowl the 36th over. Imran swung hard, the ball went between the batsman and the stumps. Border and Dyer appealed for a stumping and a catch. 'Dickie' Bird gave Imran out caught behind. Pakistan doubted the merit of the decision, although there was some evidence of a bottom edge.

A lot of responsibility now rested with Miandad. He brought up his 50 in 79 balls. It was Akram, however, who tried to acclerate the scoring. He slapped McDermott straight down the ground for six and swept Border away into the cheering masses for a second six. McDermott responded with a leg stump yorker to leave Pakistan 5-177 in the 39th over. The assignment was getting tougher and tougher. 76 runs were needed from nine overs when 19 year old Ijaz Ahmed clipped a Reid leg stump half volley in the air straight to Jones at deep square leg.

Miandad remained as the last hope. Two runs to square leg off Waugh took the total to 200 in the 43rd over and his 'invention' upward nudge shot brought two more runs straight after. Fifty-six were still required from 37 balls when he slogged at Reid and lost his off stump. He had visibly tired during his innings, fatigued by having had to wicketkeep and the looming disappointment for his team. Yousuf and Qadir fought on, getting closer if not quite within striking distance. Yousuf and then Jaffer slogged at McDermott and were caught behind.

Tauseef faced up to the last ball of the 49th over, tentative and in pain from his throbbing thumb. He hung his bat out to a McDermott delivery and feathered an edge to Dyer. The Australians ran and embraced each other, everyone else in the stadium was despondent.

At McDermott's Man of the Match presentation the smiles from the dignataries, including General Zia, were impressive but strained. This was a defeat that was not in the Pakistani script. Imran had retired in defeat. Well, retired for a while.

AUSTRALIA		PAKISTAN	
G. R. Marsh run out	31	Mansoor Akhtar b McDermott	9
D. C. Boon st Javed Miandad b Salim Malik	65	Rameez Raja run out	1
D. M. Jones b Tauseef Ahmed	38	Salim Malik c McDermott b Waugh	25
A. R. Border (capt) run out	18	Javed Miandad b Reid	70
M. R. J. Veletta b Imran Khan	48	Imran Khan (capt) c Dyer b Border	58
S. R. Waugh not out	32	Wasim Akram b McDermott	20
S. P. O'Donnell run out	0	Ijaz Ahmed c Jones b Reid	8
G. C. Dyer (wk) b Imran Khan	0	Salim Yousuf (wk) cDyer b McDermott	21
C. J. McDermott b Imran Khan	1	Abdul Qadir not out	20
T. B. A. May not out	0	Salim Jaffer c Dyer b McDermott	0
Extras b1 lb19 w13 nb1	34	Tauseef Ahmed c Dyer b McDermott	1
(50 overs)	8-267	Extras lb6 w10	16
Did not bat: B. A. Reid		(49 overs)	249
1/73 2/155 3/155 4/215 5/236 6/236 7/241 8/249		1/2 2/37 3/38 4/150 5/177 6/192 7/212 8/236 9/247	
Bowling: Imran Khan 10-1-36-3; Jaffer 6-0-57-0;		Bowling: McDermott 10-0-44-5; Reid 10-2-41-2;	
Akram 10-0-54-0; Qadir 10-0-39-0;		Waugh 9-1-51-1; O'Donnell 10-1-45-0; May 6-0-36-0;	
Tauseef Ahmed 10-1-39-1; Salim Malik 4-0-22-1		Border 4-0-26-1	

Umpires: H.D. Bird D.R. Shepherd
Toss: Australia

2ND SEMI FINAL : INDIA vs ENGLAND
WANKHEDE STADIUM, BOMBAY: ENGLAND WON BY 35 RUNS

Australia had shattered the promoters' dream of an all-subcontinental Final. That did not upset India. They fancied their chances against Australia at Eden Gardens, especially after the mauling they gave their bowlers at New Delhi. All they had to do was overcome England in the Bombay semi-final on Thursday to fulfill their dream of winning a second consecutive World Cup, this time in front of their own adoring public.

England, happy to have a few day's extra preparation because they were able to stay in India rather than travel to Lahore, looked at the Wankhede Stadium wicket and were suspicious and critical. It was about 40 metres long, devoid of grass, red brown in colour and promised a complete absence of bounce. It appeared custom made for the Indian left-arm spinners. Gooch saw it and spent an hour in the nets practising his sweep shot against local bowlers.

Bombay's big day dawned, cloudy, airless, humid and stiflingly hot. The ground's 45,000 capacity was stretched to the limit. It made for an intimidating spectacle as Wankhede's covered stands almost lean over the smallish playing arena. The noisy, seething spectators according to Eddie Hemmings were, "Breathing down your neck." The effect was increased by the wire fences. They were designed to keep the spectators out, but gave the players the feeling they were performing in a cage.

Against Zimbabwe, Manoj Prabhakar had swung the ball disconcertingly in the hot and heavy atmosphere. What to do if the toss was won? The English hierarchy was split on whether to bat or bowl. In the end it did not matter. Gatting called incorrectly. To this day he does not know what his decision would have been had he won. Kapil Dev sent England in.

India were without Dilip Vengsarkar, incapacitated with the type of stomach upset which more commonly affects visitors to the country. Wicketkeeper Kiran More returned while Chandrakant Pandit retained his place as a batsman. England's side was unchanged from their previous match.

Kapil's hoped for swing was not there and apart from a throat clearing shout for lbw, Graham Gooch and Tim Robinson were not troubled by the new-ball. Early progress was slow and after ten overs only 20 runs were on the board. Robinson twice got Prabhakar away to the boundary, a clip to square leg and a drive over cover. Then when Maninder Singh came on the fun really began.

His first ball turned a metre away from Gooch, scooting through about five centimetres above the ground. Next ball Gooch bent low and swept hard. The ball shot away to fine leg for four. Gooch's assessment was right. From then he went on sweeping, paddling and pulling against the left arm spin. Robinson's departure in the 13th over, stumped going for a drive, made no difference. The ball spinning away prodigiously, so Kapil was slow to plug up the leg-side gaps and the runs were coming freely out there.

Bill Athey battled to come to terms with the conditions. He could only contribute four runs to a 39 second wicket stand with Gooch in nine overs before inside edging Chetan Sharma to More. Then Gooch found a like minded partner in his captain and they swept the Indians to distraction. Shot after shot went onto the vacant leg-side, fine, behind and in front of square leg. Gooch had reached his 50 in the 19th over off 64 balls. He brought up the 100 with yet another bent knee sweep, taking his own score to 60.

Azharuddin came on and Gatting varied the strokeplay with a square cut for four. Gooch had reached 82 when he finally mishit a sweep only for Kris Srikkanth to miss the skied chance as he ran in the same direction as the ball. A few overs later the Essex man pushed Kapil to deep mid-on and ran the single that brought up his impressive 100 out of 3-157 in the 38th over. Next, he back cut the same bowler for four while at the other end Gatting brought out the reverse sweep and hit Ravi Shastri for four more to third man.

Gatting went to his 50 when he put Maninder fine for another boundary. It had taken 59 balls and included four fours. An edged drive through slip for four more from a full toss took the stand to 117 in 19 overs, next ball, though, Gatting went so far across to the off that his sweep only brought the ball back onto the leg-stump. England were 3-196 in the 41st over. Gooch finally went a couple of overs later, held under his chin by a relieved Srikkanth on the square leg boundary. He had hit 11 fours in 136 balls. Kapil's late wickets could not stop Allan Lamb guiding England to 6-254 by the time of their compulsory closure. On this wicket, like Australia in Lahore, England knew they were in with a big chance.

The biggest roar of the day came in response to Gavaskar's stylish leg glance to the fine leg boundary to open his scoring in Philip DeFreitas' first over. A few minutes later joy turned to horror as the little opener's off stump was sent cartwheeling. DeFreitas had nipped the ball back between bat and pad. Most Indians believed Gavaskar would bat for them one more time. As events turned out this was his final departure from the international arena and, unlike Imran, he was never called back.

It was an inspirational start by DeFreitas and it made Srikkanth and Navjot Sidhu more circumspect. Srikkanth played and missed three consecutive deliveries and was dropped by wicketkeeper Paul Downton off Gladstone Small when he was 10. He and Sidhu eventually added 51 without hitting a boundary. A missed slog at Neil Foster removed Srikkanth and 15 runs later it was 3-73 when Sidhu was caught in the covers by Athey off the same bowler.

India, like Pakistan the day before, could feel their Reliance Cup dreams slipping away. Pandit and Azharuddin responded by attacking Hemmings as soon as the off-spinner was introduced. Sweeping was again the fashion, although Azharuddin's boundary that brought up the 100 in the 25th over was nearly caught at square leg by a brave Small. The tactic worked. Hemmings conceded 27 runs from three overs and was removed from the attack.

Pandit failed to take advantage of that when a slower ball from Foster hit him on the foot on the full right in front of the stumps. That brought in the Indian captain at 4-121. He french cut Foster just past his leg stump, one of several similar shots that day on the stay down pitch. A flick to fine leg off DeFreitas got a better result.

After a few overs from Gooch, Gatting brought back Hemmings. Kapil swung him away for yet another leg-side four and India were starting to close in. Kapil and Azharuddin had put on 47 in 5.2 overs when Hemmings insisted Gatting put a fieldsman on the mid wicket boundary. He had been urging him to do so for some time and was not pleased that it took so long to get a response. Eventually Gatting himself went out there.

The very next ball Kapil hit hard and high in that very direction. The English captain said his entire cricket career flashed in front of him as he waited for the ball to descend. Nevertheless the crucial catch was safely held. Kapil had faced just 22 balls for his 30.

Azharuddin pushed John Emburey to point to bring up his 50 in 60 balls. His job was far from finished and he was still there with Shastri to raise the 200. The sweeping swipe was still popular and such a hit right off the middle by Shastri left India a very gettable 51 runs to win from nine overs with five wickets standing.

Now, though, the game changed decisively. Azharuddin was given out lbw by umpire Steve Woodward when he swept at a straight and full Hemmings top-spinner. Azharuddin hit seven fours in 74 balls. His dismissal seemed to induce an Indian panic. One run later, Kiran More chipped a catch back to Emburey who nonchalantly caught the ball one handed high to his right. Prabhakar stepped away to cut Small and was caught behind off the bottom edge. Sharma slogged his first ball from Hemmings into the deep where Lamb took an excellent outfield catch lowdown.

It was all left up to Shastri. From the non-striker's end he had witnessed the suicidal batting that had reduced his side to 9-219. India still needed 36 and only non-batsman Maninder was left with him. There were 33 deliveries remaining, but Shastri pulled out the hari kari sword as well. Another hoik off Hemmings skied the ball to square leg where Downton judged the catch perfectly. The old traditional rivals, England and Australia were through. The subcontinental rivals were out.

India had lost their last five wickets for 20 in 33 balls. Hemmings share was 4-21 in 34 balls. Thank goodness his captain had finally agreed with his field placement. Gooch won the Man of the Match Award and allowed himself the luxury of a smile.

When Kapil had been racing along with Azharuddin fireworks were being let off continously in the stands. Once things went wrong, though, Wankhede was as quiet as Gaddafi had been the day before. The fans could be blamed for the loss, too, to the extent that all through the Indian innings they were madly calling for sixes. They were drunk on the type of batting their team had exhibited at Nagpur. Kapil got the official blame.

He was relieved of the captaincy for the second time.

ENGLAND		INDIA	
G. A. Gooch c Srikkanth b Maninder	115	K. Srikkanth b Foster	31
R. T. Robinson st More b Maninder	13	S. M. Gavaskar b DeFreitas	4
C. W. J. Athey c More b Sharma	4	N. S. Sidhu c Athey b Foster	22
M. W. Gatting (capt) b Maninder	56	M. Azharuddin lbw b Hemmings	64
A. J. Lamb not out	32	C. S. Pandit lbw b Foster	24
J. E. Emburey lbw b Kapil Dev	6	Kapil Dev (capt) c Gatting b Hemmings	30
P. A. J. DeFreitas b Kapil Dev	7	R. J. Shastri c Downton b Hemmings	21
P. R. Downton (wk) not out	1	K. S. More c & b Emburey	0
Extras b1 lb18 w1	20	M. Prabhakar c Downton b Small	4
(50 overs)	6-254	Chetan Sharma c Lamb b Hemmings	0
Did not bat: N. A. Foster, E. E. Hemmings, G. C. Small		Maninder Singh not out	0 .
1/40 2/79 3/196 4/203 5/219 6/231		Extras b1 lb9 w6 nb3	19
Bowling: Kapil Dev 10-1-38-2; Prabhakar 9-1-40-0;		(45.3 overs)	219
Maninder 10-0-54-3; Sharma 9-0-41-1; Shastri 10-0-49-0;		1/7 2/58 3/73 4/121 5/168 6/204 7/205 8/218 9/219	
Azharuddin 2-0-13-0		10/219	
		Bowling: DeFreitas 7-0-37-1; Small 6-0-22-1;	
		Emburey 10-1-35-1; Foster 10-0-47-3;	
		Hemmings 9.3-1-52-4; Gooch 3-0-16-0	

Umpires: A.R. Crafter S.J. Woodward

Toss: India

SUNDAY 9 NOVEMBER 1987
THE RELIANCE CUP FINAL: AUSTRALIA vs ENGLAND
EDEN GARDENS, CALCUTTA: AUSTRALIA WON BY 7 RUNS

The absence of their own team did nothing to deter the cricket fans of Calcutta. The World Cup final was an event, whoever the combatants. And the Indians selected Australia as the team to support. The English press believed it was because they had knocked out India while Australia had eliminated India's rivals, Pakistan. They do not realise that every other country will support whoever is playing against England. Always have, always will.

So 70,000, 80,000, 90,000—or however many fill that massive stadium—were there in force for a match that whatever the result would see a new country celebrating the holding of cricket's most prestigious limited overs trophy. The scalpers had to cut their ticket prices. India's semi-final defeat had cost them thousands of rupees.

There was plenty of radio coverage worldwide. Australians, suddenly very interested in cricket again, had to be satisfied with that and some more delayed television highlights of the conclusion of the match. The only live coverage was on Sky television in hotels. Despite images to the contrary, not all Australians live in public bars. Once more the words and pictures came via the BBC. Tony Lewis, Jack Bannister and Ray Illingworth competed with buzzing voices coming from crossed telephone lines. Did this mean there were Indians not actually watching the final?

The wicket provided for the big game was still slow, but far better than the one for the Bombay semi-final. Its preparation had been overseen by Les Burdett, curator at the Adelaide Oval, who was invited over by the Bengal Cricket Association.

All players involved were impressed, excited and even overwhelmed by the atmosphere, the occasion and the vibrancy of the stadium. This was not Lord's, but everyone celebrated the difference and the most cynical doubters had to admit Eden Gardens in its own way was a venue worthy of the World Cup final.

Australian coach, Bob Simpson has rated this ground the equal of any in the world. Mike Veletta was another who was very impressed. "We had an early rise because of the 9am start," Veletta says. "It was an exciting day and the whole team were thrilled just to be involved. There were thousands of people milling around as we drove in the bus to the ground. We had worked so hard to get to the Final and this was a celebration of the success we had in the tournament.

"It was the only time I played at Eden Gardens so I only ever saw it full. It is a fantastic arena with a good surface and the Indian authorities had done a great job in getting everything organised."

The day dawned fine and hot, if far more comfortable than steamy Bombay. Border won an important toss. Both he and his counterpart had wanted to bat first. The team line-ups were unchanged from their semi-final wins. England started the match as the bookmaker's favourite.

The value of Gatting's incorrect call was emphasised when David Boon and Geoff Marsh got Australia away to a flyer. Gladstone Small and Phil DeFreitas seemed affected by the occasion and were unable to control the new-ball. Boon, in particular, took advantage. Small's first over contained two no balls and cost 11 runs.

DeFreitas dropped short. One ball had Boon in trouble, the next was pulled for four. Another shot off his toes brought four more. After nine overs the total was already 48 and Boon was outscoring his partner three to one. Between them the two West Indies-born new-ball bowlers conceded 67 runs and Gatting decided not to risk them using their full quota of overs.

Neil Foster came on first change at the pavilion end and immediately made Boon and Marsh work harder for their runs. The next nine overs realised just 27. Then Foster moved a leg cutter through Marsh's defence and Australia were 1-75. Foster's first eight overs cost him just 16 so that after 25 overs the score was just 1-95. The off-spinners John Emburey and Eddie Hemmings had been introduced. Jones pulled the latter for six and lofted a Graham Gooch medium pacer down the ground for four.

Drinks were taken at the end of the 34th over with Australia 1-150. There were wickets in hand, but the projected target was now closer to 230 than the 270 it might have been after ten overs. The break in play fortified England's attack. Jones clipped Hemmings to Bill Athey at mid wicket straight after the break.Border's concern with the run rate was clear when Craig McDermott was promoted with the sole purpose of clouting some quick runs. He slogged Gooch for consecutive fours, however a few balls later missed a straight yorker from the same bowler. Two runs later when Boon top edged a sweep off Hemmings and wicketkeeper Paul Downton held the catch running back Australia were 4-168 in the 39th over. Their innings now lay in the balance. Boon had hit seven fours in 125 balls for his fifth half century of the competition.

Border was joined by Veletta and the pair quickly re-asserted Australia's position. Busy and bustling they put on 73 in 10 overs. Veletta who made his unbeaten 45 in just 31 balls glanced, swept and ran like a terrier. His placement was a feature of perhaps the most important innings of his life.

"I had to play my shots straight away," Veletta says. "AB and I got the partnership going with singles and then we hit out and took the odd chance towards the end of the innings. The spinners bowled a straight line, so it was better to sweep them rather than back away and hit the ball to the off, which I only did a couple of times. I think the combination of a left- and right-hand batsman mucked up their line a bit."

Gooch's eighth over cost 12 and the 200 was raised in the 44th over. A total of 79 was taken from the last 10 overs, including 11 from the luckless DeFreitas in the 50th.

"Two hundred and fifty-three was 20 more than we thought we would get in the middle of the innings," Veletta says. "More than that, though, a flurry of runs at the end gives the team a lift and puts them in a positive frame of mind when they go out to field. We knew we were in with a chance with 253 on the board, but also knew that we had a lot of hard work in front of us."

It did not take much work to get rid of Tim Robinson. His first ball was the third of the innings. McDermott bowled a fullish length, the ball cut back and Robinson, immobile at the crease, was trapped right in front. There was talk the Australian and English teams had asked for Tony Crafter and 'Dickie' Bird to officiate in the final. Quite rightly the tournament officials inisisted on neutrals and Ram Babu Gupta and Mahboob Shah got the job, which they handled competently. Robinson's lbw was one of the day's easier decisions.

Border had a half chance to run out Athey in the fourth over. The Yorkshireman responded with a nice glance for four in the next over. McDermott was bowling quickly enough to extract some lift from the slow wicket, but he could do nothing about a trademark Gooch on-drive to a half volley pitched on middle stump. The opener pulled Reid for another boundary then the left-armer slid the ball past his outside edge. Veletta added to the value of his batting by saving runs with some energetic work at square leg.

Simon O'Donnell, hiding the fact that he was very ill, dived desperately at fine leg to save two runs, then in the 18th over brought a ball back into Gooch that won a second lbw decision. It was 2-66, so Athey and Gooch had consolidated well without scoring at the run rate needed to win the match.

Gatting's task was to lift that rate. He got off the mark with an off-side glide for four off Waugh then selected young off-spinner, Tim May as the object of his batting brutality. He reverse swept and drove the South Australian for a seven run return then lofted him down the ground. Waugh on the boundary judged the catch perfectly. Unfortunately the force of the hit caused him to take two steps back. Waugh looked at his feet, and threw the ball back in disgust. He had stepped over the rope and the shot would count as six. After four expensive overs May was removed from the attack.

England reached their hundred in the 25th over. Gatting and Athey had added 69 in 14 overs when Border brought himself on to bowl. England were 2-135. Without any assessment of the left-arm spinner, Gatting reverse swept Border's first ball. It flew from the top edge onto his shoulder and lollied in the air to wicketkeeper, Greg Dyer. In an instant every English scribe and follower had a scapegoat for the eventual loss. Chairman of Selectors, the late Peter May, a known opponent of the reverse sweep, watching from the pavilion, closed his eyes. An over or so later the shot may have been a worthwhile risk. The judgemental error was to try it off Border's first ball. Veletta says, "I was surprised. They were batting well and it was unnecessary."

Athey, stylish and unhurried reached his 50 in 92 balls. When he and Allan Lamb paused for the day's last break for drinks England wanted 102 from 15 overs. Upon the resumption Lamb escaped when Dyer missed a stumping off Border. England had to keep pressing desperately for runs. Going for a third run Athey failed by a whisker to beat Waugh's throw. He had become one of over 60 run out dismissals throughout the tournament. Athey, who had assumed the role of the innings cornerstone hit just two fours in 103 balls. His dismissal left England on 4-170 in the 39th over.

Downton came in ahead of Emburey. He looked uncertain as to whether he should support Lamb or hit out to reduce the deficit. He hit a four, was dropped in the deep by a diving McDermott and then holed out to O'Donnell at long off. Five for 188 in the 42nd over. All of Emburey's expertise in the unorthodox was required. He played his special step away square slash at McDermott. The ball flew over point. Veletta was well placed, but the low sun was not. A brave attempt at the catch failed.

"The sun was in my eyes," Veletta says. " But AB still was not impressed when the catch went down."

The ask was getting tougher all the time. It was down to 38 required from 24 balls. Lamb pulled hard at Waugh, missed and ran a leg bye, another single to Emburey and Lamb tried the pull again. The ball hurried through and he was bowled. England felt it was over. Two more singles at the start of the 48th over did nothing to boost their hopes. Then Emburey swatted hard to mid wicket and ran. Boon did not have to move and his throw to McDermott was spot on. England 7-220 needed 34 from 15 balls and were out of it. The Indians thought so. They were cheering and dancing to a result that pleased them.

DeFreitas just ignored all this and smashed McDermott's next ball over extra cover for four. No one took a great deal of notice. Next ball he wound up and cracked the ball over the sightscreen for six. Now people were watching. From the sixth ball the seamer stepped right away and lifted the ball over mid wicket for four more.

"I think Craig was bowling to get wickets and put the ball on the wrong length," Veletta says. "DeFreitas gave us a bit of a fright. It got pretty nerve wracking out there"

Waugh, though, was not so easy to hit. DeFreitas used the same tactics and did not connect properly once. There was laughter when an outrageous slower ball barely bounced over his stumps. Then an inside edge was caught on the half volley by Dyer. When DeFreitas did connect he merely lobbed a catch to Reid deep on the off side.

It was left to the two fast bowlers, Small and Foster to get 17 from the final over. They pushed hard and collected a brave, but forlorn nine. Australia had won the Reliance Cup by seven runs.

"I fielded the last ball and foolishly threw it back in," Veletta says. "In the end the only souvenir I got from the match was a bail from Greg Dyer. I also got all the players to sign my bat. Otherwise there are just the memories. I'm not a great watcher of cricket, so I've never even sat through a video of the game."

Within minutes the smiling mullet-haired Australians were being feted and photographed in the darkness. For the long suffering Border, carried in triumph on the shoulders of his teammates, it was his sweetest moment in the game. The crowd stayed to cheer the Australians as they displayed their trophy on a lap of honour. They were then treated to a fantastic fireworks display which signalled the close of the 1987 World Cup. It was a spectacular conclusion to a wonderful tournament. Some original doubters were now sorry the carnival was over. David Frith in *Wisden Cricket Monthly* wrote, "Australia is back! And the cricket world is better for it."

"We had plenty of plans to celebrate and there was a function put on for us back at the hotel,"Veletta says. "I remember Simon O'Donnell doing a bit of singing, but it was a big day and by midnight I had conked out. I think the majority of the team were the same. We were able to celebrate a bit more over the next couple of days."

In the Oberoi Grand Hotel most people had forgotten that David Boon won the Man of the Match Award. This was a victory for every member of the Australian team.

AUSTRALIA		ENGLAND	
D. C. Boon c Downton b Hemmings	75	G. A.Gooch lbw b O'Donnell	35
G. R. Marsh b Foster	24	R. T. Robinson lbw b McDermott	0
D. M. Jones c Athey b Hemmings	33	C. W. J. Athey run out	58
C. J. McDermott b Gooch	14	M. W. Gatting (capt) c Dyer b Border	41
A. R. Border (capt) run out	31	A. J. Lamb b Waugh	45
M. R. J. Veletta not out	45	P. R. Downton (wk) c O'Donnell bBorder	9
S. R.Waugh not out	5	J. E. Emburey run out	10
Extras b1 lb13 w5 nb7	26	P. A. J. DeFreitas c Reid b Waugh	17
(50 overs)	5-253	N. A.Foster not out	7
Did not bat: S. P.O'Donnell, G. C.Dyer (wk), T. B. A. May,		G. C.Small not out	3
B. A.Reid		Extras b1 lb14 w2 nb4	19
1/75 2/151 3/166 4/168 5/241		(50 overs)	8-246
Bowling: DeFreitas 6-1-34-0; Small 6-0-33-0;		Did not bat: E. E. Hemmings	
Foster 10-0-38-1; Hemmings 10-1-48-2;		1/1 2/66 3/135 4/170 5/188 6/218 7/220 8/235	
Emburey 10-0-44-0; Gooch 8-1-42-1;		Bowling: McDermott 10-1-51-1; Reid 10-0-43-0;	
		Waugh 9-0-37-2; O'Donnell 10-1-35-1;	
		May 4-0-27-0; Border 7-0-38-2	

Umpires: R.B. Gupta   Mahboob Shah

Toss: Australia

POST-MORTEM

Australian World Cup joy was tempered by the announcement that 24-year-old all-rounder, Simon O'Donnell was diagnosed with cancer soon after his return home. The life threatening lymphatic tumour in his ribcage had to receive exhausting chemotherapy treatment. Happily, a couple of months later O'Donnell was given the all clear, to the relief of the entire cricket community. O'Donnell successfully resumed his career at the start of the 1988-89 season, although his perspective on life had been slightly altered.

At least that saga had a positive ending. The same could not be said of Mike Gatting's clash with umpire Shakoor Rana during the acrimonious Pakistan-England Test series which immediately followed the World Cup. The petty feud between the two countries sullied the game. The finger-pointing incident went a long way towards ending Gatting's tenure as captain. It also distracted attention away from the great job India and Pakistan did as co-hosts of the 1987 Reliance Cup. The tournament was a success in virtually every aspect and did great credit to the organisers.

CHAPTER 6:

Benson and Hedges World Cup, 1992: Imran's Cornered Tigers

Nineteen ninety-two was the year coloured uniforms, replay screens, night cricket under lights and tobacco advertising came to the World Cup. It was also the year that the South African issue dominated the headlines in the lead-up to the tournament. Fortunately, this time it was for all the right reasons.

To contest the World Cup in Australasia seemed a logical progression after the success of the first migration to India and Pakistan in 1987 and as a follow-up to the exciting win by Allan Border's team in the Reliance Cup final in Calcutta. Yet there was reluctance from the Australian authorities to commit themselves. Not even a World Cup was going to interfere with their schedule of a Test series and the precious, television-friendly World Series Cup. Some even questioned the likelihood of the financial success of a World Cup in Australia and New Zealand.

New Zealand Cricket Council chairman Bob Vance showed most enthusiasm for the idea, finally convincing his Australian counterparts at an ICC meeting in London in 1987 of the merit of the proposal.

Another ICC meeting in July 1989 ratified the joint submission that the 1992 World Cup would be played with the two countries as co-hosts. A schedule of matches was drawn up which included the same eight teams that participated in the competition in 1983 and 1987, except that this time the tournament would be played as a full round robin, each side meeting all the others once and four teams progressing to the semi-finals.

This caused meant there would be 31 games, four more than previous tournaments.

Everything seemed set until the political situation South Africa began to change. When Nelson Mandela was released from jail he gave his blessing for South Africa to return to the international cricketing fold. The ICC re-admitted them at their meeting in July 1991, although chairman, Colin Cowdrey suggested they would not be able to be included in the 1992 World Cup.

Mandela's advice was sought on the matter. He wrote to Cowdrey suggesting South Africa's inclusion would assist reconciliation and be a reward for the ground-breaking racial integration by South African cricket authorities. British Prime Minister John Major and his Australian counterpart, Bob Hawke, were also involved in negotiations. Most people liked the idea and in October it was agreed that a ninth side be included in the tournament. That necessitated a redraw which increased the number of matches to 39. The publicity the move brought to the competition was invaluable.

Once all that was sorted out, the rules for the 1992 Benson and Hedges World Cup could be drawn up. Each innings was once again limited to 50 overs. Fielding restrictions were increased in the first 15 overs with only two men allowed outside the circles during that time. The players' uniforms would be coloured and would bear their names on the back. A selection of games at suitable venues were to be partially played under lights at night. Two white balls were used each innings because of a problem with the greying and fading of just one. Most controversially, the tight scheduling allowed only one day to be set aside for each fixture and if lost overs were only to be "compensated by the lowest scoring overs of their opponents". It looked a dangerous and potentially unfair rule even at its inception.

Scheduling the tournament right at the end of the southern summer in late February and March, after all the other Australian Test and limited-over commitments had been cleared, meant there was a big risk of rain.

Despite the amount of cricket they had already played that summer, the form of the Australian side in 1991-92 under Allan Border had been excellent and at the start of the Benson and Hedges World Cup they were red-hot favourites to take the trophy for the second time running. They had the measure of India and the West Indies in the World Series Cup and had thrashed India 4-0 in a five-match Test series.

David Boon was in the midst of a fantastic run of form with the bat. The consistency of the powerful Tasmanian in the short and longer versions of the game was to be marvelled at. Against India he peeled off four Test centuries and one more in a limited-over international.

Boon's opening partner, Geoff Marsh, had a leaner time and had lost his Test place, but the popular deputy had been recalled for the World Cup. Mark Taylor, Dean Jones, possibly the greatest limited-overs batsman in the world and on the verge of becoming a specialist in that form of the game, Border and the Waugh twins, Mark and Steve, suggested a line-up capable of many match-winning totals in conditions that would suit them.

Like Boon, paceman Craig McDermott had just completed a fine domestic summer with oodles of wickets. With support from Merv Hughes, Mike Whitney, a fit-again Bruce Reid, off-spinner Peter Taylor and the all-rounders it was easy to see why this unit, well drilled by Bob Simpson, began the tournament regarded as the team to beat. Sharp running between wickets and error-free fielding were keynotes to recent successes and likely to feature again.

Australia's opponent in the 1987 final, England, under manager Mickey Stewart and the Simpson ethos of discipline and hard work. After a strong showing against the West Indies and New Zealand in recent months they were very confident of a strong showing.

Since his leadership appointment in 1990, Gooch had responded with a welter of runs and was an important component at the top of the order. Although 38, his willingness to train and keep fit was standing him in good stead. Gooch's philosophy meant that no place could be found for David Gower. However, Ian Botham, who arrived late in New Zealand because he had a part to play in a children's pantomime, was included.

Botham was just one of a squad bursting with all-rounders and middle-order batsmen. There was no specialist opener selected to accompany Gooch and the word was that Botham would be used to launch the innings in an attacking style that was perhaps four years ahead of its time. Graeme Hick's reputation as a batsman with the ability to massacre mediocre bowling preceded him, while Alec Stewart, the son of the team's manager, had adopted the important dual role of wicketkeeper-batsman and had been a revelation at the end of the English season and in New Zealand. For the likes of Gooch, Allan Lamb and Ian Botham, this was a last chance at the ultimate limited-overs prize.

Winning of the World Cup was Imran Khan's final ambition in cricket, too. The all-rounder wanted to do it for himself, his team, his country and the cancer hospital he wanted to have built in Pakistan. His squad was filled with talent, not least his own which, if diminishing slightly, was still formidable. There had been plenty of comings and goings in the lead-up to the World Cup as Pakistan tried to get the balance of their squad just right. A big loss was the back injury to Wasim Akram's new ball partner Waqar Younis. On the bright side, Javed Miandad had just recovered from a back injury.

Since the disappointing loss in the 1987 semi-final, Salim Malik had become a quality performer in the Pakistani middle order and Ramiz Raja, an aggressive opener, also had an impressive record in limited-over internationals. Imran, starting the tournament with a shoulder injury, could still deliver a lethal in-swinger, while his heir apparent, Wasim Akram, swung the ball late at fast left-arm. His hitting in a tight situation was a real bonus to Pakistan.

India had been playing cricket in Australia since the previous November and by February had only a few wins in the World Series Cup to show for their efforts. Much attention centred on the wunderkind batting of Sachin Tendulkar. At 18, the youngster from Bombay had already shown the skill and temperament to flourish at the highest level.

At the other end of his career was all-rounder Kapil Dev. Like Botham and Imran, this would be the last showcase of his great talents. He had just become the second bowler in history to pass the 400 Test wicket mark. Kapil's fast-medium swingers were the cutting edge of the Indian attack. To neutral spectators, though, it was his middle-order hitting that was the greatest attraction.

Disappointed at losing the 1987 semi-final in Bombay after the triumph of 1983, the pressure was on the respected Indian captain, Mohammad Azharuddin, to get plenty of runs himself.

While holding on to their status as the best Test side in the world, the past six years had seen a decline in the West Indies as a force in the limited-overs version of the game. They, like India, were familiar with conditions in Australia, although the selectors made some changes to the World Series Cup squad to the one for the World Cup.

Viv Richards had hoped to use the tournament as his swansong, but the selectors opted to leave him out. hoping that the new captain, Richie Richardson, could establish some authority over the team. The World Cup squad was boosted with the inclusion of experienced players such as Roger Harper, Phil Simmons and Winston Benjamin. Malcolm Marshall's wise head was another asset to Richardson, although the champion fast bowler had lost a lot of his sting with the new ball.

Eagerly anticipated was the batting of the rival to Tendulkar's status as world prodigy, Brian Lara. The stylish Trinidadian left-hander had a pedigree as impressive as Tendulkar's and was at about the same stage of his career. Desmond Haynes and Richardson would be expected to be the best performed West Indian batsmen, while Curtly Ambrose remained a fearsome opponent when armed with a new ball.

Although rated only a 14-1 chance to win the World Cup, New Zealand were thrilled with their role as joint hosts, had prepared thoroughly and might be a handful on their own wickets. The Kiwis had been outclassed by England only weeks before, but Martin Crowe and his brains trust still had a few tricks up their sleeves and hoped to make an impact on the competition.

If New Zealand were to have any success, Crowe himself, a batsman among the world's elite, would have to score plenty of runs. There was some talent behind him, too, in the shape of John Wright, Ken Rutherford and Mark Greatbatch, but the best feature of the attack looked to be its steadiness, which was hardly inspiring. The medium pace of Willie Watson was supported by the fast-medium pace of Chris Cairns and Danny Morrison, the slow-medium pace of Gavin Larsen and Rod Latham and the flat darting off spin of Dipak Patel.

The possible promotion of Zimbabwe to full ICC membership and hence eventual Test status was welcomed by the Sri Lankans, as they would no longer be viewed as the underlings of the international fold. An isolated win against other countries still gave cause for special celebration in Colombo, but they gave no indication that they would have any impact on the event. As with New Zealand, their bowling looked to lack the necessary punch to restrict quality opposition to a losing total.

Aravinda de Silva was captain for the World Cup and clearly his side's classiest batsman in a well-credentialled line-up which included chunky left-hander Arjuna Ranatunga. Hashan Tillerkeratne, Sanath Jayasuriya and Asanka Gurusinha were also accomplished left-banders with their best days ahead of them, while Roshan Mahanama's style and technique at the top of the order complemented the aggression of the left-handers well.

Sri Lankan bowling resources were thin. Rumesh Ratnayake, Pramodya Wickremasinghe and Champaka Ramanayake may have been able to defend substantial totals, but not modest ones. Sri Lanka would find by the end of the tournament that their geographical knowledge of Australasia was excellent. As in 1987, they had plenty of international criss-crossing to do.

Zimbabwe had made the best possible start when they entered the competition in 1983 by defeating Australia, but that initial victory was still their only World Cup success. Dave Houghton would hope to remedy that. His individual effort against New Zealand in 1987 had brought Zimbabwe closest to their second win. Now Houghton was captain, taking on that role at the expense of his wicketkeeping duties which he had handed over to the promising left-handed opening batsman, Andy Flower. Teenager Alistair Campbell was another Zimbabwean batsman of great promise.

Eddo Brandes offered the greatest likelihood of breaking through with the new ball. The most reliable member of the Zimbabwean attack, however, was still off-spinner John Traicos, who was only a few months short of his 45th birthday. Traicos remained as lean and fit as when he played three Tests for South Africa back in 1970.

Like many others, Traicos was probably astounded when South Africa achieved sudden re-acceptance into the outside cricketing world. And he and his peers were excited by the prospect of pitting their skill against the former exiles.

The South African side was led by Kepler Wessels, who, like Traicos, had now represented two countries. Wessels had already played more than 50 limited-over internationals for Australia between 1982 and 1985.

Seven years later the selection of his team had caused an uproar in South Africa. Three favourite sons who had done themselves great credit through the years of isolation, Clive Rice, Jimmy Cook and Peter Kirsten, were all omitted from the South African side. Following much protest a spot was found for Kirsten. Cook was selected for a couple of later Tests, but Rice, a great all-rounder who captained the side in South Africa's first sanctioned match on their return in India, was finished as an international cricketer when he had hardly started.

Many of Wessels' players were new names and faces to fans outside South Africa. One whose arrival in Australasia was eagerly anticipated was fast bowler Allan Donald. 'White Lightning' had a reputation as one of the quickest bowlers in the world. An exciting spectacle as a thoroughbred in the Michael Holding and Dennis Lillee mould, Donald's bowling would be a talking point amongst the batsmen in each of the other eight sides before the tournament was over.

The teams in their vivid blues, greens, yellows and reds lined up on the deck of the *HMAS Canberra* on Sydney Harbour for the now almost traditional pre-tournament group photo. Another shot at Circular Quay with the Opera House as a backdrop featured the captains, with Border and Gooch nursing the trophy.

The weather for Sydney was a little gloomy, which summed up the attitude of some of the participants and those covering the tournament at this early stage. A complaints department would have been very busy after the black-tie dinner that launched the competition. Too expensive, poorly arranged and uninspiring was the view of the critics after the event. Ian Chappell wrote the guests would have been better off to spend their money on a harbour cruise. Wasim Akram called the photo session a shambles and the price of the dinner 'immoral'. Ray Martin hosted without the support of the type of quality offsider he had when introducing Australian television coverage of the 1999 World Cup.

The only memorable moment came when joint chairman of the organising committee, Malcolm Gray, said that the room contained the most extraordinary collection of cricketing talent, "with the possible exception of when Sir Donald Bradman dines alone". Three days later a selection of that talent, sans Bradman, was on display.

The Benson and Hedges World Cup was under way.

SATURDAY 22 FEBRUARY 1992
NEW ZEALAND vs AUSTRALIA
EDEN PARK, AUCKLAND: NEW ZEALAND WON BY 37 RUNS

Australia had only to play one of their matches in New Zealand, and after the tournament favourites were well beaten by the better-prepared Kiwis in this one they would be glad not to have to come back.

After some pre-match hype that included the distribution of thousands of party hooters to the big parochial crowd and a parade with sets of giant stumps, dancing girls and Sir Richard Hadlee being driven around holding that precious glass trophy, Martin Crowe won the toss and elected to bat. Craig McDermott opened with a wide, sent another one down second ball then bowled John Wright behind his legs with the first legal delivery of the tournament.

When Ian Healy brilliantly caught Rod Latham low to his right the home side was 3-53 after 15 overs and there was no indication the Australians would be set a difficult target. Some signs were not good for Allan Border's side, though. Tom Moody had already dropped a simple waist-high chance at first slip and the bowlers, supposedly slightly underdone in the shorter version of the game, were unwisely dropping the ball short.

This meant Martin Crowe could put his powerful pull shot and the short boundaries at backward square leg to good use. It almost brought him unstuck when a diving Dean Jones nearly brought off the catch of the season at deep square leg. Otherwise time and again, even with two fieldsmen protecting the boundary, short balls were pummelled to the fence. A Ken Rutherford version of the shot off Steve Waugh raised the 100 in the 28th over as the acceleration began.

Off-spinner Peter Taylor bowled a poor spell. Crowe belted yet another short delivery between two leg-side boundary sweepers to bring him to his 50 in the 31st over. The milestones continued. The 100 partnership arrived in the 38th over with still another pulled four by Crowe off Bruce Reid. For variety, the next ball was driven through mid off, also for four.

The deepening frown on Border's brow grew darker when the Australian captain failed to hold a swirling chance running back at square leg given by his opposite number. A direct-hit underarm throw by Mark Waugh which ran out Rutherford ended the excellent 118-run stand.

However, it failed to bring any relief for Border and the Australians. Productive little partnerships between Crowe and Chris Harris, then Crowe and Ian Smith, lifted the total above 200. Healy's second wonderful catch brought in Chris Cairns and the young all-rounder mixed the verbals with the Australians, clubbed a couple of boundaries and ran like the wind to complete the single which gave Crowe his 100 in the 50th over. The Kiwi supporters invaded Eden Park in celebration, happy at the milestone and the final team total of 6-248 which included 77 from the final 10 overs.

Crowe had been no certainty to start in the World Cup because of problems with his right knee. It was another reason why seven of his 11 fours had come from back-foot pulls. The quality and aggression of the New Zealand captain's batting, in harness with Rutherford, had taken the favourites by surprise. Now, in the field, he confused their tactics further by opening the bowling with off-spinner Dipak Patel.

The idea brought no immediate reward as David Boon and Geoff Marsh put on 62 for the first wicket. The pair, with Marsh in particular struggling, used up 18 overs which boosted the required run rate to a run per ball. Once Marsh was caught at cover driving Larsen, Jones attempted to lift the tempo only to be run out going for a two to square leg on Cairns' powerful arm. The decision by Khizar Hayat, which replays showed was a tight one, had a big impact on the Australian momentum.

Boon pulled Patel for four to raise the 100 in the 28th over. The Kiwis had reached the landmark at the same time. A few balls later, unaccountably, Border swung across the line at the off-spinner and was caught at deep square leg by Cairns. Moody struggled and soon totally mistimed a defensive push straight back to Latham. When Mark Waugh was given out lbw hitting across a full-pitched ball from Gavin Larsen Australia were 5-125 in the 34th over and in deep trouble.

Crowe kept rotating his medium pacers in one- and two-over spells which upset the rhythm of the Australian batting. When Steve Waugh joined Boon Australia needed nearly eight per over. The sixth-wicket pair also had to repair the damage caused by the collapse on a wicket playing slower and lower than in the morning. They did so to good effect, putting on 74 at a run per ball. In the 45th over Waugh stepped away and clobbered Latham straight for the only six of the match. More of the same was needed, as the ask was now up to 10 per over.

Larsen's next over decided the result. Boon, who like Crowe was starting to hobble in the later stages on his bad knee, brought up his 100. Then Waugh tried to advance on the bowler, was checked by a shorter delivery and pushed the ball in the air back along the pitch. Larsen dived and exultantly came up with the catch.

Two balls later a brilliant direct-hit throw at the bowler's end by Chris Harris ran out Boon by a metre and finished Australia's challenge. Healy and McDermott were also run out sacrifices, Taylor was caught at mid wicket and when Reid lifted Harris to Andrew Jones on the long on boundary, a worthy hit by the spindly nonbatsman, Australia had lost five wickets in 17 balls and New Zealand had completed a sensational 37-run victory.

The 25,000 strong crowd charged onto the ground again in celebration. Victory over Australia was sweet, especially so for the recently criticised, now Man of the Match New Zealand captain. He described it as one of the best days of his life.

NEW ZEALAND		AUSTRALIA	
J. G. Wright b McDermott	0	D. C. Boon run out	100
R.J. Latham c Healy b Moody	26	G. R. Marsh c Latham b Larsen	19
A. H. Jones lbw b Reid	4	D. M. Jones run out	21
M. D. Crowe (capt) not out	100	A. R. Border (capt) c Cairns b Patel	3
K. R. Rutherford run out	57	T. M. Moody c & b Latham	7
C. Z. Harris run out	14	M. E. Waugh lbw b Larsen	2
I. D. S. Smith (wk) c Healy b McDermott	14	S. R. Waugh c & b Larsen	38
C. L. Cairns not out	16	I. A. Healy (wk) not out	7
Extras (lb 6, w 7, nb 4)	17	C. J McDermott run out	1
(50 overs)	6-248	P. L. Taylor c Rutherford b Watson	1
Did not bat: D. N. Patel, G. R. Larsen, W. Watson		B. A. Reid c Jones b Harris	3
1/2 2/13 3/53 4/171 5/191 6/215		Extras (lb 6, w 2, nb 1)	9
Bowling: McDermott 10-1-43-2; Reid 10-0-39-1, Moody		(48.1 overs)	10-211
9-1-37-1; S. R. Waugh 10-0-60-0; Taylor 7-0-36-0; M. E.		1/62 2/92 3/104 4/120 5/125 6/199 7/200 8/205 9/206	
Waugh 4-0-27-0		Bowling: Cairns 4-0-30-0; Patel 10-1-36-1; Watson 9-1-39-1;	
		Larsen 10-1-30-3; Latham 8-0-35-1; Harris 7.1-0-35-1	

Umpires: Khizar Hayat, D.R Shepherd.

Toss: New Zealand.   Points: New Zealand 2, Australia 0

ENGLAND vs INDIA
WACA, PERTH: ENGLAND WON BY 9 RUNS

Same date, same tournament, but almost half a world and certainly half a day away, England won a thriller against India in Perth. The Australian section of the competition was lit up both figuratively and literally as India became the first team in the World Cup to bat at night under lights. The late finish in Perth meant that most people on the east coast of Australia and in New Zealand had to wait until the next morning to find out the result of this tight encounter.

Graham Gooch took Ian Botham out to open with him after he won the toss and batted on a typically hard and bouncy Perth wicket. The pantomime king's booming drive over mid off in the seventh over was an isolated blow in an inconsequential innings. Troubled, as many are by the steep bounce, he batted sluggishly for nine overs before edging a back foot drive off Kapil Dev through to Kiran More.

Robin Smith, a record-breaker with South Perth four years before, was altogether more comfortable and soon making up for the slow start. In his navy blue Test helmet rather than the sky blue of the World Cup, Smith spanked a couple of thrilling cover drives, then in the 24th over pulled left-arm spinner Ravi Shastri many a mile for a six over mid wicket that brought up the 100. His own half century was completed four overs later.

Gooch, much more circumspect, had only once reached the boundary when he passed 50. Hampered by a knock to his leg from his own bat and using Botham as a runner, he tried to drive Shastri inside out and spooned an easy catch to cover.

His replacement, Graeme Hick, hit one stunning lofted off drive then perished to a feeble push outside the off stump to Subroto Banerjee. Pragmatic rather than fashionable, Neil Fairbrother added 60 with the in-form Smith, who pulled Banerjee for his second six. When a vicious Smith cut was beautifully held by Mohammad Azharuddin in the gully one run later England were 5-198 in the 44th over. Their all-rounders failed to significantly add to that and the English tally for the last seven overs was 6-39 out of an eventual 9-236.

Gooch was unsure about his side's total. Any lack of confidence would have been compounded by Srikkanth's attacking approach which brought him seven thumping boundaries. In the 16th over he twice pulled Phil DeFreitas for four then, unable to calm his adrenalin rush, skyed the next ball to mid off. When Azharuddin was caught behind by a beauty from Dermott Reeve next over, 0-63 had become 2-63 and India had forfeited their advantage.

Ravi Shastri and Sachin Tendulkar doubled the score by the 30th over, the teenager looking ominously good. Then Botham put England back on top again. A perfectly pitched away cutter had Tendulkar caught behind playing forward. In the midst of a very tight spell Botham also had Tendulkar's old school chum, Vinod Kambli, chipping to a juggling Hick at mid-on.

Shastri completed a solid 50 before skying a slog off Defreitas straight up in the air. The bowler, perhaps distracted by moving batsmen, dropped the chance but retained enough composure to run out Shastri with an underarm direct hit.

The equation was reduced to 51 from seven overs. Kapil Dev smacked some powerful blows before holing out to Defreitas at long on. In the rush for runs Praveen Amre and More were run out and Manoj Prabhakar was bowled stepping away to drive Reeve. The last pair of Banerjee and Srinath had to conjure up another 36 in three overs.

To the astonishment of the healthy English contingent in the crowd, the Indian pacemen started to strike the ball well, Banerjee lifted an off drive to the boundary and smashed Derek Pringle's last ball for six over long on. India needed 11 from the last over, but from the second ball messed up their running which allowed Botham to charge in from short cover and break the stumps. England sighed with relief.

Botham was named Man of the Match ahead of Smith. Azharuddin saw Tendulkar's dismissal as the turning point in the game and also lamented the 13 wides sent down by his bowlers.

ENGLAND		INDIA	
G. A. Gooch (capt) c Tendulkar b Shastri	51	R. J. Shastri run out	57
I. T. Botham c Moore b Kapil Dev	9	K. Srikkanth c Botham b DeFreitas	39
R. A. Smith c Azharuddin b Prabhakar	91	M. Azharuddin (capt) c Stewart b Reeve	0
G. A. Hick c Moore b Banerjee	5	S. R. Tendulkar c Stewart b Botham	35
N. H. Fairbrother c Srikkanth b Srinath	24	V. G. Kambli c Hick b Botham	3
A. J. Stewart (wk) b Prabhakar	13	P. K. Amre run out	22
C. C. Lewis c Banerjee b Kapil Dev	10	Kapil Dev c DeFreitas b Reeve	17
D. R. Pringle c Srikkanth b Srinath	1	S. T. Banerjee not out	25
D. A. Reeve not out	8	K. S. More (wk) run out	1
P. J. DeFreitas run out	1	M. Prabhakar b Reeve	0
P.C.R. Tufnell not out	3	J. Srinath run out	11
Extras lb 1, lb 6, w 13)	20	Extras (lb 9, w 7, nb 1)	17
(50 overs)	9-236	(49.2 overs)	10-227

1/21 2/121 3/137 4/197 5/198 6/214 7/222 8/223 9/224

1/63 2/63 3/126 4/140 5/149 6/187 7/194 8/200 9/201

Bowling: Kapil Dev 10-0-38-2; Prabhakar 10-3-34-2; Srinath 9-1-47-2; Banerjee 7-0-45-1; Tendulkar 10-0-370; Shastri 4-0-28-1

Bowling: Pringle 10-0-53-0; Lewis 9.2-0-36-0; DeFreitas 10-0-39-1; Reeve 6-0-38-3; Botham 10-0-27-2; Tufnell 4-0-25-0

Umpires: D.P. Buultjens, P.J. McConnell.

Toss: England.   Points: England 2, India 0

SUNDAY 23 FEBRUARY 1992
SRI LANKA vs ZIMBABWE
PUKEKURA PARK, NEW PLYMOUTH: SRI LANKA WON BY 3 WICKETS

The first Sunday helping of the Benson and Hedges World Cup was not considered worthy of television coverage, so details of the extraordinary match at Pukekura Park in New Plymouth are left to those who actually attended the attractive North Island venue. If the 3000 or so spectators had put their heads together to contrive some sort of a tale to tell their friends about what they had seen, they could not have bettered this run bonanza. The joint lack of bowling penetration cancelled out any advantage to either side, so the tiny ground hosted a 625-run thriller.

Zimbabwe batted first after Aravinda de Silva had won the toss and sent them in. Their start was unremarkable as they were 3-82 when Asanka Gurusinha had Dave Houghton caught behind. Kevin Amott's run-per-ball 52 of a partnership of 85 with young opener Andy Flower was the first indication of the day's batting. Then when powerful Andy Waller joined Flower all hell broke loose during a recordbreaking unbroken stand of 145 in 13 overs. Waller raced to his 50 in 32 balls, then also a record. The Sri Lankan attack was without Rumesh Ratnayake who had a dislocated shoulder and they found it impossible to stem the run flow.

Waller crunched nine fours and three sixes, one of which landed in a nearby duck pond. Flower completed his maiden century in limited-over internationals.

Only the arrival of the 50-over limit stopped the entertainment, and then just temporarily. When the chase for 313 began, Sri Lankan openers Roshan Mahanama and Athula Samarasekera were quickly into their stride.

Samarasekera raced to his 50 at a rate just one ball slower than Waller and 128 runs were on the board before John Traicos brought some bowling sanity to the game. The 44-year-old picked up a wicket, conceded just three to 4-167, a scoreline identical to the one Zimbabwe had been.

But Traicos could only bowl 10 overs, so that even though 100 was required from the last 11 overs, the return of the medium pacers again invited all-out attack. Sanath Jayasuriya in a cameo taster for 1996 smashed two sixes and two fours in 23 balls. It was the ex-captain Arjuna Ranatunga, playing his 100th limited-over international, who became the match winner. He smashed his way to 50, bringing up the milestone with a six and, after being caught off a no ball, went on to make 88 in 61 balls, including the winning boundary, a pull off Malcolm Jarvis with three wickets and four balls to spare.

Andy Flower, unable to believe his side had lost after making 4-312, was named Man of the Match.

ZIMBABWE		SRI LANKA	
A. Flower (wk) not out	115	R. S. Mahanama c Arnott b Brandes	59
W. R. James c Tillekaratne b Wkkremasinghe	17	M. R. Samarasekera c Duers b Traicos	75
A.J. Pycroft c Ramanayake b Gurusinha	5	P.A de Silva (capt) c Houghton b Brandes	14
D. L. Houghton (capt) c Tillekaratne b Gurusinha	10	A.P. Gurusinha run out	5
K. J. Arnott c Tillekaratne b Wkkremasinghe	52	A. Ranatunga not out	88
A. C. Waller not out	30	S. T. Jayasuriya c Flower b Houghton	32
Extras (b 2, lb 6, w 13, nb 9)	30	H. P. Tillekaratne (wk) b Jarvis	18
(50 overs)	4-312	R. S. Kalpage c Duers b Brandes	11
Did not bat: L.P. Butchart, K. G. Duers, E. A Brandes,		C. P. H. Ramanayake not out	1
M. P. Jarvis, A.J. Traicos		Extras (lb 5, w 5)	10
1/30 2/57 3/82 4/167		(49.2 overs)	7-313
Bowling: Ramanayake 10-0-59-0;		Did not bat: K.l.W. Wijegunawardene, G. P. Wickremasinghe	
Wijegunawardene 7-0-59-0; Wickremasinghe 10-1-50-2;		1/128 2/144 3/155 4/167 5/212 6/273 7/309	
Gurusinha 10-0-72-2; Kalpage 10-0-51-0;		B. Wling: Jarvis 9.2-0-61-1; Brandes 10-0-70-3;	
Jayasuriya 3-0-18-0		Duers 10-0-72-0; Butchart 8-0-'53-0; Traicos 10-1-33-1;	
		Houghton 2-0-19-1	

Umpires: P.D. Reporter, S.J. Woodward.

Toss: Sri Lanka.   Points: Sri Lanka 2, Zimbabwe 0

PAKISTAN vs WEST INDIES
MCG, MELBOURNE: WEST INDIES WON BY 10 WICKETS

To top off run-making Sunday, the West Indies and Pakistan played out a match at the MCG where just two wickets fell for 441 runs from 96.5 overs. This game was entertaining enough for the 14,000 in attendance and the television viewers, but without the thrills and spills of New Plymouth as the West Indies always looked to have plenty in hand when they batted.

Such a crowd makes little impact on the 90,000 or so seats available at the MCG, so it was a fairly cold and cheerless venue that greeted Ramiz Raja and Aamir Sohail as they began the Pakistani innings after Richie Richardson had sent them in to bat. The pair certainly took some time to warm to their task. Sohail was only on Marshall away for a couple of fours before skying Winston Benjamin to Gus Logie in the covers.

The arrival of young Inzamam-ul-Haq failed to lift the tempo. The West Indies used both their off-spinners, Carl Hooper and Roger Harper, effectively. Ramiz survived a stumping chance when he was 16 and moved from 23 to 57 in singles. Harper got rid of Inzamam in the 30th over when the total was still short of 100. At that rate Pakistan would barely top 160 after 50 overs.

Javed Miandad, captaining the side in place of the injured Imran Khan even though Salim Malik had been nominated as vice-captain in the selected souad, started barking orders at Ramiz and forcing him to run for short singles.

West Indian wicketkeeper David Williams missed catching both batsmen as Miandad started improvising and Ramiz finally began to hit the ball in the middle. The opener reached his 100 in 157 balls.

Miandad, walking everywhere around the crease, glanced Marshall to the unguarded fine-leg boundary. He reached his 50 in 56 balls, was caught off an Ambrose delivery that was called a no ball because it bounced above his shoulder and was still at the crease with Ramiz when the 50 overs were completed. The unbroken stand was worth 123 and the West Indies, in stark contrast to previous sides from the Caribbean, had actually completed their overs 30 minutes ahead of time.

They also reached their target ahead of schedule on the back of a brilliant innings by Brian Lara, who made 88 in 101 balls before a Wasim Akram yorker crushed his toe. The Pakistani attack without Imran Khan and Waqar Younis lacked firepower once Akram had completed his first spell. They certainly could not afford to drop Desmond Haynes on 35 and 49, as the experienced Barbadian went on to bat until the game had reached its conclusion.

Lara's innings won him the Man of the Match award. He struck 11 boundaries, all with the flourishing backlift, exquisite timing and full follow-through that are so appealing to the eye. X-rays showed no bone damage after Lara was assisted from the field with the total on 175, just seven short of the then first-wicket World Cup record set in 1975.

Two no balled bouncers by Aaqib Javed finished the match and annoyed Miandad, as did the increasing number of fielding mistakes. His opposite number was pleased that pushing Lara up the order had been effective and that his off-spinners had bowled with such control.

PAKISTAN		WEST INDIES	
Ramiz Raja not out	102	D. L. Haynes not out	93
Aamir Sohail c Logie b Benjamin	23	B. C. Lara retired hurt	88
Inzamam-ul-Haq c Hooper b Harper	27	R. B. Richardson (capt) not out	20
Javed Miandad (capt) not out	57	Extras (b 2, lb 8, w 7, nb 3)	20
Extras (b 1, lb 3, w 5, nb 2)	11	(46.5 overs)	0-221
(50 overs)	2-220	Did not bat: C. L. Hooper, K. L. T. Arthurton, A. L. Logie,
Did not bat: Salim Malik, Ijaz Ahmed, Wasim Akram,		R. A. Harper, M. D. Marshall, W. K.M. Benjamin,
Main Khan (wk), Iqbal Sikander, Wasim Haider, Aaqib Javed		D. Williams (wk), C. E. L. Ambrose
1/45 2/97		Lara retired hurt at 0-175
Bowling: Marshall 10-1-53-0; Ambrose 10-0-40-0;		Bowling: Wasim Akram 10-0-37-0; Aaqib Javed 8.5-0-42-0;
Benjamin 10-0-49-1; Hooper 10-0-41-0; Harper 10-0-33-1		Wasim Haider 8-0-42-0; Ijaz Ahmed 6-1-29-0; Iqbal
		Sikander 8-1-26-0; Aamir Sohail 6-0-35-0

Umpires: S.G. Randell, I.D. Robinson,

Toss: West Indies.   Points: West Indies 2, Pakistan 0

TUESDAY 25 FEBRUARY 1992
NEW ZEALAND vs SRI LANKA
TRUST BANK PARK, HAMILTON: NEW ZEALAND WON BY 6 WICKETS

The most featureless match of the competition so far saw New Zealand cruise to their second win by six wickets in Hamilton. Martin Crowe's failure suggested the Kiwis were a force as a team, not just a one-man show. Sri Lanka's batsmen, on the other hand, at no stage batted with the freedom they had on Sunday and were unable to set a challenging target.

It was a humid day, so Crowe used his pacemen rather than Dipak Patel's off-spin to take the new ball after he won the toss and asked Sri Lanka to bat. Roshan Mahanama's determination and technique were the platform of a sound base to the Sri Lankan innings. His stand of 70 with Aravinda de Silva took Sri Lanka to 2-120. The run out of the Sri Lankan captain was untimely, although Mahanama and Arjuna Ranatunga put on another 52 so that at the 42-over mark a competitive score was a strong possibility.

Then, against the tight bowling of Patel and Willie Watson and bedevilled by more run outs, the innings stalled. The last eight overs produced just 34 runs for the loss of six wickets. Even though left-handed opener John Wright had hurt his shoulder while fielding, he dominated the opening stand of 77 with Rod Latham.

The two Sri Lankan spinners, Ruwan Kalpage and left-armer Don Anurasiri, reined in the scoring. Kalpage got rid of both openers and when a restrained Crowe was caught in the deep off a Pramodya Wickremasinghe long-hop the Kiwis had slipped to 3-105.

That was as close as the Sri Lankans came to winning. Ken Rutherford was dropped by Ranatunga at slip before he had scored and then put together a match-winning innings. Andrew Jones' solidity allowed Rutherford to stroke the ball with confidence and fluency. To rub salt into the Sri Lankan wound, he put Ranatunga over long on for six. When Jones was out after a stand of 81 with Rutherford victory was clearly in sight and duly achieved with 10 balls to spare.

Rutherford was named Man of the Match. Aravinda de Silva lamented his injury list; Athula Samarasekera had damaged a hamstring and Rumesh Ratnayake's shoulder injury put him out of the tournament. A request that Graeme Labrooy be included in the Sri Lankan squad in Ratnayake's place was granted.

SRI LANKA		NEW ZEALAND	
R. S. Mahanama c & b Harris	80	J. G. Wright c & b Kalpage	57
M. R. Samarasekera c Wright b Watson	9	R. T. Latham b Kalpage	20
A. P. Gurusinha c Smith b Harris	9	A. H. Jones c Jayasuriya b Gurusinha	49
P. A. de Silva (capt) run out	31	M. D. Crowe (capt) c Ramanayake b Wickremasinghe	5
A. Ranatunga c Rutherford b Harris	20	K. R. Rutherford not out	65
S. T. Jayasuriya run out	5	C. Z. Harris not out	5
H. P. Tillekaratne (wk) c Crowe b Watson	8	Extras (lb 3, w 3, nb 3)	9
R. S. Kalpage c Larsen b Watson	11	(48.2 overs)	4-210
C. P. H. Ramanayake run out	2	Did not bat: D. N. Patel, I. D. S. Smith (wk). G. R. Larsen,	
S. D. Anurasiri not out	3	D. K. Morrison, W. Watson	
G. P. Wickremasinghe not out	3	1/77 2/91 3/105 4/186	
Extras (b 1, lb 15, w 4, nb 5)	25	Bowling: Ramanayake 9.2-0-46-0; Wickremasinghe 8-1-40-1;	
(50 overs)	9-206	Anurasiri 10-1-27-0; Kalpage 10-0-33-2; Gurusinha 4-0-19-1;	
1/18 2/50 3/120 4/172 5/172 6/181 7/195 8/199 9/202		Ranatunga 4-0-22-0; Jayasuriya 2-0-14-0; de Silva 1-0-6-0	
Bowling: Morrison 8-0-36-0; Watson 10-0-37-3;			
Larsen 10-1-29-0; Harris 10-0-43-3; Latham 3-0-13-0;			
Patel 9-0-32-0			

Umpires: P.D. Reporter, D.R. Shepherd.

Toss: New Zealand.   Points: New Zealand 2, Sri Lanka 0

WEDNESDAY 26 FEBRUARY 1992
AUSTRALIA vs SOUTH AFRICA
SCG, SYDNEY: SOUTH AFRICA WON BY 9 WICKETS

South Africa's debut in the World Cup could not have gone better. In front of an initially enthusiastic and later subdued capacity SCG crowd of 40,000, Kepler Wessels' side annihilated an out-of-form and out-of-touch Australian side by nine wickets.

If Martin Crowe had a good day at Auckland at the Australian's expense on Saturday, Wessels' Wednesday was perfection. From the moment the South Africans received an enormous reception when they took the field after Allan Border had won the toss and batted to the winning nudge by the captain to third man at 9.38pm, this game was like a tribute to 22 lost years. The only act towards South Africa lacking in generosity was Brian Aldridge's not-out decision when Geoff Marsh followed Allan Donald's first ball as it lifted outside the off stump. He clearly edged it through to wicketkeeper Dave Richardson, but the umpire was unmoved.

As if wracked by guilt, Marsh scratched around for 72 balls for 25. David Boon's conscience forced him to run himself out after looking in great form for 10 overs and Allan Border so much wanted South Africa to feel at home he let himself be bowled off his pad first ball by a beautiful in-swinger by Adrian Kuiper.

The Australian acts of self-destruction continued unabated for almost the duration of their 49-over innings. Border's dismissal left his side on 3-76 in the 21st over. Donald's new-ball partner Meyrick Pringle had been punished by Boon before Richard Snell choked off the flow of runs. Dean Jones was caught behind from the full face of the bat off Brian McMillan. He still waited for Steve Bucknor to give him out. Tom Moody was clearly lbw to Donald when the speedster was recalled to bowl to his Warwickshire team-mate.

That left Australia 5-108 in the 33rd over. Steve Waugh and Ian Healy hinted at recovery when they put on 35 in six overs, at one stage taking 12 off an over from the expensive Pringle.

Healy, though, was incapacitated by a bad hamstring strain, the result of an ambitious call for a short single by Waugh. Eventually the Australian wicketkeeper skyed a lofted drive off Donald, Waugh was caught at short cover off the verbally aggressive Brian McMillan and Peter Taylor had his leg stump neatly removed by another Donald thunderbolt.

Craig McDermott underestimated the athleticism of the cover-point fieldsman, a newcomer named Jonty Rhodes, which left Mike Whitney and Bruce Reid to bolster Australia's final total. Whitney would later write of the excitement of playing in the World Cup. One highlight must have been his off-side glide that scooted for four down to third man off the previously economical Snell.

Whitney's captain, at his most solemn during the between innings break, needed the left-arm paceman to bowl with penetration rather than scrape together a few runs.

Unfortunately, neither Whitney nor his team-mates could make any impression on the South African top order. There was little excitement as Wessels and Andrew Hudson went about their business at just above the three runs per over they needed to win. The television commentators resorted to informing their viewers of the beauty of the Sydney sunset and the perfect weather. A run out chance missed by Jones and a couple of stylish cover drives by Hudson briefly roused the crowd.

An on-driven four by Wessels off Whitney raised the 50 in the 16th over, then off the last ball of the same over Boon, wicket-keeping in place of the injured Healy, put down an edged drive low to his left. Finally, in off-spinner Taylor's first over, Hudson aimed a big drive and was bowled. The crowd roared, hoping the wicket was the first of many. It was, in fact, the last of the night. Peter Kirsten was as sound as Wessels and was rarely troubled.

Border brought himself on to bowl. The SCG had on occasions been kind to his left-arm spinners. This was not one of them. In the 29th over Wessels raised the South African 100. Six overs later, a square drive to the boundary off McDermott brought him to an emotional 50.

The match was heading to an obvious conclusion, yet after 45 overs Australia had actually been one run ahead of the South Africans at the same stage. A couple of cracking off-side shots by Wessels took his side to the brink of victory. Many of the Australian fans were leaving, but not the handful of green-shirted South African fans, however. They stayed even after the game was over and the lights were out, sharing a precious moment with their victorious team.

Wessels, named Man of the Match, was also a national hero. The changes necessary to dismantle Apartheid still had to pass a referendum. It was believed the big win could have a significant influence on the result of that vote. African National

Congress official Steve Tshwete embraced Wessels in the dressing-room. President F.W. de Klerk congratulated Wessels over the phone back at the hotel, where there were also 250 faxes congratulating the team. It was a big night for South Africa.

AUSTRALIA		SOUTH AFRICA	
G. R. Marsh c Richardson b Kuiper	25	K. C. Wessels (capt) not out	81
D. C. Boon run out	27	A. C. Hudson b Taylor	28
D. M. Jones c Richardson b McMillan	24	P. N. Kirsten not out	49
A. R. Border (capt) b Kuiper	0	Extras [lb 5, w 6, nb 2)	13
T. M. Moody lbw Donald	10	(46.5 overs)	1-171
S. R. Waugh c Cronje b McMillan	27	Did not bat: W. J. Cronje, A. P. Kuiper, J. N. Rhodes,	
I. A Healy (wk) c McMillan b Donald	16	B. M. McMillan, R. P. Snell, D. J. Richardson (wk),	
P. L. Taylor b Donald	4	M. W. Pringle, A. A Donald	
C. J. McDermott run out	6	1/74	
M. R. Whitney not out	9	Bowling: McDermott 10-1-23-0; Reid 8.5-0-45-0;	
B. A. Reid not out	5	Whitney 6-0-26-0; Waugh 4-1-16-0; Taylor 10-1-32-1;	
Extras (b 2, w 11, nb 4)	17	Border 4-0-13-0; Moody 4-0-15-0	
(49 overs)	9-170		

1/42 2/76 3/76 4/97 5/108 6/143 7/146 8/156 9/161
Bowling: Donald 10-0-34-3; Pringle 10-0-52-0; Snell 9-1-15-0;
McMillan 10-0-35-2; Kuiper 5-0-15-2; Cronje 5-1-17-0

Umpires: B.L. Aldridge, SA Bucknor.

Toss: Australia.   Points: South Africa 2, Australia 0

THURSDAY 27 FEBRUARY 1992
PAKISTAN vs ZIMBABWE
BELLERIVE OVAL, HOBART: PAKISTAN WON BY 53 RUNS

Imran Khan called this a perfect day's cricket because he did not have to bat or bowl and his side still won easily.

In good weather, it was a surprise only 1101 people bothered to journey out to Bellerive Oval. They would have seen some enterprising batting from Man of the Match and century-maker Aamir Sohail, and from Javed Miandad. Much of the cricket, however, fell well short of Imran's tongue-in-cheek interpretation. In truth the Pakistani captain was still badly troubled by his injured shoulder.

Initially Pakistan struggled on a bouncy wicket after Dave Houghton had sent them in. Pakistan was 2-63 when Miandad joined Sohail. As he had done in Melbourne, Miandad brought a positive urgency to the batting. The score was still only 96 at the 30-over mark and only a low percentage of the runs were made in boundaries, yet he and Sohail were able to put on 145 at virtually a run per ball. Even John Traicos was unable to stem the flow this time. For much of the partnership the pair scored at eight runs per over. Sohail was able to go on to complete his maiden century in limited-over internationals. He had offered three clear-cut chances to the Zimbabwean fieldsmen after reaching 50, but also struck 12 fours.

Zimbabwe never looked like getting near their target of 255. Even without Waqar Younis or Imran, the Pakistani attack was too accomplished. Dave Houghton admitted after the game that his batsmen could only concentrate on survival, particularly against the pace and skill of Wasim Akram who claimed his 150th wicket in limited-over internationals. The top order didn't even manage to survive.

Zimbabwe struggled to 3-33 and after 30 overs was out of the contest at 3-69. Andy Waller and Iain Butchart gave the total a boost by adding 79 in nine overs. All that achieved against an attack which used three spinners was respectability. Pakistan and much of the small crowd by that stage had lost interest.

PAKISTAN		ZIMBABWE	
Ramiz Raja c Flower b Jarvis	9	K. J. Arnott c Wasim Akram b Iqbal Sikander	7
Aamir Sohail c Pycroft b Butchart	114	A. Flower (wk) c Inzamam-ul-Haq b Wasim Akram	6
Inzamam-ul-Haq c Brandes b Butchart	14	A. J. Pycroft b Wasim Akram	0
Javed Miandad lbw Butchart	89	D. L. Houghton (capt) c Ramiz Raja b Aamir Sohail	44
Salim Malik not out	14	A. H. Shah b Aamir Sohail	33
Wasim Akram not out	1	A. C. Waller b Wasim Akram	44
Extras (lb 9, nb 4)	13	I. P. Butchart c Javed Miandad b Aaqib Javed	33
(50 overs)	2-254	E. A. Brandes not out	2
Did not bat: Imran Khan (capt), Moin Khan (wk],		A. J. Traicos not out	8
Iqbal Sikander, Mushtaq Ahmed, Aaqib Javed		Extras (b 3, lb 15, w 6)	24
1/29 2/63 3/208 4/253		(50 overs)	7-201
Bowling: Brandes 10-1-49-0; Jarvis 10-1-52-1; Shah		Did not bat: W. R. James, M. P. Jarvis	
10-1-24-0; Butchart 10-0-57-3; Traicos 10-0-63-0		1/14 2/14 3/33 4/103 5/108 6/187 7/190	
		Bowling: Wasim Akram 10-2-21-3; Aaqib Javed 10-1-49-1;	
		Sikander 10-1-35-1; Mushtaq Ahmed 10-1-34-0;	
		Aamir Sohail 6-1-26-2; Salim Malik 4-0-18-0	

Umpires: D.P. Buultjens, S.G. Randell.

Toss: Zimbabwe.   Points: Pakistan 2 Zimbabwe 0

ENGLAND vs WEST INDIES
MCG, MELBOURNE: ENGLAND WON BY 6 WICKETS

England were launched to first-week tournament favouritism when an inept batting display by the West Indies allowed Graham Gooch's side to cruise to an easy victory.

Brian Lara was hit in the box by the first ball he faced from Chris Lewis and that seemed to knock the stuffing out of not just Lara, but the entire West Indian batting line-up.

The weather in Melbourne was as clear as in Hobart, but the amount of moisture below the surface of the wicket was indicated by the dark marks left by the bowlers' footmarks and the batsmen's scratchings at the crease. Graham Gooch read the conditions correctly and sent in the West Indies after winning the toss.

Lewis, bowling the second over of the match with a sparsely populated Great Southern Stand as his backdrop, had Lara caught behind the ball after he struck him. In the next over Derek Pringle, straight on to a perfect line, had Desmond Haynes edging an outswinger low to Ian Botham at slip. Botham claimed the catch, the batsmen and the umpires were unsure, so Haynes stayed. Botham's immediate reaction was one of disgust. Replays were inconclusive.

With the exception of Lewis' third over, which cost 11 runs, the West Indies were circumspect and their apprehension increased two overs later when Richie Richardson was too slow getting his bat out of the way of a Lewis out-swinger and edged a clear catch to Botham.

Carl Hooper coped neither with the pressure nor the conditions and skyed a pull off Botham to Dermot Reeve, moving in from cover. Haynes played a couple of elegant pulls, survived a chance behind to Alec Stewart, then pulled Phil DeFreitas shoulder high to Neil Fairbrother at backward square leg. That left the West Indies 4-55 in the 20th over. Despite a couple of brave blows by Keith Arthurton, who hit Phil Tufnell for a straight six and pulled DeFreitas for another six to raise his 50, and Gus Logie, whose leg-side scoop off Botham also went into the stand, the West Indies never recovered from their poor start.

There remained an air of self-destruction about their running between wickets. Logie went wandering after an lbw shout and Malcolm Marshall responded to an Arthurton call only to find his partner had gone back. When DeFreitas held Curtly Ambrose at third man off a misdirected slog, Lewis had his third cheap wicket and the West Indies had been dismissed for their second-lowest World Cup score.

Ambrose sorely troubled both Gooch and Botham in his opening spell. However, Malcolm Marshall was far less imposing and Gooch twice belted him through the covers for four in his fourth over.

Botham was meant to be the batsman to take the initiative, but he had only made eight of an opening partnership of 50 when he pushed forward at Winston Benjamin and was caught behind. Benjamin also got Robin Smith to badly mistime a pull to Logie at square leg 21 runs later. Gooch, though, was in command and he reached his 50 in the 25th over. Hooper bowled his off spin tidily enough. Roger Harper on the other hand was punished severely by Graeme Hick for sending down a succession of long-hops.

By the time Gooch went waltzing down the pitch to Hooper and missed, an English win was only 32 runs away. Hick hastened the end by racing to his 50 at a run per ball, the milestone being reached with a lofted drive for six over extra cover. Harper got a little revenge when he dived and claimed a caught and bowled off the Zimbabwean-born player's soft push back up the wicket.

As with the Botham slips 'catch' earlier in the day, there was some doubt as to the legitimacy of the dismissal. This time, however, the batsman walked away. It made no difference. In the next over, Fairbrother's educated edge flew past slip to the third-man boundary leaving the English fans ready to claim they would win the World Cup.

Lewis was the Man of the Match.

WEST INDIES		ENGLAND	
D. L. Haynes c Fairbrother b Defreitas	38	G. A. Gooch (capt) st Williams b Hooper	65
B. C. Lara c Stewart b Lewis	0	I. T. Botham c Williams b Benjamin	8
R. B. Richardson (capt) c Botham b Lewis	5	R. A. Smith c Logie b Benjamin	8
C. L. Hooper c Reeve b Botham	5	G. A. Hick c & b Harper	54
K. L. T. Arthurton c Fairbrother b Defreitas	54	N. H. Fairbrother not out	13
A. L. Logie run out	20	A. J. Stewart (wk) not out	0
R. A. Harper cHick b Reeve	3	Extras (lb 7, w 4, nb 1)	12
M. D. Marshall run out	3	(39.5 overs)	4-160
D. Williams (wk) c Pringle b Defreitas	6	Did not bat: D. A. Reeve, C. C. Lewis, D. R. Pringle,	
C. E. L. Ambrose c DeFreitas b Lewis	4	P. A. J. DeFreitas, P. C.R. Tufnell	
W. K.M. Benjamin not out	11	1/50 2/71 3/126 4/156	
Extras (lb 4, w 3, nb 1)	8	Bowling: Ambrose 8-1-26-0; Marshall 8-0-37-0; Benjamin	
(49.2 overs)	10-157	9.5-2-22-2; Hooper 10-1-38-1; Harper 4-0-30-1	
1/0 2/22 3/36 4/55 5/91 6/102 7/114 8/131 9/145			
Bowling: Pringle 7-3-16-0; Lewis 8.2-1-30-3;			
Defreitas 9-2-34-3; Botham 10-0-30-1; Reeve 10-1-23-1;			
Tufnell 5-0-20-0			

Umpires: K.E. Liebenberg, S.J. Woodward.

Toss: England.   Points: England 2 West Indies 0

FRIDAY 28 FEBRUARY 1992
INDIA vs SRI LANKA
HARRUP PARK, MACKAY: NO RESULT

Mackay in tropical Queensland is a long way to go for two deliveries. The first rain in a month initially delayed the match and then, after 3000 gathered in anticipation of a 20-overs-per-side slogarama, it returned in all its tropical fury to quickly stymie even that prospect. The outcome must have been heartbreaking for local officials.

Kris Srikkanth has made the only World Cup run ever scored in Mackay.

<table>
<tr><td colspan="2" align="center">**INDIA**</td><td colspan="2" align="center">**SRI LANKA**</td></tr>
</table>

INDIA			**SRI LANKA**

<table>
</table>

INDIA

K. Srikkanth not out

Kapil Dev not out

Extras 0

(0.2 overs) 0-1; Did not bat: M. Azharuddin (capt),
S. R. Tendulkar, V. G. Kambli, P. K. Amre, A. D. Jadeja,
K. S. More (wk), M. Prabhakar, J. Srinath, S. L.V. Raju

Bowling: Ramanayake 0.2-0-1-0

SRI LANKA

1   R. S. Mahanama, U. C. Hathurusingha, A. P. Gurusinha,

0   P. A. de Silva (capt), A. Ranatunga, S.J. Jayasuriya,
    H. P. Tillekaratne (wk), R. S. Kalpage, C. P. H. Ramanayake,
    K. I. W. Wijegunawardene, G. P. Wickremasinghe

Umpires: I.D. Robinson, D.R. Shepherd.

Toss: Sri Lanka.   Points: Sri Lanka 1, India 1

SATURDAY 29 FEBRUARY 1992
NEW ZEALAND vs SOUTH AFRICA
EDEN PARK, AUCKLAND: NEW ZEALAND WON BY 7 WICKETS

The uncharitable might have suggested that putting New Zealand in grey uniforms for the World Cup was appropriate because that has often been the colour of their cricket. Yet if that had ever been the case it was certainly not so during the Benson and Hedges World Cup. Another big crowd at Eden Park was treated to innovative, aggressive, entertaining and successful cricket and nearly all of it came from the home side.

Kepler Wessels later wrote of a hangover following the wonder of the win against Australia. His top-order batsmen were indeed as sluggish as someone after a big night and were totally unable to adapt to the same dry, slow Eden Park wicket that had scuppered Australia the week before.

Neither Wessels, who had won the toss, Andrew Hudson, nor young Hansie Cronje could come to terms with the accuracy and pacelessness of Willie Watson, who opened without a slip, and off-spinner Dipak Patel, once more recalled to take the new ball. When Cronje was caught behind off Chris Harris' first ball South Africa were 3-29 and into the 16th over. What they might have finished with without the contribution of Peter Kirsten is too frightening to contemplate. The 36-year-old late addition to the squad and wicketkeeper Dave Richardson shored up the middle overs of the innings with a solid partnership of 79.

Trouble loomed again when Richardson's dismissal was followed by the bizarre demise of Adrian Kuiper. He hooked at a Cairns bouncer and gloved the ball through to Ian Smith. Thinking he was out caught, Kuiper started walking away only for Kirsten to yell at him to regain his crease because umpire Piloo Reporter had called no ball for an above-the-shoulder delivery. As he tried to regain his ground the bails were removed and Kuiper was given run out.

It was much the same circumstance as when Dean Jones was controversially run out in a Test in Guyana a year earlier. On both occasions lack of clear-cut knowledge of the rules by players and umpires had affected a dismissal. Kirsten went on to hit 10 fours before becoming Watson's second victim and it took a late rally by Richard Snell and Brian McMillan, including 15 off the final over, to set the Kiwis what looked a moderately competitive target. But 191 turned out to be a simple assignment.

On the back of a stunning opening partnership of 114 in just 18 overs between Mark Greatbatch and Rod Latham, the Kiwis strolled home with more than 15 overs to spare. Greatbatch was only in the side as a replacement for the injured John Wright.

Blanking out previous poor form against England, the big left-hander took a couple of sighters, then started smashing the ball in all directions. His clean uncomplicated hitting reaped Greatbatch nine fours and three big sixes, the last of which landed on the roof of the North Stand. Latham was hardly circumspect, either, hitting seven fours and scoring at a rate just below a run per ball. When Greatbatch finally got too carried away and Latham had fallen to Snell, Crowe sent in Smith who promptly hit his first three balls for four and even had the temerity to dance out to Allan Donald and crack him down the ground for another boundary. The wicketkeeper then got out of the way so that his captain could come in and hit the winning runs to top off an almost perfect day.

It was special for Greatbatch, who had grasped his opportunity with both hands. At his Man of the Match conference he admitted his whole innings was a bit of a blur.

SOUTH AFRICA		NEW ZEALAND	
K. C. Wessels (capt) c Smith b Watson	3	M. J. Greatbatch b Kirsten	68
A. C. Hudson b Patel	1	R. T. Latham c Wessels b Snell	60
P. N. Kirsten c Cairns b Watson	90	A. H. Jones not out	34
W. J. Cronje c Smith b Harris	7	I. D. S. Smith (wk) c Kirsten b Donald	19
D. J. Richardson (wk) c Larsen b Cairns	28	M. D. Crowe (capt) not out	3
A. P. Kuiper run out	2	Extras (b 1, w 5, nb 1)	7
J. N. Rhodes c Crowe b Cairns	6	(34.3 overs)	3-191
B. M. McMillan not out	55	Did not bat: K. R. Rutherford, C. Z. Harris, D. N. Patel,	
R. P. Snell not out	11	C. L. Cairns, G. R. Larsen, W. Watson	
Extras (lb 8, nb 1)	9	1/114 2/155 3/179	
(50 overs)	7-190	Bowling: Donald 10-0-38-1; McMillan 5-1-23-0;	
Did not bat: T. Bosch, A. A. Donald		Snell 7-0-56-1; Bosch 2.3-0-19-0; Cronje 2-0-14-0;	
1/8 2/10 3/29 4/108 5/110 6/121 7/162		Kuiper 1-0-18-0; Kirsten 7-1-22-1	
Bowling: Watson 10-2-30-2; Patel 10-1-28-1;			
Larsen 10-1-29-0; Harris 10-2-33-1; Latham 2-0-19-0;			
Cairns 8-0-43-2			

Umpires: Khizar Hyatt, P.O. Reporter.

Toss: South Africa.   Points: New Zealand 2 South Africa 0

WEST INDIES vs ZIMBABWE
WOOLLOONGABBA, BRISBANE: WEST INDIES WON BY 75 RUNS

Here was another match of injuries, bumps and bruises for the West Indies. This time, though, they gave as good as they got and ended up comfortable winners over Zimbabwe.

Phil Simmons, in the side because of a back injury to Desmond Haynes, opened with Brian Lara after the West Indies had been sent in to bat by Dave Houghton. The weather that night was fine but the spectacle of maroon-verses-red only attracted 2000 local devotees.

The stay-at-homes missed another gem of an innings by Lara. The young Trinidadian featured some more sweet cover drives as he raced to 72 at a run per ball. Simmons supported him in an opening stand of 78, then Richie Richardson and Carl Hooper added 117 to take the score to 2-220 in the 43rd over. Both batsmen were caught in the deep, one straight after the other, trying to add to their sixes' tally.

Keith Arthurton showed how that was best done with two blows over the boundary in the closing overs. Otherwise the West Indian tail did little to boost the final total.

The West Indian pacemen were soon clunking, smacking and crunching the Zimbabweans into submission. Andy Pycroft was hit on the cheekbone, then caught behind next ball, and Kevin Arnott had his finger bloodied and broken and had to retire hurt. With another batsman, Wayne James, already nursing a fractured finger Zimbabwe asked permission for an addition to their squad.

There were other problems hitting the West Indian and Zimbabwean players. Richie Richardson deliberately took a catch at cover to remove Alistair Campbell one handed because of his injured digit and Houghton batted after receiving a pain-killing injection for a broken toe. It was he and Ali Shah, also his side's best bowler in this game, who restored respectability after Zimbabwe had been in effect 5-63.

They both made half centuries and ensured the innings ran its full 50-over course. Richardson admitted that at the end his side started "relaxing a bit".

Lara won his second Man of the Match award.

WEST INDIES		ZIMBABWE	
P. V. Simmons b Brandes	21	K. J. Arnott retired hurt	16
B. C. Lara c Houghton b Shah	72	A. Flower (wk) b Patterson	6
R. B. Richardson (capt) c Brandes b Jarvis	56	A. J. Pycroft c Williams b Benjamin	10
C. L. Hooper c Pycroft b Traicos	63	D. L. Houghton (capt) c Patterson b Hooper	55
K. L. T. Arthurton b Duers	26	A. C. Waller c Simmons b Benjamin	0
A. L. Logie run out	5	A. D. Campbell c Richardson b Hooper	1
M. D. Marshall c Houghton b Brandes	2	A. H. Shah not out	60
D. Williams (wk) not out	8	E. A. Brandes c & b Benjamin	6
W. K. M. Benjamin b Brandes	1	A. J. Traicos run out	8
Extras (b 1, lb 6, w 2, nb 1)	10	M. P. Jarvis not out	5
(50 overs)	2-264	Extras (lb 9, w 5, nb 8)	22
Did not bat: AC. Cummins, B. P. Patterson		(50 overs)	7-189

West Indies: 1/78 2/103 3/220 4/221 5/239 6/254 7/255 8/264

Bowling: Brandes 10-1-45-3; Jarvis 10-1-71-1; Duers 10-0-52-1; Shah 10-2-39-1; Traicos 10-0-50-1

Zimbabwe: Did not bat: K. G. Duers

1/24 2/43 3/48 4/64 5/132 6/161 7/181

K. J. Arnott retired hurt at 2/43

Bowling: Patterson 10-0-25-1; Marshall 6-0-23-0; Benjamin 10-2-27-3; Cummins 10-0-33-0; Hooper 10-0-47-2; Arthurton 4-0-25-0

Umpires: K.E. Uebenberg, S.J. Woodward.

Toss: Zimbabwe.   Points: West Indies 2 Zimbabwe 0

SUNDAY 1 MARCH 1992
AUSTRALIA vs INDIA
WOOLLOONGABBA, BRISBANE: AUSTRALIA WON BY 1 RUN

This thrilling game arrived just in the nick of time for the locals, whose campaign was on the verge of floundering. To win a thriller like this in front of a large Sunday-afternoon television audience was crucial to the future ratings of the tournament in Australia.

It was the second time in as many World Cups that Australia had beaten India by one run.

This time they were lucky on two counts. Rain took three overs off the Indian innings, but the new rain rule meant that their target was only reduced by two runs. Then, when Javagal Srinath clubbed the final ball into the outfield, the man in the hot seat was almost inevitably Steve Waugh, a cricketer noted for his ability to handle such a situation. He came through again, if only just.

The Gabba was far from full when Allan Border won the toss and elected to bat. His two openers, Mark Taylor and Geoff Marsh, made little impact and it was left to David Boon and Dean Jones to give the innings direction. Jones provided the feature Australian batting of the day. His second scoring shot was a six off Srinath over long on. However, exactly half of his 90 runs came in singles, 22 of them consecutively as Boon, Waugh and Tom Moody were made to move. Not only were Jones' batting partners kept busy. Bruce Reid and Mark Waugh had to maintain supplies of batting gloves and water throughout his 109-ball stay.

The Indian bowlers improved their figures as wickets tumbled through the final few overs and a target of 238 from 50 overs was seen as about an even money bet. They had lost Kris Srikkanth and were 1-45 in the 17th over when the rain interruption occurred. Although the mathematics of that pause was unfair on India, the damp ball at least hampered the Australians and allowed Mohammad Azharuddin to put together one of his gems.

Kapil Dev was promoted to increase the run rate, but it was Sanjay Manjrekar, in partnership with Azharuddin, who put India within reach of a win.

The requirement had moved to 77 off eight overs when the two Indians really began their assault. After 10 fours in 103 balls Azharuddin fell foul of the throwing accuracy of his opposite number at short mid wicket. Manjrekar hit Merv Hughes for a four and a six and scored at better than a run per ball before being run out with 20 still needed.

Border, who later admitted to a "monumental cock-up", found it hard to calculate the allocation each bowler was allowed with the Indian innings reduced to 47 overs and had to use Tom Moody for the final six deliveries. The tall West Australian had 12 runs to play with. After two balls he had just four left.

Wicketkeeper Kiran More put two full tosses to the boundary at square leg. Then, probably trying to win the match with another four, he was bowled backing away and hitting across the line. Manoj Prabhakar scored a single from the fourth ball and was run out from the fifth which left Srinath having to hit a four to win the match from the last ball.

Moody bowled, Srinath swung hard and connected, sending the ball soaring into the leg-side outfield. The cries from the crowd followed the ball as it neared the boundary and Steve Waugh ran around. At full tilt Waugh reached for the catch only for the ball to hit his wrist. Like an Aussie Rules footballer, he crumbed his own dropped mark, picking the ball up as it rolled parallel to the boundary. A quick throw reached wicketkeeper Boon first bounce as Venkatapathy Raju scrambled for the third run.

The substitute gloveman held his nerve enough to break the stumps with Raju short of his ground. It was an agonising loss for India, who might easily have come out of their two games in Queensland with four points, but had to be satisfied with just the one from the match in Mackay.

Jones was named Man of the Match, getting the award ahead of Azharuddin by the few centimetres that Raju was run out.

AUSTRALIA		INDIA	
M. A. Taylor c More b Kapil Dev	13	R. J. Shastri c Waugh b Moody	25
G. R. Marsh b Kapil Dev	8	K. Srikkanth b McDermott	0
D. C. Boon (wk) c Shastri b Raju	43	M. Azharuddin (capt) run out	93
D. M. Jones c & b Prabhakar	90	S. R. Tendulkar c Waugh b Moody	11
S. R. Waugh b Srinath	29	Kapil Dev lbw b Waugh	21
T. M. Moody b Prabhakar	25	S. V. Manjrekar run out	47
A. R. Border (capt) c Jadeja b Kapil Dev	10	A. D. Jadeja b Hughes	1
C. J. McDermott c Jadeja b Prabhakar	2	K. S. More (wk) b Moody	14
P. L. Taylor run out	1	J. Srinath not out	8
M. G. Hughes not out	0	M. Prabhakar run out	1
Extras (lb 7, w 5, nb 4)	16	S. L.V. Raju run out	0
(50 overs)	9-237	Extras (lb 8, w 5)	13
Did not bat: M. R. Whitney		(47 overs)	10-234
1/18 2/31 3/102 4/156 5/198 6/230 7/235 8/236 9/237		1/6 2/53 3/86 4/128 5/194 6/199 7/216 8/231 9/232	
Bowling: Kapil Dev 10-2-41-3; Prabhakar 10-0-41-3;		Bowling: McDermott 9-1-35-1; Whitney 10-2-36-0;	
Srinath 8-0-48-1; Tendulkar 5-0-29-0; Raju 10-0-37-1;		Hughes 9-1-49-1; Moody 9-0-56-3; Waugh 10-0-50-1	
Jadeja 7-0-34-0			

Umpires: B.L. Aldridge, I.D. Robinson.

Toss: Australia.   Points: Australia 2 India 0

ENGLAND vs PAKISTAN
ADELAIDE OVAL, ADELAIDE: NO RESULT

While rain was hampering India's progress in Brisbane, it saved the skin of neighbours and rivals, Pakistan. An unseasonable drenching of the driest of Australia's capital cities washed out their match with England after they had been bowled out for 74.

It had not rained in Adelaide for five weeks yet only two overs were possible after lunch, much to England's frustration of England. On such things are World Cups won and lost.

Imran Khan's bad shoulder kept him out again, so it was Javed Miandad who called incorrectly at the toss, Gooch telling him Pakistan would bat. None of them could make much of the conditions as the ball seamed and jagged around. Derek Pringle finished with astonishing figures. The Pakistanis' innings lasted 40 overs, but they were dismissed for their lowest World Cup total. It was a procession, the best stand being 15 for the ninth wicket.

The wicket had sweated under covers and soon Ramiz Raja drove to point off Phil DeFreitas and Inzamam-ul-Haq was caught behind first ball to leave Pakistan 2-5. Salim Malik hit three of the innings' five fours and Mushtaq and Wasim Haider used up what turned out to be valuable time when the scoreboard read 8-47. Mushtaq played and missed at an entire over of out-swingers from Dermot Reeve.

England was still able to bat prior to the lunch interval and Gooch was out again before he could get to a sandwich, given out caught behind off Akram. The left-arm paceman was unhappy with the condition of the wicket, although with so much rain around, how that might have been changed is hard to imagine.

In the good old days of the World Cup everyone would have come back on Monday to finish. In 1992, though, one-day cricket literally meant one day of cricket and Pakistan and England both received one point for the 'no result'.

PAKISTAN		ENGLAND	
Ramiz Raja c Reeve b DeFreitas	1	GA. Gooch (capt) c Moin Khan b Wasim Akram	3
Aamir Sohail c & b Pringle	9	I. T. Botham not out	6
Inzamam-ul-Haq c Stewart b Defreitas	0	R. A. Smith not out	5
Javed Miandad (capt) b Pringle	3	Extras (b 1, lb 3, w 5, nb 1)	10
Salim Malik c Reeve b Botham	17	(8 overs)	1-24
Ijaz Ahmed c Stewart b Small	0	Did not bat: G. A. Hick, N. H. Fairbrother, A. J. Stewart (wk),	
Wasim Akram b Botham	1	D. A. Reeve, C. C. Lewis, D. R. Pringle, P. A. J. Defreitas,	
Moin Khan (wk) c Hick b Small	2	G. C. Small	
Wasim Haider c Stewart b Reeve	13	1/14	
Mushtaq Ahmed c Reeve b Pringle	17	Bowling: Wasim Akram 3-0-7-1; Aaqib Javed 3-1-7-0;	
Aaqib Javed not out	1	Wasim Haider 1-0-1-0; Ijaz Ahmed 1-0-5-0	
Extras (lb 1, w 8, nb 1)	10		
(40.2 overs)	10-74		
1/5 2/5 3/14 4/20 5/32 6/35 7/42 8/47 9/62			
Bowling: Pringle 8.2-5-8-3; DeFreitas 7-1-22-2;			
Small 10-1-29-2; Botham 10-4-12-2; Reeve 5-3-2-1			

Umpires: SA Buckner, P.J. McConnell.

Toss: England.   Points: England 1 Pakistan 1

MONDAY 2 MARCH 1992
SOUTH AFRICA vs SRI LANKA
BASIN RESERVE, WELLINGTON: SRI LANKA WON BY 3 WICKETS

The faxes received by Kepler Wessels after this surprising defeat were a little less complimentary than those sent following the win over Australia. The condemnation was not just of the performance of his team, but also of Wessels' own batting.

The hero of Sydney struggled through 94 balls at the Basin Reserve without once reaching the boundary. He said he found the wicket even slower and lower than the one used in Auckland. He had been on three at the 10-over mark after South Africa had been sent in to bat by Aravinda de Silva. Champaka Ramanayake's first seven overs cost just seven runs.

Wessels' decision to use Adrian Kuiper as an opener instead of Andrew Hudson also failed, the all-rounder missing more deliveries than he struck before being bowled by left-arm spinner Don Anurasiri. Although the second wicket did not fall until the total was 113, Wessels and, to a lesser extent, Peter Kirsten had been so tardy that 35 overs had been completed by the time both fell within a run of each other.

The acceleration from that point was at a cost of all remaining wickets. Jonty Rhodes established himself and was batting in an enterprising fashion when Sanath Jayasuriya leapt high to hold the first of two great catches at short cover.

When Allan Donald was run out from the last ball of the innings South Africa had lost 9-81 and were all out for 195. Maybe 'White Lightning' was annoyed by his dismissal because he bowled like fury at the start of the Sri Lankan reply. They had made the long 14-hour journey from Mackay with only 12 fit players and when Donald, who sent down six wides in his two overs, yorked de Silva, Sri Lanka were 3-35. That meant an uphill fight for the pre-match underdogs, one started by the solid Roshan Mahanama and Hashan Tillekaratne who put on 52.

Omar Henry's removal of the Sri Lankan wicketkeeper was followed by a stand of 67 by Mahanama and Arjuna Ranatunga. The opener finally fell in the 43rd over with 42 runs still needed.

The result was clearly going down to the wire and the cheap dismissal of Jayasuriya meant Ranatunga would have to score the bulk of the runs. He was equal to the task. South Africa's bowlers had given Sri Lanka 17 extra runs and deliveries which left Donald, one of the worst offenders, with just five runs to spare for the 50th over. A four over mid wicket by Ranatunga and a slashing square drive by Ramanayake carried Sri Lanka to victory from the second-last ball. It was the first time the Sri Lankans had won two games in a World Cup tournament, so the onfield dancing of Ranatunga and Ramanayake, a well as the singing from the group of flag-wavers in the outer, was justified.

Ranatunga was named Man of the Match for an innings which lasted 73 balls and included six fours. Wessels was left to read his poisoned mail.

SOUTH AFRICA		SRI LANKA	
K. C. Wessels (capt) c & b Ranatunga	40	R. S. Mahanama c Richardson b McMillan	68
A. P. Kuiper b Anurasiri	18	U. C. Hathurusingha c Wessels b Donald	5
P. N. Kirsten c Hathurusingha b Kalpage	47	A. P. Gurusinha lbw Donald	0
J. N. Rhodes c Jayasuriya b Wickremasinghe	28	P. A. de Silva (capt) b Donald	7
M. W. Rushmere c Jayasuriya b Ranatunga	4	H. P. Tillekaratne (wk) c Rushmere b Henry	17
W. J. Cronje st Tillekaratne b Anurasiri	3	A. Ranatunga not out	64
B. M. McMillan not out	18	S. J. Jayasuriya st Richardson b Kirsten	3
R. P. Snell b Anurasiri	9	R. S. Kalpage run out	5
D. J. Richardson (wk) run out	0	C. P. H. Ramanayake not out	4
O. Henry c Kalpage b Ramanayake	11	Extras (b 1, lb 7, w 13, nb 4)	25
A. A. Donald run out	3	(49.5 overs)	7-198
Extras (lb 9, w 4, nb 1)	14	Did not bat: S. D. Anurasiri, G. P. Wickremasinghe	
(50 overs)	10-195	1/11 2/12 3/35 4/87 5/154 6/168 7/189	
1/27 2/113 3/114 4/128 5/149 6/153 7/165 8/165 9/186		Bowling: McMillan 10-2-34-1; Donald 9.5-0-42-3;	
Bowling: Ramanayake 9-2-19-1; Wickremasinghe 7-0-32-1;		Henry 10-0-31-1; Snell 10-1-33-0; Kuiper 5-0-25-0;	
Kalpage 10-0-38-1; Anurasiri 10-1-41-3; Ranatunga 6-0-26-2;		Kirsten 5-0-25-1	
Gurusinha 8-0-30-0			

Umpires: Khizar Havat, S.J. Woodward.

Toss: Sri Lanka.   Points: Sri Lanka 2 South Africa 0

TUESDAY 3 MARCH 1992
NEW ZEALAND vs ZIMBABWE
McLEAN PARK, NAPIER: NEW ZEALAND WON BY 48 RUNS

The stupidity of the rule for rain-reduced games was exemplified by this greasy encounter on the east coast of New Zealand's North Island. One reduction followed another until finally Zimbabwe's ask was 154 from 18 overs, which their captain Dave Houghton thought was "bizarre" and turned out to be quite unrealistic.

There were problems right from the start and a 75-minute delay meant that the contest began as one of 43 overs per side. When the game got under way Houghton won the toss and sent New Zealand in. After 11 overs, the players were interrupted again with New Zealand 2-52. When Martin Crowe and Andrew Jones resumed the innings they had an allowance of only another 76 deliveries. Of those they received just 57 before yet another shower brought the Kiwi time allocation to an end. It turned out those 9.3 overs were enough to set up a winning total.

Aided by bowlers who struggled to control a wet ball and fieldsmen who slipped all over the place on a wet outfield, Crowe and Jones created batting mayhem by adding 110 in 57 balls. Crowe, in particular, was uninhibited in his assault on the Zimbabwean attack. Much of his hitting was through and over the leg side.

When Houghton packed that half of the field Crowe stepped away and began cracking the ball over the covers. He hit Ali Shah for six over square leg and then over cover into the Centenary Stand, racing to his 50 in 31 balls which put Andy Waller's 32-ball effort earlier in the competition into second place.

The difficulties the Zimbabweans were under were highlighted when Iain Butchart slipped over twice as he ran in to bowl. He was punished as severely as anyone by Jones and Crowe, but at least had the consolation of ending the 14-over, 129 stand when Jones was beautifully caught by Waller in front of the sightscreen from another big hit.

Zimbabwe made a brave attempt to make 154 from 108 balls. Wickets kept tumbling in the overcast conditions, though, and the loss of the best hitter, Waller, to a Danny Morrison yorker was critical. Chris Cairns was belted and Dipak Patel was not used because of the wet ball. Chris Harris and Gavin Larsen could not be collared and between them took 6-31 from eight overs. Then, when light rain returned in the 13th over, a 'no result' threatened again. Alistair Campbell skyed a ball towards Crowe and the New Zealand captain later admitted he considered deliberately dropping it. He thought the umpires might have taken the players off the ground at the break in play as the rain was getting heavier.

Much to the Kiwis' relief, the officials consulted, then allowed the game to continue. The rain eased a little and the 18 overs were completed. Crowe was named Man of the Match and even allowed himself the luxury of thoughts of a semi-final berth.

NEW ZEALAND		ZIMBABWE	
M. J. Greatbatch b Duers	15	A. Flower (wk) b Larsen	30
R. T. Latham b Brandes	2	A. C. Waller b Morrison	11
A. H. Jones c Waller b Butchart	57	D. L. Houghton (capt) b Larsen	10
M. D. Crowe (capt) not out	74	I. P. Butchart c Cairns b Larsen	3
C. L. Cairns not out	1	E. A. Brandes b Harris	6
Extras (b 7, lb 6)	13	A. J. Pycroft not out	13
(20.5 overs)	3-162	A. D. Campbell c Crowe b Harris	8
Did not bat: K. R. Rutherford, C. Z. Harris, D. N. Patel,		A. H. Shah b Harris	7
I. D.S. Smith (wk), G. R. Larsen, D. K. Morrison		M. G. Burmester not out	4
1/9 2/25 3/154		Extras (lb 9, w 3, nb 1)	13
Bowling: Brandes 5-1-28-1; Duers 6-0-17-1; Shah		(18 overs)	7-105
4-0-34-0; Butchart 4-0-53-1; Burmester 1.5-0-17-0		Did not bat: A. J. Traicos, K. G. Duers	
		1/22 2/41 3/63 4/63 5/75 6/86 7/97	
		Bowling: Morrison 4-0-14-1; Cairns 2-0-27-0; Larsen 4-0-16-3;	
		Harris 4-0-15-3; Latham 3-0-18-0; Crowe 1-0-6-0	

Umpires: D.P. Buultjens, K.E. Liebenberg.

Toss: Zimbabwe.   Points: New Zealand 2 Zimbabwe 0

WEDNESDAY 4 MARCH 1992
INDIA vs PAKISTAN
SCG, SYDNEY: INDIA WON BY 43 RUNS

India's luck turned for the better in the first-ever World Cup match between cricket's biggest neighbours. The collapse of the Pakistani middle order in front of an estimated television audience of 250 million left India victorious by a comfortable margin.

After the game Imran Khan spoke optimistically about Pakistan's chances of reaching the semi-finals, even though they had only one win from four starts.

Ten thousand expatriate and visiting Indians and Pakistanis were in the SCG when Mohammad Azharuddin won the toss and batted. The Indians had left out their vice-captain Ravi Shastri for slow batting and it was his replacement, Ajay Jadeja, in only his second limited-over international, who got the Indian innings away to a positive start. Apart from the cheap removal of an out-of-touch Kris Srikkanth, who had all sorts of trouble with the accurate Aaqib Javed, there was consistency at the top of the Indian order, although no-one managed to go on to a really big score.

Sachin Tendulkar put on 46 with Vinod Kambli. Then young leg-spinner Mushtaq Ahmed had the left-hander caught, and bowled Sanjay Manjrekar first ball to leave India 5-148. There was cause for concern for the Indians that they may not have set a worthy target in such a prestigious match.

That, however, reckoned without the maturity and skill of 18-year-old Tendulkar and the smiting ability of Kapil Dev. Mushtaq had three valuable and quite cheap wickets. Kapil hit hard and to good effect to give his figures a bit of a battering while 60 runs were added in eight overs. Once Kapil put the spinner over extra cover for six on his way to 35 in 26 balls.

Tendulkar batted through to the end of the innings, called after 49 overs because of Pakistani tardiness. There were only three boundaries in an effort which still exuded class throughout its 62-ball duration.

Protecting 216 Azharuddin kept his fieldsmen in a ring around the Pakistanis to increase the pressure. It worked at the start as the absence of the injured Ramiz Raja was felt by Pakistan. A wicket each to Kapil and Manoj Prabhakar left them 2-17 and Aamir Sohail and Javed Miandad with a rebuilding assignment. It was tense stuff as they put together a partnership of 88. Javed Miandad and Indian wicketkeeper Kiran More had a tete-a-tete over the merits or otherwise of some appeals. Miandad, never one to back away from such matters, demonstrated his feelings with a high-leaping imitation of More. Both players were reported, but let off because umpires Peter McConnell and David Shepherd could not understand what the protagonists had actually said to each other.

The Pakistani innings stalled in the face of a fine spell by Prabhakar. Salim Malik responded with two boundaries, then was caught behind off a perfectly pitched leg-cutter. Prabhakar gave the batsman a fiery send-off. Imran, who had tested his shoulder with a tidy eight-over spell of medium-paced inswing, entered with his side 3-127, needing 90 in 15 overs.

It was a respectable ask yet the Pakistani middle order crumbled. Imran fell foul of a running muddle, then Wasim Akram failed to pick Venkatapathy Raju's arm ball and was stumped. Javed shouldered even more pressure as his side's last hope. His had been the innings of a determined rather than in-form batsman. When, after 113 balls he stepped away to hit Javagal Srinath through the off side and edged the ball into his stumps the elation of the Indians was obvious.

Tendulkar was named Man of the Match and Pakistan would have to wait for another opportunity to restore national pride.

INDIA		PAKISTAN	
A. D. Jadeja c Zahid Fazal b Wasim Haider	46	Aamir Sohail c Srikkanth b Tendulkar	62
K. Srikkanth c Moin Khan b Aaqib Javed	5	Inzamam-ul-Haq lbw Kapil Dev	2
M. Azharuddin (capt) c Moin Khan be Mushtaq Ahmed	32	Zahid Fazal c More b Prabhakar	2
V. G. Kambli c Inzamam b MushtaqAhmed	24	Javed Miandad b Srinath	40
S. R. Tendulkar not out	54	Salim Malik c More b Prabhakar	12
S. V. Manjrekar b Mushtaq Ahmed	0	Imran Khan (capt) run out	0
Kapil Dev c Imran Khan b Aaqib Javed	35	Wasim Akram st More b Raju	4
K. S. More (wk) run out	4	Wasim Haiderb Srinath	13
M. Prabhakar not out	2	Moin Khan (wk) c Manjrekarb Kapil Dev	12
Extras (lb 3, w 9, nb 2)	14	Mushtaq Ahmed run out	3
(49 overs)	7-216	Aaqib Javed not out	1
Did not bat: J. Srinath, S. L.V. Raju		Extras [lb 6, w 15, nb 1)	22
1/25 2/86 3/101 4/147 5/148 6/208 7/213		(48.1 overs)	10-173
Bowling: Wasim Akram 10-0-45-0; Aaqib Javed 8-2-28-2;		1/8 2/17 3/105 4/127 5/1306/141 7/141 8/161 9/166	
Imran Khan 8-0-25-0; Wasim Haider 10-1-36-1; Mushtaq		Bowling: Kapil Dev 10-0-30-2; Prabhakar 10-1-22-2; Srinath	
Ahmed 10-0-59-3; Aamir Sohail 3-0-20-0		8.1-0-37-2; Tendulkar 10-0-37-1; Raju 10-1-41-1	

Umpires: P.J. McConnell, D.R. Shepherd.

Toss: India.   Points: India 2 Pakistan 0

THURSDAY 5 MARCH 1992
SOUTH AFRICA vs WEST INDIES
LANCASTER PARK, CHRISTCHURCH: SOUTH AFRICA WON BY 64 RUNS

As it did against England, the West Indies batting let them down badly against South Africa, allowing Kepler Wessels to relax when the faxes came in after this game.

In grey weather there were few batting comforts on a bouncy pitch which encouraged fast bowling. Wessels lost the toss and was first out with the total on eight. Andrew Hudson and the consistent Peter Kirsten brought up the 50 by the 17th over before the opener was brilliantly caught by Brian Lara in the gully. Kirsten used a runner for the second half of his innings, having pulled a calf muscle on 28. He was the only one of six batsmen who reached 20 to go on to a substantial score. His 92-ball innings included just two fours before wicketkeeper David Williams took a catch to give Malcolm Marshall his second wicket.

There were few boundaries and only one six, a leg-side clout by Adrian Kuiper off Winston Benjamin which raised the South African 100, in a neat total of 200 from the 50 overs. Kuiper had become second top score before playing over a slower yorker from Curtly Ambrose, who along with Marshall was the most effective of the West Indian bowlers.

The team whose fast bowlers had inflicted such pain on other teams over the years now got a bit of their own medicine as the South African speedsters ripped through the West Indian top order. It was Meyrick Pringle, not Allan Donald, who did the damage. After a couple of square cuts, Brian Lara holed out to Jonty Rhodes at point.

Then Richie Richardson was trapped lbw and Carl Hooper and Keith Arthurton were caught by Wessels at slip while the score was stationary on 19. Pringle took four wickets in 11 balls without cost. Desmond Haynes survived the Pringle massacre, but had an already damaged finger so badly battered he retired hurt and intended to get hospital treatment.

Instead, when Richard Snell dismissed Malcolm Marshall and David Williams one after the other, he returned to the crease at 6-70. Gus Logie was going down fighting and punished Adrian Kuiper for a succession of boundaries. One of those raised his 50 and brief hopes of an unlikely West Indian win. But Kuiper got revenge when he removed Logie and Haynes caught behind driving in the same over. Eight for 117 soon became 136 all out. The West Indies had made their lowest total in a World Cup.

Pringle had not even been selected in South Africa's original World Cup squad of 20. Now he was Man of the Match in a game that revitalised South Africa's whole campaign.

SOUTH AFRICA		WEST INDIES	
K. C. Wessels (capt) c Haynes b Marshall	1	D. L. Haynes c Richardson b Kuiper	30
A. C. Hudson c Lara b Cummins	22	B. C. Lara c Rhodes b Pringle	9
P. N. Kirsten c Williams b Marshall	56	R. B. Richardson (capt) lbw Pringle	1
M. W. Rushmere st Williams b Hooper	10	C. Hooper c Wessels b Pringle	0
A. P. Kuiper b Ambrose	23	K. L. T. Arthurton c Wessels b Pringle	0
J. N. Rhodes c Williams b Cummins	22	A. L. Logie c Pringle b Kuiper	61
B. M. McMillan c Lara b Benjamin	20	M. D. Marshall c Rhodes b Snell	6
D. J. Richardson (wk) not out	20	D. Williams (wk) c Richardson b Snell	0
R. P. Snell c Haynes b Ambrose	3	C. E. L. Ambrose run out	12
M. W. Pringle not out	5	A. C. Cummins c McMillan b Donald	6
Extras (lb 8, w 3, nb 7)	18	W. K. M. Benjamin not out	1
(50 overs)	8-200	Extras [lb 9, w 1)	10
Did not bat: A. A. Donald		(38.4 overs)	10-136

1/8 2/51 3/73 4/119 5/127 6/159 7/181 8/187

Bowling: Ambrose 10-1-34-2; Marshall 10-1-26-2; Benjamin 10-0-47-1; Cummins 10-0-40-2; Hooper 10-0-45-1

1/10 2/19 3/19 4/19 5/70 6/70 7/116 8/117 9/132 10/136

Haynes retired hurt 4-50 and resumed at 6-70

Bowling: Donald 6.4-2-13-1; Pringle 8-4-11-4; McMillan 8-2-36-0; Snell 7-2-16-2; Kuiper 9-0-51-2

Umpires: B.L. Aldridge, S.8. Randell.

Toss: West Indies.　　Points: South Africa 2, West Indies 0

AUSTRALIA vs ENGLAND
SCG, SYDNEY: ENGLAND WON BY 8 WICKETS

Australia found co-hosting a World Cup did not agree with them and for the second time they were thrashed at the SCG. The chances of the home side west of the Tasman Sea reaching the semi-finals was not looking good.

What irked Australians most was that Ian Botham, a forgotten Ashes nemesis, proved a match-winner and had no trouble taking the game award. The recipe for the Australian disaster was also horribly similar to the one of the previous week: a sound start, a disastrous middle-order collapse, and a total around 170 which the bowlers could make nothing of.

Allan Border won the toss and batted in front of another capacity SCG crowd, whose spread of support was more even than it had been the previous Thursday. Mark Taylor failed again and David Boon, backing up too far, fell foul of a sharp piece of work by Neil Fairbrother at mid wicket in the 10th over.

Tom Moody had been promoted to open at the expense of the lacklustre Geoff Marsh and he responded with an important half century. He and Dean Jones took Australia to a 2-106 in 28 overs when the Victorian was brilliantly caught at point by the athletic Chris Lewis off a well-timed cut shot.

Even after Moody had gloved a ball from left-arm spinner Phil Tufnell back on to his stumps while sweeping there was no sense of imminent disaster. Border and Steve Waugh carried Australia to 4-145 in the 38th over when the ghosts of 1981 rose up from the grave. Initially it seemed Australia had been let off when Waugh was dropped at short cover, but from the fifth ball Botham duplicated Adrian Kuiper's inswinger to Border and achieved the same result.

That was only the pantomime king's warmup. In his next over, the 40th of the innings, Ian Healy clipped a catch to mid wicket. Two balls later Peter Taylor fell in the same way and for the same score as his top-of-the-order namesake.

Craig McDermott offered a soft catch to Phil DeFreitas at mid-on. Botham had 4-0 in seven balls. It was pitiful stuff by Australia and it must have caused a lot of local television viewers to switch channels. Steve Waugh's run out in the 43rd over ended any hope of a reasonable total and when Dermot Reeve captured the prized scalp of Bruce Reid Australia had lost 6-26 in 11 overs.

Botham, not satisfied with 4-31, made the Union Jacks in the Doug Walters Stand and on the refurbished Hill wave even harder when he and Graham Gooch put on a century opening partnership. They withstood a fast opening spell by a highly motivated McDermott, then took control.

Wasim Akram had complained that batting conditions under lights could be difficult. But neither England nor South Africa had much difficulty seeing the white ball at night. Botham's promotion to opener had achieved little to this point and his previous highest score in any World Cup was 22, but he had a night out in Sydney and hit six fours in his 50 before being well caught down the leg side in the 23rd over.

Gooch went on to complete his 50 as well, and was not dismissed until victory was assured. The target was reached nine comfortable overs to spare. After the humiliations of the Ashes tour in 1990-91 and talk by the Prime Minister, Paul Keating, of Australia becoming a republic, it was a sweet moment for the proud English captain.

AUSTRALIA		ENGLAND	
T. M. Moody b Tufnell	51	G.A. Gooch (capt) b Waugh	58
M. A. Taylor lbw Pringle	0	I. T. Botham c Healy b Whitney	53
D. C. Boon run out	18	R.A. Smith not out	30
D. M. Jones c Lewis b DeFreitas	22	G.A. Hick not out	7
S. R. Waugh run out	27	Extras (lb 13, w 8, nb 4)	25
A. R. Border (capt) b Botham	16	(40.5 overs)	2-173
I. A. Healy (wk) c Fairbrother b Botham	9	Did not bat: N. H. Fairbrother, A. J. Stewart (wk), D.A. Reeve,
P. L. Taylor lbw Botham	0	C.C. Lewis, D. R. Pringle, P. J. Defreitas, P.C.R. Tufnell
C. J. McDermott c DeFreitas b Botham	0	1/107 2/153
M. R. Whitney not out	8	Bowling: McDermott 10-1-29-0; Reid 7.5-0-49-0;
B. A. Reid b Reeve	1	Whitney 10-2-28-1; Waugh 6-0-29-1; P. L. Taylor 3-0-7-0;
Extras [b 2, lb 8, w 5, nb 4]	19	Moody 4-0-18-0
(49 overs)	10-171		

1/5 2/35 3/106 4/114 5/145 6/155 7/155 8/155 9/163
10/171

Bowling: Pringle 9-1-24-1; Lewis 10-2-28-0;
D. Freitas 10-3-23-1; Botham 10-1-31-4; Tufnell 9-0-52-1;
Reeve 1-0-3-1

Umpires: S.A. Buckner, Khizar Hayat.
Toss: Australia.   Points: England 2 Australia 0

SATURDAY 7 MARCH 1992
INDIA vs ZIMBABWE
TRUST BANK PARK, HAMILTON: INDIA WON BY 55 RUNS

The "if it's Saturday we must be in Hamilton" game turned out to be yet another frustrating exercise for the well-travelled Zimbabweans. The timing of the rain interruptions gave them virtually no chance of winning and poured further scorn on the rule for rain-affected games. It was threatening to undermine the validity of the whole tournament.

India was back to a swings-and-roundabouts situation, having won points and lost points because of the rule. At least they could relish another great display by Sachin Tendulkar, whose better-than-a-run-per-ball 81 dominated India's 32-over allocation. He was named Man of the Match and mastered all the Zimbabwean bowlers except John Traicos. The off-spinner was 26 years older than the young Indian master and played in South Africa's last Test three years before Tendulkar's birth. Traicos handled the wet ball as well as anyone on the day.

Tendulkar added an important 99 with Sanjay Manjrekar in 15 overs and hit eight fours and a six before becoming one of Mark Burmester's three victims.

With plenty of rain around, the players skipped their lunch break between innings and got straight on with the game. The Indians ran, slipped and fell all over the place as they tried to fit in 15 overs to avoid the 'no result' curse.

They got in 19.1 before the umpires took them off, never to return. Ali Shah, Andy Flower and Andy Waller had batted in competent fashion to that point and there was nothing to suggest Zimbabwe would not have made another 100 runs if the extra 13 overs had been delivered. But the man with the calculator told them they should have made 160 in 19 overs. Zimbabwe said nothing officially, but they were not very happy.

INDIA		ZIMBABWE	
K. Srikkanth b Burmester	32	AH. Shah b Tendulkar	31
Kapil Dev lbw Brandes	10	A. Flower (wk) not out	43
M. Azharuddin (capt) c Flower b Burmester	12	AC. Waller not out	13
S. R. Tendulkar c Campbell b Burmester	81	Extras (b l,lb 11, w 5)	17
S. V. Manjrekar c Duers b Traicos	34	(19.1 overs)	1-104
V. G. Kambli b Traicos	1	Did not bat D. L. Houghton (capt), AJ. Pycroft, I. P. Butchart,	
A. D. Jadeja c Shah b Traicos	6	AD. Campbell, E. A. Brandes, M. G. Burmester, AJ. Traicos,	
K. S. More (wk) not out	15	K. G. Duers	
J. Srinath not out	6	1/79	
Extras [lb 3, w 3]	6	Bowling: Kapil Dev 4-0-6-0; Prabhakar 3-0-14-0; Srinath	
(32 overs)	7-203	4-0-20-0; Tendulkar 6-0-35-1; Raju 2.1-0-17-0	
Did not bat M. Prabhakar, S. L.V. Raju			
1/23 2/43 3/69 4/168 5/170 6/182 7/184			
Bowling: Brandes 7-0-43-1; Duers 7-0-48-0;			
Burmester 6-0-36-3; Shah 6-1-38-0; Traicos 6-0-35-3			

Umpires: D.P. Buultjens, S.G. Randell.

Toss: India.   Points: India 2 Zimbabwe 0

AUSTRALIA vs SRI LANKA
ADELAIDE OVAL. ADELAIDE: AUSTRALIA WON BY 7 WICKETS

It was symbolic of a far better day for Australia that, even though Geoff Marsh dropped an early catch in the gully, the previously out-of-form opener made 60 on his return to the Australian side batting, after a cautious start, with his old fluency in an opening partnership of 120 with fellow Western Australian Tom Moody.

As Australia were only chasing 189 the stand settled the result and capped the co-host's best performance of the tournament. It also revived their semi-final hopes.

Allan Border won the toss, sent Sri Lanka in and, perhaps in an attempt to be innovative, opened the bowling with Steve Waugh. The medium pacer, more used to bowling at the end of the innings, made no impact but soon the Sri Lankans began to run themselves out. Roshan Mahanama was first, being slow to respond to a call from his opening partner, Athula Samarasekera.

De Silva's 62 provided the platform for a potentially competitive total. He scored 20 consecutive singles and hit only two boundaries. The Sri Lankan captain's most memorable shot was a dancing reverse sweep off Border. However, Michael Whitney, Craig McDermott, Peter Taylor and Border were so frugal the whole innings contained just eight fours and the run rate never looked likely to reach the four-per-over mark.

When Sri Lanka attempted to lift the tempo the captain was caught on the mid wicket boundary. The lower order became involved in three more run outs, including one from the final ball of the innings. The scoreline slipped from 3-123 to 9-189 at the completion of the 50 overs.

Moody and Marsh only scraped together 16 runs from the first nine overs. Certain sections of the Adelaide crowd made their feelings known about this. Marsh responded with a cover drive for four off Champaka Ramanayake and a sweep for six off left-arm spinner Don Anurasiri.

The 100 arrived in the 26th over and after the openers had been dismissed, Mark Waugh and Dean Jones hit sixes on the massively long Adelaide Oval which impressed the crowd.

Australia won by seven wickets at the end of the 44th over and Tom Moody was named Man of the Match.

SRI LANKA			AUSTRALIA	
R. S. Mahanama run out	7		T. M. Moody c Mahanama b Wickremasinghe	57
M. A. R. Samarasekera c Healy b Taylor	34		G. R Marsh c Anurasiri b Kalpage	60
A. P. Gurusinha lbw b Whitney	5		M. E. Waugh c Mahanama b Wickremasinghe	26
P. A. de Silva (capt) c Moody b McDermott	62		D. C. Boon not out	27
A. Ranatunga c Jones b Taylor	23		D. M. Jones not out	12
S. T. Jayasuriya lbw b Border	15		Extras (lb 2, w 3, nb 3)	8
H. P. Tillekaratne (wk) run out	5		(44 overs)	3-190
R. S. Kalpage run out	14		Did not bat: A. R. Border (capt), S. R Waugh, I.A. Healy (wk),
C. P. H. Ramanayake run out	5		P. L. Taylor, C. J. McDermott, M. R. Whitney
S. D. Anurasiri not out	4		1/120 2/130 3/165
Extras [b 3, lb 6, w 5, nb 1)	15		Bowling: Wickremasinghe 10-3-29-2; Ramanayake 9-1-44-0;
(50 overs)	9-189		Anurasiri 10-0-43-0; Gurusinha 6-0-20-0;
Did not bat: G. P. Wickremasinghe			Ranatunga 1-0-11-0; Kalpage 8-0-41-1

1/8 2/28 3/72 4/123 5/151 6/163 7/166 8/182 9/189

Bowling: McDermott 10-0-28-1; S. R Waugh 7-0-34-0;

Whitney 10-3-26-1; Moody 3-0-18-0; Taylor 10-0-34-2;

Border 10-0-40-1

Umpires: P.D. Reporter, I.D. Robinson.

Toss: Australia.   Points: Australia 2 Sri Lanka 0

<h2 style="text-align:center">SUNDAY 8 MARCH 1992
NEW ZEALAND vs WEST INDIES
EDEN PARK, AUCKLAND: NEW ZEALAND WON BY 5 WICKETS</h2>

The campaign of the once-mighty West Indies was falling in a heap. They were outplayed by a rampant New Zealand who completed only their second win in a limited-over international against the side once so obviously their superior.

There were plenty of frustrations for the West Indians: batting that just refused to gel as a unit, slogging by Mark Greatbatch that might have been stopped if short deliveries were allowed, a poor run out decision and some missed opportunities in the field.

In the good old days, though, none of them would have made a difference. The West Indies would still have won. The new wicket for this match looked green to Martin Crowe so he bowled after winning the toss on an overcast morning infront of a growing crowd. He opened again with the off spin of Dipak Patel and set two short mid wickets rather than slips catchers, which sedated Desmond Haynes and Brian Lara.

The West Indian openers got stuck into Gavin Larsen and Willie Watson when they came on and eventually put on 65 for the first wicket. When Lara, who went on to complete a half century in his usual stylish manner, took 14 from Larsen's first over Crowe brought his second medium pacer, Chris Harris, into the attack and switched Larsen to the other end. The move brought almost immediate reward when Harris caught and bowled Haynes and the run rate was slowed again.

Patel's economy was exceptional and when Carl Hooper tried to put him out of Eden Park, Greatbatch waited what seemed like 10 seconds under a skyed hit before completing the catch. Keith Arthurton made a worthwhile contribution, but it was the bright innings by little wicketkeeper David Williams, which included five fours and took advantage of loose bowling by Willie Watson, that pushed the West Indies score above 200.

For three overs neither Greatbatch nor Rod Latham could lay willow on leather. Then the big left-hander began smacking the ball around in what had become his accustomed style. There was great gnashing of Ambrose's significant teeth when Greatbatch hit him for six over third man. He also danced down the wicket and smote Malcolm Marshall over extra cover and onto the roof of the West Stand for a six that Martin Crowe called "the stroke of the World Cup".

Greatbatch hit seven fours and three sixes during his 77-ball innings. He swung and missed plenty of times, as well. After one unsuccessful foray Ambrose put forth a few opinions as to Greatbatch's true worth. That fired the big crowd up and Winston

Benjamin became a target for bottle throwers at third man. The game was stopped and the match referee Peter McDermott called for more police to be stationed in the offending area.

Upon the resumption Rod Latham was caught behind. Later, within three runs of each other Benjamin got rid of Andrew Jones, also caught behind, and Greatbatch caught at third man. The Kiwis were 3-100, the fall of wickets uncannily similar to the way they had fallen during the West Indian innings and their win far from a certainty.

Or it was until Crowe put together another masterpiece. The loss of Ken Rutherford and Chris Harris on the way did not stem the flow of strokes. He mastered the off spin of Carl Hooper, then with drives and pulls put Marshall out of the attack. Patel was given not out when a metre short of his ground, then two balls later the West Indies missed another blatant run out chance.

It was their last opportunity to steal the match. Crowe pressed on and when he straight drove Winston Benjamin for four from the third ball of the 49th over he had struck 12 boundaries in 77 balls. The Kiwi captain had won the Man of the Match award for the third time, had a tournament batting average of 263, and his team were unbeaten on top of the Benson and Hedges World Cup qualifying table with five wins. How many perfect days should one man have?

WEST INDIES		NEW ZEALAND	
D. L. Haynes c & b Harris	22	M.J. Greatbatch c Haynes b Benjamin	63
B. C. Lara c Rutherford b Larsen	52	R. T. Latham c Williams b Cummins	14
R. B. Richardson (capt) c Smith b Watson	29	A. H. Jones c Williams b Benjamin	10
C. L. Hooper c Greatbatch b Patel	2	M. D. Crowe (capt) not out	81
K. L. T. Arthurton b Morrison	40	K. R. Rutherford c Williams b Ambrose	8
A. L. Logie b Harris	3	C. Z. Harris c Williams b Cummins	7
M. D. Marshall b Larsen	5	D. N. Patel not out	10
D. Williams (wk) not out	32	Extras [lb 7. w 5. nb 1)	13
W. K.M. Benjamin not out	2	(48.3 overs)	5-206
Extras (lb 8, w 7, rtb 1)	16	Did not bat: I. DS. Smith (wk), G. R. Larsen. D. K. Morrison,	
(50 overs)	7-203	W. Watson	
Did not bat: C. E. L. Ambrose, A.c. Cummins		1/67 2/97 3/100 4/135 5/174	
1/65 2/95 3/100 4/136 5/142 6/156 7/201		Bowling: Ambrose 10-1-41-1; Marshall 9-1-35-0; Cummins	
Bowling: Morrison 9-1-33-1; Patel 10-2-19-1;		10-0-53-2; Benjamin 9.3-3-34-2; Hooper 10-0-36-0	
Watson 10-2-56-1; Larsen 10-0-41-2; Harris 10-2-32-2;			
Latham 1-0-14-0			

Umpires: K.E. Liebenberg, P.J. McConnell.

Toss: New Zealand.   Points: New Zealand 2. West Indies 0

PAKISTAN vs SOUTH AFRICA
WOOLLOONGABBA, BRISBANE: SOUTH AFRICA WON BY 20 RUNS

This was the sixth match to be adversely affected by rain in the first two weeks of the tournament. Pakistan were the side to suffer for choosing to bat second when they lost 14 overs from their innings while the target was reduced by just 18 runs. A Brisbane downpour stopped play at the 22-over mark when they were 2-74 chasing South Africa's 211.

At the time they required 4.84 per over to win. Upon the resumption it had leapt to 8.28, and when a flurry of shots by Imran Khan and Inzamam-ul-Haq was ended by the fielding brilliance of Jonty Rhodes Pakistan's hopes of victory quickly evaporated. Pakistan lost some sympathy because Imran Khan chose to field first even though most local forecasts and the sky itself suggested there would be rain at some stage of the match. They were hampered by injury and illness, Ramiz Raja and Javed Miandad being unavailable.

South Africa's batting, which they knew was not their strength, was again only functional. Andrew Hudson got the innings away to a flyer when he hit two off-side fours in Wasim Akram's first over. He and Mark Rushmere took the total to 1-98 in the

26th over. Then the journey from the 30th to the 40th over was a wasted one and, despite some lacklustre work in the field by the Pakistanis, South Africa slipped to 5-127.

Hansie Cronje and Brian McMillan put on 71 in 78 balls to give the South African attack something to bowl at. Cronje hit five fours as 68 were put on for the final 10 overs. There was more Pakistani fielding panic. Inzamam dropped an important catch at deep mid wicket and Moin Khan hit Aaqib Javed in the head when returning the ball to the bowler before he was ready. Aqib received treatment for the blow.

Aamir Sohail and Zahid Fazal, assisted by Allan Donald's waywardness, had a half-century opening stand before both fell at the same score. When Inzamam and Imran resumed they were able to take advantage of the damp ball and struck 61 runs in nine overs, lifting their partnership to 85.

Then Inzamam, not yet renowned as the worst runner in world cricket, went looking for a leg bye, turned and saw Jonty Rhodes, in a fair impression of a low-flying Superman, demolish all stumps in his path. It was a spectacular dismissal which turned the game decisively.

Imran was caught behind in the same McMillan over and with 58 still needed from just five overs the hitting had to be desperate. That made the risk factor too high for a new batsman and the wickets continued to tumble, three of them to Adrian Kuiper to catches in the deep. When the 36th over had been completed Pakistan were still 20 runs short of the target.

Hudson was named Man of the Match and Wessels admitted the overs reduction had helped his side.

SOUTH AFRICA		PAKISTAN	
A. C. Hudson c Ijaz Ahmed b Imran Khan	54	Aamir Sohail b Snell	23
K. C. Wessels (capt) c Moin Khan b Aaqib Javed	7	Zahid Fazal c Richardson b McMillan	11
M. W. Rushmere c Aamir Sohail b Mushtaq Ahmed	35	Inzamam-ul-Haq run out	48
A. P. Kuiper c Moin Khan b Imran Khan	5	Imran Khan (capt) c Richardson b McMillan	34
J. N. Rhodes lbw b Iqbal Sikander	5	Salim Malik c Donald b Kuiper	12
W. J. Cronje not out	47	Wasim Akram c Sneil b Kuiper	9
B. M. McMillan b Wasim Akram	33	Ijaz Ahmed c Rhodes b Kuiper	6
D. J. Richardson (wk) b Wasim Akram	5	Moin Khan (wk) not out	5
R. P. Snell not out	1	Mushtaq Ahmed run out	4
Extras (lb 8, w 9, nb 2)	19	Iqbal Sikander not out	1
(50 overs)	7-211	Extras (lb 2, w 17, nb 1)	20
Did not bat: M. W. Pringle, A. A. Donald		(36 overs)	8-173

1/31 2/98 3/110 4/111 5/127 6/198 7/207

Bowling: Wasim Akram 10-0-42-2; Aaqib Javed 7-1-36-1; Imran Khan 10-0-34-2; Sikander 8-0-30-1; Ijaz Ahmed 7-0-26-0; Mushtaq Ahmed 8-1-35-1

Did not bat: Aaqib Javed

1/50 2/50 3/135 4/136 5/156 6/157 7/163 8/170

Bowling: Donald 7-1-31-0; Pringle 7-0-31-0; Snell 8-2-26-1; McMillan 7-0-34-2; Kuiper 6-0-40-3; Cronje 1-0-9-0

Umpires: B.L. Aldridge, S.A. Bucknor.

Toss: Pakistan.   Points: South Africa 2 Pakistan 0

MONDAY 9 MARCH 1992
ENGLAND vs SRI LANKA
EASTERN OVAL, BALLARAT: ENGLAND WON BY 106 RUNS

On a beautiful public holiday Monday in front of a standing-room only crowd, England made short work of Sri Lanka. It was a big weekend in Ballarat, a town not always noted for warm sunny weather, with the opening of the annual Begonia Festival coinciding with the staging of the World Cup cricket match.

Melbourne's Sri Lankan community had made the journey to the old gold-mining city in force and added colour and spectacle to the day. Unfortunately, the greatest contribution of their team to the entertainment was to provide bowlers fit for collaring.

England built a total quite outside the scope of the Sri Lankan batsmen, their only glitch a hamstring injury to Graham Gooc, which occurred during the fourth over of the Sri Lankan innings. Gooch, who won the toss, had missed out with the bat, too, being first out after 40 minutes to Graeme Labrooy' s fourth ball in the competition. His partner, Ian Botham, had a let off on five before clubbing five fours and two sixes in 63 balls. Graeme Hick also spent some quality time in the centre.

It was the middle order, though, that provided the real excitement. Neil Fairbrother, dropped by wicketkeeper Hashan Tillekaratne on three, topscored and was a key factor in building the momentum of the final overs. He and Alec Stewart began striking the ball to all parts of the smallish Eastern Oval ground, the bowling green behind the old grandstand being an attraction to the big hitter. Stewart hit one six and Fairbrother two, but it was left to Chris Lewis right at the end of the innings to actually middle the ball with enough power to get it out of the ground.

Lewis only faced six balls for his 20 not out, his audacious strokeplay boosting the return from the last 10 overs to 106, including 73 from the last five.

For a few overs it seemed Athula Samarasekera might actually be able to lead a challenge to England's 280. He struck four boundaries within the first few overs during an opening partnership of 33.

But Lewis' form and confidence soon shattered that thought. He picked up four wickets in 18 balls as Sri Lanka slipped to 4-60. Neil Fairbrother's great catch at square leg to dismiss Aravinda de Silva was the most crucial of the four. The 5000 Sri Lankan fans, although disappointed at the collapse, would not let their spirits be dampened. They continued to provide a great atmosphere throughout the sun-drenched afternoon long after the game ceased to be a serious contest.

Chris Lewis was named Man of the Match.

ENGLAND		SRI LANKA	
G. A. Gooch (capt) b Labrooy	8	R. S. Mahanama c Botham b Lewis	9
I. T. Botham b Anurasiri	47	M. A. R. Samarasekera c Illingworth b Lewis	23
R. A. Smith run out	19	A. P. Gurusinha c & b Lewis	7
G. A. Hick b Ramanayake	41	P. A. de Silva (capt) c Fairbrother b Lewis	7
N. H. Fairbrother c Ramanayake b Gurusinha	63	A. Ranatunga c Stewart b Botham	36
A. J. Stewart (wk) c Jayasuriya b Gurusinha	59	H. P. Tillekaratne (wk) run out	4
C. C. Lewis not out	20	S. T. Jayasuriya c Defreitas b Illingworth	19
D. R. Pringle not out	0	G. F. Labrooy c Smith b Illingworth	19
Extras (b 1, lb 9, w 9, nb 4)	23	C. P. H. Ramanayake c & b Reeve	12
(50 overs)	6-280	S. D. Anurasiri lbw Reeve	11
Did not bat: D. A. Reeve, P. J. Defreitas, R. K. Illingworth		G. P. Wickremasinghe not out	6
1/44 2/80 3/105 4/164 5/244 6/268		Extras (lb 7, w 8, nb 6)	21
Bowling: Wickremasinghe 9-0-54-0; Ramanayake		(44 overs)	10-174
10-1-42-1; Labrooy 10-1-68-1; Anurasiri 10-1-27-1;		1/33 2/46 3/56 4/60 5/91 6/119 7/123 8/156 9/158	
Gurusinha 10-0-67-2; Jayasuriya 1-0-12-0		Bowling: Pringle 7-1-27-0; Lewis 8-0-30-4;	
		Defreitas 5-1-31-0; Botham 10-0-33-1; Illingworth 10-0-32-2;	
		Reeve 4-0-14-2	

Umpires: Khizar Hayat, P.O. Reporter.

Toss: England.   Points: England 2 Sri Lanka 0

TUESDAY 10 MARCH 1992
INDIA vs WEST INDIES
BASIN RESERVE, WELLINGTON: WEST INDIES WON BY 5 WICKETS

And again the stupid rain rule was needed. This time at least the side batting second was able to win, but this was a very important game in the context of the tournament and it had not been possible to let it reach a conclusion without interference. Players from all sides just shook their heads.

Mohammad Azharuddin had elected to bat on a cold, windy showery day that indicated, in Wellington at least, time for summer sports was growing short. He got the start he would have wanted, albeit that Ajay Jadeja and Kris Srikkanth were a little on the slow side during their opening partnership.

Sachin Tendulkar failed for once, Curtly Ambrose being recalled to the bowling crease and producing a peach of a leg-cutter to have him caught behind. That meant it was the captain's turn to play the major innings and he did so in style. For 85 balls he charmed spectators and sustained his side until the 43rd over when India at 3-166 looked likely to set the West Indies a target of reasonable significance.

Then a flat-batted off-drive off Anderson Cummins was caught near the boundary by Ambrose. From that point the Indian batting went nowhere. Cummins just put the ball in the right spot and the batsmen offered a succession of catches. Seven wickets went down for 31 and the innings did not even run its full course. It was a costly collapse of the type which can cause a team to miss a semi-final place.

The West Indies were confident they could get the runs. They were more uncertain about what the deteriorating weather would do to them. The clouds threatened as they began their reply so Brian Lara set out to get as many early runs as possible. Manoj Prabhakar was his target and the medium pacer was smashed for 32 in his first three overs. Desmond Haynes was lost at 57, then at 81 after 11 overs the umpires took the players off for rain.

Richie Richardson reckoned it was no more than a mist.

Fours overs and three runs were deducted for the 20-minute delay. Upon resumption, it looked as if the batsmen had lost concentration. Worried about the possible return of the rain, Lara, Phil Simmons, Richardson and Gus Logie thrashed and got out, leaving the West Indies 5-112.

Fortunately for cricket and justice it did not return and Keith Arthurton and Carl Hooper were able to put together a match-winning partnership of 83. They steadied, saw that the sky was clearing, then took control. Both batsmen hit three fours and Arthurton completed his 50 before the win was completed in perfect sunshine.

Cummins was an interesting choice as Man of the Match.

Malcolm Marshall, who had just announced he would be retiring from international cricket at the end of the World Cup, was left out of the side because of an ankle injury. His international career had already finished.

INDIA		WEST INDIES	
A. D. Jadeja c Benjamin b Simmons	27	D. L. Haynes c Manjrekar b Kapil Dev	16
K. Srikkanth c Logie b Hooper	40	B. C. Lara c Manjrekar b Srinath	41
M. Azharuddin (capt) c Ambrose b Cummins	61	P. V. Simmons c Tendulkar b Prabhakar	22
S. R. Tendulkar c Williams b Ambrose	4	R. Richardson (capt) c Srikkanth b Srinath	3
S. V. Manjrekar run out	27	K. L. T. Arthurton not out	58
Kapil Dev c Haynes b Cummins	3	A.L. Logie c More b Raju	7
P. K. Amre c Hooper b Ambrose	4	C. L. Hooper not out	34
K. S. More (wk) c Hooper b Cummins	5	Extras (lb 8, w 2, nb 4)	14
M. Prabhakar c Richardson b Cummins	8	(40.3 overs)	5-195
J. Srinath not out	5	Did not bat: D. Williams (wk), C. E. L. Ambrose, AC.
S. L.V. Raju run out	1	Cummins,
Extras [lb 6, w 5, nb 1]	12	W. K.M. Benjamin
(49.4 overs)	10-197	1/57 2/81 3/88 4/98 5/112

1/56 2/102 3/115 4/166 5/171 6/173 7/180 8/186 9/193 10/197

Bowling: Ambrose 10-1-24-2; Benjamin 9.4-0-35-0; Cummins 10-0-33-4; Simmons 9-0-48-1; Hooper 10-0-46-1; ; Arthurton 1-0-5-0

Bowling: Kapil Dev 8-0-45-1; Prabhakar9-0-55-1; Raju 10-2-32-1; Srinath 9-2-23-2; Tendulkar 3-0-20-0; Srikkanth 1-0-7-0; Jadeja 0.3-0-5-0

Umpires: S.G. Randell, S.J. Woodward.

Toss: India.   Points: West Indies 2, India 0

SOUTH AFRICA vs ZIMBABWE
MANUKA OVAL, CANBERRA: SOUTH AFRICA WON BY 7 WICKETS

Another historic encounter involving South Africa was played in the Australian capital city at the lovely Manuka Oval.

Tuesday was difficult for many, so only 3000 turned up to what turned out to be a pedestrian and one-sided encounter anyway. At least the weather was good, so the better side on the day could win unencumbered.

South Africa were that better side, keeping their northern neighbours' batting under wraps, then pacing themselves solidly, unspectacularly but inevitably to a seven-wicket victory.

Kepler Wessels won the toss and sent the slightly nervous Zimbabweans in to bat. Wayne James did not last long and Andy Flower soon had to retire with a damaged finger after misjudging a cut shot at Allan Donald. He resumed his innings later, but Dave Houghton kept wicket.

Worse than those setbacks was the loss of three wickets to Peter Kirsten's straight breaks in his first two overs while the total moved from 2-72 to 5-80. Houghton and Andy Waller both holed out unnecessarily to Hansie Cronje at deep mid wicket. Eddo Brandes got a measure of revenge when he clouted Kirsten for six and there were plenty of free offerings as Meyrick Pringle and Brian McMillan sprayed plenty of wides and no balls.

There were no partnerships; though, that were able to take advantage of batsmen getting a start.

Extras comfortably top scored. When Donald bowled Kevin Duers halfway through the 48th over, South Africa needed just 164 to win.

A partnership of 112 between Kepler Wessels and Peter Kirsten, still nursing a recovering calf strain but in superb form, ensured that win would be a straightforward one. Wessels hit six fours in 137 balls despite a sore thumb. He had lost his opening partner Andrew Hudson at 27, bowled leg stump by a full-pitched Malcolm Jarvis delivery, and was dropped at fine leg by Kevin Duers off Mark Burmester soon after. That was Zimbabwe's final sniff until victory was just 25 runs away. Kirsten remained unbeaten when the winning run was scored with five overs and seven wickets left.

Kirsten's not-out gave the 36-year-old Man of the Match a tournament batting average of 101. His side were now third.

ZIMBABWE		SOUTH AFRICA	
W. R. James lbw b Pringle	5	K. C. Wessels (capt) b Shah	70
A. Flower c Richardson b Cronje	19	A. C. Hudson b Jarvis	13
A. J. Pycroft c Wessels b McMillan	19	P. N. Kirsten not out	62
D. L. Houghton (capt-wk) c Cronje b Kirsten	15	A. P. Kuiper c Burmester b Brandes	7
A. C. Waller c Cronje b Kirsten	15	J. N. Rhodes not out	3
A. H. Shah c Wessels b Kirsten	3	Extras (lb 4, w 2, nb 3)	9
E. A Brandes c Richardson b McMillan	20	(45.1 overs)	3-164
M. G. Burmester c Kuiperb Cronje	1	Did not bat: W. J. Cronje, B. M. McMillan, M. W. Pringle,	
A. J. Traicos not out	16	R. P. Snell, D. J. Richardson (wk), A. A. Donald	
M. P. Jarvis c & b McMillan	17	1/27 2/139 3/151	
K. G. Duers b Donald	5	Bowling: Brandes 9.1-0-39-1; Jarvis 9-2-23-1;	
Extras (lb 11, w 13, nb 4)	28	Burmester 5-0-20-0; Shah 8-2-33-1; Duers 8-1-19-0;	
(48.3 overs)	10-163	Traicos 6-0-26-0	

1/7 2/51 3/72 4/80 5/80 6/115 7/117 8/123
9/151 10/163
A. Flower retired hurt 1-26, resumed at 5-80
Bowling: Donald 9.3-1-25-1; Pringle 9-0-25-1;
Snell 10-3-24-0; McMillan 10-1-30-3; Cronje 5-0-17-2;
Kirsten 5-0-31-3

Umpires: SA Bucknor, D.R. Shepherd.

Toss: South Africa.   Points: South Africa 2 Zimbabwe 0

WEDNESDAY 11 MARCH 1992
AUSTRALIA vs PAKISTAN
WACA, PERTH: PAKISTAN WON BY 48 RUNS

This was the match of Imran Khan's 'cornered tigers'; a pivotal contest in the whole competition which determined the long-term fate of these two underachieving sides.

The people of Perth knew its worth and turned out in good numbers even though the mid-week day/night fixture would keep them up late.

The Pakistani captain admitted to the pressure for both teams in what amounted to a first final. The cutthroat nature of the contest strained temperaments to the full and the WACA witnessed, not for the first time, some heated exchanges between Australians and Pakistanis.

In the final analysis, though, Australia's batting let them down and another total in the low 170s was that of a loser.

Imran won the toss and batted and Aamir Sohail was promptly caught behind off a Bruce Reid no ball before he had scored. The lanky left-arm paceman often beat the edge in his opening spell without getting a wicket. The total was 78 after 20 overs before a wicket fell when an overaggressive Ramiz Raja was caught at short mid wicket off Mike Whitney. Sohail, scoring a high percentage of his eight boundaries with the pull shot, put on another 77 with Javed Miandad, who had just returned to the side after recovering from a stomach infection, so that with several overs to go Pakistan were 3-193.

From there Steve Waugh, at his canniest, caused the batting to fall away and the last six wickets could only contribute an extra 27 runs. Despite hitting Mike Whitney into the stands, Imran batted slowly, Wasim Akram was caught first ball off a slower delivery and Ijaz Ahmed was run out second ball off a dropped catch. The Pakistanis had made 9-220, which was only as good or bad as their bowlers made it.

Aaqib Javed made it look very good when he had Tom Moody caught at first slip and David Boon taken at third slip during an excellent opening spell. Geoff Marsh survived, but little else, and was subjected to more barracking, even from his home crowd. A French cut was his only stroke to the boundary in 91 balls.

Dean Jones, however, was altogether more positive in a stand of 85 in 22 overs. The Australians found their efforts supplemented by numerous calls for wides and no balls, as indeed had the Pakistanis in their batting innings.

So frequent were the wide calls earlier in the day that at one point Border asked for clarification. What he might have been better off requesting was for some batting advice because he was at the top of another horrendous collapse. His failure, caught at square leg, left Border a World Cup aggregate on 30 from five innings. The Australian captain came and went after Jones had been caught at long off from leg spinner Mushtaq Ahmed and Marsh was caught behind from an Imran in-swinger.

Akram said the Pakistanis had their hearts in their mouths as the ball sailed towards Aqib from Jones' big hit. It was a relief to them all when an unreliable catcher held the best one-day batsman in the Australian side.

Mark Waugh showed some class, but he had precious little support as Australia lost 8-56. The latter part of the innings was not just marred by batting incompetence, but also an altercation between Mike Whitney and wicketkeeper Moin Khan, who had to be separated by Bruce Reid and umpire Piloo Reporter. It was as pointless as it was childish as Wasim Akram finished the match by bowling the Australian tailender almost immediately after.

Both players were docked a portion of their match fees, as was Man of the Match Aamir Sohail who had disagreed with a caught-behind decision in favour of David Boon in the seventh over.

Australia, who had struggled with the ball moving around in the air under lights, were not deserving of a semi-final spot according to their disappointed captain at the post-match press conference.

PAKISTAN		AUSTRALIA	
Aamir Sohail c Healy b Moody	76	T. M. Moody c Salim Malik b Aaqib Javed	4
Ramiz Raja c Border b Whitney	34	G. R. Marsh c Moin Khan b Imran Khan	39
Salim Malik b Moody	0	D. C. Boon c Mushtaq Ahmed b Aaqib Javed	5
Javed Miandad c Healy b S. R. Waugh	46	D. M. Jones c Aaqib Javed b Mushtaq Ahmed	47
Imran Khan (capt) c Moody b S. R. Waugh	13	M. E. Waugh c Ijaz Ahmed b Mushtaq Ahmed	30
Inzamam-ul-Haq run out	16	A. R. Border (capt) c Ijaz Ahmed b Mushtaq Ahmed	1
Ijaz Ahmed run out	0	S. R. Waugh c Moin Khan b Imran Khan	5
Wasim Akram c M. E. Waugh b S. R. Waugh	0	I. A. Healy (wk) c Ijaz Ahmed b Aaqib Javed	8
Moin Khan (wk) c Healy b McDermott	5	C. J. McDermott lbw Wasim Akram	0
Mushtaq Ahmed not out	3	M. R. Whitney b Wasim Akram	5
Extras (lb 9, w 16, nb 2)	27	B. A. Reid not out	0
(50 overs)	9-220	Extras (lb 7, w 14, nb 7)	28
Did not bat: Aaqib Javed		(45.2 overs)	10-172
1/78 2/80 3/157 4/193 5/194 6/205 7/205 8/214 9/220		1/13 2/31 3/116 4/122 5/123 6/130 7/156 8/162 9/167	
Bowling: McDermott 10-0-33-1; Reid 9-0-37-0;		10/172	
S. R. Waugh 10-0-36-3; Whitney 10-1-50-1; Moody		Bowling: Wasim Akram 7.2-0-28-2; Aaqib Javed 8-1-21-3;	
10-0-42-2; M. E. Waugh 1-0-13-0		Imran Khan 10-1-32-2; Ijaz Ahmed 10-0-43-0;	
		Mushtaq Ahmed 10-0-41-3	

Umpires: K.E. Liebenberg P.D. Reporter..

Toss: Pakistan.   Points: Pakistan 2 Australia 0

THURSDAY 12 MARCH 1992
NEW ZEALAND vs INDIA
CARISBROOK, DUNEDIN: NEW ZEALAND WON BY 4 WICKETS

It was no wonder India did not win at cricket's closest venue to the South Pole. Bitter winds swept the ground all day, making fingers numb, the ball hard and elusive in the air. Twice fieldsmen failed to touch chances from swirling, skyed shots. India, gloved and padded, batted well enough but could not restrain their in-form opponents who by the start of the 48th over of their innings had completed a record-equalling six consecutive World Cup wins.

Crowe admitted that his original idea was to give other players in the squad a run in games such as this. Now, in the lead-up to the semi-finals, New Zealand stuck to their strongest side to give them their best opportunity to maintain the winning habit.

Understandably fearing rain, Mohammad Azharuddin batted after he won the toss. Kris Srikkanth tried to undermine the Dipak Patel tactic and was caught on the long on boundary from the third ball of the match. His opening partner, Ajay Jadeja, soon snapped a hamstring muscle that surely was not warmed up enough. That brought together Azharuddin and Sachin Tendulkar. The two stylists did not always come off as a pair, but when they did it was a sight to behold. Their stand of 127 in 30 overs warmed the hearts of the 9000 hardy souls in attendance.

Azharuddin reached 50 by hitting Patel for six, then trying to repeat the shot was caught by Mark Greatbatch diving forward at deep mid wicket. Tendulkar went on to 84 in 105 balls with six off-side fours before becoming another of Chris Harris' growing bag of World Cup victims. Kapil Dev hit five fours in 17 balls, which lifted India to a very competitive score in the context of this competition. Mark Greatbatch sensibly used the wind assistance to hit four sixes and five fours in another belligerent onslaught during the fielding restrictions of the first 15·overs. He twice clouted Kapil Dev over square leg, got to his 50 in 47 balls and with the reliable Andrew Jones had the total up to 118 before holing out to square leg in the 25th over.

Martin Crowe looked confident when Kiran More freakishly ran him out with a backward flick from gully. The halving of the New Zealand captain's World Cup batting average had no real detrimental affect as Jones held the chase together until victory. Greatbatch chased Crowe's Man of the Match tally with his second award. India, possibly thinking of their warm homeland more this day than on any other during their marathon Antipodean tour, were now able to make plans for their return.

INDIA		NEW ZEALAND	
A. D. Jadeja retired hurt	13	M. J. Greatbatch c Banerjee b Raju	73
K. Srikkanth c Latham b Patel	0	R. I. Latham b Prabhakar	8
M. Azharuddin (capt) c Greatbatch b Patel	55	A. H. Jones not out	67
S. R. Tendulkar c Smith b Harris	84	M. D. Crowe (capt) run out	26
S. V. Manjrekar c & b Harris	18	I. D. S. Smith (wk) c sub (P. K. Amre) b Prabhakar	9
Kapil Dev c Larsen b Harris	33	K. R. Rutherford lbw b Raju	21
S. T. Banerjee c Greatbatch b Watson	11	C. Z. Harris b Prabhakar	4
K. S. More (wk) not out	2	C. L. Cairns not out	4
J. Srinath not out	4	Extras (b 4, lb 3, w 4, nb 8)	19
Extras (b 1, lb 4, w 4, nb 1)	10	(47.1 overs)	6-231
(50 overs)	6-230	Did not bat: D. N. Patel, G. R. Larsen, W. Watson	

Did not bat: M. Prabhakar, S. L. V. Raju

1/42 1/149 3/166 4/201 5/222 6/223

Jadeja retired hurt at 1/22

Bowling: Cairns 8-1-40-0; Patel 10-0-29-2; Watson 10-1-34-1; Larsen 9-0-43-0; Harris 9-0-55-3; Latham 4-0-24-0

1/36 2/118 3/162 4/172 5/206 6/225

Bowling: Kapil Dev 10-0-55-0; Prabhakar 10-0-46-3; Banerjee 6-1-40-0; Srinath 9-0-35-0; Raju 10-0-38-2; Tendulkar 1-0-2-0; Srikkanth 1.1-0-8-0

Umpires: P.J. McConnell, I.D. Robinson.

Toss: India. Points: New Zealand 2 India 0

ENGLAND vs SOUTH AFRICA
MCG, MELBOURNE: ENGLAND WON BY 3 WICKETS

England won an exciting victory, overcoming a worthy opponent in South Africa, the unfair rain regulation and a high injury attrition rate. Behind the scenes Ian Botham was beginning to grumble about the strict training routines Graham Gooch and Mickey Stewart were still forcing upon the team. The two fitness fanatics could point to a string of wins, 'Beefy' Botham to a growing casualty list.

None of those debates on cricket philosophy were evident during an entertaining afternoon and evening at the MCG. The handy Thursday crowd witnessed a great opening partnership by Kepler Wessels and Andrew Hudson after Alec Stewart, captaining England in place of the injured Gooch, won the toss and chose to bowl.

It took until Hudson's drive off Derek Pringle in the fifth over for the ball to reach the new, reduced, roped-off boundary at the MCG. However, as the stand grew, bowlers were soon falling rather than wickets. Chris Lewis could not bowl at all because of a side strain, Phil DeFreitas limped off the ground at the end of each of his spells and Dermot Reeve fell in a foothole and hurt himself in his delivery stride and could not complete his stint.

Meantime when Hudson cut the expensive Gladstone Small for four in the 15th over the opening partnership was worth 50. The milestones kept totting up at a steady rate. Hudson, by far the most fluent of the pair, reached his 50 with a clip off his toes off Botham in the 26th over.

Wessels kept on until the 32nd over, on-driving Reeve for a four that took the stand to 122. Hudson was run out by Fairbrother but the umpire, still at this time not allowed to use a television replay, had to call not out because the substantial torso of Botham blocked his view. Finally Graeme Hick, the seventh bowler used, induced a tame caught and bowled from Hudson to break the partnership in the 36th over at 151.

Peter Kirsten got off the mark by lifting Richard Illingworth over the rope at long off for six. Yet the boundaries really dried up from that point. Adrian Kuiper's back-away square drive off Pringle in the 49th over was the first four in 10 overs. South Africa had to be satisfied with 236 when for a time a total in excess of 250 had beckoned.

On the still expansive MCG it remained a worthy target, but the new English captain set about balancing the odds with a positive start. He cut and drove Meyrick Pringle for fours in the eighth over which got the embryonic 'Barmy Army' singing, then raised the 50 in the 11th over with a slashing cut off Richard Snell.

It was Man of the Match-worthy stuff, but it came to an abrupt halt when an unscheduled shower arrived at 0-62 after 12 overs.

The 43-minute interruption reduced the target by 11 runs and the number of overs by nine. When Brian McMillan smashed Botham's middle stump and had Robin Smith caught behind cutting, and Richard Snell found the outside edge of Graeme Hick's bat on the drive England were 3-64 in the 15th over and thoughts of a win suddenly seemed fanciful.

But Stewart kept playing as if the collapse had never happened. A late cut off Snell gave him his 50 in 61 balls, and with Neil Fairbrother as an ally, 68 runs were added in the next 13 overs. Jonty Rhodes' brilliance at cover point brought about a fatal hesitation in Stewart's running in the 28th over.

Fairbrother assumed the role of major run scorer, cutting, pulling and clipping the ball at varying angles to keep England within touch of the asking rate.

That rate stayed tight at about seven per over until Chris Lewis blazed 33 in 22 balls with four fours. He added 50 in six overs with Fairbrother, which took England to within 10 runs of victory.

Rhodes was again the fieldsman when Lewis was run out with two overs remaining. Fairbrother reduced the odds even further with a slash drive over point and even Pringle's tame push to mid wicket off a Snell full toss in the final over could not deny England. Stewart had captained his country to victory over South Africa in the first clash between the two nations since 1965. To top off his night he was named Man of the Match.

England joined New Zealand as confirmed semi-finalists.

SOUTH AFRICA		ENGLAND	
K. C. Wessels (capt) c Smith b Hick	85	A.J. Stewart (capt-wk) run out	77
A. C. Hudson c & b Hick	79	I. T. Botham b McMillan	22
P. N. Kirsten c Smith b Defreitas	11	R. A. Smith c Richardson b McMillan	0
J. N. Rhodes run out	18	G. A. Hick c Richardson b Snell	1
A. P. Kuiper not out	15	N. H. Fairbrother not out	75
W.J. Cronje not out	13	D. A. Reeve c McMillan b Snell	10
Extras (b 4, lb 4, w 4, nb 3)	15	C. C. Lewis run out	33
(50 overs)	4-236	D. R. Pringle c Kuiper b Snell	1
Did not bat: B. M. McMillan, D. J. Richardson (wk),		P. A. J. Defreitas not out	1
R. P. Snell, M. W. Pringle, A. A. Donald		Extras (lb 3, w 1, nb 2)	6
1/151 2/170 3/201 4/205		(40.5 overs)	7-226
Bowling: Pringle 9-2-34-0; Defreitas 10-1-41-1;		Did not bat: R. K. Illingworth, G. C. Small	
Botham 8-0-37-0; Small 2-0-14-0; Illingworth 10-0-43-0;		1/63 2/63 3/64 4/132 5/166 6/216 7/225	
Reeve 2.4-0-15-0; Hick 8.2-0-44-2		Bowling: Donald 9-1-43-0; Pringle 8-0-44-0; Snell 7.5-0-42-3;	
		McMillan 8-1-39-2; Kuiper 4-0-32-0; Cronje 3-0-14-0;	
		Kirsten 1-0-9-0	

Umpires: B.L. Aldridge, D.P. Buultjens.

Toss: England.   Points: England 2, South Africa 0

FRIDAY 13 MARCH 1992
WEST INDIES vs SRI LANKA
BERRI OVAL, BERRI: WEST INDIES WON BY 91 RUNS

Sri Lanka's extensive travelling took them to the far-flung regions of South Australia, north-east of Adelaide by the Murray River where, in contrast to Thursday in Dunedin, they met the West Indies in sweltering 38-degree temperatures. Their previous on-road experiences gave the Sri Lankans no advantage and they were outplayed by Richie Richardson's side, who still harboured ambitions to reach the semi-finals. Aravinda de Silva won the toss and, for some reason, condemned his side to a 50-over stint in the heat.

After Brian Lara was an early casualty, Phil Simmons dominated a visibly wilting Sri Lankan attack. He had substantial partnerships with Desmond Haynes and Keith Arthurton and went on to complete his highest international score. The Sri Lankans could have got rid of him on six and twice on 47, only to miss each opportunity.

The Trinidadian punished those misdemeanours with nine fours and two sixes before becoming one of Chandika Hathurusingha's four victims in the 40th over with the total 197. The medium pacer, perhaps only used because of the heat, precipitated a collapse where the West Indies lost 5-31. A final burst of 40 runs from Curtly Ambrose and Winston Benjamin re-asserted West Indian dominance and left Sri Lanka with an unlikely target of 269 for victory.

As they did against England, Roshan Mahanama and Athula Samarasekera gave the early impression that the chase was on with an opening partnership of 56.

It was an illusion.

Carl Hooper's off spin assumed Patel-like status as the runs dried up and the wickets began to fall. Ambrose, too, was exceptionally difficult to score from. Samarasekera hit five fours and a six, a greater return of boundary strokes than the rest of the batsmen put together. The demise was fairly gradual and in the end the West Indians did not have enough strength left to take the last wicket. When the 50th over was completed the Sri Lankans were still 92 runs short of what they required.

At one point Sri Lanka had been third on the qualifying table. Now they, like India and Zimbabwe, could plan their homeward journey.

Phil Simmons was named Man of the Match.

WEST INDIES		SRI LANKA	
D. L. Haynes c Tillekaratne b Ranatunga	38	R. S. Mahanama c Athurton b Cummins	11
B. C. Lara c & b Ramanayake	1	M. R. Samarasekera lbw Hooper	40
P. V. Simmons c Wickremasinghe b Hathurusingha	110	U. C. Hathurusingha run out	16
R. B. Richardson (capt) run out	8	P. A. de Silva (capt) c & b Hooper	11
K. L. T. Arthurton c Tillekaratne b Hathurusingha	40	A. Ranatunga c Benjamin b Arthurton	24
A. L. Logie b Anurasiri	0	A.P. Gurusinha c Richardson b Ambrose	10
C. L. Hooper c Gurusinha b Hathurusingha	12	H. P. Tillekaratne (wk) b Ambrose	3
D. Williams (wk) c Tillekaratne b Hathurusingha	2	R. S. Kalpage not out	13
C. E. L. Ambrose not out	15	C. P. H. Ramanayake b Arthurton	1
W. K.M. Benjamin not out	24	S. D. Anurasiri b Benjamin	3
Extras (lb 9, w 3, nb 6)	18	G. P. Wickremasinghe not out	21
(50 overs)	8-268	Extras (lb 8, w 14, nb 2)	24
Did not bat: A.C. Cummins		(50 overs)	9-177

1/6 2/72 3/103 4/197 5/199 6/219 7/223 8/228

1/56 2/80 3/86 4/99 5/130 6/135 7/137 8/139 9/149

Bowling: Wickremasinghe 7-0-30-0; Ramanayake 7-1-17-1; Anurasiri 10-0-46-1; Gurusinha 1-0-10-0; Ranatunga 7-0-35-1; Kalpage 10-0-64-0; Hathurusingha 8-0-57-4

Bowling: Ambrose 10-2-24-2; Benjamin 10-0-34-1; Cummins 9-0-49-1; Hooper 10-1-19-2; Arthurton 10-0-40-2; Simmons 1-0-3-0

Umpires: D.R. Shepherd, S.J. Woodward.

Toss: Sri Lanka.   Points: West Indies 2, Sri Lanka 0

SATURDAY 14 MARCH 1992
AUSTRALIA vs ZIMBABWE
BELLERIVE OVAL, HOBART: AUSTRALIA WON BY 128 RUNS

Australia showed they were still capable of crushing the underlings of international cricket with this emphatic win in Tasmania. It was probably too little too late, but enjoyed by the locals nevertheless.

The omission of Geoff Marsh terminated the Australian career of Allan Border's favoured lieutenant. He was not to be missed this day, though. Dave Houghton sent the Australians in after he won the toss. There were some showers around, but the interruption came early and the reduction to a 46-over contest had little impact on the pattern or worth of the game.

Local hero David Boon and Dean Jones carried Australia to a commendable 1-102 after Tom Moody was left stranded in the second over. Boon just failed to make his 50, while Jones reached his with his 22nd consecutive single.

After he played on to Mark Burmester and Border was stumped dashing at John Traicos, Australia were 5-144 and a total in the 170s was not out of the question.

Then wicketkeeper Andy Flower dropped Steve Waugh before he had scored. It was a costly miss. He and his twin brother Mark took sudden and complete control of the game by putting on 113 in 11 exhilarating overs. Steve deflected fine to the off and on and belted a caught and bowled chance back at Eddo Brandes. Mark scored faster, looked better and used a wider variety of strokes. They ran between wickets with the daring and instinct of twin brothers. Steve reached his 50 in 39 balls, Mark with a six over mid wicket in 32 balls.

Brandes got a little of his own back on Steve with a well-pitched yorker and Ian Healy was lbw to Kevin Duers second ball, but the damage had been done. The final 10 overs lifted the total by 106.

Ali Shah and Flower, making no real attempt to chase 265, survived until the total reached 47. From the moment Shah was beaten by Bruce Reid's throw the innings became a bit of a procession. The progress of 50 runs from 47 to 97 cost seven wickets, shared around between Steve Waugh, Mike Whitney, Craig McDermott and Tom Moody.

Andy Waller and Brandes struck a few isolated retaliatory blows which prolonged the afternoon's entertainment until there were just five overs left in the game. How does a number-11 batsman approach a target of 130 runs in five overs?

Steve Waugh beat Mark for the Man of the Match award. And Australia retained the slimmest hope of making the semi-finals.

AUSTRALIA		ZIMBABWE	
T. M. Moody run out	6	AH. Shah run out	24
D. C. Boon b Shah	48	A. Flower (wk) c Border b S. R. Waugh	20
D. M. Jones b Burmester	54	A. D. Campbell c M. E. Waugh b Whitney	4
A. R. Border (capt) st Flower b Traicos	22	A.J. Pycroft c M. E. Waugh b S. R. Waugh	0
M. E. Waugh not out	66	D. L. Houghton (capt) b McDermott	2
S. R. Waugh b Brandes	55	AC. Waller c Taylor b Moody	18
I. A Healy (wk) lbw Duers	0	K. J. Arnott b Whitney	8
P. L. Taylor not out	1	EA. Brandes c McDermott b Taylor	23
Extras (b 2, lb 8, w 2, nb 1)	13	M. G. Burmester c Border b Reid	12
(46 overs)	6-265	AJ. Traicos c Border b Taylor	3
Did not bat: C. J. McDermott, M. R. Whitney, BA. Reid		K. G. Duers not out	2
1/8 2/102 3/134 4/144 5/257 6/258		Extras (lb 11, w 8, nb 2)	21
Bowling: Brandes 9-0-59-1; Duers 9-1-48-1; Burmester		(41.4 overs)	10-137
9-0-65-1; Shah 9-0-53-1; Traicos 10-0-30-1		1/47 2/51 3/51 4/57 5/69 6/88 7/97 8/117 9/132 10/137	
		Bowling: McDermott 8-0-26-1; Reid 9-1-18-1; S. R.	
		Waugh 7-0-28-2; Whitney 10-3-15-2; Moody 4-0-25-1;	
		Taylor 3.4-0-14-2	

Umpires: B.L. Aldridge, S.A. Bucknor.

Toss: Zimbabwe.   Points: Australia 2 Zimbabwe 0

NEW ZEALAND vs ENGLAND
BASIN RESERVE, WELLINGTON: NEW ZEALAND WON BY 7 WICKETS

In the eyes of some, particularly English and New Zealand supporters, this was a final preview. If so, the Kiwis would have claimed title favouritism after a comfortable win in the first match of a World Cup triple-header Sunday.

The result had little impact on anything other than keeping the winning habit, as both these teams had already qualified for the semi-finals. England had more injury worries, with Neil Fairbrother, prior to the game, and Derek Pringle, during it, joining the long list of the incapacitated. Ian Botham reckoned the team was exhausted.

Certainly their batting adrenalin seemed to wane as their innings progressed after Martin Crowe had sent them in. The Basin Reserve was packed and bathed in sunshine as Ian Botham, who pre-match had promised as much, attempted to do a Mark Greatbatch job on the slowest opening attack in international cricket in the 20th century.

He and Alec Stewart, again English captain, got Chris Harris away a few times. Dipak Patel, however, was once more in total control on a patchy turning wicket. He had a stumping chance missed off Stewart and then bowled Botham, hitting across the line, in the seventh over.

Patel's five-over spell of immaculate off spin yielded just seven runs. It was not until Willie Watson started dropping short that the runs flowed. Stewart and Graeme Hick, who twice pulled Watson for four in the 12th over and later hoisted Chris Cairns for six, added 70 in 14 overs.

Then Patel returned and Stewart swept to square leg where Harris held a smart catch. Hick brought up his 50 off 62 balls and took the total to 2-135 with Robin Smith. Slowly, though, Crowe's bowlers and fieldsmen strangled the English run flow. Hick cut at Harris, far more effective in his second spell, and was caught behind by Greatbatch who was substituting for Ian Smith, who was struck down with a migraine.

Gavin Larsen, like Patel, could not be hit. Andrew Jones had fumed when Crowe announced his decision to bowl. Now, he bowled flat off breaks almost as effectively as Patel.

Allan Lamb, back in the side after a long injury lay-off, made little headway. Smith was discouraged by the low slow wicket and after he had holed out at long on Chris Lewis pushed his first ball softly back to the bowler Watson.

That left England on 5-162 in the 42nd over and try as the remaining batsmen might they could not get the bowling properly away. Attempts at big hits resulted in more outfield catches. Astonishingly, only 68 runs were scored from the final 18 overs of the innings.

Chasing 201, New Zealand were once more given an excellent start by Greatbatch, who showed Botham a thing or two about belting early fours and sixes. He had lost recalled opening partner John Wright, bowled behind legs in a carbon copy of the first legal ball of the tournament, from Phil DeFreitas' first ball.

Greatbatch had scoop-swiped Pringle over square leg for six when he picked out DeFreitas on the boundary in the 13th over. Botham was triumphant. He shouldn't have been. No more wickets fell for another 108 runs, by which time the result was a formality.

Crowe survived a caught-behind appeal off Hick, then cut the same bowler for four to raise the 100 in the 23rd over. That was no faster than England, but without the spin of Phil Tufnell, a star in the Tests in New Zealand, the attack was rendered increasingly ineffective on this Basin Reserve surface.

Jones got to his 50 in 78 balls, then brought up the 150 in the 32nd over when he cut left-arm spinner Richard Illingworth for another four. Finally Hick threw down the bowler's stumps from point to penalise Jones' hesitation. He had hit 13 fours, seven more than the unbeaten Crowe would finish with when the winning runs were scored.

The New Zealand captain had led his side to a record-breaking sequence of seven World Cup wins. Conceding the Man of the Match award to Jones would not have upset him too much.

ENGLAND		NEW ZEALAND	
A. J. Stewart (capt-wk) c Harris b Patel	41	M. J. Greatbatch c DeFreitas b Botham	35
L. T. Botham b Patel	8	J. G. Wright b DeFreitas	1
G. A. Hick c Greatbatch b Harris	56	A. H. Jones run out	78
R. A. Smith c Patel b Jones	38	M. D. Crowe (capt) not out	73
A. J. Lamb c Cairns b Watson	12	K. R Rutherford not out	3
C. C. Lewis c & b Watson	0	Extras (b 1, lb 8, w 1, nb 1)	11
D. A. Reeve not out	21	(40.5 overs)	3-201
D. R. Pringle c sub (R. T. Latham) b Jones	10	Did not bat: C. Z. Harris, I. D. S. Smith (wk), C. L. Cairns,	
P. A. J. Defreitas c Cairns b Harris	0	D. N. Patel, G. R Larsen, W. Watson	
R. K. Illingworth not out	2	1/5 2/64 3/172	
Extras (b 1, lb 7, w 4)	12	Bowling: Pringle 6.2-1-34-0; Defreitas 8.3-1-45-1;	
(50 overs)	8-200	Botham 4-0-19-1; Illingworth 9-1-46-0; Hick 6-0-26-0;	
Did not bat: G. C. Small		Reeve 3-0-9-0; Small 4-0-13-0	
1/25 2/95 3/135 4/162 5/162 6/169 7/189 8/195			
Bowling: Patel 10-1-26-2; Harris 8-0-39-2;			
Watson 10-0-40-2; Cairns 3-0-21-0; Larsen 10-3-24-0;			
Jones 9-0-42-2			

Umpires: S.G. Randell, I.D. Robinson.

Toss: New Zealand.   Points: New Zealand 2, England 0

SUNDAY 15 MARCH 1992
INDIA vs SOUTH AFRICA
ADELAIDE OVAL, ADELAIDE: SOUTH AFRICA WON BY 6 WICKETS

A rain-shortened match saw South Africa clinch the third semi-final berth, leaving Australia, West Indies and Pakistan to battle for the last promotional place.

The 59.1 overs of cricket played realised 361 runs at better than one per ball and contained at least four exciting innings. The win was a great achievement by the former isolates and might have tipped the balance in favour of reform at the following Tuesday's referendum.

Rain held up play until 1.15 pm, then Wessels won the toss and sent India in. If he expected a collapse similar to the one which Pakistan suffered against England in their rain-affected match in Adelaide, he was mistaken. This wicket was a belter and after Kris Srikkanth was brilliantly caught one-handed and high to his left by Peter Kirsten, batsmen held sway.

Indian skipper, Mohammad Azharuddin, after his team's many unsuccessful months away from home; had nothing more to play for than pride, yet he batted beautifully for 79 at better than a run per ball. He put on 78 with Sanjay Manjrekar and 71 in eight overs with Kapil Dev.

The great all-rounder bid farewell to the World Cup stage with a 29-ball extravaganza of clean hitting including one great six off Allan Donald over fine leg. Donald picked up a couple of wickets, while Brian McMillan, carrying an injured ankle, and Adrian Kuiper withstood the batting heroics best.

A few batsmen fell in the frantic closing moments of the innings, which eventually realised a neat 180 from 30 overs, including 80 from the final 10. South Africa needed exactly a run per ball plus one to reach the semi-finals.

Wessels dropped himself down the order and promoted the in-form Kirsten to open with Andrew Hudson. There were no early fireworks and at the 10-over mark the total was only 44. Then came the charge. The boundaries flowed and the required run rate decreased. Hudson survived a close run out call on 34 and a stumping chance before he completed his third 50 in four innings with four boundaries. Kirsten was even more impressive and hit seven fours in 84 balls. The score had reached 128 in 24 overs when his partner stepped away to drive Javagal Srinath and was bowled.

Seventy-five had been needed from the final 10 overs. Kirsten was bowled charging Kapil Dev, Kuiper was run out and Jonty Rhodes lasted just three balls, although he did hit Manoj Prabhakar for an invaluable six in that brief stay.

Wessels came in to oversee the final victory push with 14 required from the last two overs. It was eight off seven balls when the South African captain drove Kapil Dev through the off side for four, reducing the final over requirement to one more boundary.

A clip over mid wicket by Hansie Cronje, the youngest member of the side, secured the win from Prabhakar's first ball and led to joyous South African celebration from which they had a week to recover until their semi-final. Kirsten, once more emphasising the folly of his original omission, was Man of the Match.

INDIA		SOUTH AFRICA	
K. Srikkanth c Kirsten b Donald	0	A. C. Hudson b Srinath	53
S. V. Manjrekar b Kuiper	28	P. N. Kirsten b Kapil Dev	84
M. Azharuddin (capt) c Kuiper b Pringle	79	A. P. Kuiper run out	7
S. R. Tendulkar c Wessels b Kuiper	14	J. N. Rhodes c Raju b Prabhakar	7
Kapil Dev b Donald	42	K. C. Wessels (capt) not out	9
V. G. Kambli run out	1	W. J. Cronje not out	8
P. K. Amre not out	1	Extras (lb 10, nb 3)	13
J. Srinath not out	0	(29.1 overs)	4-181
Extras (lb 7, w 6, nb 2)	15	Did not bat: B. M. McMillan, D. J. Richardson (wk),	
(30 overs)	6-180	R. P. Snell, A. A. Donald, M. W. Pringle	
Did not bat: M. Prabhakar, K. S. More (wk), S. L. V. Raju		1/128 2/149 3/157 4/163	
1/1 2/79 3/103 4/174 5/177 6/179		Bowling: Kapil Dev 6-0-36-1; Prabhakar 5.1-1-33-1;	
Bowling: Donald 6-0-34-2; Pringle 6-0-37-1; Snell		Tendulkar 6-0-20-0; Srinath 6-0-39-1; Raju 6-0-43-0	
6-1-46-0; McMillan 6-0-28-0; Kuiper 6-0-28-2			

Umpires: D.P. Buultjens, Khizar Hayat.

Toss: South Africa.   Points: South Africa 2, India 0

PAKISTAN vs SRI LANKA
WACA, PERTH: PAKISTAN WON BY 4 WICKETS

Despite the turnaround in their fortunes against Australia, Pakistan still had no margin for error if they were to take the last semi-final spot and could not afford a lapse against Sri Lanka.

In the end they won, but without displaying the skill they had under lights against Australia. The Sri Lankans for their part, already moving in a westward direction, were probably thinking of home.

Pakistan, staying put, had a few days to prepare for the match in Perth, while Sri Lanka had winged their way straight across the Nullarbor Plain from Berri. Their bowlers could at least put their feet up for a while as Aravinda de Silva won the toss and batted. The game was only a modest local attraction and in the end turned out to have few outstanding performances.

The Pakistani pace attack misplaced its radar again and offered the Sri Lankans plenty of wides and no balls between the occasional unplayable delivery. Wasim Akram got a swinging yorker through Roshan Mahanama, then Mushtaq Ahmed's leg spin accounted for Chandika Hathurusingha and Athula Samarasekera after the opener had put on 51 in 10 overs with his captain.

The Pakistani fielding had also slipped. de Silva, who top-scored and hit 23 singles out of 43, was given one life, but some sensible batting by left-handers Asanka Gurusinha and wicketkeeper Hashan Tillekaratne lifted the total to a respectable 213.

Pakistan had early worries when Champaka Ramanayake had the in-form Aamir Sohail caught in the gully in the second over and Imran Khan, promoting himself to the troubled number three spot, took 37 balls over his first two runs. The innings was not progressing quickly enough when Imran holed out to deep mid off to his opposite number.

At 3-84 and behind the run rate, an upset was on the cards. It took a century partnership and the best batting of the match from Salim Malik and Javed Miandad to ensure that did not happen. They put on 101 in 21 overs improvising, running for anything and playing the occasional boundary stroke.

Both reached their half centuries without going any further and it took until the first ball of the last over of the game, when Ijaz Ahmed straight drove Pramodya Wickremasinghe for four, for the win to be completed. Ijaz had been involved in the run out of Inzamam-ul-Haq. It would not be the last time in their lives that the pair would have running troubles. Javed Miandad, who had top-scored and stayed until victory was only 28 runs away, was named Man of the Match.

SRI LANKA		PAKISTAN	
R. S. Mahanama b Wasim Akram	12	Aamir Sohail c Mahanama b Ramanayake	1
M. A. R. Samarasekera st Moin Khan b Mushtaq Ahmed	38	Ramiz Raja c Gurusinha b Wickremasinghe	32
U. C. Hathurusingha b Mushtaq Ahmed	5	Imran Khan (capt) c de Silva b Hathurusingha	22
P. A. de Silva (capt) c Aamir Sohail b Ijaz Ahmed	43	Javed Miandad c Wickremasinghe b Gurusinha	57
A. P. Gurusinha c Malik b Imran Khan	37	Salim Malik c Kalpage b Ramanayake	51
A. Ranatunga c sub (Zahid Fazal) b Aamir Sohail	7	Inzamam-ul-Haq run out	11
H. P. Tillekaratne (wk) not out	25	Ijaz Ahmed not out	8
R. S. Kalpage not out	13	Wasim Akram not out	5
Extras (lb 15, w 11, nb 6)	32	Extras (lb 12, w 9, nb 8)	29
(50 overs)	6-212	(49.1 overs)	6-216

Did not bat: C. P. H. Ramanayake, G. P. Wickremasinghe, K. I. W. Wijegunawardene

1/29 2/48 3/99 4/132 5/158 6/187

Bowling: Wasim Akram 10-0-37-1; Aaqib Javed 10-0-39-0; Imran Khan 8-1-36-1; Mushtaq Ahmed 10-0-43-2; Ijaz Ahmed 8-0-28-1; Aamir Sohail 4-0-14-1

Did not bat: Moin Khan (wk), Mushtaq Ahmed, Aaqib Javed

1/7 2/68 3/84 4/185 5/201 6/205

Bowling: Wijegunawardene 10-1-34-0; Ramanayake 10-1-37-2; Wickremasinghe 9.1-0-41-1; Gurusinha 9-0-38-1; Hathurusingha 9-0-40-1; Kalpage 2-0-14-0

Umpires: K.E. Liebenberg, P.J. McConnell.

Toss: Sri Lanka.   Points: Pakistan 2, Sri Lanka 0

WEDNESDAY 18 MARCH 1992
NEW ZEALAND vs PAKISTAN
LANCASTER PARK, CHRISTCHURCH: PAKISTAN WON BY 7 WICKETS

Pakistani Manager Intikhab Alam had indicated after the win over Sri Lanka in Perth that his team was very confident of ending New Zealand's winning streak. Despite having to readjust from the bouncy wickets of the WACA, Intikhab suggested Pakistani players were more than comfortable in the conditions they would find in Christchurch.

His prediction proved accurate as the Kiwis were easily beaten. The win put Pakistan in fourth spot on the qualifying table and eliminated Australia from semi-final calculations. Adding to the cross-Tasman frustration, the loss actually benefited New Zealand. Had Australia snuck into the final four, the Kiwis would have had to play their semi-final against them in Sydney. The loss allowed them to enjoy the benefits of a home tie in Auckland. Martin Crowe admitted that throwing the match had been considered, but the Kiwis eventually picked their best side. It made no difference to Imran Khan's 'cornered tigers'.

Imran won the toss and bowled on a fine but breezy morning which had players in long-sleeved jumpers vigorously rubbing their hands during the early overs. Aaqib Javed's temper quickly warmed up when Mark Greatbatch thumped the last three balls of his first over for two fours and a big six, his 12th of the tournament, over mid wicket. .

Unfortunately for the Kiwi fans, the Pakistani pacemen had other ideas. Greatbatch became inhibited as Aqib struck back to have Rod Latham, in the side again for John Wright, caught at slip in his next over. Then, from the other end, Akram's in-swinging yorker hit Andrew Jones' boot in front of middle stump.

But the biggest blow carne in the ninth over when Crowe clipped another of the left-armer's in-swingers, this time from around the wicket, to Aamir Sohail's chest at backward square leg. New Zealand were 3-39 and the middle order batted as if in shock at their captain falling so cheaply. Greatbatch hit a few shots, including a cracking square cut off Akram and Rutherford hung around while 46 runs were put on. Rutherford was struggling, however, and should have been caught by wicketkeeper Moin Khan off Imran.

Then in the 20th over Rutherford was sent back too late for a pushed single to cover. That precipitated a collapse which saw the Kiwis lose five wickets in eight overs. Chief architect of the collapse was Mushtaq Ahmed. The leg-spinner was unhittable and had Greatbatch caught sweeping and Chris Harris stumped off an offside wide.

The innings eventually almost ran its course through the doggedness of Gavin Larsen and renowned rabbit, Danny Morrison. Neither had batted in the tournament to this point, yet they managed to scrape together 44 runs in 17 overs.

Morrison, lucky to survive a stumping appeal, was finally caught at slip off Akram, who picked up his fourth wicket when he yorked the retreating Larsen. A few wides and the throw to run out Rutherford made it a busy day for the left-arm paceman. With extras equal top score on 42, the scoreboard had a strange top-to-tail look about it.

Morrison must have been excited about his batting because he bounced Aamir Sohail first ball of the Pakistani innings. The left-hander hooked the delivery down Dipak Patel's throat at fine leg, thinking he was immune because the ball was clearly above his shoulder. To Sohail's surprise and distress, Steve Randell at square leg said nothing. Sohail, not the calmest of cricketers, had to bite his tongue and leave the crease. Morrison then fired out Inzamam-ul-Haq so that Pakistan were 2-9 in pursuit of 166.

The game might have become really interesting if Patel had held a sharp caught and bowled chance off Javed Miandad not long after. The let-off allowed Javed to dig in while Ramiz Raja unleashed a fine array of shots. Patel and Watson were tight, but Harris, still the leading wicket-taker in the competition, and Larsen ineffective. Not even 15 bowling changes by Crowe could make a difference this time. Miandad only hit one boundary in 85 balls, but he stayed while 115 runs were added with Ramiz. The opener continued on to his second 100 for the tournament, then slogged the winning boundary off Rutherford in the 45th over.

He hit 16 fours in 155 balls yet was beaten for the Man of the Match award. Not by Akram, but the bouncing, whirling leg spinner Mushtaq. Straight after the game everyone sought out a television to see if Australia would defeat the West Indies.

NEW ZEALAND		PAKISTAN	
M. J. Greatbatch c Salim Malik b Mushtaq Ahmed	42	Aamir Sohail c Patel b Morrison	0
RJ. Latham c Inzamam-ul-Haq b Aaqib Javed	6	Ramiz Raja not out	119
A. H. Jones lbw Wasim Akram	2	Inzamam-ul-Haq b Morrison	5
M. D. Crowe (capt) c Aamir Sohail b Wasim Akram	3	Javed Miandad lbw Morrison	30
K. R. Rutherford run out	8	Salim Malik not out	9
C. Z. Harris st Moin Khan b Mushtaq Ahmed	1	Extras (lb 1, w 1, nb 2)	4
D. N. Patel c Mushtaq Ahmed b Aamir Sohail	7	(44.4 overs)	3-167
I. D. S. Smith (wk) b Imran Khan	1	Did not bat: Imran Khan (capt), Ijaz Ahmed, Wasim Akram,	
G. R. Larsen b Wasim Akram	37	Moin Khan (wk), Mushtaq Ahmed, Aaqib Javed	
D. K. Morrison c Inzamam-ul-Haq b Wasim Akram	12	1/0 2/9 3/124	
W. Watson not out	5	Bowling: Morrison 10-0-42-3; Patel 10-2-25-0;	
Extras (b 3, lb 23, w 12, nb 4)	42	Watson 10-3-26-0; Harris 4-0-18-0; Larsen 3-0-16-0;	
(48.2 overs)	166	Jones 3-0-10-0; Latham 2-0-13-0; Rutherford 1.4-0-11-0;	
1/23 2/26 3/39 4/85 5/88 6/93 7/96 8/106 9/150 10/166		Greatbatch 1-0-5-0	

Bowling: Wasim Akram 9.2-0-32-4; Aaqib Javed 10-1-34-1; Mushtaq Ahmed 10-0-18-2; Imran Khan 8-0-22-1; Aamir Sohail 10-1-29-1; Ijaz Ahmed 1-0-5-0

Umpires: SA Bucknor, S.G. Randell.

Toss: Pakistan.   Points: Pakistan 2, New Zealand 0

ENGLAND vs ZIMBABWE
LAVINGTON SPORTS GROUND, ALBURY: ZIMBABWE WON BY 9 RUNS

While Pakistan, New Zealand and, later in the day, Australia and the West Indies were involved in their cutthroat dramatics, in Albury England and Zimbabwe wrote their own little piece of cricketing history.

Unfortunately for England it was the story of another momentous and unexpected defeat, the type of which has become all too familiar in the past decade. According to Ian Botham the main cause of Zimbabwe's first win in the 1992 World Cup—and only their second in three tournaments—and their maiden victory over England, was the exhaustion and injuries carried into the match by the overworked English team.

This meant England's batsmen could not successfully chase a total of 134.

The conditions favoured bowlers all day and the Zimbabwean batsmen were always struggling after Graham Gooch won the toss and sent them in. England's slower bowlers, left-arm spinners Richard Illingworth and Phil Tufnell and Botham's medium pace, did most damage, picking up eight of the 10 wickets to fall. Zimbabwean captain Dave Houghton top-scored, but it took an important eighth-wicket partnership of 31 between Iain Butchart and Eddo Brandes, who came together at 7-96, to ensure a total in excess of 120.

Six thousand were in attendance at Lavington, which is on the Sydney side of Albury, the border city on the Murray River between Victoria and New South Wales. Their numbers were made up of face-painted English supporters, local enthusiasts and schoolchildren.

There was little to excite the fans while Zimbabwe batted, but when Eddo Brandes trapped Gooch lbw on the first ball of the England innings they sat up and took notice. The chicken-farming former schoolmate of Graeme Hick then hit Robin Smith's off-stump, had Allan Lamb mistiming a pull to mid-on and yorked his old school chum first ball. With Botham feathering a catch through to wicketkeeper Andy Flower off Ali Shah's mediumpaced swing England were a messy 5-43 in the 15th over.

Alec Stewart and Neil Fairbrother halted the collapse by putting on 52 for the sixth wicket. It was grim stuff and lasted 24 overs. Fairbrother, suffering a stomach ailment, did not have the strength to reach the boundary once in 77 balls.

Shah and John Traicos, at 44 finally bowing out of World Cup cricket, conceded just 33 in 20 miserly overs. When Shah had Stewart caught the tumble of wickets began again.

The pressure on the tail-end batsmen was increased by the lack of overs left available. Fifteen were needed from the last two overs. That had been reduced to 11 when Andy Pycroft's direct hit ran out Illingworth. Then from the first ball of the final over, Gladstone Small chipped Malcolm Jarvis to Pycroft at mid wicket. Schoolboys ran everywhere.

Dave Houghton, who had played in the win over Australia in 1983 spoke with great emotion at the post-match press conference and Eddo Brandes struck a blow for the chicken farmers of the world when he was named Man of the Match.

ZIMBABWE		ENGLAND	
W. R. James c & b Illingworth	13	G. A. Gooch (capt) lbw b Brandes	0
A. Flower (wk) b DeFreitas	7	I. T. Botham c Flower b Shah	18
A. J. Pycroft c Gooch b Botham	3	A. J. Lamb c James b Brandes	17
K. J. Arnott lbw Botham	11	R. A. Smith b Brandes	2
D. L. Houghton (capt) c Fairbrother b Small	29	G. A. Hick b Brandes	0
A. C. Waller b Tufnell	8	N. H. Fairbrother c Flower b Butchart	20
A. H. Shah c Lamb b Tufnell	3	A. J. Stewart (wk) c Waller b Shah	29
I. P. Butchart c Fairbrother b Botham	24	P. A. J. DeFreitas c Flower b Butchart	4
E. A. Brandes st Stewart b Illingworth	14	R. K. Illingworth run out	11
A. J. Traicos not out	0	G. C. Small c Pycroft b Jarvis	5
M. P. Jarvis lbw Illingworth	6	P. C. R. Tufnell not out	0
Extras (lb 8, w 8)	16	Extras (b 4, lb 3, w 11, nb 1)	19
(46.1 overs)	134	(49.1 overs)	125

1/12 2/19 3/30 4/52 5/65 6/77 7/96 8/127 9/127 10/134

1/0 2/32 3/42 4/42 5/43 6/95 7/101 8/108 9/124 10/125

Bowling: DeFreitas 8-1-14-1; Small 9-1-20-1; Botham 10-2-23-3; Illingworth 9.1-0-33-3; Tufnell 10-2-36-2

Bowling: Brandes 10-4-21-4; Jarvis 9.1-0-32-1; Shah 10-3-17-2; Traicos 10-4-16-0; Butchart 10-2-32-2

Umpires: B.L. Aldridge, Khizar Hayat.

Toss: England.　　Points: Zimbabwe 2, England 0

AUSTRALIA vs WEST INDIES
MCG, MELBOURNE: AUSTRALIA WON BY 57 RUNS

The time difference and the playing of this match as a day/night fixture meant that the Australians were put out of their misery quite quickly when they heard the result from Christchurch.

If anything, the disappointment seemed to galvanise them and they proved too accomplished for the West Indies in front of the biggest crowd of the tournament so far. Australia got away to an excellent start. Allan Border batted when he won the toss, a decision opening pair Tom Moody and David Boon relished. They combined for 27 overs in a partnership of 107.

It was Boon who led the way, moving on to the front foot with confidence to drive the fast bowlers on both sides of the wicket. After surviving a shout for a catch behind pulling at Anderson Cummins, he brought up his 50 in the 24th over.

Moody lofted Phil Simmons down the ground for his third boundary, then in the same over was expertly caught by a diving Winston Benjamin at deep square leg. The Australian batting spluttered along once the openers had been separated.

Boon took until the 46th over to complete his century, then immediately skyed an attempted slog to end his tournament with the same score he started it. He left the MCG with 4001 runs in limited-over internationals to his credit. He was easily Australia's best-performed batsman, in stark contrast to his captain who finished with an average of eight.

Both Boon and Border were bidding farewell to World Cup cricket.

Cummins bowled Steve Waugh with a full toss and it was left to Ian Healy and Peter Taylor, who could boast that he slogged Curtly Ambrose to mid wicket for four, to get the total up to a noncommittal 6-216 after 50 overs.

In good conditions under lights there was nothing too imposing about the task in front of the West Indies, and for seven overs Desmond Haynes and Brian Lara batted with authority.

Then Haynes clipped a Craig McDermott full toss off the middle of his bat to Dean Jones at backward square leg. Next ball, Phil Simmons, only half forward, was given out lbw to leave the West Indies struggling at 2-27.

Richie Richardson, with the unenviable task of leading a Caribbean side gradually on the decline, battled with Lara for another 12 overs, before being given out caught behind driving at Mike Whitney.

The West Indian captain indicated the ball had struck his pad rather than his bat, but Piloo Reporter was never going to change his mind. Whitney continued to make inroads into the middle order. Keith Arthurton hit a couple of powerful drives then holed out tamely to mid off. A brilliant full-length dive to his right by Healy removed the driving Gus Logie and Carl Hooper guided the ball to Mark Waugh, who had been put in place at slip.

One decent partnership would have kept the West Indies well in the contest because Lara was largely untroubled in his efforts to keep one end secure. He brought up his fifty and the team 100 in the 28th over with a swept four off Taylor, but could not find a worthy partner. Eventually, in the panic that was making the West Indies self-destruct he ran for a sharp single and Winston Benjamin didn't.

When Benjamin swung across the line at Steve Waugh and was given out lbw both sides had become World Cup spectators. Australia had beaten the West Indies for the first time in a World Cup match and for all their early poor form had missed the cut by one point.

Pakistan, by virtue of the point gained in the 'no result' in Adelaide against England, were through. David Boon was named Man of the Match.

AUSTRALIA		WEST INDIES	
T. M. Moody c Benjamin b Simmons	42	D. L. Haynes c Jones b McDermott	14
D. C. Boon c Williams b Cummins	100	B. C. Lara run out	70
D. M. Jones c Williams b Cummins	6	P. V. Simmons lbw McDermott	0
A. R. Border (capt) lbw Simmons	8	R. B. Richardson (capt) c Healy b Whitney	10
M. E. Waugh st Williams b Hooper	21	K. L. T. Arthurton c McDermott b Whitney	15
S. R. Waugh b Cummins	6	A. L. Logie c Healy b Whitney	5
I. A. Healy (wk) not out	11	C. J. Hooper c M. E. Waugh b Whitney	4
P. L. Taylor not out	10	D. Williams (wk) c Border b Reid	4
Extras (lb 3, w 3, nb 6)	12	W. K.M. Benjamin lbw b S. R. Waugh	15
(50 overs)	6-216	C. E. L. Ambrose run out	2
Did not bat: C. J. McDermott, M. R Whitney. B. A. Reid		A. C. Cummins not out	5
1/107 2/128 3/141 4/185 5/189 6/200		Extras (b 3. lb 5, w 3. nb 4)	15
Bowling: Ambrose 10-0-46-0; Benjamin 10-1-49-0;		(42.4 overs)	159
Cummins 10-1-38-3; Hooper 10-0-40-1; Simmons		1/27 2/27 3/59 4/83 5/99 6/117 7/128 8/137 9/150	
10-1-40-2		10/159	
		Bowling: McDermott 6-1-29-2; Reid 10-1-26-1;	
		Whitney 10-1-34-4; S. R Waugh 6.4-0-24-1; Taylor 4-0-24-0;	
		Moody 6-1-14-0	

Umpires: P.D. Reporter. D.R. Shepherd.

Toss: Australia.   Points: Australia 2, West Indies 0

SATURDAY, 21 MARCH and SUNDAY, 22 MARCH 1992
BENSON & HEDGES WORLD CUP SEMI-FINALS

The qualifying table' at the end of the preliminary rounds of the Benson and Hedges World Cup was as follows:

	P	W	L	NR	Pts	NR/R		P	W	L	NR	Pts	NR/R
New Zealand	8	7	1	0	14	+0.59	Australia	8	4	4	0	8	+0.20
England	8	5	2	1	11	+0.47	West Indies	8	4	4	0	8	+0.07
South Africa	8	5	3	0	10	+0.14	India	8	2	5	1	5	+0.14
Pakistan	8	4	3	1	9	+0.16	Sri Lanka	8	2	5	1	5	-0.68
							Zimbabwe	8	1	7	0	2	-1.14

21 MARCH, FIRST SEMI-FINAL: NEW ZEALAND vs PAKISTAN
EDEN PARK, AUCKLAND: PAKISTAN WON BY 4 WICKETS

On his great *John Lennon/Plastic OnoBand* album John Lennon sang, "The dream is over, what can I say?" Lennon was referring to the demise of the Beatles, but Martin Crowe, a tear in his eye, could easily have expressed the same sentiment to the majority of the Eden Park crowd as he led his team on a lap of honour after this semi-final.

The Kiwis had been part of an exciting game on a wonderful occasion. In the end, though, their bowling shortcomings were exposed by the team they feared most on their own wickets. Pakistan had the answers even chasing a target of 263 and they, not New Zealand, would be at the MCG in four days' time in an attempt to secure cricket's limited-overs Holy Grail.

A windy Saturday with scudding dark clouds building and threatening throughout the afternoon began with Crowe receiving his cash and car prizes as World Cup Champion Player.

Heavy rain was forecast and that affected Crowe's decision when he won the toss. He wanted to bat second, but understandably feared the overs-reduction rule. So New Zealand went in first. Dozens of Kiwi flags fluttered proudly amongst the thousands cramming into the Eden Park terraces as John Wright and Mark Greatbatch walked out to bat after the teams had lined up for the national anthems.

The opening pair found a hard and flat pitch that seemed to suit bashing opener Greatbatch. Wasim Akram posed their greatest threat and he twice beat Greatbatch before the left-hander slashed him over third man for six to get off the mark.

Greatbatch then on drove Aaqib Javed into the South Stand for his 14th six of the World Cup.

It was also his last. In the 10th over he motioned away, suggesting another big swing, only to be bowled leg stump on the outside, by an outrageous Aqib slower ball. Three overs later, when Wright inadvisably tried to hit Mushtaq Ahmed down the ground into the wind and was caught at deep mid-on, 0-35 had become 2-39.

Crowe was immediately into his stride, which indicated there would be no repeat of Wednesday's collapse. Andrew Jones stuck around while 48 were added. During that time he never had much idea what Mushtaq was doing and was eventually trapped in front of his stumps hitting across a top-spinner. Even Steve Bucknor, holding his hat to his chest because of the strong winds, had no hesitation.

There was no New Zealand comfort in 3-87 in the 24th over and the tension increased further when Ken Rutherford took 25 deliveries to get off the mark. He was plumb lbw to an Akram no ball. Crowe told him to go for his shots and Rutherford started lofting the spinners down the ground.

Iqbal Sikander was deposited over the boundary at long off. Crowe swept Mushtaq for a big six over square leg and the pair put on 107 in 113 balls. Akram returned and Rutherford top-edged a pull that was safely held by Moin Khan.

Worse for New Zealand was that Crowe tore a hamstring as he ran through for the skyed shot. He lay on the ground and had his thigh strapped, then hit Akram for six over fine leg. Crowe continued until the 47th over when he could only watch his runner Greatbatch fall a metre short of the crease following a mix-up with Ian Smith.

Crowe's 91 in 83 balls with seven fours and three sixes rightly received a standing ovation and with Smith, Dipak Patel and Gavin Larsen continuing the good work the total increased by 91 in the final 10 overs. Two hundred and sixty-two was New Zealand's highest score for the tournament and the whole nation was brimming with confidence despite the fact that Wright, rather than Crowe, would have to lead the team in the field.

There was no indication that Pakistan would have the batting impetus to overtake such a mountain in the early stages of their innings. Aamir Sohail swept Patel to Jones in the ninth over and although no further wickets fell for some time the progress of Imran and Ramiz Raja was sedate. Imran back in his protective number-three role, hit two big sixes, one off Patel and a big on-drive off Larsen, but took 93 balls to make his 44.

When he top-edged a sweep to fine leg off the medium pacer Harris, in the 34th over Pakistan's required run rate had crept above eight per over. Salim Malik's mistimed one-handed drive to substitute fieldsman Rod Latham at cover point in the next over left 123 runs to be made from the final 15 overs.

The rain which, if it had fallen, would have destroyed any Pakistani hopes failed to support the weather forecasters and kept blowing away. Crowe, resting in the pavilion wanted the spinners recalled. However, the bowling changes and field placings were out of his hands. Uncapped youngster, 22-year-old Inzamam-ul-Haq, took charge. In the period after a drinks break where Wright ran to the pavilion and asked Crowe for a bowling plan, Inzamam took the game by the scruff of the neck.

'Inzy' had nearly made himself unavailable for the match because of an illness the previous night. There were no signs of that as he belted Chris Harris, Danny Morrison and even Patel to all parts. A high-elevation lofted drive off Harris must have risked attracting the rain. The hit lobbed out of reach over the boundary at long off.

Inzamam reached 50 in 31 balls and put on 87 in 10 overs with Javed Miandad when Harris's dive from short cover resulted in his run out.

Harris' brilliant fielding temporarily lifted New Zealand's sinking spirits. There had been stooped shoulders and signs of panic in the field during Inzamam's onslaught.

Another 35 was needed from the last five overs. Willie Watson bowled Akram, then Moin Khan settled the issue. He pulled a tiring Watson away for four, on bent knee drove Harris over mid off for six, then from the final ball of the 49th over pulled him for the boundary that put Pakistan into their first World Cup final.

As the emotion of disappointment overwhelmed the Kiwis, so did the Pakistanis rejoice. Miandad had guided the younger players through with another of his beautifully engineered innings. When Moin struck the winning boundary the veteran kissed the turf. The New Zealand flags were put away and replaced by a few proud green and white ones. Imran and the Pakistani cricket team had their own dream.

Inzamam-ul-Haq who batted for just 37 balls, was named Man of the Match.

NEW ZEALAND		PAKISTAN	
M. J. Greatbatch b Aaqib Javed	17	Aamir Sohail c Jones b Patel	14
J. G. Wright c Ramiz Raja b Mushtaq Ahmed	13	Ramiz Raja c Morrison b Watson	44
A. H. Jones lbw b Mushtaq Ahmed	21	Imran Khan (capt) c Larsen b Harris	44
M. D. Crowe (capt) run out	91	Javed Miandad not out	57
K. R. Rutherford c Moin Khan b Wasim Akram	50	Salim Malik c sub (R. Latham) b Larsen	1
C. Z. Harris st Moin Khan b Iqbal Sikander	13	Inzamam-ul-Haq run out	60
I. D. S. Smith (wk) not out	18	Wasim Akram b Watson	9
D. N. Patel lbw Wasim Akram	8	Moin Khan (wk) not out	20
G. R. Larsen not out	8	Extras (b 4, lb 10, w 1)	15
Extras (b 4, lb 7, w 8, nb 4)	23	(49 overs)	6-264
(50 overs)	7-262		

Did not bat: D. K. Morrison, W. Watson

1/35 2/39 3/87 4/194 5/214 6/221 7/244

Bowling: Wasim Akram 10-0-40-2; Aaqib Javed 10-2-45-1; Mushtaq Ahmed 10-0-40-2; Imran Khan 10-0-59-0; Iqbal Sikander 9-0-56-1; Aamir Sohail 1-0-11-0

Did not bat: Iqbal Sikander, Mushtaq Ahmed, Aaqib Javed

1/30 2/84 3/1344 /140 5/227 6/238

Bowling: Patel 10-0-50-1; Morrison 9-0-55-0; Watson 10-2-39-2; Larsen 10-1-34-1; Harris 10-0-72-1

Umpires: SA Buckner, D.R. Shepherd.

Toss: New Zealand.

22 MARCH, WORLD CUP SECOND SEMI-FINAL: ENGLAND VS SOUTH AFRICA
SCG, SYDNEY: ENGLAND WON BY 19 RUNS

No-one questioned England's right to progress through to the final of the 1992 World Cup. What annoyed the entire global cricketing community was that 12 minutes of rain turned an exciting semi-final climax into an absurdity and condemned the wet-weather rule to eternal damnation. With South Africa requiring 21 runs off 13 balls it began to rain. The batsmen, knowing what the rain rule would do to them, wanted to stay on. England suggested to umpires Brian Aldridge and Steve Randell that it was too wet to continue. England accepted an offer to leave the SCG, much to the disappointment of the 30,000 strong crowd.

The rain soon stopped and everyone returned, but by the time the covers were removed the umpires decreed that only one-ball remained to be bowled. Brian McMillan faced that delivery. He is a big man. However, even he couldn't hit the ball far enough to score 21 from one shot.

Wessels had checked with a local weather forecaster whether there would be any rain at the SCG that Sunday. The expert predicted a brief interruption of about 10 minutes late in the evening. The South African captain wanted to bat second and thought a late five-minute shower was not a worthwhile deterrent to that decision.

Little did he know.

Allan Donald and Meyrick Pringle, perhaps nervous because of the occasion, were so wayward the total had reached 20 by the third over with the majority of the runs extras. Then a big shout for a catch behind against Graham Gooch was upheld by umpire Steve Randell. Replays showed the South Africans were lucky to get the decision in their favour. Five overs later Ian Botham played on to Pringle.

Graeme Hick, his reputation in international cricket greater than his achievement, came in at 2-39 and the first ball received more benefit of the doubt on an lbw decision than his captain did on the caught behind. The South Africans could not believe Hick survived and were incredulous when next ball he was caught at slip off a no ball.

They were key let-offs as from that point the English batsmen took charge.

Alec Stewart had been promoted to number three after Robin Smith had joined the injured list with a pinched nerve in his back. He batted sensibly and steadied the innings while the relieved Hick quickly grew in confidence. They put on 71 in 14 overs and when Stewart was caught behind, Neil Fairbrother and the Zimbabwean added a further 73, also in 14 overs. The South African bowlers were being mastered and, using a cynical old West Indian trick, slowed their over rate.

The overs were reduced to a trickle, but the runs continued to flow. Hick's ultimately impressive 90-ball innings with nine fours was finally ended by a leaping Jonty Rhodes catch at point.

Fairbrother was bowled by Pringle, the most effective of the South African bowlers. It was obvious England was not going to receive their full allocation in three and a half hours so their middle order attacked with even greater vigour.

Allan Lamb, in his only innings against the country of his birth, hit one wonderful flat-batted off drive. Chris Lewis scored at better than a run per ball and Dermot Reeve smashed 25 in 14 balls including 17 in one over from his Warwickshire team-mate, Donald. Reeve's onslaught against just about the fastest bowler in the world included three consecutive lofted on drives to the foot of the old Hill, where sky-blue shirted English fans went berserk.

South Africa were fined 20 per cent of their match fee for completing just 45 overs.

South Africa was scheduled to receive the same number in return and needed to score at 5.62 per over to overhaul England's formidable 6-252. Most of the Australians in the crowd were behind them and Wessels, back opening, got his side away to a brisk start.

However, a powerful pull was followed by a mistimed cut to Lewis at deep gully. Peter Kirsten struggled with an injured groin and had his off stump cleanly removed by a perfect Phil DeFreitas leg-cutter.

South Africa fought hard while losing wickets at crucial times. Andrew Hudson's elegant 46 was ended in the 19th over when he tried to cut Richard Illingworth's well-disguised arm ball. Adrian Kuiper hit two big straight drives off Illingworth, then three consecutive boundaries off Gladstone Small before missing a wild slog to a ball on middle stump from the left-arm spinner.

It was now 4-131, the requirement above six per over. Even though batting was not their strongest point, the South Africans kept coming.

When Hansie Cronje was caught at deep square leg by Hick the requirement was 74 off nine overs. Rhodes may have held his spot in the team with his fielding ability, now he showed his batting prowess to a television-land audience of millions. Going hell for leather he broke his bat, had it replaced and smote Botham one bounce for four to square leg next ball.

Rhodes slashed Small hard and high to the point boundary and the 200 mark had just been passed when he repeated the off-side shot only to find Lewis 10 metres inside the fence.

Streakers of various denominations momentarily diffused the tension of an equation of 40 runs from, supposedly, four overs. McMillan and Dave Richardson maintained the challenge. They hit and ran furiously, getting 18 from the next 11 balls, which had the English bowlers and fieldsmen just starting to wilt. Or was it their shirts clinging and hair becoming bedraggled? At night, rain is felt before it is seen.

A fiasco developed. The umpires were under more pressure to be fair to everyone than for a hairline run out decision. There were howls of derision as the players left the field. To all but the English supporters, Gooch's men were villains avoiding a finish where they might have come off second best.

The SCG scoreboard started flashing the altered requirement; 22 runs off 7 balls. There were more boos. The finish time had been brought forward to 10pm because South Africa had only bowled 45 overs. The scoreboard changed the requirement again. Lewis had to bowl just one more delivery.

The tribute visits by the two teams back onto the ground were given quite different receptions. The crowd lauded the departing South Africans, while many unfairly jeered England. The hosts would need to support someone in the final and, like India at Calcutta in 1987, it would be the team that opposed the old imperial masters.

There was no such ill will in the pavilion. Wessels admitted he would have left the field given the same situation. The English captain, his delight at reaching the final tempered slightly by the recent anti-climax, said his heart went out to his opponents.

They both should have demanded to know who wrote that rule.

Graeme Hick was named Man of the Match.

ENGLAND		SOUTH AFRICA	
G. A. Gooch (capt) c Richardson b Donald	2	K. C. Wessels (capt) cLewis b Botham	17
I. T. Botham b Pringle	21	A. C. Hudson lbw b Illingworth	46
A. J. Stewart (wk) c Richardson b McMillan	33	P. N. Kirsten b Defreitas	11
G. A. Hick c Rhodes b Snell	83	A. P. Kuiper b Illingworth	36
N. H. Fairbrother b Pringle	28	W. J. Cronje c Hick b Small	24
A. J. Lamb c Richardson b Donald	19	J. N. Rhodes c Lewis b Small	43
C. C. Lewis not out	18	B. M. McMillan not out	21
D. A. Reeve not out	25	D. J. Richardson (wk) not out	13
Extras (b 1, lb 7, w 9, nb 6)	23	Extras (lb 17, w 4)	21
(45 overs)	6-252	(43 overs)	6-232
Did not bat: P. A. J. DeFreitas, R. K. Illingworth, G. C. Small		Did not bat: R. P. Snell, M. W. Pringle, A. A. Donald	
1/20 2/39 3/110 4/183 5/187 6/221		1/26 2/61 3/90 4/131 5/176 6/206	
Bowling: Donald 10-0-69-2; Pringle 9-2-36-2; Snell 8-0-52-1; McMillan 9-0-47-1; Kuiper 5-0-26-0; Cronje 4-0-14-0		Bowling: Botham 10-0-52-1; Lewis 5-0-38-0; DeFreitas 8-1-28-1; Illingworth 10-1-46-2; Small 10-1-51-2	

Umpires: B.L. Aldridge, S.G. Randell.

Toss: South Africa.

WEDNESDAY 25 MARCH 1992
BENSON AND WORLD CUP FINAL
ENGLAND vs PAKISTAN
MCG, MELBOURNE: PAKISTAN WON BY 22 RUNS

Imran Khan had played for Pakistan in the very first World Cup in 1975. He and his deputy Javed Miandad were the only two men to complete the marathon five-tournament journey over nearly 17 years.

Apart from one or two moments of satisfaction, they had ultimately suffered disappointment in each of those competitions, getting no further than a place in the semi-finals.

Now under lights on what Imran later called, "the best ground in front of the best crowd", they were winners, part of an erratic and inconsistent team that when both talent and temperament were in harmony could take on and master any opposition in the world.

Here, in the Benson and Hedges World Cup, they had overcome a terrible start and, by winning their last four matches over 10 days, became the toast of the cricketing community and national heroes.

In the 1992 final, Pakistan defeated England by 22 runs. Whatever the hitches, glitches and upsets of the Australasian version of the event; the final was a wonderful occasion which did total justice to a sporting occasion now followed by a billion television viewers. What is more, the weather was impeccable and the crowd enormous, both adding to the spectacle during a quality limited-overs cricket match.

The English view was slightly more sombre. This was their third loss in World Cup finals and the second in as many tournaments. As in 1987, they were favourites and still went down. After the defeats of 1979 and 1987 they were disappointed without being despondent. The group that was obliged to watch Imran Khan being presented with the glass trophy for winning the 1992 World Cup wore a tired and haggard look.

Their long journey had just fallen short of the dreamed of success. Mature players like captain, Graham Gooch, Ian Botham and Allan Lamb had missed their last chance and the defeat hit harder for that reason.

During the match, relations between the teams were fine. It had not always been that way between Pakistan and England. That, too, might have increased the level of disappointment for the losers. Botham and Gooch did not go into the match in the friendliest frame of mind. They had walked out in disgust on Queen Elizabeth impersonator Gerry Connolly at the pre-final dinner.

Australian Prime Minister Paul Keating had his say, the republic issue was raised again, none of which had anything to do with winning a cricket match except to give the neutrals in the 87,000 strong crowd greater incentive to support Pakistan.

There were speeches, songs and marches prior to the main event. Imran won the toss and batted. Gooch said he would have bowled anyway and it was England, not Pakistan, who got the start they wanted.

Ramiz Raja, who opened with Aamir Sohail, had a let-off when he clipped a high-bouncing delivery outside the off stump from Chris Lewis to Graeme Hick at point. Ramiz began to walk away, but Steve Bucknor rightly called "no ball" for an above-the-shoulder delivery. The opener scrambled back into his crease while the ball was thrown at the stumps by Phil DeFreitas. Bucknor knew his stuff and called dead-ball.

Derek Pringle had missed the semi-final with a rib injury. Back in the side, he bowled an immaculate new-ball spell and soon had the left-hander, Sohail, caught behind by Alec Stewart low to his left as he pushed forward. Salim Malik was to be protected if 10 overs had not been bowled, so Imran came in at number three again and must have been horrified when Ramiz walked across his crease and was trapped lbw.

His side was 2-24 in the ninth over with both their tournament century-makers back in the pavilion. The two World Cup veterans, Imran and Miandad, put their heads down and tried to consume overs like it was the last day of a Test which had to be saved. The tempo dawdled along. This was colour with no movement. Pringle had two close lbw appeals rejected and three runs were added in 11 overs. When Imran on nine attempted to put DeFreitas over the onside in the 21st over he skied the ball towards deep mid wicket. Gooch ran back and under the ball and was still going full tilt when it descended and hit his hands.

For a moment, as he fell, he had the ball. Then it was down.

Halfway through the over allocation, Pakistan were a mere 2-70 and it took 107 balls for Imran and Miandad's partnership to produce 50 runs. Many wondered at the merit of the plan, then three overs later the Pakistani captain danced down the wicket to left-arm spinner Richard Illingworth and hit him for a straight six into the Members' Stand.

It was the signal for a change of intent. The scoreboard began to tick over. By the 31st over the 100 had been raised. Miandad's back got so sore he called for a runner and later he did not field. Imran cut and drove, Miandad glanced and nudged. Both batsmen reached 50, the stand was worth 100 and still the tempo built, as it did in Auckland.

Miandad stepped away and drove a Chris Lewis full toss through the covers for four, then a few balls later over-improvised and reverse swept Illingworth softly to Botham at backward point. He had put on 139 with his captain in 31 overs and even got out of the way at just the right moment so the powerful tyro, Inzamam-ul-Haq, had enough time to make his mark. He flicked Botham to square leg and dabbed him past Alec Stewart's outstretched hand for two fours in the 42nd over.

Imran's important contribution was ended when he stepped away and clubbed Botham through the lengthening shadows to Illingworth on the long on boundary. Again the timing was good. It left Wasim Akram with just enough leverage for some final-overs biffo. Inzamam traded flailing blows with the left-armpaceman while another 52 runs were put on in the last six overs.

Akram hit four boundaries, never being averse to cross-bat heaves towards cow corner. Pringle withstood the final assault well and even picked up another wicket when Inzamam missed a slog. Akram was run out going for a bye from the final ball of the innings without a hint of dissatisfaction. After 136 had been scored from the final 16 overs, he was happy to bowl at 249.

History was against England. No side batting second had won any of the other finals. Luck, too, seemed to favour Pakistan. Akram, already bowling around the wicket, bounced the ball past the outside edge of Botham's bat. There was an appeal and, responding to the ball's deviation, Brian Aldridge gave 'Beefy' out caught behind. His displeasure was matched by the crowd's joy.

Botham had repeatedly referred to the Australians as "convicts", then shown public indignation when a comedian impersonated the Queen. He should not have been surprised at the send off he received after making a duck.

When Botham's head went back and he pulled a few faces, Sohail indicated the direction he had to take to find the dressing-room. The east coast of Australia missed the drama, Channel 9, as ever, feeling obliged to interrupt the cricket coverage with news and current affairs programs.

Alec Stewart was struggling, as well, and edged an outswinger from Akram, This time umpire Aldridge ruled in favour of the batsman. It was of little benefit to either Stewart or his team as he soon edged another outswinger, this time off Aaqib Javed, and walked away before the umpire could make a decision.

England was 2-21 and Gooch was charged with putting together a captain's innings of equal merit to Imran's. He might have succeeded, too, if he only had to face a succession of finger spinners and medium pacers. Instead, Pakistan's first change bowler was a talented leg-spinner.

Mushtaq was introduced in the 11th over and was soon confusing both Gooch and Graeme Hick. They survived past the evening drinks break then Hick was palpably lbw to a Mushtaq wrong 'un which no-one had any right to say they would have picked. Nor was the 21-year-old who was often left out of his Pakistan domestic side, United Bank, finished there. Ten runs later in the 21st over he struck a bigger blow when Gooch top-edged a sweep and Aqib ran in and dived forward to hold an excellent catch at deep square leg. The bowler celebrated with a David Campese style 'goose' run.

If England had folded completely from a position of 4–69 it would not have come as a total surprise. That they did not could be put down to the fighting qualities of Allan Lamb and that underrated limited-overs batsman, Neil Fairbrother. The Lancastrian left-hander scored at nearly a run per ball with his deflections and daring dashes between wickets.

Lamb, straining his unreliable limbs, also responded well to the demands of the situation. They took 64 balls to put on 50, punished Imran severely and were scoring at the required seven per over against Ijaz Ahmed and Aamir Sohail when Akram was recalled. In a flash he all but sealed the result. Still around the wicket, he angled the ball in to Lamb then cut it away to hit the off-stump, ending the 72-run partnership.

"It's one of the best balls I've ever bowled," Akram would say later. Next ball, a perfectly pitched in-swinger to Chris Lewis, slipped between bat and pad to the top of the stumps. Akram had been instructed by his captain at the start of the competition to bowl for wickets rather than containment. He finished with the tournament's highest wide count and the most wickets.

Only boundaries would revive England's fortunes from 6-141 and, despite Fairbrother's brave efforts, they would not come. He and Dermot Reeve put on another 39 without really suggesting a miracle was about to happen. Then, in the 43rd over, after 70 balls of total dedication, Fairbrother top-edged a pull off Aqib that lobbed easily to Moin. The requirement was now up to around 10 per over. DeFreitas slogged hard before taking on Salim Malik's arm from deep mid wicket and losing. Illingworth briefly hit with power, too, and even managed a couple of fours before Imran, whose figures were none too impressive, bowled the final over of the 1992 World Cup.

He didn't get to complete it. From the second ball Illingworth top-edged an attempted smite. Ramiz ran around at mid off and held the comfortable offering, then continued in a large circle with his arms aloft. At 10.18pm Eastern Summer Time on 25 March 1992 Pakistan joined the West Indies, India and Australia as winners of the World Cup.

Ramiz's catch was followed by a session of proud men in green shirts kissing the ground. They arose with broad smiles to hug each other and anyone else who came within arm's reach.

Within an instant the media had invaded the sanctity of the Pakistani gathering. Imran's immediate reaction on television was, "You know I always felt we were going to win it. Even when we were struggling, I always knew we were going to win it."

Wasim Akram, who was named as Man of the Match offered, "This is the best moment of my life!"

Their captain accepted the glass trophy and they ran around the boundary brandishing it casually, totally confident of its safety. The giant MCG bowl still providing a fantastic spectacle under lights, even with the match over, exploded into life as the sky was filled with fireworks to close the tournament. It brought down the curtain on a disappointing finish for England who, heads held high, walked a thank-you lap, their honour intact. Gooch suggested it was not the end of the world, but Alec Stewart's arm around him during the presentation indicated that the disappointment, quite understandably, went deep.

Gooch admitted later; "To be fair, Pakistan deserved to win. They played better than us today."

There was a rousing rendition of *Allah Hoo* in the MCG dressing-room, dancing in the streets of Lahore and in the Pakistani communities in Bradford. Imran was thrilled because of the publicity and fundraising benefit to the cancer hospital he wanted to have built in Lahore.

Soon cricket would not interfere with his devotion to that cause.

PAKISTAN	
Aamir Sohail c Stewart b Pringle	4
Ramiz Raja lbw Pringle	8
Imran Khan (capt) c Illingworth b Botham	72
Javed Miandad c Botham b Illingworth	58
Inzamam-ul-Haq b Pringle	42
Wasim Akram run out	33
Salim Malik not out	0
Extras (lb 19, w 6, nb 7)	32
(50 overs)	6-249

Did not bat: Ijaz Ahmed, Moin Khan (wk), Mushtaq Ahmed, Aaqib Javed

1/20 2/24 3/163 4/197 5/249 6/249.

Bowling: Pringle 10-2-22-3; Lewis 10-2-52-0; Botham 7-0-42-1; DeFreitas 10-1-42-0; Illingworth 10-0-50-1; Reeve 3-0-22-0

ENGLAND	
G. A. Gooch (capt) c Aaqib Javed b Mushtaq Ahmed	29
I. T. Botham c Moin Khan b Wasim Akram	0
A. J. Stewart (wk) c Moin Khan b Aaqib Javed	7
G. A. Hick lbw Mushtaq Ahmed	17
N. H Fairbrother c Moin Khan b Aaqib Javed	62
A. J. Lamb b Wasim Akram	31
C. E. Lewis b Wasim Akram	0
D. A. Reeve c Ramiz Raja b Mushtaq Ahmed	15
D. R. Pringle not out	18
P. A. J. DeFreitas run out	10
R. K. Illingworth c Ramiz Raja b Imran Khan	14
Extras (lb 5, w 13, nb 6)	24
(49.2 overs)	10-227

1/6 2/21 3/59 4/69 5/141 6/141 7/180 8/183 9/208 10/227

Bowling: Wasim Akram 10-0-49-3; Aaqib Javed 10-2-27-2; Mushtaq Ahmed 10-1-41-3; Ijaz Ahmed 3-0-13-0; Imran Khan 6.2-0-43-1; Aamir Sohail 10-0-49-0

Umpires: B.L. Aldridge, S.A. Bucknor.
Toss: Pakistan

POST-MORTEM

Financially, the 1992 World Cup continued the stories of success, not least through the merchandising of coloured replica team shirts.

Unlike the previous tournaments, though, the organisers received only mixed reviews. The amount of travel involved and some of the accommodation provided were criticised by players and their countries' officials. When the weather behaved, the cricketers offered some great entertainment and there was genuine public pleasure that a team of such mercurial talent was able to time its run and overcome those whose tactics were more rigid and less dynamic.

Pakistan, true to form, rumbled about Imran's attitude to his players after the World Cup win. Officially he retired due to ongoing problems with his shoulder, unofficially the players did not want him to lead them on the 1992 tour of England. Under Javed Miandad, they won the Test series but lost the one-dayers. Waqar Younis and Wasim Akram swung the old ball late and to a full length, often scattering stumps in all directions. It made great viewing as feet rather than heads were under threat.

The Test win was sullied by accusations of ball tampering which England wanted to believe was the real reason they were beaten in the Tests and maybe even the World Cup.

The Australians were dissatisfied with their World Cup result and had a good look at where things might have gone wrong. Sri Lanka was less forgiving of those at the helm and Aravinda de Silva found he had swapped places with Arjuna Ranatunga again when he got back home.

South Africa and the West Indies went off to play a Test against each other and soon Zimbabwe joined the brotherhood of Test nations. Test cricket resumed its former eminence, but behind closed doors powerful and influential men were planning their campaigns for four years hence.

CHAPTER 7:

The Wills World Cup, 1996: Sri Lanka's Joy

India and Pakistan, with the addition of Sri Lanka, wanted to run the World Cup again. They were supported by a lot of the associate members of the ICC and Zimbabwe. However, the majority of the Test-playing nations favoured the TCCB's push for England as a venue. Eventually to break the deadlock and with the guarantee that they would host the 1998 tournament, and the World Cup be held every three years, the English contingent withdrew their bid. The ICC secretary, Lt-Col. John Stephenson, an Englishman, called the gesture, "most magnanimous" and "gentlemanly". South Africa were in line to hold the eighth competition in 2001.

The major economies of the world may have managed to hold inflation largely in check in the western world in the first half of the 1990s, however there was no such achievement on the World Cup stage. The number of participants continued to increase, this time from nine to 12. The extra three sides were to come from the first three places in the February 1994 ICC Trophy tournament in Kenya.

Eventually the United Arab Emirates, boosted by the inclusion of expatriate Indians, Sri Lankans and Pakistanis with first class experience, hosts Kenya and third placed Holland won the treasured spots. Soon after the ICC met again and agreed on the February and March dates for the World Cup in 1996, at the same time thinking better of their once-every-three years plan. On reflection the four yearly status quo had greater appeal.

There was some slight deflation in the number of matches. Yet another new structure reduced the fixtures from 39 to 37. Groups were back in fashion. Into Group A went India, Australia, West Indies, Sri Lanka, Zimbabwe and Kenya. The Bs contained Pakistan, England, New Zealand, South Africa, Holland and United Arab Emirates. The preliminary stage matches eliminated two sides from each group, the surviving eight teams progressing through to a quarter-final round, followed by semi-finals and the final. A second day was set aside for any matches that could not be finished because of rain.

Umpires were allowed to call for video replay adjudication from a third umpire for stumping and run out decisions. Otherwise the rules for the 1996 World Cup were much the same as those that had become standardised for limited-over internationals.

The greater change was in the power of sponsorship and television rights. For the second time a tobacco company was able to offer enough financial incentive to get their name attached to a cricket World Cup. Wills were able to put their name on the tournament for a contract rumoured to cost them around AU$20 million. That also bought them playing field and stump logos. The 1996 version of coloured uniforms were also to bear the tobacco company's name. Coca-Cola was named as the official World Cup soft drink. Matches at major venues were to be played under lights, including the final at Lahore. Jagmohan Dalmiya was the game's new major powerbroker and a convenor of PILCOM, the World Cup organising committee. With everyone trying to get the best deal off everyone else there were difficulties with whom was televising to whom. Not surprisingly, by the time the event began the holding out between rival companies had finished.

The South African issue had been buried by February 1996. Even members of the final 'Rebel' tour there, Mike Gatting's English team of 1989-90 had their bans lifted and were available if their selectors wanted them and had been since 1992-93. There was to be no political plain sailing, though. Two issues clouded the 1996 World Cup, one being serious enough for it to cause two matches to be forfeited.

In 1995 high-profile Australian players Mark Waugh, Tim May and Shane Warne made accusations that Pakistani batsman, Salim Malik had tried to bribe them during the 1994 Australian tour of Pakistan. The accusations created the greatest controversy the game has ever known. At the time of writing, the matter had still not been resolved. Much initial reaction on the sub-continent was disbelieving and strained relations between Australia and the co-hosts of the 1996 World Cup.

When Sri Lankan off-spinner Muttiah Muralitharan was no balled for throwing by umpire Darrell Hair in a Test in Melbourne there were some cries of a conspiracy by certain sections of the press in India and Pakistan as well as Sri Lanka.

The deterioation in relations continued when a couple of weeks prior to the lavish opening ceremony at Eden Gardens in Calcutta a terrorist bomb exploded in central Colombo, killing 80 people. The Australian Cricket Board requested that their match against Sri Lanka be relocated to a venue in India. When this was rejected by PILCOM, the Australian authorities announced that despite assurances of increased security, they would not be sending a team to play in Sri Lanka. The West Indian authorities also fearing for the safety of their players joined Australia in boycotting their scheduled match in Sri Lanka.

Although conceding two points, Australia were installed as 5-2 favourites to win the 1996 Wills World Cup. The punters were obviously not discouraged by their disappointing showing in 1992. Since Pakistan's historic win in Melbourne in 1992 Australia had gradually asserted its dominance over all other nations in Test cricket. Mark Taylor had replaced Allan Border at the helm and added freshness and enterprise to the competitiveness that Border's regime had established.

Indeed, of the side that played in the 1987 final in Calcutta only Steve Waugh and Craig McDermott remained and the big fast bowler from Queensland was destined to send down just three more overs for his country. Trump cards in the Australian attack were now paceman Glenn McGrath, a spindly mean-hearted bowler with a killer instinct and a biting tongue and high profile, blond leg-spinner, Shane Warne.

Warne, who had single handedly re-ignited the public image of leg-spin, was cautious about the reception he would receive on the subcontinent. Controversial at times himself, Warne was nothing less than a champion, easily the best Australian leg-spinner since Bill O'Reilly and sure to be a force in the World Cup.

The Waugh brothers were at the peak of their batting powers, Mark taking up the role as an aggressive opener in partnership with his more pedestrian captain. While struggling at Test level, Michael Bevan had mastered many facets of middle order batting in the shorter game. The left-hander had averaged 194 in the recently completed World Series Cup tournament in Australia, hitting the ball with precision into gaps and running with amazing speed between wickets. Tasmanian Ricky Ponting was the young batting tyro of the line-up, recently established in the team and looking to fulfil his immense potential.

The holders of the World Cup, Pakistan, had gone through various ructions and upheavals through the four years since their great victory. They retained the talent necessary to take back-to-back titles, but had to withstand many pressures including the added expectation of playing at home. Captains had come, gone and returned. Allegations of pot smoking in the West Indies followed the bribery accusations. Key fast bowling all-rounder, Wasim Akram was at the helm for the 1996 World Cup, there having been five changes at the top of the Pakistani team in a year. Akram had come a full circle since a player's revolt in South Africa.

He remained a wonderful bowler, fast and adaptable with plenty of variations, including a killer in-swinging yorker. When both he and Waqar Younis were fit, on good terms with each other and firing on both cylinders, the new-ball pair displayed speed and skills the equal of any of the legendary fast bowling duos in history. While Shane Warne received most plaudits for rejuvenating the art of wrist spin at the game's highest level, Mushtaq Ahmed, another with snapping fingers and supple wrists had actually preceded him on the world stage. Almost as accurate as the Australian star, he possessed even great variation, if anything concentrating too much on wrong 'uns.

The emergence of Saeed Anwar as an opening partner to Aamer Sohail gave Pakistan power at the start of their innings. Both left-handers approached their job with aggressive intent. Anwar was perhaps the more stylish of the two, however, Sohail lost nothing in comparison of scoring capability or entertainment value. Ijaz Ahmed, Salim Malik, Inzama-ul-Haq and the recalled veteran of six World Cups, Javed Miandad, completed Pakistan's highly credentialled middle order.

Co-hosts India faced similar pressures. One of the motivating factors behind the success of Imran Khan's 1992 side had been the desire to match the euphoria in Pakistan that India had felt in 1983. Now fans in both countries expected nothing less than a repeat of that type of joy and placed them with Australia as official tournament favourites. Mohammad Azharuddin had been subject to waves of criticism each time India's form fell below those high levels of expectation. Yet his calm self-assuredness in times of success and failure made him a very capable captain even without considering his superb batting.

Since 1992 Sachin Tendulkar had gone from strength to strength. Even Sir Donald Bradman had compared the technique of the young Indian to himself. Tendulkar also showed the same killer instinct towards bowlers, seeking total domination while exhibiting every shot available. Like Mark Waugh, Tendulkar had been promoted to open the batting in limited-over internationals.

There was plenty of talent to support Tendulkar and Azharuddin. Sanjay Manjrekar, Navjot Sidhu , Ajay Jadeja and Vinod Kambli were all accomplished run makers. They needed to be. India's bowling was weaker, despite the quality of wrist-spinner Anil Kumble and the brave determination of the medium-pace brigade, which included Javagal Srinath, the very competitive Manoj Prabahkar and Venkatesh Prasad.

Unlike 1992, England arrived to begin their World Cup campaign on a downer having lost a Test series in South Africa and the follow up one-day tournament. That summed up their fortunes for the majority of the time since their appearance in the Final against Pakistan. Under the guidance of Keith Fletcher, then with Ray Illingworth in charge, England's overseas record was poor.

Mike Atherton, after three years in the job had become a hardened 27-year-old. His own courage, dedication and concentration had earned plaudits without getting the results he or his country would have hoped. His side were bedevilled by inconsistency. No-one could doubt the occasional brilliance of the likes of Alec Stewart, Graeme Hick, Robin Smith and Graham Thorpe, yet as a collective unit they were prone to unaccountable lapses. Graham Gooch and Ian Botham were long gone and no-one of the same calibre had stepped forward take their place.

The bowling, the enthusiastic Darren Gough apart, had made limited progress. It relied again on medium-paced seamers like Phil DeFreitas, back for his third World Cup, Angus Fraser, Dominic Cork and Peter Martin. None of these threatened serious damage on batsmen friendly sub-continental wickets. Nor was the spin of Neil Smith, Mike Watkinson nor Richard Illingworth likely to create significant fear. Yet England's World Cup record was remarkably consistent, never having failed to reach at least the semi-final stage. The competitive spirit of this side again bursting with all-rounders could not be discounted.

South Africa had shown since 1992 that their achievements were based on genuine talent, not the romance of the return to international cricket. Kepler Wessels' bad knees had led to retirement, leaving the reins to young Hansie Cronje a designated leader if ever there was one. The success of the Proteas had been based on solid rather than spectacular batting, accurate pace bowling and brilliant fielding.

Allan Donald remained one of the world's premier fast bowlers and his effectiveness had been increased through the emergence of a quality partner in Shaun Pollock. The red-headed son of the Chairman of Selectors and former Test paceman, Peter Pollock, had made an immediate impression during his debut series against England. At 22 he was fast and aggressive with a batting talent more in line with his uncle Graeme than his father.

Another newcomer in the South African line-up was freakish left arm spinner, Paul Adams. The teenager with the 'frog in a blender action' had shown unorthodoxy was no obstacle to success. His meteoric rise attracted plenty of publicity, not least because, as a Cape Coloured, he set a landmark for the new direction of South African cricket.

Jonty Rhodes' athleticism and Brian McMillan's enormous safe hands set the standards for the amazingly high quality of the South African fielding. Although lacking renowned champions the Proteas' batting line-up had great depth, off-spinning all-rounder Pat Symcox at number 10 would eventually become a Test centurymaker. Importantly South Africa were coming into the tournament in prime limited-overs form.

West Indian decline had not been arrested since 1992. In addition to having limited impact on the shorter version of the game they had recently lost their crown as the world's premier Test nation to Australia. That increased the pressure on captain Richie Richardson who had already had 12 months out of the game through emotional fatigue. While Richardson recuperated, Courtney Walsh had successfully assumed the leadership role. The push from Walsh's home island, Jamaica, was that their man was the rightful captain. The Leeward Islands and more importantly the West Indian Board remained faithful to Richardson.

That created some inter-island rivalry inside the dressing room, the type of which haunted West Indian cricket prior to their halcyon days. It also had the potential to undermine the still obvious talent within the side. Richardson had not recaptured his complete pre-hiatus run-making capacity. His decline was nowhere near as severe as some people suggested, though.

Brian Lara's profile had skyrocketed after he broke the long-standing highest Test record score and the highest first class record score within weeks of each other in 1994. Since then questions had arisen over his ability to handle media pressure. That included temporarily walking out during the 1995 tour of England and making himself unavailable for the World Series Cup tournament in Australia.

Yet Lara's sublime batting talent could carry all before it and was central to the West Indies chances of success. Shivnarine Chanderpaul had emerged as a determined and consistent left-hander, and Jimmy Adams had been prolific on the tour of India 12 months earlier. Carl Hooper withdrew from the side at the last minute through illness and would be missed.

The cutting edge of Richardson's attack was his trio of big, mean fast bowlers. Curtley Ambrose, Courtney Walsh and Ian Bishop needed to stay fit and in form if the West Indies were to make an impact on the 1996 World Cup. Each, in the past, had shown the ability through strength and accuracy to overcome the slowness of wickets on the sub-continent. Both Walsh and Ambrose were the wrong side of 30 and the world waited for a diminishing of their powers and achievements. It was as well that no-one held their breath.

There was sense that New Zealand had missed their chance by not getting through to the final in 1992. Now Martin Crowe's injured knee had brought his career to an end. He departure just prior to the start of World Cup left a big gap which could not be filled despite the batting promise of Nathan Astle and Stephen Fleming.

Also into the line-up had come new captain Lee Germon, promoted to the national leadership after impressing in the role for Canterbury in New Zealand. Germon, who came in a package deal with new coach, Glenn Turner, displaced Adam Parore from behind the stumps, although the talented 24-year-old retained his place as a batsman. Like Dipak Patel before him, Roger Twose achieved instant Kiwi status by leaving England, marrying his girlfriend from New Zealand and settling there. The doughty left-hander walked straight into the side, his experience invaluable as in addition to Crowe retiring Mark Greatbatch had been omitted and Ken Rutherford, deposed as captain, had gone to play in South Africa.

Seam and medium pace was back in favour. The bulk of the New Zealand bowling responsibility would fall on Danny Morrison, Chris Cairns and Dion Nash, whose introduction to the big time had created a favourable impression. It was difficult to believe New Zealand had the talent to do any serious damage in the World Cup. However, they had a habit of reaching the semi-final stages and showed in 1992 they were very capable of causing an upset or two.

It was a pity for Sri Lanka that their first chance to showcase their home on the World Cup stage was marred by controversy. The boycotts by Australia and the West Indies curtailed the number of matches in Colombo and Kandy from four to two. If nothing else it gave Arjuna Ranatunga's side a four-point launching pad for the quarter finals.

The portents from their tour of Australia were not good. Heavy defeats were intermingled with controversy and ill-feeling. At home, though, they had always been a different proposition and they had their best ever chance to really progress. Any impact would be based on taking full advantage of their aggressive batting line-up. Ranatunga's inventiveness in the middle order was in the Javed Miandad class and extended beyond ploys whereby he would call for a runner.

Relieved of the burden of captaincy Aravinda de Silva sought opportunities to measure himself against the best batsmen in the world, while left-handers such as Hashan Tillekaratne, Asanka Gurusinha and Sanath Jayasuriya were all apporaching 30, often a batsman's peak years.

It was unfortunate that Sri Lanka's key bowler, Muttiah Muralitharan, now had to carry the stigma of being called for throwing. How that affected his form during the World Cup remained to be seen. The young off-spinner had handled the matter with a great deal of dignity and was sure to receive sympathetic treatment from fans on the sub-continent, in India and Pakistan, as well as Sri Lanka. The pressure on the umpires when Muralitharan bowled would be as great as on the bowler, himself.

His support was variable. Chaminda Vaas and Pramodya Wickremasinghe could be penetrative with the new-ball. At other times they merely removed the shine for the spinners like Muralitharan and fellow off-spinner Kumara Dharmasena.

No-one had done any favours for Zimbabwe. They were not going to benefit from forfeits, had no home ground advantage and were in Group A which had only one of the tournament underlings, fellow Africans Kenya, instead of two as in Group B. Now a Test nation they were prepared to risk playing in Sri Lanka in the search for precious points in an attempt to advance their languishing international status.

Andy Flower, like his predecessor a wicketkeeper batsman, was the captain of Zimbabwe. Eleven years Flower's senior, Dave Houghton was the original choice as vice-captain, but his hopes of finishing his career on a high note were shattered by a foot injury sustained during a century innings against New Zealand. That placed a greater responsibility on the shoulders of both Flower brothers; Andy and Grant. The duo formed a very effective brotherly opening partnership.

Alistair Campbell was a more accomplished batsman with four years' experience behind him, while Andy Waller, Dave Houghton's replacement, another former captain and a veteran of two previous World Cup campaigns was among the hardest hitters in the game as he showed in the 1992 World Cup match at New Plymouth.

Eddo Brandes had left his chickens behind for another crack at cricketing glory. He would share the new-ball with Heath Streak, a bowler of genuine pace well up to international class. Leg-spinning was now popular in Zimbabwe too, Paul Strang being the nation's top practitioner. Underdogs still, they at least could boast the tournament's richest colours on their uniform, a bright crimson number that encouraged the opposition to wear their sponsor's sun glasses at all times.

Holland, for their part, if they achieved nothing else, looked sharp in the only appearance to date of their bright orange World Cup uniform. Their outfit, like that of all other teams had taken 10 days from order to availability.

Their line-up contained plenty of experience. Barbados-born Nolan Clarke, a scorer of 159 for his island against the MCC back in 1974 was now 47 and a legend in Dutch cricket. Captain for 10 years, Steve Lubbers and Flavian Aponso were also in their 40s. That must have made the others with first-class experience, paceman Paul-Jan Bakker (38), all-rounder Roland LeFefebvre (33) and Australian Peter Cantrell (33) feel like striplings. Lefebvre was still contracted to County side, Glamorgan.

The oldest players in the Kenyan side, Dipak Chudasama, Asif Karim and Tariq Iqbal were just 32. They also had in their squad the youngest player in the tournament, 17-year-old all-rounder, Thomas Odoyo. The team's joy at participating in the prestigious World Cup was tempered by a dispute with the Kenyan authorities over the players' meagre daily allowance. That was resolved in time to avoid a fiasco. Seen as a potential future Test playing nation, Kenya's viability during the World Cup was very important.

Maurice Odumbe, like Hansie Cronje a young national captain, was a classy all-rounder. But much attention would centre on Steve Tikolo. Many were keen to see how this talented batsman, who had played first-class cricket in South Africa, acquitted himself against the world's best. With Kenya in Group A he would be up against Test class opposition in every World Cup match.

The United Arab Emiriates captain, Sultan Zarawani and vice-captain Saeed Al-Saffer were the only native members of their side. Immediately following their 1994 ICC Trophy victory the grumbles began and soon the rules for player qualification were altered so that a repeat could not occur. But for the Wills 1996 World Cup this conglomerate of former Pakistani and Indian players would have to be accepted.

Outside the UAE and Pakistan, none of the players were very well known. Their batting strength had got them through the ICC Trophy tournament and would be their best chance of picking up a win in the World Cup. Someone had to win the game between UAE and Holland. Mazhar Hussain a crouching low-gripping batsman had been on a Pakistani B tour of Zimbabwe and Saleem Raza, an opener with experience against touring sides in Pakistan were two of the batsmen Sultan Zarawani hoped would give UAE competitive totals. In their uniforms that would not have looked out of place on the 1st Alabama Musket Brigade in 1862 UAE should have set out to enjoy their few weeks in the limelight, for unlike Kenya and Holland, they definitely would not be back.

Tight security marked the lead-up to the opening ceremony at Eden Gardens in Calcutta. The terrorist attack in Colombo and the follow-up boycotts by the Australians and the West Indians made everyone a little apprehensive. Steve Waugh pointed out that the armed guards were of greater value in keeping fanatical cricket followers at bay than any need to protect them from bombers or murderers.

There were only cricket fans amongst the 120,000 crammed into Eden Gardens for the opening ceremony to the 1996 Wills World Cup. Eye-witnesses said the reaction of the crowd when the Indian team was presented to them was something to behold. The spontaneous roar overwhelmed even the most battle-hardened players in the centre. It was the climax to a night that had its share of anti-climaxes.

The major let down came when the wind knocked over a mesh screen essential to the proper working of a $2 million laser light show. The announcer, who had also confused his introduction of UAE and South Africa, told disappointed patrons to talk among themselves. There were rumblings of discontent, but the riot was saved up for a couple of weeks. At least the fireworks went off with a bang.

The occasion, as it would three years later at Lord's, fell a long way short of the extravaganzas witnessed at Olympic and even Commonwealth Games. Some local Government officials were so disgusted with the result they wanted Jagmohan Dalmiya arrested for wasting public money. It did, however, prime everyone for the start of the real thing in three days. The prize at the end would be four-kilogram 118-year-old sterling silver trophy originally made by the crown jewellers in London.

After the Final it was to be kept not by the victorious country, but by the tournament sponsors, Wills. The World Cup wins by India in 1983, Australia in 1987 and Pakistan in 1992 meant that thereafter the tournament would always be a tantalising prospect. Favouritism would only go so far towards indicating a likely victor. Richard Hutton wrote in his editorial of the March 1996 edition of *The Cricketer International*, "Such are the twists of form and fate that anyone can win the World Cup-except Holland, Kenya, the UAE, and probably Zimbabwe, Sri Lanka, New Zealand."

Well, Richard, your assessment of five out of those six sides was spot on.

WEDNESDAY 14 FEBRUARY 1996
SARDAR PATEL STADIUM, AHMEDABAD:
ENGLAND vs NEW ZEALAND; GROUP B
NEW ZEALAND WON BY 11 RUNS

New Zealand began their 1996 campaign as convincingly as they did the one in 1992. The Lee Germon-led Kiwis continued England's miserable recent run with a sound win.

The Kiwi batsmen showed greater enterprise and their fieldsmen caught their catches. On four crucial occasions England did not. In what *The Times* correspondent, Alan Lee called, "an ugly, unkempt stadium", Mike Atherton gave New Zealand first use of the Sardar Patel Stadium pitch, even though by reputation it did not wear well.

He was hoping to take advantage of the moisture still in the wicket at the 9am start. Germon said he also would have bowled first. Soon that was the least of Atherton's concerns. In the third over of the day the sole slip fieldsman, Graham Thorpe, according to television commentator, Tony Greig, "Standing too far back", dropped Nathan Astle off Peter Martin. Thorpe also put down Astle's opening partner Craig Spearman. That was not too costly because Dominic Cork held a caught and bowled chance off Spearman to complete the first dismissal of the 1996 World Cup.

The miss off Astle, though, was very expensive. He put on 96 for the second wicket in 19 overs with Stephen Fleming and went on to hit eight fours and two sixes off 132 balls while completing his third century in limited-over internationals.

There were more misses. Atherton and Cork were also culprits and England, in general, looked lacklustre. Their ground fielding also conceded unnecessary runs, enough to be significant by the end of the day. Perhaps worn down by a surfeit of cricket in South Africa, there were a number of injury problems from the outset of the tournament.

Both Fleming and Roger Twose were caught by a more sure-handed Thorpe at deep square leg off top edged sweeps. Then Chris Cairns scored at better than a run per ball striking four fours and a six. He took New Zealand to the verge of 200 with ten overs remaining. From the moment he was caught at point off the accurate left-arm spinner, Richard Illingworth the batting was pedestrian. Instead of something in the vicinity of 270, the Kiwis had to be satisfied with 239, only 43 having come from those last 10 overs.

A well-pitched in-swinging yorker from Dion Nash to Atherton in his first over got England away to a bad start. The England captain then walked to square leg rather than the pavilion. Graeme Hick had joined the growing list of the injured with a strained hamstring, sustained while fielding, and Atherton stayed on the ground as his runner. The trio of Alec Stewart, Hick and Atherton worked effectively in a partnership worth 99 runs. Hick dominated the stand, hitting nine fours in 101 balls.

At 1-100 England were reasonably placed. Once Hick watched his own demise, run out after a hesitation between Atherton and Neil Fairbrother at 144, they were always struggling. Like his 1992 predecessor, Martin Crowe, Germon was prepared to mix his bowlers around. England wanted 96 from their last 15 overs and had a spark of hope when Dominic Cork thrashed around for a couple of fours and a six. Nash extinguished that in the 47th over when he had the Derbyshire all-rounder caught behind and Danny Morrison had little trouble protecting the 16 runs available in the last over.

Atherton said after the game that he believed the poor catching had cost his side the match. Astle took the Man of the Match Award in what was really a fairly tame opening to the sixth World Cup.

NEW ZEALAND		ENGLAND	
C. M. Spearman c & b Cork	5	M. A. Atherton (capt) b Nash	1
N. J. Astle c Hick b Martin	101	A. J. Stewart c & b Harris	34
S. P. Fleming c Thorpe b Hick	28	G. A. Hick run out	85
R. G. Twose c Thorpe b Hick	17	G. P. Thorpe b Larsen	9
C. L. Cairns c Cork b Illingworth	36	N. H. Fairbrother b Morrison	36
C. Z. Harris run out	10	R. C. Russell (wk) c Morrison b Larsen	2
S. A. Thomson not out	17	C. White c Cairns b Thomson	13
L. K. Germon(wk/capt) not out	13	D. G. Cork c Germon b Nash	19
Extras b4 lb2 w4 nb2	12	D. Gough not out	15
(50 overs)	6-239	P. J. Martin c Cairns b Nash	3
Did not bat: D. J. Nash, G. R. Larsen, D. K. Morrison		R. K. Illingworth not out	3
1/12 2/108 3/141 4/196 5/204 6/212		Extras b1 lb4 w1 nb2	8
Bowling: Cork 10-1-36-1; Martin 6-0-37-1; Gough 10-0-63-0;		(50 overs)	9-228
Illingworth 10-1-31-1; Hick 9-0-45-2; White 5-0-21-0;		1/1 2/100 3/123 4/144 5/151 6/180 7/185 8/210 9/222	
		Bowling	
		Morrison 8-0-38-1; Nash 7-1-26-3; Cairns 4-0-24-0;	
		Larsen 10-1-33-2; Thomson 10-0-51-1; Harris 9-0-45-1;	
		Astle 2-0-6-0	

Umpires:B.C. Cooray S.G. Randell

Toss: England   Points: New Zealand 2 England 0

THURSDAY 15 FEBRUARY and FRIDAY 16 FEBRUARY 1996
CRICKET STADIUM, RAWALPINDI: SOUTH AFRICA vs UAE - GROUP B
SOUTH AFRICA WON BY 169 RUNS

The Emirates team would have been under no illusions as to the monumental task in front of them in trying to compete with the best cricket teams in the world after this thrashing handed out by South Africa.

Sultan Zarawani had the honour of winning the choice of innings, but nothing went right for him after that. He, like the rest of his bowlers, was flayed by the South African batsmen who complied their highest ever score in a limited-over international. Later the UAE captain was confident or foolhardy enough to face Allan Donald without a helmet and was promptly hit on the head first ball. He lasted another few balls before Brian McMillan dismissed him for a duck.

Rain had washed out the scheduled first day. This time the 'no result' was avoided because a second day had been set aside. As the covers had been on the pitch for four days in the previous week Sultan Zarawani's decision to bowl was thought a sensible one. There may have been some assistance for the bowlers if those using the conditions had been of a reasonable standard.

They did not worry Gary Kirsten. The left-handed opener batted through the innings, broke the highest individual World Cup score and at the completion of 50 overs was an agonising one run behind Viv Richards all time limited-over international record score of 189. He needed four from the last ball of the innings, but, probably starting to feel a little fatigued, had to be satisfied with two. Kirsten knew at the crease he had broken Richards' 1987 World Cup record, but was unaware of the all time limited-over international record. It was the first century for South Africa in a World Cup match. Kirsten gave one chance on 118.

He and Andrew Hudson had set the domination in motion with an opening stand of 60. Kirsten and Hansie Cronje then put on 116 for the second wicket. The South African captain although hitting only one four and one six batted for just 62 balls while scoring 57. Cronje's dismissal by his opposite number was the last Emirates success as Kirsten went to town over the last 20 overs. Daryll Cullinan, normally a very aggressive batsman, sat back while Kirsten continued on his merry way. At the completion of 50 overs he had struck 13 fours and four sixes from 159 balls. His partnership with Cullinan realised 145 runs for the third wicket.

Azhar Saeed and Ganesh Mylvaganam began the UAE reply as if they meant to get all of the 322 runs they needed. Once they had been removed brilliantly caught by wicketkeeper Steve Palframan and Brian McMillan, though, the rest of the batsmen got into a spot of bother. By the end of the 28th over UAE were 8-72. Kirsten was an easy choice as Man of the Match.

SOUTH AFRICA		UNITED ARAB EMIRATES	
A. C.Hudson b Samarasekera	27	Azhar Saeed c McMillan b Pollock	11
G. Kirsten not out	188	G. Mylvaganam c Palframan b Donald	23
W. J.Cronje(capt) st Abbasi b Zarawani	57	Mazhar Hussain b Donald	14
D. J.Cullinan not out	41	V. Mehra run out	2
Extras b1 lb1 w3 nb3	8	Mohammad Aslam b McMillan	9
(50 overs)	2-321	Arshad Laiq not out	43
Did not bat: J. H.Kallis, J. N.Rhodes, B. M. McMillan,		J. A.Samarasekera c Hudson b Donald	4
S. M.Pollock, S. J.Palframan(wk), C. R.Matthews,		Sultan M. Zarawani(capt) c Cronje b McMillan	0
A. A.Donald		Imtiaz Abbasi(wk) c Palframan b McMillan	1
1/60 2/176		S. Dukanwala not out	40
Bowling: Samarasekera 9-2-39-1; Altaf 3-0-22-0;		Extras w3 nb2	5
Laiq 6-0-52-0; Dukanwala 10-0-64-0; Azhar 7-0-41-0;		(50 overs)	8-152
Zarawani 10-0-69-1; Mazhar 5-0-32-0		Did not bat: Shahzad Altaf	
		1/24 2/42 3/46 4/60 5/62 6/68 7/70 8/72	
		Bowling: Pollock 9-2-28-1; Matthews 10-0-39-0;	
		Donald 10-0-21-3; Cronje 4-0-17-0; McMillan 8-1-11-3;	
		Kallis 6-0-27-0; Kirsten 3-0-9-0	

Umpires: S.A.Bucknor V.K.Ramaswamy

Toss: UAE   Points: South Africa 2 UAE 0

FRIDAY 16 FEBRUARY 1996
FATEH MAIDAN STADIUM, HYDERABAD: WEST INDIES vs ZIMBABWE
GROUP A WEST INDIES WON BY SIX WICKETS

The 1996 World Cup was struggling to provide exciting contests in its early stages and this one-sided affair in front of 27,000 enthusiasts in Hyderabad only raised the pulse rate in fits and starts, too. Fortunately a sparkling cameo by Brian Lara in his first match for the West Indies since his self-imposed exile gave the crowd something to cheer.

That it was no more than a 43-minute exhibition can be attributed to Zimbabwe not setting a significant challenge to the talented left-hander or his team. Andy Flower had taken first use of a sound surface, forcing the West Indies to bat under lights, but Zimbabwe were unimpressive throughout. They scored at barely three per over for the full 50 overs, losing wickets regularly along the way, three of them to unnecessary run outs.

Curtley Ambrose's opening over cost nine runs, including three of the four wides that were sent down during the innings. He was quickly back on target and soon had Andy Flower caught behind, the first of three wickets in a Man of the Match-winning performance. Once his brother had gone, Grant Flower batted with some fluency, hitting six fours in 70 minutes which took total to 1-53 with Guy Whittall.

After the second Flower had been removed by Otis Gibson, Whittall's errors of judgement got Zimbabwe into trouble. He called Alistair Campbell through for a short single to mid wicket and Lara's direct hit throw found him short of his ground. Next, Whittall went for a second run to a Gibson misfield at third man, tripped on the bowler, Ian Bishop's heel, dropped his bat and was beaten by the throw back to Courtney Browne. Three wickets had fallen for five runs between the19th and 22nd overs leaving Zimbabwe to haul themselves back from 4-58.

They did so ever so slowly. Dave Houghton had confessed after a 1992 game that sometimes against high-class bowling Zimbabwean batsmen thought of little else but survival. They were doing so again. Ian Bishop was hardly touched, Roger Harper's off-spin was almost as economical and when Amborse tried a poorly executed slower ball Eddo Brandes picked out Shivnarine Chanderpaul at deep square leg. A couple of hard chances were put down and Zimbabwe were not bowled out, but the West Indies' requirement was an unthreatening 152.

Richie Richardson opened with Sherwin Campbell and the pair moved freely to 78 before Paul Strang had Richardson caught by Alistair Campbell. That brought in Lara, who was immediately into his stride. Campbell stayed with him until, just short of his 50, he failed to pick a Paul Strang wrong 'un. The leg-spinner then picked up Chanderpaul and Arthurton with another wrong 'un.

Strang had four wickets including three in seven balls. Even Lara was troubled enough to give a chance to slip. However, 4-136 chasing 151 is hardly cause for panic and Lara already had the measure of the medium pacers. He pulled Heath Streak mightily for six, and drove Brandes in that exquisite and inimitable style twice through covers for four.

The crowd chanted for more and Lara turned his attention to Strang. He drove him down the ground for four then two balls later lofted him over mid off for six to finish the match in the most decisive fashion possible. The prodigal had returned and rushed his side to victory with 20 overs to spare.

ZIMBABWE		WEST INDIES	
A. Flower (wk/capt) c Browne b Ambrose	3	S. L. Campbell b Strang	47
G. W. Flower c & b Gibson	31	R. B. Richardson (capt) c Campbell b Strang	32
G. J. Whittall run out	14	B. C. Lara not out	43
A. D. R. Campbell run out	0	S. Chanderpaul b Strang	8
A. C. Waller st Browne b Harper	21	K. L. T. Arthurton c Campbell b Strang	1
C. N. Evans c Browne b Ambrose	21	R. A. Harper not out	5
S. G. Davies run out	9	Extras b5 lb3 w10 nb1	19
H. H. Streak lbw b Walsh	7	(29.3 overs)	4-155
P. A. Strang not out	22	Did not bat: O. D. Gibson, C. O. Browne (wk), I. R. Bishop,	
E. A. Brandes c Chanderpaul b Ambrose	7	C. E. L. Ambrose, C. A. Walsh	
A. C. I. Lock not out	1	1/78 2/115 3/123 4/136	
Extras lb10 w4 nb1	15	Bowling: Streak 7-0-34-0; Lock 6-0-23-0; Brandes 7-0-42-0;	
(50 overs)	9-151	Whittall 2-0-8-0; Strang 7.3-1-40-4	

1/11 2/53 3/56 4/58 5/91 6/103 7/115 8/125 9/142

Bowling: Ambrose 10-2-28-3; Walsh 10-3-27-1;
Gibson 9-1-27-1; Bishop 10-3-18-0; Harper 10-1-30-1;
Arthurton 1-0-11-0

Umpires:R.S. Dunne S. Venkataraghaven

Toss:Zimbabwe   Points:West Indies 2 Zimbabwe 0

SATURDAY 17 FEBRUARY 1996
I.P.C.L.SPORTS COMPLEX GROUND, BARODA: NETHERLANDS vs NEW ZEALAND
GROUP B
NEW ZEALAND WON BY 119 RUNS

The lure of World Cup cricket was apparent as 20,000 turned up to witness still another one-sided contest between a fully fledged Test nation and ICC up and comers. New Zealand and Holland probably both got out of the game what they had hoped for. One a comfortable victory and two points, the other a respectable batting performance that lasted 50 overs.

Holland made a great start after Lee Germon had won the toss and batted when Tim de Leede ran out Nathan Astle from cover point in the second over of the day. Wednesday's century maker had been disposed of for a duck and hopes of Dutch dominance flickered. They were brief. Craig Spearman and Stephen Fleming soon took control. Neither Roland Lefebvre nor Paul Jan Bakker were able to stem the run flow that realised 118 runs in 19 overs. Spearman impressed with his eight boundaries in 59 balls, developing enough confidence in the later stages to employ the reverse sweep profitably. He was the next batsman dismissed, holing out to Bas Zuiderent at long off from a Steve Lubbers off-spinner. On 155, the Dutch captain snared Fleming in identical fashion to give the 18-year-old Zuiderent his second catch. Ten runs later Roger Twose became too ambitious. Marcel Schewe completed the stumping and Lubbers had a third victim.

Chris Cairns and Adam Parore paused, consolidated, then when the time was right kick started the innings again. They hit sixes as a matter of course, five between them as 88 runs were added for the fifth wicket. Cairns got to his 50 in 38 balls. Parore took a little longer, ensuring with his captain, that 300 would be attained.

A number of the Dutch players were suffering from stomach disorders and they seemed to lack the energy for such an imposing chase, let alone the skill. Peter Cantrell and Roland Lefebvre joint top scored and handled the Kiwi attack capably enough. Cantrell, who took two excellent gully catches as a sub in the Brisbane Ashes Test of 1990-91, held the top of the innings together and hit five fours.

Chris Harris was back to his medium-paced best form of 1992 and at 5-102 the Dutch innings might have been swept away. Klaas van Noortwijk, at first supporting Lefebvre, went a long way towards ensuring it was not. The Man of the Match adjudicator considered Spearman's innings had been the best of the four half centurion contenders for the day's award.

NEW ZEALAND		NETHERLANDS	
C. M. Spearman c Zuiderent b Lubbers	68	N. E. Clarke b Kennedy	14
N. J. Astle run out	0	P. E. Cantrell c Astle b Harris	45
S. P. Fleming c Zuiderent b Lubbers	66	G. J.A. F. Aponso c Astle b Harris	11
R. G. Twose st Schewe b Lubbers	25	S. W. Lubbers(capt) run out	5
C. L. Cairns b Cantrell	52	R. P. Lefebvre b Kennedy	45
A. C. Parore c Clarke b Aponso	55	T. B.M. de Leede lbw b Harris	1
C. Z. Harris c Schewe b Bakker	8	K. J. van Noortwijk not out	36
L. K. Germon (wk/capt) not out	14	M. Schewe(wk) st Germon b Fleming	12
D. N. Patel c Schewe b Bakker	11	B. Zuiderent not out	1
D. K. Morrison not out	0	Extras b3 lb5 w8 nb2	18
Extras lb7 w1	8	(50 overs)	7-188
(50 overs)	8-307	Did not bat: E. Gouka, P. J. Bakker	

Did not bat: R. J. Kennedy

1/1 2/119 3/155 4/165 5/253 6/279 7/292 8/306

Bowling: Lefebvre 10-0-47-0; Bakker 10-0-51-2; de Leede 7-0-58-0; Aponso 10-0-61-1; Lubbers 9-0-48-3; Cantrell 4-0-35-1;

1/18 2/52 3/66 4/100 5/102 6/147 7/181

Bowling: Morrison 4-1-11-0; Kennedy 10-2-36-2; Cairns 7-1-24-0; Harris 10-1-24-3; Patel 10-0-43-0; Astle 5-0-20-0; Fleming 2-0-8-1; Twose 2-0-14-0

Umpires: Khizar Hayat I.D. Robinson

Toss: New Zealand   Points: New Zealand 2 Holland 0

R.PREMADASA STADIUM, COLOMBO: SRI LANKA vs AUSTRALIA - GROUP A
SRI LANKA WON ON FORFEIT

The Australians spent the Saturday of their first scheduled match of the World Cup at leisure in Bombay. They had held firm to their boycott after the bomb blast of January 31st in Colombo which killed 80 people. The Sri Lankan Board threatened to sue the Australian and West Indian Boards for compensation. The Sri Lankan side had net practice at the ground. It was enough to take points off Australia in the World Cup for the first time.

Umpires: Mahboob Shah C.J.Mitchley

Points: Sri Lanka 2 Australia 0

SUNDAY FEBRUARY 18th 1996
BARABATI STADIUM, CUTTACK: INDIA vs KENYA - GROUP A
INDIA WON BY 7 WICKETS

This was a day when almost everyone went home happy. The capacity crowd got the entertainment and result they wanted, the former through a great Sachin Tendulkar century, the latter through a seven-wicket win. The Kenyans, although comfortably beaten, were not disgraced and at one point in their innings had worked their way to 2-161.

Mohammad Azharuddin, in his 200th limited-over international, won the toss and sent Kenya in. As with other captains so far in this competition who elected to bowl, Azharuddin did not get the early breakthroughs he might have hoped for. Dipak Chudasama was soon in to his stride striking five boundaries in the first hour of play as Javagal Srinath and Manoj Prabhakar failed to make inroads.

Steve Tikolo, coming in at number three, was also largely untroubled and dominated the scoring in a 96 run partnership with his captain, Maurice Odumbe, for the third wicket. Tikolo hit four fours and an off driven six off left-arm spinner Venkatapathy Raju during his 83 ball innings.

When Raju finally deceived him, Tikolo left the Barabati Stadium to a standing ovation from 30,000 fans. It was Raju and fellow spinner, Anil Kumble who stemmed the run flow once Tikolo was gone.

India needed exactly 200 to win and openers Tendulkar and Ajay Jadeja got 163 of them. At times Jadeja must have felt like just another one of the 30,000 spectators as his 22-year-old partner raced to 50 in 48 balls. The 100 was up by the 20th over and the stand had lasted 33 overs when a tiring Jadeja, four fours and a six in 85 balls, was caught on the boundary off Aasif Karim. There was a slight stutter as Navjot Sidhu and Vinod Kambli failed and Tendulkar was temporarily stalled on 99. Then, once he had reached the milestone, away he went again. He had thrilled all concerned with 15 fours and a six in 134 balls, when Nayan Mongia struck the winning boundary off Odumbe with eight overs to spare.

Tendulkar in his 102nd limited-over international had completed his first World Cup century and was not a difficult choice as Man of the Match.

KENYA		INDIA	
D. Chudasama c Mongia b Prasad	29	A. D. Jadeja c Ali b Karim	53
K. O. Otieno (wk) c Mongia b Raju	27	S. R. Tendulkar not out	127
S. O. Tikolo c Kumble b Raju	65	N. S. Sidhu c Suji b S. O. Tikolo	1
M. O. Odumbe (capt) st Mongia b Kumble	26	V. G. Kambli c D. Tikolo b M. O. Odumbe	2
H. Modi c Jadeja b Kumble	2	N. R. Mongia (wk) not out	8
T. M. Odoyo c Prabhakar b Kumble	8	Extras b3 w7 nb2	12
E. Odumbe not out	15	(41.5 overs)	3-203
A. V. Karim not out	6	Did not bat: M. Azharuddin (capt) M. Prabhakar J. Srinath	
Extras b2 lb11 w7 nb1	21	A. Kumble B. K.V. Prasad S. L.V. Raju	
(50 overs)	6-199	1/163 2/167 3/182	
Did not bat: D. Tikolo, M. Suji, R. Ali		Bowling: E. Odumbe 3-0-18-0; Suji 5-0-20-0;	
1/41 2/65 3/161 4/161 5/165 6/184		Karim 10-1-27-1; Odoyo 3-0-22-0; Ali 5-0-25-0; S.	
Bowling: Prabhakar 5-1-19-0; Srinath 10-0-38-0;		O. Tikolo 3-0-26-1; M. O. Odumbe 9.5-1-41-1; D.	
Prasad 10-0-41-1; Kumble 10-2-28-3; Raju 10-2-34-2;		Tikolo 3-0-21-0	
Tendulkar 5-0-26-0			

Umpires: K.T. Francis D.R. Shepherd

Toss: India   Points: India 2 Kenya 0

SUNDAY 18 FEBRUARY 1996
SHAHI BAGH STADIUM, PESHAWAR: ENGLAND vs UAE - GROUP B
ENGLAND WON BY 8 WICKETS

It was a sad reflection of another Wills World Cup mismatch that the day's most spectacular event was the unfortunate Man of the Match, Neil Smith, being sick on the side of the pitch. It was something his father, Mike Smith, a former England captain on a tour of India, was not renowned for doing.

This one-sided affair was a throw back to the matches between the major and minor sides of 1975 and failed to attract much attention from the citizens of Peshawar who, living so close to the Khyber Pass and the North West Frontier, often have a fair bit going on in their lives anyway. The strict fast of Ramadan might have discouraged a few from going to the cricket, as well. As a mark of respect to their hosts, both teams left the field to have their drinks break.

Phil DeFreitas back in the side on his 30th birthday snared the first two wickets in an impressive opening spell after Sultan Zarawani had won the toss and batted on a dry cracked pitch. Craig White broke down with an intercostal muscle strain and Mazhar Hussain struck some boundaries so that UAE reached 2-48, but the runs dried up once the spinners could bowl to a spread field. At one stage six runs were scored off 11 overs. Vijay Mehra batted 44 minutes for 1, being the first of three victims for off-spinning Smith in eight balls.

After 25 overs, UAE were 5-49 and only hard work by Johanne Samarasekera and Shaukat Dukanwala got the total past 100 and made the innings last until the 49th over. Sultan Zarawani still refusing to wear a helmet avoided further threats to his skull, but was hardly more successful with the bat than against South Africa.

Before succumbing to the affects of a dodgy reheated pizza, Smith gave the England reply a brisk start with four boundaries in 31 balls. Even the absence of Robin Smith and Graeme Hick through injury was not going to disturb England's march to victory against the UAE attack. While Neil Smith recovered his composure and health, Graham Thorpe scored the bulk of the remaining runs needed for the two points. He hit five fours, the win coming with a comfortable 15 overs to spare.

Mike Atherton said, "These games have a strange pressure of their own." Maybe so, but only the players felt it. Perhaps he was referring to the pressure build up inside poor Neil Smith.

UNITED ARAB EMIRATES		ENGLAND	
Azhar Saeed lbw b DeFreitas	9	A. J. Stewart c Mylvaganam b Laiq	23
G. Mylvaganam c Fairbrother b DeFreitas	0	N. M.K. Smith retired ill	27
Mazhar Hussain b Smith	33	G. P. Thorpe not out	44
V. Mehra c Russell b Smith	1	M. A. Atherton (capt) b Azhar	20
Mohammad Aslam b Gough	23	N. H. Fairbrother not out	12
Arshad Laiq b Smith	0	Extras b4 lb2 w2 nb6	14
Salim Raza b Cork	10	(35 overs)	3-140
J. A.Samasekera run out	29	Did not bat: R. C.Russell (wk), C. White, D. G. Cork,	
Sultan M. Zarawani (capt) b Cork	2	P. A. J. DeFreitas, D. Gough, R. K.Illingworth	
S. Dukanwala lbw b Illingworth	15	1/52 2/109	
Imtiaz Abbasi not out	1	Smith retired at 1-57	
Extras b4 lb4 w4 nb1	13	Bowling: Samarasekera 7-1-35-0; Laiq 7-0-25-1;	
(48.3 overs)	136	Raza 5-1-20-0; Azhar 10-1-26-1; Zarawani 6-0-28-0	
1/2 2/32 3/48 4/49 5/49 6/80 7/88 8/100 9/135			
Bowling: Cork 10-1-33-2; DeFreitas 9.3-3-16-2;			
Gough 8-3-23-1; White 1.3-1-2-0; Smith 9.3-2-29-3;			
Illingworth 10-2-25-1			

Umpires: B.C. Cooray V.K. Ramaswamy

Toss: UAE   Points: England 2 UAE 0

TUESDAY 20 FEBRUARY 1996
IQBAL STADIUM, FAISALABAD: NEW ZEALAND vs SOUTH AFRICA - GROUP B
SOUTH AFRICA WON BY 5 WICKETS

This poorly attended, one-sided contest at least gave an indication of who might be the team to beat from Group B. South Africa's cool and efficient demolition of New Zealand showed their accurate and powerful bowling and brilliant outcricket was superior to anything their five preliminary-round competitors might offer. From the moment Nathan Astle was run out at the bowler's end in the third over of the day South Africa were on top and there they stayed throughout.

Even though Ramadan was officially over the players still took their drinks off the ground. In the press box they complained that the Coca-Cola was warm. Lee Germon won the toss, batted, then found one of his openers, Craig Spearmen, and possibly the TV replay umpire, burned his partner.

Astle's early sacrifice was his second in as many matches. "A couple of freak incidents, I hope," he said later.

After striking three boundaries Spearman was caught behind off Chris Matthews. His dismissal left New Zealand 2-17. A superb slips catch by Brian McMillan removed Roger Twose and made it 3-36. If that was the feature catch Gary Kirsten's pin point throw from deep square leg and Jonty Rhodes athleticism at cover were the ground fielding highlights. They resulted in the direct hit run outs of Chris Harris and Adam Parore and left New Zealand on a rather dispiriting 7-116.

Shane Thompson and Germon ensured the avoidance of total embarrassment. Germon batted through to the completion of the 50 overs, but could do no more than push towards respectability. Allan Donald allowed no freedom at the end of the Kiwi innings while off-spinner Pat Symcox had been very economical.

Any hopes New Zealand harboured of protecting 177 must have evaporated when, they had dropped both South African openers by the third over of their reply. The total was 41 in the 10th over when Danny Morrison bowled Steve Palframan.

The wicketkeeper had opened in place of Andrew Hudson. He did his job well in that when Hansie Cronje came in it seemed as if the sting had gone out of the bowling. The South African captain unleashed a brutal assault on the Kiwi attack, especially the medium pacers who had been so effective four years before. Gavin Larsen, went for 18 in an over as Cronje hit 11 fours and three sixes in 64 balls. One of those sixes off Thompson's off-spin, raised Cronje's 50 in just 36 balls.

By the time he holed out off Nathan Astle his side were within 32 runs of victory and had more than 20 overs left to get them. There were no other fireworks and a couple more wickets fell, however the result was never in doubt. The Proteas won by five wickets half way through the 38th over. Cronje, who took the time to say a few phrases to the crowd in Urdu was named Man of the Match. The South African coach, Bob Woolmer felt his side put on an awesome display, "The best since I've been in charge."

NEW ZEALAND		SOUTH AFRICA	
C. M. Spearman c Palframan b Matthews	14	G. Kirsten lbw b Harris	35
N. J. Astle run out	1	S. J. Palframan b Morrison	16
S. P. Fleming b McMillan	33	W. J. Cronje (capt) c Fleming b Astle	78
R. G. Twose c McMillan b Pollock	13	D. J. Cullinan c Thomson b Astle	27
C. L. Cairns b Donald	9	J. H. Kallis not out	11
A. C. Parore run out	27	J. N. Rhodes c & b Larsen	9
C. Z. Harris run out	8	B. M. McMillan not out	2
S. A. Thomson c Cronje b Donald	28	Extras 0	
L. K. Germon (wk/capt) not out	31	(37.3 overs)	5-178
G. R. Larsen c Cullinan b Donald	1	Did not bat: S. M. Pollock, C. R. Matthews, P. L. Symcox,	
D. K. Morrison not out	5	A. A. Donald	
Extras lb5 nb2	7	1/41 2/87 3/146 4/159 5/170	
(50 overs)	9-177	Bowling: Morrison 8-0-44-1; Cairns 6-0-24-0;	
1/7 2/17 3/36 4/54 5/85 6/103 7/116 8/158 9/165		Larsen 8-1-41-1; Harris 4-0-25-1;	
Bowling: Pollock 10-1-44-1; Matthews 10-2-30-1;		Thomson 8.3-0-34-0; Astle 3-1-10-2	
Donald 10-0-34-3; Cronje 3-0-13-0; Symcox 10-1-25-0;			
McMillan 7-1-26-1			

Umpires: S.G. Randell S. Venkataraghaven

Toss: New Zealand   Points: South Africa 2 New Zealand 0

WEDNESDAY 21 FEBRUARY 1996
SINHALESE SPORTS CLUB, COLOMBO:
SRI LANKA vs ZIMBABWE, GROUP A
SRI LANKA WON BY 6 WICKETS

At last World Cup cricket came to Sri Lanka and their fans embraced it with fervour. No wonder. Two of their batsmen turned on an exhilerating exhibition of power stroke play, which broke national records and to some extent brought the competition to life.

This was not quite the run feast of New Plymouth 1992, but by putting on 172 in 27 overs Aravinda de Silva and Asanka Gurusinha kept everyone in attendance royally entertained to a similar degree. Zimbabwe, being prepared to travel to Colombo, were popular visitors. They were given tight and vigilant security and played the game in a fine spirit. They left without two points, though, and that would have disappointed them.

Zimbabwe batted first when Andy Flower won the toss and on a good wicket it took a long time for them to get going. Unfortunately, both opening Flower brothers were run out. Andy was the first to go, victim of a direct hit throw by Chaminda Vaas. Steve Dunne, from New Zealand, who gave the decision had not been certain to travel to Sri Lanka, either. Andy Flower might have been happier if he had not come. Dunne gave the Zimbabwean captain out without checking with the replay, which suggested Flower had actually made his ground. Guy Whittall rather than the umpire was to blame for Grant Flower's run out.

A couple of other decisions indicated Dunne might not have been entirely at ease with his situation on this particular day. Alistair Campbell was, however, and it was the big left-hander who gave the Zimbabwean innings some impetus. That came after Muttiah Muralitharan had been joyously welcomed to the bowling crease by his home fans. The unorthodox off-spinner, recently called for throwing in Australia, then had Guy Whittall caught at long on to make the Zimbabwean total 3-92.

Campbell added 68 with Andy Waller and went on to finish with an accomplished 75, which contained seven fours in 102 balls. Supplemented by some effective late over work by Craig Evans, Zimbabwe were able to set Sri Lanka a respectable target of 229.

It looked more than respectable when Heath Streak removed both openers by the fifth over. The Zimbabwean paceman's first ball of the innings had gone for four wides, and indeed his opening over cost 11 runs. In the middle of it, though, Romesh Kaluwitharana, suffering from cramp but declining a runner, slogged a catch to mid-on. Sanath Jayasuriya also went cheaply before de Silva and Gurusinha began their display.

They treated all bowlers with the same disrespect. Leg-spinner Paul Strang made no impact this time, going for more than eight per over. Gurusinha was brutal at times. He struck six powerful sixes, five of them straight hits between long off and long on. He brought up the 100 with his variation on a six hitting theme, a big pull over mid wicket off Streak. Gurusinha's sixth six equalled the World Cup record held by Viv Richards and Kapil Dev.

De Silva's innings was more cultured and contained only two blows over the boundary, although the first, a trademark pull off Charlie Lock was perhaps the shot of the game and the stroke that ignited the Sri Lankans. Although still recovering from a side strain suffered in Australia, he also struck ten fours in addition to his two sixes, compiling the highest score ever by a Sri Lankan in a World Cup match.

Both batsmen missed their 100s. Gurusinha was run out because he was so exhausted he couldn't make the crease in time. De Silva was given out lbw 14 runs later to the disappointment of the crowd, although it did not deny him his Man of the Match Award. That gave Streak his third wicket, a good return spoilt by the number of wides he sent down. The Zimbabweans won more plaudits when they stayed on the field through drizzle towards the end of the game. The Sri Lankans celebrated their victory with 13 overs to spare.

ZIMBABWE		SRI LANKA	
A. Flower (wk/capt) run out	8	S. T. Jayasuriya b Streak	6
G. W.Flower run out	15	R. S. Kaluwitharana (wk) c Peall b Streak	0
G. J.Whittall c Jayasuriya b Muralitharan	35	A. P. Gurusinha run out	87
A. D. R. Campbell c Muralitharan b Vaas	75	P. A. de Silva lbw b Streak	91
A. C.Waller b Jayasuriya	19	A. Rantunga(capt) not out	13
C. N.Evans not out	39	H. P. Tillekeratne not out	7
H. H.Streak c de Silva b Vaas	15	Extras lb5 w17 nb3	25
P. A.Strang not out	0	(37 overs)	4-229
Extras b1 lb16 w4 nb1	22	Did not bat: R. S. Mahanama, H. D. P. K. Dharmasena,	
(50 overs)	6-228	W. P. U. J. C. Vaas, G. P. Wickremasinghe, M. Muralitharan	
Did not bat: S. G.Peall, E. A.Brandes, A. C. I. Lock		1/5 2/23 3/195 4/209	
1/19 2/51 3/92 4/160 5/194 6/227		Bowling: Streak 10-0-60-3; Lock 4-0-17-0; Peall 3-0-23-0;	
Bowling: Vaas 10-0-30-2; Wickremasinghe 8-0-36-0;		Brandes 8-0-35-0; Strang 5-0-43-0; Whittall 2-0-20-0; G. W.	
Ranatunga 2-0-14-0; Muralitharan 10-0-37-1;		Flower 5-1-26-0	
Dharmasena 10-0-50-0; Jayasuriya 10-0-44-1			

Umpires: R.S. Dunne Mahboob Shah

Toss: Zimbabwe   Points: Sri Lanka 2 Zimbabwe 0

CAPTAIN ROOP SINGH STADIUM, GWALIOR: INDIA vs WEST INDIES - GROUP A
INDIA WON BY 5 WICKETS

Under lights that highlighted the smoke from fireworks and torches, India secured an important victory, which kept them apace with Sri Lanka. The game was noisily supported in large numbers, the natural attraction of a contest between the co-hosts and their high-profile opponents, the West Indies being boosted to even greater levels by publicity for the 'Lara vs Tendulkar' batting shoot out.

Brian Lara, greeted on the ground by many cheers and the odd racist taunt, was an early casualty and India eventually had a comfortable win. So that turned into a 'fizzer', yet there were few complaints, thanks to a win and a Man of the Match innings by Sachin Tendulkar.

Richie Richardson won the toss, batted, said he was looking for 300 and faced the new ball himself with Sherwin Campbell. He soon lost his Barbadian partner to Javagal Srinath whose movement and bounce troubled the batsmen in an opening spell of 2-14 from seven overs. The big blow to the West Indies was the loss of Lara in the sixth over, given out caught behind down the leg-side by Pakistani umpire Khizar Hayat, a decision over which there was some doubt. Richardson and Shivnarine Chanderpaul responded with a solid stand that took the score to 2-91, then the captain's dismissal heralded the loss of three wickets in 12 balls.

Roger Harper hit a six and put on 42 with wicketkeeper, Courtney Browne before there was another three-wicket-in-12-balls collapse, Anil Kumble's leg-spin doing its share of the damage. The West Indian fast bowlers battled through until the final ball of the innings. A total of 173 was still short of Richardson's projected target.

The loss of 8-82 meant the batting frailties of 1992 still existed in the West Indian line-up and against virtually any other attack 173 on good wicket would have been quite inadequate. It would prove so again this time, bit did not appear so when Curtley Ambrose beat Ajay Jadeja for pace in the first over and did likewise to Navjot Sidhu in the third.

The West Indies could have further undermined the Indians from 2-15. Tendulkar on 12 was dropped at square leg then on 22 in the 10th over he skied a leg-side shot which dollied in the air only for wicketkeeper Browne to fumble it. That allowed the young star to put on 79 in 16 overs with Mohammad Azharuddin and another 31 with Vinod Kambli after his captain was caught in the deep. Tendulkar got to 70 in 91 balls with eight fours when he was run out following a mix-up with his old schoolmate, Kambli.

Harper caught Prabhakar off his own bowling to briefly revive West Indian hopes. Kambli and Nayan Mongia soon quashed those, taking runs with some ease off Otis Gibson and in his later overs, Ambrose.

WEST INDIES		INDIA	
S. L. Campbell b Srinath	5	A. D. Jadeja b Ambrose	1
R. B. Richardson (capt) c Kambli b Prabhakar	47	S. R. Tendulkar run out	70
B. C. Lara c Mongia b Srinath	2	N. S. Sidhu b Ambrose	1
S. Chanderpaul c Azharuddin b Kapoor	38	M. Azharuddin (capt) c Walsh b Harper	32
R. I.C. Holder b Kumble	0	V. G. Kambli not out	33
R. A. Harper b Kumble	23	M. Prabhakar c & b Harper	1
C. O. Browne (wk) b Prabhakar	18	N. R. Mongia (wk) not out	24
O. D. Gibson b Kumble	6	Extras lb3 w1 nb8	12
I. R. Bishop run out	9	(39.4 overs)	5-174
C. E. L. Ambrose c Kumble b Prabhakar	8	Did not bat: A. R.Kapoor, A. Kumble, J. Srinath,	
C. A. Walsh not out	9	B. K.V. Prasad	
Extras lb2 w5 nb1	8	1/2 2/15 3/94 4/125 5/127	
(50 overs)	173	Bowling: Ambrose 8-1-41-2; Walsh 9-3-18-0;	
1/16 2/24 3/91 4/99 5/99 6/141 7/149		Bishop 5-0-28-0; Gibson 8.4-0-50-0; Harper 9-1-34-2	
Bowling: Prabhakar 10-0-39-3; Srinath 10-0-22-2;			
Kumble 10-0-35-3; Prasad 10-0-34-0; Kapoor 10-2-41-1			

Umpires: Khizar Hayat I.D.Robinson

Toss: West Indies   Points: India 2 West Indies 0

THURSDAY 22 FEBRUARY 1996
SHAHI BAGH STADIUM, PESHAWAR: ENGLAND vs NETHERLANDS - GROUP B
ENGLAND WON BY 49 RUNS

A 500-run day was watched by a healthier Peshawar gathering than the one attending the previous Sunday when UAE were accounted for. Their reward was some energetic batting from both sides.

The first all-European World Cup cricket match saw England bat first and run up what turned out to be a match-winning total after Mike Atherton had won the toss. The captain, batting down the order, missed out again, bowled dab cutting at Steve Lubbers and Alec Stewart provided Paul Jan Bakker with an early wicket. Neil Smith was back to reasonably robust health and it was his 31 in 33 balls which took advantage of the early fielding restrictions. Once he had been caught by Nolan Clarke, Graeme Hick and Graham Thorpe tore the Dutch attack apart.

Hick gave two hard chances with flat batted drives. Otherwise he was his usual assertive self against second string bowling. He was still not quite as impressive as Thorpe who belted seven fours and a six in 82 balls on way to 89. Thorpe scored the majority of the runs in a 25 over partnership with Hick worth 143 for the third wicket. A hundred beckoned for the Surrey left-hander until Roland Lefebvre, bravely struggling against injury, had an lbw shout upheld.

It was Hick, picking up the tempo with Neil Fairbrother towards the end of the innings, who did reach three figures. He had rested his strained hamstring against UAE, and showed no ill effects here as he raised his second 100 in limited-over internationals with a big six off Bakker. It was his second six in 133 balls and came in the 50th over of the innings.

Dominic Cork, despite being too sharp for the 47-year-old opener Clarke, conceded plenty of runs, including wides and no balls and it was left to the altogether more accurate DeFreitas to reduce Holland to 4-81.

Tim de Leede had stroked his way impressively to a run per ball 41, but it was left to Klaas van Noortwijk and 18-year-old Bas Zuiderent to show the gap in class between the two sides was not so marked. They put on 114 for the fifth wicket in 27 overs. England's left-arm spinner, Richard Illingworth, had pulled out of the side with a stomach upset and the young Dutchmen relished the diet of medium pace and off-spin. They both completed half centuries, their country's first in limited-over internationals. Van Noortwijk once deposited Peter Martin deep into the cheering crowd.

Top-order batsman Flavian Alponso was another down with stomach trouble and the required run rate was always demanding. When Martin had van Noortwijk caught in the deep and Zuiderent taken by Thorpe the sting went out of the game. Hick was named Man of the Match.

ENGLAND		NETHERLANDS	
A. J. Stewart b Bakker	5	N. E. Clarke lbw b Cork	0
N. M.K. Smith c Clarke b Jansen	31	P. E. Cantrell lbw b DeFreitas	28
G. A. Hick not out	104	T. B.M. de Leede lbw b DeFreitas	41
G. P. Thorpe lbw b Lefebrve	89	S. W. Lubbers (capt) c Russell b DeFreitas	9
M. A. Atherton (capt) b Lubbers	10	K. J. van Noortwijk c Gough b Martin	64
N. H. Fairbrother not out	24	B. Zuiderent c Thorpe b Martin	54
Extras lb12 w4	16	R. P. Lefebrve not out	11
(50 overs)	4-279	M. Schewe (wk) not out	11
Did not bat: R. C. Russell (wk), D. G. Cork, D. Gough,		Extras lb4 w6 nb2	12
P. A. J. DeFreitas, P. J. Martin		(50 overs)	6-230
1/11 2/42 3/185 4/212		Did not bat: G. J. A. F. Aponso, F. Jansen, P. J. Bakker	
Bowling: Lefebvre 10-1-40-1; Bakker 8-0-46-1;		1/1 2/46 3/70 4/81 5/195 6/208	
Jansen 7-0-40-1; Aponso 8-0-55-0; Lubbers 10-0-51-1; de		Bowling: Cork 8-0-52-1; DeFreitas 10-3-31-3;	
Leede 2-0-9-0; Cantrell 5-0-26-0		Smith 8-0-27-0; Gough 3-0-23-0; Martin 10-1-42-2;	
		Hick 5-0-23-0; Thorpe 6-0-28-0	

Umpires: S.A.Bucknor K.T.Francis

Toss: England   Points: England 2 Holland 0

FRIDAY 23 FEBRUARY 1996
INDIRA PRIYADARSHINI MUNICIPAL CRICKET GROUND, VISAKHAPATNAM: AUSTRALIA vs KENYA - GROUP A
AUSTRALIA WON BY 97 RUNS

Finally, a week after the start of the Wills World Cup, Australia got themselves onto a cricket field. It was hardly a major fixture at the Indian east coast venue, which is more than a mouthful for anyone not conversant with the local dialect, but still refocused attention away from boycotts, security and various perceived threats.

Mark Taylor's side would have been grateful to be able to get rid of a few cobwebs without massive pressure being exerted upon them by Kenya. While the Kenyans at no stage looked like pulling off the surprise their fellow Africans, Zimbabwe achieved in 1983, they kept apace with their highly rated opponents at various stages of the match and went down fighting.

Maurice Odumbe decided to bowl after he won the toss and Martin Suji and Rajab Ali responded by removing Mark Taylor and Ricky Ponting by the eighth over, leaving Australia 2-26. Mark and Steve Waugh were also beaten more than once early in their innings. Once they had become accustomed to the bowling, the lack of pace in the wicket and the heat, they established what became a record-breaking and match-winning partnership.

They took a heavy toll of the second string bowlers, who conceded 159 between them from 20 overs. Mark Waugh was dropped off consecutive deliveries in the 27th over. Ali at long off spilled a lofted drive and next ball wicketkeeper Kennedy Otieno got a glove to an edge. As Mark Waugh was already on 75 the misses probably did not alter the result. They did, however, allow 'Junior' Waugh to complete his first World Cup 100 and to go on to his equal highest score in a limited-over international.

He scored his 130 at just above a run per ball, often gasping for breath in the heat and humidity and hit 14 fours and a six in the process. The partnership with Steve put on 207 for the third wicket in 32 overs, the first double-century stand in the World Cup. Steve's 82 lasted 88 balls and contained five fours and one six. He drove a catch back to Suji the over after Mark had been dismissed, leaving the task of lifting the total above 300 to Stuart Law, Michael Bevan and Ian Healy.

Craig McDermott had Deepak Chudasama caught behind with a nice out-swinger at the start of the Kenyan reply only to strain a doubtful calf muscle and walk off the ground for Australia for the last time after the fifth over. Paul Reiffel then claimed the prize wicket of Steve Tikolo to leave Kenya in trouble at 2-30.

The east Africans were still not overwhelmed by their opposition as Maurice Odumbe showed when he cover drove his first ball for four. That heralded the start of an 102-run stand between the Kenyan captain and his wicketkeeper, Otieno. Steve Waugh's medium pacers were treated with some disrespect. So effective was the strokeplay of the Kenyan pair that at the halfway point of the innings their score was comparable with Australia's at the same stage.

Odumbe got to his 50 in 53 balls with seven fours, then fell to Michael Bevan's, little-known left-arm wrist spin. That was a blow to Kenya, but not as serious as the leg cramping that caused the temporary retirement of Otieno at 3-166. The wicketkeeper batsman was suffering after 85 overs straight in the heat and had to leave the field 18 short of his 100. Although he later resumed, the Kenyans never again regained their batting momentum. Otieno added only three runs before being yorked by Glenn McGrath and Shane Warne kept the runs well in check.

Otieno had hit eight fours and a six. Mark Waugh's innings, though, was the one the Man of the Match adjudicator rated the highest.

AUSTRALIA		KENYA	
M. A. Taylor (capt) c Modi b Suji	6	K. O. Otieno (wk) b McGrath	85
M. E. Waugh c Sjui b Ali	130	D. Chudasama c Healy b McDermott	5
R. T. Ponting c Otieno b Ali	6	S. O. Tikolo c Ponting b Reiffel	6
S. R. Waugh c & b Sjui	82	M. O. Odumbe (capt) c Reiffel b Bevan	50
S. G. Law run out	35	H. Modi b Bevan	10
M. G. Bevan b Ali	12	E. Odumbe c Bevan b Reiffel	14
I. A. Healy (wk) c E. Odumbe b Karim	17	D. Tikolo not out	11
P. R. Reiffel not out	3	T. M. Odoyo st Healy b Warne	10
S. K. Warne not out	0	M. Suji not out	1
Extras b1 w10 nb2	13	Extras lb7 w6 nb2	15
(50 overs)	7-304	(50 overs)	7-207

Did not bat: C. J. McDermott, G. D. McGrath

1/10 2/26 3/233 4/237 5/261 6/301 7/301

Bowling: Suji 10-1-55-2; Ali 10-0-45-3; Odoyo 8-0-58-0; E. Odumbe 4-0-21-0; Karim 10-1-54-1; M. O. Odumbe 4-0-35-0; D. Tikolo 3-0-21-0; S. O. Tikolo 1-0-14-0

Did not bat: A. V. Karim, R. Ali

1/12 2/30 3/132 4/167 5/188 6/195 7/206

Otieno retired hurt at 5/166, resumed 5/188

Bowling: McDermott 3-0-12-1; Reiffel 7-1-18-2; M. Grath 10-0-44-1; S. R. Waugh 7-0-43-0; Warne 10-0-25-1; M. E. Waugh 5-0-23-0; Bevan 8-0-35-2

Umpires: C.J. Mitchley D.R. Shepherd

Toss: Kenya   Points: Australia 2 Kenya 0

SATURDAY 24 FEBRUARY 1996
JINAH STADIUM, GUJRANWALA: PAKISTAN vs UAE - GROUP B
PAKISTAN WON BY 9 WICKETS

Pakistan had taken even longer than Australia to get onto a cricket ground in the World Cup. Their delay was because of the fast of Ramadan rather than fear of bombs. Like the Australians, Pakistan's opening fixture almost amounted to a warm up and they had no trouble at all disposing of an inept UAE side.

Heavy overnight rain in the northern Pakistani city left the roads to the Jinah Stadium difficult and muddy and the outfield so saturated the match could not start until 12.15pm. It had to be reduced to 33 overs per side. Pakistan included Javed Miandad. The 38-year-old veteran was making his sixth appearance in a World Cup tournament being the sole survivor now from 1975. His selection was very popular at the other end of the country in Karachi.

Eventually he would not bat as Pakistan's surge to victory came very quickly at minimal cost. They had only needed 110 to win and got them in 18 overs. Sultan Zarawani had bravely suggested his side's uninhibited batting style might be suited by the overs reduction and when Salim Raza charged out of the blocks all guns blazing after UAE were sent in, it seemed he might be right. With the ball swinging around in the damp atmosphere, the opener cracked two fours and swung Wasim Akram away for a six-over square-leg in 20 balls before skying a catch to give Miandad his only real action for the game.

The only other UAE batsman to top 20 was Shaukat Dukanwala, who also hit a worthy six off Waqar Younis. In between no-one could work out the leg-spin of Man of the Match, Mushtaq Ahmed whose three wickets came in 10 balls. The first of those was his 100th in limited-over internationals. The 33rd and final over of the innings bowled by Waqar Younis was a wicket maiden.

The crowd half filled the ground and were happy at the ease of their side's progress, making plenty of wisecracks as they jumped and waved banners. They were briefly quietened when Johanne Samarasekera got through Aamir Sohail's defence in the first over. Unfortunately Samarasekera also sent down a 12-ball over as he sprayed the new ball around. Wides were plentiful and soon Saeed Anwar and Ijaz Ahmed were moving into their work. The runs began to flow with ease. They added 105 in 106 balls, Ijaz reaching his 50 just before the win was completed with 15 overs, not much less than half the allotment, to spare.

UNITED ARAB EMIRATES		PAKISTAN	
G. Mylvaganam b Mushtaq Ahmed	13	Aamir Sohail b Samarasekera	5
Salim Raza c Javed Miandad b Aaqib Javed	22	Saeed Anwar not out	40
Azhar Saeed run out	1	Ijaz Ahmed not out	50
Mazhar Hussain c Waqar Younis b Mushtaq Ahmed	7	Extras lb1 w12 nb4	17
Mohammad Aslam b Mushtaq Ahmed	5	(18 overs)	1-112
Mohammad Ishaq b Wasim Akram	12	Did not bat: Inzamam-ul-Haq, Salim Malik, Javed Miandad,
Arshad Laiq c Ijaz Ahmed b Aaqib Javed	39	Wasim Akram (capt), Rashid Latif (wk), Mushtaq Ahmed,
J. A. Samarasekera b Waqar Younis	10	Waqar Younis, Aaqib Javed
S. Dukanwala not out	21	1/7
Sultan M. Zarawani (capt) b Wasim Akram	1	Bowling: Samarasekera 3-0-17-1; Laiq 4-0-17-0;
Imtiaz Abbasi (wk) not out	0	Dukanwala 3-1-14-0; Raza 3-0-17-0; Zarawani 3-0-23-0;
Extras lb1 w5 nb2	8	Azhar 2-0-16-0
(33 overs)	9-109		

1/27 2/40 3/47 4/53 5/54 6/70 7/80 8/108 9/109

Bowling: Wasim Akram 7-1-25-2; Waqar Younis 7-0-33-1;
Aaqib Javed 6-0-18-2; Mushtaq Ahmed 7-0-16-3;
Aamir Sohail 6-0-16-0

Umpires: B.C. Cooray S. Venkataraghavan

Toss: Pakistan   Points: Pakistan 2 UAE 0

SUNDAY 25 FEBRUARY 1996
RAWALPINDI CRICKET STADIUM, RAWALPINDI: ENGLAND vs SOUTH AFRICA
GROUP B
SOUTH AFRICA WON BY 78 RUNS

Even without an incapacitated Allan Donald, the mean and lean South African bowling attack, supported by their intimidating fieldsmen, were far too good for England's batsmen who lacked confidence between bouts of carelessness. The decisive margin of defeat of 78 runs still flattered England. At one stage they had been 7-97 chasing 230.

The highest score in South Africa's 230 was 38 by opener Gary Kirsten. Yet the Proteas hardly relaxed the psychological grip they had recently built over England. It was an edge that had netted them six wins from seven starts in limited-over internationals against Mike Atherton's maligned side.

There was cloud and drizzle about when Hansie Cronje won the toss and decided to bat. Dampness had hampered England's match preparation and they had complained. That raised once more the sensitivities and disputes that raged between Pakistan and England during the 1980s and in 1992. Poor facilities had nothing to do with Robin Smith's bruised calf, which prevented him from playing yet again. Smith was struck on his unprotected leg when he decided to practice with only his front pad on.

Dominic Cork missed a skied catch off Steve Palframan, which allowed the South African openers to launch the innings with a 12-over partnership of 56. They then slipped to 3-88. Gary Kirsten was run out by Alec Stewart from mid-on and Hansie Cronje was caught behind from a Darren Gough out-swinger.

Daryll Cullinan and 20-year-old Jacques Kallis had retrieved the situation when rain held up play for 20 minutes at 3-133. Neither batsman got going again upon the resumption and it was left to Jonty Rhodes, as energetic at times with the bat as he is in the field, to ensure South Africa got above 200.

There were no easy wickets for England to the end. Fanie de Villiers, in the side for the ailing Donald, batted last and also got to double figures before falling to Gough from the last ball of the 50th over. Gough like Cork had taken two wickets, however, big Lancastrian, Peter Martin was the best performed of the English bowlers. Perhaps the cloud and drizzle made him feel like he was at home in Manchester.

Mike Atherton promoted himself back to the opening position and was promptly caught behind from the fourth ball of the innings. It was a setback from which England never really recovered. Neil Smith fell next, then the previously in-form Graeme Hick clipped a catch to Brian McMillan at mid wicket.

The recalled de Villiers had snared both of them and England were 3-33. Graham Thorpe was relishing the scrap and momentarily his Surrey teammate, Alec Stewart dug in, as well. Normal service was resumed on 52, however, when Stewart failed to ground his bat while strolling through for a single and Pat Symcox threw down the stumps from mid-on.

The off-spinner soon had Neil Fairbrother caught behind sweeping and it was 5-62. Jack Russell's determination to stay with Thorpe was already merely token resistance as the result was well in hand. Both eventually fell at 97, Thorpe at least finished with the highest individual score of the match.

DeFreitas' aggression brought him a few boundaries and allowed England to equal the score made by the UAE against South Africa 10 days earlier. He was run out when he failed to ground his bat, too. England were dismissed in the 45th over.

At the post match conference a spiky Atherton called one Pakistani journalist "a buffoon". He would have been better looking at his own team or, with no form at all, himself. He apologised the next day.

Jonty Rhodes was named Man of the Match.

SOUTH AFRICA		ENGLAND	
G. Kirsten run out	38	M. A. Atherton (capt) c Palframan b Pollock	0
S. J. Palframan (wk) c Russell b Martin	28	N. M.K. Smith b de Villiers	11
W. J. Cronje (capt) c Russell b Gough	15	G. A. Hick c McMillan b de Villiers	14
D. J. Cullinan b DeFreitas	34	G. P. Thorpe c Palframan b Symcox	46
J. H. Kallis c Russell b Cork	26	A. J. Stewart run out	7
J. N. Rhodes b Martin	37	N. H. Fairbrother c Palframan b Symcox	3
B. M. McMillan b Smith	11	R. C. Russell (wk) c Rhodes b Pollock	12
S. M. Pollock c Fairbrother b Cork	12	D. G. Cork b Matthews	17
P. L. Symcox c Thorpe b Martin	1	P. A. J. DeFreitas run out	22
C. R. Matthews not out	9	D. Gough b Matthews	11
P. S. de Villiers c Smith b Gough	12	P. J. Martin not out	1
Extras lb1 w5 nb1	7	Extras lb7 w1	8
(50 overs)	230	(44.3 overs)	152

1/56 2/85 3/88 4/137 5/163 6/195 7/199 8/202 9/213 10/230
Bowling: Cork 10-0-36-2; DeFreitas 10-0-55-1; Gough 10-0-48-2; Martin 10-0-33-3; Smith 8-0-40-1; Thorpe 2-0-17-0

1/0 2/22 3/33 4/52 5/62 6/97 7/97 8/139 9/141 10/152
Bowling: Pollock 8-1-16-2; de Villiers 7-1-27-2; Matthews 9.3-0-30-2; McMillan 6-0-17-0; Symcox 10-0-38-2; Cronje 4-0-17-0

Umpires:S.G. Randell I.D. Robinson
Toss: South Africa   Points: South Africa 2 England 0

R.PREMEDASA STADIUM, COLOMBO: SRI LANKA vs WEST INDIES- GROUP A
SRI LANKA WON ON FORFEIT

The West Indies, like Australia, held to their promise to keep away from Sri Lanka, thus handing the hosts two points and a guaranteed place in the quarter finals. They were concerned, though, that they would lack match practice as they had to wait eight days between games. The West Indies' worries centred on Brian Lara who was taking his turn to suffer stomach troubles.

MONDAY 26 FEBRUARY 1996
GADDAFI STADIUM, LAHORE: PAKISTAN vs NETHERLANDS - GROUP B
PAKISTAN WON BY 8 WICKETS

Sixteen thousand people turned up at the Gaddafi Stadium and Javed Miandad was not needed again! Perhaps it was the fault of the dodgy spaghetti that laid low half the Dutch team with diarrhoea just before the match. Their batting was very much lacking in energy. Steve Lubbers actually missed the game, but with a bad knee, not gastric difficulty. Whatever, this was a very one-sided affair that required the employment of just four Pakistani batsmen for about 30 overs to achieve the desired result for the home side.

The first mismatch after acting Dutch captain Roland Lefebvre had won the toss and batted was 47-year-old Nolan Clarke facing Wasim Akram and a fired up Waqar Younis with a swinging new ball. When Younis removed Peter Cantrell and Tim de Leede with consecutive deliveries, Holland were a desperate-looking 3-29.

A 73-run partnership between Klaas van Noortwijk and Flavian Aponso averted a rout. Both batsmen hit a six off Mushtaq Ahmed while generally batting to slow for limited-overs cricket. Aponso, a former Sri Lankan 'rebel' tourist of South Africa who worked in the Sri Lankan embassy in The Hague, went on to his half century. Younis finally bowled him and Lefebrve to make his haul four out of the seven wickets that fell.

Pakistan's ask was less than three per over and not even the enthusiastic Lefebrve claiming the early wicket of Aamir Sohail could make the task seem more than it was. After 14 overs, Pakistan were 1-34, and below the required rate. At the completion of the 15th over, the score was 1-48 and Saeed Anwar and Ijaz Ahmed had assumed control. Their urgency grew as rain clouds gathered during the afternoon. The accleration continued even when Ijaz was caught off Cantrell.

Anwar raced on to 83 off 92 balls. In addition to nine fours he hit three sixes which scattered the modest crowd as they landed. Inzamam-ul-Haq celebrated his first innings of the tournament by opening his account with a six, too. The third of Anwar's sixes, a massive strike over long on off Erik Gouka, completed the victory. The players had not long left the field when it began to rain heavily. That dampened the presentation of the Man of the Match Award to Waqar Younis.

Attendances in Pakistan remained lower than anticipated. The team may have been keeping pace with India, but their fans were behind in their commitment. With Ramadan over the blame now centred on the poor arrangements for ticket sales.

NETHERLANDS		PAKISTAN	
N. E.Clarke c Rashid Latif b Aaqib Javed	4	Aamir Sohail c Jansen b Lefebvre	9
P. E.Cantrell c Ijaz Ahmed b Waqar Younis	17	Saeed Anwar not out	83
T. B.M. de Leede c Rashid Latif b Waqar Younis	0	Ijaz Ahmed c Lefebvre b Cantrell	39
K. J. van Noortwijk c Mushtaq Ahmed b Aaqib Javed	33	Inzamam-ul-Haq not out	18
G. J.A. F.Aponso b Waqar Younis	58	Extras lb1 w1	2
R. P.Lefebvre(capt) b Waqar Younis	10	(30.4 overs)	2-151
B. Zuiderent run out	6	Did not bat: Salim Malik Javed Miandad Wasim	
E. Gouka not out	0	Akram(capt) Rashid Latif(wk)	
Extras lb7 w4 nb6	17	Mushtaq Ahmed Waqar Younis Aaqib Javed	
(50 overs)	7-145	1/10 2/104	
Did not bat: F. Jansen, M. Schewe, P. J.Bakker		Bowling: Lefebvre 7-1-20-1; Bakker 7-1-13-0;	
1/16 2/28 3/29 4/102 5/130 6/143 7/145		Jansen 2-0-22-0; de Leede 4-0-20-0; Aponso 5-0-38-0;	
Bowling: Wasim Akram 10-1-30-0; Waqar Younis 10-1-26-4;		Cantrell 4-0-18-1; Gouka 1.4-0-19-0	
Aaqib Javed 9-2-25-2; Mushtaq Ahmed 10 -2-27-0; Aamir			
Sohail 9-0-21-0; Salim Malik 2-0-9-0			

Umpires: S.A. Bucknor K.T. Francis

Toss: Holland   Points: Pakistan 2 Holland 0

MONDAY 26 and TUESDAY 27 FEBRUARY 1996
MOIN-UL-HAQ STADIUM, PATNA: KENYA vs ZIMBABWE - GROUP A
ZIMBABWE WON BY 5 WICKETS

World Cup cricket came to the city of Patna in the north-east corner of India and the locals responded with such enthusiasm that they were rewarded with two matches for price of one.

The 30,000 who turned up on the Monday only saw 95 balls bowled, but they received, at no extra charge a close encounter with a helicopter. The flying machine with the giant fan had been brought in to help the drying when rain soaked the ground after an hour's cricket. It had been a good hour for Kenya and in particular, Edward Odumbe, too.

Andy Flower had won the toss for Zimbabwe and in cloudy conditions elected to bat. He sent in Andy Waller to open with his brother, Grant Flower, probably to reduce his own onerous duties as captain, wicketkeeper and batsman. The move did not succeed as Rajab Ali quickly made the first breakthrough. Edward Odumbe then had Guy Whittall caught by brother and captain, Maurice and trapped Alistair Campbell lbw first ball. It was only the 16th over and Andy Flower had to come in, anyway. As it turned out that was as far as the cricket got on the Monday.

Once the rain stopped every effort was made to restart the game. The idea of the helicopter was a good one. Alas the execution was lacking. The wind from the rotor blades instead of drying the ground, blew the covers away and deposited the water from them onto the pitch. Play was abandoned for the day and the game was declared void. According to Wisden an ICC ruling directed abandoned matches like this to receive recognition as a limited-over international.

ZIMBABWE		KENYA
G. W. Flower not out	25	D. Chudasama, Tariq Iqbal (wk), K. O. Otieno, S. O. Tikolo,
A. C. Waller c E. Odumbe b Ali	3	M. Odumbe (capt), Hitesh Modi, E. Odumbe, T. M. Odoyo
G. J. Whittall c M. O. Odumbe b E. Odumbe	12	Asif Karim M. Suji, Rajab Ali
A. D. R. Campbell lbw b E. Odumbe	0	
A. Flower (capt/wk) not out	0	
Extras lb1 w4	5	
(15.5 overs)	3-45	

Did not bat: C. N.Evans, H. H.Streak, P. A.Strang, B. C.Strang, S. G.Peall, A. C. I. Lock

1/ 8 2/44 3/45

Bowling: Suji 5-1-11-0; Ali 5-0-14-1; Odoyo 3-0-10-0; E. Odumbe 2.5-0-8-2

Same venue, same players and umpires, seemingly same crowd; very different result. Consensus was that Kenya could have been on the verge of an upset in the Monday edition of this game. That was never an absolute certainty and on Tuesday Zimbabwe, courtesy of some brilliant Paul Strang leg-spin, were well in control for most of the game.

Andy Flower had a change of heart when he won the toss again and this time he sent Kenya in. They lost Tariq Iqbal early, but Dipak Chudasama and Kennedy Otieno lifted the total to 1-60. Then four wickets went down in a matter of moments as Kenya to slipped to 5-67. Paul Strang's brother Bryan, a left-arm medium pacer, took two of those four wickets in quick succession, including Steve Tikolo.

Maurice and Edward Odumbe looked to have restored batting sanity when they added 42. It was an illusion. Paul Strang ripped the middle and lower order apart. He took three wickets in four balls, then closed the innings in the final over with two more victims in consecutive deliveries. Kenya had lost 9-74 after their solid start.

Andy Waller and Grant Flower made as if they were going to get the entire 135 runs Zimbabwe needed by themselves. They rattled up 59 in 13 overs, quickly hitting yesterday's threat, Edward Odumbe, out of the attack. Maurice was on the spot, though, and so were Asif Karim and Rajab Ali. Once Maurice Odumbe had dismissed Waller, the Zimbabweans crawled to their victory, losing wickets here and there, mostly to Ali, along the way. The win was eventually achieved in lacklustre fashion in the 43rd over by five wickets. Paul Strang having taken the best figures ever by a Zimbabwean in a limited-overs international, was named Man of the Match.

KENYA		ZIMBABWE	
D. Chudasama run out	34	A. C. Waller c Tikolo b M. O. Odumbe	30
Tariq Iqbal (wk) b Lock	1	G. W. Flower b Ali	45
K. O. Otieno b Peall	19	A. D. R. Campbell c Tikolo b M. O. Odumbe	6
S. O. Tikolo st A. Flower b B. Strang	0	G. J. Whittall c E. Odumbe b Ali	6
M. O. Odumbe (capt) c B. Strang b P. A. Strang	30	A. Flower (capt/wk) lbw b Ali	5
H. Modi b B. Strang	3	C. N. Evans not out	8
E. Odumbe c Campbell b P. A. Strang	20	H. H. Streak not out	15
T. M. Odoyo c G. W. Flower b P. Srang	0	Extas b3 lb4 w12 nb3	22
A. V. Karim lbw b Strang	0	(42.2overs)	5-137
M. Suji c G. W. Flower b P. A. Strang	15	Did not bat: P. A. Strang, S. G. Peall, B. C. Strang,	
R. Ali not out	0	A. C. I. Lock	
Extras lb3 w8 nb1	12	1/59 2/79 3/104 4/108 5/113	
(49.4 overs)	134	Bowling: Suji 9.2-0-37-0; Ali 8-1-22-3; E. Odumbe 2-0-14-0;	

1/7 2/60 3/61 4/63 5/67 6/109 7/109 8/109 9/109
10/134

Odoyo 2-0-7-0; Karim 10-1-21-0; M. O. Odumbe 10-2-24-2;

Bowling: Streak 7-2-23-0; Lock 8-2-19-1; Whittall 5-0-21-0;

Tikolo 1-0-5-0

Peall 10-1-23-1; B. Strang 10-0-24-2; P. A. Strang 9.4-1-21-5

Umpires: Khizar Hayat C.J. Mitchley

Toss: Zimbabwe   Points: Zimbabwe 2 Kenya 0

TUESDAY 27 FEBRUARY 1996
IQBAL STADIUM, FAISALABAD: NEW ZEALAND vs UAE - GROUP B
NEW ZEALAND WON BY 109 RUNS

Grey was the colour of both teams and also the colour of the overall interest surrounding this flat contest. New Zealand emerged from the fog to complete an easy win over UAE in what Lee Germon admitted was, "a good practice for our next match against Pakistan". The two points they gained for their efforts at the Iqbal Stadium were enough to guarantee a place in the quarter finals.

Visibility was not good at the scheduled start in Faisalabad. By the time the fog had lifted an hour had been lost and three overs had been deducted from each innings. Sultan Zarawani won the toss and sent New Zealand in. First day tournament centurymaker, Nathan Astle, was bowled by Johannes Samarasekera ten minutes into proceedings. Stephen Fleming did not last long either, hitting a catch back to Shaukat Dukanwala after making his entire score in boundaries.

The Kiwi dominace of UAE began with the stand of 120 in 123 balls for the third wicket between Craig Spearman and Roger Twose. The opener was at his powerful best, striking 10 fours in 112 balls, while Twose, the former Warwickshire stalwart who may have felt some empathy with all the UAE imports, continued on towards his maiden century for New Zealand after his partner had perished to the reverse sweep.

He fell just eight runs short of the milestone after eight fours in 112 balls and it was left to Shane Thompson to give the total a final filip. Danny Morrison came in at the fall of the eighth wicket with just two balls remaining in the innings. He faced the left-arm spin of Azhar Saeed who with three wickets was the most successful of the UAE bowlers. With no time for sighters, Morrison smacked his first ball for four then ended the innings with a six over long on. His strike rate for the match was threrefore 500.

Those extra 10 runs left UAE 277 to win in 47 overs. Some handy work from the top order, including a typical early burst of strokeplay from Salim Raza hinted at respectability even though a win was never a real prospect. The limited skill of the UAE middle order was once again apparent when the score slipped from 2-65 to 7-92.

At that point an early finish seemed likely, but Samarasekera dominated stands with Arshad Laiq and Sultan Zarawani and the innings was able to run its meaningless course. Samarasekera, who had emigrated from Sri Lanka because of terrorist attacks near his home, at least had the pleasure of hitting seven fours in 59 balls from a Test standard attack.

Twose was named Man of the Match.

NEW ZEALAND		UNITED ARAB EMIRATES	
C. M. Spearman b Raza	78	Azhar Saeed c Fleming b Nash	5
N. J. Astle b Samarasekera	2	Salim Raza c Kennedy b Morrison	21
S. P. Fleming c & b Dukanwala	16	Mazhar Hussain c Cairns b Thomson	29
R. G. Twose c Mazhar b Azhar	92	V. Mehra c Cairns b Thomson	12
C. L. Cairns c Abbasi b Zarawani	6	Mohammad Ishaq c Cairns b Kennedy	8
A. C. Parore c Azhar b Zarawani	15	Mohammad Aslam c Twose b Thomson	1
S. A. Thomson not out	31	S. Dukanwala c & b Cairns	8
L. K. Germon (capt/wk) b Azhar	3	Arshad Laiq run out	14
D. J. Nash lbw b Azhar	8	J. A.Samarasekera not out	47
D. K. Morrison not out	10	Sultan M. Zarawani (capt) c Thompson b Nash	13
Extras b2 lb12 nb1	15	Imtiaz Abbasi (wk) not out	2
(47 overs)	8-276	Extras lb2 w3 nb2	7
Did not bat: R. J. Kennedy		(47 overs)	9-167

1/11 2/42 3/162 4/173 5/210 6/228 7/239 8/266

1/23 2/29 3/65 4/72 5/82 6/87 7/92 8/124 9/162

Bowling: Samarasekera 6-0-30-1; Laiq 2-0-16-0; Dukanwala 10-0-46-1; Mazhar 3-0-28-0; Azhar 7-0-45-3; Raza 9-0-48-1; Zarawani 10-0-49-2

Bowling: Morrison 7-0-37-1; Nash 9-1-34-2; Cairns 10-2-31-1; Kennedy 6-0-20-1; Thomson 10-2-20-3; Astle 5-0-23-0

Umpires:B.C. Cooray S. Venkataraghavan

Toss: UAE   Points: New Zealand 2 UAE 0

WANKHEDE STADIUM, MUMBAI (BOMBAY): INDIA vs AUSTRALIA - GROUP A
AUSTRALIA WON BY 16 RUNS

Under lights in Mumbai, nearly two weeks into the tournament, the Wills World Cup finally produced a top-draw, limited-overs cricket match. As in 1987 and 1992, Australia and India were involved in a great contest and if this one did not finish with the last over dramas of the matches in Madras and Brisbane it was still rated more highly than nearly everything else in the 1996 tournament to that point.

That Australia won would have disappointed the majority of the 40,000 noisy and enthusiatic fans who crammed into the Wankhede Stadium for the ground's debut under lights. They could not have questioned that the players gave them their money's worth, though. There were some great performances, moments of individual brilliance and a gathering tension as the climax built. For their part the players relished the knowledge of the spectators and the fantastic electric atmosphere they contributed.

With his team hungry for cricket, Mark Taylor won the toss and elected to bat. Then, unexpectedly, he took the role of chief aggressor instead of Mark Waugh in an attractive century opening partnership. The Australian captain survived shouts for lbw and testing bowling from Javagal Srinath to loft the ball over the in field during the first 15 overs. Once he put Srinath away for six and by the time the fieldsmen were allowed outside the rings in numbers Australia were 0-74.

Venkatapathy Raju and Anil Kumble were able to stem the run flow with their accurate spin and in the 22nd over the slight looking left-armer, Raju, had Taylor caught at long on. That signalled the start of Mark Waugh's dominance. He raised his 50 by sweeping Raju for six then lost Ricky Ponting at 140, the Tasmanian being brilliantly caught low and one handed by Sanjay Manjrekar off Raju at backward point. Seventeen runs later, he was indirectly responsible for the dismissal of his twin brother when Raju deflected a straight drive back onto the stumps with Steve, backing up, out of his ground.

So assured was Mark Waugh that he only needed some one to run with him. Stuart Law did that effectively as the total was taken from 157 to 232. Waugh reached his record-breaking second consecutive World Cup 100 in the 43rd over off 120 deliveries. He received a standing ovation, which he celebrated by flat batting Srinath over mid wicket for six to raise the Australian 200. Waugh was run out from square leg attempting to turn a single into two after hitting eight fours and three sixes in 135 balls. It signalled an astonishing Australian collapse where they lost 7-26 through the last five overs. Venkatesh Prasad picked up a couple of those wickets in a hectic final over where four batsmen were dismissed for just two runs. That thrilled the crowd and, of course, the television sponsors who had heaps of their advertisements crammed in during that 50th over while batsmen walked in and out.

The procession of wickets temporarily continued when India began their pursuit of Australia's 258. With Craig McDermott and Paul Reiffel out of the side with injury, Damien Fleming got to share the new ball with Glenn McGrath and he made the most of his opportunity. While McGrath sent down three maidens in four overs, Fleming trapped Ajay Jadeja lbw then bowled Vinod Kambli as the left-hander played loosely across the line.

Disaster loomed and Sachin Tendulkar's response was as brave as it was effective. McGrath paid dearly for missing a tough caught and bowled chance as Tendulkar took 27 runs from two of his overs. The Wankhede Stadium was alight in more ways than one, the spectacle of Tendulkar smashing the best Australia could offer on his home ground under lights was something special to behold. He lost his captain with the total on 70 when Mohammad Azharuddin played on a pull shot to a Fleming slower ball.

Still the crowd cheered, "Sachin! Sachin! Sachin!" He had completed his 50 from 41 balls, going from 12 to 56 in just 25 exhilerating balls. He found a solid partner in Manjrekar and paced himself in a slightly more measured fashion to build a stand of 73.

Shane Warne tested both batsmen with his variation and accuracy after conceding 10 runs in his first over, which included a straight hit for six by Tendulkar from his first ball. However, it was Mark Waugh, bowling a spell of his off-breaks, who gained the vital breakthrough. He saw Tendulkar move out of his crease and pushed the ball wide. It slid through to Ian Healy who completed the stumping in a flash. The adrenalin waned in Wankhede. Tendulkar's 84 ball innings included 14 fours and a six.

Australia were now confident of their victory and more so seven runs later when Manoj Prabhakar was run out. They still had work to do, though, as Manjrekar and wicketkeeper Nayan Mongia added 54 in nine overs. They were scoring at a run per ball as required when Taylor recalled Warne to the attack. In the 41st over the leg-spinner deceived Mongia with a flighted delivery and the wicketkeeper edged a drive to the Australian captain who had brought himself back in to slip.

When Steve Waugh fiddled out Manjrekar in the next over, India needed 54 from eight overs with only three wickets in hand.

Kumble fought hard and Srinath made to slog India home. The task was quite beyond them and Fleming returned to pick up both tailenders. He bowled Kumble through his scythe from the last ball of the 48th to complete the win and claim his fifth wicket.

Mark Waugh's 126 got the nod from the Man of the Match adjudicator.

AUSTRALIA		INDIA	
M. E. Waugh run out	126	A. D. Jadeja lbw b Fleming	1
M. A. Taylor(capt) c Srinath b Raju	59	S. R. Tendulkar st Healy b M. E. Waugh	90
R. T. Ponting c Manjrekar b Raju	12	V. G. Kambli b Fleming	0
S. R. Waugh run out	7	M. Azharuddin (capt) b Fleming	10
S. G. Law c & b Kumble	21	S. V. Manjrekar c Healy b S. R. Waugh	62
M. G. Bevan run out	6	M. Prabhakar run out	3
S. Lee run out	9	N. R. Mongia (wk) c Taylor b Warne	27
I. A. Healy (wk) c Kumble b Prasad	6	A. Kumble b Fleming	17
S. K. Warne c Azharuddin b Prasad	0	J. Srinath c Lee b Fleming	7
D. W. Fleming run out	0	B. K.V. Prasad c Bevan b S. R. Waugh	0
G. D. McGrath not out	0	S. L.V. Raju not out	3
Extras lb8 w2 nb2	12	Extras b5 lb8 w8 nb1	22
(50 overs)	258	(50 overs)	242

1/ 103 2/140 3/157 4/232 5/237 6/244 7/258 8/258 9/258 10/258

1/7 2/7 3/70 4/143 5/147 6/201 7/205 8/224 9/231 10/242

Bowling: Prabhakar 10-0-54-0; Srinath 10-1-51-0; Prasad 10-0-50-2; Kumble 10-1-47-1; Raju 10-0-48-2

Bowling: McGrath 8-3-48-0; Fleming 9-0-36-5; Warne 10-1-28-1; Lee 3-0-23-0; M. E. Waugh 10-0-44-1; Bevan 5-0-28-0; S. R. Waugh 3-0-22-2

Umpires: R.S. Dunne D.R. Shepherd

Toss: Australia   Points: Australia 2 India 0

"I have no words right now," said Richie Richardson. As the captain of the West Indian team that had just been humiliated by none other than Kenya that was no surprise. He, along with the entire Caribbean cricket community, must have been stunned. February 29 comes along every four years, but a result like this is almost once in a lifetime.

Even more surprising was the nature of the victory. Kenya batting first only set the West Indies 166, yet eventually they were able to protect that total with some comfort. So lacking in passion was the West Indian batting performance that Colin Croft called for the captain and management team to be sacked mid tournament. The Kenyans didn't care.

The match began with Dipak Chudasama hitting Curtley Ambrose for boundaries after Richardson had decided to bowl. The former dual World Cup champions looked unhappy with their lot even when early wickets fell. Courtney Walsh had claimed three victims by the 10th over and even some brave strokes by Steve Tikolo, who once pulled Walsh for six, could not halt the Kenyan slide to 6-81 on a greenish pitch.

A united West Indian side would have comfortably finished the job. This, apparently, was no such team. The tally of wide and no balls built up, Cameron Cuffy being a serious culprit. Ian Bishop kicked the ground after a hit wicket decision went in Tikolo's favour. Ambrose was at his sullen worst, grumbling and staring at anyone within eye range. Off-spinner Roger Harper, in contrast to his fast bowling teammates was on the spot and it was when he had Tikolo caught behind sweeping and Martin Suji taken at slip that the Kenyans were at their lowest point in the 23rd over. But even Harper blotted his copybook by dropping two catches.

A determined partnership of 44 between Hitesh Modi and 17-year-old Tom Odoyo seemed to provide Kenya with nothing more than respectability at the time. Modi spent nearly two hours over his runs before offering one of the four catches taken by Jimmy Adams. The Jamaican had replaced Courtney Browne and with a stumping to add to his collection on the day, he equalled Syed Kirmani's 1983 World Cup record of five dismissals for a wicketkeeper. The last of those was taken off Ambrose in the final over of the Kenyan innings.

Extras finished top score, 27 of the bonus runs coming in wides and no balls.

Michael Henderson of *The Times* called the West Indian batting response worse than an unspeakable mess. The rot set in early when Richardson was bowled by a Rajab Ali in-swinger in the fourth over.

Brian Lara, a hero to his opponents as much as the 5,000 or so spectators in the ground, was quickly off the mark with a cover driven four, but in the next over Suji bowled Sherwin Campbell behind his legs. With the West Indies 2-22 the Kenyans were beginning to enjoy themselves. A couple of overs later Lara, who had been batting recklessly, edged a ball to wicketkeeper Tariq Iqbal. There was a momentary fumble from the rotund gloveman, then excited glee as the magnitude of the dismissal of the number one West Indian batsman hit home.

Keith Arthurton joined the procession, running himself out when looking for a single to get off the mark. It was now 4-35 in the 10th over and thoughts were turning to an upset.

Briefly, Adams and young Shivnarine Chanderpaul restored batting sanity. A pull for four by Chanderpaul off Odoyo brought up the 50 in the 17th over. Then Maurice Odumbe induced a mishit to off Chanderpaul to Tikolo at backward point and normal service had been resumed. The asking rate of three runs per over at the start of the innings had crept up to over five. The Kenyan captain was getting plenty of assistance from the pitch for his off-spinners. Adams batted for nearly an hour without hitting a boundary and was then caught in close off bat and pad.

Harper hit a couple of defiant blows before Iqbal held an excellent leg side catch that gave his captain his third wicket on way to identical figures, a maiden apart, to those the departing batsman had achieved. The crowd which included a contingent of Kenyan students were now chanting for the giant killers. They did not have to continue long enough to make themselves hoarse.

From the second ball of the 36th over Cameron Cuffy lunged forward at Ali and was bowled. Kenya had defeated the West Indies by 73 runs and the cricket world was agog with perhaps the greatest upset in its history. The Kenyan players ran over to their supporters for a round of embracing. That was followed by a lap of honour.

Maurice Odumbe was named Man of the Match. "It's like winning the World Cup. It's a dream come true," said the justifiably thrilled Kenyan captain.

KENYA		WEST INDIES	
D. Chudasama c Lara b Walsh	8	S. L. Campbell b Suji	4
Tariq Iqbal (wk) c Cuffy b Walsh	16	R. B. Richardson(capt) b Ali	.5
K. O. Otieno c Adams b Walsh	2	B. C. Lara c Iqbal b Ali	8
S. O. Tikolo c Adams b Harper	29	S. Chanderpaul c Tikolo b M. O. Odumbe	19
M. O. Odumbe(capt) hit wicket b Bishop	6	K. L. T. Arthurton run out	0
H. Modi c Adams b Ambrose	26	J. C. Adams (wk) c Modi b M. O. Odumbe	9
M. Suji c Lara b Harper	0	R. A. Harper c Iqbal b M. O. Odumbe	17
T. M. Odoyo st Adams b Harper	24	I. R. Bishop not out	6
E. Odumbe b Cuffy	1	C. E. L. Ambrose run out	3
A. V. Karim c Adams b Ambrose	11	C. A. Walsh c Chudasama b Karim	4
R. Ali not out	6	C. E. Cuffy b Ali	1
Extras lb8 w14 nb13	35	Extras b5 lb6 w4 nb2	17
(49.3 overs)	166	(35.2 overs)	93

1/15 2/19 3/45 4/72 5/77 6/81 7/125 8/126 9/155 10/166

1/18 2/22 3/33 4/35 5/55 6/65 7/78 8/81 9/89 10/93

Bowling: Ambrose 8.3-3-21-2; Walsh 9-0-46-3; Bishop 10-2-30-1; Cuffy 8-0-31-1; Harper 10-4-15-3; Arthurton 4-0-15-0

Bowling: Suji 7-2-16-1; Ali 7.2-2-17-3; Karim 8-1-19-1; M. O. Odumbe 10-3-15-3; Odoyo 3-0-15-0

Umpires: Khizar Hayat V.K. Ramaswamy

Toss: West Indies   Points: Kenya 2 West Indies 0

NATIONAL STADIUM, KARACHI:
PAKISTAN vs SOUTH AFRICA - GROUP B
SOUTH AFRICA WON BY 5 WICKETS

South Africa gave another warning that they would take some beating in the 1996 World Cup with a thoroughly convincing performance against Pakistan in Karachi. If not the sensation that occurred in Poona, this was still an important cricket match; one that probably meant Pakistan would have to play their quarter final in India, something they had hoped to avoid.

Their opponents confirmed their place at the top of Group B with yet another efficient display of batting, bowling and fielding. They had the restored Allan Donald back in the team, but it was Shaun Pollock and Chris Matthews who opened the attack after Wasim Akram had won the toss and batted. Pollock had Aamer Sohail dropped by Brian McMillan in the first over and it was a costly miss. It gave the left-hander the opportunity to regain form and he so did with a vengance.

Sohail and Saeed Anwar put on 52 in 12 overs before Hansie Cronje brought himself on to bowl his medium pacers ahead of Donald. Within four balls he had Anwar caught at short cover and Ijaz Ahmed lbw. Sohail and Inzamam-ul-Haq overcame that abberation with a stand of 60 before the big man fell foul of his most common form of dismissal in World Cup matches. Cronje's throw was right on target. Sohail and Salim Malik then put on 77 as the Pakistani total grew to significant proportions.

After debutant Paul Adams had Malik caught behind, Sohail completed his worthy 100. He was not dismissed until he sliced Pollock high to point in the second last over of the innings. Sohail had hit eight fours in 139 balls. The Pakistani captain boosted the latter part of the innings which finished on a worthy, but not imposing 6-242.

It certainly did not intimidate the South African top order, who went after the bowling with real vigour in the first 15 overs. Neither Andrew Hudson nor Gary Kirsten was solely intent on holding the South African cause together. Hudson, just back in the side really went for his shots, hitting six fours while scoring at a run per minute. He was bowled by Waqar Younis who quickly followed up with the wicket of McMillan who had been promoted in the order.

The two wickets made little difference to the tempo of the South African batting. When spin replaced pace Kirsten and Daryll Cullinan brought back memories of 1987 with one sweep shot after another. Mushtaq Ahmed's leg spin was mastered, however 19-year-old off spinner Saqlain Mushtaq held firm. He bowled the left-hander Kirsten and took a caught and bowled off Jacques Kallis. The match lay in the balance at 4-125 as Cronje came to the crease to join Cullinan.

They applied themselves well, stuck to the team strategy with confidence, knowing that even behind them there was batting quality. The run rate held firm as 78 was added for the fifth wicket. When Younis came back to conclude Cullinan's 76-ball, six-boundary contribution the momentum was all with the Proteas. Pakistan were feeling the pinch. They lost their wicketkeeper, Rashid Latif to a groin strain. The wide and no ball count became significant. Pollock and his well-set captain forcefully carried their side to their impressive victory with nearly six overs to spare.

Wasim Akram admitted to misreading the pitch and that his team had been outplayed. The experts suggested Pakistan had erred by selecting an extra batsman and only two pace bowlers. The masses in the outer at the National Stadium probably thought Javed Miandad either omitted, retired or suffering from a bad back, would have made the difference.

There was less pressure on Hansie Cronje. He could have spent some of his press conference showing off his Man of the Match Award.

PAKISTAN		SOUTH AFRICA	
Aamer Sohail c Cronje b Pollock	111	A. C. Hudson b Waqar Younis	33
Saeed Anwar c McMillan b Cronje	25	G. Kirsten b Saqlain Mushtaq	44
Ijaz Ahmed lbw b Cronje	0	B. M. McMillan lbw b WaqarYounis	1
Inzamam-ul-Haq run out	23	D. J. Cullinan b Waqar Younis	65
Salim Malik c Palframan b Adams	40	J. H. Kallis c & b Saqlain Mushtaq	9
Wasim Akram(capt) not out	32	W. J. Cronje (capt) not out	45
Rashid Latif (wk) lbw b Matthews	0	S. M. Pollock not out	20
Ramiz Raja not out	2	Extras b8 lb4 w6 nb8	26
Extras b1 lb2 w4 nb2	9	(44.2 overs)	5-243
(50 overs)	6-242	Did not bat: S. J. Palframan (wk), C. R. Matthews,	
Did not bat: Mushtaq Ahmed, Waqar Younis,		A. A. Donald, P. R. Adams	
Saqlain Mushtaq		1/51 2/53 3/111 4/125 5/203	
1/52 2/52 3/112 4/189 5/233 6/235		Bowling: Wasim Akram 9.2-0-49-0; Waqar Younis 8-0-50-3;	
Bowling: Pollock 9-0-49-1; Matthews 10-0-47-1;		Mushtaq Ahmed10-0-54-0; Aamir Sohail 6-0-35-0; Saqlain	
Cronje 5-0-20-2; Donald 8-0-50-0; Adams 10-0-42-1;		Mushtaq 10-1-38-2; Salim Malik 1-0-5-0	
McMillan 8-0-31-0			

Umpires: S.A. Bucknor K.T. Francis

Toss: Pakistan   Points: South Africa 2 Pakistan 0

FRIDAY 1 MARCH 1996
VIDARBHA CA GROUND, NAGPUR: AUSTRALIA vs ZIMBABWE - GROUP A
AUSTRALIA WON BY 8 WICKETS

Although Zimbabwe were a fully fledged Test playing opponent, they gave Australia less trouble than Kenya had earlier in the tournament. Watched by one of the smallest crowds of the World Cup, the Zimbabwean batsmen could only set Australia a very mediocre target. And Mark Waugh's superb form meant the game was over with plenty of overs unused.

Andy Flower was having far more success with the coin than the bat. He took first use of what looked a wicket full of runs, but came in with his side in trouble at 3-55 and left soon after with them in worse strife at 4-68. Only the experienced Andy Waller batted with any sign of permanency, opening and lasting until the 36th over. Glenn McGrath was miserly with the new-ball while Steve Waugh got rid of Guy Whittall and Alistair Campbell.

Craig Evans and Waller took the score to 4-106, which raised the possibility of a Zimbabwean recovery. It did not eventuate. Shane Warne and Damien Fleming easily cut through the lower order.

Once Waller was run out from third man after hesitating over whether to go for a second leg bye, all worthwhile resistance ceased. Waller had hit 10 fours in 102 balls. When Warne bowled Charles Lock with what Steven Lynch in *Wisden Cricket Monthly* called a near replica of the Mike Gatting, "ball from hell", Zimbabwe had lost 6-48 to be all out in the 46th over.

Heath Streak began his new-ball spell against Mark Taylor and Mark Waugh with three maidens. However, Andy Flower would have called for wickets not economy and Lock at the other end could not even keep a hold on the run flow. Neither could Whittall, Bryan Strang or Stephen Peall make any impact as the Australian pair ran up a opening stand of 92.

Paul Strang did cause the batsmen some concern and it was the leg-spinner who eventually had Taylor caught by his brother Bryan. Fifty-eight runs later, he snared Ricky Ponting caught and bowled. It gave the leg-spinning fraternity half the wickets to fall in the game, Shane Warne's haul of four winning him the Man of the Match Award. Mark Waugh who batted through until the winning run had been scored, facing 109 deliveries and hitting 10 fours, had been Warne's main title challenger.

ZIMBABWE		AUSTRALIA	
A. C. Waller run out	67	M. A. Taylor (capt) c B. Strang b P. A. Strang	34
G. W. Flower b McGrath	4	M. E. Waugh not out	76
G. J. Whittall c & b S. R. Waugh	6	R. T. Ponting c & b Strang	33
A. D. R. Campbell c M. E. Waugh b S. R. Waugh	5	S. R. Waugh not out	5
A. Flower (capt/wk) st Healy b Warne	7	Extras b6 lb2 w1 nb1	10
C. N. Evans c Healy b Warne	18	(36 overs)	2-158
H. H. Streak c S. R. Waugh b Fleming	13	Did not bat: S. G. Law, M. G. Bevan, S. Lee, I. A. Healy (wk),	
P. A. Strang not out	16	S. K. Warne, D. W. Fleming, G. D. McGrath	
B. C. Strang b Fleming	0	1/92 2/150	
S. G. Peall c & b Warne	0	Bowling: Streak 10-3-29-0; Lock 4-0-25-0; B.	
A. C. I. Lock b Warne	5	Strang 3-0-20-0; Whittall 2-0-11-0; P. A. Strang 10-2-33-2;	
Extras lb8 w3 nb2	13	Peall 4-0-20-0; G. W. Flower 3-0-12-0	
(45.3 overs)	154		

1/21 2/41 3/55 4/68 5/106 6/126 7/140 8/140 9/145 10/154

Bowling: McGrath 8-2-12-1; Fleming 9-1-30-2; Lee 4-2-8-0; S. R. Waugh 7-2-22-2; Warne 9.3-1-34-4; M. E. Waugh 5-0-30-0; Law 3-0-10-0

Umpires: R.S. Dunne D.R. Shepherd

Toss: Zimbabwe   Points: Australia 2 Zimbabwe 0

GADDAFI STADIUM, LAHORE:
NETHERLANDS vs UAE - GROUP B
UAE WON BY 7 WICKETS

In contrast to the way these two sides had competed against the 'majors' of the competition, UAE cruised to an easy win over Holland which was a repeat of what happened in the 1994 ICC Trophy semi-final. Form had suggested Holland would easily account for the disappointing Emirates team, but it was as if the UAE had been laying low while waiting for an opportunity like this. Their bowlers restrained the Dutch batsmen from any serious runs and then, inspired by the carefree Salim Raza, they galloped home with six overs and seven wickets in hand.

Steve Lubbers, back in the side, batted after winning the toss only for Nolan Clarke to fail again. It seemed the two years between the ICC Trophy and the World Cup had taken their toll on the 47-year-old former Barbadian and his inability to get the innings away to a bright start was disappointing.

Flavian Aponso hit six boundaries as he and Peter Cantrell put on 74 for the second wicket. They had to struggle early as the new ball moved around. Shahzad Altaf, in the side for his first World Cup game, recovered from a first ball wide and an opening over tumble to be the personification of accuracy in his 10 over spell. The former Queensland Sheffield Shield player,

Cantrell, batted on after Aponso became the first of offspinner Shaukat Dukanwala's five victims. He was able to hold the innings together but batted without any urgency for more than two-and-a-half hours.

Cantrell's slow progress meant that although Holland reached 2-148, they were already past the 40th over. The need for acceleration brought about a regular loss of wickets. Sultan Zarawani had his opposite number, Lubbers caught by the only other UAE national in the side, Saeed Al-Saffer, while Dukanwala picked up four wickets from his final 11 balls.

After 15 overs, UAE were already 0-94 in reply to Holland's 9-216. Raza was making short work of Paul Jan Bakker and soon blasted Tim de Leede out of the attack. Batting in the city where he was born the 31-year-old opener belted a World Cup record equalling six sixes in addition to his seven fours in 68 fun filled balls. When he was caught on the boundary off Lubbers and the ever limping Roland Lefebvre removed Mazhar Hussain UAE had lost 2-3 to be 3-138.

If there was any concern Vijay Mehra and the bearded Mohammad Ishaq did not show it. They batted with common sense and aggression in a 99-ball match-winning partnership of 82. The boundaries flowed freely again and Ishaq, like Raza from Lahore, rejoiced at his home coming by hitting the first two balls of Aponso's eighth over for four. That raised his 50 and took UAE to their well-deserved win. Dukanwala and Raza shared the Man of the Match Award.

NETHERLANDS		UNITED ARAB EMIRATES	
N. E. Clarke c Mehra b Shahzad	0	Azhar Saeed run out	32
P. E. Cantrell c Abbasi b Azhar	47	Salim Raza c Zuiderent b Lubbers	84
G. J.A. F. Aponso c & b Dukanwala	45	Mazhar Hussain c Clarke b Lefebvre	16
T. B.M. de Leede c & b Azhar	36	V. Mehra not out	29
K. J. van Noortwijk c Zarawani b Dukanwala	26	Mohammad Ishaq not out	51
S. W. Lubbers (capt) c Al-Saffar b Zarawani	8	Extras lb7 w1	8
R. P. Lefebvre c Ishaq b Dukanwala	12	(44.2 overs)	3-220
B. Zuiderent st Abbasi b Dukanwala	3	Did not bat: J. A. Samarasekera, S. Dukanwala,	
M. Schewe (wk) b Dukanwala	6	Sultan M. Zarawani (capt), Saeed Al-Saffar, Imtiaz Abbasi,	
R. F. van Oosterom not out	2	Shahad Altaf	
P. J. Bakker not out	0	1/117 2/135 3/138	
Extras b5 lb15 w11	31	Bowling: Lefebvre 8-0-24-1; Bakker 8-0-41-0;	
(50 overs)	9-216	de Leede 4-0-33-0; Aponso 7.2-0-47-0; Lubbers 9-0-38-1;	
1/3 2/77 3/148 4/153 5/168 6/200 7/200 8/209 9/210		Cantrell 8-0-30-0	
Bowling: Shahzad 10-3-15-1; Samarasekera 9-1-35-0;			
Al-Saffar 3-0-25-0; Dukanwala 10-0-29-5;			
Zarawani 8-0-40-1; Raza 5-0-23-0; Azhar 5-0-29-2			

Umpires: Mahboob Shah S.G. Randell
Toss: UAE   Points: UAE 2 Holland 0

SATURDAY 2 MARCH 1996
FEROZE SHAH KOTLA GROUND, DELHI: INDIA vs SRI LANKA - GROUP A
SRI LANKA WON BY 6 WICKETS

In the context of the 1996 Wills World Cup this was a landmark match. It was a game filled with thrilling strokeplay which harvested 543 runs for only seven wickets. Not surprisingly nearly all the heroes were batsmen. Eventually Sri Lanka produced a couple more of those heroes which allowed them to complete a breathtaking victory against the odds in front of 25,000 dismayed Indians.

The players got better reviews than the stadium whose renovations for the tournament were hardly inspiring and actually reduced the ground's capacity. That left as many disappointed fans outside as there were squeezed into it. Clive Lloyd and Wes Hall were not allowed in, ticket accreditation being a shambles.

The lucky ones who got a seat soon had plenty to distract them from any discomfort or concern for those outside. Arjuna Ranatunga sniffing the grey morning mist offered India first use of the wicket so that Sachin Tendulkar was on show from the start. Less frenetic than during his 90 against Australia, he was just as accomplished and entertaining, building his momentum as his innings progressed. There was no batting joy for the totally out of touch Manoj Prabahakar who scratched around for 10 overs before mistiming a drive to mid off. Sanjay Manjrekar's consistency complemented Tendulkar nicely for another 14 overs while 66 runs were added. He provided an important part of the platform for Tendulkar and Mohammad Azharuddin before top edging a sweep to wicketkeeper, Romesh Kaluwitharana who had to dive in front of the batsman to complete the catch.

The following 26 overs provided another of those special Tendulkar/Azharuddin occasions. There was a 15-minute rain interruption after which the Sri Lankan spinners, Muttiah Muralitharan and Sanath Jayasuriya kept the two batsmen under relative control so that at the 40 over mark India were 2-172.

The crowd were impatient for an acceleration and called for sixes. They got more than their fair share over the final 10 overs as the two strokeplayers indulged themselves in a run feast and the Sri Lankan fielding became slipshod.

Ranatunga was obliged to bring back his medium pacers. Chaminda Vaas was punished. Ravindra Pushpakumara was slaughtered. Tendulkar reached 99 with a straight driven four off Pushpakamura in the 45th over then pushed a single to reach his 100.

Pushpakumara also bowled the 49th over from which 23 runs were taken. Tendulkar climaxed his innings with two fours and two sixes from the over which dented the confidence of the man labelled the Sri Lankan Waqar Younis. When he was run out by the bowler, Vaas, in the final over, Tendulkar had scored 137 at exactly a run per ball while hitting five sixes and eight fours. His partnership with his captain had put on 175, an all wicket record for India in the World Cup. Azharuddin remained unbeaten on 72 having seen 99 runs scored from the last 10 overs. His side had set Sri Lanka the big task of making 272 to win.

The response of their openers Jayasuriya and Kaluwitharana was devastating. After three overs they had already wiped 42 off the target. Jayasuriya assaulted Prabhakar with four fours and a six off his second over. The captain of Delhi, on his home ground, had figures of 0-33 from two overs. His own crowd booed him and the proud all-rounder was banished to the outfield a broken man, soon to announce his retirement from the game.

It was felt such batting could not continue, which seemed to be confirmed when Kumble held a sharp low catch at cover from a Kaluwitharana drive off Venkatash Prasad in the first over after he replaced Prabhakar.

Jayasuriya, though, just kept going, reaching his 50 in 36 balls. With Asanka Gurusinha providing busy support, the total had reached 1-117 by the completion of the 15th over. Then, between 129 and 141, three wickets fell as for the only time in the match a bowler got the upper hand.

Anil Kumble picked up Jayasuriya caught in the deep after nine fours and two sixes and a fretting Aravinda de Silva was stumped when the leg-spinner saw him coming. Gurusinha, who had played one lovely hook for six off Salil Ankola, had been run out going for a second run by Prasad. Only 23 overs had been bowled and Sri Lanka had lost four wickets. The Indians felt the time was right for a Mexican wave.

Their joy was premature. Kumble and suprisingly Tendulkar were the only bowlers to really cause the Sri Lankans any problems. So aggressive had been the start of the innings that Ranatunga and Hashan Tillekeratne had time to consolidate before stepping up to top gear. They put on the whole 131 Sri Lanka needed to win, only 32 of which came in boundaries.

Ranatunga did not run too many sharp singles, either. Ankola missed a sliding catch at long off. The dropping of Venkatapathy Raju left India a spinner short. Prabhakar came back for two more overs of off-spin. That didn't work.

The Mexican wave stopped. The ground went quiet. With eight balls to go empty drink containers began raining onto the outfield. Sri Lanka had won by six wickets and Jayasuriya was Man of the Match. His successful onslaught against the new-ball would impact on the rest of the tournament.

INDIA		SRI LANKA	
M. Prabhakar c Gurusinha b Pushpakumara	7	S. T. Jayasuriya c Prabhakar b Kumble	79
S. R. Tendulkar run out	137	R. S. Kaluwitharana(wk) c Kumble b Prasad	26
S. V. Manjrekar c Kaluwitharana b Dharmasena	32	A. P. Gurusinha run out	25
M. Azharuddin (capt) not out	72	P. A. de Silva st Mongia b Kumble	8
V. G. Kambli not out	1	A. Ranatunga(capt) not out	46
Extras b4 lb7 w11	22	H. P. Tillekeratne not out	70
(50 overs)	3-271	Extras b4 lb9 w3 nb2	18
Did not bat: A. D. Jadeja, N. R. Mongia (wk), A. Kumble,		(48.4 overs)	4-272
J. Srinath, S. A. Ankola		Did not bat: R. S. Mahanama, H. D. P. K. Dharmasena,	
B. K.V. Prasad		W. P. U. J.C. Vaas ,M. Muralitharan, K. R. Pushpakumara	
1/27 2/93 3/268		1/53 2/129 3/137 4/141	
Bowling: Vaas 9-3-37-0; Pushpakumara 8-0-53-1;		Bowling: Prabhakar 4-0-47-0; Srinath 9.4-0-51-0;	
Muralitharan 10-1-42-0; Dharmasena 9-0-53-1;		Prasad 10-1-53-1; Ankola 5-0-28-0; Kumble 10-1-39-2;	
Jayasuriya 10-0-52-0; Ranatunga 4-0-23-0		Tendulkar 10-0-41-0	

Umpires: C.J. Mitchley I.D. Robinson

Toss: Sri Lanka   Points: Sri Lanka 2 India 0

SUNDAY 3 MARCH 1996
NATIONAL STADIUM, KARACHI: PAKISTAN vs ENGLAND - GROUP B
PAKISTAN WON BY 7 WICKETS

Pakistan comfortably accounted for an English side palpably not in the same league as the major contenders for the World Cup. Mike Atherton's team could not make anything from the return to form of their captain and his opening partnership of 147 with Robin Smith, who finally was given a clean bill of health.

A National Stadium filled with 30,000 had to wait 28 overs for any joy after Atherton, contrary to what Wasim Akram would have done, had won the toss and batted. Smith pulled Waqar Younis for a mighty six in the fourth over, seemingly trying to make up the lost time for the matches he had missed. Atherton took to leg-spinner Mushtaq Ahmed and hit him out of the attack.

At the half way point of the innings England looked on target to reach total in excess of 300. By then the strain was starting to tell on Smith's damaged calf and Dominic Cork was running for him. Finally, after hitting that one six and eight fours in 92 balls, Smith holed out to mid-on off part-time leg-spinner Salim Malik. The stand had been the highest for England for any wicket against Pakistan in a limited-over international.

Five minutes later, Smith was joined back in the pavilion by Graeme Hick who, unaccountably, was lured out of his ground second ball by Aamir Sohail. The second string left-arm spinner followed up by removing Atherton's off stump as he tried to cut. England had lost 3-9 in three overs on an excellent batting surface and their advantage had been squandered.

Graham Thorpe and Neil Fairbrother again briefly rallied the cause, but Mushtaq returned and took 3-14 from his last five overs after 39 had been scored from his first five. When a fizzing Mushtaq wrong 'un bowled Dermot Reeve England were 7-217 and on the verge of complete collapse. That did not quite occur through the efforts of Thorpe who worked his way through the tumble of wickets to an unbeaten 52 and Darren Gough who swiped a few handy runs.

Pakistan required a neat five per over to win and on a still sound wicket did so in relative comfort. Sohail and Saeed Anwar garnered the first 81 needed in 16 overs, the two left-handers keeping pace with each other, punctuating their batting with flowing boundary strokes. Sohail chipped a catch to Thorpe at mid wicket, but there was no follow up panic as had been evident in the English batting once the openers had been separated.

Atherton made 12 bowling changes. None made any difference. Fairbrother tore a hamstring and limped out of the tournament. Neil Smith was already out injured. Cork, although expensive, bowled with enough spark to have Anwar caught behind and later repeated the dose to Ijaz Ahmed. They had, however, scored 71 and 70 respectively and by the time Ijaz was out Pakistan were within 36 runs of victory with plenty of overs in hand.

Ijaz got out in time for Javed to bat for 30 minutes which thrilled his parochial home town fans. Inzamam-ul-Haq was thumping the ball to good effect so that Miandad's cameo just involved the odd push and nudge. Inzamam in his 100th limited-over international completed the win when he clouted Reeve for his sixth four to complete a run per ball half century.

Miandad bidding farewell to the National Stadium at last after several failed attempts at retirement was mobbed as he walked off the ground. He was given a special cash award of 600,000 rupees for his participation in six World Cups over 21 years. Sohail received the Man of the Match award for his all round contribution over seven hours.

Atherton's post-match comments amazingly indicated that England were gaining confidence from their succession of defeats against the other Test-playing nations. They had still made it through to the quarter finals.

Pakistan forfeited the chance of a home quarter final by winning this game. The suggestions they might not have gone all out for victory were unfounded.

ENGLAND		PAKISTAN	
R. A. Smith c Waqar Younis b Salim Malik	75	Aamir Sohail c Thorpe b Illingworth	42
M. A. Atherton (capt) b Aamir Sohail	66	Saeed Anwar c Russell b Cork	71
G. A. Hick st Rashid Latif b Aamir Sohail	1	Ijaz Ahmed c Russell b Cork	70
G. P. Thorpe not out	52	Inzamam-ul-Haq not out	53
N. H. Fairbrother c Wasim Akram b Mushtaq Ahmed	13	Javed Miandad not out	11
R. C. Russell (wk) c & b Mushtaq Ahmed	4	Extras lb1 w2	3
D. A. Reeve b Mushtaq Ahmed	3	(47.4 overs)	3-250
D. G. Cork lbw b Waqar Younis	0	Did not bat: Salim Malik, Wasim Akram (capt),	
D. Gough b Wasim Akram	14	Rashid Latif (wk), Mushtaq Ahmed, Waqar Younis,	
P. J. Martin run out	2	Aaqib Javed	
R. K. Illingworth not out	1	1/81 2/139 3/214	
Extras lb11 w4 nb3	18	Bowling: Cork 10-0-59-2; Martin 9-0-45-0; Gough 10-0-45-0;	
(50 overs)	9-249	Illingworth 9-0-46-1; Reeve 6.4-0-37-0; Hick 2-0-17-0	

1/147 2/151 3/156 4/194 5/204 6/212 7/217 8/241 9/247
Bowling: Wasim Akram 7-1-31-1; Waqar Younis 10-1-45-1; Aaqib Javed 7-0-34-0; Mushtaq Ahmed 10-0-53-3; Aamir Sohail 10-0-48-2; Salim Malik 6-1-27-1

Umpires: B.C. Cooray S. Venkataraghavan
Toss: England   Points: Pakistan 2 England 0

MONDAY 4 MARCH 1996
SAWAI MANSINGH STADIUM, JAIPUR: AUSTRALIA vs WEST INDIES - GROUP A
WEST INDIES WON BY 4 WICKETS

This West Indian turnaround was one of the game's imponderables. How does a once-proud side lose to Kenya and then four days later master the tournament favourites? While totally bewildering it almost summed up West Indian cricket in the mid 1990s. Volatile and inconsistent, yet still capable of beating anyone when their cluster of champions click together.

Richie Richardson, whose treatment by certain members of his team often seemed totally unjustified, guided the West Indies to victory. He was named as Man of the Match, then announced he would retire from international cricket after the tournament. Unlike some others, his honour remained intact.

The Sawai Mansingh Stadium in the 'Pink City' in northern India still retained the aroma of the previous day's anti-mosquito spraying when Mark Taylor won the toss and batted. Curtley Ambrose and Courtney Walsh gave the first indication that this was a different West Indian team to Thursday's disorganised bunch. On a two-paced wicket they gave neither Taylor nor Mark Waugh any freedom against the new ball, sending down six maidens in tandem while conceding just eight runs in the first nine overs.

Mark Waugh, previously in such scintillating form, could not reach the boundary until the 17th over. By then he had already lost his captain and opening partner; caught behind off the persevering Walsh. That four was Mark Waugh's one boundary stroke in his entire 102-minute innings which used up a lot of overs while providing a necessary solid foundation.

Ricky Ponting and Steve Waugh made best use of that foundation with a third-wicket partnership of 110 from 114 balls. Although boundaries were fairly scarce, Ponting's six off Ian Bishop was one of the shots of the tournament. He danced out to the paceman and lofted him over the boundary at extra cover. The urgency of the latter overs cost the Australians wickets, including three run outs, to bring their misjudgements for the competition to nine so far. Stuart Law might have been another when he backed up too far, however the bowler, Walsh, did nothing more than offer one of his icy stares. Ponting was one of the casualties, but not before he had completed his second century in limited-overs internationals. Surviving a close run out on 96 he eventually hit five fours as well as his six in 112 balls. The Australians were able to lift the total by 135 from the final 20 overs, including 71 from the final 10.

The task confronting the West Indies appeared difficult when they had lost both their openers by the time the score was 26. They had been unable to chase 166 against Kenya and here they were in trouble against Australia needing 230 to have any hope of gaining a place in the quarter finals. Sherwin Campbell was caught behind off Damien Fleming in the second over and Courtney Browne, back in the side with the added portfolio of opening batsman as well as wicketkeeper, sacrificed himself when Brian Lara called for a single that was not there.

That brought together Richardson and Lara; the two best West Indian batsmen had not always seen eye-to-eye. That was temporarily put behind them at least in Jaipur during an important partnership of 87. Lara was the more aggressive of the two cracking seven fours in 74 balls. Shane Warne's leg-spin tested both batsmen, runs coming much more freely from the fast-medium bowlers. Eventually Warne went wicketless. It was Mark Waugh, purveying his off-spin while wearing a wide brimmed floppy hat and sunglasses, who got the breakthrough when he had Lara caught deep on the leg-side by Glenn McGrath.

He also had Richardson 'caught' by Ponting on the boundary at deep mid wicket. The Tasmanian showed excellent judgement, but fell into a soft drink advertising hoarding after holding the ball, so the shot counted for six. Waugh had genuine success when he bowled Shivnarine Chanderpaul and continued Keith Arthurton's miserable tournament with a successful lbw shout. At 6-196 the West Indies were under pressure which without their captain may have developed into something more significant. That security allowed Jimmy Adams to hit three precious boundaries. The winnings runs were scored with seven balls to spare.

"We had a long serious meeting on Sunday and were determined to play well," Richardson said after the match. It was a time for West Indian meetings apparently, because their Board of Control were convening to thrash out a post mortem following the embarrassment against Kenya.

AUSTRALIA		WEST INDIES	
M. E. Waugh st Browne b Harper	30	S. L. Campbell c Healy b Fleming	1
M. A. Taylor (capt) c Browne b Walsh	9	C. O. Browne (wk) run out	10
R. T. Ponting run out	102	B. C. Lara c McGrath b M. E. Waugh	60
S. R. Waugh b Walsh	57	R. B. Richardson (capt) not out	93
M. G. Bevan run out	2	S. Chanderpaul b M. E. Waugh	10
S. G. Law not out	12	R. A. Harper lbw b Reiffel	22
I. A. Healy run out	3	K. L. T. Arthurton lbw b Waugh	0
P. R. Reiffel not out	4	J. C. Adams not out	17
Extras lb3 w6 nb1	10	Extras lb12 w5 nb2	19
(50 overs)	6-229	(48.5 overs)	6-232
Did not bat: S. K. Warne, D. W. Fleming, G. D. McGrath		Did not bat: I. R. Bishop, C. E. L. Ambrose, C. A. Walsh	
1/22 2/84 3/194 4/200 5/216 6/224		1/1 2/26 3/113 4/146 5/194 6/196	
Bowling: Ambrose 10-4-25-0; Walsh 9-2-35-2;		Bowling: Reiffel 10-3-45-1; Fleming 7.5-1-44-1;	
Bishop 9-0-52-0; Harper 10-0-46-1; Arthurton 9-0-53-0;		McGrath 9-0-46-0; Warne 10-1-30-0; M. E.	
Adams 3-0-15-0		Waugh 10-1-38-3; Bevan 2-0-17-0	

Umpires: Mahboob Shah D.R. Shepherd

Toss: Australia   Points: West Indies 2 Australia 0

TUESDAY 5 MARCH 1996
RAWALPINDI CRICKET STADIUM, RAWALPI
NDI: NETHERLANDS vs SOUTH AFRICA - GROUP B
SOUTH AFRICA WON BY 160 RUNS

South Africa ended the preliminary rounds of the Wills World Cup as they began it, with a ruthless demolition of one of the promoted ICC teams. It meant that they and Sri Lanka were the only two teams to get through to the quarter final stage unbeaten. The Netherlands, for their part, went home with no wins, but no regrets, either.

LIke the UAE bowlers three weeks before, the Dutch attack was thoroughly mauled by the South African batsmen. The absence of Roland Lefebrve forced Steve Lubbers to share the new-ball with Paul Jan Bakker. Neither the off-spinning Dutch captain in his final game for his country, nor any of the other bowlers could make an impression on Andrew Hudson and Gary Kirsten. The pair compiled the highest opening stand in the World Cup, passing Australian pair, Rick McCosker and Alan Turner's 182 scored against Sri Lanka at The Oval in 1975.

It was Hudson who made the most of the friendly bowling this time, going on to his second century in limited-over internationals. After losing his left-handed partner at 186, he blazed his way to 161 in 132 balls with 13 fours and four sixes. Erik Gouka had conceded three consecutive sixes when he had the opener caught on the boundary going for yet another one. Hudson's departure made little difference as the Proteas topped their then record limited-over internationals score against UAE by seven.

It was thought by some critics that Hansie Cronje had erred by not giving some of his middle-order batsmen a chance to spend more time in the middle. So successful had South Africa been that the likes of Brian McMillan would enter the quarter finals badly underdone.

Cronje gave eight of his bowlers a turn during the Dutch innings. There were few significant moments in an effort that managed to get just over halfway to the target of 329. Nolan Clarke, like his captain in a farewell performance, briefly turned back the clock with a couple of great shots during his hour at the crease. He and Peter Cantrell put on 56 for the first wicket, Clarke raising the half-century stand with one of his two sixes. Once the 47-year-old had mistimed a drive to mid off much of the interest went out of the game, even though the teenager Bas Zuiderent again demonstrated his promise.

Andrew Hudson was a clear-cut Man of the Match.

SOUTH AFRICA		NETHERLANDS	
G. Kirsten c Zuiderent b Aponso	83	N. E. Clarke c Pollock b Donald	32
A. C. Hudson c Zuiderent b Gouka	161	P. E. Cantrell c & b Matthews	23
W. J. Cronje (capt) c Lubbers b Cantrell	41	T. B.M. de Leede b Donald	12
D. J. Cullinan not out	19	K. J. van Noortwijk c Palframan b Symcox	9
J. H. Kallis not out	17	G. J.A. F. Aponso c Kirsten b Symcox	6
Extras lb5 w2	7	B. Zuiderent run out	27
(50 overs)	3-328	M. Schewe (wk) b Matthews	20
Did not bat: B. M. McMillan, S. J. Palframan (wk),		E. Gouka c Kallis b Pollock	19
S. M. Pollock, C. R. Matthews, P. L. Symcox, A. A. Donald		R. F. van Oosterom not out	5
1/186 2/274 3/301		S. W. Lubbers (capt) not out	2
Bowling: Bakker 10-1-64-0; Lubbers 8-0-50-0; de		Extras lb7 w5 nb1	13
Leede 10-0-59-0; Aponso 10-0-57-1; Cantrell 10-0-61-1;		(50 overs)	8-168
Gouka 2-0-32-1		Did not bat: P. J. Bakker	
		1/56 2/70 3/81 4/86 5/97 6/126 7/158 8/163	
		Bowling: Pollock 8-0-35-1; Matthews 10-0-38-2;	
		Donald 6-0-21-2; Cronje 3-1-3-0; Symcox 10-1-22-2;	
		M. Millan 4-2-5-0; Kallis 7-1-30-0; Cullinan 2-0-7-0	

Umpires: Khizar Hayat S.G. Randell

Toss: South Africa   Points: South Africa 2 Holland 0

WEDNESDAY 6 MARCH 1996
ASGIRIYA STADIUM, KANDY: SRI LANKA vs KENYA - GROUP A
SRI LANKA WON BY 144 RUNS

An orgy of runs delighted everyone in attendance as the Wills World Cup bade farewell to Sri Lanka. It was the home side who dominated the merry making rattling up the world record limited-over international total of 5-398. Between them the Sri Lankans and Kenyans belted, smashed, lofted, drilled and clobbered a total of 21 sixes and 63 fours through 100 overs where bowlers were for the most part mere fodder. The match aggregate of 652 runs also created a new World Cup record.

Sri Lanka were subject to rumours that they would throw the match for a more favourable quarter final situation. An opening stand of 83 in 6.3 overs by Romesh Kaluwitharana and Sanath Jayasuriya dispelled that idea.

It was ridiculous stuff that could not continue. Except that it did. Asanka Gurusinha and Aravinda de Silva added 183 at a run per ball in fewer than two hours. After the all-wicket Sri Lankan limited-over international record had been terminated by the 'Guru's' dismissal, de Silva went on to complete a wonderful 100, getting to his country's highest score in a limited-over international, 145, before holing out off Martin Sjui. He had contributed 14 fours and five sixes to the day's festivities. De Silva had been involved in a second century stand, 106 with his captain, Arjuna Ranatunga, who had earlier lost the toss.

Rantunga had rattled up 75 in 40 balls by the time 50 overs were up. He hit 13 fours and one six, having reached 50 in 26 balls, yet another World Cup record. The same bowlers who had so troubled the likes of Richie Richardson and Brian Lara had gone this day as many as 10 runs per over. Kennedy Otieno, back behind the stumps in place of Tariq Iqbal, had twice missed de Silva.

The only team who might conceivably have chased eight runs run per over for 50 overs would have been Sri Lanka themselves. Kenya had no hope, but the wicket was good, the ground was small, the outfield fast so there were plenty more runs to be had.

Otieno and Dipak Chudasama got Kenya away to a good start before Muttiah Muralitharan and Chaminda Vaas inspired a collapse of 3-4. Kenya's pride would not be dimmed, however, and Steve Tikolo and Hitesh Modi earned respect with a fourth-wicket partnership of 137. Tikolo signed off from the tournament the way he opened it, with a fine innings. He was yorked by Kumara Dharmasena just four runs short of a deserved 100 having hit eight fours and four sixes. It would have been Kenya's first century at the game's top level. The team's 7-254 was the third highest score by a non-Test playing nation in the World Cup.

Among the welter of runs and records, de Silva was named as Man of the Match.

SRI LANKA		KENYA	
S. T. Jayasuriya c D. Tikolo b E. Odumbe	44	D. Chudasama b Muralitharan	27
R. S. Kaluwitharana(wk) b E. Odumbe	33	K. O. Otieno (wk) b Vaas	14
A. P. Gurusinha c Onyango b Karim	84	S. O. Tikolo b Dharmasena	96
P. A. de Silva c Modi b Suji	145	M. O. Odumbe (capt) st Kaluwitharana b Muralitharan	0
A. Ranatunga(capt) not out	75	Hitesh Modi run out	41
H. P. Tillekeratne run out	0	D. Tikolo not out	25
R. S. Mahanama not out	0	E. Odumbe c Muralitharan b Ranatunga	4
Extras b1 lb5 w11	17	L. Onyango c sub(M. S. Atapattu) b Ranatunga	23
(50 overs)	5-398	M. Suji not out	2
Did not bat: H. D. P. K. Dharmasena, W. P. U. J. C. Vaas,		Extras b1 lb9 w7 nb5	22
M. Muralitharan, K. R.Pushpakumara		(50 overs)	7-254
1/83 2/88 3/271 4/377 5/383		Did not bat: A. V. Karim, R. Ali	
Bowling: Ali 6-0-67-0; Suji 9-0-85-1; Onyango 4-0-31-0; E.		1/47 2/51 3/51 4/188 5/196 6/215 7/246	
Odumbe 5-0-34-2; Karim 10-0-50-1; D. Tikolo 2-0-13-0; M.		Bowling: Vaas 10-0-44-1; Pushpakumara 7-0-46-0;	
O. Odumbe 9-0-74-0; S. O. Tikolo 5-0-38-0		Muralitharan10-1-40-2;	
		Dharmasena 10-0-44-1; Jayasuriya 7-0-34-0;	
		Ranatunga 5-0-31-2; Tillekeratne 1-0-4-0	

Umpires: R.S. Dunne V.K. Ramaswamy

Toss: Kenya   Points: Sri Lanka 2 Kenya 0

GREEN PARK, KANPUR: INDIA vs ZIMBABWE - GROUP A
INDIA WON BY 40 RUNS

This game allowed India to finish third in their group and set up the mouth-watering prospect of a quarter final clash with Pakistan in Bangalore. Zimbabwe missed out on the big win they required to progress to the next round.

It all started promisingly for Zimbabwe, too. A clinking break back from Heath Streak shattered stumps of Tendulkar, the man with 422 tournament runs to his credit, with the total on just five. Then by the 13th over Sanjay Manjrekar and Mohammad Azharuddin had both driven catches to Alistair Campbell at short mid wicket. Campbell took both chances well, one high and the other low.

India were 3-32 and an upset loomed. Campbell had set a fielding standard that, surprisingly, the Zimbabweans were unable to maintain. With his more illustrious former schoolmate Tendulkar, gone, Vinod Kambli, who sometimes made it look as batting was a fashion statement, took a key role with Navjot Sidhu. The left-hander put on 142 in 29 overs with Sidhu, surviving two outfield chances and a sharp caught and bowled to left-armer, Bryan Strang before going on to his second 100 in limited-over internationals. At 174 Streak held on to a chance offered by Sidhu off leg-spinner Paul Strang. By then, the Sikh had struck five fours in 116 balls.

While Kambli pushed on to his 100, Ajya Jadeja unleashed an array of thrilling shots that brought him three fours and two sixes in 27 balls. With plenty of wickets in hand he wrought havoc on Charles Lock's final over, hitting two fours and a six from the first three deliveries. Kambli had finally been dismissed after hitting 11 fours in 110 balls.

Zimbabwe needed to get 248 in 40 overs if they were to progress and Grant Flower and Andy Waller showed the proper intent by rattling up 50 in the first 10 overs. Those runs were scored off the Indian pacemen and the spin of Anil Kumble and Venkatapathy Raju proved a much more difficult proposition on a wicket getting lower and slower by the minute. Azharuddin supported his spinners with close catchers. Grant Flower was taken at silly point in Raju's first over and Waller held at silly mid-on by Tendulkar in Kumble's second over.

Zimbabwe got to 2-92 at the halfway point of their innings then lost a wicket in each of the next three overs. Guy Whittall batted an hour for 10. Streak kept the game alive with some judicious hits without ever suggesting he was going to create a miracle. The damage had been done. Jadeja won the Man of the Match Award.

INDIA		ZIMBABWE	
S. R. Tendulkar b Streak	3	A. C. Waller c Tendulkar b Kumble	22
N. S. Sidhu c Streak b P. A. Strang	80	G. W. Flower c Azharuddin b Raju	30
S. V. Manjrekar c Campbell b Lock	2	G. J. Whittall run out	10
M. Azharuddin (capt) c Campbell b B. Strang	2	A. D. R. Campbell c & b Jadeja	28
V. G. Kambli c G. W. Flower b Lock	106	A. Flower (capt/wk) b Raju	26
A. D. Jadeja not out	44	C. N. Evans c Srinath b Jadeja	6
N. R. Mongia (wk) not out	6	H. H. Streak lbw b Raju	30
Extras lb1 w3	4	P. A. Strang b Srinath	14
(50 overs)	5-247	B. C. Strang lbw b Srinath	3
Did not bat: A. Kumble, J. Srinath, B. K. V. Prasad,		S. G. Peall c Raju b Kumble	9
S. L.V. Raju		A. C. I. Lock not out	2
1/5 2/25 3/32 4/174 5/219		Extras b4 lb11 w11 nb1	27
Bowling: Streak 10-3-29-1; Lock 10-1-57-2; B.		(49.4 overs)	207
Strang 5-1-22-1; P. A. Strang 10-0-55-1; Peall 6-0-35-0;		1/59 2/59 3/96 4/99 5/106 6/168 7/173 8/193 9/195	
Whittall 3-0-19-0; G. W. Flower 3-0-16-0; Campbell 3-0-13-0		10/207	
		Bowling: Srinath 10-1-36-2; Prasad 7-0-40-0; Kumble	
		9.4-1-32-2; Raju 10-2-30-3; Tendulkar 6-0-23-0;	
		Jadeja 7-0-31-2	

Umpires: S.A. Bucknor C.J. Mitchley

Toss: Zimbabwe   Points: India 2 Zimbabwe 0

GADDAFI STADIUM, LAHORE: PAKISTAN vs NEW ZEALAND - GROUP B
PAKISTAN WON BY 46 RUNS

The 30th game of the Wills World Cup, the last of the preliminary round, made a greater impact on the tournament for the injuries that players suffered during it than for the result. New Zealand fast bowler, Danny Morrison, tore a groin muscle and, even more significantly, Wasim Akram, already under a cloud with an injured thumb, strained a muscle in his side. Neither would play in the quarter finals.

Workmen on the still unfinished light towers overlooking the ground got an elevated view of a fairly energetic match. The towers were originally scheduled to be working for this fixture. Now the fans of Lahore would have to wait until the final to see their cricket at night. Lahore is not the only venue to have had problems with the installation of light towers.

Morrison's appearance was merely a cameo. He limped off the field after just two expensive overs, not returning even to bat late in the game. Lee Germon had sent Pakistan in. Aamir Sohail seemed to take that as an invitation to demolish the new-ball attack. He hit 10 fours, carving the ball through and over the off-side, and raced to his 50 in an hour. He was then caught in the most amazing fashion by Shane Thomson at square leg. Sohail pulled a Robert Kennedy delivery off the middle of his bat. Thomson leapt and at full stretch claimed the ball in his left hand as he fell back.

Inspiring as that was it had no real effect on the rest of the Pakistani batting. Only Javed Miandad, having another innings on the farewell Javed tour, missed out on making a worthwhile contribution when he was run out after struggling for 27 minutes. Chris Harris' brilliant work at cover brought about the mistake which prompted the crowd's big tribute for the departing batsman.

Saeed Anwar, Inzamam-ul-Haq and Salim Malik and Wasim Akram, who put on 81 in the last nine overs, more than compensated for the veteran's slow rate. Malik got to his 50 in just 42 balls, hitting six fours in that time. Akram grimaced after a pull shot, but kept batting even though it would have made little difference to the destiny of this game.

Half an hour into the New Zealand innings Rashid Latif's two catches had removed both openers. The Pakistani wicketkeeper would go on to equal Syed Kirmani and Jimmy Adams' World Cup record of five dismissals in an innings, but they did not come quite as quickly or regularly as those first two.

Lee Germon promoted himself to number three in the order and soon settled in, although his was a supporting role as he failed to reach the boundary in 110 minutes of batting. Stephen Fleming got there seven times during a partnership of 60 with his captain that offered the Kiwis a glimmer of hope.

There were handy contributions from the entire middle order, however only Chris Cairns really scored at a rate that would have enabled New Zealand to reach the 282 they required. He struck a six over long on and another over cover from the spin bowling of Mushtaq Ahmed and Sohail. The left armer was, like Malik and Ijaz Ahmed, filling in their injured captain's quota of overs. Sohail exacted some revenge when he had the Kiwi all-rounder caught behind.

With Malik, who bowled a wide mixture of leg spin and medium pace, picking up Fleming and Adam Parore, and Mushtaq back to his best New Zealand did not have enough runs on the board or sufficient fit batsmen left to make the 87 they required from the final 10 overs. When Aaqib Javed returned to bowl Kennedy they were still 47 runs short. Malik was named Man of the Match.

PAKISTAN

Aamir Sohail c Thomson b Kennedy	50
Saeed Anwar run out	62
Ijaz Ahmed c Spearman b Cairns	26
Inzamam-ul-Haq run out	39
Javed Miandad run out	5
Salim Malik not out	55
Wasim Akram (capt) not out	28
Extras lb5 w5 nb6	16
(50 overs)	5-281

Did not bat: Rashid Latif (wk), Mushtaq Ahmed, Waqar Younis, Aaqib Javed

1/70 2/139 3/155 4/173 5/200

Bowling: Morrison 2-0-17-0; Nash 10-1-49-0; Cairns 10-1-53-1; Kennedy 5-0-32-1; Astle 9-0-50-0; Thomson 6-0-35-0; Twose 8-0-40-0

NEW ZEALAND

C. M. Spearman c Rashid Latif b Aaqib Javed	14
N. J. Astle c Rashid Latif b Aaqib Javed	6
L. K. Germon (capt/wk) c sub (Ata-ur-Rehman) b Mushtaq Ahmed	41
S. P. Fleming st Rashid Latif b Salim Malik	42
R. G. Twose c Salim Malik b Mushtaq Ahmed	24
A. C. Parore c Mushtaq Ahmed b Salim Malik	36
C. L. Cairns c Rashid Latif b Aamir Sohail	32
S. A. Thomson c Rashid Latif b Waqar Younis	13
D. J. Nash not out	5
R. J. Kennedy b Aaqib Javed	2
D. K. Morrison absent hurt	-
Extras b4 lb9 w6 nb1	20
(47.3 overs)	235

1/23 2/23 3/83 4/132 5/138 6/182 7/221 8/228 9/235

Bowling: Waqar Younis 9-2-32-2; Aaqib Javed 7.3-0-45-2; Mushtaq Ahmed 10-0-32-2; Salim Malik 7-0-41-2; Ijaz Ahmed 4-0-21-0; Sohail 10-0-51-1

Umpires: K.T. Francis I.D. Robinson

Toss: New Zealand   Points: Pakistan 2 New Zealand 0

THE QUARTER FINALS

The draw for the quarter finals was determined by the relative positions of the sides in their Group tables. The top of Group A would play the fourth-placed side from Group B and vice versa throughout. From here on the Wills World Cup became a straight knockout tournament, every side had as much chance as the other whatever their number of wins in the preliminary round.

GROUP A	P	W	L	Pts
SRI LANKA	5	5	0	10
AUSTRALIA	5	3	2	6
INDIA	5	3	2	6
WEST INDIES	5	2	3	4
Zimbabwe	5	1	4	2
Kenya	5	1	4	2

GROUP B	P	W	L	Pts
SOUTH AFRICA	5	5	0	10
PAKISTAN	5	4	1	8
NEW ZEALAND	5	3	2	6
ENGLAND	5	2	3	4
United Arab Emirates	5	1	4	2
Holland	5	0	5	0

SATURDAY 9 MARCH 1996
FIRST QUARTER FINAL
IQBAL STADIUM, FAISALABAD: SRI LANKA vs ENGLAND
SRI LANKA WON BY 5 WICKETS

England had hoped that when they reached the business end of the tournament they might pull out something special. They didn't.

No other game marked the decline of English cricket since the 1992 tournament and the improvement in Sri Lankan cricket as clearly as this one. The Sri Lankans were simply too good. Their exuberant batting, led by the astonishing Sanath Jayasuriya totally obliterated the early England bowling and condemned them to an exit prior to the semi-finals for the first time in the history of the World Cup.

"We'll bat and try to make 300," Mike Atherton told his team after he won the toss at the Iqbal Stadium. It was the first time England had played at the ground since Mike Gatting and umpire Shakoor Rana had argued heatedly back in late 1987. The result this day would be less controversial, but in its own way even more disappointing for the English visitors. There was only a modest gathering in the ground when Robin Smith and Atherton began their confrontation with Chaminda Vaas and Pramodya Wickremasinghe.

Unike the previous match, it was Atherton, rather than Smith who batted with early aggression, the 300 a little prematurely in his sights. After half an hour he was caught behind off the left-armer Vaas.

That left the African-born pair of Smith and Graeme Hick together and they just did not gel. The clear-eyed third umpire, V.K.Ramaswamy, adjudged Smith as run out from a Jayasuriya direct hit which made England 3-66, Hick having clipped off-spinner Muttiah Muralitharan to Arjuna Ranatunga on the on-side eight runs earlier.

England were a miserable 4-95 at the half way point, so pinch-hitting Phil DeFreitas was moved up the order. The promotion worked, as the seamer hit around him in effective if unorthodox fashion. He rattled up 67 in 63 balls with five fours and two sixes, one each off Jayasuriya and Muralitharan, before perishing as did Graham Thorpe and 'Jack' Russell to the English scourge on the subcontinent, the sweep.

Despite the efforts of DeFreitas, virtual disaster threatened again when the Sri Lankan spinners reduced England to 7-173. It was left to Dermot Reeve's improvisation and Darren Gough's muscle to put on 62 in 57 balls to give the scoreline a respectable look about it.

Plenty of World Cup matches have been won with 235 on the board. However not anywhere a berserk Jayasuriya was chasing. The assault began immediately, momentarily faltered then careered away again in decisive fashion.

Jayasuriya's opening partner, Romesh Kaluwitharana's, innings lasted three balls. He smashed Richard Illingworth for two fours, then was bowled behind his legs next ball.

It made no difference to Jayasuriya. The move to open the bowling with the left-arm spin of Illingworth showed imagination and looked like it might have worked until Jayasuriya hit him for four fours off consecutive deliveries. DeFreitas was also a special target, his second over costing 22, including sixes that hit a satellite dish and another that elevated the ball near the television commentators. In 30 balls he had reached his 50.

Gurusinha had been dropped by Gough low down before he had scored. He went on to again play a perfect secondary roll to the aggressor, sharing the plaudits for a century stand that took just 65 balls.

The crowd of 2,500 had witnessed about the best hour of uninhibited batting they were ever likely to see when Jayasuriya, the ball after being bowled by a no ball, was stumped by Russell off the medium pacer, Reeve. He had made his 82 in 44 balls, being in and out by the 13th over, even before the fielding restrictions had been lifted. Jayasuriya hit 16 of those 44 balls for either a four or a six. He had offered one chance, a scorcher to square leg off Peter Martin when he was on 43.

What followed had to be a little anti-climactic. Neverthless Aravinda de Silva and Rantatunga scored freely enough while Gurusinha held firm to make sure Jayasuriya's efforts were not wasted. When Gough had an lbw shout upheld against the Sri Lankan captain and then ended Gurusinha's resistance with a display of his soccer touch Sri Lanka were 5-198. There was no pressure on Hashan Tillekeratne or Roshan Mahanama, though, as they still had 20 overs to get the further 38 their side required. They took their time and got there with 10 overs to spare. Sri Lanka were through to the World Cup semi-finals for the first time.

Having also picked up a couple of wickets with his left-arm sliders, Jayasuriya's Man of the Match Award was never in doubt. English manager, Ray Illingworth could not be so certain of his position. Sky TV conducted a post match phone poll where 94 per cent of viewers called for him to step down. His two years at the top had not been happy ones.

ENGLAND	
R. A. Smith run out	25
M. A. Atherton (capt) c Kaluwitharana b Vaas	22
G. A. Hick c Ranatunga b Muralitharan	8
G. P. Thorpe b Dharmasena	14
P. A. J. DeFreitas lbw b Jayasuriya	67
A. J. Stewart b Muralitharan	17
R. C. Russell (wk) b Dharmasena	9
D. A. Reeve b Jayasuriya	35
D. Gough not out	26
P. J. Martin not out	0
Extras lb8 w4	12
(50 overs)	8-235

Did not bat: R. K. Illingworth

1/31 2/58 3/66 4/94 5/145 6/171 7/173 8/235

Bowling: Wickremasinghe 7-0-43-0; Vaas 8-1-29-1; Muralitharan 10-1-37-2; Dharmasena 10-0-30-2; Jayasuriya 9-0-46-2; de Silva 6-0-42-0

SRI LANKA	
S. T. Jayasuriya st Russell b Reeve	82
R. S. Kaluwitharana (wk) b Illingworth	8
A. P. Gurusinha run out	45
P. A. de Silva c Smith b Hick	31
A. Ranatunga (capt) lbw b Gough	25
H. P. Tillekeratne not out	19
R. S. Mahanama not out	22
Extras lb1 w2 nb1	5-236

Did not bat: H. D. P. K. Dharmasena, W. P. U. J.C. Vaas, M. Muralitharan, G. P. Wickremasinghe

1/12 2/113 3/165 4/194 5/198

Bowling: Martin 9-0-41-0; Illingworth 10-1-72-1; Gough 10-1-36-1; DeFreitas 3.4-0-38-0; Reeve 4-1-14-1; Hick 4-0-34-1

Umpires: Mahboob Shah I.D. Robinson
Toss: England

SATURDAY 9 MARCH 1996
SECOND QUARTER FINAL
M. CHINNASWAMY STADIUM, BANGALORE: INDIA vs PAKISTAN
INDIA WON BY 39 RUNS

The organisers might have wanted this clash of the local titans to be the final, or at least the semi-final in Calcutta. Such a game would have been a very hot affair, possibly even too hot if the passion behind this quarter final was any indicator. For many of the 55,000 in the ground there was seemed more at stake in Bangalore than progress towards winning a cricket World Cup.

There is hardly a major cricket ground in India that could be further away from Pakistan than the Chinnaswamy Stadium and any piece of quality play by the Pakistanis all day and night was greeted by absolute silence.

The Pakistani noises came from across the border in the west and they were not very pleasant after India held on to win. In a sort of warm-up for the negative hysteria that greeted his team's defeat in the 1999 final, effigies of Wasim Akram were burned and people turned their guns on their televsions and themselves. Tiresome accusations of bribery also surfaced.

Akram did not even play in Bangalore, as he hadn't recovered from the side strain suffered against New Zealand. Aamir Sohail was given charge of the team for this nationally important event ahead of five other ex-captains and he got off to a bad start by losing the toss. Mohammad Azharuddin's decision to bat meant Pakistan had to bat under the lights of Chinnaswamy. At least they were supplemented by various fireworks, fires and flares during the evening.

That lay ahead. The pressure of the situation was so intense even Sachin Tendulkar was subdued, Waqar Younis sending down a testing early spell. He passed the outside edge of Navjot Sidhu's bat three times in the first over. Younis' burst only lasted four overs as he was surprisingly relieved by his captain and Tendulkar and Sidhu weathered the storm. They made steady rather than spectacular progress taking 22 overs to put on 90, Sidhu continuing to be the more aggressive of the two. He reached his 50 in 72 balls just before Tendulkar played on to Akram's replacement, Ata-ur-Rehman.

Sanjay Manjrekar also left the scoring dominance to Sidhu. India cruised along at between four and five per over looking to keep wickets in hand. The Sikh called for a runner as a muscle strain deterioated during his innings and seven runs short of a milestone 100 he was deceived, swung across the line and was bowled by a Mushtaq Ahmed flipper. Never a certain selection in the Indian team, Sidhu's impressive innings had lasted 120 balls and included 11 fours. Like Manjrekar, Mohammad Azharuddin and Vinod Kambli got starts without really taking a toll of the Pakistani attack. When the Indian captain was brilliantly caught by a diving Rashid Latif in the 42nd over India were 4-200 and well short of a strong total.

Sidhu would be named Man of the Match, but it was Ajay Jadeja's short innings that changed the game. In 27 balls he cracked four fours and two sixes ruining the figures of Younis of all people, who had been so impressive in his first spell.

Javagal Srinath and Anil Kumble contributed to the final spree so that 51 runs were added from the final three overs, including 40 from Younis' ninth and 10th overs. Jadeja had put him over long off with a mighty drive. The bowler had Jadeja caught in the deep soon after to claim his 200th wicket in limited-over internationals, however there was little cause for celebration.

Instead of chasing 250 the Pakistanis, who had been bombarded with missiles whenever they were in the outfield, now had to make 288 to win. The match referee, Raman Subba Row, also penalised them one over for their slow rate of bowling.

Those lost six balls looked unlikely to make any difference as Saeed Anwar and Sohail implemented a Jayasuriya-style assault on Srinath and Venkatash Prasad. Maintaining the momentum of the end of the Indian innings, they had 84 on the board by the end of the 10th over. Even the early introduction of Kumble could not halt the run flow and the nature of the loss against Sri Lanka became the uppermost thought of Indian fans.

After 32 balls of mayhem, the exhileration of pounding bowlers became too much for Anwar and he skied a slog off Srinath to Kumble, a local double act dismissal that thrilled the crowd. Anwar had hit five fours and two sixes and his captain for the day continued in the same vein whacking Venkatapathy Raju for six with an extraordinary flat batted drive over point that brought him to 50 and raised the Pakistani 100. Then Sohail let the emotion of the moment affect his concentration. Prasad was recalled, Sohail drove him for four and offered him some advice. Then the opener aimed somewhere deep on the on side and was bowled.

It had been a fatal error because it fired up Prasad who followed up by having Ijaz Ahmed caught in the deep and Inzamam-ul-Haq caught behind off the glove. From the comfort of 1-113, Pakistan had slipped to 4-132 and the rousing start had been wasted. The fight from there was well taken up by Salim Malik and Javed Miandad. They travelled at a more cautious rate, though, as the collapse had made wickets an issue.

The required run rate, once down to just above five per over went back out to nearly eight. Rashid Latif came in and hit two sixes off Kumble, then four wickets fell in a few minutes for just seven runs to settle the issue. In the 43rd over Latif was stumped, Mushtaq pushed a catch back to Kumble first ball, and Miandad scoring at an insufficient rate, fell foul of a Jadeja throw and the red light of the third umpire. His poignant exit from the international stage for definitely the last time momentarily distracted from the fact that India had the game in their keeping. The celebrations went outside the ground into the streets of Bangalore as car horns and whistles were over worked. There had been no second prize this day.

INDIA		PAKISTAN	
N. S. Sidhu b Mushtaq Ahmed	93	Aamir Sohail (capt) b Prasad	55
S. R. Tendulkar b Ata-ur-Rehman	31	Saeed Anwar c Kumble b Srinath	48
S. V. Manjrekar c Javed Miandad b Aamir Sohail	20	Ijaz Ahmed c Srinath b Prasad	12
M. Azharuddin (capt) c Rashid Latif b Waqar Younis	27	Inzamam-ul-Haq c Mongia b Prasad	12
V. G. Kambli b Mushtaq Ahmed	24	Salim Malik lbw b Kumble	38
A. D. Jadeja c Aamir Sohail b Waqar Younis	45	Javed Miandad run out	38
N. R. Mongia (wk) run out	3	Rashid Latif (wk) st Mongia b Raju	26
A. Kumble c Javed Miandad b Aaqib Javed	10	Mushtaq Ahmed c & b Kumble	0
J. Srinath not out	12	Waqar Younis not out	4
B. K.V. Prasad not out	0	Ata-ur-Rehman lbw b Kumble	0
Extras lb3 w15 nb4	22	Aaqib Javed not out	6
(50 overs)	8-287	Extras b1 lb3 w5	9
Did not bat: S. L.V. Raju		(49 overs)	9-248

1/90 2/138 3/168 4/200 5/226 6/236 7/260 8/279

1/84 2/113 3/122 4/132 5/184 6/231 7/232 8/239 9/239

Bowling: Waqar Younis 10-1-67-2; Aaqib Javed 10-0-67-1; Ata-ur-Rehman 10-0-40-1; Mushtaq Ahme d 10-0-56-2; Aamir Sohail 5-0-29-1; Salim Malik 5-0-25-0

Bowling: Srinath 9-0-61-1; Prasad 10-0-45-3; Kumble 10-0-48-3; Raju 10-0-46-1; Tendulkar 5-0-25-0; Jadeja 5-0-19-0

Umpires: S.A. Bucknor D.R. Shepherd

Toss: India

MONDAY 11 MARCH 1996
THIRD QUARTER FINAL
NATIONAL STADIUM, KARACHI: SOUTH AFRICA vs WEST INDIES
WEST INDIES WON BY 19 RUNS

South Africa found how much of a waste five wins on the trot can be if the fall comes at the first hurdle of the knockout stage. Their masters were the tournament enigmas, the West Indies, who were inspired by a brilliant century from the enigma king, Brian Lara. South African coach Bob Woolmer and the captain, Hansie Cronje both felt Lara was the difference between the two sides.

The first surpise came prior to Richie Richarsdon winning the toss and batting. South Africa decided to omit fast-bowling spearhead Allan Donald and played a second spinner, Paul Adams, instead. Public interest in Karachi for this game was as limited as Saturday's clash in Faisalabad, the country was still to some extent in cricket mourning for the loss in Bangalore.

Courtney Browne and Shivnarine Chanderpaul became the third opening pair used by the West Indies in as many matches. The young, slender left-hander Chanderpaul absorbed new ball thrust while Browne attacked. The ploy worked for a few overs while the wicketkeeper hit three fours before Craig Matthews broke through.

Lara's nervousness was obvious at the start of his innings. He played and missed repeatedly during his first three overs at the wicket. Then one shot came off the middle, a square drive off Hansie Cronje, and he was away.

Lara relished the Proteas' emphasis on slow bowling and put off-spinner Pat Symcox away for five fours in an over on way to completing his 50 in 45 balls. Paul Adams was also expensive. Now the pressure was on the South Africans in the field and for a while they struggled, misfields and a missed catch by Jonty Rhodes being part of an out-of-character performance.

Lara completed his splendid 100 in 83 balls and with Chanderpaul put on 138 in 25 overs. Chanderpaul perished while sweeping Brian McMillan. Symcox, changing the angle by bowling over the wicket to the left-hander and aiming at leg stump, picked up Lara when he top edged a sweep. Lara had hit 16 fours in 97 balls and set up a big total that did not quite eventuate.

The later batsmen showed far less composure against the spinners, although Keith Arthurton was able to double his tournament aggregate. A couple of hefty blows by Ian Bishop off Adams lifted the final total to a still very competitive 8-264.

It was certainly enough to inspire Curtley Ambrose and Courtney Walsh to another demanding opening salvo. It restricted South Africa to 19 runs off 10 overs and then brought about the wicket of Gary Kirsten who broke his stumps as he set off for a single.

The worst possible scenario was quickly engulfing South Africa and Andrew Hudson and Daryll Cullinan responded with a display of necessary belligerence. They put on 97 in 19 overs, Cullinan clubbing three big sixes in his innings including an inside out drive over extra cover off Jimmy Adams to take him to his 50. Hudson also reached the half-century landmark, having been recalled to the crease at one stage by Lara after being bowled by a no ball from Ian Bishop. Although Adams, bowling left-arm spin at the leg stump, had both caught on the boundary attempting straight sixes, Cronje kept his side in the hunt with two shots off Walsh that did clear the boundary.

South Africa got as far as 3-186 then Cronje picked out Arthurton at mid wicket to give the part-time spinner, part-time wicketkeeper, Adams his third wicket. It was not until the 41st over, though, that the match swung decisively in favour of the West Indies. Roger Harper had Rhodes pulling to Adams on the mid wicket boundary, then next ball Brian McMillan missed a straight ball he had tried to turn to square leg. Before the end of the over Steve Palframan hit a low drive back to the bowler which the world's most dextrous fieldsman took low and one-handed.

From a desperate position of 7-198 Symcox struck out to good but brief effect, collaring Harper twice before failing to clear the boundary with his next attempt off Arthurton.

It was South Africa's last gasp. By the time Walsh bowled Adams in the last over the task had been well beyond them. Lara was named Man of the Match. Andy Roberts attributed the win to the contrasting way the West Indians played compared to their opponents, "instinctive" cricket winning out ahead of "computerised science" in his opinion.

As he would lose his position after the tournament the former great fast bowler was fast running out of opportunities to back up his philosophy.

WEST INDIES		SOUTH AFRICA	
S. Chanderpaul c Cullinan b McMillan	56	A. C. Hudson c Walsh b Adams	54
C. O. Browne (wk) c Cullinan b Matthews	26	G. Kirsten hit wicket b Ambrose	3
B. C. Lara c Pollock b Symcox	111	D. J. Cullinan c Bishop b Adams	69
R. B. Richardson (capt) c Kirsten b Symcox	10	W. J. Cronje (capt) c Arthurton b Adams	40
R. A. Harper lbw b McMillan	9	J. N. Rhodes c Adams b Harper	13
R. I.C. Holder run out	5	B. M. McMillan lbw b Harper	6
K. L. T. Arthurton c Hudson b Adams	1	S. M. Pollock c Adams b Harper	6
J. C. Adams not out	13	S. J. Palframan (wk) c & b Harper	1
I. R. Bishop b Adams	17	P. L. Symcox c Harper b Arthurton	24
C. E. L. Ambrose not out	0	C. R. Matthews not out	8
Extras b2 lb11 w2 nb1	16	P. R. Adams b Walsh	10
(50 overs)	8-264	Extras b1 lb4 w2 nb4	11
Did not bat: C. A. Walsh		(49.3 overs)	245

West Indies: 1/42 2/180 3 /210 4/214 5/227 6/230 7/230 8/254

Bowling: Pollock 9-0-46-0; Matthews 10-0-42-1; Cronje 3-0-17-0; McMillan 10-1-37-2; Symcox 10-0-64-2; Adams 8-0-45-2

South Africa: 1/21 2/118 3/140 4/186 5/196 6/196 7/198 8/227 9/228 10/245

Bowling: Ambrose 10-0-29-1; Walsh 8.3-0-51-1; Bishop5-0-31-0; Harper 10-0-47-4; Adams 10-0-52-3; Arthurton 6-0-29-1

Umpires: K.T. Francis S.G. Randell

Toss: West Indies

CHEPAUK STADIUM, MADRAS (CHENNAI): AUSTRALIA vs NEW ZEALAND
AUSTRALIA WON BY 6 WICKETS

On a Madras curry of an afternoon and evening Australia outsweated New Zealand to progress through to the semi-finals of the Wills World Cup. To get there they had to produce their highest-ever score when batting second, the achievement of the target completing a match of loaded with runs and exciting strokes that thrilled the enthusiastic if relaxed capacity crowd in attendance.

New Zealand compiled their best total in a limited-over internationals against Australia without being able to go on and win. Chasing 286 Australia reached their objective with two overs and six wickets to spare. There was no surprise in the fact that the Waugh twins made a major contribution to the victory, Mark completing a World Cup record-breaking third century.

New Zealand were without Danny Morrison and knew they would need a lot of runs if they were to have a chance. They benefitted from Lee Germon winning the toss and batting on a grassless strip of concrete, which also condemned Australia to field in the heat and humidity of the afternoon.

The match opened with breakneck cricket. Craig Spearman smashed three fours in Paul Reiffel's first over then watched his partner, Nathan Astle dance out to Damien Fleming and edge through to Ian Healy.

As if liking what he saw, Spearman slashed at a wide delivery in Reiffel's next over so that New Zealand were 2-16 after 16 balls. Stephen Fleming holed out to Steve Waugh off Glenn McGrath without making an impact. That left the Kiwis on an unconvincing 3-44 as Chris Harris joined his captain who had bravely left himself at number three.

Neither Harris nor Germon had done anything in this tournament to suggest they would trouble the powerful Australian unit. The Aussies revised their thinking 27 overs later when the pair had put on 168. It was great batting and came out of the blue to the delight of the crowd whose sympathies lay mostly with the underdogs. No Australian bowler was spared. Shane Warne conceded 13 in an over, his most expensive in the competition. Harris twice clubbed McGrath for sixes, one over mid wicket, the other over square cover. The paceman found no assistance from the atmosphere despite the humidity and tended to drop the ball short.

Harris, with 26 runs from his previous three innings in the tournament, may not have been selected if Gavin Larsen had been fit. Steve Waugh admitted the Australians underestimated his capabilities, but they were learning quickly as the ball sailed into the outfield and the crowd. Once off Mark Waugh the ball landed in the second tier of the stands. Then Germon fell 11 short of his century after hitting 10 fours in 96 balls.

The Kiwi momentum stalled slightly from that point and they only added a further 57 runs from the last ten overs. Harris cramping through loss of fluids completed his 100 in 96 balls. He went on to 130 with 13 fours and four sixes and had given two chances before being caught in the 49th over, a one handed effort by Reiffel on the boundary from a pull off Shane Warne. Chris Cairns dismissal had been crucial to limiting the Kiwi total to something below 300. It was a bonus for Australia that Michael Bevan's left-arm wrist spin had been as economical as Warne's.

While there was no doubt as to the quality of Chris Harris' innings, and he did bowl quite tidily also, his effort was insufficient to win the Man of the Match Award. That accolade instead went to Mark Waugh, most likely because he ended on the winning side. Between innings the Australians remained confident in their own ability. They knew however that they had an enormous task in front of them.

Germon resorted to the 1992 tactic of opening the bowling with Dipak Patel's off-spin and in the sixth over he had Mark Taylor caught behind down the leg-side. Mark Waugh and Ricky Ponting consolidated the innings. When the Tasmanian was out in the 20th over the score was 2-84. The innings may have been consolidated, but the run rate was in desperate need of a boost.

Taylor sent in Warne to the surprise of most as a pinch hitter. He swung into his work immediately, only to be dropped in the deep by Patel. Nor did his innings last more than a quarter of an hour longer, however he made the 14 deliveries he faced count. Harris was clouted over cover for six and Shane Thomson was also punished, so that with Mark Waugh now scoring freely, 43 were added in four and a half overs.

Even when Nathan Astle removed the troublesome pinch hitter it was clear control of the game had been transferred. Steve joined Mark in a quality stand of 86 that lifted the Australian confidence and run rate further. In lighting the Australians felt was not totally adequate, Mark Waugh began to see the fading white ball as if it were a melon. Boundaries now puncutated the ones and twos which came at will.

Mark Waugh hit a straight six off Patel that took him to 99 then completed his century in 101 balls. His second 50 had come in just 34 balls. Steve rated his twin brother's innings one of the best of his career and when it was over he had broken the record for the highest aggregate by a batsman in a World Cup tournament.

The ask when Stuart Law joined Steve Waugh was 76 in 70 balls with six wickets standing. The batting plan was to try to score the majority of the runs in singles, edging ever closer to victory. Waugh stuck pretty well to that idea. Law, on the other hand, once he felt he had the measure of the bowlers, forgot it and opened up. The requirement was being quickly reduced when the Queenslander pulled Thomson for six. Waugh reached his 50 in 60 balls then sealed the exciting win with a leg glanced boundary off Chris Cairns. The victory songs in the Australian dressing room were sung with extra gusto that evening.

The four semi-finalists were all teams from Group A. Those eliminated, the four Group B sides, had been the semi finalists of 1992.

NEW ZEALAND		AUSTRALIA	
C. M. Spearman c Healy b Reiffel	13	M. A. Taylor (capt) c Germon b Patel	10
N. J. Astle c Healy b Fleming	1	M. E. Waugh c Parore b Nash	110
L. K. Germon (capt/wk) c Fleming b McGrath	89	R. T. Ponting c sub (R. J. Kennedy) b Thomson	31
S. P. Fleming c S. R. Waugh b McGrath	8	S. K. Warne lbw b Astle	24
C. Z. Harris c Reiffel b Warne	130	S. R. Waugh not out	59
R. G. Twose b Bevan	4	S. G. Law not out	42
C. L. Cairns c Reiffel b M. E. Waugh	4	Extras b1 lb6 w3 nb3	13
A. C. Parore lbw b Warne	11	(47.5 overs)	4-289
S. A. Thomson run out	11	Did not bat: M. G. Bevan, I. A. Healy (wk), P. R. Reiffel,
D. N. Patel not out	3	D. W. Fleming, G. D. McGrath
Extras lb6 w3 nb3	12	1/19 2/84 3/127 4/213
(50 overs)	9-286	Bowling: Nash 9-1-44-1; Patel 8-0-45-1; Cairns 6.5-0-51-0;
Did not bat: D. J.Nash		Harris 10-1-41-0;
1/15 2/16 3/44 4/212 5/227 6/240 7/259 8/282 9/286		Thomson 8-0-57-1; Astle 3-0-21-1; Twose 3-0-23-0
Bowling: Reiffel 4-0-38-1; Fleming 5-1-20-1;		
McGrath 9-2-50-2; M. E. Waugh 8-0-43-1; Warne 10-0-52-2;		
Bevan 10-0-52-1; S. R. Waugh 4-0-25-0		

Umpires: C.J. Mitchley S. Venkataraghavan
Toss: New Zealand

WEDNESDAY 13 MARCH 1996
FIRST SEMI-FINAL
EDEN GARDENS, CALCUTTA: INDIA vs SRI LANKA
SRI LANKA WON BY DEFAULT

This may well have been World Cup cricket's darkest and saddest day. A riot by sections of the crowd as India were sliding to an inevitable defeat brought an end to the game and forced Clive Lloyd, who handled a desperately sensitive situation with firmness and common sense, to award the game to Sri Lanka.

Arjuna Rantunga's team would have won anyway had the match gone its course. Perhaps the greatest pity of the disturbances was that they distracted from Sri Lanka's greatest cricketing achievement in reaching their first World Cup final.

The spectacle of 110,000 people crammed into one of cricket's greatest venues was at first an irresistible one and something special to be anticipated. Those in attendance thought so, too, with the added attraction being their belief India would march into the final. Later, it all went very wrong very quickly when the hosts collapsed from 1-98 to 8-120. That was too much for some to cope with. Their lack of control ruined what could have been the great advertisement for cricket in Calcutta. They embarrassed officals and brought players to tears.

Riotous celebration was the only thing on Bengali minds when two wickets fell in Javagal Srinath's opening over after Mohammad Azharuddin had won the toss and surprisingly to some critics, elected to bowl. His reasoning was that Sri Lanka preferred to chase and he was prepared to accept the predicted risk the wicket would turn more as the match progressed. By the fourth ball of the match Romesh Kaluwitharana a right-hander, and Sanath Jayasuriya, a left-hander had slashed hard and high towards third man only to be caught near the boundary.

Like a counter-punching boxer, Aravinda de Silva was soon returning blows, taking a boundary nudged past slip off Anil Kumble's first over. The leg-spinner shared the new ball with Srinath. In temperatures in the high 30s, de Silva continued to turn up the heat on the Indian bowlers. Even the loss of Asanka Gurusinha to a mistimed pull in the seventh over failed to break his stride. He took 22 off two overs by Venkatash Prasad, striking boundaries to all parts of the ground, clean beautifully timed strokes of neat movements.

A cover drive for his 11th four in the 11th over took him to his half century in 32 balls out of 3-63. Three more boundaries flowed from his bat before he edged a Kumble wrong 'un onto his middle stump in the 15th over. A score of 4-85 was still nothing to get excited about and it was the stand of 83 between Roshan Mahanama and Arjuna Ranatunga, which put Sri Lanka right in the match. Without resorting to de Silva-style fireworks they compiled their runs at a consistent five per over pace, getting plenty of singles with pushes to square leg and wide of cover.

That took its toll on Mahanama who began to cramp up and was allowed to use a runner. Not only Mahanama was dehydrating. The crowd had already gone through all the drinks available for sale in the outer and had to swelter until the sting went out of the heat in the evening.

It was India's best bowler at the game, Sachin Tendulkar, who broke the stand on 168, trapping Ranatunga lbw with a leg break. Fourteen runs later in the 38th over, Mahanama, who had hardly batted in the whole tournament, collapsed again with cramp and had to be carried from the ground. He had an 58 invaluable to his name. A few late over clouts by Chaminda Vaas and some steady scoring by Hashan Tillekeratne lifted the total to 8-251 which everyone viewed as just okay.

Totals of 270 and 280 had been inadequate in recent matches so there was nothing to suggest India would not get very close even when in the third over Navjot Sidhu clipped Vaas to Jayasuriya in the gully. The star in the bright spotlight, Tendulkar embarked on an innings of a quality not far short of de Silva's and of equal value. With Sanjay Manjrekar as a secure partner he reached his 50 out of 1-71 in the 17th over, 110,000 people cheering spontaneously as one.

By the 23rd over it was 1-98, the time for acceleration fast approaching. Jayasuriya replaced Muttiah Muralitharan and bowled his left arm sliding spin into the bowler's rough outside the leg stump of the right-hander. Tendulkar was struck on the pad and went looking for a leg bye. But Kaluwitharana had already gathered the ball and the third umpire showed Tendulkar's backward lunge had come too late.

At the moment the red light flashed the Indian wheels came straight off. One run and seven balls later Azharuddin pushed the ball via bat and pad back to off-spinner Kumara Dharmasena. An eerie silence overtook the crowd.

Manjrekar was next, bowled off his thigh, sweeping at Jayasuriya. The personal sting of the Sri Lankan opener's batting failure was being soothed by these key wickets. Srinath was promoted to pinch hit India out of their daze. He struck one boundary then failed to beat Muralitharan's throw to the bowler's end to make the score 5-110 in the 29th over. Collapses can be halted with common sense, but none was in evidence in the brewing mad house.

Ajay Jadeja, still not off the mark, swept at Jayasuriya and was bowled leg stump. Wicketkeeper Nayan Mongia went a sweeping too, lifting a de Silva off-spinner to none other than Jayasuriya at mid wicket. He leapt for joy having been involved in six of the seven dismissals.

Then facing his first ball which was the first delivery of the 35th over, Aashish Kapoor carbon copied Mongia's dismissal. India had lost 7-22 to be 8-120. Vinod Kambli went down on his haunches in an attitude of submission.

Now the missiles, most of them plastic water bottles, began to rain down. The players and umpires left the field. A large percentage of the crowd had already gone home in disgust. Many of those that remained were making their presence felt.

Kambli pleaded with Lloyd for the match to restart. There were no public announcements about authorities' plans. When they tried to resume the game after 20 minutes more missiles flew out. India were shamed out of the tournament. The crowd's attitude to their captain after the match was equally disgraceful and it took two years and a big Test century against Australia to heal the rift that developed.

Aravinda de Silva was named Man of the Match.

SRI LANKA		INDIA	
S. T. Jayasuriya c Prasad b Srinath	1	S. R. Tendulkar st Kaluwitharana b Jayasuriya	65
R. S. Kaluwitharana (wk) c Manjrekar b Srinath	0	N. S. Sidhu c Jayasuriya b Vaas	3
A. P. Gurusinha c Kumble b Srinath	1	S. V. Manjrekar b Jayasuriya	25
P. A. de Silva b Kumble	66	M. Azharuddin (capt) c & b Dharmasena	0
R. S. Mahanama retired hurt	58	V. G. Kambli not out	10
A. Ranatunga (capt) lbw b Tendulkar	35	J. Srinath run out	6
H. P. Tillekeratne c Tendulkar b Prasad	32	A. D. Jadeja b Jayasuriya	0
H. D. P. K. Dharmasena b Tendulkar	9	N. R. Mongia (wk) c Jayasuriya b de Silva	1
W. P. U. J.C. Vaas run out	23	A. R. Kapoor c de Silva b Muralitharan	0
G. P. Wickremasinghe not out	4	A. Kumble not out	0
M. Muralitharan not out	5	Extras lb5 w5	10
Extras lb1 b10 w4 nb2	17	(34.1 overs)	8-120
(50 overs)	8-251	Did not bat: B. K. V. Prasad	

1/1 2/1 3/35 4/85 5/168 6/206 7/236 8/244

Mahanama retried hurt at 5-182

Bowling: Srinath 7-1-34-3; Kumble 10-0-51-1;
Prasad 8-0-50-1; Kapoor 10-0-40-0; Jadeja 5-0-31-0;
Tendulkar 10-1-34-2

1/8 2/98 3/99 4/101 5/110 6/115 7/120 8/120

Bowling: Wickremasinghe 5-0-24-0; Vaas 6-1-23-1;
Muralitharan 7.1-0-29-1; Dharmasena 7-0-24-1;
Jayasuriya 7-1-12-3; de Silva 2-0-3-1

Umpires: R.S. Dunne C.J. Mitchley

Toss: India

THURSDAY 14 MARCH 1996
SECOND SEMI FINAL
MOHALI STADIUM, CHANDIGARH: AUSTRALIA vs WEST INDIES
AUSTRALIA WON BY 5 RUNS

Thankfully the Chandigarh semi-final was memorable for the right reasons. The lunacy of Eden Gardens was replaced by an astonishing cricket match which was heading in a one direction for much of its duration, only to be twisted violently back the other way in its closing moments.

The eventual result was a fantastic thrill to the Australians and their supporters, but equally a bitter disappointment to the West Indies. After forfeiting a seemingly invincible position with a dreadful batting collapse it was little consolation that they had progressed further than their previous two World Cup predecessors.

Australia had retained their rating as favourites to lift the silver trophy on Sunday 17 March throughout and they were now only one step away from fulfilling the confidence of those that had put money on them. Their date with Sri Lanka in Lahore would be their third appearance in a World Cup final.

Outside the subcontinent many believed the winner of the tournament would come from this match and soon after Mark Taylor won the toss and batted the West Indies had almost a stranglehold on the contest. By the 10-over mark, the eagles circling above the ground might as well have been vultures picking at the carcass of an Australian cricket team reeling at 4-15.

Curtley Ambrose immediately began the demolition of the Australian top order, taking full advantage of the two-paced wicket with his accuracy, pace and movement. He struck with the second ball of the match. A pinpoint off-cutter thumped into the stationary pads of Mark Waugh right in front of the stumps. It was a simple decision for umpire Venkataraghavan and a real boost for the West Indies to remove the most prolific batsman of the tournament so quickly.

Ian Bishop shared the new ball and in his second over Mark Taylor played the ball into his stumps leaving his side 2-7. Ambrose followed up by pinning Ricky Ponting as he had Mark Waugh. Then Steve Waugh drove an undriveable Bishop delivery back onto his stumps in the 10th over. The frontline had been punctured and the way to the reserves was open.

Michael Bevan had not properly established his reputation outside Australia as a top limited-overs batsman by the time of the Wills World Cup. After his fighting 69 at Chandigarh the world had a better idea of his qualities. He was not alone in forcing Australia back into the contest. Stuart Law's contribution in the face of adversity was equally noteworthy. The Australian 'young guns' put on 138 in 32 overs, running feverishly for singles and twos and occasionally playing a big shot. At 4-43 Law was caught off a no ball, an important let-off. As his confidence grew, Bevan struck off-spinner Roger Harper for the only six of the match.

After 106 balls, which included five fours, Law dabbed to point and Bevan charged. Law did not see him coming and was far too late to set off for what would have been a close call, anyway. Once Ambrose's throw was on target Law began walking towards the pavilion.

Four overs later Bevan's step away drive went straight to Richie Richardson at cover. He had faced 109 balls and hit four fours and a six. That made the score 6-171, so it was left to the wise ingenuity of Ian Healy to get the Australian total beyond the 200 mark by the end of the 50th over.

Even 207 was 25 short of what Taylor thought would be adequate on an admittedly big ground and it looked quite a modest challenge once the West Indian top order saw off the opening Australian thrust. Shane Warne brought on as early as the seventh over held a sharp caught and bowled when Courtney Browne punched his first ball, a long hop, back down the wicket.

Then Lara, still full of form and confidence, stroked his way to 45 at a run per ball. Such was his power at times he had no trouble beating fieldsmen set in defensive positions on the boundary. With the rock solid Shivnarine Chanderpaul, Lara carried the score from 1-25 to 1-60 after 15 overs, then 1-93 in 22 before Steve Waugh, bowling around the wicket, produced a peach of a delivery. The ball pitched on off-stump, held its line and clipped the outside of the stumps. Not even Lara's immaculate defensive bat could keep it out.

Australia thought that might have signalled a West Indian capitulation. They were on the right track, but premature. Richie Richardson and Chanderpaul assumed control as another 72 were added in 20 overs. Richardson was intent on playing in a World Cup final as his farewell to international cricket and no-one was to stand in his way, not even the square leg umpire. The West Indian captain timed a sweep off Warne, which banged into the head of umpire Cooray. The Australians should have been grateful. The head of the Sri Lankan official saved a couple of runs.

By the 42nd over most spectators at the ground and those dozing on their couches in front of the late night television back in Australia accepted the result as a formality. Taylor had tried eight different bowlers. Another 43 runs from eight overs and Richardson would have his dream farewell. With eight wickets in hand it had to be a certainty.

It mattered little when Chanderpaul, starting to cramp up, got a bit carried away and trying to belt Glenn McGrath down the ground only got as far as Damien Fleming at mid-on. Nor did the prompt removal of the all-rounders, Roger Harper and Otis Gibson, the former trapped lbw on the crease by McGrath, the latter caught behind off Warne, really indicate a possible West Indian loss.

The expressions of the faces of the crowd and the players really began to change once Jimmy Adams had been given out lbw hitting across Warne. That made the West Indies 6-183, needing 25 from 21 balls with four wickets standing. It was still fairly straightforward, but four runs later Keith Arthurton with two runs from his previous four innings in the tournament and scoreless from six balls in this one lifted his head and swung wildly at Fleming. His 48th over death or glory shot merely edged the ball through to Ian Healy and Richardson was left to get the runs with the three fast bowlers.

Seven runs later when Ian Bishop played back awkwardly to a Warne flipper he had two fast bowlers left. Warne had taken 3-6 in three Man of the Match Award-winning overs, however it was up to his fellow Victorian, Fleming to deliver the 50th over from which the West Indies required 10 runs with two wickets standing.

It would last just three balls, yet such was the tension the over seemed to last an eternity. With the ground in total uproar Richardson swung the first ball away to mid wicket for four. Six required from five balls. Richardson bottom edged a cut off Fleming's second ball along the ground to Healy and called Ambrose for the run. Healy threw down the stumps with the long Antiguan stretching for the crease. The third umpire, Khizar Hayat was called into action and everyone, especially the players, waited with baited breath, before to the delight of the Australians, Ambrose was shown the red light.

This semi-final at Chandigarh was another in that long line of Australia/West Indian classics and it came down to the final four deliveries to determine who would go through to Sunday's Final in Lahore.

There never will be a prouder West Indian cricketer than Courtney Walsh and his determination as he peered down the floodlit wicket at Fleming and belted the bottom of his bat into the blockhole was obvious. Six more runs in four balls would do it. His captain at the other end was well set. Fleming ran in and bowled. Walsh propped half forward and drove, the ball was through him in an instant and his stumps were shattered. Australia had won by five runs and the West Indies, so close to erasing the earlier ignominy of their defeat by Kenya had lost an inglorious 8-37. Richie Richardson unbeaten and within a whisker of glory walked away. He had played his last innings for the West Indies.

Steve Waugh said the final overs were a blur so hard was the adrenalin pumping through the Australians. Their elation and relief at so amazing a victory was all enveloping. They laughed and danced together in huddle taking in the memorable moment with the entire Australian squad. "I thought the West Indies were home and dry," Taylor said after the game.

AUSTRALIA		WEST INDIES	
M. E. Waugh lbw b Ambrose	0	S. Chanderpaul c Fleming b McGrath	80
M. A. Taylor (capt) b Bishop	1	C. O. Browne (wk) c & b Warne	10
R. T. Ponting lbw b Ambrose	0	B. C. Lara b Waugh	45
S. R. Waugh b Bishop	3	R. B. Richardson (capt) not out	49
S. G. Law run out	72	R. A. Harper lbw b McGrath	2
M. G. Bevan c Richardson b Harper	69	O. D. Gibson c Healy b Warne	1
I. A. Healy (wk) run out	31	J. C. Adams lbw b Warne	2
P. R. Reiffel run out	7	K. L. T. Arthurton c Healy b Fleming	0
S. K. Warne not out	6	I. R. Bishop lbw b Warne	3
Extras lb11 w5 nb2	18	C. E. L. Ambrose run out	2
(50 overs)	8-207	C. A. Walsh b Fleming	0
Did not bat: D. W. Fleming, G. D. McGrath		Extras lb4 w2 nb2	8
1/0 2/7 3/8 4/15 5/153 6/171 7/186 8/207		(49.3 overs)	202
Bowling: Ambrose 10-1-26-2; Bishop 10-1-35-2;		1/25 2/93 3/165 4/173 5/178 6/183 7/187 8/194 9/202	
Walsh 10-1-33-0; Gibson 2-0-13-0; Harper 9-0-47-1;		10/202	
Adams 9-0-42-0		Bowling: McGrath 10-2-30-2; Fleming 8.3-0-48-2;	
		Warne 9-0-36-4; M. E. Waugh 4-0-16-0; S. R.	
		Waugh 7-0-30-1; Reiffel 5-0-13-0; Bevan 4-0-12-0;	
		Law 2-0-13-0	

Umpires: B.C. Cooray S. Venkataraghavan
Toss: Australia

SUNDAY 17 MARCH 1996
WILLS WORLD CUP FINAL
GADDAFI STADIUM, LAHORE: AUSTRALIA vs SRI LANKA
SRI LANKA WON BY 7 WICKETS

There was a certain amount of trepidation about this World Cup Final between Australia and Sri Lanka. Disputes and on field controversy had marred their recent encounters and the ill-feeling surrounding Australia's boycott of Colombo lingered.

Arjuna Ranatunga had refused to shake Mark Taylor's hand after a World Series Cup final at the end of the Australian summer. What sort of behaviour might be on display on cricket's night of nights was cause for concern as there were members of both sides not keen to take a backward step.

In the end common sense prevailed and the behaviour of the players was as restrained as could be hoped. By far the greatest shock came with the ease by which Sri Lanka overcame the tournament favourites. Australian authorities had done a lot to assist Sri Lanka in gaining full Test-playing status in the early 1980s. That was nothing compared to what their defeat in this game did for cricket on the 'teardrop of India'.

The underdogs took control at the midway point of the Australian innings and did not release their hold from there. Theirs was a well-planned campaign that never faltered. It was a credit to the coach Dav Whatmore as well as the captain, Ranatunga.

"Dav told us, 'Let's do the little things right and we'll see what the result is at the end of the day,'" says Asanka Gurusinha. "That was our main focus and to be honest I wasn't that concious of the atmosphere and the pre-match build up."

An unimpressive Saturday night official World Cup dinner out of the way the players of Australia and Sri Lanka woke to a Sunday of overcast skies and streets with puddles everywhere. There had been heavy overnight rain and there was no guarantee the final would start on schedule. The Australian players heard that rumour and were surprised when they were told the team buses would soon be on their way.

The covers were removed and the players completed their warm-up routines. Outside the ground the police clashed with spectators desperate to get in. As the Gaddafi Stadium filled it became clear crowd support would be with Sri Lanka and there was no shortage of their flags being waved when it was announced that Ranatunga had won the toss. It was academic how the coin fell, though, as Mark Taylor wanted to bat first on the flat rock hard wicket and Ranatunga hoped to bowl.

Both teams announced unchanged sides from their semi-final wins. Englishman David Shepherd and West Indian, Steve Bucknor earned the right to officiate in cricket's showcase event. They had put on an impeccable display in the pressure-packed quarter final between India and Pakistan and were generally regarded as the best two umpires in the world. Mistakenly the South African national anthem was originally played beside *Advance Australian Fair*, the Sri Lankan anthem had to be squeezed in just before the 2.30pm start.

As if stamping his authority on the occasion, Taylor took on the Sri Lankan opening attack of Chaminda Vaas and Pramodya Wickremasinghe. From the word go the Australian captain was finding the middle of the bat and flashing the white ball to the boundary. Mark Waugh preferred to begin sedately looking to build towards a century as he had successfully done on three previous occasions in the tournament. From the first ball of the eighth over, though, his plan came unstuck as he clipped Vaas to an elated Sanath Jayasuriya at square leg.

Mark Waugh's demise had no effect on the confidence of Taylor and his new partner, Ricky Ponting. This was the Australian side that had so recently thrashed Sri Lanka in both the Tests and limited-over internationals in Australia. Bob Simpson said pre-match the team had tried to fight complacency. Now runs were coming freely again, especially from the captain who hit repeatedly to the leg-side and once lifted Vaas over square leg for six.

By the 15 over mark the total was 1-82. Taylor raced past his 50 in 52 balls and even the introduction of Muttiah Muralitharan made no difference. At the halfway stage of the innings Australia were 1-134 and the talk was of a total around 300 that might be too much for the even in form Sri Lankan batsmen. Rantunga had more than one finger spinner available to try to turn the tide and introduced Aravinda de Silva as the sixth bowler.

Taylor had made 74 in 83 balls with eight fours and a six and added 101 in 19 overs with Ponting when he swept at de Silva. He made solid contact with the top half of the blade so that the ball flew towards the square leg boundary. In place was that man Jayasuriya again and he had no trouble holding on to his second catch of the match. The dismissal of the Australian captain was the turning point of the final.

Suddenly Ponting and Steve Waugh were going nowhere against the off-spinners who kept a tight line and gained some turn. Four overs and 15 runs after Taylor's dismissal, Ponting backed away to cut a sharply turning de Silva off break and was bowled middle stump. Shane Warne strode to the wicket full of big hitting intent, only to stumble forward to his sixth ball and be neatly stumped down the leg-side by Romesh Kaluwitharana off Muralitharan.

Stuart Law and Steve Waugh joined in a worried assessment of the situation at the drinks-break score of 4-166 from 34 overs. Whatever they planned did no good as Waugh tried to chip Kumara Dharmasena over the in-field in the next over only to loft the ball to de Silva near the long on boundary. Australia had lost 4-33 in eight overs and disarray threatened. Michael Bevan and Law avoided that, but nine runs in the next five overs hardly eased the pressure. After 40 overs Australia were 5-178 and there had not been a boundary in the 13 overs since Taylor's dismissal.

The push had to come and Law pulled Dharmasena cleanly and square for six. However, it was only a half charge. Law was caught at point and Ian Healy played all over a full-pitched delivery to give de Silva a third wicket. Bevan cracked a few balls away in partnership with Paul Reiffel which included 18 from the last two overs. Ranatunga who had bowled his various combinations of spinners right through walked off content with his position. Sri Lanka required 242 to win the World Cup. "We thought they might get 270 or 280 at one stage," Gurusinha says. "But because of the way we had been batting we were still confident and would have been so even if we had wanted 300."

For a few minutes during the break between innings it became problematical whether his side would have an opportunity to pursue any runs. The stadium lights went out. There had been suggestions the amount of power used by the new floodlights, the first at a Pakistani cricket ground, could place too much strain on the supply. They soon came back on and play resumed.

As the Australians took the field they noticed something different to their games in India under lights. An evening dew had come straight down and the outfield was very damp. Australia had done their pre-match practice during the day. Sri Lanka had trained under lights. They were aware of what would happen, the Australians were not.

The ball would soon become sodden and ineffective on the wet outfield so the Australians had to take plenty of early wickets. They got two quickly. In the second over, bowled by Damien Fleming, Jayasuriya went for a two to third man on Glenn McGrath's arm and misjudged the task by the barest margin. Sri Lanka were 1-12, then 2-23 four overs later when Kaluwitharana mistimed a pull off Fleming and Michael Bevan ran around behind the square leg umpire to hold the catch. It was the last chance accepted by an Australian fieldsman, but by no means the last chance offered.

The crowd were enjoying their night at the final and got through plenty of Mexican waves. De Silva was nearly run out and McGrath sent down a pressure packed spell. Fleming's waywardness released some of that pressure at the other end so Taylor introduced Warne for the 11th over. This crucial over included three shots through the off side by de Silva and a delivery that hit the inside edge and whisked past Healy.

When the fieldsmen moved back at the end of 15 overs Sri Lanka were 2-71. Gurusinha lofted Mark Waugh down the ground and Fleming slid across the damp outfield and missed the chance. The 100 was brought up in the 21st over as Gurusinha clubbed Warne down the ground for four. The chubby-faced left-hander, who would soon settle in Australia, then belted Warne for an amazing pull for six over long off!

"It was a slow track and I when I got into position to play the pull shot the ball was still coming," Gurusinha says. "I didn't want to hit across it because I might have mistimed it. So I hit the ball with a straight bat instead and away it went. Shane Warne was not a problem for us that night. We play him fairly well anyway and he knows it. We respect him as a fine bowler, but if the ball is loose we have always have had the confidence to punish it, which is what we did in the Final."

Both batsmen reached the half century landmark as the prospect of a Sri Lankan victory became very real. It was Australia who were struggling with the pressure. Gurusinha pulled Bevan and Law at deep square leg did not have to move to take the catch. It might have been better if he had, for the ball hit his hands and went straight down. The crowd enjoyed that.

After a partnership of 125 with de Silva, Gurusinha charged Reiffel and was bowled.

"We had spent a few overs just getting singles so I told Aravinda to stay there and I would have a hit, but I swung across the ball instead of straight so I missed it," Gurusinha says.

Australia hoped the reckless-looking dismissal might bring about another Chandigarh type collapse, however lightning did not strike twice. Ranatunga came in with 95 needed from 19 overs and was as immediately assured as his partner who was progressing towards a landmark century. At first the pair batted with little urgency while ensuring the required run rate was within reach.

Then Mark Waugh conceded 10 runs from an over, which left 50 to be scored from the last 10. Ranatunga drove the ball straight for four through Warne's fingers then smashed a misdirected attempted flipper away for six and poked his tongue out at the bowler. The Sri Lankan captain was rather enjoying himself. Taylor had tried all sorts of permuatations and variations, but this time nothing would work for him.

A neat glance for four off Fleming took the little Sri Lankan maestro to his century from 119 balls, only the third to be scored in a World Cup final. He joined Viv Richards and Clive Lloyd in that exclusive club and no-one could doubt the worth of his membership.

"It was one of the best innings I have ever seen," Gursinha says. "The first ball he faced he just gently pushed at the ball and it scooted away through mid off for three. I knew then everything was all right. His feet were moving. His head was still. He gave me such confidence, too. We had already shared in a couple of century partnerships during the tournament so we were confident in each other's game."

De Silva's 100 had come as a personal bonus for he had already done enough along with Gurusinha and Ranatunga to ensure victory. That wonderful formality was completed when Ranatunga nudged McGrath through the vacant slips region along the ground to the third man boundary for four from the second ball of the 42nd over. It was the shot he will best remember for his entire life.

Ranatunga and de Silva were almost instantly surrounded by their elated teammates. The military band in attendance played a victory march. There were well wishers everywhere as the beaming Ranatunga received the World Cup trophy from Pakistani Prime Minister, Benazir Bhutto and de Silva accepted his enormous cheque for being named Man of the Match. During the presentations the evening mist that had floated in and turned to rain. The well wishers pressed their heroes so hard everyone went for a tumble, including Ranatunga and his precious trophy. For the lone survivor of Sri Lanka's inaugural Test nothing could dampen the exultation of the moment.

Both captains, one in victory, the other in defeat, were gracious at the post match conferences. Neither would be drawn into talk of previous controversies, even though Warne and the Waugh twins would later refuse to sign Sri Lankan souvenir bats sent into the Australian dressing room. In Sri Lanka most people took a holiday on the Monday to celebrate their very special achievement. Their team, who had never even got close to a semi-final berth before were the world champions of limited-overs cricket.

"It was a great feeling," Gursinha says. "Although it took some time to sink in. We hadn't expected to be that successful at the start, but we had played fantastic cricket to win and in the Final had beaten a great side in Australia. I don't think Australia were complacent. They had struggled to get in the final whereas we had played the best cricket in the tournament. Our top six batsmen were all in great form and the Australians knew that would be a problem for them.

"We flew back to Colombo the morning after the game. Normally the drive from the airport to the city is 40 minutes, but it took us two hours. There were millions of people out on the streets still celebrating.

"I think they had been up all night. We were being driven to the Presidential Palace and had full security and the Presidential fleet of cars, but there was no way we could get through all the people. They were all very happy."

AUSTRALIA		SRI LANKA	
M. A. Taylor (capt) c Jayasuriya b de Silva	74	S. T.J ayasuriya run out	9
M. E. Waugh c Jayasuriya b Vaas	12	R. S. Kaluwitharana (wk) c Bevan b Fleming	6
R. T. Ponting b de Silva	45	A. P. Gurusinha b Reiffel	65
S. R. Waugh c de Silva b Dharmasena	13	P. A. de Silva not out	107
S. K. Warne st Kaluwitharana b Muralitharan	2	A. Ranatunga (capt) not out	47
S. G. Law c de Silva b Jayasuriya	22	Extras b1 lb4 w5 nb1	11
M. G. Bevan not out	36	(46.2 overs)	3-245
I. A. Healy (wk) b de Silva	2	Did not bat: H. P. Tillekeratne, R. S. Mahanama,	
P. R. Reiffel not out	13	H. D. P. K. Dharmasena, W. P. U. J. C. Vaas, M. Muralitharan,	
Extras lb10 w11 nb1	22	G. P. Wickremasinghe	
(50 overs)	7-241	1/12 2/23 3/148	
Did not bat: D. W. Fleming, G. D. McGrath		Bowling: McGrath 8.2-1-28-0; Fleming 6-0-43-1;	
1/36 2/137 3/152 4/156 5/170 6/202 7/205		Warne 10-0-58-0; Reiffel 10-0-49-1; M. E. Waugh 6-0-35-0;	
Bowling: Wickremasinghe 7-0-38-0; Vaas 6-1-30-1;		S. R. Waugh 3-0-15-0; Bevan 3-0-12-0	
Muralitharan 10-0-31-1; Dharmasena 10-0-47-1;			
Jayasuriya 8-0-43-1; de Silva 9-0-42-3			

Umpires: S.A. Bucknor D.R. Shepherd
Toss: Sri Lanka

POST-MORTEM

Alan Lee's summation of the 1996 tournament in *Wisden Cricketers' Almanack* was that, despite a handsome profit, the organisation and spirit of the Wills World Cup was not a patch on 1987.

Some of that was out of the hands of the cricket authorities, other aspects, such as travelling arrangements and practice facilities were within their sphere of influence. There had indeed been problems and flat moments.

However, some of the cricket had been sensational and no-one would question the worth of the winners, Sri Lanka.

Surprisingly Dav Whatmore soon resigned as coach of Sri Lanka, the politics of the cricket in the country of his birth taking their toll on the former Australian batsman. He would return to the position at the end of the 1999 World Cup.

Even though Australia had barely dented their reputation as one of the world's leading cricket teams by losing the final, a dramatic policy change was made soon after the tournament. Bob Simpson was replaced as Australian coach and Mark Taylor and Ian Healy's days in the limited-overs side were also numbered. By the time the leading cricket nations of the world convened in England in 1999. Taylor and retired and Healy was a Test cricketer. I nearly wrote 'only'.

CHAPTER 8:

WORLD CUP 1999: NO SURPRISES LEFT

Twelve sides remained enough for the seventh World Cup as the competition returned to England after a 16-year break. It was still seen as necessary to tamper with the format and to increase the number of games played to a new record. The criticism that the 1996 format only eliminated the weaker countries in the preliminary group matches was overcome with only three sides progressing from their various groups through to the next round in 1999. That next round was the Super Sixes section, a little tournament of nine matches enclosed within the bigger contest. It, too, looked to have imperfections. Some sides were able to carry through points from their Round Robin games to the Super Six section. It depended upon whom they had beaten and who else got through.

Whether that format would work more satisfactorily than what went before only time would tell.

Such a big impression had been created by the New Zealand and Sri Lankan innovations of 1992 and 1996 that the world waited with baited breath for the new revolutionary and trendsetting tactics of 1999. Editorials and feature articles in newspapers, periodicals and on the internet were devoted to the prospect that some current cricket brain was at play trying to connive an unorthodox tactic that would put all opposition sides in a spin. It was easily forgotten that Imran Khan's 1992 Pakistanis had won by having brilliant skills and just peaking at the right time.

The newcomers to the program were Scotland and Bangladesh. They and Kenya won their places ahead of the United Arab Emirates and Holland by virtue of their ICC Trophy triumphs in Kuala Lumpur in 1997. The inclusion of these nations, while worthy in the cause of cricketing globalisation was hardly seen as likely to have a big impact on the popularity of the 1999 World Cup. The spreading of the cricketing gospel was considered so essential that instead of all the games being played in England there was one each in Dublin, Edinburgh and Amsterdam. Of far greater immediate import than this were the attempts by the marketing arm of the England Cricket Board to sell the World Cup product to a sceptical English populace.

This was to be the 'Carnival of Cricket' World Cup which meant lots of music and colour. Leading cricketers modelling their country's colourful uniforms were joined in photo shoots by various celebrities, notably – blonde English bombshell, Caprice. There was an official World Cup logo. Australian journalist Martin Blake called the yellow-and-green Australian uniform 'hideous' when he saw them in a warm-up game at Worcester. South Africa wore upside down Y-fronts. They had sponsors' logos, their country's emblems and were now numbered as well as named. Equally as blond as Caprice, rock guitarist Dave Stewart provided the 'hit' song *All Over the World* which was supposed to capture the hearts of the nation and lure them to the cricket grounds around the country from Friday May 14th until the final at Lord's on Sunday June 20th. Two videos accompanied the song. A Royal Albert Hall concert was mooted then cancelled due to a lack of big name attractions. Women were targetted as a prospective audience. It was a far cry from the formal receptions of 1975 and looked a lot of effort for little result as early ticket sales were slow. By the start of March the only sell out matches were the final and the England vs South Africa game at The Oval. There was no soccer World Cup to compete with, but the FA Cup and the football Premiership were still to be resolved by the time that England met Sri Lanka at Lord's on May 14th.

The ongoing mediocrity of the performances of the English team was another restraining factor on early public interest. Crowd troubles in India and the West Indies in the months before the World Cup had given the game some bad publicity. However, possibly the most significant negative influence was the lingering accusations that bookmakers from the Indian subcontinent had infiltrated player ranks.

The issue of bribes and match fixing had not been fully resolved. The revelations by Australian stars, Shane Warne and Mark Waugh, that they had taken money from bookmakers years before and that the Australian authorities after finding out and punishing the pair had covered the information up, brought the game in that country into disrepute. The ICC had met and discussed the issue in New Zealand, showing resolve but little prompt action. While in Pakistan accusations and counter accusations continued to fly in all directions inside and outside of courtrooms. None of this enhanced the good name of cricket.

The choice of the first part of the English summer for the program of matches was a risk both with ticket sales and the games themselves. The weather at that time of year was unreliable. In 1975 the gods had been kind and the Prudential Cup was unaffected. They were less co-operative in 1979 and some matches were curtailed and went into a second day. England, though, made the final. That might have been a consideration for the authorities setting up the 1999 competition.

It did not make the host team tournament favourites. That honour fell to Hansie Cronje's South Africans who began the competition at 3-1, ahead of Australia at 7-2. Scotland were rated a 500-1 chance and Bangladesh were 1000-1. This was considered to a very open World Cup, but not that open.

The Proteas who were placed along with England, India, Sri Lanka, Zimbabwe and Kenya in the tougher looking Group

A, brought form and confidence to the World Cup. Over the southern summer they had thrashed the West Indies at home in both the Test series and the Limited Overs series of matches. Then, in February and March they had made short work of New Zealand in New Zealand.

A featured strength of the South African side was the bevy of genuine all-rounders in the line-up as opposed to the bits-and-pieces cricketers touted as all-rounders by other countries. Jacques Kallis and Shaun Pollock at 23 and 25 years of age respectively were emerging as a combined powerhouse in world cricket. Either player could hold their place in the South African one-day side for their batting or bowling. More than that they were exciting and aggressive players capable of the energetic and athletic fielding, the type of which can win one-day games.

That they were rated below Jonty Rhodes only served to prove that South Africa's busy and positive middle-order batsman was rated as highly as any cover fieldsman who had ever played the game. The South African batting could have been labelled a tad colourless at times. Recent form had indicated that the problem would be resolved, especially if the powerful Daryl Cullinan could be kept away from Shane Warne. And then there was Allan Donald.

The champion paceman was reaching the late middle age of his fast bowling career. He had become a middle of the innings rather than a new ball bowler in limited-over internationals. Such was Donald's pace and skill whoever avoided his thundering, silken charges would have been very relieved. One bad day had cost South Africa dearly in 1996. Some believed they might stumble at the wrong time again. The other 11 sides hoped that would be the day the Proteas played them.

Grim-faced Steve Waugh provided a stark contrast to the receptive, friendly but all seeing countenance of the captain of the 1996 runners-up, Australia. Waugh had taken over from Mark Taylor as official captain of Australia's limited overs side in 1997-98. They were in Group B, and could be one of themselves, Pakistan, New Zealand or the West Indies to miss promotion to the Super Sixes, even presuming Scotland and Bangladesh were out of their league. Waugh's elevation seemed to correspond with a deterioration in his own form and fitness in the branch of the game where he had first established a worldwide reputation. A torn hamstring in the World Series Cup had severely curtailed his appearances during the early months of 1999. It also gave Shane Warne the opportunity to impress as a bright captain with his finger on the pulse.

Nevertheless Waugh regained his place at the helm of the Australian one-day side. In the Caribbean he had to withstand some appalling treatment by over excited and incensed crowds. His reputation as one of the game's most resilient characters and great students of the game was undiminshed by those events. Some, like Martin Crowe, felt his captaincy was a weak link, others suggested he was Australia's greatest asset.

That overlooked the brilliance of Glenn McGrath, the equal of any bowler in the world. The accuracy of Shane Warne whose powers in one-day cricket were not as diminished as at Test level. The audacious opening batting of Adam Gilchrist, which, when complimented by the grace and strokeplay of Mark Waugh, launched Australian innings at breakneck speed. Nor could the enigmatic Michael Bevan be forgotten. The batsman with the highest average in the world in limited-overs cricket was able to brilliantly control the closing overs of an innings and rarely failed to score off any ball received. It beggared belief that his techniques were found so wanting in the longer version of the game.

The holders of the trophy, Sri Lanka, arrived in England as even greater outsiders than when they snared the World Cup just over three years before. Fatigue, injury and the onset of cricketing old age were offered as reasons for Sri Lanka's inconsistency over the southern summer. They had rarely been a match for England nor Australia in the World Series Cup and with an attack based around controversial off-spinner, Muttiah Muralitharan, were thought unlikely to be suited to English wickets in May and June.

When the prospect of the MCC outlawing 'sledging' became a topical issue, Arjuna Ranatunga, whose clashes with Alec Stewart in a one-day match in Adelaide in January had been most unpleasant, had plenty to say on the matter. With Javed Miandad retired, the rotund Sri Lankan captain assumed the position as the game's leading on-field stirrer. He would have been quite prepared to annoy all cricket followers outside his own country again if it meant holding up the game's leading limited-overs trophy again in 1999.

He still had plenty of batting talent on call. Sanath Jayasuriya's left-handed belligerence would be suited to the smallest English grounds. Little Aravinda de Silva on his day was the equal of any batsman in the world and in Australia and during the Pepsi Cup, 21-year-old Mahela Jayawardene had revealed a precocious talent that suggested a budding champion. Happily, too, a return to England reduced the amount of travelling this weary team would have to complete. In 1987 and 1992 they spent more time in airports than on cricket grounds.

England had banked on experience and bowlers who might be able to take advantage of seaming wickets in their World Cup 1999 squad selection. There was as much discussion on who was left out as on who was included. Like Steve Waugh, there were those in England of the opinion that better captains were available for limited-overs matches than Alec Stewart. Unlike Australia that is the norm amongst English thinking. That Mark Ramprakash's improved consistency at Test level had not yet translated into limited-overs selection was a surprise. The extent of Graham Thorpe's recovery from back injury in cool May conditions might be an influential factor when determining England's fate. Whatever England's overall level of success, the prospect of Graeme Hick batting against Kenya was exciting. The lime tree at Canterbury had been declared unwell. An on song Hick could have demolished it even before its time was up.

Darren Gough's fitness and degree of accuracy was seen as the lynchpin as to England's bowling penetration. In the helpful dampness of May and early June, though, the old warhorse Angus Fraser threatened a few surprises as a last international hurrah.

Hot and cold and often controversial, Pakistan were capable of finishing either first last or something in between. Coach Javed Miandad resigned just before the tournament. Still haunted and taunted by such politics and the match-fixing allegations, Wasim Akram's side oozed enough variety and talent to win the World Cup if his players could keep their minds solely on cricket. The captain, reinstated after having been sacked or resigned from the position three times previously, was at about the same stage of his career as Imran Khan had been in 1992. His influence might have been just as significant.

Any pace bowling line-up that boasted Akram himself, supported by Waqar Younis and the emerging Shoaib Akhtar could conceiveably cut a swathe through opposing top orders. The cold might not suit Mushtaq Ahmed's leg-spin. It would be less of a concern to the off-spin of the talented and developing Saqlain Mushtaq.

Shahid Afridi, still not yet 20, offered the possibility of Bothamesque all-round feats. Saeed Anwar's class as a left-handed opening batsmen had been evident in all forms of cricket in every corner of the globe on all wickets. His run-making contributions could almost be taken for granted. Not so those of the lethargic looking Inzamam-ul-Haq. No-one could forget his semi-final winning innings in New Zealand in 1992. In the ensuing years his mobility might have been compromised, his power along with his size had increased to a corresponding degree.

The gloom that had descended over West Indian cricket after their tour of South Africa was partially lifted by their demonstration of fighting qualities against Australia in the Caribbean. That they were still an unknown quantity could be attributed to a perceived lack of depth. The batting totally revolved around Brian Lara during the Test series against Australia and it was hard to see the West Indies putting together match-winning scores without plenty of runs from the flawed genius from Trinidad. Carl Hooper had retired at just the wrong time in regards to this tournament and Shivnarine Chanderpaul might have found it difficult to attain top form after such a long lay off with a shoulder injury.

Injury might also be a problem for the West Indian attack if the ageing muscles of Courtney Walsh and Curtley Ambrose failed to cope with the intensity of a World Cup likely to be played in hamstring-snapping temperatures. The tall pace bowling pair had lost some speed as they reached their mid 30s, yet their skill and accuracy was something to be marvelled at. With the new white, high-seamed Dukes ball in their hand Walsh and Ambrose were as big a threat to batsmen as they had ever been.

New Zealand's record in World Cups is more than respectable considering their overall standing on the international cricketing stage. It was always within their capacity to spring some surprises and reach at least the semi-final stage of the tournament. Their young captain, Stephen Fleming and Australian coach, Steve Rixon, had given New Zealand cricket some purpose and a measure of home success in the late 1990s.

Like South Africa they boasted a couple of genuine all-rounders. Chris Cairns on his day was an explosive proposition and possible match winner. The re-emergence of Dion Nash added quality to both the Kiwi bowling and lower-order batting. Two of the dibbly dobblers of Martin Crowe's 1992 side remained. Chris Harris and Gavin Larsen might well have been suited to the greentops provided at Chelmsford, Cardiff and Southampton.

Craig McMillan had displayed attributes of a top class batsman in his short international career while Fleming himself would be hungry for runs following a lay off with a groin injury in the months prior to the competition. Hanging over his side was the shadow of a recent thrashing at the hands of South Africa and some consistency problems at the top of the batting order. They remained a country not to be underestimated, however.

Such is the style and charisma of the Indian batting line-up that most cricket fans hoped that team would acquit itself well in the 1999 World Cup. They more than anyone might offer batting approaching a carnival with Sachin Tendulkar, the world number one in the eyes of most, as the chief attraction.

The record of Mohammad Azharuddin's team outside their own country had been poor and it was thought they might also struggle in English conditions as they had in 1996. Rahul Dravid, Ajay Jadeja and Saurav Ganguly as support for Tendulkar and the charming Azharuddin suggested potential run feasting. If that occurred Javagal Srinath, Venkatash Prasad and Anil Kumble, the 10-out-of-10 man, had enough skill to give their millions of fanatical followers an exciting ride through May and June of 1999.

Zimbabwe arrived in England with just three victories in their previous four World Cups. Indications were that disappointing return would be improved upon in 1999. Their recent Test victories over India and Pakistan indicated a side growing in self-confidence and self belief. In addition the men in the red and green had reached the final of the one-day tournament in Sharjah and in late 1996 had beaten England 3-0 in a limited-overs series in Zimbabwe. They had gained full status some years before, now at last they were competing with their opponents at every turn and earning full respect from the world's best players. They started the 1999 World Cup as no more unlikely winners than Sri Lanka had been in 1996.

Alistair Campbell, at 26 equal with Stephen Fleming as the youngest captain in the tournament, led a team with plenty to prove and a real chance to prove it. The efforts of the Flower brothers, Andy and Grant and captain, Campbell, had often given Zimbabwe enough runs to be competitive in limited overs matches. That ability had been boosted by the recruitment of Murray Goodwin, a Zimbabwe born Australian product who had moved from Sheffield Shield cricket to international class with deceptive ease and no shortage of runs.

Heath Streak was a highly rated paceman with an impressive record for his country. At times much of his bowling support had been inadequate with the exception of Paul Strang's excellent leg breaks. In the previous months Streak's burden had been reduced. Henry Olonga, despite bursts of inaccuracy, had matured as a bowler without compromising his exceptional speed. Neil Johnson's record as a county bowler in England in 1997 was nothing startling, however in his first Test he claimed perhaps the most prized scalp in the world in Tendulkar. Having returned from South Africa he, like Goodwin, slotted into the team as if a spot had been waiting for him all his life.

Bangladesh should have been viewing the 1999 World Cup in the same way as Sri Lanka did the 1979 tournament and Zimbabwe the competition of 1987. It was to be seen as another stepping stone towards full Test status for a nation whose entire population of 123 million seemed to be cricket fans. The Tigers had already played their fair share of limited-over internationals.

Their captain, Aminul Islam, was rated as their best batsman leading in to the tournament, while Akram Khan had also scored some handy runs at the top level. As with most teams taking their first tentative steps at the top level, finding bowlers capable of restricting and dismissing the world's best batsmen was a problem. Mohammad Rafique and Hasibul Hussain had claimed the highest percentage of early wickets, but this was an area team coach Gordon Greenidge must have thought of as possibly inadequate in such unfamiliar surroundings.

Kenya were in a similar position to Bangladesh. The 1999 World Cup presented them with an opportunity to mix it with the big boys in the hope of increasing their status and recognition. They took to England eight of the players who had participated in the 1996 tournament when to the surprise of everyone they knocked over the West Indies. One of the heroes of that win, Maurice Odumbe, was back although he had handed over the captaincy to Aasif Karim, Kenya's leading wicket-taker. Steve Tikolo and Kennedy Otieno had already accumulated enough runs against quality opposition to be confident of their chances of handling anything their Group A opponents could send down.

It is a bit of a surprise to anyone living outside the British Isles that the weather could be tolerable enough to even contemplate cricket in Scotland, let alone put together a side to compete in the World Cup. Gavin Hamilton had originally been in the English squad and he was rated as an extremely promising all-rounder on the English County circuit. James Brinkley was favoured to take the new-ball. He was a much travelled player, having been contracted to both Worcestershire and Essex after having grown up in Australia. His birth certificate was what counted on this occasion. Seveteen-year-old John Blain, another signed up for County cricket was expected to be his side's fastest bowler.

As the rain tumbled down on the County grounds around England during the first two weeks of May the term 'warm-up matches' looked to be inappropriate. Players barely had the chance to get the newness out of their uniforms so regular were the interruptions. In five weeks' time, one captain amongst the twelve photographed posing with the cherished trophy would be holding it aloft on the evening of June the 20th at Lord's. His side would be US$300,000 richer and he and his team would be the darlings of the cricketing world. That was if the rain did not muck things up. The rain rules had been altered again. Mr Duckworth and Mr Lewis would be called upon in the event of the need for a re-calculation.

FRIDAY 14 MAY 1999
LORD'S, LONDON: ENGLAND vs SRI LANKA-GROUP A
ENGLAND WON BY EIGHT WICKETS

England got the start they wanted to their home campaign with a comfortable victory over the increasingly maligned 1996 champions. The greatest threat to Alec Stewart's team came from persistent showers, but these were always brief enough to cause only short delays or arrived during intervals. Despite the comments over poor pre-match ticket sales there was nothing wrong with this Friday attendance at the home of cricket.

The most controversial change at Lord's over the winter months had been the admission of women to membership of the MCC for the first time. Why that met with resistance and the perching of the world's largest clock radio above the bowler's arm at the Nursery End of the ground did not, cannot be imagined. One kept waiting for the thing to be plugged in and the digital clock figures to appear on its windows.

Instead there were big national flags, fireworks, a speech from British PM Tony Blair and a balloon releasing in a sort of poor man's Commonwealth Games opening ceremony on the outfield. Finally Alec Stewart and Arjuna Ranatunga, newspaper criticism of him from Shane Warne still ringing in his ears, came out to toss.

That this might be England's day was indicated by Stewart's good fortune at the fall of the coin. He had no hesitation in electing to bowl. The hesitations came a few minutes later when a shower held up the start of the World Cup by a few minutes. Soon Darren Gough opened the tournament with a no-ball to Sanath Jayasuriya and the English opening bowlers used the Dukes ball to good effect, repeatedly beating the outside edge in helpful conditions.

Sri Lanka had hidden Romesh Kaluwitharana down the order, promoting the experienced Roshan Mahanama back to open. He and Jayasuriya added 42 until left-armer Alan Mullally, coming on first change, got the ball on line. In his first over the tall fair haired speedster had Mohanama attempting a pull which steepled over gully. Graeme Hick ran back to take a well judged catch.

Mohanama and Jayasuriya had used up a lot of the early luck. Marvin Atapattu Jayasuriya and Aravinda de Silva fell in similar fashion to slips catches. With the bowlers on top Stewart employed three slips.

They were not required when Hashan Tillekeratne was caught behind down the leg-side from Mark Ealham's first ball. Sri Lanka were in desperate trouble at 5-65. Kaluwitharana and Ranatunga stemmed the decline with a bright stand of 84. The wicketkeeper batsman dominated the partnership, counterattacking with slashing drives and powerful pulls. One of his six boundaries brought up his 50 in the 32nd over from just 52 balls. Ranatunga joined in when he hit Graeme Hick straight into the pavilion which was nearly empty. MCC members were protesting at the ECB directive that they have to pay to watch World Cup matches.

Mullally came back to claim Kaluwitharana and after Ranatunga was nicely caught low down in the gully by Nasser Hussain the Sri Lankan batting gradually fell away. As England batted there was always the fear that showers would alter the direction of the contest and the requirement of the chase. A few heavy clouds dwelt around St Johns Wood, but they stayed away from Lord's.

Hussain opened with Stewart in place of the injured Nick Knight. He stayed long enough with his captain for 50 runs to be posted before dancing down at Muttiah Muralitharan and being stumped.

Hussain's departure opened the way for Stewart and Hick to win the match. They put on 125 runs in positive fashion, always keeping well up with the required run rate. Twice Hick skied the ball only for it to fall between desperate fieldsmen. Otherwise he and Stewart dominated. A front foot scoop by Hick sent the ball for six into the Grandstand crowd at square leg.

Stewart's poor form in limited-overs matches had been coming under scrutiny. This powerful reply which was not ended until his side were within 30 of victory. After he had been caught behind off the inside edge from Chaminda Vaas, Hick and Graham Thorpe carried England home with three overs to spare. Hick finished the match with another six, a calmly struck straight drive into the pavilion seats off the expensive Jayasuriya. Stewart was named Man of the Match.

SRI LANKA		ENGLAND	
S. T. Jayasuriya c Hick b Mullally	29	N. Hussain st Kaluwitharana Muralitharan	14
R. S. Mohanama c Hick b Mullally	16	A. J. Stewart (wk/capt) c Kaluwitharana b Vaas	88
M. S. Attapattu c Thorpe b Austin	3	G. A. Hick not out	73
H. P. Tillekeratne c Stewart b Ealham	0	G. P. Thorpe not out	13
P. A. de Silva c Thorpe b Mullally	0	Extras lb6 w12 nb1	19
A. Ranatunga (capt)c Hussain b Ealham	32	(46.5 overs)	2-207
R. S. Kaluwitharana (wk) c Stewart b Mullally	57	Did not bat: N. H. Fairbrother, A. J. Hollioake, A. Flintoff,
W. P. U. J. C. Vaas not out	12	M. A. Ealham, I. E. Austin, D. Gough, A. D. Mullally
K. E. A. Upashantha c Thorpe b Hollioake	11	1/50 2/175
G. P. Wickremasinghe c Stewart b Austin	11	Bowling: Vaas 10-2-27-1; Wickremasinghe 10-0-41-0;
M. Muralitharan b Gough	12	Upashantha 8-0-38-0; Muralitharan 10-0-33-1;
Extras lb9 w9 nb3	21	Jaysuriya 7.5-0-55-0 de Silva 1-0-7-0
(48.4 overs)	204		

1/42 2/50 3/63 4/63 5/65 6/149 7/155 8/174 9/190
10/204
Bowling: Gough 8.4-0-50-1; Austin 9-1-25-2; Mullally
10-1-37-4; Ealham 10-0-31-2; Flintoff 2-0-12-0;
Hick 3-0-19-0; Hollioake 6-0-21-1

Umpires: R.E.Koertzen S.Venkataraghaven

Toss: England   Points: England 2 Sri Lanka 0

SATURDAY 15 MAY 1999
COUNTY GROUND, HOVE: INDIA vs SOUTH AFRICA-GROUP A
SOUTH AFRICA WON BY 4 WICKETS

Down by the seaside at the historic County Ground in Hove, tournament favourites, South Africa won an excellent contest by four wickets with 16 balls to spare.

Umpire Steve Bucknor prepared for his day by the sea by covering his face with sun screen. It showed a responsible attitude, although it was unnecessary as the weather remained overcast and cold all day. When Venaktash Prasad fielded at fine leg he let his long sleeved jumper slip over his hands to keep his fingers warm. Azharuddin, the most experienced one-day cricketer in the world, won the toss and batted on a slow, easy wicket. Sachin Tendulkar opened with Saurav Ganguly, the latter resplendent in a light blue helmet matching his country's uniform. His attire obviously agreed with him because the left-hander got his country away to a great start with a flashing square cut for four off Shaun Pollock from the second ball of the day.

That put the thousands of Indian expatriates in the ground in a good mood, a feeling they retained while Tendulkar and Ganguly tamed the South African new-ball thrust. Tendulkar was eventually the first to go at 57, caught behind dabbing at Lance Klusener

Rahul Dravid and Ganguly kept the Indians on top with a partnership of 130 in 158 balls. They sustained an orthodox approach, concentrating on getting four or five off each over. Ganguly was the more productive partner, punctuating his innings with drives through mid-on and mid wicket and sweet cuts. A lofted drive off Nicky Boje carried for six over long off. Both batsmen passed 50 and Dravid had faced 75 balls when he was bowled behind his legs swinging at a full pitched Klusener delivery in the 42nd over.

The Indians reached their final overs with plenty of wickets in hand. However, they failed to take advantage. Ganguly just missed a deserved century when he cut Jacques Kallis wide of gully. He took off for a run only for Jonty Rhodes to elongate himself, grab the ball one handed, raise up to his knees and throw to the bowler well before Ganguly could make his ground.

It was a brilliant piece of work, only slightly superior to the catch on the cover boundary by Boje who held a well struck 'inside out' cover drive by Azharuddin. Ajay Jadeja scored at a run per ball until he skied a pull off Allan Donald whose spells were fast, accurate and economical. South African captain Hansie Cronje had been taking advice from the dressing room during the Indian innings via a small earpiece, which he was not allowed to use again.

The par-for-the-course total of 253 looked much better when Javagal Srinath sent down a penetrative new-ball spell. He was assisted by the downhill slope at Hove. After Herschelle Gibbs had scored the first boundary for the Proteas with a french cut, Srinath brought the next one back to trap the opener in front of his stumps. Fellow opener Gary Kirsten struggled for 22 deliveries then edged Srinath onto his stumps.

Wicketkeeper Mark Boucher, batting at number three, pulled two fours off Srinath then top edged a six over the wicketkeeper's head from the first ball of the next over. The Indian paceman conceded 25 runs from two overs. Anil Kumble came on in the 12th over. Boucher greeted him with a big straight drive, but was bowled in the same over cutting at a wrong 'un.

After 15 overs South Africa were 3-75. A skied slog by Daryl Cullinan in Ganguly's first over left them 4-116 with a lot of work to do on a wicket that looked to be losing its pace. Kallis, emerging as a batsman to be ranked with the best, took that work responsibility upon himself and with the assistance of Hansie Cronje and Jonty Rhodes guided his side back into the game.

Kallis and his captain put on 64 in just 13 overs. His stand of 47 in seven overs with Rhodes then made South Africa favourites to win. As with Ganguly, a run out robbed Kallis of his century, but the South African still won the Man of the Match Award.

His dismissal in the 46th over revitalised Indian hopes. Klusener quickly snuffed them out again by hitting three fours while facing just four balls. From the first ball of the 48th over Rhodes clubbed Prasad over mid off for four then pushed the next delivery to gully for the single that won the match. One upset Indian spectator who invaded the team group had to be escorted away by police.

INDIA		SOUTH AFRICA	
S. C. Ganguly run out	97	H. H. Gibbs lbw b Srinath	7
S. R. Tendulkar c Boucher b Klusener	28	G. Kirsten b Srinath	3
R. Dravid b Klusener	54	M. V. Boucher (wk) b Kumble	34
M. Azharuddin (capt) c Boje b Klusener	24	J. H. Kallis run out	96
A. Jadeja c Kirsten b Donald	16	D. J. Cullinan c Singh b Ganguly	19
R. R. Singh not out	4	W. J. Cronje (capt) c Jadeja b Agarkar	27
N. R. Mongia (wk) not out	5	J. N. Rhodes not out	39
Extras b6 lb2 w11 nb6	25	L. Klusener not out	12
(50 overs)	5-253	Extras lb4 w3 nb10	17
Did not bat: J. Srinath, A. B. Agarkar, B. K. V. Prasad, A. Kumble		(47.2 overs)	6-254
		Did not bat: S. M. Pollock, N. Boje, A. A. Donald	
1/67 2/197 3/204 4/235 5/247		1/13 2/22 3/68 4/116 5/180 6/227	
Bowling: Pollock 10-0-47-0; Kallis 10-1-43-0; Donald 10-0-34-1; Klusener 10-0-66-3; Boje 5-0-31-0; Cronje 5-0-24-0		Bowling: Srinath 10-0-69-2; Prasad 8.2-0-32-0; Kumble 10-0-44-1; Agarkar 9-0-57-1; Singh 2-0-10-0; Ganguly 4-0-16-1; Tendulkar 4-0-22-0	

Umpires: S.Bucknor D.Shepherd

Toss: India   Points: South Africa 2 India 0

COUNTY GROUND, TAUNTON: ZIMBABWE vs KENYA-GROUP A
ZIMBABWE WON BY 5 WICKETS

Zimbabwe, relishing the chance to go into a match as favourites against a local rival, cruised home with nine overs to spare Even so the Kenyans were far from disgraced or disheartened by their performance.

Kenya had to bat first after Alistair Campbell won the toss and sent them in on a wicket that played well throughout. At first he cannot have been happy when Kennedy Otieno flayed his opening bowlers. After 13 overs the total was already 62. Otieno cracked five boundaries lifting the drumbeats of the band of Kenyans who had followed their side into Somerset.

Otieno and his partner, Ravinda Shah were out within two balls of each other. Neil Johnson, coming on as first change, ripped into the middle order. When he bowled Hitesh Modi the Kenyans had lost 4-25 to be 4-87. In the good old days of the first World Cup the Kenyans might have crumbled from there. Not in 1999, though.

Maurice Odumbe held tight for 57 balls while Alpesh Vadher struck a six and five fours while reaching an invaluable half century. Paul Strang broke the 22 over 84 run partnership when he trapped Odumbe lbw. That brought young fast bowler Tom Odoyo to the wicket and he walloped the ball around for a couple of fours and two nice sixes. When he became Johnson's third victim captain Aasif Karim put one over the ropes as well so that Kenya, aided by an extra 29 deliveries and runs from no-balls and wides, finished with a commendable 7-229.

Campbell made his feelings about the performance of his bowlers quite clear, "Too many loose balls and too many four balls," which is an interesting distinction. His batsmen pleased him, though

Johnson went straight into business with the bat. He and Grant Flower opened with 81 in 14 very profitable overs. Johnson was severe on the Suji brothers, Martin and Tony, who shared the new-ball. He hit seven fours and two sixes in 70 balls. Paul Strang also made good use of the short straight boundaries at Taunton hitting two of the day's nine sixes. Wides and no-balls haunted the Kenyan attack as they had the Zimbabweans, but a couple of wickets to the O-Force, Odumbe and Odoyo reduced their opponents to 4-147.

Andy Flower and Campbell with over five thousand runs between them in limited over internationals were unphased by the losses and added a further 66 to their combined aggregate. That briskly took Zimbabwe to within a few runs of an obvious victory. Johnson's Man of the Match Award was equally clear cut.

KENYA		ZIMBABWE	
K. O. Otieno (wk) c G. W. Flower b Johnson	16	N. C. Johnson c Modi b Odoyo	59
Ravindu Shah c Strang b A. R. Whittall	37	G. W. Flower c Ravindu Shah b Aasif Karim	20
S. O. Tikolo c A. Flower b Johnson	9	P. A. Strang c A. Suji b Odoyo	29
M. O. Odumbe lbw b Strang	20	M. W. Goodwin c Aasif Karim b Odumbe	17
H. S. Modi b Johnson	7	A. Flower (wk) c Tikolo b Odumbe	34
A. Vadher c A. R. Whittall b Strang	54	A. D. R. Campbell (capt) not out	33
T. M. Odoyo b Johnson	28	G. J. Whittall not out	11
Aasif Karim (capt) not out	19	Extras lb5 w16 nb7	28
A. Suji not out	3	(41 overs)	5-231
Extras b2 lb5 w25 nb4	36	Did not bat: S. V. Carlisle, A. R. Whittall, H. H. Streak,	
(50 overs)	7-229	M. Mbangwa	
Did not bat: M. A. Suji, J. K. Kamande		1/81 2/119 3/123 4/147 5/213	
1/62 2/64 3/74 4/87 5/171 6/181 7/219		Bowling: M. Suji 7-0-47-0; A. Suji 6-1-32-0; Odoyo 9-0-40-2;	
Bowling: Streak 9-1-50-0; Mbangwa 8-0-37-0; Johnson		Kamande 9-0-38-0; Aasif Karim 3-0-30-1; Odumbe 7-1-39-2	
10-0-42-4; A. R. Whittall 9-0-51-1; G. J. Whittall 6-0-20-0;			
Strang 8-0-22-2			

Umpires: D. Cowie Javed Akhtar

Toss: Zimbabwe   Points: Zimbabwe 2 Kenya 0

SUNDAY MAY 16th 1999
PHOENIX COUNTY GROUND, BRISTOL:PAKISTAN vs WEST INDIES - GROUP B
PAKISTAN WON BY 27 RUNS

Always providers of a fascinating contest, the West Indies and Pakistan once more turned on a fluctuating cricket match from which the latter eventually triumphed. It was played before a packed house of 8,000. Many fans were unable to get tickets which drew criticism wondering why the game had not been scheduled at a venue with a larger capacity.

Despite the fact that the three Group A matches had been won by the side going in second and that the weather was grey and overcast, Wasim Akram batted when he won the toss. His openers had to face Courtney Walsh on the pitch that was his own for 14 years and they struggled. In his fourth over Walsh had Shahid Afridi caught behind and in his next Saeed Anwar who had earlier been dropped in the slips, was held by Lara at mid-on off a leading edge.

It got worse for the Pakistanis and their thousands of flag-waving fans when Mervyn Dillon bowled Abdur Razzaq between bat and pad on the drive and had Inzamam-ul-Haq top edging a pull to wicketkeeper, Ridley Jacobs first ball. Dillon was mixing leg-side wides with unplayable deliveries. Wasim Akram's decision looked sick. Pakistan were 4-42 in the 19th over.

If the West Indies had an extra quality fast bowler in their line-up they may have finished Pakistan there and then. Alas for golden years of yore. Ijaz Ahmed and Yousul Youhana were able to settle in against the support attack and added 60 in 12 overs. Brian Lara recalled Dillon and with the first ball of his second spell he hit Ijaz on the toe right in front.

Yousuf top-edged a slog 33 runs later and at 6-135 Pakistan could still have finished with an inadequate total. It was now, though, that having to use Keith Arthurton, Jimmy Adams and Ricardo Powell as bowlers became costly. Akram and Azhar Mahmood began striking the ball a long way. Between them they smashed 74 in nine overs, including two sixes apiece. Akram hit his off Adams and Powell, Azhar also struck Adams into the crowd and sent a full toss off Ambrose over the ropes at midwicket. The part-time bowlers conceded 83 runs in their combined 10 overs. A total of 23 wides and 2 no-balls added both to Pakistan's total and the balls they could face. Arthurton twisted an ankle in the outfield which would affect his batting later. Pakistan increased their score by 94 in the final 11 overs. The West Indies, so long on top in this match, now had to make 230 to win.

They had to withstand the opening burst of the young man now renowned as the fastest bowler in the world. Shoaib Akhtar excited the Pakistani spectators with his long run-up and extreme pace. He got the adrenalin of the West Indian openers, Ridley Jacobs and Sherwin Campbell going, too. His opening delivery, a short flyer, was hooked for six by Sherwin Campbell. The Bajan was late with the shot and the ball sailed over third man! Jacobs fended off another thunderbolt and it flew from his handle over the wicketkeeper for a first bounce four.

In his second over, the man tipped to be the first bowler to crack the 100mph barrier, removed Campbell's off stump. Jimmy Adams came in at number three, unusually for him, supplementing his helmet with a discretionary visor. It worked to the extent that he stayed with Jacobs until 58 runs had been added. Adams was caught at slip off the first ball of the seventeenth over to become the first of Azhar Mohammad's three victims.

Lara's entrance at 2-72 offered a tantalising prospect, one enhanced by two prompt boundaries through the covers. However the entertainment lasted a mere nine balls. Abdur Razzaq induced an on drive that skewd off a leading edge to substitute Mushtaq Ahmed at cover point. It was a fatal blow to the chances of his side.

Shivnarine Chanderpaul fought hard for the rest of the innings to get the West Indies back into the match. If he could have found one decent partner that objective would have been achieved. None were forthcoming. Jacobs became Abdur's second wicket when he was caught at slip driving at a wide ball in the 23rd over. Ricardo Powell and Phil Simmons never got going and only some resilience by Dillon, and Pakistan's generous quota of wides and a couple of missed chances allowed the total to creep past 200.

Chanderpaul was last out, caught off Shoaib with 28 runs still needed off eight deliveries. The slender, reliable left-hander was still going for the win and his 96 ball innings was by a healthy margin the best of the game. The Man of the Match Award, though, went to Azhar Mahmood.

PAKISTAN		WEST INDIES	
Saeed Anwar c Lara b Walsh	10	S. L. Campbell b Shoaib Akhtar	9
Shahid Afridi c Jacobs b Walsh	11	R. D. Jacobs (wk) c Inzamam-ul-Haq b Abdul Razzaq	25
Abdul Razzaq b Dillon	7	J. C. Adams c Inzamam-ul-Haq b Azhar Mahmood	23
Ijaz Ahmed lbw b Dillon	36	B. C. Lara (capt) c sub (Mushtaq Ahmed) b Abdul Razzaq	11
Inzamam-ul-Haq c Jacobs b Dillon	0	S. Chanderpaul c Yousuf Youhanna b Shoaib Akhtar	77
Yousuf Youhanna c & b Simmons	34	R. L. Powell c Yousuf Youhanna b Saqlain Mushtaq	4
Azhar Mahmood c sub b Ambrose	38	P. V. Simmons c Moin Khan b Azhar Mahmood	5
Wasim Akram (capt) b Walsh	43	C. E. L. Ambrose c Moin Khan b Abdul Razzaq	1
Moin Khan (wk) not out	11	K. L. T. Arthurton c Saeed Anwar b Azhar Mahmood	6
Saqlain Mushtaq not out	2	M. Dillon run out	6
Extras b1 lb12 w23 nb2	38	C. A. Walsh not out	0
(50 overs)	8-229	Extras b1 lb8 w20 nb6	35
Did not bat: Shoaib Akhtar		(48.5 overs)	202
1/22 2/23 3/42 4/42 5/102 6/135 7/209 8/217		1/14 2/72 3/84 4/101 5/121 6/141 7/142 8/161 9/195 10/202	
Bowling: Ambrose 10-1-36-1; Walsh 10-3-28-3;		Bowling: Wasim Akram 10-3-37-0; Shoaib Akhtar 9.5-1-54-2;	
Dillon 10-1-29-3; Simmons 10-0-40-1		Saqlain Mushtaq 9-0-22-1; Azhar Mahmood 10-0-48-3;	
Arthurton 1-0-10-0; Adams 8-0-57-0; Powell 1-0-16-0		Abdul Razzaq 10-3-32-3	

Umpires: D. Hair D. Orchard

Toss: Pakistan   Points: Pakistan 2 West Indies 0

COUNTY GROUND, WORCESTER:
AUSTRALIA vs SCOTLAND–GROUP B
AUSTRALIA WON BY 6 WICKETS

Worcester traditionally hosts the opening fixture to Australian Ashes tours of England. There have been many memorable performances at what is widely regarded as the most beautiful cricket ground in the world. This effort against Scotland, despite the comfortable six wicket win, will never be rated among the best by the Aussies at New Road.

To be fair, Steve Waugh's side were on a hiding to nothing against the lowly rated Scots and they certainly came up with a better result than Kim Hughes side had when they played the Zimbabwean World Cup debutants in the opening round of 1983. The Australians had to contend with a pro-Scottish crowd full of grog, decipherable and indecipherable comments and weather far better suited to Glasgow than any major Australian centre.

Shane Warne was a special target of the Scottish taunts. The ability of the great leg-spinner to tolerate their jibing was diminished by having received a fine and a two-match suspended sentence for his published comments that Sri Lanka would be better off with Arjuna Ranatunga. Warne risked further censure when he gave a single finger salute to a section of the crowd. However, Ranjan Madugalle took no action.

The cricket action began immediately after Steve Waugh had won the toss and sent Scotland in to bat. Bruce Patterson gave his country a perfect start to their first limited-over interantional when he caressed a half volley from Damien Fleming through the covers for four.

Patterson and his opening partner, 40-year-old Iain Philip, flattered to deceive with that start as they scratched around for 19 runs in 11 overs. Fleming got his revenge on Patterson, Gilchrist holding a low edge, but he was one of several players to make glaring mistakes in the field. Also the Australian bowlers had as much trouble keeping the swinging ball on a line that satisfied the umpires as had the other attacks playing that weekend. Adam Dale and Glenn McGrath were the worst culprits sending down 22 illegal deliveries between them.

Scotland battled to keep their run rate above two an over. Philip was nicely caught in the gully by the Australian captain in the 23rd over, Adam Gilchrist completed a smart stumping when Mike Allingham became too ambitious against Warne and Michael Bevan flew like a bird to his left to hold Mike Smith at full stretch at mid-on off Shane Lee.

Between those commendable efforts three catches and three run outs were missed. Fleming misjudged the break on a hit to mid-on and looked a fool as he changed direction too late and the ball ran behind him for four. Gavin Hamilton a highly rated all-rounder contracted to Yorkshire and James Brinkley, a fast bowler with connections all over Australia and Great Britain, gave the Scottish total respectability by adding 62 in ten overs. Even though the pair fell within a couple of balls of each other to Warne in the 47th over, Scotland were able to complete their innings with on a far from embarrassing 7-181.

It looked better still when Asim Butt had Gilchrist caught low down at leg gully by Nick Dyer in the sixth over. That was the last real shock and from that point Australia always looked like winning. Mark Waugh was in no mood to encourage Scotland and his was the best innings of the game. He hit five sweetly timed boundaries and his 114 ball knock won him the Man of the Match Award. Waugh had a stand of 84 in 21 overs with Ricky Ponting. The Tasmanian was out to the catch of the day by Allingham, a sprinting diving effort, coming in from the square leg boundary to hold a top edged pull.

Darren Lehmann underedged his second ball onto his stumps with the score still on 101. Forty runs later, in the 36th over, Mark Waugh chipped a return catch to give Dyer his second wicket. Then Steve Waugh, who hit seven boundaries, and Bevan saw Australia home with five overs and six wickets to spare.

Waugh, who can match his former captain, Allan Border, for grumpiness, had plenty to complain about after the game. He rated Australia's performance 4 out of 10 and felt dissatisfied at the ground security provided. It was a sensitive issue with the Australian captain after the dangerous pitch-invasion and bottle-throwing incidents in the West Indies. On two separate occasions male streakers held up play for several minutes before being removed and after the game the crowd came from all directions. Waugh was none too pleased as his players were subject to some jostling.

SCOTLAND		AUSTRALIA	
B. M. W. Patterson c Gilchrist b Fleming	10	A. C. Gilchrist (wk) c Dyer b Asim Butt	6
I. L. Philip c S. R. Waugh b McGrath	17	M. E. Waugh c & b Dyer	67
M. Allingham st Gilchrist b Warne	3	R. T. Ponting c Allingham b Blian	33
M. Smith c Bevan b Lee	13	D. S. Lehmann b Dyer	0
G. Salmond (capt) c Gilchrist b S. R. Waugh	31	S. R. Waugh (capt) not out	49
G. M. Hamilton b Warne	34	M. G. Bevan not out	11
J. E. Brinkley c Dale b Warne	23	Extras lb3 w4 ‹ nb9	16
A. G. Davies (wk) not out	8	(44.5 overs)	4-182
J. A. R. Blain not out	3	Did not bat: S. Lee, S. K. Warne, D. W. Fleming, A. C. Dale,
Extras lb9 w22 nb8	39	G. D. McGrath
(50 overs)	7-181	1/17 2/101 3/101 4/141
Did not bat: Asim Butt, N. R. Dyer		Bowling: Blain 8-0-35-1; Asim Butt 10-3-21-1;
1/19 2/37 3/52 4/87 5/105 6/167 7/169		Brinkley 8-0-43-0; Hamilton 8.5-0-37-0; Dyer 10-1-43-2
Bowling: Fleming 9-2-19-1; Dale 10-2-35-0;		
McGrath 9-0-32-1; Warne 10-0-39-3; Lee 6-1-25-1;		
Waugh 6-0-22-1		

Umpires: R. Dunne   P. Willey

Toss: Australia   Points: Australia 2 Scotland 0

MONDAY 17 MAY 1999
COUNTY GROUND, CHELMSFORD: BANGLADESH vs NEW ZEALAND - GROUP B
NEW ZEALAND WON BY SIX WICKETS

New Zealand made very short work of Bangladesh at the well appointed home of Essex County Cricket Club in Chlemsford. The capacity crowd, full of noisy expatriate Bangladeshis down from East London, saw just 70 overs of cricket as the Kiwis strolled to victory.

After Stephen Fleming had won the toss on a cool windy morning and sent Bangladesh in both openers, like named but unrelated, were back in the pavilion before the end of the third over. Each fell in identical fashion, trapped lbw by balls from left armer Geoff Allott that straightened down the line of the stumps.

For the next 10 overs Akram Khan and the captain, Aminul Islam, gave the impression that Bangladesh would recover and build a respectable total. They added 31 before being the first two victims in a startling collapse. Chirs Cairns bowled Aminul middle stump then five balls later Gavin Larsen held a caught and bowled from a hard hit drive by Akram. Cairns and Larsen continued to inflict damage. When Mohammad Rafique was caught plumb in front by Cairns from the first ball he faced Bangladesh were 7-51 in the 21st over and a complete rout was on the cards. Naimur Rahman and Enamul Hoque, at least stopped the procession temporarily, and added 34 in the process. The last couple of batsmen continued to fight hard and Hasibul Hussain took 12 off a Chris Harris over including a swipe for six that landed on the roof of the commentary box. An Allott full toss, possibly an above the waist no-ball, was hit by Hassibul straight to Matthew Horne at mid wicket in the 38th over to end the innings on 116.

New Zealand began their reply before lunch and in the second over Nathan Astle plonked an off-drive off left-armer Manjural, straight into the hands of Aminul at mid-off. The Bangladeshi bowlers were able to extract some movement and hit the pads a few times without winning an lbw decision. They had to wait until the 11th over when Craig McMillan, who had just started to hit a few boundaries completely mistimed a slower ball from Hasibul and was caught at mid wicket.

Further wickets had to follow quickly if the game was to come to life. They didn't. Fleming and Horne put on 45 in 12 overs before the New Zealand captain was caught behind and Horne lasted until his side were just a dozen runs from victory. Roger Twose enlivened the final stages of the match with a huge six over long on that landed in the back garden of one of the houses in Hayes Close and was lost.

The winning run, scored from the last ball of the 33rd over, heralded yet another energetic invasion. One spectator pilfered a stump. If Steve Waugh had been watching he would have been unimpressed. Gavin Larsen as accurate as in 1992, if a little more grey-haired, was named Man of the Match.

BANGLADESH		NEW ZEALAND	
Shahriar Hossain lbw b Allott	0	M. J. Horne lbw b Naimur	35
Mehrab Hossain lbw b Allott	2	N. J Astle c Aminul b Manjural	4
Akram Khan c & b Larsen	16	C. D. McMillan c Naimur b Hasibul	20
Aminul Islam (capt) b Cairns	15	S. P. Fleming (capt) c Khaled Mashud b Mohammad	16
Khaled Mashud (wk) b Larsen	4	R. G. Twose not out	30
Naimur Rahman lbw b Larsen	18	C. L. Cairns not out	7
Khaled Mahmud c Twose b Cairns	3	Extras lb1 w4	5
Mohammad Rafique lbw b Cairns	0	(33 overs)	4-117
Enamul Hoque b Harris	19	Did not bat: A. C. Parore (wk), C. Z. Harris, D. J. Nash,	
Hasibul Hussain c Horne b Allott	16	G. R. Larsen, G. I Allott	
Manjural Islam not out	6	1/5 2/33 3/78 4/105	
Extras lb4 w5 nb8	17	Bowling: Hasibul 10-2-33-1; Manjural 8-3-23-1;	
(37.4 overs)	116	Khaled Mahmud 7-2-12-0; Enamul 3-0-21-0;	
1/0 2/7 3/38 4/38 5/46 6/49 7/51 8/85 9/96 10/116		Mohammad 3-0-22-1; Naimur 2-0-5-1	
Bowling: Allott 8.4-0-30-3; Nash 10-1-30-0; Cairns 7-1-19-3;			
Larsen 10-0-19-3; Harris 2-0-14-1			

Umpires: I. Robinson S. Venkataraghaven

Toss: New Zealand   Points:New Zealand 2 Bangladesh 0

TUESDAY 18 MAY 1999
St LAWRENCE GROUND, CANTERBURY: ENGLAND vs KENYA-GROUP A
ENGLAND WON BY NINE WICKETS

Although Canterbury is a beautiful city and has a lovely cricket ground, it can still be a depressing place when there is rain and it is persistent enough to look like ruining the cricket.

There were showers all morning in the south east corner of England. They were bad enough to prevent play at the scheduled start time and originally showed no sign of abating. But there is no point in hosting a World Cup tournament if you can't hope for a bit of good fortune with the weather. Eventually the skies cleared enough for England to complete their win over Kenya.

As against Zimbabwe, Kenya batted better than they bowled, while England only had to use three batsmen instead of the four they required against Sri Lanka. Nasser Hussain and Graeme Hick were more concerned with the prospect of rain and bad light stopping play than innocuous Kenyan bowling hampered by a wet ball. The match was not completed until 7.52 pm.

Alec Stewart won his second toss and the game was able to get underway 90 minutes late, albeit under a sky that remained grey and threatening. Kennedy Otieno was caught at slip in the 4th over off Ian Austin, cutting too close to his body. Then Ravindu Shah and Steve Tikolo put on 100 for the second wicket in 23 overs.

Tikolo's innings was most impressive. He reached his 50 off 70 balls and hit eight fine boundaries. Darren Gough came back to break the stand having Shah caught behind off an inside edge. Two overs later he bowled Maurice Odumbe with an in-swinging yorker to claim his 100th wicket in Limited Over Internationals. England took control of the game and they never loosened it from that point.

Neil Fairbrother ran out Hitesh Modi at the bowler's end with a throw from short fine leg. Gough picked up two more wickets with in-swinging yorkers and Graham Thorpe ended the innings when he ran out Martin Suji in the final over. In the end only the successful continuation of Thomas Odoyo's policy of all out attack which brought him three fours and a six off Alan Mullally over square leg ensured the efforts of Shah and Tikolo were not wasted.

England's in form top order were never going to be challenged by that, but they had to endure more interruptions and for a time feared that the game would have to continue into a second day. According to some, the umpires decree that the between-innings interval should last an hour was incorrect. At 6.00pm rain once more stopped play. Elsewhere in the world that might have spelled the end of the day. England's one climactic advantage over other cricket nations is a lengthy twilight so an opportunity to re-start presented itself at 6.43.

Stewart had been bowled in the 10th over by a ball that cut back into him. Hick and Hussain then took command of the Kenyan attack. Hussain went to his 50 in 87 balls with seven fours, however the feature shot of his innings was a pulled six in the 37th over which sent the ball sailing into the top row of a temporary stand beside the ailing lime tree. Hick finished with nine fours in his unbeaten 61, the last of which, a square cut, completed England's win with 11 overs if not much daylight to spare. Tikolo beat Hussain, Hick and Gough for the Man of the Match Award.

As with his counterparts at Worcester, the streaker at Canterbury was more than a match for the ground security.

KENYA		ENGLAND	
K. O. Otieno (wk) c Thorpe b Austin	0	N. Hussain not out	88
Ravindu Shah c Stewart b Gough	46	A. J. Stewart (capt/wk) b Odoyo	23
S. O. Tikolo c Gough b Ealham	71	G. A. Hick not out	61
M. O. Odumbe b Gough	6	Extras b5 lb6 w13 nb8	32
H. S. Modi run out	5	(39 overs)	1-204
A. Vadher b Croft	6	Did not bat: G. P. Thorpe, N. H. Fairbrother, A. Flintoff,	
T. M. Odoyo not out	34	M. A. Ealham, R. D. B. Croft, I. E. Austin, D. Gough,	
Aasif Karim (capt) b Ealham	9	A. D. Mullally	
A. Suji b Gough	4	1/45	
Mohammad Sheikh b Gough	7	Bowling: M. Suji 9-0-46-0; A. Suji 3-0-6-0; Odoyo 10-0-65-1;	
M. A. Suji run out	0	Aasif Karim 8-0-39-0; Odumbe 6-1-23-0 Mohammad	
Extras 1 lb5 w6 nb3	15	Sheikh 3-0-14-0	
(49.4 overs)	203		

1/7 2/107 3/115 4/130 5/142 6/150 7/181 8/186 9/202
10/203
Bowling: Gough 10-1-34-4; Austin 9.4-0-41-1; Mullally
10-0-41-0; Ealham 10-0-49-2; Croft 10-1-32-1

Umpires: K. Francis R. Koertzen

Toss: England   Points: England 2 Kenya 0

WEDNESDAY 19 MAY 1999
COUNTY GROUND, NORTHAMPTON: SRI LANKA vs SOUTH AFRICA-GROUP A
SOUTH AFRICA WON BY 89 RUNS

Sri Lanka's World Cup defence was looking sick after this substantial defeat by South Africa. The reigning champions had some luck with umpiring decisions and at the start of the 49th over of the South African innings looked to have the match under control.

That was all changed by five exhilerating Lance Klusener hits. His 22-run onslaught was immediately followed by an irresistible spell of fast bowling by Jacques Kallis which swept away the Sri Lankan top order. From that point there was only going to be one winner. It is a measure of South Africa's strength in this type of cricket that their best bowling came from one of their leading batsmen and their match-winning innings was played by a frontline bowler.

Arjuna Ranatunga sent South Africa in on a cool morning at the refurbished Northampton Ground. The 7000-capacity venue soon filled up and nobody would have wanted to miss an eventful start. Gary Kirsten drove three consecutive boundaries off Pramodya Wickremasinghe's second over then played on to left hander Chaminda Vaas from the third ball of the third. Two runs later Herschelle Gibbs was given out caught behind driving at a wide ball he did not believe he hit. When Wickremasinghe bowled Mark Boucher through the gate in the next over South Africa were 3-24.

The Northampton wicket was offering assistance to the bowlers so that South Africa had battle for their runs. It was a fight they continued to lose for quite some time. Kallis fended away from his body and Hansie Cronje called for a second run that was not there. Jayawardene's perfect throw from deep square leg left the Proteas 5-69 in the 21st over.

Twelve overs later, they had progressed to 6-115 when Shaun Pollock drove at Muttiah Muralitharan. He struck the ball sweetly, but straight at Ranatunga fielding in close on the off side. The ball ricocheted off Ranatunga and lobbed up to Muralitharan. The trajectory of the ball off the bat suggested it had bounced on its way to Rantunga's ankle, but the Sri Lankans appealed and Steve Dunne, referred the matter to third umpire, Ken Palmer. Palmer, an experienced practitioner, viewed the incident from various angles for seven minutes before pronouncing to everyone's surprise that Pollock had been caught and bowled.

Two overs later Daryl Cullinan, whose innings had been the mainstay of the South African effort, lofted Muralitharan down the ground towards long off. Vaas backed back and judging the ball very well held the catch. His momentum took him back further and as he approached the rope Vaas threw the ball away. If a fielder carries the ball over the rope while completing a catch the shot counts for six. Most believed the Sri Lankan paceman had saved runs by throwing the ball back. Palmer thought he had completed the catch and astonishly ruled Cullinan out to leave South Africa 8-122.

A complete capitulation was overcome when Steve Elworthy stayed with Klusener while 44 runs were put on. When Vaas began the 50th over South Africa had worked their way to 9-177. Another 8 to 10 runs would have been valuable. Klusener got those from the first four balls. Anything extra was a bonus. The fifth ball was a waist high full toss. The big left-hander heaved that over midwicket for six. Vaas' final ball pitched on a length. Klusener gave himself a little room and swung hard and straight. That ball sailed into the crowd too. It raised Klusener's 50 from 44 balls. The final total was now a competitive 9-199.

The crowd, sitting in welcome sunshine, were buzzing. So too was Kallis when the old 1996 World Cup firm of Sanath Jayasuriya and Romesh Kaluwithara came out to begin the reply. The objective was a brisk start, however Kallis' bouncy, fast out-swingers were nigh on unplayable. His extravagent movement caused Kaluwitharana to swish and miss every ball in his first over. The wicketkeeper/batsman cracked a beautiful pull from the second ball of his next over, but followed that with an edged drive. Cullinan parried the ball before holding it at the second attempt.

Another blow came from the final ball of the same over when the ball jagged into the left handed Jayasuriya at pace. He guided it into his middle stump which splattered out of the ground. Kallis wasn't finished. Marvin Atapattu also tried to drive only to inside edge through to Boucher, who dived forward and low to his left to hold an excellent catch. Kallis had three wickets in 11 balls. It could have been four as Klusener had missed a sharp chance off Aravinda de Silva at third slip just before Atapattu's dismissal.

Pollock ensured the chance had little impact when he trapped de Silva in front with an off-cutter in his next over. The little Sri Lankan walked away shaking his head. He may not have been totally satisfied with Steve Dunne's decision. Nor could he have been happy with his form or that of his teammates. After being 0-12 Sri Lanka had collapsed to 4-14. And Allan Donald had not even been needed yet. As if peeved at missing out on the fun he had Ranatunga caught behind from his second ball. It was another rearing delivery, Sri Lanka were 5-31 and the show was over. Mahela Jayawardne showed why he is so highly rated with a couple of sumptuous drives and Roshan Mahanama demonstrated the technique that might have been able to handle the new ball more effectively. That allowed the innings to stretch out for another 20 overs before Klusener topped his day with three cheap wickets and a well deserved Man of the Match Award.

SOUTH AFRICA		SRI LANKA	
G. Kirsten b Vaas	14	S. T. Jayasuriya b Kallis	5
H. Gibbs c Kaluwitharana b Wickramasinghe	5	R. S. Kaluwitharana (wk) c Cullinan b Kallis	5
M. V. Boucher (wk) b Wickramasinghe	1	M. S. Attapattu c Boucher b Kallis	1
J. H. Kallis c Mahanama b Wickramasinghe	12	P. A.de Silva lbw b Pollock	1
D. J. Cullinan c Vaas b Muralitharan	49	R. S. Mahanama lbw b Pollock	36
W. J. Cronje (capt) run out	8	A. Ranatunga (capt) c Boucher b Donald	7
J. N. Rhodes c Jayasuriya b Muralitharan	17	D. P. M. D. Jayawardene c Kallis b Elworthy	22
S. M. Pollock c & b Muralitharan	2	U. D. U. Chandana c Cullinan b Kulsener	9
L. Klusener not out	52	W. P. U. J. C. Vaas c Pollock b Klusener	1
S. Elworthy c Kaluwitharana b Vaas	23	G. P. Wickramasinghe b Klusener	6
A. A. Donald not out	3	M. Muralitharan not out	0
Extras lb2 w7 nb4	13	Extras lb5 w10 nb2	17
(50 overs)	9-199	(35.2 overs)	10-110

1/22 2/24 3/24 4/53 5/69 6/103 7/115 8/122 9/166

1/12 2/13 3/14 4/14 5/31 6/66 7/87 8/98 9/110 10/110

Bowling: Wickramasinghe 10-1-45-2; Vaas 10-0-46-3; Jayawardene 10-0-46-0; Muralitharan 10-1-25-3 Chandana 7-0-26-0 Jayasuriya 3-1-9-0

Bowling: Pollock 8-3-10-2; Kallis 8-0-26-3; Elworthy 8-1-23-1; Donald 6-1-25-1; Klusener 5.2-1-21-3

Umpires: S. Dunne S. Bucknor

Toss: Sri Lanka   Points: South Africa 2 Sri Lanka 0

GRACE ROAD, LEICESTER: INDIA vs ZIMBABWE-GROUP A
ZIMBABWE WON BY THREE RUNS

This was a poignant and ultimately heartbreaking game for India. They had to withstand the temporary loss of their best batsmen and all sorts of mistakes in the field yet still would have won if Henry Olonga had not overcome his own bowling problems and snatched victory for Zimbabwe. Alistair Campbell's side were elated because this win gave them a real chance of progressing through to the Super Sixes round.

Some members of the Indian team had only found out on the morning of the match that Sachin Tendulkar had flown back to be with his family in India upon hearing the news of his father's sudden death. Both teams lined up for a minute's silence as a mark of respect prior to the start of the game.

There was another good crowd in at Grace Road as the weather continued to be kind, if a little on the cool side, especially for Indians and Zimbabweans. Mohammad Azharuddin won the toss and sent Zimbabwe in. On a firm evenly grassed wicket Javagal Srinath and Venkatash Prasad responded well to their captain's decision, for several overs keeping the batsmen well under control. Srinath had the left-handed Neil Johnson caught behind in the third over while Grant Flower and number three, pinch hitter Paul Strang were lucky to survive.

That, though, remained the trend of the innings. In addition, the wide and no ball count mounted and the Zimbabweans took advantage of any loose bowling. Strang was yorked by Ajit Agarkar in the 10th over and when Saurav Ganguly had Murray Goodwin caught in the gully Zimbabwe were 3-87 in the 22nd over.

The Flowers combined for a stand of 57. A percentage of the runs actually came off the bat and many of those were unbelieveably short singles. Then Campbell and Andy Flower took the total beyond 200 by adding a further 60 in nine overs.

By now the inaccuracy of the Indians was really starting to tell. Anil Kumble was an exception and he picked up the wickets of the Zimbabwean captain and Guy Whittall in quick succession. Neverthless by 2.15pm he and his pace bowling colleagues had only sent down 276 legal deliveries. This meant that they had to complete their allottment to Zimbabwe, but would receive just 46 overs in return. During the final over another wide from Prasad brought up the half century of extras. The crowd cheered.

The early dismissal of the in-form Ganguly was a further regret for the Indians as they began their pursuit of 253. Eddo Brandes held the opener at fine leg off Johnson, however the veteran copped some punishment from Rahul Dravid. Heath Streak replaced the expensive Brandes and immediately had Dravid cutting to Grant Flower in the gully. When Azharuddin edged the same bowler to his opposite number at first slip India were 3-56 at the end of the ninth over.

Stand in opener Sadagopan Ramesh and Ajay Jadeja repaired the damage to the extent of an enterprising 99 partnership in 19 overs. Ramesh pulled Johnson for six. Henry Olonga missed an easy run out then sprayed the ball about in more directions than his deadlocked hair was growing. Murray Goodwin just missed holding a skier in what would have been an early bid for catch of the tournament. Soon after Ramesh was caught at mid-on by the same fieldsman off Grant Flower whose accuracy was well appreciated by the Man of the Match adjudicator.

Five overs later Streak returned to have an lbw shout upheld. India were 5-174 and six down one run later when Goodwin ran out Agarkar from mid-on. The match was boiling up into a thriller and Nayan Mongia added to the excitement with a quickfire 28. When Srinath hit Paul Strang for six over mid wicket and then repeated the dose to Guy Whittall India needed just another nine runs from two overs with three wickets standing.

On instinct Campbell threw the ball to Olonga. The tearaway responded by having Robin Singh caught at mid-off then yorked Srinath with his fifth ball to leave India 9-249. Prasad joined Kumble to face the last ball of the penultimate over of the match. It was a full length, Prasad fell across his stumps and was struck on the pads. Up went Olonga, Andy Flower and the entire Zimbabwean nation. Up also, after the briefest of delays, went umpire Peter Willey's left index finger. There was a blur of Zimbabwean red as the players celebrated a real coming-of-age World Cup win.

For India the loss was equally significant. Azharuddin was booed by Indian supporters in the crowd. *The Hindu* newspaper called the loss 'appalling'. Neutrals might have suggested it was 'exciting'.

The jostling of Zimbabwean players by invading spectators and the stoning of the team bus after the game were genuinely appalling developments.

ZIMBABWE		INDIA	
N. C. Johnson c Mongia b Srinath	7	S. C. Ganguly c Brandes b Johnson	9
G. W. Flower c Mongia b Jadeja	45	S. Ramesh c Goodwin b G. W. Flower	55
P. A. Strang b Agarkar	18	R. Dravid c G. W. Flower b Streak	13
M. W. Goodwin c Singh b Ganguly	17	M. Azharuddin (capt) c Campbell b Streak	7
A. Flower (wk) not out	68	A. Jadeja lbw b Streak	43
A. D. R Campbell (capt) st Mongia b Kumble	24	R. R. Singh c Campbell b Olonga	35
G. J. Whittall b Kumble	4	A. B. Agarkar run out	1
S. V. Carlisle b Srinath	1	N. R. Mongia (wk) b Whittall	28
H. H. Streak c Mongia b Prasad	14	J. Srinath b Olonga	18
E. A. Brandes c Mongia b Prasad	2	A. Kumble not out	1
H. K. Olonga not out	1	B. K.V. Prasad lbw b Olonga	0
Extras lb14 w21 nb16	51	Extras b1 lb4 w24 nb10	39
(50 overs)	9-252	(45 overs)	249

1/12 2/45 3/87 4/144 5/204 6/211 7/214 8/244 9/250

Bowling: Srinath 10-1-35-2; Prasad 10-1-37-2; Agarkar 9-0-70-1; Ganguly 5-0-22-1; Singh 2-0-11-0 Kumble 10-0-41-2 Jadeja 4-0-22-1

1/13 2/44 3/56 4/155 5/174 6/175 7/219 8/249 9/249 10/249

Bowling: Brandes 3-0-27-0; Johnson 7-0-51-1; Streak 9-0-36-3; Olonga 4-0-22-3; Whittall 4-0-26-1 Strang 8-0-49-0 G. W. Flower 10-0-33-1

Umpires: D. Orchard P. Willey

Toss: India   Points: Zimbabwe 2 India 0

THURSDAY 20 MAY 1999
SOPHIA GARDENS, CARDIFF: AUSTRALIA vs NEW ZEALAND-GROUP B
NEW ZEALAND WON BY FIVE WICKETS

Nothing gives a New Zealander as much pleasure as beating Australia. Steve Waugh's much vaunted team played lacklustre cricket and were totally out-senergised by the committed Kiwis. It put a dampener on later post match celebrations by Shane Warne and friends who planned to go out and mark the occasion of the overnight birth of his son, Jackson, back in Australia.

There was bright sunshine and blue skies at Sophia Gardens in Cardiff when Steve Waugh won the toss and elected to bat. Those early fears of poor ticket sales were again unjustified as the 10,000 capacity ground was comfortably full at the start of play.

Left-armer, Geoff Allott was soon getting some swing and from the first ball of his second over he struck a massive blow. A perfectly pitched in-swinger caught Mark Waugh right in front of his stumps and umpire Javed Akhtar had no hesitation.

Adam Gilchrist and Ricky Ponting played tippety run for half a dozen overs before Allott struck again. Gilchrist's dabbing cut was guided to Nathan Astle at second slip to leave Australia 2-32 in the seventh over and Ponting and Darren Lehmann with some re-building to do. As they did so the skies darkened and at 2-61, after 15 overs, there was a 37 minute interruption for rain.

Upon the resumption Ponting and Lehmann took control. The Tasmanian was dropped by a high leaping Dion Nash at short mid wicket. He tended to play second fiddle to Lehmann who swatted Chris Harris away a few times. The South Australian brought up his 50 off 65 balls with six fours in the 30th over with another big lofted drive to mid wicket. The partnership of 94 ended an over later when Ponting sliced a drive off Nathan Astle's first over to Chris Harris at backward point.

The belief was that the Australian middle order would capitalise on the sensible batting by Ponting and Lehmann. However it was the New Zealanders who responded at this point. The Australians were never again able to bat with any kind of freedom. Harris had Steve Waugh well caught low down at mid wicket from a cross bat swipe and then during Harris' last over Lehmann miscued a drive to Astle at cover. Nash following through ran out Shane Lee with a diving throw along the pitch.

Allott came back to shatter Michael Bevan's stumps on the drive and hit Shane Warne's off stump with a ball that moved away. Gavin Larsen had been at his miserly best and Australia had to be content with a non-commital and fairly uninteresting 8-213 from their 50 overs.

The Kiwis hardly got the start they wanted in their reply. Adam Dale's second ball brought him a wicket, Matthew Horne given out caught behind to a ball that went between bat and body. Five overs later Dale's new-ball partner, Damien Fleming had Astle slicing a drive to a forward running Ponting in the gully to leave New Zealand 2-21.

The score had reached 47 when Glenn McGrath ripped a perfect tall man to tall man yorker into Fleming's leg stump. An over later Craig McMillan's poorly fashioned sweep at Warne lobbed the ball to a diving Fleming at mid-on. It was as if world order was restored with New Zealand having difficulty competing against Australia.

Slowly and imperceptibly Roger Twose and Chris Cairns asserted their dominance over the bowlers. Twose had a lucky break when he hooked a catch to Fleming at fine leg only for Akhtar to call McGrath's delivery a no ball. The first major sign of a batting revival was a lofted drive by Cairns for six off Warne in the 22nd over. The partnership had started moving and now there was no stopping it. Steve Waugh tried his full hand of bowlers.

Bevan's left arm wrist spin was introduced and Cairns struck him sweetly back over his head for another six. Twose drove and pulled to the boundary on the on-side. He reached his 50 from 72 balls with six fours. Cairns' half century was two balls faster and he complimeted his three fours with as many sixes.

Even McGrath was punished and the New Zealand win was arriving with a rush when Fleming finally terminated the 148-run fifth wicket World Cup record-breaking stand. The departure of Cairns caught at long off caused no panic as Man of the Match Twose belted some more boundaries, his 10th, the last, was another mighty pull off Fleming and it completed the Kiwi win with five overs and five wickets to spare.

Mark Waugh nearly lost his cap as the ground security did nothing to control the post-match invasion. His brother needed to put on his thinking cap to restore Australia's form and confidence. New Zealand, according to their captain, had 'hardened up'.

AUSTRALIA		NEW ZEALAND	
M. E. Waugh lbw b Allott	2	M. J. Horne c Gilchrist b Dale	5
A. C. Gilchrist (wk) c Astle b Allott	14	N. J Astle c Ponting b Fleming	4
R. T. Ponting c Harris b Astle	47	C. D. McMillan c Fleming b Warne	29
D. S. Lehmann c Astle b Harris	76	S. P. Fleming (capt) b McGrath	9
S. R. Waugh (capt) c Astle b Harris	7	R. G. Twose not out	80
M. G. Bevan b Allott	21	C. L. Cairns c Dale b Fleming	60
S. Lee run out	0	A. C. Parore (wk) not out	10
S. K. Warne b Allott	15	Extras lb2 w11 nb4	17
D. W. Fleming not out	8	(45.2 overs)	5-214
A. C. Dale not out	3	Did not bat: C. Z. Harris, D. J. Nash, G. R. Larsen, G. I. Allott
Extras lb10 w5 nb3	18	1/5 2/21 3/47 4/49 5/197
(50 overs)	8-213	Bowling: Fleming 8.2-1-43-2; Dale 5-1-18-1;
Did not bat: G. D. McGrath		McGrath 9-0-43-1; Lee 6-0-24-0; Warne 10-1-44-1 S. R.
1/7 2/32 3/126 4/149 5/172 6/175 7/192 8/204		Waugh 4-0-25-0 Bevan 3-0-15-0
Bowling: Allott 10-0-37-4; Nash 8-1-30-0; Cairns 7-0-44-0;		
Larsen 10-2-26-0; Harris 10-0-50-2; Astle 5-0-16-1		

Umpires: Javed Akhtar D. Shepherd

Toss: Australia   Points: New Zealand 2 Australia 0

RIVERSIDE GROUND, CHESTER -le-STREET: PAKISTAN vs SCOTLAND - GROUP B
PAKISTAN WON BY 94 RUNS

Scotland, following a fine start quickly, discovered the extent of Pakistan's mercurial ability. They also soon realised that their bowlers had as much trouble as everyone else controlling the much discussed Dukes ball. The India and Zimbabwe match on Wednesday had contained a 90 extras. Pakistan and Scotland topped that at Chester-le-Street by six.

By the completion of this 11th match of the tournament no batsman had made a century. Mr Extras was easily the most consistent run maker in the 'Carnival of Cricket'. It remained to been seen who would be the first to crack a ton.

Another venue making its international debut, the Riverside Stadium belied its reputation by being bathed in sunshine at the start of play when George Salmond won the toss for Scotland and sent Pakistan in. As had been its habit, the ball started moving around immediately causing problems for bowlers and batsmen alike. When James Brinkley had Abdur Razzaq lbw in the 26th over Pakistan were teetering a little at 3-55 and half the total was already extras. An over later Gavin Hamilton trapped Salim Malik lbw and it was 4-58.

Inzamam-ul-Haq struggled for 12 in 50 balls before being stumped off Nick Dye. Scotland had Pakistan 5-92, but that was the end of their fun. Yousuf Youhana and Moin Khan began the fight back with a stand of 103 in 18 overs. When Moin was caught at backward square leg on the sweep, Wasim Akram came in to take advantage of a fading attack. Asim Butt was smacked for two big sixes by the Pakistani captain while Youhana went on to complete a fine unbeaten 81 in 119 balls with six fours. Extras had contributed 59 to Pakistan's 6-261.

Scotland had lost an over through being late after having to send down an extra 48 deliveries. They needed 262 to cause an upset, but by the end of the ninth over half their side were already out for 19. The prospect of the Scottish batsmen coping with Shoaib Akhtar and Akram was a daunting one and they were not up to it.

The rout began from the fourth ball of the innings when Akram bowled Bruce Patterson and did not stop until the Pakistani captain took himself and his fellow spearhead out of the attack. Iain Phillip at least got his leg in the way of the ball. Three of the other four top order batsman had their stumps blasted.

If Akram had continued with himself and Shoaib Canada's record World Cup low of 45 may have been threatened. However against the still testing, but less pacy bowling of Azhar Mahmood, Abdur Razzaq and Saqlain Mushtaq, Gavin Hamilton and to a lesser extent James Brinkley and Alec Davies were able to flourish. Hamilton put on 59 with Brinkley in 16 overs and 61 with Davies in nine overs. He got stuck into Saqlain hitting the off-spinner for two sixes in one over then raising his 50 from 90 balls.

Davies was caught off a full toss at 139. Hamilton retaliated by clouting his third six off Shahid Afridi. It was all good fun and cheered the Scottish section of the crowd, but it meant nothing in terms of the result. When Akram bowled the tiring Yorkshire all-rounder Pakistan had won by 94 runs and Yousuf Youhana was named Man of the Match. Despite the demolition of the Scottish top order, Akram warned that Shoaib had not been at full pace.

PAKISTAN		SCOTLAND	
Saeed Anwar c Davies b Asim Butt	6	B. M. W. Patterson b Wasim Akram	0
Shahid Afridi run out	7	I. L. Phillip lbw b Shoaib Akhtar	0
Abdul Razzaq lbw b Brinkley	12	M. W. Smith b Shoaib Akhtar	3
Inzamam-ul-Haq st Davies b Dyer	12	I. M. Stanger b Wasim Akram	3
Salim Malik lbw b Hamilton	0	G. Salmond (capt) c Moin Khan b Shoaib Akhtar	5
Yousuf Youhana not out	81	G. M. Hamilton b Wasim Akram	76
Moin Khan (wk) c Brinkley b Hamilton	47	J. E. Brinkley c Moin Khan b Saqlain Mushtaq	22
Wasim Akram (capt) not out	37	A. G. Davies (wk) c sub (Wasti) b Abdul Razzaq	19
Extras b5 lb6 w33 nb15	59	J. A. R. Blain lbw b Abdul Razzaq	0
(50 overs)	6-261	Asim Butt c Moin Khan b Abdul Razzaq	1
Did not bat: Saqlain Mushtaq, Shoaib Akhtar,		N. R. Dyer not out	1
Azhar Mahmood		Extras b1 lb11 w17 nb8	37
1/21 2/35 3/55 4/58 5/92 6/195		(38.5 overs)	167
Bowling: Blain 7-0-49-0; Asim Butt 9-1-55-1; Hamilton		1/1 2/5 3/9 4/16 5/19 6/78 7/139 8/149 9/160 10/167	
10-1-36-2; Brinkley 10-0-29-1; Dyer 9-0-48-1		Bowling: Wasim Akram 7.5-0-23-3; Shoaib Akhtar 6-2-11-3;	
Stanger 5-0-33-0		Azhar Mahmood 7-2-21-0; Abdul Razzaq 10-0-38-3;	
		Saqlain Mushtaq 6-0-46-1; Shahid Afridi 2-0-16-0	

Umpires: D. Cowie I. Robinson

Toss: Scotland   Points: Pakistan 2 Scotland 0

FRIDAY 21 MAY 1999
CASTLE AVENUE, DUBLIN: WEST INDIES vs BANGLADESH- GROUP B
WEST INDIES WON BY SEVEN WICKETS

This was one of the West Indies' better performances in Dublin. Once, against Ireland in 1969, they had been bowled out for 25. Here, on a day of freezing wind and showers, they at least had a win. Whether their manager, Clive Lloyd, witnessed their success is unsure. He was so rugged up with blankets he may have been unable to see any play.

The West Indies were helped by the fact that Bangladesh hardly relished the cold either. It would almost been have a let down if there had been no rain on the day of Dublin's World Cup match. At least what came was early, causing a delay of 45 minutes at the start, but no problems after that. The West Indian pacemen, given first use of the wicket by Aminul Islam, got no response from a slow track, nor was their any evidence of warmth in their joints as they sprayed the ball around adding another 25 to the enormous pool of wides in this tournament.

The majority of Bangladeshi batsmen struggled. They had difficulty scoring at a reasonable run rate. Courtney Walsh conceded a mere 11 runs form his first seven overs. The exception was 20 year old Mehrab Hossain who batted 43 overs for his acomplished 64. He put on 85 for the fifth wicket with Naimur Rahman, the pair coming together at 4-55. Mehrab brought up his 50 off 112 balls with a single to cover off Phil Simmons in the 38th over. Bangladesh were finally all out for 182 from the second ball of their last over.

Manjurul Islam passed the edge of the West Indian openers, Sherwin Campbell and Ridley Jacobs a few times with the new ball. Once that danger was past, however, they were able to put together a 67 run stand in 20 overs. Campbell eventually mistimed a pull while Jacobs went on to just complete his half century before going for a single that was never on.

Brian Lara warmed the crowd with a run-a-ball cameo worth 25 then left it to Shivnarine Chanderpaul and Jimmy Adams, who completed his half century from 82 balls with six fours, to complete the win with 21 balls to spare. Walsh's superb bowling figures won him the Man of the Match award.

BANGLADESH		WEST INDIES	
Shahriar.Hossain c Campbell b Walsh	2	S. L. Campbell c Manjural Islam b Khaled Mahmud	36
Mehrab Hossain c Chanderpaul b Simmons	64	R. D. Jacobs(wk) run out	51
Akram Khan c Lara b Dillon	4	J. C. Adams not out	53
Aminul Islam(capt) c Jacobs b King	2	B. C. Lara c Hasibul Hussain b Minhajul	25
Minhajul Abedin c Jacobs b King	5	S. Chanderpaul not out	11
Naimur Rahman lbw b Walsh	45	Extras lb2 w5	7
Khaled Mahmud c Bryan b Walsh	13	(46.3 overs)	3-183
Khaled Mashud(wk) b King	4	Did not bat: S. C. Williams, P. V. Simmons, H. R. Bryan,	
Enamul Hoque Ge c Lara b Walsh	4	M. Dillon, R. D. King, C. A. Walsh	
Hasibul Hussain b Bryan	1	1/67 2/115 3/150	
Manjural Islam not out	0	Bowling: Hasibul Hussain 7-1-28-0; Manjural Islam 7-1-15-0;	
Extras lb8 w25 nb5	38	Khaled Mahmud 8-0-36-1; Enamul Hoque 8-1-31-0; Naimur	
(50 overs)	182	Rahman 9.3-0-43-0; Minhajul Abedin 7-0-28-1	

1/8 2/29 3/39 4/55 5/140 6/159 7/167 8/180 9/182 10/182

Bowling: Walsh 10-0-25-4; Dillon 10-0-43-1; Bryan 9.2-0-30-1; King 10-1-30-3; Simmons 10-0-46-1

Umpires: K.Francis D.Hair

Toss: Bangladesh   Points: West Indies 2 Bangladesh 0

SATURDAY 22 MAY 1999
KENNINGTON OVAL, LONDON: ENGLAND vs SOUTH AFRICA- GROUP A
SOUTH AFRICA WON BY 122 RUNS

The inability of cricket to get soccer off the back pages of English newspapers was exemplified by Alec Stewart's side's failure in their first real test of the tournament. They were badly beaten by South Africa on FA Cup Final day. A big win in front of a full house at The Oval against the World Cup favourites might have challenged the news of Manchester United's predictable win. Unfortunately, the cricketers were outclassed by their opponents.

Stewart, on his home ground, had a very bad day. He won the toss, sent South Africa in and watched the backsides of Gary Kirsten and Herschelle Gibbs as they put on an opening stand of 111. Later things got even worse for the English captain, but he would have wondered how when the total started rattling along at an uncomfortably easy pace.

Gibbs was the main aggressor and very severe on the recalled Angus Fraser. After the 50 had been raised he danced down to the medium pacer and clouted him hard and high over long on for six into the Mound Stand. Soon after drinks Gibbs and Kirsten brought up only the Proteas' second century opening stand in limited-over internationals in the previous 18 months.

Then, as if such a stand was an unnatural occurrence, three wickets fell in 14 balls. Mark Ealham picked up the two openers, Gibbs, caught deep on the leg-side by Graeme Hick and Kirsten taken behind off an inside edge. Alan Mullally topped that by ripping a beautiful cut 'im in half' ball through Jacques Kallis so that South Africa were suddenly 3-112 and Stewart's decision did not look so bad.

Mullally was in the midst of another fine spell. Daryl Cullinan got a couple of shots away then skied an attempted on drive to Fraser at mid off. When Shaun Pollock got a swinging Gough special yorker first ball South Africa were 7-168 with 10 overs still to bat.

Lance Klusener, as he had against Sri Lanka at Northampton, rescued the cause. His ally then was Steve Elworthy. This time it was wicketkeeper, Mark Boucher, demoted from number three to nine in the order. Both batted with common sense through to the end of the innings while adding an unbroken 57. Klusener tried to unleash at Ealham in the 50th over and hit one clout that cleared the boundary at mid-on. He had to be satisfied with 13 off the over which lifted South Africa to 7-225, the type of score their attack looked very capable of defending.

England's apprehension about the task in front of them was fully justified. Kallis with the new-ball was again damaging. He completed Stewart's miserable day with a lifting off-cutter that Umpire Venkataraghaven thought would have hit the stumps. The English captain was out first ball and two overs later Nasser Hussain flicked at a ball down the leg-side. It would have been a wide except Venkat thought Hussain had made contact on the way through to Boucher and gave him out, too.

England were 2-6 and the game of the round was turning into a mismatch. Graham Thorpe unleashed the shot of the innings off Donald, a flashing square drive. The champion paceman's reply was a vicious inswinger that struck Thorpe so plumb in front of middle stump not even the whinging English press could find an excuse. Then five runs later, at about the same time Paul Scholes was finishing off Newcastle, Graeme Hick's well timed pull off Steve Elworthy ended in the hands of Gibbs at mid wicket.

England were 4-44 in the 17th, then 5-45 ten balls later. Donald was on song which meant Andrew Flintoff was out of his depth, well held at gully from a tame push. There was token resistance from that point, the only real reason for continuing attention being the athleticism of the South African fielding. Rhodes made the waiting worthwhile with a leap, parry, twist, dive and hold catch at gully off a Robert Croft drive. A skied drive by Fraser off Pollock finished England on 103 after 41 overs. Klusener won a second consecutive Man of the Match award.

SOUTH AFRICA		ENGLAND	
G. Kirsten c Stewart b Ealham	45	N. Hussain c Boucher b Kallis	2
H. H. Gibbs c Hick b Ealham	60	A. J. Stewart (capt/wk) lbw b Kallis	0
J. H. Kallis b Mullally	0	G. A. Hick c Gibbs b Elworthy	21
D. J. Cullinan c Fraser b Mullally	10	G. P. Thorpe lbw b Donald	14
W. J. Cronje (capt) c Stewart b Flintoff	16	N. H. Fairbrother lbw b Donald	21
J. N. Rhodes c sub (Knight) b Gough	18	A. Flintoff c Rhodes b Donald	0
L. Klusener not out	48	M. A. Ealham c Cullinan b Donald	5
S. M. Pollock b Gough	0	R. D. B. Croft c Rhodes b Klusener	12
M. V. Boucher (wk) not out	16	D. Gough c Cronje b Elworthy	10
Extras lb7 w5	12	A. R. C. Fraser c Kirsten b Pollock	3
(50 overs)	7-225	A. D. Mullally not out	1
Did not bat: S. Elworthy, A. A. Donald		Extras lb4 w9 nb1	14
1/111 2/112 3/112 4/127 5/146 6/168 7/168		(41 overs)	103

Bowling: Gough 10-1-33-2; Fraser 10-0-54-0;
Mullally 10-1-28-2; Croft 2-0-13-0; Ealham 10-2-48-2
Flintoff 8-0-42-1

1/2 2/6 3/39 4/44 5/45 6/60 7/78 8/97 9/99 10/103
Bowling: Kallis 8-0-29-2; Pollock 9-3-13-1; Elworthy
10-3-24-2; Donald 8-1-17-4; Klusener 6-0-16-1

Umpires: S. Dunne S. Venkataraghaven

Toss: England   Points: South Africa 2 England 0

COUNTY GROUND, WORCESTER: SRI LANKA vs ZIMBABWE- GROUP A
SRI LANKA WON BY 4 WICKETS

Sri Lanka were able to get back on the winning list and modestly revitalise their hopes of staying in the 'Carnival of Cricket' with a solid four wicket win over a disappointing Zimbabwe. In a game of few individual highlights the difference in the end was Zimbabwe's greater concession of extras to Sri Lanka than they received in return. It was a very 1999-style result.

Arjuna Rantunga invited Alistair Campbell to bat after he won the toss. A top edged pull shot by Neil Johnson held by Pramodya Wickrmasinghe off Eric Upashantha in the eighth over of the day got the Sri Lankan cause moving and Wickremasinghe further built up the momentum three overs later when Paul Strang played a shortish delivery on to his wicket.

Murray Goodwin and Grant Flower were restoring the balance with a 44 runs stand when the former West Australian misjudged the power and accuracy of Sanath Jayasuriya's arm when calling for a short single. Three more wickets followed quickly so that Zimbabwe were 6-94 in the 26th over when Guy Whittall drove and edged Muttiah Muralitharan to a juggling Ranatunga at slip.

Andy Flower and Stuart Carlisle had to start over again which they did effectively for 14 overs and 68 runs before undoing the good work with another unnecessary run out. Off the next ball Flower perished to the reverse sweep, as did Heath Streak not long after. Chaminda Vaas was again caned during the final over, Eddo Brandes, hitting the left-hander out of the ground at long on as part of the 17 run indulgence.

Sri Lanka had to chase a score similar to the one that proved far too excessive against South Africa. The attack facing them this time, though, was less hostile. An out-of-form Jaysuriya was soon caught cutting to short third man, however Roshan Manhanama and Marvin Atapattu withstood the threat of the new ball and started to benefit from the inaccuracy of Heath Streak and Neil Johnson. They put on 62 before Whittall yorked Mahanama. When Aravinda de Silva and Ranatunga were dismissed Sri Lanka's position at 4-108 was not secure. It got better when Atapattu, who reached his 50 off 83 balls with four fours, and Mehela Jayawardene compiled another 42. Then Streak got them both and it was 6-157.

Rumesh Kaluwitharana's return to the middle order was vital and cheered on by a pro Sri Lankan crowd he and Vaas with a mixture of sharp singles, authentic strokes, slogs and edges were able to guide their side home with four overs and four wickets to spare. Atapattu was named as Man of the Match.

ZIMBABWE		SRI LANKA	
N. C. Johnson c Wickramasinghe b Upashantha	8	S. T. Jayasuriya c Goodwin b Johnson	6
G. W. Flower c Kaluwitharana b Wickramasinghe	42	R. S. Mohanama b G. J. Whittall	31
P. A. Strang b Wickramasinghe	5	M. S. Atapattu c Campbell b Streak	54
M. W. Goodwin run out	21	P. A. de Silva c sub (A. R. Whittall) b G. J. Whittall	6
A. Flower (wk) c Kaluwitharana b Jayasuriya	41	A. Ranatunga (capt) c & b G. J. Whittall	3
A. D. R. Campbell (capt) c Kaluwitharana b Wickramasinghe	6	D. P. M. D. Jayawardene lbw b Streak	31
G. J. Whittall c Ranatunga b Muralitharan	4	R. S. Kaluwitharana (wk) not out	18
S. V. Carlisle run out	27	C. Vaas not out	17
H. H. Streak c Atapattu b Muralitharan	10	Extras lb6 w21 nb5	32
E. A. Brandes not out	19	(46 overs)	6-198
H. K. Olonga not out	5	Did not bat: K. E. A. Upashantha, G. P. Wickramasinghe,	
Extras lb3 w6	9	M. Muralitharan	
(50 overs)	9-197	1/13 2/75 3/93 4/108 5/150 6/157	

1/21 2/34 3/78 4/81 5/89 6/94 7/162 8/162 9/176

Bowling: Vaas 10-1-47-0; Upashantha 10-1-43-1;
Wickramasinghe 10-1-30-3; Jayawardene 1-0-8-0
Muralitharan 10-2-29-2 Jayasuriya 7-0-28-1; de Silva 2-0-9-0

Bowling: Brandes 8-0- 28-0; Johnson 7-1-29-1;
Streak 8-1-30-2; G. J. Whittall 10-1-35-3; Olonga 9-0-50-0 G.
W. Flower 2-0-10-0 Strang 2-0-10-0

Umpires: S. Bucknor D. Shepherd
Toss: Sri Lanka   Points: Sri Lanka 2 Zimbabwe 0

SUNDAY 23 MAY 1999
HEADINGLEY, LEEDS: AUSTRALIA vs PAKISTAN- GROUP B
PAKISTAN WON BY 10 RUNS

The 16th match of the 'Carnival of Cricket' came the closest in atmosphere and actual play to the theme that had been set down for the 1999 World Cup. A wildly fluctuating game of sheer cricketing exhilaration, it built to a fantastic climax, one from which Wasim Akram's side triumphed to the great delight of a capacity crowd most of whom were Pakistani supporters. Not all the green shirts were inside the ground. Those on the steep rooftops surrounding Headingley were showing their unstinting devotion to cricket and their country on such a windy day.

Cool May breezes swept across the ground and there was never much sign of a warm sun, yet once again the cricket was unscathed by weather and allowed to go its full distance. It seemed at this point that the god of cricket fixture scheduling was well pleased by the supplications brought to it by the ECB authorities. May was proving strangely co-operative.

A flat and firm Headingley pitch encouraged Steve Waugh to bowl first when he won the toss. Damien Fleming was soon on target but Saeed Anwar took a liking to the recalled Paul Reiffel. Four exquisite shots and one miscue reached the boundary before a short rising delivery on leg-stump was edged by the left-hander through to Adam Gilchrist.

This signalled a period when the Australian bowlers were on top. Wajahatullah Wasti, much to the relief of the commentators, drove the first ball of Glenn McGrath's second over to Steve Waugh in the gully and Ijaz Ahmed almost walked before umpire Peter Willey could give him out lbw to an off-cutter from Fleming. Pakistan were in trouble at 3-46 in the 13th over.

Inzamam-ul-Haq announced his arrival with a clip through square leg and a cut off Fleming, which roused the recently subdued crowd back to their usual level of unrestrained excitement. This, though, was a time for consolidation and Abdur Razzaq knuckled down with his hefty partner. Shane Warne was introduced in the 24th over to a chorus of catcalls and boos.

The greatest threat to breaking the partnership was Inzamam's lumbersome running and selfish calling. Only the fact that Fleming's throw ricocheted from the stumps saved Inzamam when both batsmen were caught at the same end. Inzamam voiced his opinion of his partner's calling.

It was as if this galavnised both into action. The run rate had cruised along under four per over. When Steve Waugh was obliged to bowl himself, Damien Martyn and Darren Lehmann the batsmen went into assault mode. Razzaq, who had reached his 50 off 92 balls, launched the accleration with a flatly driven six off Warne over long off. He fell to the same shot off the same bowler ending an invaluable 118 run stand in 27 overs.

Then the fun began. The punishment of the Australian bowlers was brutal. McGrath was brought back for the 45th over and Inzamam greeted him with a mighty hooked six that landed on the roof of the old players pavilion. Youhana smashed Martyn over midwicket for a six and scored at two runs per ball before finding his quick single call totally ignored by Inzamam. There was humour when Inzamam collapsed mid pitch to tend a bruised foot while his captain, Wasim Akram scampered a single. The big man after making 81 in 104 balls had to limp away, but he was safe in the knowledge that his side were on target for a 250 plus total.

Moin Khan completed the wonderful display with three great sixes and two fours in 12 balls. When the Australians, cursing and swearing more frequently everytime the ball sailed away into the crowd, could finally retreat into the dressing room they had conceded 108 runs from their final ten overs and needed 276 to win.

Australia started disastrously. Gilchrist played crookedly and late at Akram's third ball and was clean bowled. Shoaib was quick without quite living up to his new reputation and Mark Waugh and Ricky Ponting, after the latter had been badly dropped at slip by Inzamam, were able to keep Australian fans, watching on television through Sunday night into Monday morning, interested with a 91-run partnership in 16 overs. Then it seemed the challenge had been routed. Mark Waugh dabbing outside the off stump was brilliantly held by a diving Moin and Ponting and Darren Lehmann were caught off Saqlain three balls apart, both going for the sweep. Australia were 4-101 in the 20th over and their tournament was at the crossroads.

As he had done in the West Indies, Steve Waugh led the revival of his team, himself. He settled in with Michael Bevan and in 22 overs the New South Welshmen added 113 precious runs. They were positive throughout and played their shots with freedom on a wicket that encouraged them. Bevan swiped Saqlain for six over midwicket and brought up his 50 in 66 balls.

Akram returned and Bevan was caught off a leading edge. Steve Waugh retaliated by cracking Saqlain for six, but when Shoaib seared a yorker under his driving bat the assignment was getting difficult. Light was fading and there were five overs left with 38 required. Warne and Reiffel fell during the hectic chase. Then with 10 needed off four balls Akram bowled Martyn. This prompted another invasion from spectators who cannot count to 10. Stumps, time and light were lost by the time the ground was cleared. Australian number 11, McGrath had no chance and a swinging yorker from Akram sealed the result and started another invasion.

Steve Waugh felt his side had fought the good fight this time. He denied reports of a rift between himself and his vice-captain, Warne. Rumours started that Pakistan had tampered with the ball. Inzamam was named Man of the Match.

PAKISTAN		AUSTRALIA	
Wajahatullah Wasti c SWaugh b McGrath	9	A. C. Gilchrist (wk) b Wasim Akram	0
Saeed Anwar c Gilchrist b Reiffel	25	M. E. Waugh c Moin Khan b Abdul Razzaq	41
Abdul Razzaq c Fleming b Warne	60	R. T. Ponting c Saeed Anwar b Saqlain Mushtaq	47
Ijaz Ahmed lbw b Fleming	0	D. S. Lehmann c Moin Khan b Saqlain Mushtaq	5
Inzamam-ul-Haq run out	81	S. R. Waugh (capt) b Shoaib Akhtar	49
Yousuf Youhana run out	29	M. G. Bevan c Ijaz Ahmed b Wasim Akram	61
Wasim Akram (capt) c Glichrist b Fleming	13	D. R. Martyn b Wasim Akram	18
Moin Khan (wk) not out	31	S. K. Warne run out	1
Azhar Mahmood run out	1	P. R. Reiffel c Wasim Akram b Saqlain Mushtaq	1
Saqlain Mushtaq not out	0	D. W. Fleming not out	4
Extras b1 lb5 w15 nb5	26	Extras b7 lb10 w14 nb7	38
(50 overs)	8-275	(49.5 overs)	265

Did not bat: Shoaib Akhtar

1/32 2/44 3/46 4/164 5/216 6/230 7/262 8/265

Bowling: Fleming 10-3-37-2; Reiffel 10-1-49-1; McGrath 10-1-54-1; Warne 10-0-50-1; S. R. Waugh 6-0-37-0; Martyn 2-0-25-0; Lehmann 2-0-17-0

1/0 2/91 3/100 4/101 5/214 6/238 7/248 8/251 9/265 10/265

Bowling: Wasim Akram 9.5-1-40-4; Shoaib Akhtar 10-0-46-1; Azhar Mahmood 10-0-61-0; Saqlain Mushtaq 10-1-51-3; Abdul Razzaq 10-0-50-1

Umpires: R. Koertzen P. Willey

Toss: Australia   Points: Pakistan 2 Australia 0

COUNTY GROUND, BRISTOL: INDIA vs KENYA-GROUP A
INDIA WON BY 94 RUNS

If Australia and Pakistan fought out the great contest on this Sunday, then it was Sachin Tendulkar way out west in Bristol, who offered the dazzling exhibition. Batting with a the emotional weight of his father's death, Tendulkar played the innings of the tournament to date, an 101-ball extravaganza that thrilled all who witnessed it, but especially the 8,000 Indians who filled the ground in Nevil Road. He came in at number four to help him recover from his jet lag. On reaching his 50 and then his 100, Tendulkar gazed at the sky and mouthed words of dedication.

This was also a day for the statisticians as Tendulkar's third-wicket partnership with Rahul Dravid realised a World Cup record-breaking 237 runs in 29 overs. Dravid could only have been overshadowed by one man this day, and his 104 not out in 109 balls was also a treat. The pair had come together in the 21st over of the Indian innings after Aasif Karim had won the toss and sent India in. Saurav Ganguly was lbw in the 11th over to Martin Suji and Sandagoppan Ramesh missed out on a big score when he backed up too far with the total on 92. Tendulkar and Dravid concentrated on singles and twos at first, then accelerated against a pedestrian attack. The two went neck and neck until well past their 50s, then Tendulkar surged ahead with lofted drives that peppered the boundary. An off-drive off Steve Tikolo brought up Tendulkar's 100, the first of the competition, in 84 balls.

He then toyed with the Kenyan attack, dabbing, reverse sweeping and occasionally thumping the same attack that had been mauled by the Waugh twins in 1996 for the previous record. Dravid, who had gained little strike, raised his century in the last over, then Tendulkar signed off the innings with a drive over mid wicket for his third six. India's 2-329 was their highest score ever in the World Cup. Kenya's bowlers in three matches had taken 8-764.

Kenya could hardly follow an act like that. Once again, though, their batsmen did themselves credit. After a slow start when two wickets were lost by the 12th over Kennedy Otieno and Steve Tikolo put on 118 for the third wicket. Both had shown they were not outclassed at this level and while some pressure was off they emphasised the point again. Tikolo thumped Debashish Mohanty for a pulled six and followed with a flick for four more.

Once that pair had been removed only big hitting Tom Odoyo adding a couple more sixes to his catalogue scored with any proficiency. Kenya were left 94 runs short when the overs ran out. Tendulkar was a clear cut choice for Man of the Match. He said afterwards, "I did it for my father and my country. This was a difficult, but special occasion."

INDIA		KENYA	
S. Ramesh run out	44	K. O. Otieno (wk) c Agarkar b Chopra	56
S. C. Ganguly lbw b M. Suji	13	Ravindu Shah c sub(Singh) b Mohanty	9
R. Dravid not out	104	S. K. Gupta lbw b Mohanty	0
S. R. Tendulkar not out	140	S. O. Tikolo lbw b Mohanty	58
Extras lb5 w21 nb2	28	M. O. Odumbe c sub (Singh) b Mohanty	14
(50 overs)	2-329	T. M. Odoyo b Agarkar	39
Did not bat: M. Azharuddin (capt), A. Jadeja,		Aasif Karim (capt) b Srinath	8
N. R. Mongia (wk), N. Chopra, A. B. Agarkar, J. Srinath,		A. Vadher not out	6
D. S. Mohanty		M. Suji not out	1
1/50 2/92		Extras lb10 w31 nb3	44
Bowling: M. Suji 10-2-26-1; Angara 7-0-66-0;		(50 overs)	7-235
Odoyo 9-0-59-0; Tikolo 9-1-62-0; Aasif Karim 7-0-52-0		Did not bat: H. S. Modi, J. O. Angara	
Odumbe 8-0-59-0		1/29 2/29 3/147 4/165 5/193 6/209 7/233	
		Bowling: Srinath 10-3-31-1; Agarkar 10-0-35-1; Mohanty	
		10-0-56-4; Ganguly 9-0-47-0; Chopra 10-2-33-1	
		Tendulkar 1-0-23-0	

Umpires: D. Cowie I. Robinson

Toss: Kenya   Points: India 2 Kenya 0

MONDAY 24 MAY 1999
COUNTY GROUND,SOUTHAMPTON:WEST INDIES vs NEW ZEALAND-GROUP B
WEST INDIES WON BY 7 SEVEN WICKETS

The West Indian win over New Zealand in a lacklustre affair at Southampton threw the last two promotion spots in Group B wide open. New Zealand's first setback exposed the limitations of their top order batting.

Once Nathan Astle became the first of Ridley Jacobs five victims behind the stumps in Curtley Ambrose's opening over, the Kiwi batsmen were always deep in trouble. The experienced pacemen were a difficult proposition with the new-ball. Courtney Walsh had Matthew Horne miscuing a pull to mid-on in the fifth over. When Reon King came on as first change he continued Stephen Fleming's run of outs and had Thursday's hero, Roger Twose, edging to first slip on nought. The Kiwis were 4-31 in the 17th over.

Craig McMillan and Chris Cairns batted out of character as they tried to build a competitive total. Their success was limited. Ambrose had sent down 10 superb overs in one spell and the run rate limped along at just above two per over when McMillan, having received a clunk on the head, edged Phil Simmons behind. It was no better at 6-75 as Cairns hit a catch off the leading edge.

Chris Harris and Adam Parore offered resistance for ten overs, but it summed up New Zealand's day when the wicketkeeper was caught behind down the leg-side off Mervyn Dillon. Big Merv picked up two more wickets as the Kiwi innings stuttered along until the first ball of the 49th over when Harris holed out in the deep.

The West Indies needed just 157 to win and they took nearly 45 overs to get them. Jacobs batted throughout the innings, maintaining his excellent form since coming into the West Indian team in South Africa. He lost a becalmed Sherwin Campbell to a Dion Nash off-cutter and Jimmy Adams to a fine delivery from Geoff Allott.

Lara came in at 2-49 and, in the spirit of the game, was more restrained than usual. He did, however, strike the sweetest shot of the day when a straight drive off Gavin Larsen carried for six. With Jacobs, Lara took his side to within 36 runs of victory.

This was a very important result for the West Indies and they were well pleased to obtain such an emphatic win. Some cynics suggested that as their loss jeopardised Australia's chances, the New Zealanders weren't too disappointed. Jacobs who batted for 131 balls and hit eight fours and a six while making an unbeaten 80 was named Man of the Match.

NEW ZEALAND		WEST INDIES	
M. J. Horne c Lara b Walsh	2	S. L. Campbell lbw b Nash	8
N. J Astle c Jacobs b Ambrose	2	R. D. Jacobs (wk) not out	80
C. D. McMillan c Jacobs b Simmons	32	J. C. Adams c Parore b Allott	3
S. P. Fleming (capt) c Jacobs b King	0	B. C. Lara (capt) c Nash b Harris	36
R. G. Twose c Williams b King	0	S. C. Williams not out	14
C. L. Cairns c Lara b Dillon	23	Extras lb4 w5 nb8	17
A. C. Parore (wk) c Jacobs b Dillon	23	(44.2 overs)	3-158
C. Z. Harris c Campbell b Dillon	30	Did not bat: S. Chanderpaul, P. V. Simmons,	
D. J. Nash c Williams b Dillon	1	C. E. L. Ambrose, M. Dillon, R. D. King, C. A. Walsh	
G. R. Larsen c Jacobs b Simmons	14	1/29 2/49 3/121	
G. I. Allott not out	0	Bowling: Allott 10-2-39-1; Nash 10-2-25-1; Cairns	
Extras lb6 w17 nb6	29	9.2-1-42-0; Larsen 7-1-29-0; Harris 8-2-19-1	
(48.1 overs)	156		

1/2 2/13 3/22 4/31 5/59 6/75 7/125 8/130 9/155 10/156

Bowling: Walsh 10-1-23-1; Ambrose 10-0-19-1; King
10-1-29-2; Simmons 9-2-33-2; Dillon 9.1-0-46-4

Umpires: Javed Akhtar S. Venkataraghaven

Toss: West Indies   Points: West Indies 2 New Zealand 0

RAEBURN PLACE, EDINBURGH:
SCOTLAND vs BANGLADESH - GROUP B
BANGLADESH WON BY 22 RUNS

This almost novelty encounter was never going to turn the tide of the 1999 World Cup, but it was a splendid cricket match. The innings of both teams followed a pattern of top order collapse followed by recovery. Bangladesh collapsed a little more spectacularly, however they also fought back better, a sign that they just had the edge in depth of talent.

The eventual 22-run defeat was a bitter disappointment to George Salmond's Scottish team. This was their best chance for a win, especially as all went well for Scotland during the first dozen overs after Salmond won the toss and inserted the Bangladeshis.

The wind was wicked, the pitch bumpy and John Blain and Asim Butt, while still sending down their share of wides, were a handful for the batsmen with the new ball. When Faruk Ahmed played on to give Blain his fourth wicket, Bangladesh were 5-26.

The first stage of the Bangladeshi fightback was led Naimur Rahman ably assisted by Minhajul Abedin. They put on 69 in 19 overs. It still looked insufficient when Rahman was caught at mid-on off James Brinkley and Khaled Mahmud was caught low at mid wicket off spinner Nick Dyer. That left Bangladesh in the seemingly hopeless position of 7-96 at the end of the 31st over. Fortunately Abedin was still at the crease and well settled. He batted through the innings with Enamul Hoque, Hasibul Hussain and Manjural Islam, almost doubling the total in the last 19 overs. Without resorting to fireworks Abedin reached his invaluable 50 in the 46th over, then hit two boundaries off Brinkley to crown his innings in the 48th.

Scotland now had their work cut out. They had conceded 39 wides and no-balls and had been penalised an over for their late finish. Nor was 185 a straightforward target on a wicket still favouring the bowlers. Two lbw decisions and a caught behind accounted for Scotland's first three batsmen by the middle of the sixth over with only eight runs on board. An excellent catch at backward point by Faruk Ahmed sent Salmond on his way and when Ian Stanger became the third lbw victim the home side were 5-49 and fading fast. Gavin Hamilton was the remaining hope and he responded brilliantly. He hit hard and well and raced to his 50 in 62 balls. Hamilton celebrated that milestone by sweeping Rahman for the only six of the match, but his dismissal soon after was a tragedy for Scotland. A straight drive by Alec Davies was deflected by the bowler Manjural onto the stumps with Hamilton out of his ground backing up. Even though Davies kept up the fight Scotland were battling from the moment of Hamilton's dismissal. Abedin was named Man of the Match.

BANGLADESH		SCOTLAND	
Khaled Mashud (wk) c Phillip b Blain	0	B. M. W. Patterson lbw b Hassibul Hussain	0
Mehrab Hossain c Dyer b Asim Butt	3	I. L. Philip lbw b Manjural Islam	3
Faruk Ahmed b Blain	7	M. W. Smith c Khaled Mashud b Hasibul Hussain	1
Aminul Islam (capt) lbw b Blain	0	I. M. Stanger lbw b Minhajul Abedin	10
Akram Khan c Philip b Asim Butt	0	G. Salmond (capt) c Faruk Ahmed b Manjural Islam	19
Minhajul Abedin not out	68	G. M. Hamilton run out	63
Naimur Rahman c Stanger b Brinkley	36	J. E. Brinkley c Hasibul Hussain b Khaled Mahmud	5
Khaled Mahmud c Salmond b Dyer	0	A. G. Davies (wk) c Manjural Islam b Khaled Mahmed	32
Enamul Hoque c Philip b Dyer	19	J. A. R. Blain run out	9
Hasibul Hussain c & b Blain	6	Asim Butt c Aminul Islam b Enamul Hoque	1
Manjural Islam not out	2	N. R. Dyer not out	0
Extras lb5 w28 nb11	44	Extras lb1 w13 nb6	20
(50 overs)	9-185	(46.2 overs)	163

1/6 2/12 3/13 4/24 5/26 6/95 7/96 8/133 9/164

1/0 2/8 3/8 4/37 5/49 6/83 7/138 8/158 9/163 10/163

Bowling: Blain 10-1-37-4; Asim Butt 9-1-24-2;
Hamilton 10-3-25-0; Brinkley 10-0-45-1; Stanger 4-0-23-0
Dyer 7-1-26-2

Bowling: Hasibul Hussain 8-1-26-2; Manjural Islam 9-2-27-2;
Khaled Mahmud 9-2-27-2; Minhajul Abedin 3-0-12-1
Naimur Rahman 10-0-41-0 Enamul Hoque 7.2-0-23-1

Umpires: K. Francis D. Orchard

Toss: Scotland   Points: Bangladesh 2 Scotland 0

TUESDAY 25 MAY 1999
TRENT BRIDGE, NOTTINGHAM: ENGLAND vs ZIMBABWE - GROUP A
ENGLAND WON BY 7 WICKETS

Zimbabwe sent in to bat on a cloudy, swing-inducing Nottingham morning were unable to set England a worthwhile total. Their defeat was never in doubt in a match described by *Daily Telegraph* correspondent, Michael Henderson, as 'wretched stuff'.

The winning of the toss by Alec Stewart was crucial, the cloud having swept in after a sunny morning in Nottingham. There was no sudden Zimbabwean collapse, just a gradual demise and no sign that the innings would go up a gear. All the English bowlers were difficult to attack. Angus Fraser swung the ball in and Alan Mullally got it to go both ways. Darren Gough took the first wicket then Mullally removed pinch hitter Paul Strang before he hit anything at all. He also had Murray Goodwin caught low at slip to make the score 3-47 in the 18th over.

Grant Flower, Alistair Campbell and Guy Whittall fought hard without being able to play their strokes with any freedom. Extras accumulated as effectively as did runs off the bat. Mullally bouncing and moving the ball off a good length was untouchable. Only Andrew Flintoff and Adam Hollioake conceded runs at anything like the regular rate. Zimbabwe had two wickets in hand at the end of 50 overs, however with the sun back they did not have nearly enough runs.

There was just a sniff of a turnaround when Stewart clipped a catch off Neil Johnson to Murray Goodwin at mid wicket in the ninth over and three overs later Graeme Hick wafted outside his off stump at Pommie Mbangwa. That made England 2-36 which was hardly better than Zimbabwe had been at the same time. There was nothing in the Zimbabwean attack to really trouble Nasser Hussain nor Graham Thorpe and once they got going the result was never in doubt.

For a time the pair, who have shared some important partnerships in Test cricket, traded boundary for boundary. Then the left-handed Thorpe scooted away as he brought up his 50 in 59 balls. Finally, after a stand of 123 in 22 overs, Thorpe was caught at slip slashing at Mbangwa. England required just nine from there and Hussain and Neil Fairbrother took five overs to get them. Perhaps they were trying to preserve their averages, or maybe they wanted to sedate the crowd for the end of the match. If it was the latter they failed, for when Hussain drove Strang to extra cover the hordes came charging on yet again. Mullally, championing the bowler's cause, won the Man of the Match Award ahead of Hussain and Thorpe.

ZIMBABWE		ENGLAND	
N. C. Johnson b Gough	6	N. Hussain not out	57
G. W. Flower c Thorpe b Ealham	35	A. J. Stewart (wk/capt) c Goodwin b Johnson	12
P. A. Strang c Hick b Mullally	0	G. A. Hick c A. Flower b Mbangwa	4
M. W. Goodwin c Thorpe b Mullally	4	G. P. Thorpe c Campbell b Mbangwa	62
A. Flower (wk) run out	10	N. H. Fairbrother not out	7
A. D. R. Campbell (capt) c Stewart b Fraser	24	Extras lb3 w16 nb7	26
G. J. Whittall lbw b Ealham	28	(38.3 overs)	3-168
S. V. Carlisle c Fraser b Gough	14	Did not bat: A. Flintoff, A. J. Hollioake, M. A. Ealham,
H. H. Streak not out	11	D. Gough, A. R. C. Fraser, A. D. Mullally
H. K. Olonga not out	1	1/21 2/36 3/159
Extras lb16 w17 nb1	34	Bowling: Johnson 7-2-20-1; Streak 8-0-37-0;
(50 overs)	8-167	Mbangwa 7-1-28-2; G. J. Whittall 4-0-23-0; Olonga 3-0-27-0
Did not bat: M. Mbangwa		Strang 9.3-1-30-0

1/21 2/29 3/47 4/79 5/86 6/124 7/141 8/159

Bowling: Gough 10-2-24-2; Fraser 10-0-27-1; Mullally 10-4-16-2; Ealham 10-1-35-2; Flintoff 3-0-14-0 Hollioake 7-0-35-0

Umpires: S. Bucknor D. Hair

Toss: England   Points: England 2 Zimbabwe 0

WEDNESDAY 26 MAY 1999
COUNTY GROUND, TAUNTON: INDIA vs SRI LANKA- GROUP A
INDIA WON BY 157 RUNS

It was as if the batting of Sachin Tendulkar and Rahul Dravid against Kenya had been the warm up. At Taunton the Indian batsmen turned it on again as Saurav Ganguly and Dravid broke all sorts of records and ended Sri Lanka's tournament.

Sunday had been an emotional event as millions admired and felt for the grieving Tendulkar. This 318-run partnership between Ganguly and Dravid was a celebration of pure classical batsmanship. Without mentioning a shot the list of records achieved by the pair are exciting enough; India's highest score in a one-day game, the second highest innings total in a one-day game, Ganguly's 183 was the highest score ever by an Indian in a one-day game, the second highest ever in the World Cup and the fourth highest by any country. Their second wicket partnership was the best for any wicket in a one-day game.

Chaminda Vaas bowled Sadagopan Ramesh in the day's opening over with a superb delivery. The left-arm paceman tasted no more success, nor did his teammates for 45 overs. On a beautiful batting wicket the right and left-handed combination played scarcely a stroke that was not straight out of the textbook until a position of strength had been established. The bowling of the Sri Lankan seamers was wayward and allowed Dravid the opportunity to unleash a series of gorgeous front foot drives.

After 25 overs, the two batsmen became a little more expansive in their shot selection. Dravid had gone to his 50 in 43 balls with 10 fours, Ganguly took 68 balls and hit six fours. Later, footwork and grace counted for little as the pair became dissatisfied with fours and looked to strike sixes instead. Ganguly came into his own in the second half of the stand. His 100 was reached in 119 balls, a slightly slower rate than Dravid who took just 102 balls. Dravid's effort of scoring consecutive World Cup centuries has only been equalled by Mark Waugh in 1996. Those landmarks opened the way for even faster run scoring as 128 were added in the final ten overs. Ganguly's beautiful glance brought up the 200 in the 35th over then Dravid struck an inside out six over cover off Muralitharan.

In the 45th over Ganguly smashed three fours off Upashantha to raise the 300 partnership then bettered it next ball with a dancing straight six to reach 150. Finally, in the next over, Dravid failed to beat Muralitharan's throw from long off. .

Sri Lanka were never in the hunt. From the first ball of the third over Sanath Jayasuriya pushed to the on-side and called for a quick single.

Ganguly won the toss from Dravid and was named Man of the Match.

INDIA		SRI LANKA	
S. Ramesh b Vaas	5	S. T. Jayasuriya run out	3
S. C. Ganguly c sub b Wickramasinghe	183	R. S. Kaluwitharana lbw b Srinath	7
R. Dravid run out	145	M. S. Atapattu lbw b Mohanty	29
S. R. Tendulkar b Jayasuriya	2	A. de Silva lbw b Singh	56
A. Jadeja c & b Wickramasinghe	5	D. P. M. D. Jayawardene lbw b Kumble	4
R. R. Singh c de Silva b Wickramasinghe	0	A. Ranatunga b Singh	42
M. Azharuddin(capt) not out	11	R. S. Mahanama run out	32
J. Srinath not out	1	W. P. U. J. C. Vaas c Ramesh b Singh	1
Extras lb3 w12 nb6	21	E. Upashantha c Azharuddin b Singh	5
(50 overs)	6-373	P. Wickramasinghe not out	2
Did not bat: A. Kumble, D. Mohanty, B. K. V. Prasad		M. Muralitharan c Tendulkar b Singh	4
1/6 2/324 3/344 4/349 5/349 6/372		Extras b4 lb12 w8 nb7	31
Vaas 10-0-84-1; Upashantha 10-0-80-0; Wickramasinghe		(42.3 overs)	216
10-0-65-3; Muralitharan 10-0-60-0; Jayawardene 3-0-21-0;		1/5 2/23 3/74 4/79 5/147 6/181 7/187 8/203 9/204 10/216	
Jayasuriya 3-0-37-1; de Silva 4-0-23-0		Bowling: Srinath 7-0-33-1; Prasad 8-0-41-0;	
		Mohanty 5-0-31-1; Kumble 8-0-27-1; Ganguly 5-0-37-0;	
		Singh 9.3-0-31-5	

Umpires: D. Shepherd S. Dunne

Toss: Sri Lanka   Points: India 2 Sri Lanka 0

VRA GROUND, AMSTELVEEN: KENYA vs SOUTH AFRICA- GROUP A
SOUTH AFRICA WON BY 7 WICKETS

World Cup cricket went below sea level for the first time in an exercise that could be considered a success. The Dutch weather was an improvement on what had been available in the Britain. The cricket unfortunately after the first hour was predictable.

South Africa outclassed the Kenyans without ever appearing to be at their absolute best. Only a few sixes at the end by Daryl Cullinan lifted the adrenalin level of the spectators. It hinted at being more than that when Kennedy Otieno and Ravindu Shah were opening the game with some choice shots off Shaun Pollock and in particular Jacques Kallis. They rattled up 66 in 15 overs. Shah looked in great form cracking Kallis through the covers and punishing Allan Donald in the 17th over.

Already, by then Steve Elworthy had broken the opening stand and with Donald quickly exacting revenge on Shah, the innings quickly began to totter. The runs dried up and Lance Klusener stepped in to make a mess of the middle and lower order. When he bowled Joe Angara, Kenya had lost 10-86 and had been dismissed with five and a half overs to spare.

Herschelle Gibbs and Gary Kirsten got the South African reply away to a bright start. Gibbs lifted Aasif Karim over long on for six and 55 runs were up by the end of the 11th over when Tom Odoyo had Gibbs lbw playing across the line. As it did against England, the dismissal of Gibbs slowed the South African rate of progress. Mark Boucher, back at number three, made no impression and Gary Kirsten fell foul of his own impatience. There was still no real pressure. Kallis and Cullinan took their time easing the Proteas to their fourth win, putting on 67 in 18 overs, with a mixture of the sedate and the belligerent. Klusener was able to add to his rapidly growing Man of the Match collection.

KENYA		SOUTH AFRICA	
K. O. Otieno (wk) lbw b Elworthy	26	G. Kirsten b Odumbe	27
Ravindu Shah c Boucher b Donald	50	H. H. Gibbs lbw b Odoyo	38
S. K. Gupta b Elworthy	1	M. V. Boucher (wk) c Mohammad Sheikh b Angara	3
S. O. Tikolo c Cronje b Klusner	10	J. H. Kallis not out	44
M. O. Odumbe b Donald	7	D. J. Cullinan not out	35
A. Vadher c & b Klusener	2	Extras b4 w1 nb1	6
T. M. Odoyo lbw b Klusener	0	(41 overs)	3-153
Aasif Karim (capt) lbw b Cronje	22	Did not bat: J. N. Rhodes, L. Klusener, S. M. Pollock,	
Mohammad Sheikh b Klusener	8	W. J. Cronje (capt), S. Elworthy, A. A. Donald	
M. A. Suji not out	6	1/55 2/58 3/86	
J. O. Angara b Klusener	6	Bowling: Suji 6-0-18-0; Aasif Karim 7-0-43-0;	
Extras lb5 w7 nb2	14	Angara 8-1-34-1; Odoyo 9-3-18-1; Mohammad	
(44.3 overs)	152	Sheikh 4-0-21-0 Odumbe 7-1-15-1	

1/66 2/80 3/82 4/91 5/104 6/104 7/107 8/138 9/140 10/152

Bowling: Pollock 8-1-22-0; Kallis 8-0-37-0; Donald 8-1-42-2; Elworthy 10-2-20-2; Klusener 8.3-3-21-5 Cronje 2-0-5-1

Umpires: D. Cowie P. Willey

Toss: South Africa   Points: South Africa 2 Kenya 0

THURSDAY 27 MAY 1999
RIVERSIDE GROUND, CHESTER-LE-STREET: AUSTRALIA vs BANGLADESH-GROUP B
AUSTRALIA WON BY 7 WICKETS

On a day when it was easy to believe the sun always shone in Durham, it was also easy to believe Australia were still a powerful force in this World Cup tournament. The impeccable weather at Chester-le-Street encouraged an impressive batting display by the Australians. Providing they defeated the West Indies, it would keep them in contention for promotion to the Super Six mini-tournament. Chasing a modest total of 178, they rattled along at nine per over allowing all the Bangladeshis in attendance the opportunity to beat the rush hour traffic on the A1 motorway back to East London.

When Australia were in the field after Steve Waugh sent Bangladesh in they had one ear on relayed scores from Leicester where the West Indies were decimating Scotland. There was no sign of the Australian bowlers doing anything like the same job on Animul Islam's team. The Bangladeshis never got away on the Australians. Nor did they seem likely to be bowled out in 50 overs.

For 21 overs Mehrab Hossain, looked a batsman well within his class, striking seven fine boundaries before slicing Tom Moody to backward point. That shot gave Ricky Ponting his third catch in the same position out of four dismissls, the best of the three was a forward diving effort that got rid of Faruk Ahmed. He also held Naimur Rahman there off Tom Moody. The captain of West Australia and Worcester had been brought in as an extra seamer after the fifth bowler debacle at Leeds. He came on as first change after Glenn McGrath had picked up two wickets. His splendid spell suggested the change should have been made long before.

When Shane Warne had an lbw shout upheld against Akram Khan, Bangladesh were 6-99 and there was the possibility of complete collapse. The Australian bowling, though, was tidy rather than penetrative. Minhajul Abedin, the hero of Edinburgh, was once more able to hold the second half of the order together and he went on to complete an accomplished half century with six boundaries.

Australia returned to the dressing room needing 179 to win in the knowledge that the West Indies had already completed their day's work. Steve Waugh asked for a special effort from his batsmen setting them a target of winning in 30 overs. They got there in 20.

Adam Gilchrist turned around his earlier poor form. After taking a couple of overs to settle in he clouted the ball through and over the field on both sides of the wicket. One straight drive tested the speed of umpire, Steve Bucknor's reactions. His evasive skills were just good enough to maintain his manhood. The wicketkeeper batsman raced to his half century in 34 balls and when he was stumped dancing down at Minhajul he had hit 12 fours and lifted Australia to 98 in the 12th over. Mark Waugh, who had supported Gilchrist so well must have liked what he saw for the very next over he too danced out of his crease and was stumped.

Brendan Julian, promoted to boost the scoring further, hit two boundaries before becoming the second wicket for left-arm spiner Enamul Hoque. Tom Moody had been lifted up the order, too. His pinch hitting lasted 29 balls. That was enough for him to make the fastest 50 ever in the World Cup. Moody hit six fours and two sixes to win the match for his country from the second last ball of the 20th over. The winning hit was his second six, a massive blow that cleared mid wicket. Moody's efforts easily won him the Man of the Match Award. Like Ganguly the day before, Moody's record meant that another of Kapil Dev's feats at Tunbridge Wells in 1983 had been put in to second place.

BANGLADESH		AUSTRALIA	
Khaled Mahmud lbw b McGrath	6	M. E. Waugh st Khaled Mashud b Enamul Hoque	33
Mehrab Hossain c Ponting b Moody	42	A. C. Gilchrist (wk) st Khaled Mashud b Minhajul Abedin	63
Faruk Ahmed c Ponting b McGrath	9	B. J. Julian b Enamul Hoque	9
Naimur Rahman c Ponting b Moody	2	T. M. Moody not out	56
Aminul Islam (capt) b Fleming	13	R. T. Ponting not out	18
Minhajul Abedin not out	53	Extras w2	2
Akram Khan lbw b Warne	0	(19.5 overs)	3-181
Khaled Mashud (wk) lbw b Moody	17	Did not bat: M. G. Bevan, D. S. Lehmann, S. R. Waugh (capt),	
Enamul Hoque not out	17	S. K. Warne, D. W. Fleming, G. D. McGrath	
Extras b2 w10 nb7	19	1/98 2/98 3/111	
(50 overs)	7-178	Bowling: Hasibul Hussain 4-0-24-0; Manjural Islam 3-0-23-0;	
Did not bat: Hasibul Hussain, Manjural Islam		Khaled Mahmud 2.5-0-39-0; Naimur Rahman 2-0-17-0	
1/10 2/39 3/47 4/72 5/91 6/99 7/143		Enamul Hoque 5-0-40-2 Minhajul Abedin 3-0-38-1	
Bowling: McGrath 10-0-44-2; Fleming 10-0-45-1; Moody			
10-4-25-3; Julian 10-1-44-0; Warne 10-2-18-1			

Umpires: S.Bucknor D.Orchard

Toss: Australia   Points: Australia 2 Bangladesh 0

GRACE ROAD, LEICESTER: SCOTLAND vs WEST INDIES- GROUP B
WEST INDIES WON BY 8 WICKETS

This match did not take very long. The whole affair was completed in less than 42 overs. The weather was fine at Grace Road and the crowd keen, but the wicket was lively and the Scottish batsmen were no match for the West Indian bowlers.

It surprised many that George Salmond batted when he won the toss. He placed himself at number four and by the 15th over was already trying to retrieve a dicy situation with his side on 2-18. Ridley Jacobs had taken a catch each off Curtly Ambrose and Phil Simmons. Ambrose was almost unplayable and Salmond lasted just four balls before becoming the giant Antiguan's second victim. He was also caught behind. Jacobs had four catches and Scotland were a disastrous 4-20.

Worse was to follow. Courtney Walsh came on first change and with his impeccable accuracy and variations was also far too good for the Scottish batsmen. James Brinkley was caught at second slip and two balls later when Alec Davies was given out lbw Scotland were 7-29. The ignominy of finishing with a total lower than Canada's 45 in 1979 was a real possibility. Fortunately Gavin Hamilton was a better player than anyone in that Canadian line-up and by cracking Henderson Bryan for a couple of boundaries he eased that threat.

Asim Butt hit an out-of-context six, but Reon King had almost immediate revenge and when Nick Dyer lamely pushed his second ball to second slip, Hamilton had been left stranded and Scotland were all out for 68.

It took the West Indies just 61 deliveries to get the runs. John Blain struck a couple of retaliatory blows, having Simmons caught at mid-on and trapping Stuart Williams lbw first ball. Shivnarine Chanderpaul was in an aggressive mood and struck the ball cleanly. Brian Lara, attracted to the prospect of a whole afternoon off, began flaying the Scottish bowlers upon his arrival at the crease. He targetted Hamilton taking 17 off his one over. He lifted the all-rounder for six over mid wicket with perhaps the highest hit of the tournament. The tartans in the crowd had to find some other entertainment for the afternoon. Walsh was named Man of the Match.

SCOTLAND		WEST INDIES	
M. W. Smith c Jacobs b Simmons	1	P. V. Simmons c Stanger b Blain	7
M. Allingham c Jacobs b Ambrose	6	S. Chanderpaul not out	30
I. M. Stanger c Jacobs b Walsh	7	S. C. Williams lbw b Blain	0
G. Salmond (capt) c Jacobs b Ambrose	1	B. C. Lara (capt) not out	25
G. M. Hamilton not out	24	Extras lb2 w4 nb2	8
J. G. Williamson c Williams b Bryan	1	(10.1 overs)	2-70
J. E. Brinkley c Simmons b Walsh	2	Did not bat: J. C. Adams, R. D. Jacobs (wk), S. Campbell,	
A. G. Davies (wk) lbw b Walsh	0	R. D. King, C. A. Ambrose, H. R. Bryan, C. A. Walsh	
J. A. R. Blain lbw b Bryan	3	1/21 2/22	
Asim Butt c Williams b King	11	Bowling: Blain 5.1-0-36-2; Asim Butt 4-1-15-0;	
N. R. Dyer c Williams b King	0	Hamilton 1-0-17-0	
Extras w9 nb3	12		
(31.3 over is)	68		
1/6 2/18 3/20 4/20 5/25 6/29 7/29 8/47 9/68 10/68			
Bowling: Ambrose 10-4-8-2; Simmons 7-1-15-1;			
Walsh 7-1-7-3; Bryan 6-0-29-2; King 1.3-0-9-2			

Umpires: Javed Akhtar I. Robinson

Toss: Scotland   Points: West Indies 2 Scotland 0

FRIDAY 28 MAY 1999
COUNTY GROUND, DERBY: PAKISTAN vs NEW ZEALAND- GROUP B
PAKISTAN WON BY 62 RUNS

The talented and flamboyant Pakistanis, their favoritism rising with each win in the tournament, were too good for New Zealand. The strong winds whistling across the old Racecourse Ground in Derby would have reminded the Kiwis of Wellington, but the crowd was straight out of Karachi and the tide of lime green soon became an irresistable one.

Stephen Fleming won the toss, sent Pakistan in and promptly watched his opening bowlers get flogged for 23 in their opening overs. Afridi hooked Dion Nash for six to his teammates at the front of the pavilion. The total was already 40 when Geoff Allott recovered his composure enough to have Afridi caught behind. The left-armer followed up by bowling Saeed Anwar behind his legs to make it 2-51. Allott would later bend back Saleem Malik's middle stump and have Azhar Mahmood caught. His teammates, however, made little impression on the Pakistani middle order.

Abdur Razzaq and Ijaz Ahmed began the Pakistani assertion with a 19-over stand worth 76. Both were run out, only one of which involved Inzamam-ul-Haq. Ijaz reached his 50 off 68 balls before being punished for daring to look for a short single when batting with Inzamam. He backed up too far and fell to a direct hit throw from point by Chris Harris. Inzamam maintained his fine batting form from the previous Sunday against Australia, hitting with power off the front and back foot. There was not the final mayhem of the final 10 overs at Headingley, neverthless Pakistan finished with a comparable total of 8-269.

Shoaib Akhtar ensured it would be plenty. Given the tail wind by his captain, he was genuinely fast and quickly had both Nathan Astle and Matthew Horne edging through to Moin Khan. When Craig McMillan miscued a cover drive off Wasim Akram to mid-on New Zealand were 3-35 in the 11th over and effectively out of it.

The Kiwis' pride and their all important run rate was preserved well enough by their captain who added 83 with fellow left-hander Harris in 19 overs. That, unfortunately for New Zealand came after they had been 6-71, so it had no bearing on the result. Fleming had gone to his 50 in 76 balls, one of his straight drives off Shoaib was the equal of any shot during the day.

Fleming became Azhar Mahmood's third scalp in the 39th over and Harris succumbed to Saqlain Mushtaq when he top edged a sweep. Then, sadly, with two balls to go there was another pitch invasion. Those involved displayed a counting ability and maturity lower than the teletubbies who had the common sense to stay in their seats. The ground announcer was irate calling them, "fools" and "idiots". Inzamam was voted Man of the Match for the second consecutive game. Those who run between wickets with him do not vote on the matter.

PAKISTAN		NEW ZEALAND	
Saeed Anwar b Allott	28	M. J. Horne c Moin Khan b Shoaib Akhtar	1
Shahid Afridi c Parore b Allott	17	N. J Astle c Moin Khan b Shoaib Akhtar	0
Abdul Razzaq run out	33	C. D. McMillan c Saleem Malik b Wasim Akram	20
Ijaz Ahmed run out	51	S. P. Fleming (capt) c Wasim Akram b Azhar Mahmood	69
Inzamam-ul-Haq not out	73	R. G. Twose c Inzamam-ul-Haq b Azhar Mahmood	13
Saleem Malik b Allott	8	C. L. Cairns lbw b Azhar Mahmood	0
Moin Khan (wk) c McMillan b Astle	19	A. C. Parore (wk) lbw b Azhar Mahmood	0
Wasim Akram (capt) lbw b Cairns	1	C. Z. Harris c Abdul Razzaq b Saqlain Mushtaq	42
Azhar Mahmood c Twose b Allott	14	D. J. Nash not out	21
Saqlain Mushtaq not out	0	G. R. Larsen not out	3
Extras b4 lb10 w8 nb3	25	Extras lb15 w13 nb10	38
(50 overs)	8-269	(50 overs)	8-207

Did not bat: Shoaib Akhtar

1/40 2/51 3/127 4/163 5/180 6/221 7/226 8/255

Bowling: Nash 10-1-36-0; Allott 10-0-64-4; Larsen 10-0-35-0; Cairns 7-0-46-1; Harris 8-0-47-0 Astle 5-0-27-1

Did not bat: G. I. Allott

1/2 2/12 3/35 4/70 5/71 6/71 7/154 8/200

Bowling: Wasim Akram 9-0-27-1; Shoaib Akhtar 7-1-31-2; Azhar Mahmood 10-0-38-3; Saqlain Mushtaq 10-1-34-2; Shahid Afridi 6-1-26-0; Abdul Razzaq 8-0-36-0

Umpires: K. Francis R. Koertzen

Toss:New Zealand   Points:Pakistan 2 New Zealand 0

SATURDAY 29 MAY 1999
COUNTY GROUND, CHELMSFORD: SOUTH AFRICA vs ZIMBABWE-GROUP A
ZIMBABWE WON BY 48 RUNS

Here was an upset no-one saw coming, particularly England who, as it turned out, were more upset about it than anyone else. Zimbabwe controlled the game from the first ball to the last and were deserved winners. The success gave special satisfaction to Alistair Campbell's side. They were now assured of progressing to the Super Sixes stage of the tournament with a real chance of reaching the semi-finals. To achieve all that against their highly credentialled neighbours so convincingly was all the more meritorious.

Alistair Campbell won the toss and batted on a fine morning with no suggestion of devilment in the Chelmsford wicket. Soon Neil Johnson, rediscovering the form he had lost after his Man of the Match performance against Kenya, and Grant Flower were trading in boundaries against the much vaunted Protea attack. The first of three fours off one Kallis over brought up the 50. The pair rattled up 65 in 14 overs before Flower edged Steve Elworthy to Daryl Cullinan at slip.

Murray Goodwin continued the good work with Johnson. The opener cracked Elworthy for another four through the covers to bring him to his half century and by the time Goodwin mistimed a pull off Lance Klusener Zimbabwe were already 2-131. Andy Flower flat batted Allan Donald back over his head for six. Generally, though, the early momentum was lost once Goodwin was out.

Donald terminated Johnson's fine innings when he pulled a short ball to Shaun Pollock on the mid wicket boundary. Then the South African spearhead won an lbw decision against Campbell first ball with a perfectly pitched yorker. Donald celebrated with more than his usual enthusiasm as this was his 200th wicket in limited-over internationals. When Andy Flower made a suicidal call for a second run to Pollock's arm from the point boundary the Zimbabwean innings could have fallen away. Instead Guy Whittall, who hit Klusener for a straight six, and Stuart Carlisle put together enough runs to leave Zimbabwe with a competitive 6-233.

As the Zimbabwean innings progressed the fine morning had deterioated and during lunch a heavy shower saturated the ground. It meant South Africa started their reply 25 minutes late. It was apparent the rain had livened the wicket. Johnson's first ball to Gary Kirsten lifted from a length, struck him on the gloves and lobbed to gully where Andy Whittall brought off a diving catch.

Herschelle Gibbs and Mark Boucher gave no hint that anything out of the ordinary was about to happen. Then Boucher ignored the adage, 'never run on a misfield' and left Gibbs stranded. The next over the wicketkeeper was caught off a no-ball then given out lbw essaying a pull shot at Heath Streak. South Africa were now 3-25 which hinted at serious trouble. The threat quickly intensified. On the same score Jacques Kallis drove at a widish ball and was caught behind. Then Hansie Cronje was yorked by an ecstatic Johnson and when Streak hurried a ball through onto Jonty Rhodes' pads, the Proteas were an astonishing 6-40.

At Edgbaston, as they put up their umbrellas against the incoming rain, the English fans began to squirm. It wasn't time to panic yet, though, as the depth in South African batting ensured the a battle. Pollock and Cullinan added 66, then Pollock stayed with Klusener to put on another 43. The scoring rate was now an issue, as well, and soon after Pollock reached his 50 off 78 balls he holed out in the deep off Andy Whittall. Six balls later and Steve Elworthy was gone. That left Klusener to do all the work with Donald.

He had a go at it too, reaching yet another half century and once placing Streak into the crowd near the main scoreboard at mid wicket. Another 49 were needed off three overs when Henry Olonga, the hero of the win at Leicester, had Donald caught by a high leaping Streak at cover. Zimbabwe attacked their neighbours from the start and reaped the benefit. Their success was at the expense of the loser of the England-India match. When play was washed out at Edgbaston the game lay in the balance. It would be a tense night for both those teams. Meanwhile Zimbabwe could celebrate a sweet moment in their cricket history. Neil Johnson did so with the added satisfaction of a Man of the Match Award.

ZIMBABWE		SOUTH AFRICA	
N. C. Johnson c Pollock b Donald	76	G. Kirsten c A. R. Whittall b Johnson	0
G. W. Flower c Cullinan b Elworthy	19	H. H. Gibbs run out	9
M. W. Goodwin c Kirsten b Klusener	34	M. V. Boucher (wk) lbw b Streak	8
A. Flower (wk) run out	29	J. H. Kallis c A. Flower b Johnson	0
A. D. R. Campbell (capt) lbw b Donald	0	D. J. Cullinan c & b Whittall	29
G. J. Whittall c Cullinan b Donald	20	W. J. Cronje (capt) b Johnson	4
S. V. Carlisle not out	18	J. N. Rhodes lbw b Streak	5
H. H. Streak not out	9	S. M. Pollock c Olonga b A. R. Whittall	52
Extras b1 lb15 w8 nb4	28	L. Klusener not out	52
(50 overs)	6-233	S. Elworthy c A. R. Whittall b Streak	1
Did not bat: A. R. Whittall, A. Huckle, H. K. Olonga		A. A.. Donald c Streak b Olonga	7
1/65 2/131 3/170 4/175 5/186 6/214		Extras b2 lb1 w8 nb7	18
Bowling: Pollock 10-1-39-0; Kallis 6-0-36-0; Donald		(47.2 overs)	185
10-1-41-3; Elworthy 6-0-32-1; Klusener 9-0-36-1;		1/0 2/24 3/25 4/25 5/34 6/40 7/106 8/149 9/150 10/185	
Cronje 9-0-33-0		Johnson 8-1-27-3; Streak 9-1-35-3; G. J. Whittall 4-0-20-0;	
		Olonga 4.2-0-17-1; Huckle 10-1-35-0; A. R. Whittall	
		10-0-41-2; G. W. Flower 2-0-7-0	

Umpires: D. Shepherd S. Venkataraghaven

Toss: Zimbabwe   Points: Zimbabwe 2 South Africa 0

SATURDAY 29 MAY and SUNDAY 30 MAY 1999
EDGBASTON, BIRMINGHAM: ENGLAND vs INDIA- GROUP A
INDIA WON BY 63 RUNS

This started out as a likely vehicle for England to assert their position in Group A and ended in a sudden death scamble for the last place for promotion to the Super Sixes. The host nation's nightmare eventually came true as their batsmen failed to cope with the pressure of chasing 233 runs for their World Cup survival.

India by contrast had recovered from the setbacks of their first two losses and in front of thousands of raucous supporters bowled and fielded with the passion of obvious matchwinners. Those with level heads, like outgoing coach, David Lloyd, realistically admitted that, "When we needed to stand up and be counted, we weren't up to it."

Alec Stewart won his fifth toss and on a bright, clear morning decided to bowl. There was no immediate breakthrough although Saurav Ganguly and Sandgoppan Ramesh had the standard amount of difficulty with the new ball. Thirteen overs of survival and occasional strokes brought 49 runs before the consistent Alan Mullally had Ramesh edging to slip. Ganguly and Rahul Dravid were unable to repeat the dramatics of their Wednesday onslaught against Sri Lanka, but their contribution was important.

When Dravid lofted Mark Ealham to mid off the Indian innings lost its cornerstone. Ealham had also tied down Sachin Tendulkar enough to cause him to hole out at mid wicket. He and Mohammad Azharuddin both got a start without developing their innings into something really substantial. It was Ajay Jadeja with five good boundaries in 30 balls who got the Indian total up to something that might give England some concern. After 50 overs there was virtually no difference between what India finished with and Zimbabwe's effort at Chelmsford.

Alec Stewart made a flying start to the 'Carnival of Cricket'. Since then his form had been in decline and that trend continued when he drove at the energetic Mohanty, preferred to Venkatash Prasad with the new ball, and edged the ball into the stomach of the Indian captain at second slip. Not expected to make a big impact on the tournament, India's only Orissian cricketer stunned a nation of 60 million and thrilled 900 million others when he ripped through Graeme Hick's crooked defence with his next legal delivery. England were 2-13 in the fourth over and the dark clouds were gathering in more ways than one.

Graham Thorpe, at his best a fantastic counter puncher, responded with three brilliant cover drives to bring the Indian paceman back to earth. His partner, Nasser Hussain was nowhere near as confident. He survived a perilously close lbw shout and lobbed a leading edge just out of harms way before chopping on Ganguly's innocuous looking opening delivery. The skies were closing in by now and everyone soon retreated to the dressing room. They didn't return, the rain being so persistent that not even Edgbaston's mighty 'Brumbrella' could save the day.

England's Sunday offering was 160 runs with 29.3 overs left to bowl. When the players returned after a delayed start, the sky was still overcast and the temperature chill. In contrast to the buzz of yesterday's full house, this was a near empty stadium of witnesses to a cricketing execution. It was quickly obvious England were losing their heads. Three overs into the day and Thorpe was given out lbw to Javagal Srinath bowling around the wicket to the left-hander. One shot by Andrew Flintoff that sent the ball over mid wicket for six deceptively hinted at an English revival. Two balls later he was flummoxed by Anil Kumble and out lbw. The run rate was rising and the wickets were disappearing.

Fairbrother still fought on, but there was nothing left to support his efforts. When he charged Ganguly and swung wildly to be caught behind England were 8-132 and the result inevitable. A bit of bat waving by Darren Gough and Angus Fraser just prolonged the agony. Twenty-four overs into the day's play Srinath ended England's participation by removing two of Mullally's stumps which released the Indian supporters on their joyous stampede. Ganguly, challenging Lance Klusener as the player of the tournament, secured another Man of Match Award.

Dave Stewart's World Cup song was now ready to be released in Britain. Any English supporters motivated by it now had no team to support.

INDIA		ENGLAND	
S. C. Ganguly run out	40	N. Hussain b Ganguly	33
S. Ramesh c Hick b Mullally	20	A. J. Stewart (wk/capt) c Azharuddin b Mohanty	2
R. Dravid c Ealham b Flintoff	53	G. A. Hick b Mohanty	0
S. R. Tendulkar c Hick b Ealham	22	G. P. Thorpe lbw b Srinath	36
M. Azharuddin (capt) c Hussain b Ealham	26	N. H. Fairbrother c Mongia b Ganguly	30
A. Jadeja c Fraser b Gough	39	A. Flintoff lbw b Kumble	15
N. R. Mongia (wk) b Mullally	2	A. J. Hollioake lbw b Kumble	6
J. Srinath b Gough	1	M. A. Ealham c Azharuddin b Ganguly	0
A. Kumble not out	6	D. Gough c Kumble b Prasad	19
B. K. V. Prasad not out	2	A. R. C. Fraser not out	15
Extras lb7 w10 nb4	21	A. D. Mullally b Srinath	0
(50 overs)	8-232	Extras b4 lb3 w5 nb1	13
Did not bat: D. S. Mohanty		(45.2 overs)	169

1/49 2/93 3/139 4/174 5/188 6/209 7/210 8/228

Bowling: Gough 10-0-51-2; Fraser 10-2-30-0;
Mullally 10-0-54-2; Ealham 10-2-28-2; Flintoff 5-0-28-1;
Hollioake 5-0-34-0

1/12 2/13 3/72 4/81 5/118 6/130 7/131 8/132 9/161
10/169

Bowling: Srinath 8.2-3-25-2; Mohanty 10-0-54-2;
Prasad 9-1-25-1; Ganguly 8-0-28-3; Kumble 10-1-30-2

Umpires: D. Hair Javed Akhtar

Toss: England   Points: India 2 England 0

SUNDAY 30 MAY 1999
OLD TRAFFORD, MANCHESTER: AUSTRALIA vs WEST INDIES- GROUP B
AUSTRALIA WON BY 6 WICKETS

Australian satisfaction at turning on their best form of the 1999 World Cup and reaching the Super Sixes was tempered by criticism of their go-slow batting tactics when on the verge of victory. On the streets of Auckland the attempt to keep the West Indies in the picture at the expense of New Zealand was seen as a despicable act; the equivalent of the infamous underarm 'sneak' of 1981.

Steve Waugh and Michael Bevan were trying to lift the West Indian run rate to a point that it would stay superior toNew Zealand's. If that occurred the West Indies would also make the Super Sixes and Australia would take in the two points from this match. A New Zealand promotion eliminated those points and enabled the Kiwis to take in the two from the win against Australia at Cardiff. Despite the admission from the coach, Steve Rixon, and other New Zealand officials that their side would have done the same thing given similar circumstances, the Fleet Street response was scathing. The next day it amounted to nothing anyway.

The fault lay with the rules rather than the players. Qualification for the Super Sixes had even made the AFL final-eight system seem simple and fair. Those to suffer were the fans packed into Old Trafford. As the majority of them were English, by mid afternoon they were not in a particularly happy state of mind anyway.

If the Australians were boring, the West Indies were insipid against a rejuvinated Glenn McGrath. They had no answer to his pace and movement as the champion from Narromine exposed flaws in technique and application, much as he had done a few weeks before in the Caribbean.

Like the game at Edgbaston, this clash, even without knowing the result between Scotland and New Zealand, was virtually a sudden-death play-off. McGrath was a threat from his first over after Steve Waugh had won the toss and elected to bowl saying he was, "Looking for moisture" on an overcast Manchester morning.

There were occasional puffs of dust rather than clear signs of dampness, however the Australian pacemen got the desired response from the wicket. In the fifth over, Sherwin Campbell played across a McGrath delivery and a leading edge carried to a diving Mark Waugh at second slip. Next ball Jimmy Adams pushed half forward and was struck on the pad right in front of the middle stump.

The contest between Brian Lara and McGrath might well settle the result and was eagerly anticipated for that reason. The West Indian captain looked solid and cracked Damien Fleming off his hip for the opening boundary of the innings. Then McGrath sent down an unplayable off-cutter that went past Lara's impeccable defensive shot and clipped the top of his off-stump. It was a sublime moment for the Australians who knew they had opened the door to a West Indian batting disaster.

That prospect was avoided for 14 overs as Ridley Jacobs, in no real trouble, and Shivnarine Chanderpaul carried the total to a more respectable 3-64. They took advantage of some loose stuff from Brendan Julian. The introduction of Shane Warne for the 23rd over then completely ruptured the West Indian cause. On his 'ball from hell' ground the leg-spinner forced Chanderpaul to chop his third delivery into his stumps. Next over Tom Moody, who sent down another impeccable spell, had Stuart Williams badly mistiming a pull shot to Mark Waugh at mid wicket. It was 6-69 in the 26th over when Phil Simmons played on to Fleming, 7-70 when Curtley Ambrose shuffled in front of the stumps to a Warne leg-spinner and 8-71 when Mervyn Dillon did likewise to McGrath.

Ridley Jacobs watched his side lose a 5-7 in seven overs to effectively non-bat themselves out of the World Cup. The composure of the left-handed wicketkeeper/opening batsman put his teammates to shame. The last two wickets added another 39 until McGrath came back to abruptly finish the innings. He had 5-14, Warne 3-11 and Jacobs had carried his bat through a completed innings, a rarity in one-day cricket.

The West Indies were never going to successfully defend 110, yet Ambrose did all within his extensive powers to do so. He quickly had Mark Waugh, pushing out tentatively, caught behind. Adam Gilchrist and Ricky Ponting batted positively for eight overs and 33 runs before Ambrose struck a second time, bowling Gilchrist on the crease between bat and pad. A superb diving left-handed catch in the gully by Adams removed Darren Lehmann and gave the Antiguan his third wicket.

When Ponting hooked Reon King to Chanderpaul at deep square leg Australia were 4-62 in the 20th over, a worse position than the West Indies had been in at the same stage. Ambrose, though, was finished his spell which allowed Bevan and Steve Waugh all the freedom they required. They scored the next 30 runs in brisk time, then the last 19 took 13 overs. It was painful viewing as the certain result stifled all tension.

Spectators had paid 40 pounds for a seat at this match in Manchester's famous Old Trafford. The Carnival of Cricket was short changing them badly. The torment was finished from the fourth ball of the 41st over and Glenn McGrath was named Man of the Match.

WEST INDIES		AUSTRALIA	
S. L. Campbell c M. E. Waugh b McGrath	2	A. C. Gilchrist (wk) b Ambrose	21
R. D. Jacobs (wk) not out	49	M. E. Waugh c Jacobs b Ambrose	3
J. C. Adams lbw b McGrath	0	R. T. Ponting c Chanderpaul b King	20
B. C. Lara (capt) b McGrath	9	D. S. Lehmann c Adams b Ambrose	9
S. Chanderpaul b Warne	16	S. R. Waugh (capt) not out	19
S. Williams c M. Waugh b Moody	3	M. G. Bevan not out	20
P. V. Simmons b Fleming	1	Extras lb4 w7 nb8	19
C. E. L. Ambrose lbw b Warne	0	(40.4 overs)	4-111
M. Dillon lbw b McGrath	0	Did not bat: T. M. Moody, B. J. Julian, S. K. Warne,	
R. D. King lbw b Warne	1	D. W. Fleming, G. D. McGrath	
C. A. Walsh b McGrath	6	1/10 2/43 3/53 4/62	
Extras lb3 w18 nb1	22	Bowling: Ambrose 10-0-31-3; Walsh 10-3-25-0;	
(46.4 overs)	110	Dillon 7.4-1-22-0; King 10-2-27-1; Simmons 3-2-2-0	

1/7 2/7 3/20 4/64 5/67 6/69 7/70 8/71 9/88 10/110

Bowling: McGrath 8.4-3-14-5; Fleming 7-1-12-1;

Moody 7-0-16-1; Julian 7-1-36-0

Warne 10-4-11-3; Bevan 7-0-18-0

Umpires: S. Dunne K. Francis

Toss: Australia   Points: Australia 2 West Indies 0

COUNTY GROUND, SOUTHAMPTON: KENYA vs SRI LANKA- GROUP A
SRI LANKA WON BY 45 RUNS

While the cricket world followed the dramas at Edgbaston and Old Trafford in Hampshire the Sri Lankans and Kenyans were going through the motions like a set of County players might at an end of season game at, for example, Southampton.

The game produced plenty of runs but was played out to the emptiest house of the tournament. After the Sri Lankans had been sent in by Aasif Karim, Sanath Jayasuriya finally showed glimpses of the form that had made him a star in 1996. He cut Tom Odoyo for six and dominated the opening stand with Roshan Manhanama before both openers were out within a couple of overs of each other.

Aravinda de Silva failed again before a century stand by Marvin Atapattu and Arjuna Ranatunga put Sri Lanka into a strong position. Four wickets then fell between the 40th and 43rd overs. It took a sprightly 64 partnership in seven overs by Mahela Jayawardene and Chaminda Vaas to give Sri Lanka a powerful total. The Kenyans had been hampered by a wet ball while the Sri Lankans batted and during the break between innings the drizzle became more persistent. It delayed the resumption which sent lots of spectators home.

When play started again at 4.40pm it was still cloudy and damp enough to suggest that it would be difficult to finish the match before Monday. That assessment was revised when Kenya slumped to 5-52, Vaas and Jayawardene doing a great deal of damage. However, there was to be no easy escape for the Sri Lankans as Maurice Odumbe and Alpesh Vadher took root and batted for 30 overs. They never looked likely to change the result, but had the satisfaction of going into the World Cup and limited-over interantional record books by putting on 161 for the sixth wicket. It must have annoyed the Sri Lankans who were getting saturated as the drizzle kept on and on through into the evening. Muralitharan bowled in his cap, understanding that most body heat is lost through the head.

Several times umpires Dave Orchard and Peter Willey offered the players the chance to come off. No-one wanted to return the next day so everyone kept going.

Jayasuriya finally bowled Odumbe on the drive in the 48th over. The Kenyan had done enough by that stage to receive the Man of the Match Award.

SRI LANKA		KENYA	
S. T. Jayasuriya lbw b Odoyo	39	K. O. Otieno (wk) lbw b Vaas	0
R. S. Mohanama b Odoyo	21	Ravindu Shah c Muralitharan b Jayawardene	12
M. S. Atapattu c Otieno b Angara	52	D. N. Chudasama b Vaas	3
P. A.de Silva c Chudasama b Odoyo	10	S. O. Tikolo lbw b Wickramasinghe	19
A. Ranatunga (capt) run out	50	Aasif Karim (capt) lbw b Jayawardene	4
U. D. U. Chandana c Otieno b Kamande	0	M. O. Odumbe b Jayasuriya	82
D. P. M. D. Jayawardene c Ravindu Shah b M. Suji	45	A. Vadher not out	73
R. S. Kaluwitharana (wk) c Chudasama b Angara	3	T. M. Odoyo not out	16
W. P. U. J. C. Vaas not out	29	Extras b4 lb8 w8 nb1	21
G. Wickramasinghe not out	0	(50 overs)	6-230
Extras lb7 w16 nb3	26	Did not bat: M. A. Suji, J. O. Angara, J. K. Kamande	
(50 overs)	8-275	1/0 2/10 3/33 4/36 5/52 6/213	
Did not bat: M. Muralitharan		Bowling: Vaas 7-1-26-2; Wickramasinghe 9-1-27-1;	
1/72 2/74 3/87 4/191 5/191 6/199 7/209 8/273		Jayawardene 10-0-56-2	
Bowling: M. Suji 9-1-58-1; Angara 10-0-50-2;		Muralitharan 3-0-11-0; Chandana 1-0-13-0;	
Odoyo 10-2-56-3; Aasif Karim 10-0-35-0;		Jayasuriya 10-1-39-1; de Silva 10-0-46-0	
Kamande 9-0-51-1; Odumbe 2-0-18-0			

Umpires: D. Orchard P. Willey

Toss: Kenya   Points: Sri Lanka 2 Kenya 0

MONDAY 31 MAY 1999
RAEBURN PLACE, EDINBURGH: SCOTLAND vs NEW ZEALAND
NEW ZEALAND WON BY SIX WICKETS

A vibrant performance by New Zealand overwhelmed Scotland so that the Kiwis were able to oust the West Indies from the last spot of the Group B Super Sixes. The capacity crowd would have hoped for a better effort from their team who, despite not winning a match themselves could still have affected the destiny of the 1999 World Cup. Scottish flags were prominent prior to the start of play, however they soon were put away when, after Stephen Fleming won the toss and inserted Scotland, the home side hit 3-12.

Dion Nash made the first breakthrough. It was left-arm paceman Geoff Allott who impressed again, though. He brought one back at Scottish captain, George Salmond to win an lbw decision, then moved the ball away to catch the edge of Mike Allingham's bat. For a time Gavin Hamilton, a class above England's token all-rounders, and Ian Stanger restored cricketing parity with a partnership of 54. Once Nathan Astle had Hamilton caught at mid wicket the slump was rejoined and Scotland slipped to 6-68 in the 28th over. Chris Harris cleaned up the tail, finished with astonishing figures and two thirds of a hattrick. Scotland by the 43rd over were all out for 121.

The tree-lined ground was lifted by the bright afternoon sun as New Zealand began their pursuit. They had 50 overs to win, but only 20.5 overs to tip their run rate above the West Indies'. And they made the worst possible start. Matthew Hart, a tidy left-arm spinner, had been brought in as an opening batsman to replace the out-of-form Matthew Horne. Hart lasted one ball, bowled behind his legs from a fast full pitched delivery from John Blain. New Zealand were batting in a fashion a little alien to their normal approach and the uncertainty showed at the start. Halfway through the third over Astle edged another full Blain delivery through to wicketkeeper Davies to make New Zealand 2-19. Everyone took a breather with New Zealand on 2-30 from 5 overs at lunch.

Roger Twose, who kick started the Kiwi World Cup campaign with his match-winning innings against Australia, approached his task with gay abandon. He was dropped at short cover from a firm dive, at mid wicket from a skied pull and fine leg from another top edged pull shot. The New Zealand innings might have been in some disarray if all the chances had been taken. Instead Twose survived and between mishits made some worthwhile connections. Asim Butt was clubbed over mid wicket for six and other hits travelled to the boundary, sometimes on their intended course, others at a variety of angles. He dived through the stumps at the bowler's end scrambling for a run. He lost Craig McMillan at 81 and Fleming played on 11 runs later to give the promising Blain his third wicket. Twose reached his 50 off 44 balls. Then he sat back and watched Chris Cairns pick up Hamilton and hit him way over square leg for the six that won the game. Geoff Allott was named Man of the Match.

SCOTLAND		NEW ZEALAND	
M. W. Smith c Cairns b Nash	1	M. N. Hart b Blain	0
M. Allingham c Fleming b Allott	2	N. J Astle c Davies b Blain	11
G. Salmond (capt) lbw b Allott	1	C. D. McMillan c & b Hamilton	19
G. M. Hamilton c Allott b Astle	20	R. G. Twose not out	54
I. M. Stanger c Astle b Cairns	27	S. P. Fleming (capt) b Blain	7
J. E. Brinkley c Parore b Allott	0	C. L. Cairns not out	20
J. G. Williamson c & b Harris	10	Extras b1 lb2 w5 nb4	12
A. G. Davies (wk) c sub (Vettori) b Harris	24	(17.5 overs)	4-123
J. A. R. Blain lbw b Harris	0	Did not bat: A. C. Parore (wk), C. Z. Harris, C. E. Bulfin,
Asim Butt c Twose b Harris	10	D. J. Nash, G. I. Allott	
N. Dyer not out	2	1/0 2/19 3/81 4/92	
Extras b1 lb7 w13 nb3	24	Bowling: Blain 7-0-53-3; Asim Butt 5-0-33-0; Hamilton	
(42.1 overs)	121	5.5-0-34-1	

1/2 2/11 3/12 4/66 5/68 6/68 7/100 8/100 9/110 10/121

Bowling: Allott 10-3-15-3; Nash 10-3-16-1; Bulfin 6-0-31-0;
Cairns 8-0-26-1; Astle 5-1-18-1; Harris 3.1-0-7-4

Umpires:R. Koertzen I. Robinson

Toss:New Zealand   Points:New Zealand2 Scotland 0

COUNTY GROUND, NORTHAMPTON: BANGLADESH vs PAKISTAN -GROUP B
BANGLADESH WON BY 62 RUNS

This was not expected to be a memorable cricket match. Pakistan would finish on top of Group B and Bangaldesh fifth whatever the result. So good had Pakistan's form been their fifth victory looked a mere formality. The odds on Bangladesh winning was 33-1. Anyone willing to lay out money on them would have done very well out of the day. The two teams played as if their records and positions were reversed and Bangladesh won by 62 runs. It was a fantastic win for a country working hard for Test status. In Bangladesh the government declared a half day holiday. The people of the former East Pakistan were excited to record a win over the country from whom they had to fight to win independence in 1971.

Wasim Akram sent Bangladesh in, however neither he, nor his highly rated pace bowling partners, Waqar Younis and Shoaib Akhtar could separate Shahriar Hossian and Mehrab Hossain until the total was 69. As usual the ball regularly beat the bat. Sometimes it was within close proximity to the edge, often it was a long way. Extras did as well as anyone. That is not to deny the quality or importance of the pair's batting. They were two of the seven batsmen who reached double figures and with the contribution of extras, a competent 9-223 was reached. Saqlain Mushtaq did most to restrain it from being much more by the returning the best ever figures by a Pakistani in the World Cup.

Pakistan were penalised an over for slow bowling. Shahid Afridi was penalised for not being able to handle Khaled Mahmud's fifth ball. Pakistan were 1-5, then 2-7 when Ijaz Ahmed was bowled by Shafiuddin Ahmed in the next over. Saeed Anwar was run out while batting with none other than Inzamam-ul-Haq. When Saleem Malik fell lbw halfway through the 13th over to Khaled Mahmud the favourites were 5-42 and defeat seemed inevitable. Eventually Azhar Mahmood, Wasim Akram, Moin Khan and Saqlain Mushtaq gave the Pakistani total some respectablity. Another 63 runs were required from 26 balls when Khaled Mashud's direct hit throw brought a call from Darrell Hair to the third umpire, David Shepherd to make a run out decision.

Most Bangladeshi supporters never saw the red light to confirm Saqlain's dismissal. They were already on the ground celebrating the win that their captain Aminul Islam called, "A great achievement". Khaled Mahmud was named Man of the Match.

BANGLADESH		PAKISTAN	
Shahriar Hossain lbw b Saqlain Mushtaq	39	Saeed Anwar run out	9
Mehrab Hossain st Moin Khan b Saqlain Mushtaq	9	Shahid Afridi c Mehrab Hossain b Khaled Mahmud	2
Akram Khan c Wasim Akram b Waqar Younis	42	Ijaz Ahmed b Shafiuddin Ahmed	0
Aminul Islam (capt) b Shahid Afridi	15	Inzamam-ul-Haq lbw b Khaled Mahmud	7
Naimur Rahman b Waqar Younis	13	Saleem Malik lbw b Khaled Mahmud	5
Minhajul Abedin c & b Saqlain Mushtaq	14	Azhar Mahmood run out	29
Khaled Mahmud st Moin Khan b Saqlain Mushtaq	6	Wasim Akram (capt) c Shahriar Hossain b Minhajul Abedin	29
Khaled Mashud (wk) not out	15	Moin Khan (wk) c Mehrab Hossain b Naimur Rahman	18
Mohammad Rafique c Shoaib Akhtar b Saqlain Mushtaq	6	Saqlain Mushtaq run out	21
Neeyamur Rashid lbw b Wasim Akram	1	Waqar Younis b Mohammad Rafique	11
Shafiuddin Ahmed not out	2	Shoaib Akhtar not out	1
Extras lb5 w28 nb7	40	Extras b1 lb6 w21 nb1	29
(50 overs)	9-223	(44.3 overs)	161

1/69 2/70 3/120 4/148 5/148 6/187 7/195 8/208 9/212

1/5 2/7 3/26 4/29 5/42 6/97 7/102 8/124 9/160 10/161

Bowling: Waqar Younis 9-1-36-2; Shoaib Akhtar 8-0-30-0; Wasim Akram 10-0-35-1; Azhar Mahmood 8-0-56-0; Saqlain Mushtaq 10-1-35-5; Shahid Afridi 5-0-26-1

Khaled Mahmud 10-2-31-3; Shafiuddin Ahmed 8-0-26-1; Neeyamur Rashid 5-1-20-0; Mohammad Rafique 8-0-28-1Minhajul Abedin 7-2-29-1; Naimur Rahman 6.3-2-20-1

Umpires: D. Hair D. Cowie

Toss: Pakistan   Points: Bangladesh 2 Pakistan 0

THE SUPER SIXES

Following the preliminary rounds of the 1999 World Cup the first three teams in each group were promoted to the Super Sixes. Their standings were as follows.

GROUP A	P.	W	L	Pts	RR.	GROUP B	P	W	L	Pts	RR
South Africa	5	4	1	8	+0.86	Pakistan	5	4	1	8	+0.53
India	5	3	2	6	+ 1.28	Australia	5	3	2	6	+0.73
Zimbabwe	5	3	2	6	+0.02	New Zealand	5	3	2	6	+0.58
England	5	3	2	6	-0.33	West Indies	5	3	2	6	+0.50
Sri Lanka	5	2	3	4	-0.81	Bangladesh	5	2	3	4	-0.54
Kenya	5	0	5	0	-1.20	Scotland	5	0	5	0	-1.93

The actual starting table of the Super Sixes was something else.

	Pts	NR
Pakistan	4	0.72
Zimbabwe	4	0.33
South Africa	2	-0.35
New Zealand	2	-0.40
India	-	0.03
Australia	-	-0.35

FRIDAY 4 JUNE 1999
THE OVAL, LONDON: AUSTRALIA vs INDIA; SUPER SIXES No 1.
AUSTRALIA WON BY 77 RUNS

Glenn McGrath, proving he is the better of any batsman in the world, inspired Australia to an emphatic and important 77-run win over India. Three perfect deliveries shattered the Indian top order and ruined any hope they might have entertained of chasing Australia's substantial 6-282.

Early rain promptly cleared south of the Thames into cool breezy conditions. Mohammad Azharuddin showed he had the calling ability to end Steve Waugh's unbelievable run of success with the coin. The historic ground quickly filled as Australia began batting at the invitation of the Indian captain.

The bounce in The Oval wicket encouraged Javagal Srinath to bend his back. He worked up a genuine pace and had the ball thumping into Nayan Mongia's gloves on the rise. Mark Waugh and Adam Gilchrist, despite one wicked blow in the groin, withstood that early threat and then prospered.

Waugh signalled a change of attitude when he started advancing on bowlers before they released the ball. An edged drive sailed to the third man boundary, another was smashed to the rope at cover. In other matches Saurav Ganguly had been a consistent partnership breaker. Waugh greeted him by going down on his knee and flat batting the ball onto the second level of the Barrington Stand.

A calm tickle around the corner raised his second 50 of the competition in the 19th over from 55 balls. The next milestone would be the 100 opening stand. Gilchrist, however, did not quite get there. Three short of the mark he advanced on Ganguly and his totally mistimed off-drive landed in the hands of Debashish Mohanty at mid-off. Ricky Ponting countered that blow with an audacious drive on the up that also deposited the ball over the rope at long off to get off the mark.

Ponting and Waugh rattled along at a run per ball for 10 overs until the opener's 99 ball innings ended when a leg side scoop carried to Venkatesh Prasad at fine-leg. Robin Singh made it a double breakthrough in the same over when Ponting chopped the ball onto his stumps.

Australia were 3-158 in the 31st over. Their middle order batted profitably from that point. The runs came in ones and twos as Steve Waugh and Darren Lehmann put on 60 in 11 overs. There was real urgency in the final overs which brought acceleration but also cost wickets. Steve Waugh scooped to mid-on, Lehmann got lost in the middle of the pitch as Ajay Jadeja threw down the stumps and Michael Bevan, after hitting a flat scoop for six over long off, skied a short rising ball to the wicketkeeper Nayan Mongia off Prasad in the 50th over. Tom Moody with a couple of imperious drives gave a final boost, 78 having come from the final ten overs.

The question of whether India might seriously challenge Australia's 282 was quickly settled by McGrath. From the final ball of his opening over his away swinger induced an edge from Sachin Tendulkar's defensive bat and Gilchrist made no mistake. Tendulkar had been prolific in his most recent limited-over internationals against Australia. Then, though, the attacks had been without McGrath. Tendulkar was forced to reduce the size of the label on his bat prior to the match. If the size of his bat had been reduced instead, McGrath's delivery might have missed the edge. From the fifth ball of his next over the paceman repeated the dose to Rahul Dravid. Damien Fleming joined in the demolition with the equally valuable wicket of Saurav Ganguly, who chopped on an in-swinger to the left-hander.

When Azharuddin could do nothing except parry the ball to gully off the shoulder of his bat India were 4-17 in the seventh over. McGrath had 3-8 in four brilliant overs. It was exciting stuff except for the thousands of Indians in the crowd. They were spared total humiliation by the spirited batting of Robin Singh and Ajay Jadeja who combined to put on 141 in 30 overs. It was fine batting that saved face and run rate if not the two points from this match. Both batsman got stuck into Shane Warne, who had been in doubt for this game with a sore neck and shoulder. One Warne over cost 21 as the ball sailed into the crowd three times.

Australian commentator, Bill Lawry was close to tears as two pigeons paid for their lack of cricket knowledge with their lives in two separate incidents. One was crunched out of mid air by a Paul Reiffel throw and another could not avoid a powerful shot by Jadeja. The Indian reached a fine 100 a few balls before a comical runout of Mohanty ended the match with 10 balls remaining.

India now faced an almost impossible task to qualify for the semi-finals. Australia had won their first game at The Oval for 22 years. McGrath was named Man of the Match.

AUSTRALIA		INDIA	
M. E. Waugh c Prasad b Singh	83	S. C. Ganguly b Fleming	8
A. C. Gilchrist (wk) c Mohanty b Ganguly	31	S. R. Tendulkar c Gilchrist b McGrath	0
R. T. Ponting b Singh	23	R. Dravid c Gilchrist b McGrath	2
D. S. Lehmann run out	26	A. Jadeja not out	100
S. R. Waugh (capt) c Kumble b Mohanty	36	M. Azharuddin (capt) c S. R. Waugh b McGrath	3
M. G. Bevan c Mongia b Prasad	22	R. R. Singh c Reiffel b Moody	75
T. M. Moody not out	26	N. R. Mongia (wk) run out	2
S. K. Warne not out	0	J. Srinath c Gilchrist b S. R. Waugh	0
Extras lb14 w10 nb11	35	A. Kumble c Gilchrist b S. R. Waugh	3
(50 overs)	6-282	B. K. V. Prasad lbw b Fleming	2
Did not bat: P. R. Reiffel, D. W. Fleming, G. D. McGrath		D. Mohanty run out	0
1/97 2/157 3/158 4/218 5/231 6/275		Extras lb3 w4 nb3	10
Bowling: Srinath 10-2-34-0; Mohanty 7-0-47-1;		(48.2 overs)	205
Prasad 10-0-60-1; Kumble 10-0-49-0; Ganguly 5-0-31-1;		1/1 2/10 3/12 4/17 5/158 6/181 7/186 8/192 9/204	
Singh 7-0-43-2; Tendulkar 1-0-2-0		10/205	
		Bowling: McGrath 10-1-34-3; Fleming 9-1-33-2; Reiffel	
		10-1-30-0; Moody 10-0-41-1; M. E. Waugh 1-0-7-0; Warne	
		6.2-0-49-0; S. R. Waugh 2-0-8-2	

Umpires: S. Bucknor P. Willey

Toss: India   Points: Australia 2 India 0

SATURDAY 5 JUNE 1999
TRENT BRIDGE, NOTTINGHAM: PAKISTAN vs SOUTH AFRICA-SUPER SIX No.2
SOUTH AFRICA WON BY 3 WICKETS

The two best performed teams in the tournament recovered from the shock of their recent defeats to turn on a riveting contest at Trent Bridge. In the end South Africa won with an over to spare, although the margin was tight enough to suggest the result could easily be reversed if the teams met again, which their positions and form indicated was quite possible.

South Africa's hero was Lance Klusener whose batting was attaining legendary status. Anyone able to spank Shaoib Akhtar for six has an amazing talent.

Every seat was taken at Trent Bridge as befitted one of the matches of the competition. Wasim Akram won the toss and batted against a side that had not changed for six matches. As usual, for much of the innings the Pakistanis showed no inclination to take the attack to the bowlers. Saeed Anwar and Wajahatullah Wasti provided a steady start, but like Abdur Razzaq and Ijaz Ahmed could not build upon that. Steve Elworthy was economical and when Inzamam-ul-Haq failed to ground his bat, even though he had lumbered over the line in time to beat Jonty Rhodes' throw, Paksitan were 5-118 in the 36th over and going nowhere.

Moin Khan, supported by Yousuf Youhana, back in the side but soon suffering a reoccurrence of his hamstring strain, and then Azhar Mahmood, gave the innings some substance. Youhana's runner, Ijaz Ahmed, was run out when Klusener proved an attempted short single was ill-advised.

The last four overs realised another 48 runs as Moin went berserk. He smashed Allan Donald for two fours and clipped him for six behind square leg in the 47th over. In the next over bowled by Shaun Pollock, he hit another four and a six, this time a dancing d rive which sailed high over long off. Moin had completed his 50 in 48 balls and although he became the third run out victim of the innings in the next over, he had given his vaunted bowling attack something to defend.

Allan Donald had consistently clocked 86mph on the radar gun placed in the ground to measure the pace of the fast bowlers. Shoaib Akhtar set out to top that and by his third ball was well into the 90s. His fifth delivery brought greater reward when Herschelle Gibbs guided a catch to Ijaz in the gully. Hansie Cronje surprisingly promoted himself to number three and Shoaib had him jumping as well. The speedster reached 95mph (153kmph) and in his third over Cronje was caught on the third man boundary from a top edged cut.

Not to be denied Akram trapped Gary Kirsten lbw not playing a shot and when Azhar Mahmood had Daryl Cullinan caught at cover and Rhodes lbw to an inswinger South Africa were 5-58 and heading for a heavy defeat.

However, the never-say-die attitude of the Proteas has been an obvious attribute since their return to authorised international cricket late in 1991. Jacques Kallis and Pollock showed plenty of that quality in a partnership of 77 in 16 overs. The work was mostly done in smartly taken singles and when Pollock stretched out at Azhar and was caught at slip, South Africa had just a sniff of their target at 6-135.

Klusener had the form and quality, though, to turn the scent of victory into a very powerful aroma. He and his powerful bat soon drastically reduced the run requirement. Kallis completed an essential 50 in 89 balls with just three fours. Klusener pulled a short Saqlain delivery for six over square leg then lost Kallis as he top edged an attempt at a simliar shot off the same bowler in the 45th over.

Now Klusener turned the evenly balanced match South Africa's way. Shoaib came roaring in at full steam determined to break the left-hander's sequence of not outs. Klusener swung hard and a top edge sailed to the boundary at fine leg. He followed that with a mighty hit, rocketing the ball off the bat as fast as it was sent down, over mid wicket for six. This may well have been the shot of the World Cup. When a yorker flew off Klusener's toe through Moin for four leg byes the task had been reduced to 24 runs off 27 balls.

A pull shot off Saqlain for four and a heave over mid wicket for six off Akram by the man of the moment took South Africa to 7-212. Then the silent partner Mark Boucher displayed his wares with a right hander's six over mid wicket off the suffering Saqlain. The excitement subsided as did the exhortations of the Pakistani supporters. There was one final flutter as Klusener, never likely to get the runs in singles, skied another attempted slog at Saqlain. The ball steepled over mid off. Anwar misjudged the catch which allowed the batsman to complete the two runs needed for the unlikely victory. Trent Bridge had seen a ripper and Lance Klusener had collected four Man of the Match Awards in six starts.

PAKISTAN		SOUTH AFRICA	
Saeed Anwar c Boucher b Elworthy	23	G. Kirsten lbw b Akram	19
Wajahatullah Wasti c Boucher b Donald	17	H. H. Gibbs c Ijaz b Shoaib	0
Abdur Razzaq c Kirsten b Elworthy	30	W. J. Cronje (capt) c Saqlain b Shoaib	4
Ijaz Ahmed c Cullinan b Klusener	23	D. J. Cullinan c Anwar b Azhar	18
Inzamam-ul-Haq run out	4	J. H. Kallis c Moin b Saqlain	54
Yousuf Youhana run out	17	J. N. Rhodes lbw b Azhar	0
Moin Khan (wk) run out	63	S. M. Pollock c Inzamam b Azhar	30
Azhar Mahmood not out	15	L. Klusener not out	46
Wasim Akram (capt) not out	5	M. V. Boucher (wk) not out	12
Extras b4 lb8 w11	23	Extras lb11 w14 nb13	38
(50 overs)	7-220	(49 overs)	7-221
Did not bat: Saqlain Mushtaq, Shoaib Akhtar		Did not bat: S. Elworthy, A. A. Donald	
1/41 2/58 3/102 4/11 5/118 6/150 7/206		1/7 2/19 3/39 4/55 5/58 6/135 7/176	
Bowling: Pollock 10-1-42-0; Kallis 10-0-47-0; Donald		Bowling: Akram 10-0-44-1; Shoaib 9-1-51-2; Azhar	
10-2-49-1; Elworthy 10-2-23-2; Klusener 9-0-41-1		10-1-24-3; Abdur 10-1-40-0; Saqlain 10-0-51-1	

Umpires: D. Hair D. Shepherd

Toss: Pakistan   Points: South Africa 2 Pakistan 0

SUNDAY 6 JUNE 6th and MONDAY 7 JUNE 1999
HEADINGLEY, LEEDS: NEW ZEALAND vs ZIMBABWE- SUPER SIX No.3
NO RESULT

The weather finally caught up with the World Cup and ruined a game that was not a special spectacle anyway. After an interrupted first day and a blank second New Zealand and Zimbabwe came away with a point each. For the Kiwis, who believed they would win easily, it was a frustrating time. The Zimbabweans, on the other hand, sneaked a point closer to a surprising semi-final berth.

Between showers on the Sunday, the Zimbabwean batsmen fell away badly during their final overs and set New Zealand a modest 176 for victory. Alistair Campbell had been confident enough to bat when he won the toss and his partnership of 81 for the fourth wicket with Murray Goodwin put his side in a very reasonable position. It was after the second rain interruption that things began to go astray and when Chris Cairns made short work of the tail Zimbabwe had lost 6-39 in 13 overs.

Fearing the worst with the weather Matthew Horne, who had brilliantly run out Grant Flower at the start of the day, and Nathan Astle got the Kiwi reply away to a cracking start. Between them they struck ten boundaries in nine overs before they fell one after the other to Guy Whittall and Henry Olonga. When Craig McMillan played down the wrong line to Heath Streak and was out lbw the Kiwis were 3-70 and needed a period of consolidation.

It never really got going. Soon, Dave Orchard and Srinivas Venkataraghaven were offering the light to the batsmen. When Stephen Fleming accepted that offer at ten past seven in the evening the game was all over. The next day rain started falling halfway through the morning. Everyone waited until 4.30 pm in the afternoon, but to no avail. Geoff Allott's three wickets brought his tally for the tournament up to an impressive 18. In a 'no result', though, there is no Man of the Match Award.

ZIMBABWE		NEW ZEALAND	
N. C. Johnson b Allott	25	M. J. Horne lbw b Whittall	35
G. W. Flower run out	1	N. J Astle c Streak b Olonga	20
M. W. Goodwin c Parore b Harris	57	C. D. McMillan lbw b Streak	1
A. Flower (wk) c McMillan b Allott	0	S. P. Fleming (capt) not out	9
A. D. R. Campbell (capt) c Nash b Larsen	40	R. G. Twose not out	0
G. J. Whittall c Astle b Allott	21	Extras lb1 nb4	5
S. V. Carlisle c McMillan b Astle	2	(15 overs)	3-70
H. H. Streak b Cairns	4	Did not bat: C. L. Cairns, A. C. Parore (wk), C. Z. Harris,	
A. R. Whittall c Astle b Cairns	3	G. R. Larsen, D. J. Nash, G. I. Allott	
A. G. Huckle c Twose b Cairns	0	1/58 2/59 3/65	
H. K. Olonga not out	1	Bowling: Johnson 3-0-21-0; Streak 5-0-25-1; G. J.	
Extras b4 lb11 w3 nb3	21	Whittall 3-0-9-1; Olonga 4-1-14-1	
(49.3 overs)	175		

1/10 2/35 3/45 4/136 5/148 6/154 7/163 8/174 9/174
10/175

Bowling: Allott 10-1-24-3; Nash 10-2-48-0; Larsen
10-0-27-1; Cairns 6.3-2-24-3; Harris 4-0-12-1; Astle 9-0-25-1

Umpires: D. Orchard S. Venkataraghaven

Toss: Zimbabwe   Points: Zimbabwe 1 New Zealand 1

TUESDAY 8 JUNE 1999
OLD TRAFFORD, MANCHESTER: INDIA vs PAKISTAN- SUPER SIXES No.4
INDIA WON BY 47 RUNS

India, just clinging on to their World Cup hopes, showed that Pakistan's batting inadequacies were real and could be exploited. If Mohammad Azharuddin's side were relieved to win such a crucial encounter, it was nothing compared to the relief of the Old Trafford authorities that the capacity crowd gave no cause for concern.

Much was made pre-match of the growing tensions between Pakistan and India over disputed territory in Kashmir. The possibility of trouble in a massed gathering of expatriates during a cricket match contested by the two countries led to greatly increased security at the ground. Those fans made a lot of noise, but the only time the security men were conspicuous was near the end of the game when happy Indian fans let off a few fireworks and then during the after-match invasion.

The cricket itself had few fireworks as batsmen struggled for freedom in a match of major national significance. When India batted after Azharuddin had won the toss Sachin Tendulkar laid the foundation for a strong total with an innings containing some of his best batting of the World Cup. The outfield sodden from heavy overnight rain, could not stop Tendulkar from striking five fine boundaries. He lost Ramesh at 37 then with Rahul Dravid took the score to 95 in the 21st over.

The importance of the Indian champion's wicket was shown by the fact that once he had been caught at deep mid off, playing an over ambitious drive against Azhar Mahmood, the Indian innings lost its punch. Ajay Jadeja did not last long which forced Dravid and Mohammad Azharuddin onto the defensive. Only two boundaries were struck between the 21st and 45th overs during which time Dravid completed another 50 off 70 balls. He was then caught at cover by a stretching Afridi off Akram.

Azharuddin realised quick runs were needed at the end of the innings. At first he and Robin Singh were all at sea as they tried to lift the run rate through the last overs. Then, suddenly, Singh clouted Saqlain for a big six that nearly landed in Warwick Road railway station. Azharuddin repeated the dose next over to the off-spinner then a bottom hand clip-chip and a back foot cover drive both for four off Shoaib Akhtar raised the Indian captain's 48th fifty in limited-over internationals. Both he and Singh fell in the final rush for runs leaving India 227 to protect.

Saeed Anwar pulled Javagal Srinath's first ball to the boundary, instigating an early flurry of fours by both openers. They briefly gave the impression that the chase was a straightforward one. Srinath ended that idea when he had Afridi slashing high to

Kumble in the gully and, when he changed to the Stretford end, Ijaz Ahmed edging to Azharuddin at second slip. Saleem Malik's last World Cup was turning into a personal nightmare and when Anwar drove at Venkatesh Prasad, Azharuddin's low diving slips catch left Pakistan 4-65. Azhar Mahmood fell cheaply, too. Yousuf Youhana's quality in the middle order was missed and Pakistan were heading for prompt defeat.

Inzamam-ul-Haq, sore fingers and all, held on while Moin Khan engaged in his hitting habit. The in-form wicketkeeper/ batsman connected with a swipe off Robin Singh for a six over square leg. The Pakistani supporters chanted for their hero. His aggressive response was a top-edged pull that gave Prasad his third wicket. Abdur Razzaq and big Inzamam kept the game alive for a few more overs. They were unable to reduce the run rate, however, and when Inzamam swung across the line at Prasad the contest finished.

The dismissal of the Pakistani captain, caught on the boundary to give Prasad his fifth wicket, with 48 runs still needed off 27 balls, heralded a fairly wild spectator charge and more fireworks. Only a sensationalist would have called this a riot as exuberance was the main emotion exhibited. The players, including Man of the Match, Prasad, were still glad to get off the ground quick smart.

INDIA		PAKISTAN	
S. R. Tendulkar c Saqlain Mushtaq b Azhar Mahmood	45	Saeed Anwar c Azharuddin b Prasad	36
S. Ramesh b Abdul Razzaq	20	Shahid Afridi c Kumble b Srinath	6
R. Dravid c Shahid Afridi b Wasim Akram	61	Ijaz Ahmed c Azharuddin b Srinath	11
A. Jadeja c Inzamam-ul-Haq b Azhar Mahmood	6	Saleem Malik lbw b Prasad	6
M. Azharuddin (capt) c Ijaz Ahmed b Wasim Akram	59	Inzamam-ul-Haq lbw b Prasad	41
R. R. Singh c Wasim Akram b Shoaib Akhtar	16	Azhar Mahmood c Mongia b Prasad	10
N. R. Mongia (wk) not out	6	Moin Khan (wk) c Tendulkar b Prasad	34
Extras b1 lb3 w8 nb2	14	Abdul Razzaq b Srinath	11
(50 overs)	6-227	Wasim Akram (capt) c Kumble b Prasad	12
Did not bat: J. Srinath, A. Kumble, B. K. V. Prasad,		Saqlain Mushtaq lbw b Kumble	0
D. S. Mohanty		Shoaib Akhtar not out	0
1/37 2/95 3/107 4/158 5/218 6/227		Extras lb11 w2	13
Bowling: Wasim Akram 10-0-27-2; Shoaib Akhtar 10-0-55-1;		(45.3 overs)	180
Abdul Razzaq 10-0-40-1; Azhar Mahmood 10-0-34-2;		1/19 2/44 3/52 4/65 5/78 6/124 7/146 8/175 9/176 10/180	
Saqlain Mushtaq 10-0-67-0		Bowling: Srinath 8-1-37-3; Mohanty 10-2-31-0; Prasad	
		9.3-2-27-5; Kumble 10-0-43-2; Singh 8-1-31-0	

Umpires: D. Shephard S. Bucknor

Toss: India   Points: India 2 Pakistan 0

WEDNESDAY 9 JUNE 1999
LORD'S, LONDON: AUSTRALIA vs ZIMBABWE- SUPER SIXES No.5
AUSTRALIA WON BY 44 RUNS

At Lord's in the best batting conditions of the World Cup so far two fine centuries were compiled during a day which realised 562 runs. Yet there was not much tension and despite the splendid individual efforts of Neil Johnson, never any real likelihood Australia, still on the ascent, would be beaten.

They lost Adam Gilchrist early after Alistair Campbell had won the toss and bowled. Soon, though, the runs were flowing. The advantage of bowling first on the fresh wicket was non-existent. Ricky Ponting was in an aggressive frame of mind. Trying to dominate the opposition, he scored at better than a run per ball. In the 15th over he played an off-cutter from the expensive Henry Olonga onto his stumps. Ponting had, however, set the tone of the innings and opened the way for a great partnership between the Waugh twins. First, Olonga had to get Darren Lehmann out of the way, which he did with the score on 2-97 by banging him on the forefinger of his left-hand, necessitating treatment and x-rays.

Mark Waugh had received little of the strike while batting with Ponting. Now, he and Steve went stroke for stroke, run for run for 25 entertaining overs. After the 100 had been raised in the 18th over Mark Waugh hit Olonga with a trademark on-drive for four and in the same over Steve produced a perfect example of his trademark shot, a cracking cover drive off the back foot.

Mark Waugh, who had been dropped at backward point by a leaping Grant Flower early in his innings, smashed a slog straight drive back down the pitch off leg-spinner Paul Strang. The only thing that prevented the ball crashing into the boundary was the grill on Steve Waugh's helmet. Fortunately, for future brotherly relations, injury was avoided, but Steve did have to replace his realigned grill.

Both Waughs bent their knees and swiped the spinners, often for four sometimes for six. Mark passed 50 for the third time in the tournament in 84 balls, Steve reached the milestone in 54 balls. He hit his second six towards the Tavern side of the ground then was bowled middle stump attempting to put medium pacer Guy Whittall into St John's Wood Road. The Waugh partnership had been worth 129.

Mark Waugh reached his record-breaking fourth World Cup century just before holing out at deep mid wicket off Johnson. Then, Michael Bevan and Tom Moody topped off the innings in a frantic stand of 55. In the final over Australia became the first side apart from India to top 300 runs in an innings in the 1999 World Cup.

Although containing Mark Waugh's fine 104, Australia's batting was a team effort. Zimbabwe's response relied almost totally on Neil Johnson who batted throughout the innings, topped Mark Waugh's score and pipped him for the Man of the Match Award. On the still perfect batting surface he found a worthy ally in Murray Goodwin with whom he added 114 in 18 overs. Once the number three had been caught at deep square leg sweeping at Bevan and Andy Flower was caught behind first ball off Paul Reiffel the Zimbabwean innings lapsed into the realms of interest only for statistical purists. Johnson, who had hammered Shane Warne when the leg-spinner was first introduced, completed his 100 in 118 balls and went on to finish with the second highest score by a Zimbabwean in the World Cup behind Dave Houghton's unbelievable 141 against New Zealand in 1987.

Paul Reiffel, like Warne, suffered some heavy punishment, but he returned to take three wickets as Zimbabwe finished 44 runs short of their requirement.

AUSTRALIA		ZIMBABWE	
A. C. Gilchrist (wk) lbw b Johnson	10	N. C. Johnson not out	132
M. E. Waugh c Goodwin b Johnson	104	G. W. Flower lbw b McGrath	21
R. T. Ponting b Olonga	36	M. W. Goodwin c Moody b Bevan	47
D. S. Lehmann retired hurt	6	A. Flower (wk) c Gilchrist b Reiffel	0
S. R. Waugh (capt) b G. Whittal	62	A. Campbell (capt) c Fleming b Reiffel	17
M. G. Bevan not out	37	G. J. Whittall c M. E. Waugh bReiffel	0
T. M. Moody not out	20	D. Viljoen st Gilchrist b Warne	5
Extras lb6 w13 nb9	28	H. H. Streak not out	18
(50 overs)	4-303	Extras lb6 w13	19
Did not bat: S. K. Warne, D. W. Fleming, P. R. Reiffel,		(50 overs)	6-259
G. D. McGrath		Did not bat: P. A. Strang, A. R. Whittall, H. K. Olonga	
1/18 2/74 3/226 4/248		1/39 2/153 3/154 4/188 5/189 6/200	
Bowling: Johnson 8-0-43-2; Streak 10-0-50-0;		Bowling: McGrath 10-1-33-1; Fleming 10-0-46-0;	
Olonga 7-0-62-1; G. J. Whittall 4-0-24-1; Strang 10-1-47-0;		Warne 9-0-55-1; Reiffel 10-0-55-3; Moody 6-0-38-0;	
A. R. Whittall 8-1-51-0; G. W. Flower 3-0-20-0		Bevan 5-1-26-1	

Umpires: D. Cowie R. Koertzen

Toss: Zimbabwe   Points: Australia 2 Zimbabwe 0

The nightmares of February/March returned to Stephen Fleming's side as they were totally outclassed by an efficient and talented South African unit. The Kiwis did not get a look in, failing to take a wicket for 37 overs and not getting anywhere near the 288 they required for victory. South Africa became the first side to qualify for the semi-finals. New Zealand's position was now quite precarious.

A sunny morning encouraged Hansie Cronje to bat after he won the toss. Edgbaston provides a great atmosphere, but a few empty seats suggested the contest had achieved only minor attraction status. Those who attended witnessed an enterprising South African batting display and the openers, Gary Kirsten and Herschelle Gibbs led from the front with their opening stand of 182. The left and right handed combination complemented each other perfectly. Both had feasted heavily on the same bowlers previously and they had little difficulty on a flat, slow surface in doing so again. They paced their stand well, starting quietly then gradually dominating. Kirsten reached his 50 first with a pull off Dion Nash. The left-hander's milestone took 79 balls. Gibbs required 76 balls. He had hit just three boundaries by that time, but doubled that with three more in succession off Nash in the 27th over.

Kirsten reached 4000 runs in limited-over interantionals, swung Nathan Astle for six over square leg then offered the easiest of catches to mid wicket off the same bowler with a miscued flick to leg. Lance Klusener, in such outstanding batting form, was sent in to massacre the despondent Kiwi attack. He struck one four then was bowled heaving at Gavin Larsen. Klusener's dismissal gave him a tournament batting average of 210.

When Gibbs became Geoff Allott's World Cup record-breaking 19th victim of the competition Hansie Cronje and Jacques Kallis indulged in some Klusener style hitting that had spectators running in all directions. In five overs the pair hit five sixes between them and rattled up a partnership of 54 in the process. Kallis hit 19 off Chris Harris' 10th over and Cronje pasted Chris Cairns for consecutive sixes

New Zealand barely offered a shot in reply. Kallis on way to his second Man of the Match Award had removed both openers by the 12th over and at the half way stage of the innings the Kiwis had not even brought up three figures. Stephen Fleming, Roger Twose and Chris Harris kept the innings going until its designated conclusion, but they offered little in the way of excitement.

SOUTH AFRICA		NEW ZEALAND	
G. Kirsten c Nash b Astle	82	M. J. Horne c Pollock b Kallis	12
H. H. Gibbs b Allott	91	N. J Astle c Cullinan b Kallis	9
L. Klusener b Larsen	4	C. D. McMillan c Gibbs b Cronje	23
J. H. Kallis not out	53	S. P. Fleming (capt) c Pollock b Cronje	42
D. J. Cullinan c & b Cairns	0	R. G. Twose c Cronje b Klusener	35
W. J. Cronje (capt) not out	39	C. L. Cairns b Klusner	17
Extras lb11 w3 nb4	18	A. C. Parore (wk) run out	3
(50 overs)	5-287	C. Z. Harris not out	27
Did not bat: S. M. Pollock, M. V. Boucher (wk), S. Elworthy,		D. J. Nash b Pollock	9
A. A. Donald		G. R. Larsen not out	13
1/176 2/187 3/228 4/229 5/283		Extras lb9 w11 nb3	23
Bowling: Allott 10-0-42-1; Nash 8-0-44-0; Cairns 7-0-55-1;		(50 overs)	8-213
Larsen 9-0-47-1; Harris 10-0-59-0; Astle 6-0-29-1		Did not bat: G. I. Allott	
		1/20 2/34 3/93 4/107 5/144 6/148 7/171 8/194	
		Bowling: Pollock 10-1-29-1; Kallis 6-2-15-2;	
		Elworthy 8-0-35-0; Donald 10-0-42-0; Klusener 9-0-46-2;	
		Cronje 7-0-37-2	

Umpires: S. Venkataraghaven I. Robinson

Toss: South Africa   Points: South Africa 2 New Zealand 0

FRIDAY 11 JUNE 1999
THE OVAL, LONDON: PAKISTAN vs ZIMBABWE- SUPER SIXES N0.7
PAKISTAN WON BY 148 RUNS

The ease with which Pakistan demolished Zimbabwe quickly put to rest the belief that Wasim Akram's side might be a spent force in the 'Carnival of Cricket'. It did suggest that Zimbabwe's exalted position of likely semi-finalists flattered them. Pakistan were now assured of their spot in the final four and their mercurial talent suggested two more wins were well within their capability.

Saqlain Mushtaq grabbed much of the attention when he finished the match with the second ever hattrick in the World Cup, but it was Saeed Anwar's 103 supported by some effective middle-order hitting that put Pakistan in an unassailable position against Zimbabwe. At least Zimbabwe, unlike New Zealand the previous day against South Africa, were able to let everyone get away early from Kennington by being dismissed in the 41st over. That they still might make the semi-finals even though their tournament record stood at three and a half wins from eight starts was a reflection of the serious problems with the current points system.

It was an overcast morning at The Oval, the London skyline views from the loftier perches in the ground taking on a grim grey visage. Pakistan, always well supported, were quickly into their stride after Wasim Akram won the toss and batted. Saeed Anwar, despite a few attractive cameos, still without a major innings in the tournament was quickly meting out punishment, and he found an able ally in fellow opener Wajahatullah Wasti. They rattled on 95 at five per over. Then when Wasti was caught at third man off Guy Whittall and Ijaz Ahmed fell foul of the Pakistanis inability to judge a run as a batting pair, Inzamam supported Saeed as he continued on his fluent way.

He had a life at 18, dropped at slip by Alistair Campbell, but his 11th boundary, a sumptuous cover drive off Henry Olonga completed the left-hander's fine century. He was caught soon after mistiming a pull and with regular late order hero, Moin Khan missing out for once, it was left to Shahid Afridi to provide the crowning fireworks. He hit two sixes, an astonishing hit over cover off Heath Streak and a more orthodox clout off Paul Strang over long on. Pakistan had 9-271.

Zimbabwe were never in the hunt in the chase for 272. Shoaib Akhtar, bursting to reach 100mph, got as far as 93 in his opening spell and shattered Grant Flower's stumps in the process. Only Neil Johnson, starting to suffer from his all-round exertions throughout eight big matches, was able to prosper against Pakistan's dynamic attack. He was the sixth batsmen out in the 29th over.

Eleven overs later, Saqlain bowled the first ball of his seventh over to Olonga. The paceman stepped forward, heaved, missed and was just unable to beat Moin's glovework with his massive follow through. Next ball Adam Huckle moved out to drive and was beaten by a top-spinner to make it two stumpings in two balls. 'Pommie' Mbangwa, who had been brought in the side as an extra bowler clearly only had survival on his mind as he faced Saqlain's hattrick ball.

He played back and across. It was Saqlain's arm ball. Mbangwa was beaten on the outside and struck on his bent back thigh. A thousand Pakistani screaming appeals rent the air, Steve Bucknor nodded his head and slowly raised his finger. Saqlain, the young off-spinning maestro, playing on the ground where he had done so well as Surrey's overseas professional, had joined Chetan Sharma as the only World Cup bowlers to take a hattrick.

PAKISTAN		ZIMBABWE	
Saeed Anwar c A. Flower b Olonga	103	N. C. Johnson lbw b Azhar Mahmood	54
Wajahatullah Wasti c Huckle b G. J. Whittall	40	G. W. Flower b Shoaib Akhtar	2
Ijaz Ahmed run out	5	M. W. Goodwin c Shahid Afridi b Abdul Razzaq	4
Inzamam-ul-Haq st A. Flower b Strang	21	A. Flower (wk) b Abdul Razzaq	4
Wasim Akram (capt) lbw b Huckle	0	A. D. R. Campbell (capt) c Wasim Akram b Abdul Razzaq	3
Moin Khan (wk) run out	13	G. J. Whittall c Shahid Afridi b Azhar Mahmood	16
Shahid Afridi c Johnson b Olonga	37	H. H. Streak not out	16
Azhar Mahmood c A. Flower b Streak	2	P. A. Strang c Azhar Mahmood b Shoaib Akhtar	5
Abdul Razzaq b Streak	0	H. K. Olonga st Moin Khan b Saqlain Mushtaq	5
Saqlain Mushtaq not out	17	A. G. Huckle st Moin Khan b Saqlain Mushtaq	0
Shoaib Akhtar not out	1	M. Mbangwa lbw b Saqlain Mushtaq	0
Extras b6 lb3 w20 nb3	32	Extras lb3 w7 nb4	14
(50 overs)	9-271	(40.3 overs)	123

1/95 2/116 3/183 4/194 5/195 6/228 7/231 8/231 9/260

Bowling: Streak 10-0-63-1; Mbangwa 8-0-28-0; G. J. Whittall 8-1-39-1; Olonga 5-0-38-2; Huckle 10-0-43-1; G. W. Flower 2-0-13-0; Strang 7-0 -38-1

1/12 2/28 3/46 4/50 5/83 6/95 7/110 8/123 9/123 10/123

Bowling: Wasim Akram 6-1-23-0; Shoaib Akhtar 7-1-22-2; Abdul Razzaq 9-1-25-3; Saqlain Mushtaq 6.3-1-16-3; Shahid Afridi 4-0-20-0; Azhar Mahmood 8-1-14-2

Umpires: S. Bucknor D. Orchard

Toss: Pakistan   Points: Pakistan 2 Zimbabwe 0

SATURDAY 12 JUNE 1999
TRENT BRIDGE, NOTTINGHAM: INDIA vs NEW ZEALAND- SUPER SIXES No.8
NEW ZEALAND WON BY 5 WICKETS

There was unconfined Kiwi joy at their team's win over India and promotion to the semi-finals of the 1999 World Cup. What is more they achieved it by outbatting the batting side of the tournament, India.

They had to chase a competitive total and relaunch the innings after a late afternoon rain interruption before reaching their target of 252 with just 10 balls to spare. Win or lose, India were saying their farewells at Nottingham. Neutrals would miss their sensational strokeplay, but inconsistencies had dogged them and disappointed their passionate supporters.

They had first use of the Trent Bridge wicket after Mohammad Azharuddin decided to bat after winning the toss. He was another making cricketing farewells this day. His prize opener Sachin Tendulkar got a couple of early shots away then missed a full and straight in-slanting delivery from Dion Nash. Rahul Dravid also prospered but only briefly, Stephen Fleming holding a hot gully chance. When Saurav Ganguly's slow display was ended by a Geoff Allott leg-stump yorker Ajay Jadeja, supported by his captain and Robin Singh had to be at their best to ensure the innings went its distance and reached a satisfactory conclusion of 6-251.

Jadeja's 90-ball attacking display was Man of the Match material until Matthew Horne and Roger Twose proved his equal in value to their side. Their 83 run stand quelled the uncertainty of being 3-90 in the 22nd over. Horne had been run out by substitute Nikhil Chopra when rain stopped play for 75 minutes at 4-194. That emptied most of the ground. The Indian fans had been told by the PA announcer they were making too much noise, anyway. Perhaps the ground's neighbours had complained.

New Zealand soon lost Chris Cairns when play restarted, and the threat of Kiwi jitters still existed. Their previous totals in the tournament had not been higher than 220. Roger Twose was joined by Adam Parore with 35 needed off five overs. He had hardly batted in the 'Carnival of Cricket'. Now he hit five fours in 14 balls, including three in four balls off Javagal Srinath in the 48th over to take New Zealand to the brink of victory. When Man of the Match,Twose swung Anil Kumble away to the rope at square leg next over Steve Rixon's boys had struck a blow for the solid work ethic and confirmed a treasured semi-final berth.

INDIA		NEW ZEALAND	
S. R. Tendulkar b Nash	16	M. J. Horne run out	74
S. C. Ganguly b Allott	29	N. J Astle c Dravid b Mohanty	26
R. Dravid c Fleming b Cairns	29	C. D. McMillan c Dravid b Srinath	6
A. Jadeja c Parore b Cairns	76	S. P. Fleming (capt) c Mongia b Mohanty	15
M. Azharuddin (capt) c Parore b Larsen	30	R. G. Twose not out	60
R. R. Singh run out	27	C. L. Cairns c Kumble b Singh	11
J. Srinath not out	6	A. C. Parore (wk) not out	26
N. R. Mongia (wk) not out	3	Extras b4 lb11 w16 nb4	35
Extras b4 lb8 w13 nb10	35	(48.2 overs)	5-253
(50 overs)	6-251		

Did not bat: A. Kumble, B. K V. Prasad, D. S. Mohanty

Did not bat: C. Z. Harris, D. J. Nash, G. R. Larsen, G. I. Allott

1/26 2/71 3/97 4/187 5/241 6/243

1/45 2/60 3/90 4/173 5/218

Bowling: Allott 10-1-33-1; Nash 10-1-57-1; Cairns 10-0-44-2; Larsen 10-0-40-1; Astle 7-0-49-0; Harris 3-0-16-0

Bowling: Srinath 10-1-49-1; Mohanty 10-0-41-2; Prasad 10-0-44-0; Singh 4-0-27-1; Ganguly 2-0-15-0; Kumble 9.2-0-48-0; Tendulkar 3-0-14-0

Umpires: D.Hair D.Shepherd

Toss: India   Points: New Zealand 2 India 0

SUNDAY 13 JUNE 1999
HEADINGLEY, LEEDS: AUSTRALIA vs SOUTH AFRICA - SUPER SIXES No.9
AUSTRALIA WON BY 5 WICKETS

A few English grumblers suggested after the previous day's largely featureless match at Nottingham that the tent pegs were already being loosened at the 'Carnival of Cricket', mainly because their own side was now missing from the action. If that were so Australia and South Africa banged those pegs back into concrete after this last over cliff-hanging masterpiece at Headingley.

For Steve Waugh and his team the mission was clear enough, win or tie and they would progress through to the semi-finals. A loss against the Proteas and they were on their way home, leaving Zimbabwe to take up the position of semi-eminence. In the end the Australian captain had to do the job himself. He had a few helpers but his second century in 266 limited-over internationals showed an inner strength of determination to succeed well beyond that of ordinary mortals. It even brought a tear to the eye of some hard-edged Aussies.

Tony Greig's pitch report prediction that the Headingley wicket would provide a batsman's match was accurate. There was occasional variation in the bounce. Mostly, however, batsmen hit confidently through the ball. One to take advantage was South African opener Herschelle Gibbs whose sweet strokes throughout his 44 overs at the crease brought him his country's first 100 of the competition.

South Africa, who went in first after Hansie Cronje won the toss, were without Jacques Kallis, resting strained stomach muscles. His batting was not missed. Later though, his bowling was. Even when Shane Warne, still hitting the headlines for the wrong reasons, picked up both Daryl Cullinan and Cronje in the 33rd over the Proteas looked likely to get a big total. Cullinan had come in at number three after Gary Kirsten had been caught at backward point driving Damien Fleming. He cracked Tom Moody for six over long on and added 95 with Gibbs before swinging across the line at his nemisis.

Jonty Rhodes and Gibbs ran like the speed of light "between wickets during their seven-per-over, 78-run partnership while Lance Klusener, even though his final over dismissal reduced his tournament batting average again, gave another joyous exhibition of slogging. He began the 50th over of the innings with an enormous drive that sent the ball way into the crowd at long off. A totally mistimed slice was beautifully held by Shane Warne running backwards at point a few balls later, but by then South Africa had 271 and Australia were up against it.

There was a fateful looking similiarity to this target for Australia and the one they had just failed to reach against Pakistan back on May 23rd. The comparison went even further when Steve Elworthy, going around the wicket got through Adam Gilchrist's concrete footed defence as easily and nearly as early as Wasim Akram had done three weeks before almost to the minute. The removal of the wicketkeeper batsman's stumps left Australia 1-6 and it was 2-20 a few moments later when Mark Waugh and Ricky Ponting failed to coordinate their running which left 'Junior' Waugh well short of his ground when Nicky Boje's return reached Mark Boucher. In the same over a topedged hook by Pointing carried all the way over Boucher's head to the sightscreen for six.

Damien Martyn, in the side for Darren Lehmann who still carried an injured finger, made no real impression before badly mistiming a pull. So at 3-48, Australia's World Cup campaign lay close to ruin when the captain strode to the wicket. After a period of consolidation Waugh and Ponting attacked Klusener and quickly blasted left-arm spinner Boje out of the attack. The left-arm spinner conceded 17 in one over. Cronje had to fill in the extra overs and he, too, was expensive. Ponting reached his 50 in 88 balls, Waugh brought up his half century in 47 balls with a superb cover drive off Shaun Pollock.

It was brilliant batting, however the need to maintain it was critical as the required run rate remained high. Australians gasped and South Africans cringed when Gibbs tried to throw up the ball before properly controlling an easy catch off Waugh at mid wicket when the Australian captain was 56. Finally Ponting skied a leg-side shot to end the 126 run stand. Now with Michael Bevan, Waugh pressed on. Elworthy, so damaging early, was creamed for six over mid wicket. The one knee slog putting him on his back and taking him from 91 to 97. A more restrained push to mid-on brought up the 100 in 91 balls, the innings of an utter champion.

There was little time for self congratulation as a run was needed every ball. Bevan had done his part in a stand of 73, but in Cronje's final over he sent an easy catch to Cullinan, leaving a winner impossible to pick.

There were hits and misses and oohs and ahs. In the big crowd the supporters of both country's were hard to distinguish as both were equally nervous and both were draped and painted in green and gold. The final equation came down to eight runs from the final over to be bowled by Shaun Pollock. A scrambled two from the first ball was followed by Tom Moody's backfoot slash that gave the ball just enough oomph to trickle over the point boundary ahead of the diving South African fieldsman. Two more singles and Australia had won, Steve Waugh at last showed some emotion with repeated punchings of the air as he ran the winning single.

There was joy unconfined on the Australian balcony. The captain was also Man of the Match. He said he had a point to prove. Both sides had go through it all again in just four days at Edgbaston. "If this was anything to go by it's going to be one hell of a game on Thursday," said Cronje. He didn't know the half of it.

SOUTH AFRICA		AUSTRALIA	
G. Kirsten c Ponting b Reiffel	21	M. E. Waugh run out	5
H. H. Gibbs b McGrath	101	A. C. Gilchrist (wk) b Elworthy	5
D. J. Cullinan b Warne	50	R. T. Ponting c Donald b Klusener	69
W. J. Cronje (capt) lbw b Warne	0	D. R. Martyn c Boje b Elworthy	11
J. N. Rhodes c M. E. Waugh b Fleming	39	S. R. Waugh (capt) not out	120
L. Klusener c Warne b Fleming	36	M. G. Bevan c Cullinan b Cronje	27
S. M. Pollock b Fleming	3	T. M. Moody not out	15
M. V. Boucher (wk) not out	0	Extras lb6 w7 nb7	20
Extras lb7 w8 nb6	21	(49.4 overs)	5-272
(50 overs)	7-271	Did not bat: S. K. Warne, P. R. Reiffel, D. W. Fleming,	
Did not bat: N. Boje, S. Elworthy, A. A. Donald		G. D. McGrath	
1/45 2/140 3/141 4/219 5/250 6/271 7/271		1/6 2/20 3/48 4/174 5/247	
Bowling: McGrath 10-0-49-1; Fleming 10-0-57-3;		Bowling: Pollock 9.4-0-45-0; Elworthy 10-1-46-2;	
Reiffel 9-0-47-1; Moody 8-1-56-0; Warne 10-1-33-2;		Donald 10-0-43-0; Klusener 10-0-53-1; Cronje 7-0-50-1;	
Bevan 3-0-22-0		Boje 3-0-29-0	

Umpires: S.Venkataraghaven P.Willey

Toss: South Africa   Points: Australia 2 South Africa 0

WEDNESDAY 16 JUNE 1999
OLD TRAFFORD, MANCHESTER: NEW ZEALAND vs PAKISTAN - 1st SEMI-FINAL
PAKISTAN WON BY 9 WICKETS

This rematch of the Auckland semi-final of 1992 was almost a clash of cricketing ideologies. Steady, hard-working, well-prepared New Zealand against mercurial, talented, controversial, inconsistent Pakistan. And like the memorable match at Eden Park the team selected from a population of 120 million proved too good for the one selected from three million.

Wasim Akram's star line-up still managed to confound the critics with a mixed performance by their bowlers, the branch of the game considered to be their strength, and a brilliant one by their top-order batsmen, thought to be the Pakistani weak link. The joy at their team reaching the prestigious final was too much for some lime-green fans to bear and the end of the match was once again interrupted by the over zealous.

No-one doubted the Kiwis were the underdogs against one of the best performed teams in the competition and it was the lovely Manchester weather that surprised more than Nathan Astle and Craig McMillan's struggles after Stephen Fleming decided to bat. Astle had his leg stump ripped out by Shoaib Akhtar and McMillan's tentative push at Akram gave a catch behind to Moin Khan.

Matthew Horne hit the ball as sweetly as he had against India. However Abdur Razzaq's yorker honed in and then neatly removed the opener's middle stump to leave New Zealand a shaky 3-58. Neither of the two left-handers, Roger Twose nor Fleming looked at their absolute best, however they were able to put on 94 with a mixture of edges, good shots and plenty of free offerings from the Pakistanis as the wide and no-ball count mounted.

When the Kiwis reached 3-152 in the 34th over Pakistan were just starting to slip. Inzamam-ul-Haq had had a couple of fielding fluffs on the third man boundary and Fleming had just hit two fine boundaries. Shoaib went around the wicket and sent down an unplayable in-swinging yorker than crashed the leg-stump of the New Zealand captain out of the ground.

The pattern stayed the same for the remainder of the innings. Pakistani misfields, dropped catches, wides and no balls punctuated by an occasional piece of brilliance. Ijaz Ahmed held a stunning one handed catch to his right when Twose, slashed Abdur to the gully. Chris Harris suffered the indignity and rarity of playing too early at Shoaib's slower ball. Chris Cairns used the lofted cover drive to good effect through the last few overs. As Pakistan had failed to chase India's 227 on the same ground the previous week, New Zealand's final total of 7-241, with extras top score, was quite a respectable one.

Or so it seemed until Saeed Anwar and Wajahatullah Wasti began striking the ball with complete assurance. The New Zealand attack were soon a spent force. With Geoff Allott unable to extend his record for the number of wickets in a World Cup no real pressure could be exerted on the Pakistani openers. Therefore they blossomed. Anwar showed he was back to his best form and with Wasti they were soon clocking up personal and partnership milestones.

Even as the possibility of a berth in the Final receded New Zealand maintained their enthusiasm in the field. There was little hint of a breakthough, though. When the score reached 160 Anwar and Wasti broke their country's 24-year-old World Cup first-wicket record. At 187 they bettered the overall World Cup record set in 1996 by Gary Kirsten and Andrew Hudson against Holland. A mistimed big hit by Wasti off Cairns finally terminated the partnership on 194 in the 41st over.

Ijaz kept the runs flowing while Anwar concentrated on reaching his second consecutive World Cup 100. As the victory loomed the behaviour of certain members of the crowd changed from noisy to intrusive. Repeated interruptions drew out the finale, spoiled the conclusion for the rest of the crowd and the players and drew attention again to the inadequacy of the security arrangements.

The Pakistanis were rightfully joyous at reaching the Final and at their 'Rawalpindi express' being named Man of the Match. However, it was to be wondered how some of them would restrain themselves at Sunday's emotive occasion at Lord's.

NEW ZEALAND		PAKISTAN	
M. J. Horne b Abdul Razzaq	35	Saeed Anwar not out	113
N. J. Astle b Shoaib Akhtar	3	Wajahatullah Wasti c Fleming b Cairns	84
C. D. McMillan c Moin Khan b Wasim Akram	3	Ijaz Ahmed not out	28
S. P. Fleming (capt) b Shoaib Akhtar	41	Extras lb3 w7 nb7	17
R. G. Twose c Ijaz b Abdul Razzaq	46	(47.3 overs)	1-242
C. L. Cairns not out	44	Did not bat: Inzamam-ul-Haq, Abdul Razzaq, Shahid Afridi,	
C. Z. Harris b Shoaib Akhtar	16	Moin Khan (wk), Wasim Akram (capt), Azhar Mahmood,	
A. C. Parore (wk) b Wasim Akram	0	Saqlain Mushtaq, Shoaib Akhtar	
D. J. Nash not out	6	1/194	
Extras b4 lb14 w17 nb12	47	Bowling: Allott 9-0-41-0; Nash 5-0-34-0; Larsen 10-0-40-0;	
(50 overs)	7-241	Cairns 8-0-33-1; Harris 6-0-31-0; Astle 7.3-0-41-0;	
Did not bat: G. R. Larsen, G. I. Allott		McMillan 2-0-19-0	

1/20 2/38 3/58 4/152 5/176 6/209 7/211

Bowling: Wasim Akram 10-0-45-2; Shoaib Akhtar 10-0-55-3; Abdul Razzaq 8-0-28-2; Saqlain Mushtaq 8-0-36-0; Azhar Mahmood 9-0-32-0; Shahid Afridi 5-0-27-0

Umpires: D. Hair P. Willey
Toss: New Zealand

THURSDAY 17 JUNE 1999
EDGBASTON, BIRMINGHAM: AUSTRALIA vs SOUTH AFRICA - 2nd SEMI-FINAL
MATCH TIED (AUSTRALIA QUALIFY FOR FINAL DUE TO A HIGHER FINISH IN TABLE)

Nothing, not even the extraordinary match at Leeds a couple of days before, could prepare anyone for a finish like this. In scenes of complete cricketing madness the semi-final between Australia and South Africa resulted in the World Cup's first tie.

The result was as good as a win for Australia and a loss for South Africa. As such one nation was joyous, another heartbroken. No limited-overs cricket match anywhere on the globe at any time can have matched the excruciating excitement of this game at Edgbaston where brilliance and heroism were mixed in equal doses with comic tragedy. People danced and sang in front of their televisions and winter heaters at 3.30am in Australia as if they too had been on the terraces in the Hollies Stand. Against the odds Steve Waugh's side had won five and tied one of the seven matches they had to take on the trot to win the World Cup.

The tournament favourites were now going home, shaking their head and wondering how they could have missed out on the Final. The feeling was that with Jacques Kallis back in the side and on the rebound after the thrilling loss at Leeds, South Africa might just have the edge this time.

That seemed clear cut when the South African pacemen did their work on the Australian top order. Hansie Cronje had won the toss and sent the Australians in to bat. Shaun Pollock responded with a lifting delivery in the first over which cut back and brushed Mark Waugh's retreating gloves on the way through to Mark Boucher.

Even though, the ground was only three quarters full at this stage on a cool and cloudy morning, many fans being caught up in a good old-fashioned Birmingham traffic jam outside the ground, the atmosphere inside Edgbaston was already electric, this being the only cricket ground in England to give the feel of a stadium. Ricky Ponting's response after a couple of assessment overs, captured the atmosphere perfectly when he hooked Steve Elworthy for six and followed it with another hook for four. Adam Gilchrist, a noted aggressor still out of form, concentrated on defence until he let loose at Elworthy, too, and plonked him over the rope at long on with nothing more than a short arm jab.

Ponting's habit throughout the World Cup was to play short, brilliant innings. Only at Leeds had he gone on to complete a half century. Here he greeted Allan Donald's introduction for the 14th over with a bent kneed cover drive on the rise which slapped a catch straight to Gary Kirsten. Suitably inspired, later in the same over Donald got one to lift and cut away enough to make Darren Lehmann's return to the side an unprofitable one.

That was 3-58 and just 10 runs later Gilchrist's slice to Donald off Kallis at third man left Australia in deep trouble and Steve Waugh had to do it all over again. He and Michael Bevan concentrated so hard on defence that just six runs came in nine overs. Waugh survived a precarious run out scare by a whisker then, finally, with Elworthy back in the attack for the 32nd over, hit two boundaries, one either side of the wicket. The Australian captain followed that by twice lofting Klusener straight, once for four, once for six. This was a champion batting like a millionaire and showing a mental strength the equal of any man ever to play the game. His 50, completed with a great cover drive off Pollock, kept Australia in the match. Just as quickly Pollock turned it back the Protea's way in the 40th over having Waugh caught behind on the dab and Tom Moody lbw third ball to a sharp off-cutter. Big Tom was so plumb umpire Venkataraghaven's finger almost beat the appeal.

Shane Warne slogged and sliced a few and Bevan pushed here and there to add 49 before Donald and Pollock ended the innings in a flash. They shared nine victims for the innings. Four wickets fell for six in the final two overs and Australia had to be satisfied with that same undistinguished total they had made in their defeat at the hands of New Zealand back in Cardiff, 213.

On a beautiful English summer's afternoon, the full ground a picture, Herschelle Gibbs and Gary Kirsten opened with a confidence which suggested 214 was a formality. Gibbs was in especially commanding form, and 48 had been raised in 12 overs when Steve Waugh introduced Shane Warne. His second ball shattered any Protean complacency at a stroke. A fizzing leg-break drifted inside Gibb's defensive push then bit back outside it to clip the top of the off-stump. 'Ball from hell two' was the call, and there was little difference in its lethal potency and impact on a game to the 1993 version. Warne screamed at his teammates, "Come on!" charging their adrenalin while knowing he had to kept a hold on his own emotions. In his next over the leg-spinner induced an ugly slog from Kirsten and rattled the stumps again. When Hansie Cronje was given out second ball caught at slip to a yorker length delivery South Africa had slumped to 3-53.

It was 4-61 when Daryl Cullinan fell foul of an accurate Bevan throw and his own tardy running. Like Steve Waugh and Bevan for Australia, so now did Kallis and Jonty Rhodes have to re-build the South African cause. Their 84 runs effort did just that, but the consumption of 20 overs, Warne hardly conceding a run, ensured the finish would be a tight one. When Paul Reiffel ended the partnership Warne was brought back as the requirement crept up to nine per over.

The 45th over signalled the start of the madness. Kallis was dropped at deep mid off by Reiffel. Pollock responded with clouts for six and four, then Kallis, who had changed his bat prior to this over was caught at short cover by Steve Waugh. Damien Fleming was recalled for the 46th over. Klusener greeted him with a smack to mid wicket for four then from the fifth ball Pollock played on a yorker as he backed away to drive.

Mark Boucher was troubled by the pressure. He struggled to give Klusener the strike and three dots balls in a row in the 48th over increased the pressure even more, if that were possible. Klusener, at last given the chance to swing at a couple, sliced an off drive over point for four and hoisted a ball to mid wicket for two, Moody opting against the attempt at a catch and saving the four instead.

Eighteen were needed from 12 balls as McGrath began the 49th over. Boucher lost his middle stump to the second ball backing away and never looking like coping with the situation. A gloved single to Elworthy gave Klusener the strike, but next ball the effort to keep him there meant a risky two and Reiffel's throw to the bowler's end was spot on. The agony was extended by repeated third umpire replays to ensure McGrath's hand had not broken the stumps.

Nine for 198 left South Africa needing 16 off 8 balls, seemingly out of even Klusener's league. Reiffel relieved to have made retribution for dropping Kallis may have thought so, too, but only for a moment. McGrath's second last delivery was a full toss. Klusener struck it baseball style. It flew flat and straight to Reiffel at long on. There was a suggestion that the shot had been mistimed, but when it struck Reiffel's upstretched hands he was flung back and the ball forced its way through and over the rope behind the fallen and crestfallen paceman for six. Steve Waugh chewed and cursed. Klusener took an easy single from McGrath's final delivery.

Fleming, who had bowled Courtney Walsh to give Australia a five run victory in the 1996 semi-final, had nine runs to play with this time. Two balls later it was one. He went around the wicket and bowled a full length. Klusener creamed both balls for four, one to cover point, the other extra cover. Thrilling, awesome shots, both.

Now, surely the match was won. There were four balls left and the scores were tied, although South Africa actually had to defeat Australia as they had finished below them in the Super Six table. Fleming went over the wicket. Klusener mistimed a pull to the third ball. Lehmann charged in. Donald backed up too far! There was an underarm throw and a reprieve as the ball shaved the stumps with the big South African paceman well out of his ground.

The fourth ball was a fuller delivery which Klusener mistimed again. The ball rolled up the wicket and Klusener ran. Donald was watching the ball and stayed in his crease. Mark Waugh's back hand flick went to Fleming who rolled it to Gilchrist. Donald dropped his bat and realised far too late that he must run. It is a token. He is not in the picture when the Australian wicketkeeper removes a stump and charges in to join his ecstatic teammates.

There is astonishment, bewilderment, heartbreak and uncontrolled joy, but thankfully no invasion. Australia dance off Edgbaston together in celebration. Cronje and his team are shattered. "The best cricket game I've ever played," says Steve Waugh. Cronje is gracious, but his face tells the story of the greatest disappointment of his career.

Shane Warne is named Man of the Match.

AUSTRALIA		SOUTH AFRICA	
A. C. Gilchrist (wk) c Donald b Kallis	20	G. Kirsten b Warne	18
M. E. Waugh c Boucher b Pollock	0	H. H. Gibbs b Warne	30
R. T. Ponting c Kirsten b Donald	37	D. J. Cullinan run out	6
D. S. Lehmann c Boucher b Donald	1	W. J. Cronje (capt) c M. E. Waugh b Warne	0
S. R. Waugh (capt) c Boucher b Pollock	56	J. H. Kallis c S. R. Waugh b Warne	53
M. G. Bevan c Boucher b Pollock	65	J. N. Rhodes b Reiffel	43
T. M. Moody lbw b Pollock	0	S. M. Pollock b Fleming	20
S. K. Warne c Cronje b Pollock	18	L. Klusener not out	31
P. R. Reiffel b Donald	0	M. V. Boucher (wk) b McGrath	5
D. W. Fleming b Donald	0	S. Elworthy run out	1
G. D. McGrath not out	0	A. A. Donald run out	0
Extras b1 lb6 w3 nb6	16	Extras lb1 w5	6
(49.2 overs)	213	(49.4 overs)	213

1/3 2/54 3/58 4/68 5/158 6/158 7/207 8/207 9/207 10/213

1/48 2/53 3/53 4/61 5/145 6/175 7/183 8/196 9/198 10/213

Bowling: Pollock 9.2-1-36-5; Elworthy 10-0-59-0; Kallis 10-2-27-1; Donald 10-1-32-4; Klusener 9-1-50-0; Cronje 1-0-2-0

Bowling: McGrath 10-0-51-1; Fleming 8.4-1-40-1; Reiffel 8-0-28-1; Warne 10-4-29-4; M. E. Waugh 8-0-37-0; Moody 5-0-27-0

Umpires: D. Shepherd S. Venkataraghaven
Toss: South Africa

SUNDAY 20 JUNE 1999
LORD'S, LONDON: AUSTRALIA vs PAKISTAN - WORLD CUP FINAL
AUSTRALIA WON BY 8 WICKETS

Australia, widely regarded as the strongest Test side in the world, claimed the title as the best limited-overs team, as well, with a clinical demolition of Pakistan in the most one-sided of all World Cup Finals. It was a margin of superority no-one could have expected, as Australia were brilliant and Pakistan very, very ordinary.

The game thrilled all Australians and maybe a few Indians, but no-one else. In the great cities of Pakistan, such as Lahore and Karachi, there was disappointment beyond the scope of a mere cricket match. The national shame manifested itself in burning effigies of Wasim Akram and tomato-bespattered giant screens which had been erected to watch the Final. The Pakistani captain suggested he was going to Mecca after the humiliating defeat for divine guidance and prayer. An article in an Australian paper suggested the Pakistan Prime Minister had told Akram he would be better off not coming home if Pakistan did not win the World Cup, anyway. His team, full of inexperienced if talented cricketers, failed miserably to cope with Australia's aggression and expertise. They had reached the Final on merit, but on the big day were second best by a long way.

Neutrals could only admire the great play of the Australians. There was precious little else to excite them or justify the money they had spent to attend the event. Ringside seats were expensive and the fight was over after five one-sided rounds. The decision? A knockout. It was a big let down after the two wonderful games between Australia and South Africa. As the South Africa vs Pakistan and Australia vs Pakistan matches had also been close and provided plenty of thrills and spills earlier in the competition the expectation was the Final would do the same.

What turned out to be an anti-climax began the same way with an early morning shower delaying the start by half an hour. It dampened the sense of aniticipation for a time even though there was a real buzz outside the Lord's as fans desperately sought a stray available ticket or some sort of elevated vantage point on the buildings around St Johns Wood.

Soon enough the skies cleared and the covers were removed. Both squads were introduced to the Duke of Edinburgh and announced teams unchanged from their semi-final victories. The removal of the covers revealed a flat and very hard wicket. Wasim Akram called correctly at the toss and elected to bat. Steve Waugh said he would have done the same as he like his opposite number believed chasing a substantial total would be difficult given the pressure of the occasion. However, the Australian captain also said he was not unhappy to lose the toss.

Thirty minutes after the originally scheduled start time umpires Steve Bucknor and David Shepherd, given the ultimate honour for their profession, shook hands as they walked onto the now sun bathed turf signalling that the World Cup Final was about to get underway. They were followed by Steve Waugh, proudly leading his Australians onto a cricket ground where they have rarely been beaten. Saeed Anwar took strike to Glenn McGrath who opened the bowling from the pavilion end.

After safely negotiating McGrath's two opening deliveries, which showed how much bounce was in the wicket, Saeed cracked the third for four to the Mound Stand boundary at point. Damien Fleming shared the new-ball from the Nursery End and he too got the ball to hit Adam Gilchrist's gloves while still on the rise. There was also some movement for the Victorian, but his early control was poor and Saeed took a toll in his second over. He clipped the ball off his legs down the Lord's slope then off the back foot through the covers for a second four.

Twenty-one from four overs indicated a satisfactory start for Pakistan, but Saeed's partner, Wajahatullah Wasti was far from settled. He tried to guide McGrath's fourth delivery from his third over wide of slips only to lose control of the shot as the ball lifted. It flew in the air to where third slip should have been. Mark Waugh at second slip took off in a fashion that would not have disgraced Superman and, still horizontal, held a stunning two-handed catch.

That was a setback for Pakistan. When Saeed, who had just stopped the game for several minutes to change the grip on his bat, hit a drive onto his leg, thence onto the stumps from the first ball of the Fleming's next over they were 2-21 and showing bad signs. McGrath was pin point in his accuracy and after the opening over boundary conceded just another two runs in five overs. Ijaz Ahmed and Abdur Razzaq held firm and looked to score more freely when McGrath and Fleming were relieved by Paul Reiffel and Tom Moody.

Reiffel's second ball beat Gilchrist down the leg-side and hurried away for four wides. Ijaz pulled Moody for four then cracked Reiffel through the covers to raise the Pakistani 50. Nine runs later Abdur overdid the turn of aggression when his attempted hit for six over long off off Reiffel went straight to McGrath. To the utter amazement of everyone, including the batsman and fieldsman, McGrath dropped the absolute sitter. Steve Waugh cursed and chewed harder on his gum.

Fortunately for McGrath the young Pakistani all-rounder failed to take advantage of the let-off and holed out to cover, giving a low catch to Steve Waugh off Moody. Pakistan were 3-68 in the 20th over. Shane Warne replaced Moody at the Nursery End and Steve Waugh crowded the new batsman Inzamam-ul-Haq. There was no second-ball miracle this time, however, in his next over he beat Ijaz with a big spinner then bowled him with one that hurried through his back foot defence.

Moin Khan had been Pakistan's most consistent batsman in the 1999 World Cup and he started in positive fashion. Warne, though was in irrepressible form and a lunging defensive push by the wicketkeeper batsman was edged through to Gilchrist. The first ball of the 28th over had given the leg-spinner his 200th limited-over international wicket and left Pakistan precariously placed at 5-91.

There was no evidence that they would be able to stem the tide of Australian dominance, either. When Inzamam was unluckily given out caught behind, pushing out at Reiffel the slide continued. The last recognised batsman was gone. The all-rounders Shahid Afridi, Azhar Mahmood and Wasim Akram were not able to show the brilliance they were capable of, succumbing to a combination of the pressure of the Final and Australia's on-going excellence. Afridi was lbw sweeping, Azhar well caught and bowled driving to Moody's shins and the captain after one big six to his 'scoring corner' at wide mid-on, holed out at mid wicket trying to repeat the shot. Warne had 202 wickets in limited-over interantionals

When Ricky Ponting dived to his right and held a stunning one-handed catch at third slip to remove Saqlain Mushtaq off McGrath the Pakistani innings had come to an abrupt conclusion at the 39-over mark. Last man Shoaib Akhtar had got lost in the pavilion trying to find his way to the middle. His plight was symbolic of what had happened to his team. Extras boosted by a few strays from Fleming and Reiffel was top score. Australia, through their efficiency, had made up the 30 minutes lost to the rain so that everyone could have their lunch at the originally scheduled time. They also needed just 133 to win the World Cup.

So confident were they in Australia that during the lunch break on the network telecasting the match thoughts were already turning to how well the Australians would go at Wimbledon in 1999. There was a brief scare when Gilchrist skied a hook off Shoaib's first ball. Rather than discourage him, though, the bouncy Lord's wicket reminded Gilchrist of the WACA at home and he took 13 runs off Akrams's second over following an off drive for four with a slashing cut over point.

Some throws went astray, Mark Waugh clipped Shoaib in the air just out of the reach of square leg for four. The Pakistani heads dropped and their fans went quiet. Even the old gentleman in the beard, who had lit up some games like a Pakistani version of Antigua's Gravy, couldn't make an impact. Gilchrist slashed Shoaib over slips to the Compton/Edrich Stand for six then drove the next ball to the pavilion for four more.

Akram rang in the bowling changes, but it made not the slightest difference. The 50 was raised from the first ball of the eighth over then Gilchrist cut and pulled Azhar and Abdur for a succession of boundaries, the best of which landed one bounce into the New Grandstand and raised his 50 in 33 balls with eight fours and a six. Something finally worked for the Pakistani captain when Gilchrist smashed Saqlain's first ball straight to Inzamam at mid off. The big man's fingers stung but he held the catch. Gilchrist in a matter of minutes had killed off any lingering thoughts that the Pakistani bowlers might make up for their batting shortcomings.

Ponting joined Mark Waugh. The requirement was 58 runs off 40 overs with nine wickets standing. It was hardly imposing and Ponting was soon into the spirit of the day by taking 14 off a Shoaib over then raising the 100 in just the 15th over with a dancing on-drive for four off Saqlain. David Shepherd hardly bothered with his traditional jig when the scoreboard read 1-111, although Ponting did offer a big edge to Moin off Akram one run later.

Mark Waugh went serenly on, clocking up 1000 World Cup runs in the process to join Javed Miandad, Viv Richards and Sachin Tendulkar. He timed a couple more on-drives then sat back as Darren Lehmann cracked the first ball of the 21st over to the cover boundary to complete Australia's ridiculously easy victory. Security had cleared a pointless ground invasion a few balls before and, prepared for the finish, were able to give the players a reasonably clear passage to the pavilion at the end of the game. Waugh and Lehmann grabbed a couple of stumps each, so the Pakistanis even missed out on the souvenirs. In the crowd inflated toy kangaroos were bouncing around everywhere. The stewards were setting up the presentation area and it was just after 4.30pm.

The restrained, mostly disappointed crowd gave acknowledgement to the champions who danced and waved on the pavilion balcony. Australia were in the Lord's away dressing room, an Australian cricketer's version of Earl's Court. Shane Warne, whose four wickets in the Final gave him a World Cup record-equalling 20 wickets for the tournament, was named Man of the Match and then hinted at possible retirement. Australian Prime Minister, John Howard, stopped short of declaring a national holiday in celebration of the win. A big cricket fan, he said the nation was allowed to sit up late and watch the game on television, which was extremely generous of him. His Foreign Minister, Alexander Downer, on his way home after a failed attempt to free two Australians in Yugoslavia, might have been the envy of his boss as he watched the match from the Long Room.

At 9.30pm the Australians, joined by friends like Michael Slater, Justin Langer, Mark Taylor and Ian Healy were still celebrating. They gathered on the wicket and with Ponting hoisted upon their shoulders sang one more rendition of 'Under the Southern Cross I Stand." When they returned home there would be ticker-tape parades and civic receptions, but this moment belonged just to the players.

South African all-rounder Lance Klusener got the car as the player of the World Cup. He would have swapped it for a spot in that evening singing group.

PAKISTAN			AUSTRALIA	
Saeed Anwar b Fleming	15		M. E. Waugh not out	37
Wajahatullah Wasti c M. E. Waugh b McGrath	1		A. C. Gilchrist (wk) c Inzamam-ul-Haq b Saqlain Mushtaq	54
Abdul Razzaq c S. R. Waugh b Moody	17		R. T. Ponting c Moin Khan b Wasim Akram	24
Ijaz Ahmed b Warne	22		D. S. Lehmann not out	13
Inzamam-ul-Haq c Gilchrist b Reiffel	15		Extras lb1 w1 nb3	5
Moin Khan (wk) c Gilchrist b Warne	6		(20.1 overs)	2-133
Shahid Afridi lbw b Warne	13		Did not bat: S. R. Waugh (capt), M. G. Bevan, T. M. Moody,	
Azhar Mahmood c & b Moody	8		S. K. Warne, P. R. Reiffel, D. W. Fleming, G. D. McGrath	
Wasim Akram (capt) c S. R. Waugh b Warne	8		1/75 2/112	
Saqlain Mushtaq c Ponting b McGrath	0		Bowling: Wasim Akram 8-1-41-1; Shoaib Akhtar 4-0-37-0;	
Shoaib Akhtar not out	2		Abdul Razzaq 2-0-13-0; Azhar Mahmood 2-0-20-0;	
Extras lb10 w13 nb2	25		Saqlain Mushtaq 4.1-0-21-1	
(39 overs)	132			

1/21 2/21 3/68 4/77 5/91 6/104 7/113 8/129 9/129
10/132

Bowling: McGrath 9-3-13-2; Fleming 6-0-30-1; Reiffel 10-1-29-1; Moody 5-0-17-2; Warne 9-1-33-4

Umpires: D. Shepherd S. Bucknor

Toss: Pakistan

POST-MORTEM

Steve Waugh, even now only offering a half grin, said it was the best win by an Australian side he had ever been in. There had been a few. He was the only survivor of the 11 that had surprised the cricketing world with their first World Cup triumph in 1987, although Tom Moody had also been in that squad.

Now Australia joined the West Indies as the only nations with two trophies in their cabinet. If the 1987 win had been something of a bolt from the blue, no-one was shocked by this result. Australia had started the Final as slight favourites ahead of Pakistan. Maligned at the start of the tournament and needing to speak a few home truths within their ranks, the Australians had peaked at the right time and completely vindicated the controversial policies of their selectors in separating the Australian Test and limited-overs teams.

The 1999 World Cup had its ups and downs. The early elimination of England was a disappointment and the crowd invasions were tiresome and threatened danger. In the end, though, the weather held, the crowds were excellent and the 'Carnival of Cricket' could be considered a worthy success. Certainly the eminence of the World Cup in limited-overs cricket went from strength to strength.

CHAPTER 9

World Cup 2003: Australia conquer all hurdles

A fter previous tournaments in England, the sub-continent and the Antipodes, the ICC decided the 2003 World Cup would be held in Africa for the first time. The 2003 tournament adopted the same format as the 1999 competition. As part of spreading the cricket message worldwide, the ICC expanded the number of teams from 12 to 14, which resulted in the number of matches growing from 42 to 54, to be played over six weeks. The 10 Test-playing teams automatically qualified, while Kenya, despite not having Test status, qualified automatically as a result of their full one-day international status. The remaining three places were filled by the top three finishers in the ICC Trophy competition in Canada in 2001: the Netherlands (winner), Namibia (runner-up) and Canada (third place). Namibia would make their World Cup debut in 2003, whilst it was second time around for the Netherlands (debut in 1996) and Canada (debut in 1979).

South Africa would host 46 matches while the remaining eight games would be shared between Zimbabwe (six matches) and Kenya (two matches). As was the case for 1996 co-hosts Sri Lanka, safety concerns in Zimbabwe and Kenya resulted in a real prospect that some or all of the visiting teams would forfeit their matches.

In February 2003, Australia embarked on its first World Cup campaign without a Waugh since the ill-fated 1983 tournament. After Australia failed to reach the finals of the triangular tournament in the summer of 2001/02, Trevor Hohns and his men made the shock decision to stand Steve Waugh down as captain of the one-day side and to drop both Waughs from the team altogether. Despite the exclusion of the Waughs from the one-day side, Australia were well served by several members of the 1999 World Cup squad. Adam Gilchrist, Ricky Ponting, Damien Martyn, Darren Lehmann and Michael Bevan had performed strongly since the last World Cup. Matthew Hayden, who was building a very good one-day record after inconsistent form in his early matches in the national side, replaced Mark Waugh to partner Gilchrist at the top of the order. Andrew Symonds was in the mix as a middle-order batsman who bowled useful, dartish off-spin. Symonds was a talented and powerful batsman, but had a modest record at limited-overs internationals before the tournament. Skipper Ricky Ponting was hoping that his strong faith in Symonds would reap dividends when the pressure was on.

Once again, the Australian bowling stocks were spearheaded by all-time greats Glenn McGrath and Shane Warne. Warne made a speedy recovery from a shoulder injury suffered in a one-day match against England at the MCG in December 2002. The fast-bowling contingent was bolstered by the rapid speed of Brett Lee and the fast-medium skills of Jason Gillespie, who seemed to have shaken off persistent injuries and was enjoying a good run in the side. Steve Waugh's favourite 12th man, the ebullient workhorse Andy Bichel, was a good back up seam option who also applied calm resolve and common sense with the bat. Youngster Shane Watson was selected to perform a bowling all-rounder's role after some encouraging performances with the ball in the VB Series. Unfortunately, stress fractures in the back ruled Watson out of the Cup, to be replaced by handy Victorian all-rounder Ian Harvey. In the spin department, the enthusiastic Brad Hogg provided useful bowling support to Warne.

All in all, the first choice Australian side was a formidable side with a proven track record and they were installed as favourites, slightly ahead of South Africa, to hold the eighth World Cup aloft on 23 March. Alongside the Australians in Group A were Test rivals Pakistan, India, England and Zimbabwe and minnows Netherlands and Namibia.

Capable of brilliance on their day when the planets happened to align, the mercurial Pakistan team were a dangerous adversary of Australia in Group A. The Pakistani bowling was as dangerous as ever. Although nearing the end of his illustrious career, Wasim Akram was still a brilliant bowler and the new ball was shared with the lightning fast and temperamental Rawalpindi Express, Shoaib Akhtar. Another bowler in the twilight of his career, captain Waqar Younis, was back for his first World Cup since 1996. Although not as hostile as in his halcyon days in the 1990s, opposition batsmen would underestimate Waqar at their peril. Pakistan had good spin bowling options in Shahid Afridi, a one-day veteran at 23 for this tournament, and the talented Saqlain Mushtaq. The Pakistan batting had a blend of experience, with seasoned players Afridi, Saaed Anwar, Saleem Elahi, Inzamam-ul-Haq and Yousuf Youhana joining emerging players Taufeeq Umar and Younis Khan. With a talented, albeit unpredictable, squad, coach Richard Pybus hoped his charges would go one better than in 1999.

With a highly talented squad, India looked to be a major force in Group A. Their performances since the 1999 tournament had been inconsistent, continuing a long-term trend of being difficult opponents at home but underachievers on the road. Sachin Tendulkar, Rahul Dravid and Sourav Ganguly were the well established stars with the bat. Virender Sehwag was the up-and-coming star, a batsman with a stand and deliver style capable of demoralising bowling attacks. However, the middle-order was inexperienced and had a hint of vulnerability. Yuvraj Singh, Mohammed Kaif and Dinesh Mongia appeared promising but were unproven at the top level. Intent on bolstering their batting power, India were inclined to have Dravid keep wicket and to bat him a notch or two lower than his customary number three slot in the Test team. The Indian bowling, as was often the case in previous World Cups, included skilled spinners and seamers who were capable but lacking in firepower. In their quest to succeed in 2003, much would depend on the guile of world class leg spinner Anil Kumble and feisty offie Harbhajan Singh. The dependable Javagal Srinath was approaching the end of a long international career as India's main seamer. Zaheer Khan was in the early stages of forging a successful career as a left-armer with the ability to move the ball both ways. The inconsistent Ashish Nehra and capable all-rounder Ajit Agarkar, he of the five consecutive Test ducks against Australia fame, were the support cast in the fast-medium brigade.

Hoping to claim their first World Cup after three losses in Finals, Nasser Hussain headed up an English squad that looked sound on paper. However, England's one-day performances had been mediocre at best since the previous World Cup and the team had not won a one-day series against quality opposition in that time. The batting firepower had been weakened by the decision of Graham Thorpe to not tour due to family issues. In Thorpe's absence, Michael Vaughan was the standout batsman after an outstanding 2002/03 Ashes, which included three big hundreds. Openers Marcus Trescothick, Nick Knight, up-and-coming middle-order batsman Paul Collingwood and veteran Alec Stewart provided batting quality and a good mix of attack and defence. Approaching his 40th birthday, sometime wicketkeeper Stewart was hoping to end his limited overs career on a high.

The English selectors continued their quest for a quality all-rounder by giving Andrew Flintoff, unproven and injury-prone at this point, an opportunity. Bits-and-pieces players Ronnie Irani, Ian Blackwell and Craig White would have their roles to play. The pace contingent was led by Andrew Caddick, very impressive on his day but, like Craig McDermott, a bowler who would be regarded as very good at the end of his career, rather than great. Jimmy Anderson was still learning the caper at the highest level and Flintoff had the capacity to hurry batsmen with his bustling seamers. The "King of Spain", Ashley Giles, would be called on to keep things tight with his off-spin and to take the occasional wicket.

The surprise packets of 1999, Zimbabwe, remained a competitive outfit despite a challenging political climate under the yoke of President Mugabe. In protest of the oppression of the Mugabe government, star batsman Andy Flower and paceman Henry Olonga wore black armbands to lament the death of democracy in their country. This show of defiance would ultimately lead to both players being banned by the Zimbabwe Cricket Union. Flower Power would be an important factor to the Zimbabwe batting racking up good totals. Big-hitting all-rounder Andy Blignaut gave the line-up firepower. Blignaut was a good foil to the busy style of keeper-batsman Tatenda Taibu. There was an element of unorthodoxy in the form of Doug Marillier, an off-spinner and handy batsman, who developed a shot against the fast men where he scooped the ball to fine leg. Heath Streak was again the main man in the Zimbabwean attack, with Blignaut, Guy Whittall and Douglas Hondo useful seamers. Much would need to go right for the Zimbabwean attack to restrict their opponents to moderate totals.

The Netherlands were back, resplendent in their bright orange uniforms. Captain and all-rounder Roland Lefebvre, who turned 40 the day before the opening ceremony in Cape Town, was back to lead the troops. The Dutch showed discipline in the field, conceding 200 only once in the ICC Trophy in 2001. Batsmen such as Tim de Leede, Daan van Bunge, Klaas-Jan van Noortwijk and Sussex representative Bas Zuiderent had showed ability and were hoping to impress on the big stage. Edgar Schiferli and Feiko Kloppenburg were willing medium-fast bowlers and the spin cause was led by van Bunge and Jacob-Jan Esmeijer.

Runners-up in the ICC Trophy, Namibia were making their first appearance in the upper echelon of limited-overs cricket. This squad of club cricketers had developed useful experience playing in the UCB Bowl, South Africa's second-11 championship. Although having a small pool of approximately 500 players, Namibia had begun to develop young talent. Daniel Keulder, who was replaced as Namibian skipper by Deon Kotze before the World Cup, had a productive time in the ICC tournament and their bowling ranks included double international, doctor and conservationist Rudi van Vuuren, who played fly-half for Namibia in the rugby union World Cups of 1999 and 2003. The line-up featured three Burgers, Jan-Berrie and brother Louis and Sarel. The major challenge for the future of cricket in Namibia was to appeal to the country's majority black population.

Main host of the tournament, South Africa, loomed as the main contender in Group B. It would be interesting to see how the South Africans would handle the pressure of home crowd expectations after the near misses of 1992 and 1999. The memory of the late Hansie Cronje was still on the minds of many South Africans as they embarked on this campaign. Shaun Pollock would be nearly three years into his captaincy when the tournament got underway at Cape Town on 9 February. Despite the change of leader, the South Africans were still essentially a very well drilled, formulaic team that played the percentages. The Proteas had shown vulnerability in high pressure games, seemingly unable to adapt from their blueprint in times of adversity.

The South African batting personnel were solid without being spectacular, with the exception of maverick opener Herschelle Gibbs. Gary Kirsten, Jacques Kallis and Jonty Rhodes were steady, resolute batsmen with fine records, but they were generally not attacking players. Mark Boucher would be called on to play busy, industrious hands at number six or seven, with fireworks to follow from Lance Klusener, player of the 1999 tournament, and Pollock.

The Proteas' bowling stocks were strong, although there were question marks over the lack of a world-class spinner and whether 36-year-old Allan Donald, now operating as a first- or second-change bowler, would be able to produce the goods. Pollock's performances with the white ball were outstanding and in the mould of Glenn McGrath. Makhaya Ntini would share the new ball with Pollock. Sharpish but not express, Ntini made history in 1997/98 by being the first black South African chosen at international level. His energy determination with the ball would complement Pollock's precision and professionalism. In recent years, Ntini's international cricket career had hung by a thread as he was convicted of rape in 1999, a conviction that was quashed.

Alongside the Proteas in Group B, New Zealand were plucky customers who often lifted their games against more fancied opponents, particularly Australia. The Aussies had been unsettled by one New Zealander in particular. Bond. Shane Bond. Bond showed in the 2001/02 limited-overs international series Down Under that he was seriously quick and a regular wicket taker. The Kiwis would be led astutely by Stephen Fleming. They boasted a good batting line up, including Fleming, strokemakers Nathan Astle and Scott Styris and the big hitting of keeper-batsman Brendon McCullum and Chris Cairns. Chris Harris, who was unable to transfer his one-day talents to the Test arena, played a Michael Bevan-like role in the middle-order and would be tough to dislodge. Harris would frustrate batsmen again in this tournament with his slow wobblers that often looked like boundary fodder but were difficult to get away. As Cairns was bowling less these days, the seam support for Bond came from Andre Adams, Jacob Oram and Daryl Tuffey. Daniel Vettori was likely to trouble opponents with his canny, accurate left-arm orthodox bowling.

Keep to atone for their disappointing showing in 1999, Sri Lanka were a dangerous adversary. The belligerent and prickly leadership reign of Arjuna Ranatunga had ended, to be replaced with the amiable manner and lack of gamesmanship of skipper Sanath Jayasuriya. Jayasuriya led a strong batting line up which featured proven performers Mahela Jayawardene and Aravinda de Silva and future star Kumar Sangakkara. Prolific wicket takers Muttiah Muralitharan and Chaminda Vaas were the obvious stars with the ball, whilst Jayasuriya had a happy knack of claiming victims with the white ball. Opposition batsmen would be well advised to attack the second string bowlers, such as de Silva, Dilhara Fernando and Pulasthi Gunaratne, to bump up their totals.

For once, bowling would be the weak link of the West Indian side. The retirements of all-time great quicks Curtly Ambrose and Courtney Walsh left a yawning chasm in the Caribbean attack. International batsmen would sleep more soundly and walk a little taller with these two legends happily retired. Brian Lara had a break from the captaincy and cool customer Carl Hooper made a comeback to the side to be in charge. The West Indies had a very talented, power-packed batting line-up. Lara, Hooper, Chris Gayle, Shivnarine Chanderpaul, Wavell Hinds, Ramnaresh Sarwan and Ricardo Powell had the collective firepower to destroy bowling attacks on their day. Sadly, it wasn't too often that the group fired as a whole. In the bowling area, Merv Dillon and Pedro Collins were the go-to men and bowling all-rounder Vasbert Drakes, who was recalled to the West Indies side the previous September after an absence of more than seven years, would provide useful fast-medium support. Drakes had the dubious honour of being the first man to be dismissed timed out in first class cricket, when playing for Border in South Africa in 2002/03, when his flight to South Africa had been delayed several hours. All told, the men from the Caribbean looked to have their work cut out for them in restricting opposition scoring.

Conquerors of Pakistan at the 1999 tournament, Bangladesh had found the going tough since playing their first Test match in November 2000. Coaches Mohsin Kamal and Ali Zia were hoping to continue Bangladesh's grounding in international company at the 2003 World Cup. Like many teams in their formative stages of international cricket, the Bangladeshi bowling was at best tidy at international level and unlikely to trouble batsmen. The batting ranks were determined but looked to lack the hitting power to threaten high scores. Bangladesh were led by keeper Khaled Mashud. Future captains Habibul Bashar and Mohammad Ashraful had made sound starts as batsmen at the top level and would play important roles. Mashrafe Mortaza, playing in his first World Cup, was a good fast-medium prospect and would add some much needed bite to the bowling.

Winless in England in 1999, co-hosts Kenya were keen to keep learning at the elite level and to possibly claim a win or two in Pool B. With former Indian film star and batsman Sandeep Patil calling the shots as coach, the Kenyans had continuity in their personnel, with 10 players from the 1999 campaign fronting up again in the squad for 2003. The experienced Steve Tikolo, usually regarded as Kenya's best-ever player, was captain and would play an important role in the middle-order. With capable batsmen such as Kennedy Otieno, Ravindu Shah and Maurice Odumbe, star of the upset win over the West Indies in 1996, in the mix, the Kenyans would stand up to anything served up by opposition attacks.

Former captain and Davis Cup representative Aasif Karim was a seasoned campaigner and displayed guile with his left-arm orthodox offerings. In Collins Obuya, Kenya had a capable leg-spin bowler and batsman. The Suji brothers, Tony and Martin, and the O-Force, Thomas Odoyo and Peter Ongondo were the main seam options. Although not much was expected from Kenya, they promised to delight spectators with their enthusiasm and flair.

Dressed in bright red, Canada were back at World Cup level after their third-place finish in the ICC Trophy in 2001. Their squad included John Davison, formerly of Victoria and South Australia, an off-spinner and sweet timer of the ball. As was the case in 1979, the Canadian squad had a strong presence of players born in the West Indies and the subcontinental nations. Coach Gus Logie would oversee the Canadian campaign.

The tournament was launched in style on Saturday, 8 February in a spectacular opening ceremony at Newlands in Cape Town. The glitzy event had the hallmarks of an Olympics opening ceremony and was in stark contrast to the hom-hum opening ceremony of the 1999 tournament at Lord's. It had a mainly local theme, emphasising the diversity of South Africa, featuring a host of dancers, gymnasts, bands and choirs. A few leading South African sportstars were paraded around the ground before the competing teams were introduced. The local sports identifies included Leeds soccer player Lucas Radebe, former rugby player Naas Botha and tennis player Amanda Coetzer. President Thabo Mbeki officially declared the 2003 World Cup open to the delight of fans. With the frivolities over, minds were quickly focused on the quest of landing cricket's most prestigious prize.

SUNDAY 9 FEBRUARY 2003
SOUTH AFRICA vs WEST INDIES - GROUP B
NEWLANDS, CAPE TOWN: WEST INDIES WON BY 3 RUNS

Their appetites whetted by an impressive opening ceremony the day before, over 24,000 patrons packed into Newlands to see the fancied South Africans take on the West Indies. Fortunately, the game produced an excellent start to the tournament. A matter of intrigue was how South Africa would respond in this day-night fixture to an intense local media build-up and public expectations that were sky high.

The match started slowly, with Pollock and Ntini bowling three consecutive maidens to Gayle and Hinds. Pollock claimed the first wicket of the tournament when he flicked the shoulder of Hinds' bat. When Gayle was bowled in Pollock's next over, the West Indies were in trouble at 2-7. Batting at number three, Lara made his return to international cricket since he fell ill in Sri Lanka five months prior. Lara's comeback innings was almost over before it started. He edged his first ball, bowled by Ntini, and the dependable Kallis put down the chance at second slip. It would prove to be a costly mistake, as the South Africans were given a three hour opportunity to view Lara's flourishing backlift.

Against the tight bowling of Pollock and Ntini, Lara and Chanderpaul played carefully. The West Indies were 2-30 from 15 overs and the score was edged along to a slow 2-65 at the halfway mark. With his eye in, Lara played with greater confidence and runs were scored freely from Boje and Klusener. The "Prince of Port-of-Spain" reached his 50 from 78 balls with a boundary from Klusener in the 29th over.

The century stand between Lara and Chanderpaul was ended a short time later, bring together past and present skippers Lara and Hooper together in the middle. Hooper calmly worked the ball around and left the dazzling strokeplay to Lara, who continued to be severe on Boje and Klusener. At the 40 over mark, the West Indies had worked their way to a competitive 3-168. Playing in his fourth and final World Cup, first change bowler Donald was brought back into the attack. The wisdom of selecting Donald, who appeared past his best, was exposed as Lara and Hooper ripped 22 runs from his two-over spell.

Once in the 90s, Lara began to cramp up and needed treatment. He overcame this discomfort to bring up his 100 in the 42nd over. His second 50 had taken only 43 balls. In the following over, Hooper was caught for an important 40 from as many deliveries. Realising the need for quick runs, Lara hit out and was superbly caught in the deep for a brilliant 116 from 134 balls, attempting one big hit too many. With the score at 5-215 in the 45th over, Powell and Sarwan tore into the South African bowlers with ferocity. They hammered 63 runs from the last 28 deliveries of the innings to launch the West Indies to a strong total of 278. Amazingly, the metronomic Pollock was assaulted in his penultimate over, conceding 23 runs. Powell ended up with an unbeaten 40 from a mere 18 balls and Sarwan with 32 from 15 balls. Significantly, the home side were docked an over because of their slow over rate.

Faced with a difficult challenge, South Africa were off to a reasonable start through Gibbs and Kirsten. A long innings from the attacking Gibbs would give South Africa a good chance of victory. That hope was extinguished in the 9th over when Dillon found the edge and Jacobs took a good diving catch in front of slip. The dismissal was of real concern: the required run rate was already above 5.5 per over and, with the steady Kirsten at the crease, the next three batsmen in the order were not known for their fast scoring. Boeta Dippenaar was tied down and the required rate soon crept above a run a ball. Dippenaar hit a six off Hooper and was stumped the next ball. The South African innings spluttered along as Kallis and Rhodes were dismissed cheaply. Kirsten and Boucher batted soundly for half an hour without making inroads into the required run rate. Kirsten chipped a return catch to Dillon and Pollock fell to a smart catch by Hooper in the covers. With his country in strife at 6-160 in the 33rd over, the player of the 1999 tournament, Klusener, strode to the centre with the required rate approaching seven.

Klusener and Boucher seemed well equipped for the task of getting their team over the line. The pressure was eased a fraction when Boucher plundered 15 runs from the 37th over from Hooper. With 10 overs remaining, 82 runs were still needed. Hopes that the Klusener-Boucher stand would take South Africa to within range of victory were snuffed out when Boucher played over the top of one from Gayle. Batting with Boje, the previously out of form Klusener hit a purple patch. He smote five sixes in his 57 from 48 balls, including three shots from a Gayle over that cleared the fence. Klusener's charge to the finish line was nearly ended when he was 31, but Collins, claiming a catch on the boundary, took two steps backwards without reason and stood on the rope.

With 14 needed from the last two overs, Collins had some partial redemption when he bowled a good penultimate over, conceding just five runs. As was the case in the 1999 semi-final, South Africa needed nine from the last over to win. Drakes was entrusted with the responsibility of bowling the last over. Klusener regained the strike after two balls and the requirement was eight runs from four deliveries. Klusener's lofted shot was mistimed and Hooper took the catch at deep mid wicket. Showing a lack of awareness in a pressure situation, Klusener and Boje forgot to run, which left Ntini to face Drakes. After a dot ball, a Ntini swipe outside off stump popped the ball up to deep point, where Sarwan took a comfortable catch. Remembering to cross while the ball was in mid-air, Boje had to score eight from the final ball for victory. The final ball bowled was legal and a consolation Boje boundary reduced the losing margin to three.

The Newlands faithful were stunned as South Africa faltered in a pressure match again. Lara was a clear choice for the man of the match award.

WEST INDIES		SOUTH AFRICA	
C. H. Gayle b Pollock	2	H. H. Gibbs c Jacobs b Dillon	24
W. W. Hinds c Boucher b Pollock	0	G. Kirsten c & b Dillon	69
B. C. Lara c Pollock b Ntini	116	H. H. Dippenaar st Jacobs b Hooper	20
S. Chanderpaul c Boucher b Klusener	34	J. H. Kallis c Jacobs b Collins	13
C. L. Hooper (capt) c Kallis b Ntini	40	J. N. Rhodes b Hooper	2
R. L. Powell not out	40	M. V. Boucher b Gayle	49
R. R. Sarwan not out	32	S. M. Pollock (capt) c Hooper b Gayle	4
Extras (lb 6, w 4, nb 4)	14	L. Klusener c Hooper b Drakes	57
(50 overs)	5-278	N. Boje not out	25
Did not bat: R. D. Jacobs (wk), V. C. Drakes, M. Dillon,		M. Ntini c Sarwan b Drakes	0
P. T. Collins		A. A. Donald not out	0
1/4 2/7 3/109 4/198 5/215		Extras (lb 4, w 5, nb 3)	12
Bowling: Pollock 10-2-52-2; Ntini 10-1-37-2;		(49 overs)	9-275
Donald 9-0-54-0; Kallis 10-2-52-0; Klusener 8-0-53-1;		1/46 2/79 3/104 4/117 5/155 6/160 7/204 8/271 9/271	
Boje 3-0-24-0		Bowling: Dillon 10-0-47-2; Collins 9-0-54-1; Drakes 8-1-33-2;	
		Hooper 10-0-63-2; Gayle 10-1-60-2; Powell 2-0-14-0	

Umpires: D.J. Harper, S. Venkataraghavan.

Toss: West Indies.   Points: West Indies 4, South Africa 0

MONDAY 10 FEBRUARY 2003
ZIMBABWE vs NAMIBIA - GROUP A
HARARE SPORTS CLUB, HARARE: ZIMBABWE WON BY 86 RUNS (DUCKWORTH/LEWIS METHOD)

Namibia made their World Cup debut on a warm day in Harare. Despite showing admirable commitment and enthusiasm, they were no match for co-hosts Zimbabwe. Steady rain in the 26th over curtailed the Namibian reply and the application of the Duckworth-Lewis method reduced the margin of defeat to 86 runs. The rain nearly deprived Zimbabwe of the win. Had the game-ending rain arrived two balls earlier, the match would have been a no-result. This match was the first time that the Duckworth-Lewis method had been called upon to decide a World Cup fixture.

With the possibility of rain, Namibian captain Deon Kotze asked the home side to bat first. Led by a brilliant innings from Craig Wishart, the Zimbabwe batsmen scored freely and reached an imposing 2-340, Zimbabwe's highest total in one-day cricket. As is often the case with emerging cricket nations, the Namibian bowling was pedestrian and cannon fodder to the Zimbabwean batting line-up. The Namibian attack would need serious help when up against a strong Test nation, such as Australia.

After Mark Vermeulen hit a return catch to 43 year old left-arm orthodox bowler Lennie Louw, Andy Flower strode to the wicket wearing a black armband in silent protest at the oppressive situation in his country. Paceman Henry Olonga made a similar protest when Zimbabwe took the field. After Flower made a fluent 39, Wishart and Grant Flower moved into assault mode. From the 31st over, the pair plundered the bowling and achieved an unbroken stand of 166. Wishart carried his bat for 172 from 151 balls, a national record in limited-overs matches and the fifth highest World Cup score at the time.

Namibia lost a wicket to the first ball they faced in international cricket when Riaan Walters nicked one from Streak. Some good hitting by Jan-Berrie Burger, including a six over extra cover off Streak, put Namibia on the path to a respectable score. Zimbabwe were sloppy in the field and Stephan Swanepoel and Danie Keulder were given reprieves. Light rain after 16 overs stopped play for 50 minutes and a heavier shower in the 26th over ended the game with Namibia battling at 5-104. Wishart was a clear choice for the man of the match.

ZIMBABWE		NAMIBIA	
C. B. Wishart not out	172	R. Walters c Taibu b Streak	0
M. A. Vermeulen c & b Louw	39	S. J. Swanepoel c Streak b Whittall	23
A. Flower c Karg b A. Burger	39	A. J. Burger c A. Flower b Streak	26
G. W. Flower not out	78	D. Keulder c Ebrahim b Whittall	27
Extras (lb 7, w 4, nb 1)	12	G. B. Murgatroyd c Wishart b G. W. Flower	10
(50 overs)	2-340	L. J. Burger not out	4
Did not bat: D. D. Ebrahim, G. J. Whittall, T. Taibu (wk),		D. B. Kotze (capt) not out	5
H. H. Streak (capt), B. A. Murphy, D. T. Hondo, H. K. Olonga		Extras (lb 1, w 8)	9
1/107 2/174		(25.1 overs)	5-104
Bowling: Snyman 10-0-49-0; L. Burger 10-1-70-0; B.		Did not bat: M. Karg (wk), G. Snyman, J. L. Louw, B. L. Kotze	
Kotze 10-1-75-0; Louw 10-0-60-1; D. Kotze 7-0-56-0; A.		1/0 2/40 3/80 4/94 5/98	
Burger 3-0-23-1		Bowling: Streak 5-0-35-2; Hondo 6-1-20-0; Olonga 3-1-8-0;	
		Murphy 1-0-7-0; G. W. Flower 5.1-1-13-1; Whittall 5-0-20-2	

Umpires: D.L. Orchard, S.J.A. Taufel

Toss: Namibia   Points: Zimbabwe 4, Namibia 0.

NEW ZEALAND vs SRI LANKA - GROUP B
BLOEMFONTEIN, SOUTH AFRICA: SRI LANKA WON BY 47 RUNS

At almost 1,400 metres above sea level, South Africa's judicial capital hosted an intriguing contest between two well-credentialed teams. The fixture was a critical game for New Zealand, as the Kiwis had refused to play against Kenya at Nairobi on 21 February because of security concerns. In the end, a sound defeat left the Black Caps with little margin for error in their bid to qualify for the Super Six stage.

On a pitch that seemed conducive to spin, the New Zealand selectors made an odd decision in overlooking Vettori and not playing a recognised slow bowler. A second surprise was the selection of Lou Vincent as the wicketkeeper ahead of Brendon McCullum. To complete the trifecta of unusual choices, captain Fleming sent Sri Lanka in after winning the toss.

Despite the early loss of Atapattu, Sri Lanka powered to a strong score of 7-272 from their 50 overs. Jayasuriya, who had already scored three 100s in limited-overs internationals in 2003, batted superbly to bring up his first World Cup century. The Sri Lankan skipper survived two scares en route to his milestone. Umpire Neil Mallender, the former England seamer, did not notice a faint edge from Daryl Tuffey when Jayasuriya was on 18. The second miss occurred when Jayasuriya edged one when on 86 and Vincent missed a difficult chance. Jayasuriya reached his century from 111 balls when a vicious uppercut off Bond sped through third man to the boundary.

Another veteran, Hashan Tillekeratne, played a sensible support role whilst Jayasuriya launched into the bowling. Jayasuriya continued the attack, including three fours from a Styris over, to 120 when he was trapped adjacent by the benign medium pace of Astle. Jayasuriya and Tillekeratne's stand was worth 170, with 106 of these scored by Jayasuriya.

From a platform of 1-193 in the 35th over, a score of 300 was a reasonable prospect for the Sri Lankans. However, the momentum was slowed by the steady fall of wickets. Jayawardene was leg before to Andre Adams in the over after Jayasuriya's dismissal. Astle made further inroads when he sent back de Silva and Sangakkara for modest scores. Tillekeratne, hampered by cramps and using a runner, and the middle-order were unable to force the pace in the last 10 overs. Tillekeratne saw it through to the end of the innings with a steady 81 not out from 106 deliveries. In a sign of things to come, the best bowler for the Kiwis was one who did not bowl quickly. Astle had the figures with 3-34 from seven overs.

Scoring 273 to win on a slowing wicket was always going to be a difficult assignment for the New Zealanders. Their prospects nose-dived inside the first half-hour as they crashed to 3-15. Astle was run out in the first over for a duck attempting a single that was never on. The disaster continued when Fleming and McMillan were removed, both edging the medium-fast bowling of Pulasthi Gunaratne. New Zealand needed someone to respond to the crisis and Styris delivered. He played a stylish knock of 141 from 125 deliveries, which included six sixes, three of which were slog swept over the boundary off Muralitharan in the final overs of the innings.

Unfortunately, none of Styris' teammates were able to survive long enough to build a substantial partnership. Cairns was the only other batsman to manage more than 13. The introduction of the spinners in the 15th over kept the scoring in check and the run rate hovered around four per over until late in the innings. Wickets steadily fell to the spinners and the required run rate was soon beyond reach. When Styris brought up his maiden limited-overs international hundred with an on-drive in the 40th over, the requirement was nearly 10 per over.

With part-time spinner Russel Arnold taking two wickets to reduce the Kiwis to 9-200, Styris tried in vain to blast his team to victory. Four sixes in the space of four overs excited the crowd, but served only to reduce the margin of defeat. Styris' lone hand and New Zealand's innings ended in the 45th over when a Styris slog off Arnold was caught in the deep by Vaas. Sri Lanka's spin quartet of Muralitharan, Jayasuriya, de Silva and Arnold claimed seven wickets. Muralitharan and Jayasuriya were difficult to get away until Styris' late flurry. In similar fashion to New Zealand, Sri Lanka's best figures were returned by a batsmen who bowled occasionally, Arnold, with 3-47.

Styris' score was the second best by a Kiwi in a limited-overs international, trailing Glenn Turner's 171 not out against East Africa in the 1975 World Cup. Despite scoring approximately 63 per cent of his team's total, Styris' performance was not enough for the Man of the Match award, which went to Jayasuriya for his all-round effort. The batting excellence of the two men meant that, in the first three games of the tournament, four centuries had been scored.

SRI LANKA	
M. S. Atapattu c Styris b Bond	6
S. T. Jayasuriya (capt) lbw b Astle	120
H. P. Tillekeratne not out	81
D. P. M. D. Jayawardene lbw b Adams	1
P. A. de Silva c Styris b Astle	12
K. C. Sangakkara (wk) c Adams b Astle	13
R. P. Arnold b Bond	12
W. P. U. J.C. Vaas b Adams	5
M. Muralitharan not out	4
Extras (b 3, lb 6, w 4, nb 5)	18
(50 overs)	7-272

Did not bat: C. R.D. Fernando, P. W. Gunaratne

1/23 2/193 3/196 4/213 5/240 6/256 7/263

Bowling: Tuffey 5-0-36-0; Bond 10-1-44-2; Oram 10-0-37-0; Adams 9-0-58-2; Harris 4-0-26-0; Styris 5-0-28-0; Astle 7-0-34-3

NEW ZEALAND	
S. P. Fleming (capt) c Sangakkara b Gunaratne	1
N. J. Astle run out	0
C. D. McMillan c Sangakkara b Gunaratne	3
S. B. Styris c Vaas b Arnold	141
C. L. Cairns c & b de Silva	32
L. Vincent (wk) c Muralitharan b Jayasuriya	1
C. Z. Harris b Muralitharan	13
J. D. P. Oram c Sangakkara b Muralitharan	12
A. R. Adams c sub (Mubarak) b Arnold	1
D. R. Tuffey c Sangakkara b Arnold	4
S. E. Bond not out	2
Extras (lb 10, w 5)	15
(45.3 overs)	10-225

1/1 2/2 3/15 4/93 5/94 6/150 7/179 8/182 9/200 10/225

Bowling: Vaas 7-0-22-0; Gunaratne 5-0-24-2; Fernando 3-1-19-0; Muralitharan 9-1-42-2; Jayasuriya 8-0-32-1; de Silva 5-0-29-1; Arnold 8.3-0-47-3

Umpires: S.A. Bucknor, N.A. Mallender.

Toss: New Zealand   Points: Sri Lanka 4, New Zealand 0

TUESDAY 11 FEBRUARY 2003
AUSTRALIA vs PAKISTAN - GROUP A
WANDERERS STADIUM, JOHANNESBURG: AUSTRALIA WON BY 82 RUNS

Tournament favourite Australia appeared vulnerable as they entered this important Group A clash against the mercurial Pakistan. On a wicket chock full of runs, the Australians sent a message to their rivals with a big win. In a promising sign, the victory was spearheaded by a player with hitherto untapped potential at international level and two lesser lights.

Australia were rocked on the eve of the game by the sensational news that Shane Warne had tested positive to a banned substance. Warne had failed a drugs test that was taken during the one-day tournament in Australia in January. Warne's "A" sample, later confirmed by the "B" sample, showed that he had taken two banned diuretics: hydrochlorothiazide and amiloride. Warne had taken the tablets during a rapid, six-week recovery from a dislocated shoulder suffered in mid-December. Warne's explanation was that he got the diuretic tablets from his mum. He said that he took the tablets out of vanity, wanting to lose weight before he returned to the Australian side. The difficulty for Warne was that diuretics can also mask steroids which, if taken, might have expedited his recovery from a dislocated shoulder. Warne was stood down from the squad and flew back to Australia. He received a one-year ban.

Aside from Warne's ban, the Australian ranks were challenged by the absence of Darren Lehmann and limited-overs maestro Michael Bevan. Lehmann had one match left to serve of a five game suspension for racial vilification and Bevan was inconvenienced with a groin injury. Waqar Younis opted to bowl first, giving his impressive pace arsenal of Wasim Akram, Shoaib Akhtar and Waqar Younis a crack at Australia's weakened batting line-up.

On a fast and bouncy track that offered lateral movement, Wasim and Shoaib bowled with unbridled aggression. Although scoring at a good rate, the Australians were under pressure at 3-52 in the 11th over after Wasim removed Gilchrist, Hayden and Martyn, the last batsman being dismissed first ball by a superb off-cutter. When Jimmy Maher edged one from Waqar, Australia were in the gun at 4-86. Ricky Ponting had survived this onslaught and he was joined at the wicket by Andrew Symonds. Symonds, who probably would not have played in this match if Lehmann and Bevan were available, was out of form and had yet to make an impression at international level. A failure here might have spelt doom for his Australian career.

Symonds began tentatively, while Ponting played with controlled aggression. Ponting's dismissal for 53 in the 30th over left Australia at 5-146, with Symonds left to bat with the bowling all-rounders and the tail. Pakistan had an opportunity to restrict Australia's total to a moderate level. However, the inconsistent morale of the Pakistanis failed them again, as the bowling and fielding became increasingly ragged.

Symonds hit his stride and displayed an impressive array of shots. He found a capable ally in Hogg, who sensibly turned the strike over to his on-song partner. Symonds and Hogg laid the platform for an impressive score with a rollicking stand of 70 in 9.1 overs. Afridi bore the brunt of the assault when Symonds hit him for four boundaries in the 35th over.

With his maiden one-day hundred in sight, Symonds increased the tempo in the final 10 overs. He reached the milestone in the 41st over when he struck Afridi for another four. Symonds raced to his 100 from only 92 deliveries with 15 fours, the second 50 coming off 33 balls.

Ian Harvey, who hit a quickfire 24, gave useful support as Symonds continued to pummel the bowling. In the penultimate over, two beam balls at Symonds from Waqar prompted an angry response from the Queenslander and umpire Shepherd banned the Pakistani captain from completing his over. Symonds and Jason Gillespie put the icing on the cake, hitting Wasim for 14 off the last over. Symonds struck a majestic six over Wasim's head. Symonds finished with a superb 143 not out from 125 balls, including 18 fours and two sixes. Symonds' innings was the highest individual score by an Australian in a World Cup match, surpassing Mark Waugh's 130 against Kenya in 1996. Symonds' hand was largely responsible for Australia's excellent total of 8-310. This score was Australia's highest tally in World Cup cricket and the best score achieved at the Wanderers. The Australian innings was boosted by Symonds and the tail blasting 39 runs from the final four overs. Significantly, the partnerships for the sixth and seventh wickets netted a combined total of 124 runs in only 17 overs.

Due to a slow over rate, an over was deducted from Pakistan's allotment in their chase of a formidable target of 311. Pakistan never looked like winning, as wickets fell regularly and several batsmen were dismissed after making a start. Symonds continued his dream day when he ran from the boundary to take an excellent catch a short distance from the ground to send Yousuf Youhana on his way. Pakistan had crumbled to 5-103 and it was all over bar the shouting.

From 7-147, Rashid Latif and Wasim rallied for a time in a belligerent 54 run stand from only 29 deliveries, including Rashid's three sixes off Harvey and Hogg. The innings merely served to reduce the margin of defeat to less than a triple figure tally of runs. Unexpectedly, lower profile bowlers Harvey and Hogg did the bulk of the damage, claiming a combined seven wickets. Wasim went on to be the equal top-scorer of the innings with 33. The fall of wickets continued, with Pakistan folding for 228 in the 45th over.

Another flashpoint in Australia-Pakistan cricket relations occurred during Rashid's volatile time at the crease. An appeal by Gilchrist for a catch behind off Hogg's bowling was rejected by Sri Lankan umpire Asoka de Silva. Some banter between fellow wicketkeepers ensued, which turned ugly in Gillespie's next over. At the end of that over, Rashid allegedly called Gilchrist a "white c*$#", which Gilchrist promptly reported to umpire Shepherd at square leg. After the match, the ICC hearing of the racial vilification charge was presided by Clive Lloyd. Ironically, Lloyd presided over the racial vilification hearing that resulted in Lehmann's five-match suspension. An audio clip from the stump microphone did not fully pick up what Rashid was alleged to have said. The Pakistan representatives at the hearing alleged that the tape had been tampered with. Further, Rashid made the extraordinary claim that Gilchrist had said that he'd never be given out by umpire de Soka because Rashid and de Soka were both of the same colour. The end result was that Lloyd dismissed the charge against Rashid because of a lack of evidence.

The spat did little to detract from Australia's commanding performance. Australia had turned in a polished, professional performance with key personnel missing and would be difficult to topple. In an eventful day, the breakthrough performance of Symonds netted him the man of the match award.

AUSTRALIA		PAKISTAN	
A. C. Gilchrist (wk) c Waqar Younis b Wasim Akram	1	Taufeeq Umar c Hogg b Lee	21
M. L. Hayden b Wasim Akram	27	Shahid Afridi c Gilchrist b Gillespie	1
R. T. Ponting (capt) c Taufeeq Umar b Shoaib Akhtar	53	Saleem Elahi c Lee b Harvey	30
D. R. Martyn b Wasim Akram	0	Inzamam-ul-Haq c Gilchrist b McGrath	6
J. P. Maher c Rashid Latif b Waqar Younis	9	Yousuf Youhana c Symonds b Harvey	27
A. Symonds not out	143	Younis Khan c Ponting b Hogg	19
G. B. Hogg run out	14	Abdul Razzaq c & b Hogg	25
I. J. Harvey c Waqar Younis b Shoaib Akhtar	24	Rashid Latif (wk) b Hogg	33
B. Lee c Inzamam-ul-Haq b Waqar Younis	2	Wasim Akram c Ponting b Harvey	33
J. N. Gillespie not out	6	Waqar Younis (capt) c McGrath b Harvey	6
Extras (b 1, lb 9, w 12, nb 9)	31	Shoaib Akhtar not out	0
(50 overs)	8-310	Extras (b 3, lb 9, w 10, nb 5)	27
Did not bat: G. D. McGrath		(44.3 overs)	10-228
1/10 2/52 3/52 4/86 5/146 6/216 7/270 8/292		1/9 2.38 3/49 4/81 5/103 6/125 7/147 8/201 9/223	
Bowling: Wasim Akram 10-0-64-3; Shoaib Akhtar 10-0-45-2;		10/228	
Waqar Younis 8.3-1-50-2; Abdul Razzaq 6-0-42-0; Shahid		Bowling: McGrath 10-2-39-1; Gillespie 8-1-28-1;	
Afridi 9.3-0-63-0; Younis Khan 6-0-36-0		Lee 7-0-37-1; Harvey 9.3-0-58-4; Hogg 10-0-54-3	

Umpires: E.A.R. de Silva, D.R. Shepherd.

Toss: Pakistan　　　Points: Australia 4, Pakistan 0.

TUESDAY 11 FEBRUARY 2003
BANGLADESH vs CANADA - GROUP B
DURBAN, SOUTH AFRICA (DAY/NIGHT): CANADA WON BY 60 RUNS

Canada, playing their first limited-overs international for 24 years, started as outsiders in their opening clash with Bangladesh. Bangladesh, who upset finalists Pakistan in the 1999 tournament, had hardly set the world on fire since they received Test status in 2000. The Bangladeshis had failed to win one of their first 43 Test matches and they were winless in limited-overs games since that shock defeat of Pakistan.

The Canadians had been restricted to training indoors since the previous October and they had not played together for five months until the warm-up matches. Most of Canada's line-up were born outside the country and the players had an eclectic mix of occupations, including salesmen, teachers, graphic artists, students and a plumber.

Captain Joseph Harris, a former Barbados player, opted to bat first. The men from the world's second largest country batted into the final over, but they were restricted to a moderate total of 180. The Bangladeshi spinners, left-arm orthodox Mohammad Rafiq, off-spinner Sanwar Hossain and Alok Kapali, proved difficult to get away. The trio claimed four wickets and conceded a total of only 79 runs from their 30 overs. For Canada, the St Kitts and Nevis-born David Chumney scored a fluent 28 at number three before a suicidal single ended his enterprising stay. The mainstay of the innings was Ian Billcliff, who was born in British Columbia, Canada, grew up in New Zealand and played first class cricket for Otago, Wellington and Auckland. The strongly built Billcliff made a measured 42 from 60 deliveries. From a reasonable platform of 2-70, the innings dwindled away to 8-146 before Austin Codrington and Davis Joseph lifted the score to 180.

Canada approached the task of defending their total with great vigour and commitment. Opening bowlers Joseph and Sanjay Thuraisingham were loose early, which enabled Hannan Sarkar and Al Sahariar to make inroads. The combination of a moderate target and a fast start to the innings appeared to result in overconfidence in the Bangladesh camp, a rare emotion for a team accustomed to being a whipping boy in international cricket.

In the end, enthusiasm won the day. The dreadlocked Codrington, who operated at a gentle medium pace, bowled with impressive discipline. His efforts were rewarded with 5-27, the first five wicket haul in the tournament. Codrington and John Davison, who claimed two wickets with his off-spinners, cut a swathe through the Bangladeshi batting. The favourites had collapsed to 120 all out from 28 overs, including six wickets falling for just 14 runs in 44 deliveries of panic-stricken batting.

The upset win was hailed as "the Miracle on Grass" in Canadian media and received front page headline back home. Canada's success, albeit against a developing Test nation, was a step forward for cricket's minnow teams and a step forward in the ICC's plan to spread the cricket gospel worldwide.

Codrington picked up the man of the match award. The 27-year-old apprentice plumber from Jamaica achieved the third-best figures by a player on his limited-overs international debut.

CANADA		BANGLADESH	
I. Maraj c Sanwar Hossain b Tapash Baisya	24	Hannan Sarkar c Bagai b Codrington	25
J. M. Davison b Mashrafe Mortaza	8	Al Sahariar c sub (Samad) b Joseph	9
D. Chumney run out	28	Habibul Bashar c Bagai b Thuraisingam	0
I. S. Billcliff run out	42	Ehsanul Haque c Bagai b Joseph	13
J. V. Harris (capt) c Khaled Masud b Sanwar Hossain	4	Sanwar Hossain lbw b Davison	25
N. A. de Groot c Alok Kapali b Sanwar Hossain	0	Alok Kapali lbw b Codrington	19
A. F. Sattaur lbw b Alok Kapali	13	Khaled Masud (capt/wk) c sub (Samud) b Davison	1
A. Bagai (wk) b Mashrafe Mortaza	7	Mohammad Rafiq c Davison b Codrington	12
S. Thuraisingam lbw b Mohammad Rafiq	6	Tapash Baisya c Sattaur b Codrington	0
A. Codrington c Tapash Baisya b Manjurul Islam	16	Mashrafe Mortaza c Sattaur b Codrington	0
D. Joseph not out	9	Manjurul Islam not out	0
Extras (lb 7, w 14, nb 2)	23	Extras (lb 2, w 14)	16
(49.1 overs)	10-180	(28 overs)	10-120

1/18 2/47 3/70 4/92 5/104 6/130 7/134 8/146 9/159 10/180

Bowling: Manjural Islam 8.1-1-30-1; Mashrafe Mortaza 8-0-38-2; Tapash Baisya 3-0-26-1; Mohammad Rafiq 10-2-34-1; Sanwar Hossain 10-0-26-2; Alok Kapali 10-0-19-1

1/33 2/44 3/46 4/76 5/106 6/108 7/108 8/119 9/119 10/120

Bowling: Joseph 8-1-42-2; Thuraisingam 6-0-34-1; Codrington 9-3-27-5; Davison 5-1-15-2

Umpires: Aleem Dar, B.G. Jerling.

Toss: Canada   Points: Canada 4, Bangladesh 0.

WEDNESDAY 12 FEBRUARY 2003
SOUTH AFRICA vs KENYA - GROUP B
NORTH WEST CRICKET STADIUM, POTCHEFSTROOM, SOUTH AFRICA:
SOUTH AFRICA WON BY 10 WICKETS

In this battle of the green uniformed teams, South Africa bounced back from their shock loss in the tournament opener to record a comfortable win over Kenya. The win came at a cost to the Proteas: Jonty Rhodes broke a hand when stopping a hard hit drive from Maurice Odumbe. The sunny Rhodes, a constant danger in the field, called time on his international career just two days later.

After Steve Tikolo choose to bat first, the top order found the going tough against accurate bowling by Pollock and Ntini. Tikolo's dismissal in the ninth over had Kenya in early trouble at 3-26 in the ninth over. Despite his partners falling regularly, opener Ravindu Shah played a classy knock. Shah reached an accomplished 60 halfway through the innings and dominated his team's score of 4-92 at that stage.

Shah's opportunity of putting a landmark innings together was extinguished when he was run out after being sent back by Odumbe. Inside 13 overs, the Kenyans capitulated to be all out for 140, losing the last six wickets for 48 runs. Through a combination of poor shot selection and impatient batting, the opportunity for Kenya to post a defendable total was frittered away. Through the clatter of wickers, Thomas Odoyo and the delightfully named Peter Jimmy Carter Ongondo provided some highlights material, both men hoisting Nicky Boje over the boundary. Klusener, bowling with clever changes of pace, took four of the last five wickets to fall.

The South Africans, with a straight-forward task of scoring 141, galloped to the target in the 22nd over with all 10 wickets intact. In an encouraging sign, Gibbs hammered an unbeaten 87 from just 66 balls, including four sixes. Kirsten, happy to play the support role, did his part in hitting 52 not out from 63 deliveries. In a bid to keep the scoring under control, Tikolo had his three spinners – left arm orthodox Aasif Karim, leg-spinner Collins Obuya and off-spinner Maurice Odumbe – in service by the 14th over. The slower pace of the bowling had the opposite effect on Gibbs' scoring. He whacked 20 runs from Odumbe's second over. Kirsten then joined in the carnage, striking Obuya to the boundary three times from the last four balls in the 21st over. Gibbs then hit two fours from Ongondo's next two deliveries to end the match over two hours early.

Klusener shaded Gibbs for the Man of the Match award in South Africa's clinical win.

KENYA		SOUTH AFRICA	
K. O. Otieno (wk) run out	1	H. H. Gibbs not out	87
R. D. Shah run out	60	G. Kirsten not out	52
B. J. Patel c Boucher b Pollock	1	Extras (w 2, 1 nb)	3
S. O. Tikolo (capt) c Kirsten b Pollock	3	(21.2 overs)	0-142
H. S. Modi c Pollock b Boje	9	Did not bat: H. H. Dippenaar, J. H. Kallis, J. N. Rhodes,	
M. O. Odumbe c Gibbs b Klusener	16	M. V. Boucher (wk), S. M. Pollock (capt), L. Klusener,	
T. M. Odoyo c Boucher b Ntini	22	N. Boje, M. Ntini, C. K. Langeveldt	
C. O. Obuya lbw b Klusener	0	Bowling: Suji 4-0-21-0; Odoyo 6-1-34-0; Karim 2-0-17-0;	
M. A. Suji c Pollock b Klusener	0	Obuya 5-1-32-0; Odumbe 2-0-21-0; Ongondo 2.2-0-17-0;	
P. J.C. Ongondo c Kirsten b Klusener	13		
A. Y. Karim not out	0		
Extras (b 1, lb 3, w 7, nb 4)	15		
(38 overs)	10-140		
1/4 2/7 3/26 4/62 5/92 6/105 7/105 8/120 9/139 10/140			
Bowling: Pollock 6-2-15-2; Ntini 7-1-14-1; Kallis 3-0-23-0;			
Langeveldt 5-0-24-0; Boje 9-1-44-1; Klusener 8-2-16-4			

Umpires: K. C. Barbour, T. H. Wijewardene.

Toss: Kenya   Points: South Africa 4, Kenya 0.

INDIA vs NETHERLANDS - GROUP A
PAARL, SOUTH AFRICA: INDIA WON BY 68 RUNS

India's World Cup campaign started off in a shabby fashion as they laboured to victory against the Netherlands in scorching conditions in the majestic backdrop of the Paarl Mountain. Against the gentle Dutch attach, India struggled to a poor 204 in the 49th over. The bowlers from the Netherlands adhered to the basics of bowling line and length and they were rewarded with a steady flow of wickets. Star batsman Sachin Tendulkar treated the bowling with respect and his application produced a half-century. When he reached 25, the Little Master passed Javed Miandad's record of 1,083 runs in World Cup cricket.

The medium pace of all-rounder Timotheus Bernadus Maria de Leede picked up the prized wicket of Tendulkar as his maiden international scalp. On his way to four wickets, he even beat the tight defences of Rahul Dravid. A little later, Mohammad Kaif's failure had India at 5-114 in the 32nd over. Dinesh Mongia and Yuvraj Singh salvaged some respectability with a 55-run stand for the sixth wicket. Yuvraj Singh's innings was ended when Adeel Raja managed to complete a juggling act from a sizzling drive. Mongia persevered, dealing mainly in ones and twos, and he reached 42 before he was the ninth batsman out. India edged past the 200 mark at seven wickets. The end came quickly, as the last three wickets fell in the 49th over for the addition of a solitary run.

Fortunately for the Indian contingent, they could depend on their bowling attack. From the fourth ball of the innings, Feikio Kloppenburg edged a delivery from Javagal Srinath and Virender Sehwag took a smart catch moving to his right at second slip. With this wicket, veteran seamer Srinath became the fifth bowler to take 300 wickets in limited-overs internationals. From that point, the Dutch innings plummeted to 7-54 in the 22nd over. Seven of the top eight batsmen scored three runs or less, with Hague student Dan van Bunge playing a lone hand with 62. Van Bunge formed a useful alliance with keeper Jeroen Smits. Their ninth-wicket partnership of 49 runs yielded more than a third of the team's score.

The Dutch could claim a measure of pride by the moderate losing margin of 68 runs and by the fact batted until the 49th over. The Dutch batsmen found the bounce and guile of spin duo Harbhajan Singh and Anil Kumble beyond them. One worry for Indian coach John Wright was that, after the Netherlands were floundering at 8-82, the bowlers were unable to finish the innings off quickly. The last two partnerships lingered for over 20 overs and 54 runs. De Leede was Man of the Match.

INDIA		NETHERLANDS	
S. C. Ganguly (capt) c Smits b Lefebvre	8	J. F. Kloppenburg c Sehwag b Srinath	0
S. R. Tendulkar s Smits b de Leede	52	D. L.S. van Bunge b Srinath	62
V. Sehwag c Zuiderent b Kloppenburg	6	H. J. C. Mol c Dravid b Srinath	2
R. Dravid (wk) b de Leede	17	B. Zuiderent c Sehwag b Khan	0
Yuvraj Singh c & b Adeel Raja	37	T. B.M. de Leede c Dravid b Harbhajan Singh	0
M. Kaif c Lefebvre b Adeel Raja	9	L. P. van Troost c Dravid b Kumble	1
D. Mongia run out	42	R. H. Scholte lbw b Kumble	1
Harbhajan Singh b de Leede	13	R. P. Lefebvre (capt) lbw b Kumble	3
A. Kumble run out	9	E. Schiferli c Mongia b Kumble	13
Zaheer Khan lbw b de Leede	0	J. Smits (wk) c Sehwag b Srinath	26
J. Srinath not out	0	Adeel Raja not out	0
Extras (lb 2, w 8, nb 1)	11	Extras (b 2, lb 6, w 18, nb 2)	28
(48.5 overs)	10-204	(48.1 overs)	10-136

1/30 2/56 3/81 4/91 5/114 6/169 7/186 8/203 9/204 10/204

Bowling: Schiferli 10-2-49-0; Lefebvre 9-1-27-1; de Leede 9.5-0-35-4; Kloppenburg 10-0-40-1; Adeel Raja 9-0-47-2; van Troost 1-0-4-0

1/0 2/29 3/31 4/38 5/42 6/44 7/54 8/82 9/131 10/136

Bowling: Srinath 9.1-1-30-4; Khan 8-1-17-1; Harbhajan Singh 10-1-20-1; Kumble 10-1-32-4; Ganguly 4-0-14-0; Tendulkar 4-0-9-0; Sehwag 3-0-6-0

Umpires: D.J. Harper, P. Willey.

Toss: India   Points: India 4, Netherlands 0.

THURSDAY 13 FEBRUARY 2003
ENGLAND vs ZIMBABWE - GROUP A
HARARE SPORTS CLUB, HARARE. ZIMBABWE WON ON FORFEIT

The English declined to travel to Harare for this fixture because of security concerns. Two requests by the English and Wales Cricket Board to the ICC to transfer this game to South Africa were rejected. The English contingent were worried about the unstable political situation in Zimbabwe and Harare in particular. Several weeks earlier, the England board had received letters from a group calling itself The Sons and Daughters of Zimbabwe, which threatened to send England players "back to Britain in wooden coffins". The England board had kept the letters secret from the players and their existence was disclosed to the players less than two weeks before the game at a meeting with ICC officials. The ICC, convinced the death threats were a hoax, were unable to allay English concerns about their safety in Harare.

Eventually, a technical committee of the ICC ruled that the Harare venue was safe despite England's security concerns. The ICC then awarded the match and the four points to Zimbabwe. This forfeit increased the difficulty of England's task of progressing from the group. The no-show had ramifications that were more far-reaching. The England board were open to claims for compensation for foregone television and sponsorship revenue. The ICC withheld US$3.5 million from England's share of the tournament revenue, pending settlement of the claims. The knock-on effect was that the England board reduced their financial support of the domestic competitions.

The walkover meant that Zimbabwe already had eight points in the bank, shortening their odds for progression to the Super Six stage.

Points: Zimbabwe 4, England 0.

NEW ZEALAND vs WEST INDIES - GROUP B
ST GEORGE'S PARK, PORT ELIZABETH, SOUTH AFRICA: NEW ZEALAND WON BY 20 RUNS

New Zealand, desperate to win after having foregone eight points, kept their hopes of progression alive with a gritty win against the West Indies. The charge was led by a quality all-round performance from Andre Adams, born in Auckland to a Guyanese mother and a father from Caribbean nation St Vincent and the Grenadines.

After being sent in, Fleming and Daniel Vettori, promoted to open in a pinch-hitting role, gave the innings a bright start with a stand of 42 runs from seven overs. The game was delicately poised at 3-66 after the openers and Styris had been removed. Astle and Cairns batted with authority to add 64 runs in a little over 12 overs. Astle was unlucky to be given out by umpire Rudi Koertzen when replays showed he had not touched the ball on its way through to the keeper. With the pitch gradually slowing down, captain Hooper turned to his part-timers Hinds and Gayle to slow things down. The move paid dividends as Hinds took the wickets of Astle, Vincent and Cairns in successive overs. From a reasonable position of 3-130 in the 29th over, the Kiwis had slumped to 6-147 in the 33rd over.

From this point, the recall of wicketkeeper and skilled batsman Brendon McCullum was vindicated. McCullum patiently worked the ball into the gaps and a 41 run union with Chris Harris had the Kiwis within range of 200. The fireworks began when Harris was bowled by Gayle in the 44th over. Adams and McCullum increased the tempo and 45 runs were blasted from the last five overs. With McCullum playing the support role, Adams took a shine to the off-spin of Chris Gayle. Adams hit the Jamaican into the stands twice en route to an unbeaten 35 from 24 balls. Adams' salvo included taking 15 runs from Gayle's final over. The McCullum-Adams stand realised a rapid 53 runs, propelling New Zealand to a good total of 7-241.

Adams continued his work, sharing the new ball with speedster Shane Bond. Adams and Gayle continued their personal duel. Gayle struck the next blow, belting Adams for three consecutive fours in the seventh over. Adams finished the battle in his next over when he had Gayle caught at slip for 22. The crucial stage of the match began when Brian Lara, hero of the win against South Africa on the first day of the tournament, walked to the centre. It was not to be his day. Lara was on his way back to the pavilion four balls later when he was run out attempting a third run. Lara's neat clip off the toes through mid wicket had Vincent in hot pursuit. Vincent's relay throw from near the boundary was taken by Cairns at square leg. Cairns' aim was true with Lara well short of his ground.

Lara's dismissal unsettled the West Indies and three wickets fell in the next four overs. Adams continued his red-letter day when Hinds clipped to short cover. In his next over, Adams picked up his third wicket when Hooper hit a lazy hook to long-leg. The soft dismissal of the West Indian skipper left his side in peril at 4-46. Matters became worse when Oram's first delivery had Chanderpaul adjacent.

Ramnaresh Sarwan and Ricardo Powell decided that attack was the best method of defence. They smashed 21 runs from Cairns' only over. Oram and Vettori then applied the brakes on the scoring. The West Indies were deep in trouble at 6-80 after Oram bowled Powell. Sarwan and Ridley Jacobs were brought together and they batted together for over an hour and a half, scoring a determined 98 runs for the seventh wicket. Although they were able to bat time, they were unable to stop the run rate required from steadily growing. Oram gave little away in his spell and continually asked questions of the batsmen. The partnership between Sarwan and Jacobs was a World Cup record for the seventh wicket, surpassing the stand of 83 between Fleming and Harris against Pakistan in the 1999 competition.

After Sarwan was bowled by Vettori in the 44th over for a game-high 75, the asking rate was already more than nine per over. From the final delivery of the next over, Jacobs' brave innings ended when he was superbly caught by Oram for 50. This effectively killed off the game as a context. The West Indies needed 51 runs from the last five overs with just two wickets in hand. Vasbert Drakes and his bowling colleagues managed to dent the bowling figures of Bond while never threatening to steal victory. Fittingly, Adams ended proceedings by bowling Merv Dillon in the last over, his fourth wicket of the innings. Adams' all-round performance delivered him the man of the match award.

NEW ZEALAND		WEST INDIES	
S. P. Fleming (capt) c & b Dillon	25	C. H. Gayle c Fleming b Adams	22
D. L. Vettori b Drakes	13	W. W. Hinds c Styris b Adams	14
N. J. Astle c Jacobs b Hinds	46	B. C. Lara run out	2
S. B. Styris c Powell b Drakes	5	S. Chanderpaul lbw b Oram	2
C. L. Cairns c Dillon b Hinds	37	C. L. Hooper (capt) c Bond b Adams	3
L. Vincent c Hooper b Hinds	9	R. R. Sarwan b Vettori	75
C. Z. Harris b Gayle	19	R. L. Powell b Oram	14
B. B. McCullum (wk) not out	36	R. D. Jacobs (wk) c Oram b Styris	50
A. R. Adams not out	35	V. C. Drakes not out	16
Extras (lb 10, w 4, nb 2)	16	N. A.M. McLean run out	5
(50 overs)	7-241	M. Dillon b Adams	8
Did not bat: J. D. P. Oram, S. E. Bond		Extras (b 1, lb 3, w 5, nb 1)	10
1/42 2/58 3/66 4/130 5/141 6/147 7/188		(49.4 overs)	10-221
Bowling: Dillon 10-1-30-1; McLean 6-0-38-0; Drakes		1/34 2/36 3/42 4/46 5/46 6/80 7/178 8/191 9/200	
10-1-49-2; Hinds 10-0-35-3; Hooper 9-0-42-0;		10/221	
Gayle 5-0-37-1		Bowling: Bond 10-2-43-0; Adams 9.4.-1-44-4; Oram	
		10-2-26-2; Cairns 1-0-21-0; Vettori 10-0-38-1;	
		Astle 4-0-14-0; Styris 5-0-31-1	

Umpires: D.B. Hair, R.E. Koertzen.

Toss: West Indies   Points: New Zealand 4, West Indies 0.

FRIDAY 14 FEBRUARY 2003
BANGLADESH vs SRI LANKA - GROUP B
PIETERMARITZBURG, SOUTH AFRICA: SRI LANKA WON BY 10 WICKETS

This context in KwaZulu-Natal's capital was effectively over within half an hour after a withering opening burst by Sri Lanka's Warnakulasuriya Patabendige Ushantha Joseph Chaminda Vaas.

After Jayasuriya sent Bangladesh in, Vaas achieved the unprecedented feat of taking a hat-trick from the first three deliveries of the match. Hannan Sarkar was bowled attempting an expansive drive from the first ball of the game. Next ball, Mohammad Ashraful popped up a regulation return catch to the gleeful left-armer. The hat-trick was achieved when Vaas induced an edge from Ehsanul Haque, which was pouched at second slip. The trifecta of Bangadeshi victims caused Vaas to perform an impersonation of an erratic aeroplane.

Sanwar Hossain had the audacity to hit the fourth delivery of the match to the boundary. After Vaas sent down a wide, the fourth wicket was captured when Hossain was caught on the crease. From a diabolical start of 4-5 after an over, the day deteriorated for the Bangladeshis when Vaas had Al Sahariar caught at mid-off in the fifth over by de Silva, playing in his 300th limited-overs international. The innings lay in ruins at 5-25 and Canada's record lowest score in a World Cup of 45 was under threat.

Alok Kapali and skipper Khaled Masud staged a mini-recovery. Forty-five runs were added in the partnership, with the batsmen singling out Dilhara Fernando for punishment. Fernando struck back to remove Kapali. With the lower-order exposed, Muralitharan went to work. The off-spin master took three wickets at little cost to push Bangladesh to 9-98. Some late hitting by Mashrafe Mortaza, including a six off Muralitharan, pushed the score to 128.

Vaas returned to the attack to claim Mortaza's wicket. Vaas' analysis of six for 25 was the third-best bowling performance in a World Cup.

Atapattu and Jayasuriya were not seriously challenged by the Bangladeshi bowling. The target was achieved without incident in the 22nd over. Atapattu was in good touch in compiling an unbeaten 69 from 71 balls. In the process, Atapattu reached 6,000 runs in limited-overs internationals. Jayasuriya's unbeaten 55 was scored at close to a run a ball. A boundary by the Sri Lankan captain from the first ball of the 22nd over by Mohammad Rafique secured the four points for the island nation. Vaas was a clear choice for the winner of the Man of the Match award.

BANGLADESH		SRI LANKA	
Hanna Sarkar b Vaas	0	M. S. Atapattu not out	69
Al Sahariar c de Silva b Vaas	10	S. T. Jayasuriya (capt) not out	55
Mohammad Ashraful c & b Vaas	0	Extras (w 1, nb 2)	2
Ehsanul Haque c Jayawardene b Vaas	0	(21.1 overs)	0-126
Sanwar Hossain lbw b Vaas	4	Did not bat: H.P. Tillekeratne, P. A. de Silva, D. P.M.	
Alok Kapali c Jayasuriya b Fernando	32	D. Jayawardene, K. C. Sangakkara (wk), R. P. Arnold,	
Khaled Masud (capt/wk) lbw b Muralitharan	20	W.P.U.J.C. Vaas, R. A.P. Nissanka, M. Muralitharan,	
Mohammad Rafiq c Sangakkara b Muralitharan	6	C.R.D. Fernando	
Tapash Baisya c Arnold b Muralitharan	5	Bowling: Manjurul Islam 6-1-22-0; Mashrafe	
Mashrafe Mortaza c Muralitharan b Vaas	28	Mortaza 5-0-38-0; Tapash Baisya 3-0-21-0; Mohammad	
Manjurul Islam not out	3	Rafiq 4.1-1-22-0; Sanwar Hossain 2-0-14-0; Alok	
Extras (b 1, lb 4, w 9, nb 2)	16	Kapali 1-0-9-0	
(31.1 overs)	10-124		

1/0 2/0 3/0 4/5 5/25 6/70 7/82 8/88 9/98 10/124

Bowling: Vaas 9.1-2-25-6; Nissanka 5-0-22-0;
Fernando 7-0-47-1; Muralitharan 10-4-25-3

Umpires: B.F. Bowden, R.B. Tiffin.

Toss: Sri Lanka   Points: Sri Lanka 4, Bangladesh 0.

SATURDAY 15 FEBRUARY 2003
AUSTRALIA vs INDIA - GROUP A
CENTURION, SOUTH AFRICA: AUSTRALIA WON BY 9 WICKETS

This keenly anticipated clash turned out to be a fizzer as Australia obliterated India by nine wickets. On the back of the unconvincing win against the Netherlands, this meek performance raised real concerns about India's prospects of making an impact in the tournament.

The Australian batting had a more settled feel with Bevan and Lehmann available. Harvey could consider himself unlucky to be squeezed out of the side after his strong contribution to the win against Pakistan.

Sourav Ganguly called correctly and opened the Indian innings with Tendulkar. From the outset, the Indian batsmen appeared nervous and unsettled by the intensity of the Australian bowling. Ponting chose to give Lee an opportunity with the new ball and to use Gillespie first-change. His tactics were on the money as Lee's pace and swing complemented the probing line and length of McGrath beautifully.

Lee struck in the fifth over when he had the Indian captain caught behind, slashing at a wide ball with the total on 22. Sehwag joined Tendulkar and the pair began to score freely, which included Tendulkar taking 14 runs off a McGrath over. A promising start of 1-41 in the eighth over was quickly turned on its head. Sehwag was unable to resist an undisciplined slash at Lee and became Gilchrist's second victim. The epitome of accurate seam bowling, McGrath, fought back in style, sending down three consecutive maidens to Tendulkar and Dravid to apply the brakes to the scoring.

Gillespie was brought into the attack with impressive results. From his first ball, he bowled the out of touch Dravid. McGrath struck in the next over when he won a questionable lbw verdict against Yuvraj Singh. In the next over, Gillespie forced Mohammad Kaif to play an ill-judged pull shot. Symonds claimed another athletic catch running in from near the boundary.

From a parlous 5-50, Tendulkar carried his team's hopes of a decent total. That did not materialise when the Little Master was trapped by a canny Gillespie slower ball on middle stump. Tendulkar had been subdued, his 36 runs taking more than two hours. Some belligerent batting from Harbhajan Singh and Kumble enabled India to eke out an inadequate total of 125 inside 42 overs. Harbhajan Singh was able to briefly defy the trend of slow scoring with boundaries from Lee and Hogg, including an unusual six off Lee that was slashed over deep point. Gillespie was the standout Australian bowler, bowling ten overs off the reel for the mean figures of 3-13.

For India to prevail, early wickets were the key. This never looked likely as the Indian bowlers appeared dejected from the outset. Gilchrist and Hayden batted positively and they flayed the new ball attack of Srinath and Zaheer Khan as though they were park cricketers. Srinath bowled like a man who knew his international cricket career would soon be over and Khan seemed out of his depth. The introduction of Harbhajan Singh and Kumble did not slow the Australians' progress. It wasn't until 100 runs were on the board that the first wicket fell, Gilchrist missing a wide ball from Kumble. Ponting played a chirpy innings and the target was reached within 23 overs. Hayden top scored for the Aussies with an aggressive 45 not out from 49 balls.

Gillespie took Man of the Match honours for his high quality exhibition of seam bowling. For Australia, things were going swimmingly. The first two fixtures against the main rivals in Group A had produced powerful wins that sent a message to the rival teams. Australia were going to be hard to stop, even without Warne.

INDIA		AUSTRALIA	
S. C. Ganguly (capt) c Gilchrist b Lee	9	A. C. Gilchrist (wk) st Dravid b Kumble	48
S. R. Tendulkar lbw b Gillespie	36	M. L. Hayden not out	45
V. Sehwag c Gilchrist b Lee	4	R. T. Ponting (capt) not out	24
R. Dravid (wk) b Gillespie	1	Extras (3 lb, 8 w)	11
Yuvraj Singh lbw b McGrath	0	(22.2 overs)	1-128
M. Kaif c Symonds b Gillespie	1	Did not bat: D. R. Martyn, D. S. Lehmann, M. G. Bevan,
D. Mongia c Symonds b Lee	13	A. Symonds, G. B. Hogg, B. Lee, J. N. Gillespie, G. D. McGrath.
A. Kumble not out	16	1/100
Harbhajan Singh lbw b Hogg	28	Bowling: Srinath 4-0-26-0 ; Zaheer Khan 4-0-26-0;
Zaheer Khan lbw b Lehmann	1	Harbhajan Singh 7.2-0-49-0; Kumble 7-0-24-1
J. Srinath run out	0	
Extras (5 lb, 10 w, 1 nb)	16	
(41.4 overs)	10-125	

1/22 2/41 3/44 4/45 5/50 6/78 7/80 8/120 9/125 10/125

Bowling: McGrath 8-3-23-1; Lee 9-1-36-3; Gillespie 10-2-13-3; Symonds 6-0-25-0; Hogg 4.4-0-16-1; Lehmann 4-0-7-1

Umpires: E.A.R. de Silva, D.R. Shepherd.

Toss: India   Points: Australia 4, India 0.

CANADA vs KENYA - GROUP B
NEWLANDS, CAPE TOWN, SOUTH AFRICA (DAY/NIGHT): KENYA WON BY 4 WICKETS

Kenya enjoyed the rare status of favourite in this fixture between two of cricket's emerging nations. There would be no upset here, although Canada ran the Kenyans much closer than expected.

Canada improved a little on their 180 against Bangladesh with a moderate score of 197 all out. Ian Billcliff top scored again and he was the cornerstone of the innings with a resolute 71. Billcliff had the honour of being the first Canadian player to score a 50 in a limited-overs international. He teamed up with captain Harris to put on 86 runs for the fourth wicket. From 3-134, the Canadians were able to edge the run rate to four runs per over at the end of the innings. The scoring received a little boost in the later overs when Sanjayan Thuraisingam hit a boundary from Maurice Odume, which was followed in the next over by a strike into the crowd over long on off Tony Suji. Odoyo was the pick of the Kenyan bowlers, claiming 4-28.

Kenya's assignment of scoring 198 runs suffered an early setback when Kennedy Otieno played on to Thuraisingam. Ravindu Shah continued his good form with a controlled 61 and he combined well with Steve Tikolo. The pair put on 84 for the second wicket as the Kenyans kept pace with the required run rate. From a good platform, the Kenyans wobbled to 5-154. Hitesh Modi found it difficult to hit the ball off the square, labouring to six from 48 deliveries. John Davison's off-spinners were able to halt the scoring and claim three middle-order victims. From that point, the value of Kenya's greater international experience shone through. Odoyo held his nerve and, with sensible assistance from Peter Ongondo, he guided his team home to victory with nine balls to spare. Odoyo's efforts earned him the man of the match award.

CANADA		KENYA	
I. Maraj b Odoyo	5	K. O. Otieno b Thuraisingham	4
J. M. Davison c C. Obuya b Ongondo	31	R. D. Shah c Maraj b Thuraisingham	61
D. Chumney c Shah b C. Obuya	10	S. O. Tikolo (capt) lbw b Davison	42
I. S. Billcliff b T. Suji	71	H. S. Modi c Harris b Davison	6
J. V. Harris (capt) c T. Suji b C. Obuya	31	M. O. Odumbe lbw b Davison	26
A. F. Sattaur b Odumbe	7	T. M. Odoyo not out	27
N. A. de Groot lbw b Odumbe	0	P. J. Ongondo b Codrington	16
A. Bagai c D. Obuya b Odoyo	12	D. O. Obuya not out	4
S. Thuraisingham c D. Obuya b Odoyo	13	Extras (lb 3, w 9)	12
A. Codrington b Odoyo	5	(48.3 overs)	6-198
D. Joseph not out	4	Did not bat: C. O. Obuya, T. O. Suji, M. A. Suji.	
Extras (lb 2, w 5, nb 1)	8	1/15 2/99 3/116 4/148 5/154 6/192	
(49 overs)	10-197	Bowling: Joseph 10-1-39-0; Thuraisingham 10-1-53-2;	
1/18 2/47 3/48 4/134 5/158 6/159 7/162 8/186 9/186		Codrington 10-1-44-1; Davison 10-3-15-3; de	
10/197		Groot 4-0-22-0; Maraj 4.3-0-22-0	
Bowling: M. Suji 7-1-23-0; Odoyo 10-1-28-4;			
Ongondo 6-1-12-1; C. Obuya 10-1-46-2; Odumbe 9-0-41-2;			
T. Suji 7-0-45-1			

Umpires: A.V. Jayaprakash, Nadeem Ghauri.

Toss: Canada   Points: Kenya 4, Canada 0.

SUNDAY 16 FEBRUARY 2003
ENGLAND vs NETHERLANDS - GROUP A
EAST LONDON, SOUTH AFRICA: ENGLAND WON BY 6 WICKETS

England finally made it to the field and recorded a comfortable win over the eager, but limited, Netherlands side at Buffalo Park.

The game was headed for a very early finish when the Dutch top-order were put to flight, the score an ailing 5-31 after 17 overs. Jimmy Anderson made a dream World Cup debut, ripping through the specialist batsmen to claim 4-25 from an uninterrupted spell of 10 overs. Tim de Leede, taking toll of any short deliveries, showed admirable application his unbeaten 58 which kept England in the field for the full 50 overs. He managed an unbroken 30 run stand for the tenth wicket with wicketkeeper Jeroen Smits to reach a final tally of 9-142. Andy Caddick bowled superbly and without luck. All of the English bowlers finished with tidy analyses, with only off-spinner Ian Blackwell conceding more than 30 runs from his ten over allotment.

England endeavoured to reach the target of 144 as quickly as possible to boost their net run rate. Marcus Trescothick seemed to have let this objective adversely affect his shot selection, being bowled after attempting an unsightly heave across the line off Edgar Schiferli. From 1-18, Nick Knight and Michael Vaughan soon found the groove against benign bowling and the scoring accelerated to six an over. Shortly after reaching his half-century, Vaughan edged occasional leg-spinner Dan van Bunge to slip. Two balls later, Andrew Flintoff struck a half-tracker from van Bunge to mid wicket. Knight struck van Bunge for two consecutive fours to bring put his fifty. Knight hit another van Bunge long-hop but succeeded only in giving van Bunge his third wicket within three overs. There was to be no further joy for the Netherlands as Blackwell and Paul Collingwood hit the 17 runs required in 10 minutes without incident. England managed to reach their target within 23 overs.

In an unspectacular game, Anderson was the Man of the Match.

NETHERLANDS		ENGLAND	
L. P. van Troost lbw b Anderson	8	M. E. Trescothick b Schiferli	12
D. L.S. van Bunge c White b Anderson	4	N. V. Knight c Zuiderent b van Bunge	51
N. A. Statham lbw b Flintoff	7	M. P. Vaughan c de Leede b van Bunge	51
B. Zuiderent c Hussain b Anderson	2	A. Flintoff c Lefebvre b van Bunge	0
K. J.J. van Noortwijk c Stewart b Anderson	0	I. D. Blackwell not out	22
T. B.M. de Leede not out	58	P. D. Collingwood not out	5
J. F. Kloppenburg c Knight b Blackwell	10	Extras (w 3)	3
E. Schiferli st Stewart b Blackwell	12	(23.2 overs)	4-144
R. P. Lefebvre (capt) b White	6	Did not bat: N. Hussain (capt), A. J. Stewart (wk), C. White,	
Adeel Raja lbw b White	2	A. R. Caddick, J. M. Anderson.	
J. Smits (wk) not out	17	1/18 2/107 3/107 4/126	
Extras (lb 10, w 4, nb 2)	16	Bowling: Schiferli 5-0-33-1; Lefebvre 5-0-18-0; de	
(50 overs)	9-142	Leede 4-0-29-0; Adeel Raja 5-0-34-0; van Bunge 3-0-16-3;	
1/15 2/22 3/31 4/31 5/31 6/67 7/90 8/108 9/112		Kloppenburg 1.2-0-14-0	
Bowling: Caddick 10-4-19-0; Anderson 10-1-25-4; Flintoff			
10-2-29-1; White 10-3-22-2; Blackwell 10-0-37-2			

Umpires: D.B. Hair, R.E. Koertzen.

Toss: England   Points: England 4, Netherlands 0

NAMIBIA vs PAKISTAN - GROUP A
KIMBERLEY, SOUTH AFRICA: PAKISTAN WON BY 171 RUNS

In the diamond mining town of Kimberley, Pakistan predictably made short work of Namibia in front of a small crowd of less than 3,000. The match was the seventh limited-overs international to be played at Kimberley and it was the first time that the team batting first had won the match. Pakistan's batting against the gentle Namibian attack was pedestrian and it was left to a fast-bowling barrage to secure a big win.

The Pakistan total of 9-255 was a lethargic effort. The Pakistani batsmen were unable to consistently rise above an eager and disciplined effort by the Namibians with the ball and in the field. Saeed Anwar's return to the side was not a success and Inzamam-ul-Haq failed again. Salim Elahi's measured 63 from 100 balls formed the backbone of the innings, helping Pakistan to 3-150 in the 36th over. Yousuf Youhana made a handy 43 and quickfire knocks by Rashid Latif and Wasim Akram in the latter stages lifted the scoring rate. The final 10 overs yielded 82 runs, although the steady flow of wickets was a disappointment. Opposition sides noted that Pakistan lost nine wickets against the Namibian attack.

A target of 256 runs was always going to be far too much for the Namibian part-timers against a talented Pakistani bowling line-up. And so it proved. Shoaib Akhtar bowled a rapid spell, pushing the speed gun to 99 miles per hour (approximately 159 kilometres per hour). At the other end, Wasim Akram bowled with his customary speed and late movement into the pads. The Namibian dressing room soon became a hive of activity as wickets fell with great frequency. A scoreline of 3-3 became 5-17, which reached 9-42 from 11 overs. The record low score in a World Cup of 45 was again under threat. The Namibian numbers 10 and 11, Bjorn Kotze and Rudi van Vuuren, saved their country from that embarrassment. Their brief rally of 42 for the 10th wicket took Namibia to 84 before Saqlain Mushtaq picked up the final wicket.

The Namibian innings was over inside 18 overs and extras was second top score, behind Bjorn Kotzes unbeaten 24. Wasim Akram and Shoaib Akhtar collected nine wickets between them, although Shoaib was expensive. Wasim Akram's superb figures of 5-28, his sixth five wicket haul in limited-overs internationals, earned him the man of the match award.

PAKISTAN		NAMIBIA	
Saeed Anwar c L. Burger b B. Kotze	23	R. Walters c Rashid Latif b Wasim Akram	0
Salim Elahi c D. Kotze b A. Burger	63	S. J. Swanepoel c Inzamam-ul-Haq b Shoaib Akhtar	1
Younis Khan c van Schoor b L. Burger	28	A. J. Burger c Younis Khan b Shoaib Akhtar	14
Inzamam-ul-Haq b D. Kotze	4	D. Keulder b Shoaib Akhtar	0
Rashid Latif (wk) b Snyman	36	G. B. Murgatroyd lbw b Wasim Akram	4
Wasim Akram not out	20	L. J. Burger lbw b Wasim Akram	0
Abdul Razzaq c van Schoor b Snyman	4	D. B. Kotze (capt) lbw b Wasim Akram	8
Waqar Younis (capt) run out	8	G. Snyman lbw b Shoaib Akhtar	0
Saqlain Mushtaq run out	1	M. van Schoor (wk) lbw b Wasim Akram	2
Shoaib Akhtar not out	3	B. L. Kotze not out	24
Extras (lb 11, w 10, nb 1)	22	R. J. van Vuuren c Waqar Younis b Saqlain Mushtaq	14
(50 overs)	9-255	Extras (lb 9, w 4, nb 4)	17
1/47 2/105 3/118 4/150 5/208 6/223 7/227 8/247 9/248		(17.4 overs)	10-84
Bowling: Snyman 8-0-51-2; van Vuuren 10-1-47-0; B. Kotze 10-1-51-2; L. Burger 10-0-45-1; D. Kotze 8-0-32-1; A. Burger 4-0-18-1		1/1 2/3 3/3 4/17 5/17 6/32 7/32 8/35 9/42 10/84	
		Bowling: Wasim Akram 9-1-28-5; Shoaib Akhtar 8-1-46-4; Saqlain Mushtaq 0.4-0-1-1	

Umpires: N.A. Mallender, D.L. Orchard.

Toss: Pakistan   Points: Pakistan 4, Namibia 0.

SOUTH AFRICA vs NEW ZEALAND - GROUP B
WANDERERS STADIUM, JOHANNESBURG, SOUTH AFRICA: NEW ZEALAND WON BY 9 WICKETS (DUCKWORTH-LEWIS METHOD)

South Africa's World Cup campaign was left hanging by a thread after a demoralising loss to New Zealand at the Wanderers Stadium. In the process, the home side became only the second side to lose a World Cup match after scoring 300 batting first. After a first-up loss to Sri Lanka and a forfeit to Kenya, it was also a vital game for New Zealand to win.

Herschelle Gibbs continued his sterling form with a spectacular innings of 143 from 141 balls, including three sixes. Gibbs' assault featured a gigantic six from Vettori that landed about 25 rows over the deep mid wicket fence. All of the New Zealand bowlers, apart from Styris, were punished. Unfortunately for the Proteas, none of his teammates made a substantial contribution in support, the next highest score being 33. Despite the impressive total of 6-306, 67 runs was the highest partnership, compiled by Gibbs and Kallis for the third wicket. After his century took 121 balls, Gibbs accelerated, his last 42 runs coming from a mere 20 deliveries. During the onslaught, Gibbs savaged 19 runs from Daniel Vettori's final over. Klusener played one of his characteristic innings in the last seven overs, flaying the ragged bowlers for an unbeaten 33 from 21 balls. In their pursuit for a massive total, captain Shaun Pollock pushed his hitters up the order. This left Gary Kirsten in the uncharacteristic role of batting at number eight. The batting services of Boeta Dippenaar were not required at all. This adventurous approach resulted in 98 runs being scored from the last 10 overs.

With dark clouds moving towards the vicinity of the Bull Ring, New Zealand faced a difficult assignment of scoring 307 to win. However, the short boundaries helped to make the task a little more manageable. Fleming decided to not use Vettori in an opening role, walking out to face the bowling with Craig McMillan instead. With the prospect that calculations from Messrs Duckworth and Lewis would be needed at some stage, a fast start from the Kiwi openers was crucial.

Fleming's form in the lead up to this match, an average of 24 from his last 23 matches, was no portent of what was to follow. After a steady start was made against Pollock and Ntini, Fleming and McMillan tore apart Donald and Kallis in their respective opening overs. Donald conceded 14 from his first over and Kallis was hammered for 17, including four consecutive boundaries by Fleming. After 12 overs, a 15-minute interruption due to a power cut after 12 overs slowed New Zealand's progress a little. The interruption worked in South Africa's favour. In the next over, Kallis found an edge from Fleming when he was on 53. Boucher put down a regulation catch moving high to his left. The breakthrough arrived in the next over when McMillan was caught behind off Donald.

From a good start of 1-89 in the 15th over, the Kiwis continued their positive approach. Fleming showed he was on the ball, as well as being on song with the bat, in an incident that occurred on the next legal delivery after McMillan's dismissal. New batsman Astle took a quick single from Donald and the throw to the bowler's end hit Astle's bat and continued to the boundary. Umpire Steve Bucknor decided that there was a dead ball and, following an approach from Fleming, the decision was changed to five runs. A short time later, play was delayed for 11 minutes due to rain.

These interruptions seemed to have no effect on Fleming's momentum. He played shots to all parts of the ground, each stroke beautifully timed and placed. There was not a hint of a slog. Several drives through the off side and clips through mid wicket were superb shots and worthy of inclusion in a batting coaching manual.

Fleming took a single from Klusener in the 30th over to reach his hundred from 109 balls. A few deliveries later, the rain returned, but with increased intensity on this occasion. The shower kept the patrons at the Bull Ring waiting for 52 minutes. After the Duckworth-Lewis calculations were performed, the innings was reduced to a 39-over affair. The benefit of New Zealand having nine wickets in hand at this point was that the equation became less demanding. A required run rate of 6.4 after 30 overs changed to a tick over 5.5 per over: the equation was that New Zealand needed to score 44 from 51 balls.

The hundred partnership was brought up in the next over when Fleming struck Klusener for another boundary. The body language of the South Africans spoke volumes as their bowlers continued to be battered. The brilliance of Fleming continued and allowed Astle to gather his runs almost unnoticed. The New Zealanders carted a listless Donald, who conceded nearly nine an over, while Klusener was punished heavily. With victory in sight in the 35th over, Astle reached his 50 from just 52 balls.

In the end, New Zealand reached the victory target with more than two overs to play with. Fleming continued his mauling of Donald's bowling, hitting the ageing paceman for 10 runs from the 37th over. Fleming's drive through backward point for four off Donald delivered the knockout punch to a stunned South Africa. The Fleming-Astle stand produced an unbeaten 140 runs for the second wicket. Fleming's dazzling innings of 134 not out from 132 deliveries would be his highest score in limited-overs internationals. Although he was outscored by Gibbs by nine runs, the majestic nature of Fleming's innings deservedly won him the Man of the Match award. The win kept alive New Zealand's chances of progression. On the other hand, South Africa could not afford a slip up in their last three pool matches.

SOUTH AFRICA		NEW ZEALAND	
G. C. Smith c McCullum b Bond	23	C. D. McMillan c Boucher b Donald	25
H. H. Gibbs c McMillan b Oram	143	S. P. Fleming (capt) not out	134
N. Boje b Styris	29	N. J. Astle not out	54
J. H. Kallis c Vincent b Vettori	33	Extras (lb 8, w 8)	16
M. V. Boucher (wk) c Cairns b Oram	10	(36.5 overs)	1-229
L. Klusener not out	33	Did not bat: S. B. Styris, C. L. Cairns, L. Vincent, B. B.	
S. M. Pollock (capt) c Oram by Adams	10	McCullum (wk), J. D. P. Oram, A. R. Adams, D. L. Vettori,	
G. Kirsten not out	5	S. E. Bond	
Extras (lb 6, w 11, nb 3)	20	1/89	
(50 overs)	6-306	Bowling: Pollock 8-0-36-0; Ntini 8-1-33-0; Donald	
Did not bat: H. H. Dippenaar, M. Ntini, A. A. Donald		5.5-0-52-1; Kallis 8-0-47-0; Boje 2-0-16-0; Klusener 5-0-37-0	

1/60 2/126 3/193 4/243 5/260 6/287

Bowling: Bond 10-0-73-1; Adams 9-0-57-1; Oram 8-0-52-2; Styris 10-0-44-1; Vettori 10-0-58-1; Astle 3-0-16-0

Umpires: S.A. Bucknor, P. Willey

Toss: South Africa   Points: New Zealand 4, South Africa 0.

TUESDAY 18 FEBRUARY 2003
BANGLADESH vs WEST INDIES - GROUP B
BENONI, SOUTH AFRICA: NO RESULT

Rain deprived the West Indies of the full four points in this match against the struggling Bangladesh side at Benoni. In the end, the decision to not allocate a reserve day for each match would cost the West Indians dearly. The two points collected by Bangladesh from this match would be the only points credited to them in this tournament.

After heavy overnight rain and morning drizzle, it was a surprise that play went underway on time at all. A disciplined bowling effort from Bangladesh kept the West Indian run rate hovering at four for most of the innings. After Gayle and Hinds were dismissed cheaply, Lara and Chanderpaul strengthened the innings with a 68 run stand from 16 overs. Lara was unusually subdued, batting for nearly two hours for his 46 from 76 balls. From 2-108, the West Indies were kept in check and they moved to a wobbly 5-158 in the 40th over. The men from the Caribbean moved into attack mode, striking 86 runs from the last 10 overs. The Bangladeshis wilted in the face of the onslaught in the final seven overs, which yielded an astonishing 73 runs. Hooper kept the score ticking over and hit the ball into the gaps in his clever 45. The late-innings charge was led by Ricardo Powell, who blasted 50 from just 30 balls, including four sixes.

A target of 245 looked to be too high a mountain for the Bangladeshis to climb. The top-order batsmen were given three reprieves by the West Indian catchers. The usually brilliant Hooper putting two chances to ground. Dismissed for a golden duck against Sri Lanka, Ehsanul Haque almost suffered the same fate here. Gayle missed the chance at second slip from Drakes. Ehsanul Haque was dropped again by Hooper at first slip, but his lives ran out when Dillon bowled him for 12. From 2-19, the score was pushed along to 2-32 in the ninth over before rain forced the players from the rain at 2.55 pm. The rain did not abate and the game was finally called off at 5 pm. A no result meant no man of the match.

The beneficiary of the no result was South Africa, who were two points adrift of third place in the group. With wins almost certain against Bangladesh and Canada in their next two games, the hosts' final pool match against Sri Lanka at Durban was vital to their advancement to the Super Six stage.

WEST INDIES		BANGLADESH	
W. W. Hinds c Al Sahariar b Khaled Mahmud	18	Al Sahariar c Gayle b Drakes	5
C. H. Gayle c Sanwar Hossain b Manjurul Islam	0	Ehsanul Haque b Dillon	12
B. C. Lara c Al Sahariar b Ehsanul Haque	46	Mohammad Ashraful not out	8
S. Chanderpaul lbw b Enhsnaul Haque	29	Sanwar Hossain not out	2
C. L. Hooper (capt) c & b Alok Kapali	45	Extras (lb 2, w 3)	5
R. R. Sarwan c & b Khaled Mahmud	13	(8.1 overs)	2-32
R. L. Powell c Sanwar Hossain b Majurul Islam	50	Did not bat: Tushar Imran, Alok Kapali,	
R. D. Jacobs (wk) not out	6	Khaled Masud (capt/wk), Khaled Mahmud,	
V. C. Drakes run out	0	Mohammad Rafiq, Manjurul Islam, Talha Jubair	
M. Dillon c Mohammad Ashraful	10	1/19 2/19	
C. D. Colleymore not out	0	Bowling: Dillon 4.1-0-13-1; Drakes 4-1-17-1	
Extras (b 1, lb 6, w 13, nb 7)	27		
(50 overs)	9-244		
1/19 2/40 3/108 4/130 5/158 6/217 7/231 8/231 9/242			
Bowling: Manjrul Islam 10-0-62-3; Talha Jubair 8-0-46-0;			
Khaled Mahmud 10-1-48-2; Ehsanul Haque 10-0-34-2;			
Mohammed Rafiq 10-0-44-0; Alok Kapali 2-1-3-1			

Umpires: B.G. Jerling, R.B. Tiffin.

Toss: Bangladesh   Points: Bangladesh 2, West Indies 2.

WEDNESDAY 19 FEBRUARY 2003
ZIMBABWE vs INDIA - GROUP A
HARARE SPORTS CLUB, HARARE, ZIMBABWE: INDIA WON BY 83 RUNS

After a poor start to the competition, India started down the road to recovery with a 83-run win over Zimbabwe in Harare. The hammering by Australia in the last match resulted in Ganguly shuffling the batting order around. He dropped himself to number four and Sehwag was given the role of opening the innings with Tendulkar.

Sehwag and Tendulkar saw off the new ball and played intelligently to set a good platform for the Indian innings. The run rate was marginally under a run a ball when, with the score on 99 in the 17th over, Sehwag got an edge to Whittall. The Indians lost momentum in the middle stages of the innings. In the 28th over, the left-arm orthodox spin of Grant Flower claimed two victims. The laboured innings of Mongia came to an end when he holed out to long on and, two balls later, Flower had the prized scalp of Tendulkar for 81. The delivery that bowled Tendulkar was a gem, pitching between middle and off and straightening. Unfortunately, Flower was denied the opportunity to bowl his full complement of overs when he injured a finger trying to stop a hard hit drive by Dravid.

Ganguly smashed leg-spinner Brian Murphy for a straight six and was out the next over to all-rounder Andy Blignaut. It was Blignaut's first game back in national colours after taking some time off to explore a modelling career. Another failure from Yuvraj Singh left India 5-184 with 11 overs remaining. Dravid, showing signs of returning to form, and Mohammad Kaif lifted the tempo and helped India to a good score of 7-255. Dravid contributed an unbeaten 43 and Kaif a quickfire 25.

Javagal Srinath had Zimbabwe two down by the ninth over after Vermeulen feathered one to Dravid and Wishart played on. Andy Flower was unable to get his innings moving and was bowled behind his legs by Harbhajan Singh when he failed to connect to a sweep shot. From a shaky 3-48, the Zimbabweans were in dire straits after Ganguly took three wickets in six balls. Grant Flower, Dion Ebrahim and Bliganut all fell to catches in the outfield. At 6-87 in the 26th over, Zimbabwe's hopes of an upset victory were forlorn. Guy Whittall played some good shots and he fell for 28 to an excellent catch by a diving Zaheer Khan at point off the occasional off-spin of Sehwag. From 7-124, Tatenda Taibu and Streak made some handy runs to keep the losing margin below 100 runs. Khan returned to the attack and he castled Douglas Hondo and Murphy in consecutive overs. Zimbabwe lasted less than 45 overs for their 172.

In a return to form, Tendulkar took out the Man of the Match award. An interesting footnote from the match was that the random inspections by the ICC found that players from both sides used bats that were more than the permitted width.

INDIA		ZIMBABWE	
V. Sehwag c Taibu b Whittall	36	C. B. Wishart b Srinath	12
S. R. Tendulkar b G. W. Flower	81	M. A. Vermeulen c Dravid b Srinath	0
D. Mongia c Hondo b G. W. Flower	12	A. Flower b Harbhajan Singh	22
S. C. Ganguly (capt) c Streak b Blignaut	24	G. W. Flower c Harhajan Singh b Ganguly	23
R. Dravid (wk) not out	43	D. D. Ebrahim c sub (Agarkar) b Ganguly	19
Yuvraj Singh c Taibu b Murphy	1	A. M. Blignaut c Mongia b Ganguly	2
M. Kaif lbw b Hondo	25	T. Taibu (wk) not out	29
Harbhajan Singh c Murphy b Streak	3	G. J. Whittall c Khan b Sehwag	28
Zaheer Khan not out	13	H. H. Streak (capt) c Kaif b Harbhajan Singh	20
Extras (b 4, lb 4, w 9)	17	B. A. Murphy b Khan	2
(50 overs)	7-255	D. T. Hondo b Khan	2
Did not bat: J. Srinath, A. Nehra		Extras (b 4, lb 2, w 5, nb 2)	13
1/99 2/142 3/142 4/182 5/184 6/227 7/234		(44.4 overs)	10-172
Bowling: Streak 9-0-46-1; Blignaut 10-0-54-1;		1/1 2/23 3/48 4/83 5/83 6/87 7/124 8/160 9/165 10/172	
Hondo 9-1-56-1; Whittall 6-0-37-1; G. W. Flower 6-0-14-2;		Bowling: Srinath 8-1-14-2; Khan 7.4-0-23-2; Nehra 7-0-35-0;	
Murphy 10-0-40-1		Harbhajan Singh 10-0-42-2; Ganguly 5-1-22-3;	
		Sehwag 3-0-14-1; Mongia 4-0-16-0	

Umpires: E.A.R. de Silva, R.E. Koertzen.

Toss: Zimbabwe   Points: India 4, Zimbabwe 0.

WEDNESDAY 19 FEBRUARY 2003
CANADA vs SRI LANKA - GROUP B
PAARL, SOUTH AFRICA: SRI LANKA WON BY 9 WICKETS

Cricket followers who had decided to visit Paarl's vineyards in the morning would probably have arrived at an empty cricket ground after their visit. Sri Lanka brushed minnows Canada aside with ridiculous ease. The match lasted a total of 23.2 overs, comfortably the shortest completed match in World Cup history. The aficionados who arrived at Boland Park for the first ball had a good argument for the staging of an exhibition match to give them some value for money.

Prabath Nissanka came into the side to replace the injured Gunaratne. Sharing the new ball with hat-trick man Chaminda Vaas, Nissanka had the best day of his international cricket career. His pace and bounce were beyond the capabilities of the Canadian batsmen, returning figures of 4-12 from seven overs. Vaas continued his good form, claiming three out of the first four wickets to fall.

The demolition began in the second over when Nissanka had Davison caught behind for a duck. By the 10th over, the Canadians were a dreadful 6-12 and Nissanka was on a hat-trick. One of the first six victims was Nick de Groot, who made his third duck from as many starts in the tournament. Keeper Ashish Bagai negotiated the hat-trick ball without incident. In the next over, the highlight of the innings arrived when Harris hit Vaas for two consecutive boundaries. In the next over, Nissanka set the Canadians back to 7-21 when a short ball hit Harris in the ribs, forcing the Canadian skipper to tread on his stumps. The Canadian tail were unable to hit their way out of embarrassment. Fernando and Muralitharan collected a few quick wickets as the innings folded for a mere 36 in 18.4 overs. This was the lowest score in a limited-overs international, "beating" the previous nadir of 38 by Zimbabwe in Colombo in December 2001.

The Sri Lankans had a world record in sight: the shortest victory chase in a limited-overs international of 4.2 overs. Sri Lanka set this mark in their nine-wicket win over Zimbabwe in Colombo in December 2001. Sri Lanka failed in this mission by two deliveries. In the process, the wicket of Jayasuriya was lost, ironically, to the Sri Lankan-born Thuraisingham. Including the innings break of 10 minutes, the duration of the game was just one hour and 55 minutes. Nissanka picked up the man of the match honours.

CANADA		SRI LANKA	
D. Chumney c Sangakkara b Vaas	9	M. S. Atapattu not out	24
J. M. Davison c Sangakkara b Nissanka	0	S. T. Jayasuriya (capt) lbw b Thuraisingham	9
A. F. Sattaur lbw b Vaas	0	K. C. Sangakkara not out	4
I. S. Billcliff lbw b Vaas	1	Extras	0
N. A. de Groot lbw b Nissanka	0	(4.4 overs)	1-37
J. V. Harris (capt) hit wicket b Nissanka	9	Did not bat: H. P. Tillekeratne, P. A. de Silva,	
I. Maraj lbw b Nissanka	0	D. P.H. D. Jayawardene, R. P. Arnold, W. P. U. J.C. Vaas,	
A. Bagai (wk) c Jayawardene b Fernando	6	R. A.P. Nissanka, M. Muralitharan, C. R.D. Fernando	
S. Thuraisingham lbw b Fernando	6	1/23	
A. Codrington b Muralitharan	0	Bowling: Thuraisingham 2.4-0-22-1; Davison 2-0-15-0	
B. B. Seebaran not out	0		
Extras (lb 2, w 2, nb 1)	5		
(18.4 overs)	10-36		
1/0 2/6 3/11 4/12 5/12 6/12 7/21 8/31 9/36 10/36			
Bowling: Vaas 7-4-15-3; Nissanka 7-1-12-4; Muralitharan 2.4-0-3-1; Fernando 2-0-4-2			

Umpires: N.A. Mallender, D.R. Shepherd.

Toss: Sri Lanka   Points: Sri Lanka 4, Canada 0.

ENGLAND vs NAMIBIA - GROUP A
ST GEORGE'S PARK, PORT ELIZABETH, SOUTH AFRICA: ENGLAND WON BY 55 RUNS

In this clash of teams with blue coloured uniforms, England recorded an expected, but unconvincing, win against a spirited Namibian side. The English camp had cause to be concerned with their team's moderate form as the three remaining matches were against the most difficult opponents in the pool: Pakistan, India and Australia.

Captain Hussain was a withdrawal from the side on the morning of the game with a sore neck. The selectors brought in Hussain's Essex teammate Ronnie Irani to add to the team's collection of all-rounders. With Hussain looking on from the stands, Stewart captained his country for the last time. In the Namibian camp, the selectors opted to pick three Burgers: Jan-Berrie and brothers Louis and Sarel.

Within 10 overs, Knight and Vaughan were gone, both playing ill-judged pull shots to mid wicket from Rudi van Vuuren. Trescothick and Stewart batted with authority and they put together 78 runs for the third wicket. Trescothick and Stewart both made fine half-centuries, with Stewart reaching his milestone with a six off off-spinner Deon Kotze. Useful contributions flowed through the middle- to lower-order without any batsman threatening to take the modest bowling apart. White played with the most urgency, striking 35 from 29 balls, including two sixes, before he holed out to long on off van Vuuren in the final over. Namibian rugby international van Vuuren also dismissed Irani and Caddick in the final over, resulting in him achieving the first five-wicket haul by a Namibian in the World Cup.

After Swanepoel and Louis Burger fell cheaply, Jan-Berrie Burger set Namibia's innings alight. He dominated the scoring and found the boundary with regularity en route to 85 from 86-balls. For nearly 12 overs, Namibia were actually ahead of the Duckworth-Lewis par score. With Danie Keulder playing the support role, the third wicket stand of 97 in 17 overs gave the underdogs a chance. In the 30th over, the Burger threat was averted when Collingwood took a fine diving catch at square leg from White's bowling. From there, Keulder was unable to lift the tempo with the middle-order and the required run rate spiralled out of Namibia's range. Irani chipped in with three wickets and he was on a hat-trick in the 45th over. Keeper Melt van Schoor and van Vuuren survived the last five overs, with van Vuuren putting an exclamation mark on the game with a six from the last delivery by Anderson. A winning margin of only 55 runs and the inability to bowl out the Namibians inside 50 overs were not favourable signs for England. Jan-Berrie Burger deservedly won the man of the match award.

ENGLAND		NAMIBIA	
M. E. Trescothick c L. Burger b A. Burger	58	S. J. Swanepoel c Vaughan b Anderson	8
N. V. Knight c L. Burger b van Vuuren	6	A. J. Burger c Collingwood b White	85
M. P. Vaughan c L. Burger b van Vuuren	14	L. J. Burger c & b Flintoff	5
A. J. Stewart (capt) (wk) c B. Kotze b D. Kotze	60	D. Keulder run out	46
P. D. Collingwood c Keulder b D. Kotze	38	G. B. Murgatroyd b Irani	24
A. Flintoff c Keulder b Snyman	21	G. Snyman b White	0
I. D. Blackwell c van Schoor b Snyman	16	D. B. Kotze (capt) b Flintoff	7
C. White c S. Burger b van Vuuren	35	S. F. Burger c Collingwood b Irani	5
R. C. Irani c D. Kotze b van Vuuren	12	M. van Schoor (wk) not out	11
A. R. Caddick b van Vuuren	4	B. L. Kotze lbw b Irani	0
J. M. Anderson not out	0	R. J. van Vuuren not out	12
Extras (lb 1, w 4, nb 3)	8	Extras (lb 5, w 6, nb 3)	14
(50 overs)	10-272	(50 overs)	9-217

1/26 2/43 3/121 4/159 5/202 6/205 7/242 8/264 9/268 10/272

1/12 2/42 3/139 4/174 5/174 6/188 7/190 8/200 9/200

Bowling: Snyman 10-0-69-3; van Vuuren 10-2-43-5; L. Burger 9-0-45-0; B. Kotze 3-0-24-0; D. Kotze 10-0-35-1; A. Burger 2-0-23-1; S. Burger 6-0-32-0

Bowling: Caddick 8-2-28-0; Anderson 8-0-44-1; Flintoff 10-2-33-2; White 10-0-46-2; Vaughan 6-0-31-0; Irani 8-0-30-3

Umpires: S.J.A. Taufel, S. Venkataraghavan.

Toss: Namibia   Points: England 4, Namibia 0.

THURSDAY 20 FEBRUARY 2003
AUSTRALIA vs NETHERLANDS - GROUP A
NORTH WEST STADIUM, POTCHEFSTROOM, SOUTH AFRICA: AUSTRALIA WON BY 75 RUNS
(DUCKWORTH/LEWIS METHOD)

After waiting 39 years, the Aussies finally had their chance to avenge the shock defeat suffered at The Hague by Bob Simpson's men in 1964 on their way home from a tour of England. The Netherlands gave some determined resistance before falling well short of the Australian total in a rain-affected match.

Persistent showers had dogged the academic city of Potchefstroom in the days leading up to the game. It seemed that the biggest threat to the Australians claiming the four points was the weather. On the morning of the game, a large amount of water spilt from the covers as the groundsmen uncovered the pitch. The start of play was delayed for an hour as diligent efforts were made to dry the wicket. After sacks placed under the pitch rollers and power blowers did not produce the desired result, a police helicopter was called in to hover a short distance above the deck to remove as much moisture as possible.

The coin landed the way of Dutch skipper Roland Lefebvre and he asked Ponting to bat on a wicket that was less than 100 per cent. Initially, the match was reduced to 47 overs. Two further rain interruptions during the Australian innings cut the available overs to 36. Jimmy Maher returned to the side, this time in the capacity as stand-in keeper/batsman for the resting Gilchrist. Maher and Hayden did not find the going easy in the greasy conditions, with the ball frequently darting about.

The openers put on 52 before Maher edged to slip. Martyn, yet to score a run in the tournament, settled into his work well. Hayden and Martyn constructed Australia's second half-century stand before Hayden was caught at deep mid wicket in the 23rd over. Hayden contributed an unusually subdued 33 from 60 balls. In his first innings of the tournament, Lehmann batted fluently. His partnership with Martyn yielded 67 runs at five an over, seeing Australia to its final tally of 2-170 from 36 overs. Martyn batted in a polished fashion, garnering an unbeaten 67 from 76 balls. The Australians seemed oblivious to an aspect of the Duckworth-Lewis rules: which was that the number of wickets lost at a particular stage of an innings was relevant only at the time the innings was interrupted. This was apparent in the final eight overs, as Martyn and Lehmann continually pushed for ones and twos with low-risk shots.

The application of Duckworth-Lewis resulted in the Dutch target being inflated to 198 from 36 overs. Dark clouds loomed over the North-West Stadium and threatened to deprive this match of a winner. Ponting's first objective was to wheel through 25 overs, the minimum number of overs needed to ensure a result. As a consequence, despite conditions that were conducive to seam bowling, McGrath and Gillespie were spelled after just six overs from shortened run-ups. Lehmann and Symonds were introduced into the attack and the 25 over mark was reached in good time. At one point, Lehmann bowled an over in under a minute.

Once Gillespie had sent back van Bunge and Zuiderent inside six overs, the Netherlands never looked like getting close to the target. The Dutch lost wickets at regular intervals and the highest partnership of the innings was just 26. Opener Luuk van Troost played positively for his 23 before he became Lehmann's first victim. De Leede, who top scored with 58 against England the previous Sunday, was again his country's leading scorer with a useful 24. He managed to score the first six of the match when he hit Lehmann into the crowd. The Netherlands' score of 122 was their lowest score in their country's World Cup history. However, the Dutch could take some solace from reaching three figures against high quality opposition.

Andy Bichel, playing in his first World Cup match as cover for the rested Lee, bowled impressively. His figures of 3-13 from five overs were the best for the Australians. Ian Harvey, who was selected as a result of Hogg being given a break, bowled with intelligent variations of pace and picked up three wickets. Unluckily, both Bichel and Harvey were likely to be left out for Australia's next match against Zimbabwe. In a game of solid contributions from several players, Martyn ended up with the Man of the Match award.

AUSTRALIA		NETHERLANDS	
J. P. Maher (wk) c van Bunge b de Leede	26	L. P. van Troost c Bichel b Lehmann	23
M. L. Hayden c Schiferli b de Leede	33	D. L.S. van Bunge c Martyn b Gillespie	1
D. R. Martyn not out	67	B. Zuiderent c Maher b Gillespie	5
D. S. Lehmann not out	29	K. J.J. van Noortwijk lbw b Lehmann	13
Extras (4 b, 3 lb, 8 w)	15	T. B.M. de Leede c Maher b Bichel	24
(36 overs)	2-170	R. H. Scholte lbw b Bichel	8
Did not bat: R. T. Ponting (capt), M. G. Bevan, A. Symonds,		E. Schiferli b Harvey	9
I. J. Harvey, A. J. Bichel, J. N. Gillespie, G. D. McGrath.		J. F. Kloppenburg c Ponting b Bichel	9
1/52 2/103		R. P. Lefebvre (capt) not out	14
Bowling: Schiferli 7-0-42-0; Lefebvre 8-2-19-0; de		J. Smits (wk) c Maher b Harvey	0
Leede 7-0-34-2; Kloppenburg 7-0-34-0; Esmeijer 5-0-16-0;		J. J. Esmeijer c Ponting b Harvey	0
van Bunge 2-0-20-0		Extras (4 lb, 11 w, 1 nb)	16
		(30.2 overs)	10-122

1/8 2/18 3/42 4/59 5/85 6/90 7/96 8/112 9/118 10/122

Bowling: McGrath 3-1-10-0; Gillespie 3-0-7-2; Lehmann 8-0-27-2; Symonds 7-0-36-0; Bichel 5-0-13-3; Harvey 4.2-0-25-3

Umpires: D.L. Orchard, P. Willey.

Toss: Netherlands   Points: Australia 4, Netherlands 0.

FRIDAY 21 FEBRUARY 2003
KENYA vs NEW ZEALAND - GROUP B
NAIROBI, KENYA: KENYA WON BY FORFEIT

New Zealand declined to play in Nairobi because of security concerns. Kenya collected the four points, which lifted them to second spot on the table behind Sri Lanka. Two wins from their last three matches against Sri Lanka, Bangladesh and West Indies would be sufficient for Kenya to progress to the next stage.

Points: Kenya 4, New Zealand 0.

SATURDAY 22 FEBRUARY 2003
SOUTH AFRICA vs BANGLADESH - GROUP B
BLOEMFONTEIN, SOUTH AFRICA: SOUTH AFRICA WON BY 10 WICKETS

South Africa reacted to the loss to New Zealand by dropping Allan Donald, depriving the champion of a farewell appearance in front of his home crowd. The Proteas used the game against whipping boys Bangladesh to give three squad members, Andrew Hall, Robin Peterson and Monde Zondeki, a run. Bangladesh were thrashed in another abject display, giving South Africa their second 10-wicket triumph of the tournament.

The South African seamers had Bangladesh five down in the 14th over. The two Khaleds, Mashud and Mahmud managed to survive for 10 overs, playing some positive strokes in their 35 run stand for the seventh wicket. The return of Ntini to the attack in the 31st over hastened the end for Bangladesh. Ntini claimed three out of the last four wickets as the innings folded for a paltry 108 in the 36th over. In the rout, there were nine catches snapped up, three of them in fine style by Dippenaar in the slips. Khaled Mashud and Khaled Mahmud were the only batsmen to pass 20.

The Bangladeshi bowling effort was off to an inglorious start, as 17-year-old Talha Jubair sent down three consecutive wides in the second over. The contrasting styles of the swashbuckling Gibbs and the patient Kirsten combined effectively for their second 100-opening partnership for the tournament. In fine form, Kirsten brought up his 50 from just 30 balls with a six off Mohammad Rafiq. In the next over, Gibbs hoisted Alok Kapali over the boundary to level the scores. A single from the next ball put Bangladesh out of their misery. The South Africans scored the runs in just 48 minutes from 12 overs.

In this lop-sided contest, Ntini won the Man of the Match award for his exhibition of high quality fast-medium bowling.

BANGLADESH		SOUTH AFRICA	
Al Sahariar c Peterson b Pollock	0	H. H. Gibbs not out	49
Ehsanul Haque c Zondeki b Pollock	3	G. Kirsten not out	52
Mohammad Ashraful c Boucher b Ntini	6	Extras (lb 1, w 7)	8
Sanwar Hossain c Kallis b Hall	11	(12 overs)	0-109
Alok Kapali c Dippenaar b Zondeki	2	Did not bat: J. H. Kallis, H. H. Dippenaar, M. V. Boucher	
Tushar Imran c Dippenaar b Hall	9	(wk), L. Klusener, S. M. Pollock (capt), A. J. Hall, R. J.	
Khaled Mashud (capt) (wk) c Boucher b Ntini	29	Peterson, M. Ntini, M. Zondeki	
Khaled Mahmud c Klusener b Ntini	23	Bowling: Manjurul Islam 4-0-26-0; Talha Jubair 2-0-24-0;	
Mohammad Rafiq run out	1	Khaled Mahmud 2-0-20-0; Mohammaq Rafiq 2-0-20-0;	
Manjurul Islam c Dippenaar b Ntini	0	Alok Kapali 2-0-18-0	
Talha Jubair not out	4		
Extras (lb 4, w 8, nb 8)	20		
(35.1 overs)	10-108		
1/3 2/14 3/21 4/33 5/33 6/56 7/91 8/93 9/99 10/108			
Bowling: Pollock 6-2-8-2; Ntini 7.1-1-24-4; Zondeki 5-1-17-1;			
Hall 6-2-15-2; Kallis 5-0-19-0; Peterson 6-0-21-0			

Umpires: B.F. Bowden, S. Venkataraghavan.

Toss: South Africa   Points: South Africa 4, Bangladesh 0.

ENGLAND vs PAKISTAN - GROUP A
NEWLANDS, CAPE TOWN, SOUTH AFRICA (DAY/NIGHT): ENGLAND WON BY 112 RUNS

With their best World Cup performance since 1992, England demolished the unpredictable Pakistan and kept their chances of reaching the Super Six stage alive.

There was early excitement when, in the fourth over, Shoaib Akhtar sent down a 100 miles per hour (161.3 km.h) scorcher, which was effectively parried by Nick Knight. The old firm of Wasim and Waqar made early inroads and England found themselves under pressure in the 14th over when Hussain was caught behind. Vaughan and Stewart steered England to safer waters with a 51-run partnership for the fourth wicket. Vaughan, caught behind first ball from a no-ball, scored an impressive half-century. Vaughan and Stewart fell in consecutive overs to leave England in trouble at 5-118 in the 25th over.

Paul Collingwood batted intelligently with the lower order, which yielded handy partnerships of 42, 34, 31 and an unbroken 23. Collingwood handled the situation with aplomb, putting the flagging Pakistani fielders under the pump with quick running between the wickets. His undefeated 66 from 73 balls helped England to handy score of 8-246.

Pakistan found themselves in trouble in just the fourth over, reeling at 3-17. Caddick had Afridi caught behind for six and, in the next over, Anderson sent back Inzamam-ul-Haq and Yousuf Youhana in consecutive deliveries. Inzamam was having an unhappy tournament: after edging Anderon to slip, he had only 10 runs from three innings to show for his efforts. Anderson produced another double wicket over in the 18th over when he trapped Saeed Anwar in front and, four deliveries later, he had Rashid caught by his opposite number. At 5-59, the match was effectively over. Pakistan deteriorated to 9-80 before an entertaining cameo from Shoaib lifted the tally to 134. Shoaib plundered 43 not out from only 16 balls, including three huge sixes off White and Flintoff. Pakistan's lamentable batting effort left them 112 runs in arrears and with 19 overs remaining. Their prospects of progressing beyond the pool stage looked dim.

The contrasting bowling performances off Anderson and Shoaib showed that raw pace is not everything. Anderson's four wickets netted him the Man of the Match award, his second award from England's three completed matches.

ENGLAND		PAKISTAN	
M. E. Trescothick c Rashid Latif b Wasim Akram	1	Saeed Anwar lbw b Anderson	29
N. V. Knight c Abdul Razzaq b Waqar Younis	15	Shahid Afridi c Stewart b Caddick	6
M. P. Vaughan c Younis Khan b Shoaib Akhtar	52	Inzamam-ul-Haq c Knight b Anderson	0
N. Hussain (capt) c Rashid Latif b Waqar Younis	8	Yousuf Youhana b Anderson	0
A. J. Stewart (wk) b Shahid Afridi	30	Younis Khan c Stewart b Flintoff	5
P. D. Collingwood not out	66	Abdul Razzaq b White	11
A. Flintoff st Rashid Latif b Saqlain Mushtaq	26	Rashid Latif (wk) c Stewart b Anderson	0
C. White c Younis Khan b Shahid Afridi	15	Wasim Akram c Giles b White	7
A. F. Giles c Shahid Afridi b Saqlain Mushtaq	17	Saqlain Mushtaq not out	12
A. R. Caddick not out	3	Waqar Younis (capt) c Knight b White	2
Extras (lb 1, w 7, nb 5)	13	Shoaib Akhtar not out	43
(50 overs)	8-246	Extras (b 4, lb 4, w 11)	19
Did not bat: J. M. Anderson		(31 overs)	10-134

1/7 2/45 3/59 4/110 5/118 6/160 7/194 8/223

1/13 2/17 3/17 4/52 5/59 6/59 7/71 8/78 9/80 10/134

Bowling: Wasim Akram 10-1-37-1; Shoaib Akhtar 9-1-63-1; Waqar Younis 7-0-37-2; Saqlain Mushtaq 10-0-44-2; Shahid Afridi 8-0-36-2; Abdul Razzaq 6-0-28-0

Bowling: Caddick 7-0-27-1; Anderson 10-2-29-4; Flintoff 9-2-37-2; White 5-0-33-3

Umpires: B.G. Jerling, R.E. Koertzen.

Toss: England   Points: England 4, Pakistan 0.

SUNDAY 23 FEBRUARY 2003
CANADA vs WEST INDIES - GROUP B
CENTURION, SOUTH AFRICA: WEST INDIES WON BY 7 WICKETS

Although the final result was no surprise, this match produced one of the unexpected thrills of the tournament in the form of John Davison's whirlwind hundred.

After a sedate start of 0-6 from the first three overs, Davison put on a brilliant display of clean hitting. The Victorian and South Australian all-rounder dominated the 96-run opening stand with Ishwar Maraj, which was totted up in a mere 12 overs. Davison was in scintillating touch, flaying the attack to all parts and bringing up his 50 in a World Cup record of 25 balls. At the beginning of the 18th over, Canada's score was a remarkable 1-131, 95 runs more than the whole team managed against Sri Lanka four days earlier. At that point, Davison had cleared the boundary five times. With the final ball of the next over, Davison lofted Merv Dillon over the long on fence to reach his hundred in breathtaking fashion. Davison powered to his century in a mere 67 balls, a World Cup record, beating by five balls the old mark set by Kapil Dev in his destruction of Zimbabwe at Tunbridge Wells in 1983.

Despite the enjoyable nature of the spectacle, one could not help thinking that it was not sustainable. And so it proved. In the 21st over, part-time medium-pacer Wavell Hinds ended the useful support innings of Desmond Chumney for 19. In Hinds' next over, Davison attempted one big hit too many. Vasbert Drakes, running backwards at a rate of knots, leapt in the air a few metres in from the long on boundary. The ball amazingly stuck in his outstretched right hand. Normal service resumed for Canada as the next 20 overs produced only 46 runs at a cost of eight wickets. The Canadians had sunk from 1-155 to 202 all out, including the last six wickets falling for 17 runs. Aside from Davison, no other batsman reached 20, although de Groot managed his first World Cup runs in his fourth match. During the demise of the Canadian innings, Drakes picked up five of the last seven wickets to fall, the other two being run outs. The final over of the innings, the 43rd over, produced an interesting mix of two run outs, two wickets to Drakes and a five to de Groot.

The target of 203 looked easy pickings for the talented West Indian batting. The next shock was the speed at which the men from the Caribbean reached their goal. After the early loss of Gayle, Lara and Hinds were savage on the hapless Canadian bowlers and their union realised an astonishing 102 runs from just seven overs. In the eighth over, Hinds beat Davison's record for the fastest half-century in a World Cup match, reaching 50 in 24 balls. The next over from left-arm orthodox bowler Barry

Seebaran produced carnage. Lara was ruthless, plundering a World Cup record 26 runs from the over. The sequence was 4, 6, 4, 6, 6 and a rare dot ball. In the process, Lara beat Hinds' brand new record for the fastest fifty in the World Cup by a solitary ball. A few minutes later, Hinds was stumped off Davison and the score had rocketed to 2-134 in the 12th over. Hinds' brutal knock of 64 from 31 deliveries included 58 runs in fours or sixes.

Lara's assault was only marginally less severe, with his 73 runs coming from only 40 balls, including five sixes. After de Groot bowled Lara, giving him a story to pass down to future generations, Sarwan collected several boundaries from the shell-shocked bowlers. His four off de Groot in the 21st over gave the players an early finish. Despite his team's heavy loss, Davison's lone hand won him the Man of the Match award.

CANADA		WEST INDIES	
I. Maraj c Hooper b Collins	16	C. H. Gayle c Bagai b Joseph	8
J. M. Davison c Drakes b Hinds	111	W. W. Hinds st Bagai b Davison	64
D. Chumney c Gayle b Hinds	19	B. C. Lara b de Groot	73
I. S. Billcliff c Jacobs b Drakes	16	R. R. Sarwan not out	42
N. Ifill c Jacobs b Drakes	9	C. L. Hooper (capt) not out	5
J. V. Harris (capt) c Hooper b Drakes	6	Extras (lb 5, w 8, nb 1)	14
N. A. de Groot run out	11	(20.3 overs)	3-206
A. Bagai (wk) run out	2	Did not bat: S. Chanderpaul, R. L. Powell, R. D. Jacobs (wk),	
A. Codrington c Jaobs b Drakes	0	V. C. Drakes, M. Dillon, P. T. Collins	
B. B. Seebaran lbw b Drakes	0	1/32 2/134 3/177	
D. Joseph not out	0	Bowling: Joseph 4-0-47-1; Codrington 4-0-25-0;	
Extras (lb 3, w 3, nb 6)	12	Ifill 4-0-46-0; Seebaran 1-0-26-0; Davison 5-0-36-1; de Groot	
(45.2 overs)	10-202	2.3-0-21-1	
1/96 2/155 3/156 4/174 5/185 6/190 7/197 8/202 9/202			
10/202			
Bowling: Dillon 5-0-41-0; Collins 7-1-35-1; Drakes			
9.5-1-44-5; Hooper 8-1-31-0; Gayle 9-1-29-0; Hinds 4-0-19-2			

Umpires: E.A.R. de Silva, D.B. Hair.

Toss: West Indies   Points: West Indies 4, Canada 0.

INDIA vs NAMIBIA - GROUP A
PIETERMARITZBURG, SOUTH AFRICA: INDIA WON BY 181 RUNS

A strong Indian contingent cheered their players to a resounding win over Namibia. In a positive sign before the business end of the competition, Tendulkar and Ganguly spent some quality time in the middle. Both men skilfully milked the Namibian bowling, without really taking the attack apart, for timely centuries.

A hint of moisture beneath the surface provided Deon Kotze with enough encouragement to send the Indians in. Sehwag manhandled the attack in his usual style before he was caught at mid wicket for 24 from as many balls. For the next 40 overs, Tendulkar and Ganguly held sway, gradually accelerating the scoring to a run a ball. Tendulkar reached his fourth World Cup hundred from 115 balls. Tendulkar became the first man to score limited-overs hundreds against 10 different opponents. A short time later, umpire Aleem Dar had a near-death experience when Tendulkar flat-batted a ball from Bjorn Kotze straight down the pitch at head height. Aleem Dar's sharp reflexes only just saved him, the ball missing his head by centimetres.

In the 48th over, Tendulkar reached 150 with a four off van Vuuren. Tendulkar was bowled from the next delivery, missing a swipe across the line. The Tendulkar-Ganguly stand produced 244 runs for the second wicket. In the next over, Ganguly brought up his hundred when he turned debutante Burton van Rooi to the fine leg boundary. India reached the 300 mark in the last over, Ganguly continuing to an unbeaten 112 from 119 balls, including four sixes.

Fortunately for the Indians, the rain stayed away and the four points were banked. Namibia were never in the hunt and they did well to last into the 43rd over. Zaheer Khan picked up two early wickets before Jan-Berrie Burger entertained with some lusty hitting. After the innings slumped to 5-47 from 15 overs, Deon Kotze and van Schoor provided some resistance with a 51-run stand for the sixth wicket. Ganguly gave his part-time bowlers some work, including Mongia sending down a full complement of overs for a two wicket return. Yuvraj Singh was used and he collected the final four wickets to give him the rare analysis of 4 for 6. The Namibians floundered against the Indian spinners, who took eight wickets between them. The Namibia innings ended at 130, handing India their biggest win in a World Cup match to date. Tendulkar won the Man of the Match award for his 152, the Little Master's best score in a World Cup match.

INDIA		NAMIBIA	
V. Sehwag c Keulder b van Vuuren	24	S. J. Swanepoel lbw b Khan	9
S. R. Tendulkar b van Vuuren	152	A. J. Burger b Mongia	29
S. C. Ganguly (capt) not out	112	L. J. Burger lbw b Khan	0
Yuvraj Singh not out	7	D. Keulder c Mongia b Harbhajan Singh	4
Extras (lb 2, w 13, nb 1)	16	G. B. Murgatroyd lbw b Harbhajan Singh	0
(50 overs)	2-311	D. B. Kotze (capt) c & b Mongia	27
Did not bat: D. Mongia, R. Dravid (wk), M. Kaif, Harbhajan		M. van Schoor (wk) c Dravid b Yuvraj Singh	24
Singh, Zaheer Khan, J. Srinath, A. Nehra		B. O. van Rooi c Mongia b Yuvraj Singh	17
1/46 2/290		B. L. Kotze c Dravid b Yuvraj Singh	3
Bowling: Snyman 10-0-57-0; van Vuuren 10-1-53-2; L.		G. Snyman c Srinath b Yuvraj Singh	5
Burger 6-0-49-0; van Rooi 6-0-36-0; B. Kotze 10-0-64-0; D.		R. J. van Vuuren not out	0
Kotze 8-0-50-0		Extras (lb 1, w 8, nb 3)	12
		(42.3 overs)	10-130
		1/19 2/21 3/43 4/47 5/47 6/98 7/99 8/124 9/124 10/130	
		Bowling: Srinath 6-0-25-0; Nehra 0.1-0-0-0; Khan 7.5-0-24-2; Harbhajan Singh 10-1-34-2; Mongia 10-1-24-2; Sehwag 4-0-16-0; Yuvraj Singh 4.3-2-6-4	

Umpires: Aleem Dar, D.R. Shepherd.
Toss: Namibia   Points: India 4, Namibia 0.

MONDAY 24 FEBRUARY 2003
KENYA vs SRI LANKA - GROUP B
GYMKHANA CLUB GROUND, NAIROBI, KENYA: KENYA WON BY 53 RUNS

After a series of one-sided results in the tournament, Kenya produced a refreshing change with a shock win over Sri Lanka. The triumph was a testament to the virtues of accurate bowling and energetic fielding. The win gave Kenya a reasonable chance of qualifying for the Super Six stage.

Jayasuriya made a surprise choice of bowling first on a track that appeared conducive to batting. Vaas picked up another first over wicket when he trapped Ravindhu Shah in front for a duck. Kennedy Otieno scored freely after the early setback to take Kenya to 1-46 in the seventh over. After that promising beginning, the Kenyans were unable to build a decent partnership. Otieno's entertaining innings of 60 from 88 balls, including two sixes, was ended in the 28th over. From 4-112, the Kenyan batsmen could not lift the tempo. On a pitch that played slowly, the batsmen found Muralitharan a difficult proposition and Jayasuriya was hard to get away. A late-innings cameo from Peter Ongondo, who scored 20 from 18 deliveries, allowed the home side to finish their innings with a rush. Thirty-three runs were taken from the final four overs, which enabled Kenya to finish on 9-210. The old firm of Muralitharan and Vaas claimed seven wickets between them.

A requirement of just over four runs an over against the modest Kenyan bowling seemed to be a comfortable assignment for the talented Sri Lankan batting line up. Jayasuriya failed for the second match in a row to give Kenya early hope.

A belligerent knock by Aravinda de Silva enabled Sri Lanka to reach a reasonable position of 3-87 in the 24th over. Leg-spinner Collins Obuya ran through the middle-order, achieving career best figures of 5-25. Sri Lanka fell to 7-119 from 32 overs and the victory target seemed light years away. Russel Arnold tried to eke out the remaining runs with the bowlers, but his efforts were in vain. Captain Steve Tikolo brought himself on to bowl his off-spinners and he collected the scalps of Nissanka and Muralitharan, both caught on the boundary. In the next over, Fernando missed an ungainly reverse sweep from Maurice Odumbe and was bowled. Kenya had won by 53 runs and their players danced and high-fived with great merriment. It was their finest hour since their boilover against the West Indies at Pune in the 1996 World Cup. Amid the celebrations, Obuya won the Man of the Match award.

KENYA		SRI LANKA	
K. O. Otieno (wk) c Muralitharan b de Silva	60	M. S. Atapattu b Odoyo	23
R. D. Shah lbw b Vaas	0	S. T. Jayasuriya (capt) c Patel b M. Suji	3
B. J. Patel c Sangakkara b Vaas	12	H. P. Tillekeratne c T. Suji b Obuya	23
S. O. Tikolo (capt) lbw b Muralitharan	10	P. A. de Silva c Otieno b Obuya	41
H. S. Modi b Muralitharan	26	D. P. M. D. Jayawardene c & b Obuya	5
M. O. Odumbe c Arnold b Muralitharan	26	K. C. Sangakkara (wk) c Otieno b Obuya	5
T. M. Odoyo c Sangakkara b Vaas	6	R. P. Arnold not out	25
C. O. Obuya not out	13	W. P. U. J.C. Vaas c & b Obuya	4
T. O. Suji b Muralitharan	6	R. A.P. Nissanka c Odoyo b Tikolo	2
P. J.C. Ongondo b Jayasuriya	20	M. Muralitharan c T. Suji b Tikolo	10
M. A. Suji not out	3	C. R.D. Fernando b Odumbe	7
Extras (b 5, lb 11, w 10, nb 2)	28	Extras (b 2, w 6, nb 1)	9
(50 overs)	9-210	(45 overs)	10-157

1/1 2/46 3/75 4/112 5/152 6/163 7/163 8/173 9/205

Bowling: Vaas 10-1-41-3; Nissanka 7-2-29-0; Fernando 7-0-33-0; Muralitharan 10-1-28-4; Jayasuriya 9-1-30-1; de Silva 5-1-23-1; Arnold 2-0-10-0

1/13 2/39 3/71 4/87 5/105 6/112 7/119 8/131 9/149 10/157

Bowling: M. Suji 8-1-24-1; Odoyo 7-0-33-1; Obuya 10-0-24-5; Ongondo 5-0-22-0; Odumbe 10-0-39-1; Tikolo 5-1-13-2

Umpires: D.J. Harper, R.B. Tiffin.

Toss: Sri Lanka   Points: Kenya 4, Sri Lanka 0.

MONDAY 24 FEBRUARY 2003
ZIMBABWE vs AUSTRALIA - GROUP A
QUEENS SPORTS CLUB, BULAWAYO: AUSTRALIA WON BY 7 WICKETS

After considering the prospect of not visiting Zimbabwe because of security concerns, the Australians crossed the border. The Australians were given a good hit-out after comfortable wins in their first three games. Prior to the game, the Zimbabwean selectors reneged on their intention to drop Andy Flower, who wore white sweatbands in this match as a sign of peace.

Under clear, blue skies, Streak won the toss and elected to bat. After a shaky start of 2-28, an 84 run stand between the Flower brothers put Zimbabwe in a sound position of 2-112 in the 30th over. The Flower union was ended when Grant, hesitating in his response to his brother's call for a second run off Hogg, was run out by Gilchrist's accurate throw at the stumps at the bowler's end. Two overs later, Andy Flower's innings ended at 62 when he was bowled by an excellent flipper from Hogg that sped through, flicked the pad and hit off-stump.

The Zimbabwean middle-order were tied down by Australia's slow bowlers. At 6-142 in the 37th over, a score in the low-200s looked realistic. That notion was turned on its head by a blistering innings by Andy Blignaut. Blignaut hit with great power, dishing out some severe treatment to Hogg and Gillespie. The 42nd over of the innings, bowled by Gillespie, produced 18 runs, all but one of these coming from Blignaut's blade. The onslaught continued in the next over from Hogg. Blignaut scored six, four and six from successive balls, with both sixes clobbered over long on. In the process, Blignaut brought up his 50 in a mere 25 deliveries. In the seven overs since the dismissal of Marillier, Zimbabwe's total had rocketed from 142 to 207. All of a sudden, a score of 250-plus was a realistic prospect.

Lee relieved Hogg in the 45th over and Blignaut's blistering knock was ended three balls later with the score on 208. Blignaut smashed a full toss back at Lee, whose quick reflexes saved him extensive facial surgery. Blignaut's innings yielded 54 runs from 28 balls, including eight fours and two sixes. Aided by industrious batting from Taibu, Streak hit out in the closing overs. Seventeen runs were scored from Lee in the penultimate over. Zimbabwe ended up with a solid score of 9-246, including 90 runs from the last ten overs.

Gilchrist and Hayden set out to relieve the pressure on the Australian middle-order by scoring quickly from the start. Gilchrist went for his shots from the first over and took most of the strike. A mistimed drive off Streak from the first ball of the innings raced down the ground for four. The next over, Gilchrist hit Blignaut for consecutive boundaries and he offered a difficult chance to Hondo on the fifth delivery. The opportunity for an early wicket was lost when Hondo put down the catch at third man.

Hayden was caught at fine-leg in the 15th over for 39. Gilchrist's momentum slowed after he reached his 50 from 41 deliveries. In an effort to regain the initiative, Gilchrist holed out to deep-mid wicket with the score on 113. Ponting and Martyn batted in consolidation mode, playing the percentages and keeping the score ticking over at around four an over. After Ponting chipped a regulation return catch to leg-spinner Murphy, the equation for Australia was 90 runs from 104 balls. The Australians played in a composed manner, keeping the asking rate below a run a ball and turning over the strike regularly. With 51 needed from the last 10 overs, the boundaries began to come more regularly. Streak shuffled his bowlers around in an attempt to break the partnership, but to no avail. Lehmann and Martyn reached their fifties and the win was achieved with 15 balls to spare. It almost escaped notice that the unbroken Martyn-Lehmann stand realised 92 runs from 89 deliveries.

Despite going wicketless and being outscored by three batsmen, Blignaut won the Man of the Match award.

ZIMBABWE		AUSTRALIA	
C. B. Wishart b Gillespie	10	A. C. Gilchrist (wk) c sub (Ervine) b Marillier	61
G. J. Whittall c Hogg b Gillespie	1	M. L. Hayden c G. W. Flower b Hondo	34
A. Flower b Hogg	62	R. T. Ponting (capt) c & b Murphy	38
G. W. Flower run out	37	D. R. Martyn not out	50
D. D. Ebrahim b Hogg	15	D. S. Lehmann not out	56
T. Taibu (wk) b McGrath	23	Extras (lb 1, w 8)	9
D. A. Marillier c Ponting b Hogg	0	(47.3 overs)	3-248
A. M. Blignaut c & b Lee	54	Did not bat: A. Symonds, M. G. Bevan, G. B. Hogg, B. Lee,	
H. H. Streak (capt) not out	28	J. N. Gillespie, G. D. McGrath	
B. A. Murphy b McGrath	1	1/89 2/113 3/156	
D. T. Hondo not out	1	Bowling: Streak 6-0-38-0; Blignaut 10-0-54-0;	
Extras (b 4, lb 3, w 3, nb 4)	14	Hondo 9-0-49-1; G. J. Whittall 3.3-0-26-0; Marillier	
(50 overs)	9-246	10-1-32-1; Murphy 9-0-48-1	

1/13 2/28 3/112 4/121 5/142 6/142 7/208 8/242 9/244
Bowling: McGrath 9-2-24-2; Gillespie 9-1-50-2; Symonds 10-0-35-0; Lee 10-0-63-1; Hogg 8-0-46-3; Martyn 4-0-21-0

Umpires: B.F. Bowden, D.L. Orchard.

Toss: Zimbabwe   Points: Australia 4, Zimbabwe 0.

TUESDAY 25 FEBRUARY 2003
NETHERLANDS vs PAKISTAN - GROUP A
PAARL, SOUTH AFRICA: PAKISTAN WON BY 97 RUNS

On a warm and humid day in Paarl, Pakistan's humdrum performance did little to dispel theories that they might not be up to the task in the 2003 World Cup.

Captain Roland Lefebvre opted to bowl first and he was entitled to be pleased with a committed performance in the field. Pakistan's score of 9-253 was only a fair result against an undemanding attack. Again, several of Pakistan's batsmen lost their wicket after making a start. Inzamam-ul-Haq's horror stretch continued when he was leg before for a second-ball duck. Inzi was unlucky on this occasion, as replays showed a thin edge. At one stage, Pakistan were a wobbly 5-153 in the 34th over. Yousuf Youhana's fluent 58 from 59 balls saved Pakistan's blushes. Despite running out an irate Wasim, Youhana batted well with the lower order. Shoaib, promoted to number nine after his swashbuckling effort in Cape Town, justified his elevation with an attractive, unbeaten 26.

Wasim stood at an amazing 499 wickets in limited-overs internationals when the Dutch innings began. He did not have to wait long to become the first member of the 500 club. With the first delivery of his second over, the champion left-armer disturbed the furniture defended by Nick Statham. Wasim celebrated his achievement with much gusto. He had reached the 500 wicket mark 18 years and one day after his first wicket in limited-overs matches, the wicket of Australia's Robbie Kerr at the MCG in the 1984-85 World Championship of Cricket.

The Dutch batsmen found the Pakistani quicks too hot to handle. Their hopes of emulating Kenya's upset win against Sri Lanka appeared forlorn at 5-78 when leading batsman de Leede perished in the 22nd over. Daan van Bunge was the only Dutch batsman to reach the thirties. Pakistan's fielding and bowling lacked discipline: this was exemplified by a whooping 40 in extras. As the game petered out to an easy win to the favourites, Waqar allowed Saeed Anwar a rare bowling performance. The move produced the wicket of Jacob-Jan Esmeijer. Wasim finished the game by bowling Jeroen Smits, handing Pakistan a 97 run victory. In a lacklustre affair, Youhana won the Man of the Match award.

PAKISTAN		NETHERLANDS	
Taufeeq Umar run out	48	N. A. Statham b Wasim Akram	0
Saaed Anwar c Esmeijer b de Leede	25	E. Schiferli c Abdul Razzaq b Shoaib Akhtar	9
Abdul Razzaq c Smits b van Bunge	47	B. Zuiderent lbw b Waqar Younis	8
Inzamam-ul-Haq lbw b de Leede	0	K. J. J. van Noortwijk c Rashid Latif b Wasim Akram	7
Yousuf Youhana b Lefebvre	58	T. B. M. de Leede c Shoaib Akhtar b Saqlain Mushtaq	15
Saleem Elahi c Zuiderent b van Bunge	5	D. L. S. van Bunge c Rashid Latif b Abdul Razzaq	31
Rashid Latif (wk) c van Bunge b Schiferli	24	L. P. van Troost c Rashid Latif b Shoaib Akhtar	22
Wasim Akram run out	1	H. J. C. Mol b Shoaib Akhtar	13
Shoaib Akhtar not out	26	J. J. Esmeijer lbw b Saeed Anwar	0
Waqar Younis (capt) c & b Mol	1	R. P. Lefebvre (capt) not out	4
Saqlain Mushtaq not out	3	J. Smits (wk) lbw b Wasim Akram	7
Extras (b 1, lb 8, w 6)	15	Extras (b 6, lb 11, w 17, nb 6)	40
(50 overs)	9-253	(39.3 overs)	10-156

1/61 2/106 3/108 4/143 5/153 6/192 7/196 8/238 9/245

Bowling: Schiferli 10-1-48-1; Lefebvre 10-1-39-1; de Leede 10-0-53-2; van Troost 2-0-18-0; Esmeijer 10-0-35-0; van Bunge 4-0-27-2; Mol 4-0-24-1

1/6 2/31 3/35 4/43 5/78 6/108 7/135 8/136 9/138 10/156

Bowling: Wasim Akram 8.3-2-24-3; Shoaib Akhtar 7-0-26-3; Waqar Younis 6-1-19-1; Saqlain Mushtaq 8-2-32-1; Abdul Razzaq 6-0-23-1; Saeed Anwar 4-0-15-1

Umpires: S.A. Bucknor, S. Venkataraghavan.

Toss: Netherlands   Points: Pakistan 4, Netherlands 0.

WEDNESDAY 26 FEBRUARY 2003
BANGLADESH vs NEW ZEALAND - GROUP B
KIMBERLEY, SOUTH AFRICA: NEW ZEALAND WON BY 7 WICKETS

With a 10-day break since their last completed match, New Zealand welcomed the opportunity for a tune-up against Bangladesh. Some cobwebs were evident in the field as the Kiwis dropped some chances. The end result was a comfortable win. For Bangladesh, at least they could take some solace from a more determined effort.

For the first time in the tournament, Bangladesh survived the full 50 overs. Their final score of 7-198, whilst modest, was a sound effort after the innings was listing at 6-107 in the 31st over. Mohammad Ashraful was the only Bangladeshi batsman to make a contribution of substance. In an apt summary of Bangladesh's batting woes, Mohammad Ashraful became the first Bangladeshi batsman to reach a half-century in this tournament. The Bangladeshi tail wagged: handy scores from Khaled Masud and Mohammed Rafiq enabled an unbroken 70 runs to be scored for the eighth wicket. Bond and Oram collected three wickets apiece, while Vettori gave very little away.

The Kiwis raced to the target in the 34th over. Craig McMillan welcomed the opportunity to bat himself into some form. His fast-paced 75 from 83 balls, including two sixes, laid the platform for the win. Fleming made a start and Andre Adams played a rare cameo at number three. From 3-138, Styris and Cairns attacked the bowling and the remaining 61 runs were compiled in 41 balls. One six by Cairns off Alok Kapali cleared the large grandstand straight down the ground. McMillan was named man of the match.

BANGLADESH		NEW ZEALAND	
Hannan Sarkar c McCullum b Bond	9	C. D. McMillan b Khaled Mahmud	75
Mohammad Ashraful c & b Bond	56	S. P. Fleming (capt) c & b Khaled Mahmud	32
Sanwar Hossain b Oram	5	A. R. Adams c Mohammad Ashraful b Khaled Mahmud	18
Habibul Bashar c McCullum b Oram	0	S. B. Styris not out	37
Alok Kapali c Bond b Adams	9	C. L. Cairns not out	33
Akram Khan c Fleming b Bond	13	Extras (w 3, nb 1)	4
Khaled Masud (capt/wk) not out	35	(33.3 overs)	3-199
Khaled Mahmud c McCullum b Oram	12	Did not bat: M. S. Sinclair, B. B. McCullum (wk), J. D. P.	
Mohammed Rafiq not out	41	Oram, K. D. Mills, D. L. Vettori, S. E. Bond	
Extras (b 1, lb 4, w 10, nb 3)	18	1/71 2/99 3/138	
(50 overs)	7-198	Bowling: Manjurul Islam 7-1-37-0; Tapash Baisya 8-0-56-0;	
Did not bat: Tapash Baisya, Manjurul Islam		Khaled Mahmud 10-0-46-3; Alok Kapali 6-0-38-0; Sanwar	
1/19 2/37 3/37 4/71 5/105 6/107 7/128		Hossain 2-0-19-0; Mohammad Ashraful 0.3-0-3-0	
Bowling: Bond 10-1-33-3; Mills 6-0-32-0; Adams 10-0-50-1;			
Oram 10-1-32-3; Cairns 3-0-17-0; Vettori 10-0-19-0;			
Styris 1-0-10-0			

Umpires: D.B. Hair, D.R. Shepherd.

Toss: Bangladesh   Points: New Zealand 4, Bangladesh 0.

WEDNESDAY 26 FEBRUARY 2003
ENGLAND vs INDIA - GROUP A
DURBAN, SOUTH AFRICA (DAY/NIGHT): INDIA WON BY 82 RUNS

India continued to build their form and downed a disappointing England in Durban. With concerns commonplace about the difficulty of chasing down a target under lights in this tournament, India won an important toss and batted. Sehwag and Tendulkar had their eyes in quickly and they were off to a flyer. From a steady beginning of 0-26 from the first seven overs, the Indian batsmen exploded in the next two overs. Sixteen runs were scored from each of the next two overs from Anderson and Caddick. Flintoff was brought into the attack for a quick reward: a leading edge from Sehwag popped up and was graciously accepted by the big Lancastrian. Tendulkar maintained the momentum for a few overs. India had established a useful platform of 1-75 from 11 overs.

Despite the fast start to the game, Flintoff bowled with impressive accuracy and good pace. At one stage, he only conceded nine runs from his first seven overs. Flintoff was rewarded with Tendulkar's wicket when he cut to backward point. From 2-91 in the 16th over, the Indian innings lost momentum. Dravid and Yuvraj Singh wrested back the initiative with a stand of 62 runs for the sixth wicket in ten overs. The last four deliveries of the innings, bowled by Caddick, produced a remarkable four wickets. Three batsmen were caught and there was one run out. When it was all said and done, India had a good score of 9-250 on the board.

England suffered a setback in just the second over when Nick Knight took a sharp single that was not on. Mohammad Kaif at extra cover was up to the task. England were in the gun in the seventh over when Trescothick mishooked Zaheer Khan. Left-arm seamer Ashish Nehra, returning from an ankle injury that allowed him to bowl only one ball in the win over Namibia, sent the England innings into disarray in the 17th over when Hussain nicked one and Stewart was trapped in front by the next ball. Nehra effectively extinguished England's hopes in his next five overs when Vaughan was caught behind and Collingwood nicked a superb delivery to first slip. Nehra finished off his ten over spell in style, having White caught behind on the drive and inducing a slips catch from Irani. Nehra finished with the magnificent figures of 6 for 23. It was the third-best bowling analysis in a World Cup match and the only performance in the top three to be away from Headingley.

From a hopeless position of 8-107 in the 31st over, Flintoff produced some fine hitting in his rambunctious 64 from 73 balls, including three sixes. Despite Flintoff's good all-round performance, it was simply too little, too late for England. The men from the Old Dart had to beat the Australian juggernaut in the final qualifying match to assure themselves of a Super Six berth. Nehra was a clear choice for the Man of the Match.

INDIA		ENGLAND	
V. Sehwag c & b Flintoff	23	M. E. Trescothick c Tendulkar b Khan	8
S. R. Tendulkar c Collingwood b Flintoff	50	N. V. Knight run out	1
S. C. Ganguly (capt) c Trescothick b White	19	M. P. Vaughan c Dravid b Nehra	20
D. Mongia lbw b Collingwood	32	N. Hussain (capt) c Dravid b Nehra	15
R. Dravid (wk) c Collingwood b Caddick	62	A. J. Stewart (wk) lbw b Nehra	0
Yuvraj Singh c Hussain b Anderson	42	P. D. Collingwood c Sehwag b Nehra	18
M. Kaif c Flintoff b Caddick	5	A. Flintoff c Sehwag b Srinath	64
Harbhajan Singh not out	0	C. White c Dravid b Nehra	13
Zaheer Khan run out	0	R. C. Irani c Sehwag b Nehra	0
J. Srinath c Trescothick b Caddick	0	A. R. Caddick not out	13
Extras (b 1, lb 4, w 9, nb 3)	17	J. M. Anderson lbw b Khan	2
(50 overs)	9-250	Extras (lb 5, w 7, nb 2)	14
1/60 2/91 3/107 4/155 5/217 6/250 7/250 8/250 9/250		(45.3 overs)	10-168
Bowling: Caddick 10-0-69-3; Anderson 10-0-61-1;		1/6 2/18 3/52 4/52 5/62 6/93 7/107 8/107 9/162 10/168	
Flintoff 10-2-15-2; White 10-0-57-1; Irani 6-0-28-0;		Bowling: Khan 9.3-1-29-2; Srinath 10-0-37-1; Nehra	
Collingwood 4-0-15-1		10-2-23-6; Ganguly 6-0-34-0; Harbhajan Singh 10-0-40-0	

Umpires: R.E. Koertzen, S.J.A. Taufel.

Toss: India   Points: India 4, England 0.

THURSDAY 27 FEBRUARY 2003
AUSTRALIA vs NAMIBIA - GROUP A
NORTH WEST STADIUM, POTCHEFSTROOM, SOUTH AFRICA: AUSTRALIA WON BY 256 RUNS

This match had the makings of the mismatch of the tournament. The end result was in line with the expectations. In the process, some records fell and the Namibians impressed all with their energy and enthusiasm for the game.

Ponting won his first toss of the tournament and chose to bat on what looked to be a good pitch. The Australians had not dominated the bowling to that point. Hayden and Symonds impressed with half-centuries. When the last over began, Australia were 6-273 with Lehmann and Hogg were at the crease. Lehmann, on 22 when the final over started, mauled the tired van Vuuren and took 28 runs from the over. Lehmann clobbered van Vuuren for four, four, four, six, four and six. The final delivery, a full toss outside off stump, was given the treatment over deep mid wicket. This shot gave Lehmann his half-century from a mere 31 balls. The final over carnage propelled Australia to an imposing total of 6-301. Van Vuuren's over was, at the time, the most expensive over in World Cup history. The last 10 overs had brought 87 runs and the whirlwind Lehmann-Hogg stand netted an unbeaten 70.

The Namibian batsmen didn't stand a chance against the canny bowling of McGrath and the express pace of Lee. The innings soon became a procession as McGrath put on a clinic of unplayable bowling. Following the wicket of Karg in McGrath's third over, McGrath scythed through the batting, taking a wicket in his fourth, fifth and sixth overs and two in his seventh over. McGrath joined West Indian paceman Winston Davis, who claimed 7-51 against Australia at Headingley in 1983, as the second bowler to achieve a seven wicket haul in the World Cup. Amazingly, the final 26 deliveries of McGrath's spell yielded six wickets for a solitary run.

Ponting gave Lee a spell and threw the ball to Bichel. The Queenslander did not have to wait for success with the ball. He finished with the figures of one over, one maiden, two wickets for no runs. Bichel's second wicket terminated the Namibia innings for just 45 in 14 overs.

It was a day of records. Gilchrist's six catches was a record in a World Cup match. Australia's win was their 11th consecutive victory in limited-overs internationals, which equaled the mark set by the imposing West Indian team from 1984 to 1985. Further, the colossal winning margin of 256 runs was the biggest winning margin at the time in a limited-overs encounter.

McGrath was an obvious choice of the man of the match. In the afterglow of his performance, he quipped "I'll feel better when I take eight against England."

AUSTRALIA		NAMIBIA	
A. C. Gilchrist (wk) b van Rooi	13	A. J. Burger c Ponting b McGrath	4
M. L. Hayden b L. Burger	88	S. J. Swanepoel c Ponting b Lee	2
M. G. Bevan c & b L. Burger	17	M. Karg c Gilchrist b McGrath	4
A. Symonds run out	59	D. Keulder c Gilchrist b McGrath	3
R. T. Ponting (capt) c D. Kotze b L. Burger	2	G. B. Murgatroyd lbw b McGrath	0
D. R. Martyn b B. Kotze	35	D. B. Kotze (capt) c Gilchrist b McGrath	10
D. S. Lehmann not out	50	L. J. Burger c Gilchrist b McGrath	1
G. B. Hogg not out	19	M. van Schoor (wk) c Gilchrist b Bichel	6
Extras (lb 8, w 6, nb 4)	18	B. L. Kotze b McGrath	0
(50 overs)	6-301	B. O. van Rooi not out	0
Did not bat: B. Lee, A. J. Bichel, G. D. McGrath		R. J. van Vuuren c Gilchrist b Bichel	0
1/26 2/104 3/140 4/146 5/230 6/231		Extras (lb 4, w 6, nb 5)	15
Bowling: van Vuuren 10-0-92-0; van Rooi 6-0-24-1; B. Kotze		(14 overs)	45
10-0-62-1; L. Burger 10-1-39-3; D. Kotze 10-0-54-0; A.		1/5 2/14 3/16 4/17 5/28 6/34 7/45 8/45 9/45 10/45	
Burger 4-0-22-0		Bowling: McGrath 7-4-15-7; Lee 6-1-26-1; Bichel 1-1-0-2	

Umpires: B.F. Bowden, R.B. Tiffin.

Toss: Australia   Points: Australia 4, Namibia 0.

SOUTH AFRICA vs CANADA - GROUP B
EAST LONDON, SOUTH AFRICA: SOUTH AFRICA WON BY 118 RUNS

South Africa missed this opportunity to convincingly beat Canada and send a message to their rivals that they were still a serious threat. The Proteas' performance was pedestrian and they were flattered by the final margin of 118 runs.

David Joseph and Ashish Patel had South Africa under early pressure at 3-23 in the eighth over. Smith and Dippenaar knuckled down and put on 109 in 22 overs to get things back on course. After Smith was bowled by Davison for 63, Dippenaar made his first real contribution with the bat, reaching 80 from 118 deliveries and combining well with Boucher and the bowlers. Some good hitting by South Africa's lower order boosted the score to 8-254.

Canada never threatened to reach their target and they laboured for their runs. Ishwar Maraj was the main culprit, taking 155 balls in carrying his bat for 53. In the process, he invoked memories of Sunil Gavaskar's excruciating 36 not out against England at Lord's in 1975. It was a disappointing effort by the Proteas' attack that only five Canadian wickets were winkled out. Pollock and Ntini each conceded less than two runs an over. Allan Donald's final international performance was a forgettable one.

In this humdrum match, Dippenaar was the Man of the Match.

SOUTH AFRICA		CANADA	
G. C. Smith b Davison	63	I. Maraj not out	53
H. H. Gibbs c Bagai b Patel	8	J. M. Davison c Zondeki b Ntini	1
G. Kirsten c Bagai b Joseph	0	D. Chumney c Smith b Pollock	2
J. H. Kallis c Ifill b Patel	1	I. S. Billcliff b Zondeki	9
H. H. Dippenaar c Seebaran b de Groot	80	N. A. de Groot c Boucher b Hall	16
M. V. Boucher (wk) b de Groot	21	J. V. Harris (capt) c Boucher b Ntini	15
S. M. Pollock (capt) c Bagai b Joseph	32	A. Bagai (wk) not out	28
A. J. Hall not out	22	Extras (lb 6, w 4, nb 2)	12
M. Ntini b Patel	14	(50 overs)	5-136
M. Zondeki not out	1	Did not bat: N. Ifill, A. Patel, B. B. Seebaran, D. Joseph	
Extras (lb 3, w 8, nb 1)	12	1/2 2/8 3/28 4/58 5/84	
(50 overs)	8-254	Bowling: Pollock 8-5-13-1; Ntini 10-2-19-2; Donald	
Did not bat: A. A. Donald		10-2-27-0; Zondeki 9-1-24-1; Hall 7-1-26-1; Kallis 5-1-11-0;	
1/19 2/22 3/23 4/132 5/174 6/197 7/227 8/249		Smith 1-0-10-0	
Bowling: Joseph 9-1-42-2; Patel 7-0-41-3; Ifill 7-0-35-0;			
Davison 10-1-45-1; Seebaran 10-0-43-0; de Groot 7-0-45-2			

Umpires: K.C. Barbour, D.J. Harper.

Toss: Canada   Points: South Africa 4, Canada 0.

FRIDAY 28 FEBRUARY 2003
ZIMBABWE vs NETHERLANDS - GROUP A
QUEENS SPORTS CLUB, BULAWAYO, ZIMBABWE: ZIMBABWE WON BY 99 RUNS

Zimbabwe kept their Super Six hopes alive with a sound performance against a spirited Dutch side. The threat of rain seemed to influence Dutch captain Lefebvre, who asked Heath Streak's men to bat. For the first 30 overs, Zimbabwe made good progress without dominating the Dutch bowling. Andy Flower led the way with an elegant 71 from 72 balls, with dabs, orthodox sweeps and reverse sweeps used to good effect. From 3-136 after 30 overs, Zimbabwe blazed 165 runs from the last 20 overs to reach the 300 mark. Blignaut powered to another quick 50, with the milestone achieved after 32 balls. Blignaut and Ebrahim put on 80 runs for the fifth wicket in just ten overs to take Zimbabwe to a strong position. An odd feature of the Zimbabwe innings was that, at the end of the 42nd over, Blignaut and Ebrahim swapped ends with umpires Bucknor and Wijewardene being none the wiser.

In the final five overs, Streak put the game out of the Netherlands' reach, clubbing 44 from 22 deliveries. Tim de Leede was carted to the tune of conceding 69 from seven overs, although he managed to pick up a scalp in each of his last two overs.

The Netherlands never looked like getting 302 against a workmanlike Zimbabwean attack. The best partnership of the innings of 42 was achieved by Lefebvre and Henk Mol for the eighth wicket from 41 balls. Unfortunately, the game was already beyond the reach of the visitors when this partnership began. Five batsmen reached 20 but none made it into the 40s. There was an enthusiastic cheer from the crowd when Henry Olonga took the field as a substitute fielder, replacing fellow protestor Andy Flower. The Zimbabwean seamers proved difficult to score from, paving the way for Murphy and Marillier to collect five wickets from the middle- to low-order. The Dutch squeaked past 200 for the first time in the tournament, but the game was long gone. Streak collected the Man of the Match award for his power hitting and accurate bowling.

ZIMBABWE		NETHERLANDS	
C. B. Wishart c Smits b Lefebvre	21	J. F. Kloppenburg c Streak b Hondo	18
M. A. Vermeulen b Kloppenburg	27	E. Schiferli b Streak	22
A. Flower c Esmeiher b Schiferli	71	B. Zuiderent run out	15
G. J. Whittall c Zuiderent b Kloppenburg	30	D. L.S. van Bunge lbw b Whittall	37
D. D. Ebrahim b de Leede	32	T. B.M. de Leede lbw b Murphy	1
A. M. Blignaut c Kloppenburg b Schiferli	58	L. P. van Troost c Hondo b Murphy	26
H. H. Streak (capt) c Esmeijer b de Leede	44	R. H. Scholte c Blignaut b Murphy	7
D. A. Marillier lbw b Lefebvre	1	H. J.C. Mol c sub (Olonga) b Marillier	23
T. Taibu (wk) not out	7	R. P. Lefebvre (capt) b Marillier	30
Extras (lb 3, w 7)	10	J. Smits (wk) not out	8
(50 overs)	8-301	J. J. Esmeijer not out	3
Did not bat: B. A. Murphy, D. T. Hondo		Extras (b 1, lb 7, w 3, nb 1)	12
1/24 2/82 3/135 4/165 5/245 6/274 7/281 8/301		(50 overs)	9-202
Bowling: Schiferli 10-2-43-2; Lefebvre 8-0-38-2; de		1/41 2/49 3/80 4/85 5/127 6/128 7/148 8/190 9/191	
Leede 7-0-69-2; Kloppenburg 10-0-40-2; Esmeijer 9-0-60-0;		Bowling: Blignaut 10-1-30-0; Streak 10-1-36-1;	
van Bunge 3-0-22-0; Mol 3-0-26-0		Hondo 6-1-16-1; Murphy 10-3-44-3; Marillier 9-0-49-2;	
		Whittall 5-1-19-1	

Umpires: S.A. Bucknor, T.H. Wijewardene.

Toss: Netherlands   Points: Zimbabwe 4, Netherlands 0.

SRI LANKA vs WEST INDIES - GROUP B
NEWLANDS, CAPE TOWN, SOUTH AFRICA (DAY/NIGHT): SRI LANKA WON BY 6 RUNS

This clash at Newlands resulted in the just the second close finish in the tournament to date, nearly three weeks after the opening nail-biter at this venue between South Africa and the West Indies. Sri Lanka managed to squeak through, leaving the Super Six door ajar for them. The West Indies' prospects of progression hinged on Bangladesh beating the in-form Kenyans the following day.

Jayasuriya chose to bat after winning his fifth consecutive toss in the competition. The Sri Lankans struggled for most of their innings and their final score of 6-228 was a middle-of-the-road effort. Sri Lanka's prospects were in jeopardy when they wobbled from 1-96 in the 24th over to 5-139 in the 36th over following Jayasuriya's dismissal. The Sri Lankan skipper was uncharacteristically becalmed, taking 99 balls over his 66 runs. Hashan Tillekeratne was laboured in his 36 from 68 deliveries and it was left to Russel Arnold, Sangakkara and Vaas to lift the tempo in the late overs. Vaas played a useful knock of 28 not out from 25 balls, putting on an unbroken partnership with Arnold of 50 runs from the final seven overs. Vasbert Drakes bowled with admirable control and spinners Hooper, Hinds and Gayle collected three wickets between them.

Again, Vaas struck in the early overs. By the ninth over, Vaas had the West Indies under pressure at 2-27, including the key wicket of Lara, caught behind on the drive. Calamity struck in the 15th over when Sarwan was hit on the back of the head by a Fernando bouncer. It looked as if Sarwan would take no further part in the match when he was stretchered from the field. The West Indians' plight worsened with the very next ball from Fernando, which trapped Hooper in front for a golden duck. In a contrast of styles, Gayle and Chanderpaul put their team into a reasonable position with a stand of 59 runs from 14 overs. At the end of the 28th over, the West Indies were 3-121 and needed 108 runs to win at a touch less than five an over. Vaas had been brought back into the attack for his second spell and his reverse swinging deliveries would pose questions for the batsmen.

Vaas caught Gayle in front of the stumps with an inswinger for 55 and, three balls later, Jacobs nicked one to be out for a duck. The West Indian were in turmoil in the next over when power hitter Powell was bowled by Muralitharan. The men from the Caribbean had lost three for one in seven balls.

Despite the regular fall of wickets, Chanderpaul batted with impressive resolve. Chanderpaul and Drakes stemmed the flow, combining for 47 runs from 13 overs. Chanderpaul's innings of 65 ended in the 43rd over, bringing Sarwan back to the crease to a standing ovation. At 7-169, the West Indies needed to score at 7.5 an over to win. Wearing a maroon cap, Sarwan took a few overs to settle back into the task. When Drakes was dismissed with the score on 186 in the 47th over, it was time for Sarwan to unleash. Sarwan took 13 runs from Jayasuriya in the 47th over, including a six over long on. Jayasuriya took a punt on de Silva bowling the 48th over. The move did not work out as hoped, with a further 13 runs being scored. Sarwan hit de Silva for a magnificent six over deep mid wicket to send the crowd into raptures. A few balls later, a big hit towards the backward square leg boundary was put down by Atapattu as he fell to the ground in an attempt to take the catch.

The game was definitely up for grabs, with the West Indies needing 16 runs from two overs. Muralitharan, who had spun the ball prodigiously in this innings, was asked to bowl the penultimate over. The champion off-spinner held firm under the pressure and conceded just two runs. Gunaratne, who had not bowled since the 10th over, was recalled to deliver the last over with 14 runs needed for a West Indian win. After a dot ball opening, Sarwan hit Gunaratne for a boundary. Ten runs were required from four balls. Dillon was run out from the next ball, leaving Sarwan on strike. Gunaratne held firm under the pressure as Sarwan and Pedro Collins could only manage singles from the last three balls of the match. Sarwan's brave innings ended at 47 not out from 44 deliveries.

In this interesting tussle, Vaas won his second man of the match award for the tournament.

SRI LANKA		WEST INDIES	
M. S. Atapattu run out	3	C. H. Gayle lbw b Vaas	55
S. T. Jayasuriya (capt) c Chanderpaul b Gayle	66	W. W. Hinds c Jayasuriya b Vaas	2
H. P. Tillekeratne b Hinds	36	B. C. Lara c Sangakkara b Vaas	1
P. A. de Silva run out	13	R. R. Sarwan not out	47
D. P. M. D. Jayawardene c Powell b Hooper	9	C. L. Hooper (capt) lbw b Fernando	0
R. P. Arnold not out	34	S. Chanderpaul c Atapattu b de Silva	65
K. C. Sangakkara (wk) c Lara b Drakes	24	R. D. Jacobs (wk) c Sangakkara b Vaas	0
W. P. U. J.C. Vaas not out	28	R. L. Powell b Muralitharan	1
Extras (lb 5, w 8, nb 2)	15	V. C. Drakes c Vaas b Jayasuriya	25
(50 overs)	6-228	M. Dillon run out	4
Did not bat: M. Muralitharan, C. R.D. Fernando, P. W.		P. T. Collins not out	1
Gunaratne		Extras (lb 6, w 12, nb 3)	21
1/11 2/96 3/113 4/131 5/139 6/178		(50 overs)	9-222
Bowling: Dillon 10-0-30-0; Collins 10-0-62-0; Drakes		1/10 2/27 3/62 4/121 5/121 6/122 7/169 8/186 9/219	
10-1-32-1; Hooper 6-0-30-1; Hinds 4-0-27-1; Gayle		Bowling: Vaas 10-3-22-4; Gunaratne 6-1-41-0; de Silva	
10-0-42-1		10-0-48-1; Fernando 6-0-33-1; Muralitharan 10-1-26-1;	
		Jayasuriya 8-0-46-1	

Umpires: D.L. Orchard, S. Venkataraghavan.

Toss: Sri Lanka   Points: Sri Lanka 4, West Indies 0.

SATURDAY 1 MARCH 2003
BANGLADESH vs KENYA - GROUP B
WANDERERS STADIUM, JOHANNESBURG, SOUTH AFRICA: KENYA WON BY 32 RUNS

Kenya made history with their win over Bangladesh, becoming the first non-Test playing nation to progress beyond the qualifying stage of the World Cup.

Kenya's modest total of 7-217 owed a lot to Maurice Odumbe, who made an impressive 52 not out from 46 balls. In the face of some accurate bowling from the Bangladeshi seamers, the Kenyans became tied down. After 35 overs, Kenya were struggling at 5-124 after off-spinner Mohammad Rafiq removed Tikolo and Modi in successive overs. With useful contributions from Odoyo and Obuya, Odumbe upped the ante and pushed the total past the 200 mark. The Kenyan innings gathered momentum in the last 10 overs, which produced 70 runs.

A rapid start by Al Sahariar, whose 14 runs in 12 balls consisted entirely of boundary strokes, was extinguished in the third over by Martin Suji. Suji struck again in his next over, catching Mohammad Ashraful adjacent, and Bangladesh were in early strife again at 2-17. Like the Kenyans, Bangladesh were unable to push the scoring along in the middle stages of the innings. A handy partnership of 46 for the fourth wicket between Tushar Imran and Alok Kapali had the match evenly poised with Bangladesh 3-99 in the 27th over. The introduction of off-spinner Odumbe yielded good results, as Alok Kapali and Tushar Imran were caught in consecutive Odumbe overs. From 5-111 in the 29th over, a 40-run stand between Akram Khan and Sanwar Hossain put Bangladesh in the box seat at 5-151 from 38 overs. The equation was a gettable 67 runs from 12 overs. Another double breakthrough from Odumbe swung the game back in Kenya's favour. Bangladesh needed 60 runs from 54 balls with only three wickets remaining.

Akram Khan and Mohammad Rafiq were unable to stop the required run rate from rising. They managed to push the score along to 7-180 in the 46th over. In four deliveries, Tikolo took three wickets for one run to end the Bangladeshi challenge. The Kenyans did a lap of honour in front of an appreciative Wanderers crowd. For Bangladesh, it was their fifth loss of the tournament and their 30th limited-overs international without a win. Odumbe was the Man of the Match for his all-round effort.

KENYA		BANGLADESH	
K. O. Otieno (wk) c Khaled Masud b Manjurul Islam	0	Al Sahariar c Otieno b M. Suji	14
R. D. Shah c Akram Khan b Mohammad Rafiq	37	Mohammad Ashraful lbw b M. Suji	1
B. J. Patel c Manjurul Islam b Khaled Mahmud	32	Tushar Imran c sub (Angara) b Odumbe	48
S. O. Tikolo (capt) b Sanwar Hossain	27	Khaled Masud (capt) (wk) c Shah b Obuya	14
H. S. Modi c & b Sanwar Hossain	12	Alok Kapali c Otieno b Odumbe	18
M. O. Odumbe not out	52	Akram Khan c sub (Angara) b Tikolo	44
T. M. Odoyo lbw b Sanwar Hossain	19	Sanwar Hossain c M. Suji b Odumbe	16
C. O. Obuya b Tapash Baisya	22	Khaled Mahmud st Otien b Odumbe	3
P. J. Ongondo not out	2	Mohammad Rafiq c Modi b Tikolo	5
Extras (b 1, lb 2, w 11)	14	Tapash Baisya not out	2
(50 overs)	7-217	Manjurul Islam st Otieno b Tikolo	2
Did not bat: M. A. Suji, T. O. Suji		Extras (b 2, lb 3, w 10, nb 3)	18
1/1 2/68 3/80 4/116 5/124 6/164 7/197		(47.2 overs)	10-185
Bowling: Manjurul Islam 7-0-30-1; Tapash Baisya 8-1-22-1;		1/16 2/17 3/53 4/99 5/111 6/151 7/158 8/180 9/180	
Khaled Mahmud 10-1-39-1; Mohammad Rafiq 7-0-35-1;		10/185	
Sanwar Hossain 10-0-49-3; Alok Kapali 2-0-9-0;		Bowling: M. Suji 8-1-27-2; Odoyo 4-0-9-0;	
Mohammad Ashraful 6-0-30-0		Ongondo 7-0-29-0; Obuya 9-0-40-1; T. Suji 4-0-23-0;	
		Odumbe 10-0-38-4; Tikolo 5.2-0-14-3	

Umpires: E.A.R. de Silva, N.A. Mallender.

Toss: Kenya   Points: Kenya 4, Bangladesh 0.

SATURDAY 1 MARCH 2003
INDIA vs PAKISTAN - GROUP A
CENTURION, SOUTH AFRICA: INDIA WON BY 6 WICKETS

On a hot day, old foes India and Pakistan produced a sizzling match that entranced millions of fans on the sub-continent. India won an interesting clash comfortably in the end and showed that they were hitting their form at the right time. This fixture was the first India-vs-Pakistan limited-overs match for nearly three years.

The Pakistan innings was spearheaded by a very good hundred from Saeed Anwar. In the process, Anwar compiled his 20th century in limited-overs internationals, including 2,000 runs in one-dayers against India. Anwar struck only seven boundaries in his innings. He adroitly worked the ball with wristy shots for the bulk of his runs. Anwar's innings was ended by an excellent yorker from Nehra in the 41st over.

Unfortunately for Pakistan, none of the other top-order batsmen put together an innings of substance. Inzamam-ul-Haq failed again, this time reaching six runs before he was run out. In the last 14 overs, Pakistan's total was boosted by an industrious innings from Younis Khan and productive cameos from Rashid and Wasim. Rashid was hit on the head during his innings and was unable to keep wicket. Wasim hit the last two deliveries of the innings from Nehra for four to bring the score to 7-273.

Against a hostile attack, the target of 274 looked to be a challenging assignment for India. Yet again, Tendulkar showed he was the man for the occasion. In Shoaib's first over, Tendulkar played an incredible cut shot, sending the ball several rows back from the deep point fence. From Shoaib's next two deliveries, he played a sumptuous pull shot and a drive down the ground, each shot whistling to the fence. Shoaib conceded 18 runs from his first over and was relived by Waqar. Sehwag joined the fun and, from Waqar's first delivery, he played a stunning uppercut over deep cover-point that deposited the ball into the crowd. It was breathtaking stuff as India rocketed to 0-53 in the sixth over.

Leading from the front, Waqar removed Sehwag, who mistimed a drive to cover. Waqar removed his opposite number with the very next ball, leg before to a full and straight one. Promoted to number four, Mohammed Kaif negotiated the hat-trick ball and proceeded to play a sensible support innings as Tendulkar monstered the bowling. In only the tenth over, Tendulkar reached his fifty from only 37 balls. With Tendulkar in superb touch, Kaif sensibly rotated the strike. Tendulkar unleashed a dazzling array of strokes, including some perfectly timed on-drives, keeping a huge global audience enthralled. When he reached 83, Tendulkar had achieved 12,000 runs in one-day internationals. A short time later, Tendulkar and Kaif reached their century stand from 81 balls. After Kaif dragged one on from Afridi, India had roared to 3-155 in the 22nd over. The target of 274 seemed a walk in the park, as 119 runs were required from 28 overs at a comfortable asking rate of 4.25.

These circumstances were conducive to Dravid patiently playing himself in. Afridi, Abdul Razzaq and Shoaib rallied temporarily and Tendulkar's scoring was slowed down. The master batsman was afflicted with leg cramps in the searing heat. After some stretching, he pressed on with the help of a runner. Sensing a hint of vulnerability, Shoaib bowled a vicious delivery to Tendulkar that reared up from a good length. Tendulkar was unable to fend the ball to ground and his magnificent innings was ended two short of a hundred.

With the run rate required well in hand, Yuvraj Singh crafted an attractive, unbeaten 50 from number six, featuring some elegant drives through the covers. With Dravid playing the anchor role, the two middle-order batsmen glided to the target, scoring the remaining 96 runs from 18 overs without any real alarm. India reached their goal with 26 balls to spare to the delight of their many millions of supporters. The Indians had taken on the Pakistani quicks and prevailed. In particular, severe treatment was meted out to Shoaib and Waqar, who each conceded more than 70 runs. There were no surprises with Tendulkar winning the Man of the Match award.

PAKISTAN		INDIA	
Saeed Anwar b Nehra	101	S. R. Tendulkar c Younis Khan b Shoaib Akhtar	98
Taufeeq Umar b Khan	22	V. Sehwag c Shahid Afridi b Waqar Younis	21
Abdul Razzaq c Dravid b Nehra	12	S. C. Ganguly (capt) lbw b Waqar Younis	0
Inzamam-ul-Haq run out	6	M. Kaif b Shahid Afridi	35
Yousuf Youhana c Khan b Srinath	25	R. Dravid (wk) not out	44
Younis Khan c Mongia b Khan	32	Yuvraj Singh not out	50
Shahid Afridi c Kumble b Mongia	9	Extras (b 1, lb 3, w 19, nb 5)	28
Rashid Latif (wk) not out	29	(45.4 overs)	4-276
Wasim Akram not out	10	Did not bat: D. Mongia, A. Kumble, Z. Khan, J. Srinath,	
Extras (b 2, lb 7, w 11, nb 7)	27	A. Nehra	
(50 overs)	7-273	1/53 2/53 3/155 4/177	
Did not bat: Shoaib Akhtar, Waqar Younis (capt)		Bowling: Wasim Akram 10-0-48-0; Shoaib Akhtar	
1/58 2/90 3/98 4/171 5/195 6/208 7/256		10-0-72-1; Waqar Younis 8.4-0-71-2; Shahid Afridi 9-0-45-1;	
Bowling: Khan 10-0-46-2; Srinath 10-0-41-1; Nehra		Abdul Razzaq 8-0-36-0	
10-0-74-2; Kumble 10-0-51-0; Ganguly 3-0-14-0;			
Sehwag 4-0-19-0; Mongia 3-0-19-1			

Umpires: R.E. Koertzen, D.R. Shepherd.

Toss: Pakistan   Points: India 4, Pakistan 0.

SUNDAY 2 MARCH 2003
AUSTRALIA vs ENGLAND - GROUP A:
ST GEORGE'S PARK, PORT ELIZABETH, SOUTH AFRICA: AUSTRALIA WON BY 2 WICKETS

Australia faced off against the Old Enemy for their first World Cup encounter in 11 years. The previous World Cup engagement was the "Lizard of Oz" match at the SCG in March 1992, won handsomely by England. Ricky Ponting's men were aiming to extend their sequence of consecutive limited-overs against England to 14, stretching back to January 1999.

Ponting lost his fifth toss from six matches, Hussain electing to bat on a pitch that was expected to be more challenging to bat on later in the day. To the delight of a substantial English contingent in the stands, openers Marcus Trescothick and Nick Knight were off to a flyer. For the first time since the opening game against Pakistan, Australia were under pressure and they appeared rattled. England had raced to 0-66 after nine overs, including Lee conceding 33 from his opening spell of four overs.

Ponting replaced Lee with Bichel and normal service in Anglo-Australian matches in the early-2000s was quickly resumed. Bichel, bowling a full length and straight, removed Knight with his fifth delivery. Knight steered a ball outside off stump to Martyn at a wide slip position. From 0-66, England wobbled to 3-74 at the end of Bichel's next over. Vaughan, the main success story from England's recently completed tour of Australia, nicked a pearler that moved off the seam subtly. Five balls later, Hussain was bowled for a third ball duck by a magnificent delivery that swung away from his forward defensive and collected off stump. In the next over, McGrath removed Trescothick, caught at slip. England had lost 4-8 from 16 deliveries and were under pressure at 4-74 in the 13th over.

Collingwood was dismissed cheaply and Flintoff joined Stewart in the middle at 5-87 in the 18th over. The resting of Bichel gave the English batsmen some respite and, after the fast start to the innings, time was on their side to recover the innings. Stewart and Flintoff batted responsibly, steadying the ship initially and then attacking Symonds. Their partnership of 90 runs in nearly 25 overs was ended by Bichel in his second over back when Flintoff skied one. England, now 6-177 in the 43rd over, had a respectable total within range.

With five wickets under his belt, Bichel added the scalps of Stewart and Giles to finish with the excellent figures of 7-20 from ten overs. This would have been a World Cup record but for McGrath's performance three days prior. White eked out some runs with the tail to take England's score to 8-204.

Like their English counterparts, Gilchrist and Hayden went hard at the bowling from the start. Their approach did not produce similar results. Caddick removed the top four batsmen with 48 on the board. Hayden, Gilchrist and Ponting perished playing loose shots and Martyn was trapped in front for his second duck of the tournament. The situation called for calm heads and, fortunately for Australia, Lehmann and Bevan obliged with a patient partnership of 63 from almost 20 overs.

From 5-111, Australia were beyond the half way mark with 20 overs remaining. Giles caught Symonds in his follow through and, in his next over, Hogg bottom-edged one into Stewart's gloves. Australia had declined to 7-115 and 90 runs were needed from 18 overs. Australia's saving grace was that Bevan, 25 not out at this stage, was still at the wicket.

White and Giles dried up the flow of runs with accurate, intelligent bowling. The pressure to keep the score ticking over took its toll, as Bevan's attempt at a quick single left Lee short of his ground at the keeper's end. Australia were 8-135 and, in the early hours of Monday morning on the east coast of Australia, cricket followers there could be excused for calling it a night.

With 70 runs required from the last 74 balls, Bevan and new batsman Bichel had a difficult assignment ahead of them on a low and slow pitch. Bevan, the consummate one-day international professional, had piloted Australia home in difficult run chases before. Bevan continued his strategy of working the ball around and looking to hit boundaries from any loose stuff. Although the odds were in his favour, Hussain rang the bowling changes – Flintoff and Caddick bowled one-over spells in the 44th and 45th overs in an effort to unsettle the batsmen. It seemed to only unsettle his bowlers. The expensive Anderson was recalled and the Australians continued to target him. Bevan subtly upped the ante and Bichel batted positively from the outset.

Giles was tight in his final over, the 48th of the innings, which left Australia to score 14 runs from 12 balls. The game was up for grabs and Hussain had one over in reserve from Caddick (4-35 from nine overs) and Flintoff (0-21 from nine overs). In a bizarre decision, he chose Anderson, who had conceded 54 runs from eight overs, to bowl the penultimate over. Bevan hit a single from the first ball. Thirteen needed from 11 balls. The ebullient Bichel smashed the next delivery, a slower ball outside off stump, to the top of the scoreboard over mid wicket. Bichel hit a superbly timed drive the next delivery through long on which had too much pace for Caddick to stop. The complexion of the game had changed dramatically in the space of two balls. Australia only needed three runs from the last nine deliveries. The fact that there were just the two wickets in hand was England's only hope now. That hope was dimmed when Bichel took a single from Anderson's fourth ball and Bevan played out two dot balls.

Only two runs were required in the last over, which was bowled by Flintoff. The tension rose a little when Bichel was unable to force a run from Flintoff's first two deliveries. The suspense was lifted the next ball when Bichel played a gentle drive to mid-on, only to see Vaughan commit a basic error and let the ball roll between his legs for a single. This brought Bevan back on strike with one run needed from the last three deliveries. Bevan delivered the last rites when he hit the next ball, a full toss, to the mid wicket boundary. Australia were home by two wickets with two balls to spare.

Bevan's measured knock of 74 not out from 126 balls saved the day. However, he was overshadowed by Bichel's brilliant all-round performance, which won the Queenslander the Man of the Match award. The win gave Australia a perfect 6-0 return from their pool matches and delivered them the world record of 12 consecutive wins in limited-overs internationals.

ENGLAND		AUSTRALIA	
M. E. Trescothick c Martyn b McGrath	37	A. C. Gilchrist (wk) c Vaughan b Caddick	22
N. V. Knight c Martyn b Bichel	30	M. L. Hayden c Giles b Caddick	1
M. P. Vaughan c Gilchrist b Bichel	2	R. T. Ponting (capt) c Giles b Caddick	18
N. Hussain (capt) b Bichel	1	D. R. Martyn lbw b Caddick	0
A. J. Stewart (wk) b Bichel	46	D. S. Lehmann c Stewart b White	37
P. D. Collingwood c Gilchrist b Bichel	10	M. G. Bevan not out	74
A. Flintoff c Gilchrist b Bichel	45	A. Symonds c & b Giles	0
C. White not out	16	G. B. Hogg c Stewart b Giles	1
A. J. Giles c Bevan b Bichel	2	B. Lee run out	6
A. R. Caddick not out	5	A. J. Bichel not out	34
Extras (lb 3, w 3, nb 4)	10	Extras (b 4, lb 4, w 4, 3 nb)	15
(50 overs)	8-204	(49.4 overs)	8-208

Did not bat: J. M. Anderson

1/66 2/72 3/74 4/74 5/87 6/177 7/180 8/187

Bowling: McGrath 9-2-41-1; Lee 9-0-58-0; Bichel 10-0-20-7; Hogg 10-1-28-0; Lehmann 10-0-34-0; Symonds 2-0-20-0

Did not bat: G. D. McGrath

1/15 2/33 3/33 4/48 5/111 6/112 7/114 8/135

Bowling: Caddick 9-2-35-4; Anderson 9-0-66-0; Flintoff 9.4-1-26-0; White 10-2-21-1; Giles 10-0-42-2; Vaughan 2-0-10-0

Umpires: Aleem Dar, R.B. Tiffin.

Toss: England   Points: Australia 4, England 0.

MONDAY 3 MARCH 2003
CANADA vs NEW ZEALAND - GROUP B
BENONI, SOUTH AFRICA: NEW ZEALAND WON BY 5 WICKETS

New Zealand set themselves the task of demolishing Canada in quick time to assure themselves of a Super Six place. In the end, the Kiwis achieved the win slower than hoped. Whether they would progress would depend on the results of the South Africa-Sri Lanka match to be played in Durban later that day.

Fleming inserted Canada in the hope of restricting them to a total that could be chased down quickly. Again, John Davison had other ideas. Opening the batting, he feasted on the bowling of Adams and Oram. Davison brought up his fifty in only 25 balls, clouting four sixes in the process. An exhilarating shot off Adams in the fourth over sailed over extra cover and into the crowd. The 10th over of the innings, bowled by Oram, produced three towering sixes by Davison over the deep mid wicket area. One shot landed on top of the grandstand and another was despatched out of the ground.

In a shrewd move, Fleming brought on the slower bowling of Vettori, Styris and Harris. The move worked as Davison's scoring was slowed markedly. Davison's innings ended in the 23rd over when he tried to blast Harris into the stands, Cairns taking the catch at long on. Davison had dominated the scoring, hitting 75 from 62 balls out of the team's score of 4-98 to that stage. The remaining batsmen were unable to get much momentum going. Canada were reduced to 8-153 in the 39th over. The Canadian tail wagged a little and the final score of 196 all out in 47 overs was a respectable effort. Despite being punished early by Davison and sending down seven wides, Oram had the figures with 4-52.

New Zealand aimed to score the 197 runs required in a mere 16 overs. Davison was used to open the bowling with his off-breaks. The self-imposed Kiwi target soon became an impossibility. Fleming was run out when sent back by McMillan, Davison had Astle stumped and McMillan skied a ball from Davison to the keeper. These reverses left New Zealand at 3-32 in the fourth over. Cairns and Adams got things back on course with a hectic stand of 65 runs from 40 balls. They took the long handle to Codrington, who conceded 20 runs in his first over. Adams and Cairns fell within three overs, leaving New Zealand in some strife at 5-114 in the 14th over. The calm heads of Styris and Harris saw the Kiwis home with an unbroken stand of 83 runs for the sixth wicket. The two middle-order batsmen intelligently combined working the ball into the gaps for ones and twos with the odd boundary. In the 23rd over, Styris hit Seebaran for four, six and four to bring up his half-century and to tie the scores. A comfortable single from the next ball brought up the win, achieved seven overs behind schedule.

In this fast-paced match, Davison won the Man of the Match award for his all-round performance.

CANADA		NEW ZEALAND	
I. Maraj lbw b Bond	0	C. D. McMillan c Bagai b Davison	14
J. M. Davison c Cairns b Harris	75	S. P. Fleming (capt) run out	5
N. Ifill c McCullum b Oram	7	N. J. Astle st Bagai b Davison	11
I. S. Billcliff c Fleming b Styris	8	C. L. Cairns c Maraj b Davison	31
N. A. de Groot lbw b Oram	17	A. R. Adams c sub (Thuraisingam) b Seebaran	36
J. V. Harris (capt) c McCullum b Bond	26	S. B. Styris not out	54
A. Bagai (wk) b Oram	1	C. Z. Harris not out	38
A. M. Samad lbw b Bond	12	Extras (lb 3, w 5)	8
A. Codrington b Oram	7	(23 overs)	5-197
A. Patel b Styris	25	Did not bat: J. D. P. Oram, D. L. Vettori, B. B. McCullum (wk),
B. B. Seebaran not out	4	S. E. Bond	
Extras (lb 1, w 12, nb 1)	14	1/19 2/31 3/32 4/97 5/114	
(47 overs)	10-196	Bowling: Patel 3-0-32-0; Davison 10-0-61-3;	

1/21 2/43 3/80 4/98 5/123 6/129 7/152 8/153 9/173 10/196

Bowling: Bond 10-3-29-3; Adams 6-0-38-0; Oram 10-1-52-4; Vettori 10-0-34-0; Styris 4-0-23-2; Harris 7-1-19-1

Codrington 2-0-33-0; Seebaran 7-0-61-1; Ifill 1-0-7-0

Umpires: A.V. Jayaprakash, B.G. Jerling.

Toss: New Zealand   Points: New Zealand 4, Canada 0.

MONDAY 3 MARCH 2003
NETHERLANDS vs NAMIBIA - GROUP A
BLOEMFONTEIN, SOUTH AFRICA: NETHERLANDS WON BY 64 RUNS

This clash between Group A's minnows produced an entertaining contest. In the end, the Netherlands won easily. Although both countries lost all of their matches against the Test playing nations, they could be pleased with their efforts.

Luuk van Troost stood in for injured captain Lefebvre and he chose to bat first. After the early loss of Edgar Schiferli, Kloppenburg and van Noortwijk put together a superb partnership of 228 in just under six per over. Kloppenburg became the first Dutch player to score a hundred in limited-overs internationals. Kloppenburg finished on 121 from 142 balls, including four sixes. Van Noortwijk reached figures a short time after his colleague, kicking on to bat to the end of the 50 overs and reaching an unbeaten 134 from 129 balls. After Kloppenburg top-edged to the keeper, Zuiderent and de Leede were dismissed cheaply, both bowled by Louis Burger. After de Leede was dismissed first ball, van Troost successfully negotiated the hat-trick delivery. The two "vans" combined to score 44 from the final 21 balls of the innings, pushing the final tally over 300. Amazingly, the Netherlands' score of 4-314 was more than Australia managed against the Namibian bowlers a few days prior.

Scoring 315 to win was too tall an order for Namibia, although they put forward a good effort in their total of 250. Jan-Berrie Burger and Karg had Namibia off to a flying start, scoring at around a run a ball for the first 12 overs. The introduction of Kloppenburg's medium pace in the 14th over produced a quick reward when the dangerous Burger was caught on the boundary. After Burger was dismissed for a quickfire 41 from 42 balls, Karg, Keulder and Murgatroyd made good contributions without placing the Dutch bowlers under serious pressure. Midway through the innings, the heat of the contest was unexpectedly diminished when an automatic sprinkler emerged from the ground.

Namibia had an outside chance when they reached 3-209 in the 40th over. The reintroduction of Kloppenburg to the attack resulted in the wickets of Louis Burger and Synman from consecutive balls. With the required run rate entering double figures, the Namibian lower order succumbed to the pressure. Adeel Raja picked up four wickets from 13 deliveries to end the Namibian effort. The Netherlands had their first World Cup victory.

With his hundred and four wickets, Kloppenburg was a deserving Man of the Match.

NETHERLANDS		NAMIBIA	
J. F. Kloppenburg c van Schoor b Snyman	121	A. J. Burger c sub (Nijman) b Kloppenburg	41
E. Schiferli b van Vuuren	10	M. Karg c sub (Nijman) b de Leede	41
K. J. van Noortwijk not out	134	D. Keulder b Kloppenburg	52
B. Zuiderent b L. Burger	5	G. B. Murgatroyd c Zuiderent b Mol	52
T. B.M. de Leede b L. Burger	0	D. B. Kotze (capt) lbw b Adeel Raja	25
L. P. van Troost (capt) not out	16	L. J. Burger b Kloppenburg	1
Extras (b 4, lb 2, w 18, n 4)	28	G. Snyman c de Leede b Kloppenburg	0
(50 overs)	4-314	S. F. Burger st Smits b Adeel Raja	6
Did not bat: D. L.S. van Bunge, H. J.C. Mol, J. J. Esmeijer,		M. van Schoor (wk) b Adeel Raja	15
J. Smits (wk), Adeel Raja		B. O. van Rooi not out	9
1/25 2/253 3/270 4/270		R. J. van Vuuren c Mol b Adeel Raja	0
Bowling: Snyman 10-0-55-1; van Vuuren 10-1-63-1; van		Extras (lb 5, w 2, nb 1)	8
Rooi 8-0-59-0; L. Burger 10-1-49-2; A. Burger 3-0-18-0;		(46.5 overs)	10-250
Kotze 4-0-29-0; S. Burger 5-0-35-0		1/76 2/87 3/179 4/209 5/213 6/213 7/224 8/237 9/250	
		10/250	
		Bowling: Schiferli 7-0-46-0; Esmeijer 7-0-43-0; de	
		Leede 8-0-33-1; Kloppenburg 10-0-42-4; Adeel Raja	
		8.5-0-42-4; Mol 6-0-39-1	

Umpires: D.J. Harper, Nadeem Gauri.

Toss: Netherlands   Points: Netherlands 4, Namibia 0.

SOUTH AFRICA vs SRI LANKA - GROUP B
DURBAN, SOUTH AFRICA (DAY/NIGHT): MATCH TIED (DUCKWORTH-LEWIS METHOD)

For the second World Cup running, South Africa's campaign ended with a tie in odd circumstances. On this occasion, a misunderstanding of the Duckworth-Lewis system put paid to the Proteas' campaign.

Realising that chasing a target under the Durban lights would be challenging, Jayasuriya wisely elected to bat first. The innings reached a critical juncture at 3-90 in the 23rd over after Jayasuriya, Tillekeratne and Jayawardene were returned to the pavilion. Marvan Atapattu was joined at the crease by veteran Aravinda de Silva. Their dynamic stand of 152 in 22 overs took Sri Lanka to a position of strength. Atapattu's 124 from 129 deliveries was one of his best limited-overs international hundreds and de Silva put his experience to good use in his fluent 73. Sri Lanka's progress was slowed in the last five overs. Atapattu and de Silva were dismissed in the space of three balls and none of the remaining batsmen made an impact. From the last 31 deliveries of the match, six wickets fell for 26 runs. In the last over, Jacques Kallis laughed heartily when he bowled Muralitharan, backing to square leg in an attempt to steer one through the covers. Kallis' smile was not an accurate indication of South Africa's plight. They had to win to stay alive in the tournament and scoring 269 at night would be a stern challenge.

The gathering of clouds around the port city meant that resort to the Duckworth-Lewis system was going to be necessary at some stage. Accordingly, Smith and Gibbs approached the task with a sense of urgency. They handled the Sri Lankan seamers comfortably and 65 runs were on the board after 11 overs. Jayasuriya decided to change the tempo and the spinners were brought on. The dividend was immediate: from de Silva's first delivery, Smith hit one straight down the throat of deep mid wicket. The spinners did the damage: Kirsten, Kallis and Dippenaar were out cheaply and the threat of Gibbs, who made an entertaining 73, was extinguished when he was bowled behind his legs by Muralitharan. South Africa were in trouble at 5-149 when Pollock joined Boucher in the 30th over. The pair kept the scoring ticking over without really taking control of the bowling.

With light drizzle falling, the stand had realised 63 in 13 overs when an instinctive flick of Muralitharan's flexible wrist ran out Pollock by millimetres.

After 43 overs, South Africa needed 54 to win from a maximum of seven overs. This equation would normally have had Klusener in his element. Amazingly, the fast-scoring all-rounder could not strike the ball cleanly in this pressure situation. He failed to score from his first eight deliveries. Occasional bowler Russel Arnold held his nerve, conceding just one run in the 44th over. A piece of paper was rushed from the South African dressing room to Boucher on which the critical number of 229 was written. The South Africans believed that, assuming that no wicket fell in the 45th over, 229 was the total that needed to be achieved to win the game.

With the intensity of the rain increasing, the Proteas needed 13 runs from Muralitharan's over to reach 229. From the fifth ball of the over, Boucher slogged a good length ball outside off stump to the deep mid wicket region. The ball flew into the jubilant crowd and Boucher punched the air. South Africa had reached 229. Strangely, Boucher gently pushed the final ball of the over to mid wicket and no attempt was made at a run. Panic and confusion overtook the home side when they realised that 229 was the score that had to be passed, rather than being the actual target. This meant that the game would be a tie if no further play were possible.

With Arnold in position to bowl the next over, the rain fell heavily and umpires Bucknor and Venkataraghavan took the players from the field. South African anxiety increased as the rain intensified and the minutes to the cut-off time of 10.45pm ticked away. A brief lightening of the rain encouraged the groundstaff to eagerly run to remove the covers. The umpires considered that conditions were still unfit for play and the game was abandoned.

Again, it was a case of so near, but yet so far, for South Africa. A basic error in applying the Duckworth-Lewis system had cost them a place in the Super Six stage. However, many overlooked the fact that South Africa would have progressed regardless of the result of the Sri Lanka game had the Proteas not dropped the games against the West Indies and New Zealand. After much public criticism and soul searching, Pollock lost his job as captain. On the other hand, Sri Lanka topped the group and looked forward to challenges ahead. In the midst of South Africa's post-mortems, Atapattu was named Man of the Match.

SRI LANKA		SOUTH AFRICA	
M. S. Atapattu c sub (Peterson) b Hall	124	G. C. Smith c Gunaratne b de Silva	35
S. T. Jayasuriya (capt) run out	16	H. H. Gibbs b Muralitharan	73
H. P. Tillekeratne c Boucher b Kallis	14	G. Kirsten b de Silva	8
D. P. M. D. Jayawardene c Boucher b Hall	1	J. H. Kallis b Jayasuriya	16
P. A. de Silva c Smith b Ntini	73	H. H. Dippenaar lbw b Jayasuriya	8
R. P. Arnold b Pollock	8	M. V. Boucher (wk) not out	45
K. C. Sangakkara (wk) c Pollock b Kallis	6	S. M. Pollock (capt) run out	25
W. P. U. J.C. Vaas run out	3	L. Klusener not out	1
M. Muralitharan b Kallis	4	Extras (lb 4, w 12, nb 2)	18
C. R.D. Fernando not out	1	(45 overs)	6-229
Extras (lb 2, w 11, nb 5)	18	Did not bat: A. J. Hall, M. Ntini, M. Zondeki	
(50 overs)	9-268	1/65 2/91 3/124 4/149 5/149 6/212	
Did not bat: P. W. Gunaratne		Bowling: Vaas 7-1-33-0; Gunaratne 6-0-26-0;	
1/37 2/77 3/90 4/242 5/243 6/258 7/261 8/266 9/268		Fernando 1-0-14-0; de Silva 8-0-36-2; Arnold 4-0-16-0;	
Bowling: Pollock 10-1-48-1; Ntini 10-0-49-1;		Muralitharan 9-0-51-1; Jayasuriya 10-0-49-2	
Zondeki 6-0-35-0; Kallis 10-0-41-3; Hall 10-0-62-0;			
Klusener 4-0-31-0			

Umpires: S.A. Bucknor, S. Venkataraghavan.

Toss: Sri Lanka   Points: South Africa 2, Sri Lanka 2.

ZIMBABWE vs PAKISTAN - GROUP A
BULAWAYO SPORTS CLUB, BULAWAYO, ZIMBABWE: NO RESULT

This final match from Group A would determine who would join Australia and India in progressing to the Super Six stage. There were a number of permutations. If Pakistan won by a crushing margin, then their net run rate would overhaul England's and they would progress. If Pakistan won and the margin was not of immense proportions, England would go through. Zimbabwe would advance if they won, the match was tied or there was a no result.

Pakistan chose to bat first, but persistent drizzle delayed the start. The players went off again in the second over after Dougie Hondo trapped Saleem Elahi in front. The match resumed 20 minutes later but more rain half an hour later stopped play in the 10th over. Over an hour later, play restarted. The disjointed nature of the proceedings was an anaethma to the batsmen's concentration, as Yousuf Youhana and Inzamam-ul-Haq were dismissed cheaply after the resumption. After 14 overs, the rain fell more heavily and play was suspended with Pakistan 3-73. Saeed Anwar picked up where he left off from the game against India, speeding to an unbeaten 40 from 45 balls.

The rain would not let up and the umpires decided to abandon the match. The no result was enough to secure Zimbabwe's passage and to wash away the campaigns of Pakistan and England. In the end, the controversial decision to not allocate a reserve day for matches had major consequences for Pakistan, England and the West Indies. After this game, Nasser Hussain resigned as the one-day captain of England, while Waqar and Carl Hooper were axed as skippers. It had been a disappointing tournament for Pakistan. None of the batsmen fired when it really mattered and a team ethos appeared to be lacking. In particular, Inzamam, who would become captain of Pakistan in the months ahead, had a terrible World Cup, cobbling together a paltry 19 runs in six innings.

PAKISTAN		ZIMBABWE
Saeed Anwar not out	40	D. D. Ebrahim, C. B. Wishart, A. Flower, G. W. Flower,
Salim Elahi lbw b Hondo	4	G. J. Whittall, T. Taibu (wk), A. M. Blignaut,
Yousuf Youhana c Taibu b Streak	17	H. H. Streak (capt), D. A. Marillier, S. M. Ervine, D. T. Hondo
Inzamam-ul-Haq c Whittall b Ervine	3	
Younis Khan not out	0	
Extras (b 1, lb 6, w 2)	9	
(14 overs)	3-73	

Did not bat: Azhar Mahmood, Rashid Latif (wk), Wasim Akram, Shoaib Akhtar, Waqar Younis (capt), Mohammad Sami

1/4 2/55 3/72

Bowling: Streak 7-1-25-1; Hondo 4-0-22-1; Ervine 3-0-19-1

C. B. Wishart, D. D. Ebrahim, A. Flower, G. W. Flower, G. J. Whittall, T. Taibu (wk), A. M. Blignaut, H. H. Streak (capt), S. M. Ervine, D. A. Marillier, D. T. Hond

Umpires: B.F. Bowden, E.A.R. de Silva.

Toss: Pakistan   Points: Zimbabwe 2, Pakistan 2.

KENYA vs WEST INDIES - GROUP B
KIMBERLEY, SOUTH AFRICA: WEST INDIES WON BY 142 RUNS

With their chance of progressing to the Super Six stage lost, the West Indies avenged their shock loss to Kenya in the 1996 World Cup. The final margin suggested a commanding performance, although a lack of authority in their batting suggested that the minds of some West Indian players had started to drift homeward.

The West Indian innings comprised two good scores by openers Gayle and Chanderpaul and nothing else of substance. The openers reached 50 for the first time in the tournament and they kicked on to 122. Chanderpaul was the first to go, scoring an impressive 66 from 72 balls, when he top-edged leg-spinner Collins Obuya in the 29th over. Lara struggled to middle the ball, taking 30 balls over his ten runs. With little support, Gayle applied himself to the task and brought up his hundred in the 45th over. After reaching his milestone, Gayle blasted two sixes from Odumbe and he was out in the next over when he tried to lift seamer Joseph Angara into the stands. Gayle's 119 was a good end to a disappointing tournament for him. The final tally of 246 was good on paper, but a trifle disappointing against the limited Kenyan bowling.

The Kenyans wilted in the face of some West Indian speed. Jermaine Lawson, picked for his first game of the tournament, was soon bowling at high speed, topping 150 kilometres per hour on occasions. One scorching delivery from Lawson forced Odumbe to tread on his stumps for a duck. The Kenyans battled to score from Lawson and Dillon and the resulting pressure enabled Drakes to get among the wickets. Drakes cut a swathe through the Kenyan line up, claiming five out of the first seven wickets to fall.

Kenya were unable to put together a partnership and the Drakes-Lawson combination had them in desperate trouble at 8-62 in the 25th over. Bowlers Ongondo and Martin Suji managed to hang around for ten overs and add 40 runs. Their union enabled Kenya to scrape past 100 and to reduce the losing margin to under 150 runs. Drakes got the nod over Gayle for the man of the match. Kenya's heavy defeat by a team that failed to qualify for the Super Six stage raised concerns about whether Kenya would be competitive for the remainder of the tournament.

WEST INDIES		KENYA	
C. H. Gayle c D. Obuya b Angara	119	K. O. Otieno (wk) c Dillon b Drakes	3
S. Chanderpaul c Angara b C. Obuya	66	R. D. Shah c Gayle b Dillon	12
B. C. Lara c D. Obuya b Tikolo	10	B. J. Patel c Lara b Drakes	11
M. N. Samuels c Patel b Odumbe	14	S. O. Tikolo (capt) lbw b Drakes	12
R. L. Powell c Otieno b Odumbe	8	H. S. Modi c Jacobs b Drakes	0
C. L. Hooper (capt) st Otieno b Angara	6	M. O. Odumbe hit wkt b Lawson	0
W. W. Hinds b Suji	10	D. O. Obuya c Powell b Drakes	4
R. D. Jacobs (wk) not out	9	C. O. Obuya c Powell b Lawson	13
V. C. Drakes not out	1	P. J.C. Ongondo b Powell	24
Extras (w 3)	3	M. A. Suji c Chanderpaul b Hinds	13
(50 overs)	7-246	J. O. Angara not out	0
Did not bat: M. Dillon, J. J.C. Lawson		Extras (lb 3, w 8, nb 1)	12
1/122 2/158 3/182 4/196 5/222 6/224 7/245		(35.5 overs)	10-104
Bowling: Suji 10-1-38-1; Angara 7-0-53-2;		1/8 2/26 3/34 4/34 5/43 6/43 7/54 8/62 9/102 10/104	
Ongondo 5-0-17-0; Odumbe 10-0-62-2; C. Obuya 10-0-48-1;		Bowling: Dillon 10-1-31-1; Drakes 10-2-33-5;	
Tikolo 8-0-28-1		Lawson 8-0-16-2; Powell 4-2-8-1; Chanderpaul 2-0-6-0;	
		Hinds 1.5-0-7-1	

Umpires: D.R. Shepherd, S.J.A. Taufel.

Toss: West Indies   Points: West Indies 4, Kenya 0.

At the end of the group stage, the standings were as follows, with the top three teams from each group qualifying for the Super Six stage.

		GROUP A									GROUP B					
	P	W	L	T	NR	Points	NR/R			P	W	L	T	NR	Points	NR/R
AUSTRALIA	6	6	0	0	0	24	2.04	SRI LANKA		6	4	1	1	0	18	1.20
INDIA	6	5	1	0	0	20	1.10	KENYA		6	4	2	0	0	16	-0.69
ZIMBABWE	6	3	2	0	1	14	0.50	NEW ZEALAND		6	4	2	0	0	16	0.99
ENGLAND	6	3	3	0	0	12	0.82	WEST INDIES		6	3	2	0	1	14	1.10
Pakistan	6	2	3	0	1	10	0.22	South Africa		6	3	2	1	0	14	1.73
Netherlands	6	1	5	0	0	4	-1.45	Canada		6	1	5	0	0	4	-1.98
Namibia	6	0	6	0	0	0	-2.95	Bangladesh		6	0	5	0	1	2	-2.04

Kenya were placed ahead of New Zealand because, where teams had the same number of points and the same number of wins, the next determinant was the head-to-head record. This rule was also applied to the West Indies and South Africa.

The starting table for the Super Six round had a different look.

	Points	NR. R
Australia	12	1.67
Kenya	10	1.06
India	8	-0.35
Sri Lanka	7.5	-0.06
New Zealand	4	-0.94
Zimbabwe	3.5	-0.98

FRIDAY 7 MARCH 2003
SUPER SIX No. 1: AUSTRALIA vs SRI LANKA
CENTURION, SOUTH AFRICA: AUSTRALIA WON BY 96 RUNS

In this clash between the group winners, Australia's emphatic win showed that there was much daylight between them and their rivals. The 96-run triumph by the Australians extended their winning run to 13 and secured a semi-final berth.

Australia batted first after Ponting called correctly for only the second time in the tournament. Vaas and Gunaratne, who had been successful with early wickets so far in the competition, were taken to task by the Australian top order. Australia raced to 68 after 10 overs, which forced Jayasuriya to bring Muralitharan on early. The world's best off-spinner broke through in his second over when he had Hayden caught at bat-pad. Gilchrist mauled the bowling, reaching 50 from 45 balls, and the Australians were on their way to a sizeable total at 1-131 from 20 overs.

Ponting, who was scratchy early in his innings, began to find his touch and kept the scoreboard ticking over. Gilchrist continued to reach or clear the boundary regularly and, in the 30th over, he was on the verge of his first World Cup hundred. Ponting worked Muralitharan just forward of square and Gilchrist, haring back to the bowler's end to complete the second run, was caught several centimetres short by a direct hit from Vaas. Gilchrist blazed his 99 runs from only 88 deliveries. His dismissal did not impede Australia's progress. Ponting, who took 66 balls to reach his half-century, lifted the tempo and Martyn scored at a good rate in his usual unobtrusive fashion. Vaas was clubbed for 20 runs in his eighth and final over, including sixes from consecutive balls by Ponting.

Ponting and Martyn worked the spinners around skilfully as the run rate grew to almost 6.5 per over. In his first substantial score of the tournament, Ponting batted with increased assuredness. When he leg-glanced a ball from Muralitharan for four in the 42nd over, he was rewarded with his second World Cup hundred, his 12th overall in limited-overs internationals. His second fifty was scored from only 30 deliveries. In the 46th over, Ponting was eventually caught from a skier off Fernando for a superb 114, which featured four sixes. Martyn reached his fifty in the penultimate over and was soon bowled by Fernando, who removed Lehmann two balls later. Australia's score of 5-319 was going to be a tough mountain to climb.

Brett Lee threw the cat among the pigeons in the second over when he cracked Jayasuriya's left thumb, forcing him to retire hurt. After several stabilising overs of batting by Atapattu and Tillekeratne, Lee struck again. Moving low to his left in his follow through, Lee took a very good return catch to send back Atapattu. In his next over, the out of form Jayawardene nicked one from Lee and Gilchrist took a regulation catch. Wickets followed in the next two overs: McGrath beat Tillekeratne's defences and Lee trapped Arnold in front. Within 22 balls, Sri Lanka had lost four wickets for six runs. With Jayasuriya out of action, the Sri Lankans were effectively 5-48 in the 14th over. Veteran batsman de Silva had to call on his experience to combat the rampant Australians. With Sangakkara and Vaas providing steady support, de Silva marshalled consecutive partnerships of 52 and 44. Despite de Silva's resistance, the required run rate spiralled out of control. When Muralitharan was caught slogging off Lehmann in the 38th over, Sri Lanka were 7-149 and a win was well out of range. De Silva took most of the strike and hit out, blasting Lee into the stands twice and Hogg once. De Silva and Fernando took the score past 200 with their rapid half-century stand. De Silva hit a return catch to Hogg in the 45th over which was gratefully accepted. De Silva's excellent hand of 92 from 94 balls earned him a standing ovation. Fernando and Gunaratne hit some consolation boundaries off Hogg before the supremely accurate McGrath put an end to this frivolity in the 48th over. The Man of the Match adjudicators favoured Ponting's innings over Lee's destruction of the Sri Lankan top order.

AUSTRALIA		SRI LANKA	
A. C. Gilchrist (wk) run out	99	M. S. Atapattu c & b Lee	16
M. L. Hayden c Tillekeratne b Muralitharan	22	S. T. Jayasuriya (capt) retired hurt	1
R. T. Ponting (capt) c Sangakkara b Fernando	114	H. P. Tillekeratne b McGrath	21
D. R. Martyn b Fernando	52	D. P. M. D. Jayawardene c Gilchrist b Lee	0
D. S. Lehmann c de Silva b Fernando	10	P. A. de Silva c & b Hogg	92
I. J. Harvey not out	5	R. P. Arnold lbw b Lee	1
M. G. Bevan not out	1	K. C. Sangakkara (wk) run out	20
Extras (lb 4, w 5, nb 7)	16	W. P. U. J.C. Vaas lbw b Hogg	21
(50 overs)	5-319	M. Muralitharan c Lee b Lehmann	4
Did not bat: G. B. Hogg, A. J. Bichel, B. Lee, G. D. McGrath		C. R.D. Fernando lbw b McGrath	9
1/75 2/181 3/293 4/313 5/314		P. W. Gunaratne not out	15
Bowling: Vaas 8-0-59-0; Gunaratne 6-0-46-0; de		Extras (b 6, lb 8, w 6, nb 3)	23
Silva 5-0-36-0; Muralitharan 10-0-47-1; Arnold 2-0-21-0;		(47.4 overs)	10-223
Fernando 9-0-47-3; Jayasuriya 10-0-59-0		1/42 2/46 3/47 4/48 5/100 6/144 7/149 8/203 9/223	
		10/223	
		Jayasuriya retired hurt at 6	
		Bowling: McGrath 9.4-1-25-2; Lee 10-1-52-3;	
		Harvey 7-0-29-0; Bichel 7-1-32-0; Hogg 9-1-45-2;	
		Lehmann 5-0-26-1	

Umpires: B.F. Bowden, D.R. Shepherd.

Toss: Australia   Points: Australia 4, Sri Lanka 0.

FRIDAY 7 MARCH 2003
SUPER SIX No. 2: INDIA vs KENYA
NEWLANDS, CAPE TOWN, SOUTH AFRICA (DAY/NIGHT): INDIA WON BY 6 WICKETS

India were made to work by an determined Kenya, who went some way to answering criticisms that they did not deserve their Super Six place.

Ganguly's men were given the challenge of chasing a target under lights, which had proved to be a difficult task in this tournament. The Kenyans were focused on occupying the crease and grinding out a competitive score. Kennedy Otieno and Ravindu Shah mainly dealt in singles and they rode their luck, as three reasonably straight-forward chances were spilled from Nehra's bowling. Otieno delighted the crowd with a superbly timed on-drive off Zaheer Khan for six. The Indians had to wait until 21 overs were bowled before they drew first blood with the score on 75. Shah backed up a fair way and charged down the wicket for a quick single, but the throw by bowler Khan to the bowler's end beat him home.

India had the double breakthrough a short time later when Tikolo played a loose sweep off Harbhajan Singh straight to deep backward square leg. Otieno and Odoyo crafted the key partnership of the innings, reaching 76 from 100 deliveries. Otieno's patient innings of 79 from 134 balls ended in the 40th over as he missed Harbhajan's arm ball. In contrast to his top order colleagues, Odumbe batted with aggression and he sped to an unbeaten 34 from 24 deliveries. Odumbe marshalled a late rally, as the 200 mark was reached in the 47th over and 68 runs were taken from the last ten overs. Despite his impressive strike rate, Odumbe only hit two fours. In the final tally of 6-225, the Kenyans could only muster 17 boundary strokes. Nehra bowled accurately and was unlucky to have not picked up a few wickets.

Aided by a breeze, the Kenyan seamers were able to get the ball to swing. Inside ten overs, Sehwag, Tendulkar and Kaif were back in the pavilion. After an early flurry of boundaries by Ganguly, the Indian skipper and the patient Dravid set out to repair the innings in an unhurried fashion. From 29 overs, India were 3-107, which was only five runs more than Kenya had scored at the same stage for one wicket less. Dravid's leading edge bobbled up to a delighted Collins Obuya in the next over and the Indians had a fight on their hands. The required run rate had climbed to six a few minutes later.

Sadly for the Kenyans, it would be the last time they tasted success in this match. Ganguly found a willing ally in Yuvraj Singh and the runs began to flow more freely. In a well-paced run chase, Ganguly and Yuvraj Singh gradually reduced the asking rate below five without playing many risky shots. In the 47th over, Yuvraj brought up his half-century from 57 balls. A few balls later, Ganguly pushed Tikolo to deep cover for a single to reach three figures. The Indian captain had achieved his second hundred of the tournament and his 21st in one-day internationals. The last rites were completed in the 48th over. India reached their target with 13 deliveries remaining. The Ganguly-Yuvraj Singh partnership produced an unbeaten 118 from 111 balls to see India across the line. Ganguly was the man of the match.

KENYA		INDIA	
K. O. Otieno (wk) b Harbhajan Singh	79	V. Sehwag c Tikolo b Odoyo	3
R. D. Shah run out	34	S. R. Tendulkar c T. Suji b M. Suji	5
S. O. Tikolo (capt) c Khan b Harbhajan Singh	3	S. C. Ganguly (capt) not out	107
T. M. Odoyo lbw b Mongia	32	M. Kaif lbw b Odoyo	5
M. O. Odumbe not out	34	R. Dravid c & b Obuya	32
C. O. Obuya c Mongia b Srinath	8	Yuvraj Singh not out	58
P. J.C. Ongondo c Tendulkar b Srinath	8	Extras (lb 5, w 8, nb 3)	16
M. A. Suji not out	11	(47.5 overs)	4-226
Extras (b 4, lb 8, w 4)	16	Did not bat: D. Mongia, Harbhajan Singh, Z. Khan, J. Srinath,	
(50 overs)	6-225	A. Nehra	
Did not bat: B. J. Patel, H. S. Modi, T. O. Suji		1/5 2/11 3/24 4/108	
1/75 2/81 3/157 4/165 5/191 6/206		Bowling: M. Suji 10-3-27-1; Odoyo 7-0-27-2;	
Bowling: Khan 10-1-53-0; Srinath 10-0-43-2; Nehra		Ongondo 5-0-31-0; T. Suji 7-0-25-0; Obuya 9.5-2-50-1;	
10-2-30-0; Harbhajan Singh 10-0-41-2; Yuvraj Singh 2-0-9-0		Odumbe 3-0-25-0; Tikolo 6-0-36-0	

Umpires: D.J. Harper, P. Willey.

Toss: Kenya   Points: India 4, Kenya 0.

SATURDAY 8 MARCH 2003
SUPER SIX No. 3: NEW ZEALAND vs ZIMBABWE
BLOEMFONTEIN, SOUTH AFRICA: NEW ZEALAND BY 6 WICKETS

Beginning the Super Six round in fifth position, this was a must-win game for New Zealand. The Kiwis were able to withstand a spirited fightback by Zimbabwe late in their innings to achieve the desired result.

On a benign track, Zimbabwe laboured against the steady New Zealand attack. After danger man Blignaut was run out in the 24th over, Zimbabwe had only managed 6-106. Wicketkeeper Taibu batted with determination to add 68 runs with Streak, but this important stand consumed 20 overs. Taibu reached his maiden half-century and was trapped in front by Harris in the next over. After 47 overs, Zimbabwe were 7-190 and a score in the low 200s seemed almost certain. Three overs later, Zimbabwe had passed 250. Streak and Sean Ervine went on a hitting spree, walloping 62 runs from the last three overs, including eight fours and three sixes. Harris' final over cost 23 runs whilst Adams was blasted for 26 in the final over. In the process, Streak zoomed from 37 to an unbeaten 72. At the end of the bombardment, the statisticians calculated that 151 runs were scored in the first 40 overs and 101 runs were scored in the last 10.

New Zealand's assignment of scoring 253 seemed to be a stretching target which, if achieved, would stand the Kiwis in good stead for the engagements with Australia and India. After the early loss of McMillan, Fleming continued his impressive form, scoring a quick 46 that included 40 runs in fours. Fleming's fast scoring gave Astle the scope to build a patient innings with the middle order. The dismissal of Styris at 3-97 in the 20th over brought Cairns to the crease with just over five runs per over required. Both Astle and Cairns played responsibly, shelving their attacking instincts in a bid to construct a sizeable partnership. The Zimbabweans missed a trick, substitute fielder Marillier dropping a sitter at backward square leg when Cairns was at 21.

In the 44th over, Cairns reached his half-century with a six from Ervine. He was bowled by the next delivery, ending a vital 121 run stand for the fourth wicket. New Zealand were well placed, but still had some work to do. Thirty-five runs were needed from thirty-six balls. In his fourth World Cup, Harris kept a cool head, taking two fours from Hondo in the 46th over to ease the pressure. In the next over, Astle slashed Ervine over extra cover for four to raise his second World Cup century. Harris finished the job in Hondo's next over, taking New Zealand home with 16 balls remaining. Astle's well-controlled hand of 102 not out from 122 deliveries won him the Man of the Match award.

ZIMBABWE		NEW ZEALAND	
C. B. Wishart c Styris b Cairns	30	C. D. McMillan c Taibu b Hondo	8
D. D. Ebrahim b Adams	0	S. P. Fleming (capt) lbw b Blignaut	46
A. Flower run out	37	N. J. Astle not out	102
G. W. Flower c Cairns b Oram	1	S. B. Styris c sub (Friend) b Blignaut	13
G. J. Whittall c McCullum b Cairns	0	C. L. Cairns b Ervine	54
T. Taibu (wk) lbw b Harris	53	C. Z. Harris not out	14
A. M. Blignaut run out	4	Extras (lb 5, w 10, nb 1)	16
H. H. Streak (capt) not out	72	(47.2 overs)	4-253
S. M. Ervine not out	31	Did not bat: B. B. McCullum (wk), J. D. P. Oram, A. R.	
Extras (lb 9, w 13, nb 2)	24	Adams, D. L. Vettori, S. E. Bond	
(50 overs)	7-252	1/27 2/72 3/97 4/218	
Did not bat: B. A. Murphy, D. T. Hondo		Bowling: Streak 10-0-59-0; Hondo 8.2-0-52-1; Blignaut	
1/5 2/59 3/63 4/65 5/98 6/106 7/174		10-0-41-2; G. W. Flower 10-0-33-0; Whittall 3-0-19-0;	
Bowling: Bond 10-1-37-0; Adams 5-0-54-1; Oram 10-4-28-1;		Ervine 6-0-44-1	
Cairns 4-0-16-2; Vettori 10-0-52-0; Harris 10-0-45-1;			
Astle 1-0-11-0			

Umpires: D.B. Hair, R.E. Koertzen.

Toss: Zimbabwe   Points: New Zealand 4, Zimbabwe 0.

MONDAY 10 MARCH 2003
SUPER SIX No. 4: INDIA vs SRI LANKA
WANDERERS, JOHANNESBURG, SOUTH AFRICA: INDIA WON BY 183 RUNS

India clinched a semi-final place with a mammoth victory over Sri Lanka. It was the second hammering Sri Lanka suffered in the space of 72 hours. Despite these setbacks, the prospect of a semi-final appearance still remained.

The Wanderers wicket has been conducive to high scores in this tournament. Jayasuriya made a surprise choice to bowl first, placing faith in the theory that moisture in the pitch from recent rainfall would help his seamers. India dismissed that theory, racking up an impressive total of 6-292. Like the Australians did three days before, India exposed the weaknesses of the Sri Lankan bowlers other than Vaas and Muralitharan. Tendulkar and Sehwag set the foundation for a large score with an opening stand of 153 that was broken in the 27th over. After Sehwag was caught at long on, Tendulkar pressed on to his second score in the 90s of this tournament. In the process, he reached 500 runs in the tournament, a feat he also achieved in 1996.

Ganguly played a fluent innings and kept the score ticking towards 300 after Tendulkar was dismissed. Vaas and Muralitharan once again showed their class, sharing four wickets for the match from 20 overs combined.

Sri Lanka made a total hash of the run chase. Atapattu was out for a duck in the second over when his poorly controlled cut shot from Srinath was caught at cover. Strangely, American-born Jehan Mubarak, who was playing his first game in the tournament, came in at number three. Two balls later he was on his way, edging a catch behind off Srinath. In another odd move, the struggling Jayawardene was in next, ahead of the in-form de Silva. In the end, it didn't matter, as both Jayawardene and de Silva were leg-before for ducks in successive overs. Jayasuriya, bravely soldiering on from the battering he received from Lee, lifted one to cover to leave Sri Lanka reeling at 5-40 from eight overs. Veteran seamer Srinath took four out of the first five wickets to fall.

The Sri Lankan innings plummeted to a disastrous 9-78 from 19 overs. Sangakkara hit a defiant 30, but he had no support. Fernando and Muralitharan managed a 31 run partnership for the last wicket, the highest stand of the innings. This fact neatly summed up Sri Lanka's batting woes. Nehra cleaned up the tail, finishing with four wickets. In a tale of woe, the Sri Lankan scorecard included five ducks. Srinath received the man of the match award for his destruction of the Sri Lankan top order.

INDIA		SRI LANKA	
S. R. Tendulkar c Sangakkara b de Silva	97	M. S. Atapattu c Kaif b Srinath	0
V. Sehwag c de Silva b Muralitharan	66	S. T. Jayasuriya (capt) c Kaif b Srinath	12
S. C. Ganguly (capt) b Vaas	48	J. Mubarak c Dravid b Srinath	0
M. Kaif b Muralitharan	19	D. P. M. D. Jayawardene lbw b Khan	0
Yuvraj Singh b Vaas	5	P. A. de Silva lbw b Srinath	0
R. Dravid (wk) not out	18	K. C. Sangakkara (wk) c Yuvraj Singh b Nehra	30
D. Mongia c de Silva b Muralitharan	9	R. P. Arnold lbw b Khan	8
Harbhajan Singh not out	7	W. P. U. J.C. Vaas c Tendulkar b Nehra	9
Extras (b 4, lb 9, w 7, nb 3)	23	R. A.P. Nissanka c Kaif b Nehra	0
(50 overs)	6-292	C. R.D. Fernando not out	13
Did not bat: Z. Khan, J. Srinath, A. Nehra		M. Muralitharan c Kaif b Nehra	16
1/153 2/214 3/243 4/251 5/265 6/277		Extras (b 1, lb 5, w 14, nb 1)	21
Bowling: Vaas 10-2-34-2; Nissanka 6-0-49-0; Fernando		(23 overs)	10-109
10-1-61-0; Muralitharan 10-0-46-3; Jayasuriya 3-0-27-0; de		1/2 2/2 3/3 4/15 5/40 6/59 7/75 8/78 9/78 10/109	
Silva 6-0-32-1; Arnold 5-0-30-0		Bowling: Khan 7-0-33-2; Srinath 9-1-35-4; Nehra 7-1-35-4	

Umpires: D.R. Shepherd, S.J.A. Taufel.

Toss: Sri Lanka   Points: India 4, Sri Lanka 0.

TUESDAY 11 MARCH 2003
SUPER SIX No. 5: AUSTRALIA vs NEW ZEALAND
ST GEORGE'S PARK, PORT ELIZABETH, SOUTH AFRICA: AUSTRALIA WON BY 96 RUNS

For the second time in three days, Australia fought back from a difficult position to keep their World Cup winning streak alive. New Zealand, who had the edge over their trans-Tasman rivals in recent one-day internationals, needed to beat India in their next match to progress their campaign to the semi-final round.

On another slow St George's Park wicket, Fleming chose to give his bowlers first crack at the Australians. Shane Bond continued his love of bowling to the Aussies, claiming the prize scalps of Hayden, Gilchrist and Ponting, who contributed a combined total of 25 runs. When Lehmann was caught off Adams' bowling in the 13th over, Australia were 4-47 and had a fight on their hands. After six overs, Bond was rested and Fleming made regular changes to the bowling, refusing to allow the Australians to settle into any rhythm. Martyn and Bevan found the Kiwi attack hard to get away and their stand of 33 took nearly 12 overs. Bond was recalled to the attack with spectacular results. In the second over of his second spell, he had Martyn caught behind and he trapped Hogg leg before from the next delivery. In his next over, he rearranged Ian Harvey's furniture, leaving Australia in dire straits at 7-84.

This crisis had Michael Bevan in his element. In a bid to prise out more wickets, Fleming kept Bond in the attack for one more over after Harvey's dismissal. This move did not produce the sought-after wicket and Bond had finished his 10 overs. He ended with the excellent figures of 6-23, a record for New Zealand in the World Cup. With the threat of Bond removed, Bevan and Bichel had less to worry about in salvaging the innings. It would be the second rescue operation for the pair at the same ground in the space of nine days.

Bevan and Bichel found runs hard to come by for 12 overs. Harris built up the pressure with plenty of dot balls and he conceded only 24 runs from his 10 overs. Fleming had also used up Vettori, which left Adams, Oram and the part-timers to bowl the innings out. From 7-128 after 40 overs, Bevan and Bichel gradually lifted the tempo, rotating the strike and hitting boundaries with increased frequency. On this occasion, it was Bichel who was the dominant partner. Despite giving his partner a 20-run start, Bichel beat Bevan to the half-century. Bevan reached his 50 shortly after and a respectable total was within the Australians' reach. Oram removed Bevan in the 48th over for a patient 56, ending the eighth wicket partnership at 97. Bichel continued to 64 before he became Oram's second wicket in the last over. Lee finished the innings off on a high, smashing Oram for two consecutive sixes and lifting Australia over 200 in the process. The final tally of 8-208 gave the Australian bowlers something realistic to defend.

Displaying his champion qualities, McGrath boosted Australian hopes when he removed pinch-hitter Vettori, Astle and Styris cheaply. New batsman Cairns and Fleming counter-attacked, taking several boundaries from McGrath and Lee and bumping up the run rate to nearly six. Harvey and Bichel applied the brakes and Cairns succumbed, steering a ball from Bichel to Lee at third man. Vincent was gone a few overs later and the mainstay of the innings, Fleming, had to go when he gloved a rising ball from Lee down the leg-side. It was New Zealand's turn to feel the heat at 6-102.

Sensing a weakness, Lee went in for the kill. Harris was unable to find anyone to stay with him as Lee scythed through the tail. McCullum, Oram, Adams and Bond could only manage to score four runs between them. Harris was left high and dry for 15. Lee picked up the last five wickets to fall at a personal cost of just three runs in 14 deliveries. New Zealand suffered the ignominy of being bowled out for their lowest score in a World Cup match. The innings lasted just over 30 overs. Australia's winning margin of 96 runs was one less than the runs produced by the Bevan-Bichel partnership. Despite his team's heavy defeat, Bond won the Man of the Match award.

AUSTRALIA		NEW ZEALAND	
A. C. Gilchrist (wk) lbw b Bond	18	D. L. Vettori c Gilchrist b McGrath	10
M. L. Hayden c McCullum b Bond	1	S. P. Fleming (capt) c Gilchrist b Lee	48
R. T. Ponting (capt) c Fleming b Bond	6	N. J. Astle c Ponting b McGrath	0
D. R. Martyn c McCullum b Bond	31	S. B. Styris lbw b McGrath	3
D. S. Lehmann c Astle b Adams	4	C. L. Cairns c Lee b Bichel	16
M. G. Bevan c Vincent b Oram	56	L. Vincent c Martyn b Harvey	7
G. B. Hogg lbw b Bond	0	C. Z. Harris not out	15
I. J. Harvey b Bond	2	B. B. McCullum (wk) lbw b Lee	1
A. J. Bichel c Cairns b Oram	64	J. D. P. Oram b Lee	0
B. Lee not out	15	A. R. Adams b Lee	0
G. D. McGrath not out	3	S. E. Bond c & b Lee	3
Extras (lb 1, w 4, nb 3)	8	Extras (lb 4, w 5)	9
(50 overs)	9-208	(30.1 overs)	10-112

1/17 2/24 3/31 4/47 5/80 6/80 7/84 8/181 9/192

Bowling: Bond 10-2-23-6; Adams 9-2-46-1; Vettori 10-1-40-0; Oram 7-0-48-2; Harris 10-1-24-0; Styris 3-0-18-0; Astle 1-0-8-0

1/14 2/14 3/33 4/66 5/84 6/102 7/104 8/104 9/108 10/112

Bowling: McGrath 6-1-29-3; Lee 9.1-2-42-5; Harvey 6-3-11-1; Bichel 5-0-15-1; Hogg 4-0-11-0

Umpires: S.A. Bucknor, E.A.R. de Silva.

Toss: New Zealand   Points: Australia 4, New Zealand 0.

WEDNESDAY 12 MARCH 2003
SUPER SIX No. 6: KENYA vs ZIMBABWE
BLOEMFONTEIN, SOUTH AFRICA: KENYA WON BY 7 WICKETS

In this African derby, Kenya surprised many observers by thrashing a disappointing Zimbabwe. The result was momentous for Kenyan cricket. The east African nation had qualified for the World Cup semi-finals for the first time, the first non-Test playing team to achieve this feat.

Zimbabwe were forced to find a replacement for injured opening batsman Mark Vermeulen. They turned to experienced campaigner Alastair Campbell, who had retired from international cricket after being overlooked for the national squad for the tournament. Zimbabwe were soon caught on the hop when medium pacer Martin Suji had sent back Wishart, Campbell and Grant Flower by the 15th over. The steady Kenyan bowling focused on accuracy and they were handsomely rewarded. Wickets fell regularly and only Andy Flower put up any sustained resistance. Flower's patient 63 represented nearly half the side's total and Doug Marillier was the only other batsman to pass 20. The Zimbabwean batsmen were tied down and they seemed unsure about how to play the spin of Collins Obuya and Asif Kairm. Zimbabwe failed to bat out 50 overs in their inadequate total of 133.

With a semi-final place there for the taking, Kenya stumbled early in their run chase. At 3-62 after 17 overs, the middle order was exposed. Odoyo and Odumbe rose to the occasion, playing an impressive array of shots. Both batsmen found the boundary regularly as Kenya sped towards 100. In the 23rd and 24th overs, the pair peeled off six consecutive fours from Bliganut and Grant Flower to bring Kenya close to an amazing win. Odumbe continued his blitzkrieg and Kenya reached their goal in 26 overs. Odumbe reached his unbeaten 38 from a mere 20 balls, while Odoyo was a little more restrained, scoring 43 from 60 balls. Their unbroken stand of 73 took only ten overs.

In a game bereft of outstanding contributions, Martin Suji's three wickets delivered him the Man of the Match prize. Campbell and Olonga represented Zimbabwe for the last time in this match.

ZIMBABWE		KENYA	
C. B. Wishart c Otieno b M. Suji	5	K. O. Otieno (wk) lbw b Olonga	19
A. D.R. Campbel lbw b M. Suji	7	R. D. Shah run out	14
A. Flower b Odoyo	63	S. O. Tikolo (capt) c Streak b Blignaut	2
G. W. Flower c Otieno b M. Suji	7	T. M. Odoyo not out	43
T. Taibu (wk) c Otieno b Obuya	3	M. O. Odumbe not out	38
D. D. Ebrahim st Otien b Obuya	13	Extras (lb 4, w 6, nb 9)	19
A. M. Blignaut run out	4	(26 overs)	3-135
H. H. Streak (capt) c Shah b Obuya	0	Did not bat: H. S. Modi, C. O. Obuya, P. J.C. Ongondo, T. O.	
D. A. Marillier b Tikolo	21	Suji, M. A. Suji, A. Y. Karim	
H. K. Olonga c Odumbe b Tikolo	3	1/24 2/33 3/62	
D. T. Hondo not out	0	Bowling: Streak 6-0-24-0; Blignaut 9-1-36-1;	
Extras (lb 1, w 4, nb 2)	7	Olonga 4-0-21-1; Hondo 3-1-14-0; G. W. Flower 3-0-27-0;	
(44.1 overs)	10-133	Marillier 1-0-9-0	

1/8 2/26 3/45 4/66 5/85 6/95 7/97 8/114 9/129 10/133

Bowling: M. Suji 8-2-19-3; Odoyo 10-0-43-1;

Ongondo 5-2-16-0; Obuya 10-0-32-3; Karim 9-0-20-0;

Tikolo 2.1-0-2-2

Umpires: Aleem Dar, S. Venkataraghavan.

Toss: Zimbabwe   Points: Kenya 4, Zimbabwe 0.

FRIDAY 14 MARCH 2003
SUPER SIX No. 7: INDIA vs NEW ZEALAND
CENTURION, SOUTH AFRICA: INDIA WON BY 7 WICKETS

India completed a clean sweep of their Super Six matches with a comfortable win over New Zealand. The loss meant a likely end to New Zealand's campaign. The fate of Fleming's men was now out of their hands. The Kiwis needed Zimbabwe to upset Sri Lanka the next day for their tournament to continue to the semi-final phase.

Ganguly sent New Zealand in and the rewards were immediate. McMillan and Astle fell for ducks in the first over from Zaheer Khan. Ganguly enjoyed a charmed run with his bowling changes as New Zealand's top order collapsed for the second match running. Fleming survived for a time but he was undone when Srinath, back for his second spell, had him caught at mid-off from a mistimed drive. From the perilous position of 5-60 in the 18th over, the middle order and tail showed some application to eke out a total of 146. It was another sub-standard effort from the usually determined New Zealand batsmen.

New Zealand's slim chances of victory were boosted when Bond and Tuffey had India three down in the fifth over. The opportunity of placing the middle order under real pressure was missed when wicket-keeper McCullum dropped Dravid from Bond's bowling. The miss occurred when the man known as "the Wall" was on one. With the required asking rate at a modest level, Kaif and Dravid had time to play themselves in and build an innings. Fleming flicked his bowling resources around, but the Indian batsmen were in for the long haul. Kaif, playing his first innings of substance in the tournament, took 98 balls to reach his half-century. Dravid reached his fifty as well, albeit at a slightly faster rate. The partnership continued to an unbroken 129 when victory was achieved with 56 balls left. Although Kaif finished with a game-high 68 not out, the Man of the Match adjudicators gave Zaheer Khan the nod for his four wickets.

NEW ZEALAND		INDIA	
C. D. McMillan c Harbhajan Singh b Khan	0	V. Sehwag c Styris b Bond	1
S. P. Fleming (capt) c Tendulkar b Srinath	30	S. R. Tendulkar c Oram b Tuffey	15
N. J. Astle lbw b Khan	0	S. C. Ganguly (capt) b Bond	3
S. B. Styris c Dravid b Nehra	15	M. Kaif not out	68
B. B. McCullum (wk) b Khan	4	R. Dravid (wk) not out	53
C. L. Cairns c Khan b Harbhajan Singh	20	(40.4 overs)	3-150
C. Z. Harris lbw b Khan	17	Did not bat: Yuvraj Singh, D. Mongia, Harbhajan Singh, Z.	
J. D. P. Oram b Sehwag	23	Khan, J. Srinath, A. Nehra	
D. L. Vettori c Ganguly b Harbhajan Singh	13	1/4 2/9 3/21	
D. R. Tuffey c & b Mongia	11	Bowling: Tuffey 10-1-41-1; Bond 8-2-23-2; Oram 5-0-20-0;	
S. E. Bond not out	0	Vettori 5-0-18-0; McMillan 2-1-4-0; Styris 6.4-0-29-0;	
Extras (lb 5, w 4, nb 4)	13	Harris 4-1-15-0	
(45.1 overs)	10-146		

1/0 2/0 3/38 4/47 5/60 6/88 7/96 8/129 9/144 10/146

Bowling: Khan 8-0-42-4; Srinath 8-0-20-1; Nehra
10-2-24-1; Harbhajan Singh 10-2-28-2; Ganguly 2-0-4-0;
Tendulkar 5-0-20-0; Sehwag 2-1-3-1; Mongia 0.1-0-0-1

Umpires: D.J. Harper, P. Willey.

Toss: India   Points: India 4, New Zealand 0.

SATURDAY 15 MARCH 2003
SUPER SIX No. 8: SRI LANKA vs ZIMBABWE
EAST LONDON, SOUTH AFRICA: SRI LANKA WON BY 74 RUNS

After two heavy defeats, Sri Lanka bounced back against Zimbabwe and booked a semi-final clash against the all-conquering Australians.

Atapattu's composed century, which featured only seven boundaries, was the cornerstone of Sri Lanka's score of 5-256. Atapattu accumulated his runs steadily and he received good support from his top order colleagues. His steady partnership of 83 with Avishka Gunawardene in 20 overs set the platform for an assault on the bowling in the later overs. An aggressive cameo by Sangakkara of 35 from 25 deliveries helped Sri Lanka to smash 73 runs from the final eight overs. Playing the anchor role superbly, it wasn't until the last over that Atapattu reached three figures with a single from Hondo.

Zimbabwe took the game right up to the Sri Lankans. With Andy Flower leading the way, Zimbabwe reached 3-140 in the 29th over and were on track to score the 257 required to win. Flower, who had played the spinners with aplomb, was adjudged lbw to de Silva on 38. Replays indicated he had managed to get an inside edge. Following this dismissal, Zimbabwe lost their way, losing seven wickets for 42 runs. Vaas and Jayasuriya mopped up the last four wickets for four runs. When Hondo was bowled by Vaas in the 42nd over to end the match, Vaas had taken his 20th wicket in the competition. Vaas drew level with Geoff Allott and Shane Warne, both of whom picked up 20 victims in the 1999 competition.

In the end, the margin of 74 runs flattered Sri Lanka, who would need to improve further to challenge the Australians. Atappatu was the Man of the Match.

SRI LANKA		ZIMBABWE	
M. S. Atapattu not out	103	C. B. Wishart b Jayasuriya	43
S. T. Jayasuria (capt) c Taibu b Streak	22	D. A. Marillier c Jayasuriya b Gunaratne	19
D. A. Gunawardene c & b Marillier	41	T. J. Friend b Gunaratne	21
P. A. de Silva c Taibu b Ervine	25	A. Flower lbw b de Silva	38
K. C. Sangakkara (wk) c G. W. Flower b Streak	35	G. W. Flower c & b Jayasuriya	31
R. P. Arnold c G. W. Flower b Hondo	1	T. Taibu (wk) b Muralitharan	2
W. P. U. J.C. Vaas not out	11	A. M. Blignaut c de Silva b Fernando	1
Extras (lb 3, w 15)	18	S. M. Ervine b Vaas	12
(50 overs)	5-256	H. H. Streak (capt) c Atapattu b Jayasuriya	2
Did not bat: H. P. Tillekeratne, M. Muralitharan, C. R.D.		S. Matsikenyeri not out	1
Fernando, P. W. Gunaratne		D. T. Hondo b Vaas	0
1/41 2/124 3/175 4/227 5/233		Extras (lb 5, w 4, nb 3)	12
Bowling: Streak 10-0-40-2; Blignaut 8-0-40-0;		(41.5 overs)	10-182
Friend 2-0-13-0; Hondo 5-0-36-1; G. W. Flower 10-0-44-0;		1/36 2/68 3/111 4/140 5/150 6/151 7/178 8/181 9/181	
Marillier 10-0-43-1; Matsikenyeri 2-0-13-0; Ervine 3-0-24-1		10/182	
		Bowling: Vaas 9.5-0-46-2; Gunaratne 7-0-33-2; de	
		Silva 9-1-36-1; Muralitharan 7-0-22-1; Jayasuriya 6-0-30-3;	
		Fernando 3-0-10-1	

Umpires: B.G. Jerling, R.E. Koertzen.

Toss: Sri Lanka   Points: Sri Lanka 4, Zimbabwe 0.

SUPER SIX No. 9: AUSTRALIA vs KENYA
DURBAN, SOUTH AFRICA (DAY/NIGHT): AUSTRALIA WON B 5 WICKETS

With the top four positions of the Super Six stage locked in, little hinged on this final match of the Super Six stage. After an abysmal start, Kenya showed admirable determination to persevere for a respectable total and to give the Australians a scare in their run chase.

After Ponting sent Kenya in, Lee soon had the Kenyan batsmen in all sorts of trouble. In his second over, Lee struck Kennedy Otieno on the point of his elbow and the ball deflected onto the stumps. In great pain, Otieno had to be taken to hospital for an X-ray. Luckily, there was no bone fracture and his World Cup would continue. From the next ball, Brijal Patel edged a full-length delivery to the Australian captain at second slip. David Obuya faced the hat-trick ball and his stumps were disturbed by a superb, fast yorker. Lee became the fourth bowler – and the first Australian – to take a hat-trick in World Cup matches.

The Kenyan innings was in disarray at 3-3. Captain Steve Tikolo joined Shah and the pair were able to stem the tide. They batted sensibly for a stand of 79 runs in 22 overs. Shah missed out on a well-deserved half-century when he top edged a sweep from Hogg to backward square leg. After playing himself in, Tikolo began to play some shots and he brought up his fifty in the 39th over. He was out a short time later, skying a ball from Lehmann to long off. Hitesh Modi, who did not look comfortable against the quicker deliveries, constructed an unfinished stand of 30 with Martin Suji to lift the total to a moderate 8-174. To reach 174 and bat out the full 50 overs seemed implausible about three hours earlier when Lee took his hat-trick.

Gilchrist and Hayden batted as if they had a prior engagement, walloping the tame Kenyan bowlers for 50 runs by the sixth over. Hayden was the first to go when he was caught at mid wicket after attempting to pull a delivery from Ongondo that was a fraction too full. In the next over, Gilchrist received a let-off when Martin Suji put down an easy chance at mid wicket from his brother's bowling. Gilchrist continued to flay the bowling and he reached his 50 in 37 balls. Immediately after reaching this milestone, Gilchrist twice swept Collins Obuya into the crowd, one blow sailing over a grandstand and out of the ground. Spearheaded by Gilchrist's brilliance, Australia zoomed to a frenetic 1-98 in the 12th over.

Gilchrist's assault was over when he edged one to stand-in keeper David Obuya. Australia were in a very strong position at 2-98 and the required run rate was only two per over. Evergreen left-arm orthodox bowler Aasif Karim caused a flutter in the

Australian dressing room. He trapped Ponting in front and, in his next over, he had Lehmann caught behind and he snaffled a return catch from Hogg. Australia were suddenly 5-118 in the 18th over and victory no longer seemed a formality.

Due to Martyn injuring his finger whilst fielding, Ponting was forced to reshuffle his batting order. Harvey came in at number seven to join Symonds, who had been recalled to the side after a two game absence. The pair found scoring against Karim very difficult, so they focused on scoring at the other end. Treating the good balls with respect and having a dash at anything loose, the two all-rounders put on a partnership of 61 in 13 overs to get Australia across the line.

Karim finished with the incredible analysis of 8-6-2-3, including a sequence of 29 deliveries where Symonds and Harvey failed to score off him. Despite his team's loss, Karim won the man of the match award.

KENYA		AUSTRALIA	
K. D. Otieno (wk) b Lee	1	A. C. Gilchrist (wk) c D. Obuya b Ongondo	67
R. D. Shah c sub (Hauritz) b Hogg	46	M. L. Hayden c sub (Angara) b Ongondo	20
B. J. Patel c Ponting b Lee	0	R. T. Ponting (capt) lbw b Karim	18
D. O. Obuya b Lee	0	A. Symonds not out	33
S. O. Tikolo (capt) c Bichel b Lehmann	51	D. S. Lehmann c D. Obuya b Karim	2
H. S. Modi not out	39	G. B. Hogg c & b Karim	0
C. O. Obuya c Gilchrist b Bichel	3	I. J. Harvey not out	28
P. J.C. Ongondo c Gilchrist b Bichel	1	Extras (b 4, lb 1, w 4, nb 1)	10
T. O. Suji c Ponting b Lehmann	1	(31.2 overs)	5-178
M. A. Suji not out	15	Did not bat: D. R. Martyn, A. J. Bichel, B. Lee, G. D. McGrath	
Extras (lb 10, w 6, nb 1)	17	1/50 2/98 3/109 4/117 5/117	
(50 overs)	8-174	Bowling: M. Suji 3-0-36-0; Ongondo 10-0-44-2; T.	
Did not bat: A. Y. Karim		Suji 2-0-24-0; C. Obuya 8-0-62-0; Karim 8.2-6-7-3	
1/3 2/3 3/3 4/82 5/131 6/139 7/141 8/144			
Bowling: McGrath 10-1-32-0; Lee 8-3-14-3; Bichel 9-1-42-2;			
Hogg 10-1-31-1; Harvey 7-0-23-0; Lehmann 6-0-22-2			

Umpires: B.F. Bowden, S.A. Bucknor.

Toss: Australia   Points: Australia 4, Kenya 0.

At the conclusion of the Super Six stage, the table was as set out below. The top four teams progressed to the semi-finals.

	P	PO	NTS	NR	R
Australia	5	5	0	24	1.85
India	5	4	1	20	0.88
Kenya	5	3	2	14	0.35
Sri Lanka	5	2	3	11.5	-0.84
New Zealand	5	1	4	8	-0.89
Zimbabwe	5	0	5	3.5	-1.25

TUESDAY 18 MARCH 2003
SEMI-FINAL: AUSTRALIA vs SRI LANKA
ST GEORGE'S PARK, PORT ELIZABETH, SOUTH AFRICA: AUSTRALIA WON BY 48 RUNS (DUCKWORTH/LEWIS METHOD)

Australia were back at St George's Park for their semi-final and hoping to avoid the alarms experienced in their two previous encounters there. They accounted for Sri Lanka for the second time in a fortnight to book their third consecutive World Cup final and their fifth final overall.

Australia were off to their customary flyer, with Gilchrist dishing out some rough treatment to Gunaratne. Jayasuriya removed him from the attack after just two overs and de Silva was brought on to bowl the sixth over. From de Silva's second delivery, Gilchrist swept a full length ball onto his pad, which ballooned behind the wicket into Sangakkara's gloves. After Rudi Koertzen declined to administer his slow finger of death, Gilchrist performed the rare act of walking. In the next over from Vaas, Ponting lifted a drive to his opposite number at a short mid-off. Vaas and de Silva bowled with discipline on a slow pitch and they were again rewarded in the 13th over. Hayden played a drive off Vaas a little early, flicking the ball to a short mid wicket. Australia were under early strain at 3-51. Symonds joined Lehmann and the pair settled Australian nerves with steady batting. The Sri Lankan spin quartet were kept at bay and the run rate hovered around four an over. Sri Lanka missed the opportunity to make the Aussies sweat when Sangakkara fumbled a stumping chance when Symonds was on 33.

In the 35th over, Australia had recovered to reach a sound position of 3-144. Jayasuriya found the rough outside Lehmann's off stump and the South Australian chopped it on. The Lehmann-Symonds partnership contributed a vital 93 runs to the cause. Jayasuriya's next ball seemed to narrowly miss the outside edge of Bevan's forward defensive. Umpire Shepherd thought otherwise. With Australia under pressure at 5-144, Shepherd's decision brought into question the merits of Gilchrist's magnanimous gesture.

A few overs later, Sangakkara executed a fine stumping from de Silva to send Hogg back to the pavilion. Symonds played a superb shot from de Silva, lifting him over wide mid-on and out of the ground. Harvey became Vaas' third victim, leaving Australia 7-175 with six overs left. Bichel came to the party again, hammering Gunaratne over deep mid wicket for six in the 48th over. A valiant diving effort by Atapattu at the boundary just failed to reel the catch in. A handy 37 runs were taken to end the innings at 7-212. The final tally owed much to Symonds' well-controlled innings of 91 not out from 118 balls. Vaas picked up another three wickets and Murali, though bowling well, was kept wicketless.

The in-form Atapattu looked ominous, striking three boundaries in the first four overs. Lee was bowling with great speed and he had Atapattu driving uppishly to cover, only for Hogg to spill a straight-forward chance. Lee bounced back in style the next ball. An excellent 160 km/h yorker sped through Atapattu's defences and wrecked his stumps. Jayasuriya, still struggling with his thumb injury, played an wishy-washy pull shot from McGrath straight to square leg. Like Australia, Sri Lanka were 2-37 in the early going.

Lee exposed Sri Lanka's middle order when he dismissed Tillekeratne and Gunawardene cheaply, caught behind and in the gully, respectively. The scoreline of 4-43 soon deteriorated to 5-51 when veteran de Silva was brilliantly run out by Bichel. The ebullient Queenslander bowled his first ball to Sangakkara, who pushed it to space at short mid wicket for a quick single. Bichel raced to the ball, picking it up with his left hand and throwing down the stumps from 15 metres with his right a split-second later. Seven years and a day after scoring a superb hundred in the 1996 final, de Silva left the field of an international cricket match for the last time.

Jayawardene continued his horror run when he was caught behind from Hogg after a deflection from the pad. Sangakkara and Arnold were tied down by tight bowling from Hogg and Bichel, including four consecutive maidens from Bichel. After struggling to three runs from 26 deliveries, frustration set in and Arnold slogged one from Hogg to deep square-leg. With black clouds rolling in from the west, Sri Lanka were in dire straits at 7-76 in the 25th over. Sangakkara was joined by the capable Vaas with little batting to follow. Australia were well in front on the Duckworth-Lewis calculations and a berth in the final was there for the taking. Sangakkara and Vaas batted steadily but they were unable to force the pace. As the partnership approached 50, only two fours and a six had been hit by the two batsmen. A few raindrops after 38 overs quickly became a downpour and the players and umpires raced from the field.

According to the Duckworth-Lewis charts, Australia were 48 runs to the good when the players scurried to the safety of the dressing room. The game was in limbo for the next hour as the umpires monitored the situation. The rain refused to yield and the game was declared over. Australia were through to the final in vastly different circumstances to the 1999 semi-final, a replay of which was shown on TV in the Australian viewing area during the rain delay. Symonds was adjudged the Man of the Match for his vital innings under pressure.

AUSTRALIA		SRI LANKA	
A. C. Gilchrist (wk) c Sangakkara b de Silva	22	M. S. Atapattu b Lee	14
M. L. Hayden c Tillekeratne b Vaas	20	S. T. Jayasuriya (capt) c Symonds b McGrath	17
R. T. Ponting (capt) c Jayasuriya b Vaas	2	H. P. Tillekeratne c Gilchrist b Lee	3
D. S. Lehmann b Jayasuriya	36	D. A. Gunawardene c Ponting b Lee	1
A. Symonds not out	91	P. A. de Silva run out	11
M. G. Bevan c Sangakkara b Jayasuriya	0	K. C. Sangakkara (wk) not out	39
G. B. Hogg st Sangakkara b de Silva	8	D. P. M. D. Jayawardene c Gilchrist b Hogg	5
I. J. Harvey c Sangakkara b Vaas	7	R. P. Arnold c Lee b Hogg	3
A. J. Bichel not out	19	W. P. U. J.C. Vaas not out	21
Extras (lb 3, w 3, nb 1)	7	Extras (b 4, lb 1, w 2, nb 2)	9
(50 overs)	7-212	(38.1 overs)	7-123
Did not bat: B. Lee, G. D. McGrath		Did not bat: M. Muralitharan, P. W. Gunaratne	
1/34 2/37 3/51 4/144 5/144 6/158 7/175		1/21 2/37 3/37 4/43 5/51 6/60 7/76	
Bowling: Vaas 10-1-34-3; Gunaratne 8-0-60-0; de Silva 10-0-36-2; Muralitharan 10-0-29-0; Jayasuriya 10-0-42-2; Arnold 2-0-8-0		Bowling: McGrath 7-1-20-1; Lee 8-0-35-3; Bichel 10-4-18-0; Hogg 10-1-30-2; Harvey 2.1-0-11-0; Lehmann 1-0-4-0	

Umpires: R.E. Koertzen, D.R. Shepherd.
Toss: Australia

THURSDAY 20 MARCH 2003
SEMI-FINAL: INDIA vs KENYA
DURBAN, SOUTH AFRICA (DAY/NIGHT): INDIA WON BY 91 RUNS

The fairytale run of Kenya ended with a sound defeat at the hands of India. To the delight of a billion fans back home, the Indians won their eighth match on end and reached their first World Cup final since 1983.

India reached a good total of 4-270 without dominating the Kenyan bowling. Tendulkar played the percentages, handling the good deliveries carefully and punishing anything short of a length. His innings of 83 from 101 balls was his fourth score between 80 and 99 in the tournament. Tendulkar and Ganguly put on a partnership of 103 in 19 overs, setting the platform for an assault in the latter overs. Ganguly tore into the bowling in the last 12 overs, taking only 38 balls to move from 50 to 100. He brought up three figures in style, hoisting Martin Suji into the long on grandstand. Ganguly's century was his third in this tournament, which equalled Mark Waugh's performance in 1996. Interestingly, all three of Ganguly's centuries were scored against non-Test playing nations Kenya – twice – and Namibia. Ganguly piloted the innings to its conclusion, walking back to the pavilion with an unbeaten 111 from 114 balls, including five sixes.

With clouds in the Durban skies, Ganguly insisted that his fast men get through their overs quickly. Srinath and Khan gave little away in the early overs. Shah, who laboured to one run from 17 balls, was the first to go when Khan trapped him in front. Tikolo's experiment of sending in Peter Ongondo as a pinch-hitter at number three did not come off. Ongondo survived for only five balls. Victory appeared out of Kenya's grasp when Otieno and Odoyo were sent back in the 14th and 15th overs. With their opponents in check at 4-36, Ganguly brought on Harbhajan Singh and Yuvraj Singh in an effort to race through to the critical 25 over mark. India achieved their goal and Yuvraj Singh picked up Odumbe's wicket along the way.

Ganguly reintroduced Khan to the attack in the 26th over and he had Modi caught behind four balls later. The run out of David Obuya in the 34th over effectively ended the contest, as Kenya slumped to 7-104 and the asking rate was nearly 10. Tikolo and Collins Obuya put together the only partnership of substance in the Kenyan innings. The Kenyan captain blasted Yuvraj Singh for 20 runs in an over en-route to his half-century. With the game in the bag, Ganguly had the opportunity of giving his part-timers a decent turn at the bowling crease. In consecutive overs, Tendulkar dismissed Kenya's two top-scorers before Khan finished the innings by bowling Martin Suji.

The tired Kenyan players farewelled the crowd with a lap of honour. Delighted that his side had made it to the final, Ganguly was an easy choice for the man of the match award. His mind would soon be on other things, as his contingent faced the ultimate challenge of toppling the formidable Australian side at the Wanderers three days later.

INDIA		KENYA	
V. Sehwag c Odumbe b Ongondo	33	K. O. Otieno (wk) c Dravid b Srinath	15
S. R. Tendulkar c D. Obuya b Tikolo	83	R. D. Shah lbw b Khan	1
S. C. Ganguly (capt) not out	111	P. J.C. Ongondo c Khan b Nehra	0
M. Kaif run out	15	T. M. Odoyo c Sehwag b Nehra	7
Yuvraj Singh c D. Obuya b b Odoyo	16	S. O. Tikolo (capt) b Tendulkar	56
R. Dravid (wk) not out	1	M. O. Odumbe c Khan b Yuvraj Singh	19
Extras (w 9, nb 2)	11	H. S. Modi c Dravid b Khan	9
(50 overs)	4-270	D. O. Obuya run out	3
Did not bat: D. Mongia, Harbhajan Singh, Z. Khan, J. Srinath,		C. O. Obuya lbw b Tendulkar	29
A. Nehra		M. A. Suji b Khan	1
1/74 2/177 3/233 4/267		A. Y. Karim not out	0
Bowling: Suji 10-1-62-0; Odoyo 10-1-45-1; Ongondo		Extras (b 16, lb 8, w 15)	39
10-1-38-1; Karim 4-0-25-0; Tikolo 10-0-60-1; C.		(46.2 overs)	10-179
Obuya 6-0-40-0		1/20 2/21 3/30 4/36 5/63 6/92 7/104 8/161 9/179	
		10/179	
		Bowling: Khan 9.2-2-14-3; Srinath 7-1-11-1; Nehra 5-1-11-2;	
		Harbhajan Singh 10-1-32-0; Yuvraj Singh 6-0-43-1;	
		Sehwag 3-1-16-0; Tendulkar 6-0-28-2	

Umpires: S.A. Bucknor, D.J. Harper.
Toss: India

SUNDAY 23 MARCH 2003
FINAL: AUSTRALIA vs INDIA
WANDERERS STADIUM, JOHANNESBURG, SOUTH AFRICA: AUSTRALIA WON BY 125 RUNS

The excellence and resilience of Australia's campaign was confirmed in the final with a comprehensive victory over India. Despite putting the one-day careers of the Waugh twins out to pasture a year before and losing Warne and Gillespie in recent weeks, Australia rose to the occasion and, amazingly, went through their 11 World Cup engagements undefeated.

After suffering a mauling from the Australians in their group match, India had regrouped and gradually improving form saw them build a winning streak of eight matches before the final. However, Sourav Ganguly's men lacked experience in the big occasion limited-overs matches and time would tell whether they had the mettle and firepower to conquer Australia.

The Australian selectors decided that Damien Martyn would be able to carry his finger injury into this game. He would resume his customary number four spot in the order. Ian Harvey was the unlucky teammate to give way. In a sign of confidence, the Indians named an unchanged side from the semi-final.

"I felt really good going into the final," recalls Australian left-arm wrist spin bowler Brad Hogg. "Throughout the whole tournament I cannot remember a team that was as close as we were. I just knew from that game against Pakistan that we were going to win the tournament and the rest of the team knew as well. I felt a lot more relaxed in the final than I did in the group matches. You play the group matches to make the final and when you reach the final, there are only two teams left and you want to win it."

There was some moisture in the Wanderers pitch following recent rain and dew. One school of thought was that the moisture would give the wicket some early life. On the flip side, some rain over the veldt was predicted during the afternoon. Under overcast skies, Ganguly called correctly and elected to bowl first. It was an adventurous decision considering the rough treatment that was meted out by the Australian top order to Zaheer Khan and Srinath in the group stage match. Further, India were faced with the prospect of having their run chase interrupted by rain and the uncertainty of meeting a Duckworth-Lewis target under the intense pressure of a final.

Hogg welcomed Ganguly's choice to bowl first. "I thought it was fantastic that we were batting first. In any form of cricket, I love bowling second. I love having runs on the board because I know what I have to do". He said Ponting would have batted first if he had won the toss. "We were always going to bat first. If you get runs on the board in a game like that, it really puts pressure on the opposition team. That's the way we play our cricket. It's harder to chase runs than put runs on the board".

Ganguly's decision implied faith in the abilities of Zaheer Khan and Srinath to bowl well from the outset and to extract an early wicket. Unfortunately, his opening bowlers suffered a severe case of stage fright. Zaheer Khan, bristling with aggressive intent, crumbled under the pressure in the very first over, which consisted of ten deliveries that yielded 15 runs. Khan opened with a no-ball and then had plenty to say to Gilchrist when he played and missed. Another no-ball followed and Gilchrist took a single from the second legal delivery of the over. From the next ball, a terrific straight drive by Hayden left Khan deflated. The rest of his over was a calamity, featuring another no-ball and two wides, one of which beat Dravid for four byes. Khan cut a dejected figure when he was removed from the attack after only three overs which leaked 28 runs.

Playing in his last international match, Srinath started steadily but was soon being manhandled by savage shots from Gilchrist and Hayden. Australia reached 50 without loss from seven overs and Srinath was blasted out of the attack in the next over. Gilchrist walloped India's senior seamer, who opted to bowl around the wicket, for two fours and a six over mid wicket in the eighth over. Srinath was banished to the outfield with the unflattering figures of 0-33 from four overs.

With his opening bowlers battered, Ganguly was forced to turn to left-armer Nehra and Harbhajan Singh inside the first 10 overs. Australia's progress was slowed marginally by the bowling changes. In the 13th over, Gilchrist reached his half-century from only 40 deliveries. It was the second World Cup final in succession that Gilchrist had kick-started the innings with a quick-fire 50. In the next over, Australia's left-handed openers ticked off another milestone: their century partnership from a mere 92 deliveries.

Two balls after the opening stand reached 100, Gilchrist top-edged a slog-sweep off Harbhajan Singh and Sehwag held on to the catch in the deep. Gilchrist's innings of 57 helped his team set an excellent platform of 1-105 off 14 overs. Hayden followed his partner to the pavilion a short time later for 37 from 54 deliveries. Harbhajan Singh claimed his second wicket when Hayden got a faint edge to a ball that spun sharply. The fall of wickets had slowed Australia's progress a fraction, although they were very well placed at 2-125 in the 20th over.

Martyn began confidently, clobbering Srinath to the rope with a back-foot slash. Ponting played himself in and Martyn quickly wrested the initiative. Despite the pain in his injured right hand, Martyn handled the Indian bowling with aplomb. His half-century was brought up in only 46 balls. With Ponting playing an unfamiliar supporting role, the century stand was reached in 18 overs. After reaching his fifty, Ponting savaged his old sparring partner Harbhajan Singh, hitting him for two consecutive sixes over mid wicket.

After his steady beginning, Ponting took the Indian bowlers to the cleaners. His first half-century was scored at a steady rate, from 74 deliveries. In sharp contrast, his second fifty was pummelled from a mere 29 balls, including five sixes. In a breathtaking exhibition of batting, featuring Ponting's trademark pull shot, the Australian captain plundered his last 90 runs from only 47 balls, including eight sixes.

Australia were soon on course to be the first team to reach 300 in a World Cup final. This objective soon became conservative as Ponting attacked the flagging bowlers. In an effort to disrupt the Australian's rhythm, Ganguly gave overs to his part-timers Sehwag, Tendulkar, Mongia and Yuvraj Singh. These bowlers simply joined the ranks of the punished. The 200-run stand was reached in the 48th over. Since his early period of reconnaissance, Ponting took a large share of the strike and the runs flowed rapidly. He blasted the last two balls of the innings from Srinath for four and six over long on into the second tier of the grandstand. These two blows saw Australia through to the mammoth score of 2-359 from 50 overs, an Australian record score in a limited-overs match. A colossal 109 runs were scored from the last 10 overs.

Ponting's boundary from the last ball of the innings took him past Viv Richards' record of 138 not out in a World Cup final. At the other end, Martyn finished on 88 not out. Another record to fall was that the 234-run stand between Ponting and Martyn was a record for Australia in limited-overs internationals. Amazingly, Ponting's 140 not out from 121 balls featured only four fours and no less than eight sixes.

After his initial fire and brimstone, Khan finished with the unflattering figures of 0-67 from seven overs. Srinath was crunched from 0-87 from 10 overs, the most expensive analysis in a World Cup final. It was not the swansong the veteran seamer had contemplated.

Hogg watched little of the Australian innings. "I'm superstitious and I didn't watch the Ponting-Martyn partnership," he recalls. "The only time I watched the batting was when Hayden and Gilchrist got out. They were the only two balls I watched in our innings. At the start of the innings, Brett Lee and I went out the back to have a bit of a hit, as we always did. After Haydos went out, I sat and listened to some music because I didn't want to put the mocker on the boys. It's just amazing how superstition creeps in."

If any of Australia's opponents could score the 360 needed for victory, it was India. Their array of dangerous batsmen had the firepower to reach an imposing total. No-one needed to say that the key wicket was that of Tendulkar. The master batsman already had an imposing 669 runs to his credit in the tournament.

Defending a huge total did not alter Hogg's approach to bowling. "If I'm providing pressure from one end and my teammate at the other end is applying the same pressure, the wickets will come. When you go and chase wickets, that's when things can get out of hand." He had carefully considered his approach to bowling to the Indian batsmen. "The Indians are the best players of spin, so you have got to concentrate on your length. At that stage I had a pretty good flipper and I was using the wrong-un as a defensive weapon as well as an attacking weapon. If we needed to slow the runs down, I could bowl a flipper as a yorker. I was able to mix it up like that. With the left-handers, I would attack them with a wrong-un straight away, trying to get them to back away and work one through point. While they are trying to work the ball through point, they might not see the ball which spins, comes back and raps them on the pads or bowls them. Or I would attack them with the flipper. With Ganguly and Yuvraj Singh, I've had a bit of success against them with both the wrong-un and the flipper".

Tendulkar made his intentions known from the fourth ball of the innings by McGrath. A delivery that was just short of a length was dispatched over mid wicket for a boundary. Tendulkar repeated the shot from the next delivery. However, the ball offered him less width and straightened up. The result was a top-edge skier that was held by a delighted McGrath. "When Pigeon got Tendulkar out, that was a pivotal moment", Hogg said. "It was a short ball on leg stump at his body. Tendulkar's dismissal put a few shivers through the Indian batting line-up".

The Indians hit back after the loss of Tendulkar. Although he was dropped from a Lee no-ball, Sehwag led the charge. He and Ganguly played positively, including hammering 19 runs, featuring two sixes, from the fifth over bowled by McGrath. The fifty partnership was achieved from only 52 balls. However, a target of 360 left little room for error.

Ganguly attempted to pull Lee and only succeeded in popping it up to mid-on. Kaif's poor World Cup ended when he nicked one from McGrath for a four ball duck. India were struggling at 3-59 in the 11th over. With dark clouds approaching the Wanderers, India needed to produce something exceptional if they were to have any chance to win this final. Ponting brought his spinners on to hasten the bowling of the 25 overs required to ensure that the contest would not be washed out. "The clouds came over and Ponting asked me to bowl in the first 15 overs, which I had never done before," Hogg remarks.

Sehwag fancied himself against Lehmann and Hogg. The Indian dasher whacked the spinners for three fours and a six. The score had improved to 3-107 in the 17th over when the rain began to fall. Fortunately for Australia, the rain was a passing shower. Only 25 minutes of play were lost and the action resumed at 4 pm with no over reduction. In order to keep the Indians in check, Bichel and McGrath were re-introduced to the attack.

The contrasting styles of the aggressive Sehwag and the patient Dravid combined well. Their 50 stand was achieved in 48 balls. India were scoring better at a run a ball. Their score of 3-122 after 20 overs was only four runs less than what Australia scored at the same stage. Australia were in need of a breakthrough and the opportunity was missed when Hogg, fielding at backward point, dropped a difficult chance from Sehwag on 72. It looked as if Sehwag would make the Australians pay when he hit Hogg for six and followed up with a boundary.

Hogg rated Sehwag as a major threat in the final. "Virender Sehwag was probably the bowler I hated bowling to most. He's got my measure. When he's on song, he can demolish any attack. When he's on the attack, you just think on your feet and try things. You either go wider to him or you try and tighten up on his legs. Tightening on his legs is tricky because if the ball turns a lot, you bring the wide into play. I probably tried to bowl a bit shorter, a foot shorter than I bowled to anyone else".

In the end, it took a run out to extinguish the threat of Sehwag. In attempting a quick single, Sehwag took on Lehmann at short mid-off and lost to a direct hit from the South Australian. India were under pressure at 4-147 in the 24th over. According to Hogg, Sehwag's dismissal was a crucial moment in the final. "You could sense India were a little bit nervous in the run chase, especially when Sehwag was run out by Lehmann. That run out just turned the whole game around."

Dravid and Yuvraj Singh kept the score moving along without getting on top of the Australian bowlers. Martyn, hampered by his finger injury, put a regulation high ball from Yuvraj Singh down. A storm to the east of the Wanderers renewed the prospect that the game would be decided by the Duckworth-Lewis method. In the 31st over, India were 4-178 and only 20 runs behind under the Duckworth-Lewis formula.

India fell further from the pace in the 32nd over when Dravid played on to Bichel for a steady 47. The task of the Indians became almost insurmountable when Yuvraj Singh attempted a big shot off Hogg and was caught at deep mid wicket by Lee charging in from the rope. In a sign that the cards were falling Australia's way, Lee had replaced the inconvenienced Martyn in this position a short time earlier. Hogg recalled Yuvraj Singh's dismissal. "He had a go for it. He tried to play across the line and I got him out. I remember charging over to Binga and giving him a big cuddle. He was the love of my life at that moment!"

In the next over, Martyn atoned for his drop by hanging on to a catch while back-pedalling to send Mongia back. India were 7-209 and the match was effectively over. Symonds then collected his second wicket when he had the abrasive Harbhajan Singh caught at mid-off. Lee cleaned up Srinath's stumps in the next over. Nehra hit two fours before his left-arm colleague Khan skied one from McGrath. With thunderclaps in the background, Lehmann took the catch to end the Indian innings at 234 in the 40th over. It was the second time that Lehmann performed the last act to deliver World Cup triumph to Australia. Australia's winning margin of 125 runs was a World Cup record, eclipsing the 92-run differential in the 1979 final.

"I remember India were nine down and I was fielding at gully", Hogg recounted. "I looked over to Punter at slip at Gilly behind the wicket and said 'I can't believe how good this is. This is the best moment of my life'. I just wanted that ball to last. You don't get moments like that too often."

Hogg took 1-61 from his 10 overs in the final. "I would have liked to have gone for a few runs less. But we had a big score on the board and going for six an over against India on the Jo'burg wicket where the ball does travel a little bit further when it comes off the bat, I was pretty happy with it. I was just rapt that I had the opportunity to have the spinning duties throughout the tournament. It just gave me a great lift knowing I wasn't playing second fiddle. I was always waiting for that opportunity."

Australia had become the first team since the West Indies in 1975 and 1979 to successfully defend their title. Australia joined the West Indies team of 1975 as being the only team to win a World Cup after winning every match. Ponting played the classical captain's knock and he was rewarded with the Man of the Match award.

"I remember when we were going up to get the trophy, the rain had gone away and the clouds had come over," Hogg recalls. "There was lightning in the background and you could just tell that it was going to pelt down at any moment. The people on the stage who were speaking had no idea what was happening behind them. I just wanted to run up there and get the trophy and to get out before it rains."

The Australians were jubilant and keen to celebrate. "When we got the trophy, we were probably a little bit forceful in pushing others off the stage," Hogg admitted. "Just in the enjoyment factor that you knew you had achieved something great. We had won every game in the tournament and we won the final against a formidable team in India. We just wanted to celebrate hard and fast that night."

The 2003 World Cup triumph was a landmark of Hogg's career. "The 2003 World Cup was definitely the pinnacle of my career. In terms of the defining moment of my career, the 2003 World Cup is the best by an absolute country mile. This was because of the simple fact that Shane Warne wasn't available for the tournament, the spinning duties were left up to me and I had an opportunity to make sure that I would give it the best that I possibly could."

Australia took home the ultimate prize in cricket and prize money of US$2 million. But there was no rest for the all-conquering Aussies. They had a break of only a week before travelling to the West Indies for a Test and limited-overs series. For India, the heavy defeat in the final caused great distress and soul-searching back home.

AUSTRALIA		INDIA	
A. C. Gilchrist (wk) c Sehwag b Harbhajan Singh	57	S. R. Tendulkar c & b McGrath	4
M. L. Hayden c Dravid b Harbhajan Singh	37	V. Sehwag run out	82
R. T. Ponting (capt) not out	140	S. C. Ganguly (capt) c Lehmann b Lee	24
D. R. Martyn not out	88	M. Kaif c Gilchrist b McGrath	0
Extras (b 2, lb 12, w 16, nb 7)	37	R. Dravid (wk) b Bichel	47
(50 overs)	2-359	Yuvraj Singh c Lee b Hogg	24
Did not bat: D. S. Lehmann, A. Symonds, M. G. Bevan, G. B.		D. Mongia c Martyn b Symonds	12
Hogg, A. J. Bichel, B. Lee, G. D. McGrath		Harbhajan Singh c McGrath b Symonds	7
1/105 2/125		Zaheer Khan c Lehmann b McGrath	4
Bowling: Khan 7-0-67-0; Srinath 10-0-87-0; Nehra		J. Srinath b Lee	1
10-0-57-0; Harbhajan Singh 8-0-49-2; Sehwag 3-0-14-0;		A. Nehra not out	8
Tendulkar 3-0-20-0; Mongia 7-0-39-0; Yuvraj Singh 2-0-12-0		Extras (b 4, lb 4, w 9, nb 4)	21
		(39.2 overs)	10-234
		1/4 2/58 3/59 4/147 5/187 6/208 7/209 8/223 9/226	
		10/234	
		Bowling: McGrath 8.2-0-52-3; Lee 7-1-31-2; Hogg	
		10-0-61-1; Lehmann 2-0-18-0; Bichel 10-0-57-1;	
		Symonds 2-0-7-2	

Umpires: S.A. Bucknor, D.R. Shepherd.
Toss: India

POST-MORTEM

The 2003 competition was a major financial success, bringing in a record profit of US$194 million. This was an improvement on the moderate return of US$51 million for the 1999 tournament. The tournament had a few key drawbacks. To many observers, the major failing of the competition was that there were too many matches spread over too long a period. The ICC's decision to allow an additional two associate teams to participate swelled the number of matches from 42 in 1999 to 54 in 2003. These fixtures were spread over 42 days, five more than in 1999, in an attempt to maximise television exposure and the accompanying revenues. The negative influence of politics was felt with the forfeiture of two games in Zimbabwe. Further, the failure of the South Africans to progress beyond their group put a slight dampener on the local interest in the tournament.

The excellence of the undefeated Australian team produced many memorable performances and was a highlight of the tournament. However, the Aussie juggernaut dulled the tension, as in most games it seemed highly likely that they would prevail. After capturing the World Cup, Ricky Ponting's men toured the West Indies where they extended their winning streak in limited-overs internationals to a superlative 21. In contrast, some of the Indian cricket enthusiasts reacted adversely to the thrashing suffered in the final. Despite the destruction of player effigies and photographs, Ganguly held on to his position as captain and India fought out a drawn Test series away with Australia in 2003-04.

CHAPTER 10

World Cup 2007: Confusion in the West Indies

After South Africa had its turn in 2003 it seemed on any logical rotation basis that the ninth World Cup should be played in the West Indies. Everyone knew when Ricky Ponting held the trophy aloft at Johannesburg that in four years the players would be heading for the scattered archipelago between North and South America. There were plenty of sponsors such as LG, Visa and Cable and Wireless involved in the tournament, but the World Cup was not named after a company or product. It was put on by the International Cricket Council and so it was named the ICC World Cup.

There was genuine anticipation among cricket followers that the vibrancy of the Caribbean cricketing culture would transmit itself well to the world audience. The official slogan of the tournament was, "Come for the cricket. Stay for the party."

The World Cup theme song emphasised the theme. *The Game of Love and Unity* by Shaggy was a calypso-based tune full of electronics and rhythm. It suited the era and target audience. For a day it would enhance the experience of a casual spectator. For those destined to hear it time after time day after day the experience might become a little less positive. The calypso mood was expected to attract television viewers and plenty of fans to the West Indian islands themselves. It was also seen as timely boost for West Indian cricket as their international standing as a team and integral member of the world cricketing fraternity had been in decline for some time, certainly on field since 1995. But such was the suspicion that the various small Caribbean cricketing islands and their administrators were divided and dysfunctional that there were serious doubts about whether the logistical demands of transporting teams, providing accommodation and practice facilities as they hopped from island to island would be satisfactorily met. Also, the ICC had insisted that the traditional West Indian grounds be rebuilt and in some cases relocated in order to cope with the size and importance of the World Cup.

So the West Indian Cricket Board, in no position to argue, was compliant. It was a huge and expensive undertaking. On schedule, though, with assistance from Chinese money and workers, the grounds were built. But the result were venues that although enhanced by increased capacity and more modern facilities, had lost much of their West Indian soul. The intimate little slightly ramshackle grounds that had developed their own identity and atmosphere either became almost unrecognisable or in the cases of Guyana and Antigua were abandoned and new stadiums were built in a new location.

The local organisers clearly feared that this vital 'buzz' could be lost in the newer starker venues, as each ground had been set up with a designated section called 'the party stand.' In Antigua they included a 'beach' area at the new Sir Vivian Richards Stadium. It was the Antiguan ground, though, that most raised eyebrows as it was located a long way from the city centre with very limited infrastructure access.

That the designs were a success is arguable. It is fair to say that since the World Cup, these grounds have rarely been filled. Also the inflated costs of admission, up to US$120 for a round one fixture, were designed to make the maximum amount of money from the cashed up visiting fans. It was easy to see the price of the tickets would be beyond the budgets of many locals. They would still have to make up the bulk of the crowds, and with increased capacity more local supporters needed to come through the gates, not less. If they were missing it would be a struggle to get the all important 'cricket party' atmosphere going.

No alcohol was allowed to be brought into the ground that was one break with Caribbean tradition and conch shells were banned because they were considered a lethal weapon. Perhaps in the Caribbean version of game Cluedo the Conch shell could replace the candlestick as a murder weapon. This continued to be the era of spreading the cricketing gospel and the inclusiveness of minnows in the game's most prestigious tournament. So in addition to the 10 Test-playing countries, Canada, Scotland, Bermuda, Kenya, Holland and Ireland were scheduled to play. That meant the number of participants in the 2007 World Cup had increased from 14 teams in 2003 to 16. The 2007 tournament contained therefore a neat four groups of four of whom eight would progress through to the second round called Super Eights. The top four sides from the Super Eights would progress to the semi finals and then a Final at one of cricket's great spiritual homes, Bridgetown, Barbados on April 28th.

It would be a day, final. That would suit certain television audiences better, so there was no need to build any light towers which was a huge saving.

The 2007 World Cup would contain 51 matches. That was down on the 54 from 2003, bit still more than a 300 per cent increase on 1975 and 1979. So that there would be a match available for telecast virtually every day those 51 games were spread over 47 days. The teams had arrived even earlier, right at the start of March as there were 17 warm-up matches spread over 11 days also to get through as a lead up to the opening ceremony before the first official match between the West Indies and Pakistan in Jamaica on March 13th.

If you were going to be stranded anywhere, the Caribbean would be the preference of many, but the structure of the fixtures meant that some teams had a week off between games. It was hardly an efficient use of their professional time.

The cricket world was now dividing itself up neatly in four-year intervals from World Cup to World Cup. Countries consciously developed their teams so that they would peak after the four-year lead up. Players, captains and coaches also saw it as a point under which to draw a line. So prior, during and just after the tournament a number of retirement and standing down announcements were made. The 2007 World Cup was an extremely popular stage for cricketing curtain calls.

Ricky Ponting brought over a powerful Australian team that would be striving for a record breaking third World Cup win in a row and their fourth in total. Despite their preeminence over the previous 12 years Australia had not had things all their own way in their most recent LOI outings. After smashing England 5-0 in the recently completed Ashes series they had then gone down to them in the follow-up one-day Commonwealth Bank series. Three losses in the follow up Chappell-Hadlee Trophy in New Zealand meant six losses in the past seven starts immediately prior to the World Cup. In addition Brett Lee was out with an ankle injury and Shane Warne had retired, although he had also missed the 2003 tournament, of course, and that did not seem to have too detrimental an effect. Australian coach, John Buchanan, perhaps satisfied that he had outlasted his strident critic, Warne, announced he would finish after the Caribbean tournament, while Glenn McGrath was another using this massive event as his farewell to international cricket. McGrath predicted that despite his country's recent poor white-ball form that Australia had come to dominate the World Cup once more.

Many thought the tournament was open, but Ian Chappell in typical forthright manner, wrote that Australia were the 'raging favourites'. With McGrath still in the side their chances of fulfilling yet another of the star fast bowler's jocularly arrogant predictions was quite a possibility. Another to eventually announce his goodbyes was the host's number one man, Brian Lara. Originally he said he wanted to lead the side in the follow-up Test series in England but later changed his mind and decided to finish after the World Cup. He would captain the West Indies and had shown it was within his power to dominate bowlers in the batting conditions in the Caribbean. This was one of several stints he had had as captain and at times in his own country and team he had been unpopular. But he remained a champion and there was optimism that the likes of blitzkrieg opener Chris Gayle and a new bunch of young fast bowlers including Jerome Taylor and Daren Powell, could re-establish the West Indies as a cricketing force and snare the big trophy on their home soil. To do so, though, they would have to become the first team ever to win the World Cup at home. A win would be a perfect send off for the 37 year-old champion left-hander from Trinidad who at that time topped the Test run aggregate list and had passed 10,000 Limited Over International runs, as well. If the West Indies had a successful World Cup on the field a lot of the stresses of running the tournament successfully would melt away.

Along with Ponting, the major challenger to Lara's title as 'best batsman on the world', Sachin Tendulkar arrived for the World Cup in perhaps the worst batting form of his life. Some critics suggested, like Lara, he should be announcing his retirement plans. In addition the Indian camp was split with Australian Coach, Greg Chappell being unpopular with certain members of the team. Former captain, Sourav Ganguly was singled out as one player definitely not on the same wavelength as the former Aussie batting great.

From a financial, television viewing and attendance point if view the progress of the Indian side to at least the semi-final stage was seen as crucial. The Barbados Government had booked a cruise liner to bring over 5,000 Indian and Pakistani expatriates down from the US for the anticipated Super Eight clash between the two great rivals in Bridgetown. If they were to get through to that stage, of course. With a line-up containing new captain, Rahul Dravid, VVS Laxman, Virendar Sehwag, newcomers Mohammad Kaif and Yuvraj Singh, as well as Tendulkar and the recalled Ganguly, the 2003 runners-up could easily make a huge impact.

Originally the appointment of Greg Chappell as Indian coach had borne fruit for India. Fresh blood was injected. The captain was changed. Matches were won. Things then went sour.

In Kolkata there was a huge clamour to sack Chappell and reinstate Ganguly. Matches were lost. Effigies of Chappell were made and boxes of matches were purchased. A similar pattern of initial success followed by doubt and defeat also followed the appointment of Bob Woolmer as Pakistan's coach. Those sudden fluctuations in form had been the nature of the Pakistani team since their inception in the early 1950's. The only thing predictable about them was their unpredictability.

Kersi Meher Homji in the March 2007 edition of *Inside Cricket* called them the 'Jekyll and Hyde' of one-day cricket.

There was no way of telling which team would turn up in the Caribbean, but with a line-up that included batsmen as talented as Inzamam-ul-Haq, Mohammad Yousef and Younis Khan and a fast bowler as potentially lethal as Shoaib Akhtar anything good or bad was possible from this side. It was possibly a little unfair to label the Pakistanis 'Jekyll and Hyde' when they were playing in the same tournament as England. The English side had backed up from an historic 5-0 drubbing in the recent Ashes series with a win in the triangular Commonwealth Bank one-day series in Australia. They too had leadership issues. After seven years at the helm, their Zimbabwean coach, Duncan Fletcher, was going to step down. But it was the captaincy that was causing the most consternation.

Within the previous 18 months England had almost reverted to their legendary 1988 'captain of the week' policy. Since Michael Vaughan's euphoric Ashes win his knee had prevented him from regular leadership. Initially Marcus Trescothick had assumed the role. But the Somerset opening batsman had an emotional breakdown, so big all-rounder, Andrew Flintoff filled in and led the side to an admirable Test win in India. But back in England after a tight series against Sri Lanka his knee had temporarily packed up, too. Andrew Strauss was next in line and he captained England to a series victory over Pakistan.

However he returned to the ranks when Flintoff returned fit for the Ashes tour in Australia. When that turned into a disaster it was felt that the workload might have been too much for Flintoff. Vaughan came back but was in and out of the side with injury during the Commonwealth Bank series in Australia, so Flintoff still had to fill in as captain on several occasions. Fletcher had his doubts about Flintoff's on-going suitability; Kevin Pietersen fancied the job and Strauss's batting form slumped. Some publications had Flintoff still as captain of the World Cup squad, but eventually Vaughan took charge in every game. It was enough to turn any sane man to drink. Pietersen and Flintoff on their day could overwhelm anyone with their heavy bludgeoning bats, and Paul Collingwood, soon the captain the T20 side, was also an excellent limited-overs cricketer, but no-one really expected England to go all the way.

If any side had a history of underachievement in the World Cup anything like England's it would have to be South Africa. As good as any side on paper, they had flattered to deceive in each tournament. So close to a place in the final in 1992 and 1999, they had tumbled at the wrong time, while at home in 2003 they had again succumbed to added pressure and the faulty pushing of the wrong buttons on a calculator. The premature exit had cost Shaun Pollock the captaincy and the champion bowling all-rounder now aged 33 would definitely be on his last chance to be part of a World Cup winning side. The new mantra from coach Mickey Arthur was 'brave cricket' and no side containing Herschelle Gibbs, Jacques Kallis, AB De Villiers and Graeme Smith could be discounted. But the draw meant they would have to overcome their old nemesis's, Australia, to reach their first ever World Cup Final. They had defeated them 3-2 at home in 2006 including the famous record breaking run chase of 438 at Johannesburg. Despite that, they were still rated second in world standing's behind Ricky Ponting's line-up.

One side likely to fulfill their potential was New Zealand. They had never reached a final, but had repeatedly utilised their limited resources to the full. Part of their success over an extended period was due to the astute captaincy of Stephen Fleming. Such a crucial part of the Kiwi set-up, he was also coming to the end of his captaincy of the national side. A key to New Zealand's potential progress was the fitness of Shane Bond. The big former policeman was a world-class fast bowler who had temporarily put the wind up the Australian batsmen in their Tasman clash in the Super Sixes in 2003. But he was injury prone and would have to be nursed through the tournament. He would certainly have voted for stretching out the matches over the seven-week period. Ten over bursts with lots of recuperation time suited him beautifully. Similarly Sri Lanka would place a lot of responsibility on one fast bowler.

Lasith Malinga, the fastest bowler ever produced in Sri Lanka, could turn a match around in an over. His unusual round-arm sling, unorthodox but clearly within the games rules, looked a threat to the central umpire's head as much as the batsman's. But it was quick and he could reverse swing a 90mph yorker at will. Like Australia's Shaun Tait, there was no question about his on-field effectiveness, but both their actions took a heavy toll on their bodies and they needed nursing. With the brilliant spin of Muttiah Muralitharan and a batting line-up containing Sanath Jayasuriya, Mahela Jayawardene, Kumar Sangakara and Tillakaratne Dilshan, in batting conditions closer to their World Cup winning year 1996 than 1999, they could not be discounted.

Zimbabwe and Bangladesh completed the Test playing nations list. Neither could be expected to win the tournament, although an upset or two had been achieved in the past and were quite possible, even likely, again. A Super Eights spot was probably as far as either country could expect to progress. But it was also an opportunity to establish an international reputation on the biggest stage available to either team. Zimbabwe had a bigger uphill of the two, as the on-going political turmoil in their country was having a detrimental effect on their cricket team. Many of their experienced players had walked out in 2004 and they had been removed from the Test match fixturing program for a while. It meant Prosper Utseya led a side mostly of unknowns. This latter point was also the case with the minnows, Canada, Bermuda, Kenya The Netherlands, Scotland and Ireland. They, along with Zimbabwe and Bangladesh, were spread evenly across the groups meaning they would have to eliminate one of the big teams to reach the Super Eight stage.

Boosted by outsiders who had learnt their cricket elsewhere but had some type of blood qualification these Associate Membership teams had every chance to just enjoy being in the limelight and could even have a fleeting moment of glory like Australian first-class cricketer, John Davison, had for Canada in 2003. Bermuda, possibly the only cricketers in the World Cup ever to speak with North American accents, could boast Glamorgan stalwart batsman, David Hemp, in their line-up. Ireland had a sprinkling of first-class players and in Eoin Morgan a batsman of genuine international calibre.

Scotland's side also boasted several players with English first-class experience including Gavin Hamilton who had played a Test in South Africa and Dougie Brown who had been selected for nine one-day internationals. A major difference, though, was the Irish had a young up and coming side whereas the Scottish players with first-class experience were past their best.

Canada's veteran with a past was Anderson Cummins who had played for the West Indies in the early 1990's including three games in 1992 World Cup.

Bermuda's player of note was Dwayne Leverock. A left-arm spinner Leverock, weighed in at 136kg. Bermuda only had a population of 60,000 so he may have been one of the biggest men on the whole island as well as being their best spinner.

Would they have a rotation system for sitting next to him on the various flights between the islands or would captain, Irving Romaine call for voluteers at each departure terminal.

Holland, too, contained established and up and coming first-class players like all-rounder Ryan ten Doeschate and batsman Alexei Kervezee. Their origins were Dutch, although both were born in Southern Africa.

Steve Tikolo's Kenyans had no players with such credentials, but they had shown by reaching the semi-finals in 2003 that they were perhaps the strongest of the ICC Associate countries. Their line-up would also standout with up to seven players surnames beginnings with an 'O'.

And so everyone moved to Jamaica for the opening ceremony. Not at Sabina Park in Kingston as most cricketing people would have thought, but miles away at the brand new stadium, Greenfield in Trelawney on the north-west coast near Montego Bay. It was purpose built at a huge cost including grants from the Chinese Government for... well at this stage for four warm-up cricket matches and the opening ceremony. Later the plans are for it to be used for athletics and soccer.

Sir Garfield Sobers was there, as was legendary Jamaican Reggae singer Jimmy Cliff. Sobers was 70 years old, Cliff not much younger. Ricky Ponting estimated the temperature in the stadium was close to 40 degrees Celsius. It is hoped the two venerable Caribbean gentlemen were well cared for.

TUESDAY 13 MARCH 2007
GROUP D: WEST INDIES v PAKISTAN
SABINA PARK, KINGSTON JAMAICA: WEST INDIES WON BY 54 RUNS

As they did in 2003, the West Indies were involved with the match that launched the World Cup. And, also as they did in South Africa, they got their tournament away to a great start with an important win. Four years ago they had caused a huge upset by defeating the hosts by three runs in a classic. This time they started as slight underdogs but eased home against a disappointing Pakistan by 54 runs. In front of a record Sabina Park crowd of 16,575 Pakistani captain Inzamam won the toss and bowled despite the fact his premier fast bowler, Shoaib Akhtar, had been a late withdrawl from the tournament with an injured hamstring. It was reported not all tickets had been sold. The fans had been lining up since early morning, though. They packed the ground and were rewarded with a day of unending blue sky and sunshine and committed and energetic cricket from the home side. After ICC President Percy Sonn had re-presented Clive Lloyd with the original World Cup Trophy from 1975, tall Pakistani paceman, Umar Gul, gave Pakistan an excellent start when his lifting delivery had local danger man, Chris Gayle, hanging his bat out to dry to be caught behind by wicketkeeper Kamran Akmal with the total on seven.

Shivnarine Chanderpaul, promoted to opener, and Ramnaresh Sarwan ensured there was no early collapse although they could not manufacture an innings launching run rate explosion like Gayle may have done. Sarwan did his best. He was dropped first ball by Younis Khan at slip then took boundaries off the fast bowlers with cuts drives and pulls. At 64 Chanderpaul fell in a fashion not dissimilar to Gayle while Sarwan allowed retribution from Younis at slip one short of his fifty. Rao Iftikhar Anjum took both wickets to leave the West Indies on 3/77. Brian Lara and Marlon Samuels then added 91 for the fourth wicket in the biggest partnership of the match. In the 26th over the run rate slipped below three per over. Lara was more sedate than Samuels who lifted three sixes to the short straight boundaries with sweet lofted drives. A double breakthrough by off-spinner Mohammad Hafeez: Lara sweeping and Samuels mistiming a pull to long on, followed immediately by the stumping of Denesh Ramdin left the West Indies on a precarious 6/183 in the 45th over. It was clear on the flat grassless wicket the West Indies required a boost in run rate and momentum. Barbadian all-rounder Dwayne Smith provided it.

Smith had done little to inspire confidence since his stunning Test debut century in South Africa in 2004. But his 15 ball counter attack which included three fours and two slog swept sixes lifted the total to 223 in the blink of an eye. When last man Corey Collymore clouted the final ball of the innings from Ifitkhar for another six over long on there was Caribbean mayhem in the crowd as 57 runs had been scored from the final five overs. The frenzy was contagious. Pakistan began their chase of 242 for victory with an astonishing first over. Second ball opener Imran Nazir slashed Daren Powell over gully for six. The local fast bowler then had immediate revenge when Imran edged a fuller outswinger to Ramdin next ball. The fourth ball of the innings Younis Khan guided a shorter wider delivery over slips for four. Pakistan 1/10 after four balls: at that rate the game would be decided within 16 overs.

The tempo slowed to a degree although an edged hook by Younis and a strangled drive by Mohammad Hafeez to mid-on gave a wicket to Jerome Taylor and another to Powell and left Pakistan on 3/39. Inzamam-ul-Haq and Mohammad Yousuf began a rebuilding operation. It was necessary but tedious. Neither sought singles and at one stage in nine overs only 13 runs were added.

Eventually Inzamam punched Powell for three fours, but it took 111 balls to add 60 in 111 balls. Then Dwayne Smith began the second phase of his best ever day in cricket. Yousuf wafted an edge to Ramdin then Inzamam walked across the crease, played around the ball and was trapped lbw. When Dwayne Bravo held a superb diving catch at backward point to remove Kamram Akmal first ball Pakistan were 6/116 and the Sabina Park terraces were once again a bouncing frenzy. As is often the case, the game over as contest, still took time to be completed. Facing a required run rate now of ten per over Shoaib Malik pointed his front leg to mid wicket and struck a few sixes on way to 62. Bravo held a one-handed caught and bowled off a full-toss then finally Shoaib holed out to Chanderpaul at long off to complete a result that had long been imminent.

Dwayne Smith was named a popular Man of the Match. Pakistani Coach Bob Woolmer lamented his side's poor running between the wickets. It is not recorded how many stayed for the party.

WEST INDIES		PAKISTAN	
C. H. Gayle c Kamran Akmal b Umar Gul	2	Imran Nazir c Ramdin b Powell	6
S. Chanderpaul c Kamran Akmal b Iftikhar Anjum	19	Mohammad Hafeez c Lara b Powell	11
R. R. Sarwan c Younis Khan b Iftikhar Anjum	49	Younis Khan c Ramdin b Taylor	9
M. N. Samuels c Shoaib Malik b Mhammad Hafeez	63	Mohammad Yousuf c Ramdin b Smith	37
B. C. Lara (capt) c Kamran Akmal b Mohammad Hafeez	37	Inzamam-ul-Haq (capt) lbw b Smith	36
D. J. Bravo c Naved-ul-Hasan b Iftikhar Anjum	16	Shoaib Malik c Chanderpaul b Collymore	62
D. Ramdin (wk) st Kamran Akmal b Danish Kaneria	1	Kamran Akmal (wk) c Bravo b Smith	0
D. R. Smith c Inzamam-ul-Haq b Umar Gul	32	Naved-ul-Hasan b Bravo	11
J. E. Taylor run out	2	Iftikhar Anjum c Lara b Bravo	11
D. B. Powell not out	1	Umar Gul c & b Bravo	0
C. D. Collymore not out	2	Danish Kaneria not out	0
Extras Lb2 w6 Nb3	11	Extras Lb 2 w2	4
(50 overs)	9/241	(47.2 overs)	187

1/7 2/64 3/77 4/168 5/181 6/183 7/223 8/228 9/232

1/6 2/17 3/39 4/99 5/116 6/116 7/144 8/187 9/187 10/187

Bowling Umar Gul 9-1-38-2; Naved-ul-Hasan 9-1-49-0; Iftikhar Anjum 10-3-44-3; Danish Kaneria 9-2-45-1; Mohammad Hafeez 9-0-39-2; Shoaib Malik 4-0-24-0

Bowling Powell 10-1-42-2; Taylor 10-1-38-1; Collymore 8.2-3-27-1; Smith 10-0-36-3; Bravo 9-0-42-3

Umpires: B.F. Bowden S.J.A. Taufel

Toss: Pakistan   Points: West Indies 2 Pakistan 0

WEDNESDAY 14 MATCH 2007
GROUP A: AUSTRALIA v SCOTLAND
WARNER PARK, BASSETERRE, St KITTS: AUSTRALIA WON BY 203 RUNS

If Tuesday's match between the West Indies and Pakistan showcased much of what is best about World Cup cricket then at St Kitts on the Wednesday, Australia and Scotland showed it could also be a bit lame. Australia went in with no real one-day form behind them and still managed to win by 203 runs, the second biggest World Cup wining margin of all time.

As it was always likely to be a non-contest it had little appeal to locals. As a sprinkling of mostly Australian supporters turned up they were greeted by sunshine, steel drum bands, music and colourful banners and no queues. So they may have had a pleasant intimate time. But even as a television product it had virtually nothing to recommend it. Very few in Australia were going to get up in the wee hours of the night to watch such a one-way match while in Scotland the limited number of cricket fans would also have little enthusiasm. Anyone who did make the effort saw Man of the Match Ricky Ponting make a century and later Brad Hogg belt 24 from one over off former England one-day and Warwickshire player Dougie Brown.

In a decision that looked suspiciously like he was ensuring the game lasted at least a few hours for the spectators in St Kitts and those watching on television, Scotland captain, Craig Wright won the toss and elected to bowl. After the 9.00 am start here was a rain interruption and it remained cloudy for periods. But it had little affect on Australia's progress on the small Warner Park ground. Adam Gilchrist and Matthew Hayden opened with a stand of 91 in 17 overs. After Gilchrist was lbw swinging across the line at Brown, Ponting took his time to settle in then took control. His 113 was his 23rd one-day international century. It was made off 93 balls and contained nine fours and five sixes. Many of the shots to the boundary came from the trademark Ponting pull shot, his sixes, though were straight drives. Hogg stole the later limelight. His 40 from 15 balls also included three sixes from big drives. A chase of 334 in 50 overs was clearly beyond Scotland. Glenn McGrath reduced them from 0/21 to 5/42. He took three wickets and was involved in the run out that broke the opening partnership. McGrath was relaxed enough to have some fun with the two and half thousand spectators; joking with them and wearing a big inflatable Australian flag hand at one stage.

Scottish wicketkeeper, Colin Smith, who had earlier dropped Ponting on 23, kept the game going for a time by making 51 in 76 balls. Then from the first ball of the 41st over left-arm wrist spinner Hogg spun one back through the gate to bowl Smith. With former Northants and Yorkshire seamer John Blain injured and unable to bat, Australia had sewn up their easy win.

AUSTRALIA		SCOTLAND	
A. C. Gilchrist (wk) lbw b Brown	46	D. F. Watts b McGrath	9
M. L. Hayden lbw b Haq	60	R. M. Haq run out	16
R. T. Ponting (capt) b Wright	113	N. S. Poonia b Tait	1
M. J. Clarke b Haq	15	R. R. Watson c Bracken b McGrath	6
B. J. Hodge c Hoffman b Rogers	29	G. M. Hamilton c Gilchrist b McGrath	3
M. E. K. Hussey st Smith b Hoffman	4	D. R. Brown c Watson b Hodge	19
S. R. Watson not out	18	C. J. O. Smith (wk) b Hogg	51
G. B. Hogg not out	40	C. M. Tait (capt) lbw b Tait	4
Extras B1 Lb2 W5 n-b1	9	G. A. Rogers run out	6
(50 overs)	6/334	P. J. C. Hoffman not out	0
Did not bat: N. W. Bracken, S. W. Tait and G. D. McGrath		J. A. R. Blain absent hurt	0
1/91 2/139 3/193 4/256 5/274 6/276		Extras Lb9 W6 n-b1	16
Bowling : Hoffman 10-0-57-1; Blain 4-0-29-0;		(40.1 overs)	131
Wright 10-0-58-1; Brown 9-0-86-1; Rogers 10-0-52-1;		1/21 2/27 3/32 4/37 5/42 6/89 7/104 8/131 9/131	
Haq 7-0-49-2		Bowling: Bracken 6-1-12-0; 8-0-45-2; McGrath 6-1-14-3;	
		Watson 7-1-18-0; Hogg 7.1-1-16-1; Hodge 6-0-17-1	

Umpires: S.A. Bucknor E.A.R. de Silva

Toss: Scotland   Points: Australia 2 Scotland 0

WEDNESDAY 14 MARCH 2007
GROUP C: CANADA v KENYA
BEAUSEJOUR STADIUM, GROS ISLET, St LUCIA: KENYA WON BY SEVEN WICKETS

Semi-finalists from 2003, Kenya, proved too strong for Canada in the first minnow-v-minnow clash. Their spinners out-bowled the Canadian slow men and the Kenyan captain, Steve Tikolo, compiled a fine innings to guide his side to victory with 40 balls and seven wickets to spare. Tikolo had won the toss and elected to bowl. New Zealand, Central Districts batsman, Geoff Barnett, then launched the Canadian innings with a series of powerful shots against the new ball. Kiwi-born and resident but born of a Canadian mother, the big left-hander hit nine fours as the innings initially rattled along at five runs per over. Nehemiah Odhiambo was severely punished conceding 33 runs from his three overs. Barnett took four boundaries from his second over.

Barnett was soon caught on the boundary by Tanray Mishra, then Tikolo introduced spinner, Hiren Varaiya, after the fifteenth over. Variya's first ball was hit for four but after that the left-arm spinner conceded just 15 more runs in his 10 over spell. Off-spinner Jimmy Kimande was equally frugal, the pair picking up three wickets between them, as well. Steve Tikolo, another off-spinner also joined in the wicket taking and run restriction.The innings limped and the healthy number of Canadian flags in the outer began to droop. At about the same time the computers in the press box dropped out again to add to the sense of a game badly leaking electricity.

Guyana-born Sunil Dhaniram gave the later overs substance with a close to a run per ball unbeaten 34. He hit Tikolo for one slog sweep six, however, the inadequate nature of the total is shown by the frenetic urgency of their last three overs which each included a run out. Kenya needed exactly 200 to win and wicketkeeper/opening batsman Morris Ouma on way to 58 gave the top order the momentum it needed. In the fifth over he hit Pakistan-born opening bowler Umar Bhatti miles over mid wicket for six. Ouma dominated the early scoring before easing back as his captain took control. Tikolo's batting was a class above anything else on show at Gros Islet. Tellingly he was able to score freely off the Canadian spinners whereas his opponents had no real answer to the turning ball. At one stage he put his opposite number, John Davison out of the ground as well as enchanting the 8,000 spectators with seven fours.

Ouma had fallen at 119, then Tikolo was joined in an unbroken 84 run stand by Mishra that took Kenya to victory. Mishra hit the second ball of the 44th over from Ugandan born seamer Henry Osinde for four to complete the comfortable win.

With England and New Zealand also in their group, Kenya would have to make the most of their celebrations that night in St Lucia. Barring miracles they would not be progressing as far as they did in 2003.

CANADA		KENYA	
G. E.F. Barnett c Mishra b Ongondo	41	M. A.Ouma (wk) c Mulla b Dhaniram	58
A. M. Samad c Tikolo b Odoyo	15	D. O. Obuya c Bagai b Cummins	4
A. Bagai (wk) st Ouma b Varaiya	19	R. D. Shah lbw b Bhatti	6
I. S. Billcliff c & b Tikolo	34	S. O. Tikolo (capt) not out	72
J. M. Davison (capt) b Kamande	8	T. Mishra not out	35
Qaiser Ali b Kamande	6	Extras B1 Lb2 w18 n-b2 P5	28
A. A. Mulla c Ongondo b Tikolo	25	(43.2 overs)	3/203
S. Dhaniram not out	34	Did not bat: C. O. Obuya, T. M. Odoyo, J. K. Kamande, N.	
U. Bhatti run out	1	N. Odhiambo, P. J. Ongondo, H. A. Varaiya	
A. C. Cummins run out	1	1/28 2/52 3/119	
H. Osinde run out	1	Bowling: Bhatti 9-0-44-1, Cummins 8-0-32-1, Osinde	
Extras Lb5 w3 n-b6	14	5.2-0-31-0, Davison 9-0-31-0, Samad 3-0-23-0,	
(50 overs)	199	Dhaniram 9-1-34-1	
1/40 2/73 3/102 4/115 5/127 6/146 7/175 8/185 9/187			
10/199			
Bowling: Odoyo 8-1-32-1; Ongondo 10-0-51-1;			
Odhiambo 3-0-33-0; Varaiya 10-3-19-1; Kamande 10-1-25-2;			
Tikolo 9-0-34-2			

Umpires: Asad Rauf P.D. Parker

Toss: Kenya   Points: Kenya 2 Canada 0

THURSDAY 15 MARCH 2007
GROUP B BERMUDA v SRI LANKA
QUEEN'S PARK OVAL, PORT OF SPAIN, TRINIDAD: SRI LANKA WON BY 243 RUNS

After the intensity of the opening fixture of the 2007 World Cup there was a feeling two days later the tournament was moving back again into 'warm-up' phase. Australia had made short work of Scotland, and now Sri Lanka did an even more efficient job on mini-minnows Bermuda to the tune of 243 runs. Whether this sort of fixture belonged in a World Cup was a debatable point, and clearly Trinidadians didn't think much of it as the 2,200 spectators failed to fill many corners of the large refurbished Queens Park Oval. At least Bermuda had a side of mostly Bermudans, unlike Canada who had only two native-born players in the game against Kenya.

Bermuda's troubles began soon after Sri Lankan captain Mahela Jayawardene had won the toss and elected to bat. Their opening bowler, Kevin Hurdle, suffered delayed stage fright when his second over lasted 14 deliveries and contained six no balls and two wides. Without much effort Sri Lanka had scored 24 runs from the third over of the innings. Sri Lanka's openers Sanath Jayasuriya and Upal Tharnaga failed to cash in, the latter falling to Hurdle in his second spell. Jayawardene and Kumar Sangakara did make hay, though. Sri Lanka's leading two batsmen added a neat 150 for the third wicket in 25 overs taking the total from 78 to 228. The contest lacked tension, but as a batting exhibition it was sublime as the pair traded a dozen boundaries. Jayawardene, twice also planted the ball into the outer, once at mid wicket and once at long on.

To add to the sense of mismatch Jayawardene had been dropped twice by Bermudan big man, Dwayne Leverock, the first time before he had scored. Both Sri Lankans were eventually dismissed for their World Cup highest scores. With Chamara Sliva racing to a 45 ball 55 and the wides and no balls continuing to pile up Sri Lanka were able to reach an imposing 321.Jayawardene sympathised with Bermuda saying Sri Lanka conceded 328 against Australia in their first World Cup match in 1975. But he failed to mention Sri Lanka had mustered 276 in reply. Bermuda got to 75. Chaminda Vaas trapped opener Clay Smith lbw with an in-swinger in the first over then Lasith Malinga at full tilt left Bermuda in tatters at 4/20 in the eighth over. By the 15th over the score was 7/39.

Lionel Cann finally made a few effective hits on way to 28. Farveez Maharoof eventually had Cann caught behind on way to four very cheap wickets. Jayawardene, though, received the Man of the Match award and that had the advantage of shortening the post-match speeches.

SRI LANKA		BERMUDA	
W. U. Tharanga c Minors b Hurdle	30	C. J. Smith lbw b Vaas	0
S. T. Jayasuriya c Pitcher b Mukeddem	22	O. L. Pitcher b Maharoof	6
D. P. M. D. Jayawardene (capt) c Hurdle b Cann	85	S. Mukuddem c Sangakara b Malinga	0
K. C. Sangakara (wk) c Tucker b Leverock	76	D. L. Hemp c Jayawardene b Malinga	14
L. P. C. Silva not out	55	I. H. Romaine (capt) lbw b Malinga	0
T. M. Dilshan c Tucker b Hurdle	12	J. J. Tucker b Muralitharan	4
M. F. Maharoof c Hemp b Mukeddem	9	D. A. Minors (wk) c Sangakara b Maharoof	4
R. P. Arnold not out	2	L. O.B. Cann c Sangakara b Maharoof	28
Extras Lb3 w13 n-b14	30	D. C.C. Borden c sub (K. M.D. N. Kulusekera) b Maharoof	6
(50 overs)	6/321	K. A.D. Hurdle not out	6
Did not bat: W. P. U. J.C. Vaas, S. L. Malinga, M. Muralitharan		R. D.M. Leverock lbw b Muralitharan	1
1/62 2/78 3/228 4/267 5/305 6/316		Extras Lb6 w3	9
Bowling: Hurdle 9-1-61-2; Mukuddem 10-0-50-2;		(24.4overs)	78
Tucker 10-0-50-0; Leverock 10-0-67-1; Borden 3-0-27-0;		1/0 2/2 3/20 4/20 5/25 6/29 7/39 8/64 9/77 10/78	
Cann 5-0-34-1; Romaine 3-0-29-0		Bowling: Vaas 6-3-11-1; Malinga 5-2-10-3;	
		Maharoof 7-1-23-4; Muralitharan 6.4-0-28-2	

Umpires: D.J. Harper I.J. Howell

Toss: Sri Lanka   Points: Sri Lanka 2 Bermuda 0

THURSDAY 15 MARCH 2007
GROUP D IRELAND v ZIMBABWE
SABINA PARK, KINGSTON JAMAICA: MATCH TIED

Ireland and Zimbabwe kick started a fresh wave of enthusiasm for the World Cup when they played out a thrilling tie at Sabina Park in Kingston. The third ever tie in the World Cup lifted the profile of the Associate member Ireland in their first ever World Cup match, while showcasing the effect the player exit and home political instability was having on the previously Test-credentialed Zimbabweans. Despite the two points being shared the publicity was all about the Irish who had a small but noisy and enthusiastic cluster of supporters in the ground and whose late rally against the odds brought forth all sorts of references about the luck and unquenchable spirit of the Irish.

Zimbabwe should have won. Chasing 222 for victory they reached 5/203 with six and a half overs to go. But they stumbled badly and lost their tenth wicket from the final ball of the match when their top scorer, Stuart Matsikenyeri, missed the ball and then didn't run! Prosper Utseya won the toss, elected to bowl and was rewarded when Chris Mpofu had Irish opener Will Porterfield caught at slip by Visu Sibanda via a deflection from wicketkeeper, Brendan Taylor in the first over. Elton Chigumbra was then involved in three dismissals and by the end of the 22nd over the boys in clover green were a precarious 5/89. But former Australian Under 19 star, Jeremy Bray, held firm to keep the Irish in the match. The left-handed opener who reminded observers of Matthew Hayden batted throughout the innings, hitting ten fours and a couple of powerful sixes from meaty cuts.

It took until the 48th over for the Sydneysider to reach his and Ireland's maiden World Cup century. However, he was involved in a number of key partnerships. The biggest was 56 with Andrew White for the sixth wicket, but the most important was probably with David Langford-Smith that took the total from 182 to 221 at the end of the innings. Zimbabwe's reply was also led by one of their opening batsmen. In their case, Visu Sibanda held the top order together with a soundly compiled 67. When his feet slipped and he stood on his stumps on the back stroke Zimbabwe were 4/128 in the 29th over, still with work to do. Then Matsikenyeri and Taylor added 70 for the sixth wicket in 14 overs and Zimbabwe appeared to be in total control. Kyle McCallan fortuitously deflected a powerful straight drive by Matsikenyeri onto the stumps with Taylor backing up too far. It changed the match's momentum The pressure built and Zimbabwe surrendered their ascendency, losing wickets in 48th, 49th (x2) and 50th overs. Matsikenyeri took seven runs from the final over, but why didn't he run for the last ball? Had the Leprechaun in the outer put a hex on him?

The Irish team did a lap of honour. The Zimbabweans looked as if they had lost.

IRELAND		ZIMBABWE	
W. F. S. Porterfield c Sibanda b Mpofu	0	T. Duffin c N. J. O'Brien b Rankin	12
J. T. Bray not out	115	V. Sibanda hit wicket b White	67
E. J. G. Morgan c Chigumbura b Brent	21	C. J. Chibhabha c Langford-Smith b Johnston	12
N. J. O'Brien (wk) c Taylor b Chigumbura	1	S. C. Williams c Rankin b M. Callan	14
A. C. Botha b Chigumbura	1	S. Matsikenyeri not out	73
K. J. O'Brien c Taylor b Rainsford	10	E. Chigumbura c Bray b M. Callan	4
A. R. White lbw b Brent	28	B. R.M. Taylor (wk) run out	24
D. T. Johnston (capt) run out	20	G. B. Brent lbw b Botha	3
W. K. M. Callan st Taylor b Williams	0	P. Utseya (capt) c Morgan b K. J.O'Brien	1
D. Langford-Smith c Taylor b Mpofu	10	C. B. Mpofu run out	0
Extras B1 Lb1 W5 N-b3	10	E. C. Rainsford run out	1
(50 overs)	9/221	Extras Lb1 W7 N-b2	10
Did not bat: W. B. Rankin		(50 overs)	221

1/0 2/43 3/44 4/64 5/89 6/145 7/182 8/182 9/221

Bowling: Mpofu 10-2-58-2; Rainsford 7-0-44-1; Chigumbura 6-2-21-2; Brent 10-1-40-2; Uteseya 10-0-29-0; Williams 6-1-21-1; Matsikenyeri 1-0-6-0

1/26 2/92 3/107 4/128 5/133 6/203 7/212 8/213 9/213 10/221

Bowling: Langford-Smith 9-0-34-0; Rankin 7-1-43-1; Botha 10-2-32-1; Johnston 10-2-32-1; M. Callan 9-1-56-2; White 3-1-15-1; K. J.O'Brien 2-1-8-1

Umpires: I.J. Gould B.G. Jerling

Toss: Zimbabwe   Points: Ireland 1 Zimbabwe 1

FRIDAY 16 MARCH 2007
GROUP C; ENGLAND v NEW ZEALAND
BEAUSEJOUR STADIUM, GROS ISLET St LUCIA:
NEW ZEALAND WON BY SIX WICKETS

Two days after Kenya had easily defeated Canada, World Cup cricket returned to Beausejour Stadium and saw New Zealand just as convincingly overcome England. The six-wicket defeat cancelled out the progress England's one-day team had made in Australia. But if that was bad enough the alleged misbehavior of former captain and leading all-rounder, Andrew Flintoff, on the evening after the match was worse. This was the day, or night, of 'the pedalo affair'. Flintoff overindulged after the game and was accused of being inebriated while in control of a maritime vehicle. After the Ashes debacle it was the last thing England, Flintoff or departing coach Duncan Fletcher needed. Flintoff had made a first-ball duck and failed to take a wicket during the match. He was fined, stripped of the vice-captaincy and dropped for the game against Canada.

The extraneous matters detracted from a great innings by Scott Styris. The Brisbane-born Kiwi made 87 not out, guiding his side to a target of 210, achieved with six wickets and nine overs to spare. Not that a result either way with Canada and Kenya in the same group, was likely to halt the progress of both these sides to the Super Eight stage.

England had been sent in by Stephen Fleming and made 7/209 from their 50 overs. Following a slightly delayed start, James Franklin had Ed Joyce caught behind chasing a long-hop from the first legal ball of the match, but a 73 run partnership between Kevin Pietersen and Paul Collingwood had lifted England to 3/133. Styris dibbly dobbing on a mist wicket and Shane Bond in a brilliant burst of fast bowling then took two wickets apiece in three overs as England slipped to a struggling 7/138. Wicketkeeper, Paul Nixon and fast bowler, Liam Plunkett averted further disaster to add an unbroken 71 for the eighth wicket to lift England to competitive if unimposing final total.

Plunkett and James Anderson initially set New Zealand back on their heels with the new-ball. Anderson dismissed Lou Vincent and Fleming, while Plunkett had Ross Taylor brilliantly caught at slip by Flintoff. The Kiwis were 3/19. Styris and Craig McMillan initially halted the English momentum and took the score to 72 before the latter was caught from a mistimed lofted drive against left-arm spinner Monty Panesar.

Styris, an obvious Man of the Match, said when he was joined by Jacob Oram they just set out to bat through the rest of the innings without worrying about the run rate. The move paid off handsomely as they put on 138 at virtually a run a ball. Oram got himself going with a nicely levered six off Panesar while Styris hit nine boundaries all round the wicket. It was a fine effort by a player who only received a late call up to due a back injury to Peter Fulton.

ENGLAND		NEW ZEALAND	
E. C. Joyce c McCullum b Franklin	0	L. Vincent c Nixon b Anderson	0
M. P. Vaughan (capt) b Franklin	26	S. P. Fleming (capt) c Joyce b Anderson	7
I. R. Bell c McCullum b Oram	5	L. R. P. L. Taylor c Flintoff b Plunkett	0
K. P. Pietersen c Franklin b Bond	60	S. B. Styris not out	87
P. D. Collingwood c McCullum b Styris	31	C. D. McMillan c Dalrymple b Panesar	27
A. Flintoff c Styris b Bond	0	J. D. P. Oram not out	63
J. W.M. Dalrymple c M. Ullum b Styris	3	Extras B2 Lb11 W11 Nb2	26
P. A. Nixon (wk) not out	42	(41 overs)	4/210
L. E. Plunkett not out	29	Did not bat: B. B.McCullum (wk), D. L. Vettori, J. E.C.	
Extras Lb2 W4 Nb7	13	Franklin, S. E. Bond, J. S. Patel	
(50 overs)	7/209	1/1 2/3 3/19 4/72	
Did not bat: J. M. Anderson, M. S. Panesar		Bowling: Anderson 8-0-39-2; Plunkett 7-0-43-1;	
1/1 2/30 3/52 4/133 5/133 6/134 7/138		Flintoff 8-1-17-0; Collingwood 3-0-20-0; Panesar 10-0-47-1;	
Bowling: Franklin 9-0-43-2; S. E.Bond 10-1-19-2;		Dalrymple 4-0-29-0; Pietersen 1-0-2-0	
Oram 6-0-25-1; Patel 8-0-42-0; Vettori 10-0-53-0;			
Styris 7-0-25-2			

Umpires: Asad Rauf, R.E. Koertzen,

Toss: New Zealand,   Points: New Zealand 2 England 0

FRIDAY 16 MARCH 2007
GROUP A: NETHERLANDS V SOUTH AFRICA
WARNER PARK, BASSETERRE, St KITTS: SOUTH AFRICA WON BY 221 RUNS

The 1442 souls who bothered to attend this mismatch were rewarded with a couple of a treats for their effort. Not only was there plenty of room available in the party stand but they also saw South Africa break several World Cup and one-day international batting records.

Primarily those thrills and the disparity between the sides was encapsulated in one amazing over where Herschelle Gibbs became the first batsman to hit six sixes in an over in an international cricket match. Gibbs clouted part time leg-spinner Daan van Bunge three times over long off, twice over mid wicket and once over long on, all with a smile on his face.

South Africa was on way to 3/353 from 40 overs at a record breaking rate of 8.82 runs per over. That was after they had been sent in by Luuk van Troost and initially were 1/5 from 4 overs. Three consecutive century partnerships followed. That was another record as was the 21 ball half century scored by Mark Boucher towards the end of the innings.

There were a total of 18 sixes, the last three coming from the final three balls of the innings from century maker Jacques Kallis. The increasingly sheepish Dutch captain, van Troost, conceded 59 runs from his four overs of left-arm medium pace. Heavy overnight rain had caused the overs reduction, but the wicket was fine, the bowling friendly and the boundaries short and inviting. A.B. De Villiers, caught behind off Billy Stelling from the second ball of the match, missed out badly. Once South Africa had batted there was little point in the spectators staying for the remainder of the match. The Netherlands made no attempt to chase the runs finishing on 9/132 from their 40 overs.

In a gesture more in keeping with a Sunday club fixture, Graeme Smith tried to give everyone who didn't have a bat a bowl. Except Ashwell Prince, who had to be satisfied with an involvement in the run out of opener Darron Reekers in the third over. That was one of three run outs, another confusing part of the totally confusing Dutch response to the South African innings.

South African born Essex all-rounder Ryan ten Doeschate did make 57 and hit a six for the Netherlands.

SOUTH AFRICA		NETHERLANDS	
A. B. de Villiers c Smits b Stelling	0	B. Zuiderant b Pollock	1
G. C. Smith (capt) c van Bunge b Borren	67	D. J. Reekers run out	4
J. H. Kallis not out	128	A. N. Kervezee c Pollock b Langeveldt	17
H. H. Gibbs c Szwarczynski b van Troost	72	R. N. ten Doeschate run out	57
M. V. Boucher (wk) not out	75	D. L.S. van Bunge lbw b Hall	5
Extras Lb2 W8 Nb1	11	E. S. Szwarczynski lbw b Smith	12
(40 overs)	3/353	T. B.M. de Leede b Kemp	21
Did not bat: A. G. Prince, J. M. Kemp, S. M. Pollock, A. J.		P. W. Borren run out	2
Hall, C. K. Langeveldt, A. Nel		L. P. van Troost (capt) c Smith b Kemp	5
1/0 2/114 3/219		W. F. Stelling not out	1
Bowling: Stelling 8-1-43-1; Reekers 5-1-35-0; ten		Extras Lb4 W2 Nb1	7
Doesschate 7-0-58-0; de Leede 4-0-48-0; Borren 8-0-52-1;		(40 overs)	9/132
van Bunge 4-0-56-0; van Troost 4-0-59-1		Did not bat: J. Smits (wk)	

1/5 2/6 3/33 4/47 5/72 6/114 7/124 8/131 9/132

Bowling: Pollock 6-3-4-1; Nel 6-1-19-0; Langeveldt 6-0-22-1; Hall 6-1-15-1; Smith 8-0-32-1; Kallis 4-0-18-0; Kemp 4-0-18-2

Umpires: M.R. Benson A.L. Hill

Toss: Netherlands   Points: South Africa 2 Netherlands 0

SATURDAY 17 MARCH 2007
GROUP B: BANGLADESH v INDIA
QUEENS PARK, PORT-OF SPAIN, TRINIDAD: BANGLADESH WON BY FIVE WICKETS

Still in the first week of the tournament, match eight provided a huge upset when Bangladesh defeated India by five wickets with nine balls to spare.

The Bangladeshis hit the ground running whereas India looked as if they were still thawing out in the warm-up stage. Queens Park had previously been India's most productive venue in the Caribbean and it was where they received most support from the large Indian ethnic population. Once again, though, the attendance of nine thousand was mediocre and the atmosphere a little uninspiring. The television audience, of course, was estimated at a slightly larger one billion.

This loss was India's sixth defeat in their nine opening World Cup fixtures.

The problems began when three out of four of India's revered and experienced batting maestros contributed just 23 runs between them. Virender Sehwag having a horror run played on to the impressive Mashrafe Mortaza, Tendulkar in the middle of his batting mid life crisis took 26 balls to make seven and Rahul Dravid in addition to struggling to a boundaryless 14 had misread the pitch after he elected to bat when it contained a lot of moisture.

At one stage the Indians went 88 deliveries without hitting a four.

The fourth Indian champion, Saurev Ganguly, opened the innings and battled his way to 66 in 129 balls. He added a crucial 85 runs in 18 overs with Yuvraj Singh for the fifth wicket. That seemed to set India back on course for a competitive total.

But the Bangladeshi side, chockfull of youngsters, never wavered and once the partnership was broken they ripped out five batsmen for two runs in 15 balls.

Left-arm spinners Abdur Razzak and Mohammad Rafique took four of those five wickets, benefitting from Indian misjudgment and their own accuracy. The one six Yuvraj did hit off Rafique, though, was probably the biggest in the tournament to that point. His slog sweep ended up in the second tier of the Queens Park Oval grandstand at square leg.

Finally, Zaheer Khan and Munaf Patel put on 32 for the tenth wicket before Patel holed out at cover in the 50th over to give Man of the Match, Mortaza, his fourth wicket.

Bangladesh needed a potentially tricky 192 to put a huge dent in India's World Cup prospects. Seventeen year old World Cup debutant, Tamim Iqbal didn't think it was tricky, though. Talented and clear headed the left-hander attacked at once with success. He flayed the new-ball to the boundary between mid off and point on bended knee then, despite a blow to the head from Zaheer Khan continued to blaze with dancing blows. One six was sliced over third man another, hit off the middle, went miles over long on.

Patel had him caught behind with an excellent delivery going across him in the 14th over to make Bangladesh 2/69. And when Patel struck again soon after, trapping Aftab Ahmed lbw it was 3/79.

But 18-year-old wicketkeeper batsman, Mushfiqur Rahim held firm while 19-year-old Shakib Al Hasan stole the initiative back driving and cutting anything with width through the off-side. One leg-side hit by Rahim finished up going for six over third man. The tension eased. It was going to Bangladesh's day. When Sehwag had Shakib stumped the fourth wicket partnership had realized 84 runs and the target had been reduced to 29 from 69 balls. Rahim stayed there and took his time to finish, but millions of those television sets had been switched off by the time his square drive confirmed the result.

Within 24 hours they would all be on again focusing on an event in Jamaica that made the cricket not seem so significant.

INDIA		BANGLADESH	
S. C. Ganguly c Abdur Razzak b Mohammad Rafique	66	Tamim Iqbal c Dhoni b Patel	51
V. Sehwag b Mashrafe Mortaza	2	Shahriar Nafees lbw b Khan	2
R. V. Uthappa c Aftab Ahmed b Mashrafe Mortaza	9	Mushfiqur Rahim (wk) not out	56
S. R. Tendulkar c Mushfiqur Rahim b Abdur Razzak	7	Aftab Ahmed lbw b Patel	8
R. Dravid (capt) lbw b Mohammad Rafique	14	Shakib Al Hasan st Dhoni b Sehwag	53
Yuvraj Singh c Habibul Bashar b Abdur Razzak	47	Habibul Bashar (capt) st Dhoni b Sehwag	1
M. S. Dhoni (wk) c Aftab Ahmed b Mohammad Rafique	0	Mohammad Ashraful not out	8
Harbhajhan Singh b Abdur Razzak	0	Extras Lb1 W4 Nb8	13
A. B. Agarker c Mushfiqur Rahim b Mashrafe Mortaza	0	(48.3 overs)	5/192
Z. Khan not out	15	Did not bat: Mohammad Rafique, Mashrafe Mortaza,	
M. M. Patel c Abdur razzak b Mashrafe Mortaza	15	Abdur Razzak, Syed Rasel	
Extras Lb5 W3 Nb8	16	1/24 2/69 3/79 4/163 5/175	
(49.3 overs)	191	Bowling: Zaheer Khan 9-2-41-1; Agarkar 10-0-41-0; Patel	
1/6 2/21 3/40 4/72 5/157 6/158 7/159 8/159 9/159		8.3-1-39-2; Harbhajan Singh 10-1-30-0; Tendulkar 3-0-8-0;	
10/191		Yuvraj Singh 3-0-15-0; Sehwag 5-0-17-2	
Bowling: Mashrafe bin Mortaza 9.3-2-38-4; Syed			
Rasel 10-2-31-0; Abdur Razzak 10-2-38-3; Shakib Al			
Hasan 10-0-44-0; Mohammad Rafique 10-2-35-3			

Umpires: Aleem Dar S.J.Davis

Toss: India   Points: Bangladesh 2 India 0

GROUP D: IRELAND v PAKISTAN
SABINA PARK, KINGSTON, JAMAICA: IRELAND WON BY THREE WICKETS

There has probably been no more dramatic or dark day in World Cup history as Saturday March 17th 2007. On the same afternoon that Bangladesh defeated India, Ireland ensured Pakistan would not progress through to the Super Eights, defeating them by three wickets at Sabina Park. Within 24 hours Pakistan's gloom was multiplied when their coach, Bob Woolmer, was found unconscious in his hotel room and later pronounced dead at University Hospital in Kingston. To this day the cause of his untimely death is questioned and there are those who believe he was murdered. But the official Jamaican inquiry could find no evidence of this and pronounced an open verdict. After all the conspiracy theories subsided, and Professor Plum with the snake poison had been cleared, it was revealed Woolmer did have serious health issues at the time of his death. The tragedy unfortunately took attention away from Ireland's and Bangladesh's wonderful on-field successes.

There was no question the colour that morning at Sabina Park was green. Both team uniforms were green, the outfield was a lush green and the wicket had a genuine emerald hue, as well. On St Patrick's Day it was appropriate that Trent Johnston won the toss.

His bowlers were often wayward, but when they hit the right spot on the pitch and the seam they found movement and that their speed between 78-82 mph was a handful. Mohmmad Hafeez and Younis Khan were out by the fourth over.

Imran Nazir and Mohammad Yousuf with a mixture of the sublime and the frenetic then carried the total to 2/56 by the 12th over.

The feeling was that any Pakistani score over 150 in the conditions would be too much for the Irish. But Yousuf slashed Johnston, to backward point and then Inzamam pushed tentatively at the impeccably accurate Andre Botha and was caught at slip. Botha repeated the dose to opener Imran Nazir and Pakistan had slipped to 5/66 after 18 overs.

Wicketkeeper Kamran Akmal looked to have put Pakistan back on course to some degree but he mistimed a pull off Boyd Rankin and Johnston took an inspirational catch running with the flight of the ball at mid wicket.

The Pakistan tailenders tried to slog off-spinner Kyle McCallan with poor results and Ireland needed 133 runs in 50 overs to guarantee their World Cup progression.

Chastened by their poor batting and probable tournament demise Pakistan threw everything at the Irish batsmen. Mohammad Sami, bowling fast and full brought the new-ball back into the left-handers and won two lbw decisions to leave Ireland 2/15.

Eventual Man of the Match, Niall O'Brien responded by pouncing on anything short and crashing it through point. With the Pakistani fast bowlers bursting to find extra penetration there were offerings available and O'Brien raced to 50 in 74 balls.

Botha suffered probably the worst umpiring decision of the World Cup from umpire Jerling, then rain came with Ireland 4/81 and ahead on Duckworth Lewis Scale. When the sides returned the target had been reduced to 128 from 47 overs and O'Brien resumed his attack. He lofted Shoaib Malik for six over long on, but with his side 20 runs from victory was stumped next ball trying for another six.

Iftikhar Anjum then made a prompt double breakthrough and at 7/113 the Pakistanis sniffed a steal.

Irish fans were tense. However, Kevin O'Brien responded with a perfect square cut off Iftikhar and with the scores level Johnston lofted a slower delivery by Azhar Mahmood over mid wicket for six. The resulting Irish jigs were spontaneous both on and off the field.

PAKISTAN		IRELAND	
Imran Nazir c Morgan b Botha	24	J. P. Bray lbw b Mohammad Sami	3
Mohammad Hafeez c N. J. O'Brien b Langford-Smith	4	W. T. S. Porterfield b Mohammad Hafeez	13
Younis Khan c Botha b Rankin	0	E. J. G. Morgan lbw b Mohammad Sami	2
Mohammad Yousuf c Porterfield b Johnston	15	N. J. O'Brien (wk) st Kamran Akmal b Shoaib Malik	72
Inzamam-ul-Haq (capt) c Morgan b Botha	1	A. C. Botha c Mohammad Hafeez b Mohammad Sami	0
Shoaib Malik c N. J. O'Brien b K. J. O'Brien	9	K. J. O'Brien not out	16
Kamran Akmal (wk) c Johnston b Rankin	27	A. R. White c Mohammad Hafeez b Iftikhar Anjum	4
Azhar Mahmood c Johnston b Rankin	2	W. K. M. Callan c Younis Khan b Iftikhar Anjum	0
Mohammad Sami c Bray b M. Callan	12	D. T. Johnston (capt) not out	9
Iftikhar Anjum not out	8	Extras Lb2 W11 Nb1	14
Umar Gul c sub (Mooney) b M. Callan	1	(41.4 overs)	7/133
Extras Lb3 W23 Nb3	29	Did not bat: D. Langford-Smith, W. B. Rankin	
(45.4 overs)	132	1/7 2/15 3/62 4/70 5/108 6/113 7/113	
1/7 2/15 3/56 4/58 5/66 6/72 7/103 8/105 9/130 10/132		Bowling: Umar Gul 9-0-24-0; Mohammad Sami 10-0-29-3;	
Bowling: Langford-Smith 10-1-31-1; Rankin 9-1-32-3;		Iftikhar Anjum 10-0-29-2; Azhar Mahmood 7.4-1-25-0;	
Botha 8-4-5-2; Johnston 7-1-20-1; K. J. O'Brien 6-0-29-1;		Mohammad Hafeez 4-0-15-1; Shoaib Malik 1-0-9-1	
M. Callan 5.4-1/12-2			

Umpires: B.F. Bowden B.G. Jerling

Toss: Ireland   Points: Ireland 2 Pakistan 0

SUNDAY 18 MARCH 2007
GROUP A: AUSTRALIA v NETHERLANDS
WARNER PARK,
BASSETERRE, St KITTS: AUSTRALIA WON BY 229 RUNS

The same day that the cricket world went into shock over the death of Bob Woolmer Australia quietly disposed of Holland by 229 runs. Australia must have been wondering when the World Cup was actually going to start after being scheduled this second mismatch game.

Brad Hodge, the batsman whose position was the most precarious in the side, made most of the friendly offerings this time. He took 61 balls to reach 50 then added a further 73 in the next 28 balls. Hodge's first one-day international century contained seven sixes, one less than Ricky Ponting's World Cup record eight in the 2003 final.

He had accelerated away from Michael Clarke with whom he added a World Cup record 204 for the fourth wicket in 27 overs. The pair had come together after two wickets had fallen on 116, Ponting being nicely caught and bowled by Ryan ten Doeschate.

Clarke left his hitting to the end of the innings. He planted three balls in a row over the boundary before allowing Shane Watson the honour of lifting the final delivery into the outer.

The Netherlands, to their credit and unlike their tedious effort against South Africa, did not muck around in their reply. Darron Reekers hit five early boundaries and after six overs the Dutch were 0/36. Unfortunately for those hoping for a contest, after eleven overs they were 5/46.

That did not alter their approach and with the assistance of Steve Bucknor and Tony Hill, who awarded five lbw's to Australian bowlers, the innings was finished in 27 overs. Two of the five were taken by Glenn McGrath who reached his 50 wicket milestone in World Cup matches.

Daan van Bunge and Peter Borren struck a few solid blows and kept the run rate close to five per over. But Brad Hogg bamboozled the tail with left-arm wrist spin, picking up four wickets in less than five overs.

At one stage during the afternoon drinks were brought out to the Australian players. The 12th man, Brad Haddin, relayed the news of Bob Woolmer's death. From that moment the players looked stunned and played without passion.

"When something like this happens it certainly rams home that there are other things happening around you all the time," Ponting said.

AUSTRALIA		NETHERLANDS	
A. C.Gilchrist (wk) c van Troost b de Leede	57	B. Zuiderent run out	9
M. L. Hayden c Borren b de Leede	29	D. J. Reekers c Clarke b Bracken	25
R. T. Ponting c & b ten Doeschate	23	A. N. Kervezee lbw b Bracken	0
M. J. Clarke not out	93	R. N. ten Doeschate lbw b Tait	1
B. J. Hodge b Borren	123	L. P. van Troost (capt) lbw b McGrath	0
M. E. K. Hussey c sub (M. Kashif) b ten Doeschate	2	D. L.S. van Bunge lbw b McGrath	33
S. R. Watson not out	12	T. B.M. de Leede c Hayden b Hogg	14
Extras Lb9 W8 Nb2	19	P. W. Borren c Hussey b Hogg	24
(50 overs)	5/358	J. Smits (wk) lbw b Hogg	3
Did not bat: G. B. Hogg, N. W. Bracken, G. D. McGrath		Adeel Raja not out	8
1/73 2/116 3/116 4/320 5/325		M. B.S. Jonkman st Gilchrist b Hogg	0
Bowling: Jonkman 6.1-1-35-0; Reekers 6-1-48-0; de		Extras B4 Lb3 W5	12
Leede 10-1-40-2; ten Doeschate 10-0-76-2; Adeel Raja		(26.5 overs)	129
7.5-0-61-0; Borren 10-0-89-1		1/36 2/36 3/38 4/40 5/46 6/87 7/97 8/106 9/129 10/129	
		Bowling: Bracken 7-1-33-2; Tait 7-0-29-1; McGrath 8-0-33-2;	
		Hogg 4.5-0.27-4	

Umpires: S.A. Bucknor A.L. Hill

Toss: Australia   Points: Australia 2 Netherlands 0

GROUP C: CANADA v ENGLAND
BEAUSEJOUR STADIUM, GROS ISLET, St LUCIA: ENGLAND WON BY 51 RUNS

England, perhaps grateful to be playing an associate member team, overcame the disruption of the disciplining of Andrew Flintoff and then the tragic news of Bob Woolmer's death, to defeat Canada by 51 runs in St Lucia. Sent in by Canadian captain, John Davison, England started well, faltered in the middle then recovered to reach 6/279; out of Canada's reach.

But the English attack had more difficulty dismissing Canadian batsmen than Kenya did. That did not auger well for their ability to overcome stronger teams in the days and weeks ahead. Ed Joyce, coming off a duck against New Zealand, and Michael Vaughan, began the match with a century opening stand in 20 overs.

Following the dismissal of Vaughan, Joyce and Ian Bell pushed the total up to 1/153. Then there was a bit of a stumble as three wickets fell for eight runs. John Davison bowled an accurate spell while Sunil Dhaniram had Bell chipping a slog sweep to short third man, Joyce bowled playing a reverse sweep and Kevin Pietersen popping his fourth ball straight back to the bowler.

Much to the relief of the English dominated crowd of nine thousand Paul Collingwood had the wherewithal to steady the innings and keep the scoreboard moving. He found support from Ravi Bopara, but it was Collingwood's 48 ball innings of 62 that made the difference and gain him the Man of the Match Award. It also allowed Paul Nixon's late eight ball assault that included four fours and a straight six off Anderson Cummins' final ball of the innings.

On a wicket losing pace and reliability game-by-game and hour-by-hour Canada had a steep chase. And they made an ordinary start to be 2/21 after five overs. Liam Plunkett bowled Geoff Barnett shouldering arms and had Ashish Bagai upper cutting a short ball straight to third man. They were the last two batsmen not to reach twenty until Canadian number nine, George Codrington batted out the final couple of overs.

The underdogs kept coming at England, however, they were always just behind the required run rate. They had particular trouble scoring with any freedom against the left-arm spin of Monty Panesar. Abdool Samad and Ashish Mulla added 96 for the fifth wicket in 18 overs. Mulla completed a fine half-century but just when it seemed Canada might accelerate towards challenging their target of a further 118 runs off 15 overs, both fell with the score on 161.

Desmond Chumney and Dhaniram then denied the English bowlers any more success.

"Fortunately Canada were not strong enough to take advantage of our disarray," Vaughan would write.

ENGLAND		CANADA	
E. C. Joyce b Dhaniram	66	J. M. Davison (capt) c Bell b Anderson	21
M. P. Vaughan (capt) c Davison b Samad	45	G. E.F. Barnett b Plunkett	7
I. R. Bell c Codrington b Dhaniram	28	A. Bagai (wk) c Pietersen b Plunkett	6
K. P. Pietersen c & b Dhaniram	5	I. S. Billcliff b Bopara	20
P. D. Collingwood not out	66	A. M. Samad lbw b Panesar	36
R. S. Bopara b Codrington	29	A. A. Mulla st Nixon b Bopara	58
J. W.M. Dalrymple c Bagai b Cummins	2	D. R. Chumney not out	27
P. A. Nixon (wk) not out	23	S. Dhaniram run out	30
Extras B4 Lb2 W8 Nb5	19	G. R. Codrington nout out	7
(50 overs)	6/279	Extras Lb2 W11 Nb3	16
Did not bat; L. E. Plunkett, J. M. Anderson, M. S. Panesar		(50 overs)	7/228
1/101 2/153 3/160 4/161 5/242 6/245		Did not bat: U. Bhatti, A. C. Cummins	
Bowling: Cummins 7-0-58-1; Bhatti 7.5-0-41-0;		1/8 2/22 3/51 4/65 5/161 6/161 7/217	
Davison 10-1-32-0; Samad 5.1-0-31-1;		Bowling: Anderson 10-1-40-1; Plunkett 9-0-46-2;	
Codrington 10-0-70-1; Dhaniram 10-0-41-3		Panesar 10-1-35-1; Bopara 9-0-43-2; Collingwood 9-0-41-0;	
		Dalrymple 3-0-21-0	

Umpires: B.R. Doctrove P.D. Parker

Toss: Canada   Points: England 2 Canada 0

MONDAY 19 MARCH 2007
GROUP B: BERMUDA v INDIA
QUEENS PARK, PORT-OF-SPAIN, TRINIDAD: INDIA WON BY 257 RUNS

The World Cup as a non-event resumed as India wreaked revenge for their loss to Bangladesh on a totally outclassed Bermuda.

India, sent in to bat, broke all sorts of batting and winning margin records, but there were few real thrills in an almost-empty Queens Park. Of course being a match involving India meant the television numbers on the subcontinent made the exercise more than financially worthwhile. Despite the Indian dominance one of the iconic moments of the entire 2007 World Cup was achieved by a Bermudan player in the opening phase of the game. Malachi Jones dismissed Robin Uthappa with his maiden ball in the World Cup—another record. The wicket was even more notable because of the stunning one-handed catch taken at the solitary slip by Bermudan big man Dwayne Leverock.

Equally as impressive as the catch was Leverock's posterior elevating roll, celebratory sprint and David Lloyd's television description of it. Jones also made a lot of his moment. Both were right to react that way, because there was nothing else to cheer them during the game. Virender Sehwag, reputedly out of form, was soon cutting and covering driving with complete freedom. Saurev Ganguly bided his time then began driving the ball for six straight and over long on. They added 202 in 28 overs before eventual Man of the Match, Sehwag, having raced to 114 of 87 balls skied a big hit off Kevin Hurdle.

After that the batting really got moving. Yuvraj Singh repeatedly belted the innocuous bowlers over the leg-side accelerating to 83 in 46 balls with seven sixes. He added 122 in 62 balls with Sachin Tendulkar who also hit four sixes in his 29 ball innings of 57.

India's 413 was the highest ever World Cup score. Questions again had to be asked, though, if such games devalued the cricket's premium tournament. Leverock, coming back to earth with a thump, conceded 96 runs from his ten overs.

Bermuda was able to bat 43 overs in reply, but the only real innings of note was from David Hemp. The hardened Glamorgan professional showed his pedigree by making an unbeaten 76 out of 156.

Hitting nine fours and a six, Hemp fired a few shots back at the Indians. But after being smashed for 32 from his two overs he had begun his innings in some debt.

INDIA		BERMUDA	
R. V. Uthappa c Leverock b Jones	3	O. L. Pitcher b Khan	0
S. C. Ganguly st Minors b Borden	89	S. D. Outerbridge b Khan	9
V. Sehwag c Jones b Hurdle	114	D. C.C. Borden lbw b Patel	13
M. S.Dhoni (wk) c Tucker b Borden	29	D. L. Hemp not out	76
Yuvraj Singh c Jones b Leverock	83	I. H. Romaine (capt) lbw b Kumble	0
S. R. Tendulkar not out	57	J. J. Tucker b Kumble	0
R. Dravid (capt) not out	7	D. A. Minors (wk) c sub (Kartik) b Agarkar	21
Extras Lb7 W17 Nb7	31	L. O.B. Cann c Uthappa b Agarkar	0
(50 overs)	5/413	K. A.D. Hurdle b Agarkar	0
Did not bat: A. B. Agarkar, A. Kumble, Z. Khan, M. M. Patel		R. D.M. Leverock c Dhoni b Tendulkar	9
1/3 2/205 3/238 4/269 5/391		M. O.J ones lbw b Kumble	1
Bowling: Hurdle 10-0-53-1; Jones 7-0-74-1; Tucker 9-0-67-1;		Extras Lb12 W12 Nb3	27
Hemp 2-0-32-0; Leverock 10-0-96-1; Borden 5-0-30-2;		(43.1 overs)	156
Cann 7-0-54-0		1/0 2/18 3/47 4/57 5/63 6/106 7/106 8/110 9/154 10/156	
		Bowling: Zaheer Khan 10-1-32-2; Agarkar 10-0-38-3;	
		Patel 8-2-20-1; Kumble 9.1-0-38-3; Sehwag 5-0-15-5;	
		Tendulkar 1-0-1-1	

Umpires: Aleem Dar I.L. Howell   Points: India 2 Bermuda 0
Toss: Bermuda

GROUP D: WEST INDIES v ZIMBABWE
SABINA PARK, KINGSTON JAMAICA: WEST INDIES WON BY SIX WICKETS

At a still sombre Sabina Park the West Indies did enough to comfortably defeat Zimbabwe. The match moved forward in fits and starts and the performance of the home team was rated well down on what it had been against Pakistan. With their captain, Brian Lara guiding them home the West Indies won by six wickets with 13 balls to spare.

They were in front in the match from the time Lara won the toss, inserted Zimbabwe and his new-ball bowlers, Daren Powell and Jerome Taylor had removed the stumps of both opening batsmen by the middle of the third over. Zimbabwe was 2/2, but from there the West Indies were in the words of their coach, Bennett King, 'scrappy'.

They bowled 15 wides of which Jerome Taylor was the worst offender with seven. This allowed the Zimbabweans to battle their way out of an unpromising situation.

Young wicketkeeper batsman, Brendan Taylor, took root at the crease for nearly 40 overs while compiling a steady even half-century. He and the more aggressive, Sean Williams, later named Man of the Match, put some substance into the total with their 82 run fifth wicket partnership. Then after Taylor was stranded mid pitch in a running mix up Williams and another youngster, Elton Chigumbra increased the total by 60 in the final nine overs, taking advantage of the width regularly on offer from the bowlers.

Zimbabwe reached 202, a very unlikely target at 2/2 and even later at 4/59 in the eighteenth over. But the wicket was sound and the West Indian batting had enough quality to get to 203 without anything but one or two very minor alarms.

Chris Gayle and Shivnarine Chanderpaul made a steady start before Gayle went from 18 to 36 from the first three balls of the 14th over. The lanky home town left-hander twice clouted Tawanda Mupariwa over long on, once onto the stand roof, and also smashed a shorter ball over mid wicket for six.

That lifted the spirits of the nine thousand strong crowd. Both openers fell, though, at 73. Then Ramnaresh Sarwan and Marlon Samuels also got out after getting a start and the West Indies were just wobbling slightly at 4/129 from 33 overs.

A steady Lara and a more fluent Dwayne Bravo steadied the ship and guided the West Indies to victory. The only real chances to change the result came and went when the Zimbabweans missed a couple of clear opportunities to run out Lara.

The West Indian captain, in fact, finished the match with a sweet trademark cover driven four and a lofted on-drive over mid wicket for six. The West Indies would progress to the Super Eights stage. Zimbabwe's destiny was now out of their own hands.

ZIMBABWE		WEST INDIES	
V. Sibanda b Powell	1	C. H. Gayle c Sibanda b Mpofu	40
F. Kasteni b Taylor	0	S. Chanderpaul c Sibanda b Chigumbura	21
C. J. Chibhaba b Taylor	12	R. R. Sarwan c & b Ireland	12
B. R.M. Taylor (wk) run out	50	M. N. Samuels c Chibhabha b Mupariwa	28
S. Matsikenyeri c Powell b Smith	16	B. C. Lara (capt) not out	44
S. C. Williams not out	70	D. J. Bravo not out	37
E. Chigumbura not out	30	Extras Lb10 W10 Nb2	22
Extras B1 Lb7 W15	23	(47.5 overs)	4/204
(50 overs)	5/202	Did not bat: D. R. Smith, D. Ramdin (wk) , J. E. Taylor,	
Did not bat: *P. Utseya (capt), T. Mupariwa, C. B. Mpofu, A.		D. B.L. Powell, C. D. Collymore	
J. Ireland		1/73 2/73 3/106 4/129	
1/0 2/2 3/31 4/59 5/142		Bowling: Mpofu 9-1-34-1; Ireland 7-0-38-1;	
Bowling: Powell 6-1-51-1; Taylor 10-0-42-2;		Mupariwa 9-2-34-1; Chigumbura 9.5-0-45-1;	
Collymore 9-0-29-0; Smith 5-0-28-1; Gayle 10-1-32-0;		Uteseya 10-1-26-0; Williams 3-0-17-0	
Samuels 10-1-48-0			

Umpires: I.J. Gould S.J.A. Taufel

Toss: West Indies   Points: West Indies 2 Zimbabwe 0

New Zealand guaranteed their place in the Super Eights with a very comfortable 148 run win over Kenya. They were sent in, were very briefly challenged, then compiled a ground record 7/331 from 50 overs.

There was plenty of big hitting on view from the Kiwi batsmen. Together they thumped 12 sixes, but once more it has to be said, not many people saw the match live.

After all players observed a minute's silence, Lou Vincent was caught at second slip in the first over from Thomas Odoyo. Stephen Fleming and Ross Taylor, though, were soon dominating the bowling. Fleming three times deposited short balls over the leg-side boundary while Taylor's stroke play was as exhilarating as ever. He would eventually win the Man of the Match Award for his 85. The total was advanced to 105 when from the first ball of the 21st over Fleming called a run to short fine leg that wasn't there. Not that the innings missed a beat with the departure of the New Zealand captain.

Taylor continued on his merry way and Scott Styris backed up beautifully following his great innings against England. The third wicket partnership was 87 in 14 overs.

Taylor, latterly in need of a runner due to a strained hamstring, was next to go and that brought in Craig McMillan who really took out the long handle. His 48 ball innings of 71 included three fours and five big sixes before he holed out in the final over of the innings.

Kenya's attack picked up seven wickets and when Odoyo bowled Jacob Oram he claimed his 100th one-day international victim. He became the first man to do so without playing a Test. However the Kenyans missed four catches and when Daniel Vettori scored boundaries off the final two balls of the innings Kenya needed a mountainous 332 to win.

Within a dozen overs they were 4/29 and such thoughts of victory were fanciful. Michael Mason, in the New Zealand side for Jeetan Patel, quickly trapped David Obuya in front, Lou Vincent's underarm throw from cover ran out Morris Ouma then Mason struck again having key Kenyan batsman Steve Tikolo caught by Daniel Vettori from a skied shot to mid off.

James Franklin soon picked up the fourth wicket. His next victim was the tenth of the innings, but it did not arrive for another 37 overs. Once the shine had been removed the Kenyans were much harder to shift and Ravi Shah batted very nicely while hitting eight fours and two sixes on way to 71. The heat, though, had already gone out of the match by then.

NEW ZEALAND		KENYA	
L. Vincent c Tikolo b Odoyo	0	M. A.Ouma (wk) run out	4
S. P. Fleming (capt) run out	60	D. O. Obuya lbw b Mason	1
L. R. P. L. Taylor c & b Tikolo	85	R. D. Shah c & b Vettori	71
S. B. Styris c Mishra b Onyango	63	S. O. Tikolo (capt) c Vettori b Mason	7
C. D. McMillan c Tikolo b Ongondo	71	T. Mishra c Fleming b Franklin	2
J. D. P. Oram b Odoyo	3	C. O. Obuya run out	21
B. B.McCullum (wk) c varaiya b Ongondo	6	T. M. Odoyo c Oram b Bond	42
D. L. Vettori not out	14	J. K. Kamande b Vettori	12
J. E.C. Franklin not out	0	L. N. Onyango run out	6
Extras Lb3 W21 Nb5	29	P. J. Ongondo c & b Franklin	4
(50 overs)	7/331	H. A. Varaiya not out	1
Did not bat: S. E. Bond, M. J. Mason		Extras Lb2 W2 Nb8	12
1/0 2/105 3/192 4/274 5/280 6/307 7/321		(49.2 overs)	183
Bowling: Odoyo 10-0-55-2; Ongondo 10-0-64-2;		1/4 2/8 3/26 4/29 5/76 6/122 7/149 8/167 9/179 10/183	
Onyango 8-0-63-1; Kamande 9-0-61-0; Varaiya 7-0-40-0;		Bowling: Mason 9-0-29-2; Bond 8-2-19-1; Franklin	
Tikolo 6-0-45-1		7.2-2-20-2; McMillan 10-0-39-0; Vettori 10-0-45-2;	
		Oram 5-0-29-0	

Umpires: B.R. Doctrove R.E. Koertzen

Toss: Kenya   Points: New Zealand 2 Kenya 0

GROUP A: SCOTLAND v SOUTH AFRICA
WARNER PARK, BASSETERRE, St KITTS: SOUTH AFRICA WON BY SEVEN WICKETS

It is a measure of the disparity between these sides that Scotland was assessed as having done well to bat their full 50 allocated overs against South Africa. No matter that they only compiled a mediocre 186 and that South Africa had surpassed their score within 24 overs. They had made their highest ever World Cup score and kept the game going well into the afternoon.

Graeme Smith, winning the toss against his old King Edwards Johannesburg school chum, Ryan Watson, sent Scotland in to bat. Watson, who also went to school with Mark Boucher, was standing in for the usual Scottish captain, Craig Wright, who had flown home to attend the funeral of an aunt. Smith may have hoped for a prompt removal of the opposition but he found Scotland were in a stubborn mood.

Neither Makhaya Ntini nor Shaun Pollock could make a breakthrough and it was the 12th over, Andrew Hall's first, before Majid Haq edged to slip.

Hall and Charl Langeveldt eventually picked up five of the six wickets that fell to bowlers.

Watson, after a hard fought 31, was run out by a direct hit throw from cover from A.B. de Villiers and Paul Hoffman was caught short of the crease from the final ball of the innings.

The Scottish tail, making up for the barely three runs per over lethargy of the top order and with Dougie Brown holding firm at one end, had rattled up 55 runs from the last five overs.

Possibly chastened by his side's inability to dismiss Scotland, Graeme Smith, launched South Africa's reply with a straight drive and a leg side clip that both went for four in the first over.

And that pretty much remained the rate throughout the innings. Smith and de Villiers, who hit 25 balls between them to and beyond the boundary, put on 134 in 16 overs. De Villiers finally perished at long on for 62, but Smith continued, first with Ashwell Prince, then Justin Kemp until South Africa were within eight runs of victory and he needed nine for his hundred.

But he then miscued another leg-side hit from the spinner Majid Haq, leaving Kemp to complete the game in decisive fashion by hitting left-arm spinner, Glenn Rogers for a four then a six over long on.

Graeme Smith said after the game and referring to their next match against Australia, "The World Cup is really starting for us now." Then he went fishing.

SCOTLAND		SOUTH AFRICA	
D. F. Watts c Smith b Langeveldt	24	G. C.Smith (capt) c Rogers b Haq	91
R. M. Haq c Boucher b Hall	13	A. B. de Villiers c Brown b Rogers	62
R. R. Watson (capt) run out	31	A. G. Prince c M. Callum b Haq	21
G. M. Hamilton c deVilliers b Hall	4	J. M. Kemp not out	12
N. F.I. M. Callum b Langeveldt	1	S. M. Pollock not out	0
D. R. Brown not out	45	Eztras B1 W1	2
C. J.O. Smith (wk) b Pollock	15	(23.2 overs)	3/188
J. A.R. Blain c Kemp b Hall	23	Did not bat: J. H. Kallis, H. H. Gibbs, M. V.Boucher (wk),	
P. J.C. Hoffman run out	18	A. J. Hall, C. K. Langeveldt, M. Ntini	
Extras B2 Lb4 W5 Nb1	12	1/134 2/162 3/179	
(50 overs)	8/186	Bowling: Hoffman 3-0-21-0; Blain 4-0-32-0; Nel 3-0-24-0;	
Did not bat: G. A. Rogers, J. D. Nel		Brown 2-0-20-0; Haq 6-0-43-2; Rogers 5.2-0-47-1	
1/35 2/43 3/63 4/71 5/84 6/113 7/163 8/186			
Bowling: Pollock 10-1-25-1; Ntini 9-0-25-0; Hall 10-2-48-3;			
Langeveldt 10-1-48-2; Kallis 8-0-21-0; Smith 3-0-13-0			

Umpires: M.R. Benson E.A.R. de Silva

Toss: South Africa   Points: South Africa 2 Scotland 0

WEDNESDAY 21 MARCH 2007
GROUP B: BANGLADESH v SRI LANKA
QUEENS PARK OVAL, PORT-OF-SPAIN, TRINIDAD: SRI LANKA WON BY 198 RUNS

Sri Lanka gave an indication they might be a long-term force in the 2007 World Cup when they crushed Bangladesh by 198 runs at Port of Spain.

The Bangladeshis had a huge reality check when they sent Sri Lanka in, were belted around to the tune of 318 runs and then capitulated themselves for just 112. If anything the margin flattered them as they had a small target reduction due to a rain interruption and their innings only stretched out to 37 overs after being 4/26, partly because Mahela Jayawardene thought he would share the late bowling duties amongst seven different players.

Sanath Jayasuriya did most to assert Sri Lanka's dominance with a typically aggressive century from the opening position. He did the bulk of the scoring in an opening partnership of 98 with Upal Tharanga. That stand was crucial on a wicket that gave some early assistance to the Bangladeshi new-ball attack. The powerful left-hander cut and pulled his way to his 24th ODI century, making him second on the all time list. He overcame a knee injury on 83 that required temporary retirement and treatment to hit seven sixes. That placed him highest of all time on that list.

Jayawardene, although a little scratchy, Sangakkara and a very fluent Silva all added further substance to Jayasuriya's Man of the Match performance. Bangladesh hopes of a good start to their reply were dashed when Chaminda Vaas got a perfect left-arm in-swinger through Shahriar Nafees's defences in the first over and Tamim Iqbal was caught behind off a fiery Malinga lifter in the fourth over. Bangladesh were 2/7 then after a momentary counter attack from Aftab Ahmed 3/20.

Rain arrived during the 28th over to briefly interrupt the one-sided contest, but once play resumed the game continued in the same direction. No real effort was made by Bangladesh to maintain the run rate and Muttiah Muralitharan conceded just 13 runs off the bat in his nine overs.

Mohammad Ashraful's 45 allowed the total to creep into three figures.

The attendance given for the match was exactly 9,500. That was the identical figure announced for the Bangladesh v India match, also at Queens Park. It is to be wondered if they were also the exact same people in the exact same seats or the figure was just a coincidence.

SRI LANKA		BANGLADESH	
W. U. Tharanga c Aftab Ahmed b Mohammad Rafique	26	Tamim Iqbal c Sangakkara b Malinga	6
S. T. Jayasuriya c Habibul Bashar b Abdur Razak	109	Shahriar Nafees lbw b Vaas	0
D. P. M. D. Jayawardene (c) c A. Ahmed b Shakib Al Hasan	46	Mushfiqur Rahim (wk) c Dilshan b Maharoof	6
K. C. Sangakkara (wk) c Tamim Iqbal b Syed Rasel	56	Aftab Ahmed c Jayasuriya b Malinga	12
L. P. C. Silva not out	52	Shakib Al Hasan b Muralitharan	4
R. P. Arnold not out	5	Habibul Bashar (capt) run out	18
Extras Lb11 W10 Nb3	24	Mohammad Ashraful not out	45
(50 overs)	4/318	Mashrafe Mortaza c Tharanga b Arnold	7
Did not bat: T. M. Dilshan, M. T. Maharoof, W. P. U. J.C. Vaas,		Mohammad Rafique c Maharoof b Dilshan	7
S. L. Malinga, M. Muralitharan		Abdur Razzak c Sangakkara b Malinga	0
1/98 2/202 3/261 4/300		Syed Rasel run out	0
Bowling: Mashrafe Mortaz 10-0-66-0; Syed Rasel 10-0-58-1;		Extras Lb2 W4 Nb1	7
Abdur Razzak 10-0-86-1; Mohammad Rafique 10-0-48-1;		(37 overs)	112
Shakib Al Hasan 10-0-49-1		1/1 2/7 3/20 4/26 5/41 6/66 7/80 8/101 9/111 10/112	
		Bowling: Vaas 7-4-11-1; Malinga 6-0-27-3;	
		Maharoof 7-1-26-1; Muralitharan 9-0-15-1; Jayasuriya	
		1.5-0-2-0; Arnold 3.1-0-17-1; Dilshan 3-0-12-1	

Umpires: S.J. Davis D.J. Harper

Toss: Bangladesh   Points: Sri Lanka 2 Bangladesh 0

GROUP D: PAKISTAN v ZIMBABWE
SABINA PARK, KINGSTON, JAMAICA: PAKISTAN WON BY 93 RUNS

An emotional Pakistan side signed off from the 2007 World Cup with a performance that would have made their late lamented coach proud. In what was a tearful Inzamam-ul-Haq's last one-day international, Pakistan lifted after agreeing to play despite being part of a police investigation and in mourning for Bob Woolmer.

They belted their way to 349 after being sent in by Prosper Utseya and then were untroubled to bowl out their opponents for 99 in less than 20 overs. In front of yet another small crowd Man of the Match and Pakistani opener, Imran Nazir, made an exhilarating 160 from 121 balls. It was the highest individual World Cup score by a Pakistani and the highest innings score by a Pakistani team in the premier tournament. Imran hit eight sixes, to equal the best ever effort by Ricky Ponting in the 2003 final.

He added 70 with Inzamam in 10 overs. The exiting Pakistani captain gave the fans a 32-minute departing treat, hitting three sixes with trademark shots over long on, long off and mid wicket. He then miscued to mid off and walked off to a line of handshakes from the opposition and a guard of honour from his teammates.

Pakistan hit 16 sixes and maintained a run rate of seven per over, but still managed to get bowled out by the 50th over. Gary Brent picked up three wickets with his left-arm spin as did Elton Chigumbura in less than seven overs. No one could curb Imran who pummelled the onside boundary between mid wicket and long on. Once he was caught by Chigumbra at long on, but the fieldsman' momentum just forced him back over the boundary rope.

Zimbabwe's reply was a non-event. Bowling with genuine pace and lift Umar Gul and Mohammad Sami, assisted by slips catches, two to Inzamam, had reduced Zimbabwe to 3/14 by the sixth over.

Then it rained for two hours. Upon resumption the reduced target was 163 from 58 balls. Chigumbura responded by making 27 in 11 balls before missing a straight one from Shahid Afridi whose three quick wickets included his 200th in ODI's.

Mohammad Yousef took his first and last one-day international wicket. Last man, Chris Mpofu lofted his first delivery to cover. Inzamam took the catch. Everyone including umpire Simon Taufel smiled. It was a nice little window in what had been a terrible time for the Pakistanis.

PAKISTAN		ZIMBABWE	
Kamran Akmal (wk) c Taylor b Chigumbra	15	V. Sibanda c Imran Nazir b Umar Gul	0
Imran Nazir c Matsikenyeri b Mpofu	160	C. J. Chibabha c Inzaman-ul-Haq b Umar Gul	3
Shoaib Malik c Cjibhabha b Williams	21	F. Kasteni c Inzamam-ul-Haq b Mohammad Sami	9
Inzamam-ul-Haq (capt) c Williams b Mupariwa	37	B. R.M. Taylor (wk) c Younis Khan b Danish Kaneria	13
Mohammad Yousef c & b Brent	3	S. Matsikenyeri run out	18
Younis Khan run out	28	E. Chigumbura b Shahid Afridi	27
Shahid Afridi b Brent	16	S. C. Williams c Umar Gul b Danish Kaneria	11
Mohammad Sami c Utseya b Brent	5	G. B. Brent b Shahid Afridi	9
Iftikhar Anjum c Matsikenyeri b Chigumbra	32	P. Utseya (capt) not out	4
Umar Gul b Chigumbra	10	T. Mupariwa b Shahid Afridi	0
Danish Kaneria not out	6	C. B. Mpofu c Inzamam-ul-Haq b Mohammad Yousef	1
Extras Lb2 W12 Nb2	16	Extras Lb1 W1 Nb2	4
(49.5 overs)	349	(19.1 overs)	99

1/31 2/88 3/158 4/170 5/252 6/285 7/295 8/301 9/324 10/349

Bowling: Mpofu 10-1-74-1; Mupariwa 10-1-57-1; Chigumbra 6.5-1-50-3; Brent 10-0-68-3; Williams 6-0-41-1; Utseya 6-0-46-0; Chibhabha 1-0-11-0

1/0 2/12 3/14 4/45 5/45 6/77 7/93 8/94 9/94 10/99

Bowling: Umar Gul 5-1-10-2; Mohammad Sami 5-0-15-1; Danish Kaneria 4-0-48-2; Shahid Afridi 4-0-20-3; Younis Khan 1-0-5-0; Mohammad Yousef 0.1-0-0-1

Umpires: B.G. Jerling S.J.A. Taufel

Toss: Zimbabwe   Points: Pakistan 2 Zimbabwe 0

Kiwi opener, Lou Vincent, scored his first run of the World Cup and exactly another hundred as New Zealand cruised to an easy 114 run win over Canada. In a match oozing goodwill Vincent claimed the arrival of his wife in St Lucia made the difference to his form while the resting of fast bowler, Shane Bond, meant the Canadian batsmen could go home (wherever that was in the world) with the contentment of a few more runs behind them.

The gestures of generosity were immediately evident when John Davison won the toss and sent New Zealand in to bat. Vincent and Stephen Fleming showed their gratitude by putting on 142 for the first wicket, the Kiwi's highest ever World Cup opening partnership. The innings began with two maidens then Vincent planted Anderson Cummins over cover for six to open his and New Zealand's account. Fleming actually scored the higher percentage of runs in the stand which was boosted by another generous Canadian gesture; plenty of wides.

The Kiwi captain after a run per ball 66 chipped spinner Kevin Sandher to mid wicket, but Vincent stayed with Peter Fulton for a second wicket stand of 80 in 14 overs. He then went on to his century in three hours with nine fours and a six. A leading edge from Vincent floated the ball back to a Davison off-spinner and at 6-278 from 43 overs New Zealand still had a little work to do to bat Canada out of the game. Brendan McCullum and Jacob Oram responded by putting on 85. McCullum's contribution included five sixes and he reached his half-century in 20 balls, pipping Mark Boucher's 21 ball effort against the Netherlands six days before to become the World Cup's fastest ever. The stand took New Zealand to 363, their highest World Cup total.

Davison led Canada's reply with a stunning half-century in 23 balls. He and Geoff Barnett put on 76 in less than ten overs, the ideal launching pad. Ashish Bagai and Ian Billcliff also batted well so that Canada reached 2/188.

But quick scoring from spin pair Daniel Vettori and Jeetan Patel was harder. By the time an advancing Bagai was bowled by Vettori 162 runs were required from 15 overs. Then in seven balls the score slipped from 3/201 to 6/207 and the contest was over.

It only remained for Sunil Dhaniram to get whacked on the wrist by a Jacob Oram full toss and Patel to mop up the tail. New Zealand was then able to turn their attention to more serious opponents ahead in the Super Eights. They had earned two useful points to carry across in the imminent phase two of the 2007 World Cup.

NEW ZEALAND		CANADA	
L. Vincent c & b Davison	101	J. M. (capt) Davison c & b Mason	52
S. P. Fleming (capt) c Bilcliff b Sandher	66	G. E.F. Barnett c McCullum b Vettori	40
P. G. Fulton lbw b Sandher	47	A. Bagai (wk) b Vettori	37
S. B. Styris c Bagai b Samad	28	I. S. Billcliff b Styris	50
C. D. McMillan c Samad b Davison	10	A. M. Samad run out	9
J. D. P. Oram not out	35	A. A. Mulla lbw b Vettori	0
B. B.McCullum (wk) not out	52	S. Dhaniram retired hurt	17
Extras B1 Lb5 W17 Nb1	24	U. Bhatti b Patel	10
(50 overs)	5/363	A. C. Cummins not out	9
Did not bat: D. L. Vettori, D. R. Tuffey, J. S. Patel, M. J.		K. T. Sandher b Patel	2
Mason		H. Osinde b Patel	0
1/142 2/222 3/253 4/266 5/278		Extras B4 Lb5 W5 Nb9	23
Bowling: Cummins 10-1-59-0; Bhatti 5.3-1-25-0; Samad		(49.2 overs)	249
2.3-0-31-1; Osinde 4-0-45-0; Sandher 10-0-58-2;		1/76 2/110 3/188 4/201 5/206 6/207 7/245 8/249 9/249	
Davison 10-0-67-2; Dhaniram 8-0-72-0		Bowling: Tuffey 6-0-40-0; Mason 8-0-60-1; Oram 7-1-16-0;	
		Patel 9.2-0-25-3; Vettori 10-0-57-3; Styris 6-0-21-1;	
		McMillan 3-0-21-0	

Umpires: Asad Rauf B.R. Doctrove

Toss: Canada   Points: New Zealand 2 Canada 0

GROUP A: SCOTLAND v NETHERLANDS
WARNER PARK BASSETERRE, St KITTS: NETHERLANDS WON BY EIGHT WICKETS

The Netherlands made short work of Scotland in this minnows' World Cup farewell match in St Kitts. Fortunately no-one over stayed their welcome.

The whole contest lasted less than 60 overs as the Scots were knocked over for 136 in 34 overs and the Dutch easily chased their target down in 24 overs with eight wickets in hand.

After being sent in to bat by Jeroen Smits, captain due to the self imposed omission of Luuk van Troost, Scotland made a hash of coping with the new-ball. Billy Stelling, another well travelled South African with a huge collection of caps and jumpers, bowling with accuracy and movement precipitated a top order collapse that left Scotland on 4/15 by the seventh over.

Back in the side after being out with a back injury against Australia, Stelling had Navdeep Poonia caught behind from the second ball of the match and later trapped Gavin Hamilton and Dougie Brown in front with consecutive deliveries. His pace barely reached 80 miles per hour, but he was penetrative enough to be awarded the Man of the Match prize at the end of play.

Scotland made no real recovery and at 8/83 any sort of three-figure total looked unlikely. But John Blain held firm at one end and Glenn Rogers was able to hit five boundaries in his top score 26 and get Scotland to a slightly more respectable 136.

Blain struck twice with the new-ball as the Netherlands began their chase. But the Dutch team, another to have more than half their players born elsewhere, were already scoring freely and batted with total confidence.

Bas Zuiderant, using the late cut to effect, and Ryan ten Doeschate added an unbroken 103 for the third wicket in 18 overs. The talented Essex all-rounder challenged Stelling as Man of Match with his attractive boundary laden 70.

He hit thirteen fours and also slapped a Rogers left-arm spinning delivery onto the roof of the stand at long on for good measure.

Holland completed their second ever World Cup win as they departed their third tournament. Scotland was winless as they had been in 1999 and had not reached 200 in any World Cup match.

SCOTLAND		NETHERLANDS	
N. S. Poonia c Smits b Stelling	0	B. Zuiderant not out	43
R. M. Haq b Reekers	6	D. J. Reekers c Wright b Blain	9
R. R. Watson c & b de Leede	16	E. S. Szwarczynski c Smith b Blain	12
G. M. Hamilton lbw b Stelling	4	R. N. ten Doeschate not out	70
D. R. Brown lbw b Stelling	0	Extras Lb4 W2	6
N. F.I. M. Callum c Stelling b Jonkman	24	(23.5 overs)	2/140
C. J.O. Smith (wk) b Jonkman	19	1/18 2/37	
C. M. Wright (capt) st Smits b Mohammad Kashif	1	Did not bat: D. L.S. van Bunge, T. B.M. de Leede,	
J. A.R. Blain not out	18	M. B.S. J onkman, W. F. Stelling, P. W. Borren,	
G. A. Rogers c Smits b Mohammad Kashif	26	J. Smits (capt/wk), Mohammad Kashif	
P. J.C. Hoffman c ten Doeschate b van Bunge	7	Bowling: Hoffman 4-0-26-0; J. A.R. Blain 5-0-29-2;	
Extras Lb5 W8 Nb2	15	C. M.Wright, 4-1-17-0; G. A.Rogers 3-1-15-0; D.	
(34.1 overs)	136	R.Brown 4-0-20-0; Haq 3.5-0-29-0	
1/0 2/9 3/15 4/15 5/39 6/77 7/83 8/83 9/117 10/136			
Bowling: Stelling 8-3-12-3; Reekers 6-0-23-1; de			
Leede 4-0-24-1; Jonkman 5-1-22-2; Mohammad			
Kashif 7-2-29-2; ten Doeschate 3-0-17-0; van Bunge 1.1-0-4-1			

Umpires: E.A.R.Silva A.L.Hill

Toss: Netherlands   Points: Netherlands 2 Scotland 0

FRIDAY 23 MARCH 2007
GROUP B: INDIA v SRI LANKA
QUEENS PARK, PORT-OF-SPAIN, TRINIDAD: SRI LANKA WON BY 69 RUNS

In the most important match of the 2007 World Cup to date, Sri Lanka proved too good for India, sending the game's biggest money spinners home before many of their fans had a chance to pack their bags and arrive in the Caribbean.

It was a tense and hard fought match, very much worthy of any World Cup tournament.

For the Indian team, their captain Rahul Dravid and their Australian coach, Greg Chappell, the recriminations of the media, ex-players and millions upon millions of disappointed fans weighed heavily. For Sri Lanka it was another scalp on way to a genuine tilt at the title.

Dravid, despite India's poor record when asking the opposition to go in first, sent Sri Lanka in to bat after he won the toss. He would have been pleased that Sanath Jayasuriya, Mahela Jayawardene and Kumar Sanakkara were removed by Zaheer Khan and Agit Agarkar for just 28 runs between them. It was the less heralded, Upal Tharanga, though, who provided the Sri Lanka top order with the solidity required.

The stylish left-hander concentrated on batting through overs, only occasionally punctuating the field with his cover drives. He hit nines fours before he was trapped in front by a full-pitched Sachin Tendulkar medium paced wobbler.

That made Sri Lanka 4/133 in the 33rd over. It brought together Chamara Silva and Tillakaratne Dilshan who put on a crucial 83 runs for the fifth wicket in 13 overs.

They eventually fell to catches by wicketkeeper Mahendra Singh Dhoni at the same score, 216. But enough time, confidence and momentum was left for Russell Arnold and Chaminda Vaas to lift the total by a further 38 in the last four overs.

India needed 255 runs or an unlikely win by Bermuda over Bangladesh to save their skins in the tournament. Commentators kept saying the wicket was not a factor, although, the outfield was a little on the sluggish side.

Indian opener, Robin Uthappa coped reasonably well. His partner, Saurav Ganguly, however, could not get moving. He had succeeded in a role as innings backbone against Bangladesh and Bermuda, but Sri Lanka choked off his runs completely. Uthappa fell when hit a hard drive straight back to Vaas who took a great caught and bowled, while Ganguly had only made 7 in 23 deliveries when he miscued the same bowler to an agile Muralitharan at deepish mid off.

Big paceman, Dilhara Fernando, then immediately broke through the defences of the out of form Tendulkar to leave India 3/43 in the 12th over.With Sehwag, having regained some batting mojo, and the resolute Dravid then digging in India remained in the contest.They were on the verge of bringing up the 100 in the 25th over when the match took its decisive turn.

Concentrating on bowling doosras around the wicket, Muralitharan had Sehwag caught at slip for 48. Five overs later Yuraj Singh called for a run as Dravid played the ball to short fine-leg. The Indian captain didn't respond and Yuvraj was stranded. Almost immediately Dhoni on the back foot misread a Muralitharan top-spinner and was plumb lbw.

India was now 6/112 in the 29th over. Dravid fought on and in one Lasith Malinga over hit four fours. He got to 60 then lofted Jayasuriya to Man of the Match Muralitharan at long on. The game lingered on until the 44th over of the innings, but India and lots of locals hoping to make money from their supporters, were shot.

Greg Chappell on the verge of finishing as Indian coach, and his wife Judy, were put under police guard for their own safety.

SRI LANKA			INDIA	
W. U. Tharanga lbw b Tendulkar	64		R. V. Uthappa c & b Vaas	18
S. T. Jayasuriya c Agarkar b Khan	6		S. C. Ganguly c Muralitharan b Vaas	7
D. P. M. D. Jayawardene (capt) c Dhoni b Agarkar	7		V. Sehwag c Jayawardene b Muralitharan	48
K. C. Sangakkara (wk) c Patel b Ganguly	15		S. R. Tendulkar b Fernando	0
L. P. C. Silva c Dhoni b Khan	59		R. Dravid (capt) c Muralitharan b Jayasuriya	60
T. M. Dilshan c Dhoni b Patel	38		Yuvraj Singh run out	6
R. P. Arnold not out	19		M. S.Dhoni (wk) lbw b Muralitharan	0
W. P. U. J.C. Vaas not out	19		A. B. Agarkar c Arnold b Malinga	10
Extras Lb11 W14 Nb2	27		Harbhajan Singh not out	17
(50 overs)	6/254		Z. Khan c Malinga b Muralitharan	1
Did not bat: M. Muralitharan, S. L. Malinga, C. R.D.			M. M. Patel c Vaas b Dilshan	10
Fernando			Extras Lb1 W7	8
1/33 2/53 3/92 4/133 5/216 6/216			(43.5 overs)	185
Bowling: Khan 10-0-49-2; Agarkar 8-1-33-1; Patel 10-1-46-1;			1/25 2/43 3/44 4/98 5/112 6/112 7/136 8/159 9/161	
Harbhajhan Singh 10-0-53-0; Ganguly 4-0-22-1;			10/185	
Tendulkar 8-0-40-1			Bowling: Vaas 8-1-39-2; Malinga 8-0-39-1; Fernando	
			6.2-0-32-1; Muralitharan 10-0-41-3; Jayasuriya 9-0-31-1;	
			Dilshan 2.1-1-2-1	

Umpires: Aleem Dar D.J. Harper

Toss: India   Points: Sri Lanka 2 India 0

GROUP D: WEST INDIES v IRELAND
SABINA PARK, KINGSTON, JAMAICA
WEST INDIES WON BY EIGHT WICKETS

Once again revealing his ability to adapt his game to any situation, Shivnarine Chanderpaul compiled a stunning unbeaten 102 to guide the West Indies to an easy eight wicket win over Ireland in their final group stage match.

The slight Guyanese left-hander completed his maiden World Cup ton in his fourth tournament at almost a run a ball as the hosts raced to their target of 190 in 38 overs. With both sides already assured of progression to the Super Eights, the match at Sabina Park came as close as any game to the party mode so publicized pre-tournament by the West Indian authorities.

And it was Chanderpaul who got the crowd throbbing with his ten fours and four sixes. He took four consecutive boundaries, including two pulls, a glance and a ripping straight drive, off promising young Irish fast bowler, Boyd Rankin, and lofted his sixes over long on and once, off a top edged sweep, behind third man! Chanderpaul lost opening partner, Chris Gayle, in the fifth over, but put on 119 with Ramaresh Sarwan to remove any doubt about the result.

Ireland had batted first after winning the toss. They were without their captain Trent Johnston due to a shoulder injury and lost Will Porterfield for his second duck of the tournament, caught at slip in the second over of the match.

Jeremy Bray's back foot strength was evident, but two overs were lost to a rain interruption at 6/161 in the 46th. Even before that, though, the Irish batsmen, including Bray, seemed to get out just when they were established.

Daren Powell's new-ball spell was sharp and accurate and Ian Bradshaw came into the side and kept a tight rein on the scoring with his left-arm medium pace. Gayle may have missed out with the bat, however, he had an influence on the result as the Irish batsman could make little headway against his off-spin.

Finally Marlon Samuels, on his home ground, put a full-toss from Andrew White over mid wicket for six to send the majority of the 12,000 fans home happy and optimistic that the West Indies could make an impact in the second stage of the tournament.

IRELAND		WEST INDIES	
J. P. Bray c sub (Simmons) b Taylor	41	C. H. Gayle c White b Langford-Smith	18
W. T.S. Portergfield c Gayle b Powell	0	S. Chanderpaul not out	102
E. J. G. Morgan c Ramdin b Powell	18	R. R. Sarwan c K. J. O'Brien b M. Callan	36
N. J. O'Brien (wk) c Ramdin b Bradshaw	11	M. N. Samuels not out	27
A. C. Botha c Ramdin b Gayle	28	Extras Lb1 W6	7
K. J. O'Brien c Sarwan b Gayle	17	(38.1 overs)	2/190
A. R. White b Bravo	18	Did not bat: B. C.Lara (capt), D. J. Bravo, D. R. Smith,	
W. K. M. Callan not out	20	D. Ramdin (wk), I. D.R. Bradshaw, J. E. Taylor, D. B.L. Powell	
J. F. Mooney c Ramdin b Bravo	0	1/24 2/143	
D. Langford-Smith not out	8	Bowling: Langford-Smith 9-1-33-1; Rankin 5-0-38-0;	
Extras B4 Lb10 W6 Nb2	22	Botha 6-0-35-0; Mooney 4-1-22-0; M. Callan 10-0-35-1; K.	
(48 overs)	8/183	J.O'Brien 3-0-13-0; White 1.1-0-13-0	

Did not bat: W. B. Rankin

1/3 2/61 3/76 4/82 5/129 6/139 7/163 8/163

Bowling: Taylor 8-0-37-1; Powell 9-2-24-2;

Bradshaw 9-0-27-1; Bravo 7-1-35-2; Gayle 10-0-23-2;

Samuels 5-0-23-0

Umpires: B.F. Bowden I.J. Gould

Toss: Ireland   Points: West Indies 2 Ireland 0

SATURDAY 24 MARCH 2007
GROUP A: AUSTRALIA v SOUTH AFRICA
WARNER PARK, BASSETERRE, St KITTS: AUSTRALIA WON BY 83 RUNS

Australia asserted itself as a 2007 World Cup power when it defeated South Africa by 83 runs in their Group A match at Basseterre. Prior to the tournament, Ricky Ponting's side had conceded their No.1 ranking as the top one-day side in the world to the Proteas. But a powerhouse batting display on the toy sized Warner Park ground, eventually proved too much for South Africa on this occasion.

It was a heavyweight clash worthy of the world's No.1 and No.2 teams. For a time it appeared the game might rival the classic from Johannesburg a year earlier when South Africa successfully chased 434. Recently Australia had also been unable to protect totals of over 300, but this time superior out cricket and more variety in their bowling options saw them prevail in the final phase of the match. After Graeme Smith sent Australia into to bat Adam Gilchrist quickly kick started the innings with a succession of powerful off and cover drives.

Then Matthew Hayden took over. He told his teammates pre-match that he was going to target Shaun Pollock and in fifth over of the match he upheld his promise. A square cut for four was followed by two bangs over the on-side for six. Pollock conceded 17 runs and Australia had 50 runs on the board after just five overs.

Gilchrist eventually misjudged a slower ball from Langeveldt with the total on 106. Hayden, though, continued on to complete a stunning century in 66 balls.

The big Queenslander had had to reclaim his one-day spot that very summer and went into the match with a broken toe. There were no inhibitions, however, as he hit fourteen fours and four sixes, completing the fastest ever World Cup and Australian one-day 100 in the process. Hayden was named Man of the Match, was awarded citizenship of St Kitts and given a life membership of Royal St Kitts Golf Club as a reward for his innings. It was quite a day. When he also holed out to point, Ponting and Michael Clarke maintained the run rage with a stand of 161 in 22 overs. Ponting later said he was dissatisfied with his form, although there were some sweet lofted drives in his run per ball 91. Clarke took some time to establish himself, then accelerated. Many of his most memorable strokes were completed on one knee. A signature square drive was notable and slogs between mid wicket and mid-on four times went into an enthusiastic crowd.

South Africa limited the later damage to some extent, but perhaps suffered from having 48 of the 50 overs bowled by right arm medium-fast to fast-medium bowlers.

Australia's 377 looked huge. Abraham de Villiers soon reduced its apparent magnitude. He and an equally belligerent Smith launched the Protean reply at a cracking rate. Shaun Tait was thumped and Glenn McGrath was struck for three fours from his first three balls by de Villiers; a leg glance, a cover drive and a glide through gully.

Bikini topped South African supporters, many of them girls, yelled with delight at the prospect of another historic run chase as the opening pair raced to 160 in the 21st over. Then the game changed momentum. Shane Watson saved a boundary at square leg and his brilliant direct hit throw found de Villiers short of his ground; the second man to be run out for 92 that day.

Next Graeme Smith began to cramp up so seriously he had to retire for treatment. Jacques Kallis, later criticized by Ponting, batted nicely but totally failed to keep the run rate up at seven or eight an over as required. That allowed the Australian bowlers to get on top. Brad Hogg had Herschelle Gibbs neatly stumped by Gilchrist from a well pitched wrong-un. Tait returned and yorked Mark Boucher and trapped Justin Kemp on the back foot in front of the stumps.

Smith returned but soon top edged a sweep off Hogg.

The threat had passed. By the time Nathan Bracken yorked Makhaya Ntini South Africa had lost 9/74 and Australia's hold over them in the World Cup had been re-established.

It was purely psychological, though, as both sides progressed to the Super Eights.

AUSTRALIA		SOUTH AFRICA	
A. C. Gilchrist (wk) c Gibbs b Langeveldt	42	G. C. Smith (capt) c Gilchrist b Hogg	74
M. L.Hayden c Gibbs b Kallis	101	A. B. de Villers run out	92
R. T. Ponting (capt) c de Villiers b Ntini	91	J. H. Kallis c Clarke b Hogg	48
M. J. Clarke run out	92	H. H. Gibbs st Gilchrist b Hogg	17
A. Symonds b Hall	18	A. G. Prince c Hayden b McGrath	1
M. E. K. Hussey c Kallis b Hall	5	M. V. Boucher (wk) b Tait	22
S. R. Watson not out	14	J. M. Kemp lbw b Tait	1
Extras Lb4 W9 Nb1	14	S. M. Pollock b Watson	7
(50 overs)	6/377	A. J. Hall not out	8
Did not bat: G. B. Hogg, N. W. Bracken, S. W. Tait,		C. K. Langeveldt b Bracken	0
G. D. McGrath		M. Ntini b Bracken	7
1/106 2/167 3/328 4/347 5/353 6/377		Extras W11 Nb1 Pen5	17
Bowling: Pollock 10-0-83-0; Ntini 9-0-68-1;		(48 overs)	294
Langeveldt 10-0-82-1; Hall 10-0-60-2; Smith 2-0-14-0;		1/160 2/220 2/223 4/256 5/264 6/267 7/277 8/279	
Kallis 9-0-66-1		9/280 10/294	
		Bowling: Bracken 9-0-40-2; Tait 10-0-61-2;	
		McGrath 9-0-62-1; Watson 8-1-46-1; Hogg 10-0-61-3;	
		Symonds 2-0-19-0	

Umpires: M.R. Benson S.A. Bucknor

Toss: South Africa   Points: Australia 2 South Africa 0

GROUP C: ENGLAND v KENYA
BEAUSEJOUR STADIUM, GROS ISLET, St LUCIA: ENGLAND WON BY SEVEN WICKETS

England had to win this match to progress to the Super Eight stage and did so by seven wickets without too much prolonged resistance from Kenya. Because of heavy morning rain in Gros Islet the start of the game was delayed and the match reduced to 43 overs per side.

England would have been keyed up because of the need to secure victory and having had a six-day break after their previous match. It was slightly surprising then that Steve Tikolo elected to bat after winning the toss. Not that he was in too much trouble at the crease, but his teammates battled to keep the runs ticking over sufficiently.

Tikolo came in at 2/35 in the 11th over and left at 8/165 in the 41st. He again looked a class above everyone else in the side and hit eight fours in 97 balls before being bowled by a full, fast straight ball by the recalled prodigal, Andrew Flintoff.

No Kenyan partnership reached 40 and the second half of the innings was marred by three run outs. England needed 178 and made the runs with seven wickets and ten overs to spare. The failure of Michael Vaughan at the top of the order was a disappointment and when Ian Bell mistimed a drive to mid off in the ninth over England were 2/53 and the 10,000 English fans in the outer were momentarily quietened.

They may also have 'ooed' a bit when Kevin Pietersen was dropped by wicketkeeper Maurice Ouma off young Mumbai born left-arm spinner Hiren Varaiya's first ball. England would have been 3/76 in the 14th over and in some trouble. From the next three balls from Varaiya, Pietersen hit seven runs, including a clinking cover driven four. He was away and England was troubled no more. Joyce, on way to a Man of the Match Award 75, lofted a six over square leg and a couple of overs later Pietersen swatted Varaiya against the spin over mid wicket for six more.

The Irishman and the South African added 103 for England for the third wicket in less than 20 overs. Tikolo, surely another candidate for Man of the Match, finally bowled Joyce with a doosra before Paul Collingwood settled the issue with three nicely struck boundaries.

KENYA		ENGLAND	
M. A.Ouma (wk) c Collingwood b Anderson	13	E. C. Joyce b Tikolo	75
R. D. Shah b Anderson	4	M. P. Vaughan (capt) c Obuya b Ongondo	1
A. O. Suji c Vaughan b Mahmood	14	I. R. Bell c sub (Bhudia) b Odoyo	16
S. O. Tikolo (capt) b Flintoff	76	K. P. Pietersen not out	56
T. Mishra b Collingwood	0	P. D. Collingwood not out	18
C. O. Obuya run out	10	Extras Lb2 W7 Nb3	12
T. M. Odoyo lbw b Flintoff	4	(33 overs)	3/178
J. K. Kamende b Collingwood	17	Did not bat: A. Flintoff, R. S. Bopara, P. A. Nixon (wk),	
L. N. Onyango run out	10	J. M. Anderson, M. S. Panesar, S. I. Mahmood	
P. J. Ongondo run out	3	1/12 2/52 3/155	
H. A. Varaiya not out	4	Bowling: Odoyo 6-0-27-1; Ongondo 4-0-31-1;	
Extras Lb8 W6 Nb8	22	Onyango 2-0-14-0; Suji 3-0-15-0; Varaiya 6-0-39-0;	
(43 overs)	177	Kamande 5-0-24-0; Tikolo 4-0-18-1; Obuya 3-0-8-0	
1/10 2/35 3/73 4/74 5/99 6/112 7/151 8/165 9/170			
10/177			
Bowling: Anderson 9-0-27-2; Mahmood 9-0-39-1;			
Flintoff 9-0-35-2; Bopara 1-0-7-0; Collingwood 7-0-33-2;			
Panesar 8-0-28-0			

Umpires: R.E. Koertzen P.D. Parker

Toss: Kenya   Points: England 2 Kenya 0

SUNDAY 25 MARCH 2007
GROUP B: BANGLADESH v BERMUDA
QUEENS PARK OVAL, PORT-OF-SPAIN, TRINIDAD: BANGLADESH WON BY SEVEN WICKETS

At a damp, grey and very empty Queens Park Oval, Bangladesh completed an historic victory over Bermuda that took them through for the first time to the second round of a World Cup. Their win also confirmed India's early exit. With so many rain interruptions it was barely a cricket match. The Bangladeshis did what they had to chasing the down the 95 they had been set in 21 overs by Bermuda with seven wickets and 21 balls to spare.

This last of the Group matches coughed and spluttered to an anticipated conclusion with little fanfare. It rained after the toss and the match was reduced to 41 overs. Then, after Bermuda was 1/6 from a couple of overs having been sent in, it rained again and then they returned for a 35 over match. Upon resumption Bermuda slipped and probably slithered to 3/17 and it rained again. There would even be a fourth interruption until the match was reduced to 21 overs per side.

A few effective hits from Dean Minors and Lionel Cann got the total up to 94.

Bangladesh seemingly had a straightforward task, but there were a few early stumbles. Kevin Hurdle ran in from third man and took a superb sliding catch from a Tamim Iqbal miscue, Shahrior edged to slip and Aftab Ahmed was trapped in front of off-stump. Salim Mukuddem, moving the ball both ways, had all three wickets and Bangladesh 3/37 in the 8th over was not a certainty.

There were a couple more lbw shouts and a missed chance or two before Shakib Al Hasan and Mohammad Ashraful eased the tension with an unbroken 59 run stand in 10 overs. For Bermuda Hurdle's great fielding effort was spoilt by his gift of ten wides and no balls in four overs. The damp conditions had made the condition of the ball and bowlers footholds a bit dicy, though.

Finally Shakib lofted Leverock over mid-on for four and Bangladeshi, players and their very patient spectators had something to celebrate.

BERMUDA		BANGLADESH	
S. D. Outridge c Mohammad Rafique b Mashrafe Mortaza	0	Tamim Iqbal c Hurdle b Mukuddem	1
O. L. Pitcher c Habibul Bashar b Shakib Al Hasan	22	Shahrior Nafees c Tucker b Mukuddem	12
D. C.C. Borden c Habibul Bashar b Mashrafe Mortaza	2	Aftab Ahmed lbw b Mukuddem	7
D. L. Hemp c Aftab Ahmed b Syed Rasel	0	Shakib Al Hasan not out	26
I. H. Romaine (capt) lbw b Abdur Razzak	11	Mohammad Ashraful not out	29
D. A. Minors (wk) c Tamim Iqbal b Abdur Razzak	23	Extras B4 W14 Nb3	21
L. O.B. Cann b Shakib Al Hasan	16	(17.3 overs)	3/96
J. J. Tucker c Tamim Iqbal b Mohammad Rafique	9	Did not bat: Mushfiqur Rahim (wk), Habibul Bashar (capt),	
K. A.D. Hurdle b Abdur Razzak	0	Mohammad Rafique, Mashrafe Mortaza, Abdur Razzak,	
S. Mukuddem not out	0	Syed Rasel	
Extras Lb5 W4 Nb2	11	1/6 2/30 3/37	
(21 overs)	9/94	Bowling: Hurdle 4-0-25-0; Mukuddem 5-1-19-3;	
Did not bat: R. D.M. Leverock		Tucker 3-0-14-0; Leverock 3.3-0-19-0; Borden 2-0-15-0	
1/2 2/8 3/11 4/35 5/52 6/73 7/86 8/94 9/94			
Bowling: Mashrafe Mortaza 4-0-8-2; Syed Rasel 5-0-14-1;			
Abdur Razzak 4-0-20-3; Mohammad Rafique 4-0-18-1;			
Shakib Al Hasan 3-0-12-2; Aftab Ahmed 1-0-17-0			

Umpires: S.J. Davis   I.L. Howell

Toss: Bangladesh   Points: Bangladesh 2 Bermuda 0

TUESDAY 27 MARCH 27th and WEDNESDAY 28 MARCH 2007
SUPER EIGHTS MATCH 1: WEST INDIES v AUSTRALIA
SIR VIVIAN RICHARDS STADIUM, NORTH SOUND, ANTIGUA: AUSTRALIA WON BY 103 RUNS

Another mighty century by Matthew Hayden launched Australia's Super Eights campaign with a big 103 run win over their World Cup hosts, the West Indies. Australia promptly adjusted to the move from St Kitts to Antigua and proved too good for Brian Lara's side, who arrived from Jamaica, in the first match of the tournament to be taken into the reserve day.

Ricky Ponting's team batted first at the brand new venue after being sent in by Lara. It was an overcast drizzly day and the outfield was sandy and wicket an unknown quantity. Adam Glichrist did not find out much about it, being caught behind from a lifting delivery from Daren Powell.

Eventual Man of the Match, Hayden took 18 deliveries to get off the mark, but it soon became clear to himself and Ponting that the groundsman had a provided a flat, grassless rock hard track. Less impressive, again, was the attendance. Locals, perhaps put off by the weather, the ticket prices, the unfinished roads to the ground and/or the relocation of their venue to the edge of the city only turned up in mediocre numbers.

Ponting was the first Australian batsman to get the scoring moving. The Australian captain made a run-per-ball 35 and had led the way as the total reached 76 when, as he is sometimes prone to do, he took on a good fieldsman and lost. This time it was Ramnaresh Sarwan at cover who threw down the stumps while Ponting stretched for the crease.

Hayden and Michael Clarke. put on 98 before Clarke was trapped in front by a Dwayne Bravo off-cutter. Hayden had begun bullying the bowlers. He was not distracted by Chris Gayle bowling his off-spinners in his brightly coloured West Indian World Cup 2007 cap and hit him out of the attack in four overs. The big Queenslander took his time to get the measures right on the bigger Antiguan ground and then belted a succession of fours and sixes. The first six off Marlon Samuels was a one-handed effort over long off. Hayden's first 50 took 72 balls, his second 38 balls and his third 27 balls. The 150 was raised with a six over cow corner from Marlon Samuels. When the same man caught him off Bravo at long off, Hayden had made 158, the highest score by an Australian in the World Cup.

In the still persistent drizzle, Shane Watson topped up the Australian innings with a few more boundary hits and the West Indies needed 323 to win. Rain, although never heavy, then set in. At one stage it was thought that the West Indies might chase a Duckworth Lewis target of 163 in 20 overs, but eventually that too was beyond consideration and the match resumed the next day.

On day two it soon became obvious the West Indies were not going to get anywhere near the total they required.

Nathan Bracken moved the ball on the now dampish surface with accuracy and bowled with genuine economy. Shivnarine Chanderpaul was given out lbw to Shaun Tait, while Chris Gayle, totally out of character, was immobilized at the crease. He faced 23 balls for two runs then miscued a pull off Glenn McGrath. When Samuels botched his attempt at a Hayden one handed drive on the move the West Indies was a disastrous 3/20 in the 10th over.

Whatever followed was consolation for the local supporters and the telecasters. It included a beautiful if empty 83-ball innings by Lara. The Trinidadian champion featured cover drives, pulls, delicate off side deflections and one booming straight drive for six, all with the sumptuous trademark flourish. Brad Hogg finally removed him when he advanced, yorked himself and was given out lbw. Dinesh Ramdin also got himself 52, but the left-arm Australian wrist spinner picked up another three wickets as the West Indian innings subsided to 219, putting a huge dent in their hopes of becoming the first hosts to win the World Cup.

AUSTRALIA		WEST INDIES	
A. C. Gilchrist (wk) c Ramdin b Powell	7	C. H. Gayle c Watson b McGrath	2
M. L. Hayden c Samuels b Bravo	158	S. Chanderpaul lbw b Tait	5
R. T. Ponting (capt) run out	35	R. R. Sarwan c Ponting b Hogg	29
M. J. Clarke lbw b Bravo	41	M. N. Samuels c Symonds b McGrath	4
A. Symonds c Ramdin b Samuels	13	B. C. Lara (capt) lbw b Hogg	77
M. E. K. Hussey b Powell	9	D. J. Bravo c Ponting b McGrath	9
S. R. Watson not out	33	D. Ramdin (wk) c Gilchrist b Bracken	52
G. B. Hogg not out	5	D. R. Smith lbw b Hogg	9
Extras B1 Lb9 W8 Nb3	21	J. E. Taylor lbw b Symonds	10
(50 overs)	6/322	D. B.L. Powell b Tait	5
Did not bat: N. W. Bracken, S. W. Tait, G. D. McGrath		C. D. Collymore not out	1
1/10 2/76 3/174 4/208 5/234 6/297		Extras B1 W15	16
Bowling: Powell 10-2-53-2; Taylor 10-0-67-0;		(45.3 overs)	219
Collymore 10-0-56-0; Gayle 4-0-29-0; Bravo 7-0-49-2;		1/11 2/16 3/20 4/91 5/107 6/156 7/172 8/199 9/217	
Samuels 9-0-58-1		10/219	
		Bowling: Bracken 9-1-25-1; Tait 7.3-0-43-2;	
		McGrath 8-1-31-3; Watson 7-0-31-0; Hogg 10-0-56-3;	
		Symonds 4-0-32-1	

Umpires: Aleem Dar   Asad Rauf

Toss: West Indies   Points: Australia 2 West Indies 0

WEDNESDAY 28 MARCH 2007
SUPER EIGHTS MATCH 2: SOUTH AFRICA v SRI LANKA
PROVIDENCE STADIUM, SOUTH GEORGETOWN, GUYANA: SOUTH AFRICA WON BY ONE WICKET

Despite a sensational late spell by Lasith Malinga, South Africa held on to win a thriller by one wicket against Sri Lanka as World Cup cricket moved to Providence Stadium in Guyana.

Malinga became the first bowler ever to claim four wickets in four balls in a one-day international as the Proteas chasing 210 for victory slipped from 5/206 to 9/207 in the blink of an eye. Spread over two overs, the round-arm mop topped (one commentator called it a 'mangled skunk' hairdo) speedster bowled Shaun Pollock with a slower yorker, had Andrew Hall chipping another slower ball to cover, removed the resolute Jacques Kallis caught behind with a fast full delivery outside off-stump and dispatched Makhaya Ntini's middle-stump with sheer pace.

Amazingly the latter half of the Sri Lankan batting order had earlier also crumbled away in similar fashion in the final overs. After a recovery from 5/98 to 6/195 their tailenders tried to slog the total to a higher plane and were singularly unsuccessful against Charl Langeveldt. The right-arm swing bowler claimed the first five-wicket haul of the tournament and was probably Man of the Match until Malinga's final burst. The judges then declared the award would be shared between the two bowling heroes.

Langeveldt was also at the crease when he and fellow tailender Robin Peterson faced eleven balls and eked out the last couple of runs South Africa needed to clinch the narrow win. Peterson was so relieved when he hit the winning runs, he accidently whacked the stumps at the non-strikers end with his bat and had to face Match Referee, Jeff Crowe.

Graeme Smith admitted to a nervous dressing room at the climax, but was thrilled his side had held on to win. It was unlike some of their predecessors who had lost critical World Cup matches in similar circumstances.

Mahela Jayawardene had elected to bat on the untried Providence Stadium wicket. It was slow and spongy and despite Sanath Jayasuriya hitting a few early boundaries and Kumar Sangakkara getting a start, when Chamara Silva stranded himself and was run out by a diving Herschelle Gibbs, Jonty Rhodes style, Sri Lanka were five down at the halfway point of their innings and had not reached 100.

The recovery came through the 97 run sixth wicket partnership in 22 overs between Tilakaratne Dilshan and Russel Arnold. They both scored half centuries, but this was accumulating batting on a sluggish surface. The pair shared only six boundaries. Yet those that followed attempted hefty blows rather than looking for the available singles. The approach was a failure. Langeveldt's final over was a three wicket maiden.

South Africa built their reply around Smith's early aggression and Kallis's attempt to bat right through the innings to victory. Initially Chaminda Vaas had removed Abraham de Villiers with a perfect left-arm in-swinger to the right-hander. Then Smith scored freely, particularly off Malinga, and with Kallis took the total to 95. Smith was deceived into becoming the first of Muralitharan's three victims, but with Gibbs partnering Kallis the total by the 33rd over was a very comfortable 2/160.

Kallis made 86 and batted at a pace not different to that which had seen him so criticised against Australia. But the conditions, size of the ground and target were quite different and his innings was the best on either side.

Seventeen overs left, 50 runs to win and eight wickets in hand was not a towering assignment.

However, Malinga added huge drama to the final overs and without Peterson's educated edge through the vacant second slip this game may have finished one of the World Cup's biggest ever turn ups. Although they would have seen an exciting match, the local fans again were not attracted. Exorbitant prices for grandstand seats limited the attendance to 5,000 spectators who crammed into the cheaper grassed bank area of the ground.

SRI LANKA		SOUTH AFRICA	
W. U. Tharanga c Kemp b Ntini	12	G. C. Smith (capt) st Sangakkara b Muralitharan	59
S. T. Jayasuriya c Kallis b Langeveldt	26	A. B. de Villiers b Vaas	0
D. P.M. D.Jayawardene (capt) c de Villiers b Langeveldt	12	J. H. Kallis c Sangakkara b Malinga	86
K. C. Sangakkara (wk) c Boucher b Hall	28	H. H. Gibbs c & b Muralitharan	31
L. P. C. Silva run out	9	M. V. Boucher (wk) lbw b Muralitharan	0
T. M. Dilshan c Kemp b Ntini	58	J. M. Kemp st Sangakkara b Jayasuriya	5
R. P. Arnold c Boucher b Langeveldt	50	S. M. Pollock b Malinga	13
M. F. Maharoof c Ntini b Langeveldt	5	A. J. Hall c Tharanga b Malinga	0
W. P. U. J.C. Vaas c Gibbs b Langeveldt	0	R. J. Peterson not out	4
S. L. Malinga not out	0	M. Ntini b Malinga	0
M. Muralitharan run out	1	C. K. Langeveldt not out	1
Extras Lb3 W4 Nb1	8	Extras B5 Lb4 w3 Nb1	13
(49.3overs)	209	(48.2 overs)	9/212

1/13 2/45 3/65 4/90 5/98 6/195 7/208 8/208 9/208 10/209

Bowling: Pollock 8-0-46-0; Ntini 8-0-26-2; Langeveldt 10-1-39-5; Hall 9.3-0-33-1; Kallis 6-0-24-0; Peterson 5-0-22-0

1/1 2/95 3/160 4/160 5/182 6/206 7/206 8/207 9/207

Bowling: Vaas 10-1-31-1; Malinga 9.2-0-54-4; Maharoof 7-0-41-0; Muralitharan 10-0-34-3; Jayasuriya 10-0-34-1; Dilshan 2-0-9-0

Umpires: S.A. Bucknor   D.J. Harper

Toss: Sri Lanka   Points: South Africa 2 Sri Lanka 0

THURSDAY 29 MARCH 2007
SUPER EIGHTS MATCH 3: WEST INDIES v NEW ZEALAND
SIR VIVIAN RICHARDS STADIUM, NORTH SOUND, ANTIGUA
NEW ZEALAND WON BY SEVEN WICKETS

An inadequate batting display by the West Indies allowed New Zealand to stroll to a seven-wicket victory with 64 balls to spare in Antigua. It completed a bad two days with the bat for the hosts. They had succumbed to Australia the day before, seemed unsettled by their selection changes, lost an important toss and floundered every time they seemed to get in to a competitive position.

New Zealand, led by the recalled Shane Bond and Man of the Match, Jacob Oram, were again efficient in the field and eased away with the points following another fine innings by Scott Styris. The pitch retained some morning moisture, so after Stephen Fleming won the toss Chris Gayle and Shivnarine Chanderpaul struggled for runs. Bond moved the ball away from the left-handers at pace, eventually having Chanderpaul edge to Styris at second slip in the eighth over.

The following batsmen established partnerships then took them no further. Jacob Oram bowled a magic spell that undermined the West Indian middle order. Chris Gayle had taken a sequence of boundaries off James Franklin, but then chopped on an attempted offside glide off Oram when bigger things beckoned.

Lara batted with restraint in an attempt to rebuild from 4-81 in the 23rd over. He got to 37 with the total on 5-150 with 13 overs remaining when he swung across the line at Scott Styris and bottom edged to Brendon McCullum.

The Kiwi wicketkeeper had an excellent day, having brilliantly caught an inside edge off Ramnaresh Sarwan one handed down the leg-side in the seventeenth over. Once Lara was gone the West Indies lost any semblance of batting resistance. In the next seven overs five wickets went down for 27 runs. This occurred despite the fact they had left out their fastest bowler, Jerome Taylor, and bolstered their lower order with opening batsman Lendl Simmons who came in at No.8.

Word had it that the unbalanced side was a result of a disagreement about selection between Lara and former fast bowling great and selector, Andy Roberts. Daren Powell showed what might have been when he bowled Peter Fulton with the second ball of the New Zealand innings. Then in the ninth over he had Hamish Marshall hitting a soft catch to cover to leave New Zealand 2/36.

But Powell's new-ball partner was medium paced trundler, Dwayne Smith. Stephen Fleming scored freely off him while he also swung Corey Collymore once away to the leg-side for six.

Lara ran his opposite number out with a direct hit throw from cover for 45 and at 3/77 the Black Caps were not completely secure.

But without Taylor bowling, the West Indian attack lacked firepower. As the wicket and seam flattened, Styris, on way to a comfortable match high of 80, was soon timing his shots through the on-side and Craig McMillan provided the necessary support.

With their run chase such a modest one, New Zealand knew one good partnership would take them to victory. In 18 overs Styris and McMillan had added 102, which was quite enough.

Lara lamented, "We are just not playing well as a team."

Possibly the lack of local enthusiasm was affecting them. "The boys are pretty disappointed and a lot of them have mentioned it. Maybe it's not the cricket," Lara said of another poor attendance.

WEST INDIES		NEW ZEALAND	
C. H. Gayle b Oram	44	P. G. Fulton b Powell	0
S. Chanderpaul c Styris b Bond	4	S. P. Fleming (capt) run out	45
R. R. Sarwan c McCullum b Oram	19	H. J.H. Marshall c Lara b Powell	15
M. N. Samuels c McCullum b Oram	9	S. B. Styris not out	80
B. C. Lara (capt) c McCullum b Styris	37	C. D. McMillan not out	33
D. J. Bravo c McCullum b Bond	18	Extras Lb1 W3 Nb2	6
D. Ramdin (wk) c Oram b Vettori	15	(39.2 overs)	3/179
L. M.P. V. Simmons not out	14	Did not bat: J. D. P. Oram, B. B.McCullum (wk), D. L. Vettori,
D. R. Smith b Vettori	8	J. E.C. Franklin, S. E. Bond, M. J. Mason
D. B.L. Powell lbw b Vettori	0	1/0 2/36 3/77
C. D. Collymore b Bond	0	Bowling: Powell 10-2-39-2; Smith 5-0-24-0;
Extras B1 Lb5 W3	9	Collymore 9-0-43-0; Bravo 8-0-32-0; Gayle 6.2-0-35-0;
(44.4 overs)	177	Sarwan 1-0-5-0

1/14 2/66 3/78 4/81 5/128 6/150 7/158 8/176 9/176 10/177

Bowling: Mason 6-2-14-0; Bond 8.4-0-31-3; Franklin 3-0-29-0; Oram 8-2-23-3; Styris 10-1-35-1; Vettori 9-1-39-3

Umpires: Asad Rauf R.E. Koertzen

Toss: New Zealand   Points: New Zealand 2 West Indies 0

FRIDAY 30 MARCH 2007
SUPER EIGHTS MATCH 4: ENGLAND v IRELAND
PROVIDENCE STADIUM, SOUTH GEORGETOWN, GUYANA: ENGLAND WON BY 48 RUNS

England, realistically on a hiding to nothing against small-time neighbours Ireland, did enough to win a fluctuating contest by 48 runs at Providence Stadium.

All the neutral sentiment was with the green clad underdogs, but after a poor start England were always slightly in front in the game.Michael Vaughan won the toss and batted, but in the second over he watched England's Irishman, Ed Joyce, get bowled while not playing a shot to 22-year-old farmer Boyd Rankin.

Vaughan himself was also back in the pavilion by the sixth over, caught behind off young the beanpole, Rankin, for six as England struggled to 2/23.

Ian Bell anchored down in an attempt to re-build the innings, but his 74 ball stay was quite torturous. He had Pietersen as a partner to add some degree of fluency. Pietersen scored his 48 at better than a run per ball. When he chipped off-spinner Kyle McCallan to midwicket, though, England was 4/113 in the 27th over and Ireland were still well in the contest.

Paul Collingwood was already established and Andrew Flintoff arrived determined to make up for his own lost time. They put on 81 in 17 overs before Flintoff played a cut off the bottom edge onto the stumps off Ireland's Australian captain, Trent Johnston, for 43.

By the time Flintoff departed the acceleration had begun. In the last six overs of the innings England put on 71 runs. Collingwood made many of these. He hit three sixes, one over mid wicket, two over long on, in addition to eight fours on way to his 90. Collingwood's last 39 runs took just sixteen balls. A brilliant throw by Johnston in the final over prevented his hundred but not his Man of the Match Award.

Ireland chasing 266 by the fourth over was 2/11. Jeremy Bray slashed James Anderson straight to Ravi Bopara at point and bowler Sajid Mahmood responded brilliantly in his follow through to reverse flick the ball on the stumps and run out Eoin Morgan.

After Ed Joyce dropped Niall O'Brien, the in form wicketkeeper batsman put together a composed 63 in two hours. It gave the Irish innings some substance.

But when he was stumped off Michael Vaughan in the 37th over Ireland were going at just four runs per over at 6/139, which was not enough.

Vaughan with his off-spin and Monty Panesar, left-arm spin, conceding just three runs per over, had turned the match irretrievably England's way. Trent Johnston and Andrew White would not give up. They bolstered the Irish total in the later part of the innings, putting on 58 for the seventh wicket in eight overs.

The equation, however, always remained out of reach at about fourteen per over. Then Andrew Flintoff returned. He bowled fast straight yorkers that lifted his wicket tally to four and ended the Irish resistance.

The consensus was that England was below par because Ireland was a minnow not expected to win. But supposedly this was a giant-killing Ireland side. So if England were meant to thrash them with ease, what was Ireland doing in the Super Eights when India and Pakistan had gone home?

ENGLAND		IRELAND	
E. C. Joyce b Rankin	1	W. T.S. Porterfield c Bell b Flintoff	31
M. P. Vaughan (capt) c N. J.O'Brien b Rankin	6	J. P. Bray c Bopara b Anderson	0
I. R. Bell c N. J.O'Brien b K. J.O'Brien	31	E. J. G. Morgan run out	2
K. P. Pietersen c Porterfield b M. Callan	48	N. J. O'Brien (wk) st Nixon b Vaughan	63
P. D. Collingwood run out	90	A. C. Botha c Flintoff b Panesar	18
A. Flintoff b Johnston	43	K. J. O'Brien lbw b Panesar	12
P. A. Nixon (wk) c Morgan b Botha	19	D. T. Johnston (capt) b Flintoff	27
R. S. Bopara not out	10	A. R. White c Nixon b Collingwood	38
S. T. Mahmood not out	0	W. K. M. Callan b Flintoff	5
Extras Lb2 W13 Nb3	18	D. Langford-Smith lbw b Flintoff	1
(50 overs)	7/266	W. B. Rankin not out	4
Did not bat: J. M. Anderson; M. S. Panesar		Extras Lb3 W9 Nb5	17
1/6 2/23 3/89 4/113 5/194 6/245 7/258		(48.1 overs)	218

Bowling: Langford-Smith 7-0-38-0; Rankin 7-1-28-2; Johnston 10-0-70-1; Botha 10-1-56-1; K. J.O'Brien 4-0-26-1; M. Callan 10-0-38-1; White 2-0-8-0

1/6 2/11 3/72 4/116 5/139 6/139 7/197 8/209 9/210 10/218

Bowling: Anderson 7-1-35-1; Mahmood 8-2-34-0; Flintoff 8.1-1-43-4; Collingwood 6-0-38-1; Panesar 10-1-31-2; Vaughan 9-0-34-1

Umpires: B.R.Doctrove S.J.A.Taufel

Toss: England   Points: England 2 Ireland 0

SATURDAY 31 MARCH
SUPER EIGHTS MATCH 5: AUSTRALIA v BANGLADESH
SIR VIVIAN RICHARDS STADIUM, NORTH SOUND, ANTIGUA: AUSTRALIA WON BY 10 WICKETS

The powerful and confident Australian side had an easy ten-wicket victory over Bangladesh in a match reduced by overnight rain and a damp outfield to 22 overs per side at the Sir Vivian Richards Stadium in Antigua.

All the fears that this facility was underprepared for a World Cup cricket match became a reality when the sun shone from mid morning and yet it took more than four hours for the ground to become fit for play.

Ricky Ponting would later write the outfield at fine leg was a sandy swamp, with no effective drainage. Then the only super-sopper machine broke down and there was disagreement about whether the boundary rope could be brought in past the offending area. Nor could any drying be done during the groundsmen's lunch break. The Australian captain was not impressed. He would have been pleased, though, with the performance of his side when play did get underway.

Nathan Bracken soon had Tamim Iqbal miscuing again, while Glenn McGrath, restored to using the new-ball, was devastating on a wicket that gave him a modicum of assistance. He yorked Shahriar Nafees, had Aftab Ahmed caught at mid off and Mohammad Ashraful skiing a slower ball to mid-on. The three wicket burst made McGrath the leading wicket taker in World Cups, going past Wasim Akram, gained him the Man of the Match Award and left Bangladesh in a mess at 4/37 in the eighth over.

Shakib Al Hasan, who slashed Shaun Tait over third man for six, captain, Habibul Bashar and Mashrafe Mortaza, who swung hard and clubbed Andrew Symonds for a straight six, then managed to just get Bangladesh into three figures.

Australia also had the annoyance that Shane Watson injured his calf when bowling his second over.

For the very few in the ground Adam Gilchrist and Matthew Hayden then eventually did provide some brief but exhilarating entertainment. Facing such a modest target they quickly went on the attack. Tapish Baisya was severely punished. His first over went for 10 runs, his second 14, including two stunning Gilchrist drives and the first five balls of his third went for 11, Hayden smashing one brutal six, before the hapless bowler broke down with an injured foot and limped off.

Nor did Shakib Al Hasan finish his first over, the fourteenth of the innings. Two more huge sixes by Hayden and the Australian openers had completed the run chase in less than an hour.

Ponting with a week off in front of him, before play had offered to return on the reserve day for a 50 over match. Bangladesh scheduled for their next fixture in two days declined the gesture. But once they lost the toss and were sent on against the Australian fast bowlers on a pitch retaining some moisture they were very much up against it.

BANGLADESH		AUSTRALIA	
Tamim Iqbal c Hogg b Bracken	3	A. C. Gilchrist (wk) not out	59
Shahriar Nafees b McGrath	1	M. L. Hayden not out	47
Aftab Ahmed c Bracken b McGrath	11	Extras	0
Shakib Al Hasan c Gilchrist b Tait	25	(13.5 overs)	0/106
Mohammad Ashraful c Ponting b McGrath	6	Did not bat: R. T. Ponting (capt), M. J. Clarke, A. Symonds,	
Habibul Bashar (capt) c Ponting b Bracken	24	M. E. K. Hussey, S. R. Watson, G. B. Hogg, N. W. Bracken, S.	
Mashrafe Mortaza not out	25	W. Tait, G. D. McGrath	
Mushfiqur Rahim (wk) not out	2	Bowling: Mashrafe Mortaza 4-0-20-0; Tapish Baisya	
Extras W7	7	2.5-0-35-0; Aftab Ahmed 0.1-0-1-0; Abdur Razzak 3-0-15-0;	
(22 overs)	6/104	Mohammad Rafique 3-0-21-0; Shakib Al Hasan 0.5-0-14-0	

Did not bat: Mohammad Rafique, Abdur Razzak, Tapash Baisya

1/4 2/8 3/25 4/37 5/65 6/97

Bowling: Bracken 4-0-20-2; McGrath 5-0-16-3; Tait 4-0-28-1; Watson 1.4-0-4-0; Hogg 5-0-20-0; Symonds 2.2-0-16-0

Umpires: Aleem Dar   B.F. Bowden

Toss: Australia   Points: Australia 2 Bangladesh 0

SUNDAY 1 APRIL 2007
SUPER EIGHTS MATCH 6: WEST INDIES v SRI LANKA
PROVIDENCE STADIUM, SOUTH GEORGETOWN, GUYANA: SRI LANKA WON BY 113 RUNS

The West Indies' hopes of being the most successful World Cup hosts ever hit another serious hurdle when they were easily accounted for by the in-form Sri Lankan side. The West Indies, perhaps starting to feel like a travelling Caribbean roadshow after having to quickly hop over to Guyana from Antigua fell foul to the brilliance of Sanath Jayasuriya.

The Sri Lankan pocket powerhouse gave the Man of the Match judges the easiest decision of their lives when he made a superb 115 and followed that up with 3/38, the best bowling figures of the match. Sri Lanka after a tardy start made 303 and then bowled the West Indies out for 190 to cruise home by a hefty 113 runs.

After a 45 minute delay, Brian Lara sent Sri Lanka in to bat. Daren Powell then achieved what was becoming a customary new-ball breakthrough when he bowled Upal Tharanga, cleanly removing two stumps in the process.

After the defeat against New Zealand the hosts had strengthened their attack and in the ninth over left-armer Ian Bradshaw had seemingly justified the change of heart when he found the edge of Kumar Sangakkara's bat.

Sri Lanka was 2/35 and the well patronised Providence Stadium was abuzz with anticipation. Gradually, though, Jayasuriya and Mahela Jayawardene quietened the fans. Jayasuriya had only hit one four by the middle of the seventeenth over and the total had drifted to 56 when he helped a wayward delivery from Bradshaw to the fine-leg boundary. Then he jumped out and clubbed the next one over mid off for a second four.

That got Jayasuriya going. He began pummeling the boundary between fine leg and square leg with pulls and pick-ups that quickly boosted the run rate. Jayasuriya raced to his 25th ODI century in 86 balls. When he was yorked by Powell, Jayasuriya had hit ten fours and four sixes.

Jayawardene in his 82 from 113 balls hit just two fours and a six, but he put on 183 with Jayasuriya for the third wicket and by the time he was bowled by Dwayne Bravo's slower ball at 4/251 his side were set to top 300. Tillakaratne Dilshan's 22 ball 39 not out ensured they got there.

Needing 304 the West Indies were soon struggling in reply. When Chaminda Vaas, bowling cutters, had Lara neatly stumped by Sangkkara the West Indies were 3/42 in the eleventh over.

Guyanese locals, Shivnarine Chanderpaul and Ramnaresh Sarwan, added 92 for the fourth wicket. But their compatriots in the outer never really fired up in support. The partnership took 24 overs and at one stage the West Indies innings went 103 balls without a boundary. The 30th over was completed and there were still 205 runs required.

Chanderpaul eventually whacked Muralitharn away for a few sixes over long on and mid wicket. But once Jayasuriya had a swishing Sarwan stumped, Samuels missed a straight ball from Muralitharan and Smith completed a sad personal match being run out after facing two balls.

At 6/148 it only remained for Muralitharan and Jayasuriya to do the mopping up which they duly did by the 45th over.

SRI LANKA		WEST INDIES	
W. U. Tharanga b Powell	8	C. H. Gayle c Fernando b Malinga	10
S. T. Jayasuriya b Powell	115	D. J. Bravo b Vaas	21
K. C.Sangakkara (wk) c Ramdin b Bradshaw	7	S. Chanderpaul b Malinga	76
D. P. M. D. Jayawardene (capt) b Bravo	82	B. C. Lara (capt) st Sangakkara b Vaas	2
L. P. C. Silva c Lara b Sarwan	23	R. R. Sarwan st Sangakkara b jayasuriya	44
T. M. Dilshan not out	39	M. N. Samuels lbw b Muralitharan	3
R. P. Arnold not out	4	D. R. Smith run out	0
Extras Lb7 W13 Nb5	25	Ramdin (wk) c Vaas b Jayasuriya	2
(50 overs)	5/303	I. D.R. Bradshaw not out	6
Did not bat: W. P. U. J.C. Vaas, S. L. Malinga, M.		J. E. Taylor lbw b Muralitharan	13
Muralitharan, C. R.D. Fernando		D. B.L. Powell b Jayasuriya	2
1/18 2/35 3/218 4/251 5/268		Extras (Lb1 W8 Nb2)	11
Bowling: Taylor 8-0-32-0; Powell 10-1-38-2;		(44.3 overs)	190
Bradshaw 10-0-67-1; Smith 3-0-23-0; Gayle 9-0-61-0;		1/20 2/40 3/42 4/134 5/147 6/148 7/158 8/173 9/187	
Bravo 7-0-60-1; Sarwan 3-0-17-1		10/190	
		Bowling: Vaas 8-1-19-2; Malinga 5-0-34-2;	
		Fernando 7-3-19-0; Dilshan 4-0-11-0;	
		Arnold 3-0-9-0; Muralitharan 9-0-59-2; Jayasuriya 8.3-0-38-3	

Umpires: M.R. Benson   D.J. Harper

Toss: West Indies   Points: Sri Lanka 2 West Indies 0

MONDAY 2 APRIL 2007
SUPER EIGHTS MATCH 7: BANGLADESH v NEW ZEALAND
SIR VIVIAN RICHARDS STADIUM, NORTH SOUND, ANTIGUA
NEW ZEALAND WON BY NINE WICKETS

New Zealand had little trouble accounting for a disappointing Bangladeshi side. The Kiwis cruised home by nine wickets with more than 20 overs to spare. The Black Caps ripped through a timid Bangladesh batting line-up for 174 then, with captain Stephen Fleming leading the charge, gave their net run rate a boost by making 175 in 29.2 overs.

Fleming completed an aggressive 92-ball century, but it was his big fast bowler, Shane Bond who claimed the Man of the Match honours with a quality spell of 2-15 in 10 impeccable overs. Scott Styris and Jacob Oram gave great support to Bond, sharing seven Bangladeshi wickets between them. Both were essential ingredients to the attack as Matt Mason broke down early with a calf strain and later James Franklin went off with a migraine.

Bangladesh actually made a reasonable if slightly tardy start after Fleming sent them in to bat. Javed Omar on World Cup debut eleven years after his ODI debut and Tamim Iqbal put on Bangladesh's second ever half-century World Cup opening partnership. At one stage they were 2/105, but in contrast to their reckless approach against Australia, they used up 28 overs to build that foundation. Each of the first four batsman reached 22 or more. None made it to 30. Oram made the ball lift, Bond blasted the stumps with pace while Styris varied his deliveries and induced inside edges.

Habibul Bashar's side lost 7/35 to slip to 9/140. Thankfully Mohammad Rafique struck some blows, twice putting Styris over the boundary, to lift the final total to a more respectable 174. Despite a nice spell from Syed Rasel, there was no early breakthrough, and on a flat deck New Zealand were soon in control. After the loss of Peter Fulton in the tenth over, Fleming and Marshall added 134 in 20 overs. Fleming with his long reach got his big bat arc going smoothly. He hit ten fours and three sixes, reserving special attention for left-arm spinner, Shakib Al Hasan who he hit for three sixes over mid wicket, including consecutive deliveries in the 27th over. Marshall saw his captain to three figures then slog swept Mohammad Ashraful's second ball over mid wicket for six to win the match and complete his own half-century.

It has to again be said that despite the location, not many Antiguans saw him do it.

BANGLADESH		NEW ZEALAND	
Javed Omar c McCullum b Oram	22	P. G. Fulton c Tamim Iqbal b Syed Rasel	15
Tamim Iqbal st McCullum b Oram	29	S. P. Fleming (capt) not out	102
Aftab Ahmed c sub (Gillespie) b Styris	27	H. J.H. Marshall not out	50
Shakib Al Hasan b Bond	25	Extras W11	11
Habibul Bashar (capt) run out	9	(29.2 overs)	1/178
Mohammad Ashraful b Styris	3	Did not bat: S. B. Styris, C. D. McMillan, J. D. P. Oram,	
Mushfiqur Rahim (wk) b Bond	0	B. B. McCullum (wk), D. L. Vettori, J. E.C. Franklin, S. E.	
Mashrafe Mortaza b Styris	2	Bond, M. J. Mason	
Mohammad Rafique not out	30	1/44	
Abdur Razzak c sub (Gillespie) b Styris	0	Bowling: Mashrafe Mortaza 6-0-41-0; Syed Rasel 7-0-22-1;	
Syed Rasel b Oram	10	Abdur Razzak 8-0-38-0; Mohammad Rafique 5-0-37-0;	
Extras B5 Lb10 W2	17	Shakib Al Hasan3-0-33-0; Mohammad Ashraful 0.2-0-7-0	
(48.3 overs)	174		
1/55 2/62 3/105 4/122 5/127 6/127 7/129 8/140 9/140			
10/174			
Bowling: Mason 1.3-1-4-0; Bond 10-4-15-2; McMillan			
1.3-0-6-0; Franklin 6-1-27-0; Oram 9.3-0-30-3;			
Vettori 10-0-34-0; Styris 10-1-43-4			

Umpires: Aleem Dar R.E. Koertzen

Toss: New Zealand   Points: New Zealand 2 Bangladesh 0

TUESDAY 3 APRIL 2007
SUPER EIGHTS MATCH 8: IRELAND v SOUTH AFRICA
PROVIDENCE STADIUM, SOUTH GEORGETOWN, GUYANA
SOUTH AFRICA WON BY SEVEN WICKETS

Ireland's early tournament gleam was further tarnished on a grey Tuesday in Guyana when South Africa easily defeated them by seven wickets. Sent in by Graeme Smith on a drizzly morning, rain soon came to interrupt the Irish innings at 1/23 after 11 overs. Play stopped for two hours. Upon resumption the match was reduced to 35 overs per side. The Duckworth Lewis rules were such that although Ireland made 152, South Africa needed 160 to win.

They lost an early wicket but Jacques Kallis had things under control and he moved to an unbeaten 66 that earned him the Man of the Match Award and took the Proteas to their win with a few overs and plenty of wickets to spare. Jeremy Bray, who had a couple of weeks earlier, launched Ireland's campaign with a century, fell for his second consecutive duck when trapped on the crease by Shaun Pollock prior to the rain arriving.

When it cleared Ireland had only 24 overs to bat so they had to press on. Pollock almost immediately had Will Porterfield spooning a drive to cover. Niall O'Brien and Eoin Morgan got starts, but found the need to take risks against the disciplined South African attack, in particular Charl Langeveldt, wore them down. Andrew White was the most effective hitting a run per ball 30 with five fours while David Langford-Smith and Trent Johnston each hit a six from the final two overs to lift the total from 8-124 past 150.

Ireland had reduced South Africa to 8-91 in a warm up match and now Boyd Rankin had AB de Villiers slashing a short ball straight to backward point from the third ball of the innings. The Irish bowlers got movement. So, Kallis took his time to settle in while Smith punished the occasional loose offering. Johnston took a stunning low caught and bowled to remove Smith at 2/71 and Rankin provoked a mishit from Herschelle Gibbs 14 runs later in the 17th over.

Then a couple of chances went down and Kallis began unfurling his cover drive. The ball aged which allowed Kallis and Ashwell Prince to put on 80 runs in 15 overs to take South Africa to victory in the battle of the green uniforms.

Journalists present commented on the rampant commercialism and heavy-handed security dragging down the atmosphere further in an already empty ground.

IRELAND		SOUTH AFRICA	
J. P. Bray lbw b Pollock	0	A. B. de Villiers c Porterfield b Rankin	0
W. T.S. Porterfield c Kallis b Pollock	14	G. C. Smith (capt) c & b Johnston	41
E. J. G. Morgan c Prince b Hall	28	J. H. Kallis not out	66
N. J. O'Brien (wk) c Gibbs b Langeveldt	25	H. H. Gibbs c White b Rankin	6
A. R. White c Gibbs b Smith	30	A. G. Prince not out	47
A. C. Botha c de Villiers b Hall	14	Extras W1 Nb4	5
D. T. Johnston (capt) not out	13	(31.3 overs)	3/165
W. K. M. Callan c Boucher b Langeveldt	3	Did not bat: M. V.Boucher (wk), J. M. Kemp, S. M. Pollock,	
P. J.K. Mooney c Boucher b Langeveldt	0	A. J. Hall, C. K. Langeveldt, M. Ntini	
D. Langford-Smith not out	17	1/1 2/71 3/85	
Extras B1 Lb3 W4	8	Bowling: Rankin 7-1-26-2; Langford-Smith 5-0-31-0;	
(35 overs)	8/152	Mooney 3.3-0-40-0; Johnston 3-0-15-1; Botha 6-0-18-0;	
Did not bat: W. B. Rankin		M. Callan 5-0-27-0; White 2-0-8-0	

Ireland: 1/0 2/31 3/63 4/77 5/116 6/119 7/124 8/124
Bowling: Pollock 7-2-17-2; Ntini 7-2-14-0; Langeveldt 7-0-41-3; Hall 7-0-37-2; Kemp 3-0-14-0; Kallis 3-0-20-0; Smith 1-0-5-1

Umpires: D.J. Harper   S.J.A. Taufel
Toss: South Africa   Points: South Africa 2 Ireland 0

WEDNESDAY 4 APRIL 2007
SUPER EIGHTS MATCH 9: ENGLAND v SRI LANKA
SIR VIVIAN RICHARDS STADIUM, NORTH SOUND, ANTIGUA: SRI LANKA WON BY TWO RUNS

Sri Lanka, who seemed to be attracting all the best games, overcame England by just two runs in pulsating cricket match in Antigua. Like their clash with South Africa, this was an evenly balanced contest between bat and ball from start to finish. But this time Mahela Jayawardene's side held their nerve and prevailed at the last gasp.

Dilhara Fernando who sent down the final over coped best with the stress. He had twelve runs to play with in the final over, but that was reduced to seven when Ravi Bopara paddled the second ball over short fine-leg for four. The ultimate requirement for Bopara, who had played his best ever innings for England to date, was to hit three runs from the final ball.

Fernando ran in, baulked, ran in again and honed in at the top of off stump. Bopara gave himself a little room, aimed to crash a drive through the covers and missed. Sri Lanka celebrated.

What would end the third closest ever World Cup match began with Michael Vaughan winning the toss and sending Sri Lanka in to bat. In 2006 Sri Lanka had hammered England 5-0 in a one-day series in England. Sanath Jayasuriya was dominant then and was currently also in great form. He rattled along to 25 in no time and had hit Sajid Mahmood for one top-edged six when the big Lancastrian struck back and had him playing on from a defensive bat. It signaled the start of a pattern where batsmen could get in and fight their way to a score, but never take control of the bowling.

Jayasuriya's partner, Upal Tharanga, took 79 balls to hit a boundary and batted 103 deliveries for 62. He put on 91 with Jayawardene who made a more fluent 56 in 61 balls. Tharanga eventually mistimed a pull shot off Andrew Fintoff in the middle of his penetrative spell to the Sri Lankan middle-order. Mahmood picked up his best bowling figures ever in ODI's and the Sri Lankan innings fell away from 2/160 to 235 all out.

England's reply began with what was now their almost accustomed bad start. Michael Vaughan in quite a trough, was strangled down the leg-side off Chaminda Vaas. When Ed Joyce failed to keep a Malinga slinger out of his pads England was 2/11. Kevin Pietersen and Ian Bell then rebuilt the English innings, adding 90 in 20 overs. Bell was eventually run out backing up when Pietersen powered a straight drive through Jayasuriya's hands onto the stumps.

That gave Sri Lanka a lift. They then got on top 25 runs later when Pietersen chipped a doosra back to Muralitharan. When Flintoff totally misjudged Fernando's slower ball and Paul Collingwood was trapped on the crease by his faster one England had slipped to 6/133 and were in huge difficulty.

Bopara and Paul Nixon kept their heads in the crisis. The wicketkeeper reverse swept Muralitharan for six. Both hit the ball into gaps at every angle and ran frantically for twos.

Their stand of 87 brought the game to a tremendous climax, but neither could consummate the win.

SRI LANKA		ENGLAND	
W. U. Tharanga c Pietersen b Flintoff	62	E. C. Joyce lbw b Malinga	10
S. T. Jayasuriya b Mahmood	25	M. P. Vaughan (capt) c Sangakkara b Vaas	0
K. C. Sangakkara (wk) c Collingwood b Mahmood	17	I. R. Bell run out	47
D. P. M. D. Jayawardene (capt) c Joyce b Collingwood	56	K. P. Pietersen c & b Muralitharan	58
L. P.C. Sliva b Flintoff	23	P. D. Collingwood lbw b Fernando	14
T. M. Dilshan run out	5	A. Flintoff c Malinga b Fernando	2
R. P. Arnold c Joyce b Mahmood	20	R. S. Bopara b Fernando	52
W. P. U. J.C. Vaas c Collingwood b Flintoff	4	P. A. Nixon (wk) c Jayawardene b Malinga	42
S. L. Malinga c Nixon b Mahmood	2	S. I. Mahmood not out	2
M. Muralitharan not out	2	Extras B1 Lb1 W2 Nb2	6
C. R.D. Fernando run out	2	(50 overs)	8/233
Extras B3 Lb6 W4 Nb4	17	Did not bat: J. M. Anderson, M. S. Panesar	
(50 overs)	235	1/1 2/11 3/101 4/126 5/133 6/133 7/220 8/233	
1/37 2/69 3/160 4/175 5/193 6/215 7/219 9/231 10/235		Bowling: Vaas 8-1-45-1; Malinga 10-1-50-2;	
Bowling: Anderson 10-1-38-0; Mahmood 9-0-50-4;		Fernando 9-0-41-3; Jayasuriya 8-0-31-0; Dilshan 5-1-16-0;	
Flintoff 10-0-35-3; Collingwood 10-0-44-1;		Muralitharan 10-1-48-1	
Panesar 8-0-45-0; Vaughan 3-0-14-0			

Umpires: Asad Rauf   B.F. Bowden

Toss: England   Points: Sri Lanka 2   England 0

SATURDAY 7 APRIL 2007
SUPER EIGHTS MATCH 10: BANGLADESH v SOUTH AFRICA
PROVIDENCE STADIUM, SOUTH GEORGETOWN, GUYANA: BANGLADESH WON BY 67 RUNS

As they did three weeks earlier against India, Bangladesh got everything to click into place this day allowing them to upset the highly rated South African side by 67 runs. Habibul Bashar's team made far better use of the slow grassless wicket, compiling a competitive total against an almost all pace Proteas attack. His own attack, dominated by left-arm spinners, was then able to strangle the South African batsmen. In the end they were flattered by their margin of defeat.

Graeme Smith sent the Bangladeshis in to bat and when they were wobbling at 4/84 the game appeared set on the course as predicted pre-match. After Tamim Iqbal's dancing belligerence got him to 38, Andre Nel broke through to put his side on top by the 24th over. Mohammad Ashraful then held firm while Aftab Ahmed took control. The momentum of the match changed in 36th over when Aftab twice struck Justin Kemp over the leg-side for six.

Aftab holed out to deep extra cover after a crucial stand of 75, but Mohammad Ashraful was entrenched and began to take the initiative. He reached his 50 and clouted Makhaya Ntini for 15 from one over. In addition to a number of stunning conventional shots Ashraful played a series of ramping flicks over short fine-leg that thrilled the crowd and had Smith tearing out his hair.

By the time he was became Nel's fifth victim, caught at fine-leg from another well -timed flick, Ashraful had made 87; the highest ever score by a Bangladeshi.

South Africa needed a worthy 252 to win and for the most part struggled in vain. Smith totally misjudged a cut, dab while AB de Villiers was totally out of form. Jacques Kallis showed some aggression and took South Africa to 1/63, however overs 15 to 20 became a complete mess.

Kallis gave left-arm medium pacer Syed Rasel his second wicket when he mistimed a lofted drive to mid-on. De Villiers played a right hand version of his captain's dismissal and Ashwell Prince made a poorly judged call for a run.

Mark Boucher hit one six, but like Kemp could find no fluency against the spinners. Boucher soon holed out to long on and Kemp hit the ball back to Shakib Al Hasan. By the end of the 27th over South Africa was 6/87.

More cricket was played as the injured Herschelle Gibbs and Shaun Pollock tried to muster something from the next nine overs. But there was another double breakthrough in the 130's and though Gibbs went to a stylish unbeaten 56 the contest was over.

When Ntini miscued to point off Abdur Razzak the green and gold team with a bit of red on their collar had knocked over all green and gold team for the first time in seven starts and breathed life into the Super Eights.

BANGLADESH		SOUTH AFRICA	
Javed Omar c Smith b Nel	17	G. C.Smith (capt) b Syed Rasel	12
Tamim Iqbal c Boucher b Nel	38	A. B. de Villiers b Abdur Razzak	15
Habibul Bashar (capt) c & b Nel	5	J. H. Kallis c Tamim Iqbal b Syed Rasel	32
Shakib Al Hasan c Smith b Kallis	9	J. M. Kemp c & b Shakib Al Hasan	7
Mohammad Ashraful c Langeveldt b Nel	87	A. G. Prince run out	1
Aftab Ahmed c Nel b Ntini	35	M. V. Boucher (wk) c Syed Rasel b Shakib Al Hasan	12
Mushfiqur Rahim (wk) run out	6	H. H. Gibbs not out	56
Mashrafe Mortaza b Nel	25	S. M. Pollock run out	17
Mohammad Rafique not out	3	A. Nel c & b Mohammad Rafique	1
Abdur Razzak not out	2	C. K. Langeveldt lbw b Abdur Razzak	9
Extras Lb7 W12 Nb5	24	M. Ntini c Mashrafe Mortaza b Abdur Razzak	8
(50 overs)	8/251	Extras Lb2 W12	14
Did not bat: Syed Rasel		(48.4 overs)	184
1/42 2/59 3/69 4/84 5/160 6/179 7/233 8/248		1/18 2/63 3/64 4/67 5/87 6/87 7/132 8/137 9/162	
Bowling: Pollock 10-1-25-0; Ntini 10-1-61-1; Nel 10-1-45-5;		10/184	
Langeveldt 10-0-57-0; Kallis 6-0-27-1; Smith 3-0-16-0;		Bowling: Mashrafe Mortaza 9-0-45-0; Syed Rasel 10-0-41-2;	
Kemp 1-0-13-0		Abdur Razzak 9.4-1-25-3; Mohammad Rafique 10-2-22-1;	
		Shakib Al Hasan 10-0-49-2	

Umpires: M.R. Benson   B.R. Doctrove
Toss: South Africa   Points: Bangladesh 2 South Africa 0

SUNDAY 8 APRIL 2007
SUPER EIGHTS MATCH 11: AUSTRALIA v ENGLAND
SIR VIVIAN RICHARDS STADIUM, NORTH SOUND, ANTIGUA
AUSTRALIA WON BY SEVEN WICKETS

Australia erased the memories of their three recent losses to England in the Commonwealth Bank series in Australia with a decisive seven-wicket win when it really mattered—in the World Cup. England had their chances to take the contest right up to Australia, but eventually the depth in batting consistency in Ricky Ponting's team gave them a decisive advantage.

Michael Vaughan's recent disasters continued when he was bowled playing on soon after winning the toss. Andrew Strauss, in the side for Ed Joyce, also suffered a similar fate at the hands of the furiously fast Shaun Tait to leave England 2/24 after six overs. Ian Bell and Kevin Pietersen had batted well together against Sri Lanka and now they topped that. The stylist and the brute put on 140 at a run per ball, seemingly setting up a hefty target for the Australians. Bell at one point hit McGrath for three fours in four balls. Andrew Flintoff rated Bell's knock the best by an Englishman in the tournament.

Finally McGrath had Bell lift his drive to cover. Ponting nominated a powerplay, recalled eventual Man of the Match, Tait, for a short spell and he had Paul Collingwood caught behind. When Andrew Flintoff was drawn out of his crease by a Brad Hogg wrong 'un England had lost 3/15 in six overs and the match was back in the balance.

Ravi Bopara and Pietersen combined in an important stand of 51 but the overs were dwindling. Bopara picked out Mike Hussey on the mid wicket boundary. Pietersen concentrated on completing his century. He got there and celebrated long and hard, but did not progress much further. The last over or two was a flurry of tail end English wickets and not many runs.

Australia needed a competitive if unimposing 248 to do a huge amount of damage to England's hopes of progression. Adam Gilchrist and Matthew Hayden opened with 57 in 11 overs. The former then spooned Flintoff to point. Hayden, who had dropped an easy catch off Pietersen at mid off, got to 41 with six fours but was bowled by Collingwood's first ball.

The delivery barely removed one bail, someone obviously having recently applied the necessary extra coat of varnish to the off stump. Australia was 2/89 in the 20th over. Three overs later, the score had moved on by eight when Vaughan, who later said he knew his one-day career was all but over, missed an opportunity to run out Ponting from mid wicket.

It was England's last real chance. Ponting and Michael Clarke took the match away from them with their partnership of 112 from 126 balls. Finally Collingwood, who was involved in all three Australian dismissals, took advantage of some running confusion between Ponting and Clarke.

There was no English revival, though. Andrew Symonds was caught on the boundary but the ball was thrown down by Pietersen as he crossed the rope.

Next ball Symonds swiped Collingwood for six and his pull for four off Mahmood from the second ball of the 48th over completed the win.

ENGLAND		AUSTRALIA	
I. R. Bell c Hussey b McGrath	77	A. C. Gilchrist (wk) c Collingwood b Flintoff	27
M. P. Vaughan (capt) b Tait	5	M. L. Hayden b Collingwood	41
A. J. Strauss b Tait	7	R. T. Ponting (capt) run out	86
K. P. Pietersen c Clarke b Bracken	104	M. J. Clarke not out	55
P. D. Collingwood c Gilchrist b Tait	2	A. Symonds not out	28
A. Flintoff st Gilchrist b Hogg	4	Extras B1 Lb5 W5	11
R. S. Bopara c Hussey b Bracken	21	(47.2 overs)	3/248
P. A. Nixon (wk) c Hodge b McGrath	8	Did not bat: M. E. K. Hussey, B. J. Hodge, G. B. Hogg,	
S. I. Mahmood c Hodge b Bracken	0	N. W. Bracken, S. W. Tait, G. D. McGrath	
M. S. Panesar not out	1	1/57 2/89 3/201	
J. M. Anderson lbw b McGrath	0	Bowling: Anderson 10-1-49-0; Mahmood 9.2-1-60-0;	
Extras B4 Lb4 W7 Nb3	18	Flintoff 10-1-35-1; Panesar 9-0-48-0; Collingwood 9-0-50-1	
(49.5 overs)	247		
1/10 2/24 3/164 4/167 5/179 6/230 7/240 8/240 9/246			
10/247			
Bowling: Bracken 10-1-33-3; Tait 10-0-41-3; McGrath			
9.5-0-62-3; Clarke 4-0-27-0; Hogg 10-0-36-1;			
Symonds 6-0-40-0			

Umpires: B.F. Bowden   R.E. Koertzen
Toss: England   Points: Australia 2 England 0

MONDAY 9 APRIL 2007
SUPER EIGHTS MATCH 12: IRELAND v NEW ZEALAND
PROVIDENCE STADIUM, SOUTH GEORGETOWN, GUYANA: NEW ZEALAND WON BY 129 RUNS

New Zealand, with Australia, remained the only unbeaten side in the 2007 World Cup when they defeated Ireland by 129 runs at Providence Stadium.

The Irish challenge to the Kiwis flickered a couple of times, but in the end their batting collapsed horribly against spin duo, Jeetan Patel and Daniel Vettori.

Stephen Fleming won the toss and batted, but the majority of his top order got themselves in then out against tidy bowling from Dave Langford-Smith and off-spinners Kyle McCallan and Andrew White.

Opener Peter Fulton was the exception. In and out of the side and juggled in the order this time he batted on while others fell. His 83 with nine fours in 110 balls won him the Man of the Match Award.

Fulton was fifth out at 172 in the 39th over when he went to sweep a yorker length ball from the persistent McCallan. When Daniel Vettori also fell to the sweep, caught behind off the glove in the 43rd over New Zealand was 7/189 and far from comfortable.

Brendan McCullum, though, with great support from James Franklin responded in brilliant fashion. The pair put on 71 in 43 balls, including 45 runs from the final three overs as Trent Johnston Kevin O'Brien were made to suffer. One six by McCullum off Johnston broke the press box window.

With Shane Bond in such good form 264 was always going to be a tall order for Ireland. Sure enough he promptly removed both openers with accuracy, pace and bounce. When Jacob Oram had Eoin Morgan caught behind cutting it was 3/35 in the 13th over.

The O'Brien brothers, Kevin and Niall then combined in a nice partnership of 75 in 16 overs. Kevin hit three sixes over long on, but just when it seemed they might push for a win their sibling understanding had a break down. Niall was responsible with a 'yes, no, sorry' call.

It was a tragedy that so broke Irish hearts that they lost 7/24 in 54 balls. Simon Taufel and Steve Bucknor hastened the conclusion by awarding four lbw's to the New Zealand spinners.

Vettori grabbed three of those lbw's as well as yorking Kyle McCallan with his faster ball. The left-arm spinner admitted to not getting much turn. "I mixed up my pace and used some drift," he said. It was good enough.

NEW ZEALAND		IRELAND	
P. G.Fulton lbw b McCallan	83	W. T. S. Porterfield c Styris b Bond	11
S. P. Fleming (capt) c Porterfield b Rankin	10	J. P. Bray c McCullum b Bond	1
H. J. H. Marshall c Morgan b Langford-Smith	16	E. J. G. Morgan c McCullum b Oram	15
S. B. Styris c N.J.O'Brien b Langford-Smith	10	N. J. O'Brien (wk) c Oram b Patel	30
C. D. McMillan c Johnston b McCallan	22	K. J. O'Brien run out	49
J. D. P. Oram c Morgan b White	20	D. T. Johnston (capt) lbw b Patel	13
B. B. McCullum (wk) c Morgan b Johnston	47	A. R. White lbw b Vettori	0
D. L. Vettori c N.J.O'Brien b White	5	P. G. Gillespie lbw b Vettori	2
J. E. C. Franklin not out	34	W. K. McCallan b Vettori	0
S. E. Bond not out	0	D. Langford-Smith not out	0
Extras B3 Lb1 W12	16	W. B. Rankin lbw b Vettori	0
(50 overs)	8/263	Extras Lb3 W8 Nb2	13
Did not bat: J. S. Patel		(37.4 overs)	134

1/35 2/59 3/83 4/118 5/172 6/181 7/189 8/260

Bowling: Langford-Smith 10-1-41-2; Rankin 8-0-55-1; Johnston 10-0-63-1; McCallan 10-0-35-2; White 10-0-45-2; K.J.O'Brien 2-0-20-0

1/5 2/22 3/35 4/110 5/125 6/127 7/133 8/133 9/134 10/134

Bowling: Franklin 8-1-27-0; Bond 5-0-18-2; Oram 6-2-15-1; Patel 7-1-32-2; Vettori 8.4-1-23-4; Styris 3-0-16-0

Umpires: S.A.Bucknor S.J.A.Taufel

Toss: New Zealand   Points: New Zealand 2 Ireland 0

TUESDAY 10 APRIL 2007
SUPER EIGHTS MATCH 13: WEST INDIES v SOUTH AFRICA
NATIONAL CRICKET STADIUM, St GEORGES, GRENADA: SOUTH AFRICA WON BY 67 RUNS

The West Indies hopes of progressing through to the 2007 World Cup semi-finals lay virtually in tatters when they were well beaten by South Africa in the first match of the tournament to be staged in Grenada.

The Proteas took revenge for the home defeat they suffered in 2003 at the hands of Carl Hooper's side. The final margin was 67 runs, but that totally flattered the West Indies.

With banners, musical instruments and flags allowed to be taken without written permission for the first time there was a great atmosphere in the National Cricket Stadium.

The West Indies unbeaten in the group stage had lost four matches in a row in the Super Eights. They made several changes to the side that lost to Sri Lanka, but felt no benefit.

Lara had a bad day. He sent South Africa in to bat, mucked up the Powerplay decision and after a promising start missed out with the bat. Post-game he announced his one-day international career would finish at the end of the tournament.

After Graeme Smith was caught behind in the seventh over, AB de Villiers and Jacques Kallis took control of the match with a second wicket stand of 170 at exactly a run per ball.

The pair ran so hard between wickets they both ended up lame. Kallis hit three fours and a six from one Dwayne Bravo over.

Finally, Kallis was bowled by Chris Gayle as he made room for his shot. Man of the Match, de Villiers, who not had a successful tournament to date, continued in aggressive vein to his century and beyond. He hit 12 fours and five sixes before being caught at short fine leg off the only West Indian bowler not to wilt, Corey Collymore.

De Villiers departure, Lara's late Powerplay and his bowlers' lack of competence then allowed Herschelle Gibbs and Mark Boucher to butcher another 77 runs in five overs. Between them in that time the pair hit eight sixes and six fours.

South Africa made 356 and the West Indies never looked like getting near it.

Only Ramnaresh Sarwan perhaps still believed as he raced to 92 from 75 balls with ten fours and a six.

He arrived at the crease at 3/69 in the 12th over after Chris Gayle had been run out by Ashwell Prince from short mid wicket.

He gave Smith's off-spin a thumping. However, he could not find a partner to establish a threatening a partnership. When he holed out to mid-off in the 39th over for 92 the West Indies were 8/213 and any last vestiges of local hope disappeared.

The game did linger from that point as Daren Powell made an unbeaten 48, a score that was double his entire ODI run aggregate before this match. His innings was empty entertainment, but it gave the suffering West Indian supporters something to cheer in the day's closing phase.

SOUTH AFRICA		WEST INDIES	
A. B. de Villiers c Chanderpaul b Collymore	146	C. H. Gayle run out	32
G. C. Smith (capt) c Ramdin b Collymore	7	S. Chanderpaul c Smith b Pollock	4
J. H. Kallis b Gayle	81	D. S. Smith c de Villiers b Nel	33
H. H. Gibbs not out	61	B. C. Lara (capt) b Kallis	21
M. V. Boucher (wk) c & b Bravo	52	R. R. Sarwan c Pollock b Ntini	92
S. M. Pollock not out	0	D. J. Bravo c Gibbs b Pollock	6
Extras Lb3 W6	9	K. A. Pollard b Kallis	10
(50 overs)	4/356	D. Ramdin (wk) c sub (Peterson) b Smith	4
Did not bat: A. G. Prince, L. E. Bosman, A. J. Hall, A . Nel,		I. D. R. Bradshaw c Hall b Smith	20
M. Ntini		D. B. L. Powell not out	48
1/21 2/191 3/261 4/347		C. D. Collymore not out	12
Bowling: Collymore 10-0-41-2; Powell 10-0-78-0; Bradshaw		Extras Lb4 W3	7
10-0-73-0; Bravo 7-0-69-1; Pollard 3-0-20-0; Gayle 6-0-42-1;		(50 overs)	9/289
Sarwan 4-0-30-0		1/5 2/65 3/69 4/119 5/142 6/169 7/181 8/213 9/254	
		Bowling: Pollock 8-0-33-2; Ntini 10-1-57-1; Nel 10-0-54-1;	
		Hall 9-0-49-0; Kallis 8-0-36-2; Smith 5-0-56-2	

Umpires: M.R.Benson D.J.Harper

Toss: West Indies Points: South Africa 2 West Indies 0

WEDNESDAY APRIL 11th 2007
SUPER EIGHTS MATCH 14: BANGLADESH v ENGLAND
KENSINGTON OVAL, BRIDGETOWN, BARBADOS: ENGLAND WON BY FOUR WICKETS

England won the first match at the revamped Kensington Oval against Bangladesh with barely a batsman on either side batting to their potential.

The day after English coach, Duncan Fletcher, secretly told ECB officials he would finish up at the end of the tournament, Michael Vaughan won the toss and bowled.

Both captain and coach would have been pleased with the way their fast bowlers, particularly Man of the Match, Sajid Mahmood, carved their way through the early Bangladeshi batsmen.

Initially it appeared the cricket gods were looking kindly upon the English team.

Tamim Iqbal after two lusty blows off Jimmy Anderson could only parry a Mahmood lifter in the second over.

Vaughan dropped an easy catch at mid-on from Shahriar Nafees only to run out Habibul Bashar who was coasting between wickets because of the apparent ease of the catch. Then Shahriar Nafees edged Mahmood to wicketkeeper Paul Nixon who could not hold it, but Andrew Strauss took the rebound.

That made Bangladesh 3/26 in the 8th over and it declined further to 6/65 in the sixteenth when Anderson had Aftab Ahmed caught behind.

Shakib Al Hasan stopped the rot. He batted through the last 30 overs of the innings, reaching 57 with six fours and a wonderful slashing cut shot six off Andrew Flintoff over backward point.

Mashrafe Mortaza gave him best support in a stand of 47 before Monty Panesar winkled out most of the tail.

England's requirement was just 144. They lost Ian Bell quickly though and the remaining batsmen could not progress beyond twenty or thirty. Vaughan actually top scored with a featureless 30 then chipped a sweep to short fine leg. When Mohammad Rafique got his arm ball through Flintoff and Ravi Bopara played on England had lost two wickets in the 32nd over to be a slightly precarious 6/110.

The two Pauls, Collingwood and Nixon, then held their nerve and took the time they needed to guide England home by four wickets. Nixon sealed the crucial two points by thumping a short ball from Mashrafe Mortaza over square leg for four with 31 balls to spare.

England's fans who made up the majority of the disappointing crowd celebrated. Their harder-to-please press contingent sucked in their breath and almost reluctantly acknowledged the victory.

BANGLADESH		ENGLAND	
Tamim Iqbal c Collingwood b Mahmood	8	I. R. Bell c Aftab Ahmed b Syed Rasel	0
Shariar Nafees c Strauss b Mahmood	9	M. P. Vaughan (capt) c Habibul Bashar b Abdur Razzak	30
Habibul Bashar (capt) run out	4	A. J. Strauss lbw b Syed Rasel	23
Mushfiqur Rahim (wk) b Flintoff	7	K. P. Pietersen c sub (Farhad Reza) b Abdur Razzak	10
Shakib Al Hasan not out	57	P. D. Collingwood not out	23
Mohammad Ashraful c Nixon b Anderson	1	A. Flintoff b Mohammad Rafique	23
Aftab Ahmed c Nixon b Anderson	10	R. S. Bopara b Mohammad Rafique	0
Mashrafe Mortaza b Panesar	13	P. A. Nixon (wk) not out	20
Mohammad Rafique c Strauss b Panesar	0	Extras B4 Lb8 W6	18
Abdur Razzak c Collingwood b Panesar	15	(44.5 overs)	6/147
Syed Rasel c Flintoff b Mahmood	4	Did not bat: S. I. Mahmood, J. M. Anderson, M. S. Panesar	
Extras Lb3 W10 Nb2	15	1/7 2/48 3/70 4/79, 5/110, 6/110	
(37.2 overs)	143	Bowling: Mashrafe Mortaza 8.5-3-28-3; Syed Rasel 10-3-25-2; Abdur Razzak 10-1-30-2; Mohammad Rafique 10-3-33-2; Shakib Al Hasan 6-0-19-0	
1/9 2/23 3/26 4/40 5/47 6/65 7/112 8/113 9/137 10/143			
Bowling: Anderson 8-0-30-2; Mahmood 8.2-0-27-3; Flintoff 8-0-38-1; Panesar 7-2-25-3; Collingwood 4-0-14-0; Bopara 2-0-6-0			

Umpires: S.A.Bucknor   S.J.A.Taufel

Toss: England   Points: England 2 Bangladesh 0

THURSDAY 12 APRIL 2007
SUPER EIGHTS MATCH 15: NEW ZEALAND v SRI LANKA
NATIONAL CRICKET STADIUM, St GEORGES, GRENADA: SRI LANKA WON BY 6 WICKETS

Sri Lanka, playing with a confidence beginning to resemble that which took them all the way to their first World Cup title in 1996, overcame the previously unbeaten New Zealand with plenty of wickets and overs to spare in the second match to be played in Grenada.

The Kiwis had a horror start, recovered thanks to another century from Scott Styris, but still set Sri Lanka's in form batsmen a far from adequate target.

Stephen Fleming won the toss, batted and promptly, for the fourth game against Sri Lanka in a row was trapped lbw by Chaminda Vaas for a duck.

When Ross Taylor, returning from injury edged the first ball from Vaas's second over to Kumar Sangakkara also for a duck, New Zealand were 2/4 after 13 balls.

Vaas, without the injured Lasith Malinga as a partner continued to move the ball and trouble New Zealand.

Scott Styris and Peter Fulton who began a steady recovery, struggled to score at much more than three per over. In the 20th over Fulton holed out in the deep off the veteran left-armer. Vaas, later to be named Man of the Match, was also unlucky not to win a caught behind decision against Styris.

And the battling Kiwi went on to become his main challenger for the MOM award. Styris had been batting superbly through the tournament and this time carried his bat for an unbeaten 111.

He hit eight fours in 157 balls and had partnerships of 67 with Fulton, 64 with Jacob Oram and an unbroken 64 with James Franklin that despite the ongoing difficulties with Muttiah Muralitharan allowed the total to reach a respectable 7/219.

For such a total to do anything beyond extend the duration of the match, though, Shane Bond needed to strike with the new ball.

Despite taking a wonderful catch at third man and bowling tidily, for once, however, he couldn't influence the result.

Jayasuriya was soon in control. He greeted first change bowler, Mark Gillespie by whacking him for six over square-leg, clipped him fine for another ball next ball and, after a no-ball thumped him over mid-on for another four.

Jayasuriya's stand with Sangakkara reached an even 100 before the former was caught behind off Jacob Oram for 64.

At 2/130 in the 26th over, all Sangakkara had to do was keep his head. Like Styris he batted through the rest of the innings, finishing on 69 not out in 104 balls with only three fours.

But Jayasuriya had removed the pressure, so with a trio of handy partnerships with his middle-order partners Sangakkara could guide Sri Lanka to an easy victory. He completed that task when he clipped the ball to fine-leg off Gillespie at the start of the world's shortest and most belated Powerplay ever.

NEW ZEALAND		SRI LANKA	
P. G. Fulton c Silva b Vaas	28	W. U. Tharanga c Bond b Franklin	11
S. P. Fleming (capt) lbw b Vaas	0	S. T. Jayasuriya c McCullum b Oram	64
L. R. P. L. Taylor c Sangakkara b Vaas	0	K. C. Sangakkara (wk) not out	69
S. B. Styris not out	111	D. P. M. D. Jayawardene (capt) c sub (Marshall) b Vettori	15
C. D. McMillan c Silva b Muralitharan	1	L. P. C. Silva c Bond b Vettori	23
J. D. P. Oram c Maharoof b Dilshan	31	T. M. Dilshan not out	14
B. B. McCullum (wk) lbw b Muralitharan	1	Extras B4 Lb7 W7 Nb8	26
D. L. Vettori c Silva b Muralitharan	5	(45.1 overs)	4/222
J. E. C. Franklin not out	25	Did not bat: R. P. Arnold, M. F. Maharoof, W. P. U. J. C. Vaas,
Extras B2 Lb2 W8 Nb5	17	C. R. D. Fernando, M. Muralitharan
(50 overs)	7/219	1/30, 2/130, 3/152 4/180
Did not bat: S. E. Bond, M. R. Gillespie		
1/1 2/4 3/71 4/77 5/141 6/145 7/155		Bowling: Franklin 8-0-49-1; Bond 8-0-26-0; Gillespie 6.1-1-
Bowling: Vaas 9-2-33-3; Fernando 7-2-31-0; Maharoof 6-0-		42-0; Vettori 10-0-35-2; Styris 7-1-28-0; Oram 6-0-31-1
31-0; Muralitharan 10-0-32-3; Jayasuriya 10-0-44-0; Dilshan		
8-1-44-1		

Umpires: Asad Rauf   B.R.Doctrove

Toss: New Zealand   Points: Sri Lanka 2   New Zealand 0

FRIDAY 13 APRIL 2007
SUPER EIGHTS MATCH 16: AUSTRALIA v IRELAND
KENSINGTON OVAL, BRIDGETOWN, BARBADOS: AUSTRALIA WON BY NINE WICKETS

In a match lasting just 42.2 overs, Ireland was smashed by Australia. Their batsmen could not handle Shaun Tait nor Glenn McGrath and they were bowled out for 91 in 30 overs.

Then Adam Gilchrist, and the promoted Mike Hussey and Andrew Symonds finished the batting job in 74 balls.

It did mean the schoolchildren used to fill a ground that otherwise would have been quite empty, could see the whole game rather than get on buses and leave while the match was still in progress, as usually happens when the kids are invited free to the cricket.

For Australia the two points gained from their win, guaranteed them a place in the semi-finals.

Ricky Pointing sent Ireland in and Glenn McGrath handed the new-ball in place of the rested Nathan Bracken, bowled Jeremy Bray with a full pitched in-swinger to the left-hander in the opening over.

Shaun's Tait's first ball to William Porterfield was an express pace lifter that raised eyebrows. In his next over his first ball was straight and too fast for Porterfield and next ball, full and wide and fast, to Niall O'Brien, was dragged onto the stumps.

That left Ireland on 3/2 in the fourth over and they were 4/12 in the fifth when Eoin Morgan edged McGrath to slip.

From there the Australians had to work a little harder for their wickets. Kevin O'Brien, Trent Johnston and later John Mooney scored enough runs to avoid any record breaking embarrassments.

And Tait, although still capable of an unplayable delivery, lost his radar enough to donate ten free runs to the Irish cause.

McGrath with his stunning figures of 3/17 from seven overs won the Man of the Match award. Tait, however, got a fourth wicket; the last of the innings, when he ran-out Mooney with a direct hit throw from mid-off.

Needing 92 the Australian batsmen had finished the job quickly enough to be able to enjoy their lunch without having to have their pads on.

By the time Trent Johnston going around the wicket got the ball between the bat and pad of Adam Gilchrist in the ninth over the total was already 62. Gilchrist had hit four fours, three from consecutive deliveries from Dave Langford-Smith; twice through the covers and once through point.

Symonds had just enough time to hit Mooney for four, get dropped off him by Bray and belt him for a straight six in the tenth over.

Hussey, for his part, finished the match with a six; with a trademark pull over mid wicket.

IRELAND		AUSTRALIA	
J. P. Bray b McGrath	1	A. C. Gilchrist (wk) b Johnston	34
W. T. S. Porterfield lbw b Tait	1	M. E. K. Hussey not out	30
E. J. G. Morgan c Hayden b McGrath	0	A. Symonds not out	15
N. J. O'Brien (wk) b Tait	0	Extras Lb4 W8 Nb1	13
K. J. O'Brien c Hodge b Clark	16	(12.2 overs)	1/92
A. R. White c Hogg b McGrath	6	Did not bat: M. L. Hayden, R. T. Ponting (capt), M. J. Clarke,	
D. T. Johnston (capt) b Tait	17	B. J. Hodge, G. B. Hogg, S .R. Clark, S. W. Tait,	
W. K. McCallan c Tait b Symonds	5	G. D. McGrath	
J. F. Mooney run out	23	1/62	
D. Langford-Smith c Ponting b Hogg	2	Bowling: Langford-Smith 3-0-27-0; Rankin 4.2-0-24-0;	
W. B. Rankin not out	4	Johnston 3-0-18-1; Mooney 1-0-14-0; McCallan 1-0-5-0	
Extras W15 Nb1	16		
(30 overs)	91		
1/2 2/2 3/2 4/12 5/32 6/42 7/54 8/72 9/80 10/91			
Bowling: McGrath 7-1-17-3; Tait 6-1-39-3; Clark 8-1-19-1;			
Hogg 6-2-9-1; Symonds 3-1-7-1			

Umpires: B.F.Bowden R.E.Koertzen
Toss: Australia Points: Australia 2 Ireland 0

SATURDAY 14 APRIL 2007
SUPER EIGHTS MATCH 17: NEW ZEALAND v SOUTH AFRICA
NATIONAL CRICKET STADIUM, ST GEORGE'S, GRENADA: NEW ZEALAND WON BY FIVE WICKETS

New Zealand bounced back from their defeat by Sri Lanka two days before with a five-wicket victory over South Africa that guaranteed their place in the 2007 World Cup semi-finals.

It was a hard-fought win in a match where the ball held sway over the bat for much of the time.

The win also confirmed Sri Lanka's place in the next phase, but it left South Africa facing a winner take all situation in their next match against England in three days at Bridgetown.

The Kiwis used their knowledge of the conditions from the match against Sri Lanka to give themselves an advantage this time. They selected an extra spinner, Jeetan Patel, and unlike the previous Thursday, Stephen Fleming elected to bowl after he won the toss.

Then, on a wicket clearly containing some moisture, his opening bowlers James Franklin and Shane Bond responded in the desired fashion.

In the second over Graeme Smith lifted a drive off Bond to Jacob Oram at cover. In the next over A.B. de Villiers got his leg in front of a Franklin in-swinger and was given out lbw for his fourth duck in eight World Cup innings.

From 2/3 South Africa had to scrap, which they did well enough without ever being able to lift the run rate to a desired level.

Herschelle Gibbs with assistance from Jacques Kallis and Ashwell Prince got the Proteas to 3/128 in the 37th over before playing a delivery from eventual Man of the Match, Craig McMillan, on to his stumps.

McMillan, the seventh bowler used by Fleming, then winkled out Prince and Mark Boucher making it three wickets in fifteen balls with his bustling medium pacers.

Bond and Patel, apart from one six by Shaun Pollock, kept the run rate within bounds in the closing overs so that South Africa had to be satisfied with a mediocre 193.

To get back into the game from there Graeme Smith's side had to do everything right, but they failed to hold crucial catches.

Fleming gave the New Zealand innings stability from the opening position. However, the total was on 2/54 when Prince dropped a hard hit from Scott Styris at square leg. It was a critical moment.

The in form Kiwi was in single figures at the time and was not removed until he had made 56, his fifth half-century in eight innings and New Zealand were within 18 runs of their target.

Other opportunities were not grasped, either. Fleming gave one chance on way to his 50 before a dabbed cut was edged behind. That made the total 3/120 in the 31st over and it brought McMillan to the crease. He hit Robin Peterson for six and on a lovely day for himself and his team watched from the non-strikers end as Brendan McCullum smashed his first ball from Andre Nel through the covers for four to complete the victory with 10 balls to spare.

SOUTH AFRICA		NEW ZEALAND	
G. C. Smith (capt) c Oram b Bond	1	P. G. Fulton c Hall b Ntini	16
A. B. de Villiers lbw b Franklin	0	S. P. Fleming (capt) c Boucher b Pollock	50
J. H. Kallis c Bond b Vettori	22	L. R. P. L. Taylor lbw b Nel	10
H. H. Gibbs b McMillan	60	S. B. Styris c Gibbs b Peterson	56
A. G. Prince c Patel b McMillan	37	C. D. McMillan not out	38
M. V. Boucher (wk) c Fulton b McMillan	16	J. D. P. Oram b Nel	10
S. M. Pollock not out	21	B. B. McCullum (wk) not out	4
A. J. Hall c Oram b Bond	17	Extras Lb3 W8 Nb1	12
R. J. Peterson not out	8	(48.2 overs)	5/196
Extras Lb3 W7 Nb1	11	Did not bat: D. L. Vettori, J. E. C. Franklin, S. E. Bond,	
(50 overs)	7/193	J. S. Patel	

Did not bat: A. Nel, M. Ntini

1/3 2/3 3/52 4/128 5/143 6/149 7/181

Bowling: Franklin 7-2-16-1; Bond 10-1-26-2; Oram 5-2-23-0; Patel 10-1-36-0; Vettori 10-1-50-1; Styris 3-0-16-0; McMillan 5-0-23-3

1/25 2/42 3/120 4/176 5/192

Bowling: Pollock 10-0-30-1; Ntini 10-0-42-1; Nel 9.2-0-33-2; Hall 8-0-32-0; Kallis 4-0-17-0; Peterson 7-0-39-1

Umpires: M.R.Benson D.J.Harper

Toss: New Zealand   Points: New Zealand 2 South Africa 0

As they had early in the tournament, Ireland threw the 2007 World Cup form book out the window when they defeated Bangladesh by 74 runs. The hot-and-cold Bangladeshis within a week had been able to overcome South Africa, the team rated No.1 in the world, then conclusively lose to an Associate Member minnow.

Another green vs green contest, this game, given normal form, would have been the India verses Pakistan fixture. Enough Indian and Pakistani fans still turned up to give the atmosphere a vibe and a boost, one that was pro-Ireland.

Trent Johnston won the toss and took the risk of sending his out of form openers in on the lively Kensington Oval wicket. The brave move paid off when William Porterfield and Jeremy Bray put on 92 in 25 overs.

They concentrated on keeping their wickets intact and running well between wickets. It was a stand that gave the Irish innings the foundation it needed.

The Bangladeshis missed several catches, but their throwing showed improved form as the innings wore on. Ireland had to make up for the absence of boundaries by taking short singles.

Eventually there were misjudgments. Shakib Al Hasan ran out Bray when Porterfield called for a single to reach his fifty that wasn't there. Two overs later Morgan was short when going for a tight second run.

Porterfield made sure those dismissals did not change the focus, though. He batted on to make 85 off 136 balls with just three boundaries, not being dismissed until he top edged a sweep off Mashrafe Mortaza in the 42nd over with the total on 4/176.

His stability allowed Kevin O'Brien and Trent Johnston to hit some sixes and lift the Irish total by 115 runs in the final 16 overs.

Ireland got to 243 knowing that no-one, apart for Australia against England, had successfully chased a target of over 200 in the tournament to date.

Nor were Bangladesh able to manage it. They were 3-48 by the 13th over. Boyd Rankin had Shahriar Nafees caught behind hooking off the glove, Aftab Ahmed chased Andre Botha's first ball back from a two game layoff and was caught behind, too, and Shakib Al Hasan was run out at the non-striker's end when Botha deflected a straight drive onto the stumps.

Tamim Iqbal and Mohammad Ashraful then added 45 at a run a ball to give the Bangladeshi innings some momentum. But when the opener, backing away to give himself room, was bowled by Johnston and Mohammad Ashraful picked out Dave Langford-Smith on the fine-leg boundary the score had slipped again to 5/102.

This time there was no way back. A struggling Habibul Bashar kept the innings going until the 42nd over when he was last out missing a swipe and Ireland could celebrate with a heartily cheered victory lap.

IRELAND		BANGLADESH	
W. T. S. Porterfield c Mohammad Rafique b M. Mortaza	85	Tamim Iqbal b Johnston	29
J. P. Bray run out	31	Shahriar Nafees c N.J.O'Brien b Rankin	7
E. J. G. Morgan run out	5	Aftab Ahmed c N.J.O'Brien b Botha	12
N. J. O'Brien (wk) c Tamim Iqbal b Shakib Al Hasan	10	Shakib Al Hasan run out	3
K. J. O'Brien run out	48	Mohammad Ashraful c Langford-Smith b Rankin	35
D. T. Johnston (capt) c Shahriar Nafees b M. Mortaza	30	Habibul Bashar (capt) b Johnston	32
A. R. White run out	4	Mushfiqur Rahim (wk) b McCallan	16
D. Langford-Smith not out	6	Mashrafe Mortaza c & b Langford-Smith	0
A. C. Botha not out	1	Mohammad Rafique c Johnston b Langford-Smith	2
Extras B1 Lb11 W6 Nb5	23	Abdur Razzak b McCallan	11
(50 overs)	7/243	Shahadat Hossain not out	0
Did not bat: W. K. McCallan, W. B. Rankin		Extras Lb4 W18	22
1/92 2/101 3/128 4/176 5/215 6/233 7/237		(41.2 overs)	169
Bowling: Mashrafe Mortaza 10-1-38-2; Shahadat Hossain 9-1-51-0; Abdur Razzak 9-0-48-0; Mohammad Rafique 10-0-42-0; Shakib Al Hasan 10-0-44-1; Aftab Ahmed 2-0-8-0		1/18 2/45 3/48 4/93 5/102 6/131 7/134 8/138 9/169 10/169	
		Bowling: Rankin 8-0-42-2; Langford-Smith 10-1-27-2; Botha 8-0-31-1; Johnston 7.2-0-40-2; McCallan 8-1-25-2	

Umpires: B.F.Bowden S.A.Bucknor

Toss: Ireland Points: Ireland 2 Bangladesh 0

MONDAY 16 APRIL 2007
SUPER EIGHTS MATCH 19: AUSTRALIA v SRI LANKA
NATIONAL CRICKET STADIUM, St GEORGE'S GRENADA: AUSTRALIA WON BY SEVEN WICKETS

Sri Lanka, going into the match without their three best bowlers, was easily defeated by a confident Australia by seven wickets with 44 balls to spare.

This had been considered to be one of the biggest matches of the tournament to date, but without Muttiah Muralitharan, Chaminda Vaas, both rested, and the injured Lasith Malinga they were never going to restrict Australia to a total below 226.

Mahela Jayawardene won the toss and batted. His top order got to 26 in the fifth over then lost 3/1.

Nathan Bracken bowled a superb opening spell. The left-armer slid one in off the seam to trap Sanath Jayasuriya lbw, then moved one away from Upal Tharanga who was caught at slip. In between Glenn McGrath won an lbw decision against Kumar Sangakkara.

At 3/27 Sri Lanka had to dig deep and Jayawardene and Chamara Silva did just that. Their partnership amounted to 140 in just on 31 overs. In addition to the runs made from many fine shots the total benefitted from another periodic loss of radar by Shaun Tait.

Brad Hogg eventually induced a mistimed sweep from Silva and in his next over he had Jayawardene over balance to be stumped by Gilchrist.

The Sri Lankan innings was in the midst of a new collapse that saw the score go from 3/167 to 8/184 in the middle of the 44th over. Tait had straightened himself out to get Tillakaratne Dilshan and Russel Arnold and when Bracken, who was an obvious choice for Man of the Match, had Nuwan Kulasekera caught a slip by Hayden his figures were 3/9 in his eighth over.

Farvez Maharoof hit four fours in 22 balls and Malinga Bandara thumped Glenn McGrath and Michael Clarke for a six apiece to get the total to a respectable 226.

Without Vaas or Malinga to threaten them Adam Gilchrist, after being dropped early at short cover by Arnold, and Matthew Hayden rattled up an opening partnership of 76 in 12 overs.

Both fell within three runs of each other to Arnold's off-breaks, who having done his job was removed from the attack after four overs.

Ponting and Michael Clarke reduced the target to 101, then Andrew Symonds sealed the issue. He put Jayasuriya away for two sixes, one over long on another over mid wicket and galloped to 63 in 71 balls.

Ponting went to his fourth half century of the tournament and finished the game when he dropped a Bandara leg-spinner over the boundary at long on.

At the post match press conference Jayawardene insisted his mature bowlers had niggling injuries that needed resting, not that they had secrets that were being hidden from the Australians.

Ponting said it did not matter whether they were there or not. His side were setting out to beat whoever they played by as much as possible. Throughout the 2007 World Cup to date they had certainly done that.

SRI LANKA		AUSTRALIA	
W. U. Tharanga c Hayden b Bracken	6	A. C. Gilchrist (wk) lbw b Arnold	30
S. T. Jayasuriya lbw b Bracken	12	M. L. Hayden c Dilshan b Arnold	41
K. C. Sangakkara (wk) lbw b McGrath	0	R. T. Ponting (capt) not out	66
D. P. M. D. Jayawardene (capt) st Gilchrist b Hogg	72	M. J. Clarke c Dilshan b Bandara	23
L. P. C. Silva c Clarke b Hogg	64	A. Symonds not out	63
T. M. Dilshan c Hodge bTait	7	Extras W4 Nb5	9
R. P. Arnold b Tait	3	(42.4 overs)	3/232
M. F. Maharoof c Symonds b Bracken	25	Did not bat: M. E. K. Hussey, B. J. Hodge, G. B. Hogg,	
K. M. D. N. Kulasekara c Hayden b Bracken	1	N. W. Bracken, S. W. Tait, G. D. McGrath	
H. M. C. M. Bandara c Hogg b McGrath	17	1/76 2/79 3/126	
C. R. D. Fernando not out	0	Bowling: Fernando 6-1-36-0; Maharoof 7-0-52-0; Kulasekara	
Extras Lb5 W11 nb3	19	4-0-20-0; Arnold 4-0-20-2; Bandara 9-4-0-53-1; Jayasuriya	
(49.4 overs)	226	6-0-32-0; Dilshan 6-0-19-0	
1/26 2/27 3/27 4/167 5/174 6/178 7/183 8/184 9/218			
10/226			
Bowling: Bracken 9.4-3-19-4; Tait 10-0-68-2; McGrath 9-1-			
48-2; Hogg 10-0-35-2; Symonds 3-0-15-0; Clarke 8-0-36-0			

Umpires: Aleem Dar B.R.Doctrove
Toss: Sri Lanka Points: Australia 2 Sri Lanka 0

TUESDAY 17 APRIL 2007
SUPER EIGHTS MATCH 20: ENGLAND v SOUTH AFRICA
KENSINGTON OVAL, BRIDGETOWN, BARBADOS: SOUTH AFRICA WON BY NINE WICKETS

England's ruined their last chance to make the semi-finals with an inept display against South Africa. They were cleaned up by the South African attack, then their own bowlers were hammered by the top three South African batsmen who took their side to the easiest nine wicket win.

Duncan Fletcher, whose resignation as England's coach would be announced two days after the match, partially blamed the failure on the decision at the toss.

Apparently his pitch sub-committee had repeatedly misread the daily change in the condition of the pitch at Kensington Oval. This meant that on one day it was better to bowl first and on the next bat first.

Michael Vaughan, another questioning his own place in the side, and Ian Bell made a turgid start after Vaughan elected to bat. Shaun Pollock was back to his miserly best and when Bell mistimed a pull in the eighth over the score had only limped to nine.

Vaughan struggled into the 13th over then missed a straight ball from Andre Nel. Then when Pietersen, who had dominated much of the pre-match publicity, chipped a leading edge to mid-off, off the ecstatic Nel England were in real trouble at 3/53 in the 17th.

England's premium rot stopper, Paul Collingwood, and Andrew Strauss attempted some sort of a recovery and put on 58 runs for the fourth wicket in 16 overs. Their stand suggested the match might develop into a contest.

But as soon as that thought surfaced Andrew Hall demolished it and wrecked every English supporter's day.

First, with the score still on Nelson, Jacques Kallis had Strauss cutting straight to Graeme Smith at a fourth slip. Then Hall, getting reverse in-swing had Collingwood lbw, bowled a driving Andrew Flintoff middle stump through the gate, had Paul Nixon caught behind with one going across him and Sajid Mahmood playing on to another in-swinger that again took out middle stump.

In 27 balls England lost 5/10 and were effectively out of the World Cup. Ravi Bopara scrambled England up to 154. Hall got another lbw to give him an astonishing and Man of the Match-winning 5/18 from his 10 overs.

England's humiliation wasn't quite over. Instead of putting up a fight their bowlers were blasted off the park by A. B. de Villiers and Graeme Smith. By the time de Villiers was caught behind for 42 off Flintoff in the 10th over the total was already 85.

No bowler was spared although Mahmood and Monty Panesar were particularly expensive.

Smith thumped his way to 89 not out in 58 balls with 13 fours. The last one off Mahmood down the ground completed the win with 30 overs to spare.

The English fans booed their side off the ground. Despondent after the game, Vaughan later wrote that he could understand their feelings.

ENGLAND		SOUTH AFRICA	
I. R. Bell c Prince b Langeveldt	7	A. B. de Villiers c Nixon b Flintoff	42
M. P. Vaughan (capt) lbw b Nel	17	G. C. Smith (capt) not out	89
A. J. Strauss c Smith b Kallis	46	J. H. Kallis not out	17
K. P. Pietersen c Smith b Nel	3	Extras B4 W3 Nb2	9
P. D. Collingwood lbw b Hall	30	(19.2 overs)	1/157
A. Flintoff b Hall	5	Did not bat: H. H. Gibbs, A. G. Prince, M. V. Boucher (wk),	
R. S. Bopara not out	27	J. M. Kemp, S. M. Pollock, A. J. Hall, C. K. Langeveldt	
P. A. Nixon (wk) c Boucher b Hall	1	1/85	
S. I. Mahmood b Hall	0	Bowling: Anderson 5-0-32-0; Mahmood 4.2-0-49-0; Flintoff	
M. S. Panesar c Boucher b Nel	2	6-0-36-1; Panesar 2-0-24-0; Collingwood 2-0-12-0	
J. M. Anderson lbw b Hall	0		
Extras B4 Lb4 W5 Nb3	16		
(48 overs)	154		

1/9 2/37 3/53 4/111 5/115 6/119 7/121 8/121 9/144 10/154

Bowling: Pollock 10-2-17-0; Langeveldt 7-1-38-1; Nel 10-3-35-3; Hall 10-2-18-5; Kallis 8-0-22-1; Kemp 3-0-16-0

Umpires: S.A.Bucknor S.J.A.Taufel

Toss: England Points: South Africa 2 England 0

WEDNESDAY 18 APRIL 2007
SUPER EIGHTS MATCH 21: IRELAND v SRI LANKA
NATIONAL CRICKET STADIUM, St GEORGE'S, GRENADA: SRI LANKA WON BY EIGHT WICKETS

Sri Lanka, with two key bowlers restored to the line-up, made short work of Ireland in the final match of the 2007 World Cup for everyone's favourite underdog.

The whole game lasted less than 40 overs, Ireland being bowled for 77 which the Sri Lankans ran down in just 10 overs. At one point in their innings the Irish lost 9/26.

No such humiliation looked likely when they reached 0/28 two balls into the eighth over after being sent in by Mahela Jayawardene.

Jeremy Bray hit Farvez Maharoof's first two balls for four, so the medium pacer went around the wicket. Bray then lifted a leading edge to cover, two balls later the promoted Andre Botha chased a wide ball and edged it behind then Eoin Morgan edged his first ball, one that seamed across him and was brilliantly caught again by Kumar Sangakkara.

After Will Porterfield and Niall O'Brien held on for 10 overs, taking the total to 3/46, there was another clatter of wickets.

Six batsmen fell for eight runs. Maharoof dismissed Porterfield and ran out Trent Johnston with some brilliant fielding off his own bowling. That was either side of Muttiah Muralitharan having Niall O'Brien caught behind and Kenny Carroll bowled trying to sweep a doosra second ball in over No.18.

When Kyle McCallan padded up to a Muralitharan off-break heading for the stumps Ireland were 9/54 in the 23rd over.

Finally Dave Langford-Smith hit a few shots in the middle of the bat. A couple of fours and a six over mid wicket off Maharoof took the No.10 to second top score before Chaminda Vaas hit him on the back pad and ended the fun.

Boyd Rankin picked up his 12th wicket of the tournament when Upal Tharanga slashed the last ball of the first over to gully. A couple of overs later Sangakkara mistimed his drive to cover to make the score 2/25.

But there was to be no more drama. Jayawardene and Sanath Jayasuriya raced to an unbroken 56-run partnership in 40 balls.

The Sri Lankan captain dominated, hitting one six over square leg and several fours through and over the off-side, including a back foot cover drove that finished the match.

Sri Lanka could begin preparations for their semi-final. Ireland would fly home, hopefully with greater ease than a number of fans reportedly had recently been having in some of the Caribbean airports.

IRELAND		SRI LANKA	
J. P. Bray c Arnold b Maharoof	20	W. U. Tharanga c Porterfield b Rankin	0
W. T. S. Porterfield c Jayasuriya b Maharoof	17	S. T. Jayasuriya not out	24
A. C. Botha c Sangakkara b Maharoof	0	K. C. Sangakkara (wk) c Carroll b Langford-Smith	10
E. J. G. Morgan c Sangakkara b Maharoof	0	D. P. M. D. Jayawardene (capt) not out	39
N. J. O'Brien (wk) c Sangakkara b Muralitharan	4	Extras W5 Nb3	8
K. J. O'Brien c Jayasuriya b Muralitharan	2	(10 overs)	2/81
K. E. D. Carroll b Muralitharan	0	Did not bat: L. P. C. Silva, T. M. Dilshan, R. P. Arnold,
D. T. Johnston (capt) run out	0	M. F. Maharoof, W. P. U. J. C. Vaas, K. M. D. N. Kulasekara,
W. K. McCallan lbw b Muralitharan	0	M. Muralitharan
D. Langford-Smith lbw b Vaas	18	1/1 2/25
W. B. Rankin not out	7	Bowling: Rankin 4-0-36-1; Langford-Smith 3-0-29-1; Botha
Extras Lb5 W2 Nb2	9	1-0-4-0; K.J.O'Brien 1-0-4-0; K.E.D.Carroll 1-0-8-0
(27.4 overs)	77	
1/28 2/28 3/28 4/46 5/48 6/48 7/49 8/49 9/54 10/77		
Bowling: Vaas 5.4-1-18-1; Kulasekara 7-3-10-0; Maharoof		
10-3-25-4; Muralitharan 5-0-19-4		

Umpires: M.H.Benson B.R.Doctrove

Toss: Sri Lanka   Points: Sri Lanka 2 Ireland 0

THURSDAY 19 APRIL 2007
SUPER EIGHTS MATCH 22: WEST INDIES v BANGLADESH
KENSINGTON OVAL, BRIDGETOWN, BARBDADOS: WEST INDIES WON BY 99 RUNS

This belated West Indian 99-run win over Bangladesh was overshadowed by the post-match announcement that Brian Lara would retire from all international cricket following his team's final match in the tournament against England.

Lara played as if distracted at times, hitting freely for 33 in 27 balls then messing up slips catches in the field.

The misses didn't matter as after a promising start, Bangladesh lost momentum and at the three quarter mark of the game were in batting damage control mode.

Habibul Bashar sent the West Indies in and halfway through their innings the home side were struggling at 3/67.

Mashrafe Mortaza and Syed Rasel had moved the ball in the air and off the wicket early and had removed both openers by the end of the fourth over. Marlon Samuels and Shivnarine Chanderpaul began the rebuild at less than three runs per over until the former was caught behind driving at Shakib Al Hasan's third delivery.

In form Ramnaresh Sarwan then gave the innings a lift. The Guyanan hit five fours and two sixes in his run per ball unbeaten 91 which won him the Man of the Match Award. He was given a life on 62 when Rudi Koertzen turned down an appeal for a run out and didn't call for a replay that showed Sarwan was in fact, just out.

He added 81 with Chanderpaul and 60 with Lara who hit the shot of the match, a front foot drive for six over cover point off Mashrafe Mortaza.

The West Indies finished on 5/230, a decent but not unattainable total to chase.

Third ball of the innings Lara dropped Tamim Iqbal when he tried to throw up a catch he had not quite controlled. He was spared long term, blushes though, when both Bangladeshi opening batsmen ran to the same end in the seventh over.

That was the beginning of a series of batting disasters. Daren Powell and Corey Collymore were getting the ball to lift giving the slips and wicketkeeper Dinesh Ramdin plenty of opportunities.

When Bangladeshi captain, Habibul Bashar failed to get over another sharply bouncing Powell delivery that he parried to a jumping Dwayne Bravo at third slip, his side was 6/52 in the 21st over.

Mushfiqur Rahim and Mohammad Rafique kept the game going for a bit longer without ever suggesting the result would change. The latter was the more aggressive, hitting four fours in 51 balls while putting on 58 with the young wicketkeeper batsman.

Bravo and Chris Gayle made sure the runs made by the Bangladeshi tail were nothing more than a nuisance. They finished with 2/28 apiece, Gayle getting the final wicket when last man Syed Rasel swung hard across the line and missed.

WEST INDIES		BANGLADESH	
C. H. Gayle lbw b Syed Rasel	1	Javed Omar c Gayle b Powell	16
D. S. Smith b Mashrafe Mortaza	5	Tamim Iqbal run out	7
S. Chanderpaul b Aftab Ahmed	50	Aftab Ahmed c Ramdin b Collymore	6
M. N. Samuels c Mushfiqur Rahim b Shakib Al Hasan	31	Shakib Al Hasan c Ramdin b Collymore	0
R. R. Sarwan not out	91	Mohammad Ashraful c Samuels b Powell	2
B. C. Lara (capt) c Javed Omar b Abdur Razzak	33	Habibul Bashar (capt) c Bravo b Powell	12
D. J. Bravo not out	9	Mushfiqur Rahim (wk) not out	38
Extras Lb3 W7	10	Mashrafe Mortaza b Bravo	37
(50 overs)	5/230	Mohammad Rafique lbw b Gayle	0
Did not bat: D.Ramdin (wk), D. B. L. Powell, C. D. Collymore,		Abdur Razzak c Lara b Bravo	1
J. E. Taylor		Syed Rasel b Gayle	2
1/8 2/8 3/55 4/136 5/196		Extras Lb1 W7 Nb2	10
Bowling: Mashrafe Mortaza 10-2-39-1; Syed Rasel 10-2-48-		(43.5 overs)	131
1; Abdur Razzak 10-0-44-1; Mohammad Rafique 10-0-46-0;		1/13 2/21 3/23 4/34 5/35 6/52 7/110 8/111 9/114	
Shakib Al Hasan 8-0-38-1; Aftab Ahmed 2-0-12-1		10/131	
		Bowling: Collymore 7-1-11-2; Powell 10-0-38-3; Taylor 8-0-	
		25-0; Bravo 10-3-28-2; Gayle 8.5-0-28-2	

Umpires: B.F.Bowden R.E.Koertzen

Toss: Bangladesh   Points: West Indies 2 Bangladesh 0

FRIDAY 20 APRIL 2007
SUPER EIGHTS MATCH 23: AUSTRALIA v NEW ZEALAND
NATIONAL CRICKET STADIUM, St GEORGES, GRENADA: AUSTRALIA WON BY 215 RUNS

The World Cup 2007 Australian juggernaut rolled on as fellow semi-finalist, New Zealand, were humiliated to the tune of a record-breaking 215 runs.

Australia's 27th consecutive World Cup victory was built around a brutal batting display and followed up by incisive pace and spin bowling.

New Zealand, like Sri Lanka before them, virtually conceded the match at selection when they rested Shane Bond and Jacob Oram. Australia felt no need to tamper with their winning formula.

Matthew Hayden again launched the Australian innings with a powerful century. His third hundred of the tournament equalled the World Cup record held by Saurav Ganguly in 2003 and Mark Waugh in 1996. It was also the hundredth ever World Cup ton.

After losing his opening partner Adam Gilchrist early he blasted 10 fours and two sixes in 100 balls, winning another Man of the Match Award and putting on 137 with the consistent Ricky Ponting, for the second wicket.

When the Australian captain clipped Jeetan Patel straight to mid wicket, Hayden put on a further 72 with Michael Clarke. The big Queenslander brought up his century with a drive to long on off Scott Styris, then saw the same bowler turn, run and superbly catch a miscue on the edge of the fielding circle.

Styris and Patel were the only two bowlers to keep some sort of a rein on the scoring. Australia were pleased to have Mike Hussey spend quality time in the middle and have Shane Watson come in and blitz the later overs.

The all-rounder arrived at the crease in over No.41 and in 32 balls hit four fours and four sixes on way to an unbeaten 65 as Australia raced to a final total of 348.

Ricky Ponting called it some of the cleanest hitting of a cricket ball he had ever seen.

Two months before in the Chappell-Hadlee Trophy matches New Zealand had successfully chased 336 and 346. This time they got as far as 133.

In Auckland New Zealand had been 2/66 after 11 overs and reached 340, in Hamilton they were 4/49 and made 350.

In St Georges, the Black Caps got to 2/77 at the same point. Opener, Peter Fulton was entrenched and Scott Styris had hit five fours in making 27.

There must have been some residual confidence, but within 20 balls it had evaporated. Styris heaved the first ball of the twelfth over off Glenn McGrath to mid wicket. In the next over Shaun Tait rocketed a full delivery through to Craig McMillan's pads then two overs later Shane Watson had James Franklin mistime his drive onto his stumps. New Zealand was now 5/89 with no way back.

They continued to play their shots and get out. Brad Hogg reaped the benefits of batsmen hitting and guessing at the spin.

Fulton was the exception. He got to 62 and was on the verge of carrying his bat right through the innings when he tried to sweep a flighted wrong'un from the left-armer and was tenth man out, bowled behind his legs.

The whole Kiwi innings lasted less than 26 overs.

AUSTRALIA			NEW ZEALAND	
A. C. Gilchrist (wk) c Gillespie b Franklin	1		P. G. Fulton b Hogg	62
M. L. Hayden c & b Styris	103		S. P. Fleming (capt) c Ponting b Tait	12
R. T. Ponting (capt) c Taylor b Patel	66		L. R. P. L. Taylor c Hussey b McGrath	3
M. J. Clarke b Franklin	49		S. B. Styris c Hayden b McGrath	27
M. E. K. Hussey c Styris b Franklin	37		C. D. McMillan lbw b Tait	1
A. Symonds c Mason b Patel	11		J. E. C. Franklin b Watson	6
S. R. Watson not out	65		B. B. McCullum c Hussey b Hogg	7
G. B. Hogg not out	0		D. L. Vettori c Symonds b Hogg	4
Extras Lb1 W5 Nb10	16		M. R. Gillespie c McGrath b Hogg	2
(50 overs)	6/348		M. J. Mason c Gilchrist b Tait	0
Did not bat: N. W. Bracken, S. W. Tait, G. D. McGrath			J. S. Patel not out	0
1/7 2/144 3/216 4/233 5/257 6/334			Extras W7 Nb2	9
Bowling: Mason 3-0-27-0; Franklin 8-0-74-3;			(25.5 overs)	133
Patel 10-0-48-2; Vettori 10-0-60-0;			1/21 2/29 3/77 4/80 5/89 6/111 7/117 8/127 9/133 10/133	
Styris 10-0-50-1; Gillespie 6-0-67-0; McMillan 3-0-21-0			Bowling: Bracken 4-0-27-0; Tait 6-0-32-3; McGrath 4-0-25-2;	
			Hogg 6.5-1-29-4 Watson 5-0-20-1	

Umpires: Aleem Dar Asad Rauf

Toss: Australia Points: Australia 2 New Zealand 0

SATURDAY 21 APRIL 2007
SUPER EIGHTS MATCH 24: WEST INDIES v ENGLAND
KENSINGTON OVAL, BRIDGETOWN, BARBADOS: ENGLAND WON BY ONE WICKET

The final game of the Super Eights section of the 2007 World Cup, although no more than a battle for fifth spot, proved to be one of the best matches of the tournament.

In addition to an exciting final over one-wicket victory to England, it was a match full of emotion, some poignancy and plenty of goodbyes.

Both sides were noisily supported, the atmosphere building to a crescendo of yells and screams as the runs, wickets and balls remaining equation gradually compressed together.

Much attention centred on the match being Brain Lara's last ever for the West Indies, although, there were also several other players and officials involved for the final time.

England made three changes to the side thrashed by South Africa.

Michael Vaughan won the toss and sent the West Indies in to bat.

Chris Gayle launched the day's entertainment with comfortably his best innings of the tournament. He smashed the new-ball everywhere and raced to 79 in 58 balls. Three times he lofted Liam Plunkett over the boundary at long on and long off.

Devon Smith gave the tall Jamaican great support and the pair opened the innings with a partnership of 131. Andrew Flintoff broke the stand when Gayle was well caught by Stuart Broad at third man.

If Broad's forward falling effort was good then Paul Collingwood's reverse thrust at point 37 runs later to remove Smith off the same bowler was genius. The ball flew high to his left. Collingwood leapt, swiveled and threw up his right-arm to take an absolutely classic catch.

Gayle's dismissal had brought Lara to the crease. He moved to 18 and seemed set for more when Marlon Samuels changed a call and left Lara stranded as Kevin Pietersen threw down the stumps from mid-on.

His team gave him a guard of honour as he left the ground. When Ramnaresh Sarwan was quickly caught behind off Plunkett it seemed the stuffing had been knocked out of the West Indian batting.

Their innings was revived by Samuels and Shivnarine Chanderpaul. They added 77 for the fifth wicket. By the time last man Corey Collymore became the third run out dismissal off the second last ball the West Indies had 300 on the board. Michael Vaughan, with his innocuous looking off-spin, had by far been England's most effective bowler.

Then, like Gayle, the English captain batted more impressively than in any of his previous innings in the tournament. And, also like Gayle, he made 79.

He guided the side to 2/154 then was run out by Dwayne Bravo. Ravi Bopara had suffered the exact same fate.

Vaughan's dismissal began a period when the West Indies got on top and nine overs later, when Paul Nixon joined Pietersen, England were in trouble at 6/189 with 14 overs remaining.

The big South Africa-born batsmen then turned on a brilliant batting exhibition. He accelerated as he moved into the sixties with England needing 88 from the last ten overs. He used the pace of the West Indian bowlers to deflect the ball to third man and fine leg for a series of boundaries, then went from 94 to 100 with a step away hit for six over long on off Jerome Taylor.

He was bowled next ball trying to repeat the shot and Plunkett went almost immediately after.

Nixon ensured that Man of the Match Pietersen's century was not wasted this time as had been his previous four One-Day hundreds. In the third last over the wicketkeeper three times struck Corey Collymore to the boundary at wide mid-on.

He too would fall in the final over, but an aerial drive over cover for two from Stuart Broad from the second last ball allowed England to finish their campaign on a high note.

WEST INDIES		ENGLAND	
C. H. Gayle c Broad b Flintoff	79	A. J. Strauss c Smith b Collymore	7
D. S. Smith c Collingwood b Flintoff	61	M. P. Vaughan (capt) run out	79
B. C. Lara (capt) run out	18	R. S. Bopara run out	26
M. N. Samuels c Collingwood b Vaughan	51	K. P. Pietersen b Taylor	100
R. R. Sarwan c Nixon b Plunkett	3	P. D. Collingwood b Bravo	6
S. Chanderpaul c Plunkett b Collingwood	34	A. Flintoff c Powell b Sarwan	15
D. J. Bravo c Dalrymple b Vaughan	13	J. W. M. Dalrymple run out	1
D. Ramdin (wk) not out	10	P. A. Nixon (wk) b Bravo	38
J. E. Taylor c Dalrymple b Vaughan	12	L. E. Plunkett c Bravo b Taylor	2
D. B. L. Powell run out	0	S. C. J. Broad not out	5
C. D. Collymore run out	1	J. M. Anderson not out	0
Extras Lb1 W14 Nb3	18	Extras B6 Lb11 W5	22
(49.5 overs)	300	(49.5 overs)	9/301

1/131 2/168 3/173 4/181 5/258 6/276 7/277 8/296 9/298 10/300
Bowling: Anderson 6-0-39-0; Plunkett 7-0-71-1; Broad 6-1-32-0; Flintoff 9.5-0-59-2; Dalrymple 3-0-19-0; Collingwood 8-0-40-1; Vaughan 10-0-39-3

1/11 2/101 3/154 4/162 5/185 6/189 7/269 8/271 9/298
Bowling: Collymore 10-0-61-1; Powell 10-0-58-0; Taylor 10-1-65-2; Gayle 5-0-32-0; Bravo 9.5-0-47-2; Sarwan 5-1-21-1

Umpires: R.E.Koertzen S.J.A.Taufel
Toss: England Points: England 2 West Indies 0

Super Eights

Teams	Mat	Won	Lost	Tied	N/R	Pts	Net RR	For	Against
Australia	7	7	0	0	0	14	+2.400	1725/266.1	1314/322.0
Sri Lanka	7	5	2	0	0	10	+1.483	1586/301.1	1275/337.0
New Zealand	7	5	2	0	0	10	+0.253	1378/308.0	1457/345.1
South Africa	7	4	3	0	0	8	+0.313	1561/299.1	1635/333.2
England	7	3	4	0	0	6	-0.394	1557/344.4	1511/307.4
West Indies	7	2	5	0	0	4	-0.566	1595/338.1	1781/337.1
Bangladesh	7	1	6	0	0	2	-1.514	1084/318.0	1398/284.0
Ireland	7	1	6	0	0	2	-1.730	1111/333.0	1226/242.0

TUESDAY 24 APRIL 2007
1st SEMI-FINAL: NEW ZEALAND v SRI LANKA
SABINA PARK, KINGSTON, JAMAICA: SRI LANKA WON BY 81 RUNS

Sri Lanka moved into their second World Cup Final with a conclusive 81-run win over New Zealand.

This was the Kiwis' fifth appearance in a World Cup semi-final and they had yet to make it through to the Final. In 1992 they had come closest. In truth, on this day, though, they were outclassed by quite a long way by the more consistent and versatile Sri Lankans.

The feature of the match was the unbeaten century by Sri Lankan captain, Mahela Jayawardene. He came to the crease with the game evenly poised at 2/67 in the 14th over and did not leave until he had made 115 runs and his side's overs allocation had expired. Wisden Almanack called it, "one of the finest one-day innings of all time."

Many Jamaicans missed it. Despite this once in a generation opportunity the country's cricket fans had to witness a World Cup semi-final only just over nine thousand people were in Sabina Park for the game.

Cost of admission, international cricket de-valuation through overkill and disappointment with the form of the West Indian team all took their toll. One could expect, though, a World Cup semi-final would fill probably every other cricket ground in the world outside the West Indies with the possible exception of the MCG.

Jayawardene completed the fourth ever century in a World Cup semi-final and his score of 115 equalled the highest ever innings by Graham Gooch in 1987. It would win him the Man of the match Award.

On a day when everything went right for the Sri Lankan captain, he began in the best possible fashion by winning the toss and batting.

In the third over James Franklin moved one through the defence of Sanath Jayasuriya and Sri Lanka were 1/13.

It was seemingly an important breakthrough as the departing batsman had been in form and the remaining one had made 17 runs from his previous three innings.

But Upal Tharanga was in a different place this day and runs flowed from his bat. He backed himself when he had room, driving and slashing the ball to all points on the off-side.

New Zealand after their early boost never again got on top. Even though Franklin picked up his second wicket in the 14th over when Kumar Sangakkara clipped the ball straight to mid-on, their key fast bowler, Shane Bond, was shadow of the star he had been previously.

Not that Jayawardene took any early liberties. Tharanga was moving the scoreboard forward so Jayawardene eased into his task. He was 2 after nineteen balls and 17 after 47 balls.

By the time the left-handed opener was bowled behind his legs by Daniel Vettori's faster ball he had made 73 from 74 balls. Tharanga was dismissed at virtually the exact halfway point of the innings. He had hit the shot of the match, a lofted cover drive for six off Vettori and he left Sri Lanka on 3/111.

Still Jayawardene accumulated only with gradual acceleration. There was a 41 run partnership with Chamara Silva, ended when Rudi Koertzen got an lbw appeal decision wrong.

That was in the 35th over. Now was the time to lift the run rate.

Amazingly Jayawardene singled out Shane Bond. With deft touches and deflections and occasional thumps over mid wicket the runs rattled along. Bond conceded 24 runs from 16 balls. In their final ten overs the Sri Lankans added 102.

Jayawardene and Tilerkaratne Dilshan put on 81 in 11 overs before the latter was also given a poor lbw decision this time by the normally reliable Simon Taufel. It mattered little as Russel Arnold and his captain, who completed only the second ever century by a Sri Lankan leader in the World Cup, piled up a further 56 runs in the final 29 balls.

Jayawardene crowned his innings with his third six in the 50th over, a full toss from Bond dispatched over mid wicket.

Sri Lanka had 289 on the board and New Zealand would have to bat better than previously in the entire history of their nation to score 290.

Lasith Malinga in his first spell ensured that was unlikely to happen. The man with the unorthodox round-arm action and a hairdo that looked like Harpo Marx the day before he visited his hairdresser bowled very fast and moved the ball away from the right-hander.

That was in to left-hander Stephen Fleming who altered his mode of dismissal from his last four innings against Sri Lanka from 'lbw b Vaas 0' to 'lbw b Malinga 1'.

Then Ross Taylor was so put through the wringer by Malinga that he could only grin at the inequality of the contest. He struggled through to the 11th over until he was given out lbw to Vaas. Struck on the front pad the assessment was that Taylor also had been unlucky to be sent on his way by Taufel.

Now, for the next 11 overs, New Zealand, raised a glimmer of hope that they could challenge their big target. Scott Styris, although carrying a hand injury, maintained the momentum of his wonderful form in the tournament while Peter Fulton, also at the top of his game, added 63 runs.

Both batsmen got stuck into Dilhara Fernando. Styris smacked him for two sixes and Fulton hit another. Styris also lofted a Muralitharan doosra back over the bowler's head for his third maximum and at 2-105 in the 22nd over there was a sense that the Kiwis were just about in the race.

Then in four overs the match was ended as a contest. Styris on 499 runs for the tournament, clipped Dilshan to a jumping Jayawardene. It was a tame dismissal that seemed to deflate New Zealand and it opened the door for Muralitharan to storm through.

In the 24th over the spin master took a low caught and bowled as Jacob Oram was flummoxed by another doosra. Next ball Brendon McCullum swept at yet another doosra, top edged and Silva grabbed a diving sliding catch at short fine-leg.

Next over Fulton chipped Jayasuriya to mid wicket and in the next Vettori was given lbw to yet another Muralitharan doosra.

New Zealand had lost 5/11 and any hope of reaching the final.

The match still lingered without heat for another 16 overs. Craig McMillan scored a few and last pair Franklin and Patel had 59 runs worth of fun in the sun before their participation in the 2007 World Cup finished.

SRI LANKA		NEW ZEALAND	
W. U. Tharanga b Vettori	73	P. G. Fulton c Silva b Jayasuriya	46
S. T. Jayasuriya b Franklin	1	S. P. Fleming (capt) lbw b Malinga	1
K. C. Sangakkara (wk) c Fleming b Franklin	18	L. R. P. L. Taylor lbw b Vaas	9
D. P. M. D. Jayawardene (capt) not out	115	S. B. Styris c Jayawardene b Dilshan	37
L. P. C. Silva lbw b Bond	21	J. D. P. Oram c & b Muralitharan	3
T. M. Dilshan lbw b Oram	30	B. B. McCullum (wk) c Silva b Muralitharan	0
R. P. Arnold not out	14	C. D. McMillan b Jayasuriya	25
Extras Lb3 W9 Nb5	17	D. L. Vettori lbw b Muralitharan	0
(50 overs)	5/289	J. E. C. Franklin not out	30
Did not bat: W. P. U. J. C. Vaas, S. L. Malinga,		S. E. Bond b Muralitharan	2
M. Muralitharan, C. R. D. Fernando		J. S. Patel c Fernando b Dilshan	34
1/13 2/67 3/111 4/152 5/233		Extras B5 Lb2 W8 Nb6	21
Bowling: Franklin 9-1-46-2; Bond 10-1-59-1;		(41.4 overs)	208
Oram 10-0-60-1; Vettori 10-0-51-1; Patel 10-0-62-0;		1/2 2/32 3/105 4/114 5/114 6/115 7/116 8/144 9/149	
Styris 1-0-8-0		10/208	
		Bowling: Vaas 8-1-25-1; Malinga 7-2-21-1; Fernando 5-0-45-0;	
		Muralitharan 8-0-31-4; Jayasuriya 9-0-57-2; Dilshan 4.4-0-22-2	

Umpires: R.E.Koertzen S.J.A.Taufel
Toss: Sri Lanka

WEDNESDAY 25 APRIL 2007
2nd SEMI-FINAL: AUSTRALIA v SOUTH AFRICA
BEAUSEJOUR STADIUM, GROS ISLET, St LUCIA: AUSTRALIA WON BY SEVEN WICKETS

Australia and South Africa have been involved in some of the greatest one-day internationals of all time. This one-sided World Cup semi-final was not one of them.

Basically the Proteas were blown off the park by the Australian fast bowlers and could not summon the firepower themselves to strike back with equal force.

It resulted in a seven-wicket win for Australia with nearly 25 overs of the match left unused.

Australia, on Anzac Day, marched into their fourth consecutive World Cup final, setting up a rematch with Sri Lanka to whom they lost at Lahore in 1996. This was South Africa's third semi-final, but they would have to wait at least another four years to attempt to again successfully reach a final.

The clash between two of the game's heavyweights was effectively over as a contest within ten overs. South Africa won the toss, batted, made a total shambles of their approach and was 5/27 after 59 balls.

The Proteas had received a motivational message pre-match from Bob Woolmer's widow, Gill, who said, 'Do it for Bob.'

But Ricky Ponting later wrote, 'South Africa just played dumb.' Sambit Bal on Cricinfo wrote of the Proteas, 'They batted like wrecks' and 'their batting descended to mindless adventure.'

Graeme Smith indicated his team's philosophy when he walked down the pitch to Nathan Bracken swung hard, missed, and was bowled in the third over.

Bracken accurate and moving the ball nicely was good, but Glenn McGrath, in his second last game for his country was as wonderful as he has ever been.

Ponting had to re-jig his fast bowling set up because of the strong wind blowing across the Beausejour Stadium. So McGrath took the new-ball and bowled brilliantly. Statisticians assessed 27 deliveries in his first five over spell were on a length.

Jacques Kallis tried to take the initiative off him. In the sixth over he walked down the wicket and away from the stumps and crashed McGrath through extra-cover for four. Next ball, after a brief interruption in front of the sightscreen, he moved back, bent his knee and tried to thrash the ball through point.

McGrath had tried to follow him the previous ball. This time just fired in a yorker on off stump and hit off stump.

South Africa was 2/12 in the sixth over and their plan to grab the initiative looked to be in tatters.

Still their batsmen persisted.

In the ninth over A.B. de Villiers hooked Shaun Tait's first ball to the mid wicket boundary. Then he went to drive his fifth ball, was slow in his forward weight transfer and was caught behind.

Next over was even worse. McGrath pushed the fourth ball wide across left-hander Ashwell Prince who chased it and edged just his second ball through to Adam Gilchrist. Next ball Mark Boucher half forward edged to Matthew Hayden low at first slip. McGrath had now taken 25 wickets for the tournament, a record, and would be named Man of the Match.

It was 5/27 and should have been 6/27. Umpire, Steve Bucknor, failed to spot an inside edge from Herschelle Gibbs bat as Tait ripped a brute of a delivery right through him next over.

But Gibbs and Justin Kemp survived to add 60. Gibbs had the talent to cope with the lethal Australian attack, driving Tait through the covers in stylish fashion and slapping him over point.

McGrath may have been finished. Tait wasn't, though. He had already sent down his trademark five wides down the leg-side when he got another bullet in the right place to trap Gibbs into an edge with a half fashioned nudge. Six runs later Andrew Hall swished outside off stump to give Tait his third wicket and Gilchrist his fourth catch.

At 7/93 the game was really gone. But Justin Kemp hung in at the crease and the South African tailenders helped him. Shaun Pollock, another champion on the verge of finishing his career, got the total past 100 then miscued a drive back to Brad Hogg.

Andre Nel and Charl Langeveldt did slightly better and by the time the latter was bowled by a full-pitched Shane Watson delivery the last two wickets had added 46. Despite this minor rally 149 was still South Africa's lowest ever World Cup total.

Langeveldt briefly hinted at the possibility of South African revival when he swung the ball through between the bat and pad of Adam Gilchrist with his first ball and hit the off stump.

Australia was 1/1 and Gilchrist was looking for answers to his batting slump. He had made one and one in his last two hits and had not topped 35 in his previous five innings. His answer lay in a small rubber sphere that had been his batting companion off and on in recent weeks.

More immediately Matthew Hayden and Ricky Ponting quelled any further new-ball dramas. Their partnership was worth 43. With the target only 150 it was enough to take the sting out of the Proteas. Not that Nel restrained his celebrations when he yorked Ponting after the Australian captain had hit five fours in 25 balls.

There would only be one more such opportunity for South African joy in the 2007 World Cup as Australia cruised onward and upward. Michael Clarke was at his stylish best, Hayden solid if a little more restrained than he had been in his previous outing against the same side.

Pollock had a skerrick of revenge for the Hayden onslaught of a month before when the big Queenslander tried to crunch him, got under the ball a bit and was caught at long on by Graeme Smith.

This time there was little to get excited about. Australia was within 40 runs of reaching the Final now and Smith was hobbling troubled badly by an injured knee.

Clarke and Andrew Symonds did not make them suffer much longer. In another 41 balls the 43 runs required had been scored and the match was finished. There was no flurry of boundaries. Instead the pair traded the occasional blow to the rope with lots of hits to the gaps for ones and twos. Finally, with the scores level, Symonds smacked an Andrew Hall full-toss to the square-leg fence.

Graeme Smith denied his side had 'choked'. No one was impressed. Many felt short changed by such a limp contest in a big match.

SOUTH AFRICA		AUSTRALIA	
G. C. Smith (capt) b Bracken	2	A. C. Gilchrist (wk) b Langeveldt	1
A. B. de Villiers c Gilchrist b Tait	15	M. L. Hayden c Smith b Pollock	41
J. H. Kallis b McGrath	5	R. T. Ponting (capt) b Nel	22
H. H. Gibbs c Gilchrist b Tait	39	M. J. Clarke not out	60
A. G. Prince c Gilchrist b McGrath	0	A. Symonds not out	18
M. V. Boucher (wk) c Hayden b McGrath	0	Extras Lb5 W3 Nb3	11
J. M. Kemp not out	49	(31.3 overs)	3/153
A. J. Hall c Gilchrist b Tait	3	Did not bat: M. E. K. Hussey, S. R. Watson, G. B. Hogg,
S. M. Pollock c & b Hogg	5	N. W. Bracken, S. W. Tait, G. D. McGrath
A. Nel c Clarke b Tait	8	1/1 2/44 3/110
C. K. Langeveldt b Watson	6	Bowling: Pollock 5-1-16-1, Langeveldt 6-0-34-1; Kallis 5-1-
Extras Lb4 W13	17	20-0; Nel 7-1-31-1; Hall 6.3-0-43-0; Kemp 2-0-4-0
(43.5 overs)	149	
1/7 2/12 3/26 4/27 5/27 6/87 7/93 8/103 9/130 10/149		
Bowling: Bracken 7-2-15-1; McGrath 8-1-18-3; Tait 10-0-39-4; Watson 8.5-0-49-1; Hogg 10-2-24-1		

Umpires: Aleem Dar S.A.Bucknor
Toss: South Africa

Never can a World Cup Final in any sport have had so many things go wrong and its memory be so tarnished by bad luck and incompetence. In the end there was relief that the best team won the prize and that one player at least showcased his talents to such a degree that despite all the setbacks the exercise was still a worthwhile one.

Australia won their 24th consecutive World Cup match and their fourth World Cup title. This 53-run win at Bridgetown was their third trophy in a row and, despite the merits of the Sri Lankan campaign, they surprised no-one by achieving such a record. It was the perfect send off for their retiring coach John Buchanan and champion fast bowler, Glenn McGrath,

Whether Australia's total dominance was a good thing for world cricket, 50-over cricket, or even World Cup cricket is a matter for discussion. This was one of the best sides ever to play the game. But the way they cut a swathe through the opposition, again, meant that at the time, fans moved on quickly after the result. The tournament had been going on for ages and after all 51 matches over two-and-a-half months the end result was the one that, on reflection at least, looked quite obvious at the start.

So many matches had been televised to the point where for many regular viewers and probably the players, the games must have become a disposable,blur. It is easy to make the argument that this was not the case in any of the previous World Cups.

"Two-and-a-half months is a long time to be in one location playing cricket with the same group of guys," says key Australian left-arm fast bowler Nathan Bracken. "We were lucky in two ways. We had a 10-day break in Antigua at one stage. There were some training commitments, but we had a fair bit of free time and you could refresh yourself.

"And also at the end of the Super Eights leg we played a couple of big games like the first match against Sri Lanka that we were able to build up for and maintain our focus for."

After all the misfortunes and bungles in the West Indies in the lead up, it was always the 2007 World Cup final unlike all previous eight finals, that was going to be bedevilled by the weather. Sure enough with the ground full, the toss made and won by Ricky Ponting and everything set to showcase the 50-over format of the game, down came the rain.

The match due to start at 9.30am local time, was delayed for nearly three hours. The prospect of having to use the reserve day became a reality. But 'Only if 20 overs are not bowled in each innings' mentioned the good folk of Cricinfo as they whiled away the time at their keyboards.

In Australia the rain helped turn off the televisions of those who without any live cricket to watch could not sustain consciousness through the middle of the night on the east coast. In Sri Lanka it was late afternoon and early evening. For the fans from that country it was not so difficult to be patient and stay awake.

The covers came off then were put back on again. That process was repeated several times. Eventually at 12.15pm the 2007 World Cup Final began as a 38-overs-per-side contest.

"You can't switch off when it is raining because you know if it stops you could be playing within 30 minutes. You need to stay focussed and ready," Bracken says. "We wanted the match to stay as close as we could to being a 50-over game.

"That was the format we had been playing well under and if it had been 21 overs or something of that nature then one good individual performance could decide the result for either side. After all that time we did not really want it to come down to that.

"Thirty-eight overs was not 50 but it was better than 20."

Chaminda Vaas and Lasith Malinga opened the bowling to the experienced Australian pair Matthew Hayden and Adam Gilchrist. From batting point of view Hayden had kick-started Australia's tournament while Gilchrist, out of form in his last two hits, had played more of a supporting role.

This time though it was Gilchrist who came out firing. In Vaas's second over he flicked the ball to fine leg for four then cracked him next ball over long on for the first six of the final. It sent the hefty yellow contingent in the crowd into raptures.

Vaas was targeted, but Lasith Malinga only conceded six runs in his first four overs. Australia had set up a special low-level bowling machine to try and replicate his low fast slinging action to some degree. It only partially worked as although he took no early wickets, his restriction of the run rate could have been crucial in this shortened game.

The total after 10 overs was no more than 46. The tempo changed in the 11th over bowled by Dihara Fernando. Gilchrist was dropped by the bowler second ball when he belted a straight drive at his ankles and the big quick could not hang on. The next ball was a full-toss hit to leg for four. Balls four and five were clubbed to long on, the first for four the second for six. Gilchrist was away.

Tillekaratne Dilshan's off-spin replaced Fernando. Gilchrist had reached his fifty off 43 balls when he twice lofted Dilshan back over his head for six in his second over. In between there had also been five wides down the leg-side so that the over cost 19 runs.

Gilchrist carried on. Fernando was clubbed for another 14 runs in his fourth over and 13 in his fifth. Muttiah Muralitharan was not totally butchered, nor was he spared. One hit by Gilchrist over mid wicket went ten rows back.

"Murali's just such a fantastic bowler, but he feels the pressure just like anyone else. If you can get on top of a player like that early, it just upsets the rest of the team, who will know that their main trump card is not all that confident," says Australia's leading spinner in the match, Brad Hogg.

From the third ball of the 21st over he drove Malinga over mid off for his eighth four to reach the most stunning century off 72 balls. It was a career crowning moment.

"I was glad I had a good seat to watch that innings and did not have to bowl to him," says Bracken. "It was fantastic. We knew Adam would come good on the big stage at just the right time. We had real confidence and belief in his ability. He just started timing the ball and hitting the gaps.

"He played the good balls as he should, then the bad ones would just disappear. It was world class."

As he celebrated, Gilchrist pointed to his left-hand. Inside was a squash ball that he had inserted on the advice of his batting coach, Bob Meuleman, to restrict the grip on his bottom hand. It was a decision that was taken up by the media. In the dressing room it made less impact.

"I had no idea what he was doing," Bracken says. "It was a total surprise when I found out he had a squash ball in his glove."

Gilchrist's century was the fifth by a batsman in a World Cup final. The previous four by Clive Lloyd, Viv Richards, Aravinda de Silva and Ricky Ponting were all exceptional innings by huge batting talents. It won each of them the Man of the Match Award and their team the World Cup.

Gilchrist's innings was the equal of any and maybe a degree better than some, because he did not stop at three figures. His opening partner Matthew Hayden knew he was witnessing a classic. Hayden wrote, 'I thought, "Don't worry about me today— I'm here to run, hopefully twos, so you can get back on strike."'

During their wonderful opening partnership he told Gilchrist, "Mate, just smash it. Smash it miles."

Gilchrist continued to do that. In each of the next two overs after reaching his century he hit two more fours off Vaas and Malinga. Hayden in fact became the first wicket to fall in the 2007 World Cup Final when from the second last ball of the 23rd over his cover drive off Malinga just failed to clear the leaping Jayawardene at short cover.

Australia was 1/172 and Hayden, recalled to the Australian one-day team after a spell on the sidelines, could be well satisfied with his contribution of 38 from 55 balls. Gilchrist and Ponting maintained the momentum with a partnership of 52 in 46 balls until finally the wicketkeeper/batsman gave Fernando some relief by mistiming the pull that would have brought up his 150. Ponting fell 37 runs later for 37 when Andrew Symonds called for a run to cover that was too tight and Jayawardene made a direct hit.

A few balls later Shane Watson was bowled behind his legs trying to paddle sweep Malinga then Andrew Symonds and Michael Clarke added 15 more runs from the final ten balls. Australia had made a formidable 4/281 from their 38 overs. The bowlers knew, though, they could not take it for granted that it was a winning total.

"You always believed that whatever was on the board would be enough if you bowled and fielded well," Bracken says. "But they had a quality top five in the order, the ground was small and the outfield fast. If they got a good start they could do some damage. The main way to do that was to take wickets. You might be protecting yourself against their strengths, but the objective is to build pressure and take wickets."

First ball of the Sri Lankan innings, Upal Tharanga thrashed a Bracken delivery through the covers. But from the first ball of his next over an outswinger from left-armer to left-hander was edged behind to Gilchrist.

Two more left-handed batsmen, Sanath Jayasuriya and Kumar Sangakkara, then provided Sri Lanka with their best period of the match with a partnership of 116 in 106 balls.

Wisden said their driving through the second Powerplay was "the best batting of the tournament." From overs 12 to 16 they added 51 runs. Jayasuriya took three fours off Watson's third over, over mid-on and the bowler's head with flat bat swats and then his trademark flash over point.

Sangakkara topped that in McGrath's next over with a six over mid wicket, a four over cover and a pull to square-leg from consecutive deliveries. They brought the hundred up in the sixteenth over. Even with such a batting onslaught, though, the required run rate stayed above eight per over. Both men had reached their fifties when the mood changed once more. It began to drizzle again then Sangkkara pulled Brad Hogg straight to Ponting at mid wicket.

"It was raining again that day and there was some moisture out on the oval," says Brad Hogg. "I wasn't able to grip the ball well. I had to change it up and bowl as best as I could. I think I bowled back-spinners the whole Sri Lanka innings. I remember that Jayawardene couldn't pick me and that Sangakkara was struggling to pick me. I just wasn't able to bowl my wrong-un and I only bowled the three overs. It was just because of the wet ball."

Three overs later Michael Clarke got a delivery through to Jayasuriya's off stump. Required run rate was now above nine. The writing began to appear on the wall. Not that Nathan Bracken thought that way.

"Although it was great to get those two out you still don't get ahead of yourself," Bracken said. "One goes and another comes in and you wonder, 'what will this bloke do?' When it is a World Cup Final you are not coming back next week for another crack. Everything is on the line. As someone who played mostly one-dayers for Australia, this was my Ashes."

Two overs later, with the score on 3/149 from nearly 25 overs, no 'blokes' could do anything as the persistent drizzle became heavier and everyone left the field.

The Sri Lankans needed 133 runs from 13.1 overs when they walked off.

When the players returned Mr Duckworth and Mr Lewis decreed the new target was 269 from 36 overs. That left them 67 balls to get 120 runs. Within an over Watson trapped Jayawardene lbw. The batsmen continued to play their shots. Chamara Silva clubbed Clarke over mid wicket for six.

Other factors were beginning to affect the game. The pitch and the ball were wet. The umpires changed the ball. Now the sun was beginning to set. And there were no lights to switch on. Dilshan slipped and was run out and Silva swiped at Clarke and missed a straight ball. The over after Silva was bowled, the 32nd of the innings, with everyone squinting to see, Glenn McGrath bowled a waist high full-toss to Russel Arnold. He miscued the ball in the air and Gilchrist held the catch.

It was McGrath's 26th wicket in his record-breaking tournament. It was his 381st one-day international wicket and his 949th wicket for Australia in all forms of the game. It was also his final wicket.

"We all wanted to send such a champion out as a winner," Bracken said. "It was an honour for me to share the new ball with him in that match. His imminent retirement was not something that needed to be discussed, but it was one extra motivation."

Clark bowled the 33rd over of the innings. Malinga hit the fifth ball for six. But after one more delivery the umpires offered the light to the Sri Lankan batsmen.

Malinga and Vaas saw that their side needed to score 63 runs from 18 balls with three wickets in hand in the dark. They accepted the invitations of Aleem Dar and Steve Bucknor to leave the ground.

Australia celebrated. They had won the 2007 World Cup.

Or had they?

"On the field we all knew that the game was a complete game after we had bowled 20 overs," Bracken said. "I believe Rudi Koertzen, the third umpire knew it was over, too. As a side we would always pride ourselves on knowing the rules. So we knew it was a result and we had won. That's why we began celebrating"

Match Referee, Jeff Crowe and some other officials, however, thought there were still three overs to be played.

Aleem Dar approached Ricky Ponting and the Australian team and told them the match was not over. The ground staff who brought the presentation platform out onto the ground had to take it back.

On television commentator Mark Nicholas was irate and confused in equal measures. Part of his confusion arose from not being able to see anything. Then Mahela Jayawardene came up with the best answer for a very bad situation. Australia would bowl their spinners for three overs in the dark and the game, to all intents and purposes already won and lost, would be completed.

Symonds bowled two overs and Clarke sent down one as quickly as they could. Eleven further runs were scored and Malinga was stumped having a big swing at a Symonds delivery. That is the assumed situation as it was almost impossible for anyone on or off the ground to see what was happening.

"At one stage I was at point and Chaminda Vaas cut the ball. I heard the clunk of bat on ball but could not see anything," Bracken says. "Brad Hogg and I just looked at each other. It was so dark we had absolutely no idea where the ball was.

"It was great sportsmanship by Jayawardene and the Sri Lankans to say, 'Let's get it over tonight.' No-one wanted to come back the next day for three overs."

This time the game was over. Australia was adjudged winners by 53 runs. They were allowed to celebrate and the presentations could go ahead.

"Bit dark at the moment, but loving every minute," said McGrath at the presentation of his Player of the Tournament Award.

Then the Australians did a lap of honour for their fans in the ground. The only illuminations allowing players and spectators to see each other were from the lights in the grandstand.

A light tower or two might have helped if they had been built.

AUSTRALIA		SRI LANKA	
A. C. Gilchrist (wk) c Silva b Fernando	149	W. U. Tharanga c Gilchrist b Bracken	6
M. L. Hayden c Jayawardene b Malinga	38	S. T. Jayasuriya b Clarke	63
R. T. Ponting (capt) run out	37	K. C. Sangakkara (wk) c Ponting b Hogg	54
A. Symonds not out	23	D. P. M. D. Jayawardene (capt) lbw b Watson	19
S. R. Watson b Malinga	3	L. P. C. Silva b Clarke	21
M. J. Clarke not out	8	T. M. Dilshan run out	14
Extras Lb4 W16 Nb3	23	R. P. Arnold c Gilchrist b McGrath	1
(38 overs)	4/281	W. P. U. J.C. Vaas not out	11
Did not bat: M. E. K. Hussey, G. B. Hogg, N. W. Bracken,		S. L. Malinga st Gilchrist b Symonds	10
S. W. Tait, G. D. McGrath		C. R.D. Fernando not out	1
1/172 2/224 3/261 4/266		Extras Lb1 w14	15
Bowling: Vaas 8-0-54-0; Malinga 8-1-49-2;		(36 overs)	8/215
Fernando 8-0-74-1; Muralitharan 7-0-44-0; Dilshan 2-0-23-0;		Did not bat: M. Muralitharan	
Jayasuriya 5-0-33-0		1/7 2/123 3/145 4/156 5/188 6/190 7/194 8/211	
		Bowling: Bracken 6-1-34-1; Tait 6-0-42-0; McGrath 7-0-31-1;	
		Watson 7-0-49-1; Hogg 3-0-19-1; Clarke 5-0-33-2;	
		Symonds 2-0-6-0	

Umpires: Aleem Dar S.A. Bucknor
Toss: Australia

POST-MORTEM

"I was talking to someone recently about the World Cup and we still talked mostly about what happened to Bob Woolmer," says Nathan Bracken. "There are still question marks about it and even though we got the result we wanted there is no doubt his death sits over the whole tournament." Another prominent writer, Simon Barnes, called the 2007 World Cup 'the worst sports event ever.' But the West Indies organisers had nothing to do with Woolmer's unfortunate demise. Nor could they do much about the untimely rain that upset the final.

So the 'worst ever' call is in some ways harsh, but there is no doubt the 2007 World Cup was huge disappointment for the West Indies and that their cricket and the sense of sporting unity between the small islands nations has not recovered. Financially it was only a questionable success, as well.

At the moment on the ICC future tours program there is no sign of the World Cup returning to the West Indies. So there must be some frustration in the Caribbean that they blew their once in a generation, or maybe even a lifetime, opportunity to host it.

But the ICC must share the blame. They controlled the scheduling and they did not help to get light towers built at grounds so that the fiasco at the end of the final could be simply avoided.

It was appropriate that ICC match referee, Jeff Crowe, apologised for his mistaken understanding of the rules, not realising that the game had been completed when the Sri Lankan batsmen accepted the umpires offer to go off for bad light.

One last reflection is that the 2007 World Cup should be remembered as the last hurrah for a cricket team as great as any to walk the planet. The Australian side went into slow decline after this tournament and no one since has reached that standard of excellence.

The last word goes to World Cup winner Nathan Bracken.

"It was an amazing experience to play with those guys," Bracken said. "They made it so easy for me."

CHAPTER 11:

World Cup 2011: – India Brings It Home

After a 15-year absence, the World Cup returned to the subcontinent to be hosted by India, Sri Lanka and, for the first time, Bangladesh. The bid by the original consortium of India-Pakistan-Sri Lanka was received after the ICC granted an extension of time for the Asian bid. The belated bid won the right to host the tournament after a vote of 10 votes to three.

Bangladesh stepped into the breach as co-host when, in April 2009, the ICC cancelled Pakistan's status as co-host following an attack in Lahore on the Sri Lankan team. As a result, the 14 matches originally allocated to Pakistan, including a semi-final, had to be transferred. The Pakistan Cricket Board estimated the loss of match fees to be approximately US$10.5 million.

At the time of the 2011 tournament, the Twenty20 format enjoyed great popularity. This was especially the case in India, where the Indian Premier League (IPL) competition had been a resounding success since it started in April 2008. Other countries set up their own Twenty20 leagues, such as the Friends Life T20 league in England and the Big Bash in Australia. The appeal of the Twenty20 format led to declining crowds for 50-over international matches. Some observers began to question the relevance of the 50-over format and the long-term future of the World Cup.

As in 2007, 14 teams would contest the 10th World Cup. The top four finishers in the 2009 qualification tournament—Ireland, Canada, Holland and Kenya—would join the 10 Test playing nations. The format was revised to give all teams more qualifying games. Aside from the increased number of teams, the format used for the tournament on the subcontinent in 1996 was applied here. In the two groups, each team would play six matches, with the top four sides from each group advancing to the quarter-finals. The Super Six and Super Eight concepts were disbanded for 2011, with all matches from the quarter-finals onwards being knockout. All in all, the tournament would comprise 49 matches, two fewer than in 2007, spread over six weeks from 19 February to 2 April.

India would host 29 matches, including the final in Mumbai and a semi-final. Sri Lanka was assigned 12 matches, including the other semi-final, while Bangladesh had the remaining eight games. Bangladesh had the honour of hosting the opening ceremony at Bangabandhu National Stadium in Dhaka on Thursday, 17 February. The tournament mascot Stumpy, a young elephant, welcomed the launch of cricket's finest exhibition with great enthusiasm.

With India a financial powerhouse of international cricket, it was little wonder that the 2011 tournament would attract a great deal of commercial interest. The ICC sold the broadcasting rights to ESPN Star Sports and Star Cricket for a whopping amount of approximately 2 billion US dollars. The ICC doubled the prize money pool to 10 million US dollars, including 3 million US dollars for the winning team. The competition was broadcast in high-definition format for the first time. It was also the first World Cup where interested followers would be able to view the action on-line and on mobile and smart phones.

The 2011 tournament also represented the World Cup debut for the umpire Decision Review System (DRS). It remained to be seen whether the use of the Hawk-Eye, Hot Spot and Snickometer technologies would improve the overall quality of decision making. Since the 2007 competition, the ICC had altered the powerplay rules. After the mandatory powerplay in the first 10 overs, the batting side had a powerplay and the bowling side had a powerplay. Both powerplays were blocks of five overs. The batting powerplay, which had to be activated at some point between the start of the 11th and 46th overs, required the fielding side to have no more than three fielders outside the 30-yard circle. The bowling powerplay required no more than two fielders outside the circle. International captains had grappled with the tactical decision of when to activate the powerplays for best effect.

With many millions of fans desperately hoping their team would prevail, India carried a crushing weight of expectation. They started favourites at a price of $4. Sri Lanka was well fancied at $5 and Australia and South Africa were each at $6. Holand was the longest of the longshots at $1,501.

Group A included Australia, the holders of a hat-trick of World Cups and an undefeated streak of 29 World Cup matches. The Australians had found the going tough in Test matches in recent years but their limited-overs form had been good. Australia would need to produce its best form to retain the top ranking in 50-over cricket at the conclusion of the tournament. Since 2007, there had been significant turnover in Australia's one-day personnel. Gone were Hayden, Gilchrist, Symonds, Hogg, Bracken and McGrath from the side that prevailed in the Bridgetown gloom four years ago. Ricky Ponting remained at the helm of a side in transition. Despite not producing sustained success in Tests, Shane Watson's one-day form was very good in the lead up to the competition. His opening partnership with Brad Haddin had served Australia well. David Hussey and Cameron White supplied the middle-order hitting power, although in the early matches the Australian batting would miss the calm finishing prowess of "Mr Cricket" Mike Hussey, who was inconvenienced by a hamstring injury.

The Australian bowlers, a damaging combination when on song, were inconsistent and the major uncertainty was whether they would be able to keep scoring in check on pitches that were conducive to fast runs. The 34-year-old Brett Lee led the pace contingent with support from Tait and left-armers Mitchell Johnson and Doug Bollinger. Injuries to spinners Nathan Hauritz and Xavier Doherty left the door ajar for off-spinner Jason Krejza to return to the Indian wickets where he had tasted success at the beginning of his international career.

Co-hosts Sri Lanka joined Australia in Group A. Their strong squad gave them a good chance of holding the trophy aloft for the first time since 1996. Upul Tharanga, Sangakkara, Jayawardene and Tillekeratne Dilshan formed the nucleus of a well-credentialed batting line-up. Following the retirement of Chaminda Vaas, captain Sangakkara would look to Lasith Malinga and the steady seam bowling of Nuwan Kulasekara for early breakthroughs. With 800 Test victims and over 500 limited-overs wickets on his CV, the legendary Muralitharan hoped for a happy swansong. Murali would be assisted by fellow spinners Rangana Herath, left-arm orthodox, and the versatile Ajantha Mendis, capable of bowling both leg-spin and off-spin.

As always, the performances of Pakistan in the tournament would be intriguing. Their preparation was rocked by the suspension on corruption charges of fast bowlers Mohammad Asif and Mohammad Amir and batsman Salman Butt. Despite this horror preparation, opposition sides would underestimate the prodigious talents of the Pakistanis at their peril. Misbah-ul-Haq, Younis Khan, Kamran Akmal and the new captain, the seemingly ageless Shahid Afridi, supplied the backbone of the batting. With the ball, star Twenty20 bowler Umar Gul, who had shown proficiency with reverse swing, was a dangerous prospect for opposition batting line-ups. Left-arm fast bowler Wahab Riaz had the colossal shoes of Wasim Akram to fill. On helpful pitches, Saeed Ajmal would pose awkward questions of batsmen with his doosra.

Regular World Cup semi-finalists New Zealand had wretched form leading into the World Cup, including a 0-4 away loss to Bangladesh. Much rested on the shoulders of the team's elite player, captain Daniel Vettori. The Kiwi squad was loaded with players that were at a good standard, but who lacked star quality. Brendon McCullum, Ross Taylor and Jesse Ryder led the charge with the bat. In the absence of the retired Shane Bond, New Zealand's pace attack lacked a bowler who could rip the heart out of an innings. Opening bowler Tim Southee's skill of bowling late swing at pace would keep batsmen's wits about them. Experienced campaigner Jacob Oram would play an important role in building pressure through his accurate bowling.

Five years of turmoil, including the mass player exodus in 2007 caused by contractual disputes, had severely weakened Zimbabwe's one-day line-up. The delightfully named Elton Chigumbura led a squad that included several spinners, such as left-arm orthodox Ray Price, the accurate off-spin of Prosper Utseya and leg-spinner Graeme Cremer. The batting included experienced Tatenda Taibu and Charles Coventry, who scored an unbeaten 194 in a limited-overs match against Bangladesh in August 2009. With limited resources overall, Zimbabwe's chances of promotion from the group stage seemed remote.

In the international cricket wilderness since their 2003 semi-final appearance, the tournament provided Kenya with a timely opportunity to regain lost ground. Coach Eldine Baptiste and new captain Jimmy Kamande were charged with the task of rebuilding the Kenyan side. The Kenyans could call on some handy batting with the likes of Thomas Odoyo, all-rounder Collins Obuya and former captain Steve Tikolo, saddling up for his fifth World Cup at the age of 39. The squad included three brothers: James Ngoche, Shem Ngoche and Nehemiah Odhiambo.

Rounding out the associate teams in Group A was Canada. A substantial turnover of players in the national side meant that only three players from 2007 would front up again in 2011. The form of journeyman John Davison, now 40, and captain Ashish Bagai would be crucial to Canada's chances of recording an upset win.

Many commentators liked the chances of main host India hoisting the trophy on 2 April. The Indians, who were dreadful in the 2007 tournament, had impressed on the one-day stage in the lead up to the 2011 campaign. Led by the calm authority of Mahendra Singh Dhoni, the Indians had developed a combative approach on the field in recent years that was in marked contrast to the genteel demeanour of many Indian players in years past. At 37 years of age, Tendulkar began 2011 in superb form and, in his sixth World Cup, would again be a prized scalp. Sehwag and Gautam Gambhir, who won a record contract of US$2.4 million in the IPL, formed an impressive opening combination. In recent years, India had unearthed the talents of Virat Kohli, a batsman who sometimes got under the skin of the opposition. Into the middle-order, India could call on the hitting talents of Yuvraj Singh, MS Dhoni and Yusuf Pathan. The seam bowling contingent was led by the experienced Zaheer Khan and Ashish Nehra, with support from the abrasive Shanthakumaran Sreesanth. With Anil Kumble retired, Harbhajan Singh became the senior spinner to up-and-comers Ravichandran Ashwin and Piyush Chawla.

Joining India in Group B, South Africa looked to put a litany of World Cup disappointments behind them. Graeme Smith's charges had beaten India 3-2 in a one-day series in the republic less than a month before the start of the competition. Smith was a member of a high-calibre batting order, which included Jacques Kallis, Hashim Amla, AB de Villiers and JP Duminy. Although these players boasted fine records, the Proteas' squad lacked batsmen with proven hitting power. Herschelle Gibbs was overlooked for selection and Lance Klusener was safely ensconced in retirement. Dale Steyn was the unquestioned star with the ball and the lofty Morne Morkel looked to extract awkward bounce on the subcontinental pitches. Another challenge for South Africa was the lack of a world-class spinner. The Proteas looked to fly under the radar of the publicity enjoyed by India and Sri Lanka and to find their way to their first World Cup final. Interestingly, only four members of South Africa's 15-man squad had played in a World Cup match.

It was nearly 20 years since England had reached the semi-finals of a World Cup. A 6-1 hammering at the hands of Australia in the series played in the new year was not the lead-in that captain Andrew Strauss would have wanted. Strauss oversaw a good quality group of players. Jonathan Trott, Ian Bell, Kevin Pietersen and Strauss himself were the leading lights with the bat. On pitches that were usually conducive to spin, the form of world-class off-spinner Graeme Swann would be vital. All-rounders Stuart Broad, Tim Bresnan and Michael Yardy had the skills to hurt the opposition with both bat and ball.

The West Indies embarked on their World Cup challenge in a rusty state, having played just the two limited-overs internationals in the previous eight months. Disputes between players and the West Indies Cricket Board, where some players had put the riches offered by the IPL ahead of representing their team in international fixtures, had interfered with the focus on the 2011 campaign. The rival teams in Group B would court danger if they took the men from the Caribbean lightly. Chris Gayle had made a habit of destroying new ball attacks, while Kieron Pollard and Dwayne Bravo were not far behind in their capacities to score quickly. The cool heads of Shivnarine Chanderpaul and Ramnaresh Sarwan provided the solidity in the middle-order. The express pace of the diminutive Kemar Roach was unsettling for batting line-ups, while captain Darren Sammy often bowled disciplined spells to restrain the progress of batting sides. Gayle and the giant Sulieman Benn, a left-arm orthodox spinner, had the chief responsibility of extracting turn from the subcontinental pitches. Under the guidance of coach Ottis Gibson, it would be intriguing to see whether the West Indians would gel as a team under the pressure of a World Cup.

Bangladesh entered the tournament with confidence after consecutive one-day series victories in recent months, including a 4-0 defeat of New Zealand at home. After progressing beyond their group in 2007, the Bangladeshis had a reasonable chance of repeating the feat with a home-ground advantage in the early stages of the tournament. Led by all-rounder Shakib Al Hasan, Bangladesh had a competent squad with an emphasis on youth. Young left-handers Imrul Kayes and Zunaid Siddique were likely prospects with the bat. Bangladesh's bowling stocks were diminished by the absence of Mashrafe Mortaza, who damaged knee ligaments in December and was unable to recover in time to present a convincing case for selection. His omission from Bangladesh's World Cup squad led to rioting and a half-day strike in one location. In Mortaza's absence, Shafiul Islam and Rubel Hossain would be the leading seamers. Abdur Razzak, not to be confused with his near-namesake from Pakistan, was a handy left-arm orthodox bowler who enjoyed a number three spot in the pre-tournament world rankings for bowlers in the 50-over game.

The 'Raiders of the Caribbean' from 2007 were back for another taste of World Cup action. Under the watchful eye of coach Phil Simmons, Ireland were capable of causing an upset or two. The defection of skilled batsman Eoin Morgan to England was off-set by former England player Ed Joyce returning to play for the country of his birth. Captain William Porterfield was a steady influence at the top of the order. His opening partner Paul Stirling was an exciting prospect with the bat and a useful off-spin bowler. Kevin O'Brien and all-rounder John Mooney provided the middle order with some firepower. Experienced medium pacer Andre Botha and Brisbane-born Alex Cusack were capable of bowling accurate spells to stem the tide of rising run rates.

Rank outsiders Holland qualified for their fourth World Cup in the last five attempts. Although they would be stretched to win a match in Group B, the Dutch boasted the batting talents of Ryan ten Doeschate, an Essex representative, and seasoned campaigner Bas Zuiderent. The name of 24-year-old Tom Cooper, born in Wollongong in Australia, seemed out of place on a Dutch scoresheet. Although Cooper seemed to fit in well with the team as a number-three batsman and off-spinner. The Dutch bowling resources in 2011 appeared thin and a major challenge in keeping opposition scoring to a moderate level lay ahead.

On the evening of 17 February 2011, two days before the opening match, Dhaka hosted an opening ceremony that was estimated to cost US$30 million. Various Bangladeshi singers, including popular artists Mila and Balam, sang the song *O Preethibi*, which means *Oh World!*, to an appreciative audience. Cycle rickshaws brought tournament mascot Stumpy to the field, followed by each of the 14 captains. An impressive fireworks display followed and, a little while later, Bangladesh's Prime Minister Sheikh Hasina declared the 2011 World Cup open. Canadian singer Bryan Adams delivered one of his hits, *Summer of '69*, as the opening ceremony drew to a close. Many viewers could be forgiven for being puzzled as to the connection between Adams' song and the tournament that was now underway. The thoughts of the captains in the middle of the Bangabandhu National Stadium soon shifted from fireworks and Bryan Adams to defeating their rivals and capturing one-day cricket's Holy Grail.

SATURDAY 19 FEBRUARY 2011
GROUP B: BANGLADESH vs INDIA
SHER-E-BANGLA NATIONAL CRICKET STADIUM, DHAKA, BANGLADESH (DAY/NIGHT)
INDIA WON BY 87 RUNS

The tournament was kicked off by this clash between two co-hosts in Mirpur, about 10 kilometers from the city centre of Dhaka. In the first World Cup match played in Bangladesh, more than 26,000 fans packed the Sher-e-Bangla National Cricket Stadium. Many of whom hoped that Bangladesh would repeat their 2007 shock victory over India.

A dominant batting performance by the Indians all but ruled out Bangladesh's chances of an upset win. Bangladesh's captain Shakib Al Hasan called correctly and asked MS Dhoni to bat. On what appeared to be a slow pitch, the merits of Shakib Al Hasan's decision to give the power-packed Indian batting order first use of the pitch seemed dubious. The Bangladeshi captain placed faith in the fact that, in the last 12 limited-overs games at the venue, the side chasing had won the game.

Virender Sehwag sent the first delivery of the tournament, a shortish delivery from Shafiul Islam, to the boundary for four with a well-executed cut shot. The Bangladeshi bowlers appeared overawed by the occasion and they helped the batsmen along with some loose deliveries. Observers could be excused for thinking that this was a Twenty20 match as India totted up 32 runs from the first three overs. Shakib Al Hasan was forced to bring his trump card, left-arm spinner Abdur Razzaq, into the attack in just the fifth over to control the damage. His accurate bowling curtailed India's progress a little, with Sehwag and Tendulkar bringing up the 50 partnership in the ninth over. The first wicket of the competition fell a short time later. Tendulkar worked a ball to wide mid-on and set off for the single. Unfortunately, Sehwag was caught ball-watching and he remained at the non-striker's end. The throw to the keeper's end sent Tendulkar on his way.

Gautam Gambhir's skillfully worked the ball into the gaps, his method contrasting with the power hitting of Sehwag. Stunned by the India onslaught, the Mirpur crowd found their voice again when Gambhir left a gap between bat and pad when driving to nudge Mahmudullah to leg. Gambhir and Sehwag had a productive partnership of 83 runs in 12 overs. Sehwag maintained his attack on the shell-shocked Bangladeshis, reaching his century from 94 balls in the 32nd over.

On his World Cup debut, Virat Kohli did not appear unnerved by the occasion. He was soon keeping up with Sehwag's rate. India took their batting powerplay in overs 35-40 and took full toll, smashing 44 runs. Sehwag's gigantic six over long on off Abdur Razzaq was a highlight. India reached 300 in the 42nd over. Sehwag repeated the dose against Abdur Razzaq in the 45th over with another colossal blow into the crowd over long on. With the World Cup record score of 188 not out by Gary Kirsten, coincidentally India's coach, in sight, Sehwag faltered. He bottom edged a full delivery from Shakib Al Hasan onto the stumps, finishing on a superb 175 from 140 balls, including five sixes. Sehwag and Kohli combined for a frenetic partnership of 203 in 24 overs.

From the penultimate ball of the innings, Kohli chipped the ball to mid-on to reach his century from 83 balls. His place in the Indian team, a matter of some debate in the lead up to this match, seemed assured. Yusuf Pathan edged the last ball of the innings to the keeper to leave India at an imposing 4-370. Bangladesh's bowlers had leaked 94 runs from the last ten overs.

Bangladesh faced an almost insurmountable task to start their campaign with a win. A World Cup first occurred on the fourth ball of the innings: the first DRS referral. Sreesanth's yorker crashed into Tamim Iqbal's boot. Umpire Dharmasena rejected the appeal and Dhoni's referral was unsuccessful. Television replays showed that the ball would have narrowly missed leg stump.

Despite the daunting target, Bangladesh were off to a flyer. Sreesanth bowled woefully in his opening spell and Imrul Kayes capitalized. Sreesanth's third over cost 24 runs, including four boundaries by Imrul Kayes. Dhoni brought on seamer Munaf Patel and his slower ball ended Imrul Kayes' enterprising innings. From a hectic beginning of 1-56 in the seventh over, Bangladesh's progress was slowed by intelligent bowling from Patel and Zaheer Khan.

Junaid Siddique thrilled the crowd with a superbly timed six off Patel that was whipped off the pads and over deep square leg. Pathan, frantically backpedalling to the rope to take the catch, tripped on the rope and crashed into the advertising boards. After some attention from the physio, Pathan continued. Harbhajan Singh bowled a good complement of dot balls, sending the required asking rate towards double figures. He was rewarded with the wicket of Junaid Siddique, courtesy of a slick stumping by Dhoni.

Tamim Iqbal, who struggled early in the innings, recovered to 70 before becoming Patel's second victim. Shakib Al Hasan scored a fluent half-century and the rest of the middle-order showed some promise, but the asking rate was just too much. Bangladesh lost five wickets for 35 runs in the last eight overs to finish 87 runs adrift of their fellow co-hosts. In the process, Patel impressed with his canny seamers, taking 4-48. But no-one would argue with Sehwag winning the Man of the Match award.

INDIA		BANGLADESH	
V. Sehwag b Shakib Al Hasan	175	Tamim Iqbal c Yuvraj Singh b Patel	70
S. R. Tendulkar run out	28	Imrul Kayes b Patel	34
G. Gambhir b Mahmudullah	39	Junaid Siddique st Dhoni b Harbhajan Singh	37
V. Kohli not out	100	Shakib Al Hasan (capt) c Harbhajan Singh b Pathan	55
Y. K. Pathan c Mushfiqur Rahim b Shafiul Islam	8	Mushfiqur Rahim (wk) c sub (Raina) b Khan	25
Extras (b 1, lb 2, w 16, nb 1)	20	Raqibul Hasan not out	28
(50 overs)	4-370	Mahmadullah b Patel	6
Did not bat: Yuvraj Singh, M. S. Dhoni (capt/wk), Z. Khan,		Naeem Islam lbw b Patel	2
S. Sreesanth, M. M. Patel		Abdur Razzak lbw b Khan	1
1/69 2/152 3/355 4/370		Shafiul Islam run out	0
Bowling: Shafiul Islam 7-0-69-1; Rubel Hossain 10-0-60-0;		Rubel Hossain not out	1
Abdur Razzak 9-0-74-0; Naeem Islam 7-0-54-0;		Extras (lb 10m w 13, nb 1)	24
Mahmudullah 7-0-49-1		(50 overs)	9-283

1/56 2/129 3/188 4/234 5/248 6/261 7/275 8/279 9/280

Bowling: Sreesanth 5-0-53-0; Khan 10-0-40-2;

Patel 10-0-48-0; Harbhajan Singh 10-0-41-1;

Pathan 8-0-49-1; Yuvraj Singh 7-0-42-0

Umpires: S.J. Davis, H.D.P.K. Dharmasena.

Toss: Bangladesh   Points: India 2, Bangladesh 0.

SUNDAY 20 FEBRUARY 2011
GROUP A: KENYA vs NEW ZEALAND
MA CHIDAMBARAM STADIUM, CHEPAUK, CHENNAI, INDIA
NEW ZEALAND WON BY 10 WICKETS

While the fans who attended in Mirpur the day before had witnessed an 100-over cricketing extravaganza between India and Bangladesh, the 10,000 who bothered to buy tickets for the Kenya-New Zealand match in Chennai were badly short changed.

Their entertainment was disposed of in less than 32 overs—191 balls—as Kenya, semi-finalists in 2003 capitulated to New Zealand in embarrassing fashion.

After Jimmy Kamande won the toss and batted the game looked like a regular cricket match for a dozen overs as Kenya moved to 1/40. The openers Alex Obanda and Seren Waters had been restricted to gleaning singles, but Collins Obuya hit a couple of boundaries from off-spinner Nathan McCullum that seemed to get things moving.

McCullum had been given the new-ball on a pitch devoid of grass which television commentator, Robin Jackman said would favour spin. Pitches can be deceptive in appearance.

Fast bowler, Hamish Bennett, called up to the side in place of the injured Kyle Mills, precipitated a collapse that eventually saw nine wickets fall for 29 runs in 12 processional overs. Not one of the wickets were taken by spinners.

This was the highest point of Bennett's international career. Bowling full and fast, he had shouts for lbw upheld against Waters, Obuya, and Morris Ouma and also removed the middle and off-stumps of the highly rated veteran Steve Tikolo. Bennett claimed these four wickets in his first 21 balls. This spell won him the Man of the Match award.

When he was relieved, Jacob Oram and Tim Southee continued the prompt demolition. Oram's bounce produced a catch behind, a dolly to Jesse Ryder at point and anther soft catch to short mid wicket. Southee meantime had found full and straight consecutive deliveries were too much for Nehemiah Odhiambo and Shem Ngoche.

All out for 69 the Kenyans could not even gain any consolation when they bowled. By the eighth ball the innings Martin Guptill had struck three fours; a pull, a back foot cover drive and a slashed cut over point. Guptill then hit Thomas Odoyo and Elijah Otieno for straight sixes. Guptill's partner Brendan McCullum did get to finish the match on a high. His two reverse sweeps at the end of the eight over to the boundary quickly removed everyone from the powerful Chennai heat.

KENYA			NEW ZEALAND	
A. A. Obanda lbw b Southee	6		M. J. Guptill not out	39
S. R. Waters lbw b Bennett	16		B. B. McCullum (wk) not out	26
C. O. Obuya lbw b Bennett	14		Extras B2 Lb1 W3 Nb1	7
S. O. Tikolo b Bennett	2		(8 overs)	0/72
M. A. Ouma (wk) lbw b Bennett	1		Did not bat: J. D. Ryder, L. R. P. L. Taylor, J. E.C. Franklin,	
R. R. Patel not out	16		S. B. Styris, D. L. Vettori (capt) , N. L. McCullum,	
J. K. Kamande (capt) c B. McCullum b Oram	2		J. D. P. Oram, T. G. Southee, H. K. Bennett	
T. M. Odoyo c Ryder b Oram	2		Bowling: Odoyo 3-0-25-0; Otieno 2-0-18-0;	
N. N. Odhiambo b Southee	0		Kamande 2-0-21-0; Odhiambo 1-0-5-0	
S. O. Ngoche lbw b Southee	0			
E. Otieno c Styris b Oram	0			
Extras B4 Lb3 W2 Nb1	10			
(23.5 overs)	69			

1/14 2/40 3/42 4/44 5/49 6/59 7/63 8/68 9/68 10/69

Bowling: Southee 6-0-13-3; N. McCullum 4-0-15-0;

Bennett 5-0-16-4; Vettori 6-1-16-0; Oram 2.5-1-2-3

Umpires: M. Erasmus R.J. Tucker

Toss: Kenya   Points: New Zealand 2 Kenya 0

GROUP A: SRI LANKA vs CANADA
MAHINDA RAJAPAKSA INTERNATIONAL CRICKET STADIUM, SOORIYAWEWA, HAMBANTOTA, SRI LANKA: SRI LANKA WON BY 210 RUNS

This match was no more of a contest than the one that had been played to the north in Chennai earlier in the day. But at least there was a decent amount of cricket to watch and a partnership of 179 between Kumar Sangakkara and Mahela Jayawardene is always very watchable. Their stand set up Sri Lanka's 210 runs win against a flimsy Canadian side who, as in previous tournaments, might have been better named 'The Combined Commonwealths. On the south Sri Lankan coast in front of 35,000 enthusiastic fans in a brand new stadium, Sangakkara won the toss and elected to bat.

After a minor delay, Tillekaratne Dilshan gave the innings the launch it needed. He and Upal Tharanga had put on 63 in 12 overs when the latter was run out after almost getting to the other end and having to go back again. The Canadians kept the run rate under reasonable control in the early stages and their desperation in the field was commendable.

At the halfway point of the innings the runs were still only coming at five per over and after Dilshan had holed out at point, twice Canada believed they had Jayawardene caught behind. They reviewed umpire Tarapore's not-out decision, but there was no evidence to overrule the call. From that moment the Canadians began to wilt in the steamy heat.

Jayawardene began to sweep to square, swipe to mid wicket and reverse sweep to third man, all with his trademark style. Sangakkara preferred the boundaries straight and to mid wicket as the run rate accelerated.

The pair was racing neck and neck to reach 100. Except Sangakkara, who was in the midst of a three-figure drought, didn't get there. On 92 he limply pushed the ball back to John Davison. Jayawardene got to his hundred in 80 balls, the fastest ever in the World Cup by a Sri Lankan and next ball he faced swept Davison to Balaji Rao on 45 degrees behind square-leg.

Canada's requirement was a steep 333. By the end of the fourth over they were 3/12. Thisara Perera's first ball rocketed through between Davison's bat and pad. Ruvindu Gunasekera cracked Nuwan Kulasekara straight to Dilshan at cover point and Zubin Surkari pushed his front leg across in front of his stumps and Perera hit it. It took another 30 overs for Sri Lanka to finish the game. Rizwan Cheema hit six off Muralitharan over cover and another to long on for good measure. But the champion spinner in his final tournament soon had his revenge. Five overs later last man Henry Osinda missed a swing to leg from a Ajantha Mendis googly and the off-bail was removed.

SRI LANKA		CANADA	
W. U. Tharanga run out	19	R. Gunasekera c Dilshan b Kulasekara	1
T. M. Dilshan c Davison b Rizwan Cheema	50	J. M. Davison b Perera	0
K. C. Sangakkara (capt/wk) c & b Davison	92	Z. E. Surkari lbw b Perera	6
D. P. M. D. Jayawardene c Balaji Rao b Davison	100	A. S. Hansra st Sangakkara b Samaweera	9
N. L. T. C. Perera run out	11	A. Bagai (capt/wk) c Sangakkara b Perera	22
A. D. Mathews c & b Baidwan	21	Rizwan Cheema c Jayawardene b Muralitharan	37
C. K. Kapugedera c sub (Kumar) b Baidwan	2	T. G. Gordon c Sangakkara b Kulsekara	4
T. T. Samaraweera not out	18	Kurram Chohan c Sangakkara b Kulsekara	4
K. M. D. N. Kulasekara not out	7	H. S. Baidwan not out	16
Extras Lb3 W8 Nb1	12	W. D. Balaji Rao c Tharanga b Muralitharan	6
(50 overs)	7/332	H. Osinde b Mendis	4
Did not bat: M. Muralitharan, B. A. W. Mendis		Extras Lb8 W4 Nb1	13
1/63 2/88 3/267 4/276 5/284 6/295 7/314		(36.5 overs)	122
Bowling: Kurram Chohan 8-0-62-0; Osinde 2.1-0-10-0;		1/0 2/8 3/12 4/42 5/53 6/68 7/74 8/103 9/111 10/122	
Baidwan 8.5-0-59-2; Hansra 9-0-47-0; Rizwan		Bowling: Kulasekara 6-2-16-3; Perera 7-0-24-3;	
Cheema 7-0-47-1; Balaji Rao 7-0-48-0; Davison 8-0-56-2		Mendis 7.5-3-18-1; Muralitharan 9-0-38-2; Dilshan 5-0-14-0;	
		Samaraweera 2-0-4-1	

Umpires: I.J. Gould S.K. Tarapore

Toss: Sri Lanka   Points: Sri Lanka 2 Canada 0

MONDAY 21 FEBRUARY 2011
GROUP A: AUSTRALIA vs ZIMBABWE
SARDAR PATEL STADIUM, MOTERA, AHMEDABAD, INDIA: AUSTRALIA WON BY 91 RUNS

Australia had a straightforward victory over Zimbabwe without indicating they were anywhere near as powerful as their predecessors in 1999, 2003 and 2007. Talented enigmas Shane Watson and Mitchell Johnson had good games for Australia who extended their winning World Cup run to 23 games, while Zimbabwe battled hard against insurmountable odds.

In the first match for seven years between these two sides, Ricky Ponting won the toss, batted and saw his openers restricted to 32 runs from 13 overs. Allegedly, the slow start was investigated by the ICC's Anti-Corruption and Security unit.

In a near-empty Sardar Patel stadium, Watson and Haddin were unable to score freely off experienced left-arm spinner Ray Price who often verbally reminded both batsmen of the limitations of their ability.

They finally got moving in the 14th over hitting two boundaries apiece off Chris Mpofu. Soon, though, Haddin misjudged the line of a delivery from off-spinner and Zimbabwe's 2007 World Cup captain Prosper Utseya. The shout for ldw was initially turned down but the country's first ever DRS referral was successful.

It took another referral to get rid of Watson after the Queensland-born New South Welshman via Tasmania had hit nine fours and a nice pulled six in 92 balls. That made the total 2/140 and it was three down four runs later when Ponting in his first match since breaking his finger in the recent Ashes series, was run out. Mpofu's brilliant direct throw from the mid wicket boundary found him short and he was so upset at his dismissal that he broke a television screen in the dressing room.

Michael Clarke busied himself with an unbeaten run a ball 58 that provided later over substance while David Hussey and Steve Smith provided brief but exhilarating cameos that lifted the total to a handy 262.

Charles Coventry began Zimabawe's reply with the shot of the day/night. In the fourth over he blasted a full and wide Brett Lee delivery on one knee flat and hard over point for six. The veteran quick soon had his revenge from a mistimed pull but the real damage to Zimbabwe's challenge occurred when three wickets fell in 12 balls between the eleventh and thirteenth overs.

Shaun Tait and Johnson skittled Zimbabwe from 1/40 to 4/44. Sean Williams led one minor rally, but then the total slipped again to 7/105. Then Graeme Cremer and Utseya put on an academic 49 for the eighth wicket before Johnson ended some very tame proceedings in the 47th over.

	AUSTRALIA			ZIMBABWE	
S. R. Watson lbw b Cremer		79	B. R.M. Taylor b Tait		16
B. J. Haddin (wk) lbw b Utseya		29	C. K. Coventry c & b Lee		14
R. T. Ponting (capt) run out		28	T. Taibu (wk) c Watson b Johnson		7
M. J. Clarke not out		58	C. R. Irvine lbw b Johnston		0
C. L. White b Mpofu		22	E. Chigumbra (capt) c Haddin b Krejza		14
D. J. Hussey b Price		14	S. C. Williams c Watson b Tait		28
S. P. D. Smith c Chakabva b Mpofu		11	R. W. Chakabva lbw b Krejza		6
M. G. Johnson not out		7	P. Utseya c Ponting b Hussey		24
Extras Lb7 W7		14	A. G. Cremer c Haddin b Johnson		37
(50 overs)		6/262	R. W. Price not out		5
Did not bat: S. W. Tait, J. J. Krejza, B. Lee			C. B. Mpofu c Haddin b Johnson		2
1/61 2/140 3/144 4/207 5/241 6/254			Extras B4 Lb9 W3 Nb2		18
Bowling: Mpofu 9-0-58-2; Price 10-0-43-1;			(46.2 overs)		171
Utseya 10-2-43-1; Cremer 10-0-41-1; Taylor 3-0-23-0;			1/22 2/40 3/40 4/44 5/88 6/96 7/104 8/153 9/167		
Chigumbra 2-0-18-0; Williams 6-0-29-0			10/171		
			Bowling: Tait 9-1-34-2; Lee 8-1-34-1; Johnson 9.2-2-19-4;		
			Krejza 8-0-28-2; Watson 3-0-7-0; Smith 5-0-24-0;		
			Hussey 4-1-12-1		

Umpires: E.A.R. de Silva R.A. Kettleborough

Toss: Australia   Points: Australia 2 Zimbabwe 0

TUESDAY 22 FEBRUARY 2011
GROUP B: ENGLAND vs NETHERLANDS
VIDARBA CRICKET ASSOCIATION, NAGPUR, INDIA (DAY/NIGHT)
ENGLAND WON BY SIX WICKETS

In India's City of Oranges, it was fitting that Holland would acquit themselves very well against an unimpressive England. The quality performance by the Dutch was timely in the context of a growing chorus of critics of four ICC associate countries having a seat at the World Cup table.

After Dutch skipper Peter Borren won the toss, openers Alexei Kervezee and keeper Wesley Baressi had their country off to a fluent start. Coming in at 2-58, Essex and Tasmania representative Ryan ten Doeschate turned in a brilliant perfomance. He found a capable ally in Tom Cooper and 78 runs were added for the 3rd wicket. Ten Doeschate played shots to all parts of the ground, gradually increasing his side's run rate. In the 45th over, ten Doeschate achieved the rare feat of bringing up his century with a five. He flicked a Broad delivery to fine leg for a single, with the resultant throw hitting the stumps and escaping to the boundary.

England's fielding and bowling, lacklustre throughout the innings, grew increasingly ragged towards the end of the 50 overs. Anderson bowled two beam balls in the space of three deliveries at ten Doeschate. Anderson was allowed to continue after stern words from the umpire. This worked to Holland's advantage, as Borren blasted a hat-trick of boundaries in Anderson's next over. Ten Doeschate eventually holed out in the penultimate over for a sparkling 119 from 110 deliveries. Moments later, England spared Borren with an elementary error. Broad bowled the Dutch captain, but a no ball was called because England had only three fielders inside the circle. Collingwood's concentration lapsed, as he forgot to walk into the circle from his mid wicket position. Holland profited handsomely from England's malaise, walloping 104 runs in the last ten overs, including 50 from their batting powerplay.

England needed to score 293 under lights to avoid embarrassment first up. Captain Andrew Strauss and Kevin Pietersen, opening for England for the first time in a limited-overs match, found the boundary regularly and kept up with the asking rate. The first wicket fell at 107 when Pietersen mistimed a drive off left-arm spinner Pieter Seelaar to cover. Disciplined bowling in the middle stages of the innings by seamers ten Doschate and Mudassar Bukhari limited England's progress. Strauss was caught in the deep 12 shy of his century and the match had reached an interesting juncture when Trott was stumped off Man of the

Match ten Doeschate's bowling in the 40th over. England's task became a little more challenging in the 43rd over when Bell was bowled by ten Doeschate's final delivery. Fifty-two runs were needed from the last seven overs. Paul Collingwood and Ravi Bopara kept a calm head, keeping the score ticking over by working the ball into the gaps. With 13 runs required from the last two overs, Bopara made short work of the requirement by hammering medium pacer Bernard Loots for six, two, four and four. The middle-order had saved England's blushes on this occasion with eight deliveries remaining.

NETHERLANDS		ENGLAND	
A. N. Kervezee c Prior b Bresnan	16	A. J. Strauss (capt) c Cooper b Mudassar Bukhari	88
W. Barresi (wk) st Prior b Swann	29	K. P. Pietersen c Borren b Seelaar	39
T. L.W. Cooper c Anderson b Collingwood	47	I. J. L. Trott st Barresi b ten Doeschate	62
R. N. ten Doeschate c Bopara b Broad	119	I. R. Bell b ten Doeschate	33
B. Zuiderent c Collingwood b Swann	1	P. D. Collingwood not out	30
T. N. de Grooth b Broad	28	R. S. Bopara not out	30
P. W. Borren (capt) not out	35	Extras (b 1, lb 2, w 11)	14
Mudassar Bukhari not out	6	(48.4 overs)	4-296
Extras (b 3, lb 3, w 2, nb 3)	11	Did not bat: M. J. Prior (wk), T. T. Bresnan, S. C.J. Broad,	
(50 overs)	6-292	G. P. Swann, J. M. Anderson	
Did not bat: P. M. Seelaar, B. P. Loots, B. A. Westdijk		1/105 2/166 3/224 4/241	
1/36 2/58 3/136 4/149 5/213 6/274		Bowling: Mudassar Bukhari 9-0-54-1; Westdijk 7-0-41-0;	
Bowling: Anderson 10-0-72-0; Broad 10-2-65-2;		Loots 9.4-0-74-0; Seelaar 10-0-54-1; ten	
Bresnan 10-0-49-1; Swann 10-0-35-2; Collingwood 8-0-46-1;		Doeschate 10-0-47-2; Cooper 3-0-23-0	
Pietersen 2-0-19-0			

Umpires: Asad Rauf, B.N.J. Oxenford.
Toss: Netherlands   Points: England 2, Netherlands 0.

WEDNESDAY 23 FEBRUARY 2011
GROUP A: KENYA vs PAKISTAN
MAHINDA RAJAPAKSA INTERNATIONAL CRICKET STADIUM, SOORIYAWEWA, HAMBANTOTA, SRI LANKA: PAKISTAN WON BY 205 RUNS

Pakistan took a little longer than New Zealand to polish off Kenya but they still eventually did so in record-breaking fashion.

After a poor start, Shahid Afridi's side compiled a significant 317 and then bowled out Kenya for 112 in 33 overs. Pakistan's total was boosted by 46 extras including an astonishing and one-day international record-equalling 37 wides. Their winning margin of 205 runs was their best in a World Cup and Kenya's heaviest defeat. The second half of Kenya's innings was inept, particularly against Afridi. Numbers six to 11 in the batting order contributed two runs between them.

Thomas Odoyo and Elijah Otieno were so accurate in their early overs that they had removed both Pakistan opening batsmen by the end of the seventh over with only 12 runs on the board.

Mohammad Hafeez was spectacularly caught by a diving and juggling Seren Waters at mid wicket and Jimmy Kamande took an easier catch at cover off the stagnant Ahmed Shehzad's leading edge. Soon, though, Kamran Akmal and Younis Khan wrested the initiative away from the Kenyan bowlers. They put on 98 in 107 deliveries. Akmal was the more aggressive hitting five boundaries. He was first to his fifty but then ran down the wicket to left-arm spinner Shem Ngoche and missed. Misbah-ul-Haq got off the mark with a six in his World Cup debut. He added another 45 with Younis who also reached his 50, but went no further, missing a sweep against Steve Tikolo.

Misbah assumed the secondary role as eventual Man of the Match, Umar Akmal, gave Pakistan total ascendancy while making a cracking 71 in 52 balls. The fifth-wicket pair rattled on 118 in 13 overs. The Kenyans were struck to all parts. Worse still Thomas Odoyo in the 35th over twice-gifted five wides. He later repeated the sin in the 49th over. Nor was he the lone offender. Odoyo was actually on what would have been a misleading hat-trick when the bowled his third five wider.

Pakistan, with Umar Akmal and Misbah belting 20 runs in the 45th over and 21 in the 47th had already taken Pakistan to the brink of their eventual 300 plus total.

Although no-one really believed Kenya would make 318, their innings did start promisingly. Morris Ouma and Waters put on an encouraging 37 runs in nine overs.

Once Umar Akmal had thrown out Waters from mid wicket their innings went into decline, however. Collins Obuya and Steve Tikolo got the total to 2/73 in the 23rd over then Shahid Afridi ripped through their line-up. While Obuya clubbed Mohammad Hafeez for sixes over square-leg and long on Afridi was confusing his partners with his fast skidding leg-breaks.

The Pakistani captain picked up the five wickets in eight overs, three of his victims being given out lbw. The first time against Tanmay Mishra he had to call on the DRS, the other two umpire, Nigel Llong, was convinced by the appeal.

In the game's last phase Kenya lost 8/39 in less than 11 overs.

PAKISTAN		KENYA	
Mohammad Hafeez c Waters b Otieno	9	M. A. Ouma (wk) c Kamran Akmal b Umar Gul	16
Ahmed Shehzad c Kamande b Odoyo	1	S. R. Waters run out	17
Kamran Akmal (wk) st Ouma b Ngoche	55	C. O. Obuya c Ahmed Shezad b Shahid Afridi	47
Younis Khan lbw b Tikolo	50	S. O. Tikolo b Shahid Afridi	13
Misbah-ul-Haq c Otieno b Kamande	65	T. Mishra lbw b Shahid Afridi	6
Umar Akmal c Obuya b Odoyo	71	R. R. Patel c Umar Akmal b Mohammad Hafeez	0
Shahid Afridi (capt) lbw b Odoyo	7	J. K. Kamande (capt) lbw b Shahid Afridi	2
Abdul Razzaq not out	8	T. M. Odoyo lbw b Shahid Afridi	0
Abdur Rehman not out	5	N. N. Odhiambo run out	0
Extras Lb3 W37 Nb6	46	S. O. Ngoche b Umar Gul	0
(50 overs)	7/317	E. Otieno not out	0
Did not bat: Umar Gul, Shoaib Akhtar		Extras B4 Lb3 W3 Nb1	11
1/11 2/12 3/110 4/155 5/273 6/289 7/289		(33.1 overs)	112
Bowling: Odoyo 7-2-41-3; Otieno 9-1-49-1;		1/37 2/43 3/73 4/79 5/85 6/87 7/101 8/112 9/112	
Odhiambo 7-0-65-0; Ngoche 10-0-46-1; Kamande 7-0-64-1;		10/112	
Tikolo 9-0-44-1; Obuya 1-0-5-0		Bowling: Shoaib Akhtar 5-1-10-0; Abdul Razzaq 5-1-23-0;	
		Umar Gul 4.1-0-12-2;	
		Abdur Rehman 7-1-18-0; Shahid Afridi 8-3-16-5;	
		Mohammad Hafeez 4-1-26-1	

Umpires: A.L. Hill N.J. Llong

Toss: Pakistan   Points: Pakistan 2 Kenya 0

THURSDAY 24 FEBRUARY 2011
GROUP B: SOUTH AFRICA vs WEST INDIES
FEROZ SHAH KOTLA, DELHI, INDIA (DAY/NIGHT): SOUTH AFRICA WON BY 7 WICKETS

This match was a contest between the well-drilled and -organised South Africans and the out-of-practice and mercurial West Indians.

Graeme Smith won the toss and gave his well-balanced attack first crack. After the early loss of Gayle, Darren Bravo batted skilfully and enabled the West Indies to wrest control of the match. The West Indies were well placed at 1-113 after 23 overs and a score nearing 300 was a reasonable prospect. Bravo was trapped by Johan Botha for a invaluable 73 from 82 deliveries. After the promising platform was set, the South African spin trio of Botha, Robin Peterson and limited-overs international debutante Imran Tahir put the brakes on the West Indies in the middle stages of the innings. Imran Tahir collected 4-41, figures on World Cup debut that were second only to Canada's Austin Codrington's 5-27 against Kenya in 2003. The regular fall of wickets stalled the West Indian innings. Dwayne Bravo played fluently, including hitting the spinners for three sixes.

His promising innings of 40 was cut short by a foolish run out. Chanderpaul played a reverse sweep directly to Morne Morkel at short third man. The batsmen attempted a single that was never on and Bravo was left short at the keeper's end.

Dale Steyn, by now the world's premier fast bowler, returned to the attack in the 44th over. With his third delivery, he became the first player to win an lbw verdict in the World Cup as the result of DRS overturning the on-field umpire's decision. Kieron Pollard was the unlucky batsman. Steyn collected two more victims before the West Indies were bowled out in the 48th over. The West Indians had declined to finish on a number favoured by Richie Benaud impersonators, the moderate score of 222. The last nine wickets tumbled for 109 runs in 26 overs.

The Proteas were in early trouble. Hasim Amla and Jacques Kallis had returned to the pavilion with the score a sorry 2-20 from five overs. Both batsmen perished to sharp chances behind the wicket induced by the new ball attack of Kemar Roach and left-arm orthodox spinner Sulieman Benn. Smith and AB de Villiers, who also kept wicket in this match, stabilised the innings and eventually a 119 run partnership for the third wicket was achieved. During the partnership, fast-medium Dwayne Bravo slipped in his follow-through and injured his knee. Bravo was assisted from the field and was sent to hospital. The injury would need four weeks to fully heal, which meant that Bravo's World Cup was over.

Smith's dismissal for 45 in the 29th over meant that de Villiers was joined by JP Duminy. The pair made gradual inroads, reducing the require run rate by adroitly placing the ball into vacant parts of the field. De Villiers reached his century, his second in World Cup matches, from 97 balls. An unbroken stand of 84 in 14 saw South Africa to their target with 43 deliveries remaining. De Villiers was a worthy and clear cut choice for the man of the match award.

WEST INDIES		SOUTH AFRICA	
C. H. Gayle c Kallis b Botha	2	H. M. Amla c Thomas b Roach	14
D. S. Smith c & b Imran Tahir	36	G. C. Smith (capt) b Pollard	45
D. M. Bravo lbw b Botha	73	J. H. Kallis c Sammy b Benn	4
R. R. Sarwan lbw b Imran Tahir	2	A. B. de Villiers (wk) not out	107
S. Chanderpaul c Peterson b Imran Tahir	31	J. P. Duminy not out	42
D. J. Bravo run out	40	Extras (lb 10, nb 1)	11
D. C. Thomas (wk) c Duminy b Imran Tahir	15	(42.5 overs)	3-223
K. A. Pollard lbw b Steyn	0	Did not bat: F. du Plessis, J. Botha, R. J. Peterson, M. Morkel,	
D. J. G. Sammy (capt) lbw b Steyn	0	D. W. Steyn, Imran Tahir	
S. J. Benn c Morkel b Steyn	6	1/15 2/20 3/139	
K. A. J. Roach not out	2	Bowling: Benn 10-0-51-1; Roach 8-0-42-1; D. J. Bravo	
Extras (b 1, lb 3, w 11)	15	2.1-0-12-0; Sammy 8-0-40-0; Pollard 7.5-0-37-1;	
(47.3 overs)	10-222	Gayle 6-0-26-0; Smith 0.5-0-5-0	
1/2 2/113 3/117 4/120 5/178 6/209 7/213 8/213 9/213			
10/222			
Bowling: Botha 9-0-48-2; Steyn 7.3-1-24-3; Morkel 8-0-35-0;			
Kallis 3-0-21-0; Imran Tahir 10-1-41-4; Peterson 10-0-49-4			

Umpires: A.M. Saheba, S.J.A. Taufel.

Toss: South Africa   Points: South Africa 2, West Indies 0.

FRIDAY 25 FEBRUARY 2011
GROUP A: AUSTRALIA vs NEW ZEALAND
VIDARBHA CRICKET ASSOCIATION STADIUM, JAMTHA, NAGPUR, INDIA:
AUSTRALIA WON BY SEVEN WICKETS

Australia took the breaks that fell their way and eased to a straightforward seven wicket victory over New Zealand that secured them the conveniently contested Chappell-Hadlee Trophy in addition to the two valuable World Cup points. The game was won and lost in its first period when the Black Caps were sent in to bat on a wicket that had spent a long time under cover.

The Australian fast bowlers took advantage and reduced New Zealand to 6/73. They fought back to a more respectable 206, but that was still easily overtaken in 34 overs.

The match was first since the tragic earthquake that hit in Christchurch on 22 February, killing nearly 200 people. During the minute's silence held for the earthquake victims before the match, the Australian and New Zealand players linked arms.

Later Kiwi captain, Daniel Vettori suggested this clearly emotional moment had no effect on the way his side performed in the match.

The toss may have. Whether the wicket held gremlins or not Martin Guptill was suspicious. He took 19 deliveries to get off the mark. Brendan McCullum was more positive but was first to go slashing a full and wide Shaun Tait delivery to Jason Krejza at third man. Guptill lasted until the 10th over then was bowled by a Shane Watson grubber.

Like Guptill, Ross Taylor was becalmed while Jesse Ryder hit a number of boundaries without significantly lifting the run rate. Then between the 14th and 17th overs the scoreboard declined from 2/66 to 6/73.

In an all left-hander show, Mitchell Johnson had both Ryder, prodding, and James Franklin, driving, caught behind by Brad Haddin three balls apart. When Scott Styris chased a short wide one from Tait next over three wickets had fallen for one run.

Jamie How and Nathan McCullum began the re-build, then McCullum and Vettori carried it on. McCullum got to 52 while Vettori scored his 44 at better than a run per ball and hit five fours.

Johnson's two late breakthroughs gave him four in the innings for the second match in a row and won him the Man of the Match Award. The modesty of the New Zealand total was quickly revealed by Watson and Haddin.

They immediately showed their intention and took nine runs off Tim Southee's first over including a cover driven four by Haddin. The wicketkeeper batsman dominated the early scoring hitting a boundary in four of the first five overs. Then Hamish Bennett conceded 19 runs in his second over including five wides so that Australia were 0/58 after eight overs.

Haddin clubbing drives to cover and mid wicket, raced to his fifty off 39 balls then Watson assumed control, dominating the strike and quickly lifting his total. They got to 133 in 118 balls, effectively finishing the match as contest. Both then fell to Bennett within three runs of each other.

Thirty-one runs later Ponting was brilliantly stumped by Brendan McCullum off a leg-side wide then Michael Clarke and Cameron White polished off the final 40 runs in 44 balls.

NEW ZEALAND		AUSTRALIA	
M. J. Guptill b Watson	10	S. R. Watson b Bennett	62
B. B. McCullum (wk) c Krejza b Tait	16	B. J. Haddin (wk) c Franklin b Bennett	55
J. D. Ryder c Haddin b Johnson	25	R. T. Ponting (capt) st B. B. McCullum b Southee	12
L. R. P. L.Taylor b Tait	7	M. J. Clarke not out	24
J. E.C. Franklin c Haddin b Johnson	0	C. L. White not out	22
S. B. Styris c Haddin b Tait	0	Extras Lb3 W29	32
J. M. How lbw b Smith	22	(34 overs)	3/207
N. L. McCullum lbw b Johnson	52	Did not bat: D. J. Hussey, S. P.D. Smith, M. G. Johnson, J. J.
D. L. Vettori (capt) c Haddin b Lee	44	Krejza, B. Lee, S. W. Tait
T. G, Southee c Ponting b Johnson	6	1/133 2/136 3/167
H. K. Bennett not out	0	Bowling: Southee 10-2-45-1; Vettori 7-0-39-0;
Extras B1 Lb8 W13 Nb2	24	Bennett 7-0-63-2; N. L.McCullum 3-0-22-0; Ryder 5-0-24-0;
(45.1 overs)	206	Franklin 2-0-11-0

1/20 2/40 3/66 4/66 5/67 6/73 7/121 8/175 9/206
10/206

Bowling: Lee 8-2-29-1; Tait 7-0-35-3; Johnson 9.1-3-33-4;

Watson 3-1-9-1; Krejza 9-0-47-0; Smith 9-0-44-1

Umpires: H.D.P.K. Dharmasena B.R. Doctrove

Toss: Australia   Points: Australia 2 New Zealand 0

FRIDAY 25 FEBRUARY 2011
GROUP B: BANGLADESH vs IRELAND
SHER-E-BANGLA NATIONAL STADIUM (DAY/NIGHT):
BANGLADESH WON BY 27 RUNS

Sher-e-Bangla Stadium was packed again for the battle between two of the surprise packets from 2007. Bangladesh's captain Shakib Al Hasan, mindful of the result of the game against India when he sent the opposition in, took a different tack here and elected to bat. His decision appeared to be a sound one when Tamim Iqbal and Imrul Kayes brought up 50 in just the sixth over. Under early fire, Ireland struck their first blow in the seventh over when Niall O'Brien executed a slick leg-side stumping from the bowling of John Mooney to send Imrul Kayes back to the pavilion.

After an explosive opening, the Bangladeshi innings stalled. Seamers Mooney, Trent Johnston and Andre Botha took the pace off the ball and Bangladesh's batsmen found it difficult to pierce the infield. Wickets fell steadily and, following the dismissal of Shakib Al Hasan in the 16th over, Bangladesh were under pressure at 4-86. Mushfiqur Rahim and Raqibul Hasan found the going tough on a slow pitch and against accurate bowling. Their stand of 61 for the fifth wicket was compiled in 18 overs.

On his World Cup debut, 18-year-old left arm orthodox spinner George Dockrell baffled the Bangladeshi batsmen with his well-flighted, looping deliveries. In consecutive overs, he dismissed the well-set Mushfiqur Rahim and Raqibul Hasan. After being tied down, both batsmen played tame sweepshots to short-backward square leg. From 6-151 in the 36th over, the middle- and lower-order batsmen survived to the second ball of the final over, clawing their way to a seemingly inadequate total of 9-205. Only three boundaries were scored from the last 19 overs of the innings.

The Irish made steady progress towards their target, with the run rate hovering around the required four per over. Midway through the innings, Ireland were well placed at 3-93 in the 25th over, with keeper-batsman Niall O'Brien well-established. The complexion of the contest then changed markedly within three overs. Andrew White paid the price for leaving a wide gap between bat and pad. O'Brien then played a loose leg-side shot from Bangladesh's captain and Tamim Iqbal completed a good catch just off the ground at deep square leg. At this point, Ireland were 5-110 and the game was up for grabs. Kevin O'Brien batted intelligently and kept the score moving along, including lifting Mohammad Ashraful over long off for six, the only shot to clear the boundary in this game. O'Brien batted capably against Bangladesh's array of spinners and the fast slingers of Rubel Hossain. Ireland reached 5-151 in the 37th over and the game was slipping away for the home side.

In a pivotal move, fast-medium bowler Shafiul Islam was recalled to the attack. In his second over, he removed the danger man Kevin O'Brien with a short ball that was injudiciously pulled straight to deep square leg. The floodgates had opened. The Irish innings faded away as the remaining four wickets fell for the addition of 27 runs. Shafiul Islam made short work of the tail and finished with 4-21 from eight overs, the best bowling figures by a Bangladesh player at the World Cup. He took four of the last five wickets to fall in the match. Despite Shafiul Islam's important contribution to the win, the man of the match adjudicators gave the nod to opener Tamim Iqbal.

BANGLADESH		IRELAND	
Tamim Iqbal c Porterfield b Botha	44	W. T. S. Porterfield (c) c Raqibul Hasan b Shakib Al Hasan	20
Imrul Kayes st N. O'Brien b Mooney	12	P. R. Stirling st Mushfiqur Rahim b Abdur Razzak	9
Junaid Siddique run out	3	E. C. Joyce c & b Mohammad Ashraful	16
Mushfiqur Rahim (wk) c White b Dockrell	36	N. J. O'Brien (wk) c Tamim Iqbal b Shakib Al Hasan	38
Shakib Al Hasan (capt) c & b Botha	16	A. R. White b Mohammad Ashraful	10
Raqibul Hasan run out	38	K. J. O'Brien c sub (Suhrawadi Shuvo) b Shafiul Islam	37
Mohammad Ashraful c White b Dockrell	1	A. C. Botha b Shafiul Islam	22
Naeem Islam c Dockrell b Johnston	29	J. F. Mooney b Naeem Islam	0
Shafiul Islam lbw b Botha	2	D. T. Johnston lbw b Shafiul Islam	6
Abdur Razzak b Johnston	11	G. H. Dockrell not out	4
Rubel Hossain not out	2	W. B. Rankin c Junaid Siddique b Shafiul Islam	3
Extras (b 2 w 8, nb 1)	11	Extras (lb 9, w 4)	13
(49.2 overs)	10-205	(45 overs)	10-178

1/53 2/61 3/68 4/86 5/147 6/151 7/159 8/170 9/193
10/205

1/23 2/36 3/75 4/93 5/110 6/151 7/164 8/168 9/171
10/178

Bowling: Rankin 9-0-62-0; Johnston 8.2-0-40-2; Mooney 7-0-25-1; Botha 9-1-32-3; Dockrell 10-2-23-2; Stirling 4-0-13-0; K. O'Brien 2-0-8-0

Bowling: Shafiul Islam 8-1-21-4; Abdur Razzak 8-0-30-1; Naeem Islam 9-1-36-1; Shakib Al Hasan 8-0-28-2; Mohammad Ashraful 9-0-42-2; Rubel Hossain 3-0-12-0

Umpires: Aleem Dar, R.J. Tucker.

Toss: Bangladesh   Points: Bangladesh 2, Ireland 0.

SATURDAY 26 FEBRUARY 2011
GROUP A: SRI LANKA vs PAKISTAN
R. PREMADASA STADIUM, COLOMBO, SRI LANKA; PAKISTAN WON BY 11 RUNS

In front of noisy Sri Lankan fans who were packed into the stadium Pakistan won an important group match by 11 runs. The result meant that they had beaten Sri Lanka in all their seven World Cup meetings. It was also Sri Lanka's first home loss in a World Cup match.

The game had many highlights and showcased the best aspects of 50-over World Cup cricket. But in the end the result may have been determined at the toss as in 72 matches at the R. Premadasa Stadium the side batting first had won 44 times.

Ahmed Shehzad set the game in motion with a stunning cover drive off Nuwan Kulasekara from the fourth ball of the first over. He would not progress much further, caught behind driving at Thisara Perera in the sixth over, but his initial shot indicated the quality of the cricket to come.

Mohammad Hafeez also played some superb drives and he and Kamran Akmal looked to be establishing themselves when some atrocious running left both batsmen standing beside the wicketkeeper with the total on 76. It took a video replay to determine who was out. Kamran Akmal survived that but not running down the wicket and missing the ball from a left-arm spinner for the second time in as many innings.

It was the two oldest players in the Pakistani line-up who put their team into a position of strength. Younis Khan and Misbah-ul-Haq had a third wicket partnership of 108 in 20 overs. The stand contained plenty of fine shots but there were also 65 singles.

A couple of times Misbah stepped to the off and whacked the ball over square-leg. Muttiah Muralitharan, as accurate and crafty as ever, was spared any serious punishment.

Rangana Herath was also effective and finally had Younis caught at short fine-leg sweeping. Misbah stayed until the conclusion of the 50 overs. With Umar Akmal and his captain, Shahid Afridi, providing a few late thumps the total was boosted to 277. This set Sri Lanka a ground-record run chase.

Under lights, Upal Tharanga and Tilerkaratne Dilshan responded to their challenging task in positive fashion. A near six over slips by Tharanga off Shoaib Akhtar's seventh delivery got the crowd and the batsmen going and they scored at the required rate of five per over for 14 overs.

At 76, Tharanga lifted a drive off Mohammad Hafeez to Afridi at short cover. Twelve runs later the Pakistanis took a hold of the match when three wickets fell for eight runs. Afridi again was a key.

He bowled Dilshan when he tried to cut a skidder and had Tilan Samaraweera brilliantly stumped drawn forward by a slower flighted delivery. Between those dismissals Mahela Jayawardene had been bowled by a fast full straight ball by Akhtar, so that by the middle of the 22nd over the Sri Lankans were in deep trouble at 4/96.

The skill of Kumar Sangakkara and the aggression of Chamara Silva kick started the chase again. Kamram Akmal missed two stumpings and 73 runs were added in 16 overs. But Afridi, an obvious Man of the Match, was in a rich vein of bowling form and not to be denied.

He picked up his 300th one-day international wicket when Sangakkara miscued to long on and finished with 4/34 and tournament figures so far of 9/50 when he had Mathews caught in the deep.

Still Silva and then at the death Kulasekara attacked. But the required run rate was now very steep. Eighteen were needed from the final over, then 13 runs from three balls. Kulasekara blasted an Umar Gul full-toss to long on but it failed to clear Umar Akmal allowing Pakistan to clinch the win.

PAKISTAN		SRI LANKA	
Ahmed Shehzad c Sangakkara b Perera	13	W. U. Tharanga c Shahid Afridi b Mohammad Hafeez	33
Mohammad Hafeez run out	32	T. M. Dilshan b Shahid Afridi	41
Kamran Akmal (wk) st Sangakkara b Herath	39	K. C. Sangakkara (capt/wk) c Ahmed Shehzad b Shahid Afridi	49
Younis Khan c Jayawardene b Herath	72	D. P. M. D. Jayawardene b Shoaib Akhtar	2
Misbah-ul-Haq not out	83	T. T. Samaraweera st Kamran Akmal b Shahid Afridi	1
Umar Akmal c Dilshan b Muralitharan	10	L. P. C. Silva st Kamran Akmal b Abdur Rehman	57
Shahid Afridi (capt) c Dilshan b Mathews	16	A. D. Mathews c Ahmed Shehzad b Shahid Afridi	18
Abdul Razzaq c sub (Kapugedera) b Perera	3	N. L. T. C. Perera b Shoaib Akhtar	8
Extras Lb4 W5	9	K. M. D. N. Kulasekara c Umar Akmal b Umar Gul	24
(50 overs)	7/277	H. M. R. K.B. Herath not out	4
Did not bat: Umar Gul, Abdur Rehman, Shoaib Akhtar		M. Muralitharan not out	0
1/28 2/76 3/105 4/213 5/238 6/267 7/277		Extras B1 Lb10 W16 Nb2	29
Bowling: Kulasekara 10-1-64-0; Perera 9-0-62-2;		(50 overs)	9/266
Mathews 10-0-56-1; Muralitharan 10-0-35-1;		1/76 2/88 3/95 4/96 5/169 6/209 7/232 8/233 9/265	
Herath 10-0-46-2; Dilshan 1-0-10-0		Bowling: Shoaib Akhtar 10-0-42-2; Abdul Razzaq 5-1-23-0;	
		Umar Gul 9-0-60-1; Mohammad Hafeez 6-0-33-1;	
		Shahid Afridi 10-0-34-4; Abdur Rehman 10-1-63-1	

Umpires: I.J. Gould D.J. Harper

Toss: Pakistan   Points: Pakistan 2 Sri Lanka 0

SUNDAY 27 FEBRUARY 2011
GROUP B: INDIA vs ENGLAND
M CHINNASWAMY STADIUM, BANGALORE, INDIA (DAY/NIGHT): MATCH TIED

The World Cup carnival moved to the south of India for this interesting Group B clash. On a pitch that offered encouragement to the spinners in the warm-up matches, England opted to shore up their bowling resources, selecting left-arm spinner and handy batsman Michael Yardy in place of Ravi Bopara. India also bolstered their spin contingent, bringing in leg-spinner Piyush Chawla for the out of form Sreesanth.

With the attacks of both teams leaking runs in their tournament openers, a run-fest was on the cards. And the match was off to an eventful start when second slip Swann dropped a difficult chance offered by Sehwag from Anderson's first delivery. After a promising start by the openers, Bresnan made the breakthrough in his first over when Sehwag edged one when trying to guide the ball through a vacant slip area. Apart from a maiden from Bresnan a few overs later, the English bowlers were unable to stop Tendulkar and Gambhir scoring at a good rate.

The tempo was increased midway through the innings as Tendulkar smote Swann's first ball for six over wide long on, bringing up the hundred partnership. Swann's next delivery was slog swept for another towering six. Into the 30th over, India had pushed the run rate to six an over and the momentum was theirs. A tentative Gambhir missed one from Swann with the score at 180, ending the second wicket stand at 134 from 131 balls. Tendulkar continued his imperious form and, to the delight of the crowd, he reached his century from 107 deliveries with a low trajectory six over long on from Swann's bowling. With five centuries in Word Cup matches, Tendulkar now held the record of the most World Cup hundreds in his own right.

Tendulkar continued to go for his shots and he eventually perished for a superb 120 from 115 balls. Yuvraj Singh and MS Dhoni were seeing the ball well and blasted 69 from just 46 balls. Yardy and Ajmal Shahzad, who came into the side for the ill Broad, suffered the most during this onslaught. From consecutive balls, both batsmen holed out to deep mid wicket. The bad news for England was that India had just reached the 300 mark. In the quest for quick runs, India's middle order overextended themselves and the wickets tumbled. In the penultimate over, Bresnan's good bowling was rewarded with three wickets from four balls, resulting in the Yorkshireman achieving a five wicket haul. Anderson, who went for plenty on this day, bowled the last over. From the fourth ball of the over, Chawla failed to capitalise on a free hit resulting from a no ball. Chawla mishit the ball back to Anderson and was run out by the bowler when attempting an unlikely single. The next ball produced another run out as Zaheer Khan failed in his bid to return for the second run.

Unfortunately, no run was scored from the delivery as the umpire signalled one short. Non-striker Munaf Patel failed by several centimetres to ground his bat inside the crease when turning for the second run. In the frenetic closing overs of the innings, India lost seven wickets for 44 runs, including 4/11 in the last two overs. After the match, England were fined for a slow over rate.

Facing a mammoth target of 339, England began to expose the limitations of India's bowling with a withering attack in the early overs. In the 10th over, Patel held onto a fierce return catch from Pietersen. Patel's catch was a reflex response to a full-blooded drive from Pietersen that would otherwise have knocked Patel out cold. After Trott was adjudged leg before playing back to Chawla, Strauss found a willing ally in Ian Bell. Bell had a reprieve on 17 when he was struck on the pads playing well down the pitch to Yuvraj Singh. India referred Bowden's not out decision to DRS, but the decision was referred back to umpire Bowden under the rule that the on-field umpire must decide lbw appeals when the distance between the stumps and the point of impact is more than 2.5 metres. The rationale for the 2.5 metre rule was that the accuracy of the Hawk Eye technology diminishes when the distance between the stumps and the point of impact exceeds 2.5 metres. Under the rule at the time, Bowden could only reverse the not out decision if the replay showed that the ball would have hit the exact centre of middle stump. The ICC changed the rule a week later to allow, where the 2.5 metre rule applied, the on-field umpire to reverse the not out decision where the replay showed that the ball would have hit any part of the middle stump.

The subdued Bangalore crowd looked on as Strauss drove a single in the 28th over to record an impressive hundred from 99 balls. Bell and Strauss mainly dealt in ones and twos and loose deliveries were sent hurtling to, and sometimes over, the fence. After 41 overs, Strauss and Bell had put together over 160 runs and England were in the box seat at 2-278. When Bell was 68, Kohli put down a straightforward catch at slip from Chawla in the 42nd over. Fortunately for India, the mistake only cost one run as a tired Bell mistimed a slog from Khan to be caught by Kohli at mid off. Khan made things interesting with the next ball, a yorker that caught Strauss plumb in front. Strauss departed for an outstanding 158 from 145 balls. Khan completed a triple strike for India when he knocked back Collingwood's off stump in the next over. India had fought back, claiming three wickets in a four over patch that produced a mere nine runs for England.

In the space of four overs, the required run rate had jumped from a manageable 6.77 after 41 overs to a demanding 10.40 after 45 overs. With only five specialist batsmen, the wisdom of Yardy's selection over Bopara would be put to the test. England's turmoil continued as Prior holed out to mid wicket off Harbhajan Singh. In the 48th over, Yardy lifted a slower ball from Patel to a gleeful Sehwag at short fine leg. England were 7-310 with only two overs to go and looked a beaten side.

Swann and Bresnan had other ideas. Both batsmen swept Chawla for six as 15 runs were taken from the penultimate over. In another twist, Bresnan attempted to heave the last ball of the over to the fence and was bowled.

The visitors needed 14 to win from Patel's last over. After Swann took three runs form the first two deliveries, Shahzad, facing his first ball, smashed Patel over his head for cleanly hit six. Five runs were required from three balls. Shahzad missed the next one and the batsmen scurried through for a bye. Swann waltzed down the wicket and managed to get an inside edge. The batsmen ran frantically for two as the ball trickled to the on side. With two runs required for a win from the last ball, Swann tried to force a good ball from Patel to the deep. Swann raced through for a single as the ball was fielded neatly by mid off.

The result was the fourth tie in World Cup history. Both teams rued missed opportunities. In a well-paced innings, England were well positioned to chase down the target, needing 69 runs from the last 10 overs to win with only two wickets down. Time would tell whether this failure to keep their nerve in this match would cost them at the business end of the tournament. For India, Patel's short run from the last ball of the innings was the difference between a tie and a one-run victory. In the man of the match stakes, Strauss shaded the performances of Tendulkar and Bresnan to claim the award.

INDIA		ENGLAND	
V. Sehwag c Prior b Bresnan	35	A. J. Strauss (capt) lbw b Khan	158
S. R. Tendulkar c Yardy b Anderson	120	K. P. Pietersen c & b Patel	31
G. Gambhir b Swann	51	I. J. L. Trott lbw b Chawla	16
Yuvraj Singh c Bell b Yardy	58	I. R. Bell c Kohli b Khan	69
M. S. Dhoni (capt/wk) c sub (Wright) b Bresnan	31	P. D. Collingwood b Khan	1
Y. K. Pathan c Swann b Bresnan	14	M. J. Prior (wk) c sub (Raina) b Harbhajan Singh	4
V. Kohli b Bresnan	8	M. H. Yardy c Sehwag b Patel	13
Harbhajan Singh lbw b Bresnan	0	T. T. Bresnan b Chawla	14
Z. Khan run out	4	G. P. Swann not out	15
P. P. Chawla run out	2	A. Shahzad not out	6
M. M. Patel not out	0	Extras (b 1, lb 7, w 3)	8-338
Extras (lb 3, w 7, nb 5)	15	Did not bat: J. M. Anderson	
(50 overs)	10-338	1/68 2/111 3/281 4/281 5/85 6/289 7/307 8/325	
1/46 2/180 3/236 4/305 5/305 6/327 7/327 8/328 9/338		Bowling: Khan 10-0-64-3; Patel 10-0-70-2;	
10/338		Chawla 10-0-71-2; Harbhajan Singh 10-0-58-1; Yuvraj	
Bowling: Anderson 9.5-0-91-1; Shahzad 8-0-53-0;		Singh 7-0-46-0; Pathan 3-0-21-0	
Bresnan 10-1-48-5; Swann 9-1-59-1; Collingwood 3-0-20-0;			
Yardy 10-0-64-1			

Umpires: B.F. Bowden, M. Erasmus.

Toss: India   Points: India 1, England 1.

MONDAY 28 FEBRUARY 2011
GROUP A: CANADA vs ZIMBABWE
VIDARBHA CRICKET ASSOCIATION STADIUM, JAMTHA, NAGPUR, INDIA
ZIMBABWE WON BY 175 RUNS

In the match between the two red-uniformed sides, Zimbabwe clearly exposed Canada's shortcomings with a dominating 175-run victory; the Africans' biggest World Cup-winning margin. The result was another indication that several minnows, despite a number of World Cup experiences were, even against hardly full sized fish, actually getting smaller, not bigger.

After Elton Chigumbra elected to bat Canada made a perfect start when Khurram Chohan trapped Brendan Taylor lbw from the first ball of the match. Just seven runs later Charles Coventry played across the line at Harvir Baidwan and was also lbw. Then Tatenda Taibu and Craig Ervine set up the Zimbabwean win with a partnership of 181 in 28 overs. It was the Zimbabweans' highest ever World Cup partnership. Ervine drove his second ball through mid off for four while Taibu hit two fours in each of Jimmy Hansra's opening overs.

Hansra was targeted and went for 41 from just four overs. Ervine twice hit John Davison for six while Taibu, on way to a Man of the Match Award, struck nine boundaries as he pushed the total along at a run a ball. Both missed their hundreds as leg-spinner Balaji Rao, on way to an impressive four-wicket haul, picked up three wickets in as many overs. Then Seren Williams, Prosper Utseya and Graeme Cremer pushed the total to a healthy 298 by the end of the 50 overs.

Zimbabwe had selected a hatful of spinners to befuddle the Canadians and the move worked like a treat. They made a terrible mess of trying to handle Ray Price's left-arm spin. He was again given the new-ball and by the sixth over of the innings had reduced Canada to 3/7.

From there the match lingered for another 37 overs without the Canadians ever threatening to get anywhere near their target. Cremer's leg-spin also became a challenge, particularly to the tailenders. Canada eventually only tallied 41% of their run requirement even though they used 84% of their overs.

ZIMBABWE		CANADA	
B. R.M. Taylor lbw b Khurram Chohan	0	J. M. Davison b Price	0
C. K. Coventry lbw b Baidwan	4	N. R. Kumar c & b Price	1
T. Taibu (wk) c Davison b Balaji Rao	98	R. Gunasekera b Lamb	24
C. R. Ervine c Bagai b Balaji Rao	85	A. Bagai (capt/wk) c Williams b Price	0
E. Chigumbra (capt) c Bagai b Rizwan Cheema	5	A. S. Hansra st Taibu b Utseya	20
S. C. Williams c Bagai b Balaji Rao	30	Rizwan Cheema c Cremer b Utseya	14
G. A. Lamb b Balaji Rao	11	Z. E. Surkari st Taibu b Lamb	26
P. Utseya c Hansra b Khurram Chohan	22	T. G. Gordon lbw b Cremer	7
A. G. Cremer b Baidwan	26	Khurram Chohan lbw b Cremer	8
R. W. Price not out	10	H. S. Baidwan not out	13
C. B. Mpofu not out	3	W. D. Balaji Rao b Cremer	1
Extras Lb2 W1 Nb1	4	Extras W9	9
(50 overs)	9/298	(42.1 overs)	123
1/0 2/7 3/188 4/193 5/201 6/219 7/240 8/281 9/284		1/1 2/7 3/7 4/50 5/50 6/66 7/78 8/97 9/122 10/123	
Bowling: Khurram Chohan 10-0-44-2; Baidwan 9-0-47-2; Hansra 4-0-41-0; Rizwan Cheema 9-0-51-1; Balaji Rao 10-0-57-4; Davison 8-0-56-0		Bowling: Mpofu 5-1-12-0; Price 8-4-16-3; Utseya 7-0-24-2; Lamb 8-0-29-2; Cremer 9.1-1-31-3; Williams 5-0-11-0	

Umpires: Asad Rauf B.N.J. Oxenford

Toss: Zimbabwe   Points: Zimbabwe 2 Canada 0

MONDAY 28 FEBRUARY 2011
GROUP B: NETHERLANDS vs WEST INDIES
FEROZ SHAH KOTLA, DELHI, INDIA (DAY/NIGHT): WEST INDIES WON BY 215 RUNS

The standing of the Associate teams in World Cup competition took a body blow when Holland were hammered by a middle-of-the-road West Indies combination.

Dutch captain Borren's decision to field first in this day-night fixture backfired. The West Indies rattled up a total of 8-330, their second highest tally in World Cup matches. The top five batsmen made useful contributions, including three half-centuries, without anyone continuing to a big score. Gayle batted steadily for his 80 and Kieron Pollard blazed 60 from a mere 27 deliveries, including four sixes. The batting powerplay, taken in overs 36-41, yielded an impressive 56 runs. Mudassar Bukhari conceded 20 runs in the 39th over, which featured Pollard clobbering three fours and a six. Left-arm spinner Seelaar took 3-45 and was the only Dutch bowler who conceded less than a run a ball.

Holland were all at sea in the early overs of their reply. The speed of Roach and the spin of Benn were too much for most of the Dutch batsmen to deal with. Roach and Benn destroyed the top order, as the Netherlands slumped to 5-36 in the 11th over. Despite the frequent fall of wickets, number three batsman Tom Cooper batted calmly and survived the onslaught. Cooper and Mudassar Bukhari constructed a partnership of 57 from 11 overs to take the Netherlands into three figures and to salvage some respectability. The resistance was ended by Roach, who bowled Mudassar Bukhari with a ball that kept a little low. In his next over, Roach took a hat-trick, the sixth in the history of the World Cup. Seelaar and Bernard Loots were caught in front by inducers from the first two balls of Roach's over. Berend Westdijk failed to negotiate the hat-trick ball, as another Roach inswinger beat a tentative defence and levelled middle stump. The hat-trick put an end to the Netherlands' innings, which lasted just shy of two hours. Cooper, who finished with an unbeaten 55, witnessed the collapse from the non-striker's end.

Roach finished with 6-27 and was an obvious choice for the man of the match. In a confidence boosting win, the West Indies' winning margin was their second largest margin in limited-overs internationals and the sixth highest margin in World Cup matches overall.

WEST INDIES		NETHERLANDS	
D. S. Smith c Barresi b Loots	53	A. N. Kervezee st Thomas b Benn	14
C. H. Gayle c Kervezee b ten Doeschate	80	W. Barresi (wk) c Gayle b Roach	0
D. M. Bravo c Kervezee b Seelaar	30	T. L.W. Cooper not out	55
R. R. Sarwan lbw b Westdijk	49	R. N. ten Doeschate lbw b Benn	7
K. A. Pollard c ten Doeschate b Mudassar Bukhari	60	B. Zuiderent b Roach	1
D. J. G. Sammy (capt) c Kervezee b Seelaar	6	T. N. de Grooth lbw b Benn	1
S. Chanderpaul b Seelaar	4	P. W. Borren (capt) c Pollard b Sammy	10
D. C. Thomas (wk) lbw b Mudassar Bukhari	13	Mudassar Bukhari b Roach	24
N. O. Miller not out	11	P. M. Seelaar lbw b Roach	1
S. J. Benn not out	3	B. P. Loots lbw b Roach	0
Extras (b 3, lb 3, w 14, nb 1)	21	B. A. Westdijk b Roach	0
(50 overs)	8-330	Extras (lb 2)	2
Did not bat: K. A. J. Roach		(31.3 overs)	10-115
1/100 2/168 3/196 4/261 5/278 6/290 7/312 8/326		1/2 2/26 3/34 4/35 5/36 6/56 7/113 8/115 9/115 10/115	
Bowling: Mudassar Bukhari 10-1-65-2; Westdijk 7-0-56-1;		Bowling: Benn 8-1-28-3; Roach 8.3-0-27-6; Miller 7-0-23-0;	
ten Doeschate 10-0-77-1; Loots 7-0-44-1; Cooper 6-0-37-0;		Sammy 7-0-33-1; Pollard 1-0-2-0	
Seelaar 10-1-45-3			

Umpires: A.M. Saheba, S.J.A. Taufel.

Toss: Netherlands   Points: West Indies 2, Netherlands 0.

TUESDAY 1 MARCH 2011
GROUP A: SRI LANKA v KENYA
R.PREMADASA STADIUM, COLOMBO, SRI LANKA: SRI LANKA WON BY NINE WICKETS

Lasith Malinga literally had Kenya on its knees as again in 2011 a minnow totally failed to cope with a Test-playing nation. The fast slinger from Galle ripped yorker after yorker under the sliding feet of forlorn Kenyan batsmen and into their pads and stumps, picking up his best ever figures and a record-breaking second World Cup hat-trick as Sri Lanka completed an easy nine-wicket win.

Malinga and Nuwan Kulusekara began the damage soon after Jimmy Kamande won the toss and elected to bat, trapping both openers lbw to leave Kenya 2/8.

The Obuya brothers, Collins and David, then batted gamely if luckily through 29.3 overs, putting on a partnership of 94. Both reached valuable half-centuries. Malinga warmed up for the later demolition when he broke through Collins Obuya's defences then 18 runs later Angelo Mathews had Steve Tikolo hitting a scorcher straight to Tilakaratne Dilshan at point.

That signalled the start of the fun. Kenya lost 7/22 in seven overs as Man of the Match Malinga and friends tore the second half of the batting order apart. His hat-trick was spread over two overs, so it lost some impact on the crowd. There was plenty going on, though. Tanmay Mishra was given out lbw to a ball that would have barely clipped the leg-stump from the final ball of his seventh over while from the first two balls of the next over Peter Ongondo and Shem Ngoche had their stumps violently removed. Malinga's next ball flew down the leg-side for five wides then he found the yorker radar again and bowled Elijah Otieno in as dramatic a finish to an innings as has been seen.

The boundaries began flowing from the bats of Upal Tharanga and Dilshan in the second over of Sri Lanka's pursuit of 142. Ongondo's second over went for 12 runs and in his third he conceded another 11. Kamande brought himself on and Tharanga hit three more fours. By the time Dilshan was out for 44 in the ninth over the total was already 72.

Tharanga and Kumar Sangakkara continued to entertain the big Sri Lankan crowd with a series of sumptuous strokes until the former, maybe tiring at the lack of contest, took 18 runs from five deliveries by Ngoche in the penultimate over of the match.

Things were not going well for the Kenyans but the captain, Jimmy Kamande, insisted there was no rift between the team and the coach, Eldine Baptiste.

KENYA		SRI LANKA	
M. A. Ouma (wk) lbw b Kulasekara	1	W. U. Tharanga not out	67
S. R. Waters lbw b Malinga	3	T. M. Dilshan c Ouma b Otieno	44
C. O. Obuya b Malinga	52	K. C. Sangakkara (capt/wk) not out	27
D. O. Obuya c Samaraweera b Muralitharan	51	Extras W7 Nb1	8
S. O. Tikolo c Dilshan b Mathews	7	(18.4 overs)	1/146
T. Mishra lbw b Malinga	0	Did not bat: D. P. M. D. Jayawardene, T. T. Samaraweera,	
J. Kamande run out	1	L. P. C. Silva, A. D. Mathews, K. M. D. N. Kulasekara, M.	
N. N. Odhiambo not out	8	Muralitharan, S. L. Malinga, B. A. W. Mendis	
P. J. Ongondo b Malinga	0	1/72	
S. O. Ngoche b Malinga	0	Bowling: Ongondo 3-0-28-0; Odhiambo 5-0-26-0;	
E. Otieno b Malinga	0	Ngoche 4-0-39-0; Kamande 1-0-14-0; Otieno 4-0-26-1; C.	
Extras B1 Lb6 W9 Nb3	19	O.Obuya 1.4-0-13-0	
(43.4 overs)	142		
1/4 2/8 3/102 4/120 5/127 6/128 7/137 8/137 9/137			
10/142			
Bowling: Malinga 7.4-0-38-6; Kulasekara 9-1-18-1;			
Mathews 7-0-20-1; Mendis 9-2-23-0; Muralitharan 8-0-24-1;			
Silva 3-0-12-0			

Umpires: A.L. Hill S.K. Tarapore

Toss: Kenya   Points: Sri Lanka 2 Kenya 0

WEDNESDAY 2 MARCH 2011
GROUP B: ENGLAND vs IRELAND
M CHINNASWAMY STADIUM, BANGALORE, INDIA (DAY/NIGHT): IRELAND WON BY 3 WICKETS

England returned to Bangalore for the British Isles derby against Ireland. To add colour to the occasion, Irish skipper Will Porterfield dyed his hair purple for a cancer charity on the eve of the game and some other players sported hairstyles with different hues. On the back of the disappointing loss to Bangladesh, this was a game Ireland were eager to perform well in.

Andrew Strauss chose to bat on a batsman-friendly wicket. In the space of three days, England achieved their second successive total in excess of 300. Strauss and Pietersen set the tone with another busy opening partnership, the yield on this occasion being 91 runs at a shade less than seven runs an over. The highlight of the innings was the 167 run stand in 26 overs between Trott and Bell. Both batsmen missed out on hundreds that were there for the taking. Approaching 300 with only two wickets lost, England lost several wickets in the quest for quick runs. Their push in the final ten overs produced the mixed result of 70 runs scored but six wickets lost. In the latter stages of the innings, Mooney struck four times for Ireland. England could be reasonably pleased with the final tally of 8-327, which was aided by 20 wides.

Ireland's chase began with the first-ball dismissal of Porterfield. Anderson, who leaked runs in England's opening two fixtures, bowled an innocuous ball wide of off stump, which was dragged onto the stumps by Porterfield. After this setback, Paul Stirling, Ed Joyce and Niall O'Brien departed after making starts. With Swann causing difficulties, Ireland struggled and looked dead and buried at 5-111 in the 25th over. At this point, Ireland needed to score more than eight an over for an unlikely victory.

Kevin O'Brien had other ideas. The burly, red-haired all-rounder decided that hitting out was the best policy and the runs began to flow. Swann was belted two leg-side sixes and Yardy was swept for two fine boundaries in an over. With Alex Cusack allowing O'Brien most of the strike, the pendulum began to swing Ireland's way. The pair raced to the 50-partnership in 31 balls.

Ireland put themselves firmly back in the contest with a punishing batting powerplay in overs 31-36. The five overs produced an astonishing 62 runs without loss to leave England rattled. Anderson was flayed for 17 runs in an over, which included a massive six by O'Brien over deep mid wicket that sailed 102 metres. In an impressive exhibition of hitting power, a ball from Bresnan that was only fractionally short was clobbered by O'Brien for six over mid wicket. It was O'Brien's sixth six in the innings.

With O'Brien on 93, England missed their opportunity to stem the flow of runs when Strauss was unable to hold onto a skier from Collingwood's bowling. English nerves frayed further in the next over when Yardy spilt a firmly hit return catch from Cusack. With the asking rate a manageable 6.50 per over, O'Brien reached his hundred when he hit a Yardy full toss for two. O'Brien created history, setting a new World Cup-mark of 50 balls for the fastest 100.

After a mix-up running between the wickets, Cusack made the sacrifice and was run out for 47. With a moment available for observers to regain their breath, the scoreboard showed that O'Brien and Cusack combined for an amazing 162 runs from a mere 103 deliveries. For Ireland, a possible victory was some way off and one of the lower-order would need to stay with O'Brien to keep their hopes alive. The equation was challenging but realistic: 55 runs required from 8.3 overs with four wickets in hand.

With O'Brien's innings reaching a post-century lull, Mooney stepped up to maintain the rate of scoring. Mooney started in unconvincing style, edging two balls for four, before he crashed Broad and Anderson through the point to cover region for boundaries. In the penultimate over, O'Brien's exhilarating innings ended at 113 when he was run out attempting an unlikely second run from a ball that was worked to mid wicket. Only 11 runs were required from 11 deliveries with three wickets standing.

Trent Johnston drove a Broad full toss to the rope and, with the first ball of the final over, Mooney flicked the ball to the mid wicket boundary to deliver the Irish an improbable win. Ireland had climbed the mountain of scoring 328 runs inside 50 overs to topple their neighbours. The result threw open the prospects of progression in Group B. To the delight of the Irish supporters, Kevin O'Brien won the man of the match award.

ENGLAND		IRELAND	
A. J. Strauss (capt) b Dockrell	34	W. T.S. Porterfield (capt) b Anderson	0
K. P. Pietersen c N. O'Brien b Stirling	59	P. R. Stirling c Pietersen b Bresnan	32
I. J. L. Trott b Mooney	92	E. C. Joyce st Prior b Swann	32
I. R. Bell c Stirling b Mooney	81	N. J. O'Brien (wk) b Swann	29
P. D. Collingwood c K. O'Brien b Mooney	16	G. C. Wilson lbw b Swann	3
M. J. Prior (wk) b Johnston	6	K. J. O'Brien run out	113
T. T. Bresnan c Johnston b Mooney	4	A. R. Cusack run out	47
M. H. Yardy b Johnston	3	J. F. Mooney not out	33
G. P. Swann not out	9	D. T. Johnston not out	7
Extras (b 1, lb 2, w 20)	23	Extras (b 5, lb 16, w 12)	33
(50 overs)	8-327	(49.1 overs)	7-329
Did not bat: S. C.J. Broad, J. M. Anderson		Did not bat: G. H. Dockrell, W. B. Rankin	
1/91 2/111 3/278 4/288 5/299 6/312 7/317 8/327		1/0 2/62 3/103 4/106 5/111 6/273 7/317	
Bowling: Rankin 7-0-51-0; Johnston 10-0-58-2;		Bowling: Anderson 8.1-1-49-1; Broad 9-0-73-0;	
Cusack 4-0-39-0; Mooney 9-0-63-4; Stirling 10-0-45-1		Bresnan 10-0-64-1; Yardy 7-0-49-0; Swann 10-0-47-3;	
		Collingwood 5-0-26-0	

Umpires: Aleem Dar, B.F. Bowden.

Toss: England   Points: Ireland 2, England 0.

Mohali Stadium, scene of the epic World Cup semi-final in 1996, was about one-third full for the clash between the Netherlands and South Africa. Unlike Ireland's win the night before, this would not be an occasion when an Associate team upstaged a Test-playing nation.

For the second time within three days, Dutch captain Borren won the toss, sent the opposition in and watched them score well over 300. Under overcast skies, the Dutch had some early success. South African captain Smith played across the line to Loots and was bowled. Kallis fell in single figures for the second match in a row, nicking a delivery outside off stump to a delighted Wesley Barresi. From 2-58 in the 16th over, Amla and de Villiers made steady progress before unleashing an assault on the Dutch bowlers. A modest score of 2-108 at the halfway point of the innings gave no indication of the havoc that was to follow. In his usual calm and assured manner, Amla scored at a steady rate and he reached his hundred from 121 balls. At the other end, de Villiers batted in an almost cavalier fashion, reaching his hundred three overs after Amla despite giving him a 15 over start.

The real action began in the 44th over from Loots. De Villiers hammered the first three balls of the over for giant sixes. The over produced 25 runs for the Proteas. De Villiers continued his blazing strokeplay in the next over from ten Doeschate, hitting a hat-trick of boundaries. The batting clinic ended as Amla was caught at point and, in the next over, de Villiers was caught well short attempting a second run. The Amla and de Villiers partnership realised a monumental 221 runs from 29.2 overs. Their battering of the Dutch part-timers included a powerplay in overs 41-46 of 69 runs.

JP Duminy continued the blitz in the closing overs, mauling 40 from just 15 deliveries, including four sixes. South Africa finished with a daunting score of 5-351, featuring an incredible 136 runs from the last 10 overs, which included 54 runs from the final three overs. An impressive feature of the Proteas late-innings assault was that, even when the batsmen were unable to score fours and sixes, dot balls were kept to a minimum. In the eye of this ferocious storm, Mudassar Bukhari was the one Dutch bowler to emerge with some credit. He conceded only 44 runs from his ten over allotment.

Morne van Wyk took the place of de Villiers behind the stumps on account of de Villers straining his back whilst batting. The Dutch made reasonable early progress, with the scoreboard reading 2-81 after 21 overs. South Africa were 2-92 at the same stage. However, this was where the similarity ended. The South African bowlers scythed through the rest of the order, capturing eight for 39 in 13.3 overs to extinguish the Dutch challenge in the 35th over. The last six wickets collapsed for only 17 runs. Barresi was the sole batsman to put up prolonged resistance with his 44. Interestingly, it was not Steyn or Morkle who engineered the destruction of the innings. The spin attack of Imran Tahir, Robin Petersen and Duminy picked up a combined six for 57 in 17.5 overs. Imran Tahir claimed the last three wickets to fall and four Dutch batsmen were out lbw.

AB de Villiers' back pain was soothed by his team's huge win and his man of the match award. The margin of 231 runs was the fourth highest in World Cup history. De Villiers became the fifth batsman, after Mark Waugh, Saeed Anwar, Rahul Dravid and Matthew Hayden, to have scored back-to-back hundreds at the World Cup.

SOUTH AFRICA		NETHERLANDS	
H. M. Amla c Cooper b ten Doeschate	113	A. N. Kervezee c & b Kallis	10
G. C. Smith (capt) b Loots	20	W. Barresi (wk) st van Wyk b Duminy	44
J. H. Kallis c Barresi b ten Doeschate	2	T. L.W. Cooper c Steyn b Kallis	9
A. B. de Villiers (wk) run out	134	B. Zuiderent lbw b Peterson	15
F. du Plessis not out	18	R. N. ten Doeschate lbw b Steyn	11
J. P. Duminy c Borren b ten Doeschate	40	T. N. de Grooth run out	12
M. N. van Wyk not out	0	P. W. Borren (capt) lbw b Peterson	3
Extras (b 2, lb 5, w 16, nb 1)	24	Mudassar Bukhari b Imran Tahir	0
(50 overs)	5-351	P. M. Seelaar not out	2
Did not bat: R. J. Peterson, M. Morkel, D. W. Steyn,		B. P. Loots lbw b Imran Tahir	6
Imran Tahir		B. A. Westdijk lbw b Imran Tahir	0
1/51 2/58 3/279 4/283 5/349		Extras (w 8)	8
Bowling: Mudassar Bukhari 10-0-44-0; Westdijk 9-0-76-0;		(34.5 overs)	10-120
ten Doeschate 10-0-72-3; Loots 9-0-60-1; Seelaar 10-0-74-0;		1/26 2/46 3/81 4/83 5/100 6/109 7/109 8/110 9/120	
Cooper 2-0-18-0		10/120	
		Bowling: Steyn 6-1-26-1; Morkel 5-0-18-0; Kallis 6-0-19-2;	
		Imran Tahir 6.5-0-19-3; Peterson 5-0-22-2; Duminy 6-0-16-1	

Umpires: E.A.R. de Silva, R.A. Kettleborough.

Toss: Netherlands   Points: South Africa 2, Netherlands 0.

THURSDAY 3 MARCH 2011
GROUP A: CANADA vs PAKISTAN
R.PREMADASA STADIUM, COLOMBO, SRI LANKA: PAKISTAN WON BY 46 RUNS

Pakistani captain, Shahid Afridi, in the midst of a stunning run of form, lifted his side to an unconvincing 46 run win over Canada. In their usual disregard for the form guide Pakistan might have lost to the lowly Canadians just five days after their wonderful win over Sri Lanka if their captain had not bowled so brilliantly again.

Afridi's Man of the Match spell of 5/23 brought his tournament return to an amazing 14/93 and he ran out Balaji Rao with a direct hit throw from mid off for good measure.

It turned around his team's precarious position as Canada, previously a tournament easybeat, had at one stage been 3/104 chasing 184. Afridi's bowling, fielding and effective use of the DRS saw the Canadians lose 7/34 and any chance of causing an upset.

He had also won the toss and batted, but his batsmen were unimpressive. By the middle of the 16th over, Pakistan were 4/67 and it took 20 overs for the steady Misbah-ul-Haq and the talented Umar Akmal to restore the innings with a stand of 73 for the fifth wicket.

Rotund leg-spinner Balaji Rao removed them both. Then as Pakistan lost their last four wickets for three runs he brought back memories of Bermudan big man, Dwayne Leverock's slips catch in 2007 with a between the thighs effort off Jimmy Hansra to dismiss Wahab Riaz. Pakistan were bowled out in 43 overs with extras third top score.

Umar Gul and Abdul Razzaq removed an opener apiece to leave Canada on 2/16 by the end of the fifth over. But Zubin Surkari, and Hansra fought hard and effectively to lift their side into the match.

They put on 60 for the fourth wicket and were not separated until Surkari was dismissed lbw by Saeed Aljmal's quicker ball and only then after Daryl Harper's not-out call was overturned by the DRS, one of four decisions by the Australian found to be incorrect by technology during this game.

That opened the door for Afridi and he stormed through. He bowled Rizwan Cheema with a wrong 'un. That made the score 5/111 and seven overs later the game was over.

Canada had batted only one ball less than Pakistan and had been gifted even three more wides than the 16 they had offered, but in the end they remained signifiantly short of their run requirement.

PAKISTAN		CANADA	
Mohammad Hafeez lbw b Osinde	11	R. Gunasekera lbw b Umar Gul	8
Ahmed Shehzad c Gordon b Baidwan	12	N. R. Kumar b Abdul Razzaq	2
Kamran Akmal (wk) c Kumar b Rizwan Cheema	16	Z. E. Surkari lbw b Saeed Ajmal	27
Younis Khan lbw b Baidwan	6	A. Bagai (capt/wk) lbw b Shahid Afridi	16
Misbah-ul-Haq c Bagai b Balaji Rao	37	A. S. Hansra b Shahid Afridi	43
Umar Akmal lbw b Balaji Rao	48	Rizwan Cheema b Shahid Afridi	4
Shahid Afridi (capt) c Kumar b Rizwan Cheema	20	T. G. Gordon c Wahab Riaz b Shahid Afridi	9
Abdul Razzaq lbw b Hansra	8	H. S. Baidwan b Shahid Afridi	0
Umar Gul not out	2	Khurram Chohan not out	5
Wahab Riaz c Balaji Rao b Hansra	0	W. D. Balaji Rao run out	1
Saeed Ajmal b Baidwan	0	H. Osinde b Wahab Riaz	0
Extras B4 Lb3 W16 Nb1	24	Extras Lb4 W19	23
(43 overs)	184	(42.5 overs)	138

1/16 2/42 3/55 4/67 5/140 6/165 7/181 8/181 9/181 10/184

1/16 2/16 3/44 4/104 5/111 6/114 7/114 8/130 9/134 10/138

Bowling: Khurram Chohan 3.3-0-10-0; Osinde 7-1-25-1; Gordon 0.3-0-1-0; Baidwan 8-1-35-3; Rizwan Cheema 8-0-33-2; Balaji Rao 10-0-50-2; Hansra 6-1-23-2

Bowling: Abdul Razzaq 7-2-16-1; Umar Gul 7-1-20-1; Shahid Afridi 10-0-23-5; Wahab Riaz 5.5-0-23-1; Saeed Ajmal 8-0-31-1; Mohammad Hafeez 5-0-21-0

Umpires: D.J. Harper N.J. Llong

Toss: Pakistan   Points: Pakistan 2 Canada 0

FRIDAY 4 MARCH 2011
GROUP A: NEW ZEALAND vs ZIMBABWE
SARDAR PATEL STADIUM, MOTERA, AHMEDABAD, INDIA: NEW ZEALAND WON BY 10 WICKETS

These two sides began the match level on points in Group A, but New Zealand's 10-wicket victory in front of a very small crowd showed there was little similarity in terms of ability.

The Zimbabweans were let down by their top-order batsmen after Elton Chigumbura won the toss and batted and when they bowled their idea of loading the side with spinners made no impact. There were few highlights in the match once Zimbabwe had slipped to 5/46. Their batting issues began in the second over when Charles Coventry called for a single to mid-on and Hamish Bennett's direct hit under arm throw found him short of the crease.

Coventry's opening partner, Brendan Taylor, was the exception in the top order as he held things together until he missed a straight floaty from Scott Styris in the 22nd over. He only hit four fours but one of them was freakish. A Tim Southee bouncer followed him and turned an upper cut over slips into a limbo position ramp shot to fine leg.

Daniel Vettori's first over of left-arm spin was a double-wicket maiden. He dented the middle order and stymied the run rate to such an extent the Zimbabweans could not get it to four an over. When they were 7/89 it seemed possible that New Zealand would not have chase much over 100. But Prosper Utseya batted soundly enough to keep the innings going until the 47th over when he was last out, yorked by Southee.

Needing 163 Martin Guptill launched the Black Caps' innings with two fours and a six over long on off Tinashe Panyangara's opening over. Then he and Brendon McCullum kept the score ticking along against the supposed threat of Ray Price's new-ball spin.

The 50 was raised in the 12th over, and Guptill on way to a Man of the Match award reached his half-century milestone off his 68th ball. McCullum took 74 balls to attain the same landmark.

The two openers allowed no maidens during the innings yet after the first over the most runs conceded in an over was 10. It had the effect of the result being inevitable without any sense of excitement or climax.

Finally Guptill bashed the third ball of the 34th over from Panyangara over mid-on for four to claim the two points and add his and McCullum's name into the record books with New Zealand's highest ever World Cup opening partnership.

ZIMBABWE		NEW ZEALAND	
B. R.M. Taylor lbw b Styris	44	M. J. Guptill not out	86
C. K. Coventry run out	0	B. B. McCullum (wk) not out	76
T. Taibu (wk) lbw b Southee	8	Extras Lb1 W1 Nb2	4
C. R. Ervine c Ryder b Mills	11	(33.3 overs)	0/166
E. Chigumbura (capt) lbw b Vettori	1	Did not bat: J. D. Ryder, L. R. P. L. Taylor, J. E.C. Franklin,	
R. W. Chakabva c Taylor b Vettori	0	S. B. Styris, N. L. McCullum, D. L.Vettori (capt) , K. D. Mills,	
G. A. Lamb run out	18	T. G. Southee, H. K. Bennett	
P. Utseya b Southee	36	Bowling: Panyangara 5.3-0-42-0; Price 7-0-23-0;	
A. G. Cremer c B. B. McCullum b Mills	22	Utseya 6-0-23-0; Lamb 5-0-18-0; Cremer 7-0-38-0;	
R. W. Price lbw b Southee	11	Chigumbura 3-0-21-0	
T. Panyangara not out	4		
Extras Lb4 W3	7		
(46.2 overs)	162		
1/2 2/27 3/42 4/46 5/46 6/86 7/89 8/122 9/157 10/162			
Bowling: Mills 10-0-29-2; Southee 9.2-3-29-3;			
Bennett 8-0-37-0; Vettori 10-3-25-2; Styris 4-0-13-1; N.			
L.McCullum 3-0-15-0; Ryder 2-0-10-0			

Umpires: Aleem Dar M.Erasmus

Toss: Zimbabwe   Points: New Zealand 2 Zimbabwe 0

FRIDAY 4 MARCH 2011
GROUP B: BANGLADESH vs WEST INDIES
SHER-E-BANGLA NATIONAL STADIUM, DHAKA, BANGLADESH
WEST INDIES WON BY NINE WICKETS

Bangladesh, who flattered to deceive in their opening two games, were given a jolting reality check by the West Indies in front of another capacity crowd at Dhaka's main venue.

The home side chose to bat first. Ninety minutes later, the innings was complete for an abysmal score of 58. The West Indies only used three bowlers, including the medium-paced wobblers of captain Sammy, who collected three wickets. Benn's 4-18 were his best figures in a limited-overs international. Roach continued his good form, sending three batsmen to the pavilion. Junaid Siddique and Mohammad Ashraful were the only Bangladeshi batsmen to reach double figures and to stay at the crease for 20 deliveries. Bangladesh's tally was the fourth lowest in World Cup history.

The West Indies made short work of their target, realising their goal in 12.2 overs for the loss of Devon Smith. The Bangladeshi crowd had every right to feel short-changed, as only 31.1 out of the maximum of 100 overs were used in this match. Some more passionate members of the crowd at Sher-e Bangla National Stadium took things further. Mistaking the bus carrying the West Indian contingent for the bus carrying Bangladesh's team, some fans hurled stones at the bus as it made its way from the ground to the West Indies' team hotel. Fortunately, no one was hurt and the only damage suffered was a few shattered bus windows.

Despite taking one less wicket than Benn, Roach collected his second man of the match award in a row.

BANGLADESH		WEST INDIES	
Tamim Iqbal c Sammy b Roach	0	D. S. Smith b Naeem Islam	6
Imrul Kayes c Thomas b Sammy	5	C. H. Gayle not out	37
Junaid Siddique lbw b Roach	25	D. M. Bravo not out	9
Mushfiqur Rahim (wk) c Sarwan b Sammy	0	Extras (b 2, w 5)	7
Shakib Al Hasan b Benn	8	(12.2 overs)	1-59
Raqibul Hasan c Pollard b Sammy	4	Did not bat: R. R. Sarwan, S. Chanderpaul, K. A. Pollard,	
Mohammad Ashraful (capt) c Thomas b Roach	11	D. C. Thomas (wk), D. J. G. Sammy (capt), N. O. Miller,	
Naeem Islam c Thomas b Benn	1	S. J. Benn, K. A. J. Roach	
Shafiul Islam c Pollard b Benn	0	1/29	
Abdur Razzak not out	2	Bowling: Shafiul Islam 2-0-11-0; Naeem Islam 6-1-14-1;	
Rubel Hossain b Benn	0	Rubel Hossain 1-0-12-0; Abdur Razzak 1-0-8-0; Mohammad	
Extras (w 1, nb 1)	2	Ashraful 2-0-11-0; Shakib Al Hasan 0.2-0-1-0	
(18.5 overs)	10-58		
1/0 2/16 3/25 4/36 5/41 6/51 7/56 8/56 9/58 10/58			
Bowling: Roach 6-0-19-3; Benn 5.5-2-18-4; Sammy 7-0-21-3			

Umpires: S.J. Davis, H.D.P.K. Dharmasena.

Toss: Bangladesh   Points: West Indies 2, Bangladesh 0.

SATURDAY 5 MARCH 2011
GROUP A: SRI LANKA vs AUSTRALIA
R.PREMADASA STADIUM, COLOMBO, SRI LANKA: NO RESULT

Sri Lanka brought Australia's great World Cup winning run to an end, but it was their weather, not the cricketers that did the trick.

The rematch between the two sides that played off in the 1996 and 2007 Finals was just getting going when a solid bout of several hours of tropical rain ended any hope of a continuation of play.

Australia made a good start. Kumar Sangakkara had restored parity by the time the match was washed out, though. No cricket match, however short, is a total waste of time if it contains an innings of 73 by the stylish Sri Lankan captain including seven fours.

There was a rebuild phase after Brett Lee and Shaun Tait removed an opener apiece. Then he expanded with those stunning cover drives. Mahela Jayawardene was lost when Steve Smith removed a bail with his throw from cover and Jayawardene having called for a single was short of his ground.

Smith had also taken an impressive leaping catch at point to remove Upal Tharanga.

Sangakkara and Tilan Samaraweera had put on 71 in seventeen overs when the rain came.

On a new wicket square that Ricky Ponting assessed as rolled mud, Sangakkara believed Australia would have had difficulty reaching 250 against his spinners.

We will never know.

SRI LANKA		AUSTRALIA	
W. U. Tharanga c Smith b Lee	6	S. R. Watson, B. J. Haddin (wk), R. T. Ponting (capt) ,	
T. M. Dilshan c White b Tait	4	M. J. Clarke, D. J. Hussey, C. L. White, S. P.D. Smith,	
K. C. Sangakkara (capt/wk) not out	73	M. G. Johnson, J. J. Krejza, B. Lee, S. W. Tait	
D. P. M. D. Jayawardene run out	23		
T. T. Samaraweera not out	34		
Extras Lb1 W5	6		
(32.5 overs)	3/146		

Did not bat: L. P. C. Silva, A. D. Mathews, H. M. R. K.B. Herath, S. L. Malinga, M. Muralitharan, B. A. W. Mendis

1/6 2/31 3/75

Bowling: Lee 5-0-27-1; Tait 5-0-23-1; Watson 7-0-29-0; Johnson 4-0-15-0; Krejza 7.5-0-34-0; Smith 4-0-17-0

Umpires: I.J. Gould A.L. Hill

Toss: Sri Lanka   Points: Sri Lanka 1 Australia 1

SUNDAY 6 MARCH 2011
GROUP B: ENGLAND vs SOUTH AFRICA
MA CHIDAMBARAM STADIUM, CHENNAI, INDIA: ENGLAND WON BY 6 RUNS

The scene of the 1986 Tied Test hosted another exciting finish in this intriguing Group B match. The game was a low scoring affair, a stark contrast to the rapid scoring of runs in most of the tournament matches to date. Despite projecting a confident and combative veneer, the Proteas again wilted in a tight finish.

South Africa opened up with the contrasting styles of Peterson and Steyn. The move paid off handsomely. Strauss was caught at mid wicket from the third ball of the match for a duck. On the last ball of the over, Peterson removed Pietersen, who edged to slip. The pressure was intensified in the fifth over when Bell chipped a well-flighted ball from Peterson straight back to the bowler, leaving England in peril at 3-15. The in-form Trott was joined by Bopara to perform a gradual repair to the innings. Trott was reprieved on 20 by a successful DRS review of an lbw verdict in Imran Tahir's favour. Trott, who missed a sweep shot, was given not out after Hawk Eye showed that the ball was turning enough to miss off stump. Trott did the hard yards to reach 50, but he soon hit a return catch to Imran Tahir, who did well moving low to his right. After the 99-run partnership, the innings was delicately placed at 4-115 in the 30th over.

Aside from a determined 60 from Bopara, the remaining English batsmen offered little, struggling against the leg-breaks of Imran Tahir. In a tournament where scores well above 250 were *de rigueur*, England's score of 171 seemed manifestly inadequate. After Peterson did the early damage, Imran Tahir collected his second four wicket haul in three matches.

On a pitch that offered the spinners plenty of assistance, England followed South Africa's lead and opened the bowling with Yardy. South Africa progressed at a good rate in the early overs. Amla's intelligent and fluent strokeplay compensated for Smith's laboured progress, especially against Swann. In the 15th over, the openers had accounted for more than a third of the target. Swann struck, removing Smith with a superb delivery that spat off the pitch and flicked a glove on the way to Prior. The umpires had to refer to the third umpire to determine whether the ball touched Smith's glove. With the game at risk of drifting out of England's grasp, Strauss threw the ball to Broad. The Nottinghamshire all-rounder took wickets in successive overs. Amla played on for 42 and Kallis' lean run continued when he chased a wide one. In a refreshing move, Kallis accepted Prior's word that the ball had carried to his gloves.

At 3-82, South Africa still had some work to do. A composed stand between AB de Villiers and Faf du Plessis took the Proteas to 3-124, 48 runs from the target with 18 overs left. The scoreboard suggested that the Proteas were home and hosed, although their tendency to seize defeat from the jaws of World Cup victory could not be discounted completely. Anderson, under pressure to hold his place in the side after indifferent performances in the tournament to date, was recalled to the attack. Anderson conjured some reverse swing, causing a ball that pitched outside de Villiers' off stump to break back and nudge the bails.

The game changed radically in the next five overs. South Africa, in a position of comfort at 3-124, were soon 7-127. Two balls after the dismissal of de Villiers, du Plessis was run out by a sharp piece of work by Bell at short leg. In the next over, Duminy successfully challenged the umpire's decision that he edged a leg side ball from Anderson. The decision under DRS of not out raised some eyebrows, as Snicko was inconclusive and it was dubious whether there was sufficient evidence for the third umpire to overrule the original verdict. It became a moot point two balls later, as a magnificent, reverse swinging delivery by Anderson levelled Duminy's off stump. With the compulsory change of ball occurring after 34 overs, Strauss spelled Anderson and used his spinners. From a shaky 6-124, van Wyk and Peterson were bogged down and eked out just three runs from three overs. Consternation became panic as Peterson nicked a drive outside off stump from Yardy.

Strauss elected to keep one over from his trump card Swann in reserve, choosing to operate Yardy and Pietersen. Steyn restored some momentum, hitting three fine boundaries off Yardy and Pietersen. This late-order rally pushed South Africa to 20 runs from the target with seven overs left. In the 44th over, it seemed as if England had missed their chance when Anderson spilled a firmly hit drive from Steyn. In desperation, Strauss brought back Swann for his final over. Van Wyk and Steyn successfully negotiated the six balls, increasing the pressure on Anderson to prise out the remaining wickets. South Africa's batting powerplay was activated with five overs remaining, bringing the field up and presenting the opportunity for the batsmen to loft over the top. Anderson was kept at bay in the next over, leading to Bresnan bowling the 47th over. South Africa only needed 13 runs to win.

Van Wyk erred in his shot selection, playing on to Bresnan from a shortish ball that was too close to the body to cut. Steyn and new batsman Morne Morkel added four invaluable runs from the remainder of the over, keeping the hopes of victory alive. Only eight runs were required from 18 balls. Broad was back in the attack and his first delivery, a full delivery that seamed in a fraction, rapped Steyn on the pads directly in front. An attempted slog by number 11 Imran Tahir trickled to mid wicket for a single and brought Morkel back on strike. With seven runs needed to win, the giant South African attempted a big drive, only to get a thin edge that was comfortably held by Prior. South Africa had again failed in a close finish. Broad had the figures with 4-15. Each of Broad's four wickets were taken at crucial times and he played an important part in England's six-run win.

England's victory was a very good response to the loss to Ireland and it kept their quarter-final hopes alive. This tension-filled game was a salient reminder that limited-overs excitement does not have to involve large scores. The decision of the Man of the Match adjudicators to favour Bopara over Broad was a questionable one. Sadly, DRS was not available to review this verdict.

ENGLAND		SOUTH AFRICA	
A. J. Strauss (capt) c de Villiers b Peterson	0	H. M. Amla b Broad	42
K. P. Pietersen c Kaills b Peterson	2	G. C. Smith (capt) c Prior b Swann	22
I. J. L. Trott c & b Imran Tahir	52	J. H. Kallis c Prior b Broad	15
I. R. Bell c & b Peterson	5	A. B. de Villiers b Anderson	25
R. S. Bopara lbw b Morkel	60	F. du Plessis run out	17
M. J. Prior (wk) c van Wyk b Morkel	10	J. P. Duminy b Anderson	0
M. H. Yardy c Peterson b Imran Tahir	3	M. N. van Wyk (wk) b Bresnan	13
T. T. Bresnan lbw b Steyn	1	R. J. Peterson c Prior b Yardy	3
G. P. Swann c Duminy b Imran Tahir	16	D. W. Steyn lbw b Broad	20
S. C.J. Broad lbw b Imran Tahir	0	M. Morkel c Prior b Broad	1
J. M. Anderson not out	2	Imran Tahir not out	1
Extras (b 1, lb 7, w 12)	20	Extras (lb 2, w 4)	6
(45.4 overs)	10-171	(47.4 overs)	10-165

1/1 2/3 3/15 4/114 5/134 6/148 7/149 8/161 9/161 10/171

1/63 2/75 3/82 4/124 5/124 6/124 7/127 8/160 9/164 10/165

Bowling: Peterson 8-2-22-3; Steyn 9-0-37-1; Morkel 7-0-16-2; Kallis 4-1-14-0; Imran Tahir 8.4-1-38-4; du Plessis 5-0-16-0; Duminy 4-0-20-0

Bowling: Yardy 9-1-46-1; Anderson 6-0-16-2; Bresnan 8-1-27-1; Swann 10-2-29-1; Broad 6.4-0-15-4; Pietersen 8-0-30-0

Umpires: A.M. Saheba, S.J.A. Taufel.

Toss: England   Points: England 2, South Africa 0.

GROUP B: INDIA vs IRELAND
M CHINNASWAMY STADIUM, BANGALORE, INDIA (DAY/NIGHT)
INDIA WON BY FIVE WICKETS

In India's Garden City, it was fitting that the green of Ireland rose to the occasion and pushed the hosts hard for a win. Despite their Associate colleagues suffering heavy defeats on a regular basis, Ireland put a strong foot forward for the minnow teams.

MS Dhoni's decision to bowl first seemed vindicated when Zaheer Khan took a wicket in each of his first two overs, reducing the Irishmen to 2-9. Porterfield and the elder O'Brien batted with great determination, playing each ball on its merits and hitting the occasional boundary. They found the bowling of Chawla more to their liking. Fifteen runs were scored from Chawla's first over, including an imperious swept six by O'Brien from a free hit delivery that resulted from a no ball. Chawla's leg-breaks were shelved when the fourth over of his spell included three wides and a no ball. At the halfway mark, the century stand had been passed and the Irish score was a useful 2-118.

In light of the pedestrian Indian bowling to that point of the innings, it was apt that it took a run out to separate Porterfield and O'Brien. After Porterfield worked the ball to the covers, O'Brien was caught short by a fast reaction from Kohli and the swift removal of the bails by Dhoni. The partnership realised a vital 113 runs from 127 balls.

As is often the case, a stubborn stand was followed by a steady flow of wickets. In his finest hour as an international bowler, Yuvraj Singh took the next five wickets with his slow left-arm spin. Andrew White edged one and Kevin O'Brien was unable to repeat his heroics against England, perishing on this occasion by tamely patting the ball back to Yuvraj Singh. In the first ball of the 38th over, immediately after the drinks break, a lapse of concentration by Porterfield cost him a shot at a century. On 75, Porterfield rocked back to dispatch a short long-hop from Yuvraj Singh, but the ball was hit straight to cover. Mooney was unable to make an impression and the dismissal of Alex Cusack, Yuvraj Singh's final wicket, caused some interest. Prior to the match, the 2.5 metre rule under DRS required, if there was at least 2.5 metres between the stumps and the point of impact, that the Hawk Eye technology show that the ball would have hit the middle stump dead centre in order for a not out verdict to be overturned. This was refined to allow, where the 2.5 metre prerequisite applied, the umpire to reverse a not out verdict if the replay showed that the ball would have hit any part of the middle stump.

Adrian Tucker changed his original not out decision when TV umpire Marais Erasmus advised that the ball would have struck off and middle.

From 8-184, Trent Johnston helped the tail to squeeze out another 23 runs, setting a moderate target of 208. At first blush, this seemed to be a Sunday evening stroll for India's vaunted top six. Accurate bowling and committed fielding by Ireland meant that events did not transpire in this way. Yuvraj Singh was the only batsman to pass 40 and the target was not achieved until 46 overs had been bowled.

Former skipper Johnston made early inroads and India were soon 2-24. Sehwag's leading edge was comfortably taken in the second over and Gambhir clumsily executed a leg glance directly to short fine-leg. Tendulkar and Kohli made starts without going on. Tendulkar missed a ball that was well pitched up by Dockrell and Kohli paid the price for indecisive running between the wickets. India were under pressure at 4-100 in the 24th over, an inferior scoreline to Ireland's 2-108 at the corresponding stage. However, as is frequently the case with up-and-coming international sides, Ireland's bowling lacked the firepower and stamina to go on with it. Yuvraj Singh and Dhoni batted patiently, content to play out dot balls from the better deliveries and to wait for anything loose. Dockrell won a lbw decision against Dhoni after the Indian captain unsuccessfully sought a review of Tucker's out verdict. India were 5-167 in the 40th over, needing 41 runs to win.

Yusuf Pathan's hard hitting soon eased the mild tension in the Indian camp. Pathan spoiled the figures of Dockrell, hammering the young left-arm orthodox prodigy for 16 runs in his final over, including two huge sixes. Pathan repeated the dose against Stirling, hitting him out of the ground to bring the number of runs required into single figures. In the 46th over, a Mooney full toss and leg stump bouncer were crunched to the fence. Pathan's final boundary delivered victory to the Indians by the unconvincing margin of five wickets. The cameo performance of Pathan netted an unbeaten 30 from 24 balls.

Yuvraj Singh reached his 50 in the final over of the run chase. He became the first man to score a fifty and take five wickets in the same World Cup match.

His all-round performance won him the man of the match award.

IRELAND		INDIA	
W. T.S. Porterfield (capt) c Harbhajan Singh b Yuvraj Singh	75	V. Sehwag c & b Johnston	5
P. R. Stirling b Khan	0	S. R. Tendulkar lbw b Dockrell	38
E. C. Joyce c Dhoni b Khan	4	G. Gambhir c Cusack b Johnston	10
N. J. O'Brien (wk) run out	46	V. Kohli run out	34
A. R. White c Dhoni b Yuvraj Singh	5	Yuvraj Singh not out	50
K. J. O'Brien c & b Yuvraj Singh	9	M. S. Dhoni (capt/wk) lbw b Dockrell	34
A. R. Cusack lbw b Yuvraj Singh	24	Y. K. Pathan not out	30
J. F. Mooney lbw b Yuvraj Singh	5	Extras (lb 4, w 5)	9
D. T. Johnston lbw b Patel	17	(46 overs)	5-210
G. H. Dockrell c Dhoni b Khan	3	Did not bat: Harbhajan Singh, P. P. Chawla, Z. Khan, M. M.	
W. B. Rankin not out	1	Patel	
Extras (lb 4, w 8, nb 6)	18	1/9 2/24 3/87 4/100 5/167	
(47.5 overs)	10-207	Bowling: Rankin 10-1-34-0; Johnston 5-1-16-2;	
1/1 2/9 3/122 4/129 5/147 6/160 7/178 8/184 9/201		Dockrell 10-0-49-2; Mooney 2-0-18-0; Stirling 10-0-45-0;	
10/207		White 5-0-23-0; K. O'Brien 1-0-3-0; Cusack 3-0-18-0	
Bowling: Khan 9-1-30-3; Patel 4.5-0-25-1; Pathan 7-1-32-0;			
Harbhajan Singh 9-1-29-0; Chawla 8-0-56-0; Yuvraj			
Singh 10-0-31-5			

Umpires: B.F. Bowden, R.J. Tucker.

Toss: India   Points: India 2, Ireland 0.

MONDAY 7 MARCH 2011
GROUP A: CANADA v KENYA
FEROZ SHAH KOTLA, DELHI, INDIA: CANADA WON BY FIVE WICKETS

Ashish Bagai, back in the city of his birth, led Canada to their first win of the 2011 World Cup in the clash of the battlers in Delhi. In what could easily be assessed as a 'division three' clash Bagai himself compiled an important responsible innings that guided the Canadians to a five-wicket victory with 27 balls to spare.

There were not many extra locals in the ground to see their proud expat play when Ugandan expat Henry Osinde opened the bowling to Morris Ouma and had him caught at second slip from the second ball of the match as he tried to pull his bat away.

Man of the Match, Osinde delivered an excellent opening spell and when he had David Obuya caught behind at the end of the seventh over Kenya were in trouble at 3/21.

It was hardly any better in the fifteenth either when they were 5/57. That forced Tanmay Mishra, Jimmy Kamande and Thomas Odoyo to spend part of their time at the crease consolidating rather than accelerating. Mishra and Kamande's 52 run stand took 84 balls and contained mostly singles on the slow, low turning wicket, while Mishra and Odoyo needed 13 overs to add a further 57 runs.

Odoyo hit five fours, reached 51, as did Mishra, then was yorked by Harvir Baidwan from the final ball of the innings.

Canada needed 199 for their second ever win in any World Cup tournament and after eleven overs they were struggling at 3/48. Ruvindu Gunasekera was third man out, stumped from a leg-side wide when he thought the ball had gone away for runs. It was the third Ngoche brother, James', first ever delivery in World Cup cricket.

Two balls later, though, Jimmy Hansra was dropped from a straight forward catch at mid-on by Seren Waters and Kenya's chance for a win was gone.

Hansra and Bagai consequently added a match-winning 132 in 32 overs, taking Canada to within 19 runs of victory. Hansra was the more aggressive of the pair hitting seven fours and two dancing straight driven sixes in 99 balls.

Bagai saw his team through hitting two fours in the 46th over to clinch the result.

KENYA		CANADA	
M. A. Ouma (wk) c Baidwan b Osinde	0	R. Gunasekera st Ouma b Ngoche	18
S. R. Waters b Osinde	2	Rizwan Cheema b Otieno	17
C. O. Obuya b Baidwan	31	Z. E. Surkari run out	10
D. O. Obuya c Bagai b Osinde	2	A. Bagai (capt/wk) not out	64
S. O. Tikolo lbw b Rizwan Cheema	12	A. S. Hansra c Ngoche b Oghiambo	70
T. Mishra c Surkari b Davison	51	T. G. Gordon b Odhiambo	3
J. Kamande (capt) c Bagai b Balaji Rao	22	J. M. Davison not out	4
T. M. Odoyo b Baidwan	51	Extras B1 W11 Nb1	13
N. N. Odhiambo b Osinde	4	(45.3 overs)	5/199
E. Otieno c Hansra b Rizwan Cheema	8	Did not bat: H. S. Baidwan, P. A. Desai, H. Osinde, W. D.	
J. O. Ngoche not out	1	Balaji Rao	
Extras Lb4 W10	14	1/19 2/37 3/48 4/180 5/186	
(50 overs)	198	Bowling: Odoyo 5-1-18-0; Otieno 8.3-0-45-1;	
1/0 2/7 3/21 4/41 5/57 6/109 7/166 8/171 9/193 10/198		Odhiambo 10-0-45-2; Ngoche 10-2-26-1;	
Bowling: Osinde 10-2-26-4; Baidwan 10-1-41-2;		Kamande 5-0-25-0; C. Obuya 2-0-15-0; Tikolo 5-1-24-0	
Desai 3-0-20-0; Rizwan Cheema 9-1-30-2; Hansra 3-0-15-0;			
Balaji Rao 10-0-36-1; Davison 5-0-26-1			

Umpires: Asad Rauf B.R. Doctrove

Toss: Kenya   Points: Canada 2 Kenya 0

TUESDAY 8 MARCH 2011
GROUP A: NEW ZEALAND v PAKISTAN
PALLEKELLE INTERNATIONAL CRICKET STADIUM, SRI LANKA
NEW ZEALAND WON BY 110 RUNS

Pakistan who had some flaws exposed by Canada had their bubble properly burst by New Zealand who, led by an inspiring century by Ross Taylor, romped home by 110 runs.

The margin in the first ever one-day international played at Pallekelle, actually flattered Pakistan. At one point they were 6/66 in pursuit of 302, but their tail rallied somewhat allowing the scoreboard to build a degree of respectability.

In many ways New Zealand's first World Cup win over Pakistan since 1983 was Taylor's day. He won the Man of the Match Award on his 27th birthday, was gifted chances by wicketkeeper Kamran Akmal first ball and fourth ball of his innings and went on to strike 55 runs from his last 13 balls as New Zealand added a stunning 92 in their final four overs. Taylor's 131 not out from 124 balls was his highest ever score.

The game began in sensational fashion when after Shoaib Akhtar bowled a no ball Brendon McCullum plastered the free hit over wide mid-on for six. He was bowled next ball as Akhtar took revenge with a ripping break-back delivery. Jamie How calmed down the noisy colourful crowd of 30,000 by taking 27 balls to make four before playing around a full straight delivery from Umar Gul.

Martin Guptill looked the best of the early Black Cap batsmen. He reached 50 in 71 balls before he played across the line to Afridi and yorked himself. Pakistan continued to make mistakes in the field and bowl wides and no balls.

But at the end of the 46th over New Zealand were 6/210 and the game seemed evenly poised. Then Taylor hit Akhtar for 28 runs in the 47th over going from 76 to 102 with two fours and three sixes, the third a brutal pull over mid wicket to raise his hundred. It would be Akhtar's final over in international cricket as he soon announced his retirement.

At the other end Abdur Rehman went for 15 and 19 runs from his last two overs as Jacob Oram also cashed in, but Abdul Razzaq even topped Akhtar's effort conceding 30 runs in over No.49. In that wonderful final onslaught as every attempted yorker became a juicy full toss, Taylor hit six sixes. From nowhere New Zealand had topped 300.

Pakistan needed 303 to guarantee their quarter-finals place. After the first ball of the eighth over they were 4/23. Tim

Southee and Kyle Mills got the ball to move nicely. Kamran Akmal was fourth out, nicely caught low down at first slip by none other than Taylor off a Southee outswinger.

New Zealand did have one setback when in the sixth over Daniel Vettori dived to catch Kamran Akmal at mid-on, missed the chance and hurt his right knee. It had little impact on this match, though. Scott Styris filled in a few of the missing overs and picked up a couple of late wickets.

In a close match Abdul Razzaq's 74 ball innings of 62 and Umar Gul's big hitting 34 might have made a difference. Here they just kept the crowd entertained until the inevitable New Zealand win.

NEW ZEALAND		PAKISTAN	
M. J. Guptill b Shahid Afridi	57	Mohammad Hafeez lbw b Southee	5
B. B. McCullum (wk) b Shoaib Akhtar	6	Ahmed Shehzad lbw b Mills	10
J. M. How lbw b Umar Gul	4	Kamran Akmal (wk) c Taylor b Southee	8
L. R. P. L. Taylor not out	131	Younis Khan b Mills	0
J. E. C. Franklin lbw b Mohammad Hafeez	1	Misbah-ul-Haq c Styris b Southee	7
S. B. Styris lbw b Umar Gul	28	Umar Akmal c Oram b N. McCullum	38
N. L. McCullum b Umar Gul	19	Shahid Afridi (capt) b Oram	17
J. D. P. Oram c Umar Gul b Abdur Rehman	25	Abdul Razzaq c Oram b Styris	62
K. D. Mills not out	7	Abdur Rehman lbw b N. McCullum	1
Extras Lb10 W11 Nb3	24	Umar Gul not out	34
(50 overs)	7/302	Shoaib Akhtar c N. McCullum b Styris	0
Did not bat: D. L. Vettori (capt), T. G. Southee		Extras Lb6 W4	10
1/8 2/55 3/112 4/113 5/175 6/210 7/295		(41.4 overs)	192
Bowling: Shoaib Akhtar 9-0-70-1; Abdur Rehman 10-0-60-1;		1/5 2/23 3/23 4/23 5/45 6/66 7/102 8/125 9/191 10/192	
Umar Gul 10-1-32-3; Abdul Razzaq 4-0-49-0; Shahid		Bowling: Mills 8-1-43-2; Southee 8-1-25-3; Oram 10-1-47-1;	
Afridi 10-0-55-1; Mohammad Hafeez 7-0-26-1		Franklin 5-0-26-0; N. McCullum 6-0-28-2; Styris 4.4-0-17-2	

Umpires: D.J. Harper N.J. Llong

Toss: New Zealand   Points: New Zealand 2 Pakistan 0

WEDNESDAY 9 MARCH 2011
GROUP B: INDIA vs NETHERLANDS
FEROZ SHAH KOTLA STADIUM, DELHI, INDIA (DAY/NIGHT): INDIA WON BY FIVE WICKETS

In their second game in a row against an Associate side, a comfortable winning margin failed to disguise a humdrum performance by India. Borren won his fourth toss from as many starts, opting to bat first in front of a vociferous crowd of about 43,000.

Seemingly operating in second gear, India's struggle to take a wicket in the early overs was similar to the challenges faced by some commentators in pronouncing and finding a vowel in the surname of Eric Szwarczynski, playing his first World Cup match. Szwarczynski and Barresi worked their way to an opening stand of 56, which equalled the highest partnership of the Netherlands in World Cup cricket to date. Szwarczynski fell in the 16th over when he was beaten by Chawla's googly.

Despite this start, the Dutch batsmen applied a subdued approach to their batting until the closing overs. After starts from Szwarczynski, Barresi and Cooper, there was little forthcoming from the middle-order. From a useful platform of 2-99 in the 29th over, the Dutch innings spluttered as four wickets fell for nine runs across six overs. Zuiderent failed again, bringing his sequence of scores in the tournament to 1, 1, 15 and 0. The Dutch laboured to 7-134 from 40 overs and a late flurry of runs pushed the tally towards 200. Seventeen runs were thumped from Chawla's last over, including two consecutive powerful blows from Borren that sailed into the crowd. Mudassar Bukhari followed suit, teeing off for six from both Nehra and Harbhajan Singh. From the beginning of the batting powerplay after 42 overs to the end of the innings, the Netherlands plundered 42 runs from 4.4 overs. Zaheer Khan put a stop to the leakage of runs, removing Borren and Mudassar Bukhari in the space of four deliveries.

The Netherlands' score of 189 was unlikely to be enough to force an upset. Their batsmen had become bogged down and they failed to rotate the strike with enough regularity. The statistical boffins pointed out that the Netherlands played out an amazing 181 dot balls from the 277 deliveries faced. The Dutch were not alone with their concerns. Harbhajan Singh, whose bowling in this tournament had been pedestrian to date, was flat again and he failed to take a wicket for the second match running.

India continued where the Dutch left off, blasting 69 runs before Sehwag was the first to go in the eighth over. The momentum was continued by Tendulkar and Yusuf Pathan, who was promoted to bat at number three for quick runs. Both batsmen scored at better than a run a ball, but fell in the same over to left-arm orthodox bowler Pieter Seelaar. After Kohli was bowled through the gate by Borren, India were feeling the pinch at 4-99 in the 15th over. Gambhir and Yuvraj Singh reigned in the adventurous shots for about half an hour. When Mudassar Bukhari bowled Gambhir in the 24th over, India were 5-139 and the Dutch players had a glimmer of hope.

Experienced one-day campaigners Yuvraj Singh and Dhoni took their time and the remaining 51 runs were accumulated in 13.2 overs. Yuvraj Singh reached his third half-century from his last three World Cup matches. Including his two victims with the ball, Yuvraj Singh had a good day and he picked up back-to-back man of the match awards. Despite India's mediocre performance, they remained unbeaten and at the top of the Group B table.

NETHERLANDS		INDIA	
E. S. Szwarczynski b Chawla	28	V. Sehwag c Kervezee b Seelaar	39
W. Barresi (wk) lbw b Yuvraj Singh	26	S. R. Tendulkar c Kruger b Seelaar	27
T. L.W. Cooper c Dhoni b Nehra	29	Y. K. Pathan c & b Seelaar	11
R. N. ten Doeschate c Khan b Yuvraj Singh	11	G. Gambhir b Mudassar Bukhari	28
A. N. Kervezee c Harbhajan Singh b Chawla	11	V. Kohli b Borren	12
B. Zuiderent lbw b Khan	0	Yuvraj Singh not out	51
T. N. de Grooth run out	5	M. S. Dhoni (capt/wk) not out	19
P. W. Borren (capt) c Nehra b Khan	38	Extras (w 4)	4
B. P. Kruger run out	8	(36.3 overs)	5-191
Mudassar Bukhari b Khan	21	Did not bat: Harbhajan Singh, P. P. Chawla, Z. Khan, A.	
P. M. Seelaar not out	0	Nehra	
Extras (b 6, lb 3, w 2, nb 1)	12	1/69 2/80 3/82 4/99 5/139	
(46.4 overs)	10-189	Bowling: Mudassar Bukhari 6-1-33-1; ten	
1/56 2/64 3/99 4/100 5/101 6/108 7/127 8/151 9/189		Doeschate 7-0-38-0; Seelaar 10-1-53-3; Borren 8-0-33-1;	
10/189		Cooper 2-0-11-0; Kruger 3.3-0-23-0	
Bowling: Khan 6.4-0-20-3; Nehra 5-1-22-1; Pathan 6-1-17-0;			
Harbhajan Singh 10-0-31-0; Chawla 10-0-47-2; Yuvraj			
Singh 9-1-43-2			

Umpires: S.J. Davis, B.N.J. Oxenford.

Toss: Netherlands   Points: India 2, Netherlands 0.

THURSDAY 10 MARCH 2011
GROUP A: SRI LANKA vs ZIMBABWE
PALLEKELLE INTERNATIONAL CRICKET STADIUM, SRI LANKA: SRI LANKA WON BY 139 RUNS

A World Cup-record opening partnership of 282 by Tillakaratne Dilshan and Upal Tharanga set up an easy 139 run win for Sri Lanka over Zimbabwe. The home side's two points guaranteed them a berth in the 2011 quarters.

The 30,000-strong Pallekelle faithful were once more treated to a wonderful batting display, although the match again, as it had on the Tuesday, developed into a one-sided contest.

Elton Chigumbura won the toss and elected to field so his spinners did not have to bowl under lights with a ball made slippery by the evening dew. The ball may have remained dry for them but neither they nor the Zimbabwean seamers could make the slightest impression on Dilshan or Tharanga.

Dilshan was faster out of the blocks than Tharanga. He hit the second over of the day from Tinashe Panyangara for 18 runs. After 11 overs the total was 84. Tharanga scored at just under a run per ball throughout the entire stand while Dilshan was always a bit ahead of that rate. He reached his hundred in 95 balls. Tharanga was only 67 from 88 balls at that stage so in the final phase of the partnership he did the bulk of the fast scoring. He caught up to Dilshan to the extent that by the end of each of their innings both had hit the ball to and over the boundary seventeen times.

The pair did have the occasional break go their way that seemed to peg them back against the spinners slightly and particularly annoyed Ray Price.

They broke the World Cup opening record when they passed 194 in the 33rd over. Tharanga reached his ton from 122 balls in the 41st over, then broke loose. Finally in the 45th over Tharanga miscued Chris Mpofu to Chigumbura at deep cover and Zimbabwe had their first wicket in the tournament for 78 overs.

Then as the later batsmen thrashed they picked up five more victims in the next 20 balls. Mpofu benefitted most from their recklessness taking four wickets.

Zimbabwe still required 328. That looked beyond their capability.

Their innings was kind of a copy of the Sri Lankan innings in reduced form. There was a big opening partnership then a huge tumble of wickets. But it lasted only 39 overs, not 50.

Brendan Taylor out batted Dilshan and Tharanga in terms of charm and style if not substance. He and Regis Chakabva put on 116 in 20 overs, with Taylor dominating on way to 80.

With the required run rate pressing the Zimbabweans lost all their ten wickets in 19 overs. Muttiah Muralitharan broke through initially bowling Chakabva with a perfect doosra. Then Angelo Mathews had Tatenda Taibu brilliantly caught behind by Kumar Sangakkara.

Soon after Taylor's fine innings ended, caught at mid wicket from Mathews slower ball. Up stepped Dilshan to ensure his Man of the match Award with a stunning bowling cameo.

Backing up from his 144 he took four wickets in three overs as the Zimbabwean innings disintegrated.

Muralitharan was given the honour of dismissing the final batsman, Mpofu, another to be bowled by a doosra.

SRI LANKA		ZIMBABWE	
W. U. Tharanga c Chigumbura b Mpofu	133	B. R.M. Taylor c Jayawardene b Mathews	80
T. M. Dilshan c Panyangara b Utseya	144	R. W. Chakabva b Muralitharan	35
N. L. T. C. Perera c Chigumbura b Price	3	T .Taibu (wk) c Sangakkara b Mathews	4
D. P. M. D. Jayawardene c Chakabva b Mpofu	9	P. Utseya st Sangakkara b Dilshan	4
K. C. Sangakkara (capt/wk) not out	11	C. R. Ervine lbw b Dilshan	17
A. D. Mathews c Chigumbura b Mpofu	0	E. Chigumbura (capt) c Perera b Muralitharan	6
L. P. C. Silva c Panyangara b Mpofu	4	G. A. Lamb c Jayawardene b Dilshan	0
T. T. Samaraweera not out	8	A. G. Cremer not out	14
Extras B2 lb3 W9 Nb1	15	R. W. Price c Samaweera b Perera	11
(50 overs)	6/327	T. Panyangara lbw b Dilshan	0
Did not bat: K. M. D. N. Kulasekara, S. L. Malinga, M.		C. B. Mpofu b Muralitharan	1
Muralitharan		Extras B2 Lb2 W12	16
1/282 2/289 3/296 4/300 5/302 6/308		(39 overs)	188
Bowling: Mpofu 7-0-62-4; Panyangara 6-0-51-0;		1/116 2/125 3/132 4/150 5/156 6/156 7/165 8/185	
Price 9-1-46-1; Chigumbura 3-0-20-0; Utseya 10-0-50-1;		9/185 10/188	
Cremer 7-0-42-0; Lamb 8-0-51-0		Bowling: Malinga 8-0-51-0; Kulasekara 8-0-33-0;	
		Perera 6-0-33-1; Muralitharan 9-0-34-3; Mathews 5-0-29-2;	
		Dilshan 3-1-4-4	

Umpires: M. Erasmus N.J. Llong

Toss: Zimbabwe   Points: Sri Lanka 2 Zimbabwe 0

FRIDAY 11 MARCH 2011
GROUP B: IRELAND vs WEST INDIES
CHANDIGARH, INDIA: WEST INDIES WON BY 44 RUNS

In this game between two unremarkable teams, Ireland failed to topple another Test nation. The Irish, who faltered at crucial stages of the contest, would be well advised to learn the lessons from this game in developing a successful national team culture.

Boyd Rankin and Alex Cusack kept the West Indian openers in check with accurate opening spells. On 10, Devon Smith played an airy drive off Cusack to extra cover. Paul Stirling spilled a difficult chance. Sadly for Ireland, this miss would be at a cost of 97 runs. Smith and Chanderpaul batted in an unconvincing fashion and only 87 runs were on the board as the 25th over began. This over produced a double strike for Kevin O'Brien. Chanderpaul drove to extra cover, with the catch being taken on this occasion, and Darren Bravo fell for a third ball duck when he failed to connect with a big swing of the bat.

The West Indies were unable to force the pace and the score was a modest 3-142 after 35 overs. Sammy activated the batting powerplay, which was the catalyst for some power batting. The 37th over of the innings was an odd affair, featuring two sixes by Pollard and four dot balls. The West Indies received another reprieve in the following over, with Pollard being dropped at long on with his score on 19. In a resolute effort, Smith overcame periods of streakiness in his innings, persevering and improving his form en route to his first hundred in limited-overs internationals. With the frequency of boundaries increasing, the powerplay was successful for the West Indies, yielding 55 runs without loss.

Pollard brought up his 50 from 35 balls and a big score was in range. In the next over, Kevin O'Brien took his second brace of wickets, hitting when Smith missed and inducing a top edge from Sammy. Smith and Pollard combined for a crucial partnership of 78 runs from 10.3 overs and Smith finished with 107 from 133 balls. Pollard mauled the bowling in the closing stages, smashing 20 runs from O'Brien's last over. Pollard finished the over with two sixes, the second of which was a remarkable one-handed swipe over deep mid wicket. With a century seemingly at his mercy, Pollard holed out off Mooney in the next over for an explosive 94 from 55 balls, featuring five sixes. The last two overs were eventful, the West Indies losing four wickets for eight runs. When Pollard mishit to point from the final ball of the innings, the Caribbean cricketers had been bowled out for a strong total of 275. The scorecard had an odd look: only three West Indian batsmen passed 10 and Kevin O'Brien had the unusual analysis of 4-71 from nine overs. After good batting from Smith and Pollard, the West Indies had lost seven for 57.

The Irish innings had a few things in common with the West Indian batting performance. There was a steady start, followed by a surge of runs, culminating in a rush of wickets and with only two batsmen making scores of substance. At one stage, Sammy bowled three consecutive maidens of medium pace. Ed Joyce and Gary Wilson batted fluently and gradually increased the run rate. Wilson dealt out some punishment to Nikita Miller, hitting a huge six from a slog sweep and, in Miller's next over, scoring two consecutive boundaries using the reverse sweep. Joyce and Wilson took the score to 3-177 in the 38th over. From this position, the required run rate was about 7.5 an over and Ireland had a reasonable prospect of victory with wickets in hand.

Joyce fell to a superb yorker from debutante Andre Russell, scoring a fine 84 from 106 balls. The Joyce-Wilson stand was productive, netting 91 runs from 99 deliveries. Kevin O'Brien fell soon after and, in the 42nd over, Ireland's prospects dimmed when Wilson was adjudged lbw to Sammy for 61 in an incident of minor controversy. The delivery pitched outside off stump and came in, striking Wilson's front pad. On the scoreboard replay, it was debatable whether Wilson was attempting to dab the ball as his bat was behind his front pad on impact. Umpire Asoka de Silva's lbw verdict was reviewed by a perplexed Wilson. Hawk Eye showed that the ball had pitched outside off stump and it would have struck the outside of the off stump. Wilson protested that he was attempting to play a shot, so de Silva referred the decision upstairs again to check. De Silva confirmed his view that Wilson had not offered a shot, so the original decision stood. An irate Wilson marched to the pavilion with a consoling arm from Sammy around his shoulder.

The remaining Irish batsmen contributed little and the innings petered out 44 runs in arrears. Similar to the West Indian innings, the last seven wickets tumbled for 54 runs. Benn collected his second consecutive four wicket return and Sammy impressed with his economy. In the post-match press conference, Irish captain Porterfield criticised de Silva's decision and received an official reprimand. The ICC elected to assign de Silva to only one more match in the tournament, a low profile Group A fixture between Kenya and Zimbabwe. Observers could draw their own inference about the ICC's view on how de Silva dealt with the Wilson incident.

Pollard won the man of the match award for his exhibition of big hitting.

WEST INDIES		IRELAND	
D. S. Smith b K. O'Brien	107	W. T.S. Porterfield (capt) c sub (Rampaul) b Sammy	11
S. Chanderpaul c Porterfield b K. O'Brien	35	P. R. Stirling c Sammy b Benn	5
D. M. Bravo b K. O'Brien	0	E. C. Joyce b Russell	84
R. R. Sarwan c Mooney b Dockrell	10	N. J. O'Brien b Benn	25
K. A. Pollard c Rankin b Mooney	94	G. C. Wilson lbw b Sammy	61
D. J. G. Sammy (capt) c Dockrell b K. O'Brien	4	K. J. O'Brien c Pollard b Sammy	5
D. C. Thomas (wk) c N. O'Brien b Rankin	2	A. R. Cusack st Thomas b Benn	2
A. D. Russell b Mooney	3	J. F. Mooney b Roach	6
N. O. Miller not out	5	A. C. Botha run out	0
S. J. Benn run out	2	G. H. Dockrell b Benn	19
K. A. J. Roach c Stirling b Botha	1	W. B. Rankin not out	5
Extras (b 3, lb 6, w 3)	12	Extras (lb 4, w 3, nb 1)	8
(50 overs)	10-275	(49 overs)	10-231

1/89 2/89 3/130 4/218 5/222 6/228 7/267 8/267 9/272
10/275

Bowling: Rankin 10-1-35-1; Cusack 7-1-22-0;
Mooney 9-0-58-2; Botha 10-0-56-1; K. O'Brien 9-0-71-4;
Stirling 2-0-9-0; Dockrell 3-0-15-1

1/6 2/42 3/86 4/177 5/187 6/199 8/201 9/215 10/231
Bowling: Roach 8-0-34-1; Benn 10-0-53-4;
Sammy 10-3-31-3; Russell 10-2-37-1; Pollard 5-0-32-0;
Miller 6-0-40-0

Umpires: E.A.R. de Silva, S.K. Tarapore.

Toss: Ireland   Points: West Indies 2, Ireland 0.

GROUP B: BANGLADESH vs ENGLAND
ZOHUR AHMED CHOWDURY STADIUM, CHITTAGONG, BANGLADESH (DAY/NIGHT):
BANGLADESH WON BY TWO WICKETS

Group B continued to produce an interesting mix of results with this surprise packet in Chittagong. England continued their Jekyll-and-Hyde run, acquitting themselves well against the heavyweights but struggling against the lesser lights.

England had personnel worries in the lead-in. The World Cup campaigns of Kevin Pietersen and Stuart Broad were over with hernia and side strain ailments, respectively. With Broad's absent, England again overlooked spinner James Tredwell. This decision meant that Strauss would need to look to part-timers Collingwood and Bopara to combine for the fifth-bowler role.

Pietersen's absence allowed the talented Eoin Morgan to return to the side. Prior replaced Pietersen as Strauss' opening partner. Seven overs in, Prior's innings was over in odd circumstances. Prior missed a leg side wide from Abdur Razzaq and dragged his back foot out of the batting crease. Prior returned his foot to safety shortly before Mushfiqur Rahim removed the bails. Inexplicably, Prior drifted from his crease again and Mushfiqur Rahim pulled the stumps out of the ground to effect the stumping. After a tame dismissal from Bell, England were under strain at 3-53 in the 17th over.

Morgan upped the tempo with a fluent half-century and Trott made it four fifties from five starts in the tournament. Their partnership was worth 109 runs from 22 overs and they took England to 4-162 with more than 11 overs and the batting powerplay in hand.

The remainder of the batting failed to cash in from this position, as England were bowled out in the last over for the addition of 63 runs. Bangladesh's spin quarter took seven wickets between them.

Tamim Iqbal launched the reply in a hectic fashion. He had scored 38 of the first 52 runs of the innings before he missed a full ball from Bresnan. Bangladesh faltered, progressing to 3-73 in the 14th over after Anderson ran out Junaid Siddique with a direct hit from the non-striker's end and Shahzad bowled Raqibul Hasan with a peach of a delivery. Imrul Kayes and Shakib Al Hasan brought Bangladesh into serious contention with a stand of 82 runs from 104 balls. English discontent, especially from excitable spinner Swann, rose as the ball became more difficult to grip with the evening dew.

From 3-154, the home side needed 71 runs from 19 overs to win. This manageable task became much more difficult as five wickets fell within nine overs. Top-scorer Imrul Kayes was run out by Shahzad's rocket arm from deep square leg when attempting a second run. Shahzad struck twice more, having Mushfiqur Rahim caught behind and Naeem Islam bowled with superb deliveries.

The home side were eight down and the game was nearly gone, as 57 runs were required from 62 balls. Mahmudullah and Shafiul Islam attacked the tiring English bowlers to keep Bangladeshi hopes alive. Sixteen runs were flayed from Swann's last over, the 42nd, to keep the equation for Bangladesh to more manageable proportions. Anderson, expensive again in this match, bowled two wides in an over and Shafiul Islam blazed two boundaries from one Bresnan over. Mahmudullah smote a Bresnan full toss through the covers for four to deliver a remarkable victory with an over to spare. Number 10 batsman Shafiul Islam played his role with aplomb, scoring an unbeaten 24 from as many balls. The English bowlers struggled with their radar, bowling 23 wides.

Imrul Kayes won the man of the match award. It was now make or break for England, as a victory from their last group match against the West Indies was needed to progress to the quarter-finals.

ENGLAND		BANGLADESH	
A. J. Strauss (capt) c Junaid Siddique b Naeem Islam	18	Tamim Iqbal b Bresnan	38
M. J. Prior (wk) st Mushfiqur Rahim b Abdur Razzak	15	Imrul Kayes run out	60
I. J. L. Trott c Junaid Siddique b Shakib Al Hasan	67	Junaid Siddique run out	12
I. R. Bell c Naeem Islam b Mahmudullah	5	Raqibul Hassan b Shahzad	0
E. J. G. Morgan c Imrul Kayes b Naeem Islam	63	Shakib Al Hasan (capt) b Swann	32
R. S. Bopara c Naeem Islam b Abdur Razzak	16	Mushfiqur Rahim (wk) c Prior b Shahzad	6
G. P. Swann c & b Shakib Al Hasan	12	Mahmudullah not out	21
P. D. Collingwood run out	14	Naeem Islam b Shahzad	0
T. T. Bresnan c Shafiul Islam b Rubel Hossain	2	Abdur Razzak c Bresnan b Swann	1
A. Shahzad b Shafiul Islam	1	Shafiul Islam not out	24
J. M. Anderson not out	2	Extras (b 1, lb 9, w 23)	33
Extras (lb 2, w 8)	10	(49 overs)	8-227
(49.4 overs)	10-225	Did not bat: Rubel Hossain	

1/32 2/39 3/53 4/162 5/182 6/195 7/209 8/215 9/217 10/225

Bowling: Shafiul Islam 8-0-43-1; Rubel Hossain 8.4-0-40-1; Naeem Islam 8-0-29-2; Abdur Razzak 10-2-32-2; Mahmudullah 5-0-30-1; Shakib Al Hasan 10-0-49-2

1/52 2/70 3/73 4/155 5/162 6/166 7/166 8/169

Bowling: Amderson 9-0-54-0; Shahzad 10-0-43-3; Bresnan 10-1-35-1; Swann 10-1-42-2; Bopara 3-0-19-0; Collingwood 7-0-24-0

Umpires: D.J. Harper, R.J. Tucker.

Toss: Bangladesh   Points: Bangladesh 2, England 0.

SATURDAY 12 MARCH 2011
GROUP B: INDIA vs SOUTH AFRICA
JAMTHA, NAGPUR, INDIA (DAY/NIGHT): SOUTH AFRICA WON BY THREE WICKETS

India's topsy-turvy form continued with a last over defeat by South Africa. The Proteas went against the trend of previous World Cups and prevailed in this humdinger.

The dynamic combination of Sehwag and Tendulkar were brutal in their attack, dishing out severe treatment to top-line quicks Steyn and Morkel. Observers could be forgiven for mistaking this fixture as a Twenty20 game as the 100 was brought up in the 12th over. Desperately searching for a wicket, Graeme Smith threw the ball to part-timer Faf du Plessis. Du Plessis broke the opening stand at 140 in the 18th over when Sehwag played on, cutting while cramped for room. Tendulkar continued to a polished hundred from 92 deliveries, his sixth in World Cups and his 99th overall at international level. With Gambhir playing a supporting role well, India continued the onslaught, powering to 267 in the 40th over. When Tendulkar skied one to point, India had posted their second century partnership of the innings.

India failed to progress from this launching pad to a score well above 300. In another batting collapse, the last nine wickets fell for 29 runs. Apart from the top three, the remaining eight batsmen could muster only 28 runs between them. Steyn fought back after his early troubles, firing out five batsmen. India's implosion saw them bowled out for 296 in the 49th over. This score seemed at least 30 runs short of expectations during the 40th over.

A good omen for South Africa was that it was five years to the day since they overhauled Australia's 434 in Johannesburg. South Africa scored with less alacrity in the early going, reaching 41 in the 9th over before Smith drove Khan to mid off. The calm and confident styles of Amla and Kallis steadily built the score to 127 in the 28th over. Harbhajan Singh picked up his first wicket in three matches when Amla edged a cut shot into the gloves of the vigilant Dhoni. Although a sound platform had been built, South Africa really needed to get a wriggle on, as the required run rate had climbed to over 7.5 runs an over.

AB de Villiers provided the required impetus. Despite losing his partner Kallis to a run out and seeing the asking rate reach nearly nine per over, de Villiers put the middle-order on the right path. De Villiers reached his half-century from 38 balls, but perished from the next ball from Harbhajan Singh. De Villiers speared a sweep straight to forward square-leg and the combative off-spinner kindly reminded him of the way back to the pavilion. Productive cameos from Duminy – who broke his bat when launching a slower ball from Khan into the sightscreen – du Plessis, Botha and Peterson kept the Proteas in with a chance. Still, they needed to score 13 runs from the last over from Nehra, who hadn't bowled since the 37th over.

Peterson was the man on strike. He swung hard at Nehra's first delivery and the resultant inside edge flew to the fine leg fence. Peterson made much better contact with the next shot, blasting the ball into the crowd over deep mid wicket. Victory was within reach as three runs were needed from the remaining four balls. Nehra responded with a yorker and found Peterson equal to the ask. Peterson was able to dig out the sandshoe crusher and the batsmen ran hard for the two runs, which tied the scores, as the ball trickled to fine leg. Peterson hammered the next ball through the covers for four, delivering South Africa the win with two balls to spare.

With numerous contributions of note from their ranks, Steyn's five wickets stood out and won him the Man of the Match award.

INDIA		SOUTH AFRICA	
V. Sehwag b du Plessis	73	H. M. Amla c Dhoni b Harbhajan Singh	61
S. R. Tendulkar c Duminy b Morkel	111	G. C. Smith (capt) c Tendulkar b Khan	16
G. Gambhir c Kallis b Steyn	69	J. H. Kallis run out	69
Y. K. Pathan c Smith b Steyn	0	A. B. de Villiers c Kohli b Harbhajan Singh	52
Yuvraj Singh c Botha b Kallis	12	J. P. Duminy st Dhoni b Harbhajan Singh	23
M. S. Dhoni (capt/wk) not out	12	F. du Plessis not out	25
V. Kohli c & b Peterson	1	M. N. van Wyk (wk) lbw b Patel	5
Harbhajan Singh b Steyn	3	J. Botha c sub (Raina) b Patel	23
Zaheer Khan c Morkel b Peterson	0	R. J. Peterson not out	18
A. Nehra c Smith b Steyn	0	Extras (lb 7, w 1)	8
M. M. Patel b Steyn	0	(49.4 overs)	7-300
Extras (lb 2, w 12, nb 1)	15	Did not bat: D. W. Steyn, M. Morkel	
(48.4 overs)	10-296	1/41 2/127 3/173 4/223 5/238 6/247 7/279	
1/142 2/267 3/268 4/268 5/283 6/286 7/293 8/294		Bowling: Khan 10-0-43-1; Nehra 8.4-0-65-0;	
9/296 10/296		Patel 10-0-65-2; Pathan 4-0-20-0; Yuvraj Singh 8-0-47-0;	
Bowling: Steyn 9.4-0-50-5; Morkel 7-0-59-1; Kallis 8-0-43-1;		Harbhajan Singh 9-0-53-3	
Peterson 9-0-52-2; Duminy 3-0-29-0; Botha 9-0-39-0;			
du Plessis 3-0-22-1			

Umpires: I.J. Gould, S.J.A. Taufel.

Toss: India   Points: South Africa 2, India 0.

SUNDAY 13 MARCH 2011
GROUP A: CANADA v NEW ZEALAND
WANKHEDE CRICKET STADIUM, MUMBAI INDIA: NEW ZEALAND WON BY 97 RUNS

Canada compiled its best ever total in the World Cup, but that was in response to New Zealand's second best ever score, so the Kiwis still won easily by 97 runs to qualify for the next phase of the 2011 tournament. It was therefore a run feast in the renovated Wankhede Stadium with initially bowlers and fieldsmen and later even batsman suffering in extreme heat and humidity.

Ashish Bagai sent the Kiwis in and watched his bowlers get belted for 358. The main protagonists were Brendan McCullum who completed his third World Cup century and won the Man of the Match Award, and Ross Taylor who rollicked along to 74 in just 44 balls. In his 109-ball innings, McCullum hit 12 fours and two sixes. Then Taylor and the later batsmen turned on the fireworks.

John Davison bowled a tidy spell in the middle overs and removed Jesse Ryder, but the final ten overs were a run feast. The Black Caps put on 122 runs as six followed six. Taylor had clobbered five maximums in his innings while in the final over, which cost 31 runs, James Franklin on way to 31 in 8 balls three times lobbed the ball over the boundary.

The suffering bowler, Rizwan Cheema, in one of the most expensive spells ever in the World Cup couldn't finish his final over as he was banned after delivering a second beamer.

Canada required a fanciful 359 to win and by the middle of the fourth over were 2/4.

But New Zealand had developing issues of its own. Kyle Mills claimed the first two wickets then limped off with a strained knee. Daniel Vettori was already missing from the attack and the tougher elimination matches were looming.

New Zealand's constant issue with depth was again evident as Bagai and Jimmy Hansra put on 125 for the fourth wicket in 24 overs.

In terms of this match it was academic, but it gave Canada some heart and raised question marks about New Zealand's ability to go any further than in previous World Cups.

Acting captain, Taylor took three good catches and used eight bowlers. Nathan McCullum broke the fourth wicket partnership having a tiring Bagai caught behind by his brother Brendan. Jacob Oram was the biggest threat and claimed three important wickets.

But with Hansra back at the crease after recuperating from cramp in the dressing room for a time, Canada had 261 on the board were still only nine down when the game's 100 overs were completed.

NEW ZEALAND		CANADA	
M. J. Guptill c Bagai b Baidwan	17	R. Gunasekera c Taylor b Mills	2
B. B. McCullum (wk) c Gunasekera b Baidwan	101	H. Patel c B. McCullum b Oram	31
J. D. Ryder c Osinde b Davison	38	Z. E. Sukari c Taylor b Mills	1
L. R. P. L. Taylor (capt) c Hansra b Balaji Rao	74	A. Bagai (capt/wk) c B. McCullum b N. McCullum	84
N. L. McCullum c & b Balaji Rao	10	A. S. Hansra not out	70
K. S. Williamson not out	34	Rizwan Cheema c B. McCullum b Oram	2
S. B. Styris c Davison b Baidwan	35	J. M. Davison run out	15
J. E. C. Franklin not out	31	W. D. Balaji Rao c N. McCullum b Oram	9
Extras B2 Lb3 W11 Nb2	18	H. S. Baidwan c Franklin b Southee	8
(50 overs)	6/358	Khurram Chohan c Taylor b Ryder	22
Did not bat: J. D. P. Oram, K. D. Mills, T. G. Southee		H. Osinde not out	0
1/53 2/149 3/185 4/254 5/259 6/318		(50 overs)	9/261
Bowling: Khurram Chohan 7-0-40-0; Osinde 7-0-52-0;		1/2 2/4 3/50 4/175 5/179 6/205 7/213 8/222 9/261	
Baidwan 9.1-0-84-3; Rizwan Cheema 4.5-0-64-0; Balaji		Bowling: Mills 2.4-1-2-2; Southee 10-1-36-2; Ryder	
Rao 10-0-62-2; Davison 10-1-30-1; Hansra 2-0-21-0		1.2-0-15-1; Oram 10-0-47-3; Franklin 4-0-31-0; N.	
		McCullum 8-0-56-1; Styris 10-0-41-0; Williamson 4-0-26-0	

Umpires: B.N.J. Oxenford S.K. Tarapore

Toss: Canada   Points: New Zealand 2 Canada 0

GROUP A: AUSTRALIA v KENYA
M.CHINNASWAMY STADIUM, BANGALORE, INDIA: AUSTRALIA WON BY 60 RUNS

On the same day that their Tasman neighbours, New Zealand, defeated Canada, Australia, possibly a trifle rusty after an eight-day break between matches, accounted for Kenya in similar fashion, but perhaps with a little less panache and a smaller margin of 60 runs.

There was some fine batting in the Australian innings of 324, but nothing to compare with New Zealand's brutal hitting in Mumbai while Kenya's 264 was their highest ever World Cup total and Collins Obuya's 98 not out their highest individual World Cup score.

Ricky Ponting won the toss and batted and his batsmen responded with a strong display. Brad Haddin, despite one quiet period against spin, did best amongst the top order with nine fours and a six in 79 balls, while Ponting himself once more looked below his best before being given out lbw to Collins Obuya after the Kenyans called for a review. Australia was then guaranteed a significant total when Michael Clarke and Mike Hussey put on 114 in 16 overs for the fifth wicket.

Hussey had been controversially drafted into the squad when he had recovered from an operation on a hamstring tear and Doug Bollinger, a bowler, had withdrawn through injury. He then took his brother, David's place in the final eleven.

Mike Hussey eventually fell to Kenya's best bowler, Nehemiah Odhiambo as did Michael Clarke in the 49th over, caught at long on seven short of his maiden World Cup century.

With a wicket apiece with the new-ball Brett Lee and Shaun Tait soon had Kenya reeling at 2/21 after four overs.

For the next 46 overs, though, only one more wicket fell to the bowlers. Batting with his brother, Collins, David Obuya was the first of three eventual run out victims.

But his departure galvanized his brother and he found an able ally in Tanmay Mishra. They made no real effort to actually reach their large target, but they did expose some of Australia's bowling limitations while putting on 115 for the fourth wicket in 25 overs. Mishra's highest one-day score ended when Michael Clarke threw down the stumps from backward point as the batsmen raced for a quick single.

The later overs were academic as Ponting did not even use any bowlers for their full spell. There was even anti-climax when Collins Obuya could not score the three runs he needed for his country's first World Cup hundred from the final two balls of the match.

AUSTRALIA		KENYA	
S. R. Watson c Ouma b Odhiambo	21	M. A. Ouma (wk) c Haddin b Lee	4
B. J. Haddin (wk) c Patel b Kamande	65	A. A. Obanda b Tait	14
R. T. Ponting (capt) lbw b C. Obuya	36	C. O. Obuya not out	98
M. J. Clarke c Patel b Odhiambo	93	D. O. Obuya run out	12
C. L.White b Kamande	2	T. Mishra run out	72
M. E. K. Hussey c D. Obuya b Odhiambo	54	T. M. Odoyo b Tait	35
S. P. D. Smith not out	17	R. R. Patel run out	6
M. G. Johnson not out	12	J. K. Kamande (capt) not out	0
Extras B2 Lb5 W16 Nb1	24	Extras B2 Lb6 W12 Nb3	23
(50 overs)	6/324	(50 overs)	6/264
Did not bat: B. Lee J. J. Krejza S. W. Tait		Did not bat: N. N. Odhiambo, E. Otieno, J. O. Ngoche	
1/38 2/127 3/131 4/143 5/257 6/304		1/12 2/21 3/46 4/161 5/247 6/263	
Bowling: Odoyo 10-0-50-0; Otieno 8-0-75-0;		Bowling: Lee 8-1-26-1; Tait 8-0-49-2; Johnson 8-1-40-0;	
Odhiambo 10-1-57-3; Ngoche 8-0-56-0;		Smith 6-0-36-0; Krejza 8-0-36-0; Clarke 5-0-21-0;	
Kamande 10-0-46-2; C. Obuya 4-0-33-1		Watson 7-0-48-0	

Umpires: Asad Rauf R.A. Kettleborough

Toss: Australia   Points: Australia 2 Kenya 0

MONDAY 14 MARCH 2011
GROUP B: BANGLADESH vs NETHERLANDS
ZOHUR AHMED CHOWDURY STADIUM, CHITTAGONG, BANGLADESH
BANGLADESH WON BY SIX WICKETS

Three days after toppling England, Bangladesh did not suffer a let down in a comfortable win over the Dutch.

Peter Borren continued his remarkable run with the coin, winning his fifth consecutive toss in the tournament. As was the case in the game against India five days earlier, the Dutch batsmen failed to consistently rotate the strike, allowing too many dot balls to dry up scoring opportunities. There were 185 scoreless deliveries in the 46.2 overs of the innings, four more dot balls than in the fixture against India. Fresh from his batting cameo against the English, Shafiul Islam consistently asked questions of the batsmen with his probing deliveries. He ended up conceding just 15 runs from 9.2 overs. It seemed unfair that he was not rewarded with a single wicket. Bangladesh's triumvirate of left-arm orthodox spinners – Abdur Razzak, Shakib Al Hasan and Suhrawadi Shuvo – did most of the damage with the ball, collecting five out of the six wickets to fall to bowlers.

The inability of the Dutch batsmen to score ones and twos regularly was exacerbated by indifferent running between the wickets. Four wickets were lost to run outs, including the wasteful dismissals of Szwarczynski and Cooper, both of whom had made starts. The batting powerplay, taken in overs 44 to 48, was a non-event. Only 19 runs were scored for the loss of a wicket.

Chasing a modest target of 161, Bangladesh were rocked when Tamim Iqbal was bowled by the fourth delivery of the innings. Imrul Kayes and Junaid Siddique took their time to get established and control was gradually re-asserted. The pair took the score to 92 in the 21st over before Junaid Siddique hit a short and wide delivery from Borren straight to extra cover. From this point, the home side needed less than 2.5 runs an over to secure the win. Shahriar Nafees, playing his first game of the tournament, played some well-placed shots. He combined with Imrul Kayes to register Bangladesh's second fifty partnership of the innings. After Shahriar Nafees was bowled around his legs by Cooper and Shakib Al Hasan was caught playing a loose shot, victory had been assured with less than eight runs required. Keeper Mushfiqur Rahim finished the run chase off in style in the 42nd over, steering the first ball of Cooper's over through extra cover for four and signing off with catching practice for the patrons over deep mid wicket. Imrul Kayes won the man of the match award again for his well-constructed, unbeaten 73.

Bangladesh now needed to upset South Africa in their final group game to progress to the quarter-finals.

NETHERLANDS		BANGLADESH	
E. S. Szwarczynski run out	28	Tamim Iqbal b Mudassar Bukhari	0
W. Barresi (wk) lbw b Shakib Al Hasan	10	Imrul Kayes not out	73
Mudassar Bukhari c Mushfiqur Rahim b Abdur Razzak	6	Junnaid Siqqique c Seelaar b Borren	35
T. L. W. Cooper run out	29	Shahriar Nafees b Cooper	37
R. N. ten Doeschate not out	53	Shakib Al Hasan (capt) c ten Doeschate b Cooper	1
A. N. Kervezee st Mushfiqur Rahim b Suhrawadi Shuvo	18	Mushfiqur Rahim (wk) not out	11
T. N. de Grooth lbw b Abdur Razzak	4	Extras (b 2, lb 3, w 3, nb 1)	9
A. F. Buurman c Imrul Kayes b Abdur Razzak	0	(41.2 overs)	4-166
P. W. Borren (capt) run out	3	Did not bat: Mahmudullah, Suhrawadi Shuvo, Shafiul Islam,	
P. M. Seelaar lbw b Rubel Hossain	0	Abdur Razzak, Rubel Hossain	
Adeel Raja run out	0	1/0 2/92 3/151 4/153	
Extras (lb 9)	9	Bowling: Mudassar Bukhari 6-2-14-1; Adeel Raja 7-0-31-0;	
(46.2 overs)	10-162	ten Doeschate 6-1-30-0; Seelaar 10-1-25-0; Borren 5-0-28-1;	
1/28 2/37 3/66 4/79 5/113 6/127 7/127 8/139 9/141		Cooper 7.2-2-33-2	
10/160			
Bowling: Shafiul Islam 9.2-3-15-0; Abdur Razzak 10-2-29-3;			
Shakib Al Hasan 8-0-38-1; Rubel Hossain 9-0-36-1;			
Suhrawadi Shuvo 10-1-33-1			

Umpires: Aleem Dar, R.J. Tucker.

Toss: Netherlands   Points: Bangladesh 2, Holland 0.

GROUP A: PAKISTAN v ZIMBABWE
PALLEKELE INTERNATIONAL CRICKET STADIUM, KANDY, SRI LANKA
PAKISTAN WON BY SEVEN WICKETS

Pakistan qualified for the quarter-finals with a comfortable seven-wicket win over Zimbabwe at a damp and subdued Pallekelle stadium in a match with enough rain for Duckworth Lewis to have an influence.

The sun was actually shining when Elton Chigumbura won the toss and elected to bat, but his side made a poor start and then twice had their innings length readjusted.

Pakistan left out Shoaib Akhtar, but he was not missed as eventual Man of the Match, Umar Gul, and his moderately paced new-ball partner, Abdul Razzaq reduced the Zimbabweans to 3/13. Razzaq claimed the key wicket of the in form Brendan Taylor in the first over, caught behind from a delivery that moved nicely away.

Craig Ervine did the best job of rebuilding the innings after such a poor start, but his momentum was interrupted at the 28 over mark by the first of the afternoon's downpours.

Almost more impressive than the cricket was the worker ant-like army of groundstaff who covered virtually the whole playing surface in a matter of moments when the skies opened.

Upon resumption Zimbabawe were supposed to have another 15 overs, but the rain came back after 11.4 overs. Ervine reached 52 off 82 balls before playing back to a skidding delivery from Mohammad Hafeez when he should have gone forward.

Chigumbura in his best innings of the tournament to date and Prosper Utseya then put on 48 to get the total just above 150 before the rain sneakily returned against the darkened skies and terminated their innings.

It meant Pakistan with all ten wickets available had 38 overs to get 162.

Ahmed Shehza played one great shot. Soon, though, he waltzed down the wicket recklessly to the wily Ray Price, again given the new-ball, and was swiftly stumped by Tatenda Taibu.

Mohammad Hafeez and World Cup debutant Asad Shafiq then settled the game as a contest with a second wicket partnership of 82 in 19 overs. Price got involved again catching Mohammad Hafeez low at slip and bowling Shahid Afridi.

However Asad Shafiq remained. He played the innings of the match, cutting sweetly when given width. With Younis Khan providing class and stability Pakistan eased home with 23 balls to spare.

ZIMBABWE		PAKISTAN	
B. R.M. Taylor c Kamran Akmal b Abdul Razzaq	4	Mohammad Hafeez c Price b Utseya	49
R. W. Chakabva lbw b Umar Gul	0	Ahmed Shehzad st Taibu b Price	8
T. Taibu (wk) c Shahid Afridi b Wahab Riaz	19	Asad Shafiq not out	78
V. Sibanda c Misbah-ul-Haq b Umar Gul	5	Shahid Afridi (capt) b Price	3
C. R. Ervine b Mohammad Hafeez	52	Younis Khan not out	13
G. A. Lamb c & b Shahid Afridi	16	Extras W13	13
E. Chigumbura (capt) not out	32	(34.1 overs)	3/164
P. Utseya c Kamran Akmal b Umar Gul	18	Did not bat: Misbah-ul-Haq, Abdul Razzaq,	
A. G. Cremer not out	0	Kamran Akmal (wk) , Abdur Rehman, Umar Gul, Wahab Riaz	
Extras Lb2 W2 Nb1	5	1/17 2/99 3/110	
(39.4 overs)	7/151	Bowling: Masakadza 6-1-44-0; Price 8-1-21-2;	
Did not bat: S. W. Masakadza, R. W. Price		Utseya 7-1-24-1; Lamb 7-0-44-0; Cremer 6.1-0-31-0	
1/5 2/5 3/13 4/43 5/84 6/103 7/151			
Bowling: Abdul Razzaq 7-1-24-1; Umar Gul			
7.4-1-36-3; Wahab Riaz; Shahid Afridi 8-0-33-1; Abdur			
Rehman 8-1-24-0; Mohammad Hafeez 3-0-11-1			

Umpires: A.L. Hill N.J. Llong

Toss: Zimbabwe   Points: Pakistan 2 Zimbabwe 0

TUESDAY 15 MARCH 2011
GROUP B: IRELAND vs SOUTH AFRICA
EDEN GARDENS, KOLKATA, INDIA (DAY/NIGHT): SOUTH AFRICA WON BY 131 RUNS

"Cricket's answer to the Colosseum" was less than half-full for this all-green battle. South Africa, who were expected to win comfortably, were sent in to bat and found themselves in a spot of bother at 5-117 in the 27th over when du Plessis edged Mooney to slip. It could have been much worse for the Proteas, as regulation catches were dropped when makeshift number three Morne van Wyk was on four and 23.

Duminy played intelligently, minimising risks with his shot selection and rotating the strike frequently in the first half of his innings. Duminy and Colin Ingram, playing his first innings of the tournament, kept the score ticking over and guided their team to safer waters. Ingram played across to Johnston when he was four short of a half-century. The partnership yielded a crucial 87 runs from 13.1 overs and South Africa now had a score of 250-plus in their sights.

With the pressure reduced, Duminy, who scored only two boundaries in reaching 50, started to play more adventurously. Duminy let fly in the penultimate over from Johnston, hoisting him well over the deep square leg fence and striking two boundaries. On 99 and with three balls remaining in the innings, Duminy put some extra runs for the team ahead of reaching his hundred with a minimum of risk. Duminy's attempt at hitting Mooney down the ground resulted in a steepling high ball that was caught one-handed by a diving Kevin O'Brien. Duminy's 99 used 103 deliveries and, with Botha batting sensibly at the other end, 65 runs were added for the seventh wicket in good time.

A target of 273 was a mountain for the Irish to climb against Steyn, Morkel, Kallis and company. Morkel made the early breakthroughs, inducing edges that were snaffled by the slip cordon in each of his first two overs. Niall O'Brien and Gary Wilson gave short-lived resistance with a fifth wicket partnership of 41. Peterson effectively ended the match as a contest with three middle order wickets in 15 deliveries. Ireland slumped to 7-107 and, even if the Irish tail were to wag, the required run rate was much too high. The Irish bowlers made a few runs and ended up giving van Wyk some catching practice. The blond, reserve keeper from Bloemfontein ended a good day personally with four catches. Ireland's innings ended in the 34th over before they had a chance to use their batting powerplay.

South Africa's landslide win meant that a win over Bangladesh in the last group match would secure the Proteas top spot in Group B. Duminy's important innings earned him the man of the match award.

SOUTH AFRICA		IRELAND	
H. M. Amla c Dockrell b Rankin	18	W. T.S. Porterfield (capt) c Smith b Morkel	6
G. C. Smith (capt) run out	7	P. R. Stirling c Kallis b Morkel	10
M. N. van Wyk (wk) b Dockrell	42	E. C. Joyce lbw b Botha	12
J. H. Kallis run out	19	N. J. O'Brien (wk) c van Wyk b Kallis	10
J. P. Duminy c K. O'Brien b Mooney	99	G. C. Wilson lbw b Peterson	31
F. du Plessis c Johnston b Stirling	11	K. J. O'Brien c Amla b Peterson	19
C. A. Ingram b Johnston	46	A. R. Cusack c Smith b Peterson	7
J. Botha not out	21	J. F. Mooney c van Wyk b Kallis	14
R. J. Peterson not out	0	D. T. Johnston c van Wyk b Duminy	12
Extras (b 2, lb 3, w 4)	9	G. H. Dockrell c van Wyk b Morkel	16
(50 overs)	7-272	W. B. Rankin not out	0
Did not bat: D. W. Steyn, M. Morkel		Extras (4 w)	4
1/24 2/52 3/84 4/95 5/117 6/204 7/269		(33.2 overs)	10-141
Bowling: Rankin 10-0-59-1; Johnston 10-0-76-1;		1/8 2/19 3/35 4/51 5/92 6/92 7/107 8/123 9/137 10/141	
Mooney 8-0-36-1; Dockrell 10-0-37-1; Stirling 10-0-45-1;		Bowling: Steyn 4-1-13-0; Morkel 5.2-0-33-3; Kallis 6-1-20-2;	
Cusack 2-0-14-0		Botha 8-0-32-1; Peterson 8-0-32-3; Duminy 2-0-11-1	

Umpires: H.D.P.K. Dharmasena, B.R. Doctrove.

Toss: Ireland   Points: South Africa 2, Ireland 0.

WEDNESDAY 16 MARCH 2011
GROUP A: AUSTRALIA v CANADA
M CHINNASWAMY STADIUM, BANGALORE, INDIA: AUSTRALIA WON BY SEVEN WICKETS

Canada exited the 2011 World Cup with one of their better performances, but Australia were still able to eventually cruise home by seven wickets with 15 overs to spare. The North Americans may have been motivated pre-match at the announcement of former captain John Davison that this game would his last. There was a neatness to the closure of his career as his 32nd and final one-day international was his first against the country where he played most of his formative and serious cricket.

After Ashish Bagai won the toss and batted, Davison returned to the position of opener. He was caught behind off Brett Lee before the end of the fourth over for 14, but the total by then was already 41. Davison's young partner Hiral Patel had begun the innings with a series of blazing shots that continued even after Davison's departure. He had taken 16 runs from Brett Lee's opening over, then in the next over, on one leg, smashed Shaun Tait over extra cover for six. A slash off Mitchell Johnson over third man and a hook off Lee also went for six as Canada rattled along to 1/62 from six overs. The 19-year-old was finally caught at third man off Shane Watson for 54, however, Bagai and Zubin Zurkari then carried the total to an extremely threatening 2/150 in the 29th over.

But Tait and Lee were much more effective in their second spells and Jason Krejza's off-spin was quite frugal. Runs dried up and wickets fell. Canada lost 8/61 in 17 overs to be all out for 211. Shane Watson and Brad Haddin had a couple of lucky breaks against the new ball. Soon they were striking the ball cleanly. After 20 overs the total was 90, They then doubled that figure in the next eight and a half overs going on to break Australia's previous best World Cup opening stand of 182 since way back in 1975.

Watson clouted Davison for what reputedly was the longest six of the tournament, 104 metres over long on, although there were not too many eye witnesses to the event in the M Chinnaswamy Stadium. That was one of six maximum blows traded by the pair as they raced neck and neck towards their hundreds. Then neither of them got there.

Haddin put Davison out of the ground to break the partnership record but three balls later tickled an off-spinner down the leg-side to Bagai and was out for 88. Two runs later Watson, adrenalin still flowing, tried to pull a six off Harvir Baidwan to reach his ton and skied a catch to long on. Ponting had earlier in the day built on his growing captain 'grumpy' image by taking a catch then throwing the ball into the turf after a territorial dispute with Steve Smith while the ball was in the air. Now, he miscued a pull when he was on seven with Australia just five runs from victory. There were no follow-up reports of dressing room damage.

In the same over Cameron White hit a four and a single and the game was over.

CANADA		AUSTRALIA	
H. Patel c Johnson b Watson	54	S. R. Watson c Osinde b Baidwan	94
J. M. Davison c Haddin b Lee	14	B. J. Haddin (wk) c Bagai b Davison	88
Z. E. Surkari b Tait	34	R. T. Ponting (capt) c Davison b Osinde	7
A. Bagai (capt/wk) c Haddin b Tait	39	M. J. Clarke not out	16
A. S. Hansra c Lee b Krejza	3	C. L. White not out	4
Rizwan Cheema b Lee	2	Extras Lb1 W2	3
N. R. Kumar c Tait b Johnson	7	(34.5 overs)	3/212
K. Whatham b Lee	18	1/183 2/185 3/207	
H. S. Baidwan c Ponting b Krejza	17	Did not bat: M. E. K. Hussey, S. P.D. Smith, M. G. Johnson,	
W. D. Balaji Rao b Lee	5	B. Lee, J. J. Krejza, S. W. Tait	
H. Osinde not out	2	Bowling: Osinde 9.5-0-53-1; Baidwan 10-1-41-1; Balaji	
Extras Lb4 W11 Nb1	16	Rao 7-0-46-0; Rizwan Cheema 3-0-23-0; Davison 4-0-29-1;	
(45.4 overs)	211	Patel 1-0-19-0	
1/41 2/82 3/150 4/157 5/157 6/161 7/169 8/195 10/211			
Bowling: Tait 8-1-34-2; Lee 8.4-0-46-4; Johnson 10-0-43-1;			
Watson 6-0-22-1; Krejza 10-0-44-2; Smith 3-0-18-0			

Umpires: B.F. Bowden A.M. Saheba

Toss: Canada   Points: Australia 2 Canada 0

THURSDAY 17 MARCH 2011
GROUP B: ENGLAND vs WEST INDIES
MA CHIDAMBARAM STADIUM, CHENNAI, INDIA: ENGLAND WON BY 18 RUNS

With their campaign on the brink, England displayed resilience under pressure to shade the West Indies in this encounter. England's win owed much to the performances of their spinners, Swann and James Tredwell, who played in his first World Cup match.

England's score of 243 all out seemed a little light-on against an explosive Caribbean batting talent. After Strauss and Prior gave the innings early momentum, Trott pressed the accelerator. The Cape Town-born batsman continued his excellent form and on this occasion the runs flowed at a faster rate. Six boundaries were scored from Trott's first nine balls and England soon found themselves at a promising 2-121 in the 22nd over. Trott's rapid scoring was extinguished when was caught at mid wicket from the bowling of debutante leg-spinner Devendra Bishoo from Guyana.

Trott's lapse triggered a mid-innings slump. Bishoo's accurate beginning to international cricket produced the key wickets of Trott, Morgan and, eventually, Luke Wright. A score of 2-121 had become a much less palatable 6-151 within 11 overs. Wright dominated a 41-run stand with Tredwell to take England on the verge of 200 with just over ten overs remaining. For England to post a sizeable total from this point, it was important that Wright bat through the remaining overs. Unfortunately, Wright exited the action in the 44th over. A mistimed slog by Wright was caught at deep mid wicket, cutting short his useful innings and leaving the bowlers with some work to do. Bresnan and his bowling colleagues lasted into the 49th over. Playing in his second match, Andre Dwayne Russell collected four wickets and Bishoo three.

Chris Gayle launched the pursuit of 244 in style, lacing four boundaries from Bresnan's second over. Chris Tremlett, bowling a fraction too full in his first over, also paid a heavy penalty as Gayle struck three boundaries and deposited one blow several rows back over mid-on. The 50 was on the board in just 29 deliveries. Theories that the West Indians could not sustain such a frenetic pace were validated a short time later. Playing in his fourth limited-overs international, Tredwell collected his first one-day scalp when he trapped Gayle in front for a hectic 43 from 21 balls.

Sammy picked up where Gayle left off, clobbering Tredwell for three sixes, including two down the ground. Sammy's star also burned brightly, but briefly. His cameo innings of 41 was over in just 29 balls. Bowling military medium pace, Ravi Bopara's accuracy resulted in both Sammy and Thomas dragging the ball onto their stumps. The West Indies seemed out of the game at 5-118 in the 20th over.

Russell had other ideas. With Sarwan playing the sheet anchor role, Russell unleashed a sparkling array of strokes that belied his number eight position, including a low trajectory, inside-out cover drive off Tredwell for six. The West Indies only needed 40 runs to win from 13 overs and England's World Cup hopes were slipping away. England's morale was challenged a few balls later. Russell swung hard at a Swann delivery and the ball sailed towards the long on boundary rope. Running backwards at a rate of knots, Trott caught the ball perilously close to the rope, possibly brushing it with his shoulder or sun hat. Although Trott vehemently argued that the catch had been taken inside the field of play, the third umpire did not agree, and Russell was awarded his third six.

Tredwell and Bopara pressed on and succeeded in arresting the scoring. Perhaps overawed by the occasion, Russell was unable to press home the advantage and he scored only four runs from 16 deliveries after the Trott incident. Tredwell had his revenge for being hit into the crowd thrice by Russell when he trapped Russell, playing back, in front of his stumps. The game had reached an interesting stage: 52 deliveries was ample time for Sarwan and company to hit the 22 runs required, but there were only three wickets in reserve.

With the score on 223, England's chances soared when Swann extracted extra bounce from the wicket and Sarwan's attempt to work it to leg resulted in a catch to short leg. Two balls later, Roach ambitiously tried to hit Swann down the crowd and only succeeded in hitting a catch to mid off. The West Indies last wicket pairing of Roach and Bishoo needed 20 runs from the last six overs. Benn scored one of them when he edged Bopara to fine leg, but he took on Trott's arm in going for the second run and lost. England were home by 18 runs and the West Indies had crumbled in the late stages of their run chase, losing four wickets for three runs in 21 balls.

For England, it was a day to remember for their spinners, who took seven wickets between them. On his return to the side, Tredwell was the star with 4-48. The Kent off-spinner won the man of the match award. England would be in the quarter-finals, unless Bangladesh upset South Africa or the West Indies bounced back to beat India in the last round of Group B matches.

ENGLAND		WEST INDIES	
A. J. Strauss (capt) c Gayle b Russell	31	D. S. Smith st Prior b Tredwell	10
M. J. Prior (wk) b Russell	21	C. H. Gayle lbw b Tredwell	43
I. J. L. Trott c Gayle b Bishoo	47	D. J. G. Sammy (capt) b Bopara	41
I. R. Bell b Roach	27	D. M. Bravo c Strauss b Tredwell	5
E. J. G. Morgan c Thomas b Bishoo	7	D. C. Thomas (wk) b Bopara	9
R. S. Bopara b Russell	4	R. R. Sarwan c Bell b Swann	31
L. J. Wright c Russell b Bishoo	44	K. A. Pollard lbw b Swann	24
J. C. Tredwell run out	9	A. D. Russell lbw b Tredwell	49
T. T. Bresnan not out	20	S. J. Benn run out	2
G. P. Swann b Russell	8	K. A. J. Roach c Tremlett b Swann	0
C. T. Tremlett c Thomas b Roach	3	D. Bishoo not out	0
Extras (b 1, lb 4, w 15, nb 2)	22	Extras (lb 8, w 3)	11
(48.4 overs)	10-243	(44.4 overs)	10-225

1/48 2/79 3/121 4/134 5/134 6/151 7/192 8/216 9/238 10/243

1/58 2/67 3/91 4/113 5/118 6/150 7/222 8/223 9/223 10/225

Bowling: Roach 9.4-2-34-2; Benn 10-0-56-0; Russell 8-0-49-4; Sammy 3-0-28-0; Bishoo 10-0-34-3; Pollard 8-0-37-0

Bowling: Bresnan 7-1-46-0; Swann 10-1-36-3; Tremlett 5-0-47-0; Tredwell 10-2-48-4; Bopara 8.4-2-22-2; Wright 4-0-18-0

Umpires: S.J. Davis, B.N.J. Oxenford

Toss: England   Points: England 2, West Indies 0.

FRIDAY 18 MARCH 2011
GROUP B: IRELAND vs NETHERLANDS
EDEN GARDENS, KOLKATA, INDIA: IRELAND WON BY SIX WICKETS

Ireland showed that they were a cut above the other Associate teams with a comfortable win in this inconsequential fixture. On a benign pitch full of runs, Ireland chased down a 300-plus score for the second time in the tournament.

For the first time in the competition, Borren called incorrectly and the Dutch were sent in to bat on a surface with some early morning moisture. The headaches started early for the Dutch, as Wesley Barresi was struck in the back of the head in the second over by a return throw from Kevin O'Brien. With the Netherlands under pressure at 3-53, Barresi returned to the crease and contributed to a handy partnership of 60 with ten Doeschate. The Netherlands' leading batsman was in good touch, pacing his innings intelligently and building the team's run rate towards six an over. Ten Doeschate combined with Borren for a key stand of 121 in 18 overs. Ireland's chances took a blow when promising left-arm spinner Dockrell landed heavily on his shoulder in fielding from his own bowling. Dockrell appeared to have dislocated his shoulder and he was unable to complete the over.

Borren reached his half-century from 56 balls and, in the next over, ten Doeschate reached three figures, only requiring 104 balls to attain the milestone. It was ten Doeschate's second century of the tournament. Ten Doeschate hit Stirling for six over mid wicket and, from the next delivery, he hit the ball straight down the throat of long off. Borren, back-up keeper Atse Buurman and Mudassar Bukhari batted with a sense of urgency in the latter overs. Borren's excellent innings ended in the 47th over when he was caught at extra cover for 84 from 82 deliveries.

The last two overs of the Dutch innings produced some bizarre cricket. In the penultimate over, Rankin bowled Buurman, but the delivery was a no ball. With the next delivery a free-hit, Rankin overstepped again and Atse Buurman was unable to make contact. The next delivery caused Buurman's middle stump to cartwheel, but the umpire's call of no ball meant that Buurman would remain at the crease. In the final over, a leg-side wide and the last three legal deliveries of the innings produced four consecutive run outs.

A target of 307, whilst challenging, always seemed to be well within Ireland's reach. In the third over, the Dutch missed the opportunity for a vital early breakthrough when Adeel Raja spilled a catch from Porterfield at third man. Porterfield and Stirling were soon in their stride and 81 runs were flayed from the first 10 overs without loss. Stirling reached his 50 in a mere 25 balls and it took his opening partner 70 balls to reach the milestone.

The openers put on an impressive 177 runs for the first wicket. Porterfield edged a cut shot to the keeper and the next delivery saw Stirling reach a century from 70 balls. Stirling seemed to lose his focus and he pulled the next delivery, a rank long hop, to a gleeful deep mid wicket.

The Irish openers had set a good platform for the remaining batsmen, easing the required scoring rate to less than a run a ball. Ed Joyce and Niall O'Brien combined for a useful stand of 54 for the third wicket, although the required run rate drifted above six an over. Wilson evened up the equation, hitting two consecutive sixes and a four from Cooper's seventh and final over. Wilson's 27 came from only 21 balls, keeping Ireland in a good position to reach their target.

It was now over to the O'Brien brothers. With 14 required from 18 balls, two sixes from Kevin O'Brien and a single apiece for each batsman delivered Ireland their second win of the competition with 14 deliveries remaining.

Stirling's fast-paced hundred won him the man of the match award.

The result of the match meant that the Netherlands finished the tournament without winning a game.

NETHERLANDS		IRELAND	
E. S. Szwarczynski c N. O'Brien b Johnston	1	W. T.S. Porterfield (capt) c Buurman b Cooper	68
W. Barresi lbw b Stirling	44	P. R. Stirling c Kervezee b Seelaar	101
T. L.W. Cooper c Porterfield b Rankin	5	E. C. Joyce c Buurman b Cooper	28
R. N. ten Doeschate c Mooney b Stirling	106	N. J. O'Brien (wk) not out	57
A. N. Kervezee c K. O'Brien b Mooney	12	G. C. Wilson c Buurman b ten Doeschate	27
P. W. Borren (capt) c Porterfield b Mooney	84	K. J. O'Brien not out	15
A. F. Buurman (wk) run out	26	Extras (lb 10, w 1)	11
Mudassar Bukhari run out	11	(47.4 overs)	6-307
P. M. Seelaar run out	0	Did not bat: A. R. Cusack, J. F. Mooney, D. T. Johnston, G. H.
Adeel Raja run out	0	Dockrell, W. B. Rankin	
B. P. Loots not out	0	1/177 2/179 3/233 4/279	
Extras (b 1, lb 8, w 5, nb 3)	17	Bowling: Mudassar Bukhari 7-0-42-0; Adeel Raja 8-1-44-0;	
(50 overs)	10-306	Loots 2-0-29-0; ten Doeschate 9-1-58-1; Seelaar 9.4-1-55-1;	

1/7 2/12 3/53 4/113 5/234 6/287 7/305 8/305 9/305
10/306

Bowling: Rankin 9-0-74-1; Johnston 10-1-50-1;
Mooney 10-0-59-2; Dockrell 3.4-0-15-0; Stirling 10-0-51-2;
Cusack 2.2-0-15-0; K. O'Brien 5-0-33-0

Borren 5-0-38-0; Cooper 7-1-31-2

Umpires: B.R. Doctrove, I.J. Gould.

Toss: Ireland   Points: Ireland 2, Holland 0.

GROUP A: NEW ZEALAND v SRI LANKA
WANKHEDE STADIUM, MUMBAI, INDIA: SRI LANKA WON BY 112 RUNS

Sri Lanka had a decisive 112-run win over New Zealand which gave them a higher placing in their group than the Kiwis for the quarter-finals, a possible psychological boost for the next round and not much else.

The match contained some umpiring controversies, but as is more common in the modern era, it took place on a television screen replay rather than on the ground itself.

For the 32,000 watching there was the enjoyment of Kumar Sangakkara's first ODI hundred for three years, a fine partnership of 145 between the Sri Lankan captain and Mahela Jayawardene and the spin wizardry of a slightly lame Muttiah Muralitharan.

Sangakkara won the toss and batted and he and Jayawardene were at the wicket by the fifth over as Tim Southee claimed two fortuitous wickets. Upal Tharanga was run out backing up too far when Southee deflected a straight drive from Tillakaratne Dilshan on to the stumps at the non-strikers end. Then it was 2/19 when Dilshan slashed a cut to Oram at deep third man.

Sri Lanka were 2/87 in the 24th over when Jayawardene, who had battled to 26, chipped the ball low back to off-spinner Nathan McCullum. McCullum dived and appeared to get his fingers under the ball. Jayawardene stayed. The catch was referred to the third umpire, Amiesh Saheba. 99 frames showed McCullum had caught the ball. One frame questioned that. The decision was not out.

New Zealand fumed. Everyone who has ever taken a low catch knows that the pictures give the wrong impression but the not out 'policy' on such occasions remains.

Sangakkara and Jayawardene were then on their way, scoring freely and lifting the run rate. Finally Southee trapped Jayawardene lbw from the first ball of the 37th over.

Sangakkara continued on. He hit Scott Styris for six back over the bowler's head and Southee over backward point for a second six. He reached his hundred in the 40th over.

After he was bowled in the 42nd over there was a tumble of wickets. Angelo Mathews, though, was an exception. He made an unbeaten 41 in 35 balls that lifted Sri Lanka to a very competitive 265.

It proved far too many for a lacklustre New Zealand batting line-up. The top four all reached double figures and that took the Black Caps to 2/82. But only Ross Taylor with 33 passed twenty.

The Sri Lankan spinners did the damage. Jesse Ryder was caught behind driving at Ajantha Mendis and Muralitharan, despite his strained hamstring, had 2/7 after three overs. Kane Williamson was stumped on the forward defensive lunge and Taylor missing a straight one. Both were doosras.

New Zealand was 5/93 in the 22nd over and there was no way back.

A light tower at the ground went out. The match continued. Muralitharan picked up two more wickets. Jacob Oram, batting very low and No.9, dragged the total beyond 150. Lasith Malinga finished the game with a straight yorker to Hamish Bennett from the final delivery of the 35th over.

Skipper Sangakkara was named Man of the Match.

SRI LANKA		NEW ZEALAND	
W. U. Tharanga run out	3	M. J. Guptill lbw b Kulasekara	13
T. M. Dilshan c Oram b Southee	3	B. B. McCullum (wk) c Jayawardene b Mathews	14
K. C. Sangakkara (capt/wk) b N. McCullum	111	J. D. Ryder c Sangakkara b Mendis	19
D. P. M. D. Jayawardene lbw b Southee	66	L. R. P. L.Taylor (capt) lbw b Muralitharan	33
A. D. Mathews not out	41	K. S. Williamson st Sangakkara b Muralitharan	5
T. T. Samaraweera c B. McCullum b Styris	5	S. B. Styris c & b Muralitharan	6
L. P. C. Silva c & b N. McCullum	3	J. E. C. Franklin c Dilshan b Muralitharan	20
K. M. D. N. Kulasekara c Guptill b Southee	1	N. L. McCullum c Jayawardene b Dilshan	4
S. L. Malinga c B. McCullum b Oram	6	J. D. P. Oram not out	20
M. Muralitharan run out	7	T. G. Southee lbw b Mendis	8
B. A. W. Mendis not out	0	H. K. Bennett b Malinga	0
Extras Lb4 W12 Nb3	19	Extras Lb4 W6 Nb1	11
(50 overs)	9/265	(35 overs)	153

1/13 2/19 3/164 4/210 5/219 6/224 7/232 8/239 9/260

1/29 2/33 3/82 4/88 5/93 6/102 7/115 8/129 9/144 10/153

Bowling: Southee 10-0-63-3; Oram 10-1-57-1; Bennett 4.1-0-16-0; Ryder 3.5-0-18-0; Franklin 3-0-11-0; Styris 8-0-44-1; N. McCullum 10-0-48-2; Williamson 1-0-4-0

Bowling: Malinga 5-0-38-1; Kulasekara 7-0-19-1; Mathews 3-0-19-1; Mendis 6-0-24-2; Dilshan 6-0-24-1; Muralitharan 8-0-25-4

Umpires: Asad Rauf R.A.Kettleborough

Toss: Sri Lanka   Points: Sri Lanka 2 New Zealand 0

SATURDAY 19 MARCH 2011
GROUP B: BANGLADESH vs SOUTH AFRICA
SHER-E BANGLA NATIONAL STADIUM, DHAKA, BANGLADESH
SOUTH AFRICA WON BY 206 RUNS

Bangladesh's World Cup campaign ended unceremoniously with a hammering at the hands of South Africa. The co-hosts suffered their heaviest defeat in terms of runs in a World Cup fixture. The defeat meant that England and the West Indies would go through to the quarter-finals regardless of the outcome of the final group game between India and the West Indies.

Most of the South African batsmen spent valuable time in the middle, tuning them up for their quarter-final in five days' time. Smith batted carefully while Amla, Kallis and du Plessis scored at good speed in their half-centuries. Against Bangladesh's spin-centric attack, none of the Proteas went on to post a big score. In any event, South Africa's final score of 284 would be difficult to overhaul.

With speedsters Steyn and Morkel enjoying a well-earned rest, the South Africans gave left-arm seamers Lonwabo Tsotsobe and Wayne Parnell, who converted to Islam a short time before the competition, their first taste of World Cup action. Tsotsobe was incisive with the new ball and had the home side on the back foot. In his first four overs, Tsotsobe had Tamim Iqbal caught behind; Imrul Kayes was bowled shouldering arms and Shahriar Nafees was bowled from an inside edge. Bangladesh were 4-21 after eight overs and a good case had been presented for the introduction of a mercy rule in international cricket contests.

No mercy was forthcoming from the Proteas, who were determined to secure top position in Group B. After Tsotsobe and Botha did the early damage, Peterson continued his impressive bowling form with a four wicket performance. The home side were given a Bronx cheer when they passed 58, which was the inglorious total scored against the West Indies over a fortnight ago. Bangladesh were fired out for a paltry 78 in 28 overs. Captain Shakib Al Hasan batted for an hour and scored nearly half the team's total. Only two of his teammates – the number 8 and 11 batsmen – could muster eight runs.

Time would tell whether the ease of the win would keep the South Africans at their battle-hardened best for the matches of greater significance. Tsotsobe received the nod over Peterson for the man of the match award. For Bangladesh, three crushing defeats and group stage elimination meant that it was back to the drawing board.

SOUTH AFRICA		BANGLADESH	
H. M. Amla b Abdur Razzak	51	Tamim Iqbal c van Wyk b Tsotsobe	5
G. C. Smith (capt) st Mushfiqur Rahim b Mahmudullah	45	Imrul Kayes b Tsotsobe	4
J. H. Kallis c & b Shakib Al Hasan	69	Junaid Siddique lbw b Botha	2
J. P. Duminy c Mushfiqur Rahim b Rubel Hossain	17	Shahriar Nafees b Tsotsobe	5
F. du Plessis c Tamim Iqbal b Rubel Hossain	52	Mushfiqur Rahim (wk) c Smith b Peterson	3
M. N. van Wyk (wk) b Shakib Al Hasan	5	Shakib Al Hasan (capt) c van Wyk b Peterson	30
J. Botha run out	12	Mahmudullah run out	5
R. J. Peterson not out	22	Naeem Islam b Peterson	8
W. D. Parnell b Rubel Hossain	0	Shafiul Islam b Peterson	0
L. L. Tsotsobe not out	4	Abdur Razzak c Peterson b Imran Tahir	0
Extras (lb 3, w 4)	7	Rubel Hossain not out	8
(50 overs)	8-284	Extras (lb 5, w 3)	8
Did not bat: Imran Tahir		(28 overs)	10-78
1/98 2/107 3/141 4/223 5/245 6/249 7/273 8/280		1/14 2/15 3/21 4/21 5/36 6/58 7/61 8/61 9/62 10/78	
Bowling: Shafiul Islam 5-0-44-0; Rubel Hossain 8-0-56-3;		Bowling: Botha 7-1-23-1; Tsotsobe 5-2-14-3; Parnell 4-1-4-0;	
Abdur Razzak 10-1-47-1; Naeem Islam 7-0-42-0;		Peterson 7-3-12-4; Imran Tahir 5-0-20-1	
Mahmudullah 10-0-46-1; Shakib Al Hasan 10-0-46-2			

Umpires: Aleem Dar, D.J. Harper.

Toss: South Africa   Points: South Africa 2, Bangladesh 0.

GROUP A: AUSTRALIA v PAKISTAN
R PREMADASA STADIUM, COLOMBO, SRI LANKA: PAKISTAN WON BY FOUR WICKETS

Finally, at the 35th time of asking, a team was able to find a way to defeat Australia in a World Cup match. It was the Shahid Afridi-led Pakistan side who claimed the almighty Australian scalp, his team easing to victory after a jitter or two by four wickets with nine overs to spare.

Twelve years before at Leeds it was also Pakistan who had inflicted Australia's most recent World Cup defeat. That win in 1999 was set up by brilliant Pakistani batting. This time, with only Ricky Ponting and Abdul Razzaq still in the line-ups, it was their bowlers, led by the worthy fast bowler Umar Gul, who turned the tables on the Australians.

Although the result had no effect on either side's participation in the quarters, Australia's loss in their first completed clash against serious opposition raised questions about their ability to defend their title.

Ricky Ponting won the toss and batted. He said the wicket looked good, but it was never easy to score freely on. Umar Gul bowled Shane Watson on the drive in the fifth over then Brad Haddin and Ponting struggled for proper batting rhythm while putting on 63 in 14 overs.

Mohammad Hafeez choked off the runs with his off-spin and had Ponting caught behind cutting. It was given not out, referred, the batsmen and a few of the Pakistanis had a bit to say to each other, then the video evidence sent the Australian captain on his way.

No other Australian batting pair could get a proper partnership going. Haddin's top score of 42 took 80 balls. Michael Clarke got to 34 then misjudged a pull and Steve Smith batted through with the tail, until chopping Afridi onto his stumps with a miscued back foot drive. In the next over, the 47th, Brett Lee lobbed Umar Gul to cover and Australia had been bowled out for 176. It was their lowest World Cup score since 1992.

Brett Lee had not given up. He bowled fast outswing and took a running sliding caught and bowled as the ball skewed off the front shoulder of Mohammad Hafeez's bat. Six overs later he slid a delivery through Kamran Akmal's defence and, despite a batsman's review, had an lbw appeal upheld.

The other Australian bowlers were less threatening. Asad Shafiq played his second important innings and he added 53 with Younis Khan. But Lee returned and had Younis caught behind off a dabble and Misbah-ul-Haq edging to slip first ball.

At 4-98 the match lay in the balance.

Young, talented, precocious, inconsistent, Umar Akmal, however, came in and played the innings that won the match and himself the Man of the Match Award. In 59 balls he hit four fours and a six.

There was one more tremor as Mitchell Johnson and Jason Krejza took wickets in the 32nd and 33rd overs. But Umar Akaml and the experienced Abdul Razzaq held their nerves, Ponting failed to bring Lee back for his last two overs and Pakistan at the end of the 41st over could celebrate a famous victory.

Australia's loss meant they had to face India in Ahmedabad for their quarter-final.

AUSTRALIA		PAKISTAN	
S. R. Watson b Umar Gul	9	Kamran Akmal (wk) lbw b Lee	23
B. J. Haddin (wk) c Kamran Akmal b Wahab Riaz	42	Mohammad Hafeez c & b Lee	5
R. T. Ponting (capt) c K. Akmal b M. Hafeez	19	Asad Shafiq c Watson b Johnson	46
M. J. Clarke b Abdul Razzaq	34	Younis Khan c Haddin b Lee	31
C. L. White run out	8	Misbah-ul-Haq c Haddin b Lee	0
M. E. K. Hussey c Misbah-ul-Haq b Abdur Rehman	12	Umar Akmal not out	44
S. P. D. Smith b Shahid Afridi	25	Shahid Afridi (capt) c Lee b Krejza	2
M. G. Johnson c Kamran Akmal b Abdul Razzaq	0	Abdul Razzaq not out	20
J. J. Krejza b Umar Gul	7	Extras B2 Lb1 W4	7
B. Lee c Misbah-ul-Haq b Umar Gul	5	(41 overs)	6/178
S. W. Tait not out	0	Did not bat: Abdur Rehman, Umar Gul, Wahab Riaz	
Extras Lb5 W10	15	1/12 2/45 3/98 4/98 5/139 6/142	
(46.4 overs)	176	Bowling: Lee 8-1-28-4; Tait 8-1-37-0; Johnson 9-1-40-1;	
1/12 2/75 3/90 4/117 5/134 6/144 7/147 8/169 9/176		Watson 6-0-26-0; Krejza 10-0-44-1	
10/176			
Bowling: Umar Gul 7.4-1-30-3; Abdur Rehman 10-0-34-1;			
Shahid Afridi 9-0-34-1; Wahab Riaz 6-0-39-1; Mohammad			
Hafeez 10-0-26-1; Abdul Razzaq 4-0-8-2			

Umpires: M.Erasmus A.L. Hill

Toss: Australia   Points: Pakistan 2 Australia 0

SUNDAY 20 MARCH 2011
GROUP A: KENYA v ZIMBABWE
EDEN GARDENS, KOLKATA, INDIA: ZIMBABWE WON BY 161 RUNS

Zimbabwe easily defeated Kenya in a match mainly notable for the retirement 39-year old Kenyan legend, Steve Tikolo. He was made captain for his 134th and final one-day international, but that failed to lift his side who were totally outplayed.

The Zimbabweans were on good terms with themselves anyway as their return to Test cricket had just been announced. The celebrated by topping 300 for the first time in the tournament after Elton Chigumbura won the toss and elected to bat.

That total was built around two century partnerships. The first between Tatenda Taibu and Vusi Sibanda put on 110 in 20 overs for the third wicket after a lacklustre start to the innings.

Sibanda was the more aggressive hitting seven fours and a six off Tikolo over long on before a 'yes/no' call from Taibu left him stranded at the wrong end.

Then, after Taibu went for 53, Craig Ervine and Chigumbura put on 105 for the fifth wicket in 14 overs to ensure Zimbabwe made a total that would be too big for Kenya. Ervine's 66 was scored in just 54 balls and earned him the Man of the Match Award.

Kenya's chase of 308 was a largely featureless affair as they succumbed to the accuracy of the Zimbabwean spinners for 147 in 36 overs. Half of the batsmen were given out lbw. One was Steve Tikolo whose departure from the crease was emotional and acknowledged by both sides.

Nehemiah Odhiambo hit five fours late in the innings to reduce the losing margin on way to an unbeaten 44.

The game mildly entertained the crowd of, it was officially announced, 25,000. One wondered if at Eden Gardens some official had run around the turnstiles shouting 'close the gates!' when the numbers inside exactly reached that round number.

They may well have done as at most games in the 2011 World Cup the attendance figure given often was an exact even number of thousands.

ZIMBABWE			KENYA		
B. R.M. Taylor c Ngoche b Otieno		26	A. A. Obanda lbw b Price		23
R. W. Chakabva c D. Obuya b Odhiambo		9	D. O. Obuya (wk) lbw b Mpofu		0
T. Taibu (wk) lbw b Ngoche		53	C. O. Obuya run out		1
V. Sibanda run out		61	S. O. Tikolo (capt) lbw b Price		10
C. R. Ervine b Otieno		66	T. Mishra c Cremer b Utseya		4
E. Chigumbura (capt) c Mishra b Ongondo		38	T. M. Odoyo lbw b Lamb		14
G. A. Lamb not out		17	R. R. Patel c Chakabva b Lamb		24
P. Utseya not out		19	N. N. Odhiambo not out		44
Extras B2 Lb3 W14		19	P. J. Ongondo lbw b Cremer		6
(50 overs)		6/308	E. Otieno run out		5
Did not bat: A. G. Cremer, R. W. Price, C. B. Mpofu			J. O. Ngoche c Mpofu b Cremer		9
1/32 2/36 3/146 4/165 5/270 6/276			Extras Lb4 W3		7
Bowling: Ongondo 10-0-53-1; Otieno 10-0-61-2;			(36 overs)		147
Odhiambo 10-1-58-1; Ngoche 10-0-68-1; C. Obuya 3-0-14-0;			1/3 2/10 3/27 4/44 5/44 6/73 7/95 8/101 9/124 10/147		
Tikolo 7-0-49-0			Bowling: Mpofu 6-0-27-1; Price 7-1-20-2; Utseya 9-0-47-1;		
			Lamb 7-0-21-2; Cremer 7-0-28-2		

Umpires: E.A.R. Silva H.D.P.K. Dharmasena

Toss: Zimbabwe   Points: Zimbabwe 2 Kenya 0

GROUP B: INDIA vs WEST INDIES
MA CHIDAMBARAM STADIUM, CHENNAI, INDIA (DAY/NIGHT): INDIA WON BY 80 RUNS

The combatants of the 1983 World Cup final squared off in the final group game in the draining heat of Chennai. Although both teams had booked themselves into the quarter-finals, the winner of the match would take second place in the group and face Australia in a quarter-final. If India won, the West Indies would remain in fourth place and would do battle with Pakistan in the next phase of the competition. Before the game started, the West Indies had every right to think that their opponents had been given an unfair advantage. The West Indies played their last game three days before, whereas India had an eight-day break leading into this clash.

As bowling and fielding in the afternoon heat would be exhausting, MS Dhoni wisely chose to bat when he won the toss. Ravi Rampaul, who was brought in for his first match of the tournament as a result of Roach feeling unwell, started off with a high bouncer that evaded Thomas and raced to the boundary for five wides. Rampaul engineered a sensational dismissal with the last ball of the first over. Rampaul bowled a delivery to Tendulkar that was just short of a length outside off stump. The Indian maestro probed at the delivery and umpire Steve Davis handed down his not out verdict to the appeal for a catch behind. Tendulkar walked, prompting great jubilation from Rampaul.

India set their innings up with an enterprising partnership between Kohli and Yuvraj Singh of 122 in 23.5 overs. Yuvraj Singh, who made productive use of the sweep shot, offered catching opportunities on nine and 13 to Sammy. The West Indian skipper missed the two chances.

The let-offs by the captain proved to be very costly to the West Indies in the final analysis. Yuvraj Singh reached his century from 112 balls in the 41st over and another sizeable Indian total was in the offing. It was a fine effort from Yuvraj Singh, who was labouring with a stomach bug. India again stumbled and lost several wickets at little cost. The last seven wickets fell for 50 runs over 45 deliveries. Rampaul bowled well and was handsomely rewarded with the figures of 5-51. A highlight of the West Indian bowling performance was a superb leg-break from Bishoo that deceived Dhoni in the air and enabled Thomas to execute the stumping.

Under lights, Devon Smith and the steady Sarwan batted with calm assurance. The Indian bowling lacked bite and the West Indian top order were 2-154 in the 31st over, leaving less than a run a ball needed for the win. Dhoni recalled Zaheer Khan to the attack for his second spell, which ended up being the turning point of the match. On 81, Smith played a loose shot off Khan and paid the ultimate price. This breakthrough precipitated the second batting collapse of the game. The West Indian decline was starker as eight wickets fell for only 34 runs. A meagre total of 15 runs were contributed by batsmen five to 11 in the order. Khan was again among the wickets and two victims apiece were collected by Yuvraj Singh and off-spinner Ravichandran Ashwin, who made his first World Cup appearance in this match.

In light of the lack of resistance shown by the West Indian batsmen, it was difficult to assess the Indian bowling and whether it would stand up to sustained pressure in the later stages of the tournament. Yuvraj Singh bagged his third man of the match award in the 2011 competition.

INDIA		WEST INDIES	
G. Gambhir c Russell b Rampaul	22	D. S. Smith b Khan	81
S. R. Tendulkar c Thomas b Rampaul	2	K. A. Edwards lbw b Ashwin	17
V. Kohli b Rampaul	59	D. M. Bravo c Harbhajan Singh b Raina	22
Yuvraj Singh c & b Pollard	113	R. R. Sarwan c Ashwin b Khan	39
M. S. Dhoni (capt/wk) st Thomas b Bishoo	22	K. A. Pollard c Pathan b Harbhajan Singh	1
S. K. Raina c Rampaul b Sammy	4	D. C. Thomas (wk) st Dhoni b Yuvraj Singh	2
Y. K. Pathan b Rampaul	11	D. J. G. Sammy (capt) run out	2
Harbhajan Singh c Pollard b Russell	3	A. D. Russell c Pathan b Yuvraj Singh	0
R. Ashwin not out	10	S. J. Benn c Patel b Khan	3
Z. Khan b Rampaul	5	D. Bishoo not out	6
M. M. Patel b Russell	1	R. Rampaul b Ashwin	1
Extras (b 5, lb 2, w 9)	16	Extras (lb 8, w 6)	14
(49.1 overs)	10-268	(43 overs)	10-188

1/8 2/51 3/173 4/218 5/232 6/240 7/251 8/259 9/267 10/268

1/34 2/91 3/154 4/157 5/160 6/162 7/165 8/179 9/182 10/188

Bowling: Rampaul 10-0-51-5; Benn 4-0-32-0; Russell 9.1-1-46-2; Sammy 6-0-35-1; Bishoo 10-0-48-1; Pollard 10-0-49-1

Bowling: Ashwin 10-0-41-2; Khan 6-0-26-3; Harbhajan Singh 9-1-35-1; Pathan 7-0-28-0; Raina 2-0-12-1; Yuvraj Singh 4-0-18-2; Patel 5-0-20-0

Umpires: S.J. Davis, S.J.A Taufel.

Toss: India   Points: India 2, West Indies 0.

At the end of the group stage, the final group tables were as set out below. The top four teams in each group proceeded to the quarter-finals, with the first placed team in Group A playing the fourth placed team in Group B, the second placed team in Group A playing the third placed team in Group B, and so on.

GROUP A							GROUP B						
	P	W	L	T	NR	Points	NR/R		P	W	L	T	NR	Points	NR/R
PAKISTAN	6	5	1	0	0	10	0.75	SOUTH AFRICA	6	5	1	0	0	10	2.02
SRI LANKA	6	4	1	0	1	9	2.58	INDIA	6	4	1	1	0	9	0.90
AUSTRALIA	6	4	1	0	1	9	1.12	ENGLAND	6	3	2	1	0	7	0.07
NEW ZEALAND	6	4	2	0	0	8	1.13	WEST INDIES	6	3	3	0	0	6	1.06
Zimbabwe	6	2	4	0	0	4	0.03	Bangladesh	6	3	3	0	0	6	-1.36
Canada	6	1	5	0	0	2	-1.98	Ireland	6	2	4	0	0	4	-0.69
Kenya	6	0	6	0	0	0	-3.04	Netherlands	6	0	6	0	0	0	-2.04

WEDNESDAY 23 MARCH 2011
1st QUARTER-FINAL: PAKISTAN vs WEST INDIES
SHER-E BANGLA NATIONAL STADIUM, DHAKA, BANGLADESH (DAY/NIGHT)
PAKISTAN WON BY 10 WICKETS

Pakistan, impressive in heading Group A, were too strong for the West Indies, who only beat Bangladesh and the minnows in Group B.

The day started off well for the men from the Caribbean when Smith square cut the first ball of the match from Umar Gul for a boundary. Gayle, back in the side, hammered two boundaries but was soon back in the pavilion when a loose drive to Umar Gul went straight to mid off. Handy off-spinner and Man of the Match Mohammad Hafeez, opening the bowling in a limited-overs international for the first time, struck twice in his third over, winning lbw verdicts with his arm-ball against Smith and Darren Bravo. From a perilous 3-16, Sarwan and Chanderpaul struggled to score, eking out 42 from 111 deliveries. Sarwan hit a square drive from Shahid Afridi to point, leaving the West Indies innings in limbo at 4-58 in the 25th over.

Shahid Afridi and off-spinner Saeed Ajmal wrecked the innings, claiming five wickets inside four overs. The West Indies were in a spin at 8-71 in the 28th over. Chanderpaul, who witnessed the collapse from the non-striker's end, found a willing ally in Roach. The pair stayed together and added 40 runs. Chanderpaul was left stranded on 44 from 106 balls when the last wicket fell at 112 in the 44th over. The Pakistani spinners prospered against the West Indies' array of left-handers, collecting eight wickets at an aggregate cost of 64 in 27.3 overs. Mohammed Hafeez was almost unplayable at times and Shahid Afridi took four wickets for the fourth time in the tournament, a unique feat.

Kamran Akmal and Mohammad Hafeez set about hauling in the 113 runs required. Roach and Rampaul conceded 11 and 14 runs, respectively, from the first two overs. In the third over, Kamran Akmal unleased a savage cut that flew to Pollard at point. The Trinidadian was lucky to not have his hand taken off. Despite some pace being taken off the ball, it rolled to the boundary. Mohammad Hafeez found the boundary regularly, hitting nine fours in reaching 50 from 55 balls. When Kamran Akmal creamed a boundary in front of point from Roach in the 21st over, Pakistan finished off a devastating performance without losing a wicket.

The win was just the second occasion in World Cup history that a non-group stage match had been decided by 10 wickets. Australia were the first to achieve this feat with their victory over Bangladesh in the Super Eights in 2007. Surprisingly, Shahid Afridi did not win the man of the match award. That honour befell Mohammad Hafeez.

WEST INDIES		PAKISTAN	
D. S. Smith lbw b Mohammad Hafeez	7	Kamran Akmal (wk) not out	47
C. H. Gayle c Shahid Afridi b Umar Gul	8	Mohammad Hafeez not out	61
R. R. Sarwan c Umar Akmal b Shahid Afridi	24	Extras (lb 4, w 1)	5
D. M. Bravo lbw b Mohammad Hafeez	0	(20.5 overs)	0-113
S. Chanderpaul not out	44	Did not bat: Asad Shafiq, Younis Khan, Misbah-ul-Haq,	
K. A. Pollard c Kamran Akmal b Shahid Afridi	1	Umar Akmal, Abdul Razzaq, Shahid Afridi (capt),	
D. C. Thomas (wk) lbw b Shahid Afridi	0	Wahab Riaz, Umar Gul, Saeed Ajmal	
D. J. G. Sammy (capt) lbw b Saeed Ajmal	1	Bowling: Roach 5.5-0-39-0; Rampaul 5-1-28-0;	
D. Bishoo b Saeed Ajmal	0	Bishoo 5-1-24-0; Sammy 5-1-18-0	
K. A. J. Roach c Younis Khan b Abdul Razzaq	16		
R. Rampaul b Shahid Afridi	0		
Extras (lb 2, w 7, nb 2)	11		
(43.3 overs)	10-112		

1/14 2/16 3/16 4/58 5/69 6/69 7/71 8/71 9/111 10/112

Bowling: Umar Gul 7-1-13-1; Mohammad Hafeez 10-3-16-2; Wahab Riaz 6-0-29-0; Shahid Afridi 9.3-1-30-4; Saeed Ajmal 8-1-18-2; Abdul Razzaq 3-1-4-1

Umpires: B.F. Bowden, S.J. Davis.

Toss: West Indies

THURSDAY 24 MARCH 2011
2nd QUARTER-FINAL: INDIA vs AUSTRALIA
SARDAR PATEL STADIUM, MOTERA, AHMEDABAD, INDIA (DAY/NIGHT)
INDIA WON BY FIVE WICKETS

A meeting between heavyweights India and Australia was expected to take place a little later than the quarter-final stage. Both sides looked to be in second gear and were slightly disappointing in the group matches. The 51,000 patrons who rolled in to Motera hoping to see a titanic struggle were not disappointed.

Ponting won the toss and made first use on a hot afternoon. Ashwin opened the bowling and extracted sharp turn and bounce early on. Watson and Haddin were unable to force the pace in the early overs. India struck the first blow after 10 overs when Watson missed a slog sweep off Ashwin and was bowled. By the 16th over, Dhoni had introduced Harbhajan Singh and Yuvraj Singh to the attack to maintain the pressure. In the midst of several low-scoring overs, Australia managed to attack seamer Patel, Haddin belting three boundaries in an over.

Ponting, who had endured a lean run in the World Cup, played himself in while the in-form Haddin kept the score ticking over. Haddin reached his third half-century of the competition and was out shortly after when he mistimed a drive to cover from a slower delivery from Yuvraj Singh. The Haddin-Ponting stand was worth 70 runs from 12.5 overs. From a reasonable position of 2-110 in the 23rd over, the Australian innings lost momentum. Middle-order batsmen Clarke, Mike Hussey and White struggled to get the bowling away and their unproductive innings stalled Australia's progress in the middle stages of the innings. Clarke perished to an unsightly heave off Yuvraj Singh that was caught at mid wicket and Mike Hussey became another victim of Zaheer Khan's slower ball.

Despite the struggles of his colleagues, Ponting passed 50 and managed to score at a good rate, including a powerful six over extra cover off Yuvraj Singh. With the Australians looking hard-pressed to score 240, David Hussey gave the innings a much needed boost. The younger Hussey hit Khan for two superbly placed boundaries in an over and he clobbered the tidy Ashwin for six over long on. Ponting continued on his determined way and a single to leg in the 47th over brought up his century from 113 balls. It was Ponting's fifth World Cup hundred and his 30th in limited-overs internationals. Sadly for Australia's all-time leading scorer in Tests and one-day matches, the century was Ponting's first at international level for over a year. Ponting's last international hundred was in a limited-overs match against the West Indies at Brisbane in February 2010.

Ponting's defiant innings ended in the penultimate over when he reverse-swept Ashwin to third man. David Hussey and Johnson took 13 from the last over from Harbhajan Singh, taking Australia to a good score of 6-260. India's bowling and fielding had improved markedly from the lacklustre performances in the group matches. Yuvraj Singh continued his excellent form with bat and ball, taking 2-44 from his ten overs.

The Australian opening bowlers were in sharp contrast. Lee began bowling accurately and with some movement away from the right-handers. On the other hand, Tait bowled waywardly at top pace, mixing wides with deliveries that beat the bat. The South Australian paceman, who made himself available for selection in the shorter formats of the game only, was spelled after two overs that cost 17 runs. Watson engineered the first wicket, inducing a cramped pull shot by Sehwag that ballooned to square leg.

Tendulkar batted well and gradually increased his frequency of boundaries as he approached 50. India managed to score at around five an over, despite some accurate overs from Lee and Johnson. Tendulkar had a life in the 16th over when he hit an airy late cut off Lee towards third man. The ball landed just short of Krejza, who seemed to have it covered but slowed as he neared the ball, possibly due to the glare of the light towers. Tendulkar's joy at reaching his 94th half-century in limited-overs games was short-lived as he nicked one from Tait in the 19th over.

India's progress was slowed in the middle stages, courtesy of several accurate overs from spinners Krejza, Clarke and David Hussey. Kohli threw away his innings after making a start, hitting a David Hussey full toss straight to mid wicket. Gambhir reached his fifty and a few balls later he narrowly avoided being run out when Ponting's throw from mid wicket missed. In the next over, Gambhir ran himself out when he charged from the non-striker's end attempting a single that was never on. The game was evenly poised with India 4-168 in the 34th over, requiring a further 93 runs to win.

A few overs later, the odds shifted to Australia's favour when Clarke at point held onto a sizzling cut from Dhoni. The home side were under pressure at 5-187 in the 38th over with only Raina and the tail to come. India counter-attacked and soon pushed the asking rate to less than a run a ball. In the 40th over, three boundaries were taken from Lee. Full of confidence,

Yuvraj Singh managed to guide an excellent Lee yorker to third man for four and, two balls later, he hit an imperious front foot drive to the cover point boundary from a ball that was just short of a length. Australian nerves frayed in the next over as Tait bowled a wide that Haddin was unable to stop and two errant throws allowed the batsmen to scamper through for an additional two runs. India now looked the better side, needing 41 runs from the last nine overs.

In the 43rd over, Yuvraj Singh hit a pull shot off Watson that raced towards the fine leg boundary. Lee valiantly attempted to cut the ball off and, during his desperate dive, the ball collected him above the eye and opened up a nasty cut. Yuvraj Singh and Raina kept the score ticking over during the next few overs, which included Yuvraj Singh reaching 50 for the fifth time in the tournament. After receiving running repairs, Lee was back on in the 46th over as Ponting strove to break this partnership and to expose the tail. Raina dented Australian hopes when he hoisted the first delivery of Lee's spell over the long on fence. Raina successfully negotiated a Johnson bouncer in the next over, glancing the ball to the fine leg boundary. India whittled the required runs down to four from the last three overs. Yuvraj Singh played the first three balls for dot balls before thrashing the fourth through the covers for the boundary that saw India home with 14 balls to spare.

India's victory booked them a semi-final clash against arch-rivals Pakistan. Yuvraj Singh collected his fourth man of the match award from the last five matches. For the Australian camp, they would be onlookers for the Final on 2 April 2011 for the first time since 1992. Indeed, the last time the Aussies were forced to fly home early from a World Cup was after their ill-fated 1983 campaign. In the fall-out of their early exit, Ponting resigned his captaincy of both the Test and one-day sides, handing over the reigns in both formats to Clarke.

AUSTRALIA		INDIA	
S. R. Watson b Ashwin	25	V. Sehwag c M. Hussey b Watson	15
B. J. Haddin (wk) c Raina b Yuvraj Singh	53	S. R. Tendulkar c Haddin b Tait	53
R. T. Ponting (capt) c Khan b Ashwin	104	G. Gambhir run out	50
M. J. Clarke c Khan b Yuvraj Singh	8	V. Kohli c Clarke b D. Hussey	24
M. E. K. Hussey b Khan	3	Yuvraj Singh not out	57
C. L. White c & b Khan	12	M. S. Dhoni (capt/wk) c Clarke b Lee	7
D. J. Hussey not out	38	S. K. Raina not out	34
M. G. Johnson not out	6	Extras (lb 3, w 16, nb 2)	21
Extras (lb 2, w 9)	11	(47.4 overs)	5-261
(50 overs)	6-260	Did not bat: Harbhajan Singh, R. Ashwin, Z. Khan,	
Did not bat: J. J. Krejza, B. Lee, S. W. Tait		M. M. Patel	
1/40 2/110 3/140 4/150 5/190 6/245		1/44 2/94 3/243 4/168 5/187	
Bowling: Ashwin 10-0-52-2; Khan 10-0-53-2; Harbhajan		Bowling: Lee 8.4-1-45-1; Johnson 8-0-41-0;	
Singh 10-0-50-0; Patel 7-0-44-0; Yuvraj Singh 10-0-44-2;		Watson 7-0-37-1; Krejza 9-0-45-0; Clarke 3-0-19-0; D.	
Tendulkar 2-0-9-0; Kohli 1-0-6-0		Hussey 5-0-19-1	

Umpires: M. Erasmus, I.J. Gould.
Toss: Australia

FRIDAY 25 MARCH 2011
3rd QUARTER FINAL: NEW ZEALAND v SOUTH AFRICA
SHERE BANGLA NATIONAL STADIUM, MIRPUR, BANGLADESH: NEW ZEALAND WON BY 49 RUNS

After finishing top of Group B and with as good a chance as at anytime in their history to win their first World Cup, South Africa crumbled at the first time of asking in an elimination match in the 2011 tournament, being comprehensively outplayed by a supposedly out-of-form New Zealand side.

There was nothing to suggest the confident, talented and well-drilled South Africans would not go through to the semi-finals. Except for their tendency on big cricketing occasions to not, according to their captain 'choke', but to do something that really closely resembles 'choking'. Perhaps Robert Houwing's, 'knockout-phase monkey' was a more apt description of their repeated underperformance in pressure matches. New Zealand's famous victory was completed after protecting a merely adequate total of 221. Their batting hero was hefty left-hander Jesse Ryder. Daniel Vettori, back in the side after injury, won the toss and batted. After six overs his side were in trouble at 2/16. Brendan McCullum was brilliantly caught and bowled from a miscued drive by Robin Peterson and Martin Guptill went nowhere for 24 balls before mistiming a lofted drive from a Dale Steyn slower ball.

Ryder responded with sound technique and a series of clumping drives and cuts through point and cover off both pace and spin. His stand of 114 in 27 overs with Ross Taylor provided the most substantial run making in what turned into a bowlers match. Even the normally fluent Taylor only managed one four and a six in 72 balls before holing out at deep square-leg off Imran Tahir's leg-spin.

Ryder was fifth out at 156 for a match high 83 from 121 balls in the 39th over, also caught from a mistimed hit off Imran Tahir. The Black Caps' innings never properly gained any momentum in its later stages but young Kane Williamson's almost run per ball unbeaten 38, including one sweet six off Peterson over long on, ensured the New Zealand innings lasted the full 50 over distance.

Daniel Vettori, as had Graeme Smith earlier, opened the bowling with a spinner. He used Nathan McCullum's off-spin, instead of himself and was rewarded immediately when Hashim Amla chopped the last ball of the first over onto Brendan McCullum's foot and thence on to Vettori at slip.

For the next 20 overs, though, the South Africans appeared to be moving surely towards their target of 222. Smith and Jacques Kallis had added 61 for the second wicket in 13 overs. Then the South African captain had sliced a wide Jacob Oram delivery to backward point, Kallis and A.B. De Villiers had carried the score to 2/108 with 26 overs remaining. From the first ball of the 25th over Kallis belted a short Tim Southee delivery to deep mid wicket. Oram sprinted to his left, leapt and pulled in a wonderful outfield catch. It turned the mood of the game. J.P. Duminy totally mistimed a cut off Nathan McCullum. On the same score De Villiers was run out after an ambitious call to mid wicket by Faf Du Plessis.

Between the 28th and 34 overs South Africa went from 3/121 to 7/132, once more shattering their World Cup hopes in an inexplicable show of batting ineptitude. Du Plessis briefly rallied the cause before he was ninth out at 172, becoming Man of the Match Oram's fourth victim when he under hit a lofted drive to Southee at cover point. Three balls later Morne Morkel lifted a deliver from Luke Woodcock to substitute Jamie How at long off. New Zealand was ecstatic, South Africa equally distraught.

NEW ZEALAND		SOUTH AFRICA	
M. J. Guptill c Botha b Steyn	1	H. M. Amla c Vettori b N. McCullum	7
B. B. McCullum (wk) c & b Peterson	4	G. C. Smith (capt) c sub (How) b Oram	28
J. D. Ryder c sub (Ingram) b Imran Tahir	83	J. H. Kallis c Oram b Southee	47
L. R. P. L. Taylor c Kaillis b Imran Tahir	43	A. B. de Villiers (wk) run out	35
S. B. Styris b Morkel	16	J. P. Duminy b N. McCullum	3
K. S. Williamson not out	38	F. du Plessis c Southee b Oram	36
N. L. McCullum c Duminy b Steyn	6	J. Botha b Oram	2
J. D. P. Oram b Morkel	7	R. J. Peterson c B. McCullum b Oram	0
D. L. Vettori (capt) b Morkel	6	D. W. Steyn c Oram b N. McCullum	8
L. J. Woodcock not out	3	M. Morkel c sub (How) b Woodcock	3
Extras B4 Lb4 W6	14	Imran Tahir not out	0
(50 overs)	8/221	Extras Lb2 W1	3
Did not bat: T. G.Southee		(43.2 overs)	172
1/5 2/16 3/130 4/153 5/156 6/188 7/204 8/210		1/8 2/69 3/108 4/121 5/121 6/128 7/132 8/146 9/172	
Bowling: Peterson 9-0-49-1; Steyn 10-0-42-2;		10/172	
Botha 9-0-29-0; Morkel 8-0-46-3; Imran Tahir 9-0-32-2;		Bowling: McCullum 10-1-24-3: Vettori 10-0-39-0;	
Kallis 3-1-6-0; Duminy 2-0-9-0		Southee 9-0-44-1; Oram 9-1-39-4; Woodcock 5.2-0-24-1	

Umpires: Aleem Dar, R.J. Tucker.

Toss: New Zealand

SATURDAY 26 MARCH 2011
4th QUARTER FINAL: SRI LANKA vs ENGLAND
R PREMADASA STADIUM, COLOMBO, SRI LANKA: SRI LANKA WON BY 10 WICKETS

An unduly regimented and mentally fatigued England was no match for a jubilant aggressive Sri Lanka. Recalling the joke about the two Welshman in the fog being the equal of a whole English army, Sri Lanka only needed their two opening batsmen to trounce England by 10 wickets, after Andrew Strauss's side had battled their way to 229.

It was eight more runs than New Zealand's match-winning total the previous night in Mirpur, but Upal Tharanga and Tillakaratne Dilshan overtook it without being separated with 63 balls to spare.

The 100th ever ODI at R Premadasa Stadium was England's first World Cup elimination match since 1996. But, after all their thrilling encounters in the Group stage, their inspiration evaporated as Tharanga and Dilshan rode some early luck to each compile unbeaten centuries. Dilshan's bowling contribution eased him ahead in the Man of the Match race with his opening partner.

Andrew Strauss won the toss and batted, then was first out when, after a scratchy 30 balls, he missed a pull shot off a skidding off-break from Dilshan in the eighth over.

Jonathon Trott joined Ian Bell and saw it as his role to occupy the crease through the innings to ensure his side batted 50 overs. Two runs later he lost his Warwickshire teammate, Bell who chipped a straightforward catch to mid wicket off Angelo Mathews.

Trott and Bopara dug in to add 64 for the third wicket in 18 overs then when the man from Essex was lbw sweeping at Muttiah Muralitharan, Trott and Eoin Morgan put on a further 91 in 16 overs.

England was 3/186 in the 43rd over and Morgan, benefitting from three chances, had registered his 50 at close to a run per ball.

With eight overs to go England had taken their batting Powerplay, but their plans went askew as they tried to accelerate past 250. Morgan lifted Lasith Malinga to cover and next over Graeme Swann tried to reverse sweep his first ball and was lbw to Ajantha Mendis.

Matt Prior hit a couple of boundaries, but Trott was so locked into his role he hit only two fours in 115 balls before sweeping Muralitharan to Mahela Jayawardene at deep backward leg to be out for 86.

England had to be satisfied with 229.

They thought they were in with a chance on a ground noted for the difficulty of chasing a decent target under lights. And their early indicators were good. Tim Bresnan and Chris Tremlett moved the new-ball and passed the edge of the Sri Lankan opening batting pair on a number of occasions.

But both Tharanga and Dilshan were prepared to take the occasional risk while backing themselves to play their shots. Dilshan was soon striking any ball with width to the boundary either side of point off both front and back foot.

Swann caused some trouble and turned the ball, but in the fourth over Tharanga danced down the wicket and hit him back over his head for six. In the ninth over Dilshan crunched Tremlett to the point boundary to raise the fifty.

For a couple of overs the run rate would drop then a boundary would ease the pressure. By the nineteenth over the total had reached 100. The total continued to click along at five runs per over as the pair went neck and neck, playing shots with discretion. In the thirtieth over, on cue, the 150 milestone was passed.

Then James Tredwell was clubbed for 14 from the 31st over and the end was on the horizon.

Both batsmen reached 80 at the same time but Dilshan then moved ahead reaching his hundred with a trademark cut off Swann for four. Three overs later, with Dilshan trying to assist his partner by maneuvering the strike, Tharanga raised his century and scored the winning runs by clouting Tremlett through the covers for four.

ENGLAND		SRI LANKA	
A. J. Strauss (capt) b Dilshan	5	W. U. Tharanga not out	102
I. R. Bell c Samaraweera b Mathews	25	T. M. Dilshan not out	108
I. J. L. Trott c Jayawardene b Muralitharan	86	Extras B9 Lb6 W6	21
R. S. Bopara lbw b Muralitharan	31	(39.3 overs)	0/221
E. J. G. Morgan c Mathews b Malinga	50	Did not bat: K. C. Sangakkara (capt/wk),	
G. P. Swann lbw b Mendis	0	D. P. M. D. Jayawardene, T. T. Samaraweera, L. P.C. Sliva,	
M. J. Prior (wk) not out	22	A. D. Mathews, S. L. Malinga, H. M. R. K.B. Herath,	
L. J. Wright not out	1	B. A. W. Mendis, M. Muralitharan	
Extras Lb3 W6	9	Bowling: Bresnan 8-1-40-0; Swann 9-0-61-0; Tremlett	
(50 overs)	6/229	7.3-0-38-0; Bopara 5-1-22-0; Tredwell 6-0-38-0;	
Did not bat: T. T. Bresnan, J. C. Tredwell, C. T. Tremlett		Wright 4-0-17-0	
1/29 2/31 3/95 4/186 5/186 6/212			
Bowling: Malinga 10-0-46-1; Dilshan 6-1-25-1;			
Mathews 5-0-20-1; Herath 10-1-47-0; Mendis 10-0-34-1,			
Muralitharan 9-0-54-2			

Umpires: B.R. Doctrove S.J.A. Taufel

Toss: England

TUESDAY 29 MARCH 2011
1st SEMI-FINAL-SRI LANKA vs NEW ZEALAND
R PREMADASA STADIUM, COLOMBO, SRI LANKA
SRI LANKA WON BY FIVE WICKETS

Sri Lanka survived a late tremble to march into their second consecutive World Cup Final at the expense of New Zealand.

In front of their adoring fans the Sri Lankans eased home by five wickets with 13 balls to spare leaving the Black Caps to ponder their sixth loss in as many World Cup semi-finals.

Daniel Vettori won the toss and batted on the same pitch that had been used for the Sri Lanka-England quarter-final. The New Zealand captain indicated his surprise at the re-use of the same wicket before the match. A key indicator to the flavour of the game was that the home side used four spinners during the New Zealand innings while the Kiwis only had Nathan McCullum and Vettori giving the ball a proper tweak when Sri Lanka batted.

"We felt confident in the quarter-final and semi-final, playing at home," says Sri Lankan batsman Tilan Samaraweera. "We played three quality spinners—Murali, Herath and Mendis—and one fast bowler.

"Both games were at R Premadasa Stadium with long boundaries of about 80-85 yards from the bat. We knew that England and New Zealand would bat slowly until the 40th over and they would try to attack the bowling in the last 10 overs.

"To counter that, our plan was that our spinners and Malinga would bowl in the final ten overs because the long boundaries would be hard to clear against those quality bowlers. Both England and New Zealand could only manage around 220-230."

One of the Sri Lankan spin quartet, Rangana Herath took the new-ball and claimed the first wicket when he bowled Brendan McCullum with the first ball of the eighth over as the wicketkeeper batsman, who had earlier played a similar shot for six, swept across the line of a quicker ball.

New Zealand's hero from the quarter-final, Jesse Ryder, carried the total to 69 with Martin Guptill, but then became Muttiah Muralitharan's first victim in the great man's final spell in his own country, caught behind from a big spinning off-break.

Guptill played some nice drives to the onside of straight. However he was another Kiwi to get in and then get out, perfectly yorked on 39 by Lasith Malinga.

All the New Zealand batsmen battled to score freely against the Sri Lankan spinners. Ross Taylor and Scott Styris had the biggest partnership of the innings, but took 18 overs to increase the total by 77.

Kane Williamson eventually provided some brief acceleration and at 4/192 in the 44th New Zealand could still have set up challenging target.

In the final six and half overs, though, they crumbled badly losing 6/25. Malinga got another straight yorker through, this onto the pads of Williamson. Then he messed with Nathan McCullum's timing and had him caught behind with a well disguised slower ball.

The biggest blow was delivered by Muralitharan 11 balls and nine runs later when Styris after a worthy 57 from 77 balls misjudged an off-break on the back foot and was lbw It was Muralitharan's final ball in an international cricket match in Sri Lanka.

The DRS gave Styris no reprieve and his three remaining lower order teammates were removed in eleven balls for four runs by the spin of Ajantha Mendis and Tillakaratne Dilshan.

New Zealand's 217 was only four runs short of the 221 that had been more than adequate against South Africa in the quarter final. But the feeling soon developed here that such a total was well short of the competitive requirements of this game.

Upal Tharanga made a strong statement in favour of that theory when he danced down the wicket and sweetly drove the third ball of the innings from Nathan McCullum back over the off-spinner's head for six. Then three wides and two exquisite drives for four by Tharanga off front and back foot had the crowd roaring and the total on 18 after two overs.

The left-handed opener continued in the same aggressive vein, hitting two more fours before after a run per ball 30 he thrashed the previously expensive Tim Southee to point where Ryder, perhaps the biggest man in the tournament, took a brilliant diving catch to his left.

It was the catch if the match, but did not appear to have any effect on the game's destiny as Dilshan and Kumar Sangakkara established a big partnership.

Their stand amounted to 120 for the second wicket in 25 overs. Boundaries were scored at opportune times. In the 24th over Dilshan planted a short delivery from Jacob Oram into the crowd at midwicket for six. Three overs later Sangakkara, eventually named Man of the Match, used his feet and lifted Nathan McCullum for six on the straight drive.

That came straight after Dilshan had raised his fifty from 71 balls with an upper edged cut for four. Then, in the 33rd over, with 58 runs required from 105 balls and nine wickets in hand, Dilshan sliced Southee to Ryder at point.

That dismissal hardly changed the mood of the game, but when Mahela Jayawardene was given out lbw to Vettori three balls later the noise level in the crowd subsided noticeably.

Seven runs later when Sangakkara guided a short delivery from left-armer, Andy McKay to Styris at third man the silence of the 32,000 was deafening. The Sri Lankan batsmen had lost three wickets for a paltry nine runs and the home side still needed 49 runs to win.

"We were travelling well at 1-160 chasing 218," Samaraweera says. "I came in at 3-161 and it was the highest pressure situation I have had to bat in.

"We lost three quick wickets and we were worried because our batting line up included four players – Malinga and our spinners Herath, Mendis and Muralitharan – who could not bat very well.

"Myself, Angelo Mathews and Chamara Silva managed to get through that difficult period and we lost only one more wicket. Hitting the winning runs in the semi-final was certainly the highlight of my career."

Initially Samaraweera and Chamara Silva added to the tension by scoring only nine runs in six overs. After a message from the dressing room, Silva struck Ryder for consecutive boundaries to point and third man. He was bowled soon after cutting at Southee, but the run making momentum had been restored.

Samaraweera whacked Ryder over mid wicket for four, then next over scored another four with a flick for three to square-leg with a bonus overthrow. In the 46th over the inexperienced McKay sprayed the ball down the leg-side for five wides. New Zealand's brave fight back was over.

Angelo Mathews, who was carrying an injury that would keep him out for the final, hit a four and a six off Southee's next over. Then a cultured edge for four from Samaraweera completed the five wicket win from the second last ball of the 48th over.

The ecstatic crowd celebrated the win. They cheered their team and the smiling spinner who said goodbye as he led a lap of honour around the R Premadasa Stadium.

NEW ZEALAND		SRI LANKA	
M. J. Guptill b Malinga	39	W. U. Tharanga c Ryder b Southee	30
B. B. McCullum (wk) b Herath	13	T. M. Dilshan c Ryder b Southee	73
J. D. Ryder c Sangakkara b Muralitharan	19	K. C. Sangakkara (capt/wk) c Styris b M. Kay	64
L. R. P. L. Taylor c Tharanga b Mendis	36	D. P. M. D. Jayawardene lbw b Vettori	1
S. B. Styris lbw b Muralitharan	57	T. T. Samaraweera not out	23
K. S. Williamson lbw b Malinga	22	L. P. C. Silva b Southee	13
N. L. McCullum c Sangakkara b Malinga	9	A. D. Mathews not out	14
J. D. P. Oram c Jayawardene b Dilshan	7	Extras Lb2 W10	12
D. L. Vettori (capt) not out	3	(47.5 overs)	5/220
T. G. Southee c Sangakkara b Mendis	0	Did not bat: S. L. Malinga, H. M. R. K.B. Herath,	
A. J. M. Kay b Mendis	0	B. A. W. Mendis, M. Muralitharan	
Extras Lb5 W6 Nb1	12	1/40 2/160 3/161 4/169 5/185	
(48.5 overs)	217	Bowling: N. McCullum 6-0-33-0; Southee 10-2-57-3;	
1/32 2/69 3/84 4/161 5/192 6/204 7/213 8/215 9/217		Vettori 10-0-36-1; Oram 8-1-29-0; M. Kay 9.5-1-37-1;	
10/217		Styris 2-0-12-0; Ryder 2-0-14-0	
Bowling: Malinga 9-0-55-3; Herath 9-1-31-1;			
Mathews 6-0-27-0; Mendis 9.5-0-35-3;			
Muralitharan 10-1-42-2; Dilshan 5-0-22-1			

Umpires: Aleem Dar S.J.Davis
Toss: New Zealand

WEDNESDAY, 30 MARCH 2011
2nd SEMI-FINAL: INDIA vs PAKISTAN
PUNJAB CRICKET ASSOCIATION STADIUM, MOHALI, CHANDIGARH, INDIA (DAY/NIGHT)
INDIA WON BY 29 RUNS

Millions of viewers and the 35,000 patrons who crammed into the Punjab Cricket Association Stadium were enthralled by the match that stopped a subcontinent. The contest between cricket's fiercest rivals produced an atmosphere and intensity worthy of a World Cup final.

India, brimming with confidence after disposing of Australia, set their sights on improving their World Cup record against Pakistan to five wins from five starts. With Harbhajan Singh in indifferent form, Ashwin could consider himself unlucky to be omitted as the Indian selectors increased the emphasis on seam bowling. Left-armer Nehra came back into the side to replace Ashwin. Pakistan made no change from the side that thumped the West Indies in the quarter-final.

Dhoni won a vital toss and elected to bat. Once again, Sehwag smacked the first ball of the match for four. Sehwag took Umar Gul to the cleaners in the third over, walloping five boundaries. Despite the mauling Umar Gul received, Afridi kept him in the attack, which led to Sehwag continuing to punish a mixture of half-volleys and short and wide deliveries. Left-armer Wahab Riaz bowled first change, relieving Abdul Razzaq, and his fifth delivery landed the scalp of Sehwag. Wahab Riaz's delivery pitched on leg stump and skidded through, wrapping Sehwag on the pads. Simon Taufel ruled that Sehwag was lbw and, following a review to DRS, it was confirmed that the ball had pitched on leg stump and would have collected middle stump.

India had made a fast start, reaching 1-48 in the sixth over when Gambhir joined Tendulkar. After Umar Gul's first spell cost 41 runs in just four overs, Afridi turned to his spinners to put the batsmen under greater pressure. Saeed Ajmal was able to achieve considerable assistance from the pitch, which brought the decision to drop Ashwin into question. The Mohali crowded were stunned into silence in the 11th over when umpire Ian Gould upheld Saeed Ajmal's lbw appeal against Tendulkar. The technology saved Tendulkar, a critic of DRS, as replays showed that the ball would have narrowly missed leg stump. Perhaps unnerved by his narrow escape, Tendulkar had a close shave from Saeed Ajmal's next delivery, a doosra that beat the outside edge of Tendulkar's forward lunge. Kamran Akmal smartly removed the bails but Tendulkar had moved his back foot to safety a split-second earlier.

Over the next 25 overs, Pakistan made life difficult for themselves as Tendulkar was dropped four times when on 27, 45, 70 and 81. Shahid Afridi was deprived of the opportunity to add to his collection of 21 wickets in the tournament as he was the unlucky bowler on three of these occasions. Despite Tendulkar's good fortune, the Indian innings was looking vulnerable at 4-141 in the 26th over. Gambhir was beaten in flight by Mohammad Hafeez and was stumped and Kohli, in two minds about playing Wahab Riaz to leg, deflected the ball to backward point. Wahab Riaz was on a hat-trick when he knocked back Yuvraj Singh's off stump with a superb inswinger.

Tendulkar and Dhoni found it difficult to increase the scoring rate against some disciplined bowling from Pakistan's three-pronged spin attack. With his 100th international level hundred in sight, Tendulkar hit a low drive from Saaed Ajmal and Shahid Afridi took an impressive catch at extra cover. India's progress had slowed and their score of 5-200 after 40 overs seemed a fraction short. In his second spell, Wahab Riaz bowled well in the cauldron of the final 10 overs, trapping Dhoni in front and getting Zaheer Khan to edge one to Kamran Akmal. For the second match running, Raina kept a cool head and gathered an unbeaten 36 from 39 balls. His late contribution helped India to boost their total a little to a competitive 9-260. Wahab Riaz enjoyed his finest day in international cricket, collecting a five wicket haul and kissing the pitch on achieving this feat.

Kamran Akmal and Mohammad Hafeez scored at a reasonable rate without getting on top of the bowling. Khan claimed another wicket with his slower ball as Kamran Akmal mistimed a square drive to point in the ninth over. Pakistan progressed to 1-70 in the 16th over and a lapse in concentration resulted in Mohammad Hafeez throwing his wicket away after a useful start. Inexplicably, Mohammad Hafeez attempted a paddle sweep shot against the fast-medium bowling of Munaf Patel and only succeeded in producing an edge to Dhoni.

Yuvraj Singh's happy knack of picking up wickets continued. He bowled Asad Shafiq, who missed a cut shot from a full-length ball, and he lured Younis Khan with a slower delivery into playing an airy drive to cover. The double strike left Pakistan under duress at 4-106 in the 26th over. With the game in danger of slipping away, Umar Akmal counter-attacked, belting a Yuvraj Singh delivery over the deep mid wicket boundary and lifting another over the sightscreen. Although Misbah-ul-Haq looked out of sorts, Umar Akmal's assault on the bowling gave Pakistan hope. At the drinks break, a lot of work still had to be done. Pakistan needed 119 runs from the last 17 overs with six wickets in hand.

Umar Akmal's salvo was cut short when he missed an arm ball from Harbhajan Singh that beat him for pace. Three overs later, all-rounder Abdul Razzaq played down the wrong line to a Patel slower ball and was bowled, the ball clipping the top of off stump. At 6-150 in the 37th over, Pakistan needed something special from their fast-scoring captain. Unfortunately, he added only 19 runs from 17 balls and became Harbhajan Singh's second victim. The combative off-spinner sent down a knee-high full toss that was top-edged to Sehwag at cover. In light of the poor quality of the delivery, Harbhajan Singh's prolonged roar and raised arms celebration looked particularly foolish.

It now all seemed too much for Pakistan, who needed 77 runs from the last eight overs. Within three deliveries, Nehra had Wahab Riaz caught and trapped Umar Gul plumb in front. After a tardy start, Misbah-ul-Haq played some eye-catching shots, including a stylish clip off his pads to send a Khan half-volley to the square leg boundary. Fifty-one runs were needed from three overs and Misbah-ul-Haq kept Pakistan's faint hopes flickering with two boundaries off Khan in the 48th over. Pakistan needed 37 runs from the last two overs, but India were never going to let this one slip. Hitting his form after the horse had bolted, Misbah-ul-Haq hoisted Patel down the ground for six to bring up his 50 from 68 balls. In the last over, Misbah-ul-Haq was unable to score from Khan's first four deliveries. On the fifth ball, he skied a catch to long on to end the game. In the end, Pakistan's specialist batsmen failed to deliver. Four of their top six batsmen made starts without going on to a substantial score and the highest partnership of the innings was the opening stand of 44. In an unusual occurrence, each of the Indian bowlers collected two wickets. The two bowlers perceived to be capable of leaking runs, Nehra and Patel, were the most economical, conceding only 73 runs between them from 20 overs.

Pakistan never seriously threatened in their run chase and India ended up winning the game comfortably. India were through to their second World Cup final in three tournaments. The eagerly anticipated, first all-Asian World Cup final on Saturday was only three days away.

Tendulkar broke Yuvraj Singh's hegemony over the man of the match award.

INDIA		PAKISTAN	
V. Sehwag lbw b Wahab Riaz	38	Kamran Akmal (wk) c Yuvraj Singh b Khan	19
S. R. Tendulkar c Shahid Afridi b Saeed Ajmal	85	Mohammad Hafeez c Dhoni b Patel	43
G. Gambhir st Kamran Akmal b Mohammad Hafeez	27	Asad Shafiq b Yuvraj Singh	30
V. Kohli c Umar Akmal b Wahab Riaz	9	Younis Khan c Raina b Yuvraj Singh	13
Yuvraj Singh b Wahab Riaz	0	Misbah-ul-Haq c Kohli b Khan	56
M. S. Dhoni (capt/wk) lbw b Wahab Riaz	25	Umar Akmal b Harbhajan Singh	29
S. K. Raina not out	36	Abdul Razzaq b Patel	3
Harbhajan Singh st Kamran Akmal b Saeed Ajmal	12	Shahid Afridi (capt) c Sehwag b Harbhajan Singh	19
Z. Khan c Kamran Akmal b Wahab Riaz	9	Wahab Riaz c Tendulkar b Nehra	8
A. Nehra run out	1	Umar Gul lbw b Nehra	2
M. M. Patel not out	0	Saeed Ajmal not out	1
Extras (lb 8, w 8, nb 2)	18	Extras (w 8)	8
(50 overs)	9-260	(49.5 overs)	10-231
1/48 2/116 3/141 4/141 5/187 6/205 7/236 8/256 9/258		1/44 2/70 3/103 4/106 5/142 6/150 7/184 8/199 9/208	
Bowling: Umar Gul 8-0-69-0; Abdul Razzaq 2-0-14-0;		10/231	
Wahab Riaz 10-0-46-5; Saeed Ajmal 10-0-44-2; Shahid		Bowling: Khan 9.5-0-58-2; Nehra 10-0-33-2; Patel 10-1-40-2;	
Afridi 10-0-45-0; Mohammad Hafeez 10-0-34-1		Harbhajan Singh 10-0-43-2; Yuvraj Singh 10-1-57-2	

Umpires: I.J. Gould, S.J.A. Taufel.

Toss: India

SATURDAY 2 APRIL 2011
ICC WORLD CUP FINAL: INDIA v SRI LANKA
WANKHEDE STADIUM, MUMBAI, INDIA: INDIA WON BY SIX WICKETS

India, the off-field financial kings of cricket, became the on-field 50 over Champions, as well, when they defeated Sri Lanka by six wickets with 10 balls to spare in front of 42,000 delirious, cheering and dancing fans in Wankhede Stadium, Mumbai.

In doing so India became the first side to win the World Cup on home soil.

Purely as a 50-over cricketing contest, the first World Cup final since 1992 not to include Australia was one of the best. One special feature were the two innings to go into the pantheon of World Cup greats.

For Sri Lanka Mahela Jayawardene charmed the entire world cricketing community with his 88-ball unbeaten 103. He then obtained the unenviable record of becoming the first batsman to score a century in a World Cup Final and end up on the losing side. As did Sri Lanka with the equal highest ever losing total in a final, their 274 replicating Australia's total in 1975 at Lord's.

Eventually Mahindra Singh Dhoni trumped Jayawardene's innings. The Indian captain smashed a match winning 91 not out in 79 balls to secure his country the coveted trophy and himself the Man of the Match Award.

Kumar Sangakkara won the toss, after Match Referee Jeff Crowe, back again despite being at the centre of the problems in the 2007 World Cup Final, called for a second throw of the coin, and elected to bat.

He hoped to set a big target that would add even more to the huge amount of local pressure on the home side. But he did condemn his bowlers to having to use a wet ball as the April dew came down late in the evening.

"When you reach the knockout stages, batting first is more crucial," says Sri Lanka's No.5 in the 2011 World Cup Final, Tilan Samaraweera. "That's because runs are harder to chase in a big game. I think we did the right thing batting first. Our target batting first was to score 280 and we managed 274."

Zaheer Khan began the final with an almost perfect spell. His first three overs were maidens then he had Upal Tharanga caught by Virender Sehwag diving to his right at first slip from the first ball of his fourth over. It had taken Tharanga 20 balls to make two. At the other end Tillkaratne Dilshan pulled and cut Sreesanth for fours to kick-start he Sri Lankan innings.

"We tried to dominate Sreesanth's bowling because he was the quickest of that lot," Samaraweera says. "We thought we had a chance against his bowling and we did well against him."

Sreesanth, in for the injured Ashish Nehra, was one of a number of changes to the two sides. Sri Lanka had four different players in the line-up compared to their semi-final team. They were unfortunate to lose top all-rounder Angelo Mathews to injury and the balance of the side was, according to the Sri Lankan selectors, so compromised that they omitted spinners Rangana Herath and Ajantha Mendis and brought in bowling all-rounders Chamara Kapugedera and Nuwan Kulasekara. That weakened the spin bowling department. Chamara Silva, whose family had suffered a tragedy just prior to the tournament, was also left out.

"I thought we picked the best side available," Samaraweera says. "Unfortunately, Mathews' injury really hurt us. His loss threw out our team balance. He is a smart bowler who can bowl five or six overs every game very well and a good batsman."

Their spin bowling limitations were further compounded by the question mark over the fitness of Muttiah Muralitharan, playing in his last international cricket match.

The next wicket Sri Lankan wicket fell to spin when Dilshan gloved his sweep again Harbhajan Singh back onto his stumps. That left Sri Lanka were 2/60. Their prospects were in the balance.

Runs from Sangakkara and Jayawardene were always going to be essential if Sri Lanka were to be competitive and they tantalised with a stand of 62 in 11 overs. They lifted the total to 122 and the run rate above four, but just when they seemed set as a pair to take total control, the Sri Lankan captain was caught behind cutting at Yuvraj Singh's skidding left arm spin.

Jayawardene remained, though. He used the angles beautifully behind point cutting with precision and timing. A paddle sweep off Yuvraj raised his 50 in 49 balls. Samaraweera provided handy support and another stand reached fifty, this one for the fourth wicket in 57 balls, but it went no further than 57 when Samaraweera was out lbw to another Yuvraj slider after moving across his stumps and missing a paddle sweep. Simon Taufel said not out, however his decision was reversed when the review showed Samaraweera had been struck in line with the off stump and the ball would have hit middle.

"Yuvraj Singh bowled well in the middle parts of the innings and he took two wickets," Samaraweera says. "We lost some momentum when Yuvraj was bowling. He bowled very cleverly.

"Against Harbhajan Singh and Yuvraj, we wanted to rotate the strike. Sri Lankans are not normally big hitters, so rotating the strike was important. Mahela said that we had to play positive cricket in the final and we had to get 250."

Three runs later Kapugedera totally miscued a slower delivery from Zaheer Khan and was caught at cover. It gave the experienced left-arm fast bowler his 21st wicket for the tournament equal top with Shahid Afridi.

Sri Lanka at 5/182 in the 40th over was again at the crossroads. Now, though, the acceleration came from Jayawardene and his new partner, Kulasekera. Jayawardene continued to glide and caress the ball with finesse while Kulasekera was more belligerent. He survived a DRS shout for a caught behind and hooked boundaries. When Zaheer Khan returned Kulasekara lofted him over for six over mid wicket. Jayawardene lifted the fifth ball of the 48th over for four over mid off to reach his hundred in 84 balls.

"It was one of the fantastic hundreds," Samaweera says. "His placement was excellent. He is a lovely touch player and not a big, hard hitter of the ball. His execution is brilliant when he is on song."

Seventeen runs came from that Zaheer Khan over, but Kulasekera was run out by a Dhoni under arm from the final ball as the batsmen tried to steal a single to short fine-leg. The partnership had been worth 66 in eight overs.

Jayawardene was now quite de-energised by the heat and humidity. Thisara Perera filled the void well, though. He took 16 runs from the final four balls of the innings including a last ball six over square from now heavily suffering Zaheer Khan. He conceded 39 runs from his final 13 deliveries. Sri Lanka scored 91 from their last 10 overs including 63 in the batting powerplay.

"Full credit to Kulasekara and Thisara for their batting at the end of the innings," Samaraweera says. "They batted very well."

Sri Lanka had 274 on the board and plenty of momentum.

"We thought we had to attack the top four: Sehwag, Tendulkar, Gambhir and Kohli," Samaraweera says. "Before the final, MS Dhoni had a quiet run, so we thought the middle- to late-order may be vulnerable if we could take early wickets.

"Against India in India, you have to take early wickets. India have one of the best top-seven batsmen in the world, who can hit a lot of fours and sixes. So it's crucial to take your chances when they come.

"We picked three off-spinners for the team (Muralitharan, Randiv and Dilshan) because India had three left-handers in their top seven (Gambhir, Yuvraj Singh and Raina)."

Virender Sehwag, who had hit six first ball of the innings fours in eight matches, began India's reply by playing the opening delivery to extra cover. The second from Lasith Malinga skidded on sharply from short of a length and hit Sehwag in front of middle and leg. Aleem Dar upheld the unanimous appeal for lbw. Sehwag challenged to no avail. Wankhede went very quiet.

They stirred again when Gautam Gambhir clipped his first ball to square leg for four and returned to full volume when Sachin Tendulkar straight drove Kulasekera and then cut him both for fours in the fourth over.

The perfect day for India would have included a win in the World Cup final while Mumbai's favourite son, Tendulkar, made his 100th century for India.

From the first ball of the seventh over the crowd of exactly 42,000 was stunned to silence again, however, when Tendulkar drove on the up at Malinga and was caught behind low down and to his right by Sangakkara. At that seemingly critical moment Sri Lanka believed they would win the final.

Gambhir and the youngster, Kohli, then dragged the match back onto an even keel. Gambhir lofted Kulasekera over cover in the 12th over to raise his 4000th ODI run. Two overs later in Randiv's first over the left-handed opener had a life when a difficult low chance at long off was missed.

The 50 run partnership was raised in the 18th over. Muralitharan came on to bowl the 19th over of the innings. India was 2/96.

Like Tendulkar for India he could have been Sri Lanka's ultimate hero, but wasn't. His action because of his sore hamstring was marginally compromised, the pitch was not turning and the dew was starting to dampen the ball.

"Murali was not at his best in the final," Samaraweera says. "He bowled brilliantly in the semi-final. He picked up a hamstring niggle during the tournament, which may have affected him and the team during the final.

"He didn't take a wicket in the final. His figures of 0-39 from eight overs were okay, but not the best by his exceptional standards. If he took one or two wickets in the final, I think it would have been a different story."

Kohli and Gambhir, who had reached his 50 in 56 balls, built their third-wicket partnership to 83 in 15 overs. Then Dilshan grabbed the catch of the match. Kohli cut him for four then forcing to the on-side chipped a leading edge back towards the bowler. He dived and caught the ball spectacularly in his right hand.

Dhoni promoted himself to No.5, entering at 3/114 in the 22nd over. He quickly moved into his work striking the ball cleanly with drives and clips on the back foot through the off-side. He and Gambhir were able to score at a required rate that kept the target at almost exactly a run per ball. They raised the 200 in the 38th over and Dhoni cut Muralitharan for four to reach his first half-century of the tournament in 52 balls.

Gambhir moved into the 90s. A wide from Muralitharan in the 39th over raised the 100 partnership. India was winning the Premiership quarter.

"That was the time we thought we were in trouble, but we still believed that if we could get one or two wickets, we were still in the game," Samaraweera says. "India had a long tail too, with four bowlers who were not the best with the bat: Harbhajan, Zaheer Khan, Patel and Sreesanth. We tried to get that breakthrough wicket by bringing Malinga back into the attack, but MS handled him very well.

"I thought it would have been a different story if the Gambhir chance was taken. But full credit to the Indian batters.

MS Dhoni helped India to the win with a fabulous knock. I think he is one of the greatest finishers in limited-overs cricket. He controlled the game very well."

Then Perera struck one blow back for Sri Lanka. Gambhir ,within three runs of the second century of the match, stepped away to cut and was bowled middle stump.

It was another skidder. The dew was clearly an issue more for the Sri Lankan bowlers now, though, than for the batsmen. They repeatedly tried to dry the ball. At one stage it became so wet it had to be changed.

Yuvraj Singh pulled Perera for four and seven balls later Dhoni cut the same bowler for six. "The crowd goes mental," said the Cricinfo commentator. India was 37 runs away from glory.

Then Kulasekara had 11 runs taken from the 47th over and the target was down to 16 runs from three overs with six wickets in hand. The faces of the Sri Lankan players glazed over. The combined bowling figures of the two extra bowling all-rounders Perera and Kulasekara were 1/119 from 17 overs.

Dhoni now finished it. He hit Malinga for two fours to square leg-then sealed India's second World Cup success with a lofted on-drive for six off Kulasekara with 10 balls left.

The fireworks instantly filled the sky. The celebration of all things Indian cricket had begun.

"A super game of cricket," said David Lloyd on television. Indian coach, Gary Kirsten celebrated with his team. Like Muralitharan he was finishing this night.

There were honourable speeches from both captains. Yuvraj Singh was named as player of the tournament. Then he and

Suresh Raina chaired a happy, tearful Sachin Tendulkar around the ground. He had his hands on a World Cup trophy after a record-equalling six attempts. Not one of the exactly 42,000 spectators admitted had left the Wankhede Stadium.

"That loss was the biggest disappointment of my career," Samaraweera says. "We were disappointed to have played in two losing World Cup finals and two losing Twenty20 finals.

"In 2011, I felt we had a good chance of victory. It was different to the 2007 final, when we were just outplayed by a brilliant Australian team. Gilchrist's innings of 149 in a 38 overs per side match was one of the most magnificent hundreds in one-day cricket.

"Speaking personally, I had a fear of failure going into the final. With high expectations back home, we were worried about what people may say if we lost. Fear of failure affected us, especially in light of our history of losses in other finals.

"Honestly, it took me a good two to three weeks to recover from losing the final. It really hurts. It's a terrible feeling when you have people asking you every day what happened. We were really disappointed that Murali's international career finished on a losing note."

SRI LANKA		INDIA	
W. U. Tharanga c Sehwag b Khan	2	V. Sehwag lbw b Malinga	0
T. M. Dilshan b Harbhajan Singh	33	S. R. Tendulkar c Sangakkara b Malinga	18
K. C. Sangakkara (capt/wk) c Dhoni b Yuvraj Singh	48	G. Gambhir b Perera	97
D. P. M. D. Jayawardene not out	103	V. Kohli c & b Dilshan	35
T. T. Samaraweera lbw b Yuvraj Singh	21	M. S. Dhoni (capt/wk) not out	91
C. K. Kapugedera c Raina b Khan	1	Yuvraj Singh not out	21
K. M. D. N. Kulasekara run out	32	Extras B1 Lb6 W8	15
N. L. T. C. Perera not out	22	(48.2 overs)	4/277
Extras B1 Lb3 W6 Nb2	12	Did not bat; S. K. Raina, Harbhajan Singh, Z. Khan,	
(50 overs)	6/274	M. M. Patel, S. Sreesanth	
Did not bat: S. L. Malinga, S. Randiv, M. Muralitharan		1/0 2/31 3/114 4/223	
1/17 2/60 3/122 4/179 5/182 6/248		Bowling: Malinga 9-0-42-2; Kulasekara 8.2-0-64-0;	
Bowling: Khan 10-3-60-2; Sreesanth 8-0-52-0;		Perera 9-0-55-1; Randiv 9-0-43-0; Dilshan 5-0-27-1;	
Patel 9-0-41-0; Harbhajan Singh 10-0-50-1; Yuvraj		Muralitharan 8-0-39-0	
Singh 10-0-49-2; Tendulkar 2-0-12-0; Kohli 1-0-6-0			

Umpires: Aleem Dar S.J.A. Taufel

Toss: Sri Lanka

POST MORTEM

There are a couple of interesting parallels between India's 2011 World Cup win and Australia's in 2007.

Although India, even after their victory, were only rated the world's second-best one-day side, by becoming the first side to in the World Cup on their own soil they had clearly become the most celebrated team in the 50-over format. The pre-eminence of this trophy, after all, is what the World Cup and indeed this very book is all about.

India also in 2011 carried the mantle of the most prestigious title, the world's No.1 Test nation. But they, like Australia four years before, had begun their transition period by the time of the World Cup.

Within a few months they were thrashed by England and then in early 2012 also by Australia 0-4. Dravid and Laxman of the old guard had already gone from the ODI line-up and Sehwag and even Tendulkar would not last much longer.

It meant the 2015 tournament was wide open and that India, despite some more blossoming batting talent, were at reasonably long odds to repeat Australia's triple success.

There were the usual number of farewells and goodbyes after the 2011 World Cup. The four year gap means that the World Cup continues to be a tournament that countries try to build their 50-over cricket towards and many players see it as a finishing point for their careers.

With the development of and current infatuation for the T20 format the 50-over game would be of very little worth without the World Cup.

India's awesome financial clout and desire/threat to expand the IPL theoretically could eventually hold the World Cup to ransom as much as it might compromise Test cricket. Dedicated followers of the game will continue to follow the political toings and froings at the ICC with intense interest.

One last thought from this coverage the 2011 World Cup arose during research. It was a pleasure to hear the distinctive voice of Tony Greig as a television commentator again. His untimely death from cancer came barely 20 months after the conclusion of the tournament.

Greig was a pioneer player of the 50-over format, day/night cricket and loved by many on the sub-continent. The thread of fun and his enthusiasm for the game could still be heard loud and clear in his voice throughout his coverage of the 2011 World Cup. He is missed.

CHAPTER 12:

2015 World Cup

I n February and March 2015, the World Cup will return to Australia and New Zealand after a 23-year hiatus.

In the bidding for the 2011 World Cup, the Australasian proposal was well received but lost out at the final vote on 30 April 2006 to the joint bid from India, Pakistan and Sri Lanka. After approving the Asian bid for 2011, the ICC decided at the same meeting to award the 2015 edition to Australia and New Zealand. Important factors in the decision were the high calibre of the trans-Tasman venues and the quality infrastructure. On a roll, the ICC also elected to award the hosting rights for 2019 to England and Wales.

The format of the 2015 World Cup will be the same as for 2011. The number of participants, 14, and the number of matches, 49, will stay constant. The ICC decided in July 2013 that Australia will host 26 matches and New Zealand 23 matches across seven venues in each country. The traditional Melbourne-Sydney rivalry resumed when deciding on the venue for the final. In the end, Melbourne prevailed, with the final scheduled for Sunday, 29 March 2015. Sydney and Auckland were granted hosting rights for the semi-final matches.

The 10 Test teams will be joined by qualifiers Ireland, Scotland, United Arab Emirates and Afghanistan, making their World Cup debut. For a while, the 2015 tournament was to be restricted to the Test nations. The ICC reached this decision in the aftermath of the 2011 tournament. The decision came under heavy fire from Cricket Ireland and the boards of other associate countries. The ICC reversed its decision in June 2011 and the qualification format for the four associate spots was revamped.

The new qualification system worked like this. The top eight associate teams played in the ICC World Cricket League Championship from June 2011 to October 2013, with the top two teams qualifying for the 2015 World Cup. Ireland and Afghanistan secured their passage by going one-two in this competition. The remaining six associate teams from the tournament entered a repechage competition, the 2014 World Cup Qualifier, held in New Zealand in January-February 2014. The six teams were joined by four countries from the second and third divisions of the 2011 ICC World Cricket League: Papua New Guinea, Hong Kong, Nepal and Uganda. Scotland and United Arab Emirates reached the final of the 2014 World Cup Qualifier, thus filling the last two places for the 2015 World Cup. Multiple World Cup qualifiers the Netherlands, Kenya and Canada failed to reach the top four of the 2014 World Cup Qualifier and lost their one-day international status until 2018 as a result. Hong Kong and Papua New Guinea gained one-day international status as a reward for finishing third and fourth.

In contrast to 1992, the 2015 tournament will not include matches at some non-capital cities around Australia. The six main Australian Test venues will cover 23 games, with the remaining three to be played at Canberra's Manuka Oval. In New Zealand, 17 out of the 23 games will be held at mainstream Test venues. Hagley Oval in Christchuch, which hosted its first limited-overs international in January 2014, will host three matches. Saxton Oval in Nelson, a ground that first hosted a cricket match in 2010, will be the venue for three contests.

The opening ceremony will be held on Thursday, 12 February 2015, two days before the first match. At the time of writing, Hagley Oval was slated as the venue for the party to usher in the 2015 tournament. The New Zealand government agreed to pour $5 million into the hosting coffers, with a substantial proportion of the funds expected to be used for the opening ceremony. On Valentine's Day, hostilities will begin when New Zealand take on Sri Lanka at Hagley Oval and, a few hours later, Australia and England will do battle at the MCG in a day-night match.

The broadcasting rights for the tournament were awarded to ESPN Star Sports and Star Cricket for 2 billion US dollars. It remains to be seen whether the ICC will boost the total prize money pool from 2011 of 10 million US dollars, including 4 million US dollars for the winners.

The 2015 World Cup promises to be an exciting event and should uphold the fine tradition that began in England in 1975. The main details of the fixture are set out below. The top four teams from each group will advance to the quarter-finals.

GROUP A – matches from 14 February to 14 March, inclusive

Afghanistan
Australia
Bangladesh
England
New Zealand
Scotland
Sri Lanka

GROUP B – matches from 15 February to 15 March, inclusive

India
Ireland
Pakistan
South Africa
United Arab Emirates
West Indies
Zimbabwe

Quarter-finals

18 March – QF 1 – A1 vs B4, Sydney
19 March – QF 2 – A2 vs B3, Melbourne
20 March – QF 3 – A3 vs B2, Adelaide
21 March – QF 4 – A4 vs B1, Wellington

Semi-finals

24 March – SF 1 - winner QF 1 vs winner QF 4, Auckland
26 March – SF 2 - winner QF 2 vs winner QF 3, Sydney

Final

29 March – winner SF 1 vs winner SF 2, Melbourne

Statistics:
Cricket's World Cup

1975

Leading Run Scorers

Player	Runs	Highest Score	Average
1. G.M. Turner (NZ)	333	171*	166.50
2. D.L. Amiss (Eng)	243	137	60.75
3. Majid J. Khan (Pak)	209	84	69.66
4. K.W.R. Fletcher (Eng)	207	131	69.00
5. A. Turner (Aus)	201	101	40.20
6. A.I. Kallicharran (WI)	197	78	49.25
7. R. Edwards (Aus)	166	80	55.33
8. C.H. Lloyd (WI)	158	102	52.66
9. Zaheer Abbas (Pak)	136	97	45.33
10. G.S. Chappell (Aus)	129	50	25.80

Leading Wicket Takers

Player	Wickets	Average	Best Bowling
1. G.J. Gilmour (Aus)	11	5.63	6-14
2. B.D. Julien (WI)	10	17.70	4-20
3. K.D. Boyce (WI)	10	18.50	4-50
4. D.R. Hadlee (NZ)	8	20.25	3-21
5. A.M.E. Roberts (WI)	8	20.62	3-39
6. D.K. Lillee (Aus)	8	27.87	5-34
7. C.M. Old (Eng)	7	12.28	3-29
8. J.A. Snow (Eng)	6	10.83	4-11
9. A.W. Greig (Eng)	6	14.83	4-45
10. Abid Ali (Ind)	6	19.16	2-22

Individual Batting Performances

Player	Score	
1. G.M. Turner (NZ)	171*	vs East Africa
2. D.L. Amiss (Eng)	137	vs India
3. K.W.R. Fletcher (Eng)	131	vs New Zealand
4. G.M. Turner (NZ)	114*	vs India
5. C.H. Lloyd (WI)	102	vs Australia (final)
6. A. Turner (Aus)	101	vs Sri Lanka
7. Zaheer Abbas (Pak)	97	vs Sri Lanka (semi-final)
8. D.L. Amiss (Eng)	88	vs East Africa
9. Majid Khan (Pak)	84	vs Sri Lanka
10. R. Edwards (Aus)	80*	vs Pakistan

Individual Bowling Performances

Player	Analysis	
1. G.J. Gilmour (Aus)	6-14	vs England
2. D.K. Lillee (Aus)	5-34	vs Pakistan
3. G.J. Gilmour (Aus)	5-48	vs West Indies
4. B.D. Julien (WI)	4-20	vs Sri Lanka
5. A.W. Greig (Eng)	4-45	vs New Zealand
6. Sarfraz Nawaz (Pak)	4-44	vs West Indies
7. J.A. Snow (Eng)	4-11	vs East Africa
8. K.D. Boyce (WI)	4-50	vs Australia (final)
9. B.D. Julien (WI)	4-27	vs New Zealand (semi-final)
10. Imran Khan (Pak)	3-15	vs Sri Lanka
10. Madan Lal (Ind)	3-15	vs East Africa

Team Batting Performances

Team	Score	
1. England	4-334	vs India
2. Pakistan	6-330	vs Sri Lanka
3. Australia	5-328	vs Sri Lanka
4. New Zealand	5-309	vs East Africa
5. West Indies	8-291	vs Australia (final)
6. England	5-290	vs East Africa
7. Australia	7-278	vs Pakistan
8. Sri Lanka	4-276	vs Australia
9. Australia	10-274	vs West Indies (final)
10. West Indies	9-267	vs Pakistan

1979

Leading Run Scorers

Player	Runs	Highest Score	Average
1. C.G. Greenidge (WI)	253	106*	84.34
2. I.V.A. Richards (WI)	217	128*	108.50
3. G.A. Gooch (Eng)	210	71	52.50
4. G.M. Turner (NZ)	176	83'	58.67
5. J.G. Wright (NZ)	166	69	41.50
6. J.M. Brearley (Eng)	161	64	32.20
7. Majid J. Khan (Pak)	150	81	37.50
8. Zaheer Abbas (Pak)	148	93	37.00
9. D.L. Haynes (WI)	144	65	36.00
10. A.M.J. Hilditch (Aus)	143	72	47.67

Leading Wicket Takers

Player	Wickets	Average	Best Bowling
1. M. Hendrick (Eng)	10	14.90	4-15
2. B.J. McKechnie (NZ)	9	15.67	3-24
3. C.M. Old (Eng)	9	17.44	4-8
4. Asif Iqbal (Pak)	9	17.44	4-56
5. M.A. Holding (WI)	8	13.25	4-33
6. Sikander Bakht (Pak)	8	13.50	3-32
7. C.E.H. Croft (WI)	8	17.50	3-29
8. J. Garner (WI)	8	21.50	5-38
9. R.G.D. Willis (Eng)	7	15.57	4-11
10. Majid J. Khan (Pak)	7	16.71	3-27

Individual Batting Performances

Player	Score	
1. I.VA Richards (WI)	138*	vs England (final)
2. C.G. Greenidge (WI)	106*	vs India
3. Zaheer Abbas (Pak)	93	vs West Indies (semi-final)
4. C.L. King (WI)	86	vs England (final)
5. B.A. Edgar (NZ)	84*	vs India
6. G.M. Turner (NZ)	83*	vs Sri Lanka
7. Majid J. Khan (Pak)	81	vs West Indies
8. G.R. Viswanath (Ind)	75	vs West Indies
9. C.H. Lloyd (WI)	73*	vs New Zealand
10. C.G. Greenidge (WI)	73	vs Pakistan (semi-final)

Individual Bowling Performances

Player	Analysis	
1. A.G. Hurst (Aus)	5-21	vs Canada
2. J. Garner (WI)	5-38	vs England (final)
3. C.M. Old (Eng)	4-8	vs Canada
4. R.G.D. Willis (Eng)	4-11	vs Canada
5. M. Hendrick (Eng)	4-15	vs Pakistan
6. M.A. Holding (WI)	4-33	vs India
7. Asif Iqbal (Pak)	4-56	vs West Indies (semi-final)
8. B.J. McKechnie (NZ)	3-24	vs India
9. B.J. McKechnie (NZ)	3-25	vs Sri Lanka
10. Sarfraz Nawaz (Pak)	3-26	vs Canada

Team Batting Performances

Team	Score	
1. West Indies	6-293	vs Pakistan (semi-final)
2. Pakistan	7-286	vs Australia
3. West Indies	9-286	vs England (final)
4. Pakistan	10-250	vs West Indies (semi-final)
5.. West Indies	7-244	vs New Zealand
6. Sri Lanka	5-238	vs India
7. England	8-221	vs New Zealand (semi-final)
8. New Zealand	9-212	vs England (semi-final)
9. New Zealand	9-212	vs West Indies
10. Australia	10-197	vs Pakistan

1983

Leading Run Scorers

	Runs	Highest Score	Average
1. D.I. Gower (Eng)	384	138	76.80
2. I.V.A. Richards (WI)	367	119	73.40
3. G. Fowler (Eng)	360	81*	72.00
4. Zaheer Abbas (Pak)	313	103*	62.60
5. Kapil Dev (Ind)	303	175*	60.60
6. Imran Khan (Pak)	283	102*	70.75
7. A.J. Lamb (Eng)	278	102	69.50
8. H.A. Gomes (WI)	258	78	64.50
9. C.G. Greenidge (WI)	250	105*	41.66
10. D.L Haynes (WI)	240	88*	34.28
10. Yashpal Sharma (Ind)	240	89	34.28

Leading Wicket Takers.

Player	Wickets	Average	Best Bowling
1. R.M.H. Binny (Ind)	18	18,66	4-29
2. A.L.F. de Mel (SL)	17	15.59	5-32
3. S. Madan Lal (Ind)	17	17.76	4-20
4. R.J. Hadlee (NZ)	14	12.86	5-25
5. V.J. Marks (Eng)	13	18.92	5-39*
6. M.D. Marshall (WI)	12	14.58	3-28
7. M.A. Holding (WI)	12	19.58	3-40
8. Kapil Dev (Ind)	12	20.41	5-43
9. R.G.D. Willis (Eng)	11	18.73	4-41
10. A.M.E. Roberts (WI)	11	21.63	3-32

Individual Batting Performances

Player	Score	
1. Kapil Dev (Ind)	175	vs Zimbabwe
2. D.I. Gower (Eng)	130	vs Sri Lanka
3. I.V.A Richards (WI)	119	vs India
4. T.M. Chappell (Aus)	110	vs India
5. C.G. Greenidge (WI)	105*	vs Zimbabwe
6. Zaheer Abbas (Pak)	103*	vs New Zealand
7. Imran Khan (Pak)	102*	vs Sri Lanka
8. A.J. Lamb (Eng)	102	vs .New Zealand
9. M.D. Crowe (NZ)	97	vs England
10. I.V.A. Richards	95*	vs Australia

Individual Bowling Performances

Player	Analysis	
1, W.W. Davis (WI)	7-51	vs Australia
2. K.H. Macleay (Aus)	6-39	vs India
3. R.J. Hadlee (NZ)	5-25	vs Sri Lanka
4, A.L.F. de Mel (SL)	5-32	vs Pakistan
5. A.L.F. de Mel (SL)	5-32	vs New Zealand
6. V.J. Marks (Eng)	5-39	vs Sri Lanka
7. Kapil Dev (Ind)	5-43	vs Australia
8. Abdul Qadir (Pak)	5-44	vs Sri Lanka
9. S. Madan Lal (Ind)	4-20	vs Australia
10. Abdul Qadir (Pak)	4-21	vs New Zealand

Team Batting Performances

Team	Score	
1. Pakistan	5-338	vs Sri Lanka
2. England	9-333	vs Sri Lanka
3. England	6-322	vs New Zealand
4. Australia	9-320	vs India
5. Sri Lanka	9-288	vs Pakistan
6. Sri Lanka	10-286	vs England
7. West Indies	9-282	vs India
8. West Indies	9-276	vs Australia
9. Australia	6-273	vs West Indies
10. Australia	7-272	vs Zimbabwe

1987

Leading Run Scorers

Player	Runs	Highest Score	Average
1. G.A. Gooch (Eng)	471	115	58.88
2. D.C. Boon (Aus)	447	93	55.88
3. G.A. Marsh (Aus)	428	126*	61.14
4. I.V.A Richards (WI)	391	181	65.17
5. M.W. Gatting (Eng)	354	60	50.57
6. Ramiz Raja (Pak)	349	113	49.86
7. Salim Malik (Pak)	323	100	53.83
8. D.M. Jones (Aus)	314	58*	44.86
9. S.M. Gavaskar (Ind)	300	103*	50.00
10. A.J. Lamb (Eng)	299	76	59.80

Leading Wicket Takers

Player	Wickets	Average	Best Bowling
1. C.J. McDermott (Aus)	18	18.94	5-44
2. Imran Khan (Pak)	17	13.06	4-37
3. B.P. Patterson (WI)	14	18.07	3-31
4. Maninder Singh (Ind)	14	20.00	3-21
5. E.E. Hemmings (Eng)	13	21.08	4-52
6. Abdul Qadir (Pak)	12	20.17	4-31
7. P.A.J. DeFreitas (Eng)	12	23.58	3-28
8. S.A. Waugh (Aus)	11	26.18	2-36
9. J.R. Ratnayake (SL)	10	31.30	3-41
10. C.A. Walsh (WI)	9	25.44	4-40

Individual Batting Performances

Player	Score	
1. I.V.A. Richards (WI)	181	vs Sri Lanka
2. D.L. Houghton (Zim)	141	vs New Zealand
3. G.R. Marsh (Aust)	126*	vs New Zealand
4. G.A. Gooch (Eng)	115	vs India (semi-final)
5. Ramiz Raja (Pak)	113	vs England
6. R.B. Richardson (WI)	110	vs Pakistan
7. G.R. Marsh (Aus)	110	vs India
8. D.L. Haynes (WI)	105	vs Sri Lanka
9. S.M. Gavaskar (Ind)	103*	vs New Zealand
10. Javed Miandad (Pak)	103	vs Sri Lanka

Individual Bowling Performances

Player	Analysis	
1. C.J. McDermott (Aus)	5-44	vs Pakistan (semi-final)
2. M. Prabhakar (Ind)	4-19	vs New Zealand
3. Abdul Qadir (Pak)	4-31	vs England
4. Imran Khan (Pak)	4-37	vs England
5. Imran Khan (Pak)	4-37	vs West Indies
6. S.P. O'Donnell (Aus)	4-39	vs Zimbabwe
7. C.A. Walsh (WI)	4-40	vs Pakistan
8. E.E. Hemmings (Eng)	4-52	vs India
9. C.J. McDermott (Aus)	4-56	vs India
10. M. Azharuddin (Ind)	3-19	vs Australia

Team Batting Performances

Team	Score	
1. West Indies	4-360	vs Sri Lanka
2. India	7-297	vs Sri Lanka
3. England	4-296	vs Sri Lanka
4. India	6-289	vs Australia
5. Australia	6-270	vs India
6. England	5-269	vs West Indies
7. India	10-269	vs Australia
8. Pakistan	6-267	vs Sri Lanka
9. Australia	8-267	vs Pakistan (semi-fina)
10. Australia	5-266	vs Zimbabwe

Leading Run Scorers

Player	Runs	Highest Score	Average
1. M.D. Crowe (NZ)	456	100*	114.00
2. Javed Miandad (Pak)	437	89	62.43
3. P.N. Kirsten (SA)	410	90	68.33
4. D.C. Boon (Aus)	368	100	52.57
5. Ramiz Raja (Pak)	349	119*	58.17
6. B.C. Lara (WI)	333	88	47.57
7. M. Azharuddin (Ind)	332	93	47.43
8. Aamir Sohail (Pak)	326	114	32.60
9. A.H. Jones (NZ)	322	78	46.00
10. M.J. Greatbatch (NZ)	313	73	44.71
10. K.C. Wessels (SA)	313	85	44.71

Leading Wicket Takers

Player	Wickets	Average	Best Bowling
1. Wasim Akram (Pak)	18	18.78	4-32
2. I.T. Botham (Eng)	16	19.13	4-31
3. Mushtaq Ahmed (Pak)	16	9.44	3-41
4. C.Z. Harris (NZ)	16	21.38	3-15
5. E.A. Brandes (Zim)	14	25.36	4-21
6. A. A. Donald (SA)	13	25.31	3-34
7. M. Prabhakar (Ind)	12	20.42	3-41
8. A.C. Cummins (WI)	12	20.50	4-33
9. W. Watson (NZ)	12	25.80	3-37
10. B.M. McMillan (SA)	11	27.82	3-30

Individual Batting Performances

Player	Score	
1. Ramiz Raja (Pak)	119*	vs New Zealand
2. A. Flower (Zim)	115*	vs Sri Lanka
3. Aamir Sohail (Pak)	114	vs Zimbabwe
4. P.V. Simmons (WI)	110	vs Sri Lanka
5. Ramiz Raja (Pak)	102*	vs West Indies
6. M.D. Crowe (NZ)	100*	vs Australia
7. D.C. Boon (Aus)	100	vs New Zealand
7. D.C. Boon (Aus)	100	vs West Indies
9. D.L. Haynes (WI)	93*	vs Pakistan
10. M. Azharuddin (Ind)	93	vs Australia

Individual Bowling Performances

Player	Analysis	Bowling
1. M.W. Pringle (SA)	4-11	vs West Indies
2. E.A. Brandes (Zim)	4-21	vs England
3. C.C. Lewis (Eng)	4-30	vs Sri Lanka
4. I.T. Botham (Eng)	4-31	vs Australia
5. Wasim Akram (Pak)	4-32	vs New Zealand
6. A.C. Cummins (WI)	4-33	vs India
7. M.R. Whitney (Aus)	4-34	vs West Indies
8. U.C. Hathurusinghe (SL)	4-57	vs West Indies
9. D.R. Pringle (Eng)	3-8	vs Pakistan
10. C.Z. Harris (NZ)	3-15	vs Zimbabwe

Team Batting Performances

Team	Score	
1. Sri Lanka	7-313	vs Zimbabwe
2. Zimbabwe	4-312	vs Sri Lanka
3. England	6-280	vs Sri Lanka
4. WestIndies	8-26a	vs Sri Lanka
5. Australia	6-265	vs Zimbabwe
6. Pakistan	6-264	vs New Zealand (semi-final)
7. West Indies	8-264	vs Zimbabwe
8. New Zealand	7-262	vs Pakistan
9. Pakistan	4-254	vs Zimbabwe
10. England	6-252	vs South Africa (semi-final)

1996

Leading Run Scorers

Player	Runs	Highest Score	Average
1. S.R. Tendulkar (Ind)	523	137	87.17
2. M.E. Waugh (Aus)	484	130	80.67
3. P.A. de Silva (SL)	448	145	89.60
4. G. Kirsten (SA)	391	188*	78.20
5. Saeed Anwar (Pak)	329	83*	82.25
6. A.P. Gurusinha (SL)	307	87	51.17
7. W.J. Cronje (SA)	276	78	55.20
8. A.C. Hudson (SA)	275	161	68.75
9. Aamir Sohail (Pak)	272	111	45.33
10. B.C. Lara (WI)	269	111	53.80

Leading Wicket Takers

Player	Wickets	Average	Best Bowling
1. A.R. Kumble (Ind)	15	18.73	3-29
2. Waqar Younis (Pak)	13	19.46	4-26
3. P.A. Strang (Zim)	12	16.00	5-21
4. RA Harper (WI)	12	18.25	4-47
5. D.W. Fleming (Aus)	12	18.42	5-36
6. S.K. Warne (Aus)	12	21.92	4-34
7. C.E.L. Ambrose (WI)	10	17.00	3-28
8. Mushtaq Ahmed (Pak)	10	23.80	3-16
9. R.W. Ali (Ken)	9	21.11	3-17
10. A. A. Donald (SA)	8	15.75	3-21

Individual Batting Performances

Player	Score	
1. G. Kirsten (SA)	188*	vs UAE
2. A.C. Hudson (SA)	161	vs Netherlands
3. P.A. de Silva (SL)	145	vs Kenya
4. S.R. Tendulkar (Ind)	137	vs Sri Lanka
5. M.E. Waugh (Aus)	130	vs Kenya
6. C.Z. Harris (NZ)	130	vs Australia
7. S.R. Tendulkar (Ind)	127*	vs Kenya
8. M.E. Waugh (Aus)	126	vs.India
9. Aamir Sohail (Pak)	111	vs South Africa
10. B.C. Lara (WI)	111	vs South Africa

Individual Bowling Performances

Player	Analysis	
1. P.A. Strang (Zim)	5-21	vs Kenya
2. Shaukat Dukanwala (UAE)	5-29	vs Netherlands
3. D.W. Fleming (Aus)	5-36	vs India
4. Waqar Younis (Pak)	4-26	vs Netherlands
5. S.K. Warne (Aus)	4-34	vs Zimbabwe
6. S.K. Warne (Aus)	4-36	vs West Indies (semi-final)
7. P.A. Strang (Zim)	4-40	vs West Indies
8. R.A. Harper (WI)	4-47	vs South Africa
9. B. M. McMillan (SA)	3-11	vs UAE
10. S.T. Jayasuriya (SL)	3-12	vs India (semi-final)

Team Batting Performances

Team	Score	
1. Sri Lanka	5-398	vs Kenya
2. South Africa	3-328	vs Netherlands
3. South Africa	2-321	vs UAE
4. New Zealand	8-307	vs Netherlands
5. Australia	7-304	vs Kenya
6. Australia	4-289	vs New Zealand
7. India	8-287	vs Pakistan
8. New Zealand	9-286	vs Australia
9. Pakistan	5-281	vs New Zealand
10. England	4-279	vs Netherlands

1999

Leading Run Scorers

Player	Runs	Highest Score	Average
1. RS. Dravid (Ind)	461	145	65.85
2. S.R. Waugh (Aus)	398	120*	79.60
3. S.C. Ganguly (Ind)	379	183	54.14
4. M.E. Waugh (Aus)	375	104	41.66
5. Saeed Anwar (Pak)	368	113*	40.88
6. N.C. Johnson (Zim)	367	132*	52.42
7. RT. Ponting (Aus)	354	69	39.33
8. H.H. Gibbs (SA)	341	101	37.88
9. R.G.Twose (NZ)	318	80*	79.50
10. J.H. Kallis (SA)	312	96	52.00

Leading Wicket Takers

Player	Wickets	Average	Best Bowling
1. G.I. Allott (NZ)	20	16.25	4-37
2. S.K. Warne (Aus)	20	18.05	4-29
3. G.D. McGrath (Aus)	18	20.38	5-14
4. L. Klusener (SA)	17	20.58	5-21
5. Saqlain Mushtaq (Pak)	17	22.29	5-35
6. A.A. Donald (SA)	16	20.31	4-17
7. Shoaib Akhtar (Pak)	16	24.50	3-11
8. Wasim Akram (Pak)	15	22.80	4-40
9. D.W. Fleming (Aus)	14	25.85	3-57
10. Abdur Razzaq (Pak)	13	23.15	3-24

Individual Batting Performances

Player	Score	
1. S.C. Ganguly (Ind)	183	vs Sri Lanka
2. R.S. Dravid (Ind)	145	vs Sri Lanka
3. S.R. Tendulkar (Ind)	140*	vs Kenya (semi-final)
4. N.C. Johnson (Zim)	132*	vs Australia
5. S.R. Waugh (Aus)	120*	vs South Africa
6. Saeed Anwar (Pak)	113*	vs New Zealand
7.R.S. Dravid (Ind)	104*	vs Kenya
8.M.E. Waugh (Aus)	104	vs Zimbabwe
9.Saeed Anwar (Pak)	103	vs Zimbabwe
10. H.H. Gibbs (SA)	101	vs Australia

Individual Bowling Performances

Player	Analysis	
1.G.D. McGrath (Aus)	5-14	vs West Indies
2.L. Klusener (SA)	5-21	vs Kenya
3. B.K.V. Prasad (Ind)	5-27	vs Pakistan
4. R.R. Singh (Ind)	5-31	vs Sri Lanka
5. Saqlain Mushtaq (Pak)	5-35	vs Bangladesh
6. C.Z. Harris (NZ)	4-7	vs Scotland
7. A. A. Donald (SA)	4-17	vs England
8. C.A. Walsh (WI)	4-25	vs Bangladesh
9. S.K. Warne (Aus)	4-29	vs South Africa (semi-final)
10. S.K. Warne (Aus)	4-33	vs Pakistan (final)

Team Batting Performances

Team	Score	
1. India	6-373	vs Sri Lanka
2. India	2-329	vs Kenya
3. Australia	4-303	vs Zimbabwe
4.South Africa	5-287	vs New Zealand
5. Australia	6-282	vs India
6.Pakistan	8-275	vs Australia
7.Sri Lanka	8-275	vs Kenya
8.Australia	5-272	vs South Africa
9.South Africa	7-271	vs Australia
10. Pakistan	9-271	vs Zimbabwe

2003

Leading Run Scorers

Player	Runs	Highest Score	Average
1. S.R. Tendulkar (Ind)	673	152	61.18
2. S.C. Ganguly (Ind)	465	112*	58.12
3. R.T. Ponting (Aus)	415	140*	51.87
4. A.C. Gilchrist (Aus)	408	99	40.80
5. H.H. Gibbs (SA)	384	143	96.00
6. M.S. Atapattu (SL)	382	124	54.57
7. A. Flower (Zim)	332	71	47.42
8. M.L. Hayden (Aus)	328	88	32.80
9. A. Symonds (Aus)	326	143*	163.00
10. D.R. Martyn (Aus)	323	88*	64.60

Leading Wicket Takers

Player	Wickets	Average	Best Bowling
1. W.P.U.J.C. Vaas (SL)	23	14.39	6-25
2. B. Lee (Aus)	22	17.90	5-42
3. G.D. McGrath (Aus)	21	14.76	7-15
4. Z. Khan (Ind)	18	20.77	4-42
5. S.E. Bond (NZ)	17	17.94	6-23
6. M. Muralitharan (SL)	17	18.76	4-28
7. A.J. Bichel (Aus)	16	12.31	7-20
8. V.C. Drakes (WI)	16	13.00	5-33
9. J. Srinath (Ind)	16	23.06	4-30
10. A. Nehra (Ind)	15	19.26	6-23

Individual Batting Performances

Player	Score	
1. C.B. Wishart (Zim)	172*	vs Namibia
2. S.R. Tendulkar (Ind)	152	vs Namibia
3. A. Symonds (Aus)	143*	vs Pakistan
4. H. H. Gibbs (SA)	143	vs New Zealand
5. S.B. Styris (NZ)	141	vs Sri Lanka
6. R.T. Ponting (Aus)	140	vs India (final)
7. S.P Fleming (NZ)	134*	vs South Africa
7. K-J.J. van Noortwijk (Neth)	134*	vs Namibia
9. M.S. Atapattu (SL)	124	vs South Africa
10. J.F. Kloppenburg (Neth)	121	vs Namibia

Individual Bowling Performances

Player	Analysis	
1. G.D. McGrath (Aus)	7-15	vs Namibia
2. A.J. Bichel (Aus)	7-20	vs England
3. A. Nehra (Ind)	6-23	vs England
3. S.E. Bond (NZ)	6-23	vs Australia
5. W.P.U.J.C. Vaas (SL)	6-25	vs Bangladesh
6. C.O. Obuya (Ken)	5-24	vs Sri Lanka
7. A. Codrington (Can)	5-27	vs Bangladesh
8. Wasim Akram (Pak)	5-28	vs Namibia
9. V.C. Drakes (WI)	5-33	vs Kenya
10. B. Lee (Aus)	5-42	vs New Zealand

Team Batting Performances

Team	Score	
1. Australia	2-359	vs India (final)
2. Zimbabwe	2-340	vs Namibia
3. Australia	5-319	vs Sri Lanka
4. Netherlands	4-314	vs Namibia
5. India	2-311	vs Namibia
6. Australia	8-310	vs Pakistan
7. South Africa	6-306	vs New Zealand
8. Australia	6-301	vs Namibia
9. Zimbabwe	8-301	vs Netherlands
10. India	6-292	vs Sri Lanka

Leading Run Scorers

Player	Runs	Highest Score	Average
1. M.L. Hayden (Aus)	659	158	73.22
2. D.P.M.D. Jayawardene (SL)	548	115*	60.88
3. R.T. Ponting (Aus)	539	113	67.37
4. S.B. Styris (NZ)	499	111*	83.16
5. J.H. Kallis (SA)	485	128*	80.83
6. S.T. Jayasuriya (SL)	467	115	46.70
7. A.C. Gilchrist (Aus)	453	149	45.30
8. K.P. Pietersen (Eng)	444	104	55.50
9. G.C. Smith (SA)	443	91	49.22
10. M.J Clarke (Aus)	436	93*	87.20

Leading Wicket Takers

Player	Wickets	Average	Best Bowling
1. G.D. McGrath (Aus)	26	13.73	3-14
2. M. Muralitharan (SL)	23	15.26	4-19
3. S.W. Tait (Aus)	23	20.30	4-39
4. G.B. Hogg (Aus)	21	15.80	4-27
5. S.L. Malinga (SL)	18	15.77	4-54
6. N.W. Bracken (Aus)	16	16.12	4-19
7. D.L. Vettori (NZ)	16	27.93	4-23
8. A. Flintoff (Eng)	14	21.28	4-43
9. A.J. Hall (SA)	14	23.92	5-18
10. C.K. Langeveldt (SA)	14	25.78	5-39

Individual Batting Performances

Player	Score	
1. Imran Nazir (Pak)	160	vs Zimbabwe
2. M.L. Hayden (Aus)	158	vs West Indies
3. A.C. Gilchrist (Aus)	149	vs Sri Lanka (final)
4. A.B. de Villiers (SA)	146	vs West Indies
5. J.H. Kallis (SA)	128*	vs Netherlands
6. B.J. Hodge (Aus)	123	vs Netherlands
7. J.P. Bray (Ire)	115*	vs Zimbabwe
7. D.P.M.D. Jayawardene (SL)	115*	vs New Zealand (semi-final)
9. S.T. Jayasuriya (SL)	115	vs West Indies
10. V. Sehwag (Ind)	114	vs Bermuda

Individual Bowling Performances

Player	Analysis	
1. A.J. Hall (SA)	5-18	vs England
2. C.K. Langeveldt (SA)	5-39	vs Sri Lanka
3. A. Nel (SA)	5.45	vs Bangladesh
4. N.W. Bracken (Aus)	4-19	vs Sri Lanka
4. M. Muralitharan (SL)	4-19	vs Ireland
6. M.F. Maharoof (SL)	4-23	vs Bermuda
6. D.L Vettori (NZ)	4-23	vs Ireland
8. M.F. Maharoof (SL)	4-25	vs Ireland
9. G.B. Hogg (Aus)	4-27	vs Netherlands
10. G.B. Hogg (Aus)	4-29	vs New Zealand

Team Batting Performances

Team	Score	
1. India	5-413	vs Bermuda
2. Australia	6-377	vs South Africa
3. New Zealand	5-363	vs Canada
4. Australia	5-358	vs Netherlands
5. South Africa	4-356	vs West Indies
6. South Africa	3-353	vs Netherlands
7. Pakistan	10-349	vs Zimbabwe
8. Australia	6-348	vs New Zealand
9. Australia	6-334	vs Scotland
10. New Zealand	7-331	vs Kenya

2011

Leading Run Scorers			
Player	Runs	Highest Score	Average
1. T.M. Dilshan (SL)	500	144	62.50
2. S.R. Tendulkar (Ind)	482	120	53.55
3. K.C. Sangakkara (SL)	465	111	93.00
4. I.J.L. Trott (Eng)	422	92	60.28
5. W.U. Tharanga (SL)	395	133	56.42
6. G. Gambhir (Ind)	393	97	43.66
7. V. Sehwag (Ind)	380	175	47.50
8. Yuvraj Singh (Ind)	362	113	90.50
9. A.B. de Villiers (SA)	353	134	88.25
10. A.J. Strauss (Eng)	334	158	47.71

Leading Wicket Takers			
Player	Wickets	Average	Best Bowling
1. Shahid Afridi (Pak)	21	12.85	5-16
2. Z. Khan (Ind)	21	18.76	3-20
3. T.G. Southee (NZ)	18	17.33	3-13
4. R.J. Peterson (SA)	15	15.86	4-12
5. M. Muralitharan (SL)	15	19.40	4-25
6. Yuvraj Singh (Ind)	15	25.13	5-31
7. Imran Tahir (SA)	14	10.71	4-38
8. Umar Gul (Pak)	14	19.42	3-30
9. K.A.J. Roach (WI)	13	15.00	6-27
10. B. Lee (Aus)	13	18.07	4-28

Individual Batting Performances		
Player	Score	
1. V. Sehwag (Ind)	175	vs Bangladesh
2. A.J. Strauss (Eng)	158	vs India
3. T.M. Dilshan (SL)	144	vs Zimbabwe
4. A.B. de Villiers (SA)	134	vs Netherlands
5. W.U. Tharanga (SL)	133	vs Zimbabwe
6. L.R.P.L. Taylor (NZ)	131*	vs Pakistan
7. S.R. Tendulkar (Ind)	120	vs England
8. R.N. ten Doeschate (Neth)	119	vs England
9. K.J. O'Brien (Ire)	113	vs England
9. H.M. Amla (SA)	113	vs Netherlands
9. Yovraj Singh (Ind)	113	vs West Indies

Individual Bowling Performances		
Player	Analysis	
1. K.A.J. Roach (WI)	6-27	vs Netherlands
2. S.L. Malinga (SL)	6-38	vs Kenya
3. Shahid Afridi (Pak)	5-16	vs Kenya
4. Shahid Afridi (Pak)	5-23	vs Canada
5. Yuvraj Singh (Ind)	5-31	vs Ireland
6. Wahab Riaz (Pak)	5-46	vs India (semi-final)
7. T.T. Bresnan (Eng)	5-48	vs India
8. D.W. Steyn (SA)	5-50	vs India
9. R. Rampaul (WI)	5-51	vs India
10. T.M. Dilshan (SL)	4-4	vs Zimbabwe

Team Batting Performances		
Team	Score	
1. India	4-370	vs Bangladesh
2. New Zealand	6-358	vs Canada
3. South Africa	5-352	vs Netherlands
4. England	8-338	vs India
5. India	10-338	vs England
6. Sri Lanka	7-332	vs Canada
7. West Indies	8-330	vs Netherlands
8. Ireland	7-329	vs England
9. England	8-327	vs Ireland
10. Australia	6-324	vs Kenya

Records for all World Cups 1975-2011

Individual Batting Performances

Player	Score		Year
1. G. Kirsten (SA)	188*	vs UAE	1996
2. S.C. Ganguly (Ind)	183	vs Sri Lanka	1999
3. I.V.A. Richards (WI)	181	vs Sri Lanka	1987
4. Kapil Dev (Ind)	175*	vs Zimbabwe	1983
5. V. Sehwag (Ind)	175	vs Bangladesh	2011
6. C.B. Wishart (Zim)	172*	vs Namibia	2003
7. G.M. Turner (NZ)	171*	vs East Africa	1975
8. A.C. Hudson (SA)	161	vs Netherlands	1996
9. Imran Nazir (Pak)	160	vs Zimbabwe	2007
=10. M.L. Hayden (Aus)	158	vs West Indies	2007
=10. A.J. Strauss (Eng)	158	vs India	2011

Individual Bowling Performances

Player	Analysis		Year
1. G.D. McGrath (Aus)	7-15	vs Namibia	2003
2. A.J. Bichel (Aus)	7-20	vs England	2003
3. W.W. Davis (WI)	7-51	vs Australia	1983
4. G.J. Gilmour (Aus)	6-14	vs England (semi-final)	1975
=5. A. Nehra (Ind)	6-23	vs England	2003
=5. S.E. Bond (NZ)	6-23	vs Australia	2003
7. W.P.U.J.C. Vaas (SL)	6-25	vs Bangladesh	2003
8. K.A. Roach (WI)	6-27	vs Netherlands	2011
9. S.L. Malinga (SL)	6-38	vs Kenya	2011
10. K.H. MacLeay (Aus)	6-39	vs India	1983

Highest Team Totals

Player	Score		Year
1. India	5-413	vs Bermuda	2007
2. Sri Lanka	5-398	vs Kenya	1996
3. Australia	6-377	vs South Africa	2007
4. India	6-373	vs Sri Lanka	1999
5. India	4-370	vs Bangladesh	2011
6. New Zealand	5-363	vs Canada	2007
7. West Indies	4-360	vs Sri Lanka	1987
8. Australia	2-359	vs India (final)	2003
9. Australia	5-358	vs Netherlands	2007
10. New Zealand	6-358	vs Canada	2011

Lowest Team Totals

Player	Score		Year
1. Canada	36	vs Sri Lanka	2003
=2. Canada	45	vs England	1979
=2. Namibia	45	vs Australia	2003
4. Bangladesh	58	vs West Indies	2011
5. Scotland	68	vs West Indies	1999
6. Kenya	69	vs New Zealand	2011
7. Pakistan	74	vs England	1992
8. Ireland	77	vs Sri Lanka	2007
=9. Bangladesh	78	vs South Africa	2011
=9. Bermuda	78	vs Sri Lanka	2007

Highest Run Scorers

Player	Runs	Matches
1. S.R. Tendulkar (Ind)	2,278	45
2. R.T. Ponting (Aus)	1,743	46
3. B.C. Lara (WI)	1,225	34
4. S.T. Jayasuriya (SL)	1,165	38
5. J.H. Kallis (SA)	1,148	36
6. A.C. Gilchrist (Aus)	1,085	31
7. Javed Miandad (Pak)	1,083	33
8. S.P. Fleming (NZ)	1,075	33
9. H.H. Gibbs (SA)	1,067	25
10. P.A. de Silva (SL)	1,064	35

Highest Wicket Takers

Player	Wickets	Matches
1. G.D. McGrath (Aus)	71	39
2. M. Muralitharan (SL)	68	40
3. Wasim Akram (Pak)	55	38
4. W.P.U.J.C. Vaas (SL)	49	31
=5. Z. Khan (Ind)	44	23
=5. J. Srinath (Ind)	44	34
7. A.A. Donald (SA)	38	25
8. J.D.P. Oram (NZ)	36	23
9. B. Lee (Aus)	35	17
=10. G.B. Hogg (Aus)	34	21
=10. Imran Khan (Pak)	34	28
=10. S.W. Tait (Aus)	34	18

Highest Partnership for Each Wicket

1. 282 W.U. Tharanga, T.M. Dilshan	SL vs Zim	2011
2. 318 S.C. Ganguly, R. Dravid	Ind vs SL	1999
3. 237* R. Dravid, S.R. Tendulkar	Ind vs Ken	1999
4. 204 M.J. Clarke, B.J. Hodge	Aus vs Neth	2007
5. 148 R.G. Twose, C.L. Cairns	NZ vs Aus	1999
6. 162 K.J. O'Brien, A.R. Cusack	Ire vs Eng	2011
7. 98 R.R. Sarwan, R.D. Jacobs	WI vs NZ	2003
8. 117 D.L. Houghton, I.P. Butchart	Zim vs NZ	1987
9. 126* Kapil Dev, S.M.H. Kirmani	Ind vs Zim	1983
10. 71 A.M.E. Roberts, J. Garner	WI vs Ind	1983

Leading Fielders (excluding wicketkeepers)

Player	Catches	Matches
1. R.T. Ponting (Aus)	28	46
2. S.T. Jayasuriya (SL)	18	38
=3. C.L. Cairns (NZ)	16	28
=3. Inzamam-ul-Haq (Pak)	16	35
=3. B.C. Lara (WI)	16	34
=6. G.C. Smith (SA)	15	20
=6. D.P.M.D. Jayawardene	15	33
=8. A. Kumble (Ind)	14	18
=8. S.R. Waugh (Aus)	14	33
=8. P.A. de Silva (SL)	14	35

Leading Wicketkeepers

Player	Dismissals	Matches
1. A.C. Gilchrist (Aus)	52	31
2. K.C. Sangakkara (SL)	46	30
3. B.B. McCullum (NZ)	32	25
4. M.V. Boucher (SA)	31	25
5. Moin Khan (Pak)	30	20
6. A.J. Stewart (Eng)	23	25
=7. R.D. Jacobs (WI)	22	11
=7. Wasim Bari (Pak)	22	14
=9. I.A. Healy (Aus)	21	14
=9. A. Bagai (Can)	21	15

BIBLIOGRAPHY

Books

James Alter, The History of World Cup Cricket 1975-2011, Roli Books, New Delhi, 2011

Geoff Armstrong and Mark Gately, *The People's Game*, Ironbark, Sydney 1994

Peter Arnold, The Illustrated Encyclopedia of World Cricket, Golden Press, Sydney, 1986

Trevor Bailey (ed.), *World of Cricket 1980*, Queen Anne Press, London 1980

Sambit Bal (ed.), Sealed with a Six: The Story of the 2011 World Cup, ESPN Cricinfo, Hachette India, New Delhi, 2011

Mark Baldwin, The History of the Cricket World Cup, Sanctuary Publishing Limited, London, 2003

Simon Barnes, Phil Edmonds *A Singular Man*, Kingswood Press, London 1986

Scyld Berry, *A Cricket Odyssey*, Pavilion Books, London 1988

Dickie Bird, *That's Out!*, Arthur Barker, London 1985

Henry Blofeld, *My Dear Old Thing*, Stanley Paul, London 1988

Allan Border, *An Autobiography*, Methuen, Sydney 1986

Mihir Bose, *All in a Day*, Robin Clark, London 1983

—*A History of Indian Cricket*, Andre Deutsch, London 1990

Ian Botham, *Botham: My Biography*, Collins Willow, London 1994

Mike Brearley, *The Art of Captaincy*, Hodder and Stoughton, London 1985

Mark Browning, A Complete History of World Cup Cricket 1975-1999, Kangaroo Press, Sydney, 1999

Greg Chappell, Fierce Focus, Hardie Grant Books, Sydney, 2011

Ian Chappell, *Chappelli: The Cutting Edge*, Swan Publishing, Perth 1992

Denis Compton, *Compton On Cricketers Past and Present*, Cassell, London 1980

John Crace, *Wasim and Waqar: Imran's Inheritors*, Boxtree, London 1992

Martin Crowe, *Out on a Limb*, Reed, Auckland 1995

Mike Denness, *I Declare*, Arthur Barker, London 1977

Kapil Dev, *By God's Decree*, Harper and Row, Sydney 1985

—Kapil, *The Autobiography of Kapil Dev*, Sidgwick and Jackson, London 1987

Duncan Fletcher, Behind The Shades: The Autobiography, Simon and Schuster, London, 2007

Andrew Flintoff, Andrew Flintoff: Ashes to Ashes, Hodder & Stoughton, London, 2009

Bill Frindall and Victor H. Isaacs, *The Wisden Book of One Day International Cricket 1971–1985*, John Wisden & Co., London 1985

Mike Gatting, *Leading From the Front*, Queen Anne Press, London 1988

Adam Gilchrist, Walking to Victory, Pan Macmillan, Sydney, 2003

Adam Gilchrist, True Colours: My Life, Macmillan, Sydney 2008

Graham Gooch and Frank Keating, *My Autobiography*, Collins Willow, London 1995

Gordon Greenidge, *The Man in the Middle*, David and Charles, Newton Abbot 1980

Edward Griffiths, *Kepler: The Biography*, Pelham Books, London 1994

Chris Harte, *A History of Australian Cricket*, Andre Deutsch, London 1993

Gideon Haigh, *The Cricket War*, Text, Melbourne 1993

Matthew Hayden, Standing My Ground, Michael Joseph, Melbourne, 2010

Eddie Hemmings, *Coming of Age*, Stanley Paul, London 1991

Graeme Hick, *My Early Life*, Macmillan, London 1991

Derek Hodgson (ed.), *Cricket World Cup 83*, Unwin Paperbacks, London 1983

David Hookes, *Hookesy*, ABC Books, Sydney 1993

Michael Hussey, Underneath the Southern Cross, Hardie Grant Books, Melbourne, 2013

Imran Khan, *Imran*, Pelham Books, London 1983

—*All Round View*, Chatto and Windus, London 1988

Martin Johnson and Henry Blofeld, *The Independent World Cup Cricket '87*, The Kingswood Press, London 1987

Jim Laker, *One Day Cricket*, Batsford, London 1977

Allan Lamb and Peter Smith, *Lamb's Tales*, George Allen and Unwin, London 1985

Brett Lee and James Knight, My Life, Ebury Press, Sydney, 2011

David Lemmon (ed.), Pelham *Cricket Year-First Edition*, Pelham Books, London 1979

David Lemmon, *Great One-Day Matches*, Pelham Books, London 1982

—*Benson and Hedges Cricket Year*, Pelham Books, London 1983

Tony Lewis, *A Summer of Cricket*, Pelham Cricket, London 1976

Clive Lloyd, *Living For Cricket*, Stanley Paul, London 1980

Steven Lynch (ed.), The Wisden Guide to International Cricket 2011, 2010, John Wisden & Co Ltd, London, England

Syed Khalid Mahmood, Spotlight on World Cup 2003, Jumbo Publishing, Karachi, 2003

Trevor McDonald, *Clive Lloyd*, Granada, London 1985

Glenn McGrath and Daniel Lane, Line and Strength, William Heinemann, Sydney, 2008

Mike Marqusee, *War Minus the Shooting*, William Heinemann, London 1996

Rod Marsh, *Gloves Sweat and Tears*, Penguin Books, Melbourne 1984

Malcolm Marshall, *Marshall Arts*, Q1ueen Anne Press, London 1987

Suresh Menon, Champions! How the World Cup was won, HarperCollins Publishers, New Delhi, 2011

Peter Murray (ed.), World Cup Cricket 1983: India Wins, Wide World of Sports Publications, Sydney, 1983

Ricky Ponting and Brian Murgatroyd, Ricky Ponting's World Cup Diary, HarperCollins Publishers Pty Limited, Sydney, 2003

Ricky Ponting, Captain's Diary 2007, HarperSports, Sydney, 2007

Ricky Ponting, At The Close of Play, HarperCollins, Sydney, 2013

Bob Simpson, *The Reasons Why*, Harper Sports, Sydney 1996

Patrick Smith (ed.), *The Age World Cup Cricket, 1992*, Five Mile Press, Melbourne 1992

Andrew Symonds, Roy On The Rise: A Year of Living Dangerously, Hardie Grant Books, Melbourne, 2008

Iva Tennant, *Imran Khan*, RF. and G. Witherby, London 1994

Michael Vaughan, Time To Declare: My Autobiography, Hodder & Stoughton, London, 2009

K.R. Wadhwaney, Scandals, Controversies & World Cup 2003, Diamond Pocket Books, New Delhi, 2003

Steve Waugh, *Steve Waugh's World Cup Diary*, Harper Sports, Sydney 1996

Newspapers. Journals and Periodicals

Cricketer, World Cup Special, 1975

Daily Telegraph

The Cricketer, July and August 1975, August 1983, November and December 1987, April and May 1992, March and April 1996

Inside Cricket, various issues from 2011

The Times

Wisden Cricket Monthly, July and August 1979, August 1983, December 1987, April and May 1992, March and April 1996

The Wisden Cricketer, various issues from 2007

Yearbooks

The A. C Australian Cricket Almanac, 1992

The Australian Cricket Almanac, 1996

Cricket Yearbook, 1988

Wisden Cricketer's Almanack, 1976, 1980, 1984, 1988, 1993, 1997, 2002, 2004, 2008, 2012

Wisden Cricketer's Almanack – Australia, 2003-04

Internet

Crick Info-The Home of Cricket on the Internet

ESPN Cricinfo website – www.espncricinfo.com

UK £16.99